MW00637840

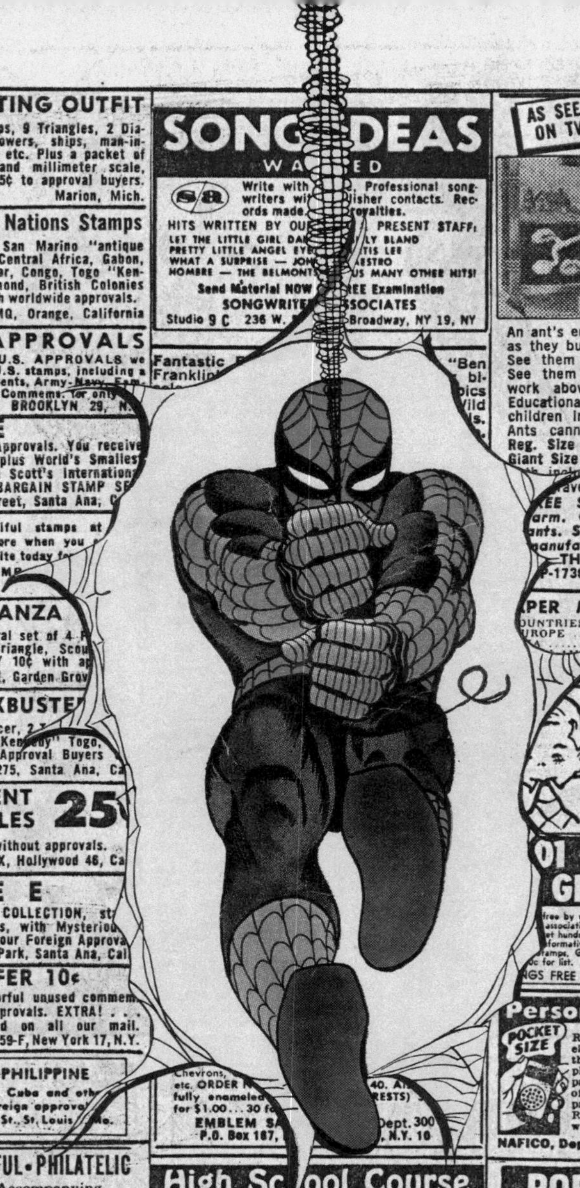

Roy Thomas

THE MARVEL AGE OF COMICS 1961-1978

TASCHEN

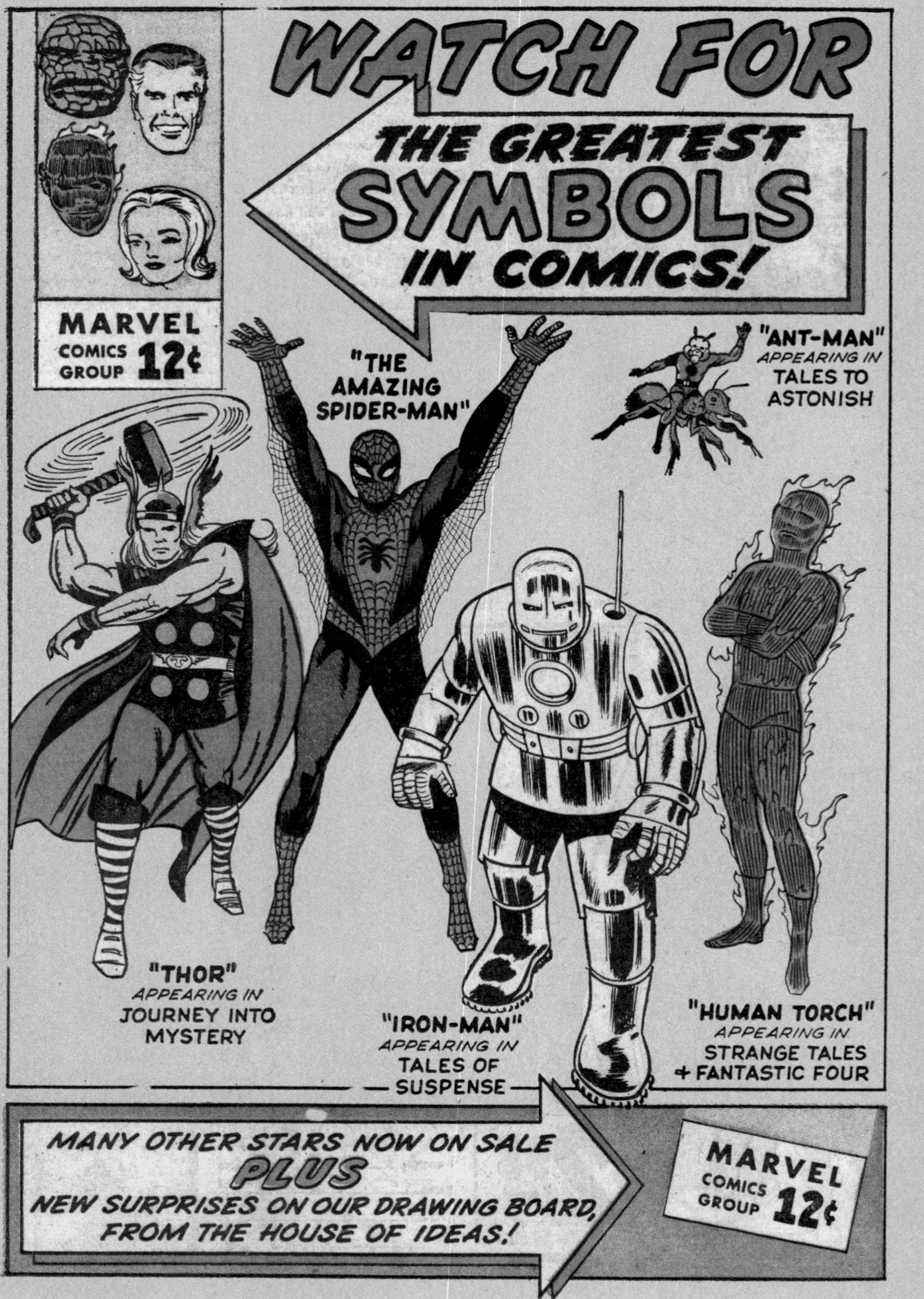
WATCH FOR
THE GREATEST
SYMBOLS
IN COMICS!
MARVEL
COMICS GROUP 12¢
"THE AMAZING SPIDER-MAN"
"ANT-MAN"
APPEARING IN
TALES TO ASTONISH
"THOR"
APPEARING IN
JOURNEY INTO MYSTERY
"IRON-MAN"
APPEARING IN
TALES OF SUSPENSE
"HUMAN TORCH"
APPEARING IN
STRANGE TALES + FANTASTIC FOUR
MANY OTHER STARS NOW ON SALE
PLUS
NEW SURPRISES ON OUR DRAWING BOARD, FROM THE HOUSE OF IDEAS!
MARVEL
COMICS GROUP 12¢

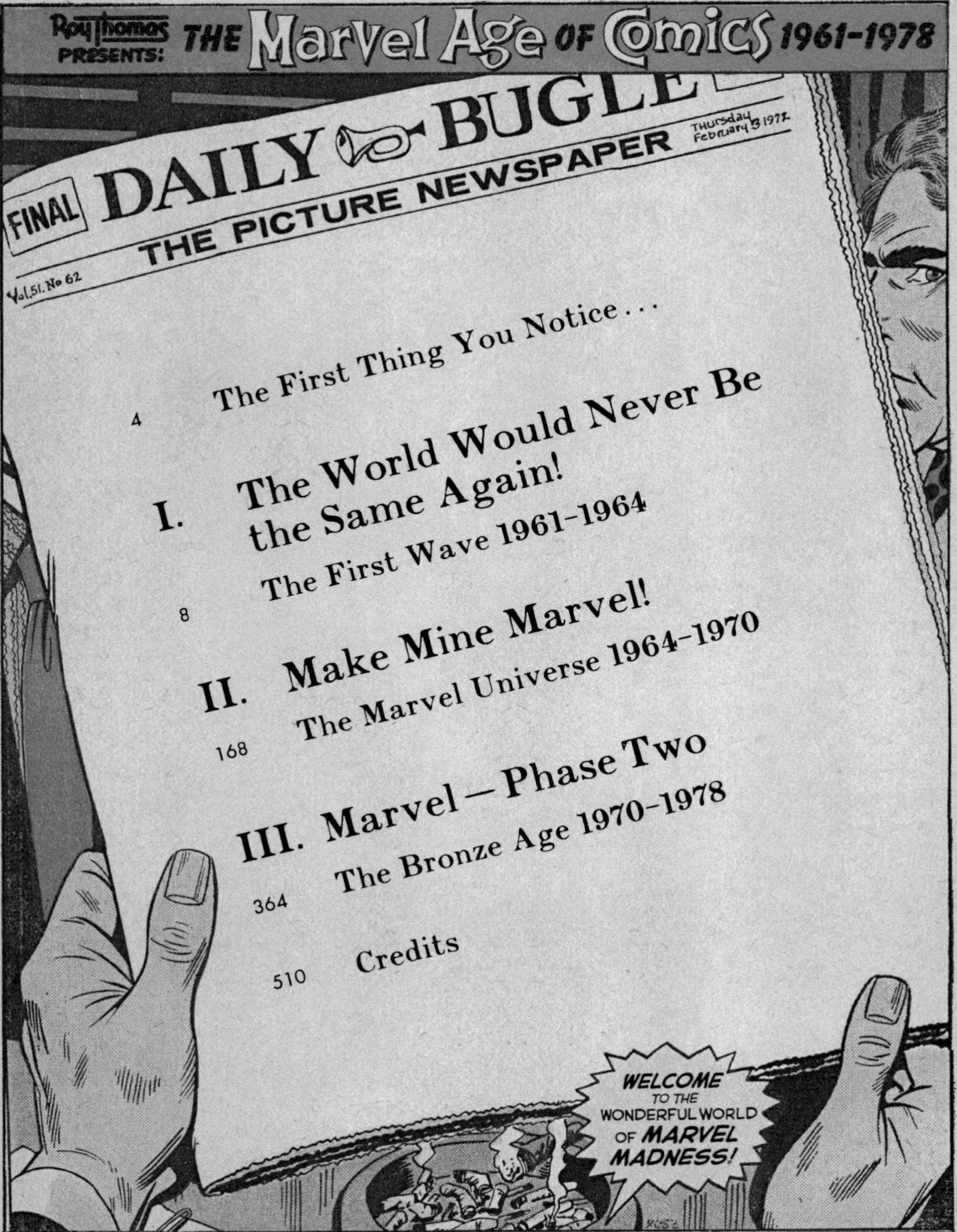
Roy Thomas PRESENTS: THE Marvel Age OF Comics 1961-1978
FINAL
DAILY BUGLE
THE PICTURE NEWSPAPER
Thursday February 3 1977
Vol. 51. No 62
WELCOME TO THE WONDERFUL WORLD OF MARVEL MADNESS!

CAPTIONS BY NICK CAPUTO, BLAKE HENNON, ANDY LEWIS, BARRY PEARL, JOHN RHETT THOMAS, AND MICHAEL VASSALLO WITH JOSH BAKER, GEOFF BOUCHER, DANNY FINGEROTH, MAURENE GOO, JESS HAROLD, AND NINA WIENER

BOMBASTIC BULLPEN BULLETIN Great effort was made to present these historic artifacts as they now appear, giving readers a glimpse at what it might be like to hold one of these imperfect treasures in their hands. Readers wishing to know more about the practices employed in reproducing and identifying the works reproduced herein may peruse the editorial note on page 511.

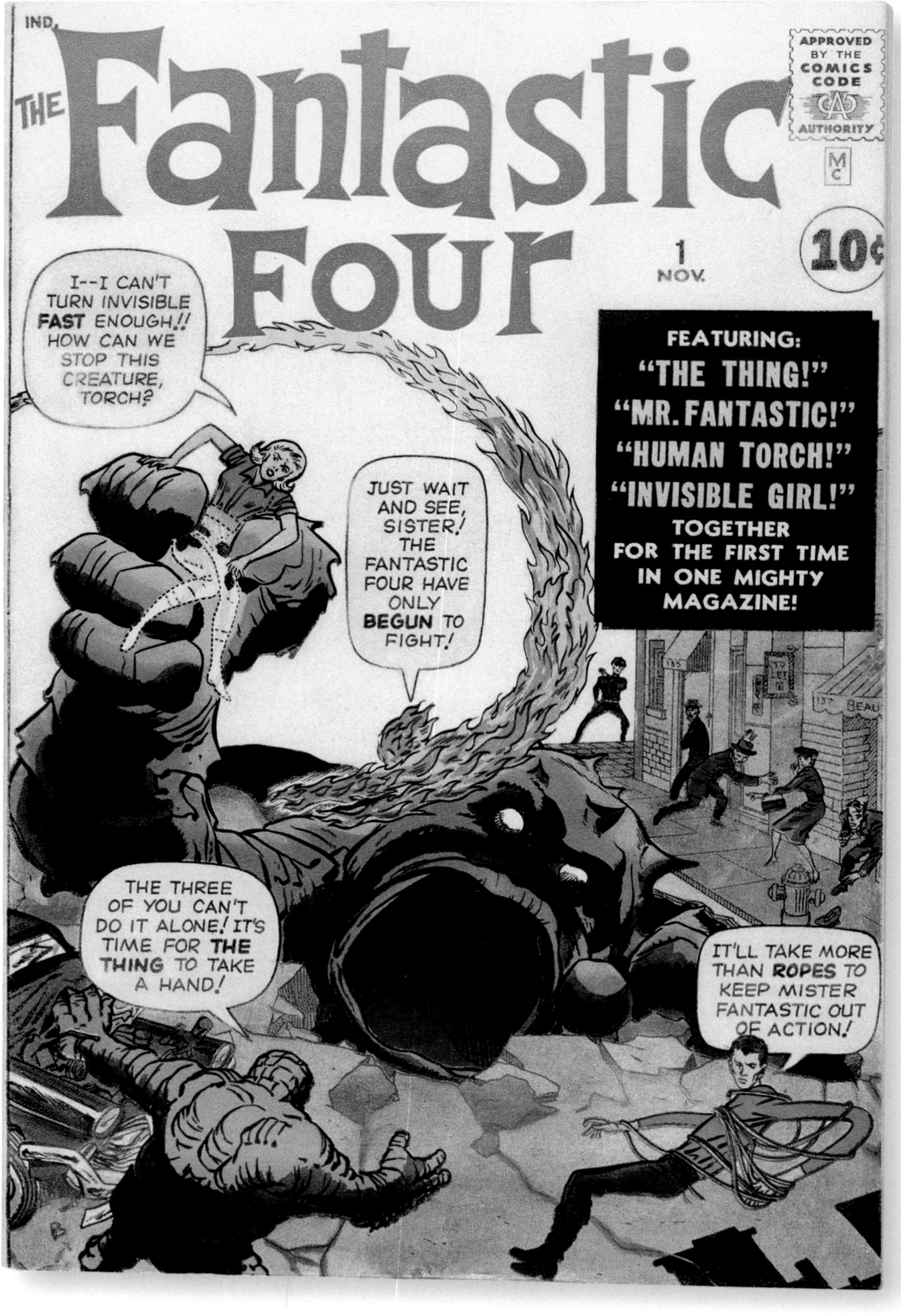

IND.
THE Fantastic FOUR
APPROVED BY THE COMICS CODE AUTHORITY
MC
1 NOV.
10¢
I--I CAN'T TURN INVISIBLE FAST ENOUGH!! HOW CAN WE STOP THIS CREATURE, TORCH?
FEATURING:
"THE THING!"
"MR. FANTASTIC!"
"HUMAN TORCH!"
"INVISIBLE GIRL!"
TOGETHER FOR THE FIRST TIME IN ONE MIGHTY MAGAZINE!
JUST WAIT AND SEE, SISTER! THE FANTASTIC FOUR HAVE ONLY BEGUN TO FIGHT!
THE THREE OF YOU CAN'T DO IT ALONE! IT'S TIME FOR THE THING TO TAKE A HAND!
IT'LL TAKE MORE THAN ROPES TO KEEP MISTER FANTASTIC OUT OF ACTION!

THE FIRST THING YOU NOTICE is the humongous monster.

Gargantuan bod — spiny, armored hide — eyeball-less white eyes — a mouth like a colossal vacuum-cleaner nozzle. And, oh yeah, he's green. Plus did I mention he's clawing his way up from beneath a big-city street?

Only then do you spot the other people on the comic book cover. No, not the cop — and not the four terrified civilians cowering on the sidewalk.

The other four guys.

One of 'em is a good-looking blonde, her lower half transparent as she squirms in the creature's gigantic paw. Like turning invisible is gonna help!

Then there's this living hunk of fire, with no features beyond a vaguely humanoid shape, flying around the monster's head like a man-sized firefly.

Plus another male, extricating himself from some ropes by bending and stretching his limbs, so that the bonds fall off him like limp spaghetti.

As for the fourth guy — he's as clearly a monster as the pavement-buster, but not that much bigger than the humans. Still, he looks strong. Maybe because he's absentmindedly crunching an automobile like an accordion to push it out of his way.

The bright red, upper-and-lower-case title at the top of the cover tells us who these four guys are, even before we read the accompanying blurb:

The Fantastic Four!

Then, in that box, their names: "The Thing!" "Mr. Fantastic!" "Human Torch!" "Invisible Girl!"—

"Together for the First Time in One Mighty Magazine!"

If something tells you it won't be the last time — you'd be right.

And before long — they'll have friends.

— ROY THOMAS, 2017

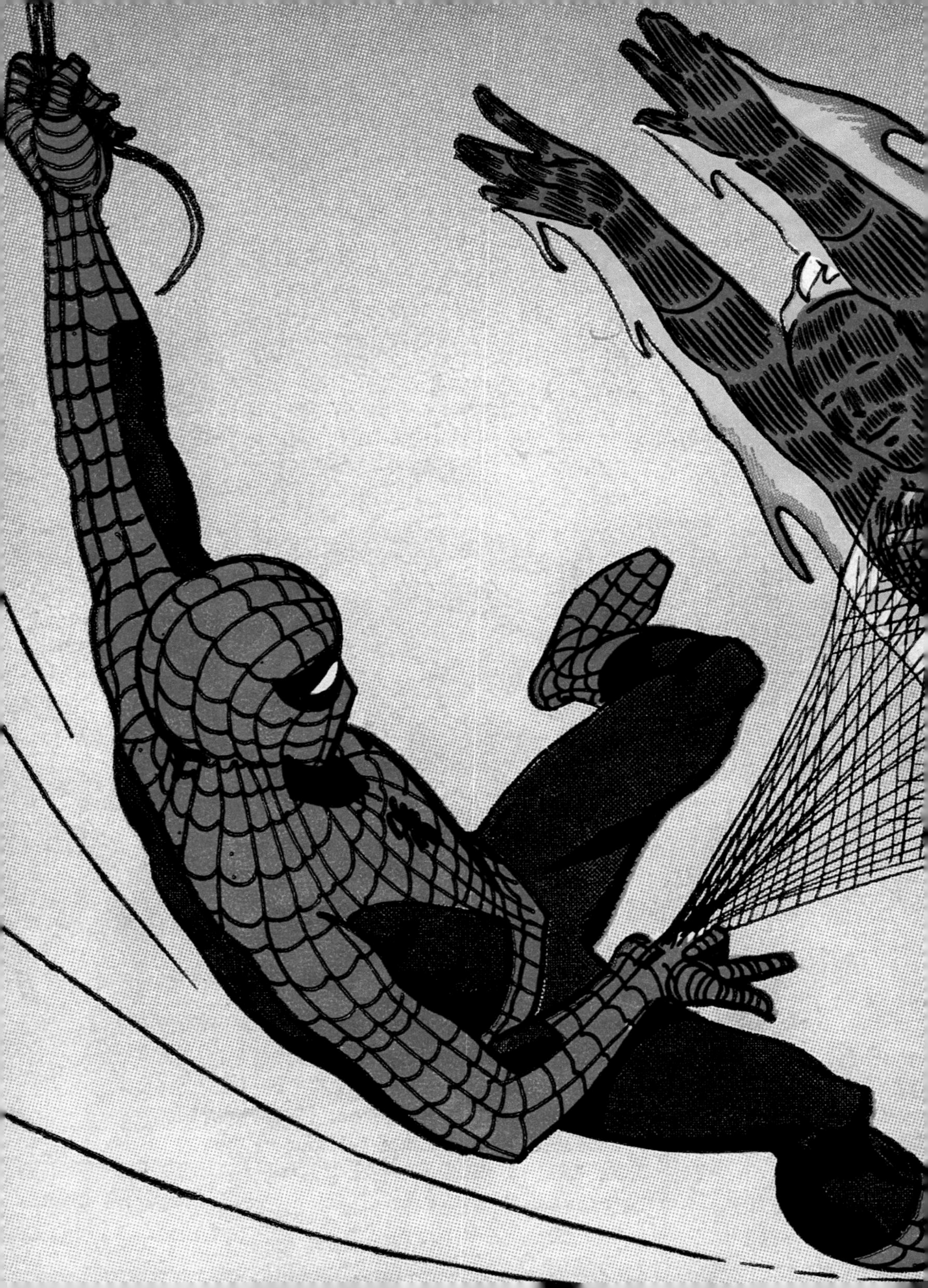

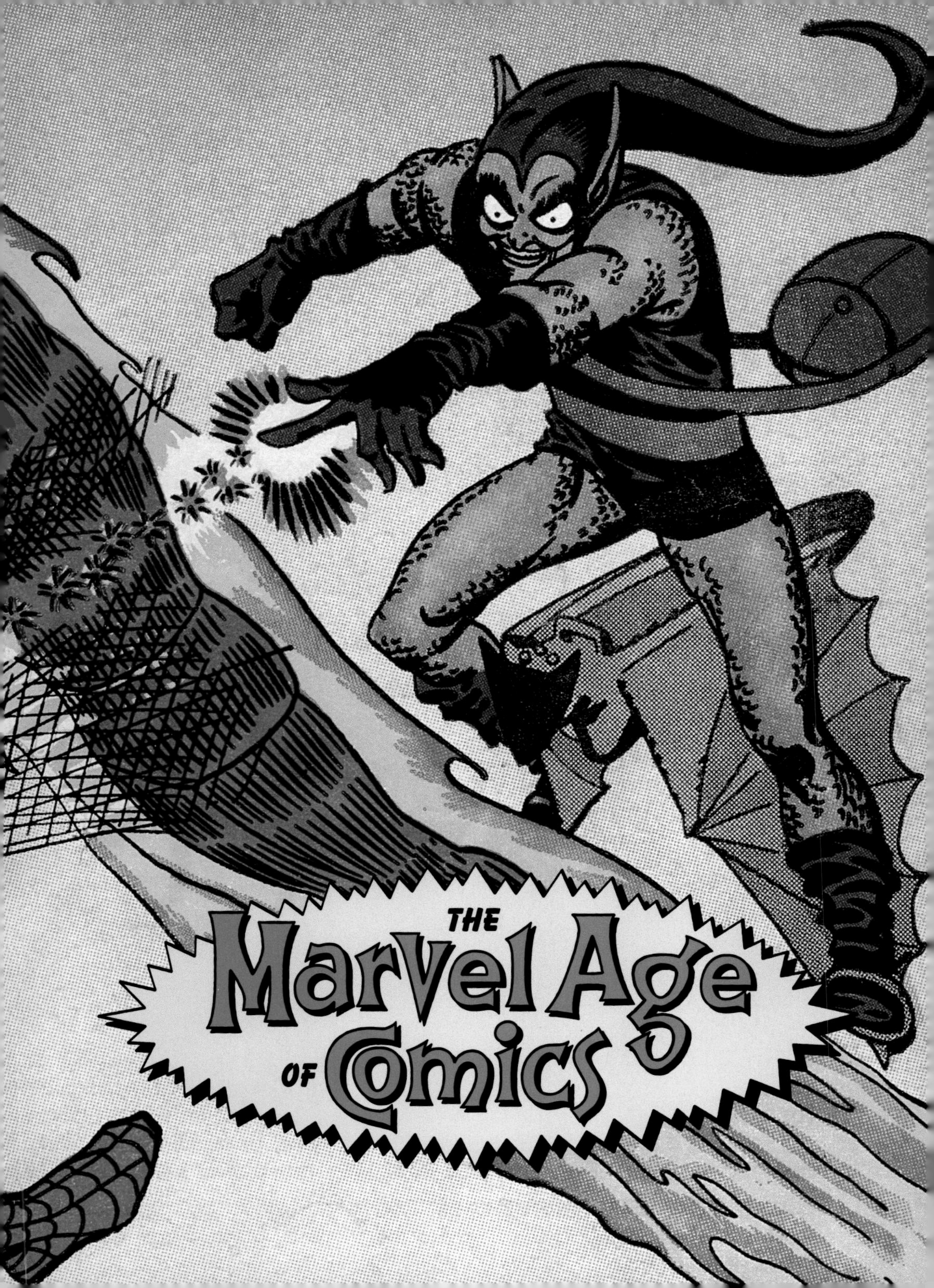
THE
Marvel Age
OF Comics

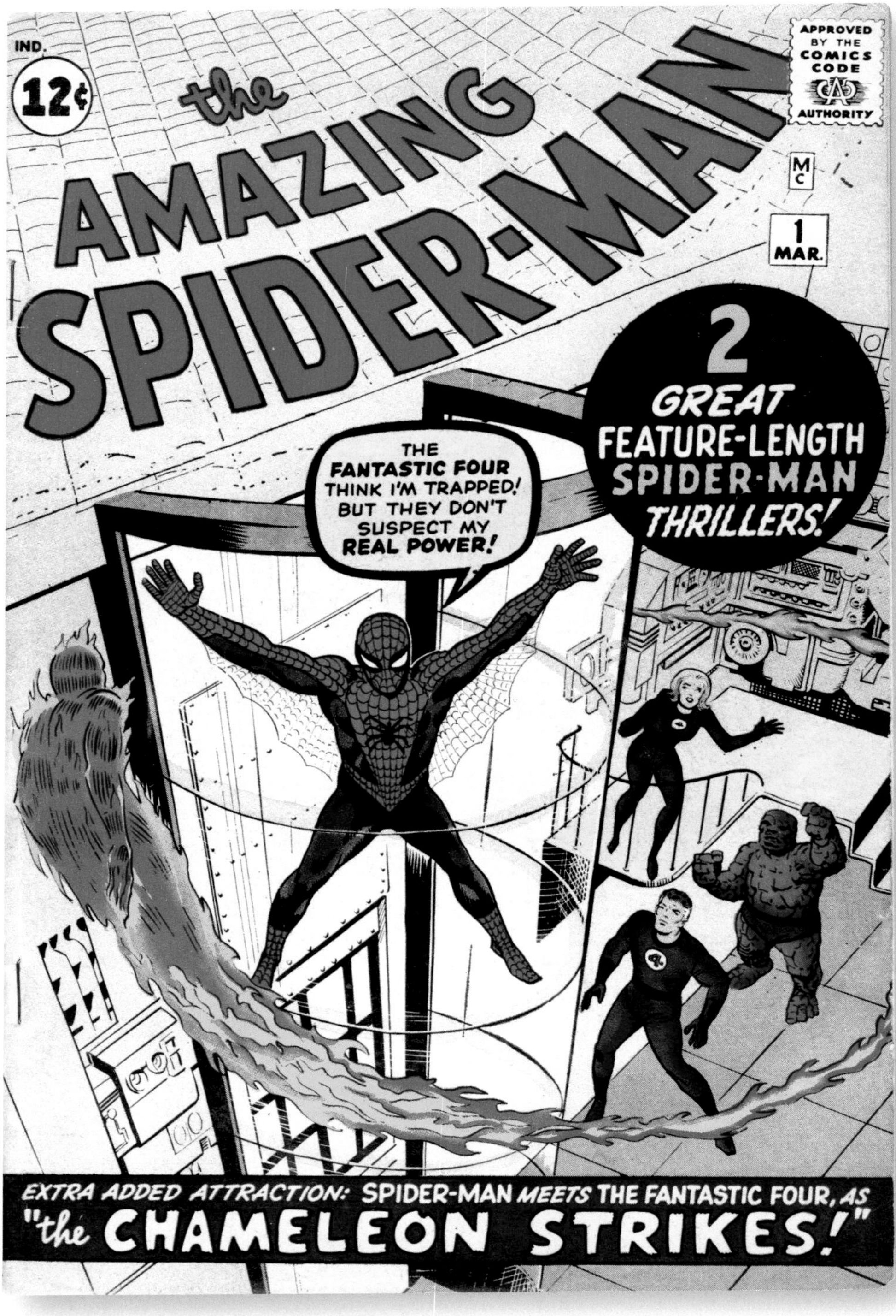
IND.
12¢
the AMAZING SPIDER-MAN
APPROVED BY THE COMICS CODE AUTHORITY
MC
1 MAR.
2 GREAT FEATURE-LENGTH SPIDER-MAN THRILLERS!
THE FANTASTIC FOUR THINK I'M TRAPPED! BUT THEY DON'T SUSPECT MY REAL POWER!
EXTRA ADDED ATTRACTION: SPIDER-MAN MEETS THE FANTASTIC FOUR, AS
"the CHAMELEON STRIKES!"

The World Would Never Be the Same Again!

THE FIRST WAVE 1961–1964

INTRODUCING THE FANTASTIC FOUR

The first Lee-Kirby hero creation of the seminal year 1961 (although Larry Lieber may have written the actual script from a synopsis by his brother) had its premiere in *Amazing Adventures* No. 1, in the five-page tale "I Am the Fantastic Dr. Droom!" An American doctor journeys to the Himalayas and becomes the disciple of a mysterious dying lama, who names him his heir in fighting evil. For five issues, Dr. Droom fought weird menaces, mostly via super hypnosis; his exploits, however, always played second fiddle to cover-featured monsters like Sserpo, the Creature Who Crushed the Earth.

But changes were brewing.

One of the changes involved Stan Lee. He complained to his wife, Joan, about how tired he was of being allowed to write only simple, unrealistic stories with elementary dialogue because comic books were "just for kids." After two decades, his job at Timely seemed to be in a slow death spiral. Maybe it was time to see what else might be out there for a facile writer in his late 30s with 20 years of editorial experience.

Then came a legendary game of golf. (That's "legendary" as in "legend-creating," not as in "apocryphal" — because there is at least anecdotal evidence that this fabled encounter on the back nine actually happened.)

Sometime in early 1961, Martin Goodman reportedly played golf with a top executive of either DC Comics or of Timely's DC-owned distributor, Independent News. His companion boasted about the sales figures on a new title, *Justice League of America*, in which DC's super heroes fought as a team. Besides the long-running Superman, Batman, Wonder Woman, and

AMAZING SPIDER-MAN No. 17
(Previous pages) Cover; pencils and inks, Steve Ditko; October 1964. "Marvel Comics. Not so much a name as a special state of mind. Not so much a group of magazines as a mood, a movement, a mild and momentary madness." — Stan Lee

THE AMAZING SPIDER-MAN No. 1
(Opposite) Cover; pencils, Jack Kirby; inks, Steve Ditko; March 1963.

AMAZING ADVENTURES No. 1

(Below) Interior, "I Am the Fantastic Dr. Droom!"; plot, attributed Stan Lee; script, attributed Larry Lieber; pencils, Jack Kirby; inks, Steve Ditko; June 1961.

Aquaman, the group included revived, updated versions of 1940s stars the Flash and Green Lantern. The debuts of the latter two, in 1956 and 1959 respectively, had jump-started what is now celebrated as comic books' "Silver Age" — but *Justice League* was outselling even the two solo heroes!

The first chance he got, Goodman directed Lee to come up with a super hero team comic, telling his editor he could revive Captain America, Human Torch, and/or Sub-Mariner, if he wanted: "That'll save you from having to dream up any new characters."

Lee, however, saw super heroes as a concept that had already failed twice. He told Joan he'd rather hand in his notice than waste time on another dead end. She was supportive, and suggested this might be the time for him to do a comic book the way *he* wanted. Why not write more substantial stories, create characters who spoke "like real people"? He had nothing to lose. If Goodman fired him — well, he wanted to quit anyway!

Convinced, Lee developed heroes who were "real, living, breathing people whose personal relationships would be of interest to the readers and, equally important, to me." So he began work on a synopsis for the first issue of the new series.

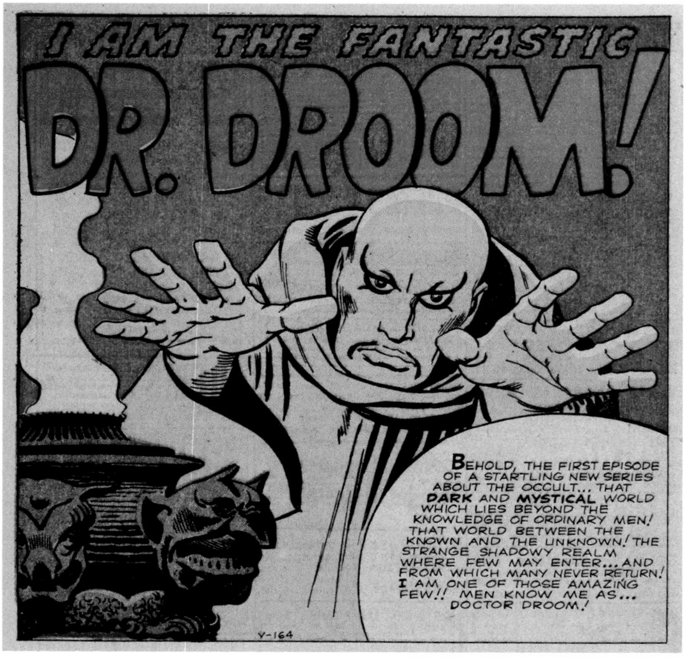
I AM THE FANTASTIC
DR. DROOM!
BEHOLD, THE FIRST EPISODE OF A STARTLING NEW SERIES ABOUT THE OCCULT... THAT DARK AND MYSTICAL WORLD WHICH LIES BEYOND THE KNOWLEDGE OF ORDINARY MEN! THAT WORLD BETWEEN THE KNOWN AND THE UNKNOWN! THE STRANGE SHADOWY REALM WHERE FEW MAY ENTER... AND FROM WHICH MANY NEVER RETURN! I AM ONE OF THOSE AMAZING FEW!! MEN KNOW ME AS... DOCTOR DROOM!
V-164

IND.
AMAZING
APPROVED BY THE COMICS CODE AUTHORITY
MC
ADVENTURES
10¢
6
NOV.
SEE HIM GROW BEFORE YOUR EYES!!
SSERPO, THE CREATURE WHO CRUSHED THE WORLD!!
HE'S STILL GROWING!! NOTHING CAN STOP HIM! BY TOMORROW HIS WEIGHT WILL CRUSH THE WHOLE PLANET!! EARTH IS DOOMED!!

AMAZING ADVENTURES No. 6

(Above) Cover; pencils, Jack Kirby; inks, attributed George Klein; November 1961. The last *Amazing Adventures*. The next issue would be entitled *Amazing Adult Fantasy*.

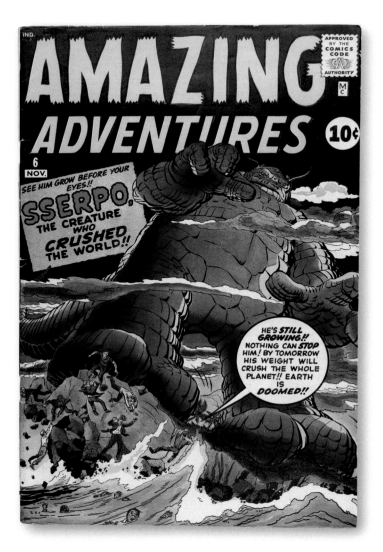

Why merely a synopsis, and not a full script with panel-by-panel descriptions, dialogue, and captions? At some time during this period, Lee had begun the practice of sometimes giving artists brief synopses ("plots") to work from, rather than full scripts. The reason: At this point, he was very nearly the company's sole writer, and it was the only way he could avoid becoming a human bottleneck if two or three artists happened to need assignments at the same time. Two synopses — maybe three — could be written in the time it might take to type out one full, detailed script; and this method prevented one artist

AND THEN THERE WERE FOUR

(Below) Fantastic Four *synopsis, Stan Lee, 1961.* "We are trying, (perhaps vainly?)," Lee wrote shortly after the issue hit newsstands, "to reach a slightly older, more sophisticated group." Lee's treatment for the first Fantastic Four story focused on character development rather than dialogue—that would be added after Jack Kirby penciled the pages.

from being left high and dry without work (or a paycheck) until Lee finished writing a script for another artist.

As he outlined the first story for the new super hero team series, four seemed like a good number of members for it to have: not so large as to be unwieldy. Reed Richards, a "young, handsome scientist"…his "actress" girlfriend, Susan Storm…"husky, brutish" Ben Grimm, a pilot "who falls for Susan also"…and Johnny Storm, her teenage "star athlete" brother—these are partial descriptions from the two-page synopsis Lee wrote, typing as always with two fingers. Reed builds a spaceship and hopes to become "the first man to Mars." (This was, after all, four years after the orbiting of the first Soviet Sputnik, with the U.S. moon landing still eight years in the future.) Richards hires Grimm, "who doesn't want any part of the project until he sees Susan."

The foursome blast off and *ZAP!*—they're bombarded by cosmic rays, right through the rocket's hull. They crash-land, and each finds him/herself changed by the radiation. Sue "has become invisible" and "can not become visible again"…Johnny

They think Reed Richards, the pilot; is unaffected by cosmic rays, as he seems normal-- UNTIL he tries to reach for something. Then they realize his arm has STRETCHED toward the thing he reached for. After awhile they realize Reed's body has become like RUBBER. He can get skinny, elongated, anything that you can do with rubber. He can squeeze thru key-holes, etc. Of course, the more stretched-out he gets, the weaker he gets-- but the point remains that he can twist and stretch his body into almost any shape. (He can even alter the appearance of his face to make himself look like someone else) BUT it is quite pain-ful to do all this, so he can only maintain the strange shapes for a very short period of time until the pain gets to be unbearable.

Finally, Ben Grimm steps out of the shadows. They all gasp-- his body has changed in the most grotesque way of all. He's sort of shapeless-- he's become a THING. And, he's grown more fantastically powerful than any other living thing. He is stronger than an elephant. BUT, he is so heavy that he moves very slowly-- he's very ponderous, and those slow, pon-derous movements should make him look very dramatic. He cannot alter his appearance as the others can, so he must wear a coat with turned-up collar, sunglasses, slouch hat, and glove when he goes out in public. But when he takes 'em off, he is a THING!

So much for who they are and how they got that way. Now, here's a gimmick I think we might play up to advantage: Let's make The Thing the heavy- in other words, he's not really a good guy. He's part of the Fantastic Four because they all got that way together and they decide to remain a team, and also because he has a crush on Susan-- but actually, he is jealous of Mr. Fantastic and dislikes Human Torch because Torch always sides with Fantastic. Let's treat him so that reader is always afraid he will sabotage the Fantastic Four's efforts at whatever they are doing-- he isn't interested in helping man-kind the way the other three are-- he is more interested in winning Susan away from Mr. Fantastic. (We might indicate that he feels he may return to his normal self at any time, because none of them know how long their strange powers will last- or whether or the effect of the cosmic rays will one day-wear off them).

Anyway, the four of them decide to form a unit-- they think it is an act of Fate which made them as they are and they think they owe it to fate to use their powers to help mankind. So they adopt their new names: HUMAN TORCH, MR. FANTASTIC, INVISIBLE GIRL, and THE THING, and vow to spend their lives fighting all sorts of evil menaces which the normal forces of the world cannot cope with. And, to keep it all from getting too goody-goody, there is always friction between Mr. Fantastic and The Thing, with Human Torch siding with Mr. F. Also, the other three are always afraid of The Thing getting out of their control some day and harming mankind with his amazing strength. Occasionally also, you might have the Thing wanting to do something for personal profit- and the other 3 try to stop him. In other words, the Thing doesn't have the ethics that the other three have, and consequently he will probably be the most interesting one to the reader, because he'll always be unpredictable.

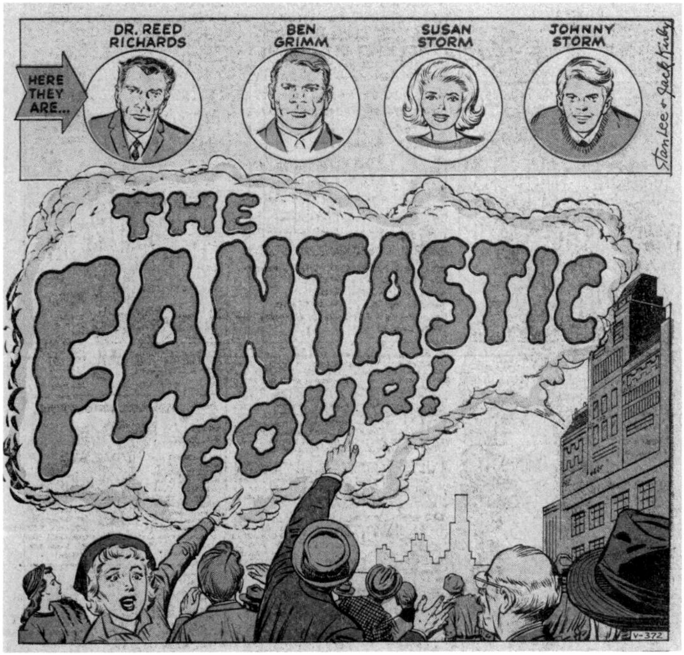
HERE THEY ARE...
DR. REED RICHARDS
BEN GRIMM
SUSAN STORM
JOHNNY STORM
THE FANTASTIC FOUR!
V-372

FANTASTIC FOUR No. 1

(Left) Interior, "The Fantastic Four"; script, Stan Lee; pencils, Jack Kirby; inks, attributed George Klein; November 1961. With the Cold War space race starting to heat up at the close of the Atlas era, Reed Richards leads a crew of four to beat the Russians into space. A storm bombards them with cosmic rays, giving them super powers. The brilliant Richards gains the power to stretch his body, and takes the name Mr. Fantastic; Susan Storm gains the power to disappear, becoming the Invisible Girl; Sue's teenage brother Johnny can become a Human Torch at will (reminiscent of the 1940s character); and Ben Grimm, the pilot and Reed's brash, outspoken college buddy, transforms into a super-strong, orange monster, appropriately named the Thing.

"becomes a Human Torch, and can fly"...Reed stretches "like rubber," but doing so causes him great pain. And Ben Grimm? He's now "sort of shapeless—he's become a THING," the "heavy" in the group, staying only because of his "crush" on Susan. Agreeing they must use their new powers to help mankind, the quartet adopts new names: Mr. Fantastic, Invisible Girl, the Human Torch, and the Thing.

THE FANTASTIC FOUR

This origin tale was to take up roughly half the issue's 20-plus story pages. At some point, Lee called in artist Jack Kirby, who had cocreated many a costumed hero over the years. For his part, Kirby sparked to the idea of doing the new series. He particularly identified with one of the Fantastic Four: "The Thing is really Jack Kirby...He has my manners, he has my manner of speech, and he thinks the wayI do...He can muscle his way through a crowd. I find I'm that sort of person."

In penciling the story, Kirby introduced each of its four heroes in a separate sequence of his/her own, letting the reader witness the strange powers of each one, before the team's origin was related as a flashback. He turned his

MINUTES LATER, JOHNNY STORM'S FLAME SUBSIDED AND HE LANDED NEAR THE OTHER THREE! SILENTLY THEY WATCHED THE SMALL FIRE HE HAD STARTED IN THE UNDERBRUSH BURN ITSELF OUT!! SILENTLY THEY WERE EACH OCCUPIED WITH THEIR OWN STARTLING THOUGHTS!
WE'VE CHANGED! ALL OF US! WE'RE MORE THAN JUST HUMAN!
LISTEN TO ME, ALL OF YOU! THAT MEANS YOU TOO, BEN! TOGETHER WE HAVE MORE POWER THAN ANY HUMANS HAVE EVER POSSESSED!
YOU DON'T HAVE TO MAKE A SPEECH, BIG SHOT! WE UNDER-STAND! WE'VE GOTTA USE THAT POWER TO HELP MANKIND, RIGHT?
RIGHT, BEN, RIGHT!

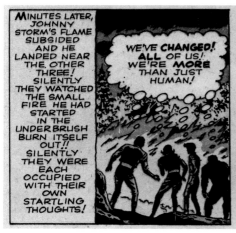

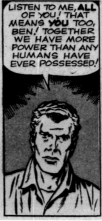

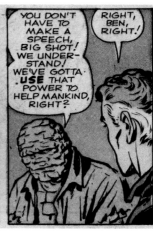

13 pages of artwork in to his editor, who once again put on his writing hat.

The differences between Lee's synopsis and Kirby's art, apart from the upfront action sequences, were minor, and at this distance it's impossible to say *which* of them instituted a given change if a certain aspect of the synopsis wasn't reflected in the artwork: Susan's actress career was dropped... the art didn't suggest that Reed and Ben had only just met... nor was there any hint of Ben lusting after Susan... she doesn't stay invisible for long... and her kid brother is presented as a skinny hot-rod enthusiast rather than a "star athlete." Squeezed into half the pages originally intended for it, the "origin" part of the story had gotten streamlined, first when Kirby penciled it, then still further when Lee added dialogue. In short, it was a true collaboration, one that brought out the best in both talented comics veterans.

FANTASTIC FOUR No. 1
(Above and opposite) Interiors, "The Fantastic Four"; script, Stan Lee; pencils, Jack Kirby; inks, attributed George Klein; November 1961. As Lee and Kirby begin developing their characters, the depraved, pathetic Mole Man becomes rather sympathetic. He would not be the last Marvel character to suffer as a result of his looks.

The second half of *Fantastic Four* No. 1 recounts the team's first full-blown mission, battling the repulsive Mole Man and his Godzilloid creatures beneath Monster Isle. That episode—and Kirby's related cover illustration—is basically a head-on collision between a super hero adventure and a standard Timely monster epic.

From the outset, however, the "FF" were as different from previous superheroes as Lee wanted them to be. They had no secret identities or costumes, or even uniforms like DC's Challengers. They squabbled amongst themselves in deadly seriousness, with the Thing blaming Richards for his grotesque

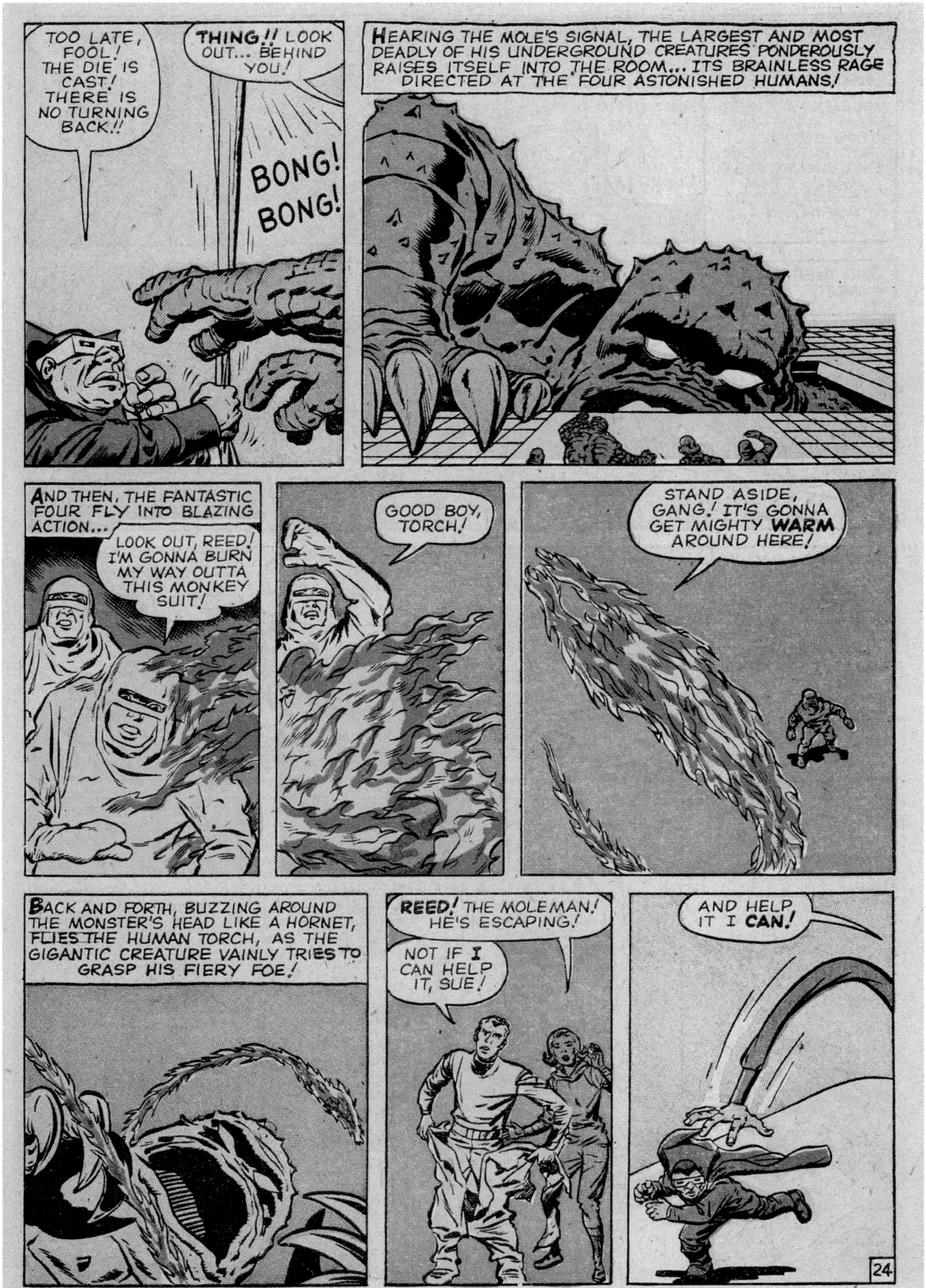
TOO LATE, FOOL! THE DIE IS CAST! THERE IS NO TURNING BACK!!
THING!! LOOK OUT... BEHIND YOU!
BONG! BONG!
HEARING THE MOLE'S SIGNAL, THE LARGEST AND MOST DEADLY OF HIS UNDERGROUND CREATURES PONDEROUSLY RAISES ITSELF INTO THE ROOM... ITS BRAINLESS RAGE DIRECTED AT THE FOUR ASTONISHED HUMANS!
AND THEN, THE FANTASTIC FOUR FLY INTO BLAZING ACTION...
LOOK OUT, REED! I'M GONNA BURN MY WAY OUTTA THIS MONKEY SUIT!
GOOD BOY, TORCH!
STAND ASIDE, GANG! IT'S GONNA GET MIGHTY WARM AROUND HERE!
BACK AND FORTH, BUZZING AROUND THE MONSTER'S HEAD LIKE A HORNET, FLIES THE HUMAN TORCH, AS THE GIGANTIC CREATURE VAINLY TRIES TO GRASP HIS FIERY FOE!
REED! THE MOLEMAN! HE'S ESCAPING!
NOT IF I CAN HELP IT, SUE!
AND HELP IT I CAN!
24

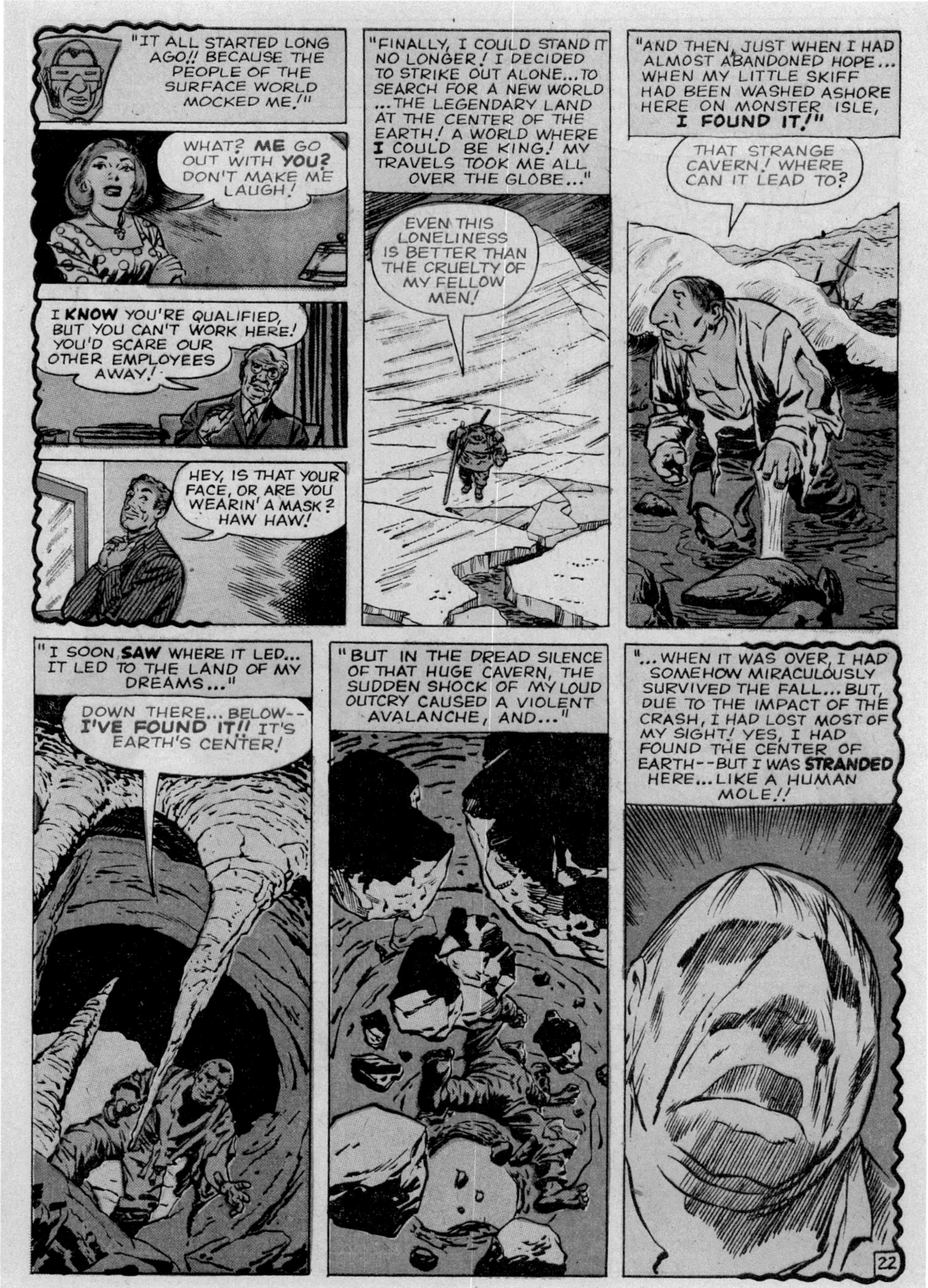
"IT ALL STARTED LONG AGO!! BECAUSE THE PEOPLE OF THE SURFACE WORLD MOCKED ME!"
WHAT? ME GO OUT WITH YOU? DON'T MAKE ME LAUGH!
I KNOW YOU'RE QUALIFIED, BUT YOU CAN'T WORK HERE! YOU'D SCARE OUR OTHER EMPLOYEES AWAY!
HEY, IS THAT YOUR FACE, OR ARE YOU WEARIN' A MASK? HAW HAW!
"FINALLY, I COULD STAND IT NO LONGER! I DECIDED TO STRIKE OUT ALONE...TO SEARCH FOR A NEW WORLD ...THE LEGENDARY LAND AT THE CENTER OF THE EARTH! A WORLD WHERE I COULD BE KING! MY TRAVELS TOOK ME ALL OVER THE GLOBE..."
EVEN THIS LONELINESS IS BETTER THAN THE CRUELTY OF MY FELLOW MEN!
"AND THEN, JUST WHEN I HAD ALMOST ABANDONED HOPE... WHEN MY LITTLE SKIFF HAD BEEN WASHED ASHORE HERE ON MONSTER ISLE, I FOUND IT!"
THAT STRANGE CAVERN! WHERE CAN IT LEAD TO?
"I SOON SAW WHERE IT LED... IT LED TO THE LAND OF MY DREAMS..."
DOWN THERE...BELOW-- I'VE FOUND IT!! IT'S EARTH'S CENTER!
"BUT IN THE DREAD SILENCE OF THAT HUGE CAVERN, THE SUDDEN SHOCK OF MY LOUD OUTCRY CAUSED A VIOLENT AVALANCHE, AND..."
"...WHEN IT WAS OVER, I HAD SOMEHOW MIRACULOUSLY SURVIVED THE FALL...BUT, DUE TO THE IMPACT OF THE CRASH, I HAD LOST MOST OF MY SIGHT! YES, I HAD FOUND THE CENTER OF EARTH--BUT I WAS STRANDED HERE...LIKE A HUMAN MOLE!!"
22

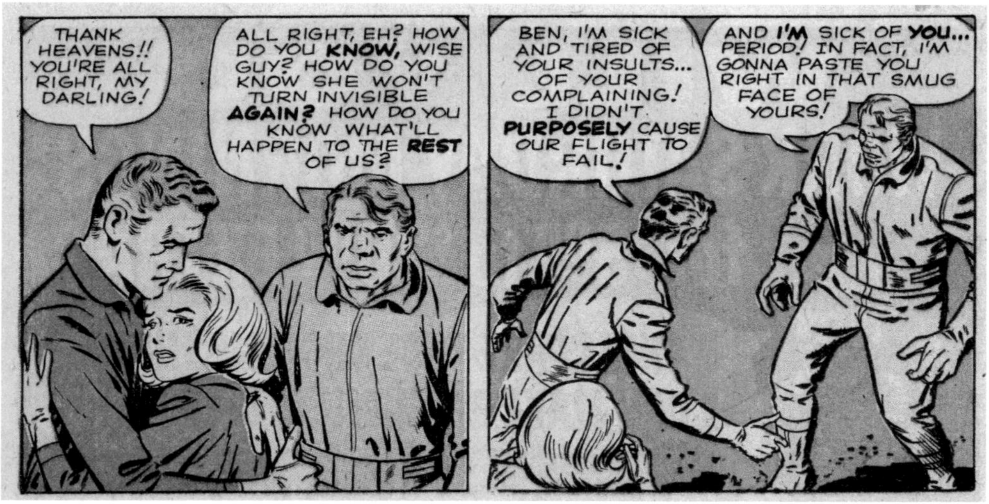
THANK HEAVENS!! YOU'RE ALL RIGHT, MY DARLING!
ALL RIGHT, EH? HOW DO YOU KNOW, WISE GUY? HOW DO YOU KNOW SHE WON'T TURN INVISIBLE AGAIN? HOW DO YOU KNOW WHAT'LL HAPPEN TO THE REST OF US?
BEN, I'M SICK AND TIRED OF YOUR INSULTS... OF YOUR COMPLAINING! I DIDN'T PURPOSELY CAUSE OUR FLIGHT TO FAIL!
AND I'M SICK OF YOU... PERIOD! IN FACT, I'M GONNA PASTE YOU RIGHT IN THAT SMUG FACE OF YOURS!

appearance (a cross between a pile of rocks and a dinosaur's hide). The four called each other by their real names, not super hero monikers. The issue's splash page even carried credits: "Stan Lee & Jack Kirby."

One question seldom asked is, how did Martin Goodman feel about all this? When he got his first glimpse of the story, or perhaps of Kirby's cover, did he wonder why the heroes weren't wearing colorful costumes like the Justice Leaguers? Lee has no memory of Goodman commenting on anything whatsoever about the issue. Perhaps that's because its cover spotlighted a gigantic lumpy monster, as did most of Timely's

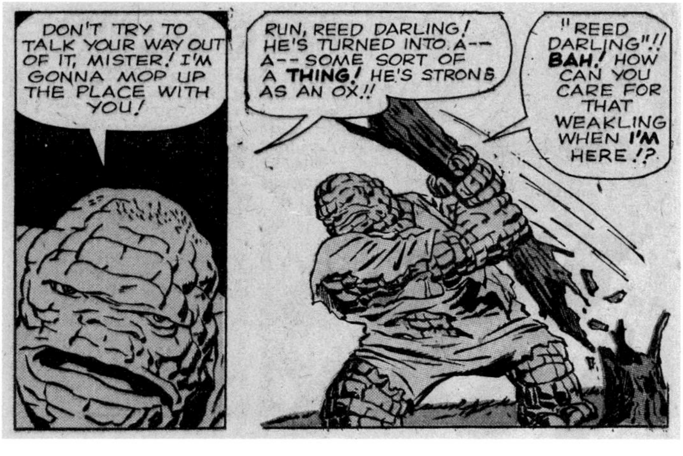
DON'T TRY TO TALK YOUR WAY OUT OF IT, MISTER! I'M GONNA MOP UP THE PLACE WITH YOU!
RUN, REED DARLING! HE'S TURNED INTO A-- A-- SOME SORT OF A THING! HE'S STRONG AS AN OX!!
"REED DARLING"!! BAH! HOW CAN YOU CARE FOR THAT WEAKLING WHEN I'M HERE!?

FANTASTIC FOUR No. 1
(Opposite, above, and below) Interiors, "The Fantastic Four"; script, Stan Lee; pencils, Jack Kirby; inks, attributed George Klein; November 1961. While Atlas comics' "Monster Age" had been populated with creatures like Gruto and the Glob, the first star of the Marvel Age was a very different kind of monster. Ben Grimm, who became the Thing, was a sympathetic, conflicted hero whose strength was only overshadowed by his rage over being transformed into a monster. His tragic plight, combined with a down-to-earth, Lower East Side manner quickly won the hearts of fans, and as the character continued to evolve, he became less angry, funnier, and his features solidified into a quasi-heroic, "lovable" look.

FANTASTIC FOUR No. 3
(Opposite) Cover; pencils, Jack Kirby; inks, Sol Brodsky. (Right) Interior, "The Menace of the Miracle Man!"; script, Stan Lee; pencils, Kirby; inks, Brodsky. March 1962. From the beginning the FF were different. Usually, super heroes gained their powers and costumes in their very first story. Not so Stan and Jack's foursome, who received costumes only after fans wrote in demanding them.

SHOWCASE No. 7
(Below) Cover; pencils and inks, Jack Kirby; DC Comics; April 1957. Four years before the Fantastic Four appeared, DC had four adventurers survive a plane crash. "Living on borrowed time," these Challengers of the Unknown decided to risk their lives and help people in need. Since the team was drawn by Jack Kirby, some readers have looked for similarities to the Fantastic Four.

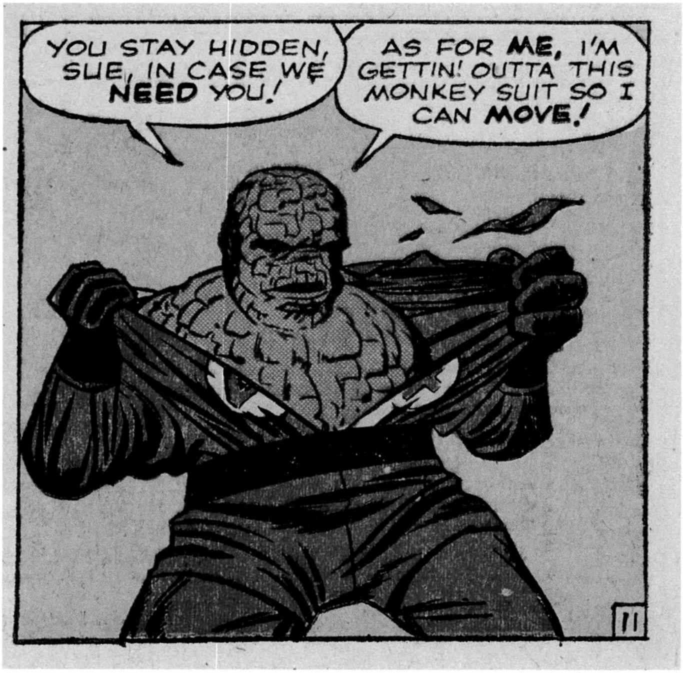
YOU STAY HIDDEN, SUE, IN CASE WE NEED YOU!
AS FOR ME, I'M GETTIN' OUTTA THIS MONKEY SUIT SO I CAN MOVE!
11

covers back then, with the Human Torch flying around (even if he resembled a living fireball more than he did Carl Burgos's character), plus, a woman turning invisible, a man twisting like a pretzel, and, as a bonus, a *smaller* but equally lumpy monster. Yes, the cover of *Fantastic Four* No. 1 probably looked just fine to the publisher of that month's "Creature from Krogarr" over in *Tales to Astonish*!

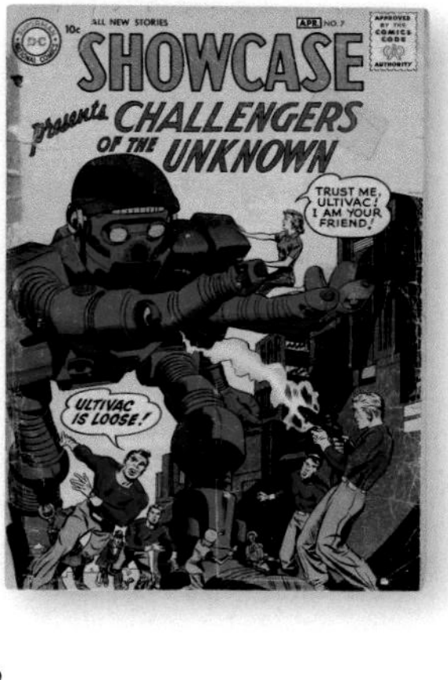
ALL NEW STORIES
SHOWCASE
presents CHALLENGERS OF THE UNKNOWN
TRUST ME, ULTIVAC! I AM YOUR FRIEND!
ULTIVAC IS LOOSE!

FIRST FRUITS

Almost immediately after *Fantastic Four* No. 1 went on sale at the turn of August 1961 (with a November cover date), Lee and Goodman began to realize they had struck a nerve.

Even before they could receive preliminary sales figures, letters poured in to the Timely offices—from children, from teenagers, even from adults—most lauding the virtues of the FF! Oh, there were a few complaints—*demands* that the heroes get costumes and (from older readers, who remembered the original Torch) for a return to that hero's classic look—but mostly the comments were wildly positive. Readers were knocked out by the interplay between the characters, so much

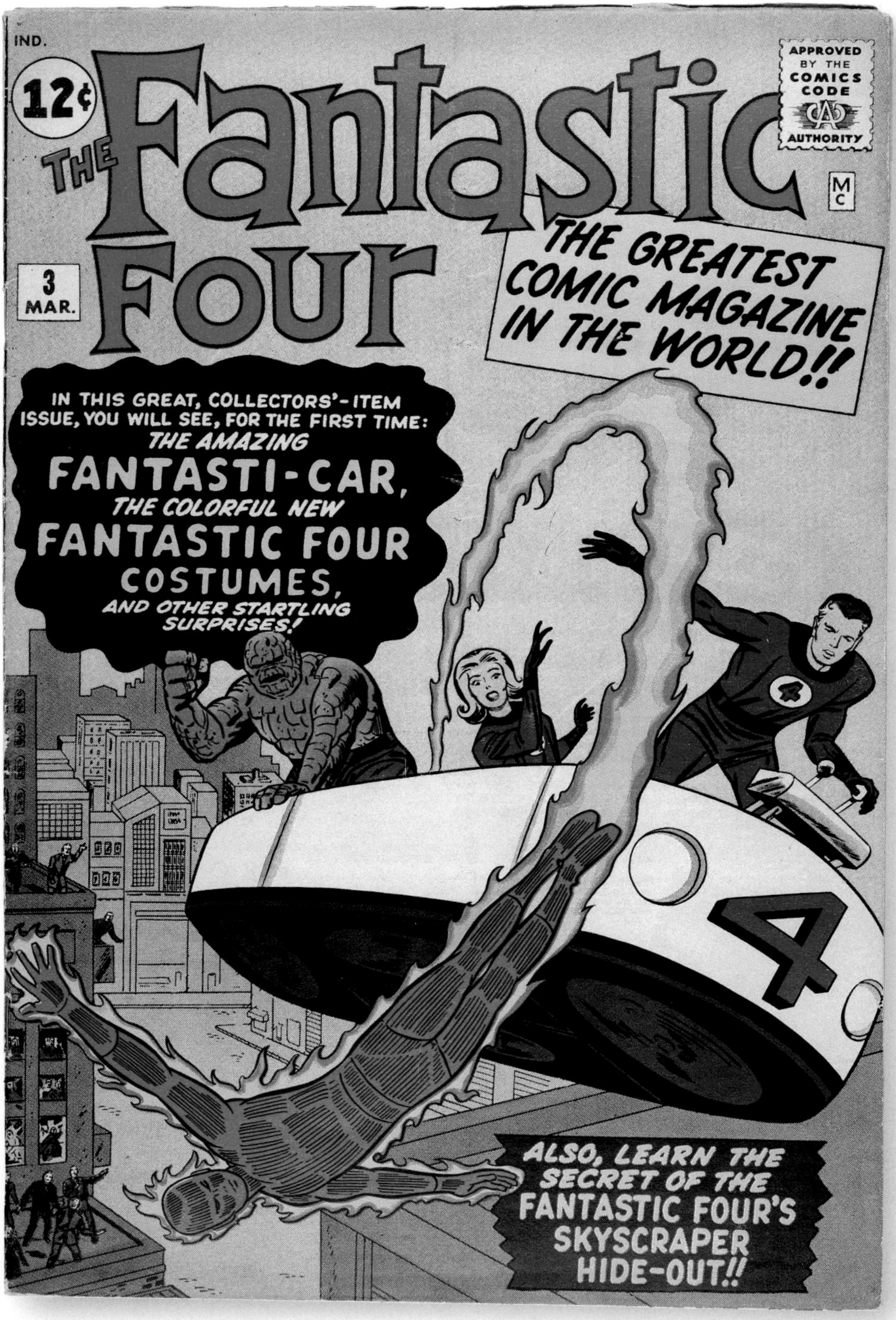
IND.
12¢
THE Fantastic Four
3
MAR.
APPROVED BY THE COMICS CODE AUTHORITY
MC
THE GREATEST COMIC MAGAZINE IN THE WORLD!!
IN THIS GREAT, COLLECTORS'-ITEM ISSUE, YOU WILL SEE, FOR THE FIRST TIME:
THE AMAZING
FANTASTI-CAR,
THE COLORFUL NEW
FANTASTIC FOUR
COSTUMES,
AND OTHER STARTLING SURPRISES!
ALSO, LEARN THE SECRET OF THE
FANTASTIC FOUR'S SKYSCRAPER HIDE-OUT!!

DEAR EDITOR...
(Below) Interior, fan page, Fantastic Four *No. 3, 1962.* The outpouring of unsolicited FF fan mail prompted the "Fantastic 4 Fan Page" in issue No. 3, beginning a tradition of personal interaction with the fans. While some early letters were fabricated in the office to promote the entire comics line (S. Brodsky was, in reality, Marvel's production man) most were genuine, including one by future Marvel writer and editor, Roy Thomas (in *FF* No. 5), and future Marvel artist Alan Weiss. Lee's informal manner and wisecracking replies were in opposition to the authoritarian tone used by Marvel's competitors. Lee soon changed the opening greetings from "Dear Editor" to the more casual "Dear Stan and Jack."

more realistic than they got in *Superman* or *Batman*. Even the dastardly Mole Man elicited their sympathy, for what kid or teenager couldn't identify with a man who was spurned and hated because he didn't fit into society? Unaccustomed to receiving fan mail, writer/editor Lee made plans to print some of these comments in the first available issue. There were plenty of letters from youngsters, but clearly this new series was reaching beyond the Peanut Gallery. Perhaps his notions about writing comics from a more sophisticated approach were bearing fruit. Of course, he was keenly aware that Kirby's dynamic art was also crucial, while the inspiration to have one of the heroes be a grotesque monster had clearly been the most brilliant stroke of all.

When the mail started cascading in, the second issue, wherein the foursome battled aliens called Skrulls, was already on the presses. But, in No. 3, the heroes donned, if not exactly costumes, uniforms at least, complete with chest symbols à la Superman, Batman, even Captain America. But, by having the Thing refuse to wear the helmet and costume ("monkey suit") that Sue designed for him, Lee and Kirby took one of the more juvenile aspects of super hero comics—the color-splashed costumes—and stood it on its head. In addition, starting with No. 3, the Torch would be drawn much more like the 1940s–50s rendition. From the outset, Lee paid attention to the fan

FANTASTIC 4 FAN PAGE

DEAR EDITOR:
I think the Fantastic Four will become a great success. The Thing and the Torch are very new and different. I would also like to know what the name of your artist is.
Alan Weiss
Pardee Place
Las Vegas, Nevada

It'll *become* a success?? What do you think it is NOW? Chicken liver?? Considering that our artist signs the name JACK KIRBY on everything he can get his greedy little fingers on, I think we can safely claim that that's his name!

4.

DEAR EDITOR:
The best thing about the comic is the character conflicts. It's nice to see a group of super-heroes who aren't unnaturally buddy-buddy. The cover of #1 was pretty poor, it didn't stand out. I wish the name of Mr. Fantastic were different. It sounds too much like Mr. Clean.
Rick Wood
Ames St.
Cambridge, Mass.

Rick, no two fans ever seem to agree on what cover is best. Same thing applies to characters' names. So, let's hear from you other readers. What type of covers do YOU prefer, and how do you feel about the name Mr. Fantastic? (We'll bet at least ONE joker writes that he'd prefer Mr. Clean!)

4.

DEAR EDITOR:
You've got a heckuva nerve making a doll like Susan Storm invisible!
Unsigned
Dallas
Texas

No WONDER you thought the mag was great, George, after reading it fifty times, brother, you've been BRAINWASHED! As for seeing more of the Torch, you've got a treat coming in the next issue!

4.

DEAR EDITOR:
Just fiinshed reading Fantastic Four and must admit to being disappointed. I expect better things from the team of Lee-Kirby. Jack is capable of better art work, and the Thing ought to revert to human form at will as his teammates do. The story also suffers from "Creeping Monsterism" to paraphrase Jean Shepard, that has dominated most, if not all, of your comics for some time.
Bill Sarill
Colorado Street
Boston, Mass.

See how fair we are? We print the knocks as well as the boosts! (The next time anyone around this office opens another one of Bill's letters, he's thrull) As for the Thing reverting to human form, it's not that easy, pal. If you don't believe us, take a dose of cosmic rays yourself and see what happens!

4.

DEAR EDITOR:
Are you the same one who also puts out STRANGE TALES, TALES TO ASTONISH, JOURNEY INTO

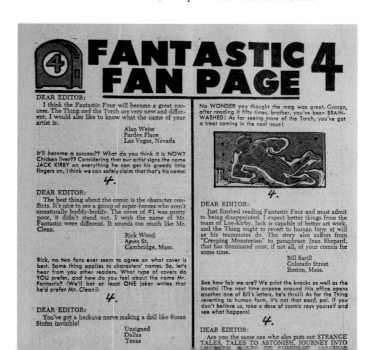

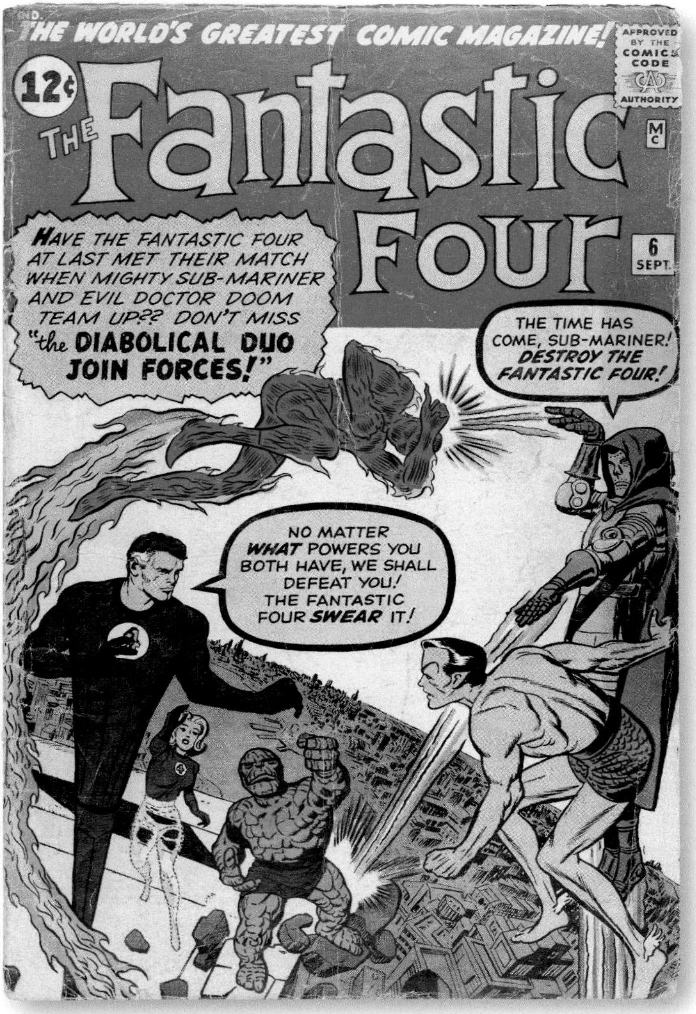
THE WORLD'S GREATEST COMIC MAGAZINE!
APPROVED BY THE COMICS CODE AUTHORITY
12¢
THE Fantastic Four
MC
6 SEPT.
HAVE THE FANTASTIC FOUR AT LAST MET THEIR MATCH WHEN MIGHTY SUB-MARINER AND EVIL DOCTOR DOOM TEAM UP?? DON'T MISS "the DIABOLICAL DUO JOIN FORCES!"
THE TIME HAS COME, SUB-MARINER! DESTROY THE FANTASTIC FOUR!
NO MATTER WHAT POWERS YOU BOTH HAVE, WE SHALL DEFEAT YOU! THE FANTASTIC FOUR SWEAR IT!

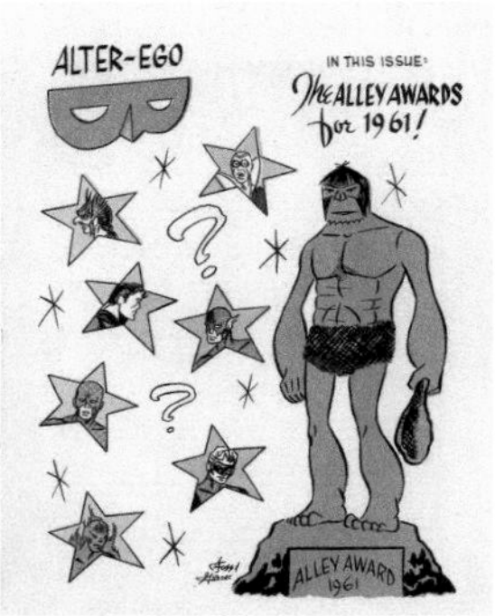
ALTER-EGO
IN THIS ISSUE:
The ALLEY AWARDS for 1961!
ALLEY AWARD 1961

FANTASTIC FOUR No. 6
(Left) Cover; pencils, Jack Kirby; inks, Dick Ayers; September 1962.

THE PEOPLE'S CHOICE
(Above) Fanzine cover, Alter-Ego *No. 4; art, Ronn Foss and Richard "Grass" Greene; Fall 1962.* Founded by Jerry Bails, and later taken over by future Marvel pro Roy Thomas, *Alter-Ego* was devoted to comic heroes. Fans voted for the industry's best in the fanzine's Alley Awards. The *FF* was a hit in 1962, winning in four categories for the previous year — even though only one issue of FF had seen print in 1961!

mail — and to the amateur comic-book "fanzines," published by and for older comics enthusiasts. His finely tuned ear would pay big dividends over the next few years.

In that first year of bimonthly publication, every issue of *Fantastic Four* brought some new milestone. The fourth issue brought back the Sub-Mariner — not a new version like the Torch but the *original* Namor, as misanthropic as Bill Everett had created him in 1939, and now Reed's rival for Sue's affections, to boot. Issue No. 5 introduced Dr. Doom, destined to become *the* iconic bad guy of the 1960s: the Man in the Iron Mask as a super villain. By No. 6, Sub-Mariner and Doom

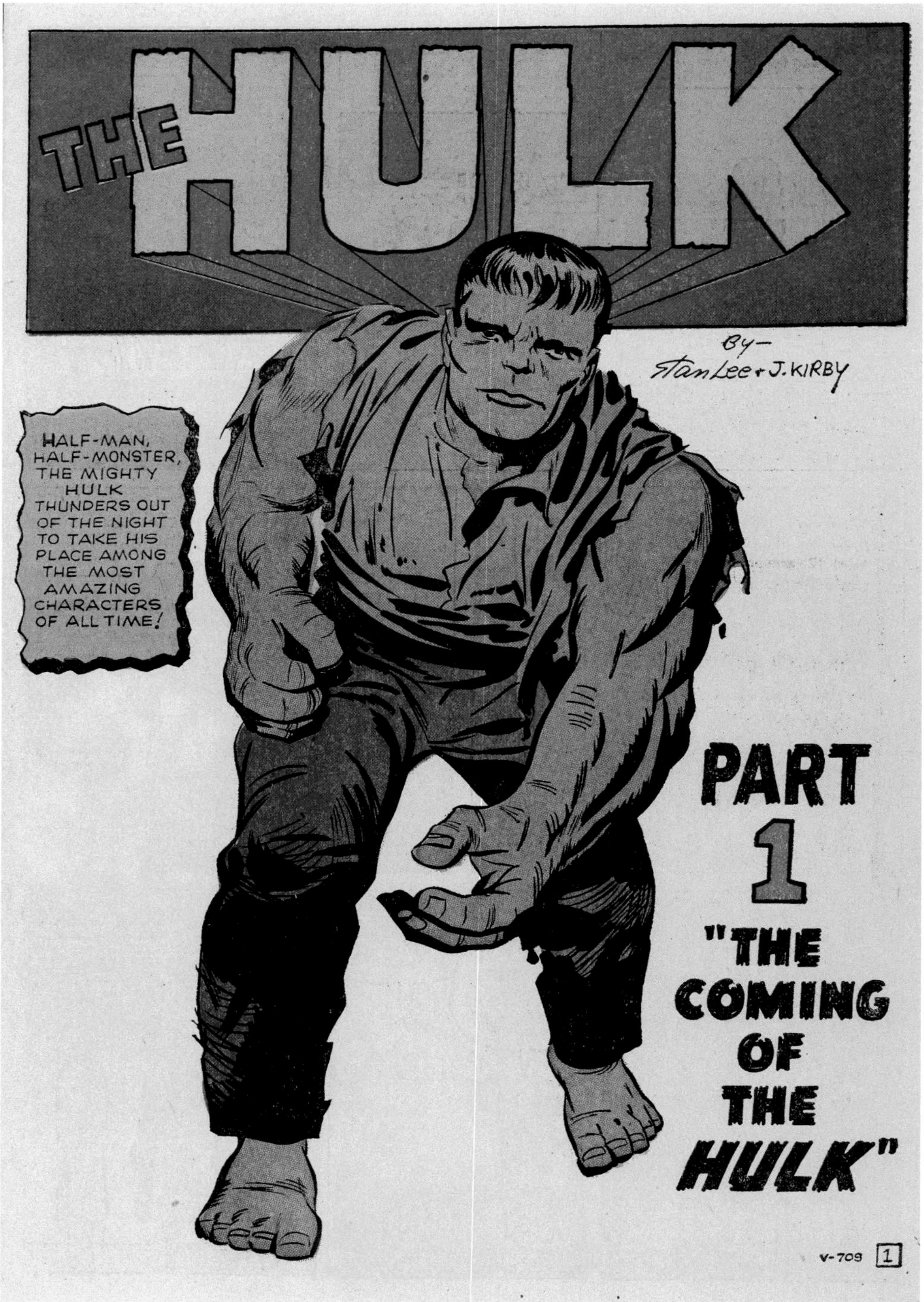
THE HULK
By— Stan Lee + J. KIRBY
HALF-MAN, HALF-MONSTER, THE MIGHTY HULK THUNDERS OUT OF THE NIGHT TO TAKE HIS PLACE AMONG THE MOST AMAZING CHARACTERS OF ALL TIME!
PART 1
"THE COMING OF THE HULK"
V-709
1

joined forces against the heroes. Things were heating up—at which point the magazine went monthly.

Naturally, as soon as the fan mail was supported by good (and dependable) sales figures, Goodman wanted a follow-up to *Fantastic Four*. Since it was clear that the breakout character in the comic was Ben Grimm, the second new title starred not a costumed super hero but another grotesquerie. *The Incredible Hulk* combined elements of *Frankenstein* and *Dr. Jekyll and Mr. Hyde*. But this time, the scientist hero *became* the monster… the romantic interest (Betty Ross) was not a super heroine… and Rick Jones was just a teenager who befriended the brute. *The Incredible Hulk* No. 1 (May 1962) shook up the key elements of *Fantastic Four* in a blender and combined them for a somewhat different result.

In the first issue, the Hulk was colored gray, but the resulting look was muddy and dull. With No. 2, his hue was altered to green. His personality also changed from issue to issue, and his vocabulary level went up and down. In one story he was controlled by Rick; in most he was totally *out* of control. Perhaps hampered by this lack of consistency, sales were just so-so. After six issues, Goodman pulled the plug on *The Incredible Hulk*.

THE INCREDIBLE HULK No. 1

(Opposite and below) Interiors, "The Coming of the Hulk!"; script, Stan Lee; pencils, Jack Kirby; inks, Paul Reinman; May 1962. The Hulk was only gray for the first issue. Stan Goldberg—a longtime Lee collaborator on *Millie the Model* and Marvel's primary colorist—has said that he wanted the Hulk to be green from the start, but writer/editor Stan Lee opted for gray. Gray did not print consistently in the comics at that time, and "Stan G." recalled that the Hulk even appeared green in one panel of this first issue, before the giant became emerald for good.

THE HEROES TAKE OVER

But, if monster heroes pure and simple didn't do the trick, then would playing up the *super hero* element perhaps appeal to more readers? From summer of 1962 till year's end, since his distribution contract limited how many comics he could

...AND WHEN THE SUN SETS, HOW DO I KNOW I WON'T CHANGE ONCE MORE? HOW DO I KNOW I WON'T KEEP CHANGING...
...INTO THAT BRUTAL, BESTIAL MOCKERY OF A HUMAN--THAT CREATURE WHICH FEARS NOTHING--WHICH DESPISES REASON AND WORSHIPS POWER!
SOON, THE SUN WILL SET AGAIN! AND HERE I SIT, HELPLESSLY, FEARING I MAY AGAIN BECOME--THE HULK!!
14

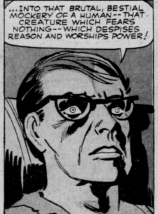

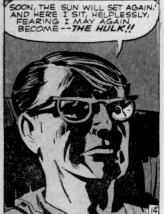

TALES TO ASTONISH No. 35

(Right) Interior, "The Return of the Ant-Man!"; plot, Stan Lee; script, Larry Lieber; pencils, Jack Kirby; inks, Dick Ayers. (Opposite) Cover; pencils, Jack Kirby; inks, Dick Ayers. September 1962. Based on sales figures for *Tales to Astonish* No. 27, it was decided that a shrinking super hero would be a worthwhile addition to the line. With his cybernetic helmet, Henry Pym gains the ability to communicate with ants. While not the typical lovable comic book companions—like dogs and horses that even replaced their human masters at times—at least they were obedient, assisting Ant-Man on many astonishing adventures.

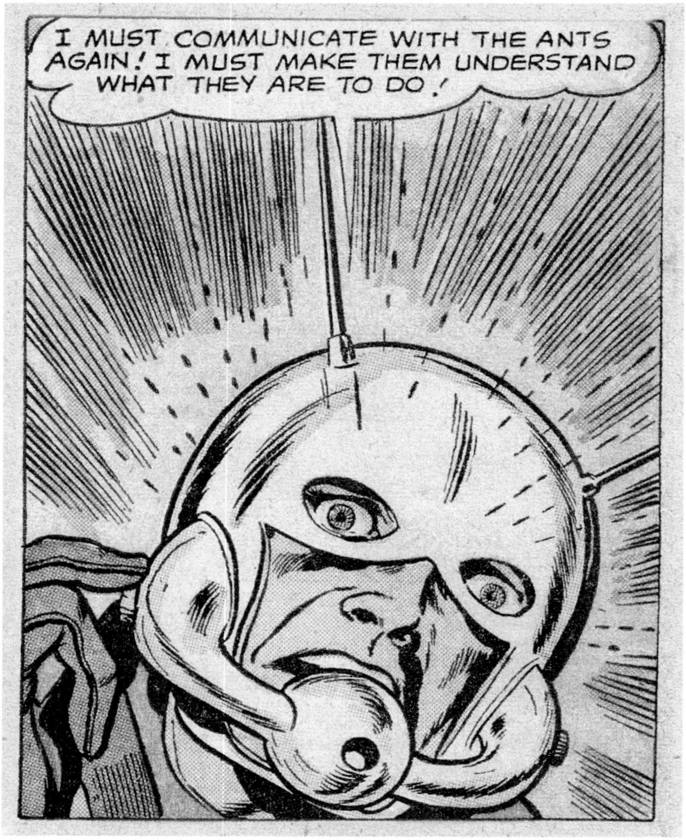
I MUST COMMUNICATE WITH THE ANTS AGAIN! I MUST MAKE THEM UNDERSTAND WHAT THEY ARE TO DO!

publish in a given month, Goodman had Lee add super hero lead features to the company's five remaining mystery titles.

Jack Kirby's cover for *Journey into Mystery* No. 83 (August 1962, on sale by June) depicted stone monster men—but they were battling the comic's new star, the mighty Thor. A crippled physician named Donald Blake finds a walking stick that, when struck on the ground, transforms itself into an ancient pagan hammer and him into Thor, visually a cross between the Norse god of thunder and a more traditional-looking super hero than the Fantastic Four (though his long golden hair wouldn't be in fashion for a few more years). Larry Lieber adapted Stan Lee's synopsis into a full script for Kirby to pencil. In most ways, this series was a step back from the avant-garde nature of the Fantastic Four; even so, Thor proved instantly popular. Lee and Kirby were proving that they could take even the more

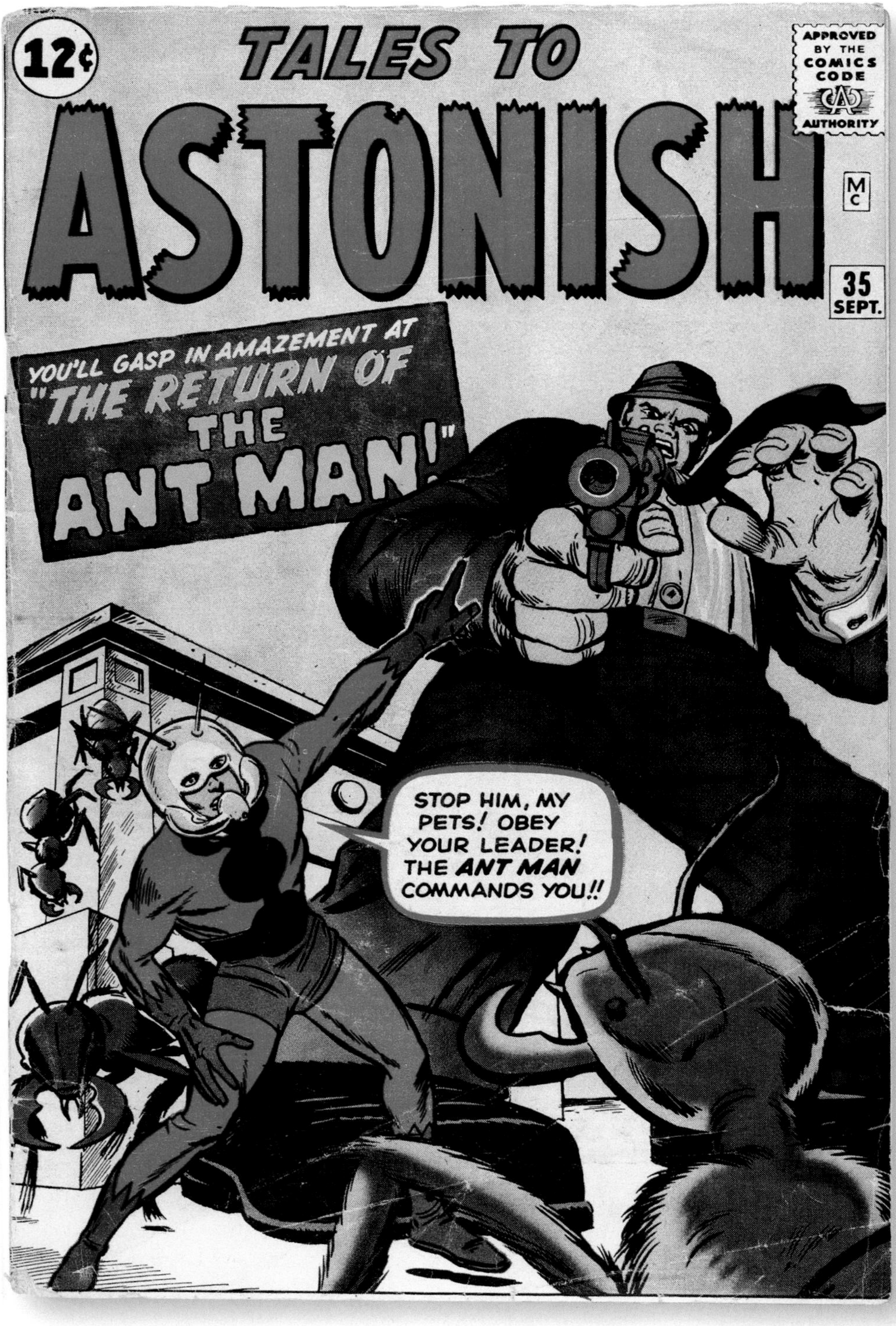
12¢
TALES TO
ASTONISH
APPROVED BY THE COMICS CODE AUTHORITY
MC
35
SEPT.
YOU'LL GASP IN AMAZEMENT AT "THE RETURN OF THE ANT MAN!"
STOP HIM, MY PETS! OBEY YOUR LEADER! THE ANT MAN COMMANDS YOU!!

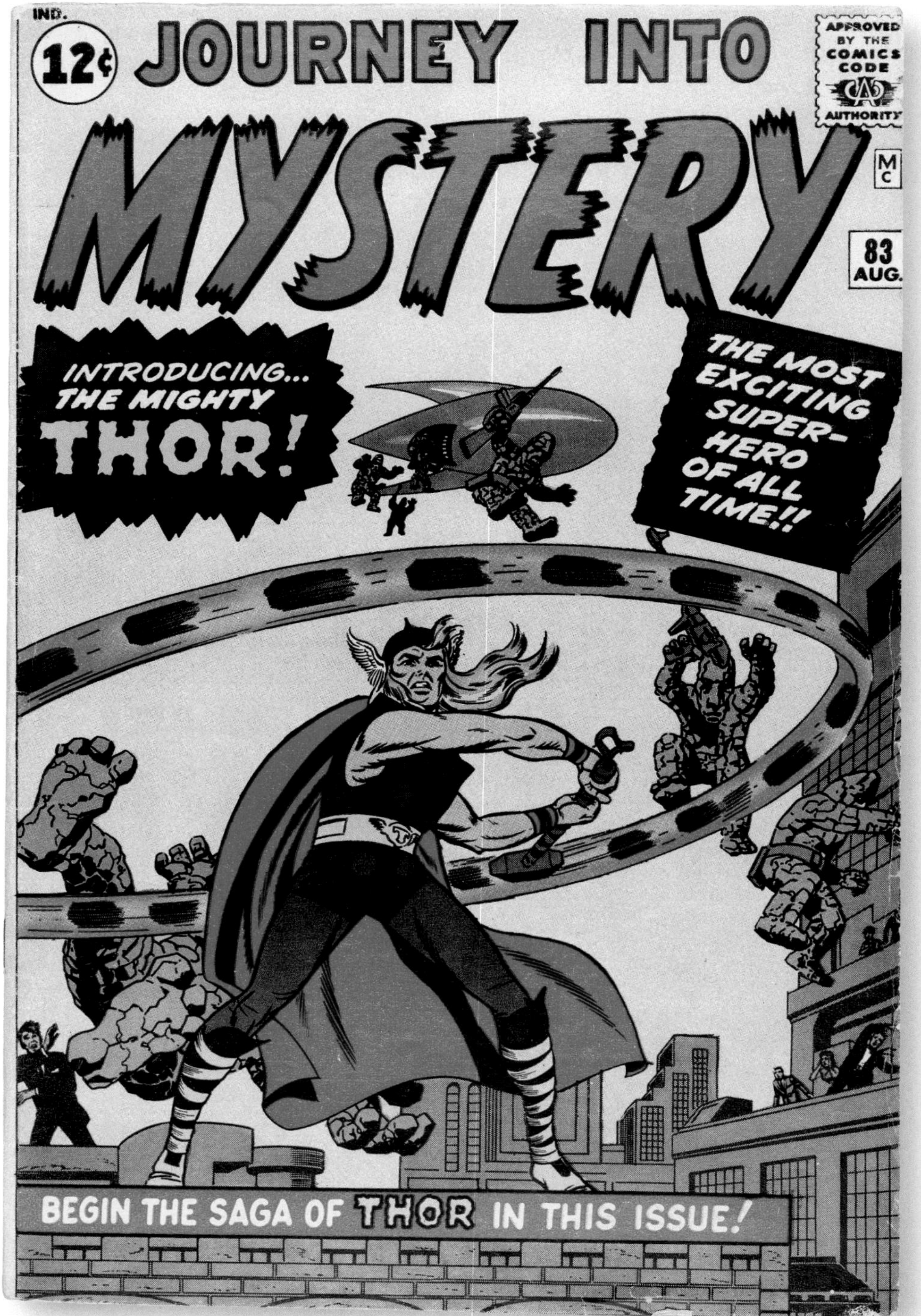
IND.
12¢
JOURNEY INTO
MYSTERY
APPROVED BY THE COMICS CODE AUTHORITY
MC
83
AUG.
INTRODUCING... THE MIGHTY THOR!
THE MOST EXCITING SUPER-HERO OF ALL TIME!!
BEGIN THE SAGA OF THOR IN THIS ISSUE!

standard elements of the super hero formula — big handsome guy with a blue-and-red costume, a billowing cape, tremendous strength, and (virtual) flight — and turn it into something new and exciting.

A week or two later, Kirby's cover for *Tales to Astonish* No. 35 (September 1962) portrayed a close-up of an ant (in effect, the issue's "giant monster") and a towering human gunman, confronting a costumed, insect-sized man in a silvery mask/helmet complete with antennae. "Return of the Ant-Man!" introduced a new super hero, but it was also a sequel to "The Man in the Ant Hill," the monster cover story of *TTA* No. 27 (January 1962). In the earlier of these two yarns, both from the Lee-Lieber-Kirby team, scientist Henry Pym had reduced himself to ant size and been promptly attacked by — aw, you guessed! He was no match physically for the insects, but slowed them down with brainpower — and judo. Befriended by one particular ant for no discernible reason, he managed to reach his enlarging potion and regained his normal size.

With that issue having sold better than the average Goodman monster comic, and with the publisher eager to transmute those titles into super hero vehicles, Pym in No. 35 dons an outfit whose headgear enables him to *control* ants; he marshals them to help fight Communist agents trying to steal his formula. The series' main strength is Kirby's forced

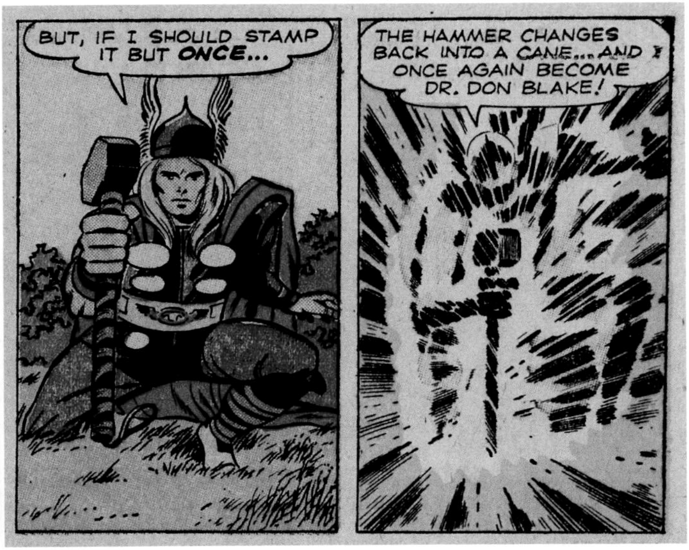
BUT, IF I SHOULD STAMP IT BUT ONCE...
THE HAMMER CHANGES BACK INTO A CANE... AND I ONCE AGAIN BECOME DR. DON BLAKE!

JOURNEY INTO MYSTERY No. 83

(Opposite) Cover; pencils, Jack Kirby; inks, Joe Sinnott. (Below) Interior, "The Stone Men From Saturn!"; plot, Stan Lee; script, Larry Lieber; pencils, Kirby; inks, Sinnott. August 1962. Dr. Don Blake turns from feeble human to powerful god by whacking his walking stick on the ground. The first of many physically impaired characters — later to include Daredevil and the X-Men's Professor X — Blake would soon stop fighting hoodlums and Cold War enemies and leave Earth for ever more epic Asgardian escapades.

IND.
APPROVED BY THE COMICS CODE AUTHORITY
Amazing
ADULT Fantasy
7
DEC.
10¢
5 FANTASTIC THRILLERS FOR THE MORE MATURE READER
"THE LAST MAN ON EARTH"
"THE ICY FINGERS OF FEAR"
"JOURNEY'S END"
"WHY WON'T THEY BELIEVE ME?"
"WITCH HUNT"
THE MAGAZINE THAT RESPECTS YOUR INTELLIGENCE.
Stan Lee + S. DITKO

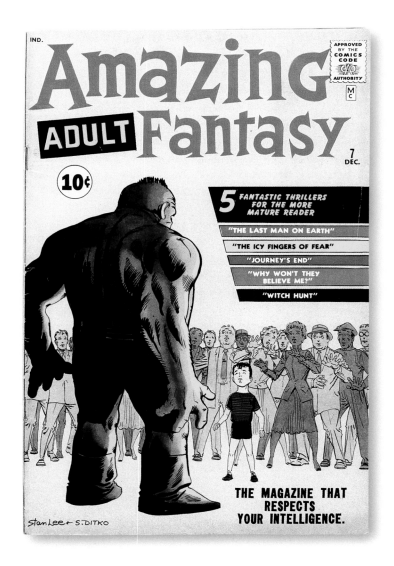

AMAZING ADULT FANTASY No. 7

(Above) Cover; pencils and inks, Steve Ditko; August 1961. Billed as "The Magazine That Respects Your Intelligence," *AAF* became a showcase for the Lee-Ditko team's popular O. Henry–style stories with a twist ending.

perspective, which plays fast and loose with the precise proportions of Ant-Man and his six-legged friends compared to normal-sized humans, but is always dramatic and engaging.

WITH GREAT POWER . . .

That summer's third new hero had actually premiered a bit earlier, at the same time as Thor. Lee enjoyed scripting the short fantasy stories with twist endings (in the vein of TV's hit *Twilight Zone*) on which he collaborated with artist/coplotter

Steve Ditko. So he had talked Goodman into changing the title and format of the unsuccessful *Amazing Adventures* — dropping giant monsters and Dr. Droom in favor of such offbeat tales — commencing with *Amazing Adult Fantasy* No. 7 (December 1961). It debuted only a week after *Fantastic Four* and was billed on covers as "The Magazine That Respects Your Intelligence."

AAF's eight issues are fondly remembered, but sales were disappointing. So with No. 15 the title was changed *again*, this time to just *Amazing Fantasy* — and it introduced a teenage super hero called Spider-Man. (As a teen himself in the 1930s, Stan Lee had been a fan of a pulp-magazine hero called the Spider, who, except for his name, had absolutely nothing spiderlike about him.)

From the get-go, Martin Goodman hated everything about the notion, telling Lee: "People don't like spiders!" and "Teenagers can only be sidekicks, not heroes!" Still, because *Fantastic Four* was off to a strong start, the publisher went along with the idea... for the moment.

Lee's first choice for penciler of the new series was Jack Kirby, just as he had been for *Fantastic Four*, *The Incredible Hulk*, Thor, and Ant-Man. He and Lee kicked around ideas, and the artist went home and began drawing. However, before Kirby had penciled more than a few pages, Lee decided that

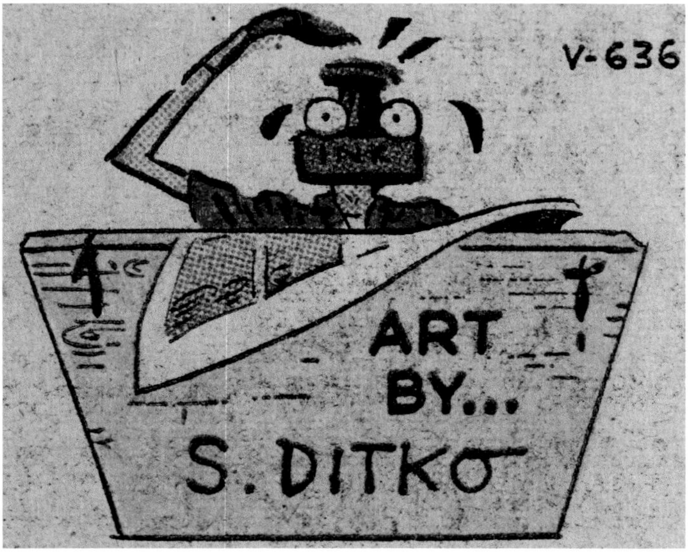
V-636
ART BY...
S. DITKO

OUT OF THE INKWELL

(Below) Interior, Amazing Adult Fantasy *No. 12; pencils and inks, Steve Ditko; May 1962.* Steve Ditko's early "self-portrait" reveals a surprisingly humorous side to the most private — and serious-minded — member of Marvel's burgeoning artistic roster. Ditko rarely agreed to interviews, once saying "It's not what I'm like that counts; it's what I did and how well it was done." Ditko did attend the first NY Comic Convention in 1964, though not as a guest, but a member of the audience.

. CRACKERS AND MILK! BLESS 'EM-- IF THEY ONLY KNEW!
NOW LET'S SEE-- A SPIDER NEEDS A WEB! THIS LITTLE DEVICE SHOULD JUST DO THE TRICK!
I'LL FASTEN ONE TO EACH ARM-- IT'LL OPERATE BY THE SLIGHTEST PRESSURE OF ANY FINGER!
I'LL NEED A NAME --WELL, GUESS SPIDERMAN IS AS GOOD AS ANY! LOOKS PRETTY GOOD, IF I DO SAY SO MYSELF!

AMAZING FANTASY No. 15

(Above) Interior, "Spider-Man"; script, Stan Lee; pencils and inks, Steve Ditko. (Opposite) Cover; pencils, Jack Kirby; inks, Ditko. August 1962. Science buff Peter Parker invents a device to shoot webbing and designs a unique costume—a productive afternoon to say the least! Unlike most artists, Ditko drew the teenage Parker (and his alter ego) with a less-than-heroic build.

the two of them simply weren't on the same wavelength regarding the way to portray a high schooler who gains arachnid powers. Lee wanted an awkward, unheroic youngster, treated more realistically than teenagers were usually portrayed in comics, but Kirby's work was full of his trademark dynamism and heroism. His Spider-Man costume, as visually recollected years later by Steve Ditko, was very simple and un-spiderly. Ditko inherited the series, and he and Lee pretty much started from the ground up.

Ditko turned out to have the perfect temperament and technique for handling a thin, socially awkward young man who acquires the proportionate powers of a spider. His design for the costume was brilliant, with the hero's features hidden behind a full-face cobweb-design mask.

Lee and Ditko's origin tale centers on Peter Parker, "Midtown High's only professional wallflower." He's Clark Kent, complete with glasses but no Superman abilities...raised by a loving aunt and uncle...a miserably insecure high schooler. At a science exhibit, he's bitten by a (momentarily) radioactive spider, in what amounts to a parody of super hero origins, and he gains "spider powers," including great strength and the ability to climb up a wall or cling to ceilings—as well as a "spider sense" that seems to have no parallel in nature.

Wearing a mask to protect his identity in case he messes up, he tries to use his new qualities for monetary gain, but shows

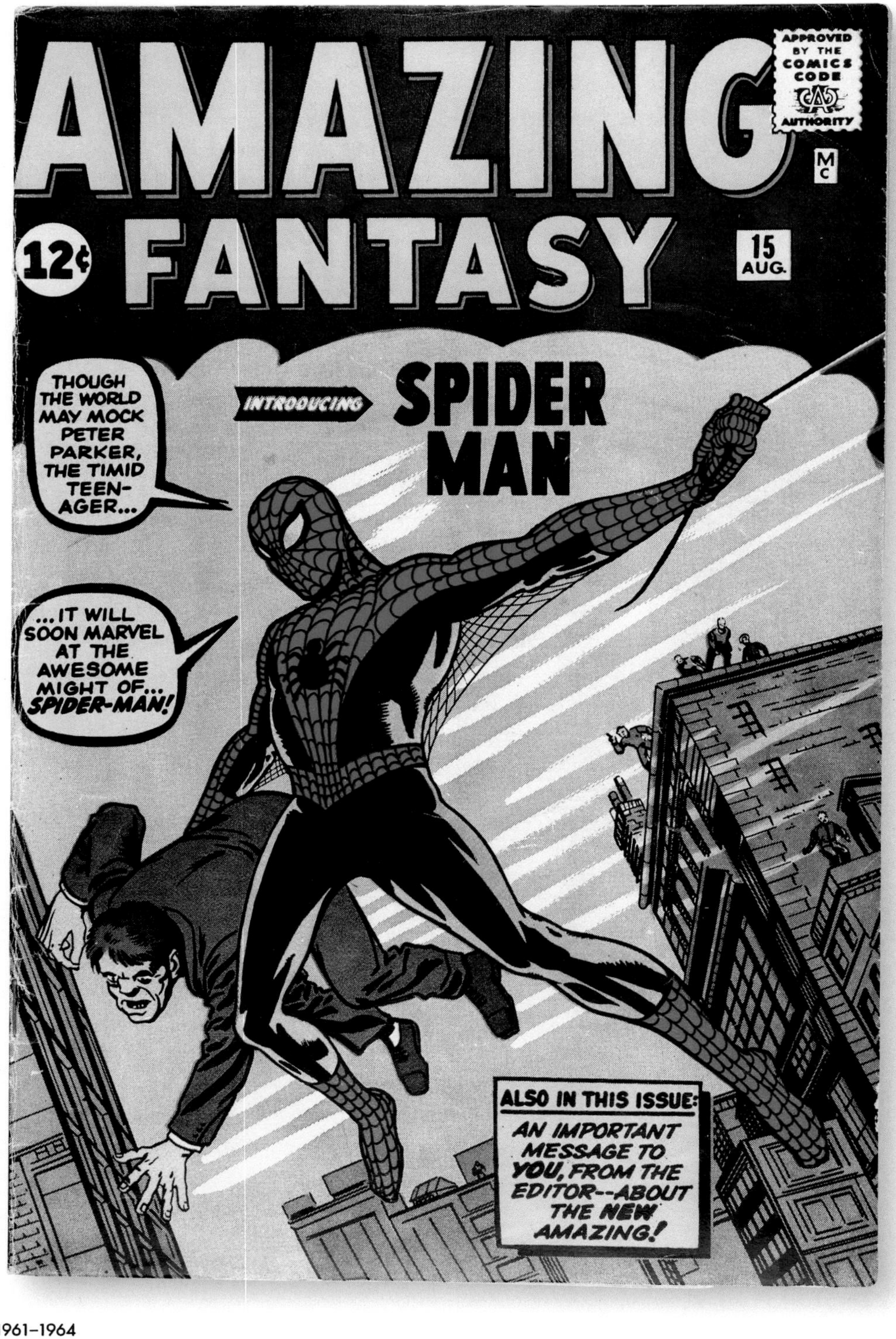
APPROVED BY THE COMICS CODE AUTHORITY
AMAZING
MC
12¢
FANTASY
15 AUG.
INTRODUCING
SPIDER MAN
THOUGH THE WORLD MAY MOCK PETER PARKER, THE TIMID TEEN-AGER...
...IT WILL SOON MARVEL AT THE AWESOME MIGHT OF... SPIDER-MAN!
ALSO IN THIS ISSUE:
AN IMPORTANT MESSAGE TO YOU, FROM THE EDITOR--ABOUT THE NEW AMAZING!

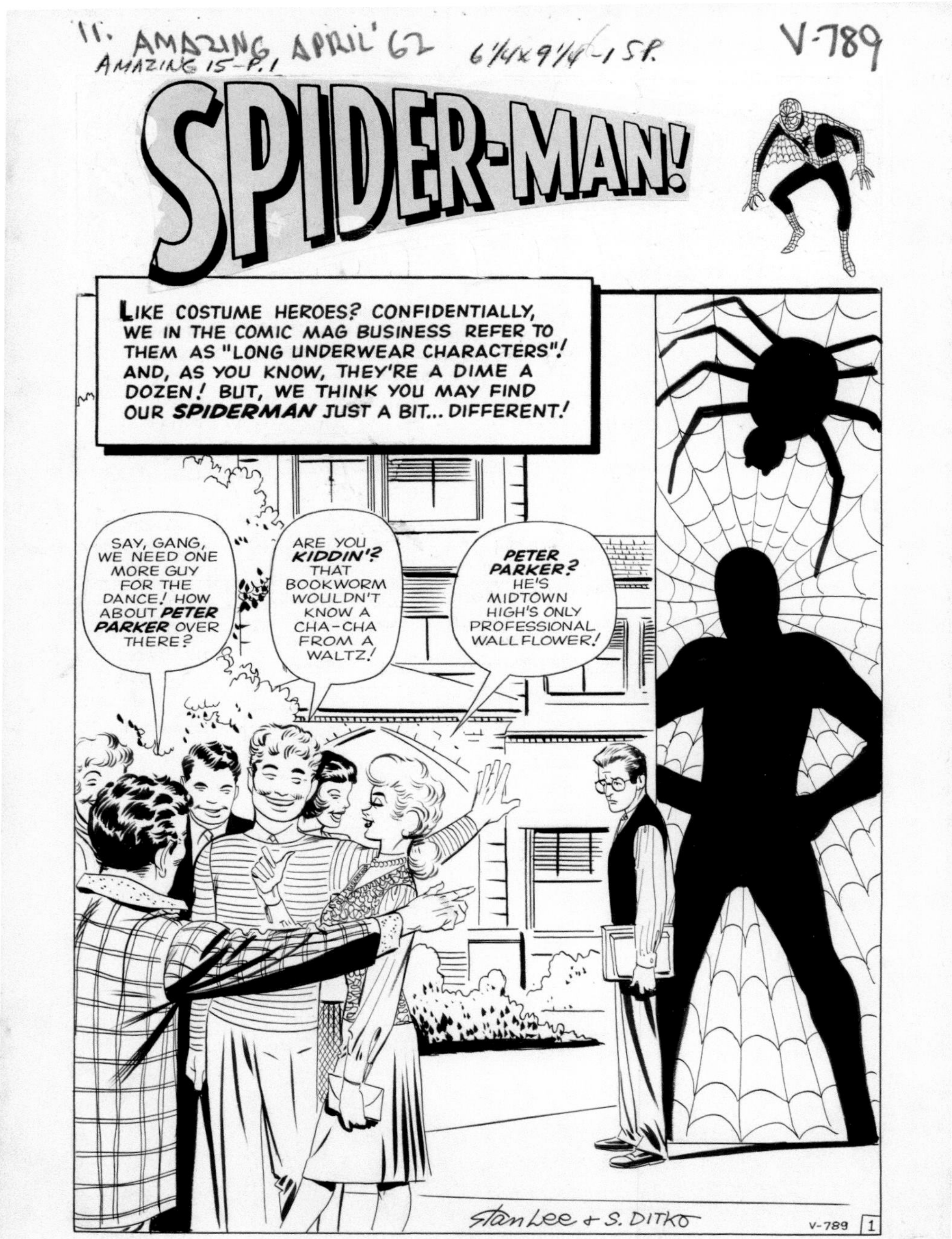

11. AMAZING, APRIL '62 6¼x9¼ -1 SP.
AMAZING 15-P.1
V-789
SPIDER-MAN!
LIKE COSTUME HEROES? CONFIDENTIALLY, WE IN THE COMIC MAG BUSINESS REFER TO THEM AS "LONG UNDERWEAR CHARACTERS"! AND, AS YOU KNOW, THEY'RE A DIME A DOZEN! BUT, WE THINK YOU MAY FIND OUR SPIDERMAN JUST A BIT... DIFFERENT!
SAY, GANG, WE NEED ONE MORE GUY FOR THE DANCE! HOW ABOUT PETER PARKER OVER THERE?
ARE YOU KIDDIN'? THAT BOOKWORM WOULDN'T KNOW A CHA-CHA FROM A WALTZ!
PETER PARKER? HE'S MIDTOWN HIGH'S ONLY PROFESSIONAL WALLFLOWER!
Stan Lee + S. DITKO
V-789 1
1.

no great aptitude for doing so. He sews himself a Spider-Man costume and develops wrist devices that shoot out sticky webbing to augment his arachnid qualities. When a thief flees past him at a TV studio where he's making an appearance, the disguised Peter sees no profit in stopping him. Only later, when that same criminal coincidentally kills his uncle, does the wall-crawling teenager realize that "With great power, there must also come—great responsibility!" It's easily one of the best origin stories in the history of comic books, all in 11 compact pages.

The issue's 1962 cover, ironically, would be penciled by Jack Kirby, who'd been taken off the series. (An earlier version of that cover, drawn by Ditko, was rejected. Ditko did, however, wind up inking the Kirby one. Go figure.)

Neither story nor cover, however, made any impression on Martin Goodman. Acting on sales figures for recent issues of *Amazing Adult Fantasy*, he canceled the rechristened title around the time Spider-Man's debut went on sale, with Lee and Ditko already at work on further episodes. But, as in the case of *Marvel Comics* No. 1 two decades earlier, the publisher had acted too hastily. When sales reports came in, *AAF* No. 15 had sold exceptionally well, so a comic book titled *Amazing Spider-Man* was quickly added to the schedule. Unlike Timely's other newly renovated mystery mags, which retained a fantasy backup tale in each issue, this one would focus entirely on the title hero. Chances are that the

NATIONAL TREASURE

(Opposite) Original art, Amazing Fantasy *No. 15, Steve Ditko, 1962.* In 2008 the original interior art for this issue—all 24 perfectly preserved pages, with pencil erasures and opaquing fluid still intact—was donated for posterity to the Library of Congress.

AMAZING FANTASY No. 15

(Below) Interior, "Spider-Man"; script, Stan Lee; pencils and inks, Steve Ditko; August 1962. The story that introduced Spider-Man to the world didn't have a happy ending. With those closing panels Stan Lee and Steve Ditko set the tone for a groundbreaking super hero series—perhaps the most haunting comic book origin of all time.

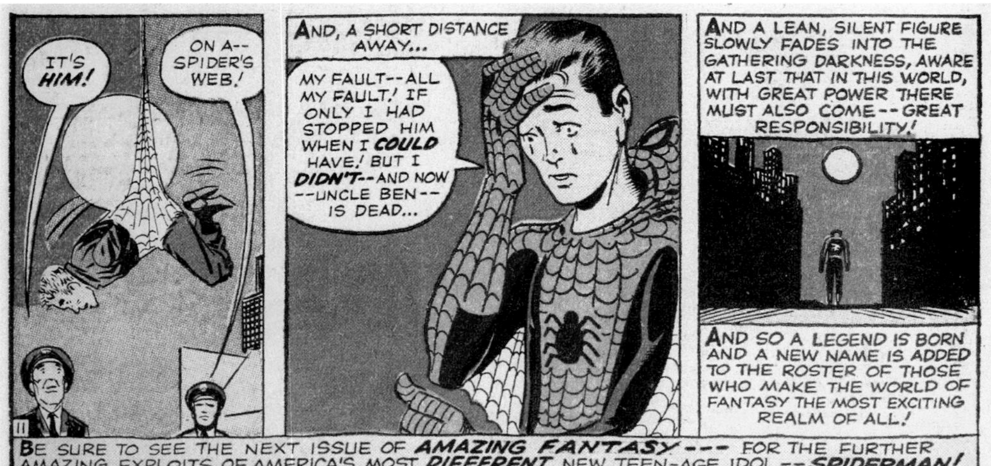

IT'S HIM!
ON A-- SPIDER'S WEB!
AND, A SHORT DISTANCE AWAY...
MY FAULT--ALL MY FAULT! IF ONLY I HAD STOPPED HIM WHEN I COULD HAVE! BUT I DIDN'T--AND NOW --UNCLE BEN-- IS DEAD...
AND A LEAN, SILENT FIGURE SLOWLY FADES INTO THE GATHERING DARKNESS, AWARE AT LAST THAT IN THIS WORLD, WITH GREAT POWER THERE MUST ALSO COME--GREAT RESPONSIBILITY!
AND SO A LEGEND IS BORN AND A NEW NAME IS ADDED TO THE ROSTER OF THOSE WHO MAKE THE WORLD OF FANTASY THE MOST EXCITING REALM OF ALL!
BE SURE TO SEE THE NEXT ISSUE OF AMAZING FANTASY--- FOR THE FURTHER AMAZING EXPLOITS OF AMERICA'S MOST DIFFERENT NEW TEEN-AGE IDOL--SPIDERMAN!

AMAZING SPIDER-MAN No. 2
(Right) Cover; pencils and inks, Steve Ditko; May 1963.

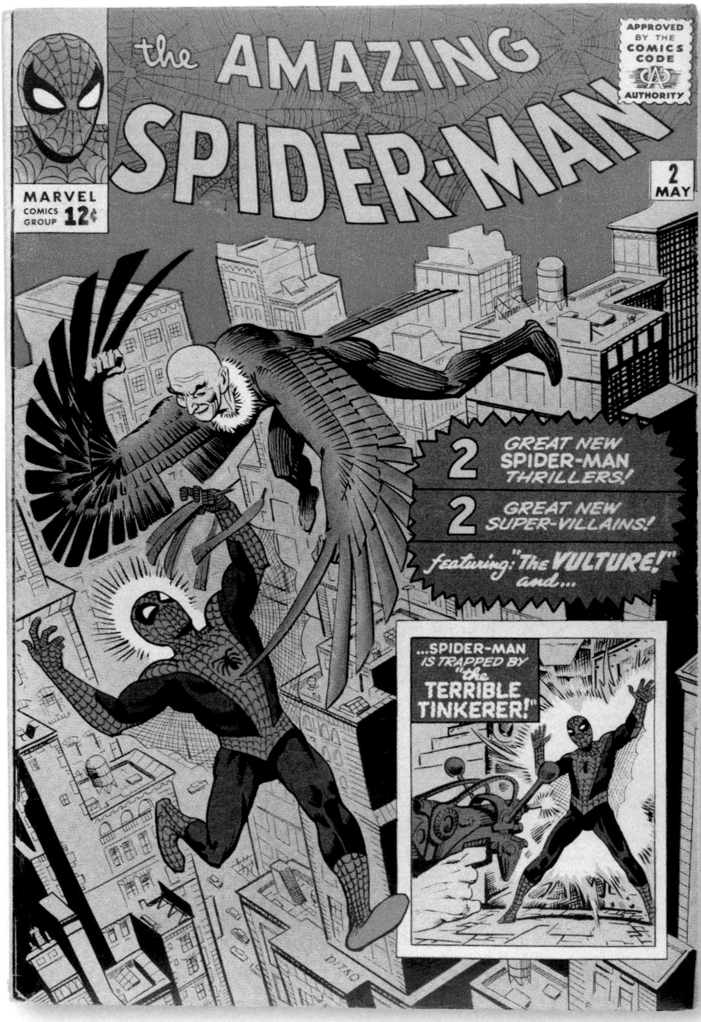
APPROVED BY THE COMICS CODE AUTHORITY
the AMAZING SPIDER-MAN
MARVEL COMICS GROUP 12¢
2 MAY
2 GREAT NEW SPIDER-MAN THRILLERS!
2 GREAT NEW SUPER-VILLAINS!
featuring: "The VULTURE!" and...
...SPIDER-MAN IS TRAPPED BY "the TERRIBLE TINKERER!"
DITKO

half-issue-length stories in its first two issues had originated for *Amazing Fantasy* No. 16 and beyond.

Over the next couple of years, Lee and Ditko introduced a formidable rogues' gallery of villains: the Vulture, Sandman, the Lizard, Electro, Dr. Octopus — "Doc Ock," for short. (How many previous super villains had nicknames that became nearly as well known as their "real" ones?)

But, most of all, it was the tension between the hero's two personas — Peter Parker and Spider-Man — that turned his title into an instant hit, which over the next three years would grow to become the company's second-best-selling comic, right behind *Fantastic Four*. The situation was, in many ways, the same basic dichotomy that had always existed between Clark Kent and Superman—but, in that instance, the real person was always the Man of Steel, with the "mild-mannered reporter" merely an identity he assumed to hide behind. However, in the Peter Parker / Spider-Man duality, Peter was the real thing: a high school nerd who lived with his aunt and had trouble getting a date or spare cash, but who, in his head-to-toe costume, became a wise-cracking, capable, seemingly self-assured *man*. Not a Spider-Boy…not even just a Spider…but a Spider-*Man*! No one in the stories ever suspected the gawky youthfulness of

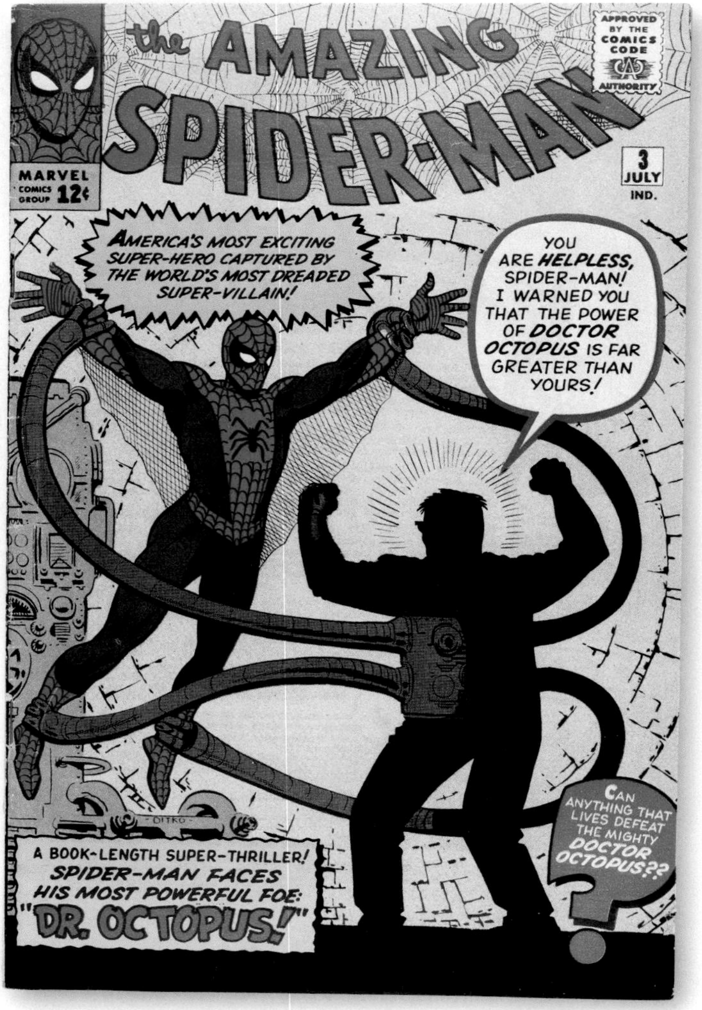
the AMAZING SPIDER-MAN
APPROVED BY THE COMICS CODE AUTHORITY
MARVEL COMICS GROUP 12¢
3 JULY IND.
AMERICA'S MOST EXCITING SUPER-HERO CAPTURED BY THE WORLD'S MOST DREADED SUPER-VILLAIN!
YOU ARE HELPLESS, SPIDER-MAN! I WARNED YOU THAT THE POWER OF DOCTOR OCTOPUS IS FAR GREATER THAN YOURS!
DITKO
A BOOK-LENGTH SUPER-THRILLER! SPIDER-MAN FACES HIS MOST POWERFUL FOE: "DR. OCTOPUS!"
CAN ANYTHING THAT LIVES DEFEAT THE MIGHTY DOCTOR OCTOPUS??

AMAZING SPIDER-MAN No. 3

(Left) Cover; pencils and inks, Steve Ditko; July 1963. Ditko designed an equally atypical rogues' gallery. The Vulture was older and gawky, and like the heavyset Doctor Octopus, he was a threat because of his scientific inventions. Full-length stories began with No. 3 and introduced Dr. Octavius, whose inventions gave him long, extended metal arms.

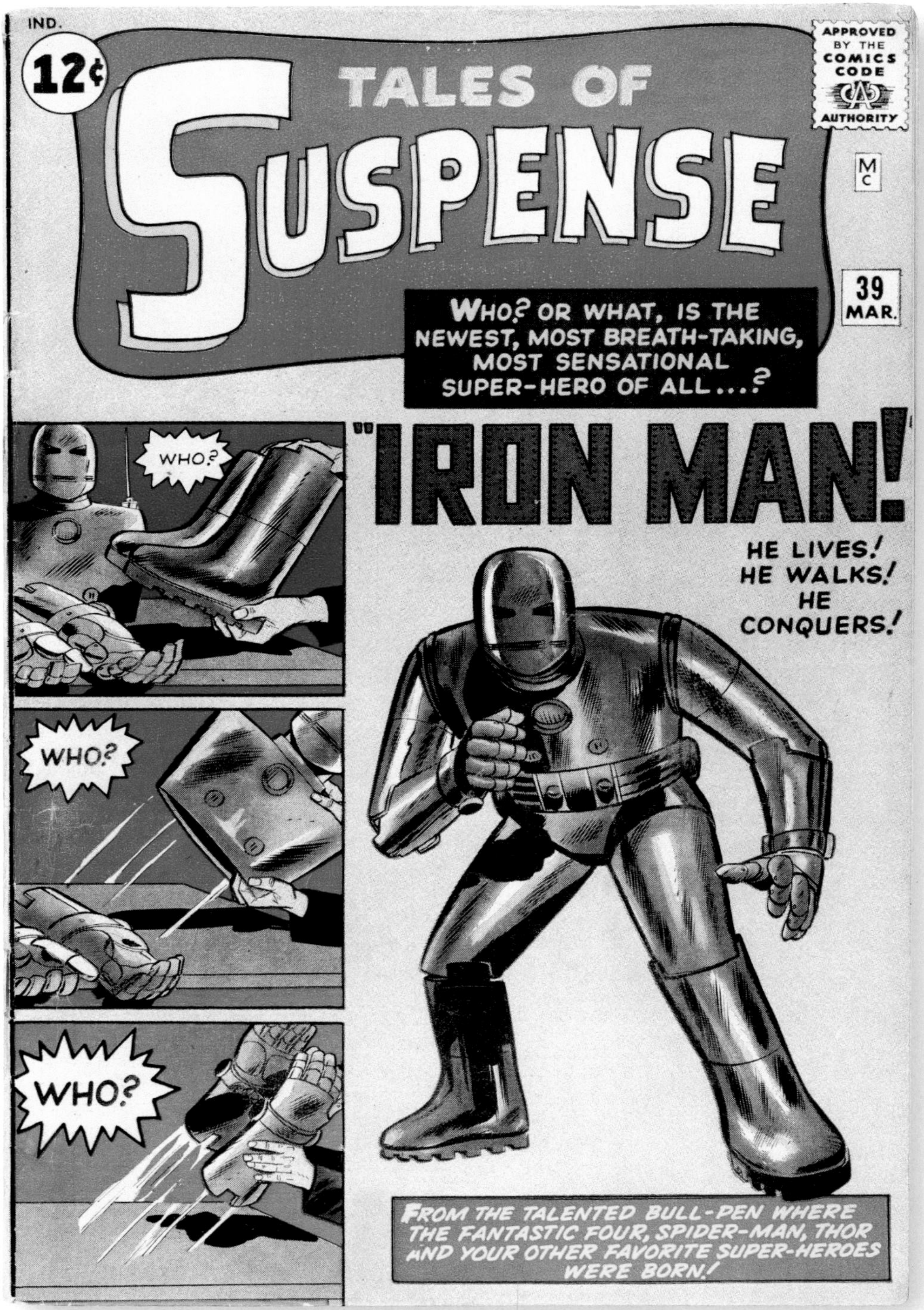
IND.
12¢
TALES OF SUSPENSE
APPROVED BY THE COMICS CODE AUTHORITY
MC
39 MAR.
WHO? OR WHAT, IS THE NEWEST, MOST BREATH-TAKING, MOST SENSATIONAL SUPER-HERO OF ALL...?
"IRON MAN!
HE LIVES! HE WALKS! HE CONQUERS!
WHO?
WHO?
WHO?
FROM THE TALENTED BULL-PEN WHERE THE FANTASTIC FOUR, SPIDER-MAN, THOR AND YOUR OTHER FAVORITE SUPER-HEROES WERE BORN!

ANTHONY STARK IS A MAN WHO LEADS THREE LIVES! HE IS RECOGNIZED THROUGHOUT THE WORLD AS A MECHANICAL GENIUS! AT A SCIENTIFIC CONFERENCE IN GENEVA...
MR. STARK, IN THE NAME OF OUR INTERNATIONAL SOCIETY OF PHYSICISTS, I AWARD YOU OUR ANNUAL MEDAL OF HONOR FOR YOUR OUTSTANDING CONTRIBUTION TO MICRO-TRANSISTOR RESEARCH!
THANK YOU, PROFESSOR!
THE "SECOND" ANTHONY STARK IS A SOPHISTICATED MILLIONAIRE PLAYBOY WHOM BEAUTIFUL WOMEN ADORE...
I'M MAD ABOUT YOU, TONY! WHY DON'T YOU COME TO MONTE CARLO MORE OFTEN SO I CAN SEE MORE OF YOU?
ER-- BUSINESS REASONS, MY SWEET! I'VE GOT INVESTMENTS ALL OVER THE WORLD THAT NEED LOOKING AFTER!

the face and figure beneath that webbed outfit. Ditko's genius in giving the hero a full face mask that revealed not one square inch of flesh—not even around his eyes!—made certain of that. As Stan Lee has always said, "Spider-Man could be *anybody* behind that mask!"

Three giant-monster comics down...two to go.

GROWING PAINS

Only weeks after the debuts of Thor, Spider-Man, and Ant-Man, *Strange Tales* No. 101 (October 1962) added a series starring the Human Torch, minus the rest of the FF. At first the art was by Kirby, who, getting busier and busier, soon handed it over to Dick Ayers, an industry veteran who had drawn the original Torch in 1954. Burgos's flamethrower had been a big solo star back in the 1940s, so maybe lightning would strike again.

And, by year's end, the fifth and final mystery/monster comic, *Tales of Suspense,* introduced its own super hero: Iron Man. Playboy industrialist Tony Stark, gravely wounded and captured by Communist guerrillas in war-torn Vietnam (where the U.S. commitment was still in its early stages), designs a metal chest plate to stay alive: something about magnetically keeping shrapnel from reaching his heart, or some such tech speak. Stark, a Howard Hughes–level inventor, constructs a cumbersome suit of metal armor; its tiny transistors turn

TALES OF SUSPENSE No. 39

(Opposite) Cover; pencils, Jack Kirby; inks, Don Heck; March 1963. The Cold War influences continue as millionaire munitions inventor Tony Stark travels to South Vietnam to test new weapons. Injured by the guerrillas, Stark creates a bulky gray costume to aid his damaged heart and protect himself from his enemies. As with the Hulk, the gray coloring lasts but a single issue.

TALES OF SUSPENSE No. 40

(Above) Interiors, "Iron Man versus Gargantus!"; plot, Stan Lee; script, Robert Bernstein; pencils, Jack Kirby; inks, Don Heck; April 1963.

...AND LO! THEY REFORM THEMSELVES INTO A GLASS CAGE... POROUS ENOUGH FOR AIR TO PASS THROUGH, BUT NOTHING ELSE!
LOOK! WHAT'S HAPPENED TO MANHATTAN?
MAYBE WE'VE BEEN UP IN THE AIR TOO LONG! WE'RE SEEING THINGS!
USAF

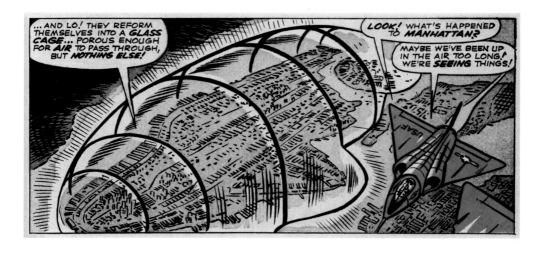

FANTASTIC FOUR No. 20
(Above) Interior, "The Mysterious Molecule Man!"; script, Stan Lee; pencils, Jack Kirby; inks, Dick Ayers; November 1963. Setting Marvel apart from the competition, New York City takes a central role as the home base for most of its heroes beginning with *Fantastic Four* No. 4. The heroes bumping into each other in a recognizable location made Lee's alternate world that much more real to fans.

him into the mechanically powered Iron Man, who defeats the Reds and returns to civilization. Lee and Lieber furnished the script and Don Heck the art, although the first cover (and, according to Heck, the iron suit's design) was by the ubiquitous Kirby. For the first year, Iron Man had the look of a big, clunky robot, formidable but off-putting even when his original gray armor was covered over with gold paint. Then, with a redesign by Steve Ditko, overnight the super hero gained a more streamlined armor of red and yellow, and it became a lot easier to remember that there was a *man* inside that metal suit.

With fewer non-hero yarns needed, several of Timely's freelance artists had to content themselves with inking pencils by Kirby, Heck, or Ditko. With *Fantastic Four* No. 6, Dick Ayers became the flagship title's regular inker, but he was also drawing the Human Torch over in *Strange Tales*. Sol Brodsky (who had inked *FF* No. 3–4), Paul Reinman, and George Roussos (moonlighting from DC as "George Bell") were other pencilers who found themselves adding ink to pencil illustrations by others.

One factor adding to the realism of Timely's various series was that most took place in the New York City area where Goodman, Lee, Kirby, and all the staff lived and worked. No Metropolis or Gotham City for *these* super heroes! The Fantastic Four rented space in the (made-up) Baxter Building in Manhattan... Spider-Man lived across the bridge in Forest Hills, Queens... Donald (Thor) Blake, Henry (Ant-Man) Pym, and Tony (Iron Man) Stark all spent most of their civilian time in the City That Never Sleeps or its immediate environs. The New York setting reinforced the feeling that all these characters existed in the same world, and might run into each other at any time. Even the Hulk soon journeyed from the southwestern desert to the Big Apple to battle the Fantastic Four.

By 1961, Independent News had slowly and quietly eased its earlier restriction on how many comics Timely could publish per month, from eight to at least 10 or even slightly more. By mid-1962, the now-monthly *Fantastic Four* joined the four monster-to-super-hero monthlies, a quartet of Westerns, six career-girl titles, *Love Romances*, and, by year's end, the

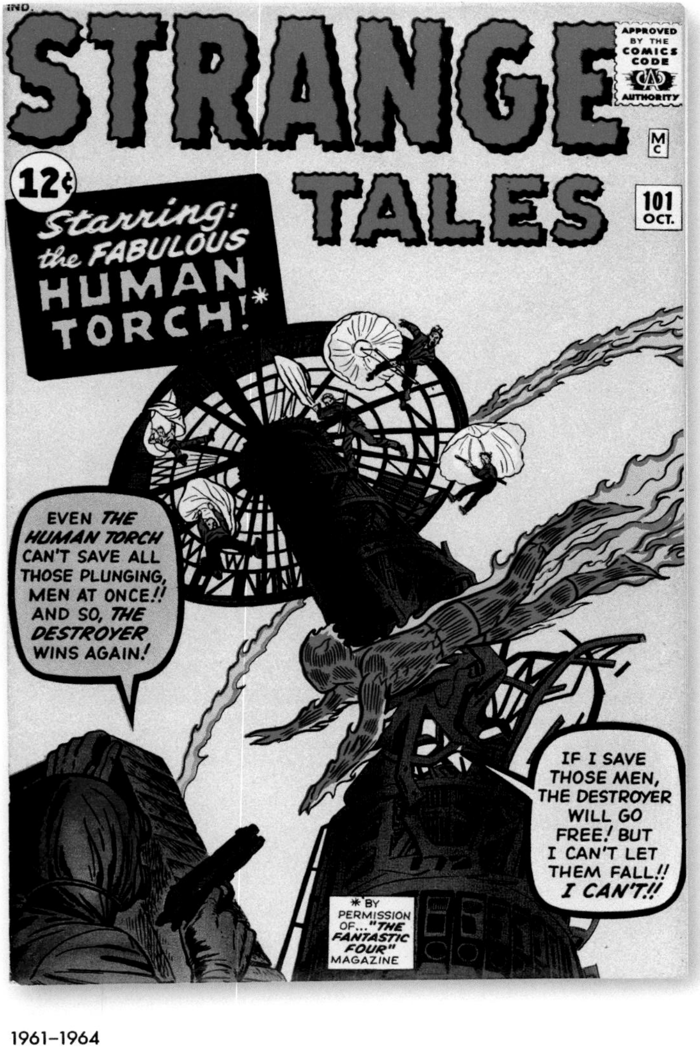
IND.
STRANGE
APPROVED BY THE COMICS CODE AUTHORITY
MC
12¢
TALES
101 OCT.
Starring: the FABULOUS HUMAN TORCH!*
EVEN THE HUMAN TORCH CAN'T SAVE ALL THOSE PLUNGING, MEN AT ONCE!! AND SO, THE DESTROYER WINS AGAIN!
IF I SAVE THOSE MEN, THE DESTROYER WILL GO FREE! BUT I CAN'T LET THEM FALL!! I CAN'T!!
*BY PERMISSION OF... "THE FANTASTIC FOUR" MAGAZINE

STRANGE TALES No. 101

(Left) Cover; pencils, Jack Kirby; inks, Dick Ayers; October 1962. The Human Torch received the first spin-off series in the Marvel Age, likely due to the success of the original Human Torch of the 1940s. Marvel did not revive *that* Torch (yet), although Johnny Storm could be considered an updated Toro the Flaming Kid.

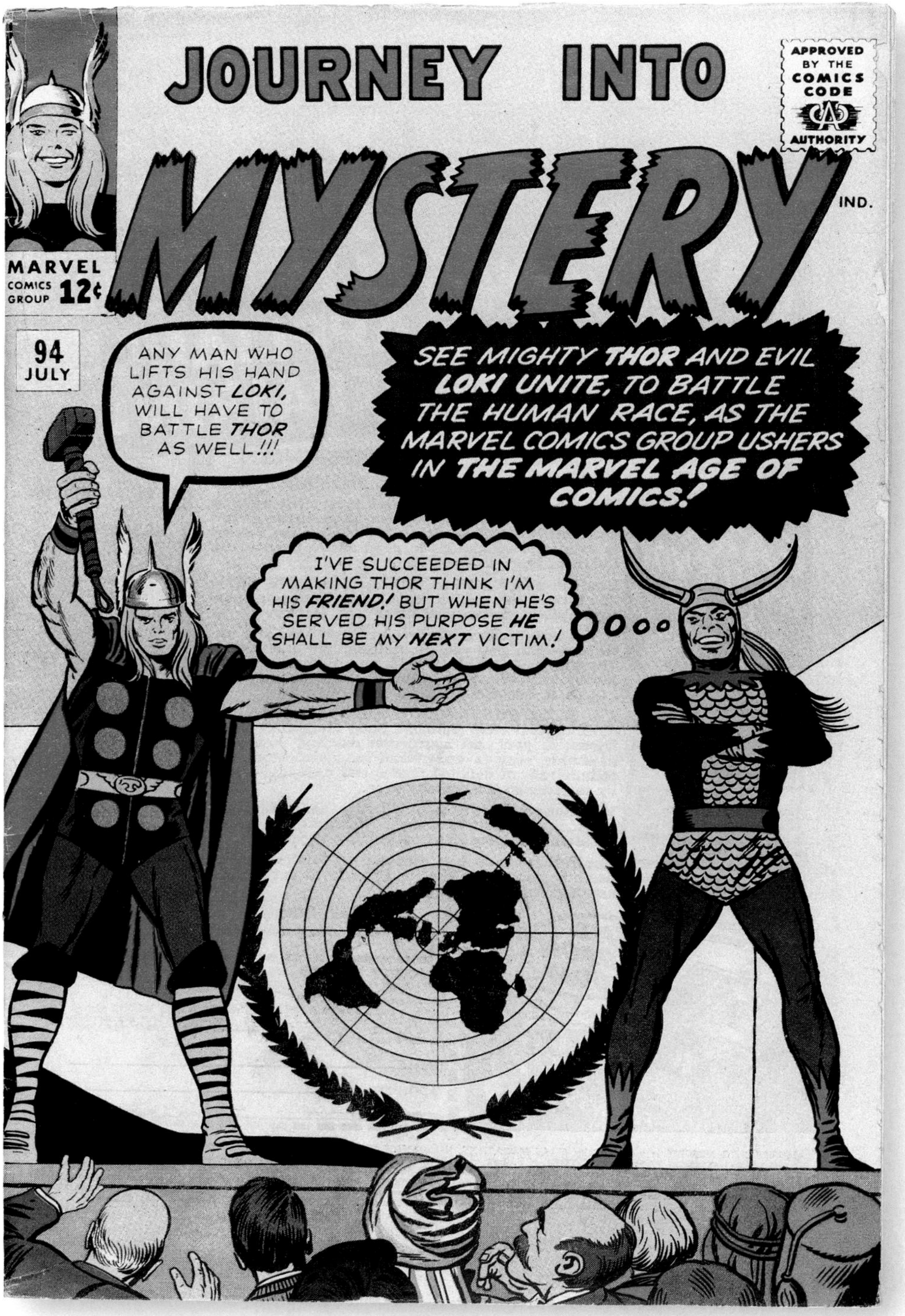
JOURNEY INTO MYSTERY
IND.
APPROVED BY THE COMICS CODE AUTHORITY
MARVEL COMICS GROUP 12¢
94 JULY
ANY MAN WHO LIFTS HIS HAND AGAINST LOKI, WILL HAVE TO BATTLE THOR AS WELL!!!
SEE MIGHTY THOR AND EVIL LOKI UNITE, TO BATTLE THE HUMAN RACE, AS THE MARVEL COMICS GROUP USHERS IN THE MARVEL AGE OF COMICS!
I'VE SUCCEEDED IN MAKING THOR THINK I'M HIS FRIEND! BUT WHEN HE'S SERVED HIS PURPOSE HE SHALL BE MY NEXT VICTIM!

bimonthly *Amazing Spider-Man* and *Incredible Hulk*—although the latter mag was then on its last green legs. Timely's in-house staff began to grow again. Most work was still done by freelancers, but Brooklynite Sol Brodsky, who'd been a staffer in the 1950s, was soon doing so much production work at the Madison Avenue offices—art corrections, paste-ups of logos and text pages, sending material to engraver and printer, and so on—that by 1963 he was appointed production manager.

Larry Lieber had been cowriting Human Torch and other super hero stories from Lee's outlines, but soon happily segued into writing and drawing backup fantasy stories and Westerns, especially *Rawhide Kid*.

Lee tried out various scribes on the super hero series. Superman cocreator Jerry Siegel scripted two Torch exploits as "Joe Carter." Others pseudonymous authors were 1950s *Crime Does Not Pay* writer Robert Bernstein ("R. Berns"), 1940s Super Rabbit creator Ernie Hart ("H.E. Huntley"), and 1950s Timely writer/artist/editor Don Rico ("N. Korok").

However, with the issues cover-dated November and December 1963, Lee took back the writing of the super hero

JOURNEY INTO MYSTERY No. 94

(Opposite) Cover; pencils, Jack Kirby; inks, Dick Ayers; July 1963. This is the first cover—though certainly not the last—to include the phrase "The Marvel Age of Comics."

FANTASTIC FOUR No. 10

(Below) Interior, "The Return of Dr. Doom!"; script, Stan Lee; pencils, Jack Kirby; inks, Dick Ayers; January 1963. In tried-and-true comic book fashion, Lee and Kirby playfully inject themselves into their own stories, something each of them had been doing since the 1940s.

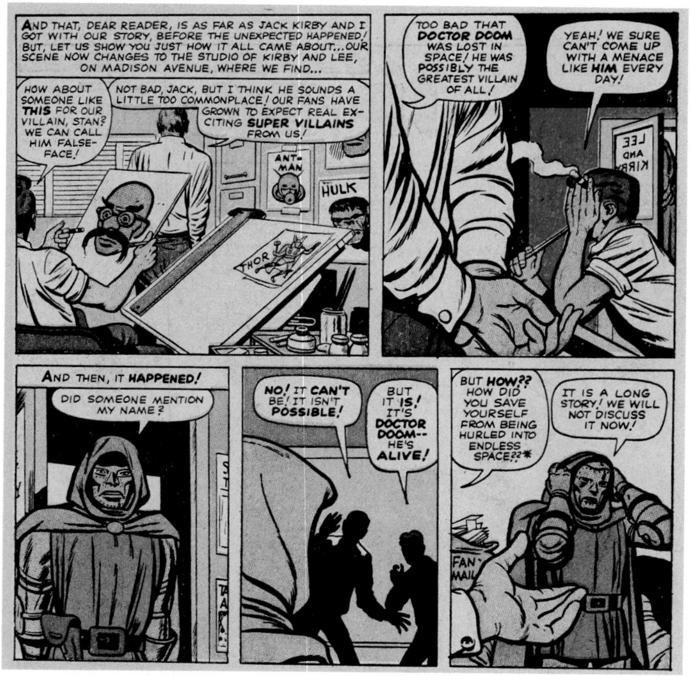
AND THAT, DEAR READER, IS AS FAR AS JACK KIRBY AND I GOT WITH OUR STORY, BEFORE THE UNEXPECTED HAPPENED! BUT, LET US SHOW YOU JUST HOW IT ALL CAME ABOUT... OUR SCENE NOW CHANGES TO THE STUDIO OF KIRBY AND LEE, ON MADISON AVENUE, WHERE WE FIND...
HOW ABOUT SOMEONE LIKE THIS FOR OUR VILLAIN, STAN? WE CAN CALL HIM FALSE-FACE!
NOT BAD, JACK, BUT I THINK HE SOUNDS A LITTLE TOO COMMONPLACE! OUR FANS HAVE GROWN TO EXPECT REAL EXCITING SUPER VILLAINS FROM US!
ANT-MAN
HULK
THOR
TOO BAD THAT DOCTOR DOOM WAS LOST IN SPACE! HE WAS POSSIBLY THE GREATEST VILLAIN OF ALL!
YEAH! WE SURE CAN'T COME UP WITH A MENACE LIKE HIM EVERY DAY!
LEE AND KIRBY
AND THEN, IT HAPPENED!
DID SOMEONE MENTION MY NAME?
NO! IT CAN'T BE! IT ISN'T POSSIBLE!
BUT IT IS! IT'S DOCTOR DOOM-- HE'S ALIVE!
BUT HOW?? HOW DID YOU SAVE YOURSELF FROM BEING HURLED INTO ENDLESS SPACE??*
IT IS A LONG STORY! WE WILL NOT DISCUSS IT NOW!
FAN MAIL

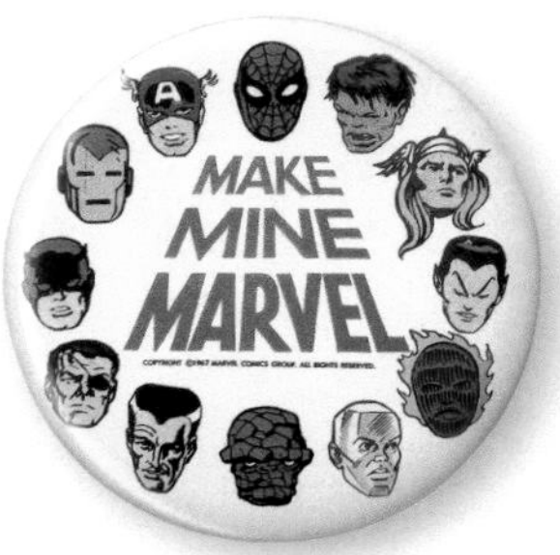
MAKE MINE MARVEL

MAKE MINE MARVEL
(Above) Promotional button, 1967. Stan Lee first used this phrase in Marvel's "Bullpen Bulletins" page in June/July 1965. It became so popular that it was used on a button for Marvel's first fan club, the Merry Marvel Marching Society (M.M.M.S.).

THE SAME INIMITABLE STYLE . . .
(Opposite) Sgt. Fury *house ad; cover; pencils, Jack Kirby; inks, Dick Ayers; lettering, Artie Simek; 1963.* Stan Lee put his promotional skills to work with bombastic slogans to encourage brand — and creative team — recognition.

books in one fell swoop. Talented storytellers like Kirby, Ditko, Heck, and Ayers were fully capable of drawing good, exciting stories from written (or even verbal) synopses, adding colorful incident and thrilling action, a fact that enabled Lee to handle the scripting of all nine hero series in a given month. Even considering the sizable contributions of artists who doubled as de facto coplotters, it was a *tour de force* rarely matched in terms of volume and sales success. To handle the load, Lee gradually convinced his publisher to let him come into the office three days a week, rather than five, and to write at home the other two days.

On the comics' letters pages (still more writing that he handled himself), Lee began referring to the artists, writers, letterers, and colorists as "the Bullpen," reviving the old 1940s–50s term. This, added to his and Kirby's fleeting cameos in the story in *Fantastic Four* No. 10 and his chatty prose style in text pages (leavened with such catchphrases as "'Nuff said!," "Face front!," and "Excelsior!") made it seem to fans as if Lee and his cohorts all sat around some Manhattan loft, having enormous fun as they turned out the comics. Readers came to feel they actually *knew* Lee and Kirby and Ditko and the rest. By now, the splash page credits had expanded to include inkers, even letterers, though not colorists.

By spring of 1963, Lee hired a full-time "corresponding secretary" — Flo Steinberg, a young and attractive one-time art history major, recently arrived from Boston. Sharing a small office with Brodsky, she handled the mail, interfaced with readers, and made certain that overeager fans didn't storm the offices in search of Lee and the Bullpen gang. When Lee christened her "Fabulous Flo" in Marvel's text pages, she soon became nearly as well known as the super heroes.

THE MARVEL AGE OF COMICS

His company was on a roll, and Martin Goodman knew it. Abruptly, the upper-left corners of some covers dated April 1963 and all with later dates sported the phrase "Marvel Comics." Though the name came (literally) out of left field to anyone who'd started reading comics after 1949, it gave the line an instant identity.

The word *Marvel* lent itself to alliterative epithets like "Make Mine Marvel!" *Journey into Mystery* No. 91 was

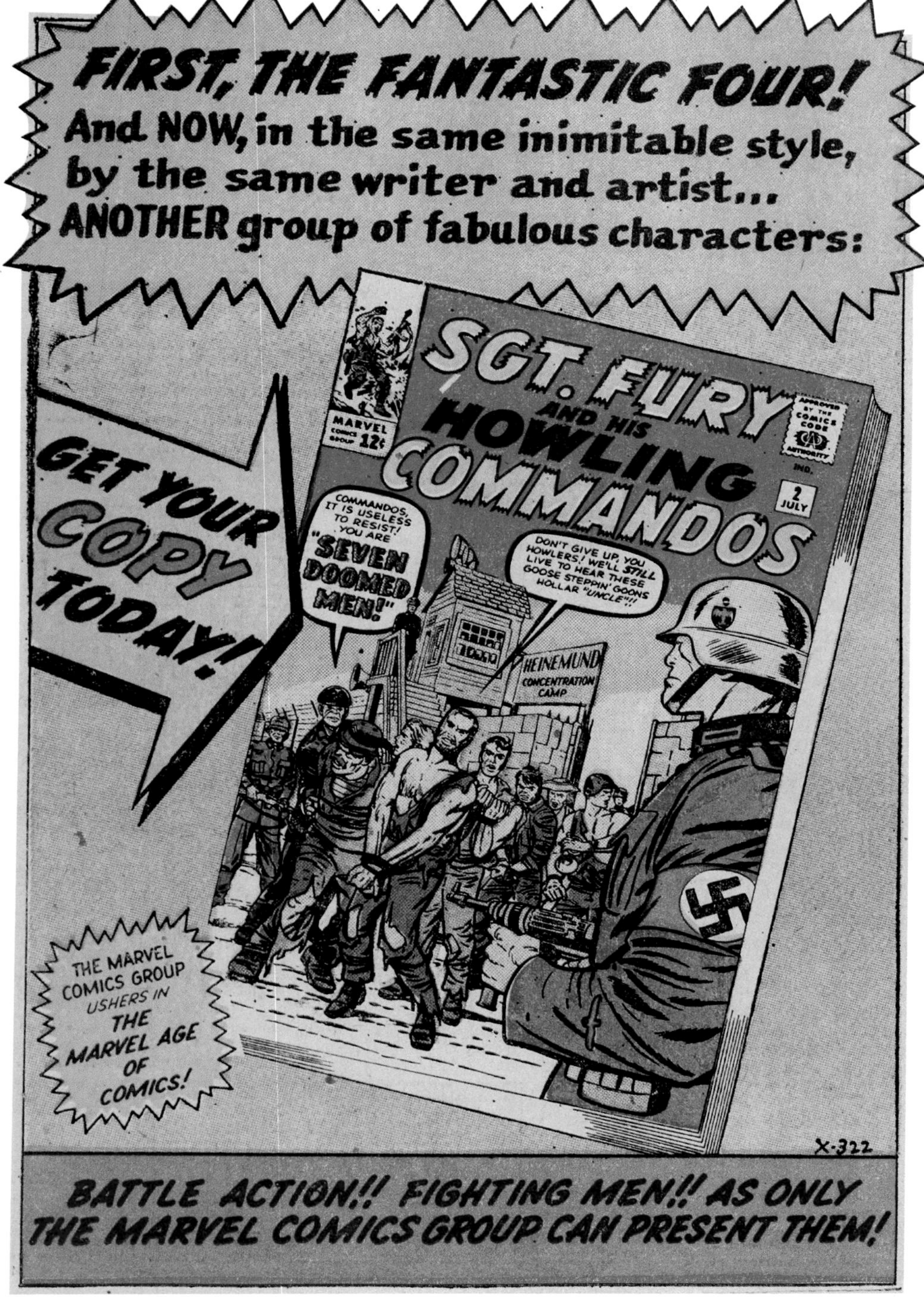
FIRST, THE FANTASTIC FOUR!
And NOW, in the same inimitable style, by the same writer and artist... ANOTHER group of fabulous characters:
SGT. FURY AND HIS HOWLING COMMANDOS
MARVEL COMICS GROUP 12¢
APPROVED BY THE COMICS CODE AUTHORITY
IND.
2 JULY
COMMANDOS, IT IS USELESS TO RESIST! YOU ARE "SEVEN DOOMED MEN!"
DON'T GIVE UP, YOU HOWLERS! WE'LL STILL LIVE TO HEAR THESE GOOSE STEPPIN' GOONS HOLLAR "UNCLE"!!
HEINEMUND CONCENTRATION CAMP
GET YOUR COPY TODAY!
THE MARVEL COMICS GROUP USHERS IN THE MARVEL AGE OF COMICS!
X-322
BATTLE ACTION!! FIGHTING MEN!! AS ONLY THE MARVEL COMICS GROUP CAN PRESENT THEM!

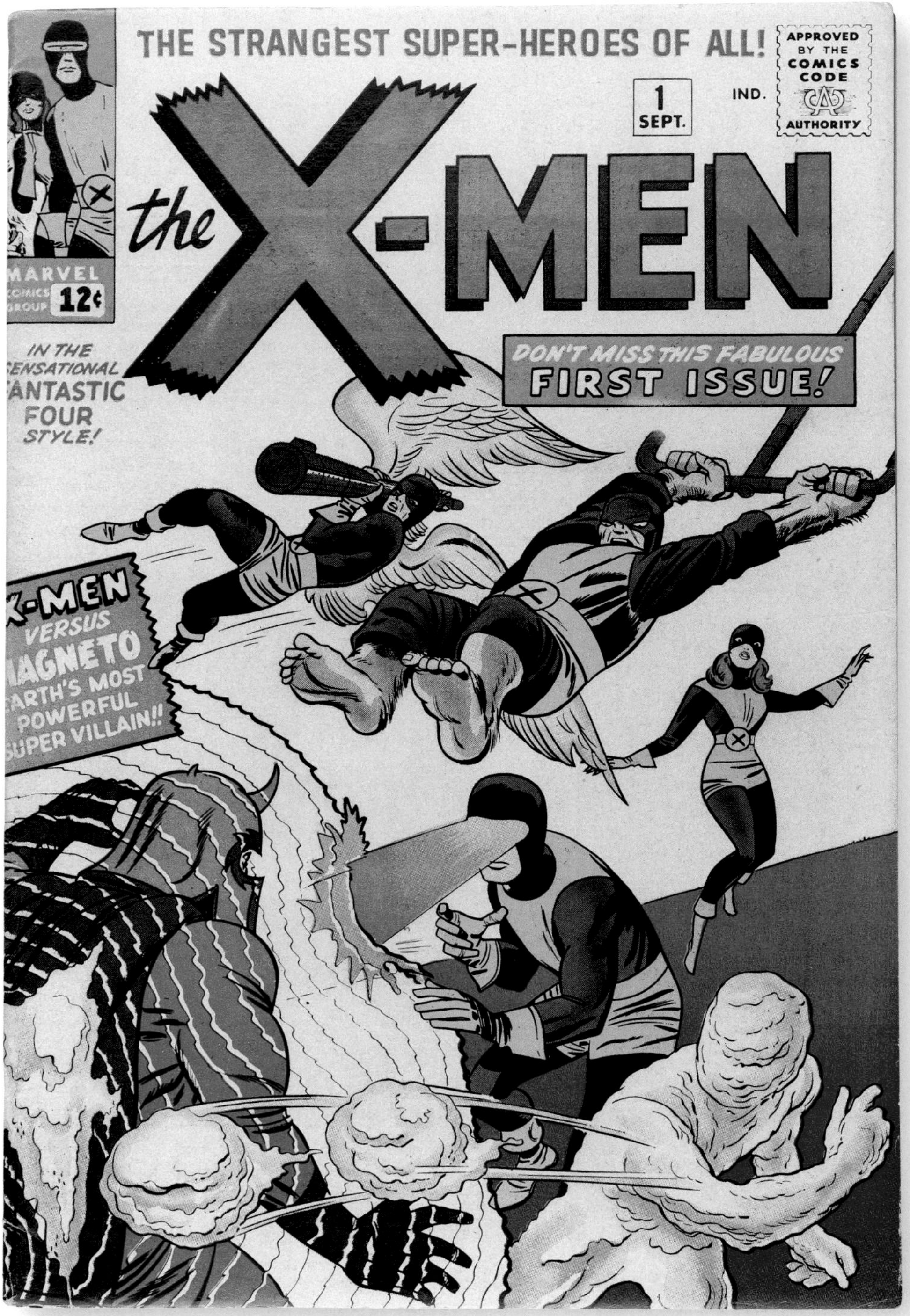
THE STRANGEST SUPER-HEROES OF ALL!
APPROVED BY THE COMICS CODE AUTHORITY
1 SEPT.
IND.
MARVEL COMICS GROUP 12¢
the X-MEN
IN THE SENSATIONAL FANTASTIC FOUR STYLE!
DON'T MISS THIS FABULOUS FIRST ISSUE!
X-MEN VERSUS MAGNETO EARTH'S MOST POWERFUL SUPER VILLAIN!!

the first adventure title whose cover carried the "Marvel Comics" imprimatur; three months later, a cover blurb on No. 94 proclaimed: "The Marvel Comics Group ushers in the Marvel Age of Comics!" Lee was making an audacious effort to differentiate the company's output from that of DC and Archie — not just in the more realistic, character-driven stories and in the more dynamic art, but in the way those stories, that art, were presented — and ballyhooed!

The first series to premiere under the new Marvel banner was, incongruously, a war mag. Lee, confident it was the new approach to characterization and action that was making the comics sell, made his publisher a wager that it would even sell a war comic, a genre whose last Timely specimen had been canceled in 1960. The result was *Sgt. Fury* — a series by Lee and Kirby set in World War II, usually called by its longer cover title, *Sgt. Fury and His Howling Commandos*. The seven Howlers battled the Nazis in escapist episodes seasoned with verbal sparring — with each other *and* with the enemy. Hoping to attract super hero fans, the cover proclaimed: "Another Big One from the Talented Team That Brings You the Famous 'Fantastic Four'!"

One intended and long-overdue milestone in the new series: one of the Commandos, Gabriel Jones, was an African American. Blacks had been all but invisible in American comics, except in menial roles, usually voicing primitive speech patterns. Actually, it turned out they were *still* invisible in 1963 to the firm that engraved the four-color plates from which *Sgt. Fury* No. 1 was printed. Even though Marvel colorist Stan Goldberg indicated gray skin tones for "Gabe," the plate-preparers decided that must be a mistake — so he wound up in print with the same pinkish flesh tones as the other Howlers. It took until issue No. 2, and a pointed written reminder to the engravers, before he was rendered correctly.

For *Strange Tales* No. 110 (July 1963), Steve Ditko conceived the five-page tale that introduced Dr. Strange, a costumed mystic; Lee provided dialogue and captions. A man is haunted in his dreams by a sinister, steed-riding entity whose very *name* is Nightmare, in a story much in the vein of the pair's *Amazing Adult Fantasy* shorts, but with a hero to bring everything to a resolution. Oddly, though, when Lee and Ditko gave Dr. Strange an origin in *Strange Tales* No. 115, it bore a distinct similarity

X-MEN No. 1

(Opposite) Cover; pencils, Jack Kirby; inks, Sol Brodsky; September 1963. Lee recounts telling Goodman, in an interview from the Archives of American Television: "'They're mutants. They were born that way. I don't have to explain any-thing.' [Goodman] said, 'Nobody is gonna know what a mutant is.'...So I said to him, 'Okay. Instead of *The Mutants* we're gonna call it *The X-Men*.' And he said, 'Yeah, that's a good name.' I thought to myself, 'If nobody is gonna know what a mutant is, how is anybody gonna know what an X-Man is?'"

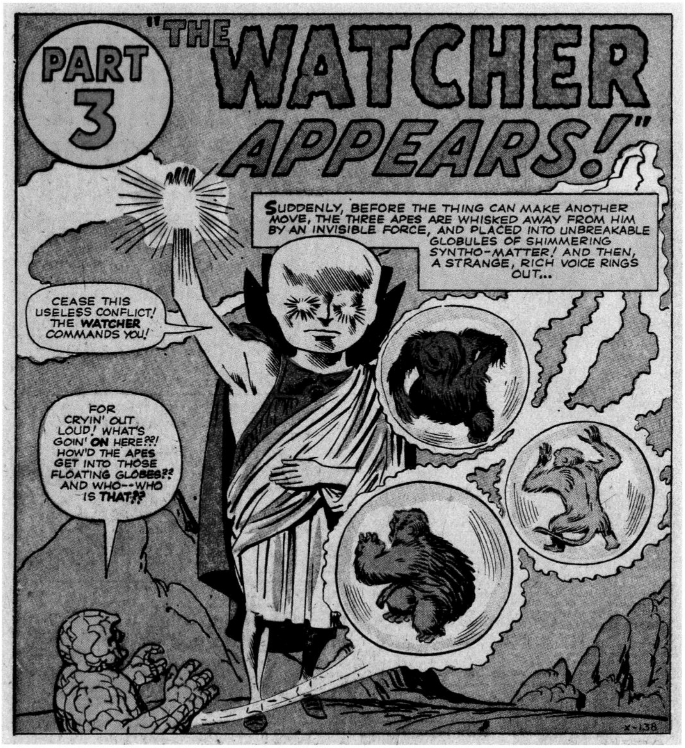
PART 3
"THE WATCHER APPEARS!"
SUDDENLY, BEFORE THE THING CAN MAKE ANOTHER MOVE, THE THREE APES ARE WHISKED AWAY FROM HIM BY AN INVISIBLE FORCE, AND PLACED INTO UNBREAKABLE GLOBULES OF SHIMMERING SYNTHO-MATTER! AND THEN, A STRANGE, RICH VOICE RINGS OUT...
CEASE THIS USELESS CONFLICT! THE WATCHER COMMANDS YOU!
FOR CRYIN' OUT LOUD! WHAT'S GOIN' ON HERE?!! HOW'D THE APES GET INTO THOSE FLOATING GLOBES?? AND WHO--WHO IS THAT??

FANTASTIC FOUR No. 13

(Above) Interior, "... Versus the Red Ghost and His Indescribable Super Apes!"; script, Stan Lee; pencils, Jack Kirby; inks, Steve Ditko; February 1963. The Watcher—an incredibly powerful alien who lives on the moon and tracks all Earthly events—has pledged not to interfere. Give him time....

to that of Lee and Kirby's Dr. Droom in *Amazing Adventures* No. 1, two years earlier. The once-haughty American surgeon Stephen Strange, his hands badly damaged in an auto accident, travels to the inscrutable East, hoping their skill can be restored by the mysterious Ancient One. Erelong, Strange becomes that aged mystic's new pupil and takes up a far nobler calling than high-society surgery: battling evil sorcery, including that of his mentor's treacherous earlier disciple, Baron Mordo.

Fantastic Four continued to innovate and to set the tone for the company. Lee and Kirby devoted half of one issue (No. 11) to "A Visit with the Fantastic Four": "the type of story most requested by your letters and postcards." On the dark side of the moon, in No. 13, the heroes encountered the Watcher, a toga-wearing giant whose cosmic duty was to observe the Earth without ever interfering. The summer of '63 saw the extra-size *Fantastic Four Annual* No. 1, in which the Sub-Mariner's undersea race invaded the surface world. It set a high mark for future specials and regular issues alike.

IN UNION THERE IS STRENGTH

That same summer witnessed the launching of not one but two additional super hero groups. Goodman wanted, in essence, "another *Fantastic Four* and another *Spider-Man*," so Lee worked with Kirby on a series about a group of teenage mutants...and with newly returned Sub-Mariner creator Bill Everett.

The mutants concept brought together five teens whose parents had been affected by radiation while working on the Manhattan Project during World War II: Cyclops, whose eyes shoot laser beams...the winged, flying Angel...the Beast,

FANTASTIC FOUR No. 11

(Below) Interior, "A Visit with the Fantastic Four!"; script, Stan Lee; pencils, Jack Kirby; inks, Dick Ayers; February 1963. This story acknowledges the growing fan support for the comic while giving new readers a chance to catch up.

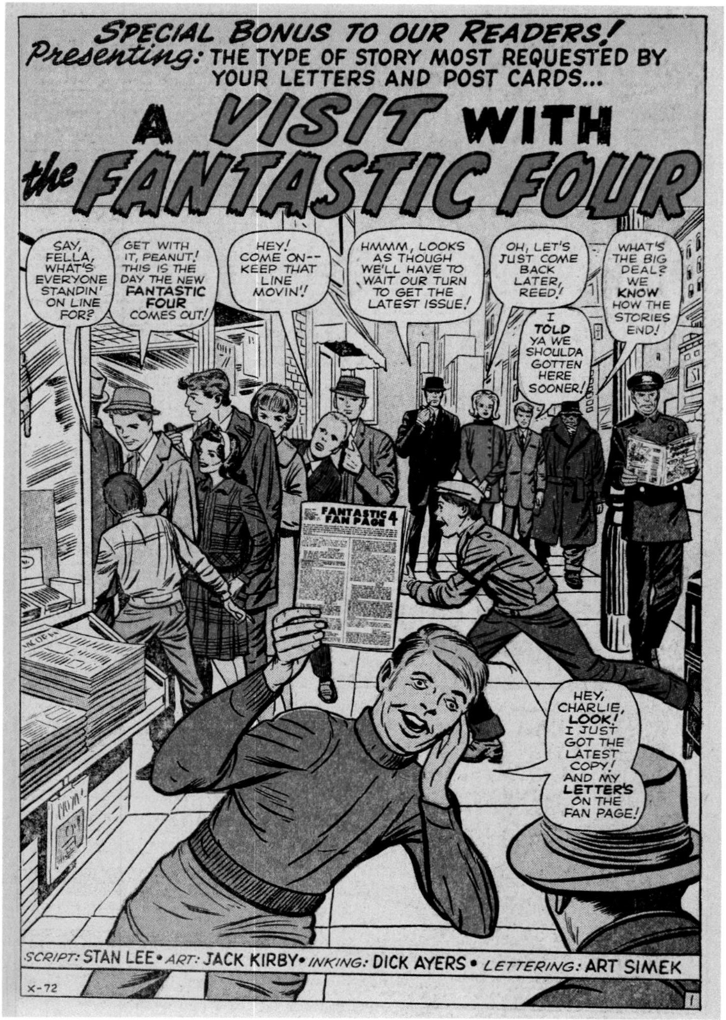

SPECIAL BONUS TO OUR READERS! Presenting: THE TYPE OF STORY MOST REQUESTED BY YOUR LETTERS AND POST CARDS...
A VISIT WITH the FANTASTIC FOUR
SAY, FELLA, WHAT'S EVERYONE STANDIN' ON LINE FOR?
GET WITH IT, PEANUT! THIS IS THE DAY THE NEW FANTASTIC FOUR COMES OUT!
HEY! COME ON-- KEEP THAT LINE MOVIN'!
HMMM, LOOKS AS THOUGH WE'LL HAVE TO WAIT OUR TURN TO GET THE LATEST ISSUE!
OH, LET'S JUST COME BACK LATER, REED!
I TOLD YA WE SHOULDA GOTTEN HERE SOONER!
WHAT'S THE BIG DEAL? WE KNOW HOW THE STORIES END!
FANTASTIC 4 FAN PAGE
HEY, CHARLIE, LOOK! I JUST GOT THE LATEST COPY! AND MY LETTER'S ON THE FAN PAGE!
SCRIPT: STAN LEE • ART: JACK KIRBY • INKING: DICK AYERS • LETTERING: ART SIMEK
X-72

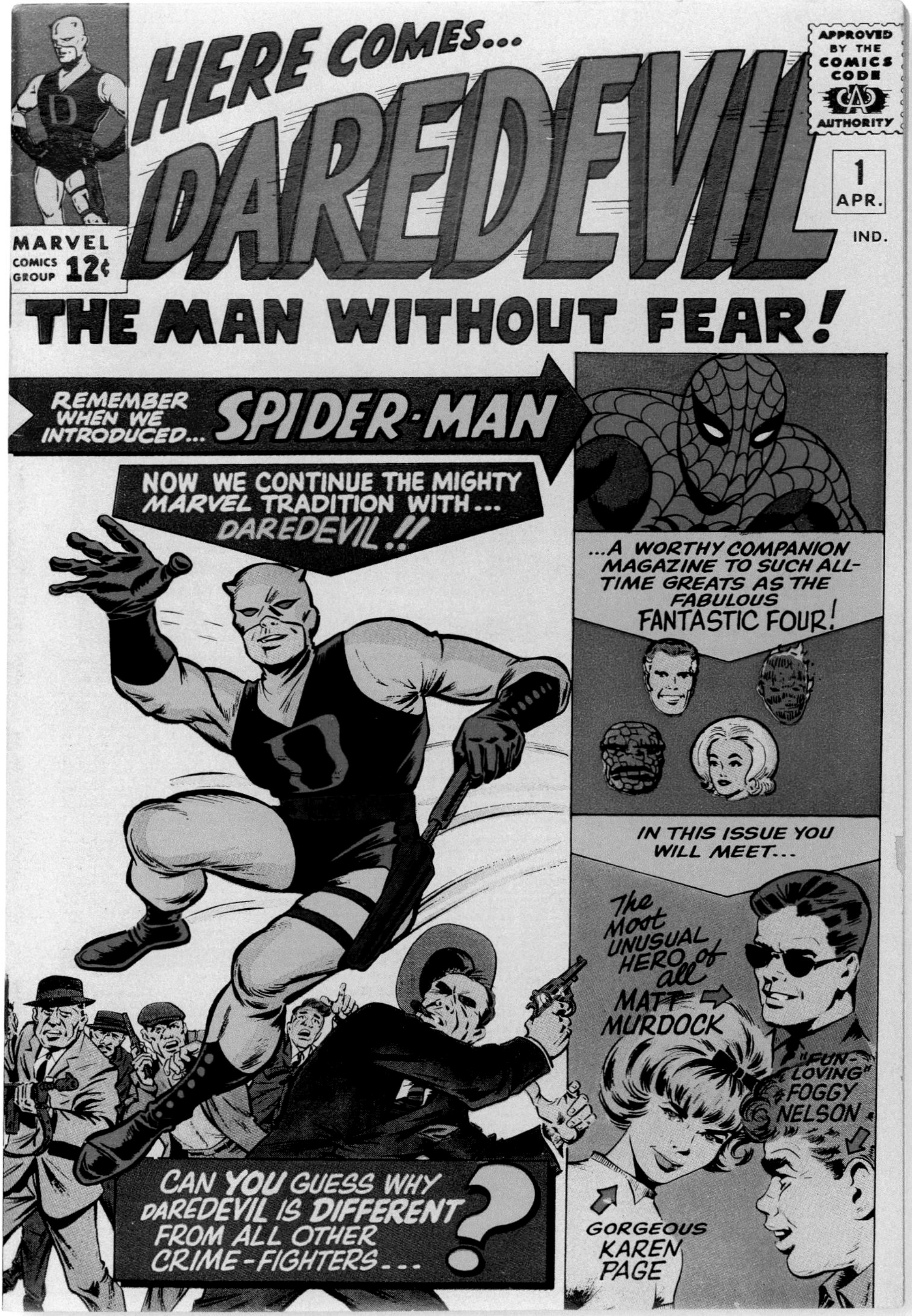
HERE COMES...
DAREDEVIL
APPROVED BY THE COMICS CODE AUTHORITY
1
APR.
IND.
MARVEL COMICS GROUP 12¢
THE MAN WITHOUT FEAR!
REMEMBER WHEN WE INTRODUCED... SPIDER-MAN
NOW WE CONTINUE THE MIGHTY MARVEL TRADITION WITH... DAREDEVIL!!
...A WORTHY COMPANION MAGAZINE TO SUCH ALL-TIME GREATS AS THE FABULOUS FANTASTIC FOUR!
IN THIS ISSUE YOU WILL MEET...
The Most UNUSUAL HERO of all MATT MURDOCK
"FUN-LOVING" FOGGY NELSON
GORGEOUS KAREN PAGE
CAN YOU GUESS WHY DAREDEVIL IS DIFFERENT FROM ALL OTHER CRIME-FIGHTERS...?

super-agile of hands and feet... Iceman, a frozen echo of the Human Torch...and Marvel Girl, with telekinetic powers. At a private school in New York's Westchester County, older mutant Professor X (short for "Xavier") trains them for protection both of and *from* normal humans, and to combat vicious specimens of their own *homo superior* species. The sinister Magneto, introduced in the first issue, would soon assemble a Brotherhood of Evil Mutants, including the super-fast Quicksilver and his sister, the Scarlet Witch, who wields a "hex power." Lee wanted to call this comic *The Mutants*, but Goodman feared younger readers wouldn't know what mutants were. He did approve his editor's second suggestion—*X-Men*, for their "extra" powers—so Lee tactfully neglected to point out that *nobody* would know what "X-Men" meant.

Meanwhile, Lee and Everett created Matt Murdock, a youth rendered blind in an accident (radiation, again!) that heightens his four remaining senses—and gives him a "radar sense" that functions as a substitute for sight. These abilities, plus years of gym workouts, turn him into a lithe acrobat who, in adulthood, dons a costume to avenge the murder of his prizefighter father. Kirby, called in for advice on developing the character, seemed to have devised the gimmick-laden billy club that became the equivalent of Spider-Man's web-shooters.

Everett, however, fell behind in drawing the debut issue because he was moonlighting from his day job in the greeting card industry. To buy time, the new title was replaced on the schedule by a last-minute substitute, a series for which Lee and

DAREDEVIL No. 1

(Opposite) Cover; pencils, Jack Kirby; inks, Bill Everett. (Below) Interior, "The Origin of Daredevil"; script, Stan Lee; pencils, Everett; inks, Everett, Steve Ditko, Sol Brodsky. April 1964. Matt Murdock joins the Marvel ranks of super heroes overcoming disabilities. After losing his vision, Murdock's other senses become super sensitive, allowing full awareness of the world around him.

"MY HEARING IS SO ACUTE, THAT I CAN TELL IF SOMEONE IS IN A ROOM WITH ME JUST BY HEARING THE HEARTBEAT!
"AND I NEVER FORGET AN ODOR ONCE I SMELL IT! I COULD RECOGNIZE ANY GIRL BY HER PERFUME... OR ANY MAN BY HIS HAIR TONIC..."
"EVEN MY FINGERS HAVE BECOME INCREDIBLY SENSITIVE! I CAN TELL HOW MANY BULLETS ARE IN A GUN JUST BY THE WEIGHT OF THE BARREL!"
"WHILE MY SENSE OF TASTE HAS BECOME SO HIGHLY DEVELOPED THAT I CAN TELL EXACTLY HOW MANY GRAINS OF SALT ARE ON A PIECE OF PRETZEL..."
PLUS!
10.

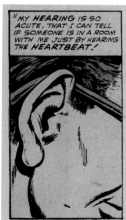

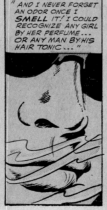

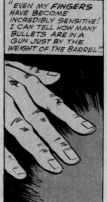

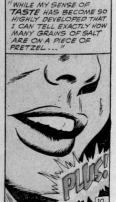

Kirby (surprise, surprise) threw together a *third* hero group, composed of all the Marvel stalwarts not already in teams except for loner Spider-Man and the brand-new Dr. Strange. *The Avengers* consisted of Thor, Iron Man, the (recently canceled) Hulk, and Ant-Man... plus the Wasp, the latter's minute but winged female partner, who'd just debuted in his *Tales to Astonish* feature. The first issues of *Avengers* and *X-Men* went on sale the very same day. (Because Ant-Man was so obviously lacking in power alongside Thor, Iron Man, and the Hulk, by issue No. 2 he had added 10 feet of stature and two letters to the

TALES TO ASTONISH No. 49

(Right) Cover; pencils and inks, Don Heck; November 1963. In response to disappointing sales, two letters were added to Ant-Man's name. Kirby, relieving Heck, made the change, which meant more work for the Living Eraser, who was tasked with transporting the new Giant-Man to Dimension Z.

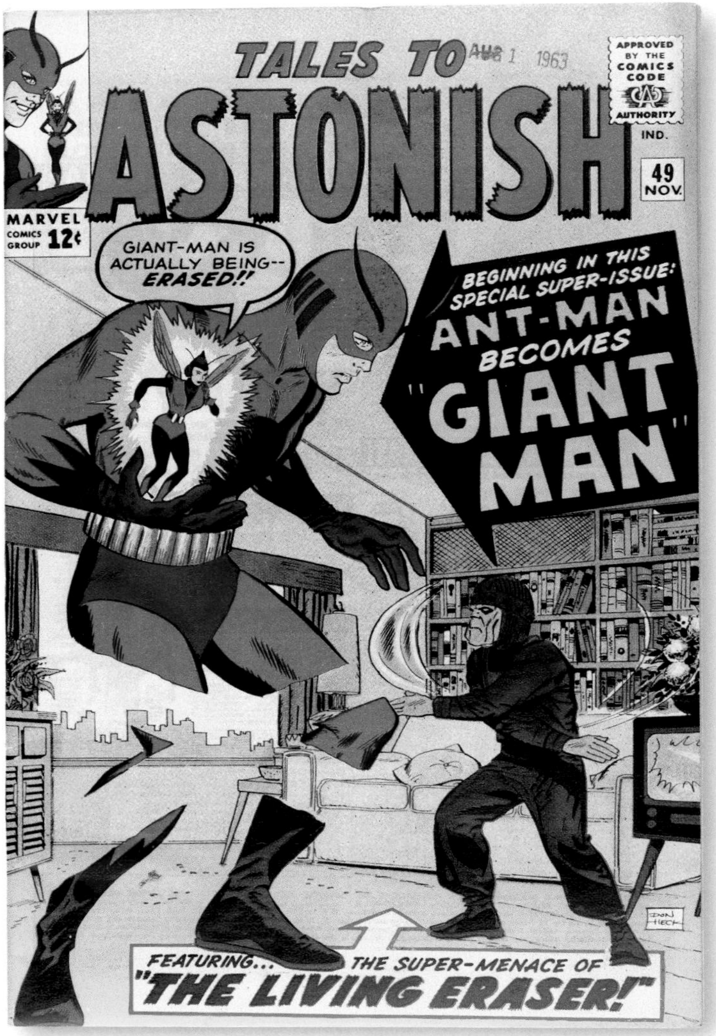
TALES TO ASTONISH
AUG 1 1963
APPROVED BY THE COMICS CODE AUTHORITY
IND.
49 NOV.
MARVEL COMICS GROUP 12¢
GIANT-MAN IS ACTUALLY BEING-- ERASED!!
BEGINNING IN THIS SPECIAL SUPER-ISSUE: ANT-MAN BECOMES "GIANT MAN"
DON HECK
FEATURING... THE SUPER-MENACE OF "THE LIVING ERASER!"

In the comic panel:

THE MIRACULOUS VAPOR ENGULFS THEM AND THEY SHRINK... SMALLER... SMALLER... SMALLER...

OH! IT FEELS SO--SO *WEIRD!*

YOU'LL GET USED TO IT, JANET!

TALES TO ASTONISH No. 44

(Left) Interior, "The Creature from Kosmos!"; plot, Stan Lee; script, Robert Bernstein; pencils, Jack Kirby; inks, Don Heck; June 1963. When her father is killed by an alien, Janet Van Dyne accepts Henry Pym's offer of partnership. Exposure to Pym particles gave her powers similar to his, and the ability to sprout wings. The Wasp added romantic interest and a dose of humor to the strip.

front of his name to become the far more substantial Giant-Man, though the Wasp was left at insect size.)

The delayed *Daredevil* No. 1 by Lee and Everett — with 11th-hour art assists from Ditko and Brodsky, and a cover/splash page penciled by Kirby — finally appeared with a cover date of April 1964. Matt Murdock becomes a brand-new lawyer in Manhattan, with a slightly buffoonish legal partner and a secretary who secretly loves Murdock. Daredevil's costume of red, yellow, and black was not one of Marvel's most visually impressive, but not to worry: It wouldn't be around long.

Neither *X-Men* nor *Daredevil* would, in the 1960s, become sales rivals to *FF* or *Spider-Man*, but they were solid titles. It would take them until the '70s and '80s, respectively, to reach their full potential under a new generation of Marvel creators.

Only weeks before *Daredevil* finally premiered, another super athlete erupted out of the past — when *The Avengers* No. 4 (March 1964) brought back Captain America, once the company's top-selling character. Ignoring all Cap stories published between 1945 and 1954, it was "revealed" that, somewhere in the "European Theater of Operations" near the end of World War II, he and his kid partner Bucky had boldly leaped onto an "explosive-filled drone plane" launched by a

THE AVENGERS No. 4
(Below) Interior, "Captain America Joins the Avengers!"; script, Stan Lee; pencils, Jack Kirby; inks, George Roussos; March 1964. Ignoring his brief resurgence in 1953, Stan and Jack revived Captain America, who had now been frozen in ice since the tail end of World War II.

THE AVENGERS No. 1
(Opposite) Cover; pencils, Jack Kirby; inks, Dick Ayers; September 1963. It took nearly two years for Marvel to introduce enough heroes to create a real counterpart to DC's Justice League.

saboteur. Seconds later, it had exploded, apparently killing Bucky outright and somehow plunging Cap into icy waters "off the coast of Newfoundland"—although attempts to reconcile the logistics of the sequence would short-circuit anybody's GPS.

By happy coincidence, nearly two decades later, the Avengers are cruising Arctic waters looking for the Hulk and/or Sub-Mariner, both of whom have recently gone rogue, when they spot Captain America floating in a cake of ice. He awakens with his athletic abilities and World War II gung-ho mentality intact, just in time to encounter the accelerating societal changes of the post–John F. Kennedy assassination 1960s. Despite being played as "a man out of his time" and tormented by guilt over Bucky's death, he quickly becomes a key Avenger.

With the premiere of *Daredevil* and the return of Captain America, the elements of Marvel's "first wave" of creation—a virtual tsunami, really—were finally all in place.

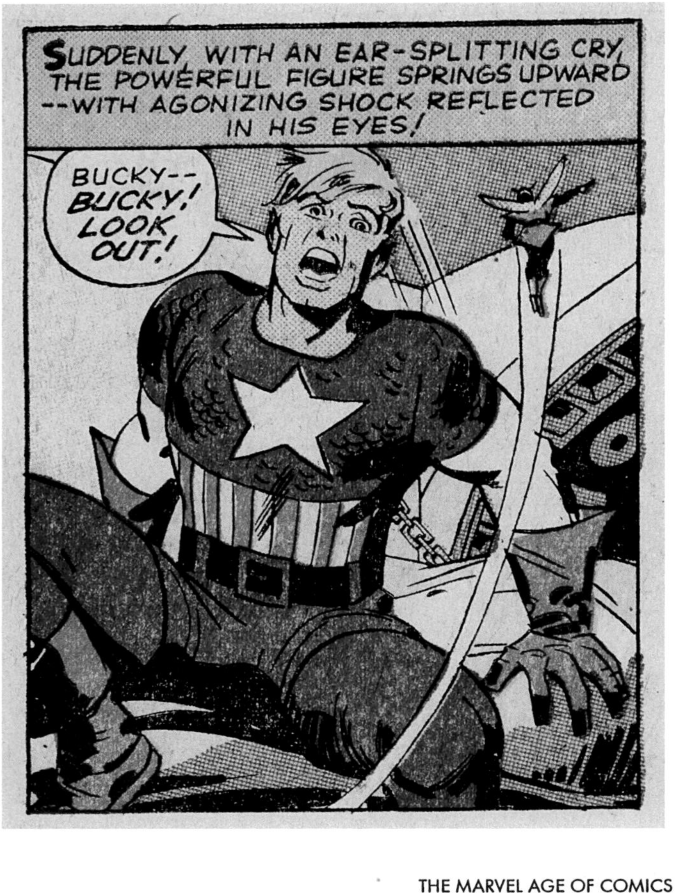
SUDDENLY, WITH AN EAR-SPLITTING CRY, THE POWERFUL FIGURE SPRINGS UPWARD --WITH AGONIZING SHOCK REFLECTED IN HIS EYES!
BUCKY-- BUCKY! LOOK OUT!

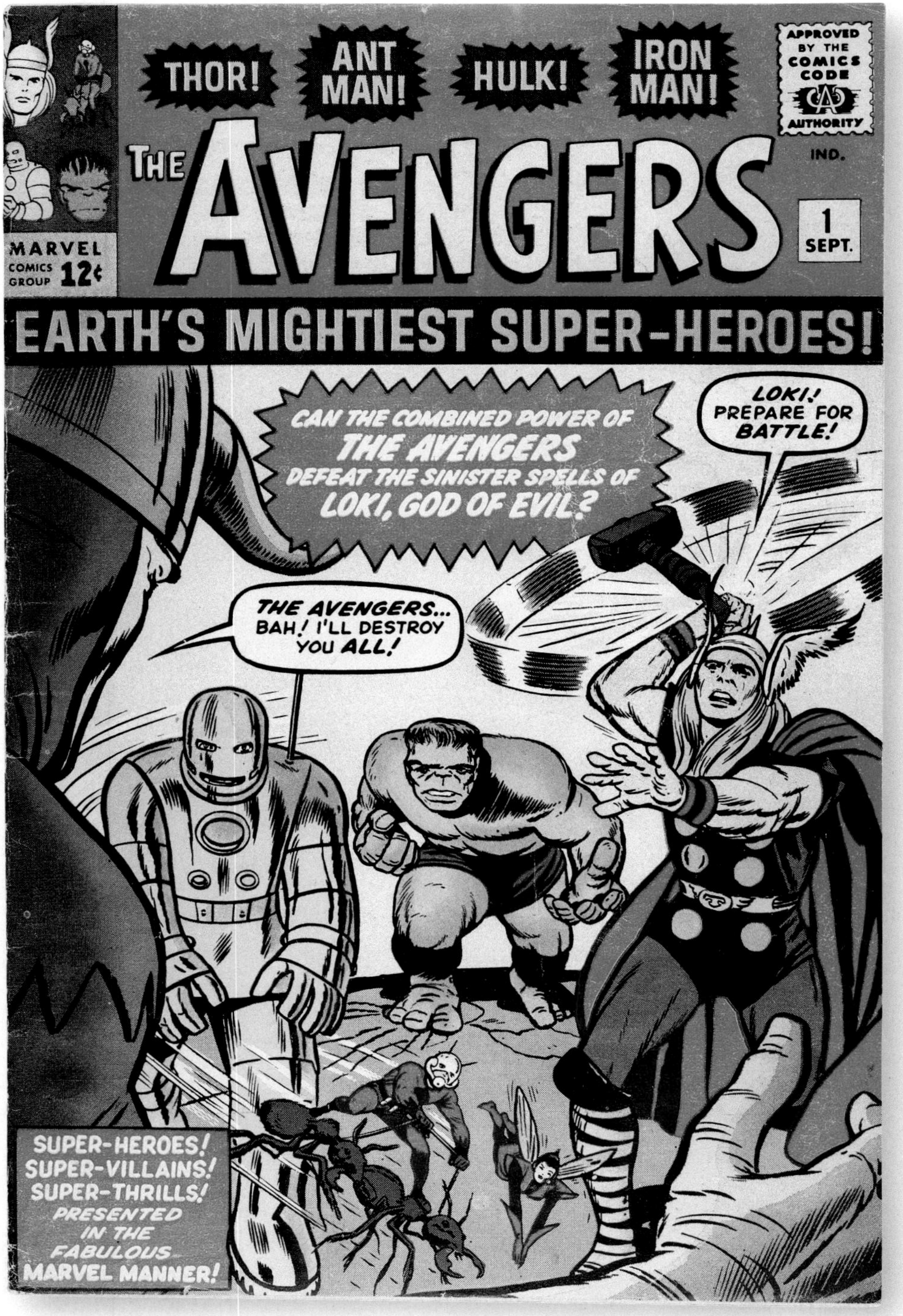
THOR!
ANT MAN!
HULK!
IRON MAN!
APPROVED BY THE COMICS CODE AUTHORITY
THE AVENGERS
IND.
MARVEL COMICS GROUP 12¢
1 SEPT.
EARTH'S MIGHTIEST SUPER-HEROES!
CAN THE COMBINED POWER OF THE AVENGERS DEFEAT THE SINISTER SPELLS OF LOKI, GOD OF EVIL?
LOKI! PREPARE FOR BATTLE!
THE AVENGERS... BAH! I'LL DESTROY YOU ALL!
SUPER-HEROES! SUPER-VILLAINS! SUPER-THRILLS! PRESENTED IN THE FABULOUS MARVEL MANNER!

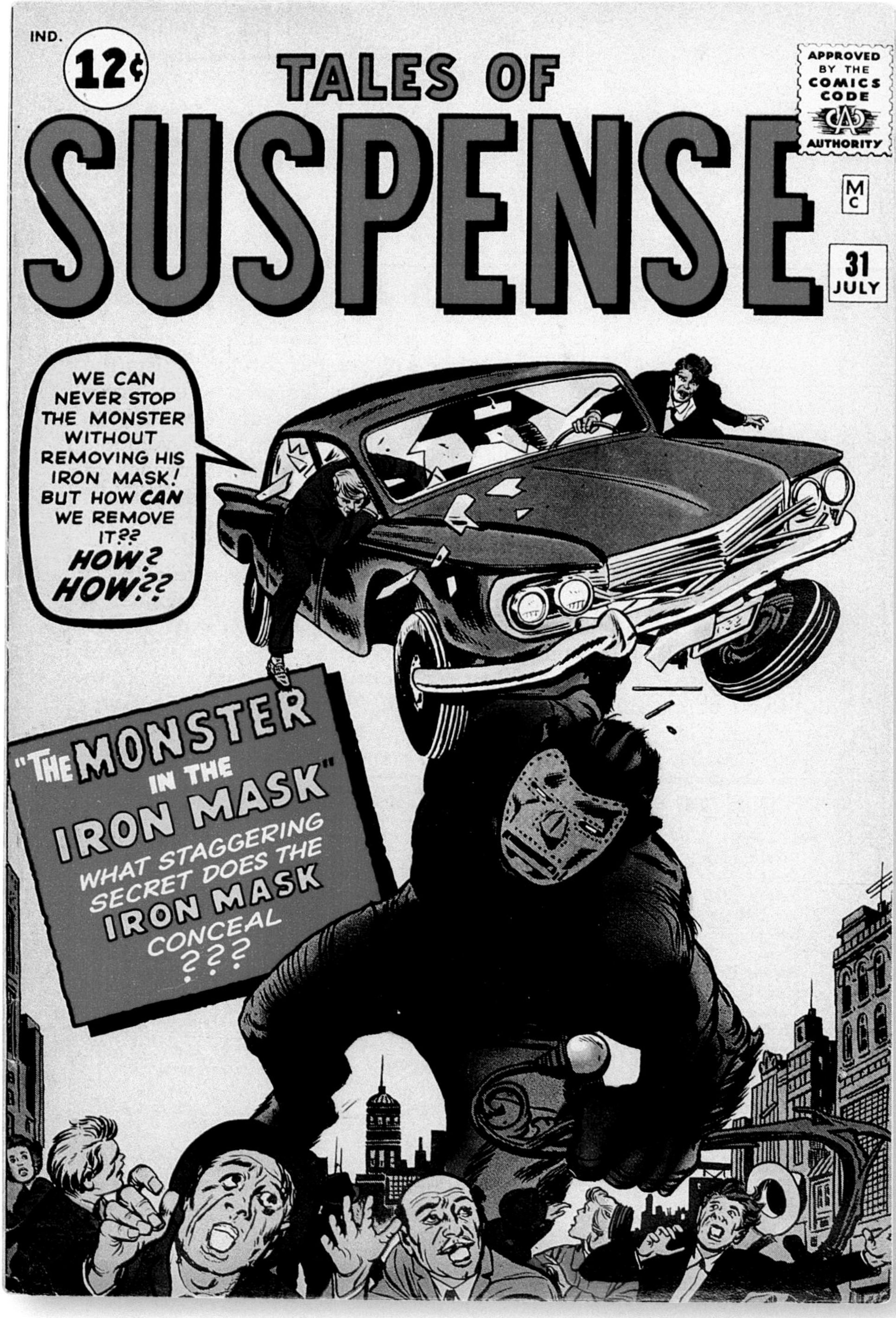
IND.
12¢
TALES OF
SUSPENSE
APPROVED BY THE COMICS CODE AUTHORITY
MC
31
JULY
WE CAN NEVER STOP THE MONSTER WITHOUT REMOVING HIS IRON MASK! BUT HOW CAN WE REMOVE IT?? HOW? HOW??
"THE MONSTER IN THE IRON MASK"
WHAT STAGGERING SECRET DOES THE IRON MASK CONCEAL ???

TALES OF SUSPENSE No. 31

(Opposite) Cover; pencils, Jack Kirby; inks, Dick Ayers; July 1962. It was no doubt coincidence (or fatigue) that made Jack Kirby adorn the Monster in the Iron Mask with the same faceplate as Dr. Doom, who debuted the same month in *Fantastic Four* No. 5.

AMAZING ADVENTURES No. 1

(Below) Interior, "I Am the Fantastic Dr. Droom!"; plot, attributed Stan Lee; script, attributed Larry Lieber; pencils, Jack Kirby; inks, Steve Ditko; June 1961. Dr. Droom passes the tests of his aged mystic master and pledges to fight sinister forces on Earth. Dr. Strange's path to mystic power will also include an elderly Asian in his origin. Since the 1920s American movies, radio, comics, and the pulps had seated the Orient as the center of mysticism, and Marvel was no exception.

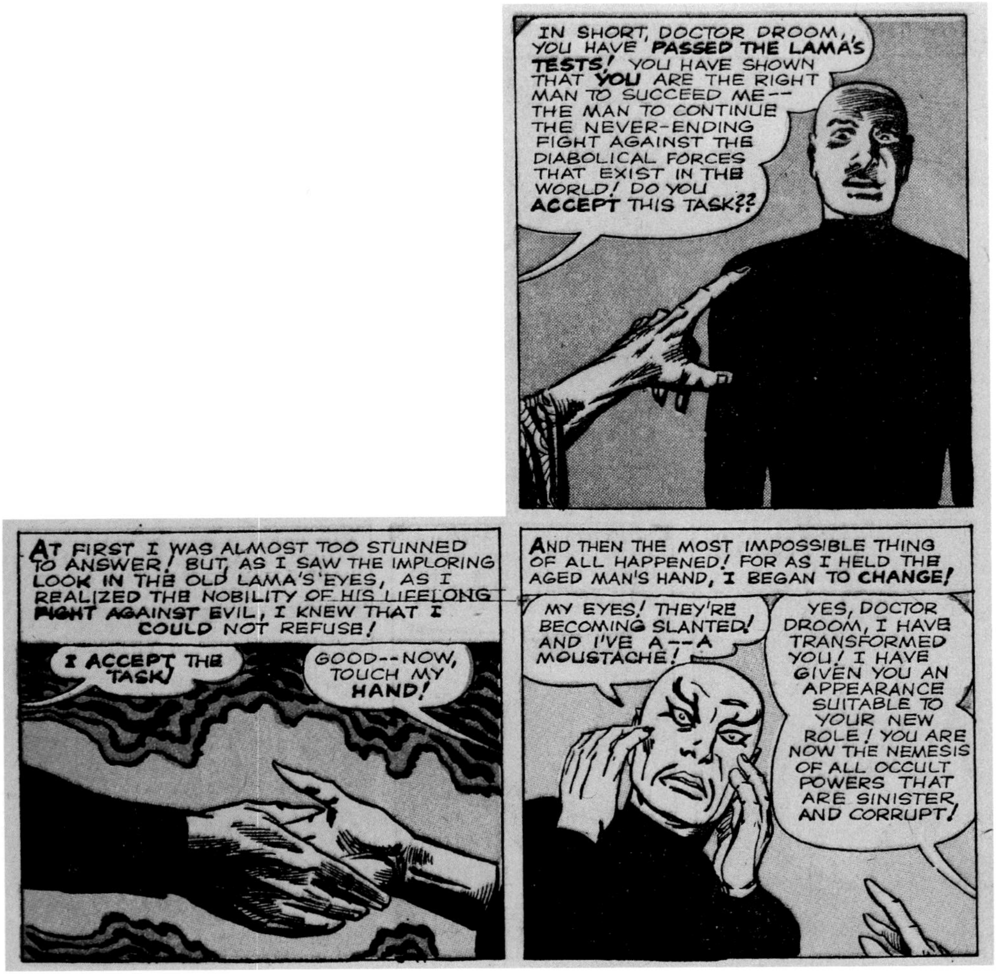
IN SHORT, DOCTOR DROOM, YOU HAVE PASSED THE LAMA'S TESTS! YOU HAVE SHOWN THAT YOU ARE THE RIGHT MAN TO SUCCEED ME-- THE MAN TO CONTINUE THE NEVER-ENDING FIGHT AGAINST THE DIABOLICAL FORCES THAT EXIST IN THE WORLD! DO YOU ACCEPT THIS TASK??
AT FIRST I WAS ALMOST TOO STUNNED TO ANSWER! BUT, AS I SAW THE IMPLORING LOOK IN THE OLD LAMA'S EYES, AS I REALIZED THE NOBILITY OF HIS LIFELONG FIGHT AGAINST EVIL, I KNEW THAT I COULD NOT REFUSE!
I ACCEPT THE TASK!
GOOD--NOW, TOUCH MY HAND!
AND THEN THE MOST IMPOSSIBLE THING OF ALL HAPPENED! FOR AS I HELD THE AGED MAN'S HAND, I BEGAN TO CHANGE!
MY EYES! THEY'RE BECOMING SLANTED! AND I'VE A--A MOUSTACHE!
YES, DOCTOR DROOM, I HAVE TRANSFORMED YOU! I HAVE GIVEN YOU AN APPEARANCE SUITABLE TO YOUR NEW ROLE! YOU ARE NOW THE NEMESIS OF ALL OCCULT POWERS THAT ARE SINISTER AND CORRUPT!

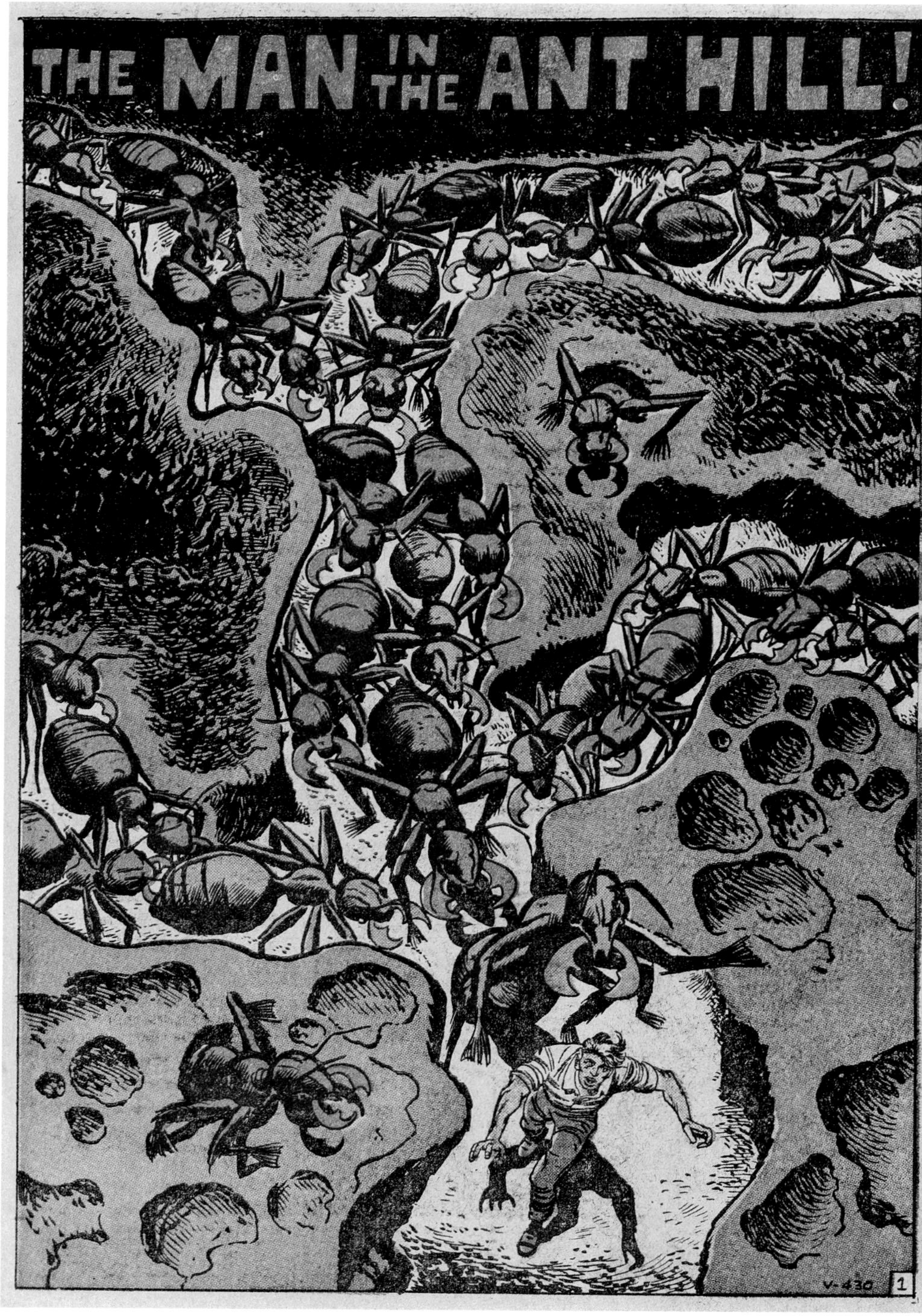
THE MAN IN THE ANT HILL!
V-430
1

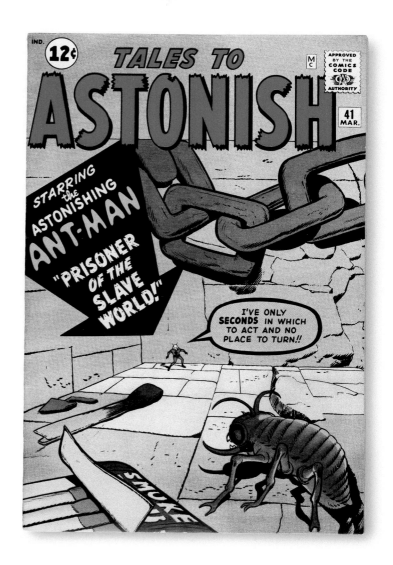

IND.
12¢
TALES TO
ASTONISH
MC
APPROVED BY THE COMICS CODE AUTHORITY
41
MAR.
STARRING the ASTONISHING
ANT-MAN
"PRISONER OF THE SLAVE WORLD!"
I'VE ONLY SECONDS IN WHICH TO ACT AND NO PLACE TO TURN!!

TALES TO ASTONISH No. 27

(Opposite) Interior, "The Man in the Ant Hill"; plot, Stan Lee; script, Larry Lieber; pencils, Jack Kirby; inks, Dick Ayers; January 1962. Henry Pym was one of many scientist protagonists of the pre-hero monster era, although he was the only character incorporated into the hero line. A man trapped at insect size was the source of much imaginative fiction, most notably the 1957 SF movie thriller *The Incredible Shrinking Man.*

TALES TO ASTONISH No. 41

(Above) Cover; pencils, Jack Kirby; inks, Dick Ayers; March 1963.

"I loved Ant-Man, but the stories were never really successful. In order for Ant-Man to be interesting, he had to be drawn *this small* next to big things.... The artists who drew him, no matter how much I kept reminding them, they kept forgetting... I would say, 'Draw a matchbook cover next to him, so we see the difference in size.'" —STAN LEE

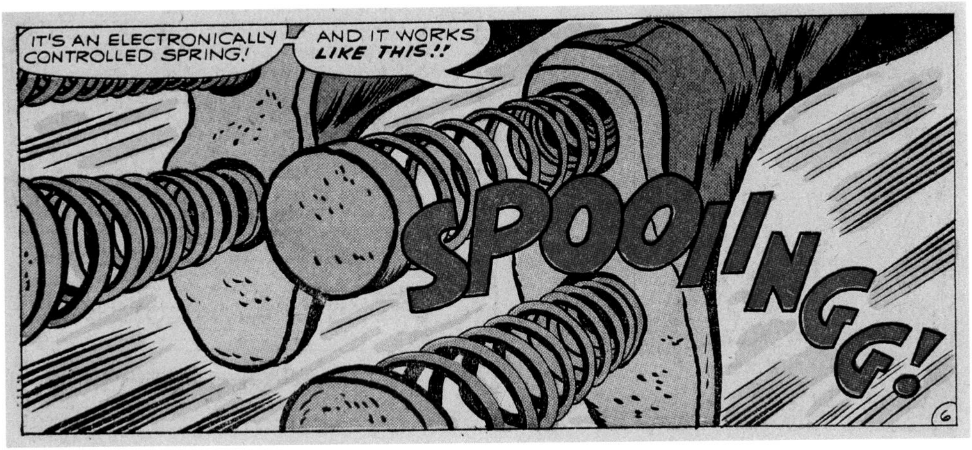

IT'S AN ELECTRONICALLY CONTROLLED SPRING!
AND IT WORKS LIKE THIS!!
SPOOIINGG!

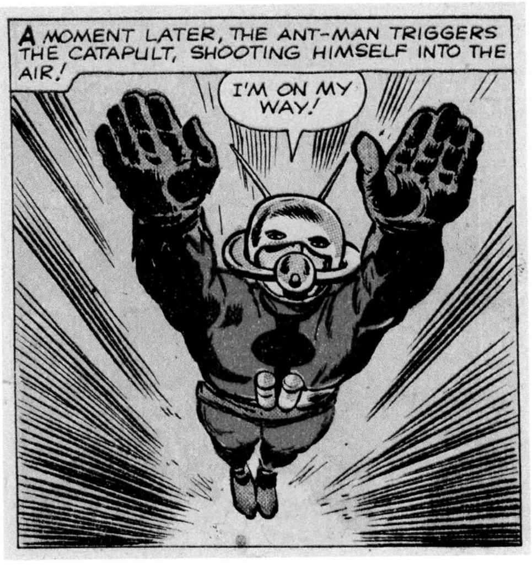

A MOMENT LATER, THE ANT-MAN TRIGGERS THE CATAPULT, SHOOTING HIMSELF INTO THE AIR!
I'M ON MY WAY!

TALES TO ASTONISH No. 37

(Above and left) Interiors, "Trapped by the Protector!"; plot, Stan Lee; script, Larry Lieber; pencils, Jack Kirby; inks, Dick Ayers; November 1962.

TALES TO ASTONISH No. 35

(Opposite) Interior, "Return of the Ant-Man!"; plot, Stan Lee; script, Larry Lieber; pencils, Jack Kirby; inks, Dick Ayers; September 1962. Scientist Henry Pym appeared in a pre-hero fantasy story eight months before his return as Marvel's second costumed super hero in *Tales to Astonish* No. 35.

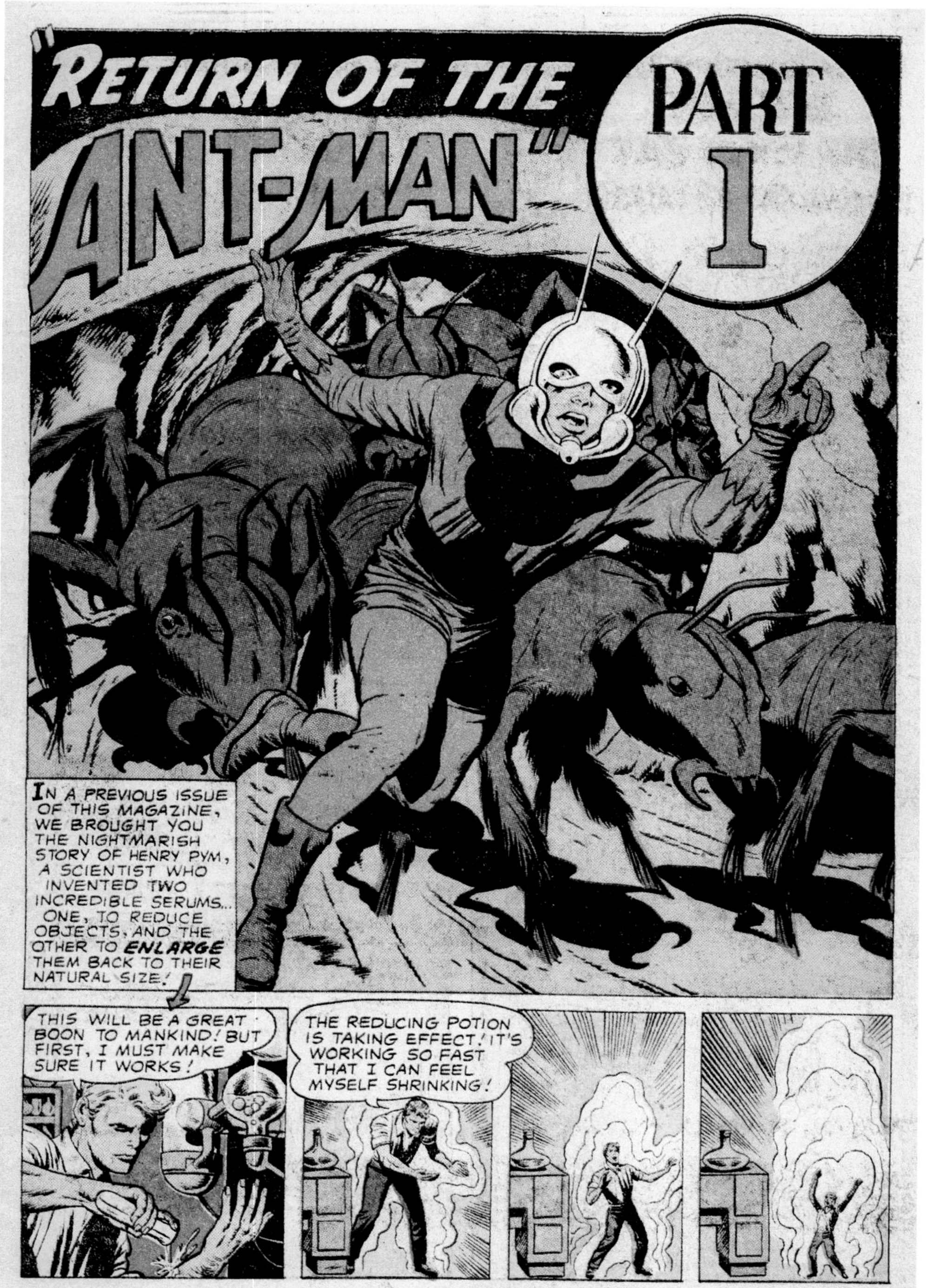
"RETURN OF THE ANT-MAN"
PART 1
IN A PREVIOUS ISSUE OF THIS MAGAZINE, WE BROUGHT YOU THE NIGHTMARISH STORY OF HENRY PYM, A SCIENTIST WHO INVENTED TWO INCREDIBLE SERUMS... ONE, TO REDUCE OBJECTS, AND THE OTHER TO ENLARGE THEM BACK TO THEIR NATURAL SIZE!
THIS WILL BE A GREAT BOON TO MANKIND! BUT FIRST, I MUST MAKE SURE IT WORKS!
THE REDUCING POTION IS TAKING EFFECT! IT'S WORKING SO FAST THAT I CAN FEEL MYSELF SHRINKING!

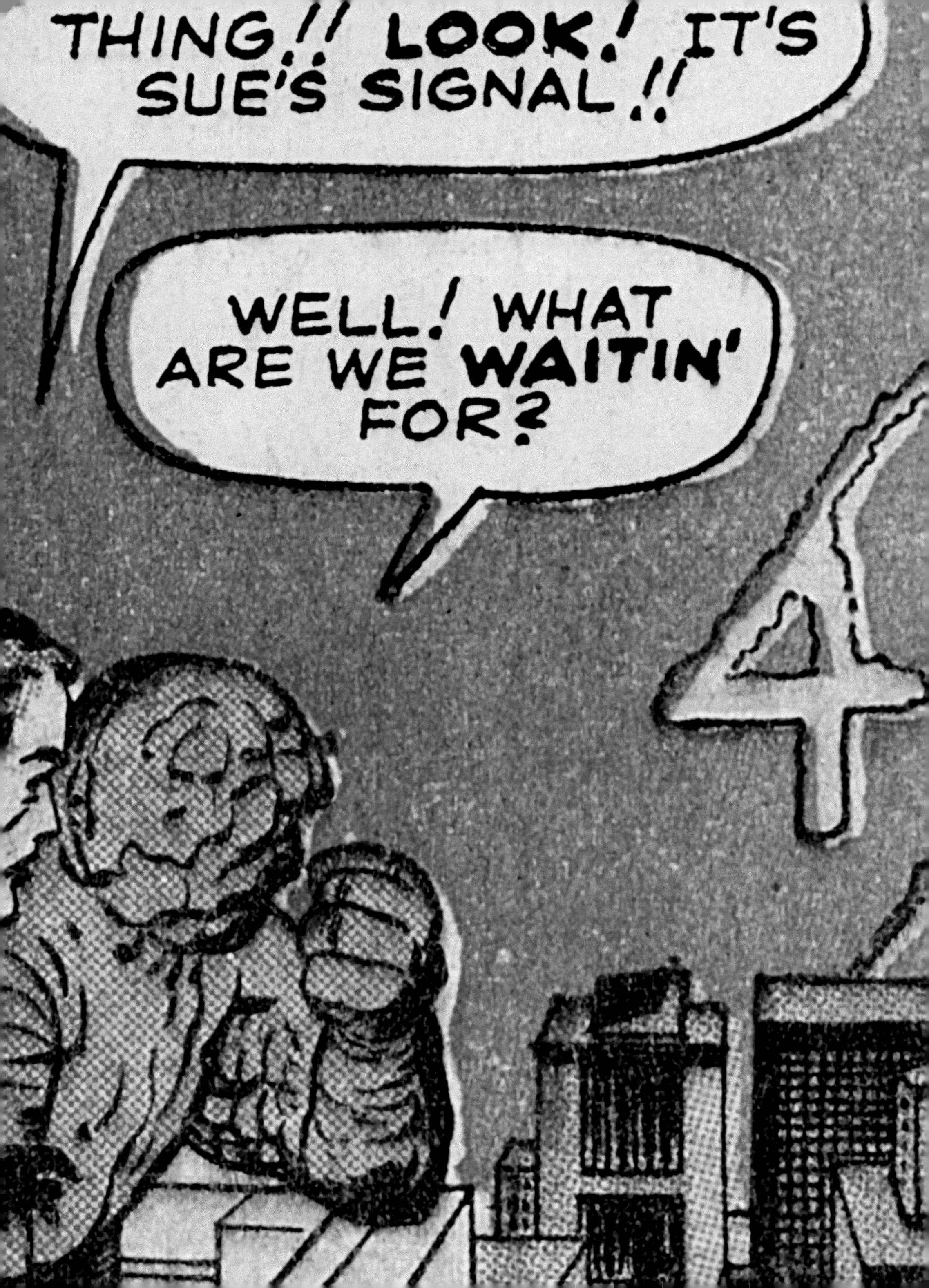
THING!! LOOK! IT'S SUE'S SIGNAL!!
WELL! WHAT ARE WE WAITIN' FOR?

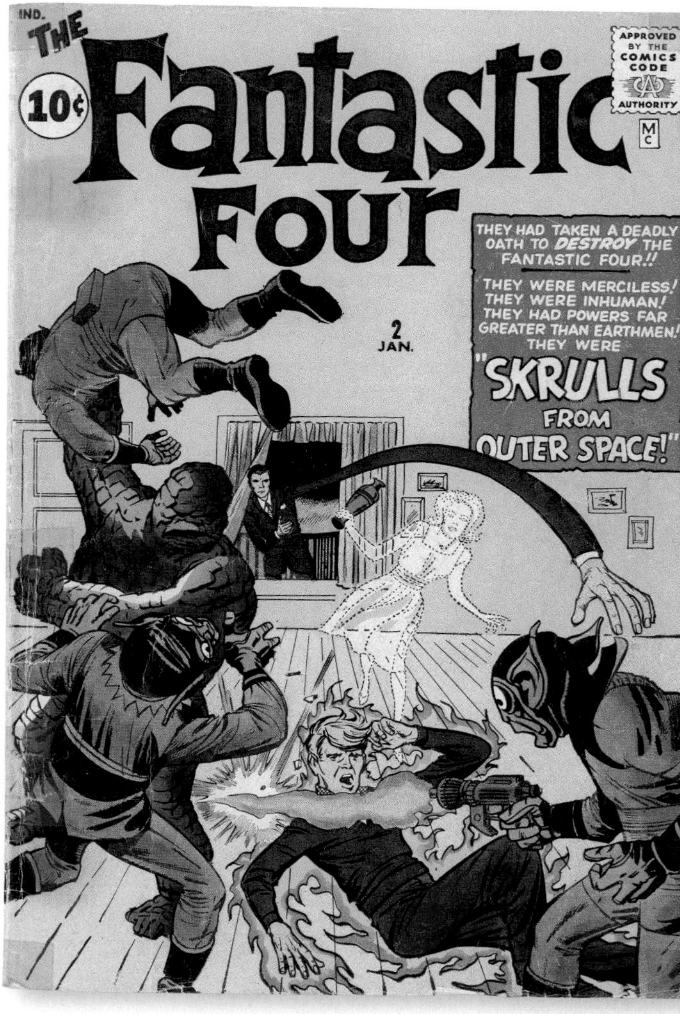
IND.
THE
10¢
Fantastic
FOUR
APPROVED BY THE COMICS CODE AUTHORITY
MC
THEY HAD TAKEN A DEADLY OATH TO DESTROY THE FANTASTIC FOUR!!
THEY WERE MERCILESS! THEY WERE INHUMAN! THEY HAD POWERS FAR GREATER THAN EARTHMEN! THEY WERE
"SKRULLS FROM OUTER SPACE!"
2
JAN.

FANTASTIC FOUR No. 3

(Opposite) Interior, "The Menace of the Miracle Man!"; script, Stan Lee; pencils, Jack Kirby; inks, Sol Brodsky; March 1962.
The "4" symbol, a simple and iconic design by Kirby and Lee, has weathered the decades far better than the costumes that debuted in this issue. The pair had also planned on giving the FF masks, but changed their minds before the final art was published. It proved a wise decision, further differentiating the FF from the usual masked heroes who hid their identities.

FANTASTIC FOUR No. 2

(Above) Cover; pencils, Jack Kirby; inks, George Klein; January 1962.

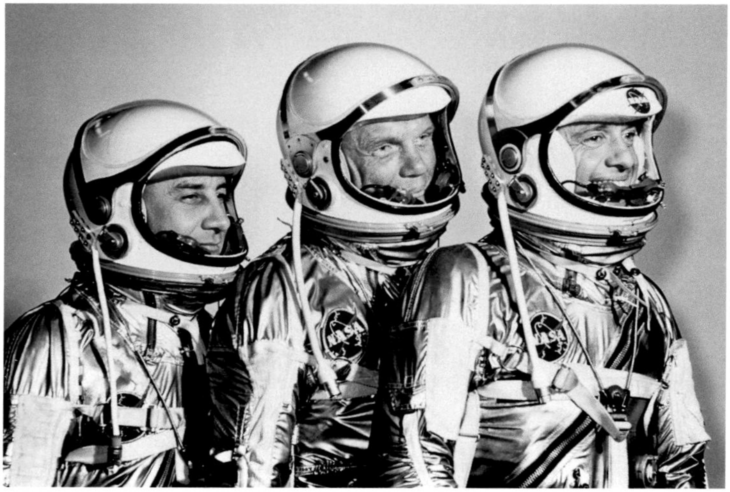

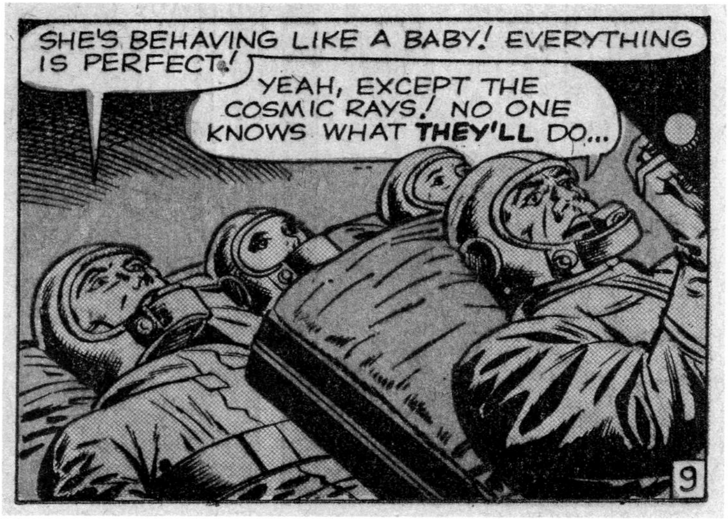
SHE'S BEHAVING LIKE A BABY! EVERYTHING IS PERFECT!
YEAH, EXCEPT THE COSMIC RAYS! NO ONE KNOWS WHAT **THEY'LL** DO...
9

SPACE-AGE HEROES

(Top) Photograph; Mercury astronauts Virgil Grissom, John Glenn, and Alan Shepard; 1960. Manned spaceflights started in April of 1961, and astronauts were heroes for many at the dawn of the optimistic Kennedy era.

FANTASTIC FOUR No. 1

(Opposite) Interior, "The Fantastic Four"; script, Stan Lee; pencils, Jack Kirby; inks, attributed George Klein; November 1961. Where once they were the quiet and reclusive warriors of two World Wars, America's heroes were changing in the early 1960s. The country looked now to a youthful president and its anointed space travelers — and Lee and Kirby used this new template to present their own vision for the future.

FANTASTIC FOUR No. 14

(Below) Interior, "The Sub-Mariner Strikes!"; script, Stan Lee; pencils, Jack Kirby; inks, Dick Ayers; May 1963. Comic book artists were cinematographers, choreographers, and directors all wrapped in one. Overhead shots displayed the influence of the movie screen on avid filmgoer Jack Kirby.

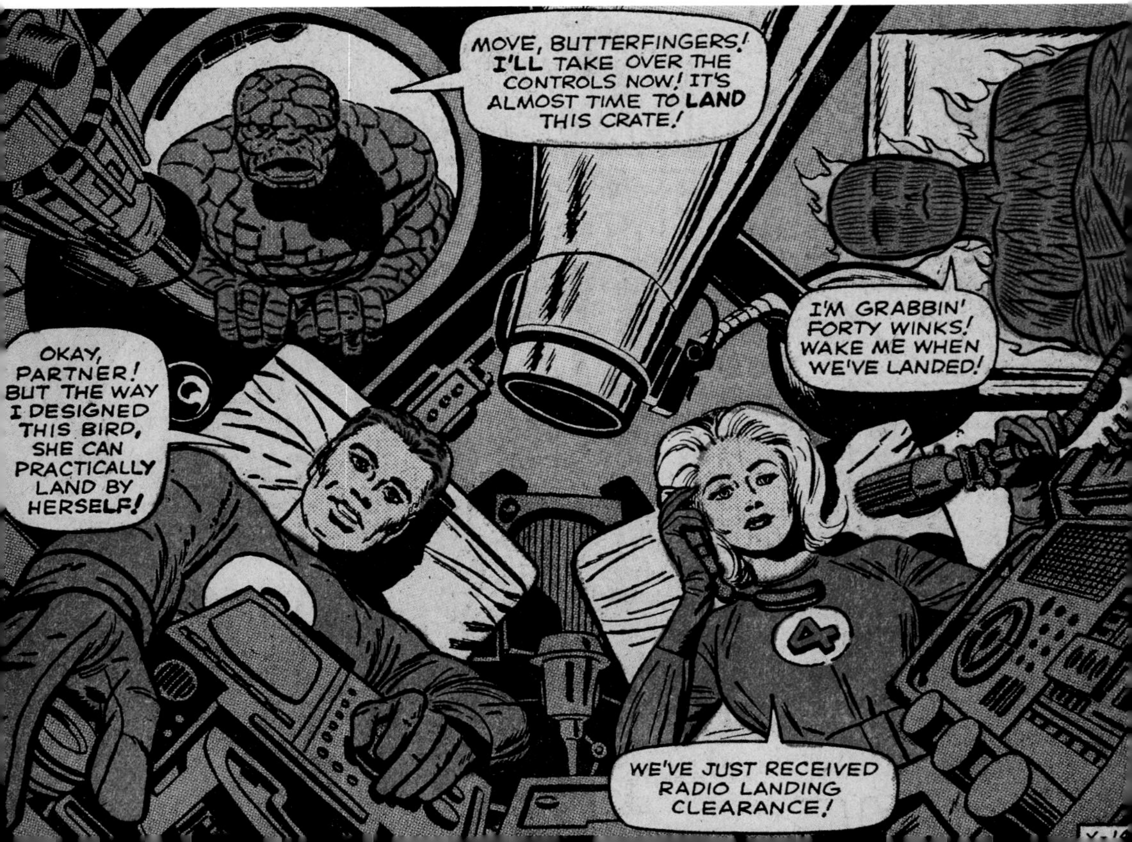

MOVE, BUTTERFINGERS! I'LL TAKE OVER THE CONTROLS NOW! IT'S ALMOST TIME TO LAND THIS CRATE!
OKAY, PARTNER! BUT THE WAY I DESIGNED THIS BIRD, SHE CAN PRACTICALLY LAND BY HERSELF!
I'M GRABBIN' FORTY WINKS! WAKE ME WHEN WE'VE LANDED!
WE'VE JUST RECEIVED RADIO LANDING CLEARANCE!

"In the beginning Marvel created the Bullpen and the Style.
And the Bullpen was without form, and was void;
and darkness was upon the face of the Artists.
And the Spirit of Marvel moved upon the face of the Writers.
And Marvel said, Let there be the Fantastic Four.
And there was the Fantastic Four.
And Marvel saw the Fantastic Four.
And it was good."
— STAN LEE

FANTASTIC FOUR No. 7

(Opposite) Interior, "Twenty-Four Hours till Zero!"; script, Stan Lee; pencils, Jack Kirby; inks, Dick Ayers; October 1962.

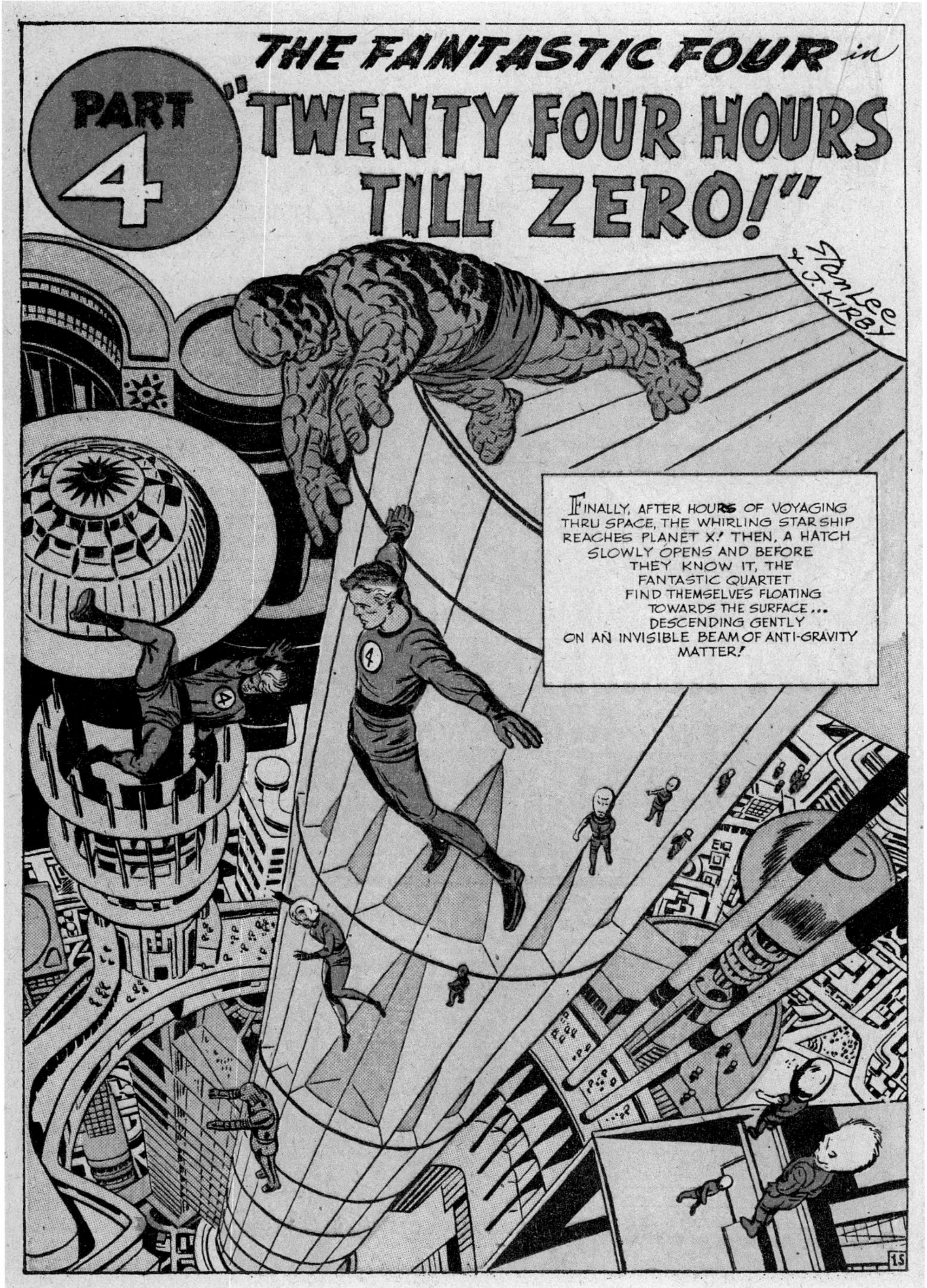
THE FANTASTIC FOUR in
PART 4
"TWENTY FOUR HOURS TILL ZERO!"
Stan Lee & J. Kirby
FINALLY, AFTER HOURS OF VOYAGING THRU SPACE, THE WHIRLING STARSHIP REACHES PLANET X! THEN, A HATCH SLOWLY OPENS AND BEFORE THEY KNOW IT, THE FANTASTIC QUARTET FIND THEMSELVES FLOATING TOWARDS THE SURFACE... DESCENDING GENTLY ON AN INVISIBLE BEAM OF ANTI-GRAVITY MATTER!
15

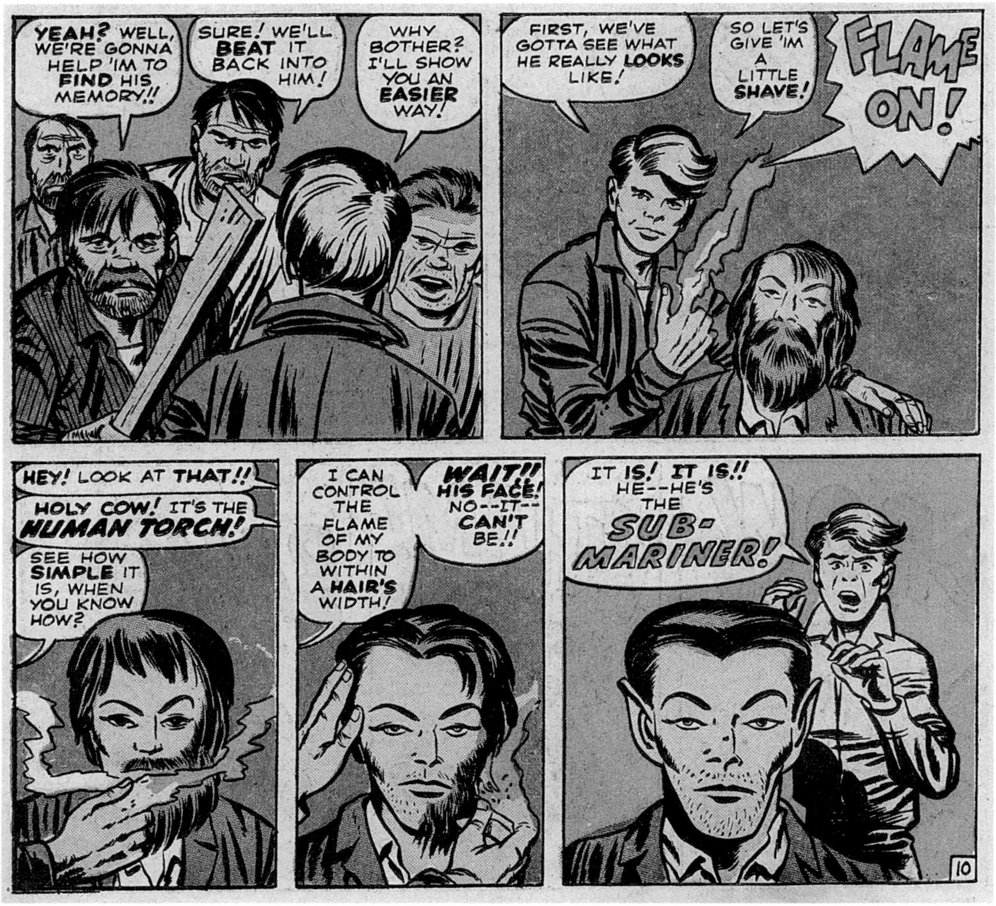
YEAH? WELL, WE'RE GONNA HELP 'IM TO FIND HIS MEMORY!!
SURE! WE'LL BEAT IT BACK INTO HIM!
WHY BOTHER? I'LL SHOW YOU AN EASIER WAY!
FIRST, WE'VE GOTTA SEE WHAT HE REALLY LOOKS LIKE!
SO LET'S GIVE 'IM A LITTLE SHAVE!
FLAME ON!
HEY! LOOK AT THAT!!
HOLY COW! IT'S THE HUMAN TORCH!
SEE HOW SIMPLE IT IS, WHEN YOU KNOW HOW?
I CAN CONTROL THE FLAME OF MY BODY TO WITHIN A HAIR'S WIDTH!
WAIT!! HIS FACE! NO--IT--CAN'T BE!!
IT IS! IT IS!! HE--HE'S THE SUB-MARINER!
10

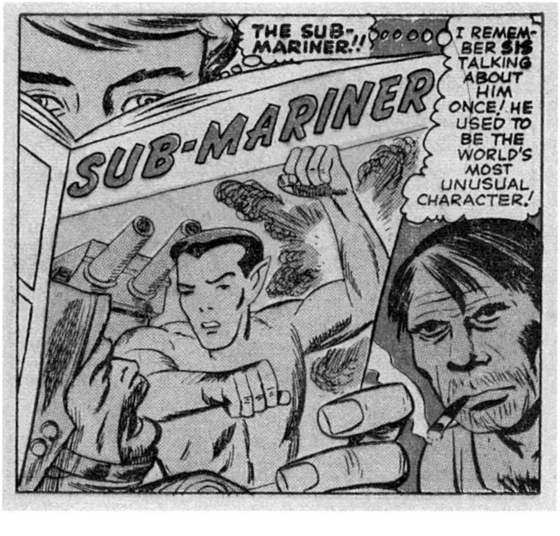
THE SUB-MARINER!!
I REMEMBER SIS TALKING ABOUT HIM ONCE! HE USED TO BE THE WORLD'S MOST UNUSUAL CHARACTER!
SUB-MARINER

FANTASTIC FOUR No. 4

(Above and left) Interiors, "The Coming of Sub-Mariner!"; script, Stan Lee; pencils, Jack Kirby; inks, Sol Brodsky; May 1962. In a brilliant marketing move, Lee cast popular teenage hero Johnny Storm — the "rebooted" Human Torch — as a comics fan who learns about the Sub-Mariner from a vintage comic book! Namor's own reboot is handled with panache: Having spent years on the street in New York's Bowery, Namor is teased about his super-strength before the slumming super-fan Torch recognizes him through a derelict's beard!

FANTASTIC FOUR No. 33

(Opposite) Cover; pencils, Jack Kirby; inks, Chic Stone; December 1964.

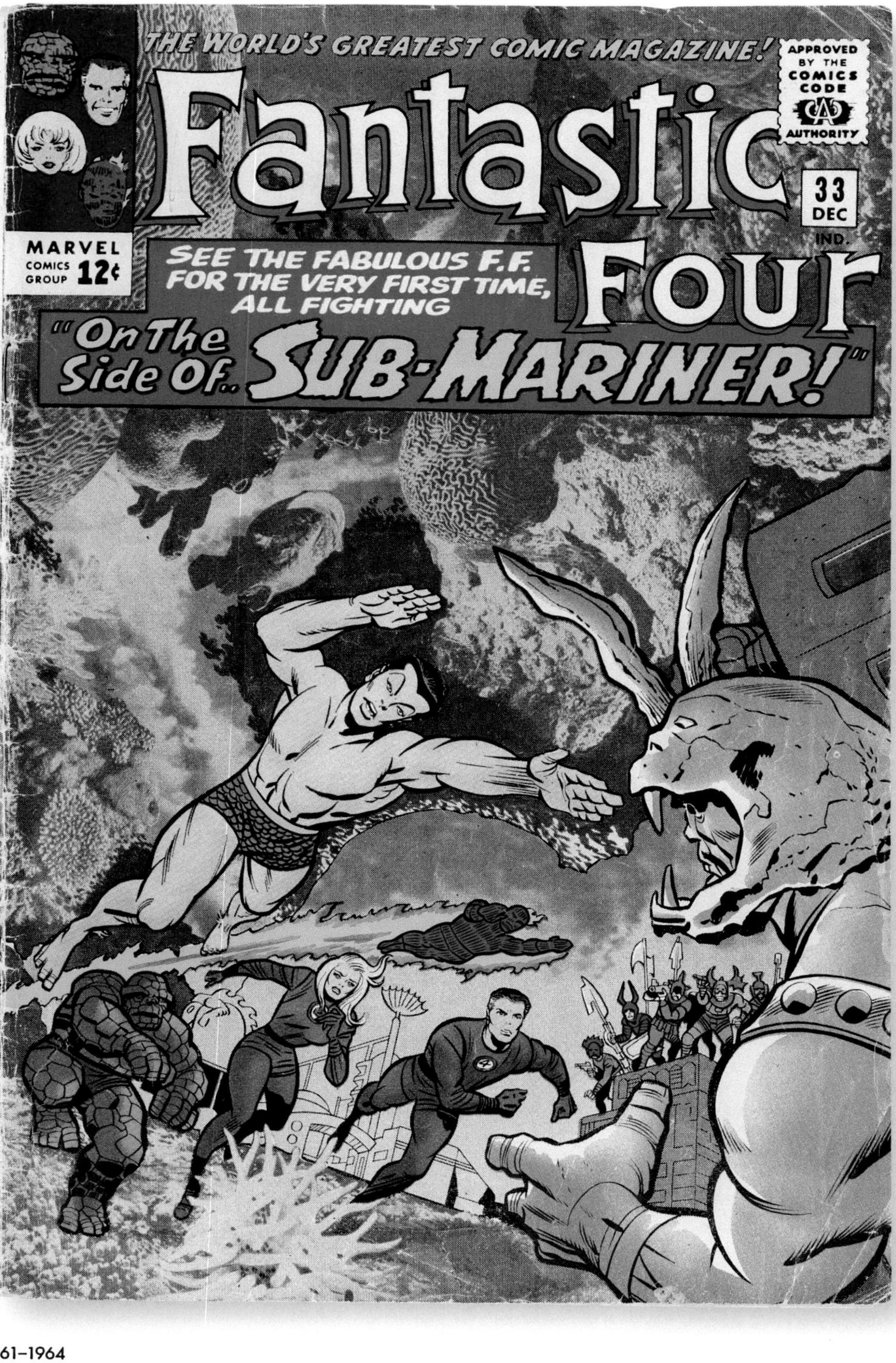
THE WORLD'S GREATEST COMIC MAGAZINE!
APPROVED BY THE COMICS CODE AUTHORITY
Fantastic Four
33 DEC
IND.
MARVEL COMICS GROUP 12¢
SEE THE FABULOUS F.F. FOR THE VERY FIRST TIME, ALL FIGHTING
"On The Side Of.. SUB-MARINER!"

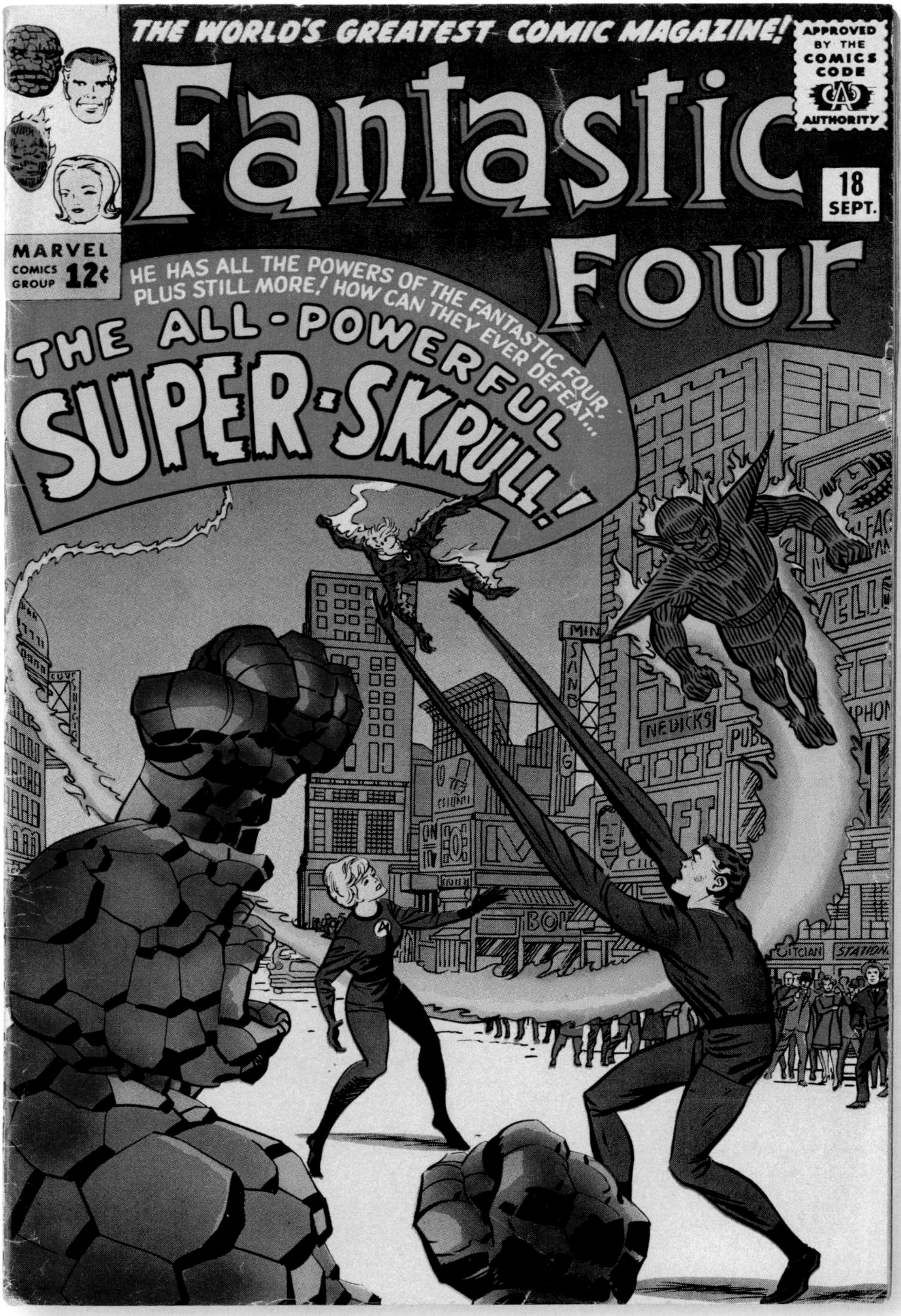
THE WORLD'S GREATEST COMIC MAGAZINE!
APPROVED BY THE COMICS CODE AUTHORITY
Fantastic Four
18 SEPT.
MARVEL COMICS GROUP 12¢
HE HAS ALL THE POWERS OF THE FANTASTIC FOUR, PLUS STILL MORE! HOW CAN THEY EVER DEFEAT...
THE ALL-POWERFUL SUPER-SKRULL!
NEDICKS

FANTASTIC FOUR No. 18

(Opposite) Cover; pencils, Jack Kirby; inks, Paul Reinman; September 1963. The Skrulls, introduced in *FF* No. 2, were the first aliens in the new Marvel Universe, and unlike villains in the earlier pre-hero stories, these little green monsters were recurring antagonists. The Super-Skrull was tailor-made wish fulfillment for the era's young readers — he had *all* the FF's powers! Stan Goldberg's distinctive coloring used gradations and dark colors, helping create a unique look for Marvel on the newsstands.

FANTASTIC FOUR No. 2

(Below) Interior, "The Fantastic Four Meet the Skrulls from Outer Space!"; script, Stan Lee; pencils, Jack Kirby; inks, George Klein; January 1962. A Skrull impersonating Reed Richards resumes his original shape.

AS FOR ME, I NEEDED NO SPECIAL DEVICES! FOR IT'S AN EASY MATTER FOR ME TO ALTER MY BODY IN ANY WAY I DESIRE!
JUST AS IT IS EASY FOR ALL OF US TO DO SO!
WHICH IS WHY THE UNSUSPECTING EARTHMEN WILL NEVER KNOW THAT WE SKRULLS HAVE IMPERSONATED THEIR FAMOUS FANTASTIC FOUR!

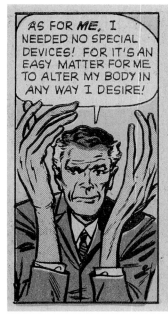

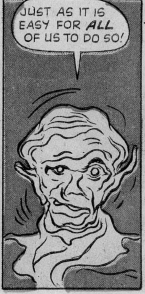

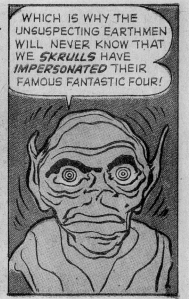

"Dr. Doom is a lovable villain. He thinks of himself as a guy who wants to rule the world 'cause he thinks he can do a better job than anyone else. And he is amazed that people try to stop him. There's no law against wanting to take over the world. You can be arrested for being a litterbug, but you're not breaking the law if you try to take over mankind."

— STAN LEE

FANTASTIC FOUR No. 5

(Opposite) Cover; pencils, Jack Kirby; inks, Joe Sinnott; July 1962. Dr. Doom was the FF's primary — and most popular — antagonist. Introduced in this issue, Doom was a complex, fascinating character that many see as the visual prototype of George Lucas's Darth Vader. Stan Goldberg, the staffer responsible for coloring most of Marvel's comics in the 1960s, would recall, "Jack gave them this long underwear with the letter '4' on their chest.... I made the '4' blue and kept a little area around it white, and then when the villains came in — the villains get the burnt umbers, dark greens, purples, grays, things like that — they can bounce off it."

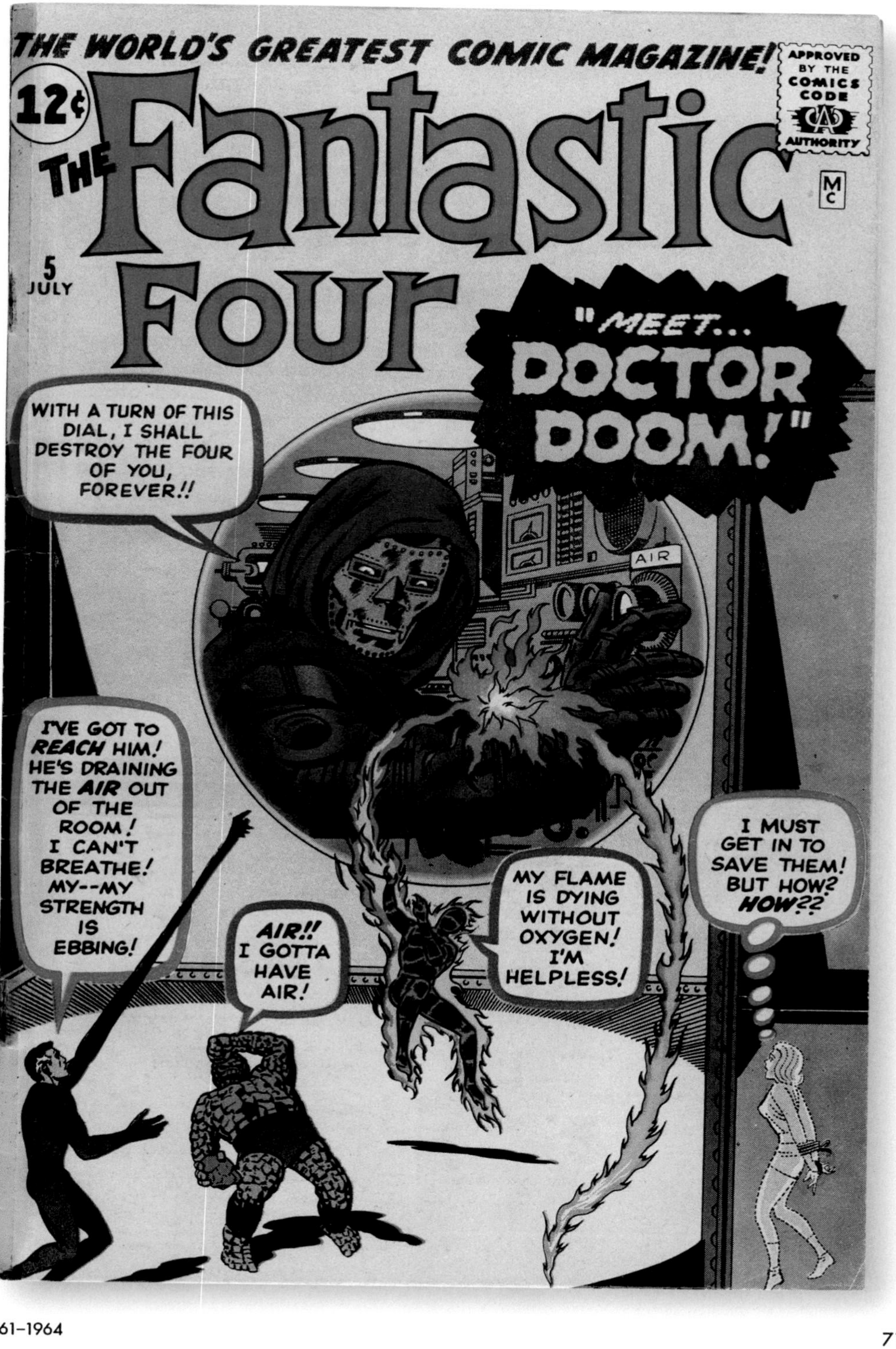
THE WORLD'S GREATEST COMIC MAGAZINE!
12¢
THE Fantastic Four
5 JULY
APPROVED BY THE COMICS CODE AUTHORITY
MC
"MEET... DOCTOR DOOM!"
WITH A TURN OF THIS DIAL, I SHALL DESTROY THE FOUR OF YOU, FOREVER!!
AIR
I'VE GOT TO REACH HIM! HE'S DRAINING THE AIR OUT OF THE ROOM! I CAN'T BREATHE! MY--MY STRENGTH IS EBBING!
AIR!! I GOTTA HAVE AIR!
MY FLAME IS DYING WITHOUT OXYGEN! I'M HELPLESS!
I MUST GET IN TO SAVE THEM! BUT HOW? HOW??

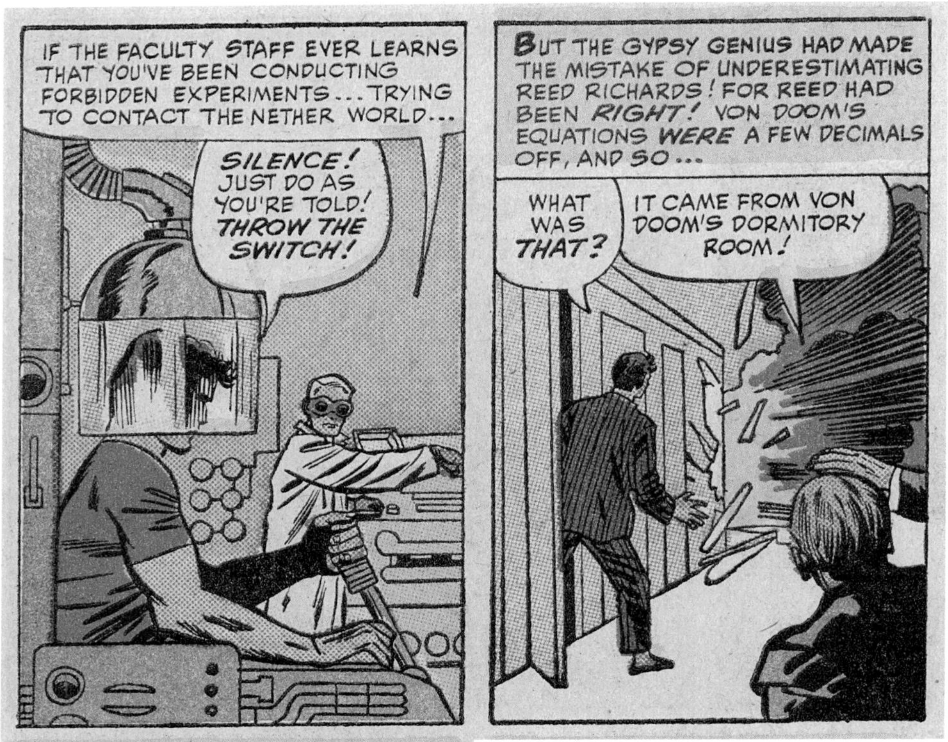
IF THE FACULTY STAFF EVER LEARNS THAT YOU'VE BEEN CONDUCTING FORBIDDEN EXPERIMENTS... TRYING TO CONTACT THE NETHER WORLD...
SILENCE! JUST DO AS YOU'RE TOLD! THROW THE SWITCH!
BUT THE GYPSY GENIUS HAD MADE THE MISTAKE OF UNDERESTIMATING REED RICHARDS! FOR REED HAD BEEN RIGHT! VON DOOM'S EQUATIONS WERE A FEW DECIMALS OFF, AND SO...
WHAT WAS THAT?
IT CAME FROM VON DOOM'S DORMITORY ROOM!

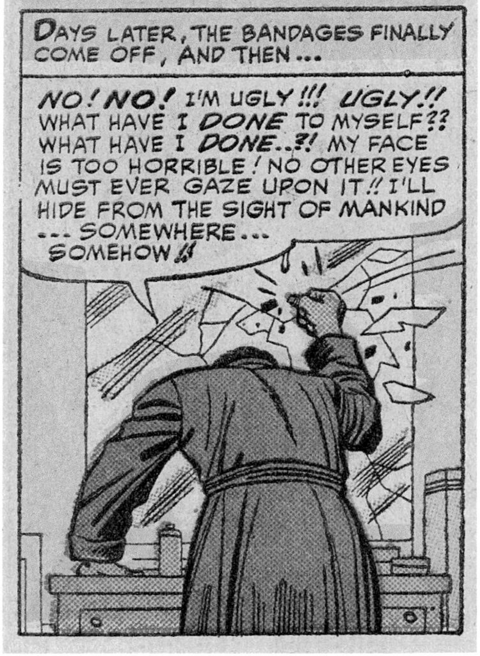
DAYS LATER, THE BANDAGES FINALLY COME OFF, AND THEN...
NO! NO! I'M UGLY!!! UGLY!! WHAT HAVE I DONE TO MYSELF?? WHAT HAVE I DONE..?! MY FACE IS TOO HORRIBLE! NO OTHER EYES MUST EVER GAZE UPON IT!! I'LL HIDE FROM THE SIGHT OF MANKIND ... SOMEWHERE... SOMEHOW!!

FANTASTIC FOUR ANNUAL No. 2

(Above and opposite) Interiors, "The Fantastic Origin of Dr. Doom"; script, Stan Lee; pencils, Jack Kirby; inks, Chic Stone; Summer 1964. Unlike most comics publishers, Lee and Kirby felt no rush to tell origin stories. They took their time revealing the pasts of popular characters like Dr. Doom. What did the face behind the mask look like? Lee and Kirby each offered different interpretations: Lee maintained that Victor Von Doom had a terribly scarred face; Kirby, a decade after Doom's introduction, said it was just a small cut that Doom couldn't accept because he was a perfectionist.

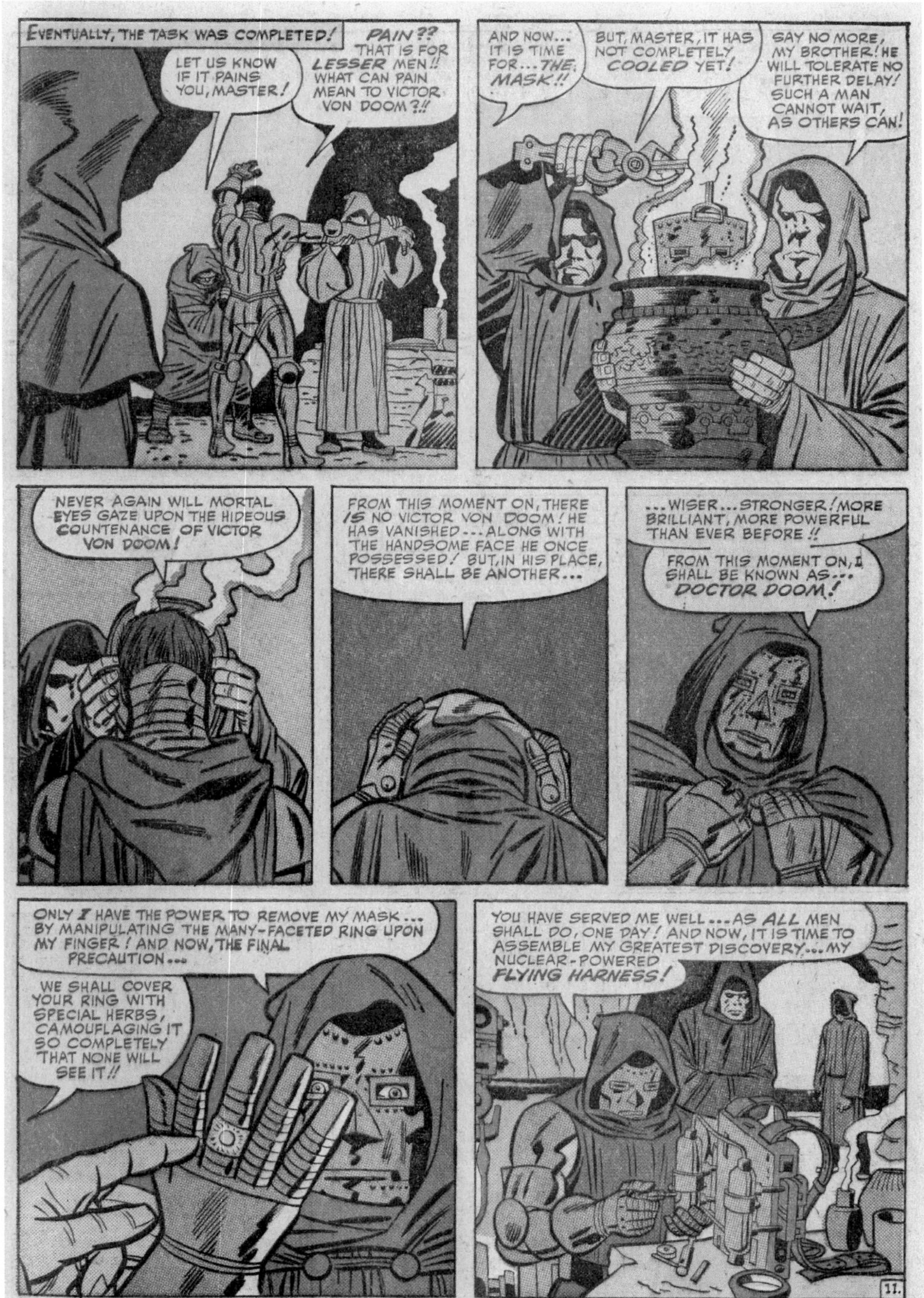
EVENTUALLY, THE TASK WAS COMPLETED!
LET US KNOW IF IT PAINS YOU, MASTER!
PAIN?? THAT IS FOR LESSER MEN!! WHAT CAN PAIN MEAN TO VICTOR VON DOOM?!!
AND NOW... IT IS TIME FOR... THE MASK!!
BUT, MASTER, IT HAS NOT COMPLETELY COOLED YET!
SAY NO MORE, MY BROTHER! HE WILL TOLERATE NO FURTHER DELAY! SUCH A MAN CANNOT WAIT, AS OTHERS CAN!
NEVER AGAIN WILL MORTAL EYES GAZE UPON THE HIDEOUS COUNTENANCE OF VICTOR VON DOOM!
FROM THIS MOMENT ON, THERE IS NO VICTOR VON DOOM! HE HAS VANISHED---ALONG WITH THE HANDSOME FACE HE ONCE POSSESSED! BUT, IN HIS PLACE, THERE SHALL BE ANOTHER...
...WISER...STRONGER! MORE BRILLIANT, MORE POWERFUL THAN EVER BEFORE!!
FROM THIS MOMENT ON, I SHALL BE KNOWN AS... DOCTOR DOOM!
ONLY I HAVE THE POWER TO REMOVE MY MASK... BY MANIPULATING THE MANY-FACETED RING UPON MY FINGER! AND NOW, THE FINAL PRECAUTION...
WE SHALL COVER YOUR RING WITH SPECIAL HERBS, CAMOUFLAGING IT SO COMPLETELY THAT NONE WILL SEE IT!!
YOU HAVE SERVED ME WELL...AS ALL MEN SHALL DO, ONE DAY! AND NOW, IT IS TIME TO ASSEMBLE MY GREATEST DISCOVERY...MY NUCLEAR-POWERED FLYING HARNESS!
11.

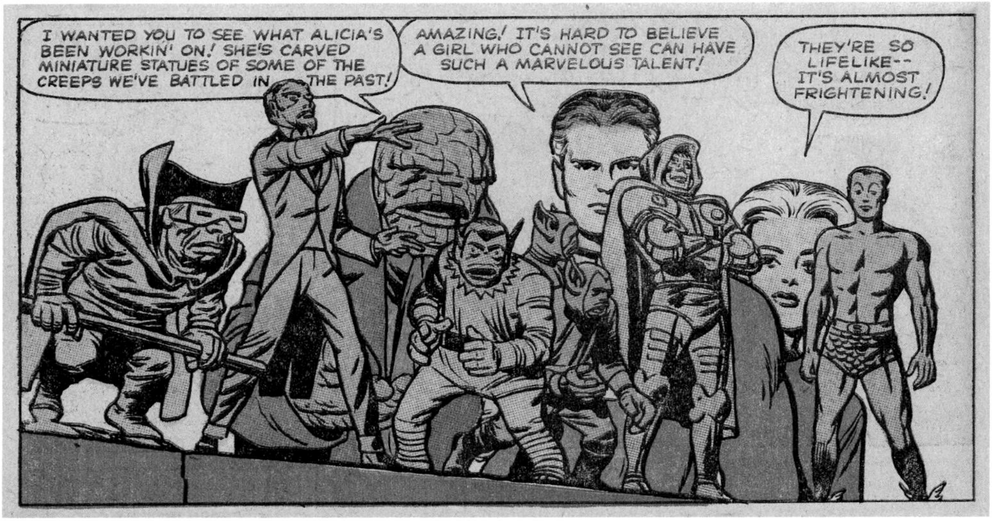
I WANTED YOU TO SEE WHAT ALICIA'S BEEN WORKIN' ON! SHE'S CARVED MINIATURE STATUES OF SOME OF THE CREEPS WE'VE BATTLED IN THE PAST!
AMAZING! IT'S HARD TO BELIEVE A GIRL WHO CANNOT SEE CAN HAVE SUCH A MARVELOUS TALENT!
THEY'RE SO LIFELIKE-- IT'S ALMOST FRIGHTENING!

FANTASTIC FOUR No. 10

(Above) Interior, "The Return of Dr. Doom!"; script, Stan Lee; pencils, Jack Kirby; inks, Dick Ayers; January 1963.

JERRY TODD & POPPY OTT

(Below) Book cover; author, Leo Edwards; art, Bert Salg; Grosset & Dunlap; 1930. "There were two . . . series that nobody ever heard of except me," recalled John Romita in a 2000 interview. "Jerry Todd, and the other was Poppy Ott . . . they had more humor than *The Hardy Boys* or *The Boy Allies* or *Tom Swift*, or any of them. And they were interspersed with gags and fun, even though they were exciting stories." Stan Lee remembered them, too, as he would cite their serial "letter pages" as the inspiration for Marvel's revolutionary dialogue with readers.

FANTASTIC FOUR ANNUAL No. 1

(Opposite) Interior; script, Stan Lee; pencils and inks, Jack Kirby; Summer 1963. The Marvel Annuals, later called King-Size Specials, often contained great features including pinups, comedic stories, and insights into the characters—a reward of sorts for Marvel's increasingly dedicated fanbase. In this first *FF Annual,* Lee and Kirby unveiled the complete layout of the Baxter Building. A tantalizingly abbreviated diagram had already appeared in issue 3.

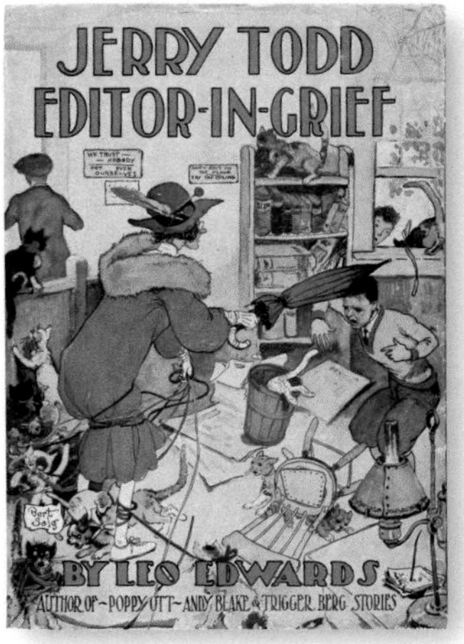
JERRY TODD
EDITOR-IN-GRIEF
BY LEO EDWARDS
AUTHOR OF—POPPY OTT—ANDY BLAKE & TRIGGER BERG STORIES

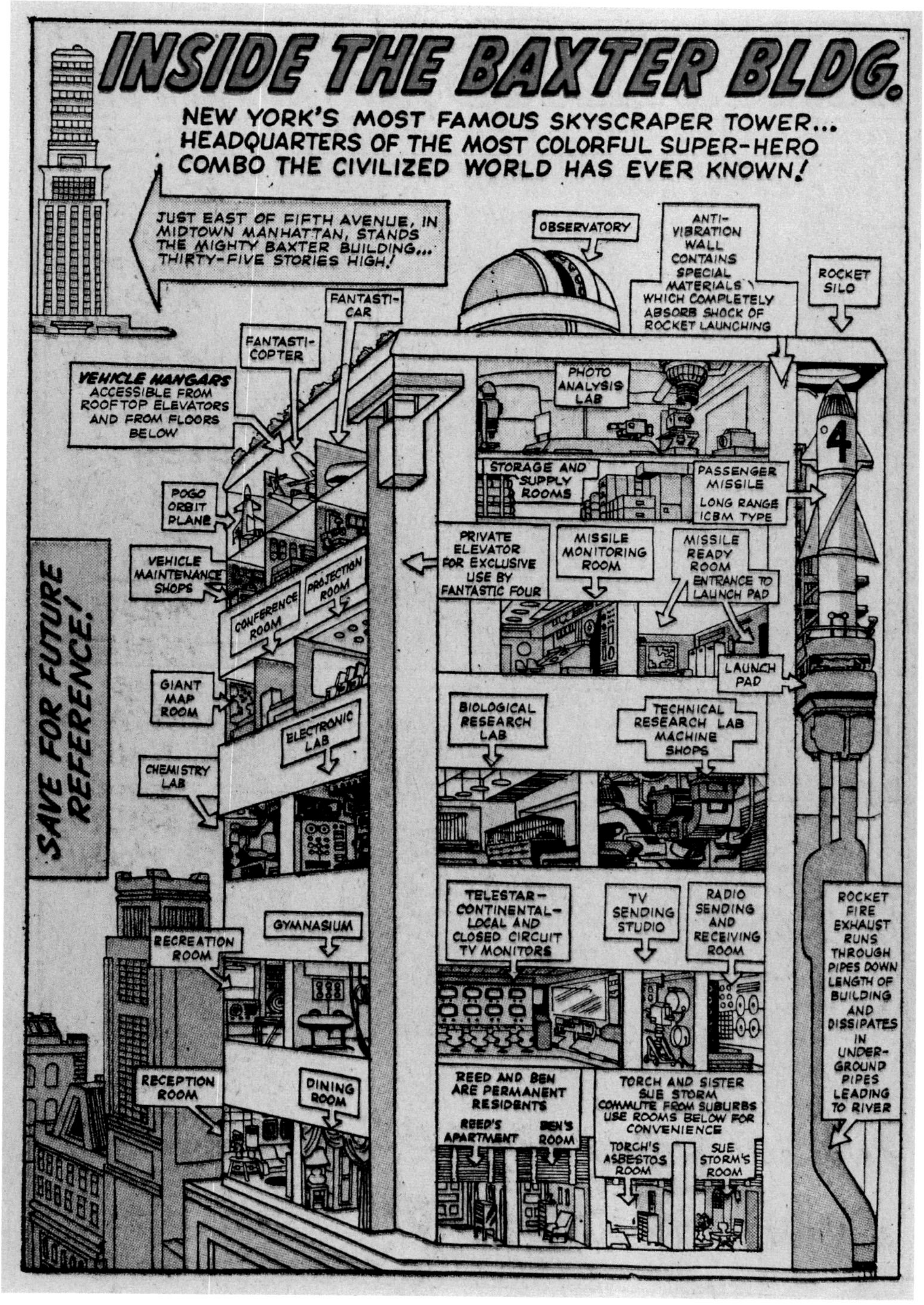
INSIDE THE BAXTER BLDG.
NEW YORK'S MOST FAMOUS SKYSCRAPER TOWER... HEADQUARTERS OF THE MOST COLORFUL SUPER-HERO COMBO THE CIVILIZED WORLD HAS EVER KNOWN!
JUST EAST OF FIFTH AVENUE, IN MIDTOWN MANHATTAN, STANDS THE MIGHTY BAXTER BUILDING... THIRTY-FIVE STORIES HIGH!
OBSERVATORY
ANTI-VIBRATION WALL CONTAINS SPECIAL MATERIALS WHICH COMPLETELY ABSORB SHOCK OF ROCKET LAUNCHING
ROCKET SILO
FANTASTI-CAR
FANTASTI-COPTER
VEHICLE HANGARS ACCESSIBLE FROM ROOFTOP ELEVATORS AND FROM FLOORS BELOW
PHOTO ANALYSIS LAB
STORAGE AND SUPPLY ROOMS
PASSENGER MISSILE
LONG RANGE ICBM TYPE
4
POGO ORBIT PLANE
PRIVATE ELEVATOR FOR EXCLUSIVE USE BY FANTASTIC FOUR
MISSILE MONITORING ROOM
MISSILE READY ROOM ENTRANCE TO LAUNCH PAD
VEHICLE MAINTENANCE SHOPS
CONFERENCE ROOM
PROJECTION ROOM
SAVE FOR FUTURE REFERENCE!
LAUNCH PAD
GIANT MAP ROOM
ELECTRONIC LAB
BIOLOGICAL RESEARCH LAB
TECHNICAL RESEARCH LAB MACHINE SHOPS
CHEMISTRY LAB
TELESTAR-CONTINENTAL-LOCAL AND CLOSED CIRCUIT TV MONITORS
TV SENDING STUDIO
RADIO SENDING AND RECEIVING ROOM
ROCKET FIRE EXHAUST RUNS THROUGH PIPES DOWN LENGTH OF BUILDING AND DISSIPATES IN UNDER-GROUND PIPES LEADING TO RIVER
GYMNASIUM
RECREATION ROOM
RECEPTION ROOM
DINING ROOM
REED AND BEN ARE PERMANENT RESIDENTS
REED'S APARTMENT
BEN'S ROOM
TORCH AND SISTER SUE STORM COMMUTE FROM SUBURBS USE ROOMS BELOW FOR CONVENIENCE
TORCH'S ASBESTOS ROOM
SUE STORM'S ROOM

FANTASTIC FOUR No. 22

(Below) Interiors, "The Return of the Mole Man!"; script, Stan Lee; pencils, Jack Kirby; inks, George Roussos; January 1964. Lee and company often referenced popular-culture figures and topical events, as evidenced by these two pages. Panels one and two include a caricature of Fred Gwynne as Officer Muldoon from the then-current TV comedy *Car 54, Where Are You?* The deadpan humor contrasted Marvel's world with that of its more straight-laced competitors. ("It's that I.C.B.M. you keep on the premises…" "Oh, is *that* all?") And Marvel often poked fun at itself, too. This sendup of "abstract art" is in reality a satire of a picture drawn by Jack Kirby.

FANTASTIC FOUR No. 29

(Opposite) Cover; pencils, Jack Kirby; inks, Chic Stone; August 1964. Many of the best *FF* covers eschewed the traditional super hero fight scenes and opted for a more subtle air of mystery…a sense of tension and the unknown. Here, the team walks through a deserted city with the Watcher looking down on them. Yancy Street was the fictional double for New York City's Delancey Street, in the heart of the Lower East Side neighborhood where Jack Kirby grew up.

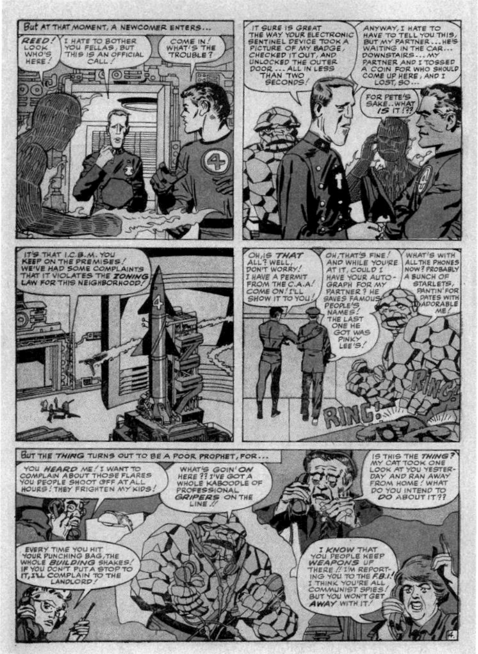

But AT THAT MOMENT, A NEWCOMER ENTERS...
REED! LOOK WHO'S HERE!
I HATE TO BOTHER YOU FELLAS, BUT THIS IS AN OFFICIAL CALL!
COME IN! WHAT'S THE TROUBLE?
IT SURE IS GREAT THE WAY YOUR ELECTRONIC SENTINEL DEVICE TOOK A PICTURE OF MY BADGE, CHECKED IT OUT, AND UNLOCKED THE OUTER DOOR... ALL IN LESS THAN TWO SECONDS!
ANYWAY, I HATE TO HAVE TO TELL YOU THIS, BUT MY PARTNER... HE'S WAITING IN THE CAR... DOWNSTAIRS... MY PARTNER AND I TOSSED A COIN FOR WHO SHOULD COME UP HERE, AND I LOST, SO...
FOR PETE'S SAKE..WHAT IS IT!??
IT'S THAT I.C.B.M. YOU KEEP ON THE PREMISES! WE'VE HAD SOME COMPLAINTS THAT IT VIOLATES THE ZONING LAW FOR THIS NEIGHBORHOOD!
OH, IS THAT ALL? WELL, DON'T WORRY! I HAVE A PERMIT FROM THE C.A.A! COME ON! I'LL SHOW IT TO YOU!
OH, THAT'S FINE! AND WHILE YOU'RE AT IT, COULD I HAVE YOUR AUTOGRAPH FOR MY PARTNER? HE SAVES FAMOUS PEOPLE'S NAMES! THE LAST ONE HE GOT WAS PINKY LEE'S!
WHAT'S WITH ALL THE PHONES NOW? PROBABLY A BUNCH OF STARLETS, PANTIN' FOR DATES WITH ADORABLE ME!
RING!
RING!
BUT THE THING TURNS OUT TO BE A POOR PROPHET, FOR...
YOU HEARD ME! I WANT TO COMPLAIN ABOUT THOSE FLARES YOU PEOPLE SHOOT OFF AT ALL HOURS! THEY FRIGHTEN MY KIDS!
WHAT'S GOIN' ON HERE?? I'VE GOT A WHOLE KABOODLE OF PROFESSIONAL GRIPERS ON THE LINE!!
IS THIS THE THING? MY CAT TOOK ONE LOOK AT YOU YESTERDAY AND RAN AWAY FROM HOME! WHAT DO YOU INTEND TO DO ABOUT IT??
EVERY TIME YOU HIT YOUR PUNCHING BAG, THE WHOLE BUILDING SHAKES! IF YOU DON'T PUT A STOP TO IT, I'LL COMPLAIN TO THE LANDLORD!
I KNOW THAT YOU PEOPLE KEEP WEAPONS UP THERE!! I'M REPORTING YOU TO THE F.B.I.! I THINK YOU'RE ALL COMMUNIST SPIES! BUT YOU WON'T GET AWAY WITH IT!
4.

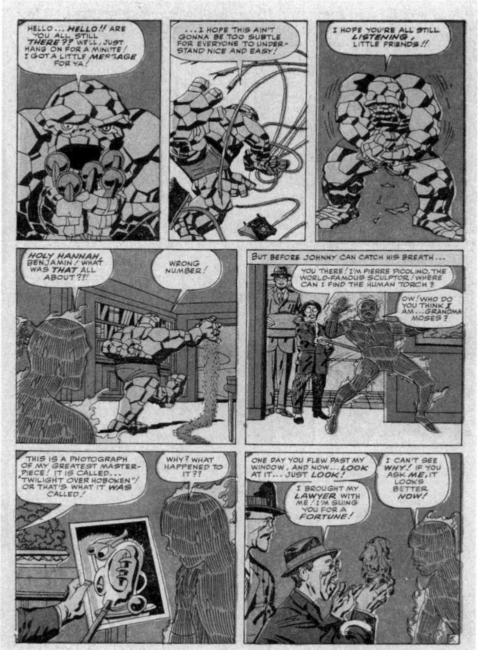

HELLO... HELLO!! ARE YOU ALL STILL THERE?? WELL, JUST HANG ON FOR A MINUTE! I GOT A LITTLE MESSAGE FOR YA!
...I HOPE THIS AIN'T GONNA BE TOO SUBTLE FOR EVERYONE TO UNDERSTAND NICE AND EASY!
I HOPE YOU'RE ALL STILL LISTENING, LITTLE FRIENDS!!
HOLY HANNAH, BENJAMIN! WHAT WAS THAT ALL ABOUT??!
WRONG NUMBER!
BUT BEFORE JOHNNY CAN CATCH HIS BREATH...
YOU THERE! I'M PIERRE PICOLINO, THE WORLD-FAMOUS SCULPTOR! WHERE CAN I FIND THE HUMAN TORCH?
OW! WHO DO YOU THINK I AM...GRANDMA MOSES?
THIS IS A PHOTOGRAPH OF MY GREATEST MASTERPIECE! IT IS CALLED... "TWILIGHT OVER HOBOKEN"! OR THAT'S WHAT IT WAS CALLED!
WHY? WHAT HAPPENED TO IT??
ONE DAY YOU FLEW PAST MY WINDOW, AND NOW... LOOK AT IT... JUST LOOK!
I BROUGHT MY LAWYER WITH ME! I'M SUING YOU FOR A FORTUNE!
I CAN'T SEE WHY! IF YOU ASK ME, IT LOOKS BETTER NOW!
5.

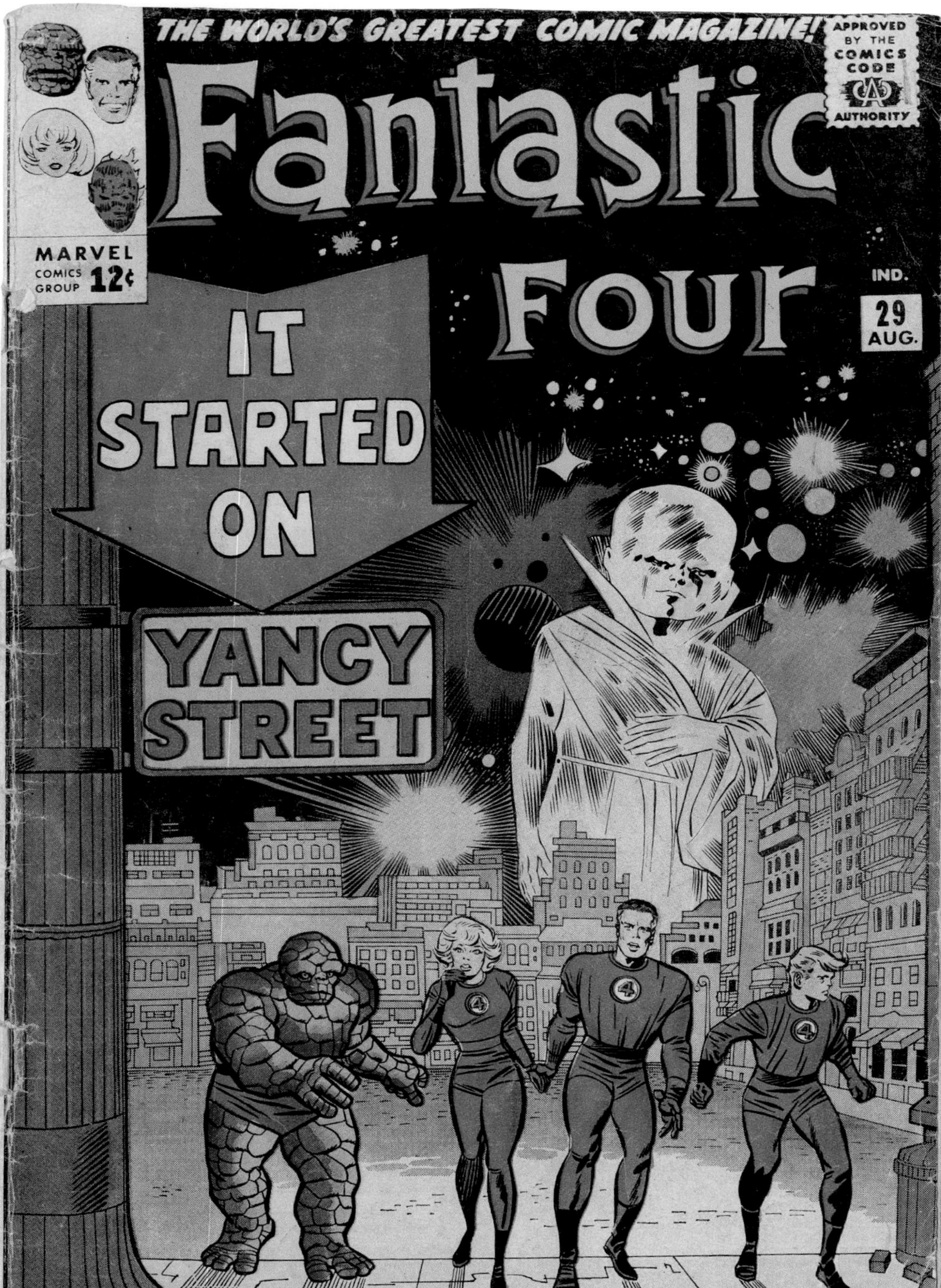
THE WORLD'S GREATEST COMIC MAGAZINE!
APPROVED BY THE COMICS CODE AUTHORITY
Fantastic Four
MARVEL COMICS GROUP 12¢
IND.
29 AUG.
IT STARTED ON
YANCY STREET

FANTASTIC FOUR No. 30

(Right) Interior, "The Dreaded Diablo!"; script, Stan Lee; pencils, Jack Kirby; inks, Chic Stone; September 1964. Kirby's mastery of his craft — in this case his signature use of foreshortening — created a 3-D effect that reached out and grabbed readers. No matter how impossible they were, in the hands of the King, characters like the Human Torch and the Thing looked nothing but real.

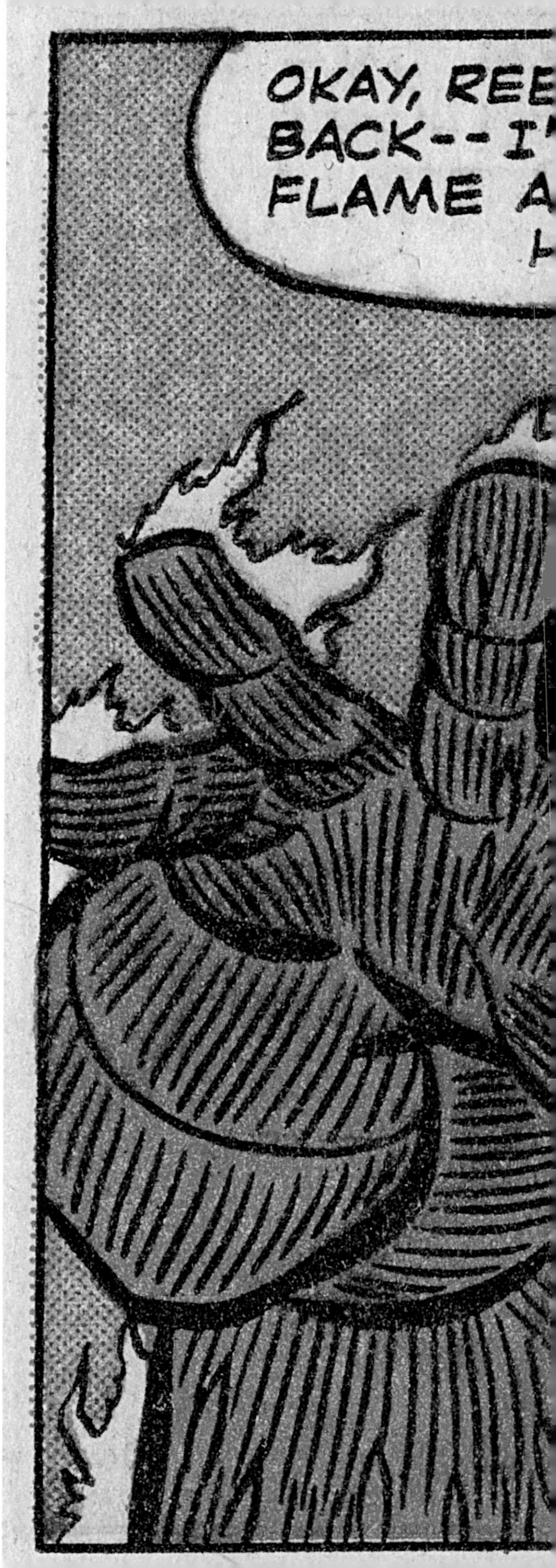
OKAY, REE
BACK--I'
FLAME A

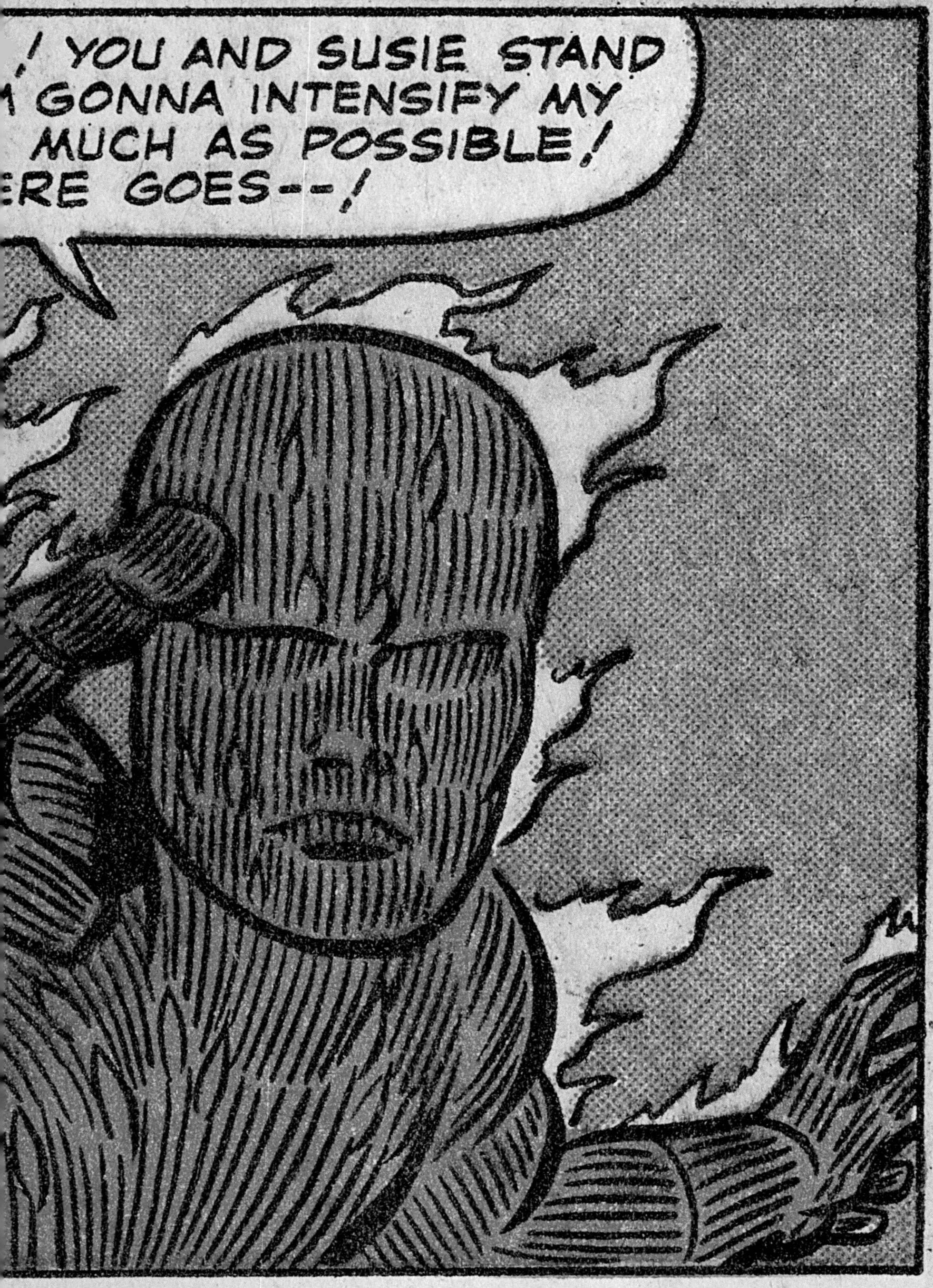
! YOU AND SUSIE STAND
GONNA INTENSIFY MY
MUCH AS POSSIBLE!
ERE GOES--!

FRANKENSTEIN
by MARY W. SHELLEY
ILLUSTRATED WITH SCENES FROM THE UNIVERSAL PHOTOPLAY PRESENTED BY CARL LAEMMLE

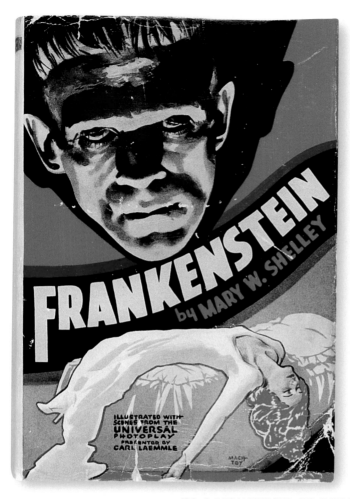

TO A NEW WORLD OF GODS AND MONSTERS

(Above) Book cover; author, Mary Shelley; Frankenstein*; Grosset & Dunlap; 1931.* Lee and Kirby's Hulk was clearly influenced visually by the classic Frankenstein movies, in particular Mary Shelley's monster as portrayed by Boris Karloff. Complemented by the brilliant makeup of Jack Pierce, the monster was a sympathetic character, much like the Hulk.

THE INCREDIBLE HULK No. 1

(Opposite) Cover; pencils, Jack Kirby; inks, attributed Kirby; May 1962. Marvel continues the monster motif popularized by the Thing. Stan Lee's cover copy playfully teases his audience with questions on exactly what kind of character the Hulk would be. Robert Bruce Banner—whose full name resulted from Stan Lee occasionally calling him "Bob"—is struck by the gamma rays of an atomic bomb while rescuing teenager Rick Jones.

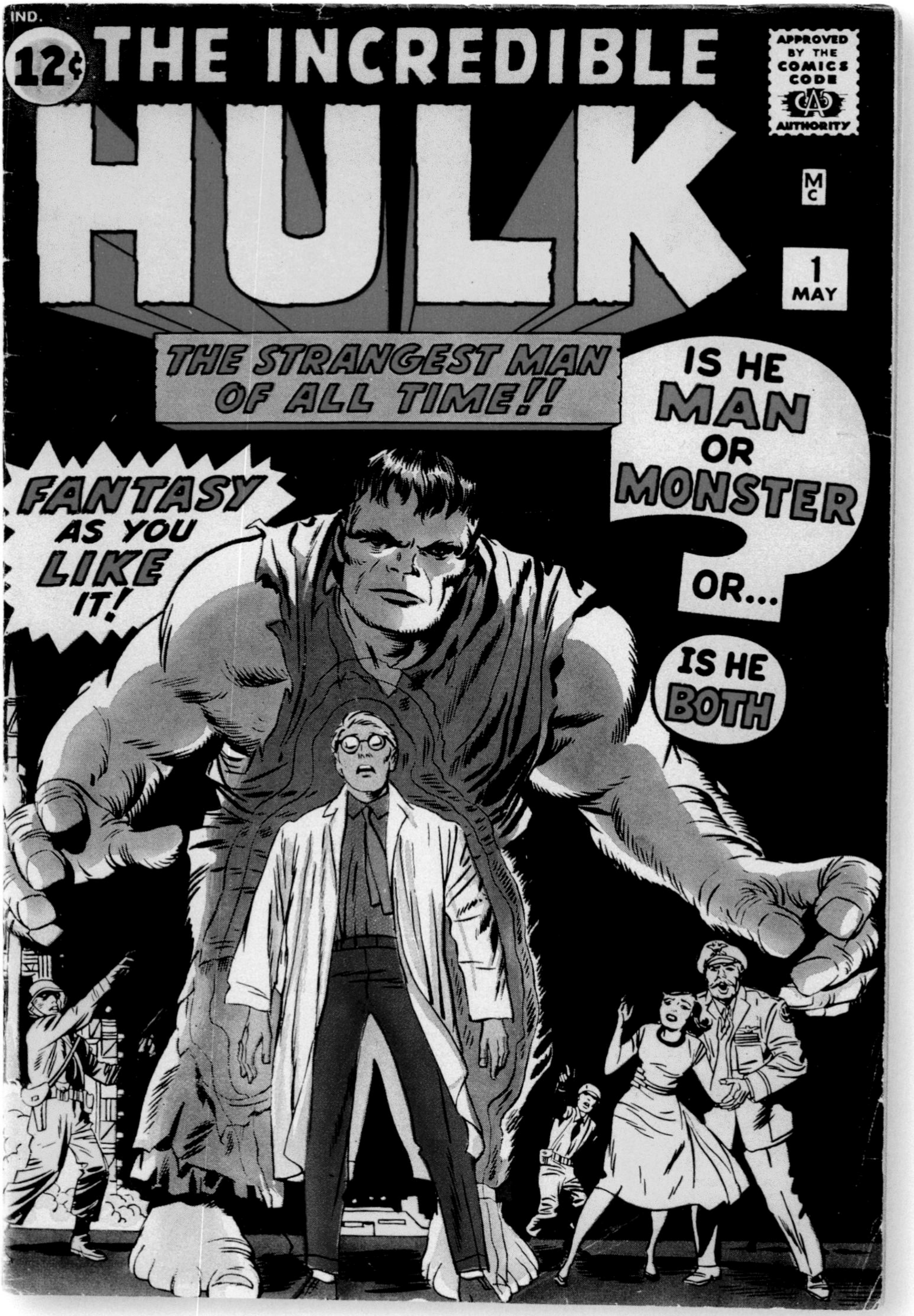
IND.
12¢
THE INCREDIBLE
HULK
APPROVED BY THE COMICS CODE AUTHORITY
MC
1
MAY
THE STRANGEST MAN OF ALL TIME!!
IS HE MAN OR MONSTER OR...
IS HE BOTH
FANTASY AS YOU LIKE IT!

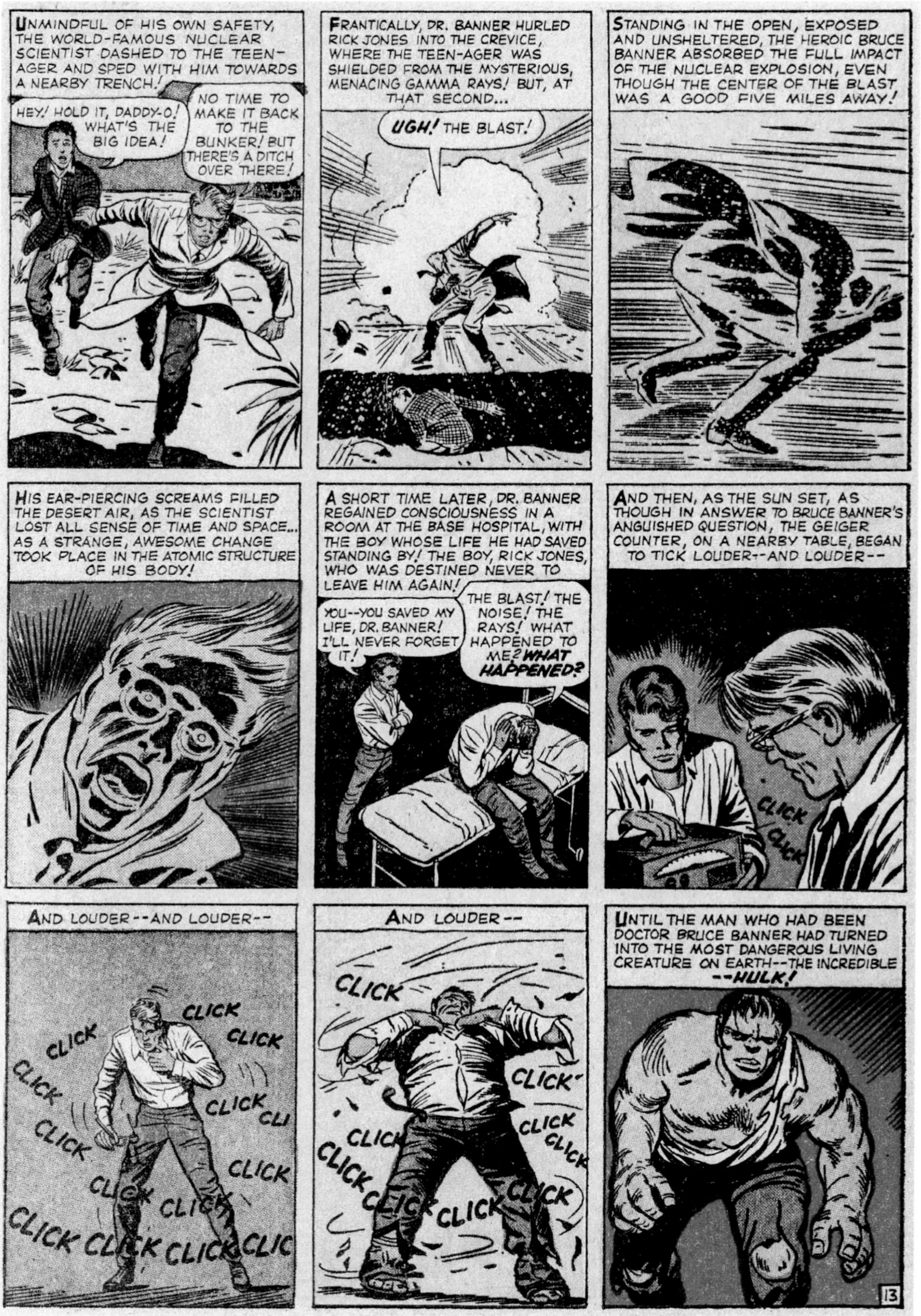
UNMINDFUL OF HIS OWN SAFETY, THE WORLD-FAMOUS NUCLEAR SCIENTIST DASHED TO THE TEEN-AGER AND SPED WITH HIM TOWARDS A NEARBY TRENCH!
HEY! HOLD IT, DADDY-O! WHAT'S THE BIG IDEA!
NO TIME TO MAKE IT BACK TO THE BUNKER! BUT THERE'S A DITCH OVER THERE!
FRANTICALLY, DR. BANNER HURLED RICK JONES INTO THE CREVICE, WHERE THE TEEN-AGER WAS SHIELDED FROM THE MYSTERIOUS, MENACING GAMMA RAYS! BUT, AT THAT SECOND...
UGH! THE BLAST!
STANDING IN THE OPEN, EXPOSED AND UNSHELTERED, THE HEROIC BRUCE BANNER ABSORBED THE FULL IMPACT OF THE NUCLEAR EXPLOSION, EVEN THOUGH THE CENTER OF THE BLAST WAS A GOOD FIVE MILES AWAY!
HIS EAR-PIERCING SCREAMS FILLED THE DESERT AIR, AS THE SCIENTIST LOST ALL SENSE OF TIME AND SPACE... AS A STRANGE, AWESOME CHANGE TOOK PLACE IN THE ATOMIC STRUCTURE OF HIS BODY!
A SHORT TIME LATER, DR. BANNER REGAINED CONSCIOUSNESS IN A ROOM AT THE BASE HOSPITAL, WITH THE BOY WHOSE LIFE HE HAD SAVED STANDING BY! THE BOY, RICK JONES, WHO WAS DESTINED NEVER TO LEAVE HIM AGAIN!
YOU--YOU SAVED MY LIFE, DR. BANNER! I'LL NEVER FORGET IT!
THE BLAST! THE NOISE! THE RAYS! WHAT HAPPENED TO ME? WHAT HAPPENED?
AND THEN, AS THE SUN SET, AS THOUGH IN ANSWER TO BRUCE BANNER'S ANGUISHED QUESTION, THE GEIGER COUNTER, ON A NEARBY TABLE, BEGAN TO TICK LOUDER--AND LOUDER--
CLICK CLICK
AND LOUDER--AND LOUDER--
CLICK CLICK CLICK CLICK CLICK CLICK CLI CLICK CLICK CLICK CLICK CLICK CLICK CLICK CLIC
AND LOUDER--
CLICK CLICK CLICK CLICK CLICK CLICK CLICK CLICK CLICK CLICK
UNTIL THE MAN WHO HAD BEEN DOCTOR BRUCE BANNER HAD TURNED INTO THE MOST DANGEROUS LIVING CREATURE ON EARTH--THE INCREDIBLE --HULK!
13

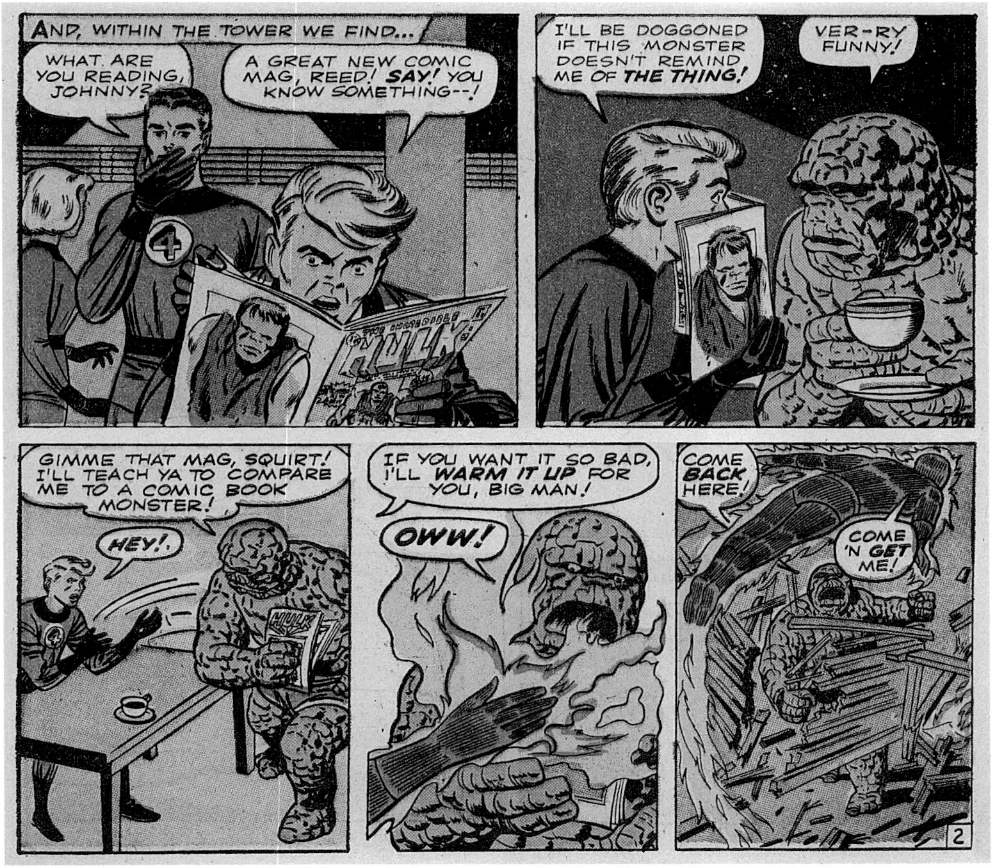
AND, WITHIN THE TOWER WE FIND...
WHAT ARE YOU READING, JOHNNY?
A GREAT NEW COMIC MAG, REED! SAY! YOU KNOW SOMETHING--!
I'LL BE DOGGONED IF THIS MONSTER DOESN'T REMIND ME OF THE THING!
VER-RY FUNNY!
GIMME THAT MAG, SQUIRT! I'LL TEACH YA TO COMPARE ME TO A COMIC BOOK MONSTER!
HEY!
IF YOU WANT IT SO BAD, I'LL WARM IT UP FOR YOU, BIG MAN!
OWW!
COME BACK HERE!
COME 'N GET ME!
2

THE INCREDIBLE HULK No. 3

(Opposite) Interior, "The Origin of The Hulk!"; script, Stan Lee; pencils, Jack Kirby; inks, Dick Ayers; September 1962. A Marvel tradition begins: updating new readers on the abilities and history of a character in a short story a few months after their debut.

FANTASTIC FOUR No. 5

(Above) Interior, "Prisoners of Dr. Doom!"; script, Stan Lee; pencils, Jack Kirby; inks, Joe Sinnott; July 1962. "Say! You know something—! I'll be doggoned if this monster doesn't remind me of the Thing!" Once again, Johnny Storm learns about a super hero by keeping up with Marvel comics. In *Strange Tales* No. 114, not too far in the future, the Torch will rediscover Captain America through a comic book as well!

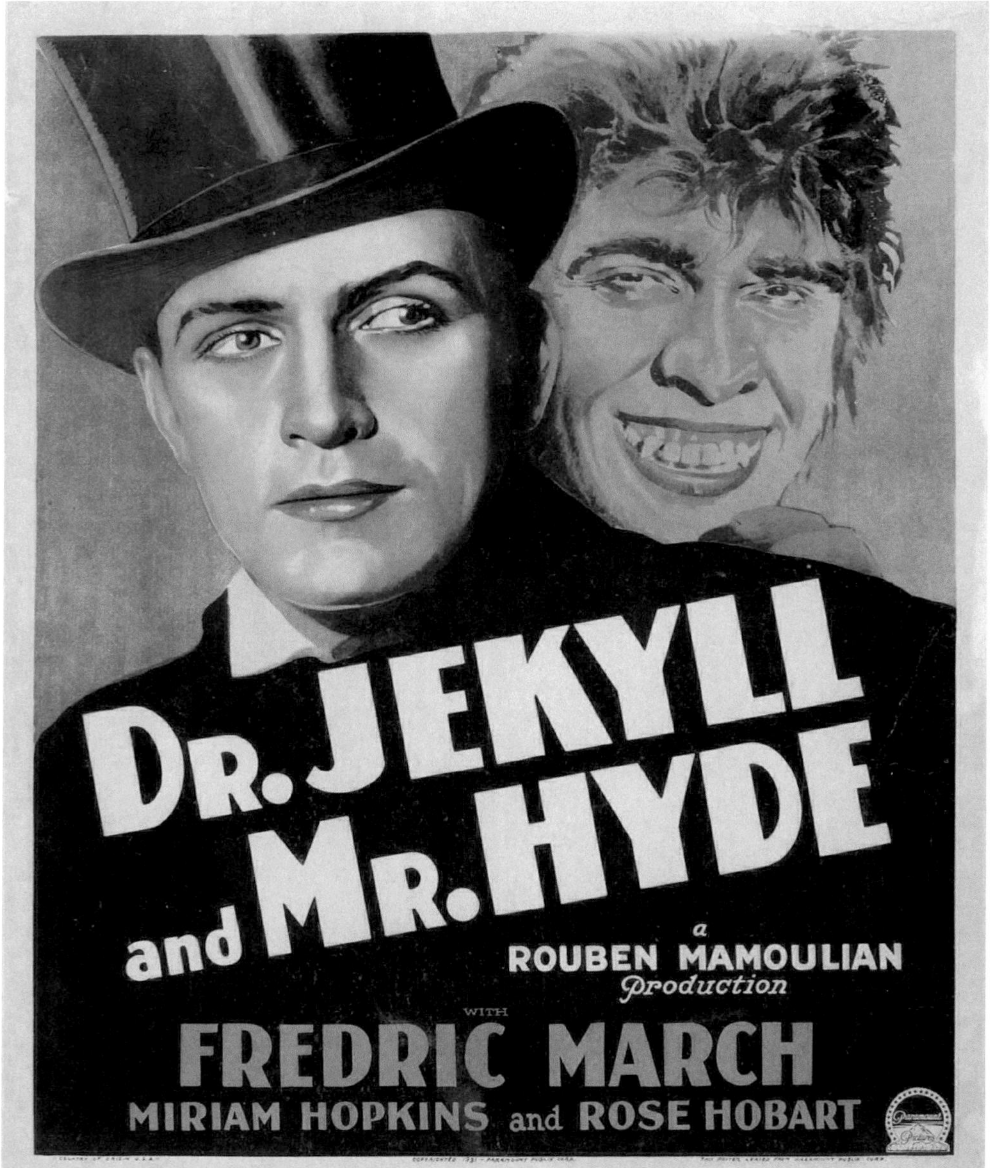
DR. JEKYLL
and MR. HYDE
a
ROUBEN MAMOULIAN
Production
WITH
FREDRIC MARCH
MIRIAM HOPKINS and ROSE HOBART

SPLIT PERSONALITY

(Above) Poster, Dr. Jekyll and Mr. Hyde, *Paramount Pictures, 1931.* Based on the novel by Robert Louis Stevenson, the 1931 movie starring Fredric March was one of numerous versions to hit the silver screen. The dichotomy between Bruce Banner and his terrible alter ego was clearly influenced by the classic story.

THE INCREDIBLE HULK No. 1

(Below) Interior, "The Coming of The Hulk!"; script, Stan Lee; pencils, Jack Kirby; inks, Paul Reinman; May 1962. The Hulk was not an instant success when his series debuted. In fact, his book was canceled after only six issues. Perhaps it was the inconsistent nature of his metamorphosis — initially tied to external forces such as the sunrise, then a machine. His battleship-gray hide lasted but one issue, the reproduction of which, Stan Goldberg lamented, fluctuated so much that it even appeared green in this fateful panel. Whatever the reason, Lee saw the potential in the emerald goliath, and for 18 months he fought his way through the rest of Marvel's titles until finally landing his own feature in *Tales to Astonish,* where Ditko added the anger management issues, along with a strong supporting cast.

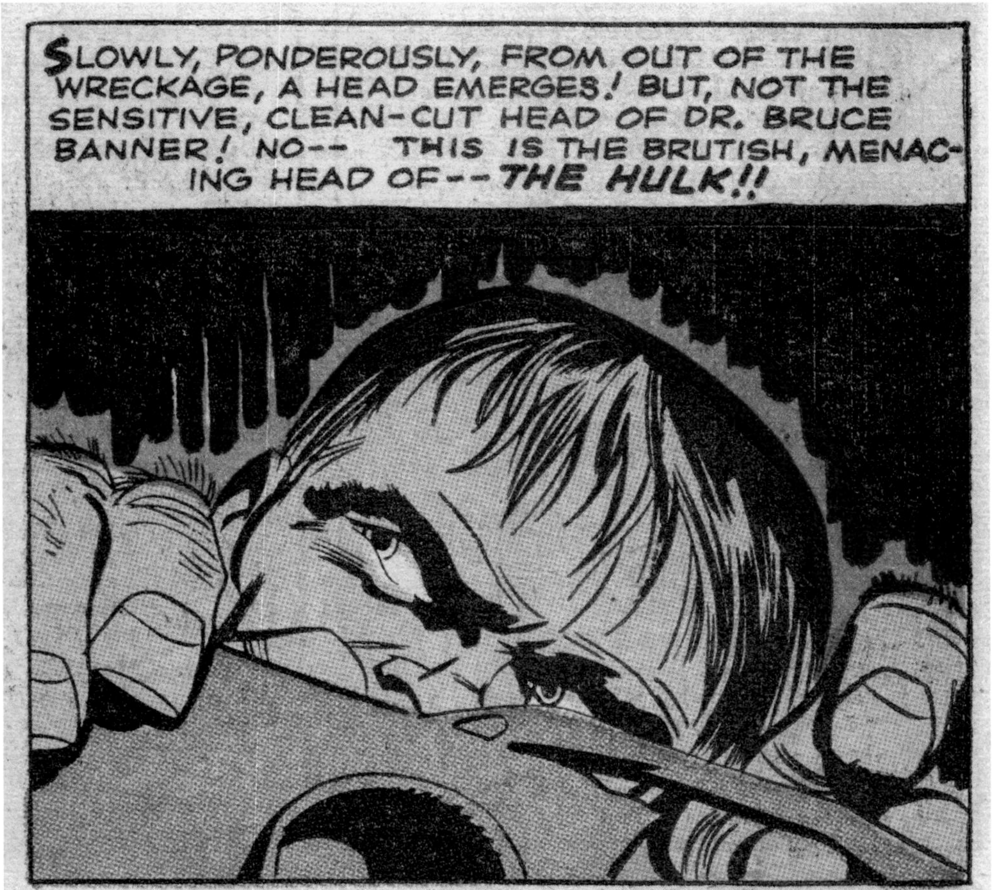
SLOWLY, PONDEROUSLY, FROM OUT OF THE WRECKAGE, A HEAD EMERGES! BUT, NOT THE SENSITIVE, CLEAN-CUT HEAD OF DR. BRUCE BANNER! NO-- THIS IS THE BRUTISH, MENACING HEAD OF--THE HULK!!

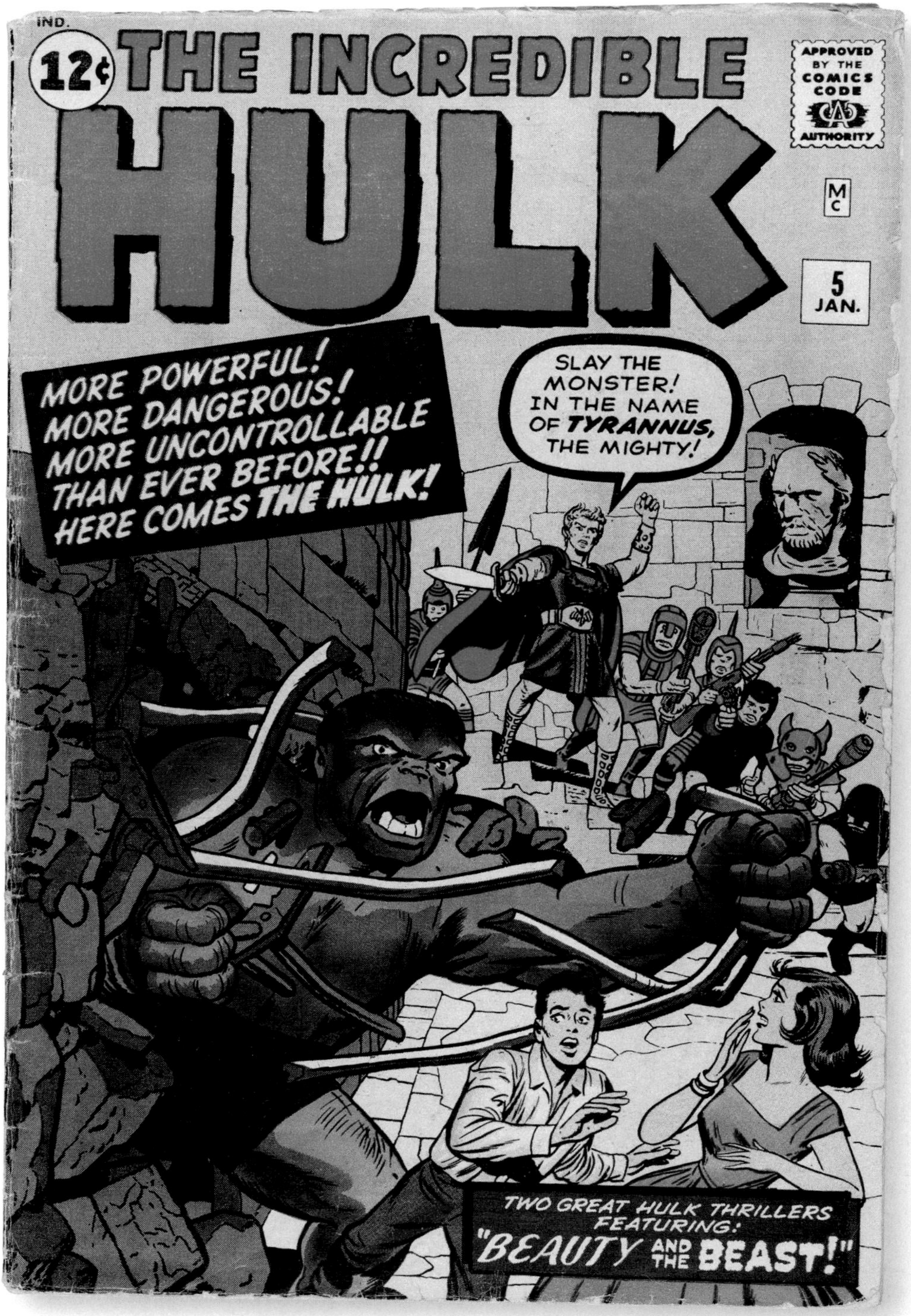
IND.
12¢
THE INCREDIBLE HULK
APPROVED BY THE COMICS CODE AUTHORITY
MC
5 JAN.
MORE POWERFUL! MORE DANGEROUS! MORE UNCONTROLLABLE THAN EVER BEFORE!! HERE COMES THE HULK!
SLAY THE MONSTER! IN THE NAME OF TYRANNUS, THE MIGHTY!
TWO GREAT HULK THRILLERS FEATURING: "BEAUTY AND THE BEAST!"

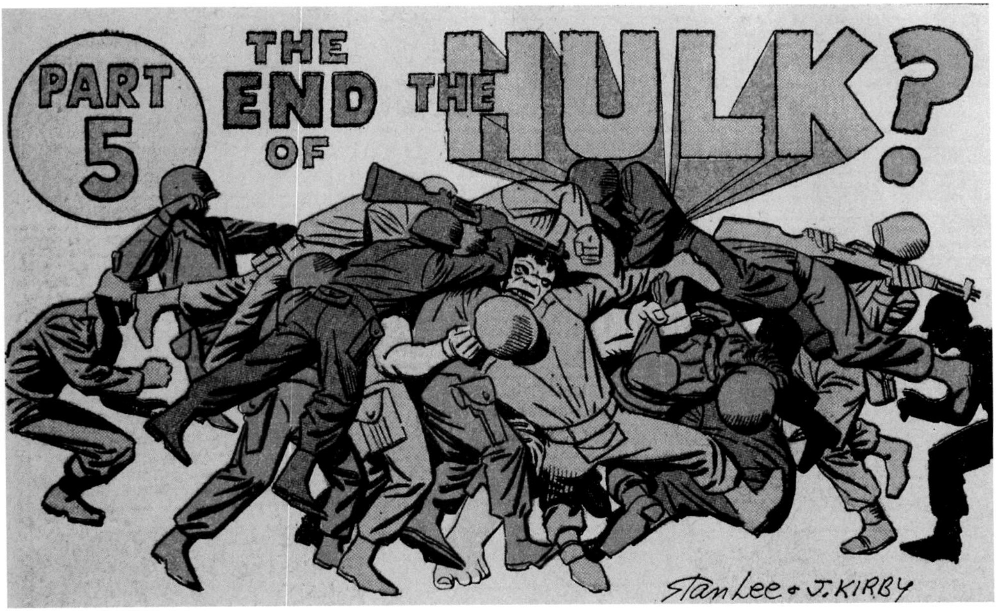
PART 5
THE END OF THE HULK?
STAN LEE + J. KIRBY

THE INCREDIBLE HULK No. 5

(Opposite) Cover; pencils, Jack Kirby; inks, Dick Ayers; January 1963.

THE INCREDIBLE HULK No. 2

(Above) Interior, "Terror of the Toad Men!"; script, Stan Lee; pencils, Jack Kirby; inks, Steve Ditko; July 1962. Ditko's detailed inking brings a sense of dread to the proceedings—in this case a classic Kirby slugfest, the likes of which hadn't been seen since Captain America's glory days in the early 1940s. Ditko was one of Kirby's early inkers in the pre-hero Atlas era, an all-star team that continued occasionally into the Marvel Age.

"We figure that, as Jack said, we don't have to be that accurate, because we think we can do better. After all, mythology is mythology, and who's to say that we can't make up our own myths? Which is what we're doing, just basing them on the past ones, and having a heck of a good time doing it."

— STAN LEE

THE MIGHTY THOR

(Opposite) Original interior art, "Thor vs. the Executioner!" Journey into Mystery *No. 84; plot, Stan Lee; script, Larry Lieber; pencils, Jack Kirby; inks, Dick Ayers; September 1962.* A common practice in the new world of Marvel heroes: A quick recap of the previous issue brings new readers up to date. More than just a stopgap in case readers missed an issue on the newsstand, this technique offered the added bonus of allowing the artists and writers to play with — and perfect — key moments in each character's fictional life, just like the retelling of the classical mythologies that came before them.

13. JRNY into MYSTERY. JUNE '62 V-831

JOURNEY INTO MYSTERY 84 6 1/4 x 9 1/4 1 S.P. P.1.

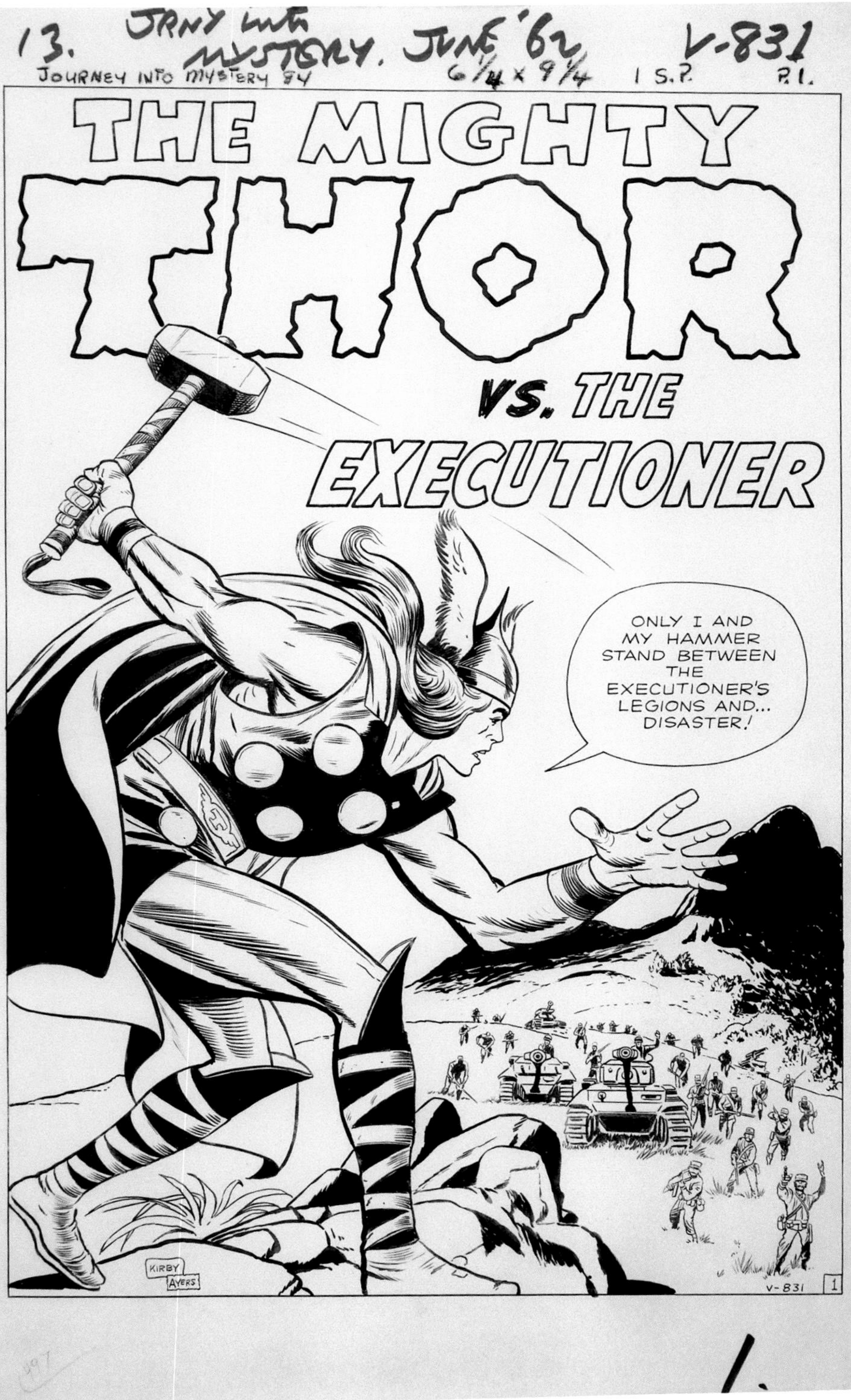
THE MIGHTY
THOR
VS. THE
EXECUTIONER
ONLY I AND MY HAMMER STAND BETWEEN THE EXECUTIONER'S LEGIONS AND... DISASTER!
KIRBY
AYERS
V-831
1

1.

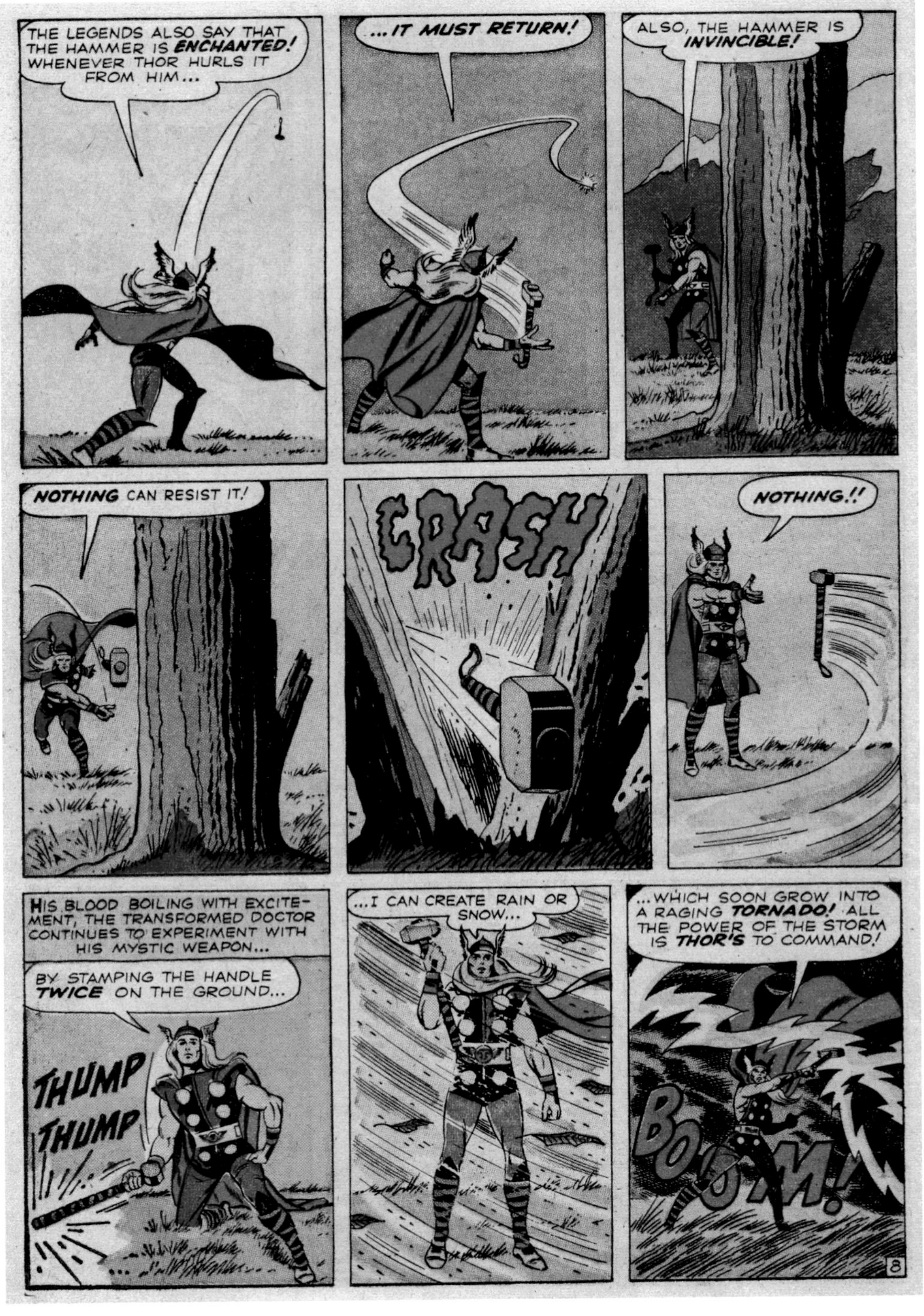
THE LEGENDS ALSO SAY THAT THE HAMMER IS ENCHANTED! WHENEVER THOR HURLS IT FROM HIM...
...IT MUST RETURN!
ALSO, THE HAMMER IS INVINCIBLE!
NOTHING CAN RESIST IT!
CRASH
NOTHING!!
HIS BLOOD BOILING WITH EXCITEMENT, THE TRANSFORMED DOCTOR CONTINUES TO EXPERIMENT WITH HIS MYSTIC WEAPON...
BY STAMPING THE HANDLE TWICE ON THE GROUND...
THUMP
THUMP
...I CAN CREATE RAIN OR SNOW...
...WHICH SOON GROW INTO A RAGING TORNADO! ALL THE POWER OF THE STORM IS THOR'S TO COMMAND!
BOOM!
8

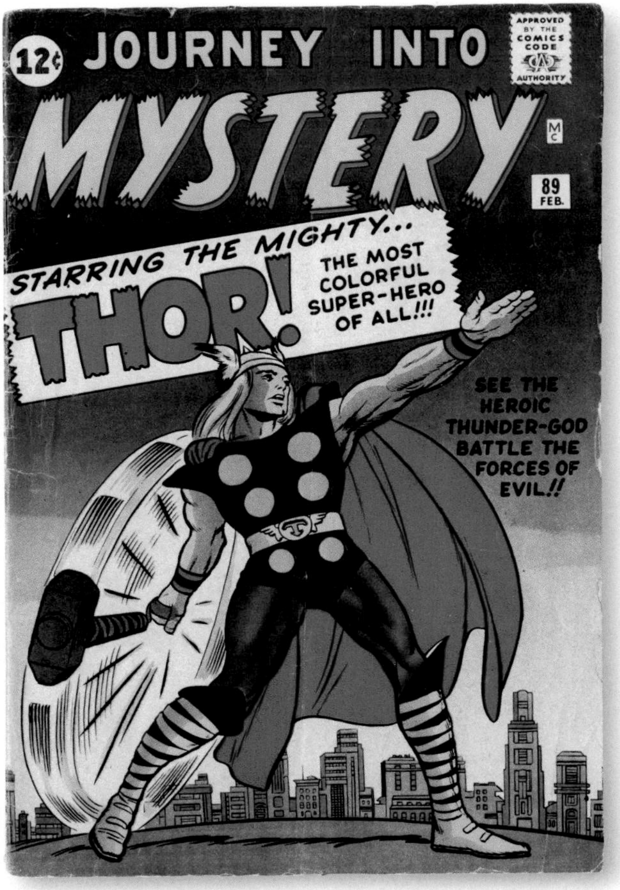
12¢
JOURNEY INTO
APPROVED BY THE COMICS CODE AUTHORITY
MYSTERY
MC
89 FEB.
STARRING THE MIGHTY...
THOR!
THE MOST COLORFUL SUPER-HERO OF ALL!!!
SEE THE HEROIC THUNDER-GOD BATTLE THE FORCES OF EVIL!!

JOURNEY INTO MYSTERY No. 84

(Opposite) Interior, "Thor vs. the Executioner!"; plot, Stan Lee; script, Larry Lieber; pencils, Jack Kirby; inks, Dick Ayers; September 1962. "How do you make someone stronger than the strongest person?" Stan Lee asks rhetorically in his autobiography. "It finally came to me: Don't make him human — make him a god."

JOURNEY INTO MYSTERY No. 89

(Above) Cover; pencils, Jack Kirby; inks, Dick Ayers; February 1963. Dreamed up by Lee and Kirby, and primarily written by Lee's brother Larry Lieber, the early issues often took place on Earth, with Thor combating Communists and even mobsters such as the Edward G. Robinson–inspired "Thug" Thatcher. Lee and Kirby teamed up on a continuous "Tales of Asgard" feature beginning in issue No. 97 and became the producers of the entire book beginning with issue No. 101.

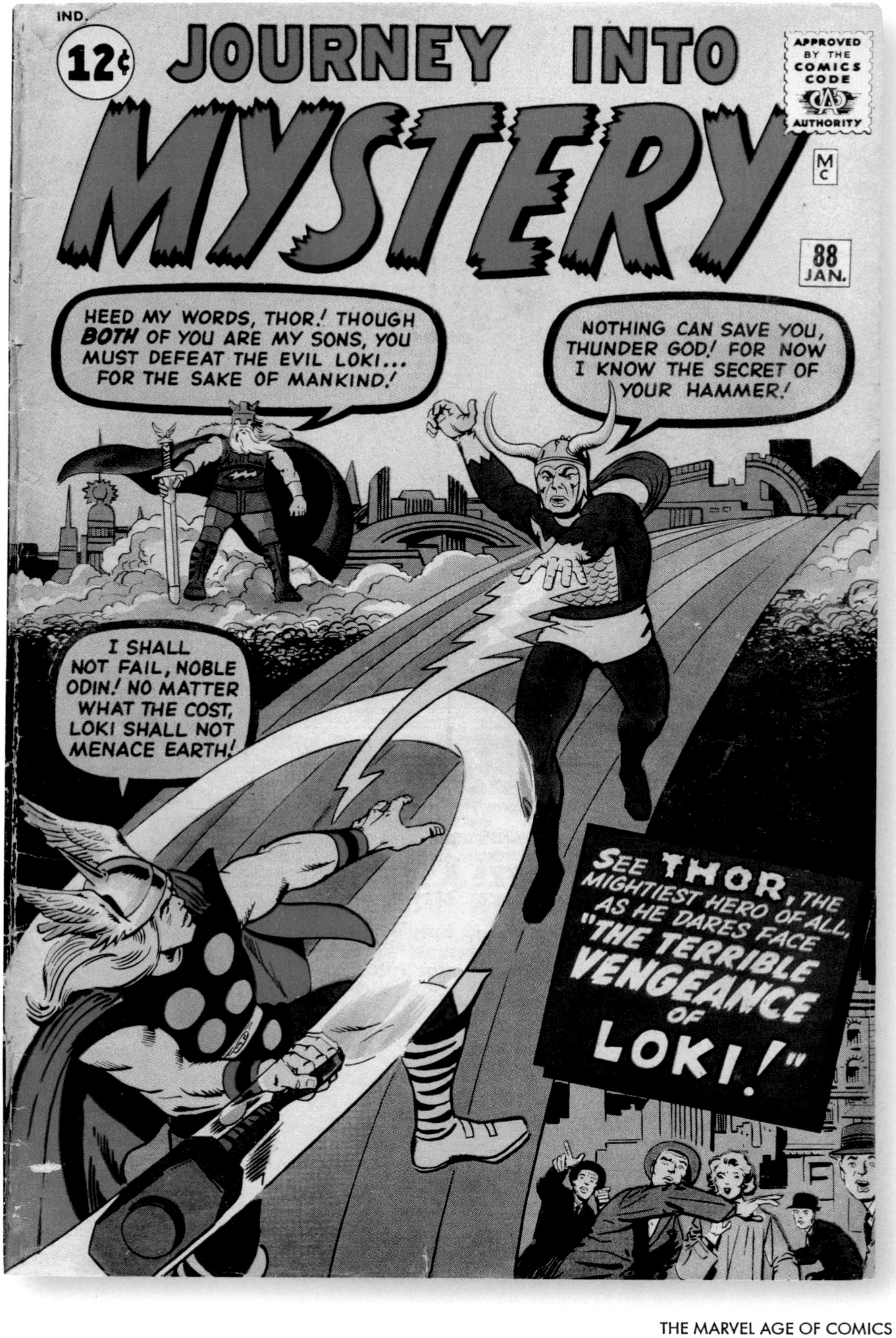
IND.
12¢
JOURNEY INTO
MYSTERY
APPROVED BY THE COMICS CODE AUTHORITY
MC
88
JAN.
HEED MY WORDS, THOR! THOUGH BOTH OF YOU ARE MY SONS, YOU MUST DEFEAT THE EVIL LOKI... FOR THE SAKE OF MANKIND!
NOTHING CAN SAVE YOU, THUNDER GOD! FOR NOW I KNOW THE SECRET OF YOUR HAMMER!
I SHALL NOT FAIL, NOBLE ODIN! NO MATTER WHAT THE COST, LOKI SHALL NOT MENACE EARTH!
SEE THOR, THE MIGHTIEST HERO OF ALL, AS HE DARES FACE "THE TERRIBLE VENGEANCE OF LOKI!"

JOURNEY INTO MYSTERY No. 88

(Opposite) Cover; pencils, Jack Kirby; inks, Steve Ditko; January 1963. Lee clearly had great fun writing the dialect of Asgard, which began in issue No. 110, something no other writer was able to do as well. "I had to give Odin authentic supreme-god expressions. Odin couldn't say, 'Hey, Thor, knock it off, would you.' He had to say things like 'Cease and desist, thou base varlet.'"

JOURNEY INTO MYSTERY No. 85

(Below) Interior, "Trapped by Loki, God of Mischief!"; plot, Stan Lee; script, Larry Lieber; pencils, Jack Kirby; inks, Dick Ayers; October 1962. Thor's mystic background is emphasized here, when in a bit of comic relief, mere humans find they cannot pick up his hammer.

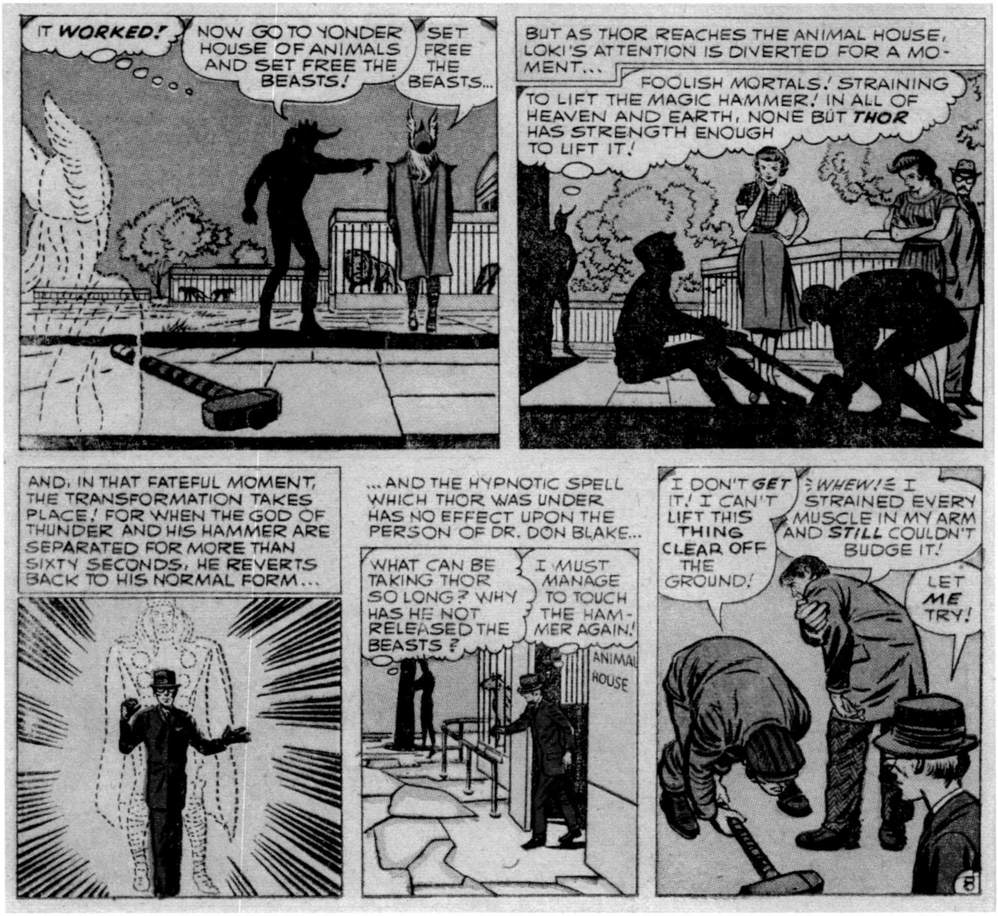

IT WORKED!
NOW GO TO YONDER HOUSE OF ANIMALS AND SET FREE THE BEASTS!
SET FREE THE BEASTS...
BUT AS THOR REACHES THE ANIMAL HOUSE, LOKI'S ATTENTION IS DIVERTED FOR A MOMENT...
FOOLISH MORTALS! STRAINING TO LIFT THE MAGIC HAMMER! IN ALL OF HEAVEN AND EARTH, NONE BUT THOR HAS STRENGTH ENOUGH TO LIFT IT!
AND, IN THAT FATEFUL MOMENT, THE TRANSFORMATION TAKES PLACE! FOR WHEN THE GOD OF THUNDER AND HIS HAMMER ARE SEPARATED FOR MORE THAN SIXTY SECONDS, HE REVERTS BACK TO HIS NORMAL FORM...
...AND THE HYPNOTIC SPELL WHICH THOR WAS UNDER HAS NO EFFECT UPON THE PERSON OF DR. DON BLAKE...
WHAT CAN BE TAKING THOR SO LONG? WHY HAS HE NOT RELEASED THE BEASTS?
I MUST MANAGE TO TOUCH THE HAMMER AGAIN!
ANIMAL HOUSE
I DON'T GET IT! I CAN'T LIFT THIS THING CLEAR OFF THE GROUND!
WHEW! I STRAINED EVERY MUSCLE IN MY ARM AND STILL COULDN'T BUDGE IT!
LET ME TRY!
8

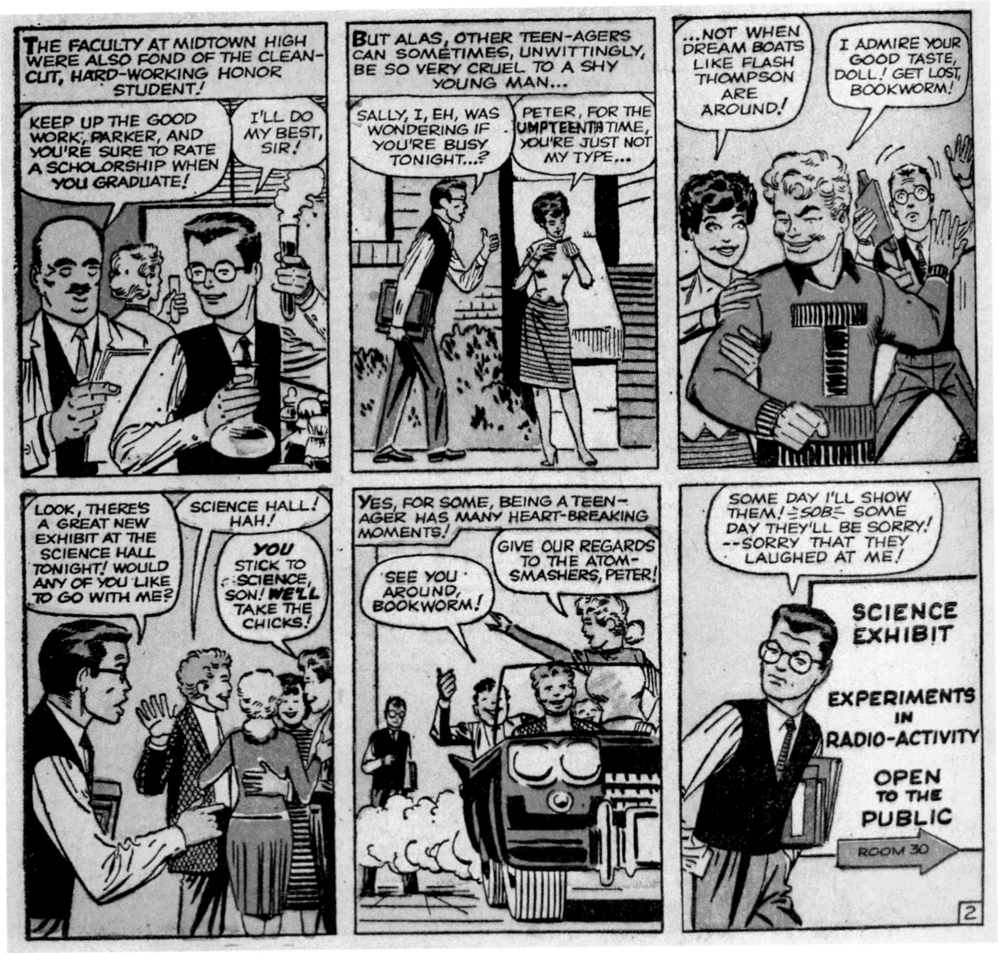
THE FACULTY AT MIDTOWN HIGH WERE ALSO FOND OF THE CLEAN-CUT, HARD-WORKING HONOR STUDENT!
KEEP UP THE GOOD WORK, PARKER, AND YOU'RE SURE TO RATE A SCHOLORSHIP WHEN YOU GRADUATE!
I'LL DO MY BEST, SIR!
BUT ALAS, OTHER TEEN-AGERS CAN SOMETIMES, UNWITTINGLY, BE SO VERY CRUEL TO A SHY YOUNG MAN...
SALLY, I, EH, WAS WONDERING IF YOU'RE BUSY TONIGHT...?
PETER, FOR THE UMPTEENTH TIME, YOU'RE JUST NOT MY TYPE...
...NOT WHEN DREAM BOATS LIKE FLASH THOMPSON ARE AROUND!
I ADMIRE YOUR GOOD TASTE, DOLL! GET LOST, BOOKWORM!
LOOK, THERE'S A GREAT NEW EXHIBIT AT THE SCIENCE HALL TONIGHT! WOULD ANY OF YOU LIKE TO GO WITH ME?
SCIENCE HALL! HAH!
YOU STICK TO SCIENCE, SON! WE'LL TAKE THE CHICKS!
YES, FOR SOME, BEING A TEEN-AGER HAS MANY HEART-BREAKING MOMENTS!
GIVE OUR REGARDS TO THE ATOM-SMASHERS, PETER!
SEE YOU AROUND, BOOKWORM!
SOME DAY I'LL SHOW THEM! -SOB- SOME DAY THEY'LL BE SORRY! --SORRY THAT THEY LAUGHED AT ME!
SCIENCE EXHIBIT
EXPERIMENTS IN RADIO-ACTIVITY
OPEN TO THE PUBLIC
ROOM 30
2

GIVE OUR REGARDS TO THE ATOMSMASHERS

(Above) Interior, Amazing Fantasy *No. 15; "Spider-Man"; script, Stan Lee; pencils and inks, Steve Ditko; August 1962.* Rejected teenager Peter Parker displays his hurt feelings and desire for revenge against his classmates. It seemed honest. Many outsider kids who sought refuge in the world of comic books finally found someone they could relate to. When publisher Martin Goodman studied the sales figures for *Amazing Fantasy*, canceled immediately after Spider-Man's debut, he realized that the odd-looking character he thought so little of had struck a nerve! No fool, Goodman told Stan Lee to reinstate the wall-crawler, this time in his own title.

AMAZING FANTASY No. 15

(Opposite) Interior, "Spider-Man"; script, Stan Lee; pencils and inks, Steve Ditko; August 1962.

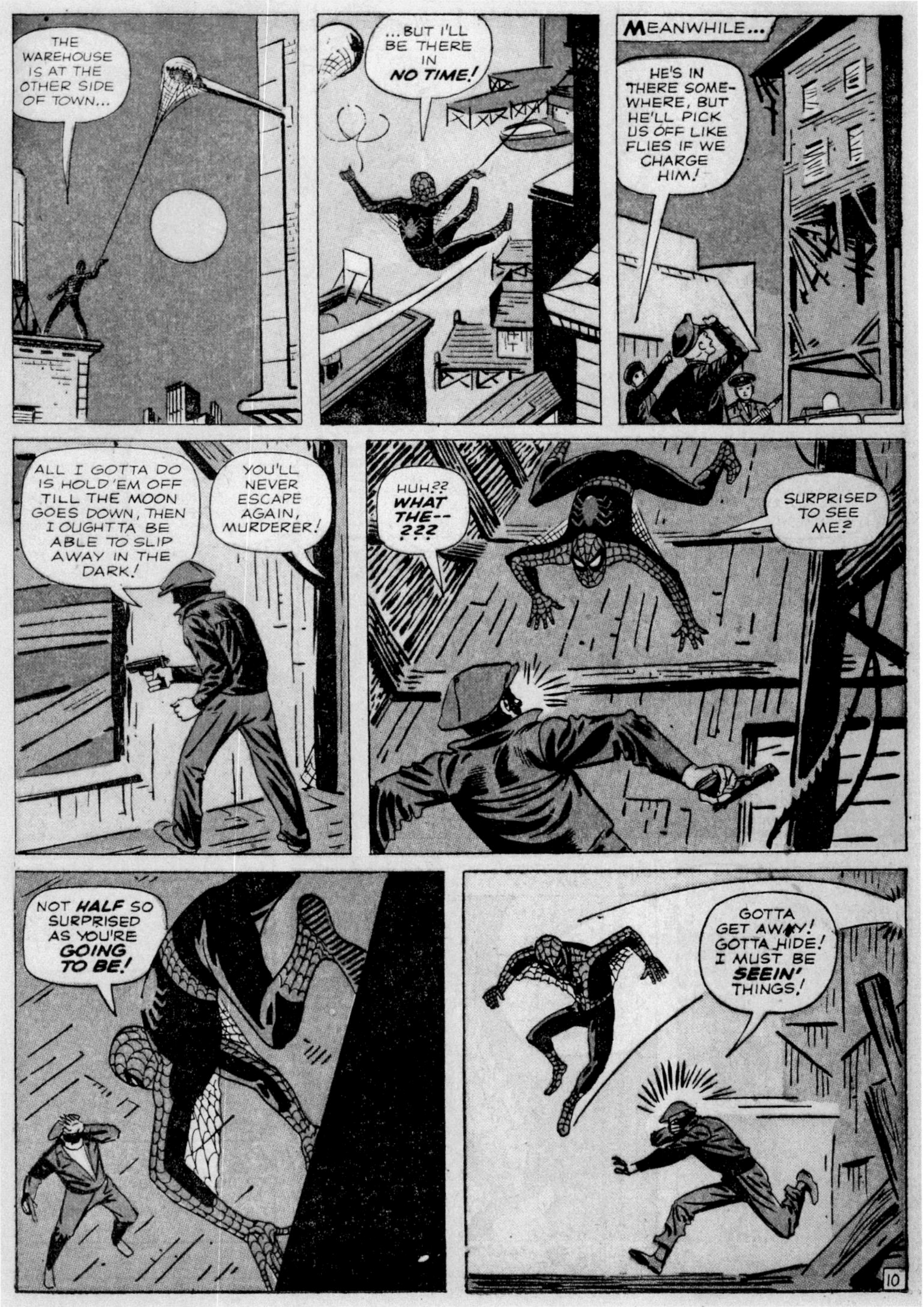
THE WAREHOUSE IS AT THE OTHER SIDE OF TOWN...
...BUT I'LL BE THERE IN NO TIME!
MEANWHILE...
HE'S IN THERE SOMEWHERE, BUT HE'LL PICK US OFF LIKE FLIES IF WE CHARGE HIM!
ALL I GOTTA DO IS HOLD 'EM OFF TILL THE MOON GOES DOWN, THEN I OUGHTTA BE ABLE TO SLIP AWAY IN THE DARK!
YOU'LL NEVER ESCAPE AGAIN, MURDERER!
HUH?? WHAT THE--???
SURPRISED TO SEE ME?
NOT HALF SO SURPRISED AS YOU'RE GOING TO BE!
GOTTA GET AWAY! GOTTA HIDE! I MUST BE SEEIN' THINGS!
10

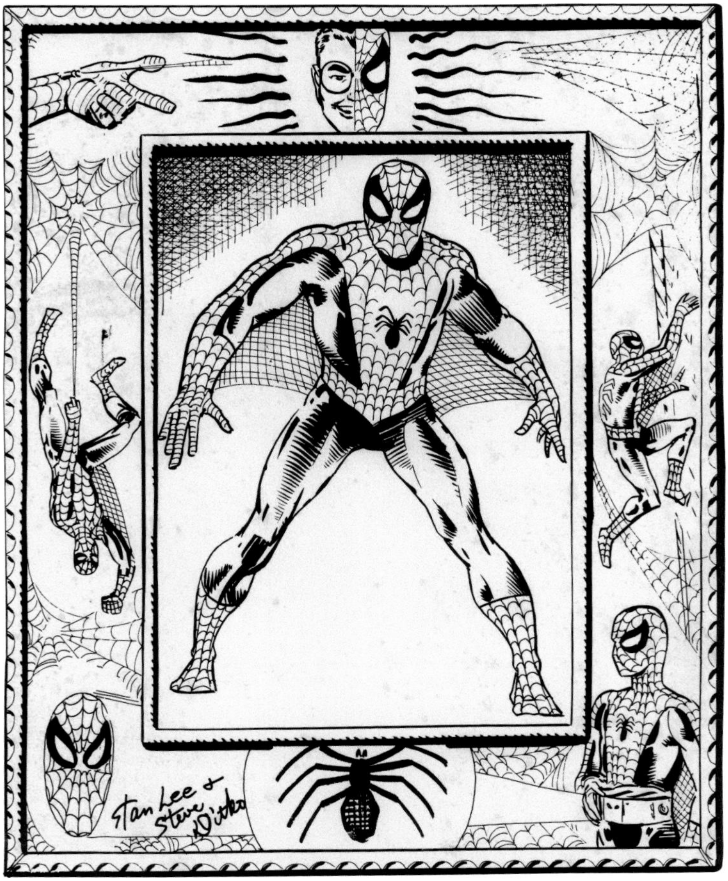
Stan Lee &
Steve Ditko

SELLING SPIDEY

(Above) Original art, Steve Ditko, ca. 1963. This pinup drawing of Spider-Man, signed by Stan Lee and Steve Ditko, was reportedly given away to the earliest fans who wrote letters.

AMAZING SPIDER-MAN No. 2

(Opposite) Interior, "Duel to the Death with the Vulture!"; script, Stan Lee; pencils and inks, Steve Ditko; May 1963. Ditko's detailed rendering of office buildings puts the reader high above the streets of Manhattan. The lean, lithe figure of Spider-Man was another appealing aspect of the character. Unlike most super heroes, who were bursting with muscles, Spider-Man had a body that suited a teenager. The menacing Vulture provided a true contrast of types: young, inexperienced kid against an older and deadlier foe.

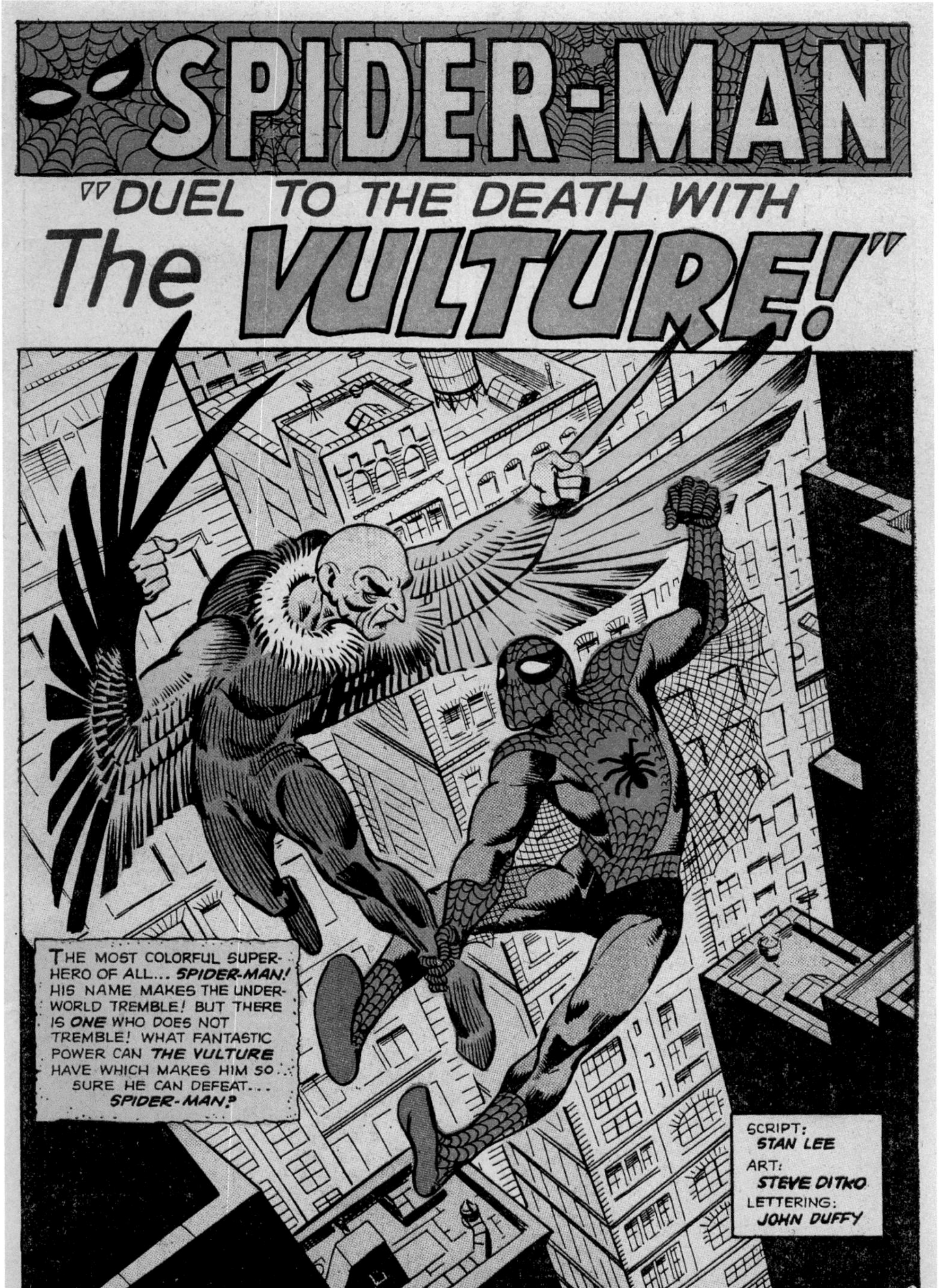
SPIDER-MAN
"DUEL TO THE DEATH WITH The VULTURE!"
THE MOST COLORFUL SUPER-HERO OF ALL... SPIDER-MAN! HIS NAME MAKES THE UNDERWORLD TREMBLE! BUT THERE IS ONE WHO DOES NOT TREMBLE! WHAT FANTASTIC POWER CAN THE VULTURE HAVE WHICH MAKES HIM SO SURE HE CAN DEFEAT... SPIDER-MAN?
SCRIPT: STAN LEE
ART: STEVE DITKO
LETTERING: JOHN DUFFY

AMAZING SPIDER-MAN No. 4

(Below and opposite) Interiors, "Nothing Can Stop . . . the Sandman!"; script, Stan Lee; pencils and inks, Steve Ditko; September 1963. The Sandman was one of Spider-Man's early rogues. Like many of Peter Parker's enemies, Flint Marko started as a common crook. But when he was caught in a nuclear explosion — in yet another Marvel Age tongue-in-cheek endorsement of the wonders of nuclear power — his body chemistry changed, giving him the power to turn to sand or harden like concrete. Spidey had to find a way to beat him and used — of all things — a vacuum cleaner to do the job! The four-panel sequence below is a perfect example of Steve Ditko's ability to visually tell a story.

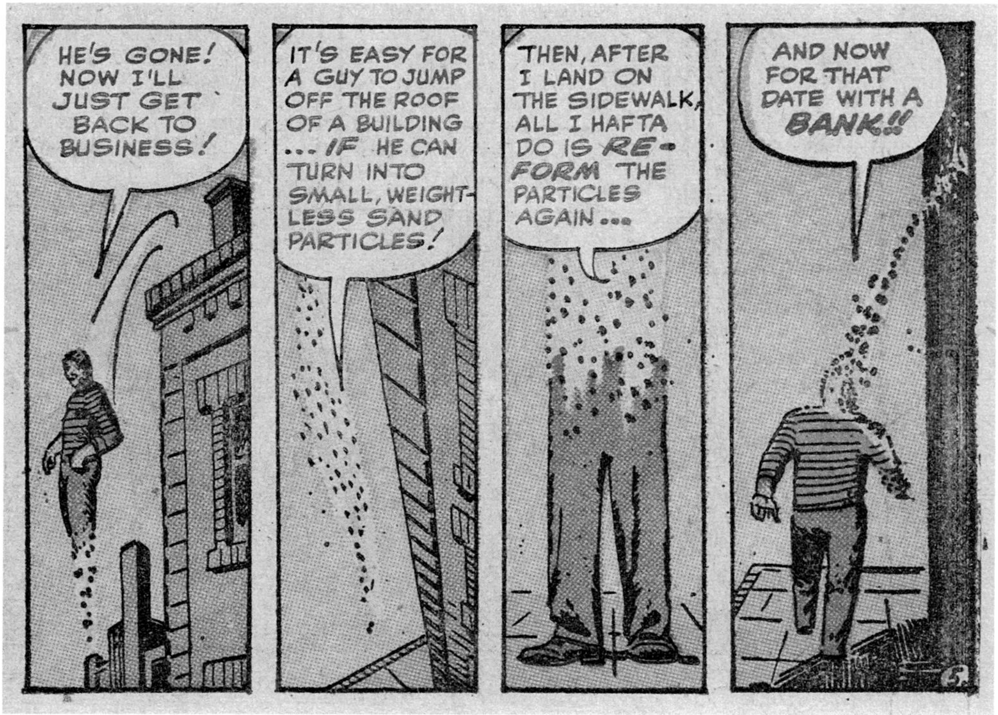
HE'S GONE! NOW I'LL JUST GET BACK TO BUSINESS!
IT'S EASY FOR A GUY TO JUMP OFF THE ROOF OF A BUILDING ... IF HE CAN TURN INTO SMALL, WEIGHT-LESS SAND PARTICLES!
THEN, AFTER I LAND ON THE SIDEWALK, ALL I HAFTA DO IS RE-FORM THE PARTICLES AGAIN ...
AND NOW FOR THAT DATE WITH A BANK!!
5

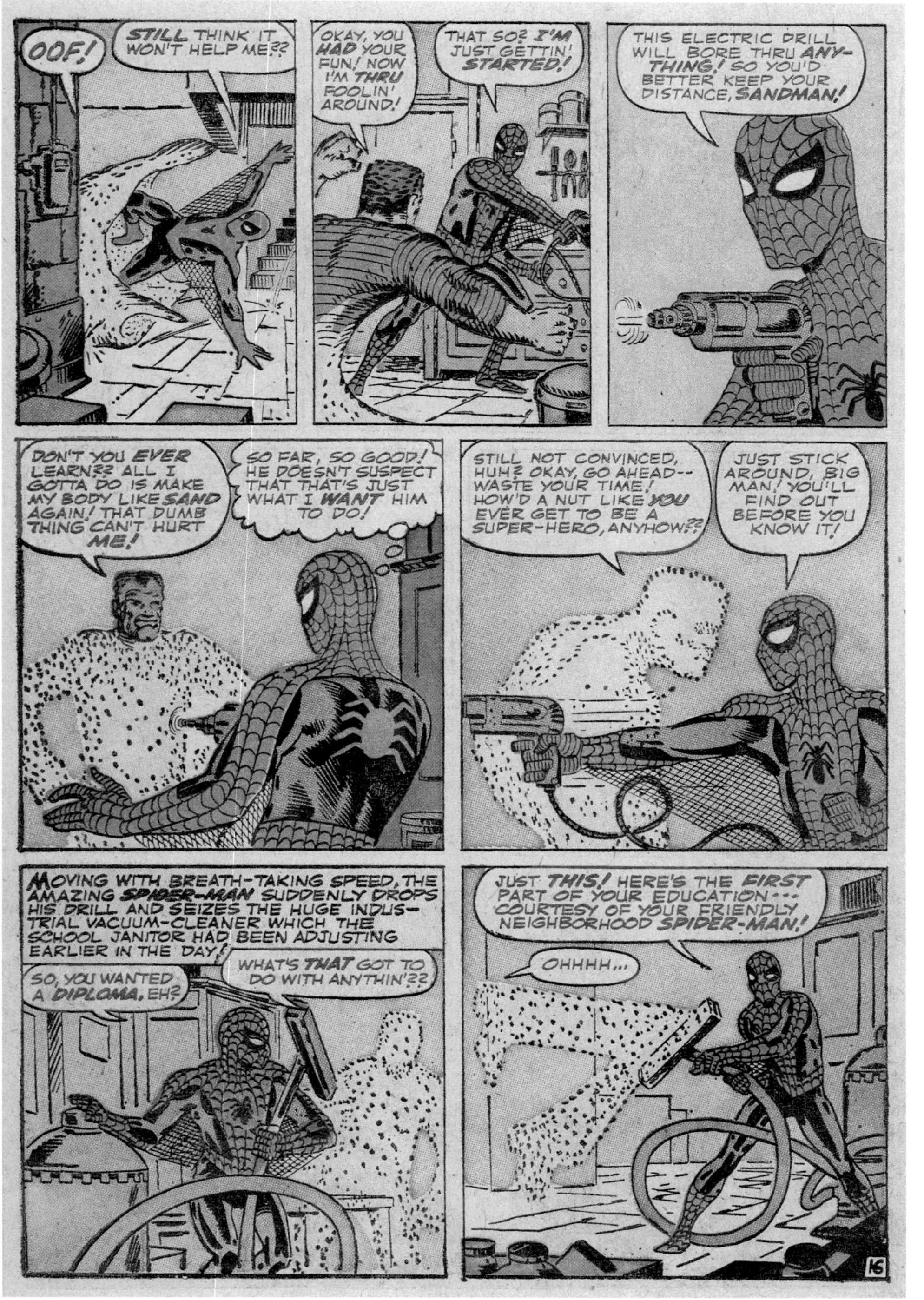
OOF!
STILL THINK IT WON'T HELP ME??
OKAY, YOU HAD YOUR FUN! NOW I'M THRU FOOLIN' AROUND!
THAT SO? I'M JUST GETTIN' STARTED!
THIS ELECTRIC DRILL WILL BORE THRU ANY-THING! SO YOU'D BETTER KEEP YOUR DISTANCE, SANDMAN!
DON'T YOU EVER LEARN?? ALL I GOTTA DO IS MAKE MY BODY LIKE SAND AGAIN! THAT DUMB THING CAN'T HURT ME!
SO FAR, SO GOOD! HE DOESN'T SUSPECT THAT THAT'S JUST WHAT I WANT HIM TO DO!
STILL NOT CONVINCED, HUH? OKAY, GO AHEAD-- WASTE YOUR TIME! HOW'D A NUT LIKE YOU EVER GET TO BE A SUPER-HERO, ANYHOW??
JUST STICK AROUND, BIG MAN! YOU'LL FIND OUT BEFORE YOU KNOW IT!
MOVING WITH BREATH-TAKING SPEED, THE AMAZING SPIDER-MAN SUDDENLY DROPS HIS DRILL AND SEIZES THE HUGE INDUS-TRIAL VACUUM-CLEANER WHICH THE SCHOOL JANITOR HAD BEEN ADJUSTING EARLIER IN THE DAY!
SO, YOU WANTED A DIPLOMA, EH?
WHAT'S THAT GOT TO DO WITH ANYTHIN'??
JUST THIS! HERE'S THE FIRST PART OF YOUR EDUCATION--- COURTESY OF YOUR FRIENDLY NEIGHBORHOOD SPIDER-MAN!
OHHHH...
16

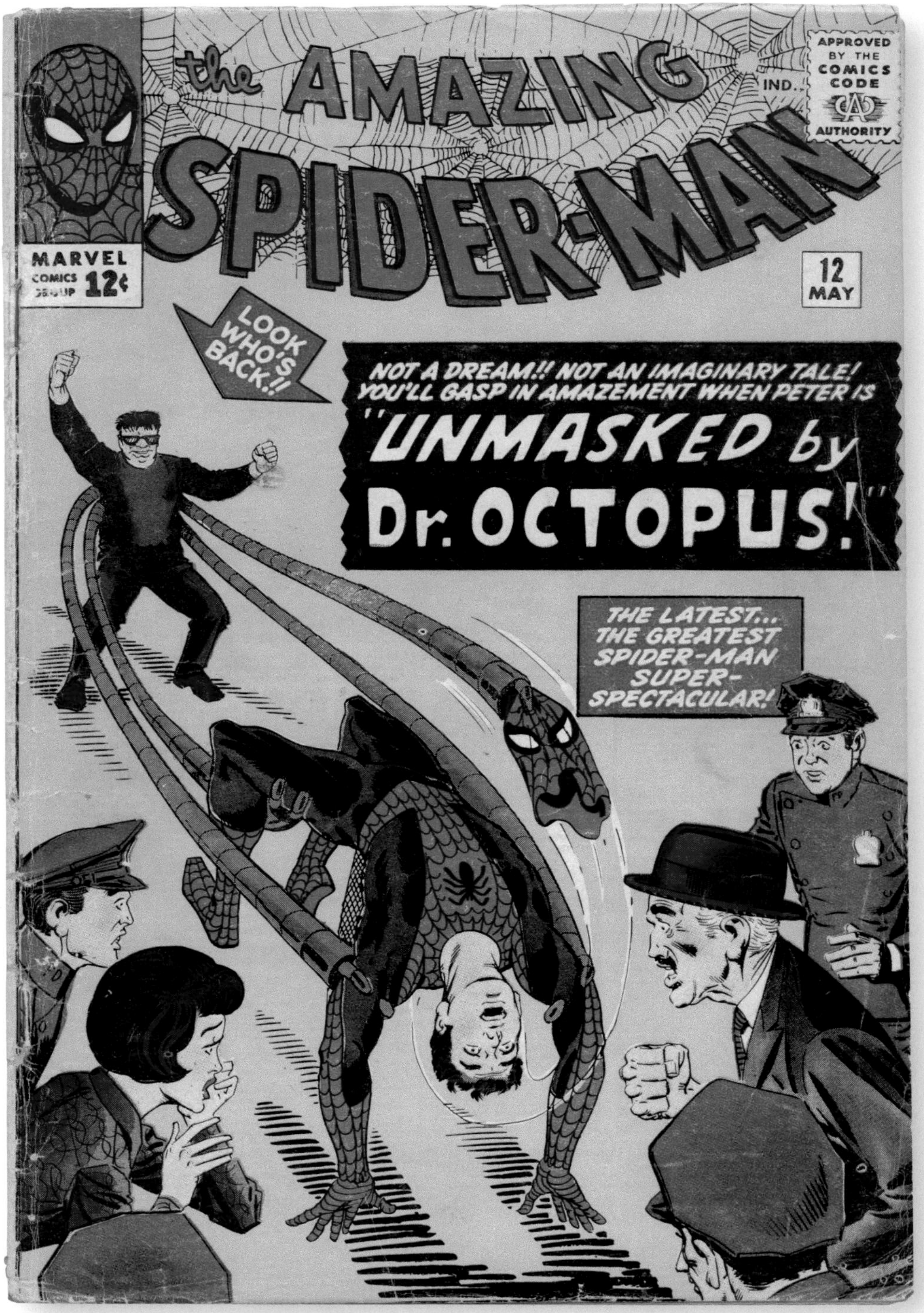
APPROVED BY THE COMICS CODE AUTHORITY
the AMAZING SPIDER-MAN
IND.
MARVEL COMICS GROUP 12¢
12 MAY
LOOK WHO'S BACK..!!
NOT A DREAM!! NOT AN IMAGINARY TALE! YOU'LL GASP IN AMAZEMENT WHEN PETER IS
"UNMASKED by Dr. OCTOPUS!"
THE LATEST... THE GREATEST SPIDER-MAN SUPER-SPECTACULAR!

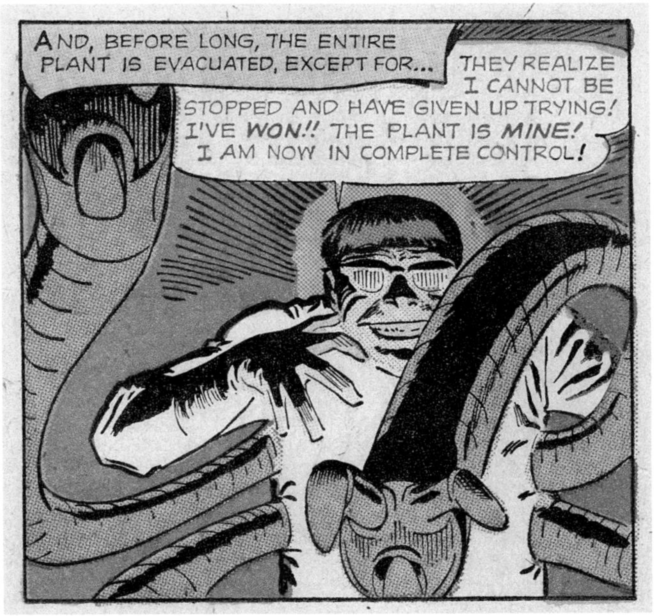
AND, BEFORE LONG, THE ENTIRE PLANT IS EVACUATED, EXCEPT FOR...
THEY REALIZE I CANNOT BE STOPPED AND HAVE GIVEN UP TRYING! I'VE WON!! THE PLANT IS MINE! I AM NOW IN COMPLETE CONTROL!

AMAZING SPIDER-MAN No. 12

(Opposite) Cover; pencils and inks, Steve Ditko; May 1964. Stan Lee's cover copy emphasized that the story was "Not a Dream!" and "Not an Imaginary Tale!"—a direct dig at the Distinguished Competition's "imaginary stories" for Superman and company. Ill with the flu, Peter Parker tries to save his girl, Betty, from Doc Ock. In his weakened state he is easily defeated, and the villain is convinced Parker is only a lovesick kid imitating the real Spider-Man—one benefit of not being taken seriously due to his age!

AMAZING SPIDER-MAN No. 3

(Above) Interior, "Doctor Octopus!"; script, Stan Lee; pencils and inks, Steve Ditko; July 1963. Doc Ock was the first super villain to defeat Spider-Man, who made the mistake of being overconfident. After a bout of depression and self-doubt, Peter learns a lesson about "never giving up" from fellow teenage hero Johnny Storm. In his next encounter, Spidey uses his scientific knowledge to defeat his enemy. Lee and Ditko made it clear that their hero was not perfect and still had a lot to learn.

"Why do I do it? Why don't I give the whole thing up? And yet, I can't! I must have been given this great power for a reason! No matter how difficult it is, I must remain Spider-Man! And I pray that some day the world will understand!"
— PETER PARKER

AMAZING SPIDER-MAN No. 11

(Opposite) Original cover art; pencils and inks, Steve Ditko; April 1964. Ditko's cover is one of the rarest artifacts of the Marvel Age, a pre-1965 original cover. Fewer than ten are known to have circulated in the collector's marketplace. The rest are lost, presumably destroyed. Fabulous Flo Steinberg has repeatedly — and apologetically — admitted that part of her job was to throw out stacks of original art when space became an issue. It's difficult to believe today, but for most of the artists and writers of the period, the comics remained a job, their original artwork merely a by-product of the paycheck. And for the publisher, the originals just took up space. What remains a mystery that pains collectors to this day is, why only the covers? Most original interior pages exist from this period, leading to speculation that it may simply have been that a separate printing plant handled the covers, returning the originals in envelopes containing several months' issues — ensuring that the priceless artwork would be neatly packaged together ... for disposal.

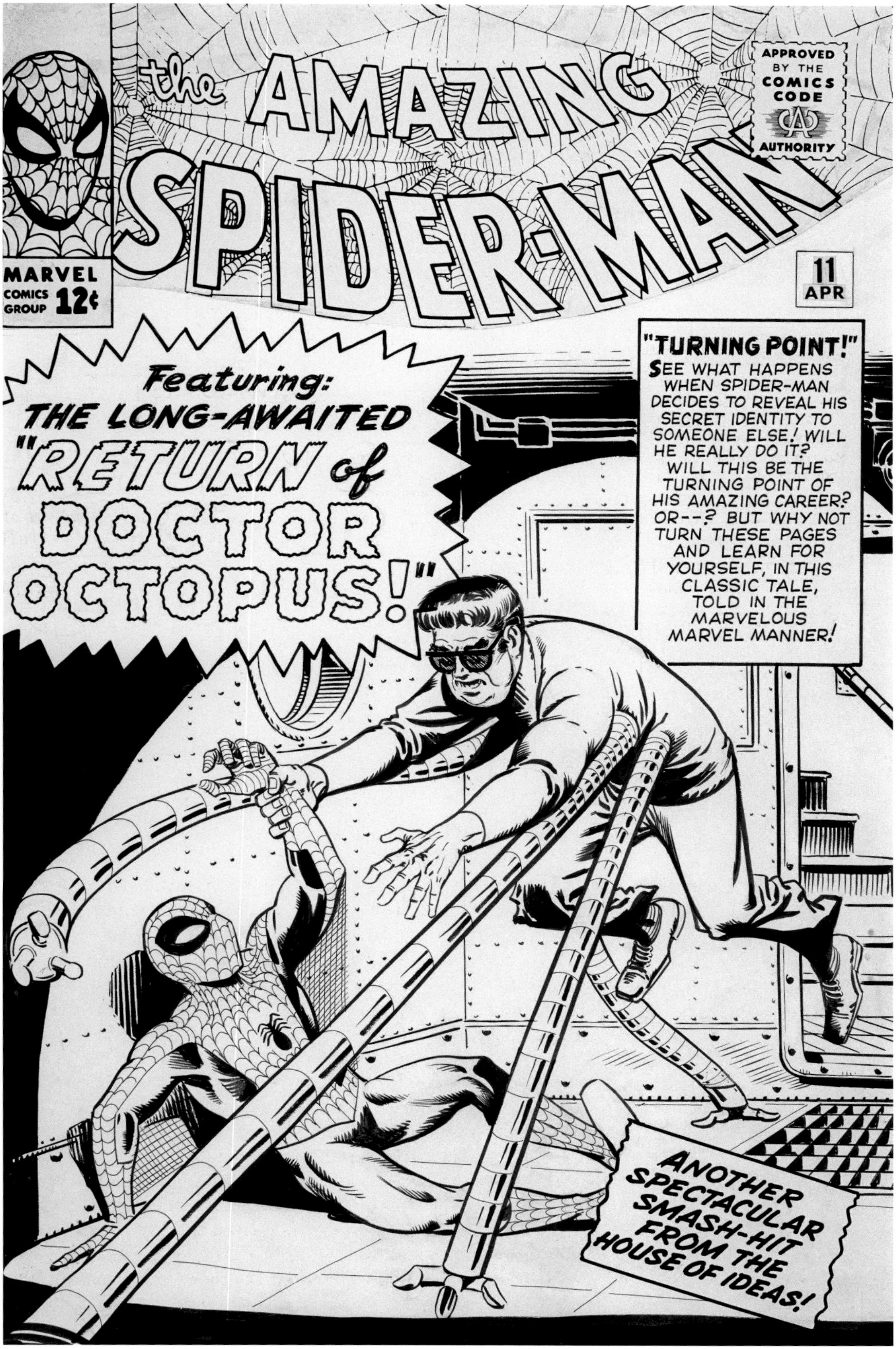

the AMAZING SPIDER-MAN
APPROVED BY THE COMICS CODE AUTHORITY
MARVEL COMICS GROUP 12¢
11 APR
Featuring: THE LONG-AWAITED "RETURN of DOCTOR OCTOPUS!"
"TURNING POINT!" SEE WHAT HAPPENS WHEN SPIDER-MAN DECIDES TO REVEAL HIS SECRET IDENTITY TO SOMEONE ELSE! WILL HE REALLY DO IT? WILL THIS BE THE TURNING POINT OF HIS AMAZING CAREER? OR--? BUT WHY NOT TURN THESE PAGES AND LEARN FOR YOURSELF, IN THIS CLASSIC TALE, TOLD IN THE MARVELOUS MARVEL MANNER!
ANOTHER SPECTACULAR SMASH-HIT FROM THE HOUSE OF IDEAS!

AMAZING SPIDER-MAN No. 14

(Below) Interior, "The Grotesque Adventure of the Green Goblin!"; script, Stan Lee; pencils and inks, Steve Ditko; July 1964. According to Ditko, Stan Lee originally wanted the Goblin to be a supernatural villain, but Ditko argued that the idea would be too far out for a hero rooted in more realistic adventures. Over the decades, the Green Goblin has captured the imaginations of children and adults alike not only in comics, but also in toys, games, animation, and movies.

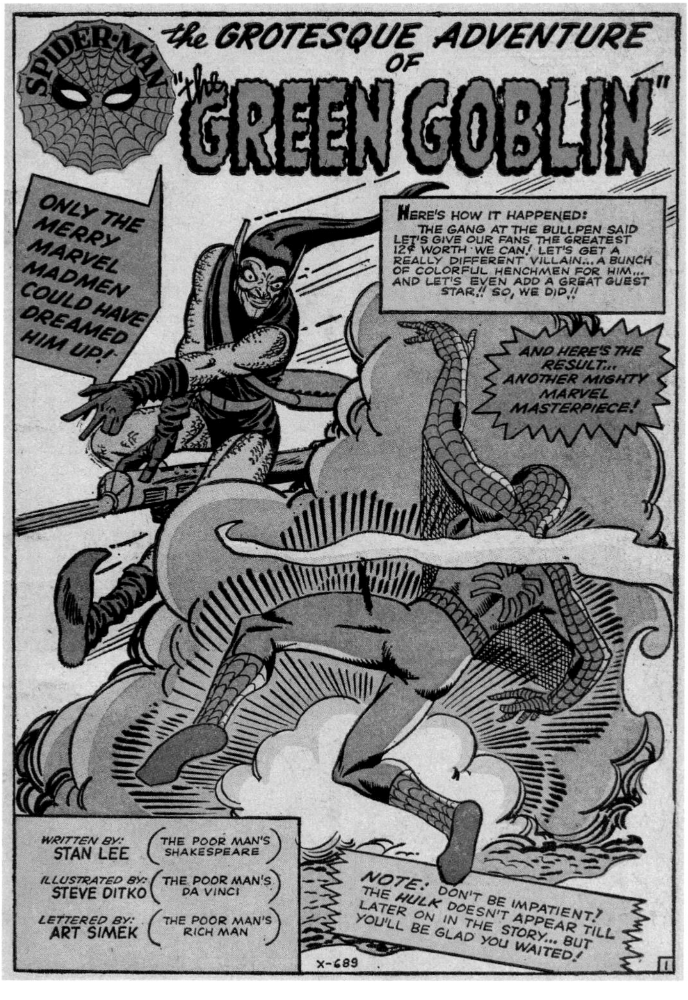
SPIDER-MAN
the GROTESQUE ADVENTURE OF "the GREEN GOBLIN"
ONLY THE MERRY MARVEL MADMEN COULD HAVE DREAMED HIM UP!
HERE'S HOW IT HAPPENED: THE GANG AT THE BULLPEN SAID LET'S GIVE OUR FANS THE GREATEST 12¢ WORTH WE CAN! LET'S GET A REALLY DIFFERENT VILLAIN... A BUNCH OF COLORFUL HENCHMEN FOR HIM... AND LET'S EVEN ADD A GREAT GUEST STAR!! SO, WE DID!!
AND HERE'S THE RESULT... ANOTHER MIGHTY MARVEL MASTERPIECE!
WRITTEN BY: STAN LEE (THE POOR MAN'S SHAKESPEARE)
ILLUSTRATED BY: STEVE DITKO (THE POOR MAN'S DA VINCI)
LETTERED BY: ART SIMEK (THE POOR MAN'S RICH MAN)
NOTE: DON'T BE IMPATIENT! THE HULK DOESN'T APPEAR TILL LATER ON IN THE STORY... BUT YOU'LL BE GLAD YOU WAITED!
X-689
1

AMAZING SPIDER-MAN No. 9

(Opposite) Interior, "The Man Called Electro!"; script, Stan Lee; pencils and inks, Steve Ditko; February 1964. Ditko composed the splash page like a movie poster: a panorama of images telling a story in pantomime. As a teenage hero Peter Parker faced a deluge of problems. Taunting classmates, an abusive boss, and concerns for his dangerously ill Aunt May made Spider-Man a very human and believable character. It wasn't all bleak, though: Betty Brant was Peter's first love, although his dual identity would soon cause problems in that area, as well. Peter retained a sense of humor, throughout, thanks to Stan Lee's witty dialogue.

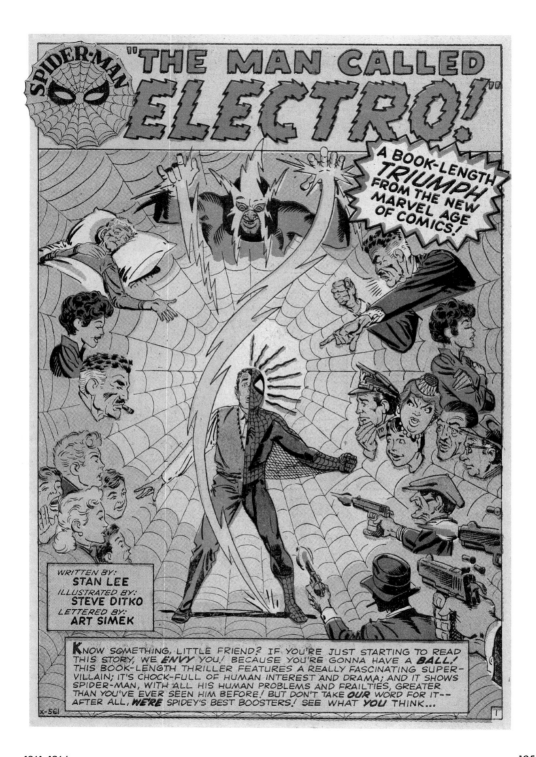

SPIDER-MAN "THE MAN CALLED ELECTRO!"

A BOOK-LENGTH *TRIUMPH* FROM THE NEW MARVEL AGE OF COMICS!

WRITTEN BY:
STAN LEE
ILLUSTRATED BY:
STEVE DITKO
LETTERED BY:
ART SIMEK

KNOW SOMETHING, LITTLE FRIEND? IF YOU'RE JUST STARTING TO READ THIS STORY, WE *ENVY* YOU! BECAUSE YOU'RE GONNA HAVE A *BALL!* THIS BOOK-LENGTH THRILLER FEATURES A REALLY FASCINATING SUPER-VILLAIN; IT'S CHOCK-FULL OF HUMAN INTEREST AND DRAMA; AND IT SHOWS SPIDER-MAN, WITH ALL HIS HUMAN PROBLEMS AND FRAILTIES, GREATER THAN YOU'VE EVER SEEN HIM BEFORE! BUT DON'T TAKE *OUR* WORD FOR IT-- AFTER ALL, *WE'RE* SPIDEY'S BEST BOOSTERS! SEE WHAT *YOU* THINK...

X-561

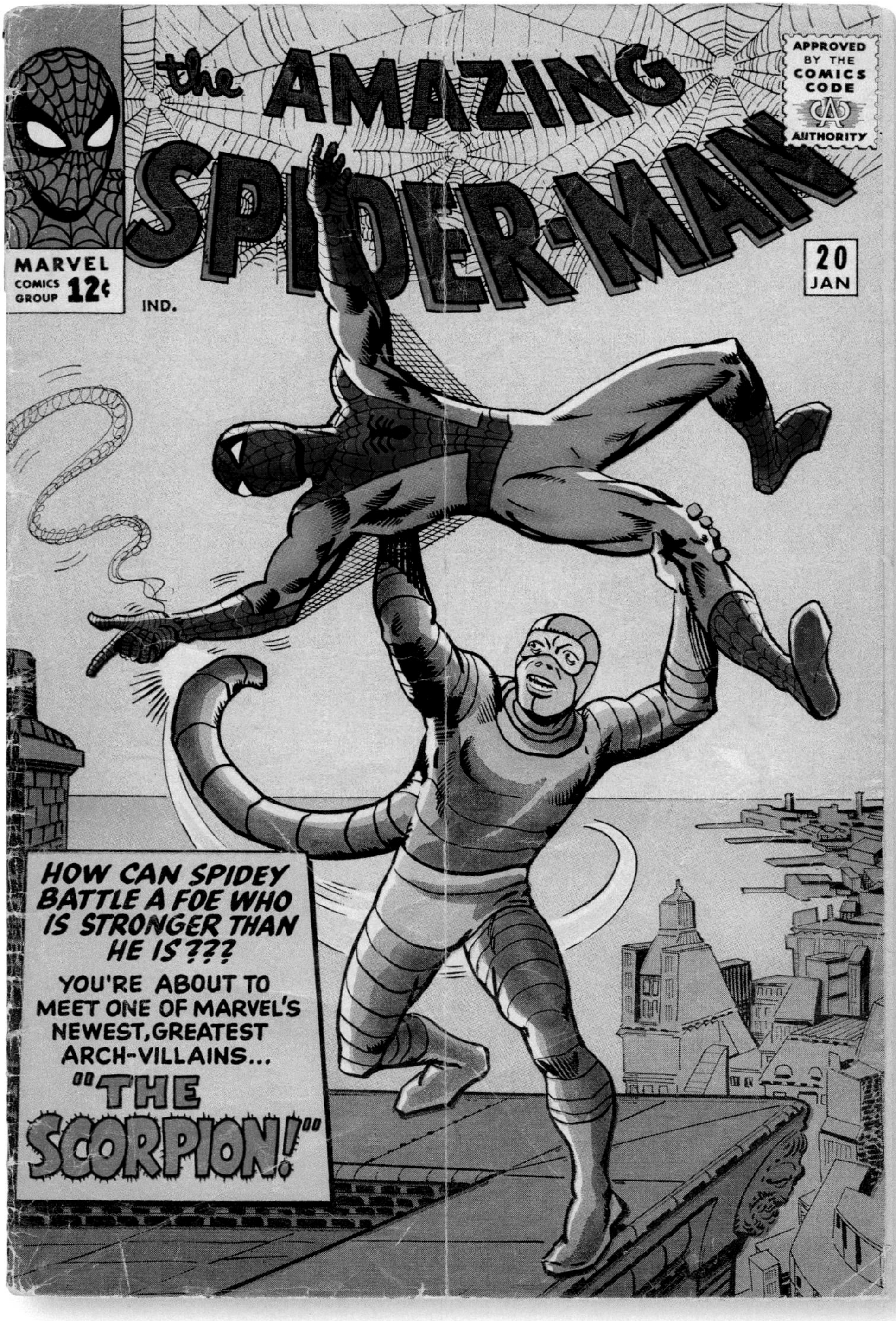
APPROVED BY THE COMICS CODE AUTHORITY
the AMAZING SPIDER-MAN
MARVEL COMICS GROUP 12¢
IND.
20 JAN
HOW CAN SPIDEY BATTLE A FOE WHO IS STRONGER THAN HE IS???
YOU'RE ABOUT TO MEET ONE OF MARVEL'S NEWEST, GREATEST ARCH-VILLAINS...
"THE SCORPION!"

ge Six THE COLGATE MAROON Wednesday, November 13, 1963

Caught in the Web of Modern Frustrations,

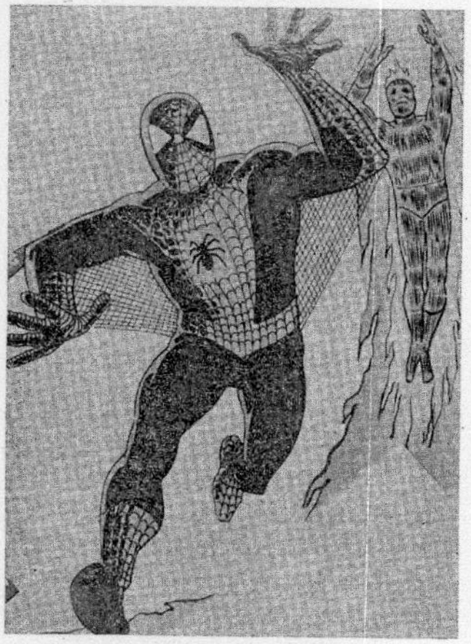

The Newest Hero, Spiderman

Spiderman Strives For Status In Competitive Comic Book World Of Insincere Superheroes

by John Butterworth '64

Will Spiderman, prime example of the realistic super hero, replace Superman and the others so-called sentimentalists? This is the question posed by a recent trend in the comic book industry. What good is it, Spiderman's supporters ask, to be faster than a speeding bullet if one is not sincere?

Certain publishers seem to feel that Superman is too superior for the literary generation of Holden Caulfield. The former seems to take too much for granted, and it is possible that quick witted, successful Superman is a phony.

There is evidence to support this. Recently, after an adventure in the ancient past with Hercules and Samson, Superboy (Superman as a boy) bid these two heroes farewell with a quick, "'Bye now, Hercules and Samson."

It was clear that Superboy was not only showing falseness of emotion, but also running out of super conversation.

In contrast to this, Spiderman's publishers have tried to drive the money lenders out of the temple. The foundation of their realistic treatment can be expressed in one word: Failure. The new breed of super heroes is unable to cope with society, outside the narrow world of criminals and perverted scientists.

One band of such superheroes nearly went out of business recently because of the failure of their stock investments. Another superhero finds that his girl assistant slows him down because she always puts on fresh lip stick before going on an assignment.

Consistently Fails

But Spiderman always fails, even when he succeeds. His career is hampered by his frustrations, neuroses, and sometimes even an inferiority complex, all of them intensified because he is a teen ager.

One recent panel shows the left-out Spiderman enviously watching a rival superhero lounging in a Sting Ray, surrounded by pretty girls. One is left with the feeling that if Charlie Brown wore a skin-tight costume and fought crime, he would be Spiderman.

Spiderman's main problem is his inability to reconcile his career as a superhero with his desire to make money. Of course he needs the money, for in real life he is timid lower middle class teen ager Peter Parker, struggling to support himself and a widowed aunt. When he first became Spiderman he hoped to be rich and famous, and so went to show business.

He almost did it, but in order to keep his identity a secret he had his pay check made out to Spiderman. When he tried to cash it the following scene ensued:

Bank Clerk: Do you have any identification?

Spiderman: What about by costume?

Bank Clerk: Don't be silly. Anyone can wear a costume. Do you have a Social Security card or a driver's license in the name of Spiderman?

No Place to Go

That was only the beginning. His attempt to join a group of superheroes also met defeat because they were a non-profit organization. As one member put it, "You came to the wrong place, pal. This isn't General Motors."

At the present time Peter Parker earns a precarious living as a newspaper photographer, taking pictures of the criminals Spiderman captures. Would Plasticman consent to such a rat race?

Spiderman is also vulnerable — in a recent adventure he broke his arm. He could certainly be the pioneer customer for a superhero's Blue Cross. Small wonder that the illustration shows him running away.

But not even Spiderman's public is on his side. The editor of Peter Parker's newspaper takes a highly reactionary stand, lecturing against Spiderman as a freak who takes the law into his own hands. He wants people to pay more attention to real heroes like his son, a test pilot. Perhaps only the Lone Ranger is conservative enough to be safe.

Pete Revolts

Peter Parker is also an outcast among his fellow high school students, because he is a good student and seems so puny. But his acceptance of this is not as stoic as young Clark Kent's.

Recently he said that he was getting tired of this "weak and timid stuff" and that if things didn't change, "Somebody's gonna lose a few teeth." But his best revenge so far has been to spread the rumor that his arch enemy, high school bully Flash Jonson, was in reality Spiderman. This is certainly not the most satisfying outlet for hostility.

It will be interesting to see what effects this defeatism has on the comic book field. Perhaps in time Spiderman will develop into more than just Superman with a negative attitude. But for now his publishers may consider this motto as the best expression of their philosophy: "Spiderman suffers for you."

AMAZING SPIDER-MAN No. 20

(Opposite) Cover; pencils and inks, Steve Ditko; July 1964. Month after month, Lee and Ditko kept coming up with new and different opponents for Spidey to battle. The Scorpion starts as private investigator Mac Gargan, who agrees to being experimented on. As if given an early version of steroids Gargan grows stronger and, with the help of his mechanical tail, defeats Spider-Man more than once.

BACK TO SCHOOL

(Above) Newspaper clipping, "Spiderman Strives for Status in Competitive Comic Book World of Insincere Superheroes," The Colgate Maroon, *November 13, 1963.* An early example of the attention being paid to the new style of comics at Marvel on college campuses and by an older, more mature audience. Stan Lee would soon become Marvel's spokesperson, being quoted in newspapers and radio and television broadcasts, and making appearances on college campuses.

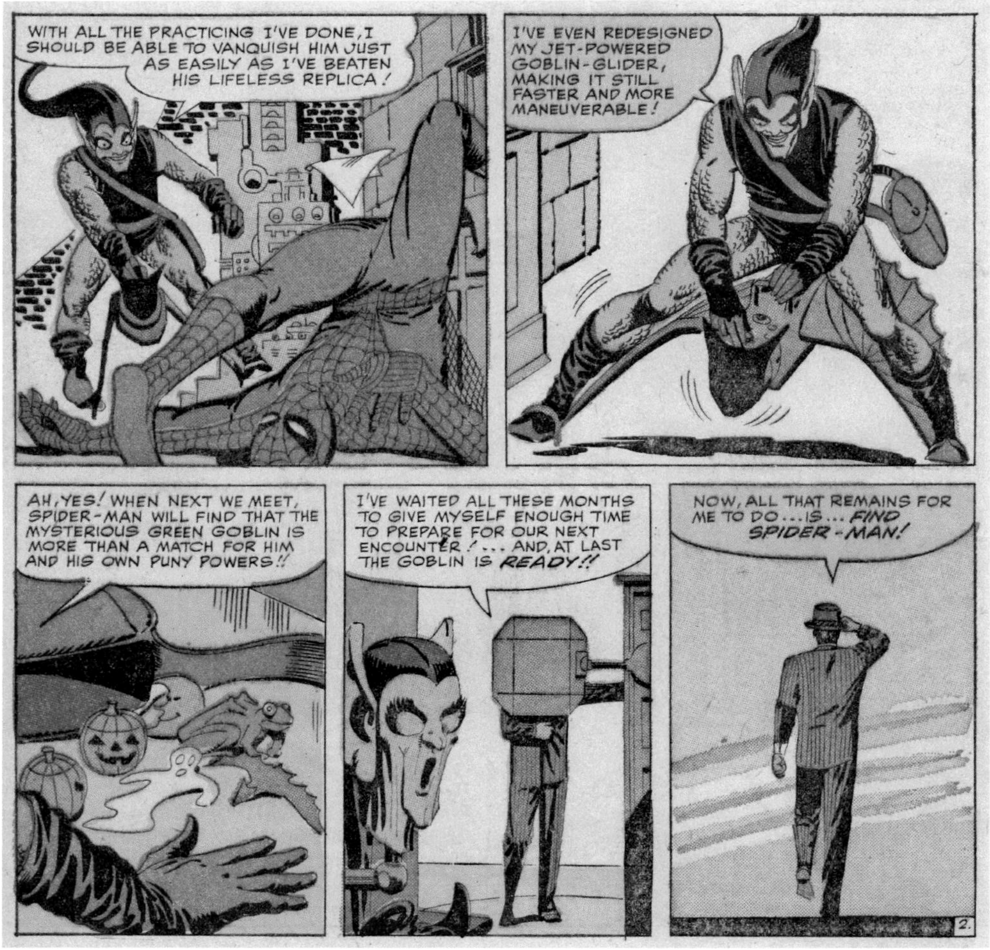

WITH ALL THE PRACTICING I'VE DONE, I SHOULD BE ABLE TO VANQUISH HIM JUST AS EASILY AS I'VE BEATEN HIS LIFELESS REPLICA!
I'VE EVEN REDESIGNED MY JET-POWERED GOBLIN-GLIDER, MAKING IT STILL FASTER AND MORE MANEUVERABLE!
AH, YES! WHEN NEXT WE MEET, SPIDER-MAN WILL FIND THAT THE MYSTERIOUS GREEN GOBLIN IS MORE THAN A MATCH FOR HIM AND HIS OWN PUNY POWERS!!
I'VE WAITED ALL THESE MONTHS TO GIVE MYSELF ENOUGH TIME TO PREPARE FOR OUR NEXT ENCOUNTER! ... AND, AT LAST THE GOBLIN IS READY!!
NOW, ALL THAT REMAINS FOR ME TO DO ... IS ... FIND SPIDER-MAN!
2.

AMAZING SPIDER-MAN No. 17

(Above) Interior; script, Stan Lee; pencils and inks, Steve Ditko; October 1964.

AMAZING SPIDER-MAN No. 6

(Opposite) Cover; pencils and inks, Steve Ditko; November 1963. When benevolent scientist Curt Connors's experimental attempt to rejuvenate his missing arm goes awry, he transforms into the deadly Lizard. The plot is similar to that of the low-budget movie *The Alligator People* (1959), but Lee and Ditko's sympathetic treatment of Connors, and the fearsome, cunning strength of his alter ego transcend comics' typical gimmicky one-shot villain.

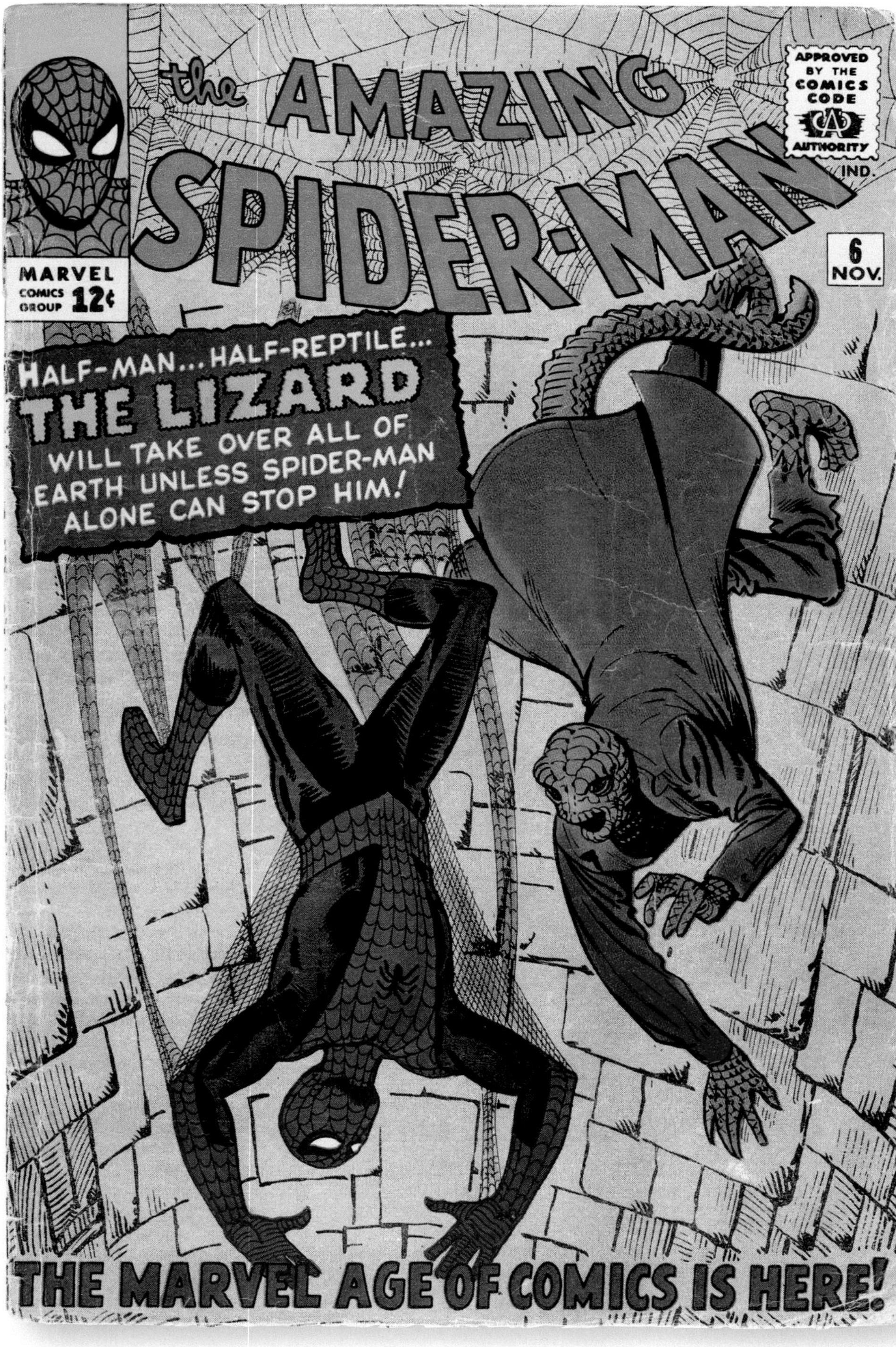
the AMAZING SPIDER-MAN
APPROVED BY THE COMICS CODE AUTHORITY
IND.
MARVEL COMICS GROUP 12¢
6 NOV.
HALF-MAN... HALF-REPTILE... THE LIZARD WILL TAKE OVER ALL OF EARTH UNLESS SPIDER-MAN ALONE CAN STOP HIM!
THE MARVEL AGE OF COMICS IS HERE!

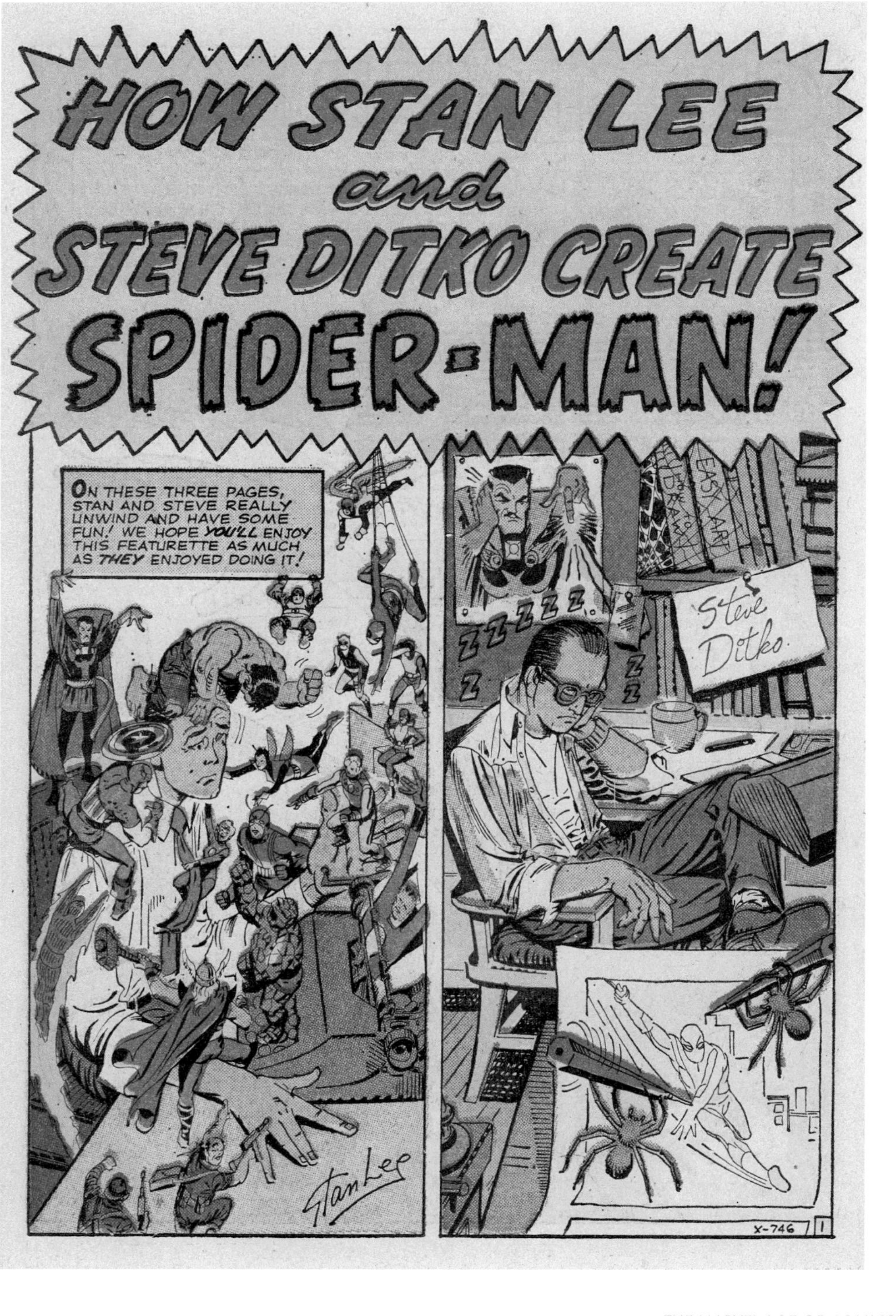
HOW STAN LEE and STEVE DITKO CREATE SPIDER-MAN!
ON THESE THREE PAGES, STAN AND STEVE REALLY UNWIND AND HAVE SOME FUN! WE HOPE YOU'LL ENJOY THIS FEATURETTE AS MUCH AS THEY ENJOYED DOING IT!
EASY ART
Z Z Z Z Z Z
Steve Ditko
Stan Lee
X-746
1

ANNUAL
72 BIG PAGES
ANNUAL
APPROVED BY THE COMICS CODE AUTHORITY
the AMAZING
SPIDER-MAN
IND.
#1
1964
MARVEL COMICS GROUP 25¢
FEATURING: SPIDEY'S BIGGEST LONGEST, GREATEST BATTLE, AS HE ATTACKS:
"THE SINISTER SIX!"
WITH A GALAXY OF THE MOST GOL-DARNED GUEST-STARS THAT YOU CAN SHAKE A WEB AT!
JAM-PACKED WITH SPECIAL SURPRISE FEATURES

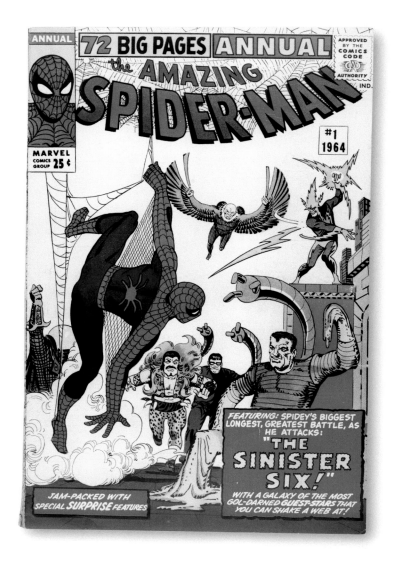

AMAZING SPIDER-MAN ANNUAL No. 1

(Opposite and above) Cover and interior, "How Stan Lee and Steve Ditko Create Spider-Man!"; script, Stan Lee; pencils and inks, Steve Ditko; Summer 1964. Spider-Man's first *Annual* included a potpourri of pinups, diagrams, and special features, including this satirical look at Lee and Ditko's creative process. The splash-page caricatures of both himself and Lee exemplify Ditko's keen sense of humor. While Lee makes self-deprecating jibes throughout, the three-page vignette includes an informative segment of Ditko at his drawing board, explaining how he pencils and inks the strip.

"I...[asked] my little daughter, seven years old, reading an issue of *Spider-Man*..., 'Do you like that?' She said, 'Yes, I like it, daddy.' 'But the heads are too big,' I said, 'and the drawing is out of proportion.' She said, 'I like it, daddy. He's worried about his homework. He's worried that his Aunt May is going to get mad because he tore his pants.' I thought, 'Oh, my God, Stan hit it!...He gave them human interest.'" — MIKE ESPOSITO

AMAZING SPIDER-MAN No. 19
*(Opposite) Cover: pencils and inks,
Steve Ditko; December 1964.*

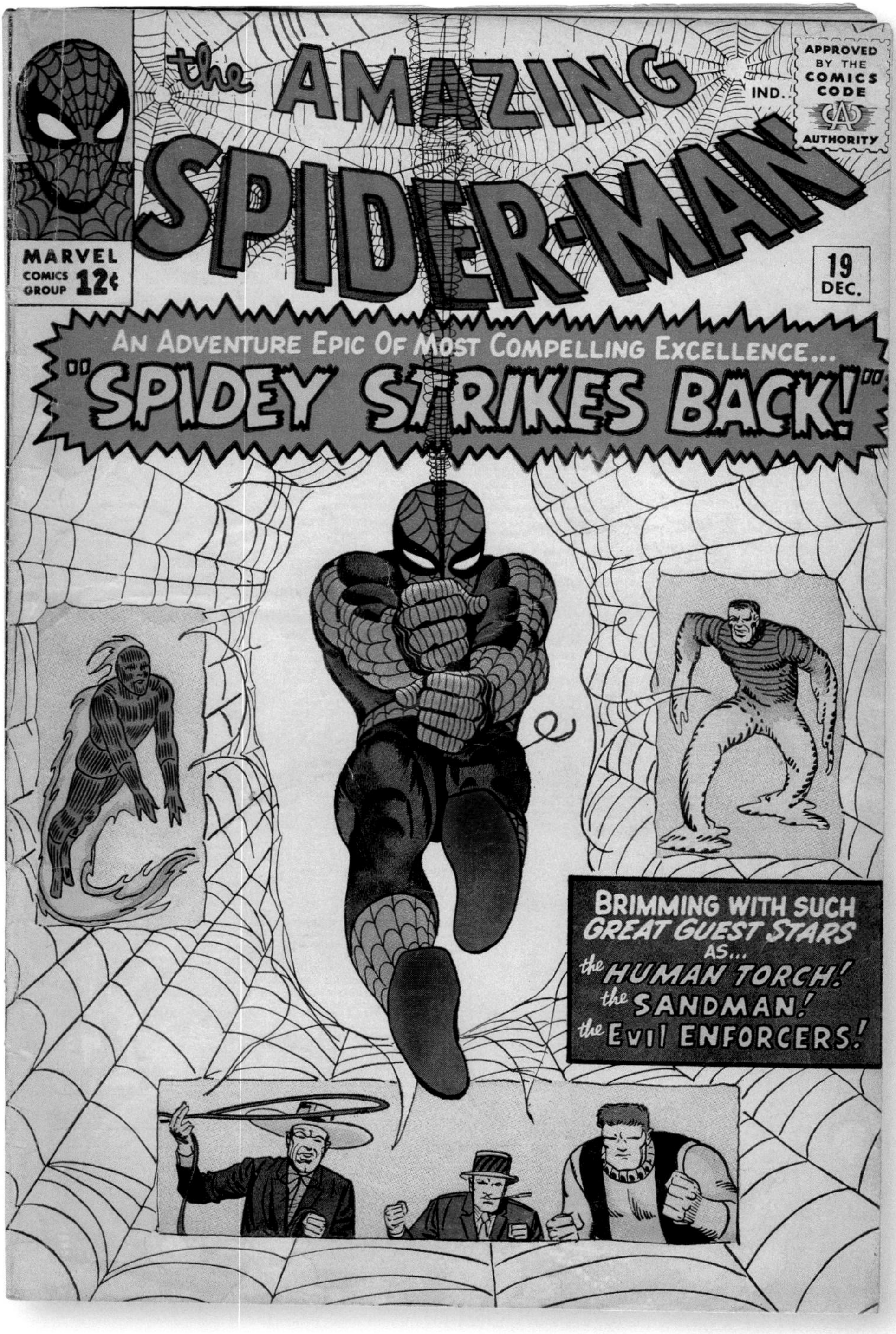
APPROVED BY THE COMICS CODE AUTHORITY
the AMAZING SPIDER-MAN
IND.
MARVEL COMICS GROUP 12¢
19 DEC.
AN ADVENTURE EPIC OF MOST COMPELLING EXCELLENCE...
"SPIDEY STRIKES BACK!"
BRIMMING WITH SUCH GREAT GUEST STARS AS...
the HUMAN TORCH!
the SANDMAN!
the EVIL ENFORCERS!

THE FIRST MAGICIAN

(Below) Book cover, Mandrake the Magician; *author, Lee Falk; illustrations, Phil Davis; Big Little Book; 1935.* Created in 1934 by Lee Falk (who also brought the world *The Phantom*), Mandrake was the first magician hero with his own comic strip. Mandrake soon graduated to other media, including radio, movie serials—even musicals—and his success inspired the look of many other magicians, usually adorned in top hats, capes, and pencil-thin mustaches much like Falk's own.

STRANGE TALES No. 128

(Opposite) Interior; pencils and inks, Steve Ditko; January 1965. Doctor Strange was as far out from Mandrake as Ditko's graphic sense was from his peers. Artist Walt Simonson celebrates the difference in a 2000 interview: "One of the things I loved about Ditko's Dr. Strange was the rather wonderful job he did creating a graphic system of magic. The dialogue was cool, but Steve created a complete visual system of magic.... Magic in comics is often depicted either verbally: 'Oh, by the bristling hair of Flear; In my hand I find a beer!' with some rhyming baloney, or else guys are shooting special effects force blasts at each other. Could just be ray guns. There's no sense, really, of an underlying reality to the magic."

Mandrake
the
MAGICIAN
THE
BIG LITTLE
BOOK

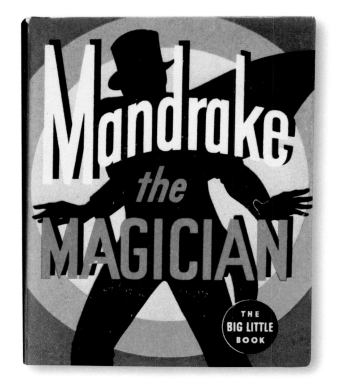

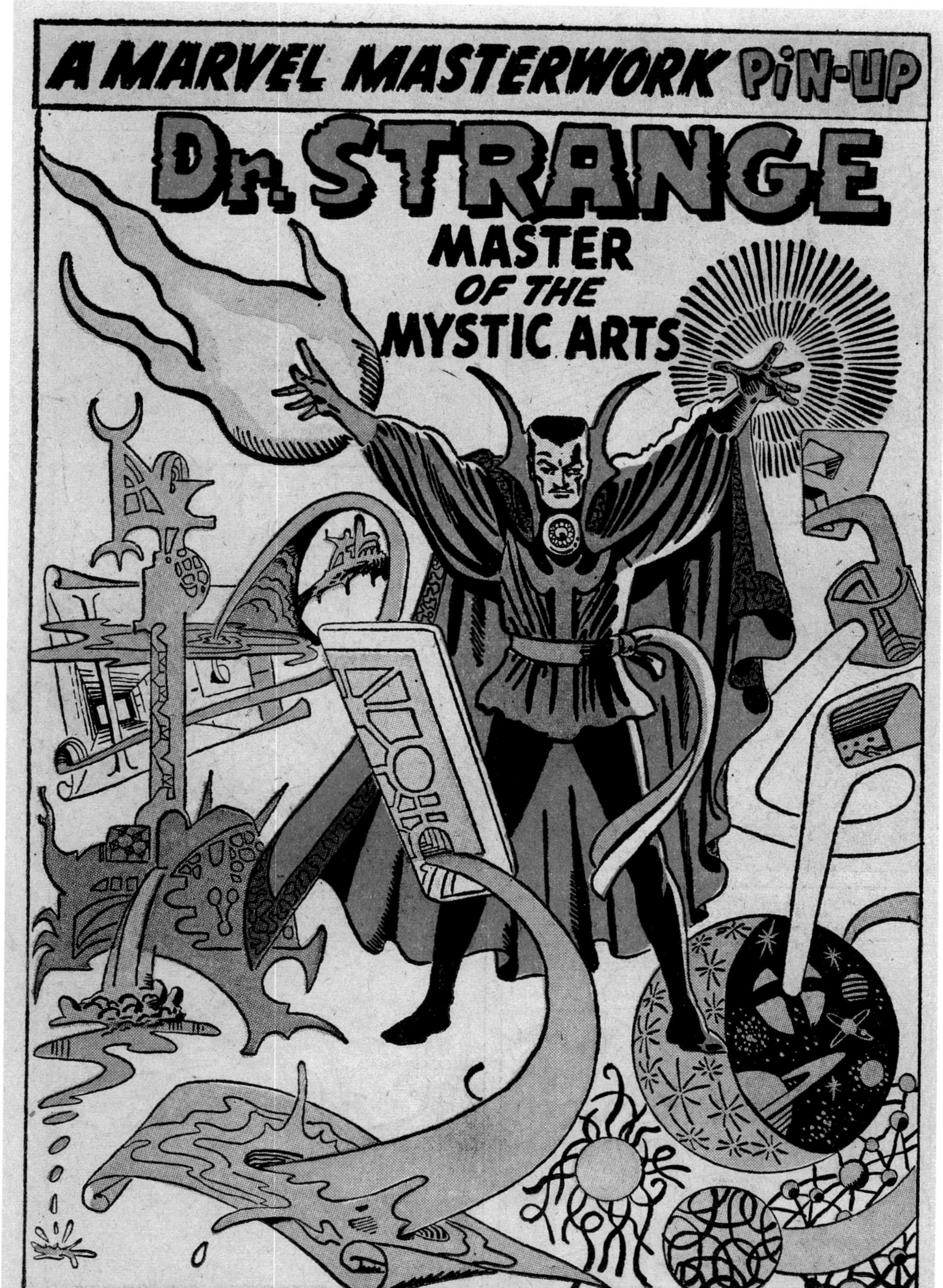
A MARVEL MASTERWORK PiN-UP
Dr. STRANGE
MASTER
OF THE
MYSTIC ARTS

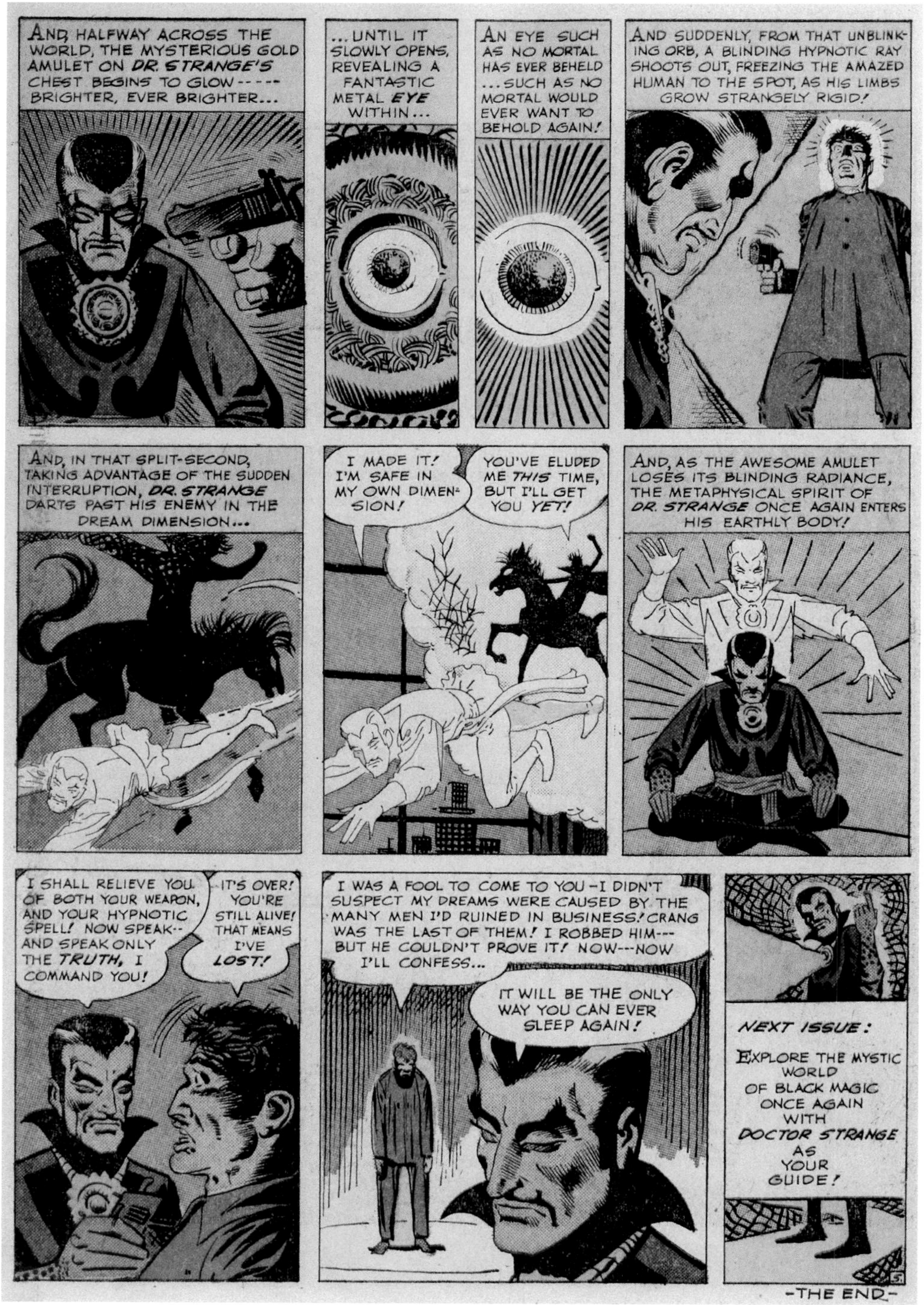
AND, HALFWAY ACROSS THE WORLD, THE MYSTERIOUS GOLD AMULET ON DR. STRANGE'S CHEST BEGINS TO GLOW ----- BRIGHTER, EVER BRIGHTER...
...UNTIL IT SLOWLY OPENS, REVEALING A FANTASTIC METAL EYE WITHIN...
AN EYE SUCH AS NO MORTAL HAS EVER BEHELD ...SUCH AS NO MORTAL WOULD EVER WANT TO BEHOLD AGAIN!
AND SUDDENLY, FROM THAT UNBLINKING ORB, A BLINDING HYPNOTIC RAY SHOOTS OUT, FREEZING THE AMAZED HUMAN TO THE SPOT, AS HIS LIMBS GROW STRANGELY RIGID!
AND, IN THAT SPLIT-SECOND, TAKING ADVANTAGE OF THE SUDDEN INTERRUPTION, DR. STRANGE DARTS PAST HIS ENEMY IN THE DREAM DIMENSION...
I MADE IT! I'M SAFE IN MY OWN DIMENSION!
YOU'VE ELUDED ME THIS TIME, BUT I'LL GET YOU YET!
AND, AS THE AWESOME AMULET LOSES ITS BLINDING RADIANCE, THE METAPHYSICAL SPIRIT OF DR. STRANGE ONCE AGAIN ENTERS HIS EARTHLY BODY!
I SHALL RELIEVE YOU OF BOTH YOUR WEAPON, AND YOUR HYPNOTIC SPELL! NOW SPEAK-- AND SPEAK ONLY THE TRUTH, I COMMAND YOU!
IT'S OVER! YOU'RE STILL ALIVE! THAT MEANS I'VE LOST!
I WAS A FOOL TO COME TO YOU -I DIDN'T SUSPECT MY DREAMS WERE CAUSED BY THE MANY MEN I'D RUINED IN BUSINESS! CRANG WAS THE LAST OF THEM! I ROBBED HIM--- BUT HE COULDN'T PROVE IT! NOW---NOW I'LL CONFESS...
IT WILL BE THE ONLY WAY YOU CAN EVER SLEEP AGAIN!
NEXT ISSUE:
EXPLORE THE MYSTIC WORLD OF BLACK MAGIC ONCE AGAIN WITH DOCTOR STRANGE AS YOUR GUIDE!
-THE END-

STRANGE TALES No. 110

(Opposite) Interior, "Doctor Strange, Master of Black Magic!"; script, Stan Lee; pencils and inks, Steve Ditko; July 1963. Even for Marvel, the debut of Dr. Strange was an oddity. Appearing with little fanfare in the back pages of *Strange Tales*, the mystic hero had the ability to leave his body and travel via astral projection, employing an amulet that became an "all-seeing eye." In his initial story Strange journeyed into a man's dream to combat the lord of that dimension, Nightmare.

STRANGE TALES No. 115

(Below) Interior, "The Origin of Dr. Strange!"; script, Stan Lee; pencils and inks, Steve Ditko; December 1963. After three appearances Dr. Strange is given a backstory, partly inspired by the 1937 movie *Lost Horizon* (the Doctor resembles actor Ronald Colman). Stephen Strange is a brilliant surgeon whose hands are damaged in a car accident. Plunged into depression, he takes a desperate trip to Tibet, where he meets the Ancient One and agrees to study the mystic arts, thereafter protecting Earth from unknown forces.

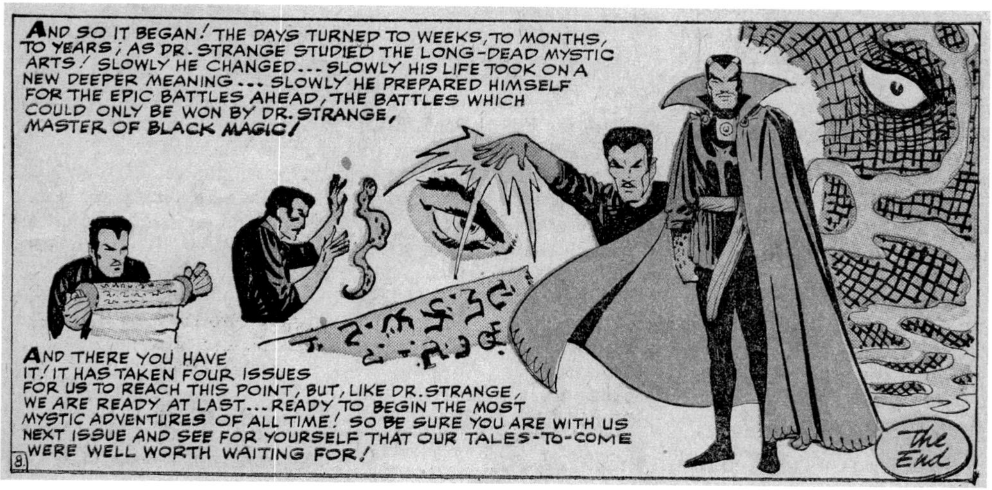
AND SO IT BEGAN! THE DAYS TURNED TO WEEKS, TO MONTHS, TO YEARS; AS DR. STRANGE STUDIED THE LONG-DEAD MYSTIC ARTS! SLOWLY HE CHANGED... SLOWLY HIS LIFE TOOK ON A NEW DEEPER MEANING... SLOWLY HE PREPARED HIMSELF FOR THE EPIC BATTLES AHEAD, THE BATTLES WHICH COULD ONLY BE WON BY DR. STRANGE, MASTER OF BLACK MAGIC!
AND THERE YOU HAVE IT! IT HAS TAKEN FOUR ISSUES FOR US TO REACH THIS POINT, BUT, LIKE DR. STRANGE, WE ARE READY AT LAST... READY TO BEGIN THE MOST MYSTIC ADVENTURES OF ALL TIME! SO BE SURE YOU ARE WITH US NEXT ISSUE AND SEE FOR YOURSELF THAT OUR TALES-TO-COME WERE WELL WORTH WAITING FOR!
8
The End

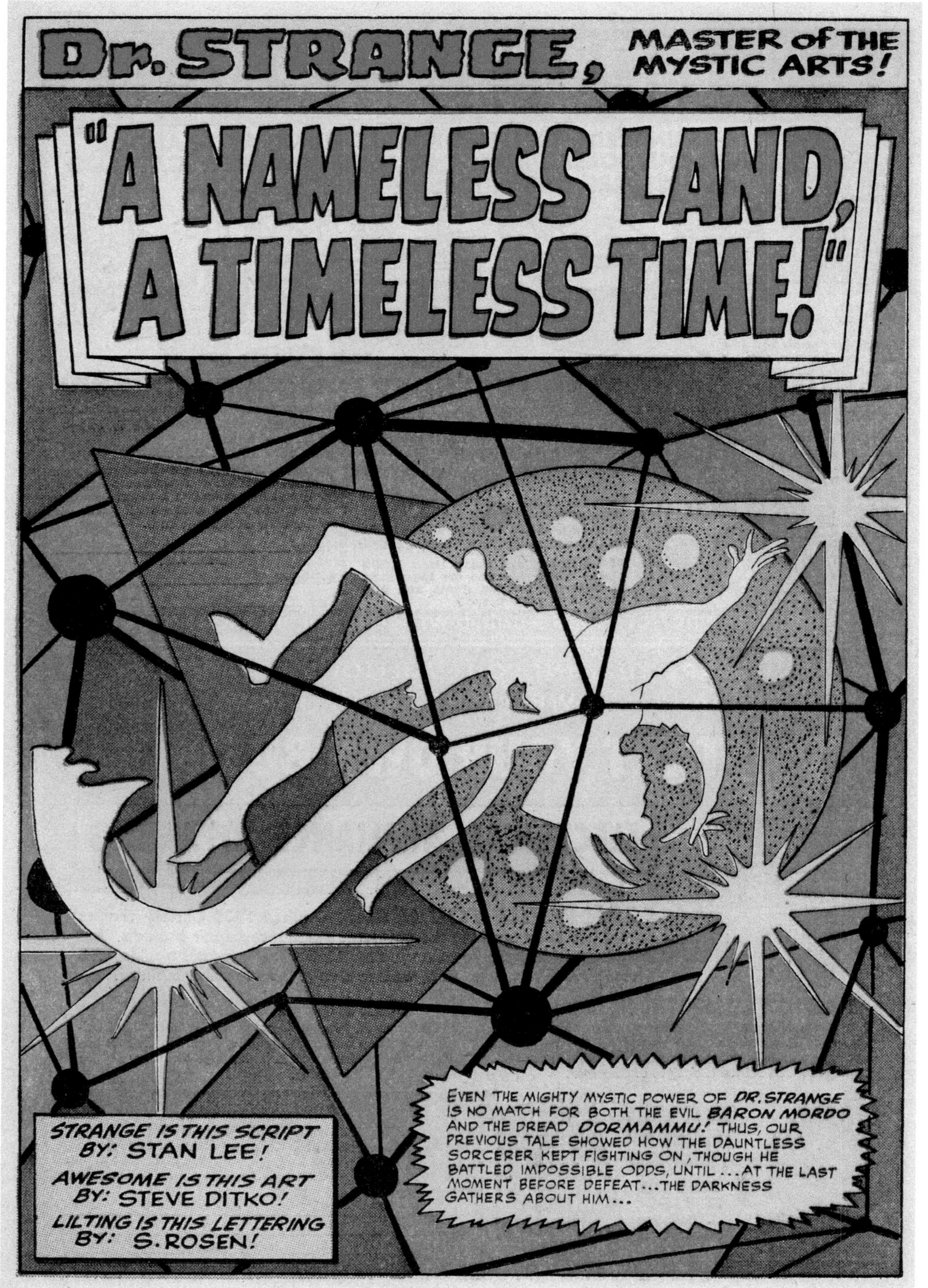
Dr. STRANGE, MASTER of THE MYSTIC ARTS!
"A NAMELESS LAND, A TIMELESS TIME!"
EVEN THE MIGHTY MYSTIC POWER OF DR. STRANGE IS NO MATCH FOR BOTH THE EVIL BARON MORDO AND THE DREAD DORMAMMU! THUS, OUR PREVIOUS TALE SHOWED HOW THE DAUNTLESS SORCERER KEPT FIGHTING ON, THOUGH HE BATTLED IMPOSSIBLE ODDS, UNTIL ...AT THE LAST MOMENT BEFORE DEFEAT...THE DARKNESS GATHERS ABOUT HIM...
STRANGE IS THIS SCRIPT BY: STAN LEE!
AWESOME IS THIS ART BY: STEVE DITKO!
LILTING IS THIS LETTERING BY: S. ROSEN!

STRANGE TALES No. 133

(Opposite) Interior, "A Nameless Land, a Timeless Time!"; script, Stan Lee; pencils and inks, Steve Ditko; June 1965. By this point Ditko's visual vocabulary for the feature was fully realized: mystical dimensions, the fully formed hero floating by means of his cloak of levitation, and battles between magicians whose hand gestures and "bolts" of energy were unlike anything previously seen in comics.

STRANGE TALES No. 119

(Below) Interior, "Beyond the Purple Veil"; script, Stan Lee; pencils and inks, Steve Ditko; April 1964. Ditko's groundbreaking imagery has inspired many moviemakers, particularly in recent decades, as the technology finally exists to duplicate some of his concepts.

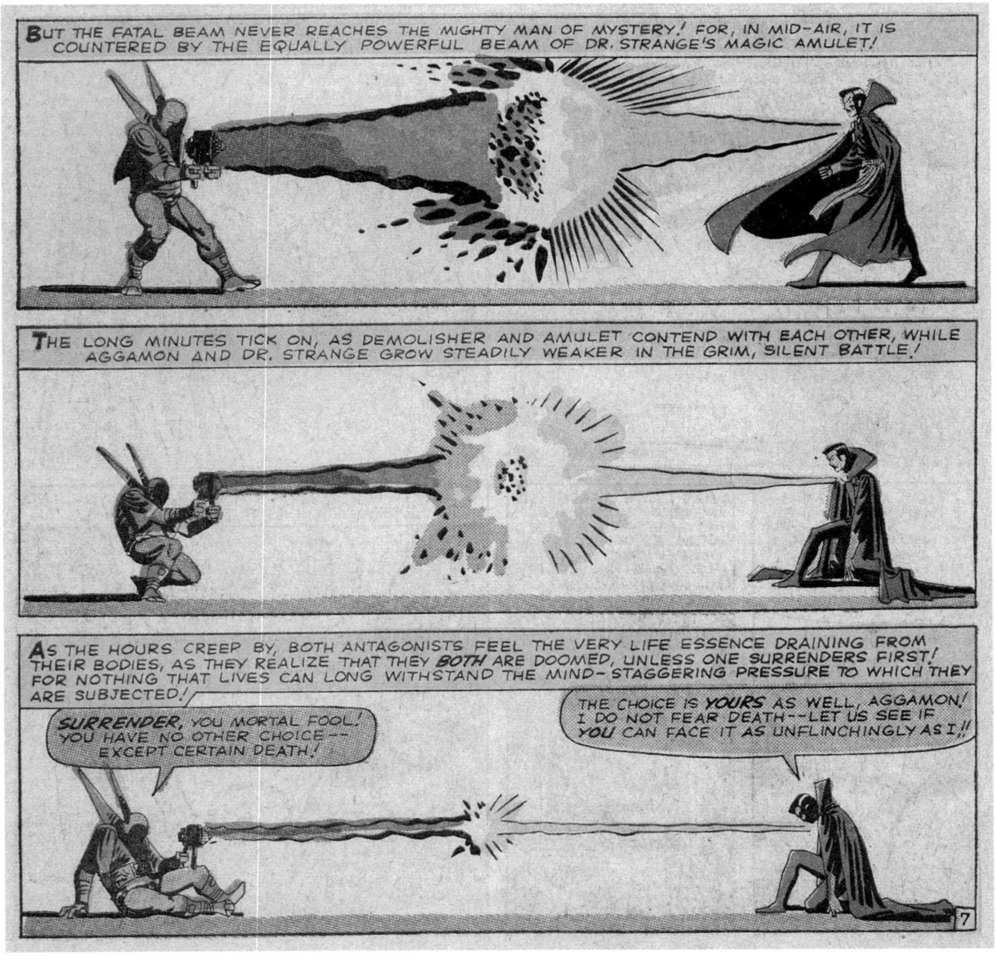

BUT THE FATAL BEAM NEVER REACHES THE MIGHTY MAN OF MYSTERY! FOR, IN MID-AIR, IT IS COUNTERED BY THE EQUALLY POWERFUL BEAM OF DR. STRANGE'S MAGIC AMULET!
THE LONG MINUTES TICK ON, AS DEMOLISHER AND AMULET CONTEND WITH EACH OTHER, WHILE AGGAMON AND DR. STRANGE GROW STEADILY WEAKER IN THE GRIM, SILENT BATTLE!
AS THE HOURS CREEP BY, BOTH ANTAGONISTS FEEL THE VERY LIFE ESSENCE DRAINING FROM THEIR BODIES, AS THEY REALIZE THAT THEY BOTH ARE DOOMED, UNLESS ONE SURRENDERS FIRST! FOR NOTHING THAT LIVES CAN LONG WITHSTAND THE MIND-STAGGERING PRESSURE TO WHICH THEY ARE SUBJECTED!
SURRENDER, YOU MORTAL FOOL! YOU HAVE NO OTHER CHOICE--EXCEPT CERTAIN DEATH!
THE CHOICE IS YOURS AS WELL, AGGAMON! I DO NOT FEAR DEATH--LET US SEE IF YOU CAN FACE IT AS UNFLINCHINGLY AS I!!
7

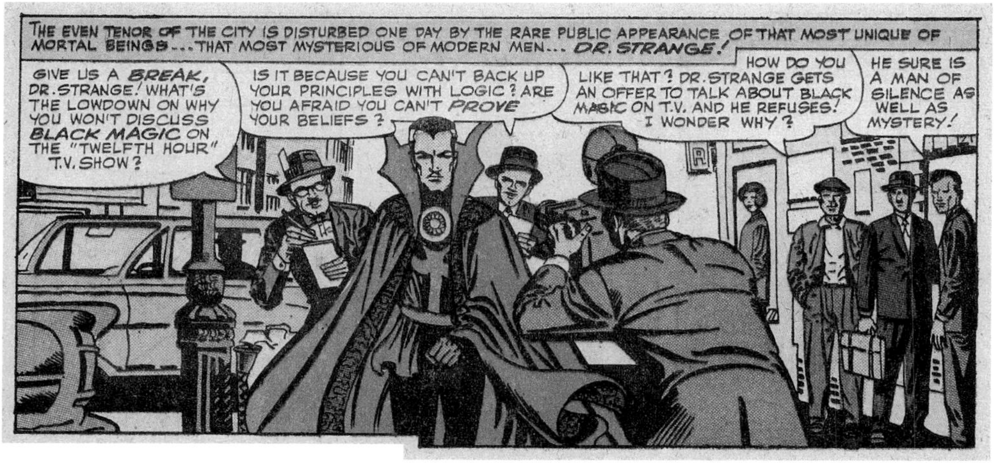
THE EVEN TENOR OF THE CITY IS DISTURBED ONE DAY BY THE RARE PUBLIC APPEARANCE OF THAT MOST UNIQUE OF MORTAL BEINGS... THAT MOST MYSTERIOUS OF MODERN MEN... DR. STRANGE!
GIVE US A BREAK, DR. STRANGE! WHAT'S THE LOWDOWN ON WHY YOU WON'T DISCUSS BLACK MAGIC ON THE "TWELFTH HOUR" T.V. SHOW?
IS IT BECAUSE YOU CAN'T BACK UP YOUR PRINCIPLES WITH LOGIC? ARE YOU AFRAID YOU CAN'T PROVE YOUR BELIEFS?
HOW DO YOU LIKE THAT? DR. STRANGE GETS AN OFFER TO TALK ABOUT BLACK MAGIC ON T.V. AND HE REFUSES! I WONDER WHY?
HE SURE IS A MAN OF SILENCE AS WELL AS MYSTERY!

STRANGE TALES No. 129

(Above) Interior, "Beware, Tiboro! The Tyrant of the Sixth Dimension!"; script, Don Rico; pencils and inks, Steve Ditko; February 1965. Dr. Strange has more important things to do than chitchat with reporters! All of Ditko's characters were determined individuals who went their own way.

STRANGE TALES No. 138

(Opposite) Interior, "If Eternity Should Fail!"; script, Stan Lee; pencils and inks, Steve Ditko; November 1965. "Unless I shatter this web of wonderment, all is lost! My mission will be forgotten— I will be doomed to a life of aimless imagery!" —Dr. Strange

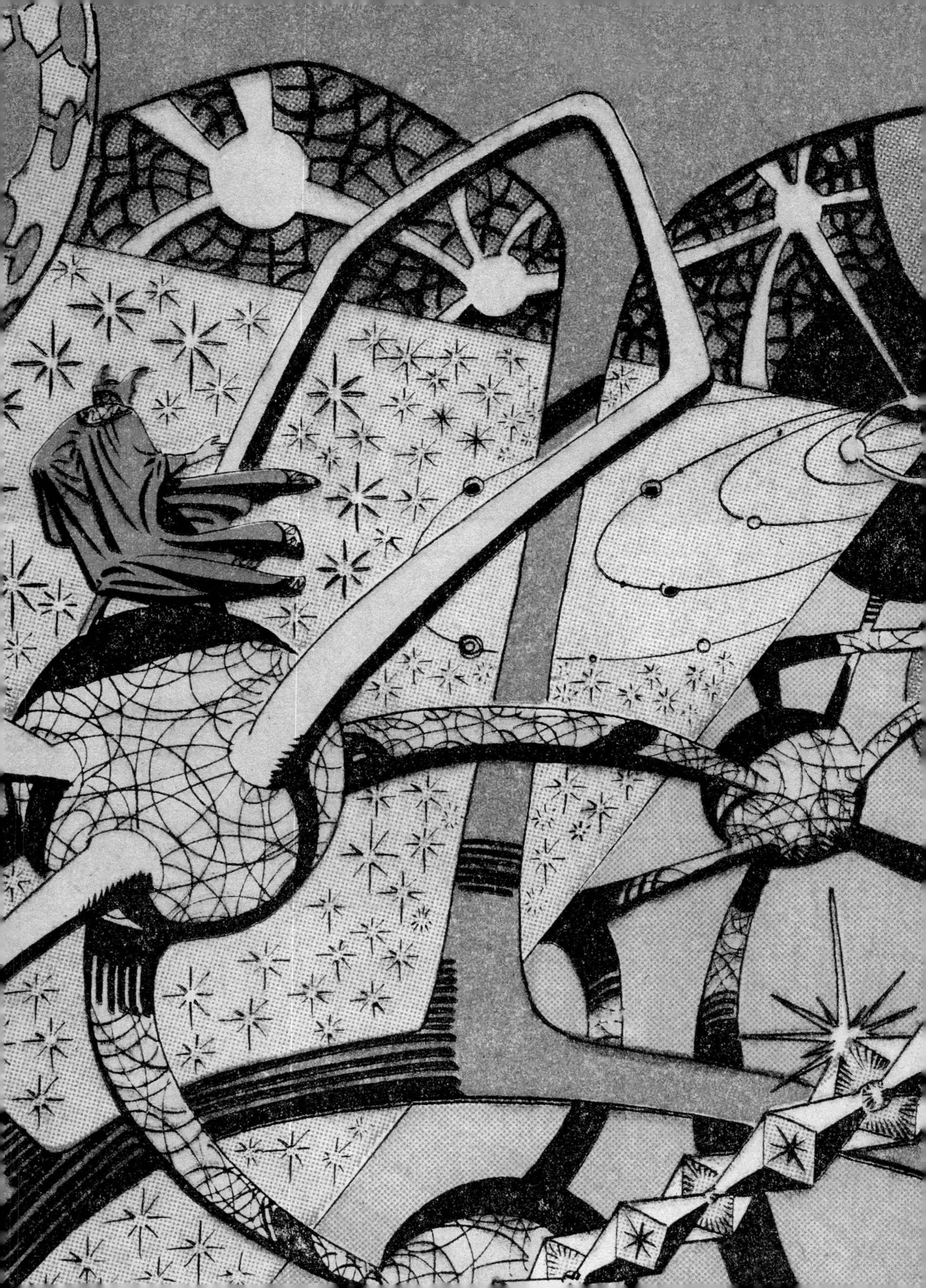

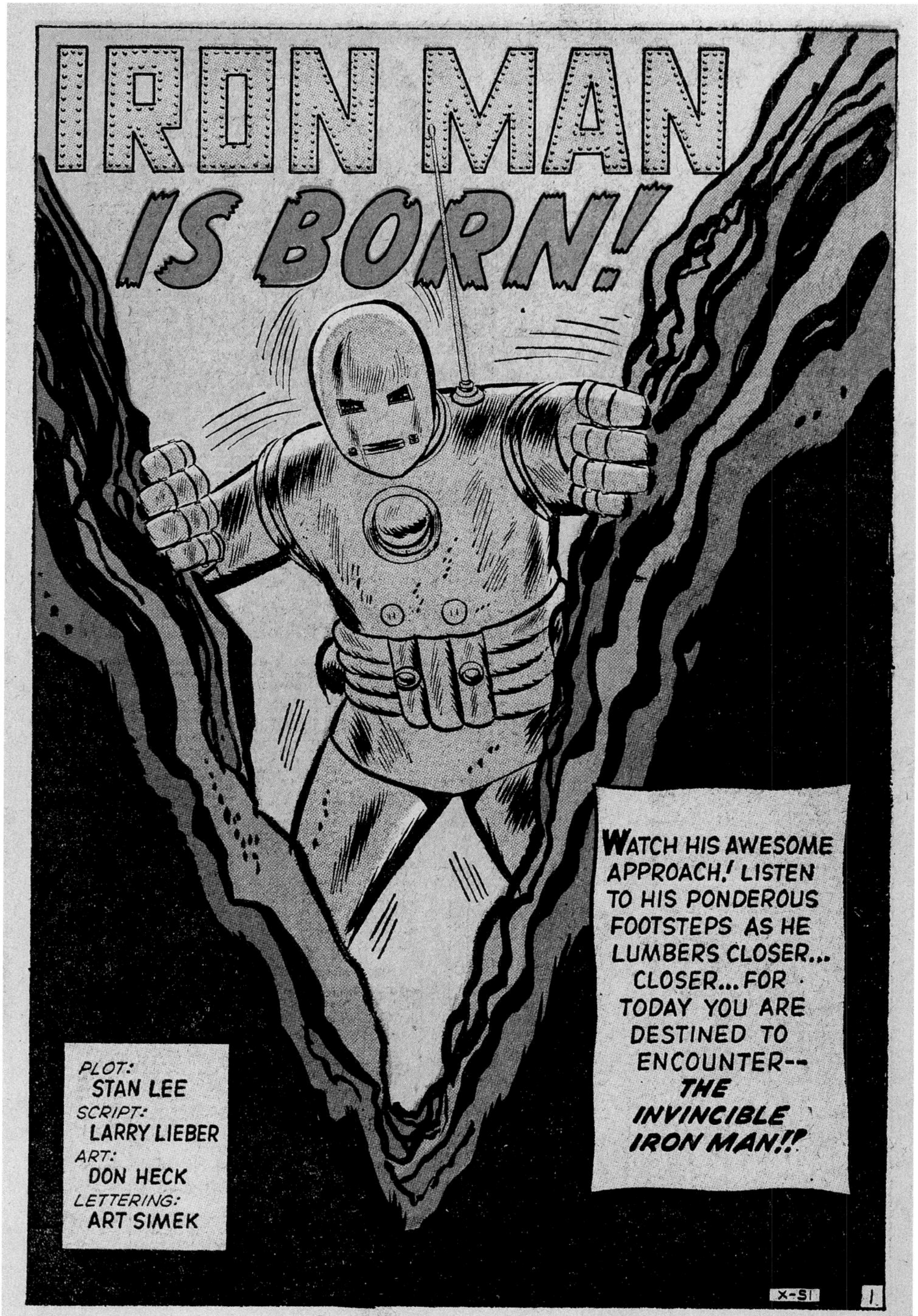
IRON MAN IS BORN!
WATCH HIS AWESOME APPROACH! LISTEN TO HIS PONDEROUS FOOTSTEPS AS HE LUMBERS CLOSER... CLOSER... FOR TODAY YOU ARE DESTINED TO ENCOUNTER-- THE INVINCIBLE IRON MAN!!
PLOT: STAN LEE
SCRIPT: LARRY LIEBER
ART: DON HECK
LETTERING: ART SIMEK
X-51
1.

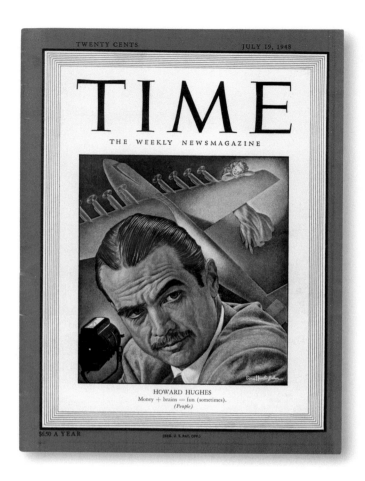

TWENTY CENTS
JULY 19, 1948
TIME
THE WEEKLY NEWSMAGAZINE
HOWARD HUGHES
Money + brains = fun (sometimes).
(People)
$6.50 A YEAR

TRAGICALLY FLAWED

(Opposite) Interior, "Iron Man," Tales of Suspense *No. 39; plot, Stan Lee; script, Larry Lieber; pencils and inks, Don Heck; April 1963.* Iron Man was unique among Marvel heroes in that he did not have special powers; anyone could become an Iron Man. Stan Lee felt that this was the reason that Iron Man was never a top seller for Marvel.

THE ORIGINAL GENIUS BILLIONAIRE PLAYBOY PHILANTHROPIST

(Above) Magazine cover, Time; *art, Ernest Hamlin Baker; July 19, 1948.* In Marvel's *Son of Origins*, Stan Lee dishes on Iron Man's inspiration: "I could envision a Howard Hughes type with almost unlimited wealth—a man with holdings and interests in every part of the world—envied by other males and sought after by glamorous females from every walk of life. But, like virtually all the mixed-up Marvel heroes, he'd have to be flawed...."

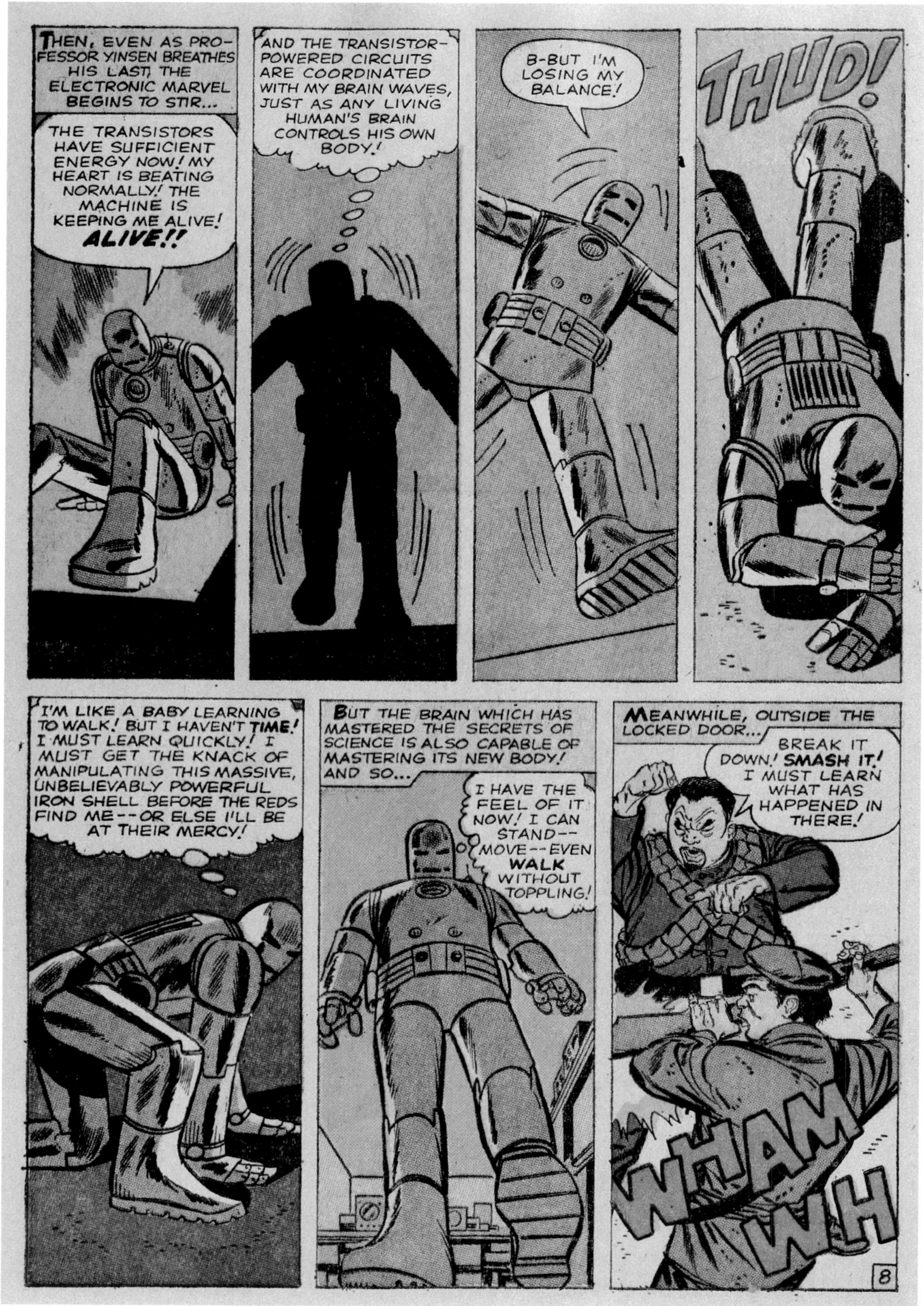
THEN, EVEN AS PROFESSOR YINSEN BREATHES HIS LAST, THE ELECTRONIC MARVEL BEGINS TO STIR...
THE TRANSISTORS HAVE SUFFICIENT ENERGY NOW! MY HEART IS BEATING NORMALLY! THE MACHINE IS KEEPING ME ALIVE! ALIVE!!
AND THE TRANSISTOR-POWERED CIRCUITS ARE COORDINATED WITH MY BRAIN WAVES, JUST AS ANY LIVING HUMAN'S BRAIN CONTROLS HIS OWN BODY!
B-BUT I'M LOSING MY BALANCE!
THUD!
I'M LIKE A BABY LEARNING TO WALK! BUT I HAVEN'T TIME! I MUST LEARN QUICKLY! I MUST GET THE KNACK OF MANIPULATING THIS MASSIVE, UNBELIEVABLY POWERFUL IRON SHELL BEFORE THE REDS FIND ME--OR ELSE I'LL BE AT THEIR MERCY!
BUT THE BRAIN WHICH HAS MASTERED THE SECRETS OF SCIENCE IS ALSO CAPABLE OF MASTERING ITS NEW BODY! AND SO...
I HAVE THE FEEL OF IT NOW! I CAN STAND--MOVE--EVEN WALK WITHOUT TOPPLING!
MEANWHILE, OUTSIDE THE LOCKED DOOR...
BREAK IT DOWN! SMASH IT! I MUST LEARN WHAT HAS HAPPENED IN THERE!
WHAM
WH
8

TALES OF SUSPENSE No. 39

(Opposite and right) Interiors, "Iron Man"; plot, Stan Lee; script, Larry Lieber; pencils and inks, Don Heck; April 1963. Here we see a mighty figure, learning, almost childishly, how to use his new abilities. Tony Stark could no longer lead the life of a playboy, although that remained his image. He had to wear his Iron Man chest armor all the time to stay alive — and remained a recluse to hide his secret identity. Thus Iron Man became a tragic character. He faced death frequently, not just at the hands of villains but also because the power cells that kept his heart pumping would run out. He was pictured as powerful and victorious; but just as often, he was shown as helpless, needing rest and a charge. It was quite a contrast.

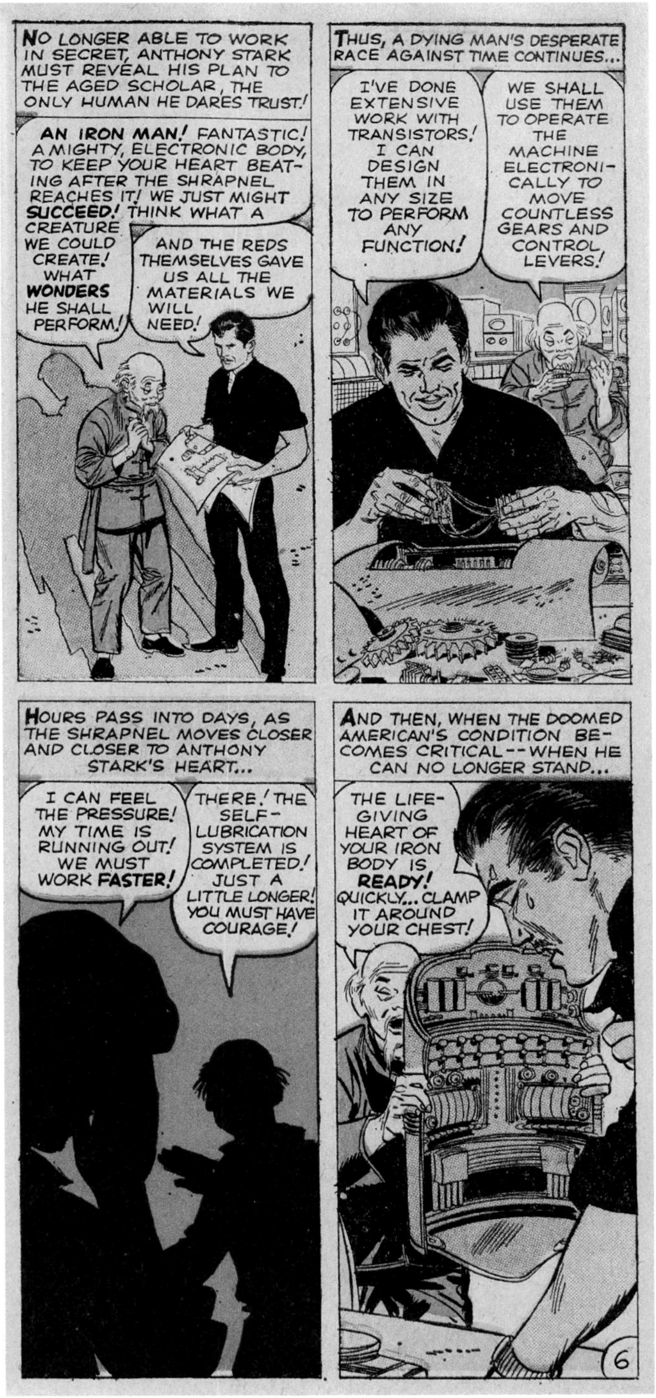

NO LONGER ABLE TO WORK IN SECRET, ANTHONY STARK MUST REVEAL HIS PLAN TO THE AGED SCHOLAR, THE ONLY HUMAN HE DARES TRUST!
AN IRON MAN! FANTASTIC! A MIGHTY, ELECTRONIC BODY, TO KEEP YOUR HEART BEATING AFTER THE SHRAPNEL REACHES IT! WE JUST MIGHT SUCCEED! THINK WHAT A CREATURE WE COULD CREATE! WHAT WONDERS HE SHALL PERFORM!
AND THE REDS THEMSELVES GAVE US ALL THE MATERIALS WE WILL NEED!
THUS, A DYING MAN'S DESPERATE RACE AGAINST TIME CONTINUES...
I'VE DONE EXTENSIVE WORK WITH TRANSISTORS! I CAN DESIGN THEM IN ANY SIZE TO PERFORM ANY FUNCTION!
WE SHALL USE THEM TO OPERATE THE MACHINE ELECTRONICALLY TO MOVE COUNTLESS GEARS AND CONTROL LEVERS!
HOURS PASS INTO DAYS, AS THE SHRAPNEL MOVES CLOSER AND CLOSER TO ANTHONY STARK'S HEART...
I CAN FEEL THE PRESSURE! MY TIME IS RUNNING OUT! WE MUST WORK FASTER!
THERE! THE SELF-LUBRICATION SYSTEM IS COMPLETED! JUST A LITTLE LONGER! YOU MUST HAVE COURAGE!
AND THEN, WHEN THE DOOMED AMERICAN'S CONDITION BECOMES CRITICAL--WHEN HE CAN NO LONGER STAND...
THE LIFE-GIVING HEART OF YOUR IRON BODY IS READY! QUICKLY... CLAMP IT AROUND YOUR CHEST!
6

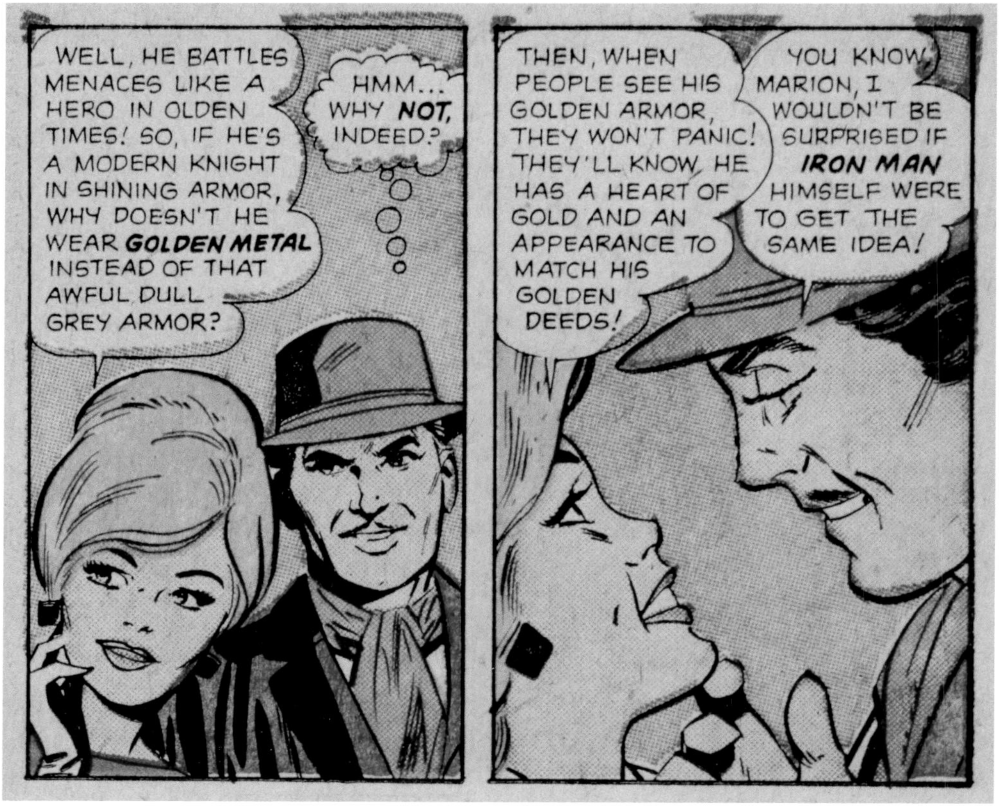
WELL, HE BATTLES MENACES LIKE A HERO IN OLDEN TIMES! SO, IF HE'S A MODERN KNIGHT IN SHINING ARMOR, WHY DOESN'T HE WEAR GOLDEN METAL INSTEAD OF THAT AWFUL DULL GREY ARMOR?
HMM... WHY NOT, INDEED?
THEN, WHEN PEOPLE SEE HIS GOLDEN ARMOR, THEY WON'T PANIC! THEY'LL KNOW HE HAS A HEART OF GOLD AND AN APPEARANCE TO MATCH HIS GOLDEN DEEDS!
YOU KNOW, MARION, I WOULDN'T BE SURPRISED IF IRON MAN HIMSELF WERE TO GET THE SAME IDEA!

TALES OF SUSPENSE No. 40

(Above) Interior, "Iron Man Versus Gargantus!"; plot, Stan Lee; script, Robert Bernstein; pencils, Jack Kirby; inks, Don Heck; April 1964.

TALES OF SUSPENSE No. 45

(Opposite) Interior, "The Icy Fingers of Jack Frost!"; plot, Stan Lee; script, Robert Bernstein; pencils and inks, Don Heck; September 1963. In the story that introduces both Pepper Potts and Happy Hogan, Tony Stark takes time to acquaint new readers to his golden armor and powers. Don Heck's lush inking was inspired here by comic art master Alex Toth.

TALES OF SUSPENSE No. 48

(Following spread) Interior, "The Mysterious Mr. Doll!"; script, Stan Lee; pencils, Steve Ditko; inks, Dick Ayers; December 1963. Steve Ditko redesigns the bulky Iron Man armor, making Tony Stark's alter ego a sleek product of the jet age. It was Ditko who opened the door to showing the character's emotion through his mask with the inclusion of wider, transparent eyeholes.

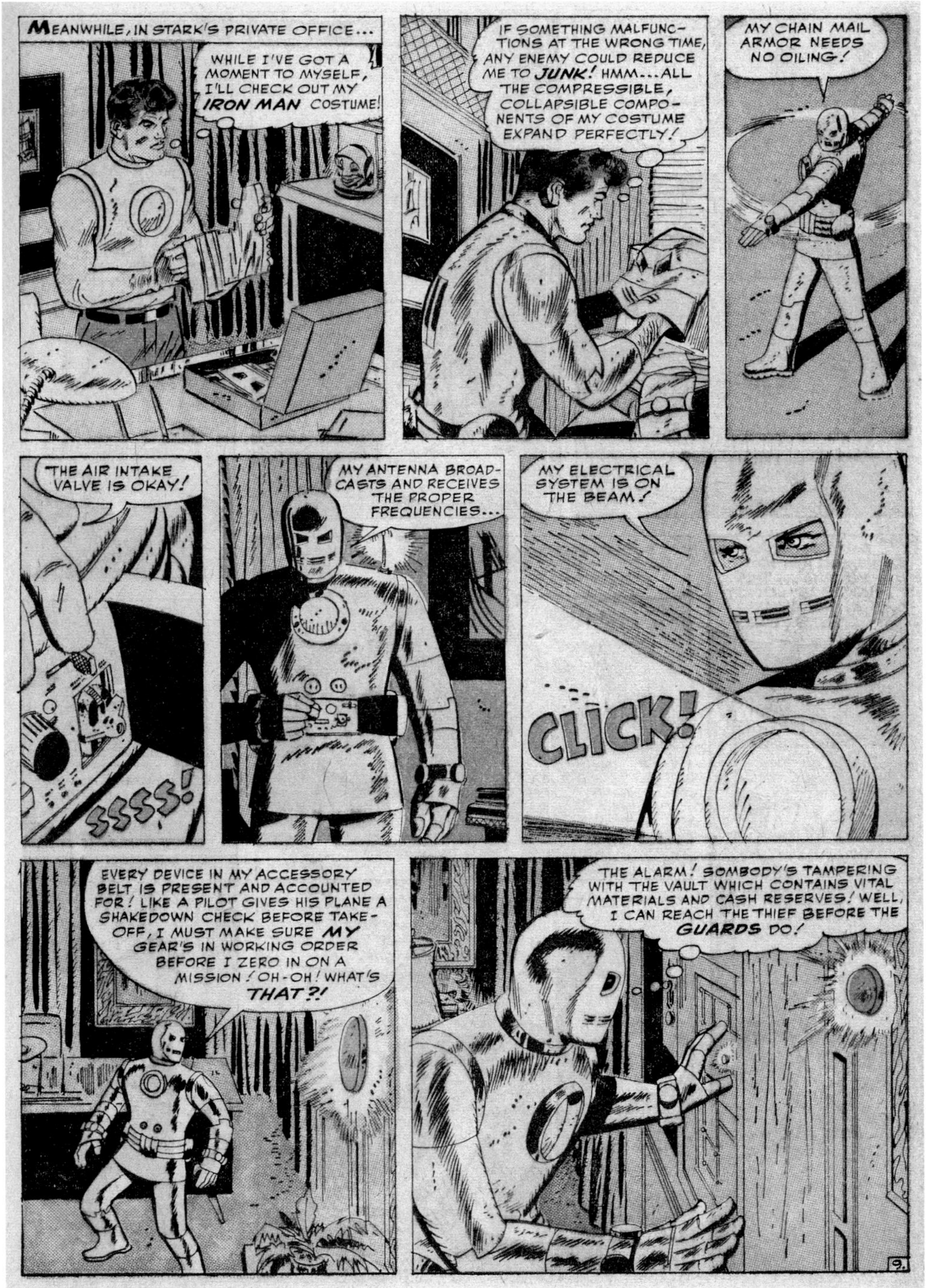
MEANWHILE, IN STARK'S PRIVATE OFFICE...
WHILE I'VE GOT A MOMENT TO MYSELF, I'LL CHECK OUT MY IRON MAN COSTUME!
IF SOMETHING MALFUNCTIONS AT THE WRONG TIME, ANY ENEMY COULD REDUCE ME TO JUNK! HMM...ALL THE COMPRESSIBLE, COLLAPSIBLE COMPONENTS OF MY COSTUME EXPAND PERFECTLY!
MY CHAIN MAIL ARMOR NEEDS NO OILING!
THE AIR INTAKE VALVE IS OKAY!
SSSSS!
MY ANTENNA BROADCASTS AND RECEIVES THE PROPER FREQUENCIES...
MY ELECTRICAL SYSTEM IS ON THE BEAM!
CLICK!
EVERY DEVICE IN MY ACCESSORY BELT IS PRESENT AND ACCOUNTED FOR! LIKE A PILOT GIVES HIS PLANE A SHAKEDOWN CHECK BEFORE TAKE-OFF, I MUST MAKE SURE MY GEAR'S IN WORKING ORDER BEFORE I ZERO IN ON A MISSION! OH-OH! WHAT'S THAT?!
THE ALARM! SOMBODY'S TAMPERING WITH THE VAULT WHICH CONTAINS VITAL MATERIALS AND CASH RESERVES! WELL, I CAN REACH THE THIEF BEFORE THE GUARDS DO!
9.

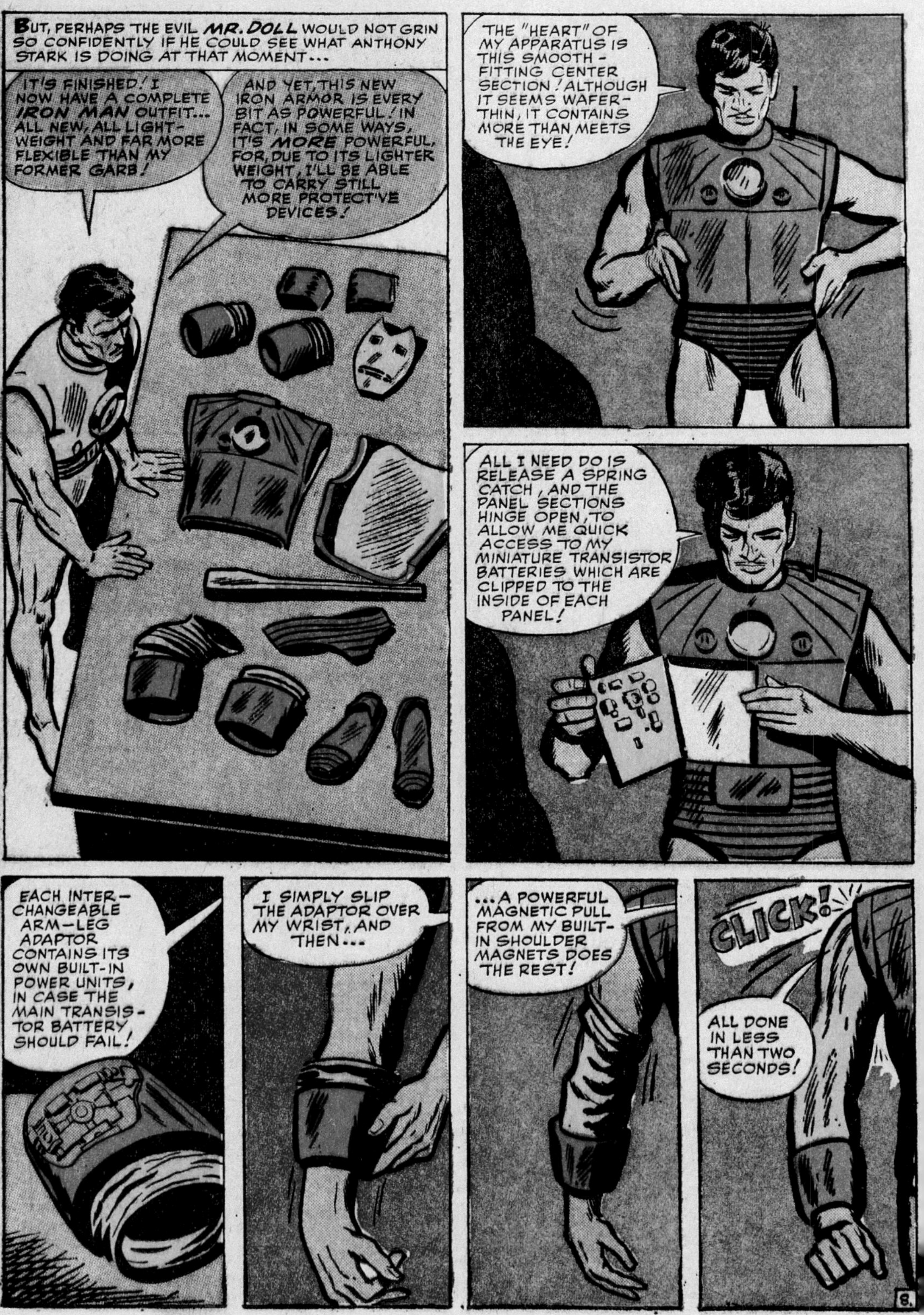
BUT, PERHAPS THE EVIL MR. DOLL WOULD NOT GRIN SO CONFIDENTLY IF HE COULD SEE WHAT ANTHONY STARK IS DOING AT THAT MOMENT...
IT'S FINISHED! I NOW HAVE A COMPLETE IRON MAN OUTFIT... ALL NEW, ALL LIGHT-WEIGHT AND FAR MORE FLEXIBLE THAN MY FORMER GARB!
AND YET, THIS NEW IRON ARMOR IS EVERY BIT AS POWERFUL! IN FACT, IN SOME WAYS, IT'S MORE POWERFUL, FOR, DUE TO ITS LIGHTER WEIGHT, I'LL BE ABLE TO CARRY STILL MORE PROTECTIVE DEVICES!
THE "HEART" OF MY APPARATUS IS THIS SMOOTH-FITTING CENTER SECTION! ALTHOUGH IT SEEMS WAFER-THIN, IT CONTAINS MORE THAN MEETS THE EYE!
ALL I NEED DO IS RELEASE A SPRING CATCH, AND THE PANEL SECTIONS HINGE OPEN, TO ALLOW ME QUICK ACCESS TO MY MINIATURE TRANSISTOR BATTERIES WHICH ARE CLIPPED TO THE INSIDE OF EACH PANEL!
EACH INTER-CHANGEABLE ARM-LEG ADAPTOR CONTAINS ITS OWN BUILT-IN POWER UNITS, IN CASE THE MAIN TRANSIS-TOR BATTERY SHOULD FAIL!
I SIMPLY SLIP THE ADAPTOR OVER MY WRIST, AND THEN...
...A POWERFUL MAGNETIC PULL FROM MY BUILT-IN SHOULDER MAGNETS DOES THE REST!
CLICK!
ALL DONE IN LESS THAN TWO SECONDS!
8.

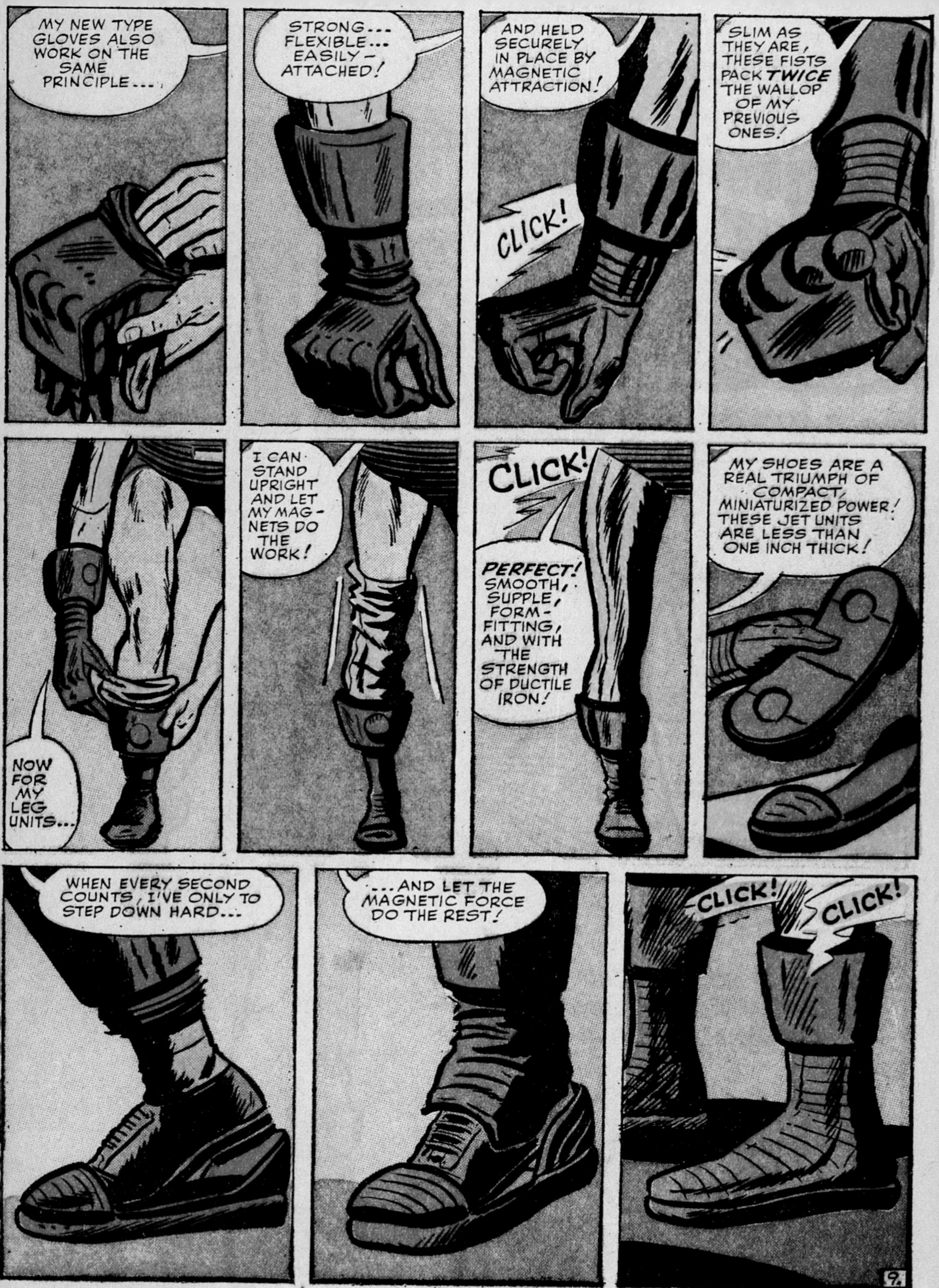
MY NEW TYPE GLOVES ALSO WORK ON THE SAME PRINCIPLE...
STRONG... FLEXIBLE... EASILY-ATTACHED!
AND HELD SECURELY IN PLACE BY MAGNETIC ATTRACTION!
CLICK!
SLIM AS THEY ARE, THESE FISTS PACK TWICE THE WALLOP OF MY PREVIOUS ONES!
NOW FOR MY LEG UNITS...
I CAN STAND UPRIGHT AND LET MY MAGNETS DO THE WORK!
CLICK!
PERFECT! SMOOTH, SUPPLE, FORM-FITTING, AND WITH THE STRENGTH OF DUCTILE IRON!
MY SHOES ARE A REAL TRIUMPH OF COMPACT, MINIATURIZED POWER! THESE JET UNITS ARE LESS THAN ONE INCH THICK!
WHEN EVERY SECOND COUNTS, I'VE ONLY TO STEP DOWN HARD...
...AND LET THE MAGNETIC FORCE DO THE REST!
CLICK!
CLICK!
9.

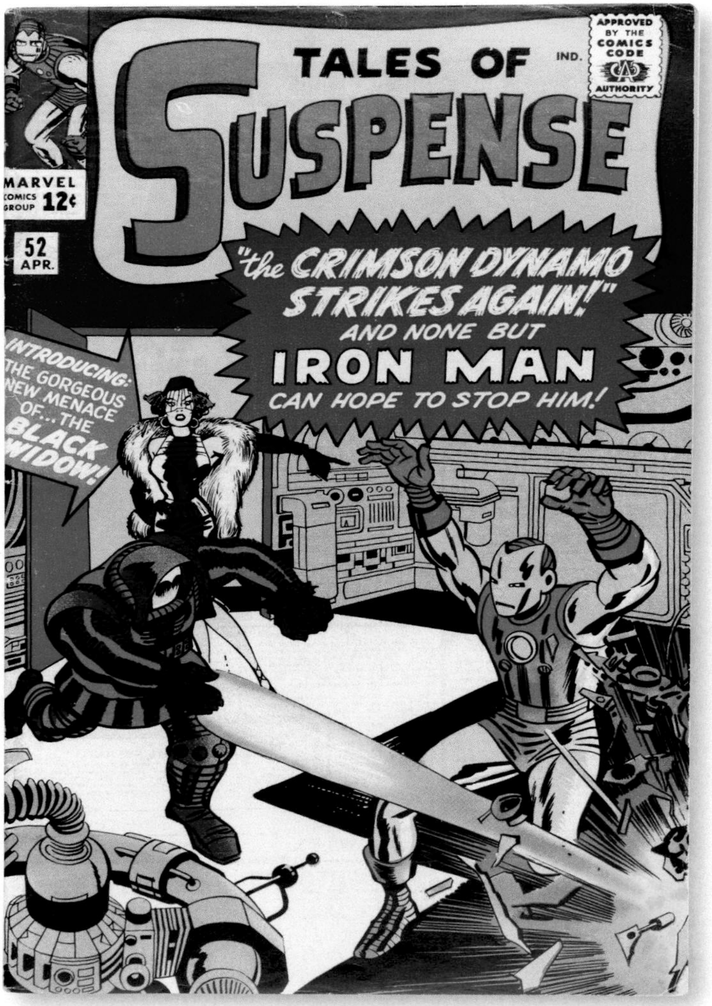
TALES OF
SUSPENSE
IND.
APPROVED BY THE COMICS CODE AUTHORITY
MARVEL COMICS GROUP 12¢
52 APR.
"the CRIMSON DYNAMO STRIKES AGAIN!"
AND NONE BUT
IRON MAN
CAN HOPE TO STOP HIM!
INTRODUCING: THE GORGEOUS NEW MENACE OF...THE BLACK WIDOW!

TALES OF SUSPENSE No. 52

(Above) Cover; pencils, Jack Kirby; inks, Paul Reinman; April 1964. It was very common in this era for heroes to have villainous counterparts with similar powers. With the Cold War at its height, many such villains came from behind the Iron Curtain.

TALES OF SUSPENSE No. 53

(Opposite) Interior, "The Black Widow Strikes Again!"; plot, Stan Lee; script, Don Rico; pencils and inks, Don Heck; May 1964. Natasha Romanoff, the Black Widow, is hiding from her leaders, including then-Premier Khrushchev. Naturally, Tony Stark pays no attention to the man behind the Iron Curtain.

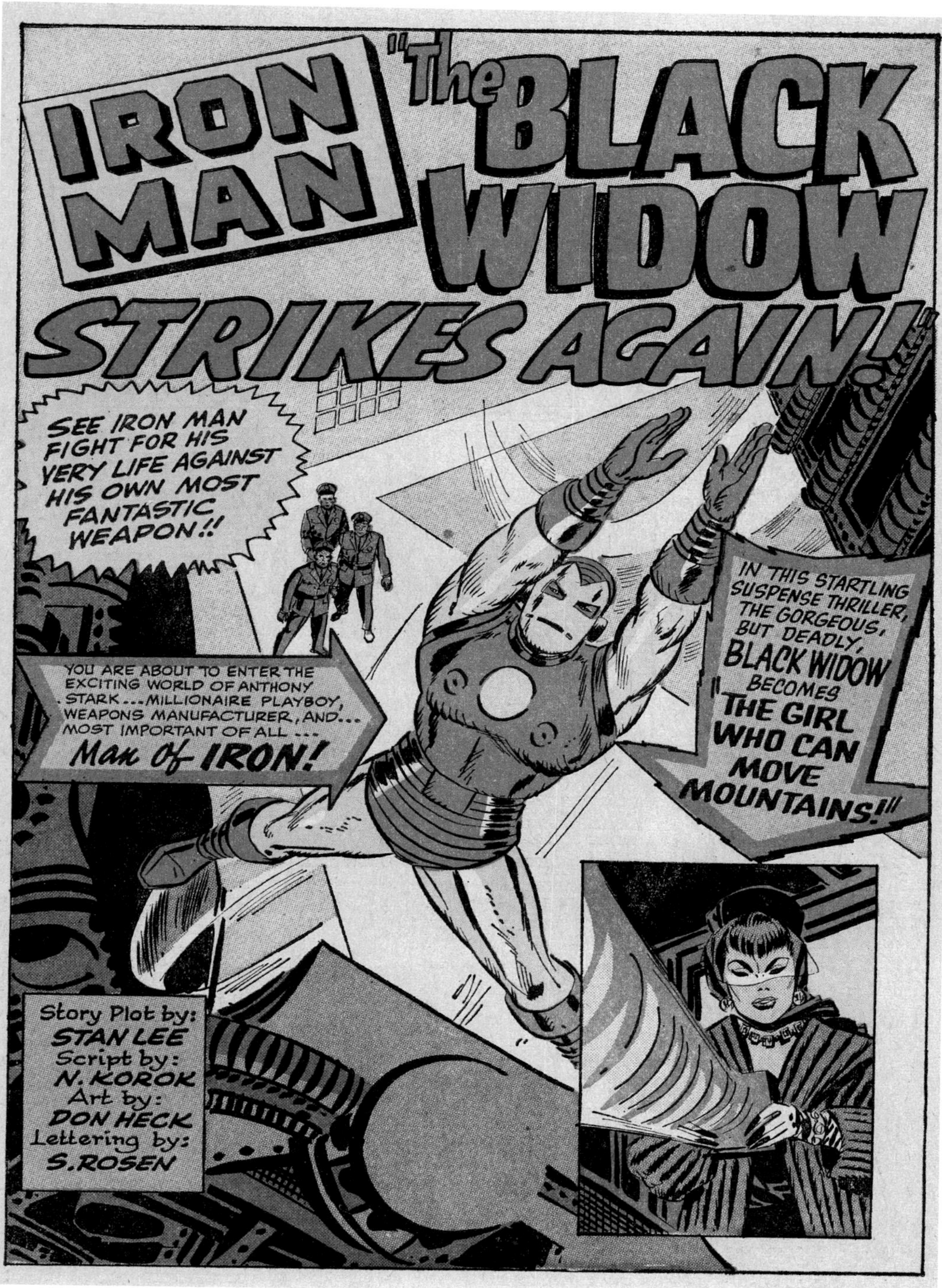
IRON MAN
"The BLACK WIDOW STRIKES AGAIN!"
SEE IRON MAN FIGHT FOR HIS VERY LIFE AGAINST HIS OWN MOST FANTASTIC WEAPON!!
IN THIS STARTLING SUSPENSE THRILLER, THE GORGEOUS, BUT DEADLY, BLACK WIDOW BECOMES "THE GIRL WHO CAN MOVE MOUNTAINS!"
YOU ARE ABOUT TO ENTER THE EXCITING WORLD OF ANTHONY STARK... MILLIONAIRE PLAYBOY, WEAPONS MANUFACTURER, AND... MOST IMPORTANT OF ALL... Man of IRON!
Story Plot by: STAN LEE Script by: N. KOROK Art by: DON HECK Lettering by: S. ROSEN

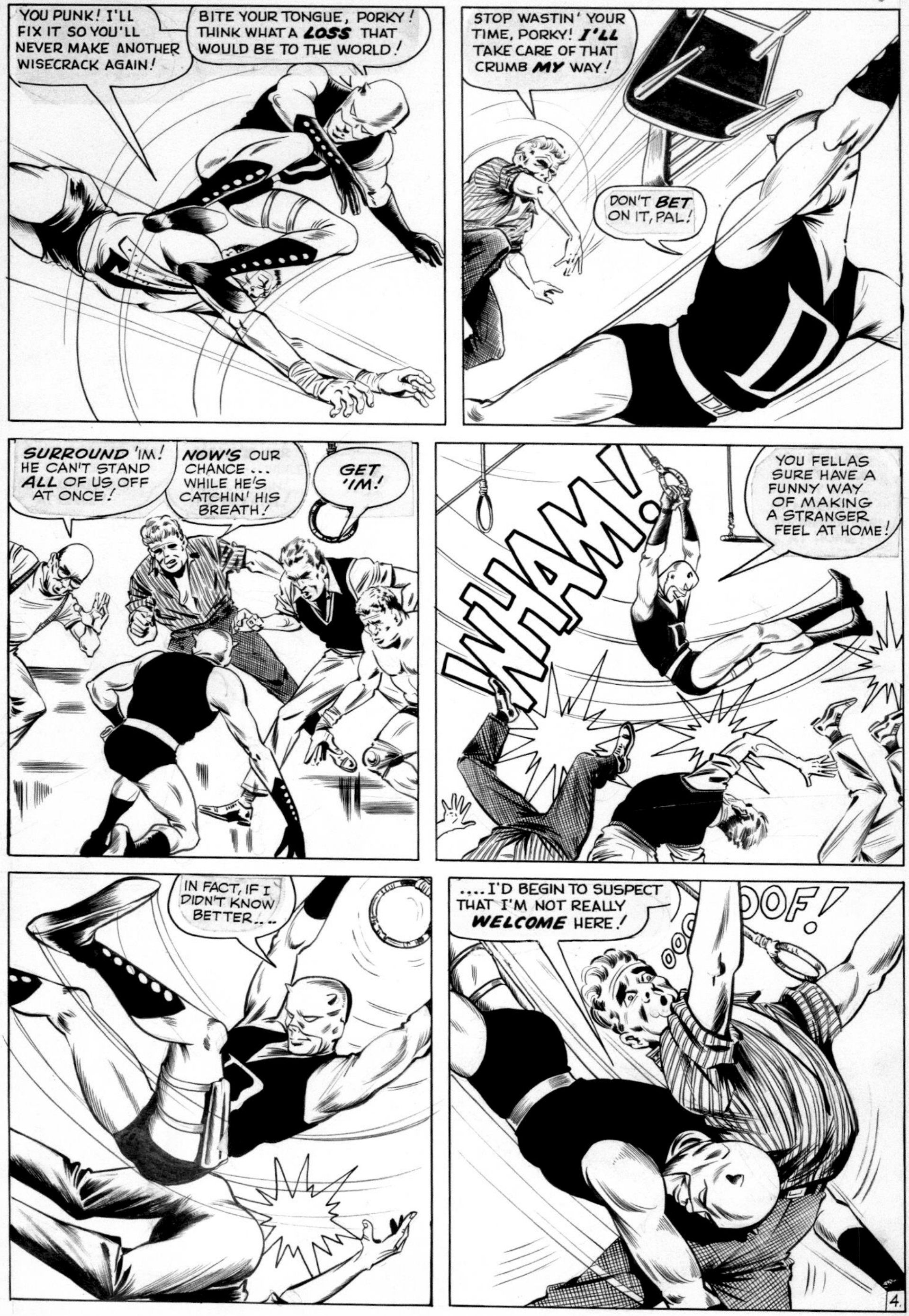
YOU PUNK! I'LL FIX IT SO YOU'LL NEVER MAKE ANOTHER WISECRACK AGAIN!
BITE YOUR TONGUE, PORKY! THINK WHAT A LOSS THAT WOULD BE TO THE WORLD!
STOP WASTIN' YOUR TIME, PORKY! I'LL TAKE CARE OF THAT CRUMB MY WAY!
DON'T BET ON IT, PAL!
SURROUND 'IM! HE CAN'T STAND ALL OF US OFF AT ONCE!
NOW'S OUR CHANCE... WHILE HE'S CATCHIN' HIS BREATH!
GET 'IM!
WHAM!
YOU FELLAS SURE HAVE A FUNNY WAY OF MAKING A STRANGER FEEL AT HOME!
IN FACT, IF I DIDN'T KNOW BETTER...
....I'D BEGIN TO SUSPECT THAT I'M NOT REALLY WELCOME HERE!
OOOOOF!

"'There is no such thing as the isolated Marvel event';
Marvel 'gives all of itself in each of its fragments.'
These quotations are from Roberto Calasso's book
about the Greek myths, *The Marriage of Cadmus
and Harmony*: I have simply substituted the word
'Marvel' for 'myth'..." — GEOFF DYER

THE ORIGIN OF DAREDEVIL

*(Opposite) Original interior art, "The Origin of Daredevil,"
Daredevil No.1; script, Stan Lee; pencils, Bill Everett; inks, Everett,
Steve Ditko, and Sol Brodsky; April 1964.* Daredevil takes on
the mob. The original artwork differs from the published
version. The effects of age reveal that Bill Everett originally
lettered the story, but Sam Rosen pasted new balloons
over Everett's. Rosen, along with Artie Simek, lettered and
designed logos for nearly every Marvel comic in the 1960s.

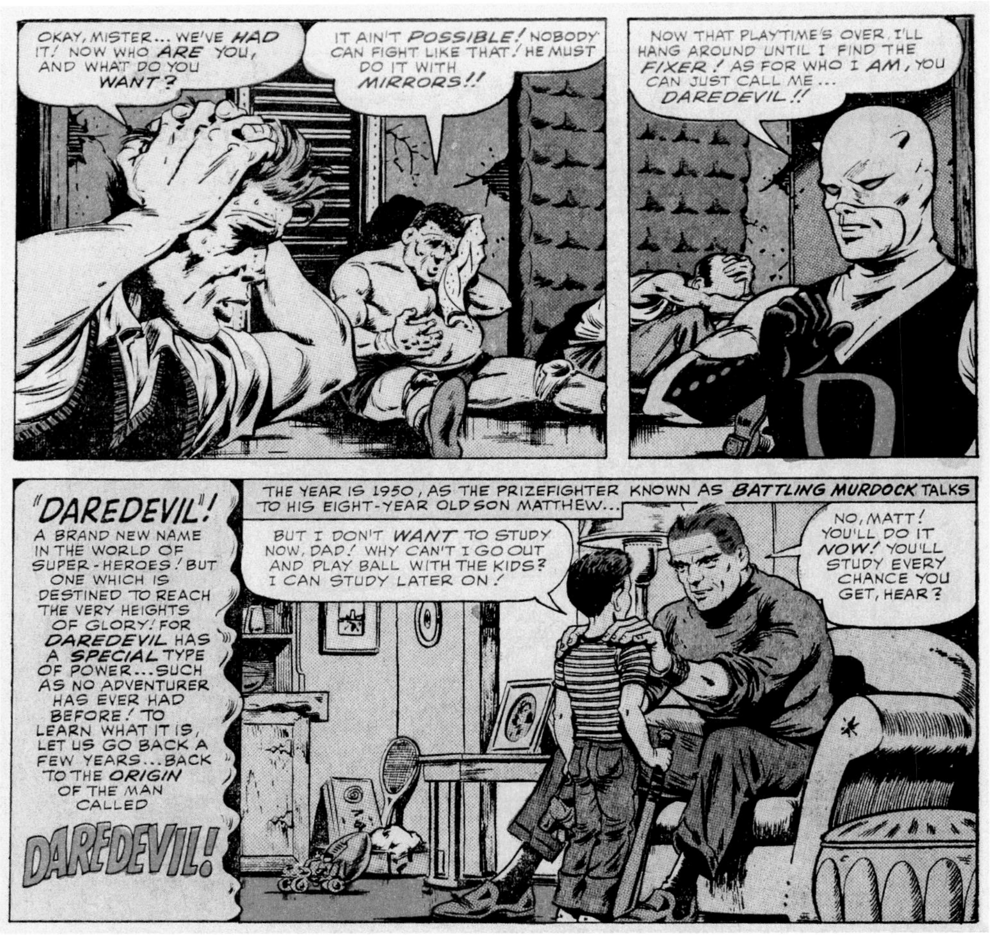
OKAY, MISTER... WE'VE HAD IT! NOW WHO ARE YOU, AND WHAT DO YOU WANT?
IT AIN'T POSSIBLE! NOBODY CAN FIGHT LIKE THAT! HE MUST DO IT WITH MIRRORS!!
NOW THAT PLAYTIME'S OVER, I'LL HANG AROUND UNTIL I FIND THE FIXER! AS FOR WHO I AM, YOU CAN JUST CALL ME... DAREDEVIL!!
"DAREDEVIL"! A BRAND NEW NAME IN THE WORLD OF SUPER-HEROES! BUT ONE WHICH IS DESTINED TO REACH THE VERY HEIGHTS OF GLORY! FOR DAREDEVIL HAS A SPECIAL TYPE OF POWER... SUCH AS NO ADVENTURER HAS EVER HAD BEFORE! TO LEARN WHAT IT IS, LET US GO BACK A FEW YEARS... BACK TO THE ORIGIN OF THE MAN CALLED
DAREDEVIL!
THE YEAR IS 1950, AS THE PRIZEFIGHTER KNOWN AS BATTLING MURDOCK TALKS TO HIS EIGHT-YEAR OLD SON MATTHEW...
BUT I DON'T WANT TO STUDY NOW, DAD! WHY CAN'T I GO OUT AND PLAY BALL WITH THE KIDS? I CAN STUDY LATER ON!
NO, MATT! YOU'LL DO IT NOW! YOU'LL STUDY EVERY CHANCE YOU GET, HEAR?

DAREDEVIL No. 1

(Above) Interior, "The Origin of Daredevil"; script, Stan Lee; pencils, Bill Everett; inks, Everett, Steve Ditko, and Sol Brodsky; April 1964. By the 1960s, radiation has all but replaced the Golden Age standard chemical methods of acquiring super powers. Joining the Fantastic Four, Spider-Man, the Hulk, many X-Men, and quite a few villains, Daredevil gains his powers (and likely one heck of a headache) when he is struck in the head by a radioactive canister. Before the Marvel Age, it was common for heroes to acquire their powers and then immediately come to the world's aid. At Marvel, characters needed a motivation, and often sought redemption to set right what once went wrong.

DAREDEVIL No. 4

(Opposite) Cover; pencils, Jack Kirby; inks, Vince Colletta; October 1964.

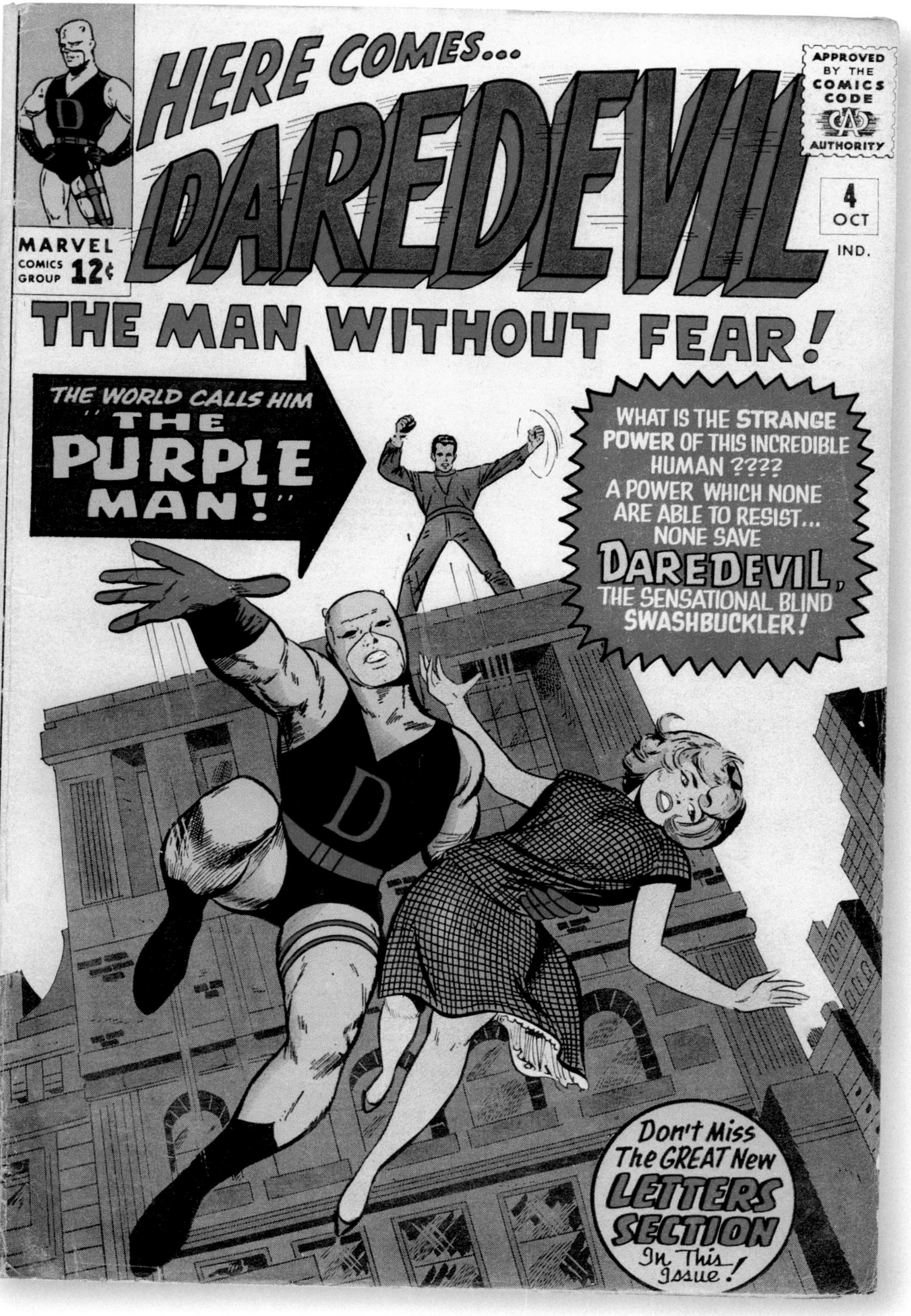
HERE COMES...
DAREDEVIL
APPROVED BY THE COMICS CODE AUTHORITY
4 OCT
IND.
MARVEL COMICS GROUP 12¢
THE MAN WITHOUT FEAR!
THE WORLD CALLS HIM "THE PURPLE MAN!"
WHAT IS THE STRANGE POWER OF THIS INCREDIBLE HUMAN ???? A POWER WHICH NONE ARE ABLE TO RESIST... NONE SAVE DAREDEVIL, THE SENSATIONAL BLIND SWASHBUCKLER!
Don't Miss The GREAT New LETTERS SECTION In This Issue!

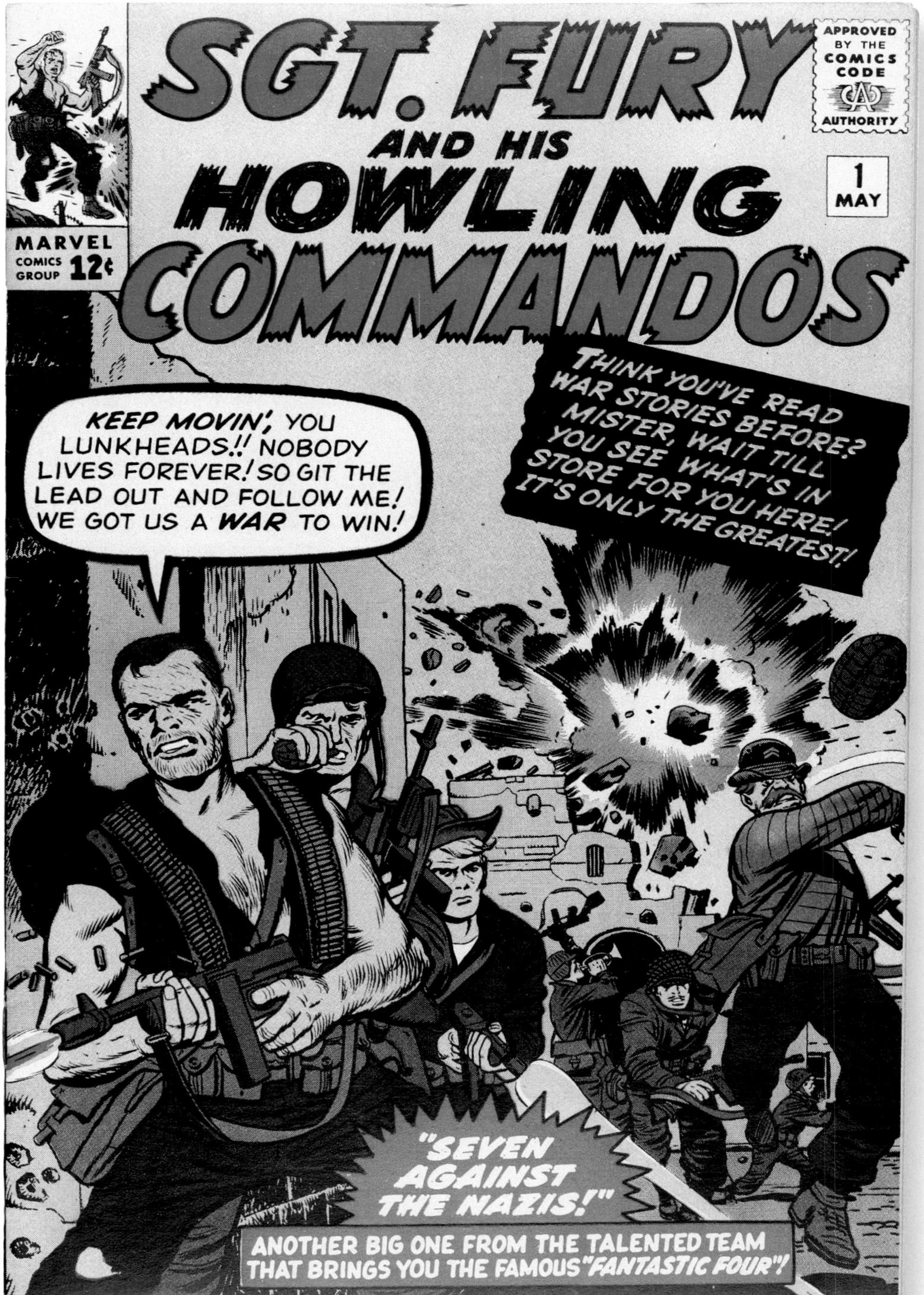
SGT. FURY
AND HIS
HOWLING
COMMANDOS
APPROVED BY THE COMICS CODE AUTHORITY
1
MAY
MARVEL
COMICS GROUP 12¢
THINK YOU'VE READ WAR STORIES BEFORE? MISTER, WAIT TILL YOU SEE WHAT'S IN STORE FOR YOU HERE! IT'S ONLY THE GREATEST!
KEEP MOVIN', YOU LUNKHEADS!! NOBODY LIVES FOREVER! SO GIT THE LEAD OUT AND FOLLOW ME! WE GOT US A WAR TO WIN!
"SEVEN AGAINST THE NAZIS!"
ANOTHER BIG ONE FROM THE TALENTED TEAM THAT BRINGS YOU THE FAMOUS "FANTASTIC FOUR"!

MEET THE HOWLING COMMANDOS
SGT. NICK FURY: SIX FOOT TWO OF STEEL-MUSCLED, IRON-NERVED FIGHTING MAN! FURY BELIEVES IN MAKING HIS MEN FEAR HIM SO MUCH THAT THEY WOULD RATHER FACE HOPELESS ODDS THAN FACE HIS ANGER! IT'S RUMORED THAT HE'S REALLY GOT A HEART, BUT NO ONE CAN PROVE IT!
ROBERT "REBEL" RALSTON: THIS LEAN EX-JOCKEY FROM THE BLUE-GRASS COUNTRY OF KENTUCKY IS A LOT TOUGHER THAN HIS SMALL SIZE MAKES HIM APPEAR! AND THERE ARE PLENTY OF MISSING-IN-ACTION NAZIS AND FASCISTS TO PROVE IT!
CORPORAL "DUM-DUM" DUGAN: THIS ONE-TIME CIRCUS STRONGMAN IS SGT. FURY'S GOOD RIGHT ARM! POWER-FUL, FEARLESS, AND EASY-GOING, HE'S A ROARING TIGER WHEN THE CHIPS ARE DOWN!
JONATHAN "JUNIOR" JUNIPER: FRESH OUT OF AN IVY-LEAGUE COLLEGE, JUNIOR IS THE CHEERFUL EAGER-BEAVER OF THE GROUP! BUT DON'T LET HIS YOUTHFUL SMILE FOOL YOU! HE'S FAST AS A PANTHER, AND JUST AS DANGEROUS!
GABRIEL JONES: "GABE" USED TO BLOW THE SWEETEST TRUMPET THIS SIDE OF CARNEGIE HALL! NOW HE GIVES OUT WITH THE HOT LICKS ON THE FIELD OF BATTLE ...BUT HIS NOTES ARE JUST AS TRUE, AND HIS HAND AND HEART AS STEADY AS EVER!
IZZY COHEN: THIS SCRAPPY, TOUGH MASTER MECHANIC LOVES MACHINERY THE WAY SOME MEN LOVE FAME AND FORTUNE! HE CAN REPAIR ANYTHING... EXCEPT THE SORROW IN HIS SOUL WHEN HE REMEMBERS THE FATE OF HIS RELATIVES IN EUROPE AT THE HANDS OF THE MAD LITTLE MAN WITH THE MOUSTACHE!
DINO MANELLI: YOU MIGHT HAVE SEEN HIM IN THE MOVIES, UNDER ANOTHER NAME; FOR THIS HANDSOME SWASHBUCKLER GAVE UP A PROMISING CAREER AS AN ACTOR IN ORDER TO REPAY THE COUNTRY HE LOVES FOR ALL IT HAS GIVEN HIM!.

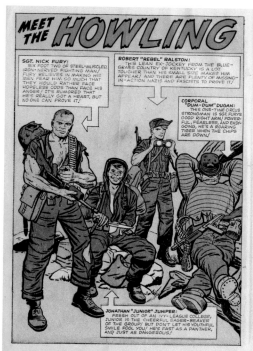

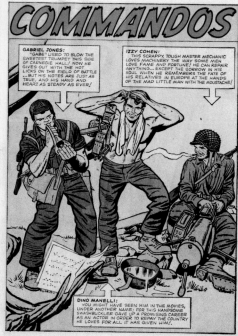

SGT. FURY No. 1

(Opposite) Cover; pencils, Jack Kirby; inks, Dick Ayers. (Above) Interior, "Sgt. Fury and His Howling Commandos!"; script, Stan Lee; pencils, Jack Kirby; inks, Dick Ayers. May 1963. Loosely based on the 101st Airborne Division — known as the Screaming Eagles — the Howling Commandos faced the most difficult missions. Led by Nick Fury and including Rebel Ralston, a southerner; Izzy Cohen, a Jew from Brooklyn; Dum Dum Dugan, an Irishman; Dino Manelli, an Italian; Junior Juniper, the youngest member; and Gabe Jones, the first African American to get a costarring role in a mainstream comic. The *Sgt. Fury* timeline begins about a year before D-Day (June 6, 1944). Though still in compliance with the Comics Code ban on showing the horrors of war, the Howlers nevertheless often confronted the terrible losses that combat entailed. Amid a war against racism, the Howlers showed that all Americans can come together when they really need to.

SGT. FURY No. 3

(Below) Interior, "Midnight at Massacre Mountain!"; script, Stan Lee; pencils, Jack Kirby; inks, Dick Ayers; September 1963. "Wah-Hoo" becomes the Howlers' battle cry. Lee, Kirby, and Ayers were all in the service during World War II, with both Kirby and Ayers seeing action in Europe.

SGT. FURY No. 9

(Opposite) Cover; pencils and inks, Dick Ayers; August 1964. "Even war and Western comics were super-hero comics in drag... It's something that's omnipresent—you don't even think about it. You don't even notice it. It's there like air is there." —Alan Moore

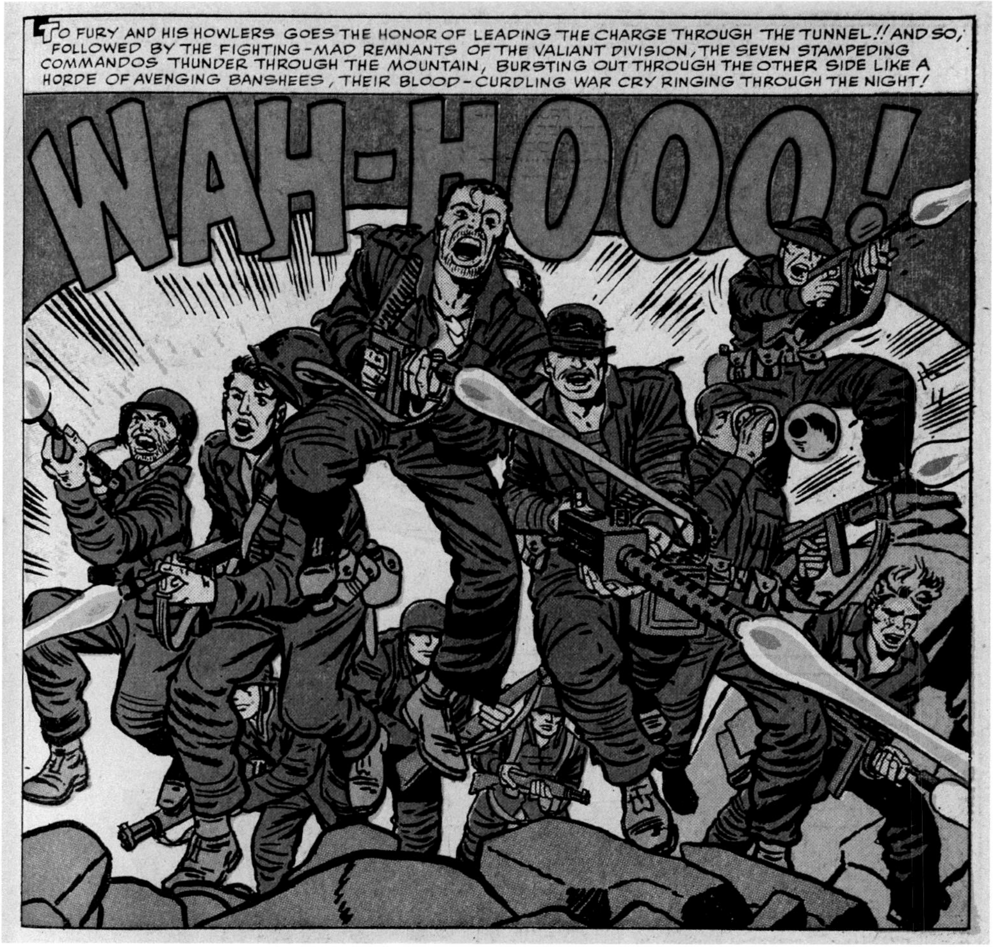
TO FURY AND HIS HOWLERS GOES THE HONOR OF LEADING THE CHARGE THROUGH THE TUNNEL!! AND SO, FOLLOWED BY THE FIGHTING-MAD REMNANTS OF THE VALIANT DIVISION, THE SEVEN STAMPEDING COMMANDOS THUNDER THROUGH THE MOUNTAIN, BURSTING OUT THROUGH THE OTHER SIDE LIKE A HORDE OF AVENGING BANSHEES, THEIR BLOOD-CURDLING WAR CRY RINGING THROUGH THE NIGHT!
WAH-HOOO!

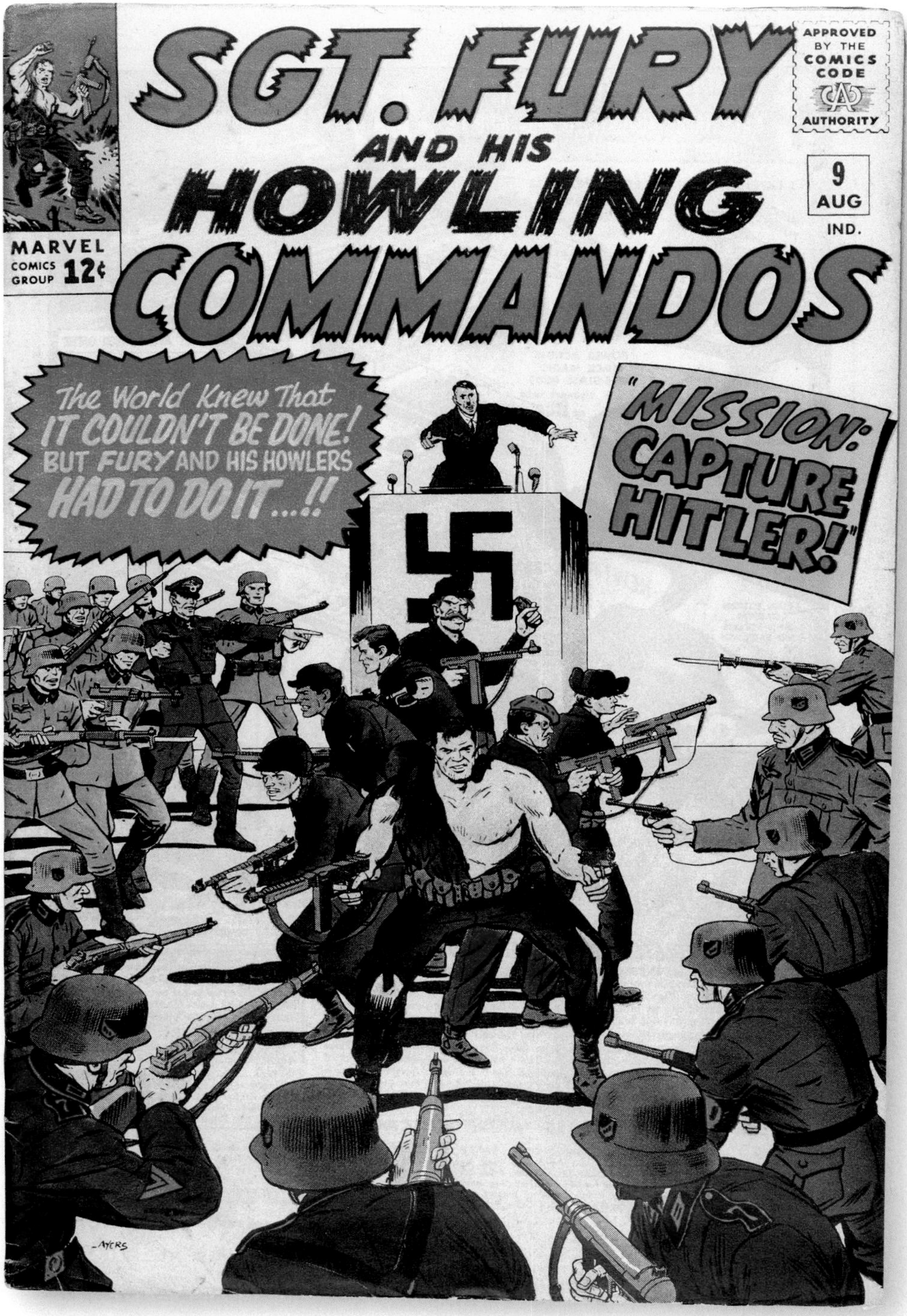
SGT. FURY
AND HIS
HOWLING
COMMANDOS
APPROVED BY THE COMICS CODE AUTHORITY
9
AUG
IND.
MARVEL COMICS GROUP 12¢
The World Knew That IT COULDN'T BE DONE! BUT FURY AND HIS HOWLERS HAD TO DO IT...!!
"MISSION: CAPTURE HITLER!"
AYERS

"Fury was the toughest son of a bitch I ever created...
Kirby did a wonderful job with him."
— STAN LEE

FANTASTIC FOUR NO. 21

(Opposite) Cover; pencils, Jack Kirby; inks, Paul Reinman; December 1963. Ex-Sgt. Nick Fury survived the war to become a CIA agent in Marvel's 1960s. He shows up to help old buddy Reed Richards and his team against the Hate-Monger, who turns out to be... Adolf Hitler?! Fury's own book got some of the Bullpen's most memorable mail, Flo Steinberg remembers: "We got a letter to Sgt. Fury from out of somewhere, maybe Texas, saying that we were Communist pinkos because...there were different races and ethnic groups in Sgt. Fury.... He was going to come to New York and take care of us. Everybody panicked. We were all running around wondering what to do! We called the FBI. In those days, you could just call and they would respond. An FBI agent came to the office, he was really nice. He looked at the letter and said, 'Well, how many people have handled this letter?' We said, 'Oh, about 50.' Everybody had handled it! So he took the letter — after we gave him a bunch of comics — and after that, no one in the Bullpen wanted to go out to the front area where people would come into the office!"

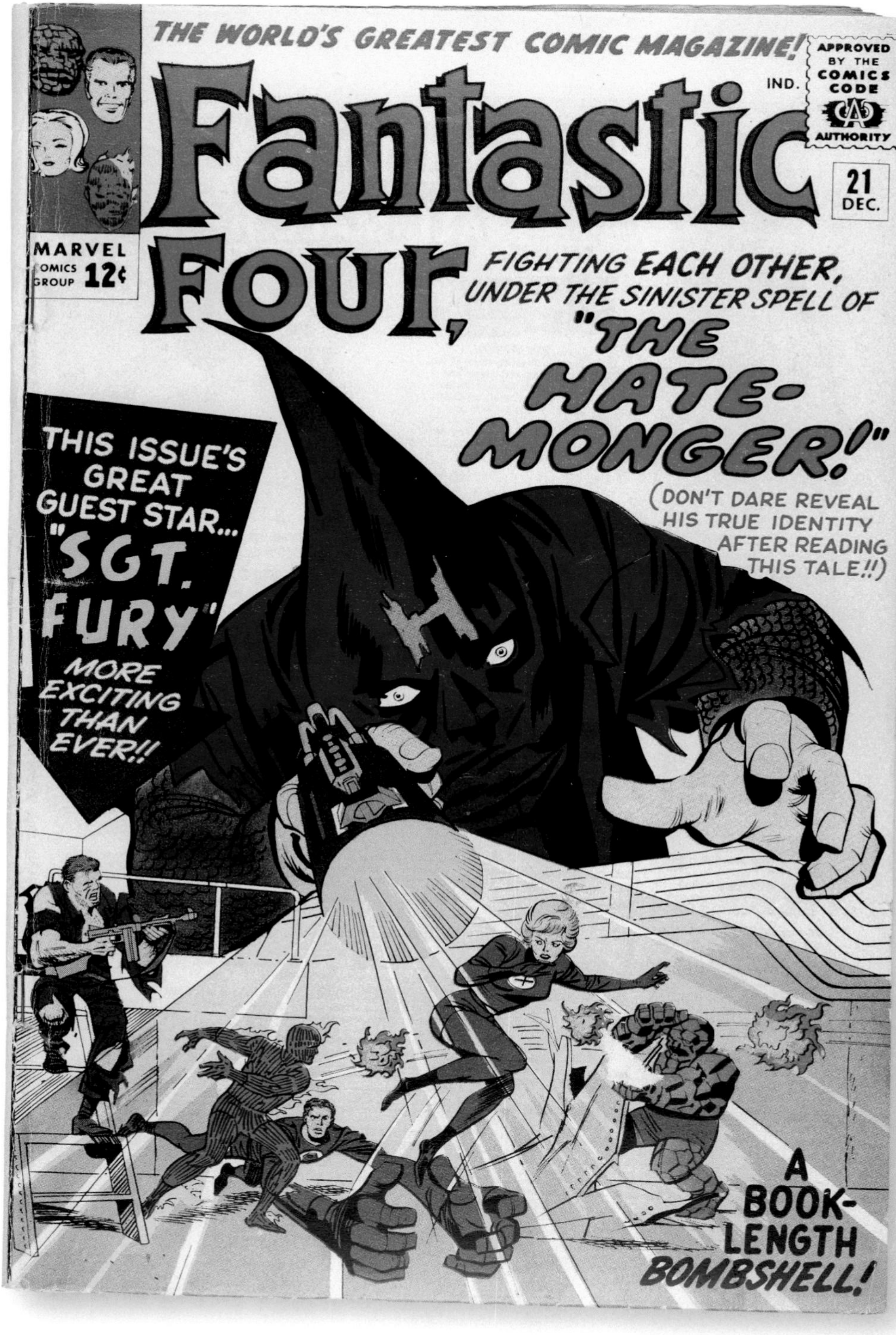
THE WORLD'S GREATEST COMIC MAGAZINE!
APPROVED BY THE COMICS CODE AUTHORITY
IND.
Fantastic Four,
21 DEC.
MARVEL COMICS GROUP 12¢
FIGHTING EACH OTHER, UNDER THE SINISTER SPELL OF "THE HATE-MONGER!"
(DON'T DARE REVEAL HIS TRUE IDENTITY AFTER READING THIS TALE!!)
THIS ISSUE'S GREAT GUEST STAR... "SGT. FURY"
MORE EXCITING THAN EVER!!
A BOOK-LENGTH BOMBSHELL!

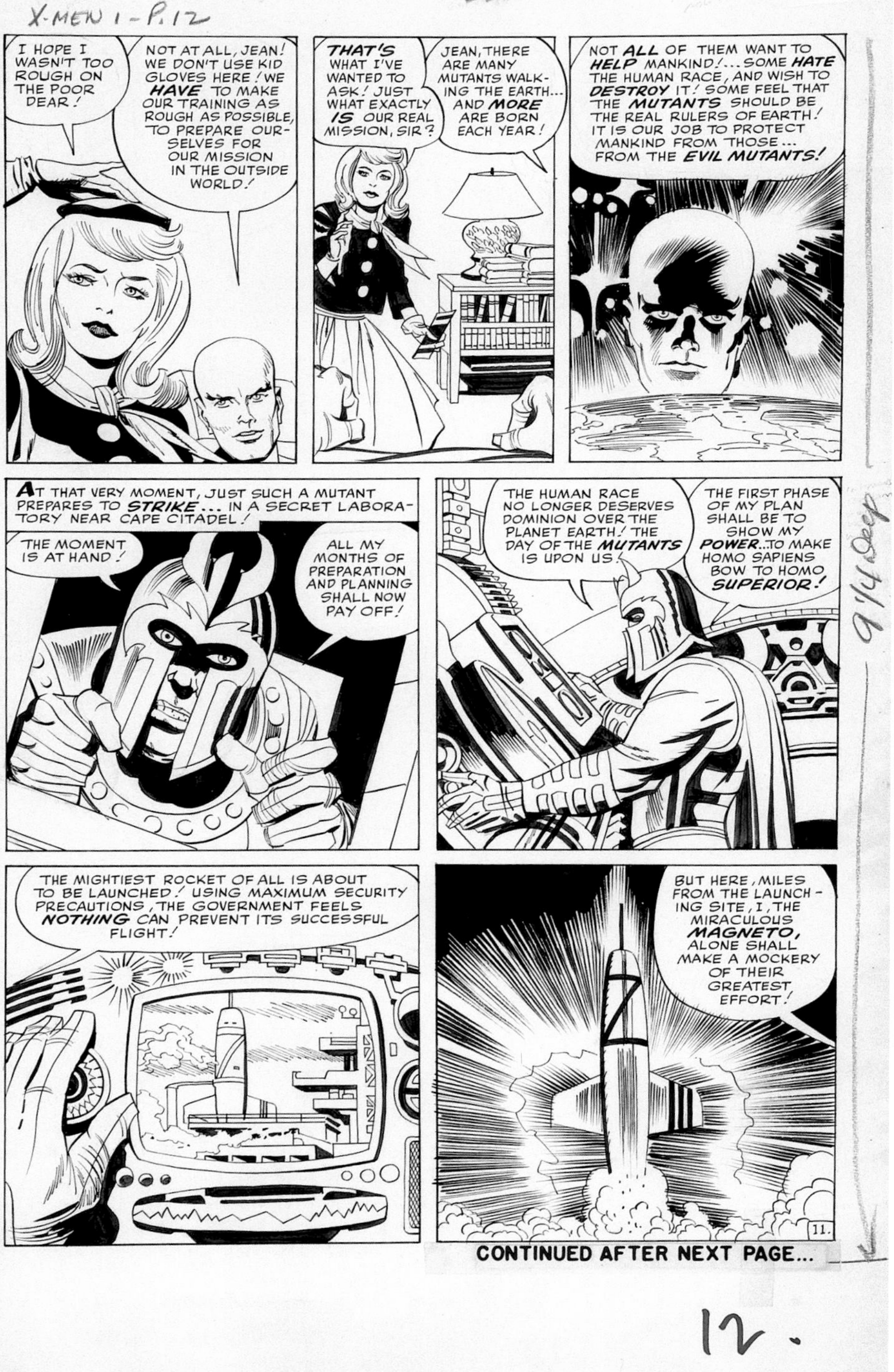
X-MEN 1 - P. 12
I HOPE I WASN'T TOO ROUGH ON THE POOR DEAR!
NOT AT ALL, JEAN! WE DON'T USE KID GLOVES HERE! WE HAVE TO MAKE OUR TRAINING AS ROUGH AS POSSIBLE, TO PREPARE OURSELVES FOR OUR MISSION IN THE OUTSIDE WORLD!
THAT'S WHAT I'VE WANTED TO ASK! JUST WHAT EXACTLY IS OUR REAL MISSION, SIR?
JEAN, THERE ARE MANY MUTANTS WALKING THE EARTH... AND MORE ARE BORN EACH YEAR!
NOT ALL OF THEM WANT TO HELP MANKIND!... SOME HATE THE HUMAN RACE, AND WISH TO DESTROY IT! SOME FEEL THAT THE MUTANTS SHOULD BE THE REAL RULERS OF EARTH! IT IS OUR JOB TO PROTECT MANKIND FROM THOSE... FROM THE EVIL MUTANTS!
AT THAT VERY MOMENT, JUST SUCH A MUTANT PREPARES TO STRIKE... IN A SECRET LABORATORY NEAR CAPE CITADEL!
THE MOMENT IS AT HAND!
ALL MY MONTHS OF PREPARATION AND PLANNING SHALL NOW PAY OFF!
THE HUMAN RACE NO LONGER DESERVES DOMINION OVER THE PLANET EARTH! THE DAY OF THE MUTANTS IS UPON US!
THE FIRST PHASE OF MY PLAN SHALL BE TO SHOW MY POWER... TO MAKE HOMO SAPIENS BOW TO HOMO SUPERIOR!
THE MIGHTIEST ROCKET OF ALL IS ABOUT TO BE LAUNCHED! USING MAXIMUM SECURITY PRECAUTIONS, THE GOVERNMENT FEELS NOTHING CAN PREVENT ITS SUCCESSFUL FLIGHT!
BUT HERE, MILES FROM THE LAUNCHING SITE, I, THE MIRACULOUS MAGNETO, ALONE SHALL MAKE A MOCKERY OF THEIR GREATEST EFFORT!
11.
CONTINUED AFTER NEXT PAGE...
12.

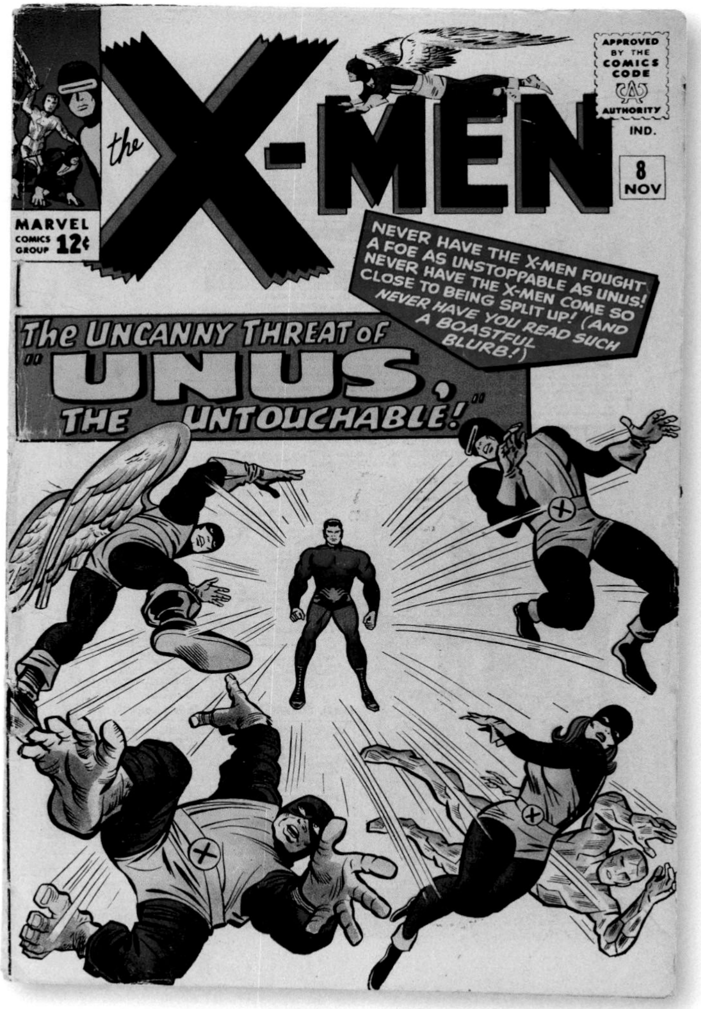
APPROVED BY THE COMICS CODE AUTHORITY
IND.
8
NOV
MARVEL
COMICS GROUP
12¢
the X-MEN
NEVER HAVE THE X-MEN FOUGHT A FOE AS UNSTOPPABLE AS UNUS! NEVER HAVE THE X-MEN COME SO CLOSE TO BEING SPLIT UP! (AND NEVER HAVE YOU READ SUCH A BOASTFUL BLURB!)
The UNCANNY THREAT of "UNUS, THE UNTOUCHABLE!"

HOMO SUPERIOR

(Opposite) Original interior art, "X-Men!," X-Men *No. 1; script, Stan Lee; pencils, Jack Kirby; inks, Paul Reinman; September 1963.* The X-Men are a group of five teenage mutants who live in Westchester, New York. They call themselves *Homo Superior*. They are Cyclops (Scott Summers), who has incredibly powerful energy beams streaming constantly from his eyes; Marvel Girl (Jean Grey), who has the power of telekinesis; the Beast (Hank McCoy), who has great strength and even greater agility; the Angel (Warren Worthington III), who has wings and can fly; and the Iceman (Bobby Drake), who has the power to create cold. Xavier's old friend, the X-Men's nemesis Magneto, also debuts.

X-MEN No. 8

(Above) Cover; pencils, Jack Kirby; inks, Chic Stone; November 1964.

X-MEN No. 1

(Below) Interior, "The X-Men!"; script, Stan Lee; pencils, Jack Kirby; inks, Paul Reinman; September 1963. Cyclops shows his great power, which will soon become his biggest fear: He has the power to accidentally injure someone close to him!

X-MEN No. 2

(Opposite) Interior, "No One Can Stop the Vanisher"; script, Stan Lee; pencils, Jack Kirby; inks, Paul Reinman; November 1963. The team goes into action! Issue by issue, Marvel introduces a host of new mutant villains with imaginative powers to pit against the X-Men.

CYCLOPS! ATTENTION!! THIS IS YOUR TEST! ASSUME THE BEAST AND ICEMAN ARE YOUR ENEMIES! PUT THEM OUT OF ACTION, WITHOUT CAUSING SERIOUS INJURY!
AS YOU SAY, SIR!
SLOWLY, SILENTLY, CYCLOPS ADJUSTS THE SMALL LEVER AT THE SIDE OF HIS HEAD-SHIELD! AND, AS HE DOES SO, HIS EYE VISOR OPENS WIDER AND WIDER ... UNTIL ...
YOU'RE THE OLDEST, BEAST, SO YOU'RE FIRST!
YEOW!

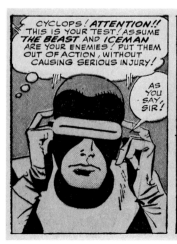

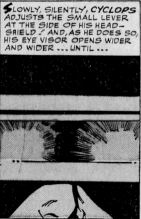

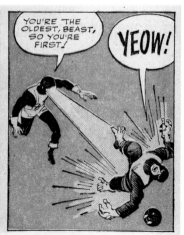

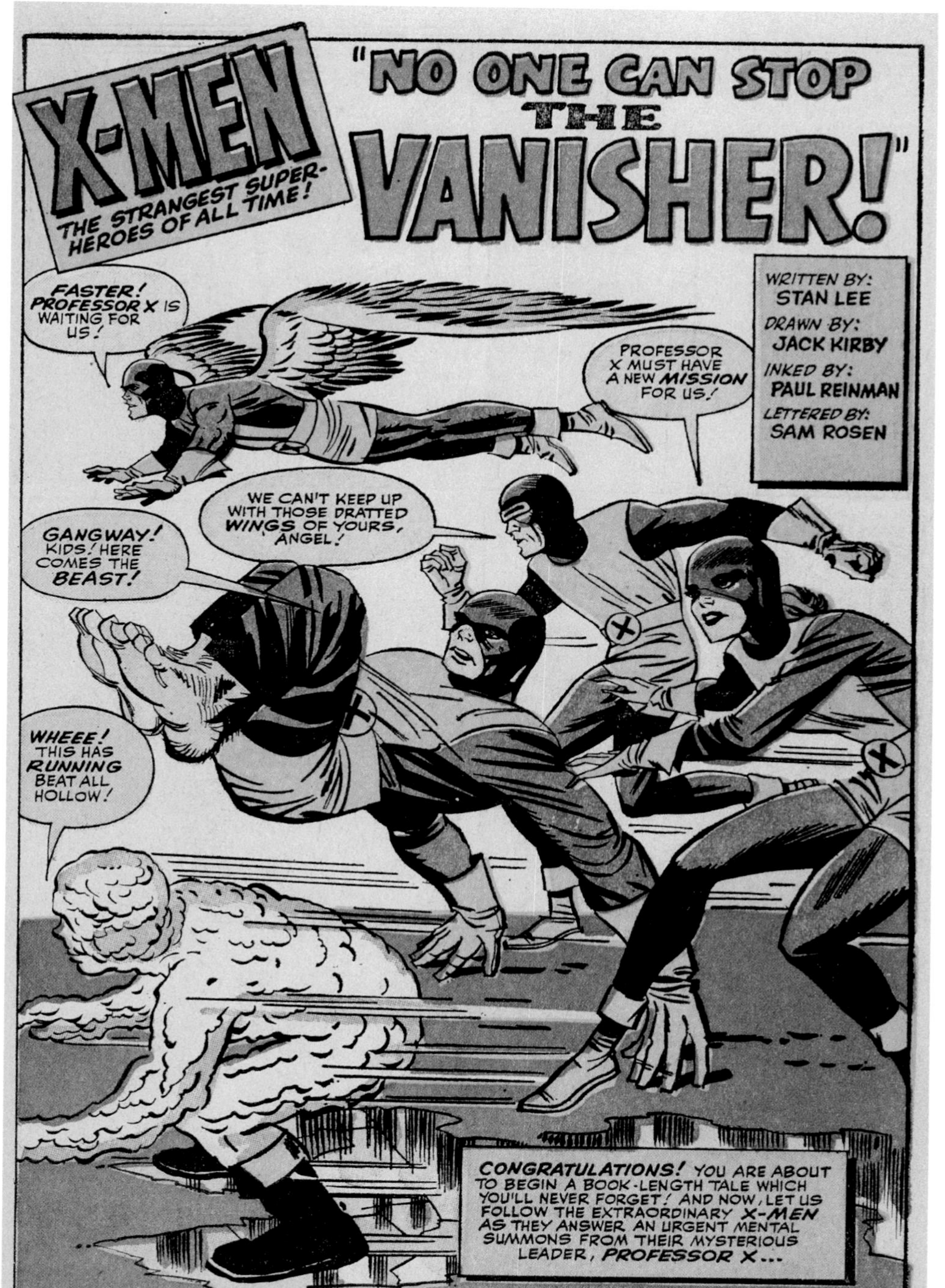

X-MEN
THE STRANGEST SUPER-HEROES OF ALL TIME!
"NO ONE CAN STOP THE VANISHER!"
WRITTEN BY: STAN LEE
DRAWN BY: JACK KIRBY
INKED BY: PAUL REINMAN
LETTERED BY: SAM ROSEN
FASTER! PROFESSOR X IS WAITING FOR US!
PROFESSOR X MUST HAVE A NEW MISSION FOR US!
WE CAN'T KEEP UP WITH THOSE DRATTED WINGS OF YOURS, ANGEL!
GANGWAY! KIDS! HERE COMES THE BEAST!
WHEEE! THIS HAS RUNNING BEAT ALL HOLLOW!
CONGRATULATIONS! YOU ARE ABOUT TO BEGIN A BOOK-LENGTH TALE WHICH YOU'LL NEVER FORGET! AND NOW, LET US FOLLOW THE EXTRAORDINARY X-MEN AS THEY ANSWER AN URGENT MENTAL SUMMONS FROM THEIR MYSTERIOUS LEADER, PROFESSOR X...

"The comic strip is no longer a comic strip but in reality an illustrated novel. It is new and raw just now, but material for a limitless, intelligent development. And eventually, and inevitably, it will be a legitimate medium for the best of writers and artists."
— WILL EISNER

X-MEN No. 4
(Opposite) Cover: pencils, Jack Kirby; inks, Paul Reinman; March 1964. Gaining two new villains (the Scarlet Witch and Quicksilver), the X-Men follow in the Marvel tradition of having an evil team with a makeup similar to their own. The Brotherhood of Evil Mutants has five members, one of whom is female—just like the X-Men.

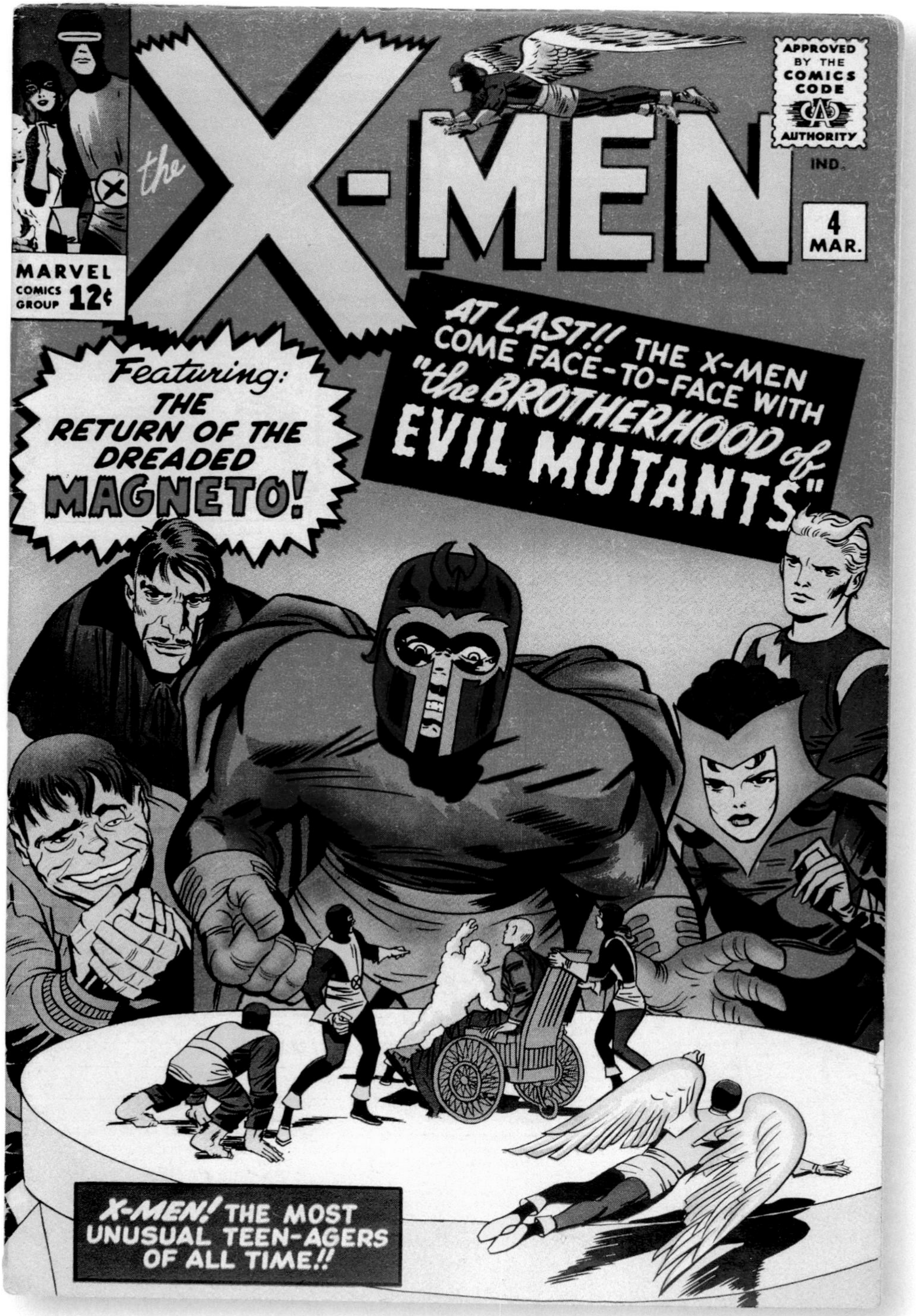
APPROVED BY THE COMICS CODE AUTHORITY
the X-MEN
IND.
4 MAR.
MARVEL COMICS GROUP 12¢
AT LAST!! THE X-MEN COME FACE-TO-FACE WITH "the BROTHERHOOD of EVIL MUTANTS"
Featuring: THE RETURN OF THE DREADED MAGNETO!
X-MEN! THE MOST UNUSUAL TEEN-AGERS OF ALL TIME!!

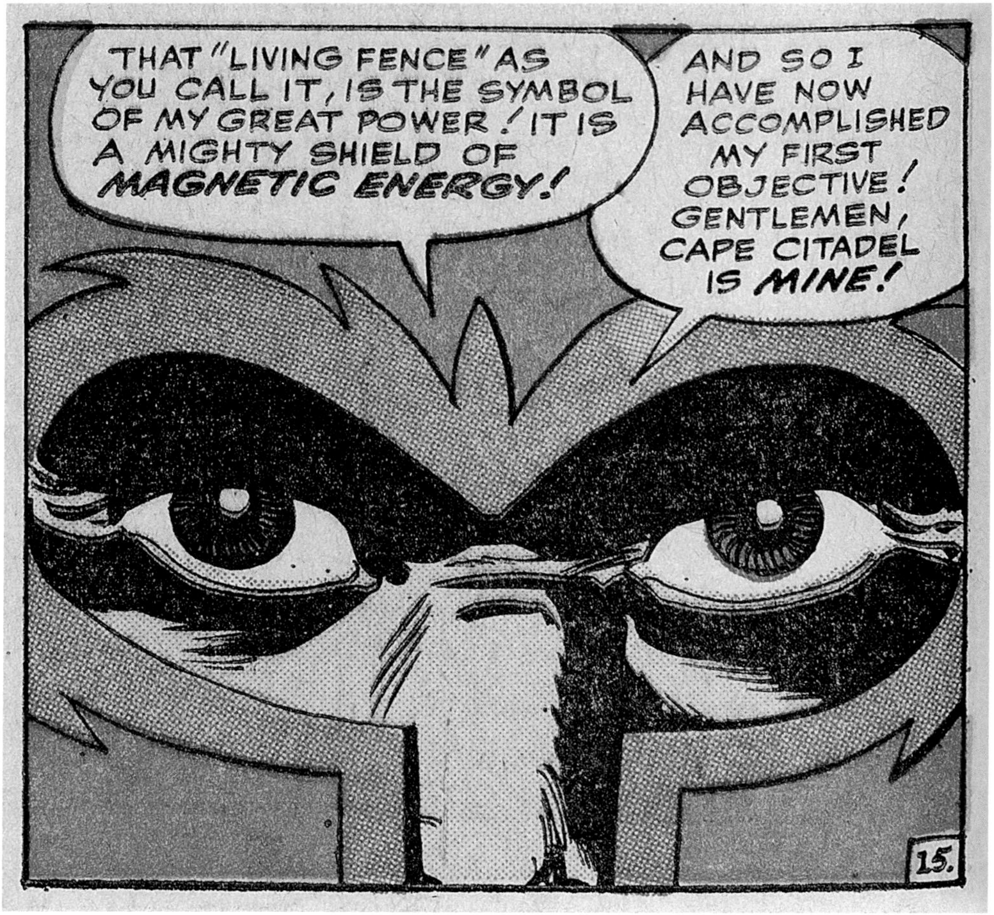
THAT "LIVING FENCE" AS YOU CALL IT, IS THE SYMBOL OF MY GREAT POWER! IT IS A MIGHTY SHIELD OF MAGNETIC ENERGY!
AND SO I HAVE NOW ACCOMPLISHED MY FIRST OBJECTIVE! GENTLEMEN, CAPE CITADEL IS MINE!
15.

X-MEN No. 1

(Above) Interior, "X-Men!"; script, Stan Lee; pencils, Jack Kirby; inks, Paul Reinman; September 1963. "[Lichtenstein] was not a fan of comics and cartoons," his widow Dorothy told the media following a 2013 retrospective of his work. "When people think of Roy, they think of those cartoon images from the early '60s. But he had another close to 40 years after that working on other imagery." It is perhaps a fitting end to the story for comic fans, who love to hate Pop Art and its blatant, celebrated co-opting of their heroes' artwork, in this case Kirby's Magneto from *X-Men* No. 1.

X-MEN No. 7

(Opposite) Interior, "The Return of the Blob!"; script, Stan Lee; pencils, Jack Kirby; inks, Chic Stone; September 1964. No, not Steve McQueen's Blob. Here, the professor develops Cerebro, a machine that can track down mutants. Apparently it isn't set to detect Inhumans.

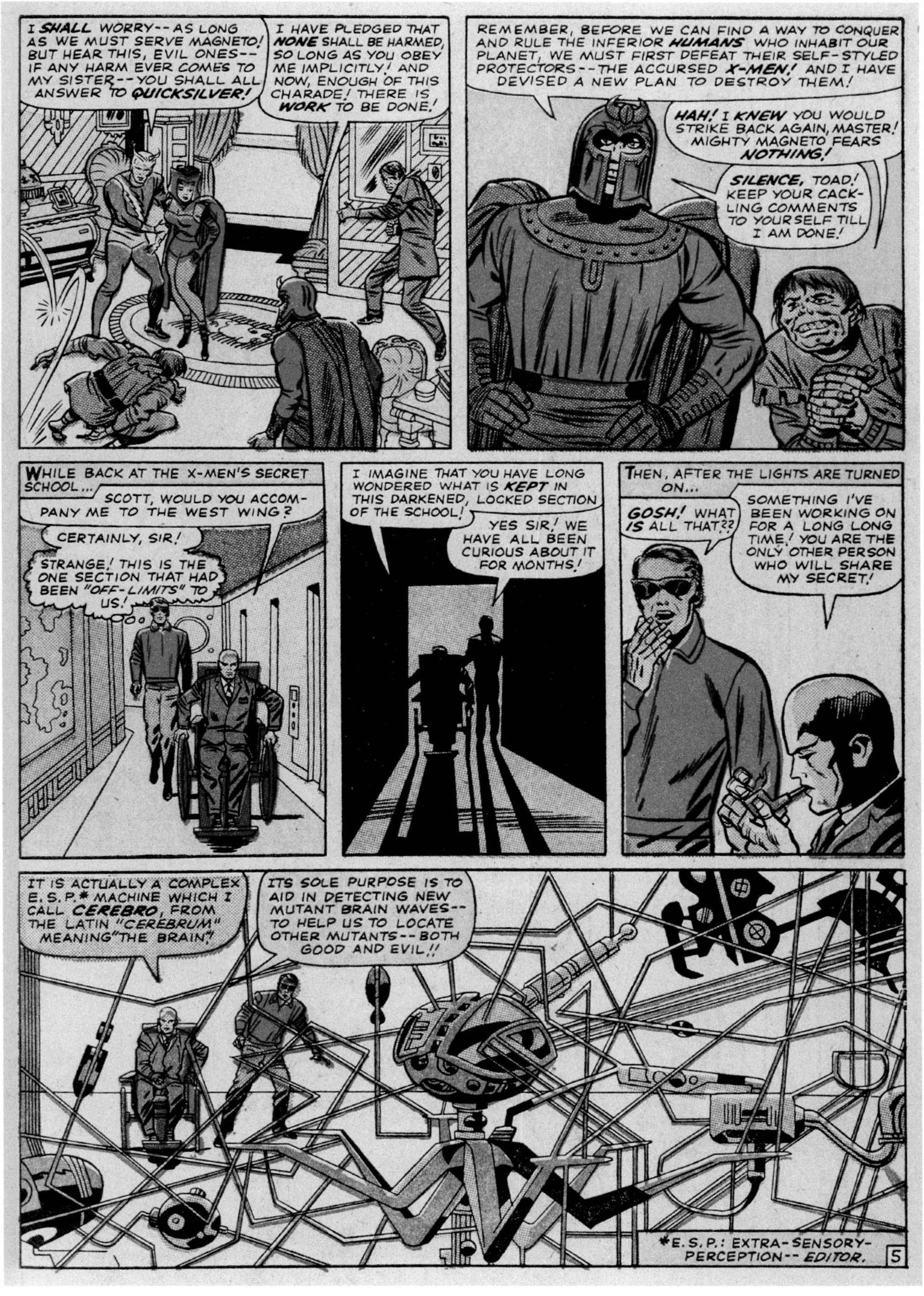
I SHALL WORRY--AS LONG AS WE MUST SERVE MAGNETO! BUT HEAR THIS, EVIL ONES--IF ANY HARM EVER COMES TO MY SISTER--YOU SHALL ALL ANSWER TO QUICKSILVER!
I HAVE PLEDGED THAT NONE SHALL BE HARMED, SO LONG AS YOU OBEY ME IMPLICITLY! AND NOW, ENOUGH OF THIS CHARADE! THERE IS WORK TO BE DONE!
REMEMBER, BEFORE WE CAN FIND A WAY TO CONQUER AND RULE THE INFERIOR HUMANS WHO INHABIT OUR PLANET, WE MUST FIRST DEFEAT THEIR SELF-STYLED PROTECTORS--THE ACCURSED X-MEN! AND I HAVE DEVISED A NEW PLAN TO DESTROY THEM!
HAH! I KNEW YOU WOULD STRIKE BACK AGAIN, MASTER! MIGHTY MAGNETO FEARS NOTHING!
SILENCE, TOAD! KEEP YOUR CACKLING COMMENTS TO YOURSELF TILL I AM DONE!
WHILE BACK AT THE X-MEN'S SECRET SCHOOL...
SCOTT, WOULD YOU ACCOMPANY ME TO THE WEST WING?
CERTAINLY, SIR!
STRANGE! THIS IS THE ONE SECTION THAT HAD BEEN "OFF-LIMITS" TO US!
I IMAGINE THAT YOU HAVE LONG WONDERED WHAT IS KEPT IN THIS DARKENED, LOCKED SECTION OF THE SCHOOL!
YES SIR! WE HAVE ALL BEEN CURIOUS ABOUT IT FOR MONTHS!
THEN, AFTER THE LIGHTS ARE TURNED ON...
GOSH! WHAT IS ALL THAT??
SOMETHING I'VE BEEN WORKING ON FOR A LONG LONG TIME! YOU ARE THE ONLY OTHER PERSON WHO WILL SHARE MY SECRET!
IT IS ACTUALLY A COMPLEX E.S.P.* MACHINE WHICH I CALL CEREBRO, FROM THE LATIN "CEREBRUM" MEANING "THE BRAIN"!
ITS SOLE PURPOSE IS TO AID IN DETECTING NEW MUTANT BRAIN WAVES--TO HELP US TO LOCATE OTHER MUTANTS--BOTH GOOD AND EVIL!!
*E.S.P.: EXTRA-SENSORY-PERCEPTION--EDITOR.
5

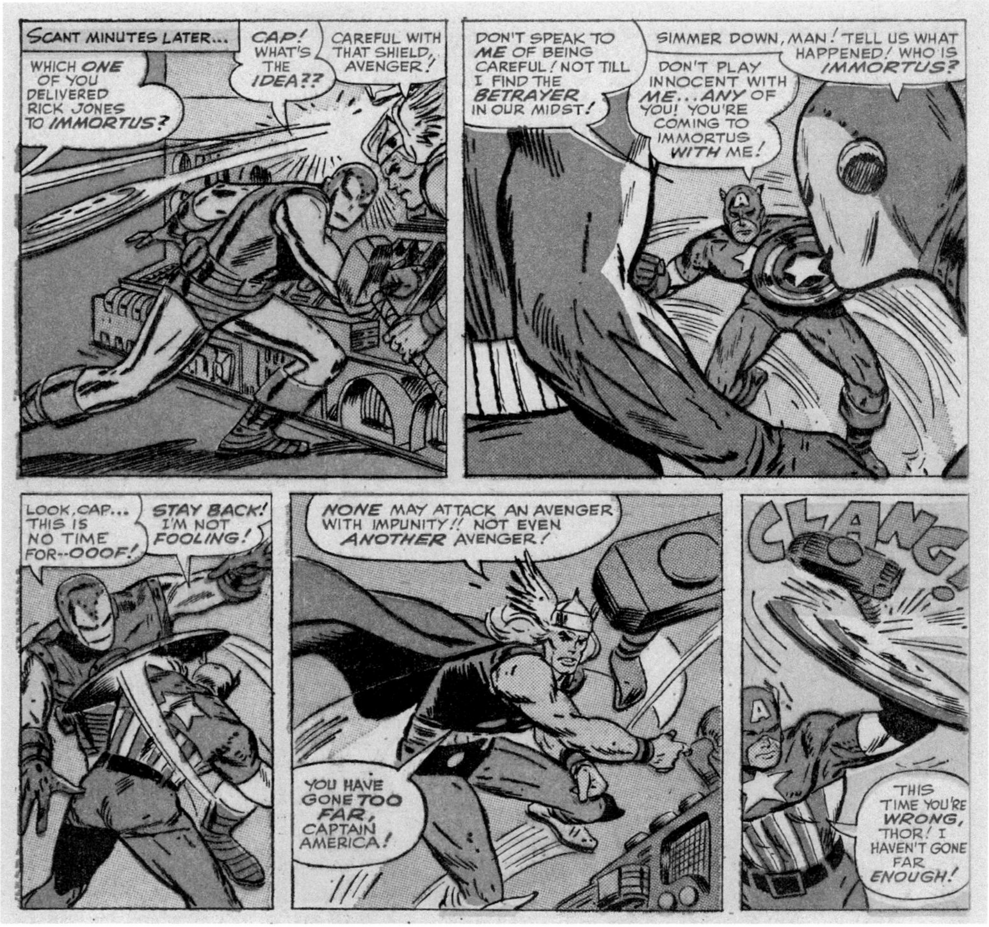
SCANT MINUTES LATER...
WHICH ONE OF YOU DELIVERED RICK JONES TO IMMORTUS?
CAP! WHAT'S THE IDEA??
CAREFUL WITH THAT SHIELD, AVENGER!
DON'T SPEAK TO ME OF BEING CAREFUL! NOT TILL I FIND THE BETRAYER IN OUR MIDST!
SIMMER DOWN, MAN! TELL US WHAT HAPPENED! WHO IS IMMORTUS?
DON'T PLAY INNOCENT WITH ME...ANY OF YOU! YOU'RE COMING TO IMMORTUS WITH ME!
LOOK, CAP... THIS IS NO TIME FOR--OOOF!
STAY BACK! I'M NOT FOOLING!
NONE MAY ATTACK AN AVENGER WITH IMPUNITY!! NOT EVEN ANOTHER AVENGER!
YOU HAVE GONE TOO FAR, CAPTAIN AMERICA!
CLANG!
THIS TIME YOU'RE WRONG, THOR! I HAVEN'T GONE FAR ENOUGH!

THE AVENGERS No. 10

(Above) Interior, "The Avengers Break Up!"; script, Stan Lee; pencils, Don Heck; inks, Dick Ayers; November 1964.

THE AVENGERS No. 4

(Opposite) Cover; pencils, Jack Kirby; inks, George Roussos; March 1963. On the splash page inside this issue, Marvel trumpets Cap's return: "Jack Kirby drew the original Captain America during the Golden Age of Comics...and now he draws it again. Stan Lee's first script during those fabled days was in Captain America—and now he authors it again, in this, The Marvel Age." Forgetting Captain America's postwar appearances (he was published by Timely until 1949 and revived in the Atlas era for a few adventures in 1953–54) we learn that *this* Captain America was frozen in ice since 1944.

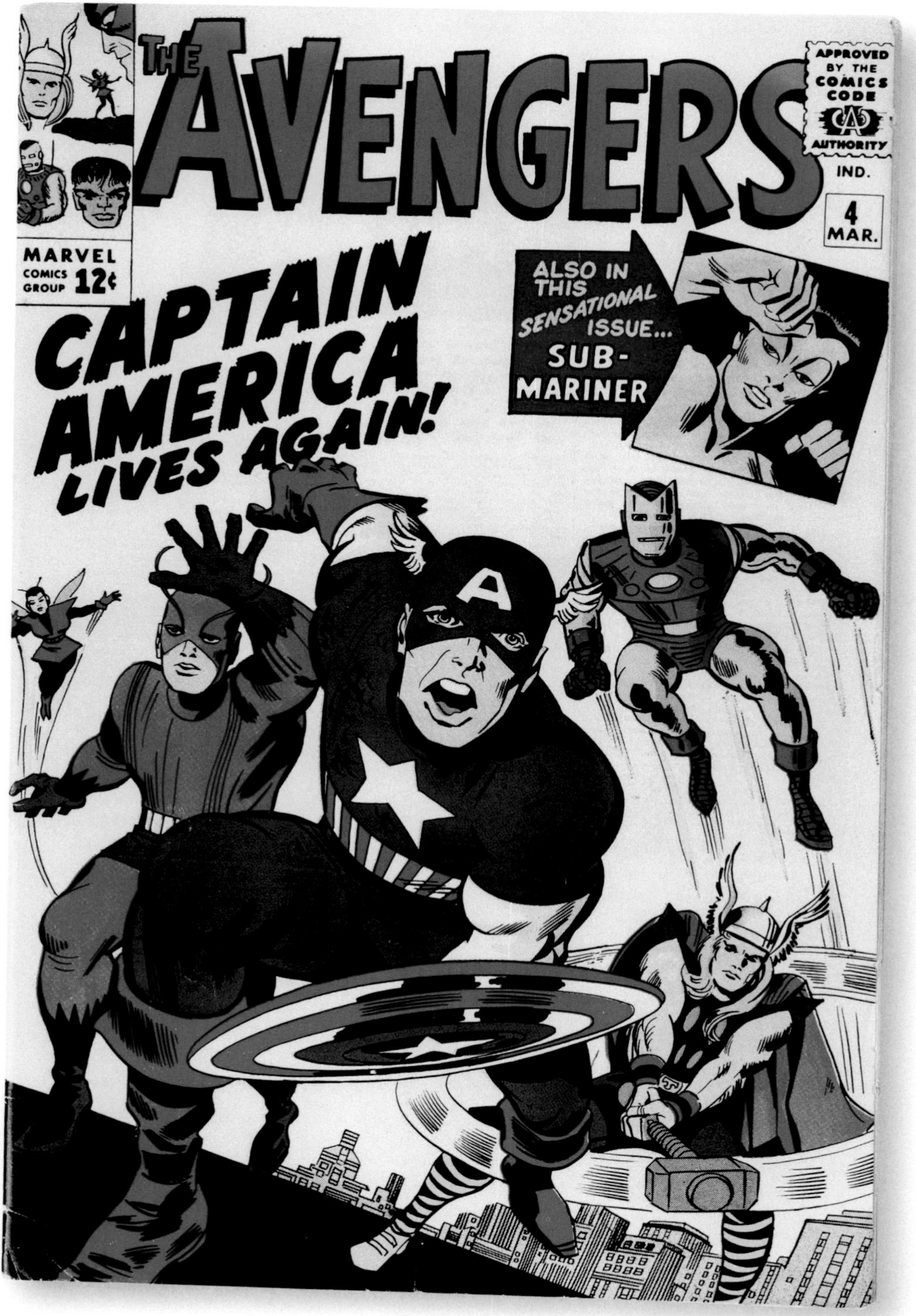
THE AVENGERS
APPROVED BY THE COMICS CODE CA AUTHORITY
IND.
4 MAR.
MARVEL COMICS GROUP 12¢
CAPTAIN AMERICA LIVES AGAIN!
ALSO IN THIS SENSATIONAL ISSUE... SUB-MARINER

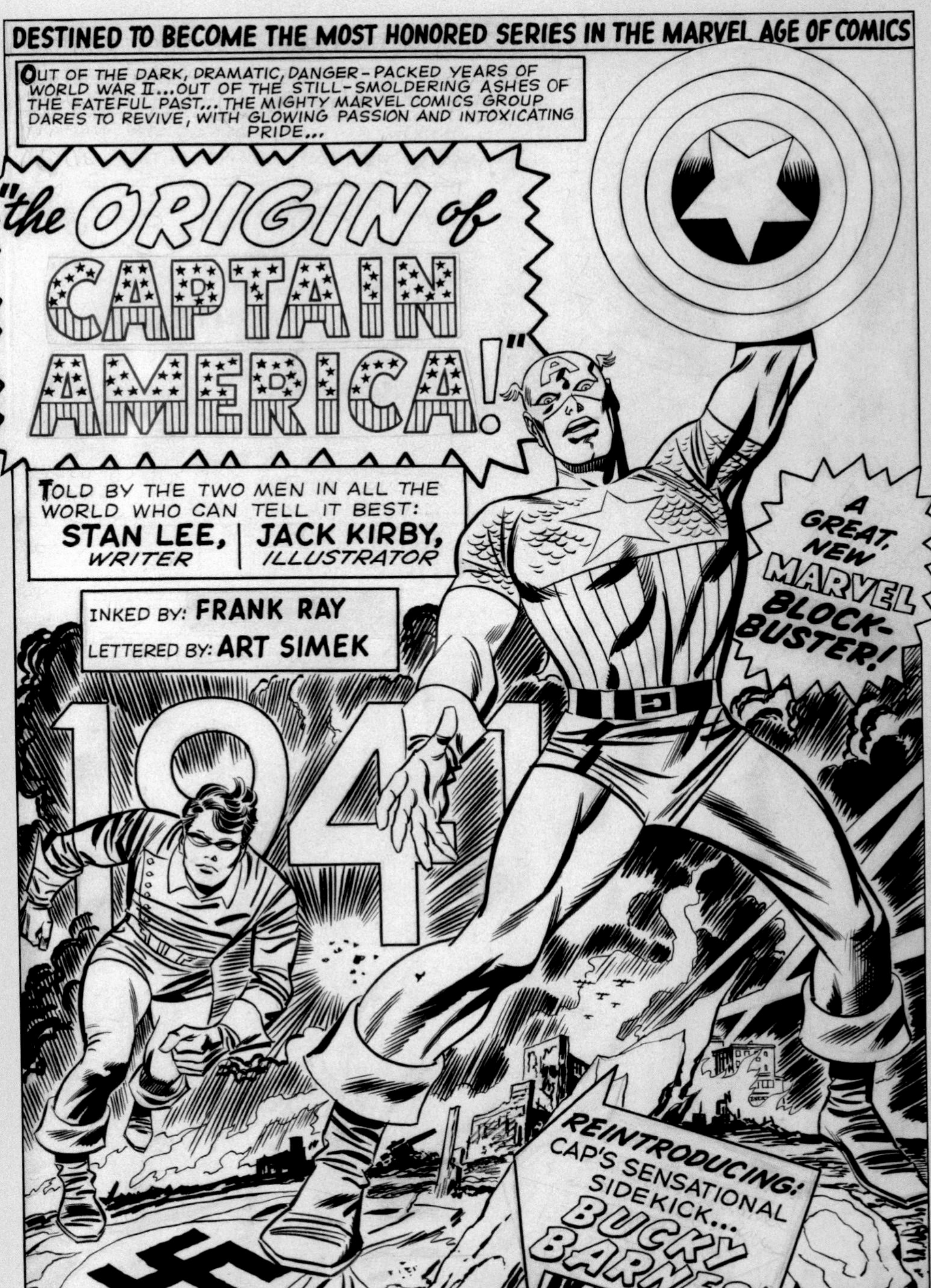
DESTINED TO BECOME THE MOST HONORED SERIES IN THE MARVEL AGE OF COMICS
OUT OF THE DARK, DRAMATIC, DANGER-PACKED YEARS OF WORLD WAR II...OUT OF THE STILL-SMOLDERING ASHES OF THE FATEFUL PAST... THE MIGHTY MARVEL COMICS GROUP DARES TO REVIVE, WITH GLOWING PASSION AND INTOXICATING PRIDE...
"the ORIGIN of CAPTAIN AMERICA!"
TOLD BY THE TWO MEN IN ALL THE WORLD WHO CAN TELL IT BEST:
STAN LEE, WRITER
JACK KIRBY, ILLUSTRATOR
INKED BY: FRANK RAY
LETTERED BY: ART SIMEK
A GREAT, NEW MARVEL BLOCK-BUSTER!
1941
REINTRODUCING: CAP'S SENSATIONAL SIDEKICK... BUCKY BARNES!
1

STRIKING TERROR TO THE HEARTS OF ENEMY AGENTS, THE MAN NOW KNOWN THRUOUT THE WORLD AS CAPTAIN AMERICA NEVER PAUSES IN HIS RELENTLESS BATTLE AGAINST THE FOES OF FREEDOM!
CRASH!
ALONE AND UNAIDED, ARMED WITH NAUGHT SAVE HIS DAUNTLESS COURAGE, HIS FIGHTING SKILL, AND HIS SHINING SHIELD, THE MIGHTY SENTINEL OF LIBERTY SEEMS TO BE EVERY-WHERE, GUARDING OUR VITAL DEFENSE PLANTS AGAINST THOSE WHO WOULD DESTROY THEM!
THWOOM!
6

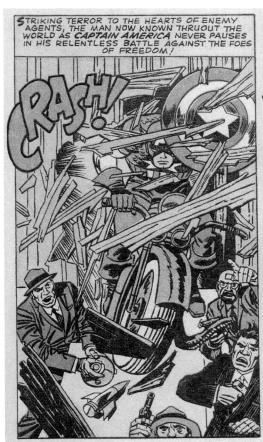

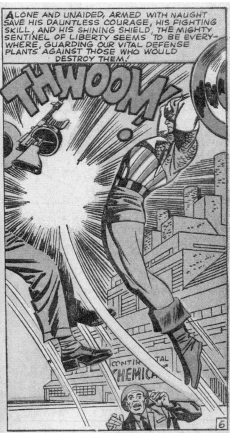

THE ORIGIN OF CAPTAIN AMERICA!

(Opposite) Original interior art, "The Origin of Captain America!," Tales of Suspense *No. 63; script, Stan Lee; pencils, Jack Kirby; inks, Frank Giacoia; March 1963.* "When you look at the earliest great directors—D.W. Griffith or Eisenstein, their work—you can't touch and even see anymore how radical it was, how extraordinary and trippy it was to encounter for the first time, because everything rests on those innovations, everyone's followed them. Early John Ford films, everything looks like that now. It became the language of cinema. And Kirby's accomplishments, I think, reside in that same kind of relationship to the culture at large." —Jonathan Lethem

TALES OF SUSPENSE No. 63

(Above) Interior, "The Origin of Captain America!"; script, Stan Lee; pencils, Jack Kirby; inks, Frank Giacoia; March 1963. "I'll have a sort of choreographed action…like a ballet…if Captain America hits a man and he falls on the floor and some guy is coming up behind, he'll already know what he's going to do.…it's acted out on the paper."—Jack Kirby

YOU'RE ONE OF US NOW

(Below) Membership welcome package, Merry Marvel Marching Society (M.M.M.S.), 1964. Flo Steinberg recalled the fan club's beginnings in a 2002 interview: "Bags and bags of mail would come and we would have to open them up and—this was before computers—we had to write down everybody's name and make labels for each one, and pull out all these hundreds of dollar bills. We were throwing them at each other there were so many!"

THE AVENGERS No. 11

(Opposite) Cover; pencils, Jack Kirby; inks, Chic Stone; alterations, attributed Steve Ditko; December 1964. Beginning in the early 1940s, the Marvel Universe was cemented with regularly occurring crossovers. Stan Lee even had characters such as Millie the Model meeting Patsy Walker or Linda Carter, Student Nurse, perhaps influenced by earlier radio and later TV shows that cross-promoted their programming.

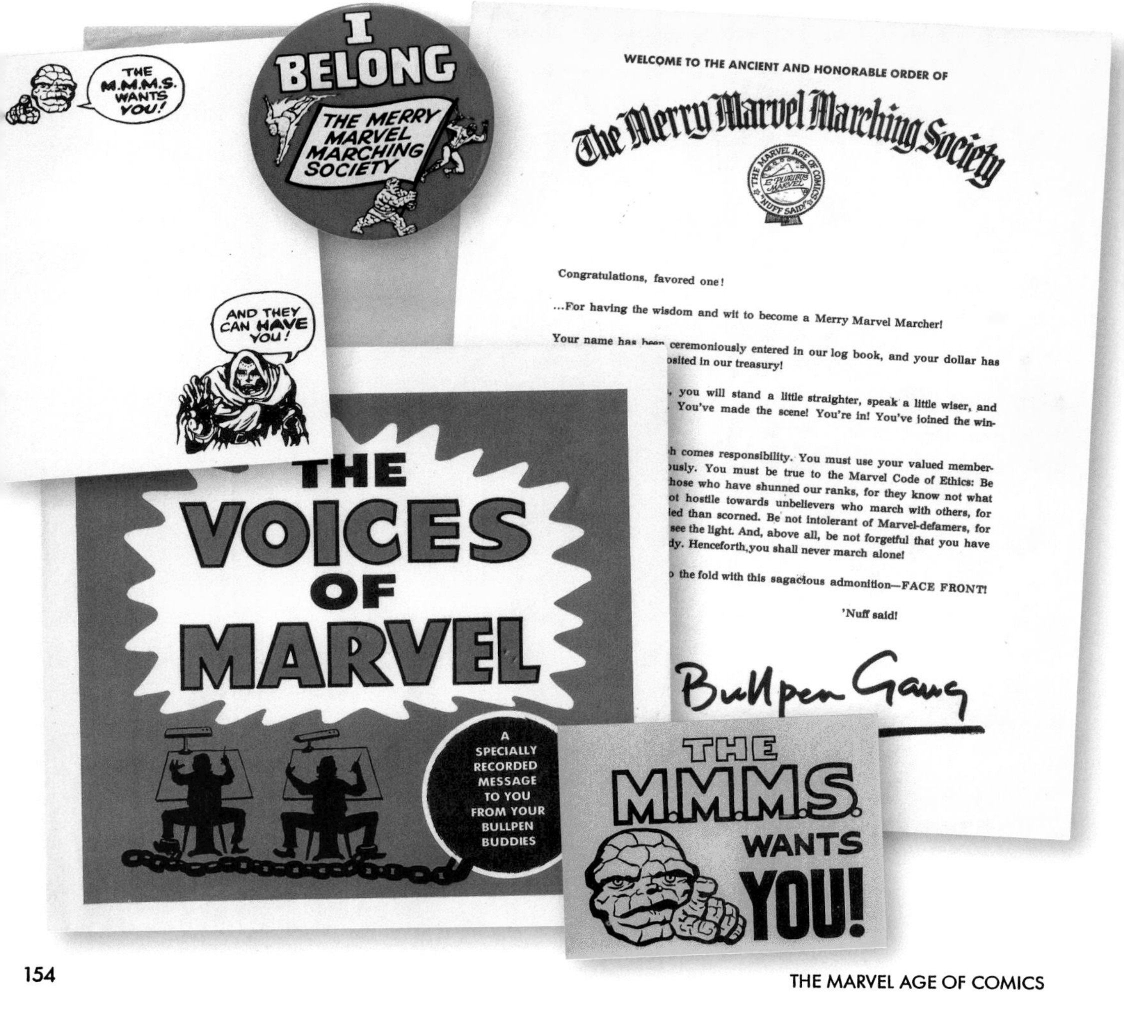
THE M.M.M.S. WANTS YOU!
AND THEY CAN HAVE YOU!
I BELONG
THE MERRY MARVEL MARCHING SOCIETY
WELCOME TO THE ANCIENT AND HONORABLE ORDER OF
The Merry Marvel Marching Society
THE MARVEL AGE OF COMICS
E PLURIBUS MARVEL
'NUFF SAID!
Congratulations, favored one!
...For having the wisdom and wit to become a Merry Marvel Marcher!
Your name has been ceremoniously entered in our log book, and your dollar has
osited in our treasury!
you will stand a little straighter, speak a little wiser, and
You've made the scene! You're in! You've joined the win-
h comes responsibility. You must use your valued member-
usly. You must be true to the Marvel Code of Ethics: Be
hose who have shunned our ranks, for they know not what
ot hostile towards unbelievers who march with others, for
ied than scorned. Be not intolerant of Marvel-defamers, for
see the light. And, above all, be not forgetful that you have
dy. Henceforth, you shall never march alone!
the fold with this sagacious admonition—FACE FRONT!
'Nuff said!
Bullpen Gang
THE VOICES OF MARVEL
A SPECIALLY RECORDED MESSAGE TO YOU FROM YOUR BULLPEN BUDDIES
THE M.M.M.S. WANTS YOU!

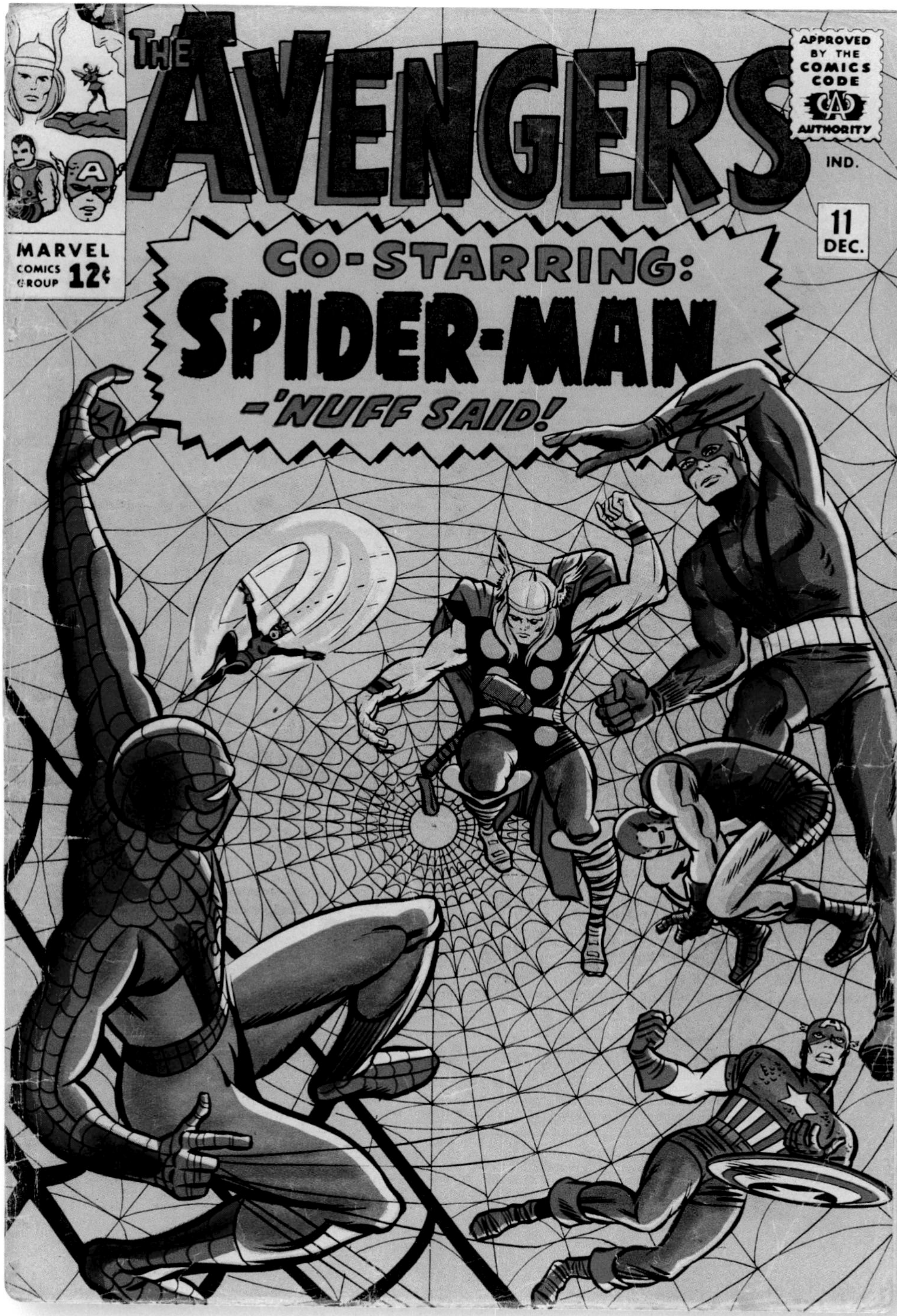
THE AVENGERS
APPROVED BY THE COMICS CODE AUTHORITY
IND.
11 DEC.
MARVEL COMICS GROUP 12¢
CO-STARRING:
SPIDER-MAN
-'NUFF SAID!

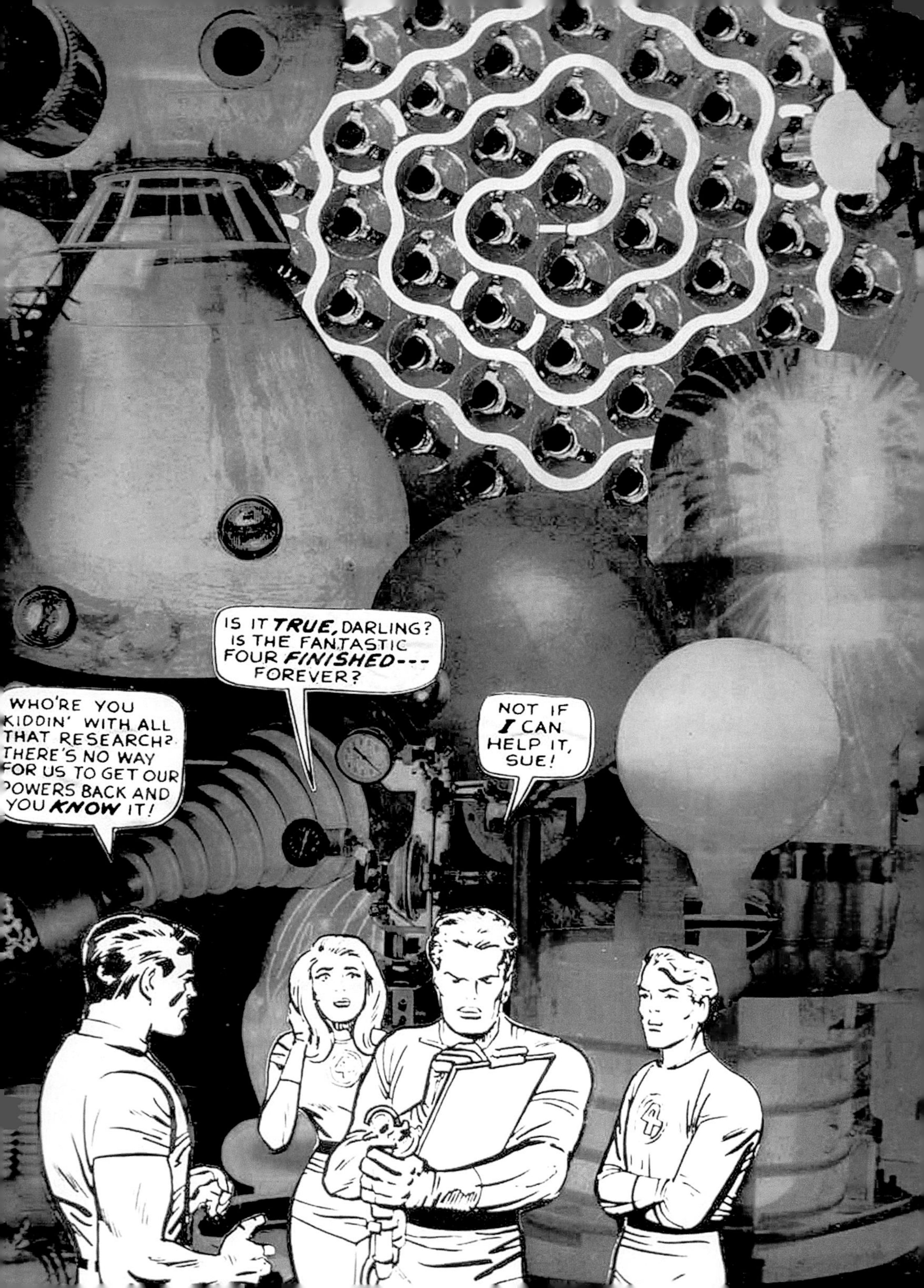
WHO'RE YOU KIDDIN' WITH ALL THAT RESEARCH? THERE'S NO WAY FOR US TO GET OUR POWERS BACK AND YOU KNOW IT!
IS IT TRUE, DARLING? IS THE FANTASTIC FOUR FINISHED--- FOREVER?
NOT IF I CAN HELP IT, SUE!

THE KIRBY LAB

(Opposite) Original interior art, Fantastic Four *No. 39; pencils and collage, Jack Kirby; inks, attributed Carl Hubbell; June 1965.* Kirby's techniques were ahead of their time, and the current technology was typically unable to reproduce his photo collages anywhere near how he intended them. For one thing, they were printed in black-and-white!

FANTASTIC FOUR No. 39

(Below and following page) Interiors, "A Blind Man Shall Lead Them!"; script, Stan Lee; pencils, Jack Kirby; inks, Frank Giacoia, Wally Wood (Matt Murdock and Daredevil figures); June 1965. This is the start of the Marvel's two-year *annus mirabilis,* arguably the best years in comics history. The *FF* alone brought the world the Inhumans, the Silver Surfer, Galactus, and the Black Panther. Read on!

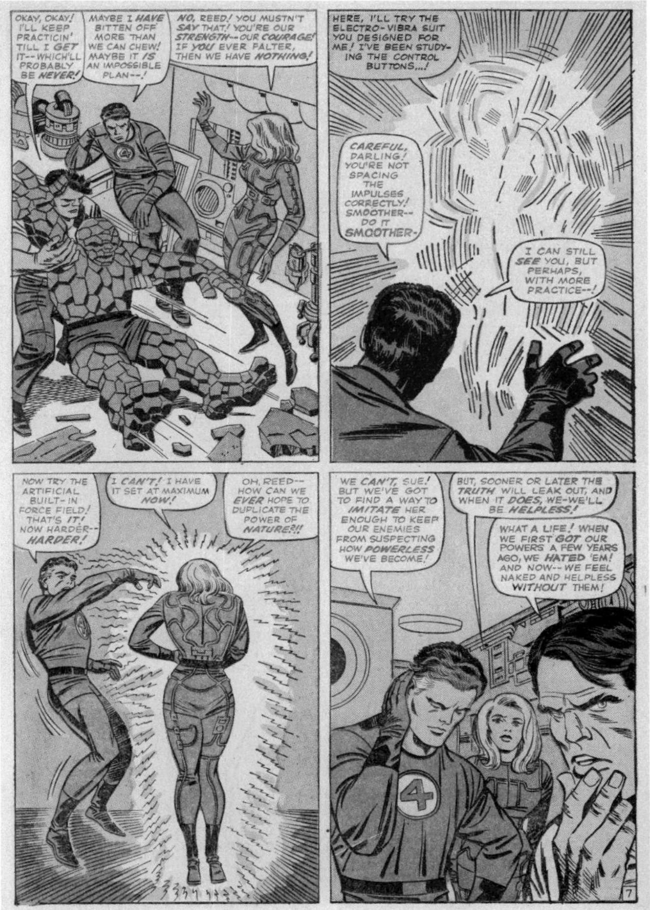
OKAY, OKAY! I'LL KEEP PRACTICIN' TILL I GET IT--WHICH'LL PROBABLY BE NEVER!
MAYBE I HAVE BITTEN OFF MORE THAN WE CAN CHEW! MAYBE IT IS AN IMPOSSIBLE PLAN--!
NO, REED! YOU MUSTN'T SAY THAT! YOU'RE OUR STRENGTH--OUR COURAGE! IF YOU EVER FALTER, THEN WE HAVE NOTHING!
HERE, I'LL TRY THE ELECTRO-VIBRA SUIT YOU DESIGNED FOR ME! I'VE BEEN STUDYING THE CONTROL BUTTONS...!
CAREFUL, DARLING! YOU'RE NOT SPACING THE IMPULSES CORRECTLY! SMOOTHER-- DO IT SMOOTHER-
I CAN STILL SEE YOU, BUT PERHAPS, WITH MORE PRACTICE--!
NOW TRY THE ARTIFICIAL BUILT-IN FORCE FIELD! THAT'S IT! NOW HARDER-- HARDER!
I CAN'T! I HAVE IT SET AT MAXIMUM NOW!
OH, REED-- HOW CAN WE EVER HOPE TO DUPLICATE THE POWER OF NATURE?!!
WE CAN'T, SUE! BUT WE'VE GOT TO FIND A WAY TO IMITATE HER ENOUGH TO KEEP OUR ENEMIES FROM SUSPECTING HOW POWERLESS WE'VE BECOME!
BUT, SOONER OR LATER THE TRUTH WILL LEAK OUT, AND WHEN IT DOES, WE-WE'LL BE HELPLESS!
WHAT A LIFE! WHEN WE FIRST GOT OUR POWERS A FEW YEARS AGO, WE HATED 'EM! AND NOW-- WE FEEL NAKED AND HELPLESS WITHOUT THEM!
7

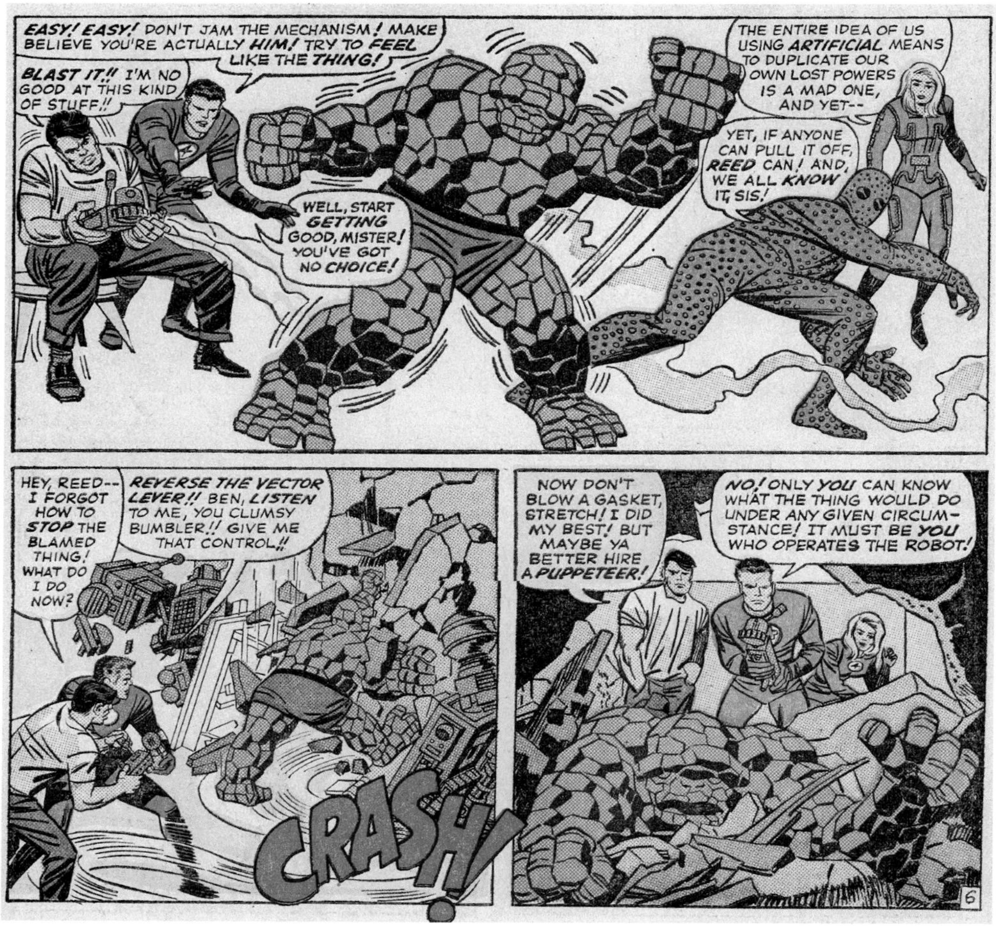
EASY! EASY! DON'T JAM THE MECHANISM! MAKE BELIEVE YOU'RE ACTUALLY HIM! TRY TO FEEL LIKE THE THING!
BLAST IT!! I'M NO GOOD AT THIS KIND OF STUFF!!
WELL, START GETTING GOOD, MISTER! YOU'VE GOT NO CHOICE!
THE ENTIRE IDEA OF US USING ARTIFICIAL MEANS TO DUPLICATE OUR OWN LOST POWERS IS A MAD ONE, AND YET--
YET, IF ANYONE CAN PULL IT OFF, REED CAN! AND, WE ALL KNOW IT, SIS!
HEY, REED-- I FORGOT HOW TO STOP THE BLAMED THING! WHAT DO I DO NOW?
REVERSE THE VECTOR LEVER!! BEN, LISTEN TO ME, YOU CLUMSY BUMBLER!! GIVE ME THAT CONTROL!!
CRASH!
NOW DON'T BLOW A GASKET, STRETCH! I DID MY BEST! BUT MAYBE YA BETTER HIRE A PUPPETEER!
NO! ONLY YOU CAN KNOW WHAT THE THING WOULD DO UNDER ANY GIVEN CIRCUMSTANCE! IT MUST BE YOU WHO OPERATES THE ROBOT!
6

FANTASTIC FOUR No. 37

(Opposite) Original interior art; pencils, Jack Kirby; inks, Chic Stone; April 1964. Chic Stone was Kirby's primary inker ca. 1964–65, giving the early Marvel line a cohesive look. Stone's bold, solid blacks were a perfect fit, adding weight and dimension to Kirby's pencils. Stone was a comics veteran dating as far back as 1939, drawing for outfits such as Fawcett, Lev Gleason, and Timely, and he found satisfaction in being Kirby's primary inker, calling the King's pencils "magnificent."

FANTASTIC FOUR ~~36~~ APR 6¼x9¼. No5P5 1.

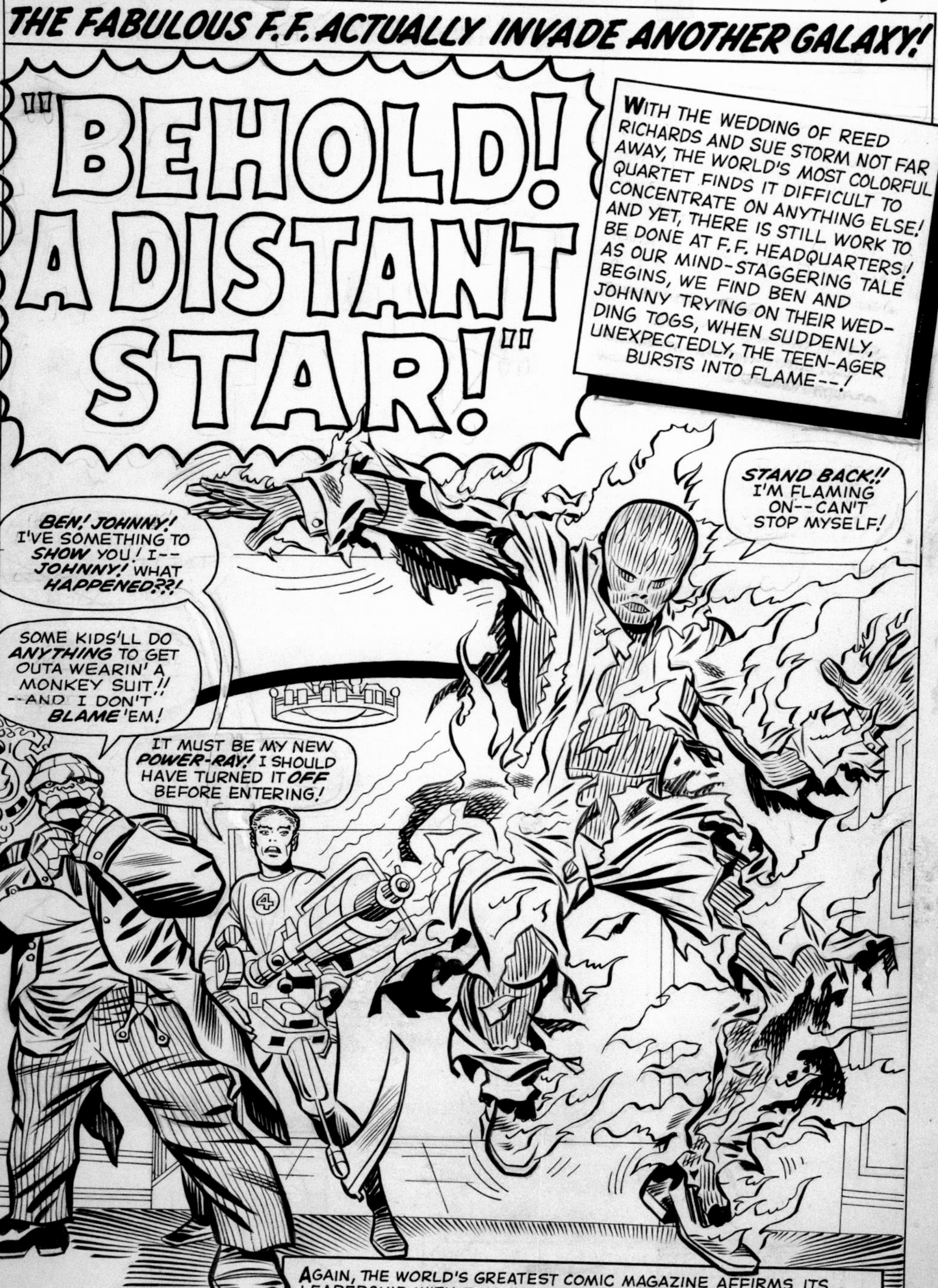

THE FABULOUS F.F. ACTUALLY INVADE ANOTHER GALAXY!
"BEHOLD! A DISTANT STAR!"
WITH THE WEDDING OF REED RICHARDS AND SUE STORM NOT FAR AWAY, THE WORLD'S MOST COLORFUL QUARTET FINDS IT DIFFICULT TO CONCENTRATE ON ANYTHING ELSE! AND YET, THERE IS STILL WORK TO BE DONE AT F.F. HEADQUARTERS! AS OUR MIND-STAGGERING TALE BEGINS, WE FIND BEN AND JOHNNY TRYING ON THEIR WEDDING TOGS, WHEN SUDDENLY, UNEXPECTEDLY, THE TEEN-AGER BURSTS INTO FLAME--!
BEN! JOHNNY! I'VE SOMETHING TO SHOW YOU! I-- JOHNNY! WHAT HAPPENED??!
STAND BACK!! I'M FLAMING ON--CAN'T STOP MYSELF!
SOME KIDS'LL DO ANYTHING TO GET OUTA WEARIN' A MONKEY SUIT!! --AND I DON'T BLAME 'EM!
IT MUST BE MY NEW POWER-RAY! I SHOULD HAVE TURNED IT OFF BEFORE ENTERING!
AGAIN, THE WORLD'S GREATEST COMIC MAGAZINE AFFIRMS ITS LEADERSHIP WITH THIS EYE-FILLING SPECTACLE, WRITTEN BY MARVEL'S INIMITABLE STAN LEE! DRAWN BY MARVEL'S UNMATCHABLE JACK KIRBY! INKED BY MARVEL'S IMPECCABLE CHIC STONE! LETTERED BY MARVEL'S UNBEARABLE ARTIE SIMEK!
1.

469

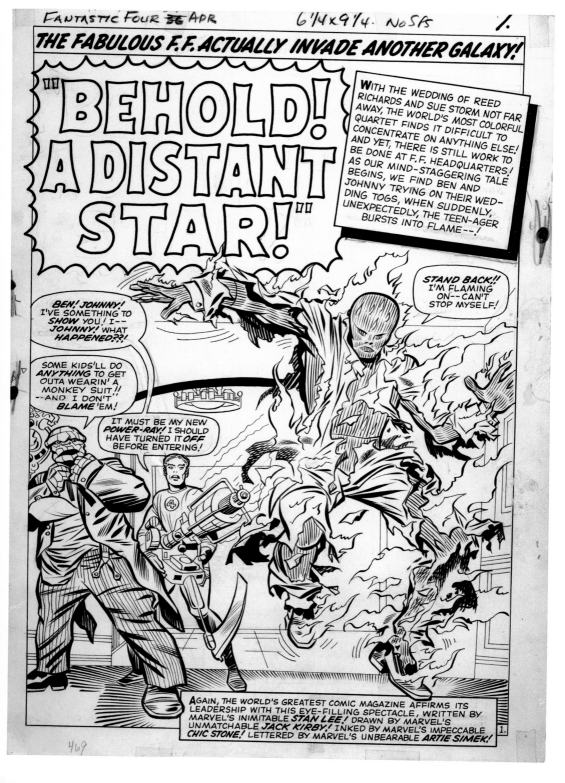

"I think Kirby was a figure like Dylan, one where you couldn't be the same after you'd encountered him as you'd been before." — JONATHAN LETHEM

FANTASTIC FOUR No. 36
(Opposite and following spread) Interiors, "The Frightful Four!"; script, Stan Lee; pencils, Jack Kirby; inks, Chic Stone; March 1965. Unlike most other heroes in the Marvel Universe, the Fantastic Four were adored by the public and treated as Hollywood royalty or rock stars, so the announcement of an engagement between Reed and Sue would naturally bring out the paparazzi. When the Elongated Man at DC got married, it was "off camera" and between issues. Here, everyone celebrates and it brings the Universe closer.

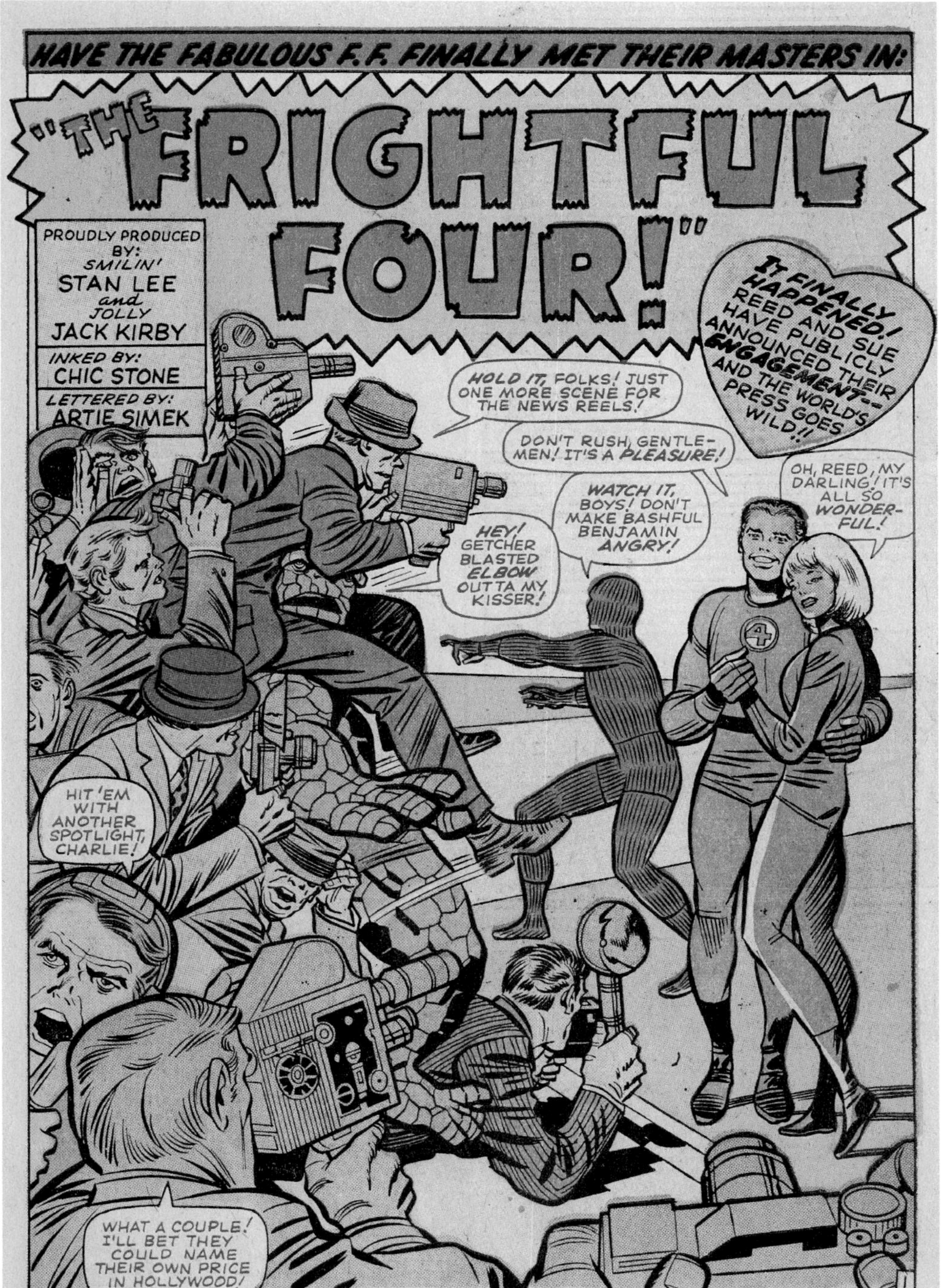
HAVE THE FABULOUS F.F. FINALLY MET THEIR MASTERS IN:
"THE FRIGHTFUL FOUR!"
PROUDLY PRODUCED BY: SMILIN' STAN LEE and JOLLY JACK KIRBY
INKED BY: CHIC STONE
LETTERED BY: ARTIE SIMEK
IT FINALLY HAPPENED! REED AND SUE HAVE PUBLICLY ANNOUNCED THEIR ENGAGEMENT-- AND THE WORLD'S PRESS GOES WILD!!
HOLD IT, FOLKS! JUST ONE MORE SCENE FOR THE NEWS REELS!
DON'T RUSH, GENTLEMEN! IT'S A PLEASURE!
WATCH IT, BOYS! DON'T MAKE BASHFUL BENJAMIN ANGRY!
HEY! GETCHER BLASTED ELBOW OUTTA MY KISSER!
OH, REED, MY DARLING! IT'S ALL SO WONDERFUL!
HIT 'EM WITH ANOTHER SPOTLIGHT, CHARLIE!
WHAT A COUPLE! I'LL BET THEY COULD NAME THEIR OWN PRICE IN HOLLYWOOD!
1

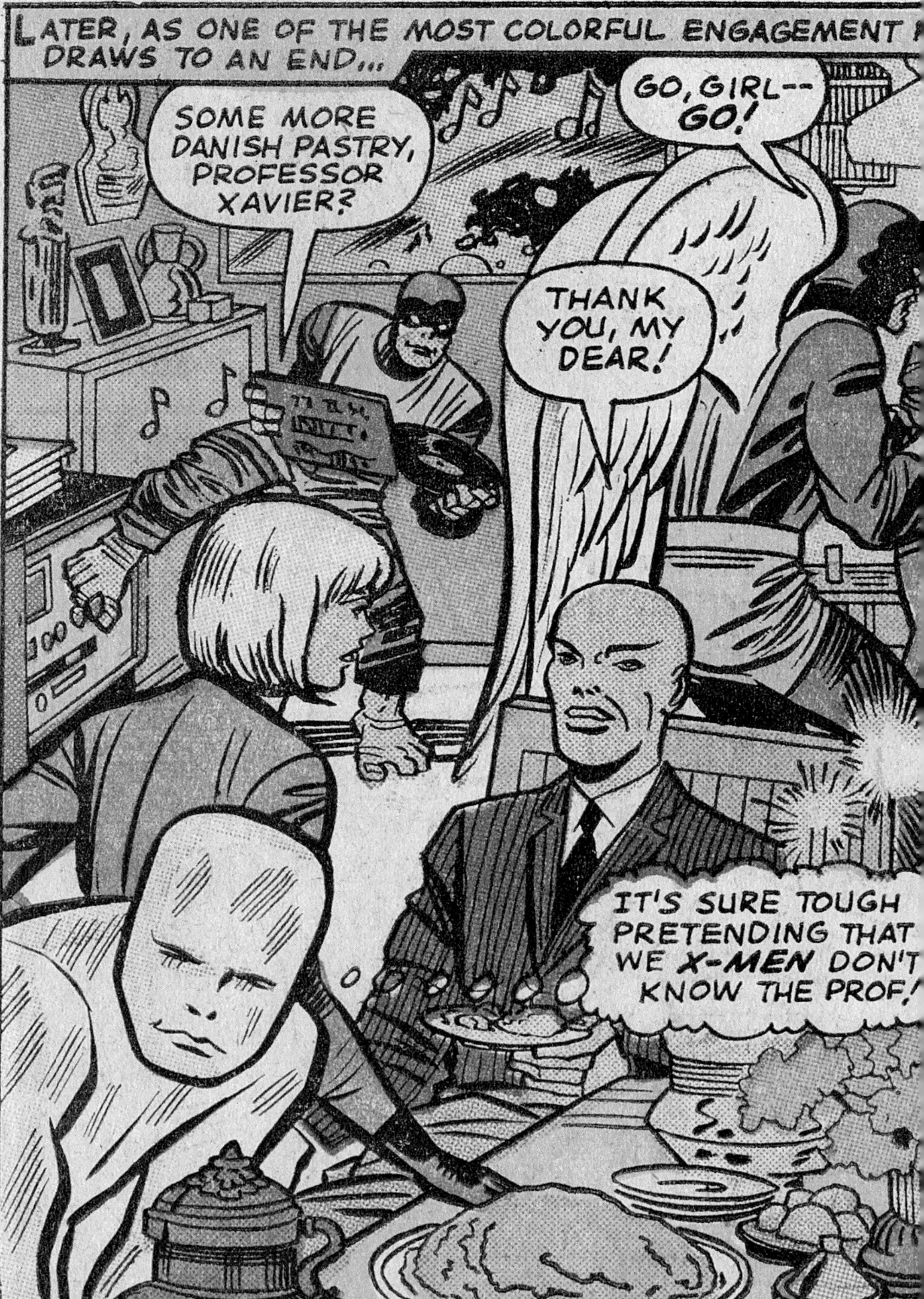
LATER, AS ONE OF THE MOST COLORFUL ENGAGEMENT P
DRAWS TO AN END...
SOME MORE DANISH PASTRY, PROFESSOR XAVIER?
GO, GIRL-- GO!
THANK YOU, MY DEAR!
IT'S SURE TOUGH PRETENDING THAT WE X-MEN DON'T KNOW THE PROF!

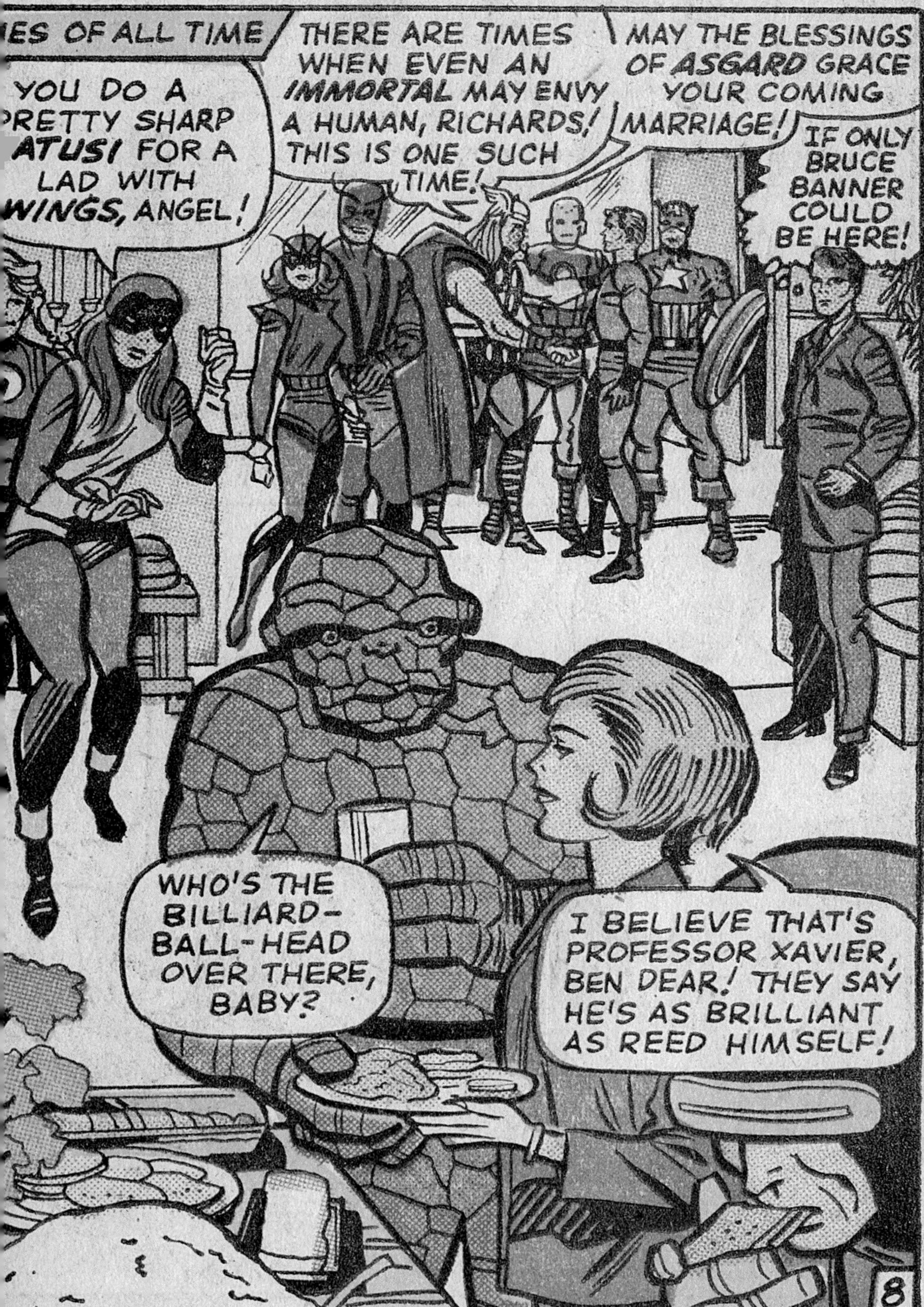

...ES OF ALL TIME
YOU DO A PRETTY SHARP ...ATUSI FOR A LAD WITH ...WINGS, ANGEL!
THERE ARE TIMES WHEN EVEN AN IMMORTAL MAY ENVY A HUMAN, RICHARDS! THIS IS ONE SUCH TIME!
MAY THE BLESSINGS OF ASGARD GRACE YOUR COMING MARRIAGE!
IF ONLY BRUCE BANNER COULD BE HERE!
WHO'S THE BILLIARD-BALL-HEAD OVER THERE, BABY?
I BELIEVE THAT'S PROFESSOR XAVIER, BEN DEAR! THEY SAY HE'S AS BRILLIANT AS REED HIMSELF!
8

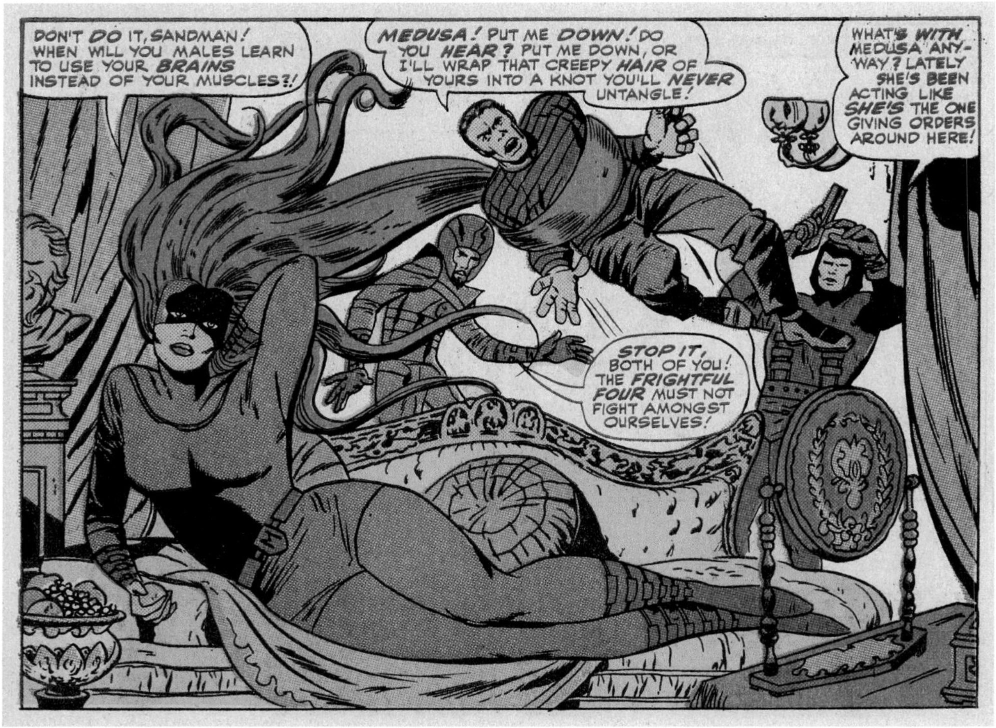
DON'T DO IT, SANDMAN! WHEN WILL YOU MALES LEARN TO USE YOUR BRAINS INSTEAD OF YOUR MUSCLES?!
MEDUSA! PUT ME DOWN! DO YOU HEAR? PUT ME DOWN, OR I'LL WRAP THAT CREEPY HAIR OF YOURS INTO A KNOT YOU'LL NEVER UNTANGLE!
WHAT'S WITH MEDUSA ANY-WAY? LATELY SHE'S BEEN ACTING LIKE SHE'S THE ONE GIVING ORDERS AROUND HERE!
STOP IT, BOTH OF YOU! THE FRIGHTFUL FOUR MUST NOT FIGHT AMONGST OURSELVES!

FANTASTIC FOUR No. 36

(Above) Interior, "The Frightful Four!"; script, Stan Lee; pencils, Jack Kirby; inks, Vince Colletta; March 1965. Marvel's villains usually played fair against their heroic counterparts. Hence we got the Frightful Four, and not the Frightful Six, and they always had an equal number of women as well. Medusa filled the Wizard's quota, despite the reservations of Sandman and Paste-Pot Pete. Madame Medusa started out as a criminal, but her character would soon evolve and she would be part of a larger storyline. A powerful female as dangerous as the male members of the Frightful Four was a rarity in the early 1960s. Even more surprising was how, even under the watchful eye of the Comics Code Authority, Jack Kirby was able to imbue Medusa (posed like an Ingres odalisque or Manet's *Olympia*) with an air of sensuality.

FANTASTIC FOUR No. 45

(Opposite) Cover; pencils, Jack Kirby; inks, Joe Sinnott; December 1965.

AVENGERS ANNUAL No. 2

(Following spread) Interior; script, Roy Thomas; pencils, John Buscema; inks, Bill Everett; Summer 1968.

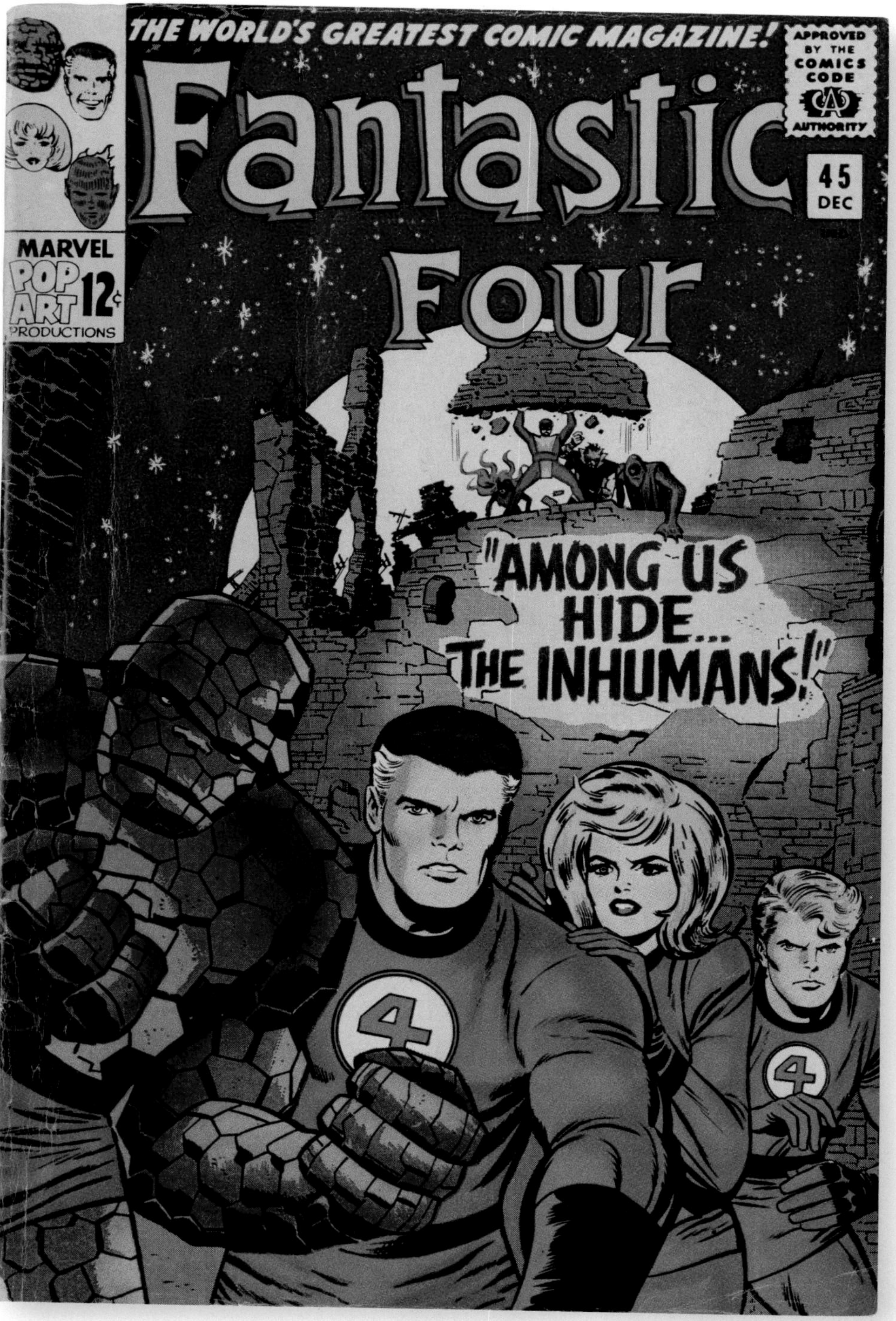
THE WORLD'S GREATEST COMIC MAGAZINE!
APPROVED BY THE COMICS CODE AUTHORITY
Fantastic Four
45
DEC
MARVEL
POP ART
12¢
PRODUCTIONS
"AMONG US HIDE... THE INHUMANS!"
4
4

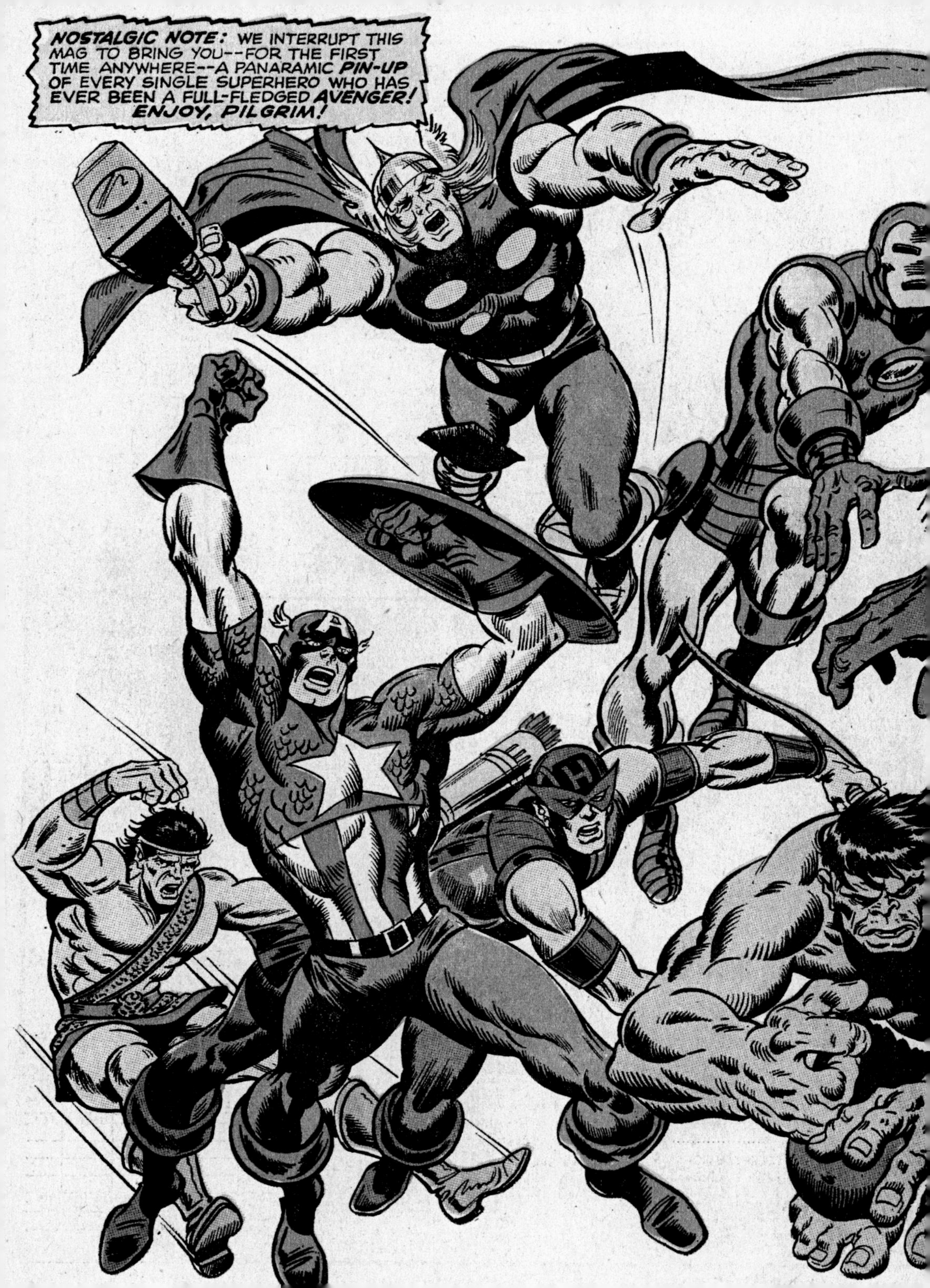
NOSTALGIC NOTE: WE INTERRUPT THIS MAG TO BRING YOU--FOR THE FIRST TIME ANYWHERE--A PANARAMIC PIN-UP OF EVERY SINGLE SUPERHERO WHO HAS EVER BEEN A FULL-FLEDGED AVENGER! ENJOY, PILGRIM!

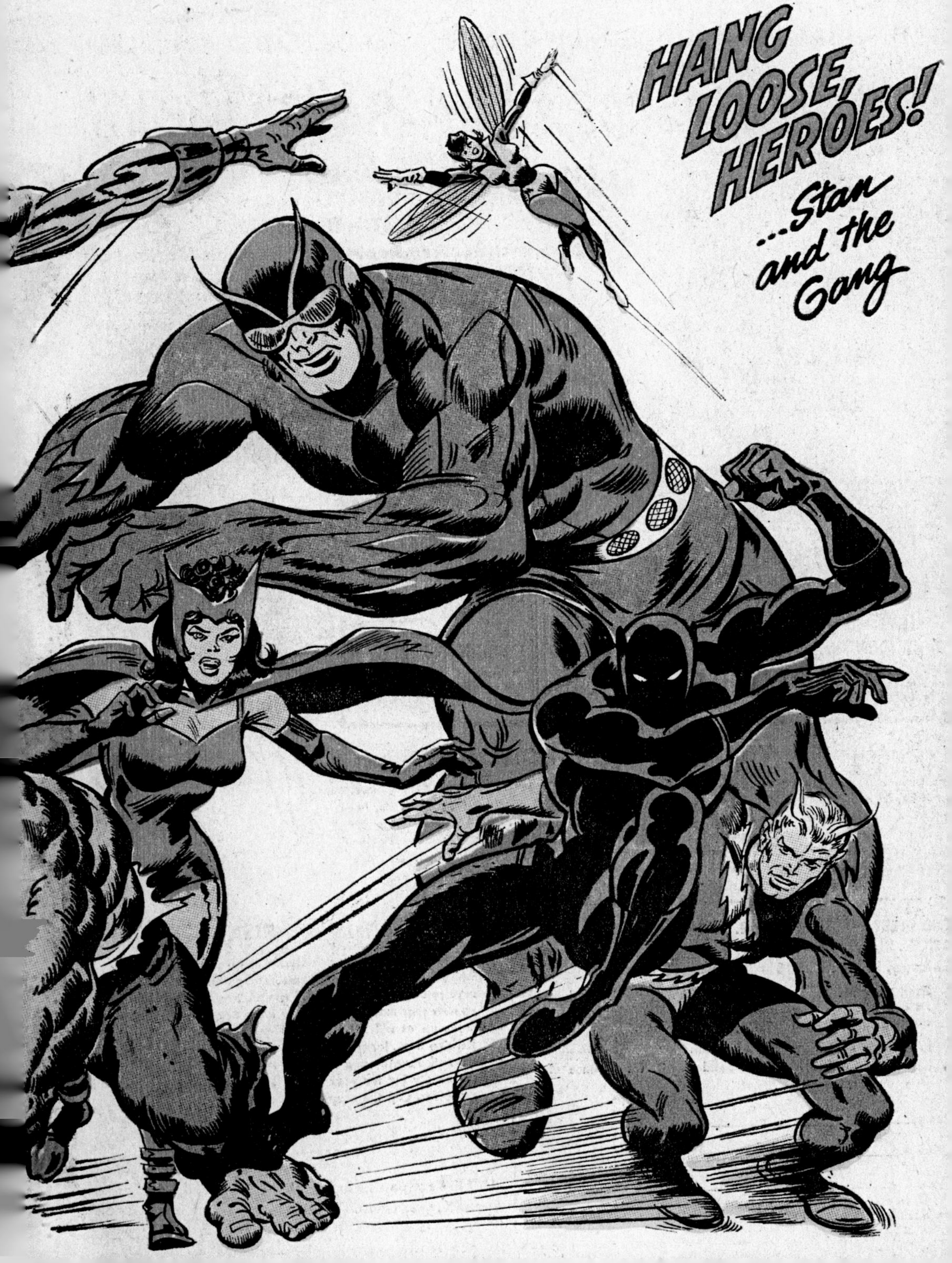
HANG LOOSE, HEROES!
...Stan and the Gang

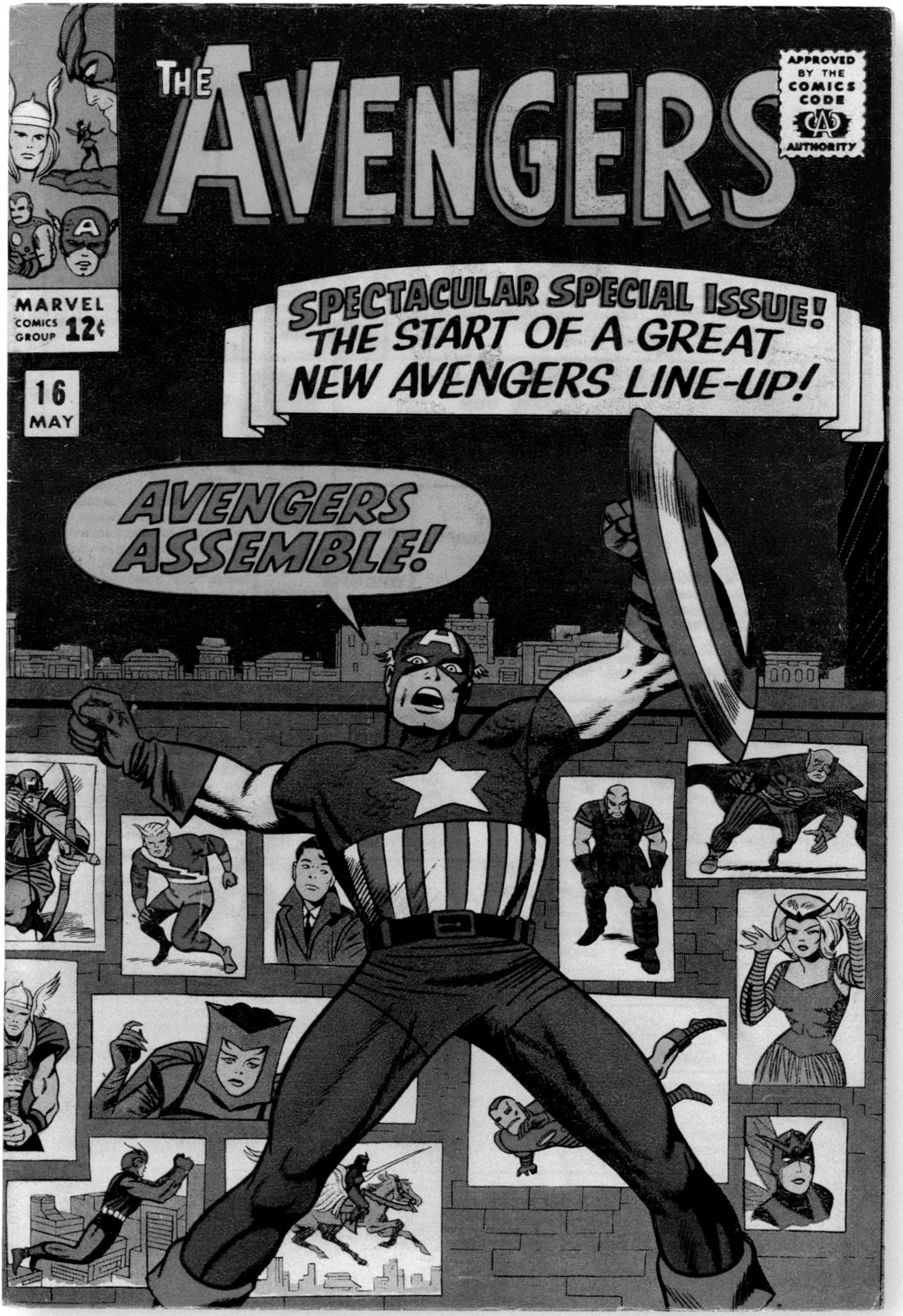
THE AVENGERS
APPROVED BY THE COMICS CODE AUTHORITY
MARVEL COMICS GROUP 12¢
16 MAY
SPECTACULAR SPECIAL ISSUE!
THE START OF A GREAT NEW AVENGERS LINE-UP!
AVENGERS ASSEMBLE!

Make Mine Marvel!
THE MARVEL UNIVERSE 1964–1970

MORE MARVEL MASTERPIECES

Now it was time to fine-tune the comics line, adding a color-ful supporting character here, an unexpected story theme or plot innovation there. Marvel would soon discover that, even if for the immediate present it couldn't further increase its number of titles, it could use the existing magazines to expand and deepen what would before long be hailed as "the Marvel Universe."

For instance, 1964 Iron Man stories would witness the arrival of the masked archer Hawkeye and the Russian spy known as the Black Widow, both destined soon to evolve from villains into heroes. The Hulk would regain a solo feature, sharing *Tales to Astonish* with Giant-Man and the Wasp, while henceforth Iron Man and Captain America would split *Tales of Suspense* between their separate features.

Cementing the unity of the Marvel titles, one hero was liable at any time to wander into another's adventure. The Hulk's second tussle with the Fantastic Four in their comic spilled over into *The Avengers* and became the first of many tales continued not merely from one issue to another, but from one *series* into another. Spider-Man tried to join the FF, but changed his mind when he learned that team didn't pay a salary. The Angel ditched his X-Men schoolmates long enough to share an episode with Iron Man. Thor was helped on one mission by Dr. Strange. The Human Torch spoke at Peter Parker's high school. Even the villains "crossed over," with Dr. Doom taking on Spider-Man, and Sub-Mariner fighting the X-Men.

Whenever Marvel heroes ran into each other, they didn't just shake hands, then rush off to fight criminals side by side like Superman and Batman or the Justice League.

THE AVENGERS No. 16
(Opposite) Cover; pencils, Jack Kirby; inks, Sol Brodsky; May 1965.

THE MAN AND THE KING
(Above) Photograph, Stan Lee and Jack Kirby, 1966.

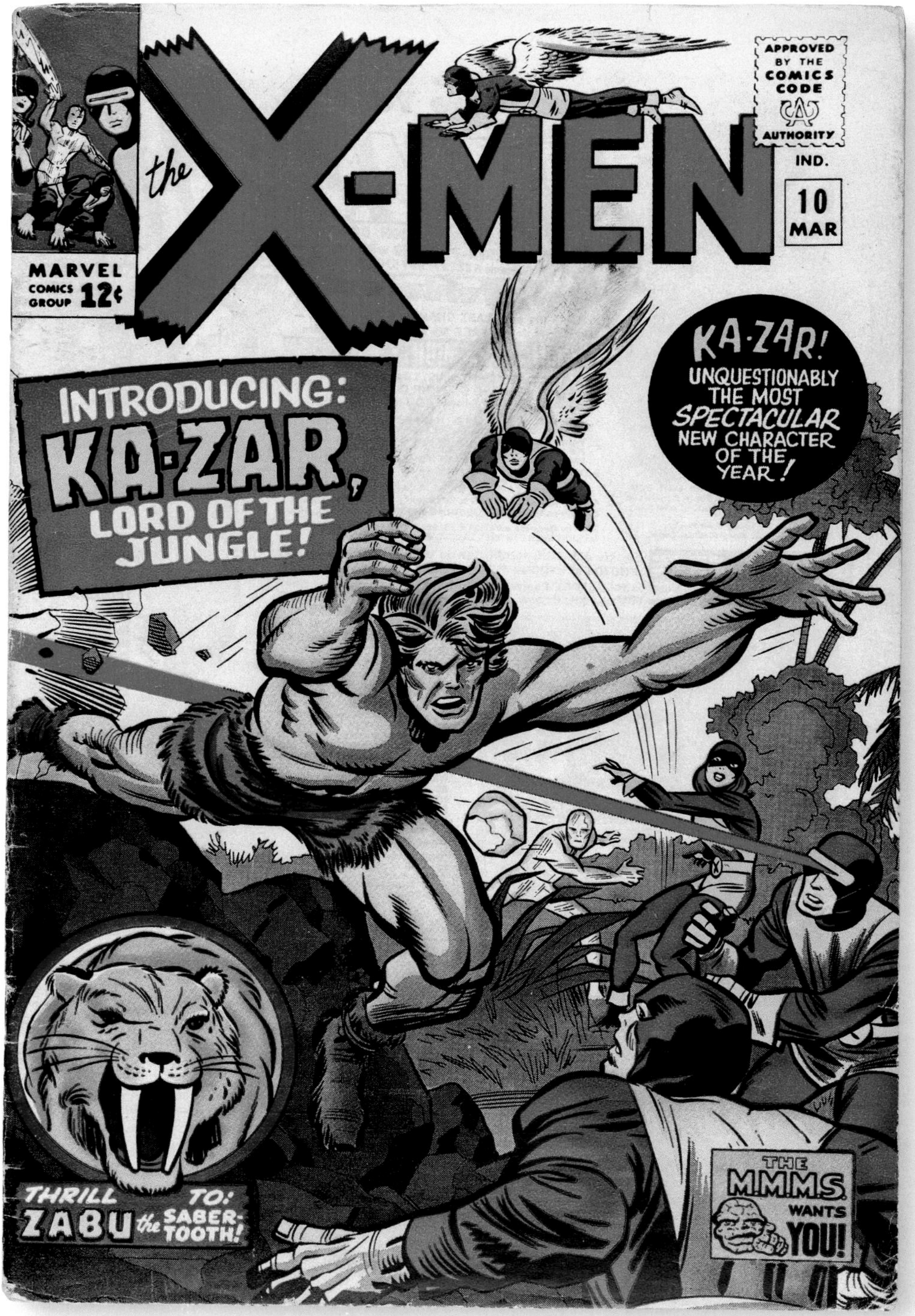
APPROVED BY THE COMICS CODE AUTHORITY
MARVEL COMICS GROUP 12¢
the X-MEN
IND.
10 MAR
INTRODUCING:
KA-ZAR,
LORD OF THE JUNGLE!
KA-ZAR!
UNQUESTIONABLY THE MOST SPECTACULAR NEW CHARACTER OF THE YEAR!
THRILL TO: ZABU the SABER-TOOTH!
THE M.M.M.S. WANTS YOU!

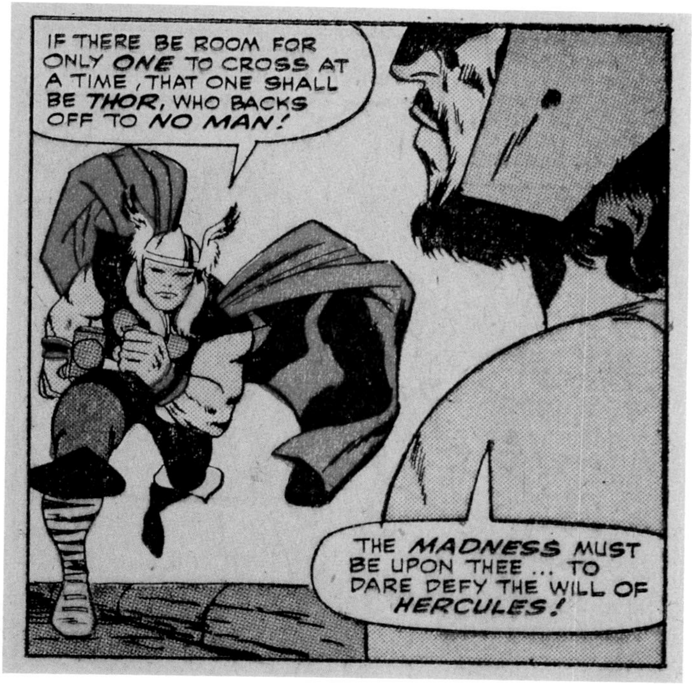
IF THERE BE ROOM FOR ONLY ONE TO CROSS AT A TIME, THAT ONE SHALL BE THOR, WHO BACKS OFF TO NO MAN!
THE MADNESS MUST BE UPON THEE ... TO DARE DEFY THE WILL OF HERCULES!

X-MEN No. 10
(Opposite) Cover; pencils, Jack Kirby; inks, Chic Stone; March 1965.

JOURNEY INTO MYSTERY ANNUAL No. 1
(Left) Interior, "When Titans Clash!"; script, Stan Lee; pencils, Jack Kirby; inks, Vince Colletta; Summer 1965.

Almost invariably, they first got embroiled in some sort of misunderstanding and came to super-powered blows before coming to accept each other. Lee found this more dramatic, and also a rolling response to a constant stream of readers' letters demanding to know which was strongest: the Hulk... or the Thing... or Thor... or Sub-Mariner... or Spider-Man... or even Iron Man.

Late in 1964, Marvel's letters pages, in between plugs for that month's Marvel comics, began tossing around the mysterious initials "M.M.M.S." Soon, a full-page ad heralded the Merry Marvel Marching Society, a "lighthearted, tongue-in-cheek" approach to a fan club. For one thin dollar, readers received a membership button, card, and certificate, some humorous illustrated stickers, a note pad, and, best of all, a 33 1/3 r.p.m. vinyl recording of "the actual voices of the Bullpen gang clowning around and welcoming you to the good ol' M.M.M.S.!"

The M.M.M.S. soon had 50,000 members, and Marvel began printing their names on the comics' text pages, though it never even came close to squeezing everyone's moniker in. In time, the club instituted honorary "ranks," with a "Q.N.S."

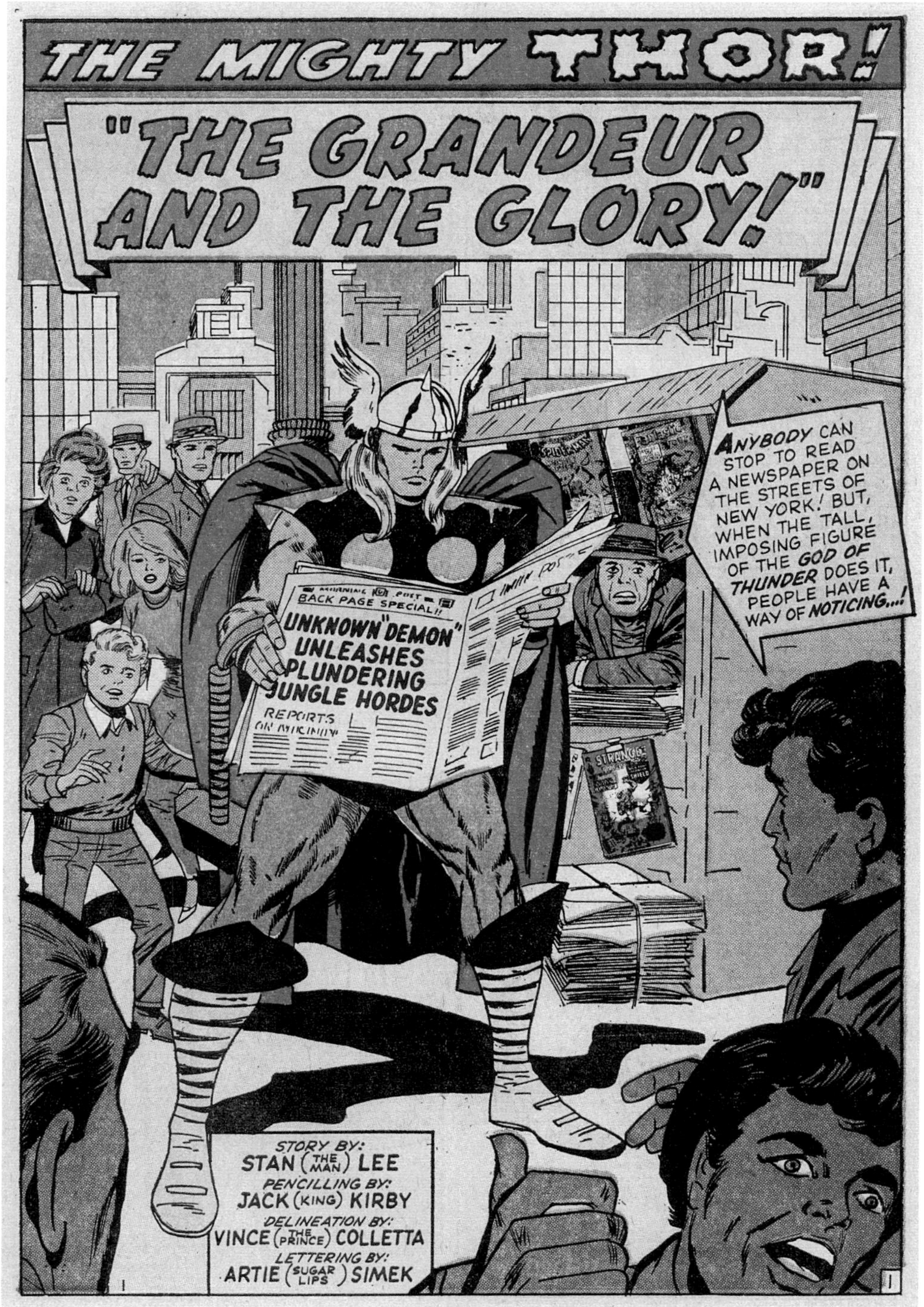
THE MIGHTY THOR!
"THE GRANDEUR AND THE GLORY!"
ANYBODY CAN STOP TO READ A NEWSPAPER ON THE STREETS OF NEW YORK! BUT, WHEN THE TALL, IMPOSING FIGURE OF THE GOD OF THUNDER DOES IT, PEOPLE HAVE A WAY OF NOTICING...!
BACK PAGE SPECIAL!!
UNKNOWN "DEMON" UNLEASHES PLUNDERING JUNGLE HORDES
REPORTS
STORY BY: STAN (THE MAN) LEE
PENCILLING BY: JACK (KING) KIRBY
DELINEATION BY: VINCE (THE PRINCE) COLLETTA
LETTERING BY: ARTIE (SUGAR LIPS) SIMEK
1

(Quite Nuff Sayer) being anyone who'd had a letter published in a Marvel comic, etc.

And more serious Marvel merchandising was in the air. Lee inaugurated a "Merry Marvel Bullpen Page" that hawked Marvel stationery and character T-shirts, as well as a "checklist" of current Marvel comics and breathless paragraphs that combined unabashed plugs with "gossip" about the artists and writers. Before long, the text material would take over the entire Bullpen Page, giving readers an added feeling of belonging to a privileged club whether or not they belonged to the M.M.M.S.

Over the course of 1964–65, Lee, who wrote each story's credit box, began to add a touch of humor (and often mock grandiosity) to the bylines: "Incredible story by Stan Lee! Incomparable penciling by Jack Kirby! Invincible inking by Joe Sinnott! Inevitable lettering by Artie Simek!" Soon he was putting colorful adjectives in front of proper names on splashes and in letters sections. "Smilin' Stan Lee," "Jolly Jack Kirby," and "Sturdy Steve Ditko" led the pack—augmented by "Dashin' Donnie Heck," "Larrupin' Larry Lieber," and so on. The former

JOURNEY INTO MYSTERY No. 124
(Opposite) Interior, "The Grandeur and the Glory!"; script, Stan Lee; pencils, Jack Kirby; inks, Vince Colletta; January 1966. Thor was often placed in ordinary settings, such as a newsstand where crowds would gather around him.

AMAZING SPIDER-MAN ANNUAL No. 1
(Below) Interior, "The Sinister Six!"; script, Stan Lee; pencils and inks, Steve Ditko; Summer 1964. Originally, the Annuals had few ads, so at 72 pages they were twice the size of a regular comic with three times the original material.

HAVING THE PROPORTIONATE STRENGTH OF A SPIDER, SPIDER-MAN IS ONE OF THE MOST POWERFUL SUPER-HEROES! ONLY THOR, THE HULK AND THE THING HAVE GREATER STRENGTH! (AND WE MUST REMEMBER THAT PETER PARKER IS STILL A TEEN-AGER, NOT HAVING QUITE REACHED HIS FULL MATURITY YET.)

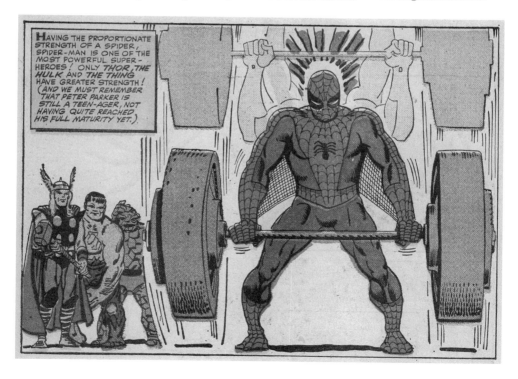

two soon became, as well, "Stan (the Man) Lee" and "Jack (King) Kirby."

With a solid lineup of super heroes in place, Lee and his artists began sculpting Marvel around the edges. Examples:

I. In *X-Men* No. 10, he and Kirby introduced a new Ka-Zar, who shared only a name with his pulp and *Marvel Mystery Comics* predecessor; this one chummed around with a saber tooth named Zabu in an Antarctic jungle inhabited by cavemen and dinosaurs. A few issues later, a fanatical scientist created huge robots called the Sentinels to render all mutants harmless, allegedly to protect humanity.

II. A Marvel version of the Greco-Roman god Hercules clashed with Thor in the latter's 1965 *Annual*, and would soon return — eventually joining the Avengers.

III. Reed and Sue got married in *Fantastic Four Annual* No. 3, with virtually every Marvel hero and villain in attendance — not to mention Lee and Kirby (who got turned away at the door because they didn't have invitations). An intriguing new group of costumed characters, the Inhumans, began to pop up, first one by one, then all together, in the monthly *FF*.

IV. A mysterious red-tressed teenager named Mary Jane Watson, niece of a neighbor of Peter Parker's Aunt May, wandered in and out of *Amazing Spider-Man*, her face never shown... while, in No. 33 (February 1966), Ditko teased and

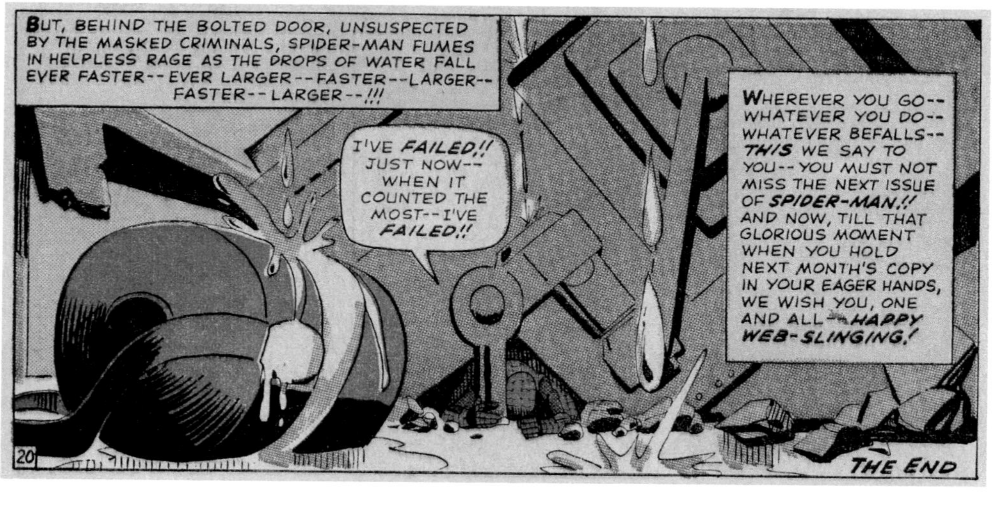
BUT, BEHIND THE BOLTED DOOR, UNSUSPECTED BY THE MASKED CRIMINALS, SPIDER-MAN FUMES IN HELPLESS RAGE AS THE DROPS OF WATER FALL EVER FASTER--EVER LARGER--FASTER--LARGER--FASTER--LARGER--!!!
I'VE FAILED!! JUST NOW-- WHEN IT COUNTED THE MOST--I'VE FAILED!!
WHEREVER YOU GO-- WHATEVER YOU DO-- WHATEVER BEFALLS-- THIS WE SAY TO YOU--YOU MUST NOT MISS THE NEXT ISSUE OF SPIDER-MAN!! AND NOW, TILL THAT GLORIOUS MOMENT WHEN YOU HOLD NEXT MONTH'S COPY IN YOUR EAGER HANDS, WE WISH YOU, ONE AND ALL--HAPPY WEB-SLINGING!
20
THE END

AMAZING SPIDER-MAN No. 32
(Below) Interior, "Man on a Rampage!"; script, Stan Lee; pencils and inks, Steve Ditko; January 1966. Ditko's Spider-Man reached its creative pinnacle in issues 31–33.

STRANGE TALES No. 135
(Opposite) Cover; pencils, Jack Kirby; inks, Frank Giacoia; August 1965. From James Bond to *The Man from U.N.C.L.E.*: With spies all the rage, Marvel reintroduced the former Sgt. Nick Fury as a present-day CIA agent recruited to head up new super-spy agency S.H.I.E.L.D. The live-action spies would take decades to catch up with Fury's array of inspired Kirby SF gadgetry.

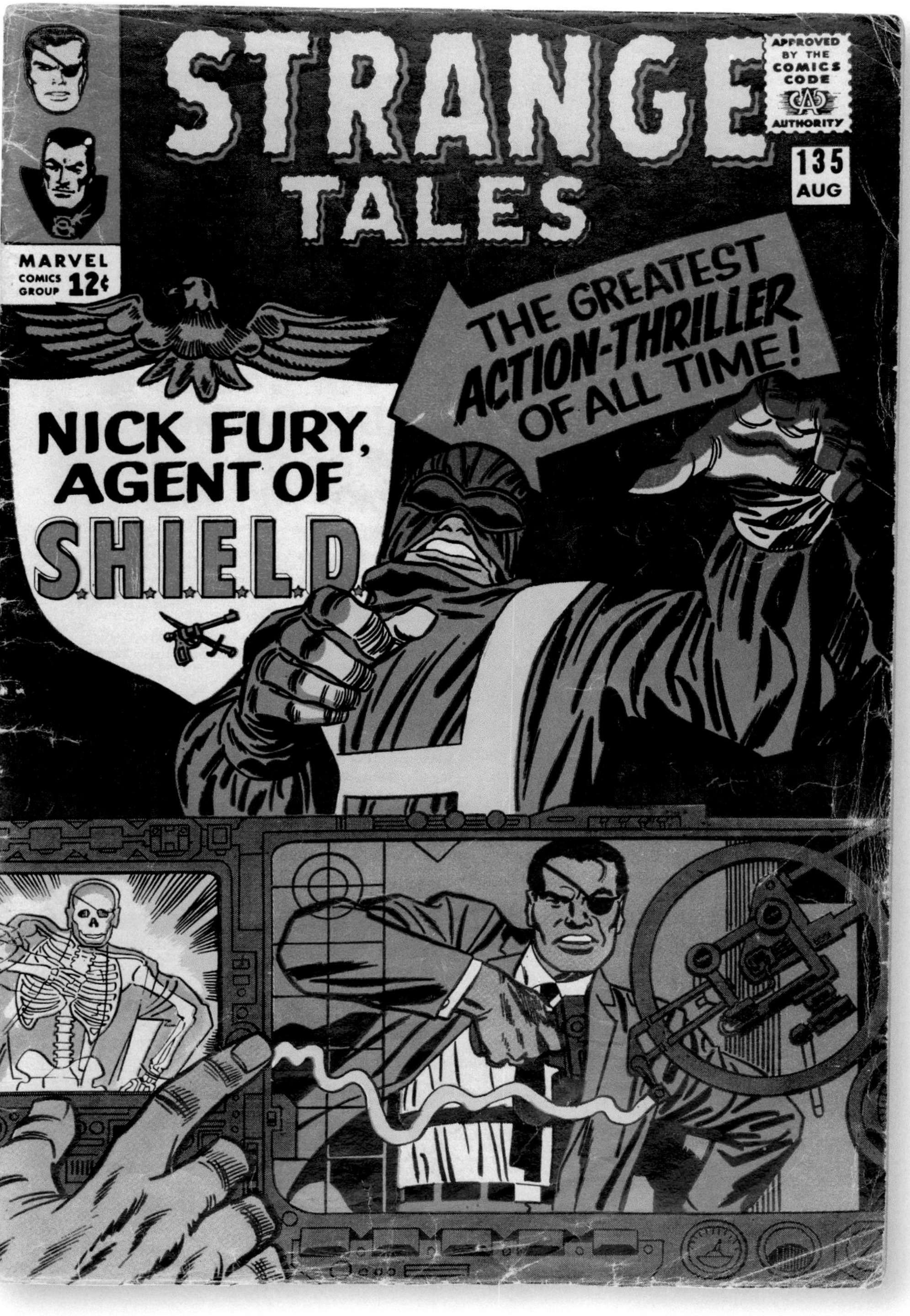
STRANGE TALES
APPROVED BY THE COMICS CODE AUTHORITY
135
AUG
MARVEL COMICS GROUP 12¢
THE GREATEST ACTION-THRILLER OF ALL TIME!
NICK FURY, AGENT OF S.H.I.E.L.D.

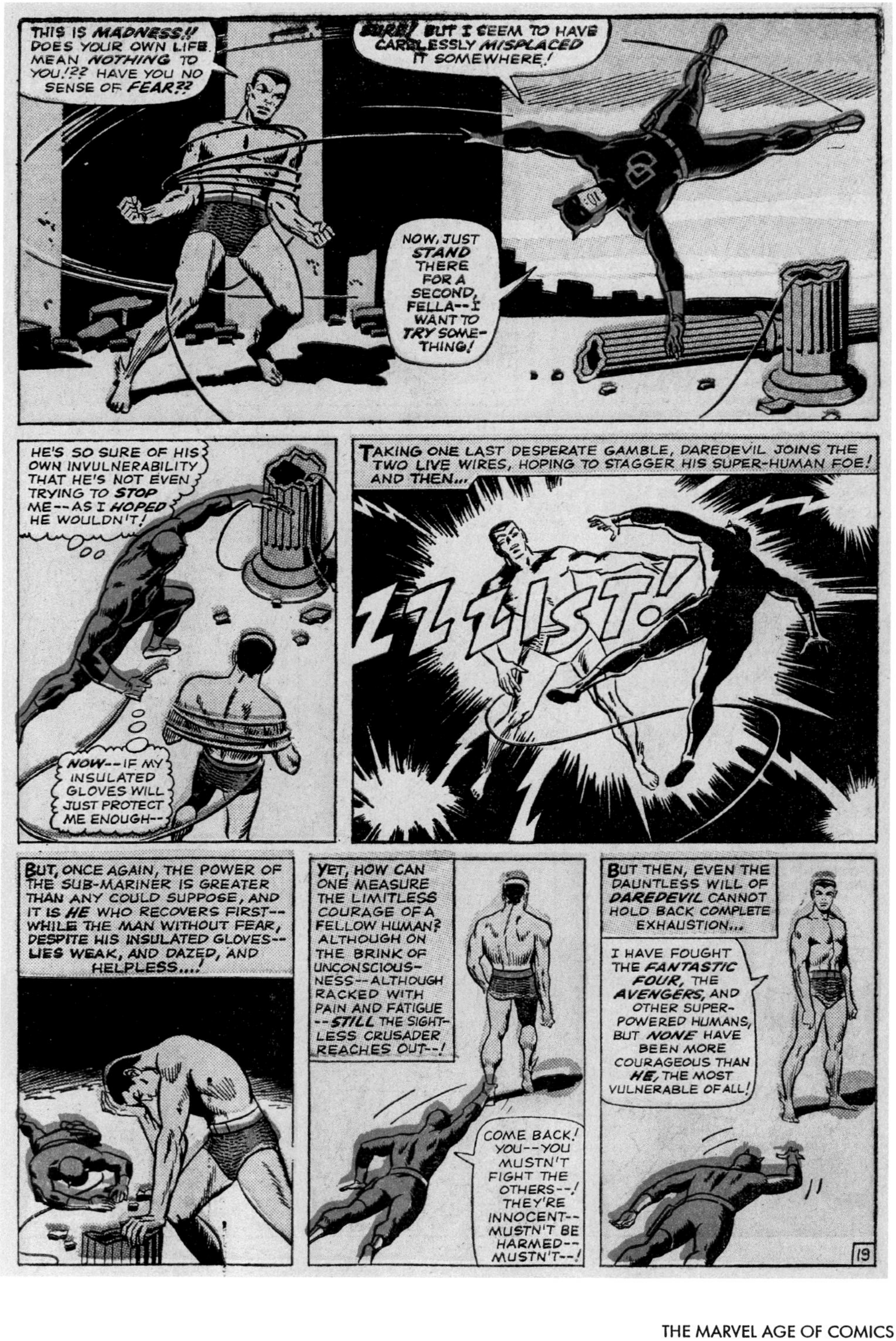
THIS IS MADNESS!! DOES YOUR OWN LIFE MEAN NOTHING TO YOU!?? HAVE YOU NO SENSE OF FEAR??
SURE! BUT I SEEM TO HAVE CARELESSLY MISPLACED IT SOMEWHERE!
NOW, JUST STAND THERE FOR A SECOND, FELLA--I WANT TO TRY SOMETHING!
HE'S SO SURE OF HIS OWN INVULNERABILITY THAT HE'S NOT EVEN TRYING TO STOP ME--AS I HOPED HE WOULDN'T!
NOW--IF MY INSULATED GLOVES WILL JUST PROTECT ME ENOUGH--
TAKING ONE LAST DESPERATE GAMBLE, DAREDEVIL JOINS THE TWO LIVE WIRES, HOPING TO STAGGER HIS SUPER-HUMAN FOE! AND THEN...
ZZZIST!
BUT, ONCE AGAIN, THE POWER OF THE SUB-MARINER IS GREATER THAN ANY COULD SUPPOSE, AND IT IS HE WHO RECOVERS FIRST--WHILE THE MAN WITHOUT FEAR, DESPITE HIS INSULATED GLOVES--LIES WEAK, AND DAZED, AND HELPLESS...!
YET, HOW CAN ONE MEASURE THE LIMITLESS COURAGE OF A FELLOW HUMAN? ALTHOUGH ON THE BRINK OF UNCONSCIOUSNESS--ALTHOUGH RACKED WITH PAIN AND FATIGUE --STILL THE SIGHTLESS CRUSADER REACHES OUT--!
COME BACK! YOU--YOU MUSTN'T FIGHT THE OTHERS--! THEY'RE INNOCENT--MUSTN'T BE HARMED--MUSTN'T--!
BUT THEN, EVEN THE DAUNTLESS WILL OF DAREDEVIL CANNOT HOLD BACK COMPLETE EXHAUSTION...
I HAVE FOUGHT THE FANTASTIC FOUR, THE AVENGERS, AND OTHER SUPER-POWERED HUMANS, BUT NONE HAVE BEEN MORE COURAGEOUS THAN HE, THE MOST VULNERABLE OF ALL!
19

ultimately thrilled readers with a five-page sequence in which Spider-Man, trapped beneath tons of "fallen steel" while the clock was ticking away Aunt May's life, strained for several pages before finally managing to lift the massive weight off himself with a desperate surge of strength.

Changes were also made to the monthly anthologies. A Sub-Mariner series, drawn by Gene Colan (who had been a Timely staff artist in the late 1940s), replaced Giant-Man in *Tales to Astonish*. The Human Torch was bumped from *Strange Tales* by Nick Fury, Agent of S.H.I.E.L.D., which exploited the craze for acronymical spy organizations set off by James Bond and TV's *The Man from U.N.C.L.E.* Originated by Lee and Kirby, it starred an older and allegedly wiser Fury—now out of uniform and sporting an eye patch—leading the Supreme Headquarters International Espionage Law-Enforcement Division against sinister conclaves like Hydra ("Cut off one head, and two more will take its place!"). With these two new series and the inauguration of a Thor-starring Tales of Asgard feature in the back pages of *Journey into Mystery*, all of Marvel's former mystery/monster titles had finally reached their ultimate form.

Along the way, Lee and his artists jettisoned one staple of the first few years of the company's resurgence: anti-Communism. From *Fantastic Four* No. 1 ("Ben, we've *got* to take that chance...unless we want the Commies to beat us to it!") through the origin of Iron Man "in a South Vietnam jungle"—from Red agents in Hungary murdering Hank (Ant-Man) Pym's first wife, through an early 1965 Captain America foray against the Viet Cong on "the battlefield of Viet Nam"—the Soviets, Red Chinese, and North Vietnamese had made convenient foes for Marvel's heroes to battle and best. There had even been a trio of allegedly Communistic "Super-Apes," led by a Marxist super villain known as the Red Ghost. Much of this ambience had carried over from the heady Axis-baiting of Timely's World War II comics, and even Atlas's brief super hero fling from 1953 to 1955.

The majority of the new breed of readers, though, let Stan Lee know through letters that they didn't want to see the Cold War—or the escalating struggle soon to be known as the Vietnam War—fought in Marvel's four-color pages. As a result,

DAREDEVIL No. 7

(Opposite) Interior, "In Mortal Combat with the Sub-Mariner!"; script, Stan Lee; pencils and inks, Wally Wood; April 1965. Bill Everett's first creation, the Sub-Mariner, defeats Everett's last creation, Daredevil. Wood's unparalleled, deep-black inking style lends the conflict a sense of high drama that underscores the appeal of Marvel's new generation of humanized heroes. Stan Lee has said all his stories were his favorites, but if he had to pick one, this would be it.

by 1965, villains hailing from behind the Iron Curtain had all but disappeared from the company's comics — and the Vietnam War became merely subtle background music, represented by an occasional generic protest or a character who happened to be a combat veteran.

Perhaps the biggest story bombshell of 1965 occurred in *The Avengers* No. 16: "The Old Order Changeth!" (Lee was developing a taste for grandiose, often archaic story titles.) Though Don Heck was now that title's regular artist, Lee had Kirby coplot and do pencil layouts for this pivotal issue, wherein Thor, Iron Man, Giant-Man, and the Wasp take indefinite leaves of absence

DAREDEVIL No. 12
(Right) Interior, "Sightless, in a Savage Land!"; script, Stan Lee; layouts, Jack Kirby; finished art, John Romita; January 1966.

DAREDEVIL No. 16
(Opposite) Cover; pencils and inks, John Romita; May 1966. Suspecting that Steve Ditko was about to jump ship, Lee had Spider-Man guest-star in *Daredevil* to test how artist John Romita would handle the character. Romita passed with flying colors and began drawing Spider-Man with issue No. 39.

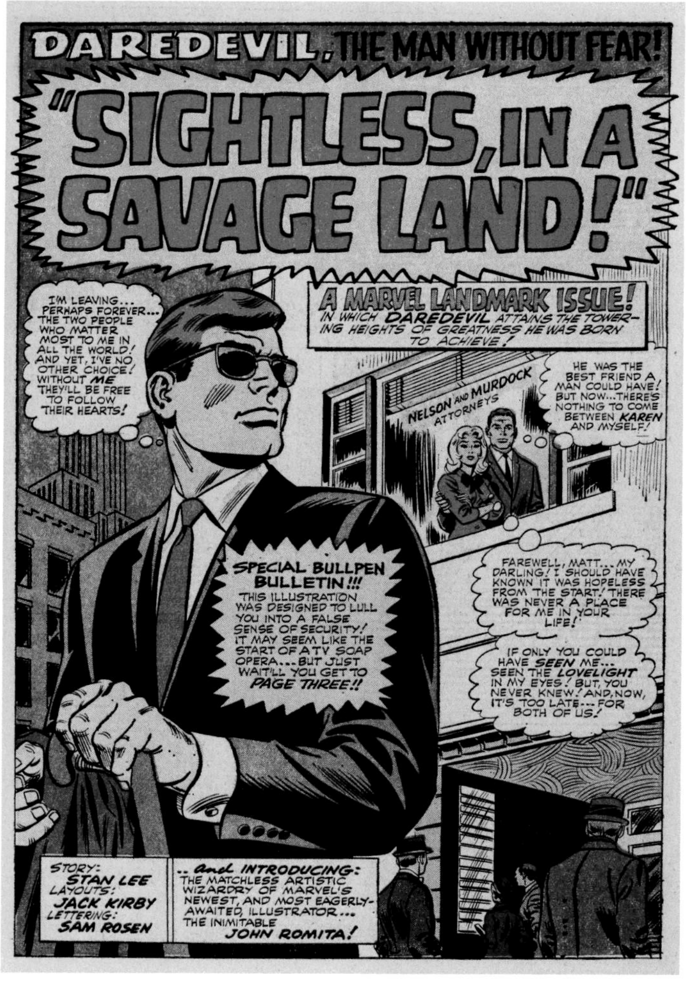
DAREDEVIL, THE MAN WITHOUT FEAR!
"SIGHTLESS, IN A SAVAGE LAND!"
A MARVEL LANDMARK ISSUE! IN WHICH DAREDEVIL ATTAINS THE TOWERING HEIGHTS OF GREATNESS HE WAS BORN TO ACHIEVE!
I'M LEAVING... PERHAPS FOREVER... THE TWO PEOPLE WHO MATTER MOST TO ME IN ALL THE WORLD! AND YET, I'VE NO OTHER CHOICE! WITHOUT ME THEY'LL BE FREE TO FOLLOW THEIR HEARTS!
NELSON AND MURDOCK ATTORNEYS
HE WAS THE BEST FRIEND A MAN COULD HAVE! BUT NOW... THERE'S NOTHING TO COME BETWEEN KAREN AND MYSELF!
SPECIAL BULLPEN BULLETIN!!! THIS ILLUSTRATION WAS DESIGNED TO LULL YOU INTO A FALSE SENSE OF SECURITY! IT MAY SEEM LIKE THE START OF A TV SOAP OPERA... BUT JUST WAIT'LL YOU GET TO PAGE THREE!!
FAREWELL, MATT... MY DARLING! I SHOULD HAVE KNOWN IT WAS HOPELESS FROM THE START! THERE WAS NEVER A PLACE FOR ME IN YOUR LIFE!
IF ONLY YOU COULD HAVE SEEN ME... SEEN THE LOVELIGHT IN MY EYES! BUT, YOU NEVER KNEW! AND, NOW, IT'S TOO LATE... FOR BOTH OF US!
STORY: STAN LEE LAYOUTS: JACK KIRBY LETTERING: SAM ROSEN
..And INTRODUCING: THE MATCHLESS ARTISTIC WIZARDRY OF MARVEL'S NEWEST, AND MOST EAGERLY-AWAITED, ILLUSTRATOR... THE INIMITABLE JOHN ROMITA!

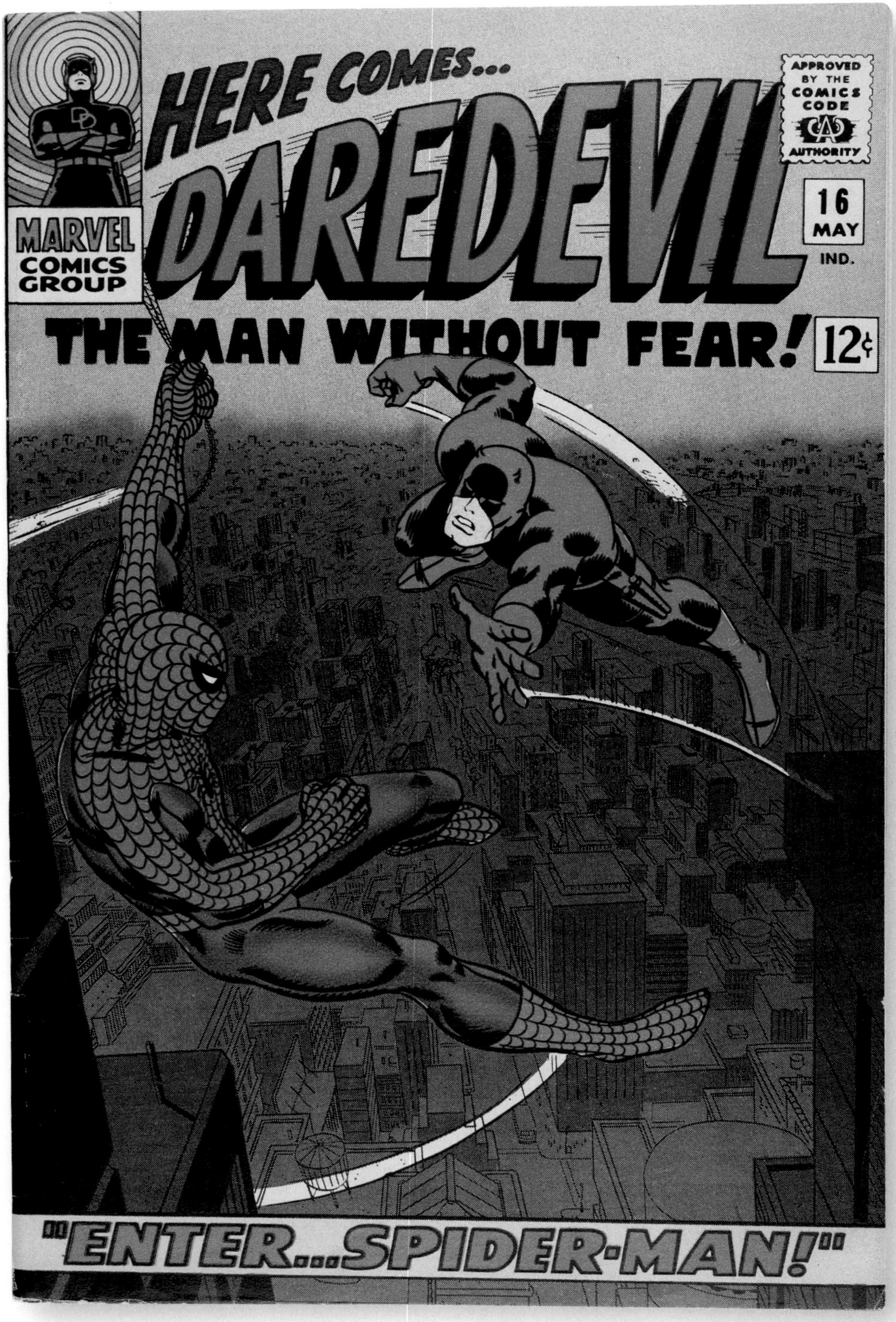
HERE COMES...
DAREDEVIL
THE MAN WITHOUT FEAR!
MARVEL COMICS GROUP
APPROVED BY THE COMICS CODE AUTHORITY
16
MAY
IND.
12¢
"ENTER...SPIDER-MAN!"

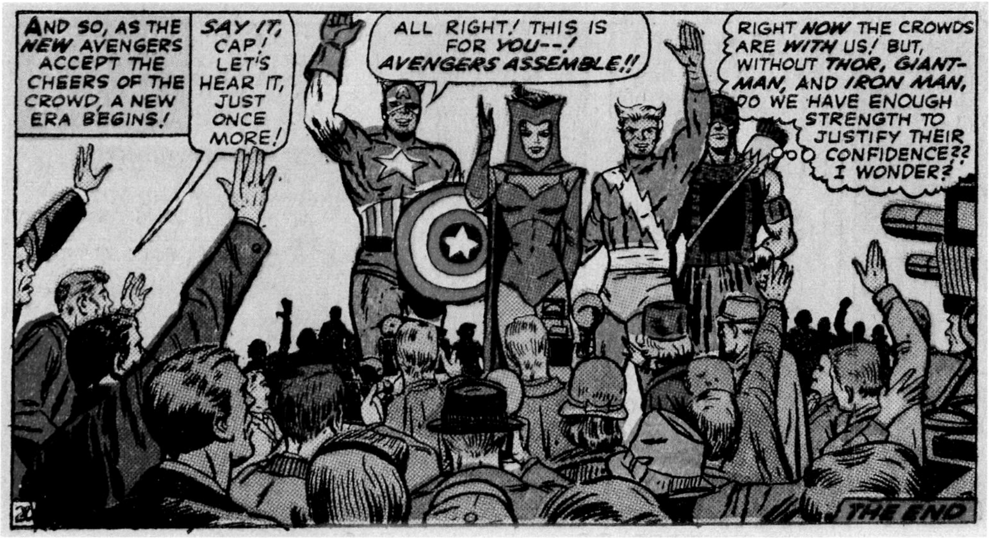
AND SO, AS THE NEW AVENGERS ACCEPT THE CHEERS OF THE CROWD, A NEW ERA BEGINS!
SAY IT, CAP! LET'S HEAR IT, JUST ONCE MORE!
ALL RIGHT! THIS IS FOR YOU--! AVENGERS ASSEMBLE!!
RIGHT NOW THE CROWDS ARE WITH US! BUT, WITHOUT THOR, GIANT-MAN, AND IRON MAN, DO WE HAVE ENOUGH STRENGTH TO JUSTIFY THEIR CONFIDENCE?? I WONDER?
THE END

THE AVENGERS No. 16
(Above) Interior; script, Stan Lee; layouts, Jack Kirby; finished art, Dick Ayers; May 1965. "Did you know the real reason we changed the Avengers lineup? Iron Man, Thor and Giant-Man were all starring in their own mags. After a while it didn't seem right to have one of them captured in Transylvania in his own mag while he might be taking in the Late Show on TV in the Avengers. The truth is it seemed to kill all the realism." —Stan Lee

from the team. Lee removed Thor and Iron Man because he felt that trying to coordinate their activities in *Avengers* with their solo series undermined the realism of both. Replacing the departed assemblers were Hawkeye, Quicksilver, and the Scarlet Witch, each recently rehabilitated from villain to hero. Thrust into leadership, Captain America shepherded these new recruits through a series of missions. Amazingly, sales of *The Avengers* actually went *up*, with readers eager to see how "Cap and the misfits" would fare compared to the original team.

Equally explosive was the impact of artist Wallace (Wally) Wood on *Daredevil*. His lush inking style, in particular—plus his ability to render mouthwateringly lovely ladies—made him an immediate favorite of a growing Marvel fandom, even if they had never seen his celebrated work for EC Comics' science-fiction titles or even for *Mad* magazine. With issue No. 7, Wood redesigned the hero's costume to a devilish red lush with black shadows—and he and Lee cast him as the underdog against a rampaging Sub-Mariner, with DD proving himself more valiant in defeat than he could possibly have been in victory. After *Daredevil* No. 11, however, Wood left Marvel to launch a super hero team book, *T.H.U.N.D.E.R. Agents*, for a new company, Tower Comics.

He had barely departed, however, when in strolled another veteran talent to take his place. John Romita had been a

Timely/Atlas artist for years before the 1957 collapse forced him to find safe harbor drawing DC romance comics. In July 1965, Lee persuaded him to return — officially acceding to his desire only to ink, not pencil — then promptly wangled him into drawing *Daredevil*. That series, already popular under Wood, would swiftly soar under Romita to sell a higher percentage of its print run than any other Marvel comic (though naturally *Daredevil*'s print run was lower than that of the company's top titles). And even greater things were in store for Romita a few months down the line.

That summer, Lee was making a renewed attempt to get out from scripting every Marvel adventure title. In June, he hired recent college graduate Steve Skeates as a potential scripter, on the strength of a letter written to Marvel in the format of a comic book.

Two weeks later, enter fanzine writer/editor (and former English teacher) Roy Thomas. (Yes, the same person who has written the book you now hold in your fevered hands — but he hopes you'll understand if he continues to write about himself in the third person, 'cause otherwise all those *I*'s would soon get

COMING TO A TV NEAR YOU

(Below) Advertisement; pencils and inks, Jack Kirby and Gene Colan; ca. 1966. Marvel Super-Heroes was a syndicated cartoon that landed on television screens across America in fall 1966. Five nights a week, Iron Man, Captain America, the Sub-Mariner, the Hulk, and Thor starred in stories adapted (and utilizing artwork) from the comics. The Grantray-Lawrence series had very limited, rudimentary animation, but it brought greater recognition to Marvel's line, and the shows did have catchy theme songs!

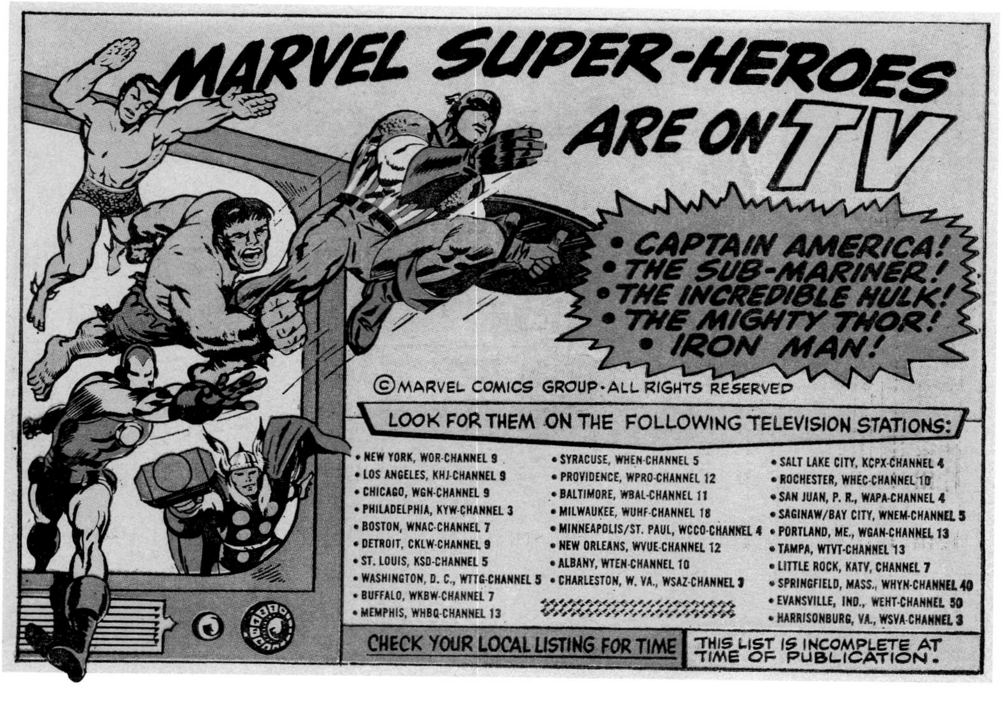

MARVEL SUPER-HEROES ARE ON TV
• CAPTAIN AMERICA!
• THE SUB-MARINER!
• THE INCREDIBLE HULK!
• THE MIGHTY THOR!
• IRON MAN!
©MARVEL COMICS GROUP • ALL RIGHTS RESERVED
LOOK FOR THEM ON THE FOLLOWING TELEVISION STATIONS:
• NEW YORK, WOR-CHANNEL 9
• LOS ANGELES, KHJ-CHANNEL 9
• CHICAGO, WGN-CHANNEL 9
• PHILADELPHIA, KYW-CHANNEL 3
• BOSTON, WNAC-CHANNEL 7
• DETROIT, CKLW-CHANNEL 9
• ST. LOUIS, KSD-CHANNEL 5
• WASHINGTON, D. C., WTTG-CHANNEL 5
• BUFFALO, WKBW-CHANNEL 7
• MEMPHIS, WHBQ-CHANNEL 13
• SYRACUSE, WHEN-CHANNEL 5
• PROVIDENCE, WPRO-CHANNEL 12
• BALTIMORE, WBAL-CHANNEL 11
• MILWAUKEE, WUHF-CHANNEL 18
• MINNEAPOLIS/ST. PAUL, WCCO-CHANNEL 4
• NEW ORLEANS, WVUE-CHANNEL 12
• ALBANY, WTEN-CHANNEL 10
• CHARLESTON, W. VA., WSAZ-CHANNEL 3
• SALT LAKE CITY, KCPX-CHANNEL 4
• ROCHESTER, WHEC-CHANNEL 10
• SAN JUAN, P. R., WAPA-CHANNEL 4
• SAGINAW/BAY CITY, WNEM-CHANNEL 5
• PORTLAND, ME., WGAN-CHANNEL 13
• TAMPA, WTVT-CHANNEL 13
• LITTLE ROCK, KATV, CHANNEL 7
• SPRINGFIELD, MASS., WHYN-CHANNEL 40
• EVANSVILLE, IND., WEHT-CHANNEL 50
• HARRISONBURG, VA., WSVA-CHANNEL 3
CHECK YOUR LOCAL LISTING FOR TIME
THIS LIST IS INCOMPLETE AT TIME OF PUBLICATION.

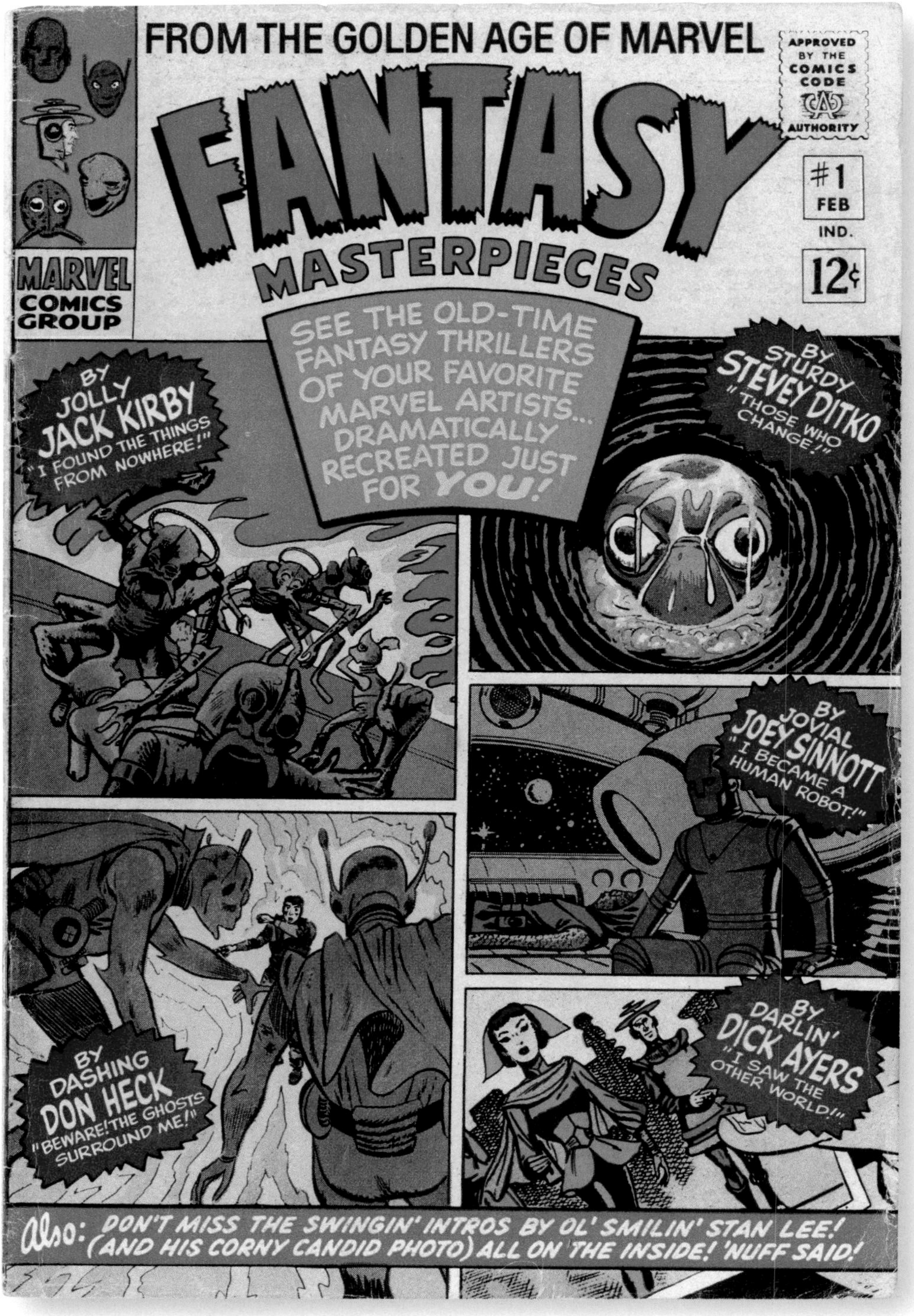
FROM THE GOLDEN AGE OF MARVEL
APPROVED BY THE COMICS CODE AUTHORITY
FANTASY MASTERPIECES
#1 FEB IND.
12¢
MARVEL COMICS GROUP
SEE THE OLD-TIME FANTASY THRILLERS OF YOUR FAVORITE MARVEL ARTISTS... DRAMATICALLY RECREATED JUST FOR YOU!
BY JOLLY JACK KIRBY "I FOUND THE THINGS FROM NOWHERE!"
BY STURDY STEVEY DITKO "THOSE WHO CHANGE!"
BY JOVIAL JOEY SINNOTT "I BECAME A HUMAN ROBOT!"
BY DASHING DON HECK "BEWARE! THE GHOSTS SURROUND ME!"
BY DARLIN' DICK AYERS "I SAW THE OTHER WORLD!"
Also: DON'T MISS THE SWINGIN' INTROS BY OL' SMILIN' STAN LEE! (AND HIS CORNY CANDID PHOTO) ALL ON THE INSIDE! 'NUFF SAID!

FANTASY MASTERPIECES No. 1

(*Opposite*) *Cover; pencils, Jack Kirby, Steve Ditko, and Don Heck; inks, Dick Ayers, Ditko, and Joe Sinnott; February 1966.* With few exceptions — notably Bill Gaines's classic EC line in the 1950s — comic book artists seemed doomed to toil in obscurity. Stan Lee changed all that. He systematically splashed artists' and writers' names on covers, even placing their photos inside at times, along the way heaping praise on their storytelling techniques. By mid-decade Marvel's artists were well on the way to becoming celebrities themselves.

confusing. This is the story of Marvel Comics, after all, not the tale of any one person. Now, back to our regularly scheduled volume.) Thomas had come to New York from Missouri to be the editorial assistant on DC's Superman titles, but was hired away from the larger company by Lee after taking a Marvel "writer's test" that consisted of adding dialogue to four wordless Kirby *FF* pages.

By late September, another test-taker, Thomas's newspaper-reporter friend and fellow Missourian, Dennis O'Neil, would be hired after Skeates had moved on.

Lee started out first Thomas, then O'Neil, scripting the exploits of Millie the Model and Patsy Walker, followed by Westerns and a handful of Ditko-plotted Dr. Strange tales.

Working with his artists, especially Kirby and Ditko, Lee was clearly guiding the creation of this cosmos of Marvel heroes. But Martin Goodman, meanwhile, discovered...*reprints*. After a few specials, he had Lee put together regular series titled *Marvel Collectors' Item Classics*, then also *Marvel Tales*, to rerun tales of the FF, Hulk, et al. *MCIC*, *Marvel Tales*, and third entry *Fantasy Masterpieces* (which soon began reprinting 1940s and '50s stories of Captain America, et al., from mediocre Photostats) enabled fans to read adventures they had missed. Presumably, any increased sales generated by reader enthusiasm would eventually trickle down to freelancers in the form of page-rate increases.

NOT JUST FOR KIDS

(*Above*) *Photograph, 1966.* Since at least 1947, Goodman's empire was called the Magazine Management Company, which along with comics and crosswords, still included pulp-derived men's magazines including *Man, Male, Swank,* and *Stag.* The rarely photographed Goodman appears at an event honoring long-time editor — and celebrated novelist and playwright — Bruce Jay Friedman.

Given Timely's late-1950s collapse, at this stage its rates were considerably lower than DC's. Even so, several DC artists did some moonlighting for Marvel, using fake names to prevent DC's editors from retaliating. Gene Colan, of late a DC romance artist, became "Adam Austin" when penciling Sub-Mariner and Iron Man... Frank Giacoia, Mike Esposito, and Jack Abel inked as "Frankie Ray," "Mickey Demeo," and "Gary Michaels," respectively... and *Green Lantern* artist Gil Kane penciled a Hulk story as "Scott Edward." Most often, the pseudonyms were the names of the artists' children, their wives' maiden names, or some such.

STRANGE TALES No. 144

(Right) Interior, "Where Man Hath Never Trod!"; script, Roy Thomas; pencils and inks, Steve Ditko; May 1966. In just two issues Steve Ditko would leave the world of Dr. Strange behind him. Stan Lee had already given up dialoguing the strip, giving newcomers Roy Thomas and Denny O'Neil a chance to work with the master.

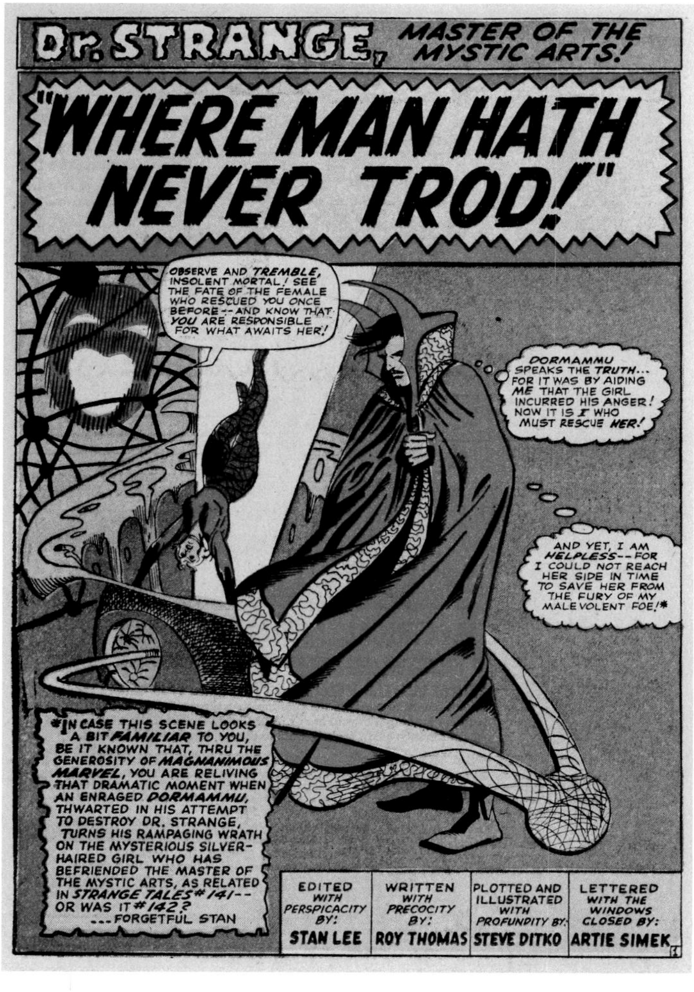
Dr. STRANGE, MASTER OF THE MYSTIC ARTS!
"WHERE MAN HATH NEVER TROD!"
OBSERVE AND TREMBLE, INSOLENT MORTAL! SEE THE FATE OF THE FEMALE WHO RESCUED YOU ONCE BEFORE--AND KNOW THAT YOU ARE RESPONSIBLE FOR WHAT AWAITS HER!
DORMAMMU SPEAKS THE TRUTH... FOR IT WAS BY AIDING ME THAT THE GIRL INCURRED HIS ANGER! NOW IT IS I WHO MUST RESCUE HER!
AND YET, I AM HELPLESS--FOR I COULD NOT REACH HER SIDE IN TIME TO SAVE HER FROM THE FURY OF MY MALEVOLENT FOE!*
*IN CASE THIS SCENE LOOKS A BIT FAMILIAR TO YOU, BE IT KNOWN THAT, THRU THE GENEROSITY OF MAGNANIMOUS MARVEL, YOU ARE RELIVING THAT DRAMATIC MOMENT WHEN AN ENRAGED DORMAMMU, THWARTED IN HIS ATTEMPT TO DESTROY DR. STRANGE, TURNS HIS RAMPAGING WRATH ON THE MYSTERIOUS SILVER-HAIRED GIRL WHO HAS BEFRIENDED THE MASTER OF THE MYSTIC ARTS, AS RELATED IN STRANGE TALES #141--OR WAS IT #142? ...FORGETFUL STAN
EDITED WITH PERSPICACITY BY: STAN LEE
WRITTEN WITH PRECOCITY BY: ROY THOMAS
PLOTTED AND ILLUSTRATED WITH PROFUNDITY BY: STEVE DITKO
LETTERED WITH THE WINDOWS CLOSED BY: ARTIE SIMEK

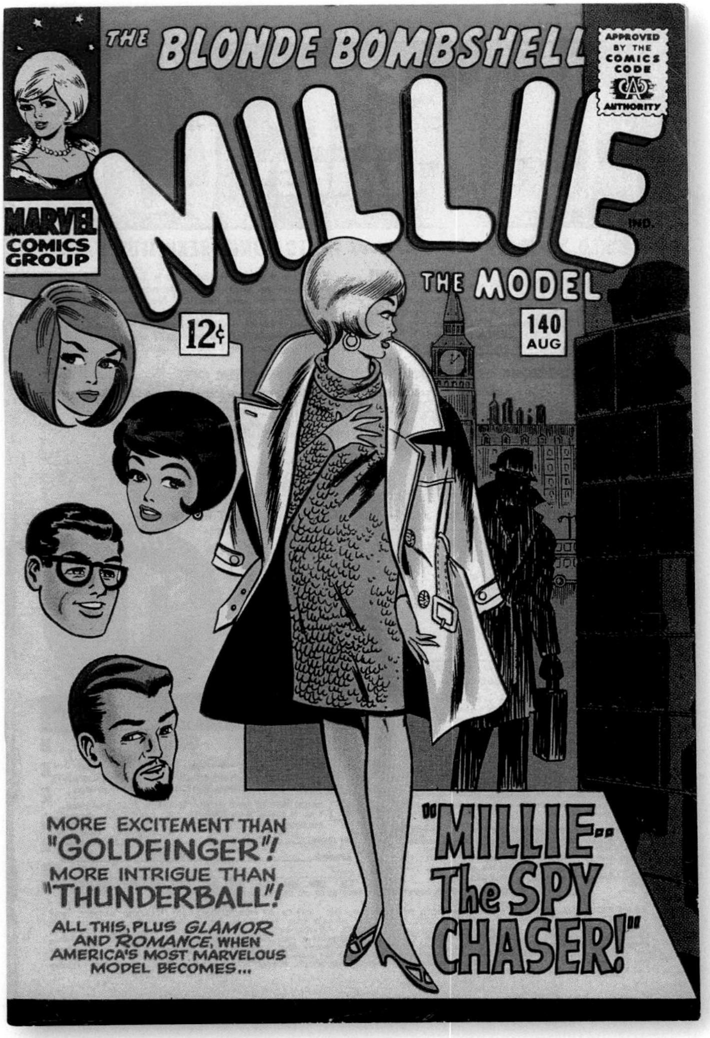
THE BLONDE BOMBSHELL
APPROVED BY THE COMICS CODE AUTHORITY
MILLIE THE MODEL
MARVEL COMICS GROUP
12¢
140 AUG
MORE EXCITEMENT THAN "GOLDFINGER"! MORE INTRIGUE THAN "THUNDERBALL"!
ALL THIS, PLUS GLAMOR AND ROMANCE, WHEN AMERICA'S MOST MARVELOUS MODEL BECOMES...
"MILLIE... The SPY CHASER!"

MILLIE THE MODEL No. 140

(Left) Cover; pencils and inks, Stan Goldberg; August 1966. After several decades and more than one hundred consecutive issues, Stan Lee used the Westerns and Marvel's "girl comics" as a training ground for new scripters, beginning with Roy Thomas and Dennis O'Neil.

MARVEL ARRIVES—BUT ONE DEPARTS

The year 1965 was also the year the media finally began to discover what one college student christened "the Marvel Universe"—a term that immediately stuck. Both Spider-Man and Hulk popped up on *Esquire* magazine's list of two dozen-plus "revolutionary icons," alongside Bob Dylan, John F. Kennedy, and Che Guevara.

Since Goodman almost never granted interviews to the press, and, at this point, Kirby and Ditko were content to keep drawing at a frantic pace, editor/writer Stan Lee inevitably became the face of Marvel, and he reveled in the role. Publications from the *Wall Street Journal*, which concentrated on increased sales figures, to *Castle of Frankenstein*, which interviewed Lee as "the man behind Marvel Comics," each found what they wanted to find in the company's color-splashed pages. The Greenwich *Village Voice* newspaper pronounced Marvel's titles the "first comic books in history" for the "post-adolescent escapist."

And then, in January 1966, the *Batman* live-action TV series hit like an A-bomb, with its "camp" approach to super heroes. Overnight, several comics companies added costumed-hero

FANTASTIC FOUR No. 52
(Right) Cover; pencils, Jack Kirby; inks, Joe Sinnott; July 1966.

FANTASTIC FOUR No. 49
(Opposite) Cover; pencils, Jack Kirby; inks, Joe Sinnott; April 1966.
"Galactus was God, and I was looking for God. When I first came up with Galactus, I was very awed by him. I didn't know what to do with the character. Everybody talks about God, but what the heck does he look like? Well, he's supposed to be awesome, and Galactus is awesome to me." —Jack Kirby

THE WORLD'S GREATEST COMIC MAGAZINE!
APPROVED BY THE COMICS CODE AUTHORITY
Fantastic Four
52 JULY
MARVEL COMICS GROUP
12¢
Introducing: THE SENSATIONAL BLACK PANTHER!

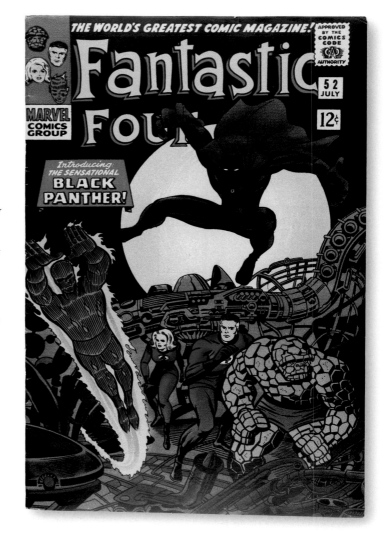

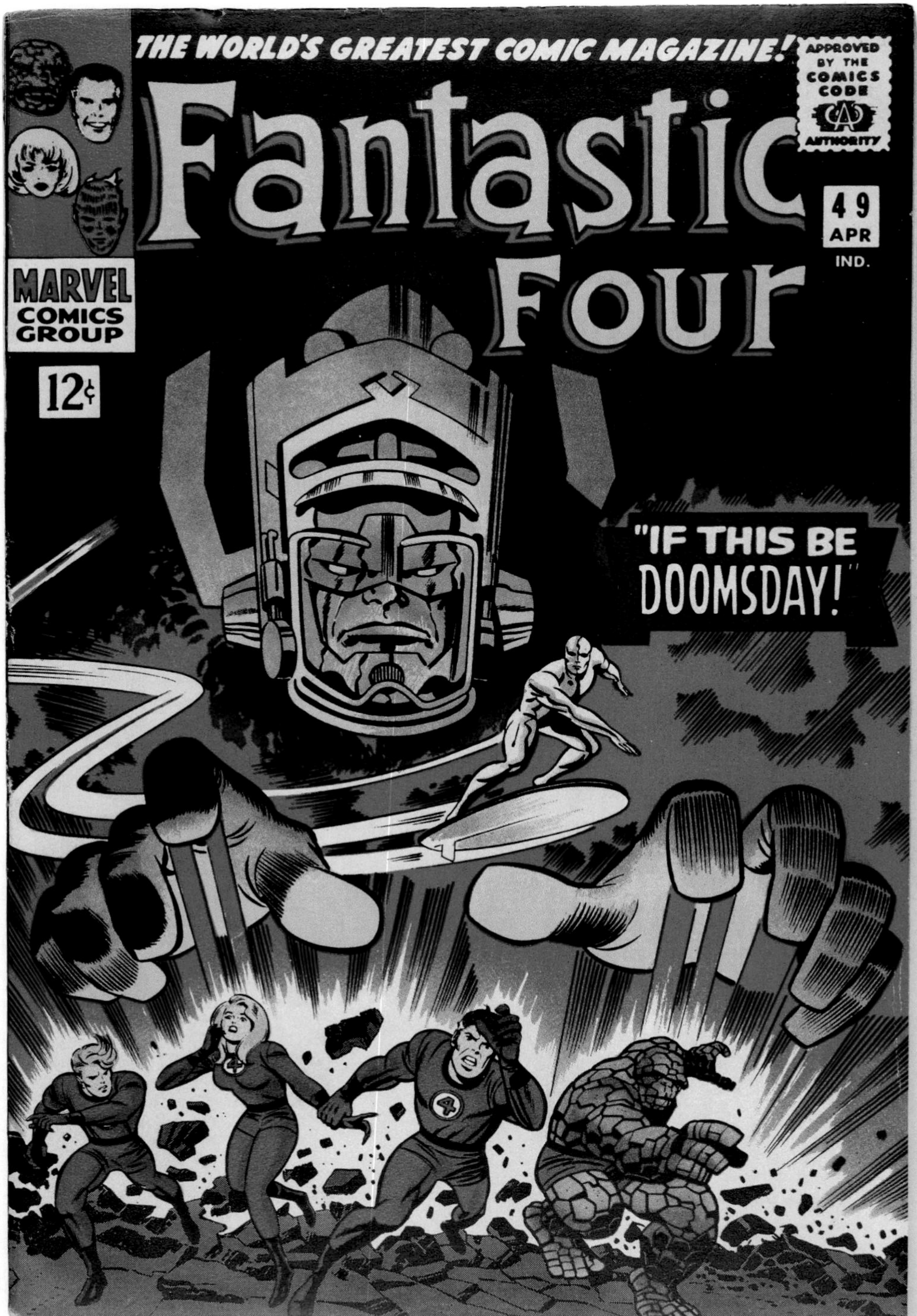
THE WORLD'S GREATEST COMIC MAGAZINE!
APPROVED BY THE COMICS CODE AUTHORITY
Fantastic Four
49 APR
IND.
MARVEL COMICS GROUP
12¢
"IF THIS BE DOOMSDAY!"

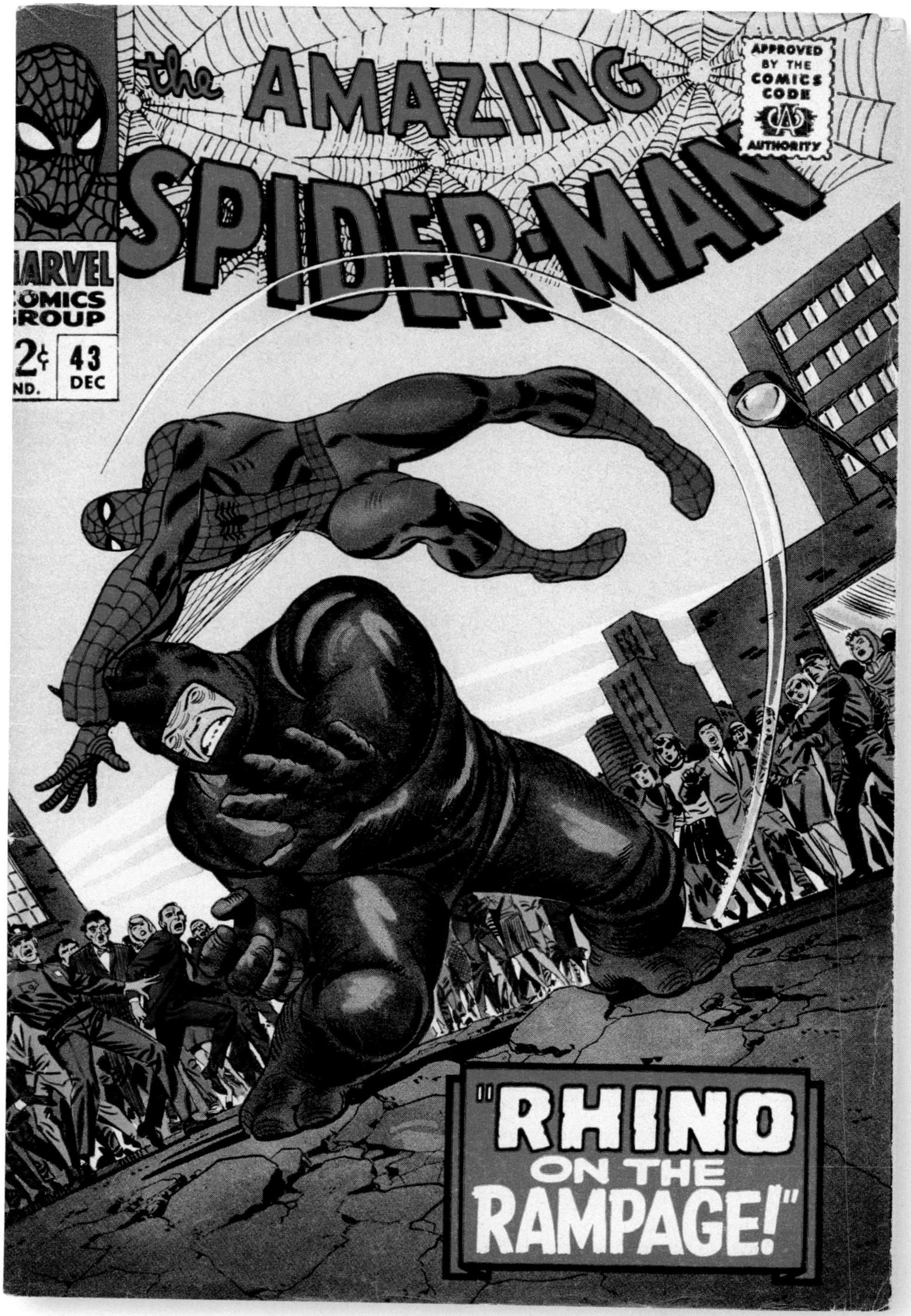
the AMAZING SPIDER-MAN
APPROVED BY THE COMICS CODE AUTHORITY
MARVEL COMICS GROUP
12¢ IND.
43 DEC
"RHINO ON THE RAMPAGE!"

titles, relying in part on so-called "camp" qualities to sell them, but also often imitative of Marvel. Goodman and Lee were particularly annoyed by Archie's "Mighty Comics Group," for which writer Jerry Siegel and recent Marvel artist Paul Reinman revived hordes of costumed characters as *The Mighty Crusaders*. Kirby's former partner, Joe Simon, edited new super hero titles for Harvey. Carl Burgos, creator of the original Human Torch, developed a new *Captain Marvel*—usurping the name of the ultra-popular Fawcett Publications hero of the 1940s and at the same time managing to use the word *Marvel* in a title (which couldn't hurt). Goodman's normal response to this competition would have been to add more titles of his own—but for the present he was still constrained by the limitations set by Independent News.

During this period, celebrities began to come calling at Marvel's offices: Italian film director Federico Fellini…English pop stars Peter and Gordon. And right down the hall, editing for Goodman's Magazine Management publications, was future best-selling novelist, playwright, and screenwriter Bruce J. Friedman. One of that division's writers, Mario Puzo, briefly considered scripting for Marvel while he was completing his next novel, but, after reading some sample comics, he returned them to Lee, saying that, given their complex backstory, it would be far easier for him to continue writing prose for Goodman's pulps while he finished his book—which, incidentally, would be titled *The Godfather*.

AMAZING SPIDER-MAN No. 43
(Opposite) Cover; pencils and inks, John Romita; December 1966.

AMAZING SPIDER-MAN No. 42
(Below) Interiors, "The Birth of a Super-Hero!"; script, Stan Lee; pencils and inks, John Romita; November 1966. Face it: We all hit the jackpot. No one cares that Spider-Man rescued astronaut John Jameson in this issue, because readers finally got to meet the gorgeous Mary Jane Watson after years of obstructed views! John Romita has said that she was modeled after movie star Ann-Margret.

I'VE SPENT MONTHS TRYING TO AVOID MEET-ING MRS. WATSON'S NIECE!
BUT, IT LOOKS AS IF THIS IS ONE CONTEST SPIDEY'S GONNA LOSE! AUNT MAY MANAGED TO OUT-MANEUVER ME AT LAST!
OH, WELL.. I GUESS I MIGHT AS WELL MEET HER AND GET IT OVER WITH!
SHE MAY NOT BE AS BAD AS I EXPECT!
SHE'LL PROBABLY BE WORSE!
19

PETER PARKER, I'D LIKE YOU TO MEET MY NIECE---
YOU MEAN... THAT'S MARY JANE..?!!
FACE IT, TIGER...
YOU JUST HIT THE JACKPOT!
NOTE: LETTERS PAGE APPEARS AFTER THE NEXT PAGE...
20

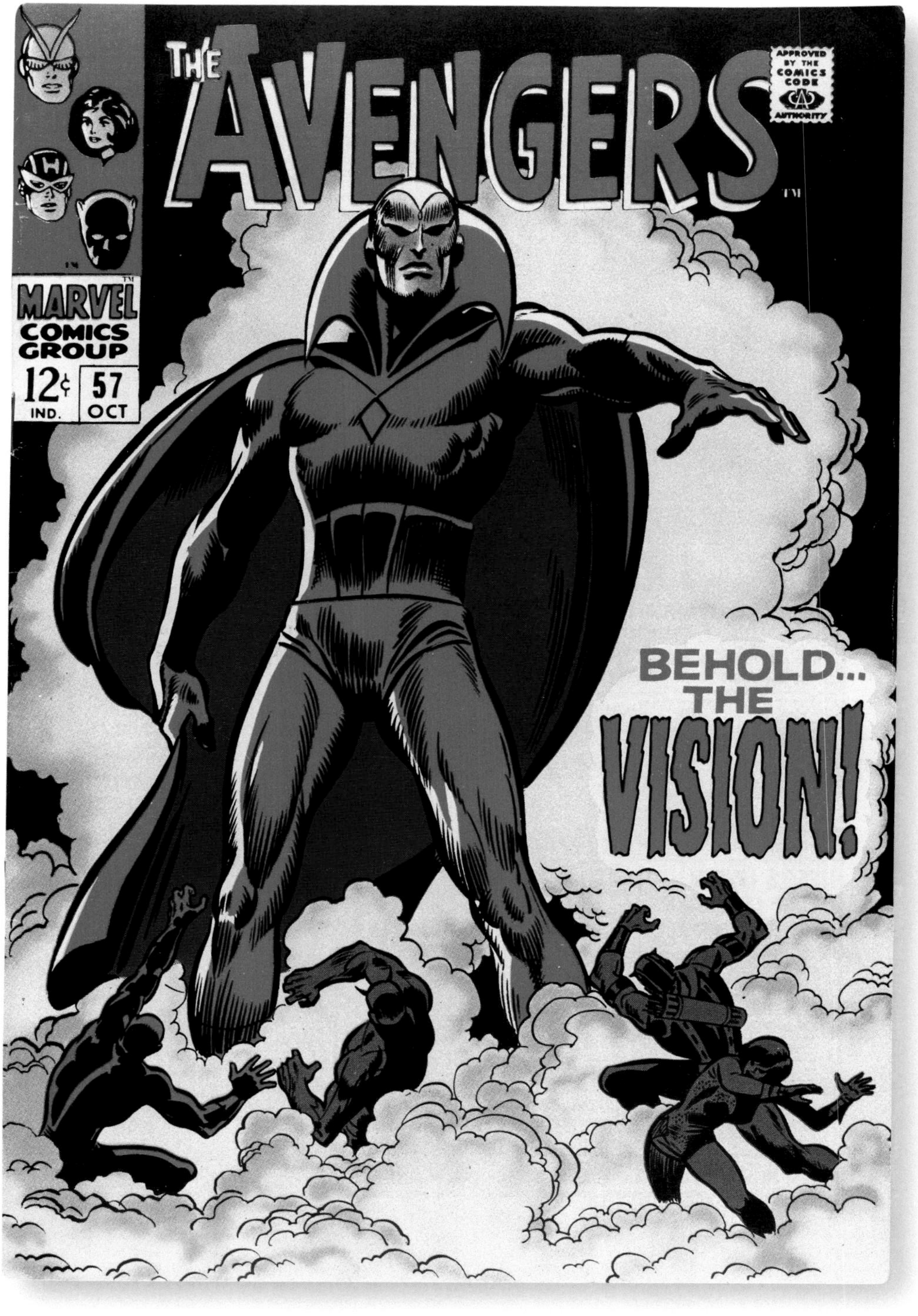
THE AVENGERS
APPROVED BY THE COMICS CODE AUTHORITY
MARVEL COMICS GROUP
12¢ IND.
57 OCT
BEHOLD... THE VISION!

Television soon came sniffing around as well. In 1966 Grantray-Lawrence Animation arranged to rotate Captain America, Iron Man, Thor, the Hulk, and Sub-Mariner in a five-days-a-week series called *Marvel Super-Heroes,* which turned actual art from the comics into (very) limited animation. Spider-Man and Fantastic Four would follow the next year, with somewhat better animation but with less fidelity to the Marvel spirit.

All was not as tranquil at the company, however, as the jaunty prose of the stories, letters pages, and "Bullpen Bulletins" might suggest.

On January 9, 1966, the *New York Herald Tribune* newspaper carried an interview with Lee and Kirby, wherein the reporter played up Lee and casually denigrated Kirby — who blamed Lee for the shabby journalistic treatment. Tensions between artist/coplotter and editor/writer, long swept under the rug, began to bubble increasingly to the surface. Lee soon changed the "writer" and "penciling" credits on their stories to reflect that they were joint "Stan Lee & Jack Kirby productions," without spelling out precisely who did what in a given story, but that only tamped the flames for a little while.

At almost the same time, *Spider-Man* and Dr. Strange artist/cocreator Steve Ditko abruptly announced he was leaving Marvel, for reasons never fully revealed. For some time, Ditko had been credited in print for the full plotting of both series, with Lee merely adding captions and dialogue; for the previous year, after too many arguments over story elements, the two men had ceased any kind of personal interaction. After departing, Ditko drew briefly for Tower, Dell, and Warren. In addition, for DC, he came up with new titles *Beware the Creeper* and *The Hawk and the Dove,* but neither lasted long. He spent most of his time drawing for Charlton.

To John Romita's chagrin, with Ditko's departure, Lee immediately moved him from *Daredevil* to drawing *Amazing Spider-Man.* Starting with *ASM* No. 39 (August 1966), the new creative team pulled out all the stops, revealing the identity of the Green Goblin (the father of Peter Parker's best friend) and, in No. 42's final panel, finally showing the full face (and killer figure) of redhead Mary Jane Watson. Romita's luscious art and her saucy entrance line, addressed to Peter — "Face it, tiger... you just hit the jackpot!" — made that panel one of

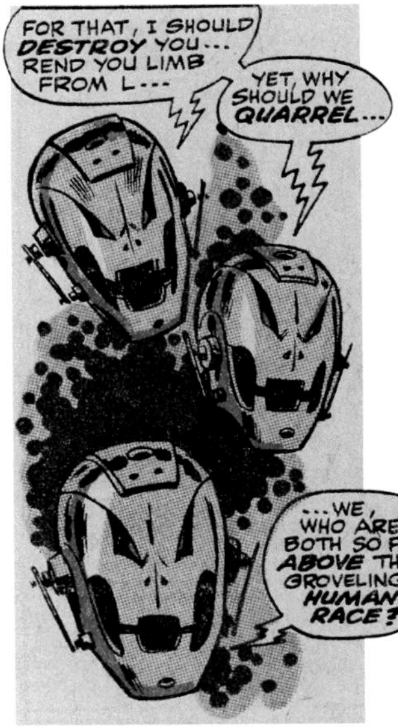
FOR THAT, I SHOULD DESTROY YOU... REND YOU LIMB FROM L---
YET, WHY SHOULD WE QUARREL...
...WE, WHO ARE BOTH SO FAR ABOVE THE GROVELING HUMAN RACE?

THE AVENGERS No. 57
(Opposite) Cover; pencils, John Buscema; inks, George Klein. (Above) Interior, "Behold... the Vision"; script, Roy Thomas; pencils, Buscema; inks, Klein. October 1968. Created by Henry Pym, the robot Ultron-5 goes on to create his *own* android — the Vision. Thomas's Vision, influenced in name and coloration by an obscure 1940s Kirby character, is revealed several years later to be an updated version of the android form of the original Human Torch... although that revelation itself was undermined a few years after that.

MARVEL SUPER-HEROES No. 12
(Right) Cover; pencils, Gene Colan; inks, Frank Giacoia; December 1967. Martin Goodman hated when people thought that Marvel Comics published the original (1940s) Captain Marvel. When the name fell out of copyright, he quickly commissioned Stan Lee to use it. Alien Captain Mar-Vell would be Stan Lee's last hero of this era.

MARVEL SUPER-HEROES
FEATURING:
CAPTAIN MARVEL
APPROVED BY THE COMICS CODE AUTHORITY
MARVEL COMICS GROUP
25¢ IND.
12 DEC
MCG
ALL NEW! NEVER SEEN BEFORE!
"THE COMING OF CAPTAIN MARVEL!"
PLUS: FIVE ALL-TIME GREATS FROM THE GOLDEN AGE!
THE BLACK KNIGHT!
THE DESTROYER!
CAPTAIN AMERICA!
THE HUMAN TORCH!
THE SUB-MARINER!
FACE IT, TIGER! THIS IS THE BIGGEST ONE YET FROM THE HOUSE OF IDEAS!
MARVEL SUPER-HEROES
MARVEL COMICS GROUP

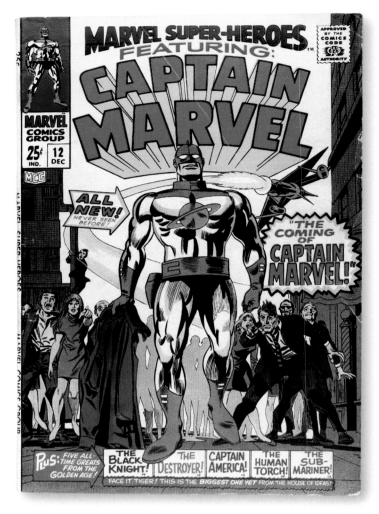

comics' most memorable. At first, Romita attempted to imitate Ditko's style, but his own soon came inevitably to the fore, with Peter and the series' other denizens gradually getting handsomer, prettier...reflecting his years as a romance artist. Over the course of the following year, *Amazing Spider-Man* went from being Marvel's second-best-selling title to its biggest, passing *Fantastic Four*.

MILESTONES AT MID-DECADE

Despite the papered-over friction between Lee and Kirby, however, 1966 also produced the most celebrated *Fantastic Four* story arc ever, in issues No. 48–50. Galactus, a King Kong–size alien, lands in Manhattan intent on absorbing all of Earth's life force for his own sustenance, leaving it a barren husk—and only the uncharacteristic intervention of the Watcher enables the FF to save this world's billions. Just as precedent-shattering as Galactus, however, was the character Jack Kirby added to the story to serve as the destroyer's herald: the Silver Surfer, a shiny-skinned alien who rides from planet to planet on a gleaming surfboard. Readers quickly dubbed this sequence of issues "The Galactus Trilogy," and it set the mark for cosmically oriented storylines from that day forward.

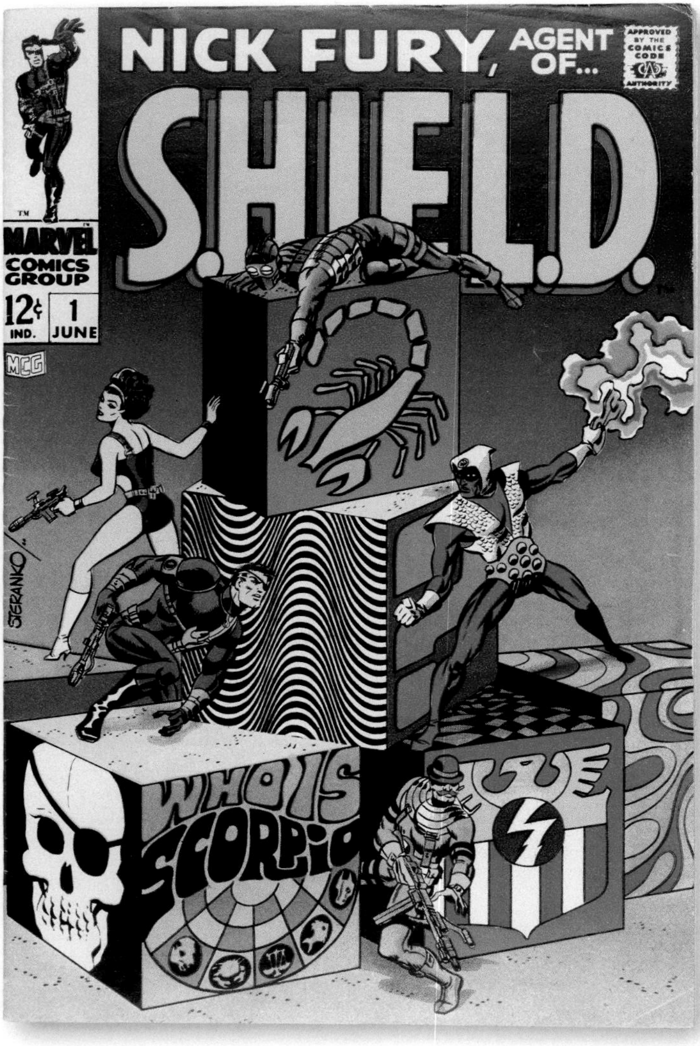

NICK FURY, AGENT OF...
S.H.I.E.L.D.
APPROVED BY THE COMICS CODE AUTHORITY
MARVEL COMICS GROUP
12¢ IND.
1 JUNE
MCG
STERANKO
WHO IS SCORPIO

NICK FURY, AGENT OF S.H.I.E.L.D. No. 1
(Left) Cover; pencils and inks, Jim Steranko; June 1968. Freed from a decade of draconian distribution restrictions, Marvel quickly expands its line, with Nick Fury, Dr. Strange, the Sub-Mariner, the Hulk, Iron Man, and Captain America each receiving his own title.

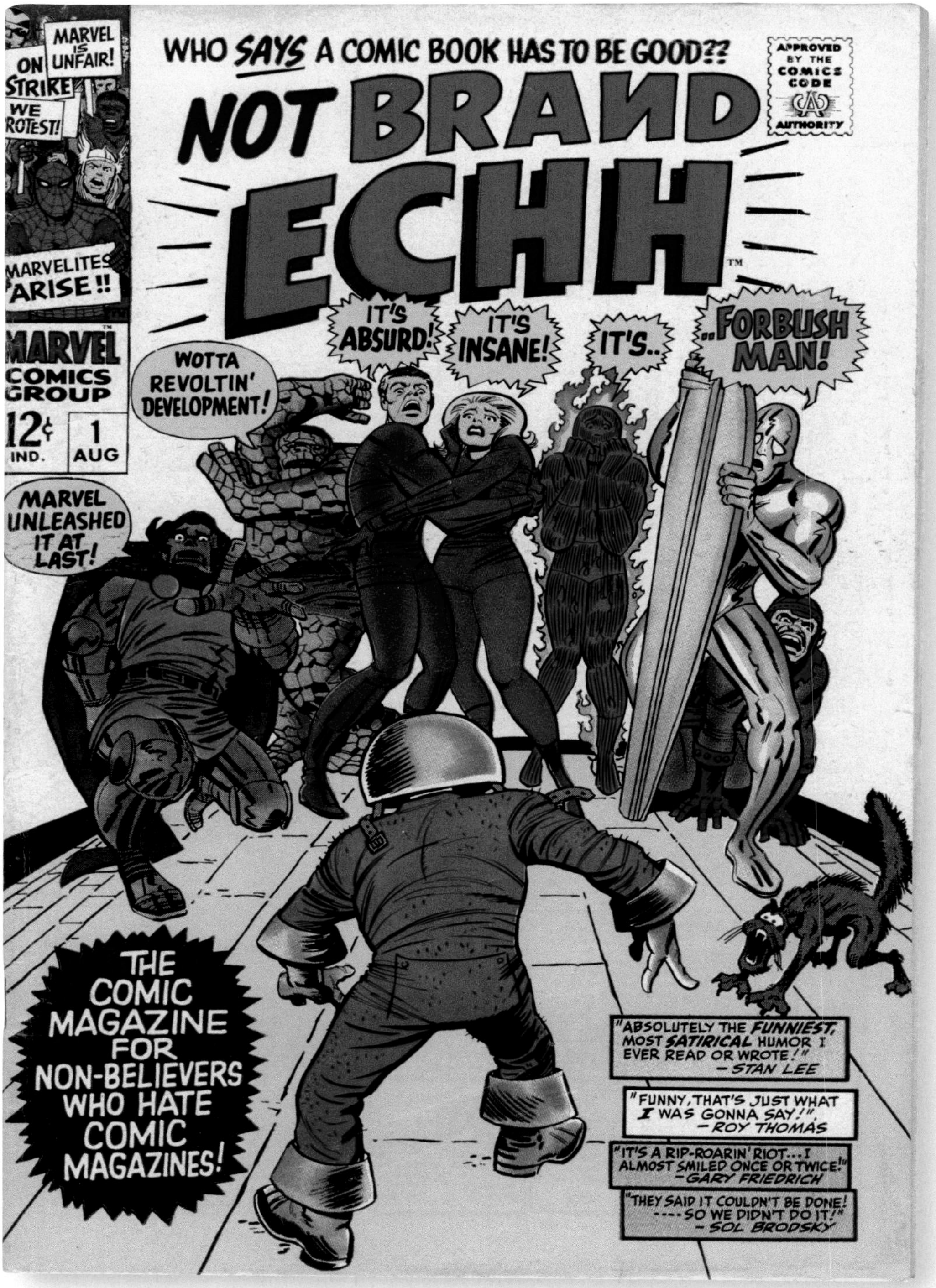
MARVEL IS UNFAIR!
ON STRIKE
WE PROTEST!
MARVELITES ARISE!!
MARVEL COMICS GROUP
12¢ IND.
1 AUG
WHO SAYS A COMIC BOOK HAS TO BE GOOD??
APPROVED BY THE COMICS CODE AUTHORITY
NOT BRAND ECHH
IT'S ABSURD!
IT'S INSANE!
IT'S..
..FORBUSH MAN!
WOTTA REVOLTIN' DEVELOPMENT!
MARVEL UNLEASHED IT AT LAST!
THE COMIC MAGAZINE FOR NON-BELIEVERS WHO HATE COMIC MAGAZINES!
"ABSOLUTELY THE FUNNIEST, MOST SATIRICAL HUMOR I EVER READ OR WROTE!" - STAN LEE
"FUNNY, THAT'S JUST WHAT I WAS GONNA SAY!" - ROY THOMAS
"IT'S A RIP-ROARIN' RIOT... I ALMOST SMILED ONCE OR TWICE!" - GARY FRIEDRICH
"THEY SAID IT COULDN'T BE DONE! ---- SO WE DIDN'T DO IT!" - SOL BRODSKY

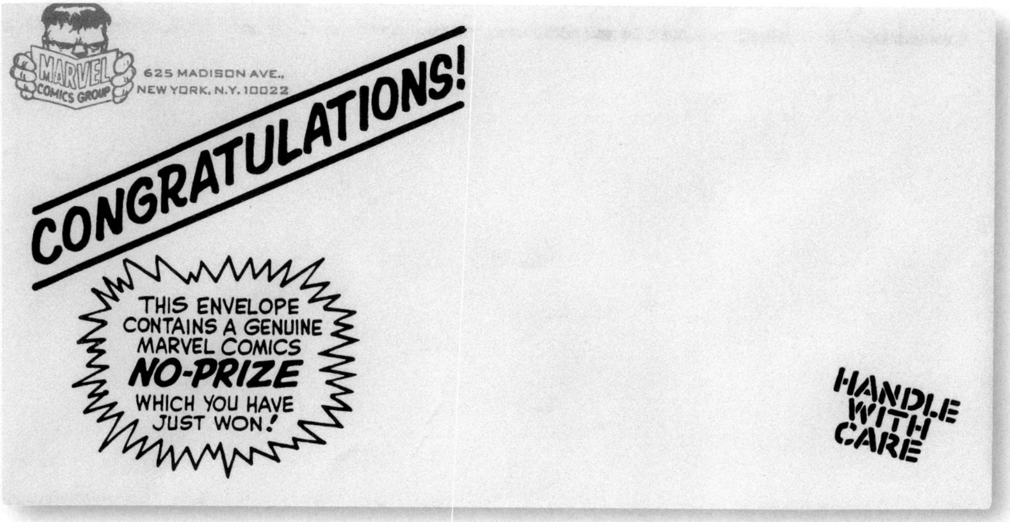
MARVEL COMICS GROUP
625 MADISON AVE., NEW YORK, N.Y. 10022
CONGRATULATIONS!
THIS ENVELOPE CONTAINS A GENUINE MARVEL COMICS NO-PRIZE WHICH YOU HAVE JUST WON!
HANDLE WITH CARE

Only two issues later, the Lee-Kirby team introduced the Black Panther, a super hero who ruled the super-technological African kingdom of Wakanda—and the first black costumed hero in American comic books. In the year's *FF Annual,* the 1940s Human Torch returned just long enough to have a heated battle with his young successor, Johnny Storm.

Lee and Kirby also generated milestones in other Marvel titles in '66: the Red Skull, Captain America's greatest Nazi foe in 1940s stories, returned in full fettle. Thor shared a truly epic adventure with Hercules and the Roman god Pluto, followed by one featuring an entire Living Planet called Ego, just as *Journey into Mystery* was renamed for its Asgardian star. In *The Avengers,* Lee and artist Don Heck introduced the Sons of the Serpent (essentially the Ku Klux Klan in multicolor dress), in a story that went further in dealing with racial and ethnic prejudice than any super hero storyline up to that time.

In the summer of '66, a young writer/artist (and former stage magician) named Jim Steranko showed up at the Marvel offices—and walked away with the assignment to draw the S.H.I.E.L.D. feature, originally over Kirby's layouts but quickly assuming the full penciling and even the writing. While heavily influenced by Kirby, Steranko also brought in visual influences from movies, Op Art, Pop Art, and Daliesque surrealism. He was a new star on the horizon...and the first new artist hired by Goodman's comics company in more than a decade.

BRAND ECHH No. 1
(Opposite) Cover; pencils, Jack Kirby; inks, Mike Esposito; August 1967.

CONGRATULATIONS!
(Above) No-Prize, 1960s. If you caught a mistake in a Marvel comic or your fan letter was published in a comic, you received this wonderful envelope, complete with "no prize" inside. (In other words, it was empty!)

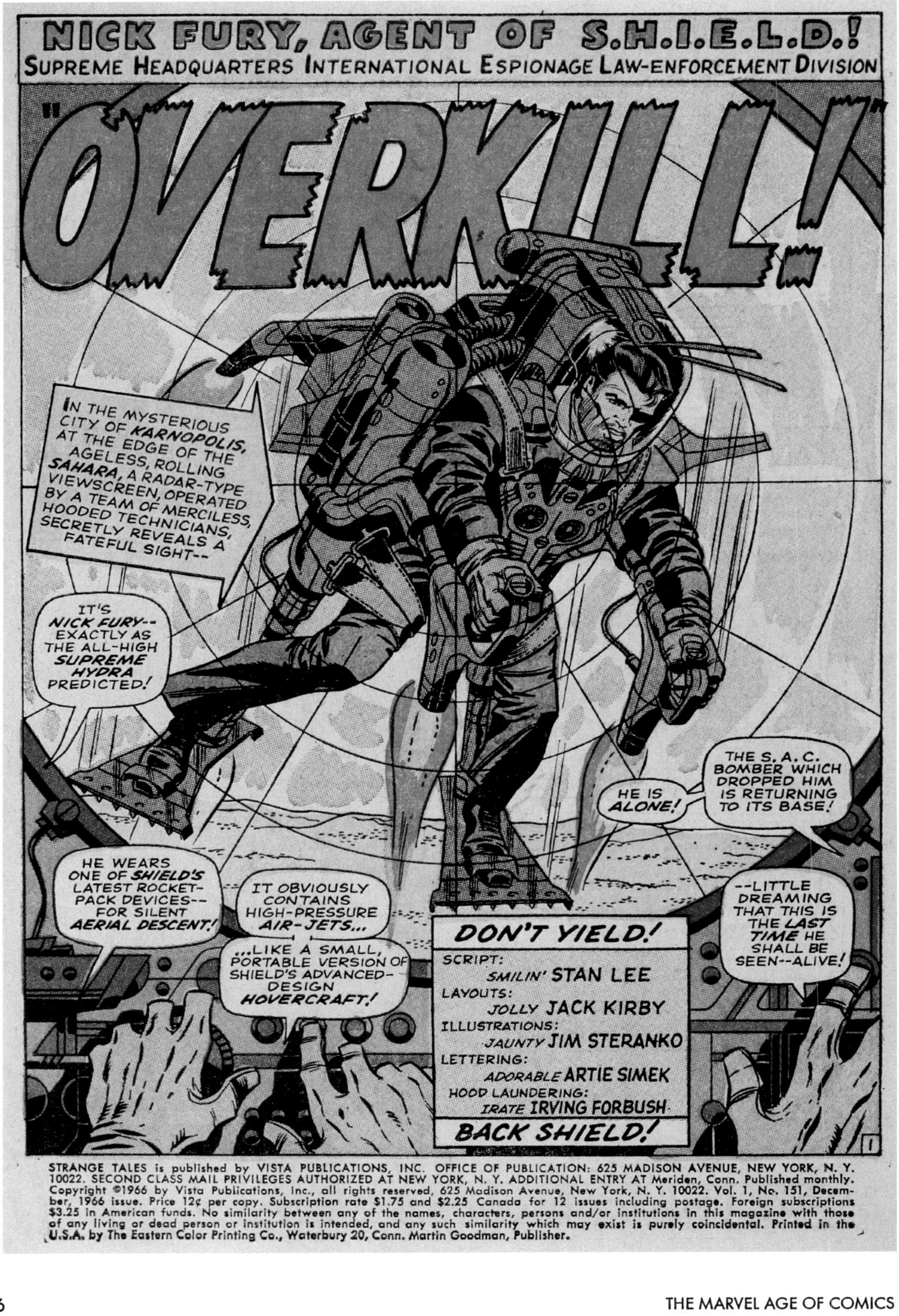
NICK FURY, AGENT OF S.H.I.E.L.D.!
SUPREME HEADQUARTERS INTERNATIONAL ESPIONAGE LAW-ENFORCEMENT DIVISION
"OVERKILL!"
IN THE MYSTERIOUS CITY OF KARNOPOLIS, AT THE EDGE OF THE AGELESS, ROLLING SAHARA, A RADAR-TYPE VIEWSCREEN, OPERATED BY A TEAM OF MERCILESS, HOODED TECHNICIANS, SECRETLY REVEALS A FATEFUL SIGHT--
IT'S NICK FURY--EXACTLY AS THE ALL-HIGH SUPREME HYDRA PREDICTED!
HE IS ALONE!
THE S.A.C. BOMBER WHICH DROPPED HIM IS RETURNING TO ITS BASE!
HE WEARS ONE OF SHIELD'S LATEST ROCKET-PACK DEVICES--FOR SILENT AERIAL DESCENT!
IT OBVIOUSLY CONTAINS HIGH-PRESSURE AIR-JETS...
...LIKE A SMALL, PORTABLE VERSION OF SHIELD'S ADVANCED-DESIGN HOVERCRAFT!
--LITTLE DREAMING THAT THIS IS THE LAST TIME HE SHALL BE SEEN--ALIVE!
DON'T YIELD!
SCRIPT: SMILIN' STAN LEE
LAYOUTS: JOLLY JACK KIRBY
ILLUSTRATIONS: JAUNTY JIM STERANKO
LETTERING: ADORABLE ARTIE SIMEK
HOOD LAUNDERING: IRATE IRVING FORBUSH
BACK SHIELD!
1
STRANGE TALES is published by VISTA PUBLICATIONS, INC. OFFICE OF PUBLICATION: 625 MADISON AVENUE, NEW YORK, N. Y. 10022. SECOND CLASS MAIL PRIVILEGES AUTHORIZED AT NEW YORK, N. Y. ADDITIONAL ENTRY AT Meriden, Conn. Published monthly. Copyright ©1966 by Vista Publications, Inc., all rights reserved, 625 Madison Avenue, New York, N. Y. 10022. Vol. 1, No. 151, December, 1966 issue. Price 12¢ per copy. Subscription rate $1.75 and $2.25 Canada for 12 issues including postage. Foreign subscriptions $3.25 in American funds. No similarity between any of the names, characters, persons and/or institutions in this magazine with those of any living or dead person or institution is intended, and any such similarity which may exist is purely coincidental. Printed in the U.S.A. by The Eastern Color Printing Co., Waterbury 20, Conn. Martin Goodman, Publisher.

One veteran artist who returned around this time was John Buscema, a burly bear of a man who'd left comics for advertising but had now changed his mind. He despised drawing super heroes and cityscapes (two Marvel staples), and it took him a few tryout stories—and a month or two of working over those ever-helpful Kirby layouts—to learn what Stan Lee wanted in terms of storytelling and action. But he was a fast learner. Soon he was teamed up with relative newcomer writer Roy Thomas on *The Avengers*; together they would cocreate the Red Guardian (a Russian response to Captain America), the Vision (an android Avenger based visually on an early Simon and Kirby hero in *Marvel Mystery Comics*), Ultron (a living robot dedicated to conquering the human race), and Yellowjacket (the latest incarnation of Ant-Man/Giant-Man, who finally married the Wasp).

The M.M.M.S. continued to grow, though with less emphasis placed on it in the mags than before; even so, T-shirts, sweatshirts, posters, and the like proliferated. Lee inaugurated a "forensic new feature" on the "Bullpen Bulletins" page: "Stan's Soapbox," in which he would address the reader in first person, writing about whatever he felt like talking about that month. In addition, for some time, he had used letters sections to award verbal "No-Prizes" to readers who spotted a mistake in a story or made some similar deathless contribution. Now, actual No-Prize envelopes were printed up and mailed—though of course the envelopes were completely empty. Well, what else should Marvel fans have expected from a "No-Prize?"

STRANGE TALES No. 151

(Opposite) Interior, "Overkill!"; script, Stan Lee; layouts, Jack Kirby; finished art, Jim Steranko; December 1966. Take a deep breath as Steranko enters the picture. Marvel's Universe will never be the same!

STRANGE TALES No. 159

(Below) Interior, "Spy School!"; script, pencils, and inks, Jim Steranko; August 1967. "I look at Kirby as being the architect, Steranko building the framework, and the rest of us doing the finish work," artist Paul Gulacy described Steranko's impact in 2009. Steranko was the first artist at Marvel allowed to both write and draw a super hero series. As a result, his stories began to flow differently, becoming more like an—as-yet-unnamed—"graphic novel."

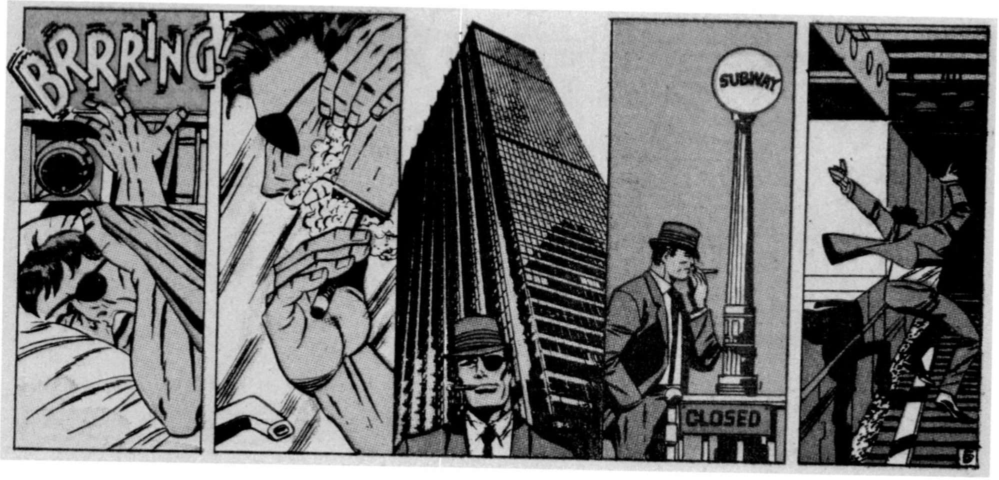
BRRRING!
SUBWAY
CLOSED

SILVER SURFER No. 4
(Opposite) Cover; pencils, John Buscema; inks, Sal Buscema; February 1969.
"Like Jack Kirby before him, John thought big as an artist, but where Jack's imagination was without bounds, John always anchored his in a very physical sense of reality. His figurework was superb, his layouts and storytelling were efficient and expansive, and his world-building was as solid as the ground under our feet."
— Gerry Conway

If milestones were perhaps slightly fewer and farther between at this juncture, they nonetheless existed. Surprisingly, Nurse Jane Foster was replaced overnight as Thor / Don Blake's love interest by the goddess Sif, who in Norse myth was the thunder god's wife... Steranko went from strength to strength on S.H.I.E.L.D., with each issue a new treat for the eye... new writer Gary Friedrich spun offbeat war yarns in *Sgt. Fury*, in tandem with artists Dick Ayers and John Severin... *Not Brand Echh* parodied both Marvel's own heroes and those of the competition and quickly became a showcase for the breakout humorous artistry of Marie Severin... "Wild Bill" Everett returned to drawing the Sub-Mariner strip he'd originated in 1939... Archie Goodwin, respected editor and writer of Warren's black-and-white horror mags, began scripting for Marvel... one-time prominent Timely/Atlas artists George Tuska and Syd Shores rejoined the company...

...and Marvel finally launched its own *Captain Marvel*. After the demise of the campy Burgos character and even a lawsuit or two between its publisher and Marvel, Goodman decided it was time Marvel itself acquired rights to that once-iconic moniker. Reportedly, a TV producer suggested that Goodman develop a science-fictional hero with that name so he could be licensed. If that's true, nothing ever came of any possible TV deal, but Lee worked with artist Gene Colan to create a super hero who was one of the Kree, an alien race recently introduced in *Fantastic Four*. The spaceman's given name was Mar-Vell, and his Kree military rank was, of course, Captain.

FREE AT LAST!

Around this time, DC Comics and its distribution arm, Independent News, were purchased by the conglomerate Kinney National. Now part of a larger corporation, Independent had new incentive to seek to increase its profits, so it allowed Marvel to add even further to its number of titles. Marvel responded in 1968 by splitting the three remaining "anthology" comics — *Tales of Suspense*, *Tales to Astonish*, and *Strange Tales* — into six solo-hero mags: *Iron Man*; *Captain America*; *Sub-Mariner*; *The Incredible Hulk*; *Nick Fury, Agent of S.H.I.E.L.D.*; and *Doctor Strange*. Simultaneously, the company also launched *Captain Marvel* and a second war title, *Captain Savage and His Leatherneck Raiders*.

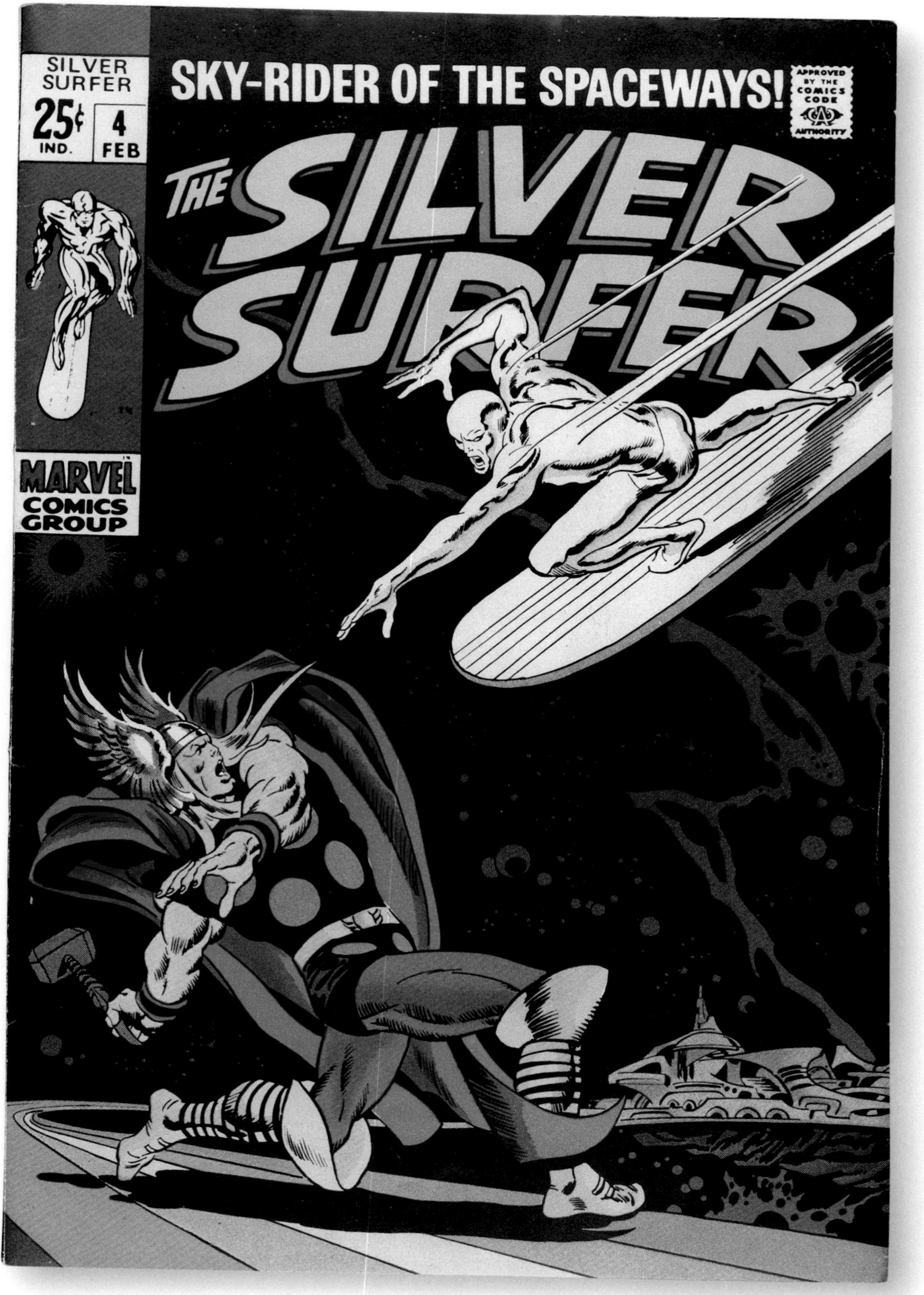
SILVER SURFER
25¢ IND.
4 FEB
SKY-RIDER OF THE SPACEWAYS!
APPROVED BY THE COMICS CODE AUTHORITY
THE SILVER SURFER
MARVEL COMICS GROUP

STRANGE TALES No. 164

(Right) Interior, "Nightmare!"; script, Jim Lawrence; pencils and inks, Dan Adkins; January 1968. After Ditko's exit, many talented artists continued to experiment with Dr. Strange's visual mindscape, like Bill Everett, Marie Severin, and Dan Adkins.

TOWER OF SHADOWS No. 1

(Opposite) Cover; pencils and inks, John Romita; September 1969. The mystery-anthology format was popular at the time, perhaps inspired by the phenomenal ratings of the supernatural daytime soap opera *Dark Shadows*.

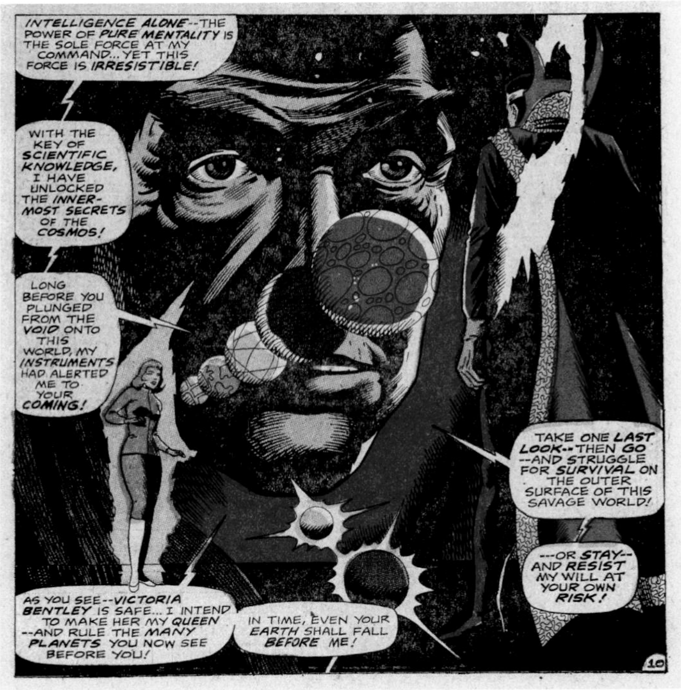
INTELLIGENCE ALONE--THE POWER OF PURE MENTALITY IS THE SOLE FORCE AT MY COMMAND... YET THIS FORCE IS IRRESISTIBLE!
WITH THE KEY OF SCIENTIFIC KNOWLEDGE, I HAVE UNLOCKED THE INNER-MOST SECRETS OF THE COSMOS!
LONG BEFORE YOU PLUNGED FROM THE VOID ONTO THIS WORLD, MY INSTRUMENTS HAD ALERTED ME TO YOUR COMING!
TAKE ONE LAST LOOK--THEN GO --AND STRUGGLE FOR SURVIVAL ON THE OUTER SURFACE OF THIS SAVAGE WORLD!
---OR STAY-- AND RESIST MY WILL AT YOUR OWN RISK!
AS YOU SEE--VICTORIA BENTLEY IS SAFE... I INTEND TO MAKE HER MY QUEEN --AND RULE THE MANY PLANETS YOU NOW SEE BEFORE YOU!
IN TIME, EVEN YOUR EARTH SHALL FALL BEFORE ME!

Following soon afterward was *The Silver Surfer*, done as an extra-length comic. Surprisingly, however, instead of assigning Kirby as its artist, Lee realized that he and Kirby had divergent views on how to handle the Surfer, whom Galactus had exiled to Earth after he turned against his master; so he tapped John Buscema as penciler. The latter's flawless draftsmanship spurred Lee to new heights of grandiloquent language and philosophizing. Older readers, in particular, heaped praise on the magazine. *Silver Surfer* No. 3 introduced Mephisto, an other-dimensional stand-in for Satan, whose attempts to persuade the Surfer to join him echoed the Temptation of Christ in the Gospels. Issue No. 4, wherein the gleaming alien journeys to Asgard to battle Thor, represents yet another apex of Marvel art—for a second issue in a row.

Marvel was achieving other highs in quality around that time, too. Steranko had turned the full-length *Agent of S.H.I.E.L.D.* title into a one-man tour de force (except for the mag's inkers), though he soon left the title due to the difficulty of producing 20 pages of art and story a month on top of his day job as a commercial artist. Thomas, Colan, and inker/

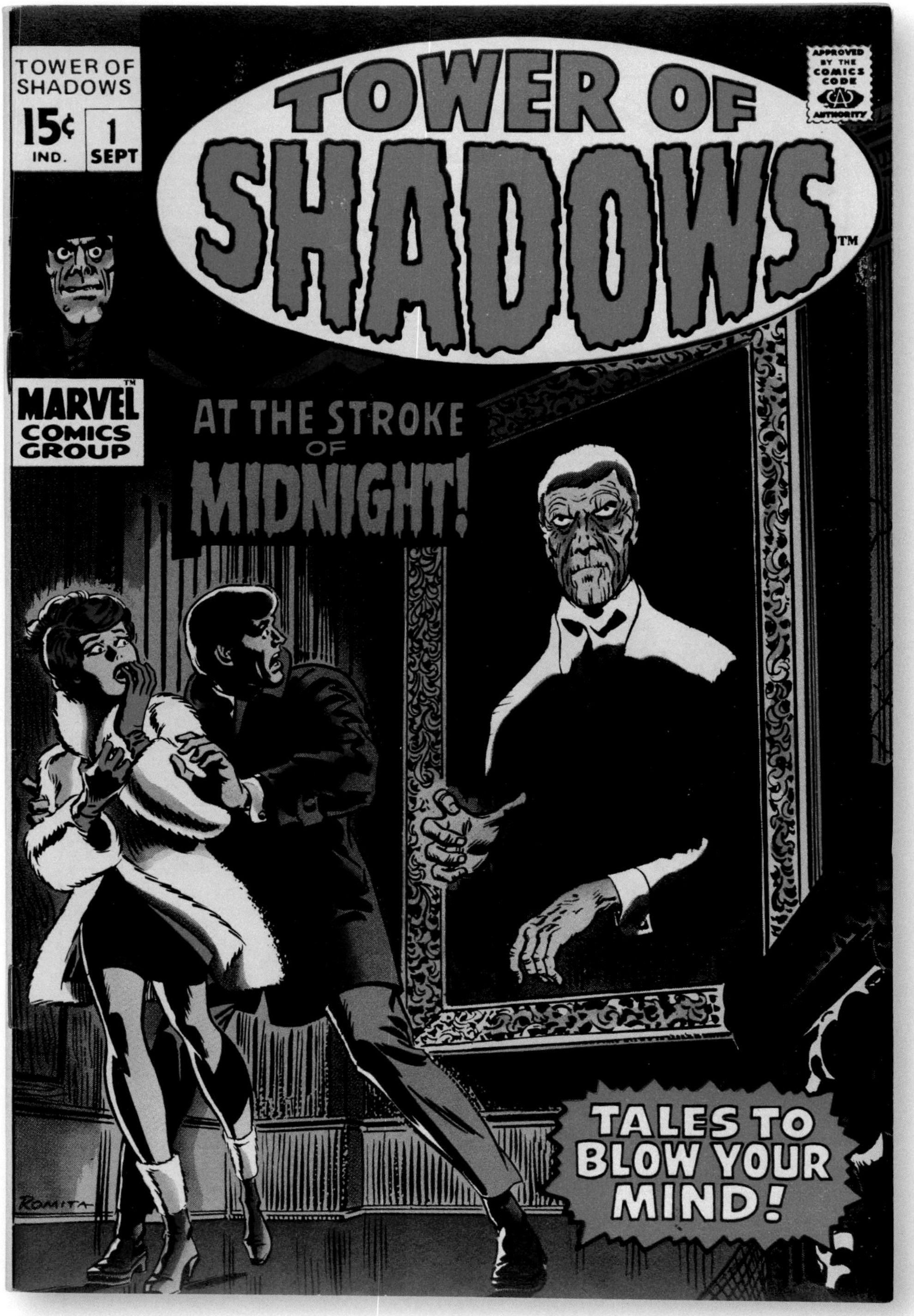
TOWER OF SHADOWS
15¢
IND.
1
SEPT
APPROVED BY THE COMICS CODE AUTHORITY
TOWER OF SHADOWS™
MARVEL™
COMICS GROUP
AT THE STROKE OF MIDNIGHT!
TALES TO BLOW YOUR MIND!
ROMITA

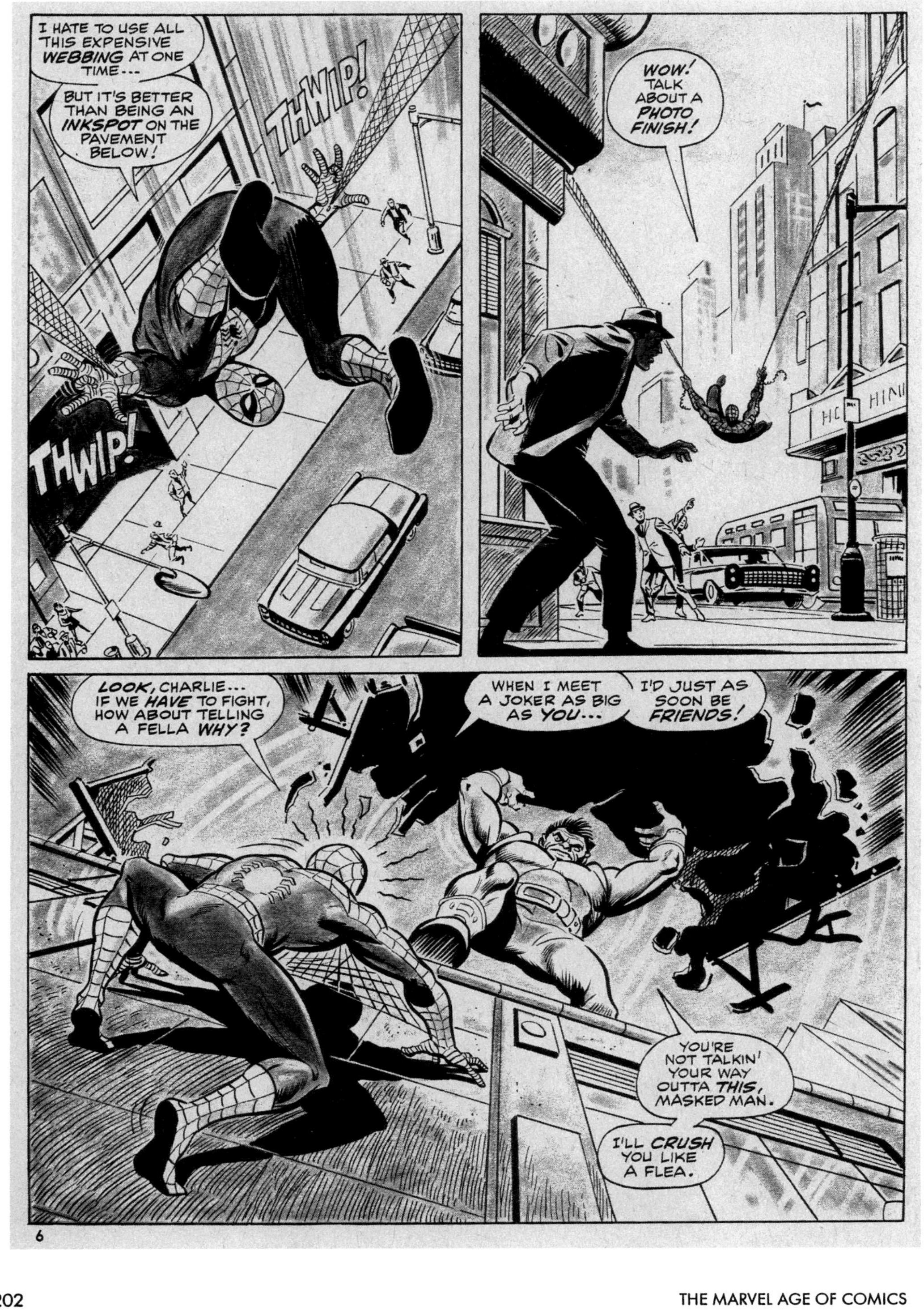

I HATE TO USE ALL THIS EXPENSIVE WEBBING AT ONE TIME---
BUT IT'S BETTER THAN BEING AN INKSPOT ON THE PAVEMENT BELOW!
THWIP!
THWIP!
WOW! TALK ABOUT A PHOTO FINISH!
LOOK, CHARLIE... IF WE HAVE TO FIGHT, HOW ABOUT TELLING A FELLA WHY?
WHEN I MEET A JOKER AS BIG AS YOU...
I'D JUST AS SOON BE FRIENDS!
YOU'RE NOT TALKIN' YOUR WAY OUTTA THIS, MASKED MAN.
I'LL CRUSH YOU LIKE A FLEA.
6

colorist Tom Palmer transformed *Dr. Strange* into an artistic showcase, moving it for the first time beyond slavish imitation of Ditko. And the phenomenally talented young Neal Adams, the first new artist hired by DC in a decade, began drawing the ailing *X-Men* title for Marvel. His bravura style married violent action to a heightened realism that emphasized detailed faces and volcanic emotions. With Thomas scripts and Palmer inks, the trio quickly made the mutant comic one of Marvel's most noteworthy, although the sales improved only slowly.

A less splashy new arrival was the Guardians of the Galaxy, a team originally composed of a time-displaced

MARVEL SUPER-HEROES
25¢ IND.
18 JAN
MARVEL SUPER-HEROES!
PRESENTS:
GUARDIANS
OF THE GALAXY
MARVEL COMICS GROUP
MARVEL SUPER-HEROES
MARVEL COMICS GROUP

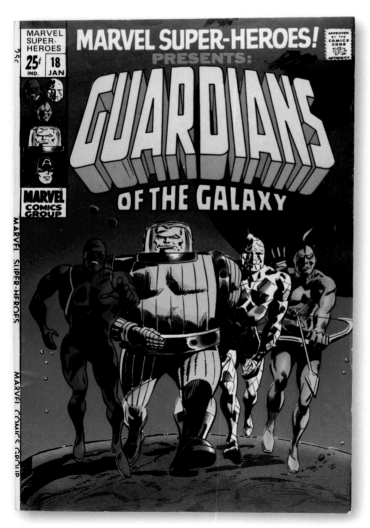

THE SPECTACULAR SPIDER-MAN No. 1
(Opposite) Interior, "Lo, This Monster!"; script, Stan Lee; art, John Romita and Jim Mooney; July 1968. Lee was eager to break out of the standard comic book format, with *Spectacular Spider-Man* planned as the first in a line of high-quality magazines featuring higher production values — and real advertisers such as Kawasaki Motorcycles. Unfortunately, Goodman had second thoughts and the title was both converted to color and canceled with the second issue.

MARVEL SUPER-HEROES No. 18
(Left) Cover; pencils, Gene Colan; inks, Mike Esposito; January 1969. A thousand years in the future, four men from vastly different planets unite to fight their common oppressors. They are the Guardians of the Galaxy.

MY LOVE No. 1 & OUR LOVE STORY No. 1
(Right and opposite) Covers; art, John Romita; September and October 1969. After toiling away on scores of DC romances in the 1950s, Romita was well-prepared to cover Marvel's short-lived romance revival.

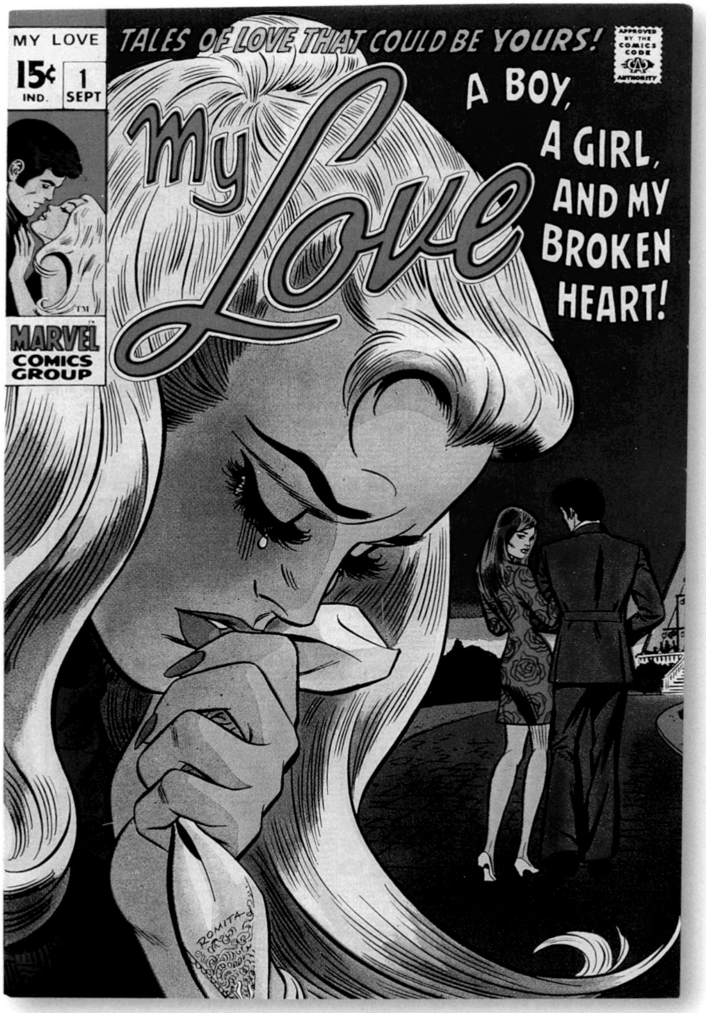
MY LOVE
15¢
IND.
1
SEPT
TALES OF LOVE THAT COULD BE YOURS!
APPROVED BY THE COMICS CODE AUTHORITY
My Love
A BOY, A GIRL, AND MY BROKEN HEART!
MARVEL COMICS GROUP
ROMITA

human explorer and three colorful aliens fighting the worlds-conquering Badoon from *Silver Surfer* No. 2. The series had a one-shot tryout story in the partly-reprint *Marvel Super-Heroes* No. 18 (December 1967), courtesy of writer Arnold Drake (creator of DC's Doom Patrol super hero team) and artist Gene Colan. This "science-fiction version of the group from the movie *Dirty Dozen*," as one Internet blogger called it, would metamorphose into a more popular form a decade later.

Lee also persuaded the reluctant Goodman to venture into the realm of non-Comics-Code-approved black-and-white "magazines"—which were actually still comic books, with slightly larger pages. This field had been pioneered in the mid-1960s by Warren Publishing's *Creepy* and *Eerie*. Lee and Romita produced *The Spectacular Spider-Man Magazine* No. 1 (1968). By its second issue, however, the publication had added color and had become basically an enlarged edition of *Amazing Spider-Man*. Moreover, Goodman probably got grief from his fellow publishers in the Comics Magazine Association of America for putting out a comic book without the Code seal, which might have led to repercussions among retailers and the public at large. There was no third issue.

That year, Martin Goodman sold Magazine Management, including Marvel Comics, to a conglomerate. Since the buyer, Perfect Film & Chemical Corporation, had also recently

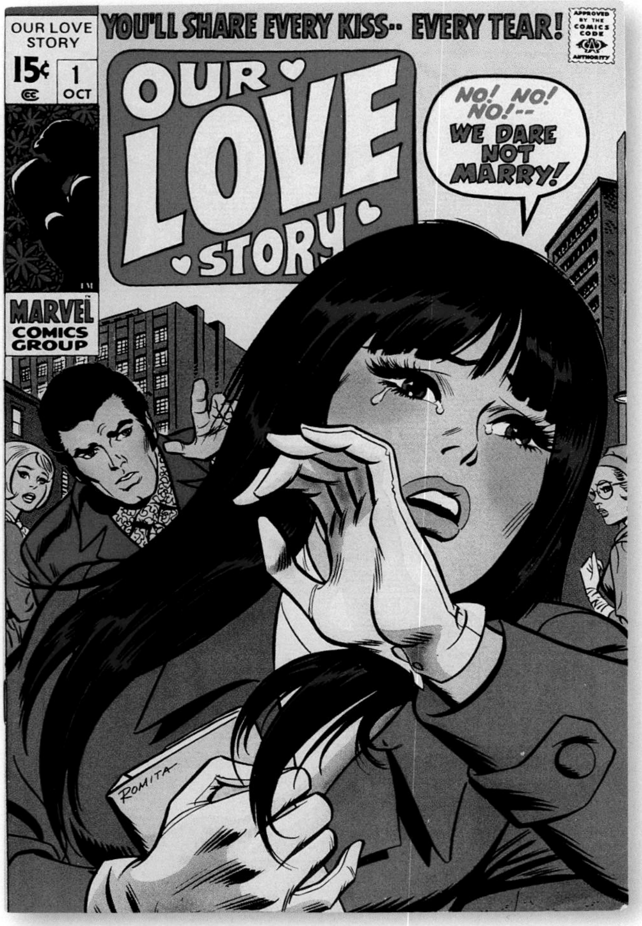
OUR LOVE STORY
15¢
1 OCT
YOU'LL SHARE EVERY KISS-- EVERY TEAR!
APPROVED BY THE COMICS CODE AUTHORITY
OUR LOVE STORY
NO! NO! NO!-- WE DARE NOT MARRY!
MARVEL COMICS GROUP
ROMITA

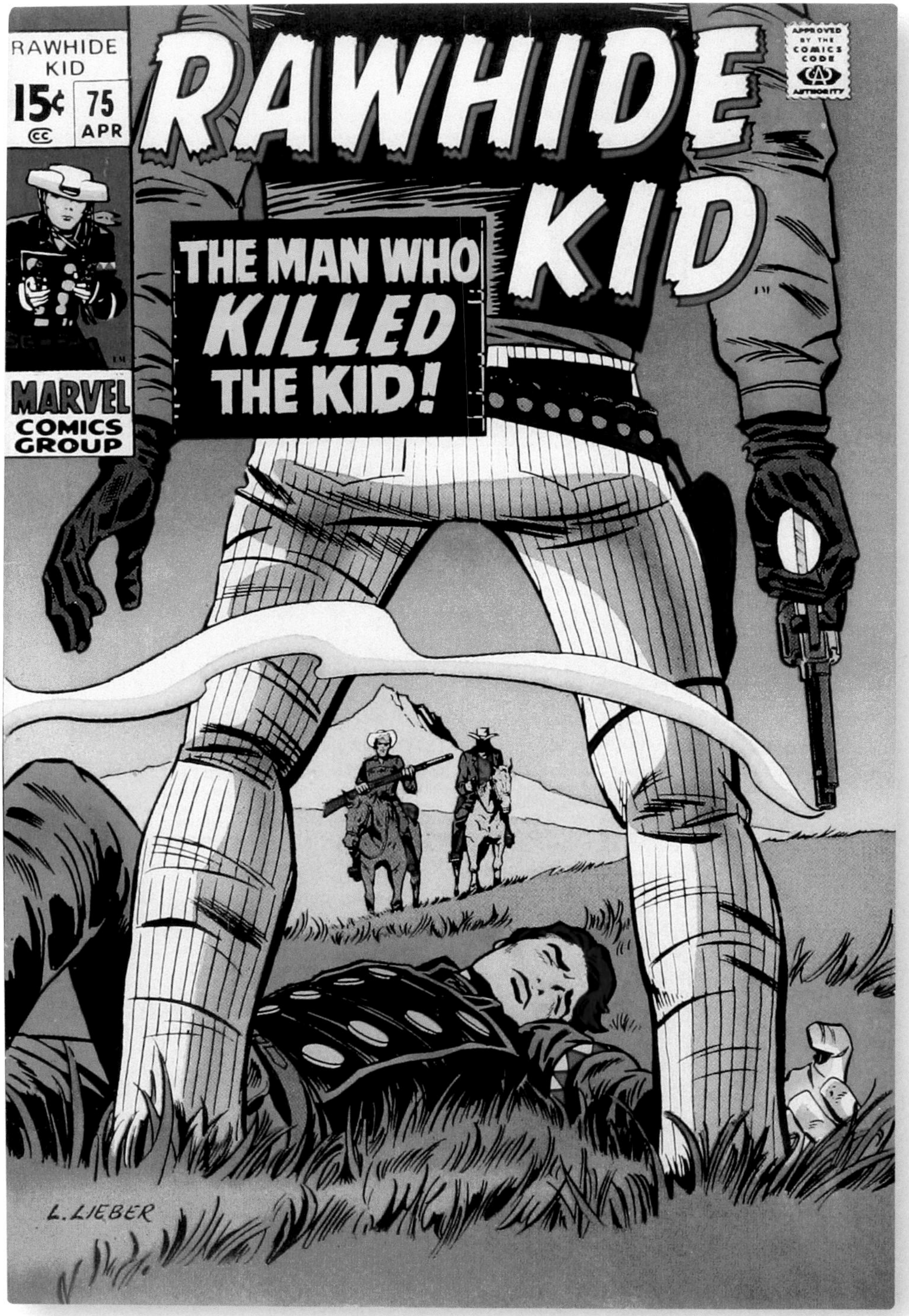
RAWHIDE KID
15¢
75
APR
CC
RAWHIDE KID
APPROVED BY THE COMICS CODE AUTHORITY
THE MAN WHO KILLED THE KID!
MARVEL COMICS GROUP
L. LIEBER

acquired a distribution arm, Curtis Circulation, the handwriting was on the wall: As soon as its contract expired, Marvel's titles would no longer be distributed by a company owned by its largest competitor. Goodman, asked to stay on as publisher, began grooming his son, Charles (Chip), to succeed him. The sale, reportedly for $15 million, was made contingent upon Stan Lee signing a several-year contract; Perfect Film was determined not to lose the man it saw as the mastermind behind Marvel, since the comics were the major reason for its purchase. To Jack Kirby's chagrin, no similar arrangements were made with him. Perfect Film would soon change its name, becoming Cadence Industries.

Unfortunately, the timing of Marvel's increase in number of titles had been poor. Whether the reason was pure overexpansion or perhaps the increasing campus turmoil over the Vietnam War and civil rights (which gave students something other than super hero fantasies to think about), the entire industry suffered a sales downturn in 1968 — Marvel's first since the upsurge begun seven years earlier. *Dr. Strange*, *S.H.I.E.L.D.*, *Not Brand Echh*, and *Captain Savage* were all canceled in 1969, replaced by reprints of 1950s Western and kiddie comics. *X-Men*, *Silver Surfer*, and *Captain Marvel* (despite a major overhaul by writer Thomas and artist Gil Kane, this time under his own name) would follow them in 1970. Mercifully, for most of these seven titles, the oblivion would be only temporary.

Stan Lee argued to Goodman that, though super heroes might have peaked, Marvel should try putting out comics in other genres. His reasoning resonated with the publisher. *Tower of Shadows* No. 1 (September 1969) became the company's first new "mystery" series in a decade, with *Chamber of Darkness* swiftly following. These were developed to compete with DC's successful line of mystery titles, but Marvel was by now so geared toward recurring characters that it lavished insufficient attention on these two outliers, which were soon relegated to reprinting giant-monster yarns. With *My Love* No. 1 (also September 1969), Lee even experimented to see if a romance comic drawn by Marvel's star artists (Romita, Buscema, Steranko, Colan, Heck, et al.) might sell. However, neither it nor sister title *Our Love Story* created much of a ripple. *Spoof*, a color *Mad* wannabe, went nowhere; neither did

RAWHIDE KID No. 75
(Opposite) Cover; pencils and inks, Larry Lieber; April 1970.

CAPTAIN AMERICA No. 117

(Right) Interior, "The Coming of the Falcon!"; script, Stan Lee; pencils, Gene Colan; inks, Joe Sinnott; September 1969. Sam Wilson was the Falcon, Harlem's airborne defender. Wilson was Marvel's second black super hero — but the first African *American*, as the Black Panther was from the fictional African nation of Wakanda. The Falcon would team up with Captain America just in time to embark on the new decade's "relevant" comic book adventures.

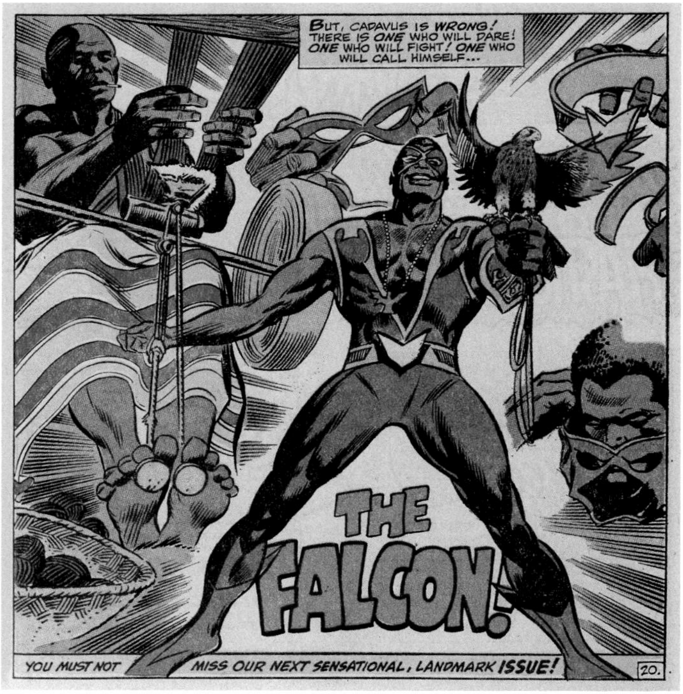
BUT, CADAVUS IS WRONG! THERE IS ONE WHO WILL DARE! ONE WHO WILL FIGHT! ONE WHO WILL CALL HIMSELF...
THE FALCON!
YOU MUST NOT MISS OUR NEXT SENSATIONAL, LANDMARK ISSUE!
20.

a new multistory cowboy comic (*Western Gunfighters*) or an Archie-style teenager (*Harvey*).

Readers reserved their adrenaline rushes during this period for such events as Lee and Steranko teaming up on *Captain America*. After three issues, however, Steranko basically left mainstream comics, except for drawing the occasional cover. To keep the favorable buzz about Cap going, Lee and replacement artist Colan introduced the Falcon, the first African American super hero, as the Star-Spangled Avenger's partner. The Falcon, who would later gain artificial wings, was "dedicated to protecting the people of Harlem." Lee and fledgling artist Herb Trimpe meanwhile turned around the dipping sales of *The Incredible Hulk* and started it on a long march upward.

Meanwhile, the Merry Marvel Marching Society had been allowed to languish; and in 1969, Chip Goodman (now Marvel's "editorial director" under his father) sold merchandising rights to the company's characters to California mail-order businessman Don Wallace. The M.M.M.S. was folded into a new and independent company, Marvelmania, which began churning out posters, art portfolios, sweatshirts, and the like. *Marvelmania* even became the name of a new fan magazine published by Wallace to plug the heroes—and, of course, the merchandise. Edited by Mark Evanier (the fan who'd once suggested that M.M.M.S. members be given ranks), it sadly lasted only seven issues in 1970–71. Unfortunately, Marvelmania ultimately proved far too ambitious an undertaking, and the whole enterprise collapsed.

KIRBY NO MORE

Lee, for his part, was too busy dreaming up new comics projects to concern himself overmuch with fan clubs. He felt it was time, after two years, to revive the concept of the "anthology" comic containing two super hero features. *Astonishing Tales* No. 1

THE INCREDIBLE HULK No. 108

(Below) Interior, "Monster Triumphant!"; script, Stan Lee; layouts, Marie Severin; pencils, Herb Trimpe; inks, John Severin; October 1968. The arrival of Vietnam vet Herb Trimpe began a virtually unbroken seven-year run, leading the emerald giant to a new level of acclaim in the 1970s.

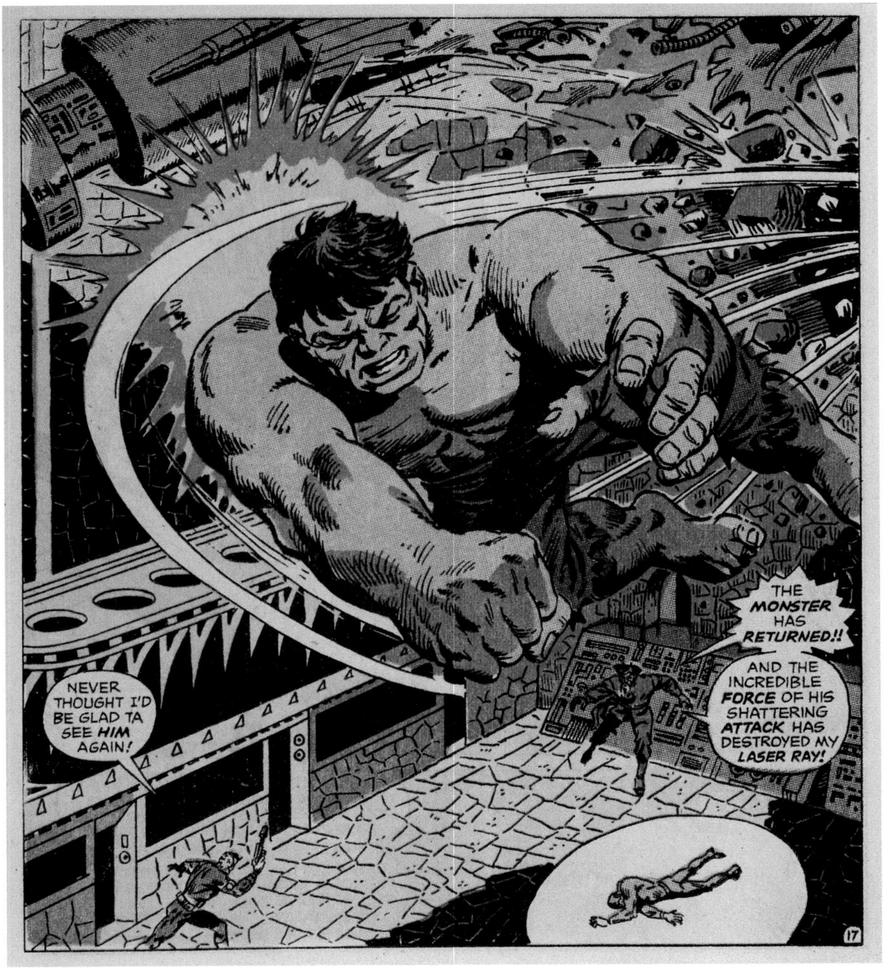
THE MONSTER HAS RETURNED!!
AND THE INCREDIBLE FORCE OF HIS SHATTERING ATTACK HAS DESTROYED MY LASER RAY!
NEVER THOUGHT I'D BE GLAD TA SEE HIM AGAIN!
17

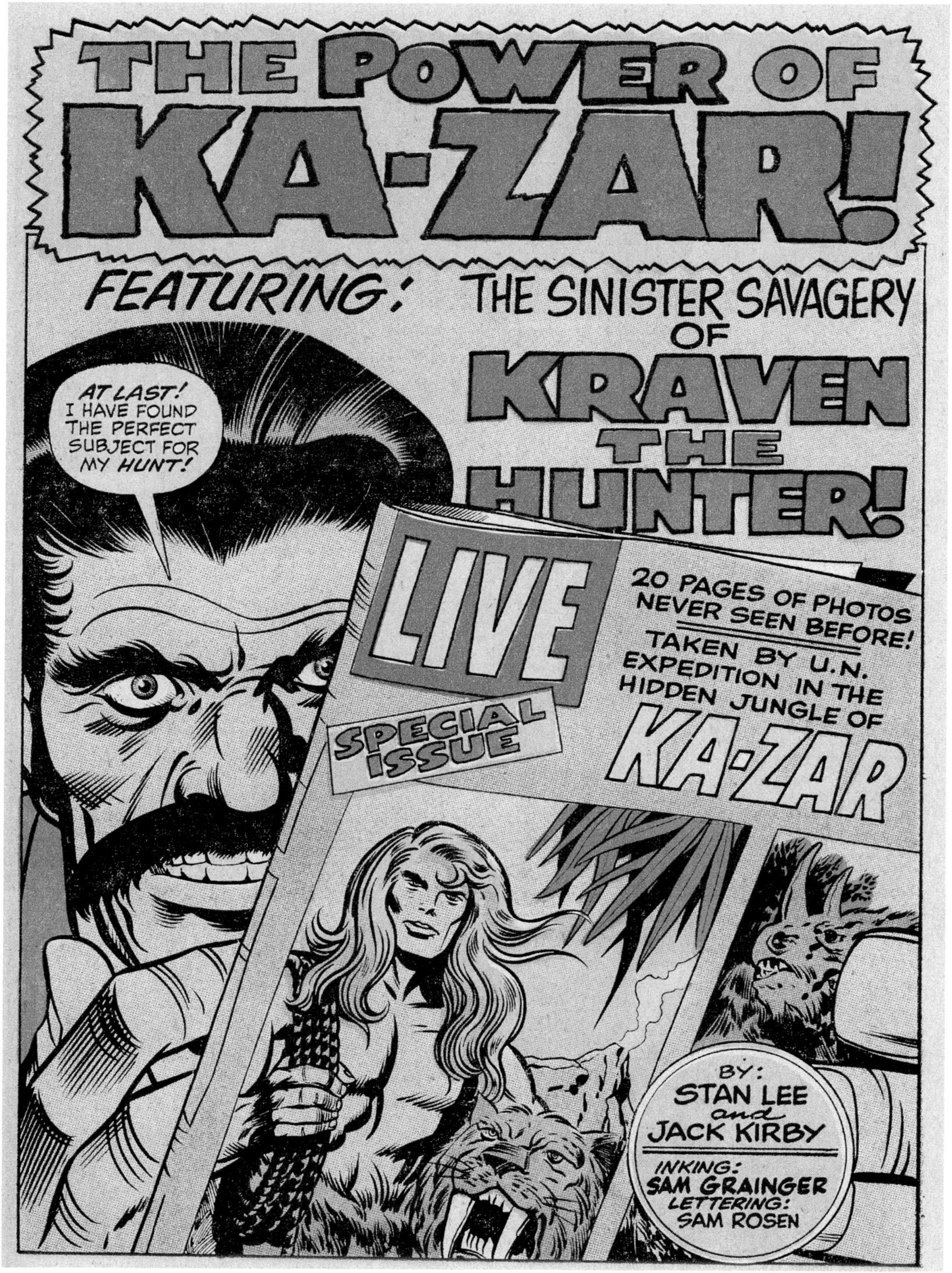
THE POWER OF KA-ZAR!
FEATURING: THE SINISTER SAVAGERY OF KRAVEN THE HUNTER!
AT LAST! I HAVE FOUND THE PERFECT SUBJECT FOR MY HUNT!
LIVE
SPECIAL ISSUE
20 PAGES OF PHOTOS NEVER SEEN BEFORE!
TAKEN BY U.N. EXPEDITION IN THE HIDDEN JUNGLE OF
KA-ZAR
BY: STAN LEE and JACK KIRBY
INKING: SAM GRAINGER
LETTERING: SAM ROSEN

teamed Lee and Kirby on Ka-Zar, while Wally Wood drew Dr. Doom, the first Marvel series to star an out-and-out villain. A new *Amazing Adventures* No. 1 showcased the Russian-spy-turned-costumed-heroine Black Widow and an Inhumans series penciled *and* written by Kirby. Lee hoped that having Kirby handle both aspects of a feature on a continuing basis would keep his disgruntled key artist contented... but it was too late for that.

In fact, while working on stories for the second issues of the two new anthologies, Kirby, who had moved to California a year earlier, had the last of several unpleasant run-ins with Perfect Film. Rejecting the contract he was offered, Kirby instead signed one with DC Comics, which was now spearheaded by an old friend of his, master artist Carmine Infantino.

Lee was, of course, downhearted at Kirby's departure. However, there were still comic books to be put out—and someone had to try to fill Kirby's very big shoes. Just as he'd done when Ditko had left, Lee immediately threw John Romita

ASTONISHING TALES No. 1

(Opposite) Interior, "The Power of Ka-Zar!"; script, Stan Lee; pencils, Jack Kirby; inks, Sam Grainger; August 1970.

THE INHUMANS ARE COMING!

(Below) House ad; art, Jack Kirby, John Romita, and Chic Stone; lettering, Sam Rosen; August 1970. 1970 saw a short-lived return to the split-book format, with Black Widow becoming the first female hero to be awarded her own strip since the jungle queens of the 1950s.

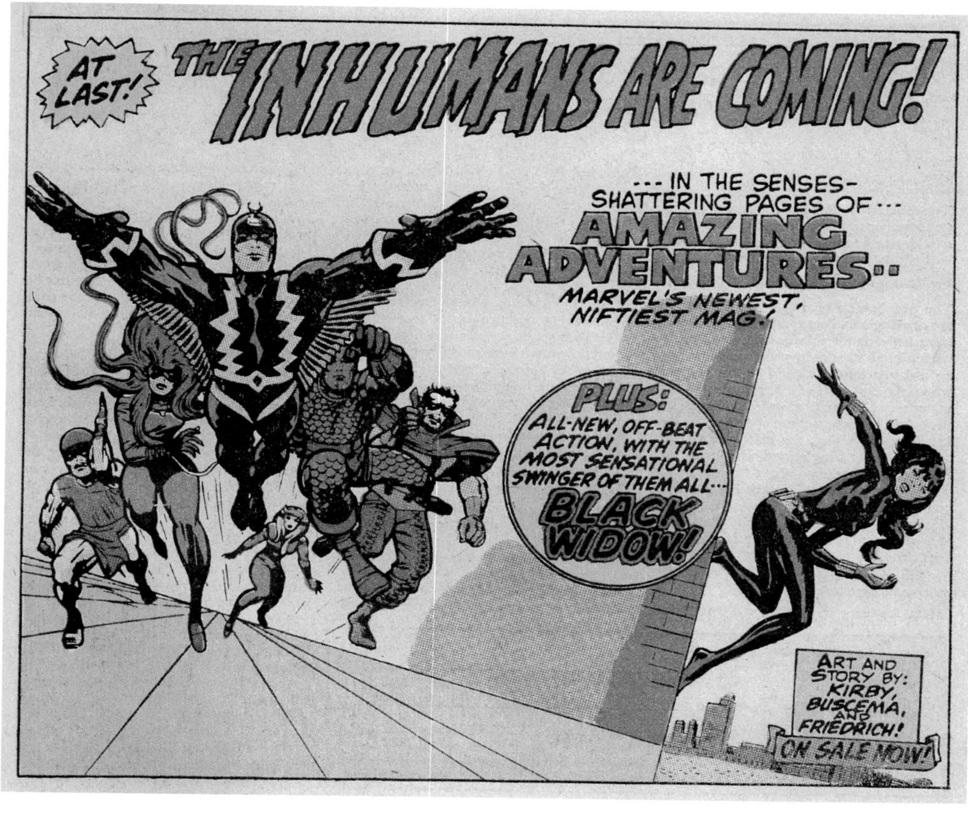
AT LAST!
THE INHUMANS ARE COMING!
... IN THE SENSES-SHATTERING PAGES OF...
AMAZING ADVENTURES..
MARVEL'S NEWEST, NIFTIEST MAG.!
PLUS: ALL-NEW, OFF-BEAT ACTION, WITH THE MOST SENSATIONAL SWINGER OF THEM ALL... BLACK WIDOW!
ART AND STORY BY: KIRBY, BUSCEMA, AND FRIEDRICH!
ON SALE NOW!

into the breach, yanking him off *Spider-Man* to draw the next few issues of *Fantastic Four*. (Amazingly, sales of Marvel's flagship title actually went up during that sequence.) Neal Adams, very much a fan favorite, drew two issues of *Thor*, the only other full-book title Kirby had been illustrating when he quit. Another major artist, Gil Kane, who had come over from DC, was assigned to *Spider-Man*. Soon, however, Lee, who scripted all three titles, restored Romita for a time to *Spider-Man*, and John Buscema began a long run on both *FF* and *Thor*.

Even as Marvel's most important artist left the fold, a new genre was about to be unleashed... one that would succeed where revived anthologies and romances had not.

THOR No. 180
(Right) Interior, "When Gods Go Mad!"; script, Stan Lee; pencils, Neal Adams; inks, Joe Sinnott; September 1970. "I'll never forget when I walked into Stan's office and heard that Jack left. I thought they were going to close up! As far as I was concerned, Jack was the backbone of Marvel." —John Buscema

CHAMBER OF DARKNESS No. 4
(Opposite) Interior, "The Sword and the Sorcerers!"; script, Roy Thomas; pencils and inks, Barry Smith; April 1970. Little did Thomas and Smith guess that only a few months after producing this sword-and-sorcery tale, they would be collaborating on a new Marvel comic starring the foremost S&S hero of them all—Conan the Barbarian!

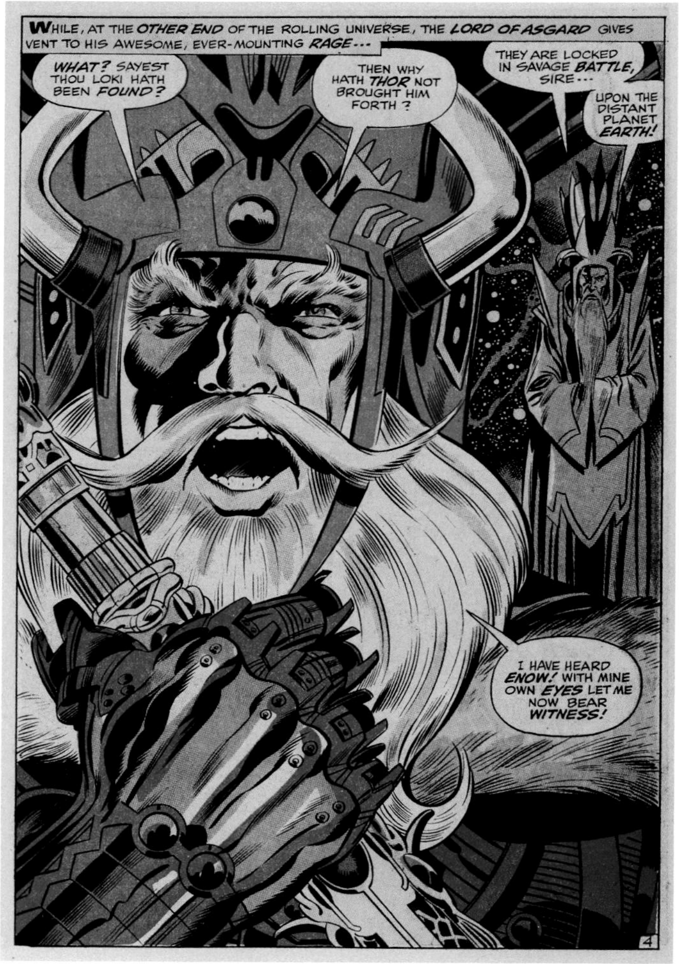
WHILE, AT THE OTHER END OF THE ROLLING UNIVERSE, THE LORD OF ASGARD GIVES VENT TO HIS AWESOME, EVER-MOUNTING RAGE...
WHAT? SAYEST THOU LOKI HATH BEEN FOUND?
THEN WHY HATH THOR NOT BROUGHT HIM FORTH?
THEY ARE LOCKED IN SAVAGE BATTLE, SIRE...
UPON THE DISTANT PLANET EARTH!
I HAVE HEARD ENOW! WITH MINE OWN EYES LET ME NOW BEAR WITNESS!
4

THE SUN TURNED CRIMSON AS THE HARD-FOUGHT BATTLE RAGED... AS STARR THE SLAYER STRUCK BLOW AFTER BLOW TO SAVE THE CITY HE RULED FROM THE SCARLET BEHEMOTH WHICH MENACED IT! AND ON THE PURPLE PLAIN ABOVE MANY-TOWERED ZARDATH, THE EVIL WIZARD TRULL RECITED HIS MOST POTENT SPELLS... FOR, THIS DAY WOULD MARK THE FINAL ENCOUNTER OF...
THE SWORD AND THE SORCERERS!
BY ALL THE GODS OF THE GREAT ABYSS!
MY MIGHTIEST BLOWS HAVE NO EFFECT ON THE FIRE-BREATHING MAN-DRAGON CONJURED UP BY TRULL!
YET, I MUST FIGHT ON... FOR THE CITY OF ZARDATH!
IF YOU YOU CAN'T QUITE FIGURE OUT WHAT'S GOING ON, FRIEND, JUST KEEP READING! SO SAY:
STAN LEE EDITOR • ROY THOMAS WRITER • BARRY SMITH ARTIST
JEAN IZZO, LETTERER
CONTINUED AFTER NEXT PAGE

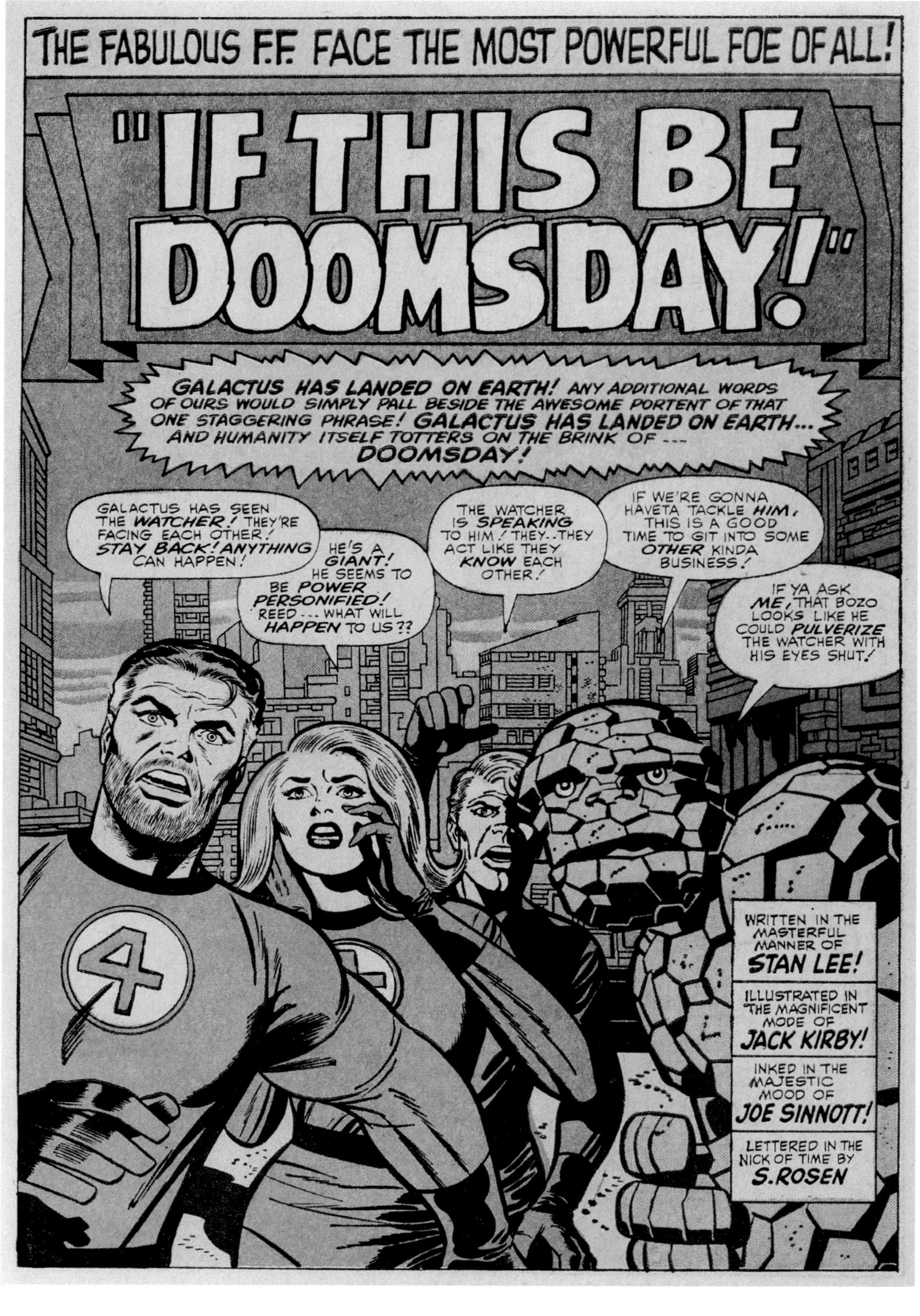

THE FABULOUS F.F. FACE THE MOST POWERFUL FOE OF ALL!
"IF THIS BE DOOMSDAY!"
GALACTUS HAS LANDED ON EARTH! ANY ADDITIONAL WORDS OF OURS WOULD SIMPLY PALL BESIDE THE AWESOME PORTENT OF THAT ONE STAGGERING PHRASE! GALACTUS HAS LANDED ON EARTH... AND HUMANITY ITSELF TOTTERS ON THE BRINK OF --- DOOMSDAY!
GALACTUS HAS SEEN THE WATCHER! THEY'RE FACING EACH OTHER! STAY BACK! ANYTHING CAN HAPPEN!
HE'S A GIANT! HE SEEMS TO BE POWER PERSONIFIED! REED --- WHAT WILL HAPPEN TO US??
THE WATCHER IS SPEAKING TO HIM! THEY--THEY ACT LIKE THEY KNOW EACH OTHER!
IF WE'RE GONNA HAVETA TACKLE HIM, THIS IS A GOOD TIME TO GIT INTO SOME OTHER KINDA BUSINESS!
IF YA ASK ME, THAT BOZO LOOKS LIKE HE COULD PULVERIZE THE WATCHER WITH HIS EYES SHUT!
WRITTEN IN THE MASTERFUL MANNER OF STAN LEE!
ILLUSTRATED IN THE MAGNIFICENT MODE OF JACK KIRBY!
INKED IN THE MAJESTIC MOOD OF JOE SINNOTT!
LETTERED IN THE NICK OF TIME BY S. ROSEN

"Confusing enough for you, faithful one?
Well, hold on tight — we've only begun!!"
— STAN LEE

FANTASTIC FOUR No. 49

(Opposite) Interior, "If This Be Doomsday!"; script, Stan Lee;
pencils, Jack Kirby; inks, Joe Sinnott; April 1966. In part two
of comics' most famous trilogy, Galactus and his herald, the
Silver Surfer, have landed on Earth. The looks of fear and
terror are so well defined on the faces of the Four that even
the staunchest fans wonder how they will defend this planet.

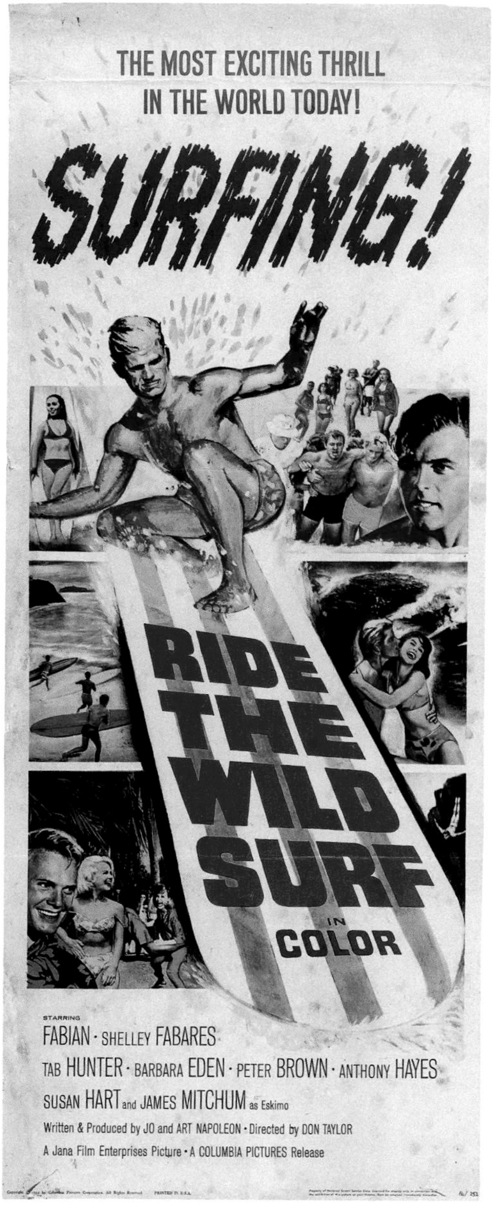
THE MOST EXCITING THRILL
IN THE WORLD TODAY!
SURFING!
RIDE THE WILD SURF
IN COLOR
STARRING
FABIAN · SHELLEY FABARES
TAB HUNTER · BARBARA EDEN · PETER BROWN · ANTHONY HAYES
SUSAN HART and JAMES MITCHUM as Eskimo
Written & Produced by JO and ART NAPOLEON · Directed by DON TAYLOR
A Jana Film Enterprises Picture · A COLUMBIA PICTURES Release

SURFIN' U.S.A.

(Left) Poster, Ride the Wild Surf, *Columbia Pictures, 1964.* In the early 1960s surfing invaded popular culture in movies and music. "I know nothing about surfers! Then one day I saw it in the paper. There was a guy standing on a wooden plank out in California. I was still in New York at the time, OK? And there's this guy standing on a plank and he's riding the wave! And that's fantastic to me! And I said, 'Suppose there was a surfer who surfed the universe?'" —Jack Kirby

FANTASTIC FOUR No. 50

(Opposite) Cover; pencils, Jack Kirby; inks, Joe Sinnott; May 1966. "And somewhere in the deep vastness of outer space, an incredible figure hurtles thru the Cosmos! A being whom we shall call the Silver Surfer, for want of a better name!" This story is not just the development of the Surfer and his discovery of his humanity. It is also about the maturation of Johnny Storm as he enters college—as will Peter Parker and the X-Men in their own magazines.

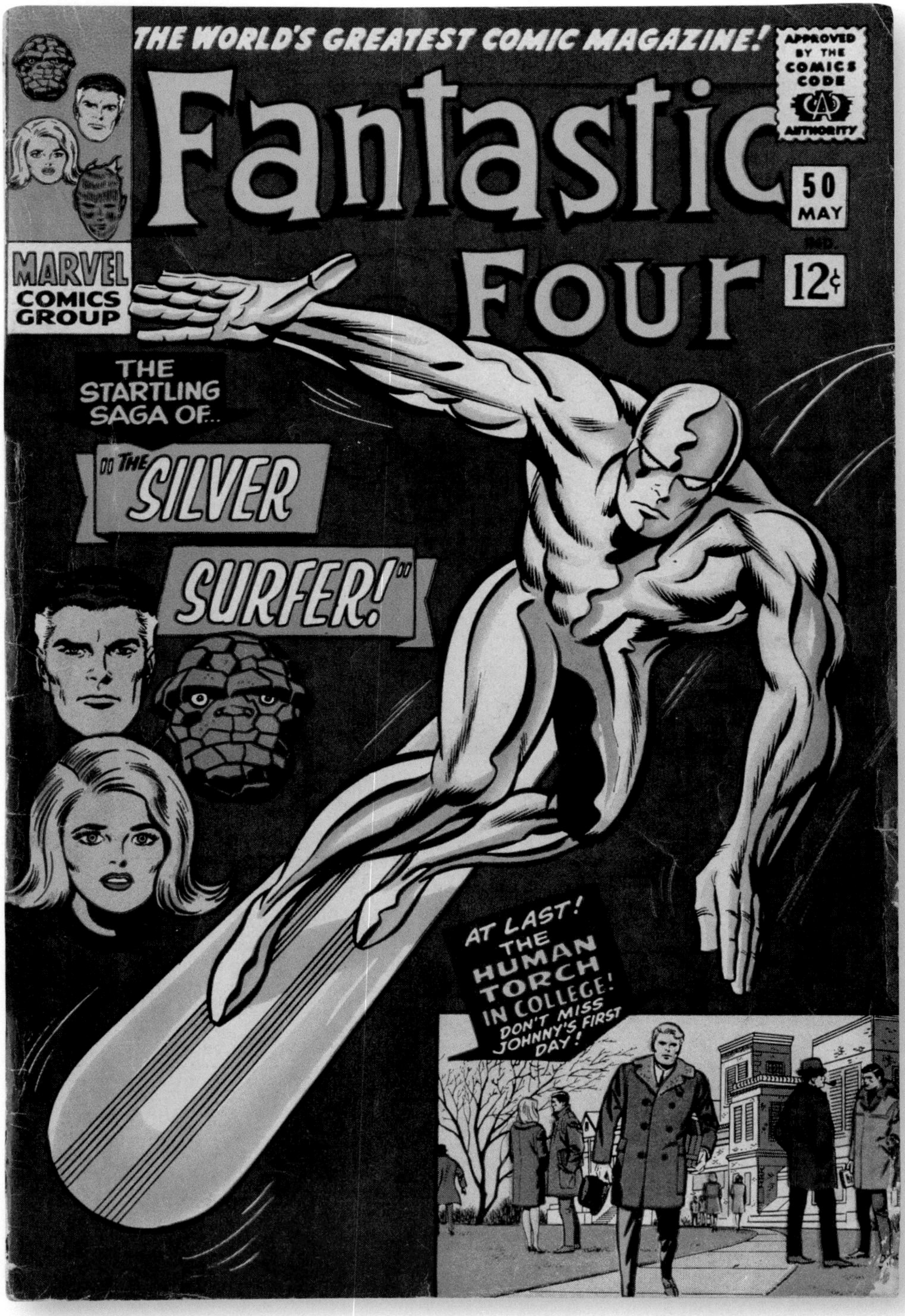
THE WORLD'S GREATEST COMIC MAGAZINE!
APPROVED BY THE COMICS CODE AUTHORITY
Fantastic Four
50 MAY
12¢
MARVEL COMICS GROUP
THE STARTLING SAGA OF...
"THE SILVER SURFER!"
AT LAST! THE HUMAN TORCH IN COLLEGE! DON'T MISS JOHNNY'S FIRST DAY!

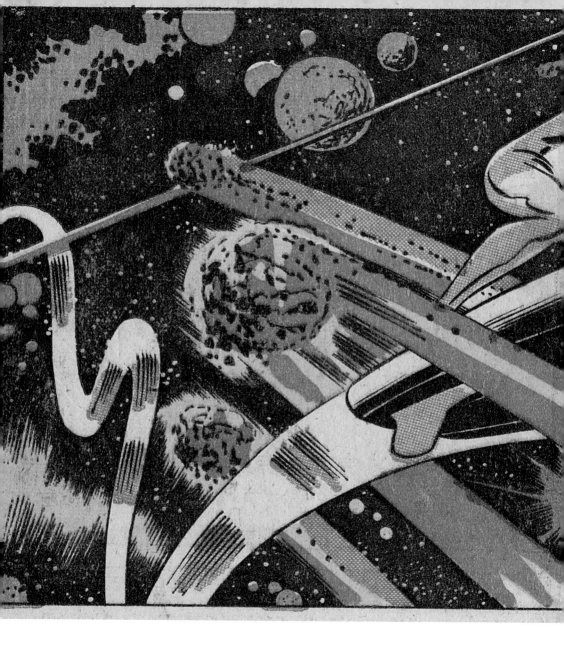

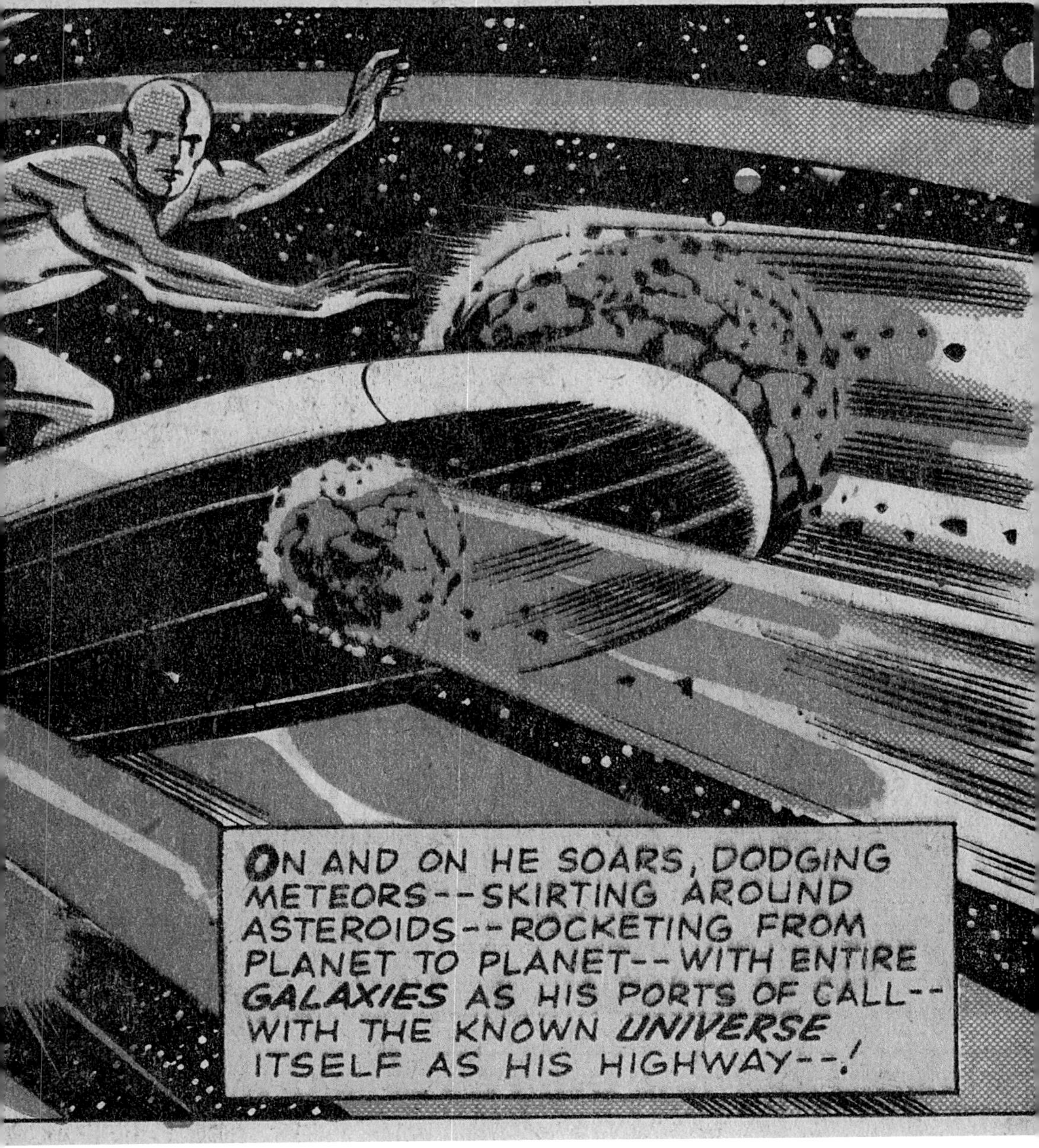
ON AND ON HE SOARS, DODGING METEORS--SKIRTING AROUND ASTEROIDS--ROCKETING FROM PLANET TO PLANET--WITH ENTIRE GALAXIES AS HIS PORTS OF CALL--WITH THE KNOWN UNIVERSE ITSELF AS HIS HIGHWAY--!

FANTASTIC FOUR No. 48

(Above) Interior, "The Coming of Galactus!"; script, Stan Lee; pencils, Jack Kirby; inks, Joe Sinnott; March 1966. After their adventure with the Inhumans, life goes on and the Silver Surfer searches through space. Kirby gave him form and Lee gave him substance, but no one gave him pants. The Surfer is, at first, a blank slate.

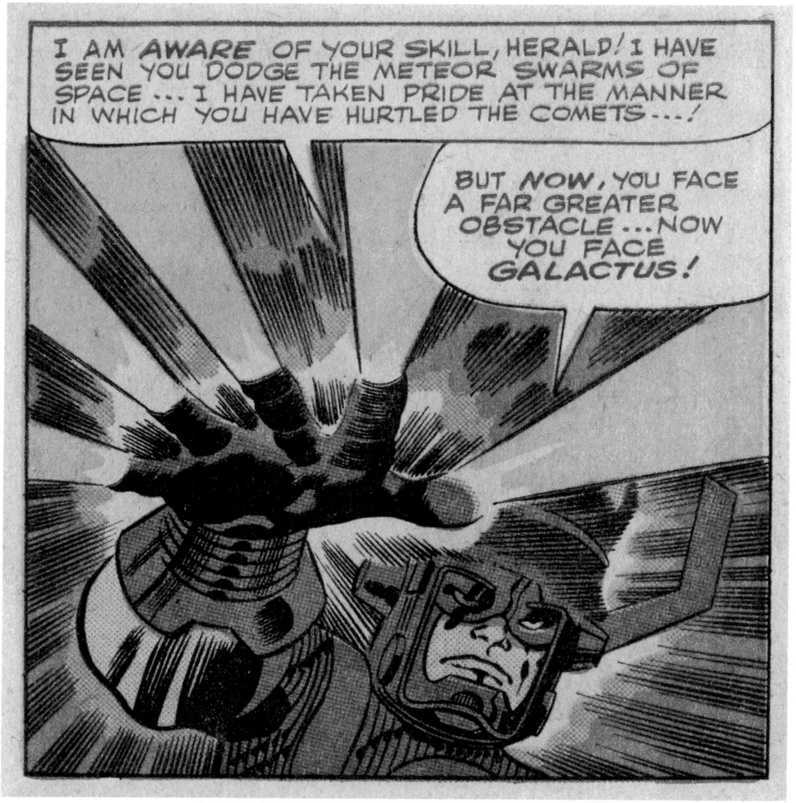
I AM AWARE OF YOUR SKILL, HERALD! I HAVE SEEN YOU DODGE THE METEOR SWARMS OF SPACE ... I HAVE TAKEN PRIDE AT THE MANNER IN WHICH YOU HAVE HURTLED THE COMETS...!
BUT NOW, YOU FACE A FAR GREATER OBSTACLE ... NOW YOU FACE GALACTUS!

FANTASTIC FOUR No. 50

(Above) Interior, "The Startling Saga of the Silver Surfer!"; script, Stan Lee; pencils, Jack Kirby; inks, Joe Sinnott; May 1966. "One other thing I think we've innovated that has been pretty successful is overlapping characters and books," Stan Lee told WBAI Radio in 1967. "In fact, all our books are one big continued story. And in the mail we received from so many college kids, they now refer to those books. They'll say, 'By the way, regarding your "Galactus Trilogy"...' And, you know, they're referring to this as though it's *The Rise and Fall of the Roman Empire,* which I love! "

BEYOND THE PALE

(Opposite) Original interior art, "This Man, This Monster!," Fantastic Four *No. 51; script, Stan Lee; pencils, Jack Kirby; inks, Joe Sinnott; June 1966.* Kirby's photo collages were part of his attempts to push the comics form—despite its inherent production limitations—as far beyond the norm as Marvel's cosmic storylines in *FF* and Thor.

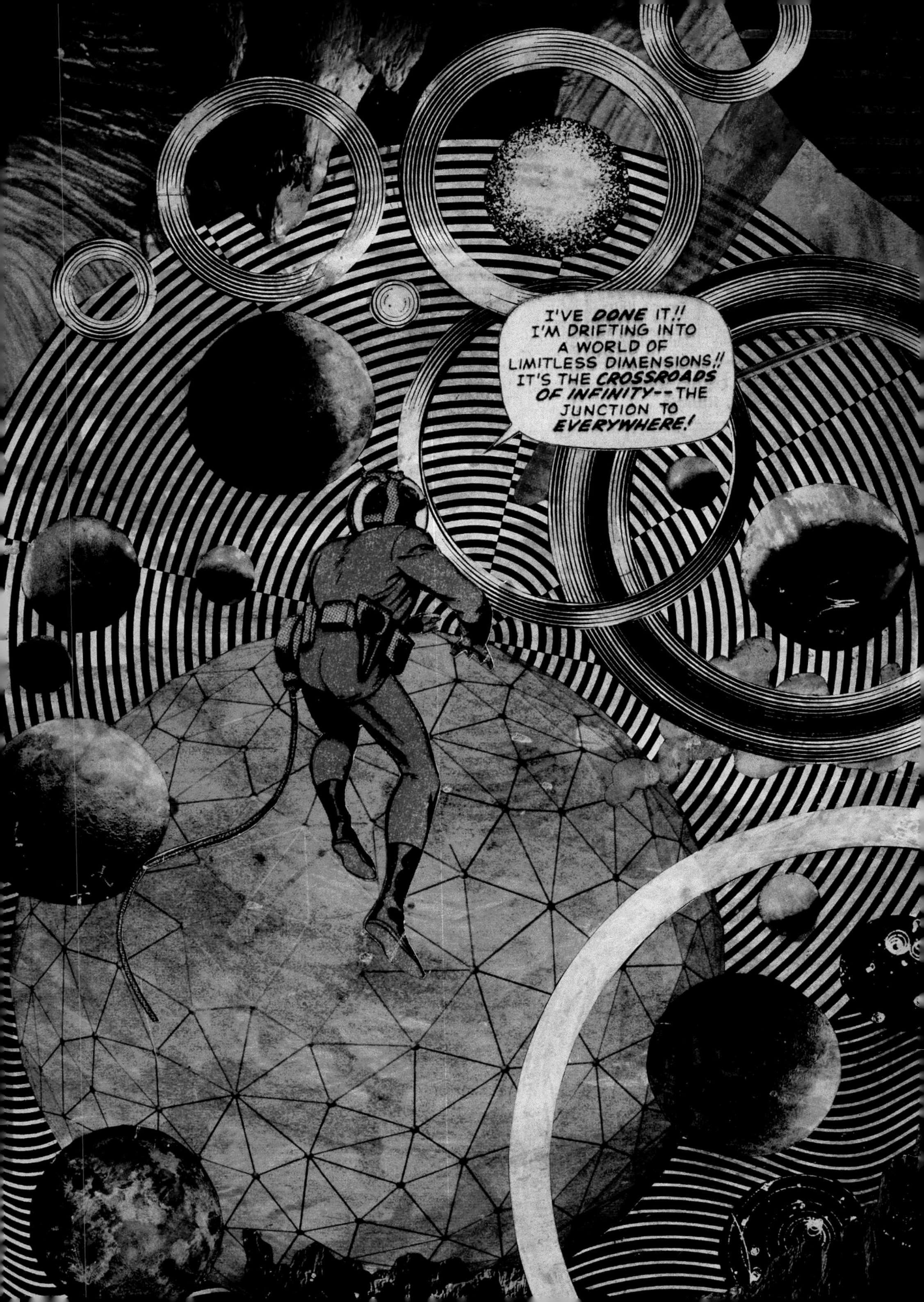
I'VE DONE IT!! I'M DRIFTING INTO A WORLD OF LIMITLESS DIMENSIONS!! IT'S THE CROSSROADS OF INFINITY--THE JUNCTION TO EVERYWHERE!

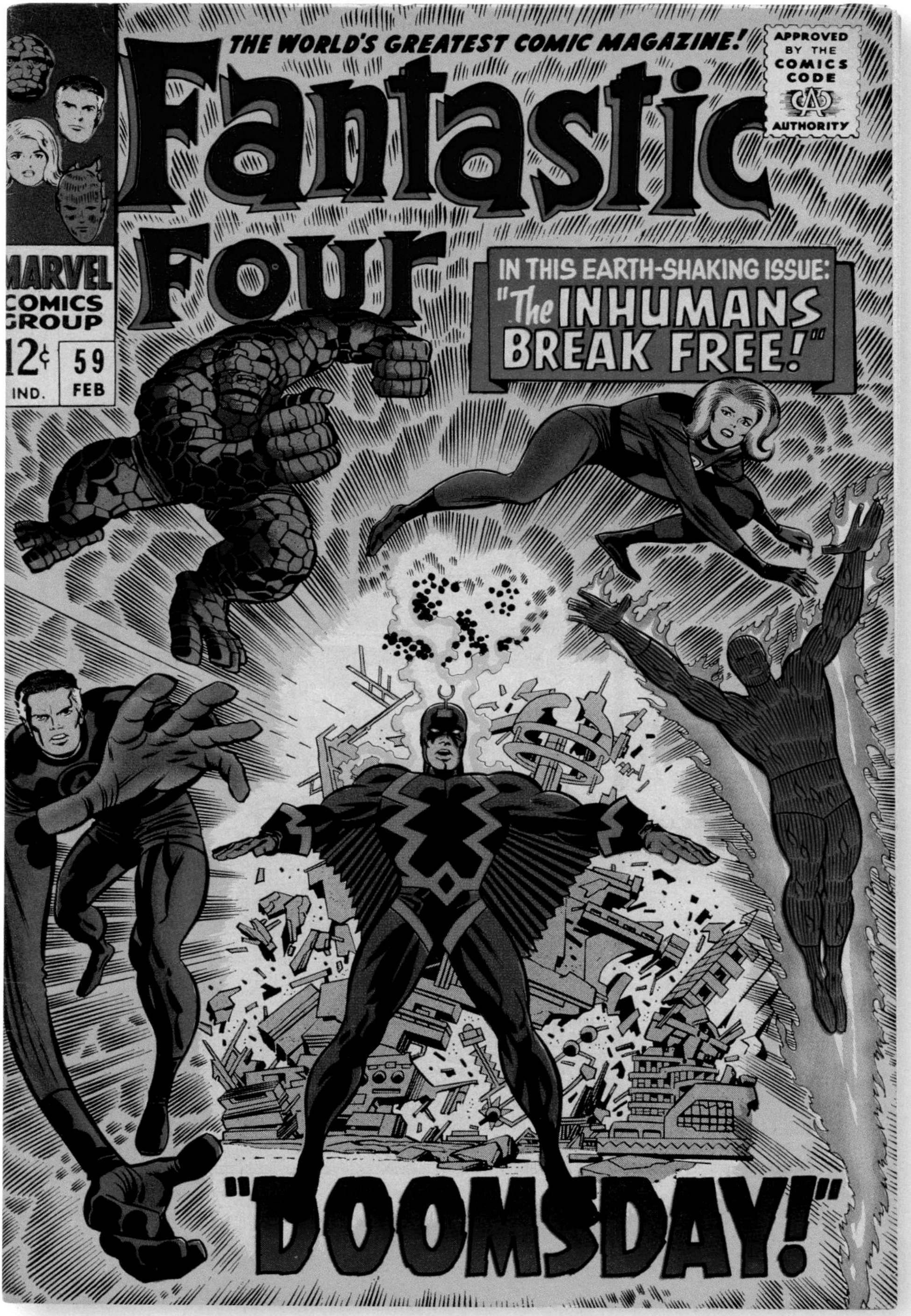
THE WORLD'S GREATEST COMIC MAGAZINE!
Fantastic Four
MARVEL COMICS GROUP
12¢ IND.
59 FEB
APPROVED BY THE COMICS CODE AUTHORITY
IN THIS EARTH-SHAKING ISSUE:
"The INHUMANS BREAK FREE!"
"DOOMSDAY!"

FANTASTIC FOUR No. 59

(Opposite) Cover; pencils, Jack Kirby; inks, Joe Sinnott; February 1967. "Jack's point of view ... became the governing philosophy of the entire publishing company and, beyond the publishing company, of the entire field," veteran artist Gil Kane told *The Comics Journal* in 1986. "[Marvel] would get artists, regardless of whether they had done romance or anything else and they taught them the ABCs, which amounted to learning Jack Kirby.... Jack was like the Holy Scripture."

FANTASTIC FOUR No. 59

(Below) Interior, "Doomsday"; script, Stan Lee; pencils, Jack Kirby; inks, Joe Sinnott; February 1967. Black Bolt, ruler of the Inhumans, is one of the most tragic characters to enter the Marvel pantheon. Possessed of sonic powers so great that his newborn cries destroyed the Inhumans' city, he lives his first eighteen years in isolation — and must vow to spend his entire life in absolute silence. Thus the Inhumans always knew he had the means to escape their captivity, but the price to pay was great. In the end, noble Black Bolt protects his evil brother, Maximus — the Inhuman Cain to his Abel — who was the cause of all of this.

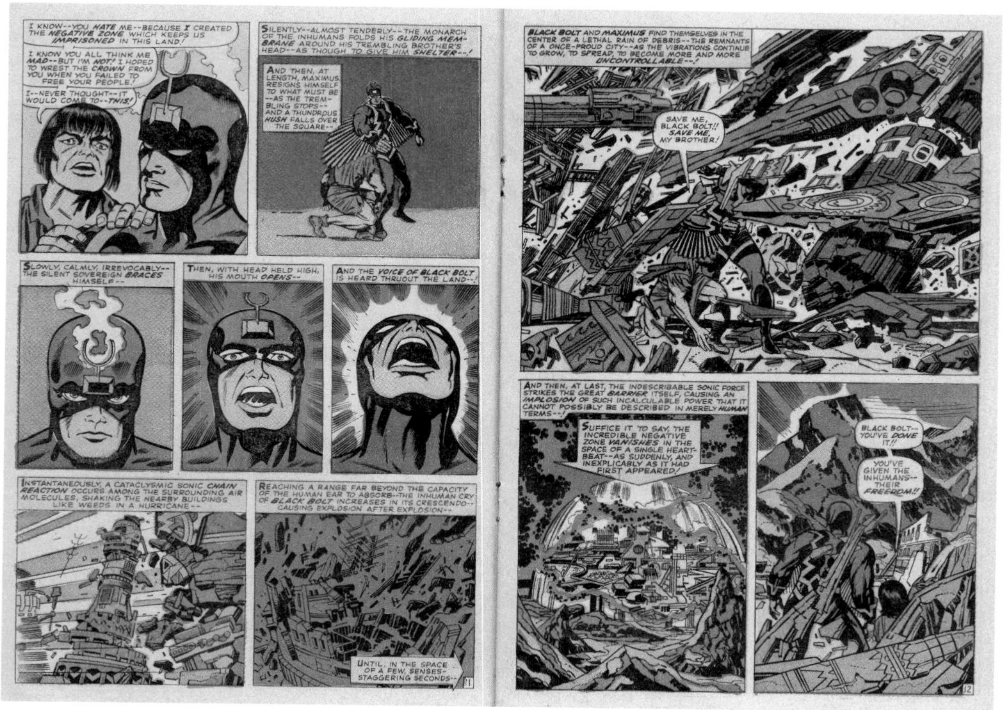

I KNOW--YOU HATE ME--BECAUSE I CREATED THE NEGATIVE ZONE WHICH KEEPS US IMPRISONED IN THIS LAND!
I KNOW YOU ALL THINK ME MAD--BUT I'M NOT! I HOPED TO WREST THE CROWN FROM YOU WHEN YOU FAILED TO FREE YOUR PEOPLE!
I--NEVER THOUGHT--IT WOULD COME TO--THIS!
SILENTLY--ALMOST TENDERLY--THE MONARCH OF THE INHUMANS FOLDS HIS GLIDING MEMBRANE AROUND HIS TREMBLING BROTHER'S HEAD--AS THOUGH TO GIVE HIM SHELTER--!
AND THEN, AT LENGTH, MAXIMUS RESIGNS HIMSELF TO WHAT MUST BE --AS THE TREMBLING STOPS-- AND A THUNDROUS HUSH FALLS OVER THE SQUARE--
SLOWLY, CALMLY, IRREVOCABLY-- THE SILENT SOVEREIGN BRACES HIMSELF--
THEN, WITH HEAD HELD HIGH, HIS MOUTH OPENS--
AND THE VOICE OF BLACK BOLT IS HEARD THRUOUT THE LAND--!
INSTANTANEOUSLY, A CATACLYSMIC SONIC CHAIN REACTION OCCURS AMONG THE SURROUNDING AIR MOLECULES, SHAKING THE NEARBY BUILDINGS LIKE WEEDS IN A HURRICANE--
REACHING A RANGE FAR BEYOND THE CAPACITY OF THE HUMAN EAR TO ABSORB--THE INHUMAN CRY OF BLACK BOLT INCREASES IN ITS CRESCENDO-- CAUSING EXPLOSION AFTER EXPLOSION--
UNTIL, IN THE SPACE OF A FEW, SENSES-STAGGERING SECONDS--
11
BLACK BOLT AND MAXIMUS FIND THEMSELVES IN THE CENTER OF A LETHAL RAIN OF DEBRIS--THE REMNANTS OF A ONCE-PROUD CITY--AS THE VIBRATIONS CONTINUE TO GROW, TO SPREAD, TO BECOME MORE AND MORE UNCONTROLLABLE--!
SAVE ME, BLACK BOLT!! SAVE ME, MY BROTHER!
AND THEN, AT LAST, THE INDESCRIBABLE SONIC FORCE STRIKES THE GREAT BARRIER ITSELF, CAUSING AN IMPLOSION OF SUCH INCALCULABLE POWER THAT IT CANNOT POSSIBLY BE DESCRIBED IN MERELY HUMAN TERMS--!
SUFFICE IT TO SAY, THE INCREDIBLE NEGATIVE ZONE VANISHES IN THE SPACE OF A SINGLE HEART-BEAT--AS SUDDENLY, AND INEXPLICABLY AS IT HAD FIRST APPEARED!
BLACK BOLT-- YOU'VE DONE IT!!
YOU'VE GIVEN THE INHUMANS-- THEIR FREEDOM!!
12

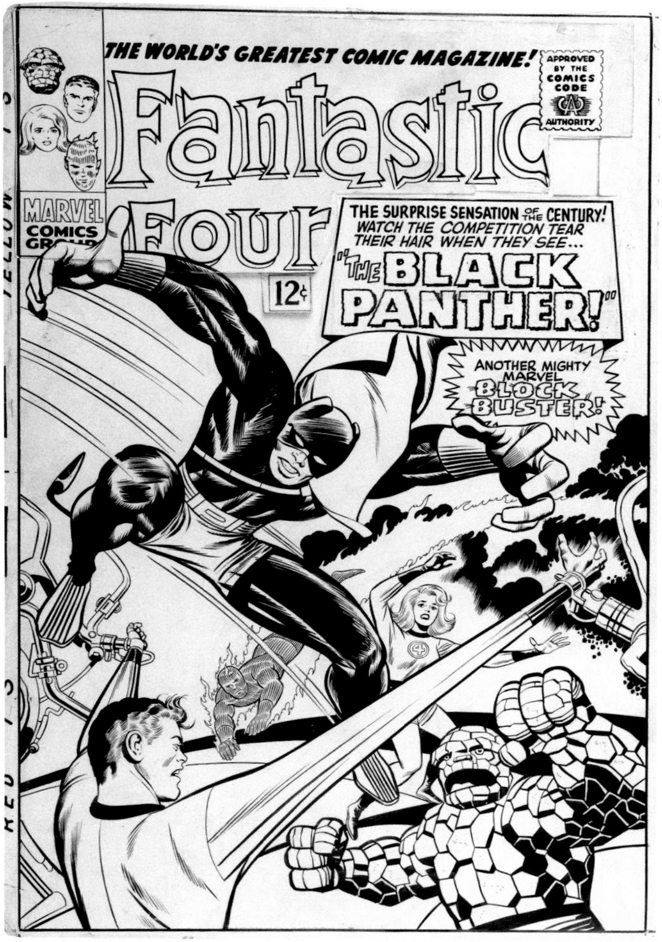
THE WORLD'S GREATEST COMIC MAGAZINE!
APPROVED BY THE COMICS CODE AUTHORITY
Fantastic Four
MARVEL
COMICS
12¢
THE SURPRISE SENSATION OF THE CENTURY!
WATCH THE COMPETITION TEAR THEIR HAIR WHEN THEY SEE...
"THE BLACK PANTHER!"
ANOTHER MIGHTY MARVEL BLOCK BUSTER!

FANTASTIC FOUR No. 53

(Opposite) Cover; pencils, Jack Kirby; inks, Joe Sinnott; August 1966. This issue tells the origin of the Black Panther, king of Wakanda. In the story Stan Lee and Jack Kirby treat T'Challa as an equal to the Fantastic Four, a dignified, intelligent, and resourceful man. He could be compared to actor Sidney Poitier, upon whom Kirby based his appearance. Only three issues earlier Lee and Kirby had also introduced Wyatt Wingfoot, a Native American who became friends with fellow college student Johnny Storm, and shared in many of the FF's adventures.

THE BLACK PANTHER

(Above) Original cover art (unpublished), Fantastic Four *No. 52; pencils, Jack Kirby; inks, Joe Sinnott; July 1966.* The Black Panther's debut was important enough to warrant Stan Lee tinkering with the hero's costume and cover layout. Originally designed with a half-mask, the published version had the Panther's face completely covered. But was the change made to make him look more mysterious, or was it a directive of the publisher, who may have feared the title would not be distributed by dealers in the American South of the mid-1960s?

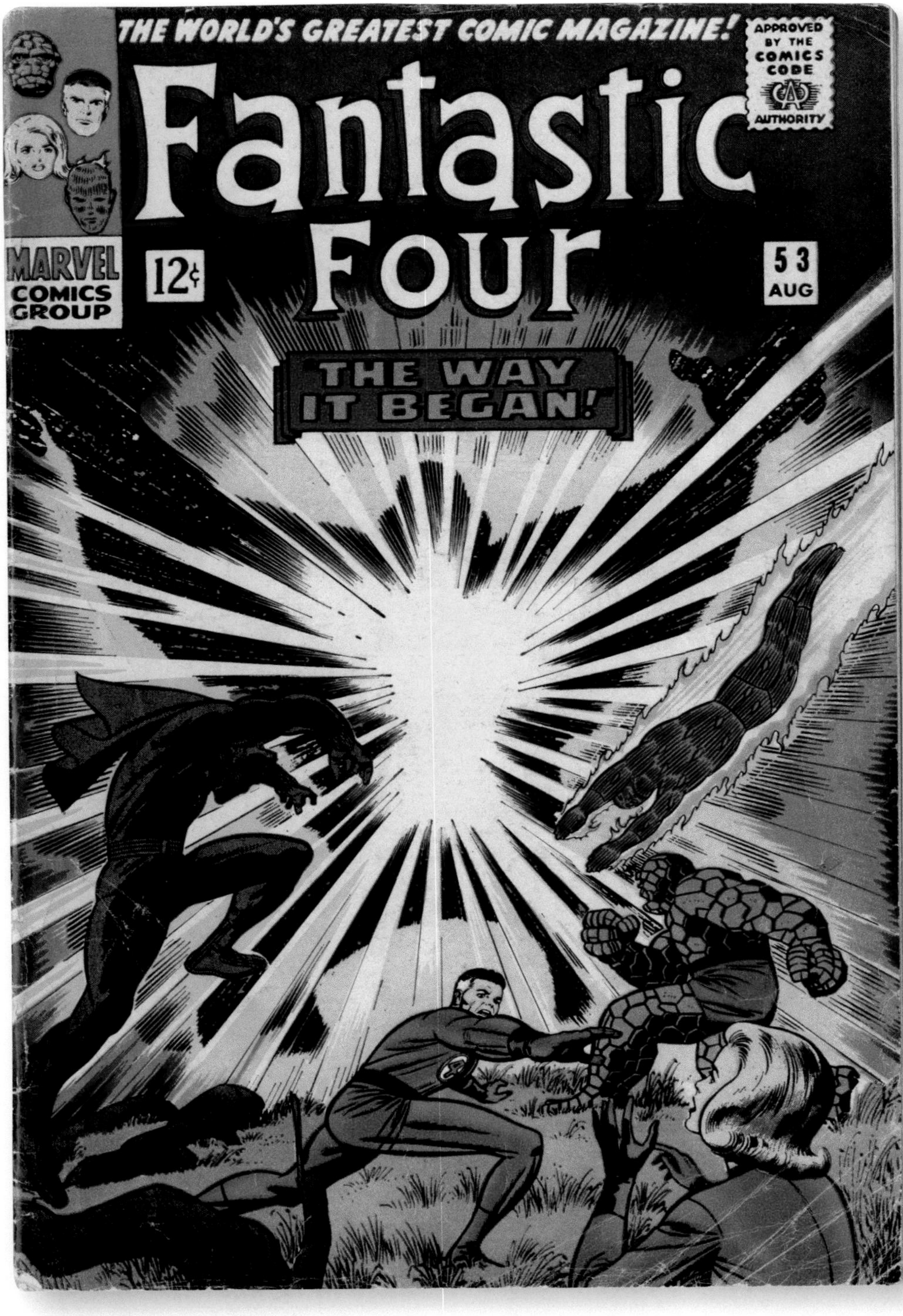
THE WORLD'S GREATEST COMIC MAGAZINE!
APPROVED BY THE COMICS CODE AUTHORITY
Fantastic Four
MARVEL COMICS GROUP
12¢
53 AUG
THE WAY IT BEGAN!

FANTASTIC FOUR No. 52

(Below and opposite) Interiors, "The Black Panther!"; script, Stan Lee; pencils, Jack Kirby; inks, Joe Sinnott; July 1966. "If ever there was a compelling black superhero that appeared directly drawn from the political moment yet presented an Afrofuturist sensibility, T'Chall[a], the Black Panther superhero of Marvel comics, is such a character. In 1966 the Lowndes County Freedom Organization first used an image of a black panther to symbolize their black political independence and self-determination in opposition to the Alabama Democratic Party's white rooster. In October of the same year the Black Panther Party for Self-Defense was created and adopted the black panther emblem as the namesake." —Adilifu Nama

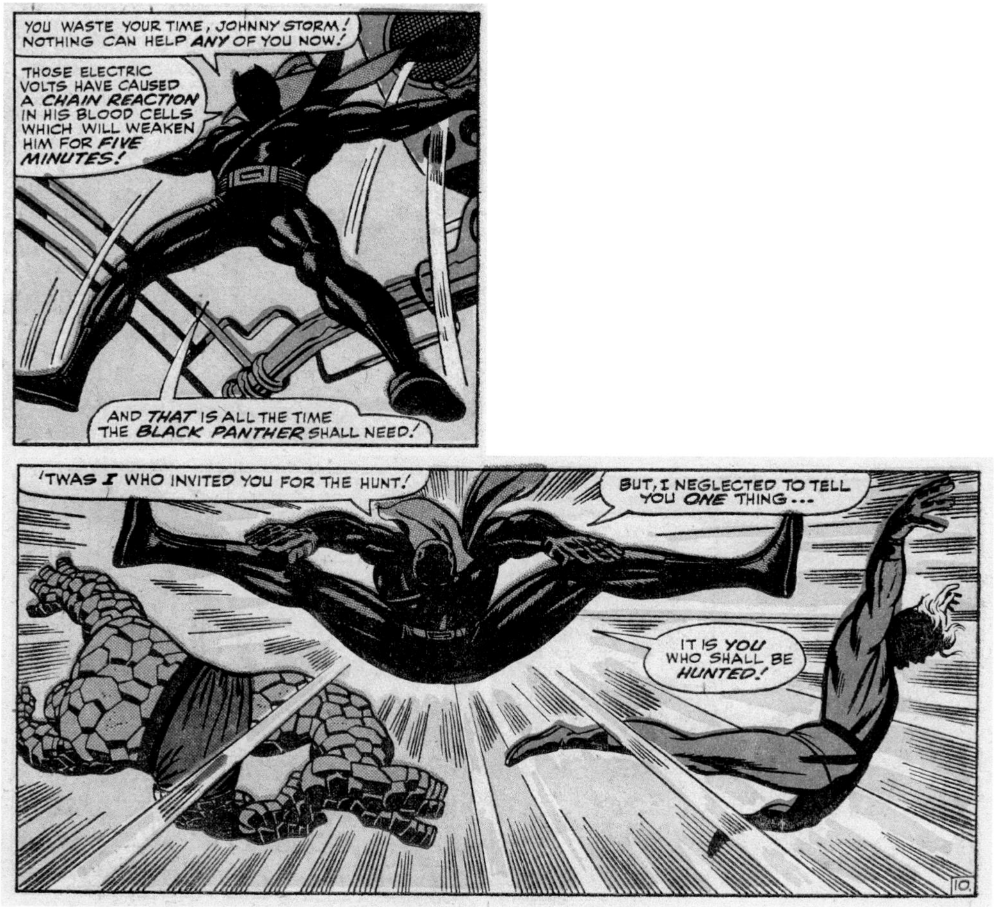
YOU WASTE YOUR TIME, JOHNNY STORM! NOTHING CAN HELP ANY OF YOU NOW!
THOSE ELECTRIC VOLTS HAVE CAUSED A CHAIN REACTION IN HIS BLOOD CELLS WHICH WILL WEAKEN HIM FOR FIVE MINUTES!
AND THAT IS ALL THE TIME THE BLACK PANTHER SHALL NEED!
'TWAS I WHO INVITED YOU FOR THE HUNT!
BUT, I NEGLECTED TO TELL YOU ONE THING...
IT IS YOU WHO SHALL BE HUNTED!
10

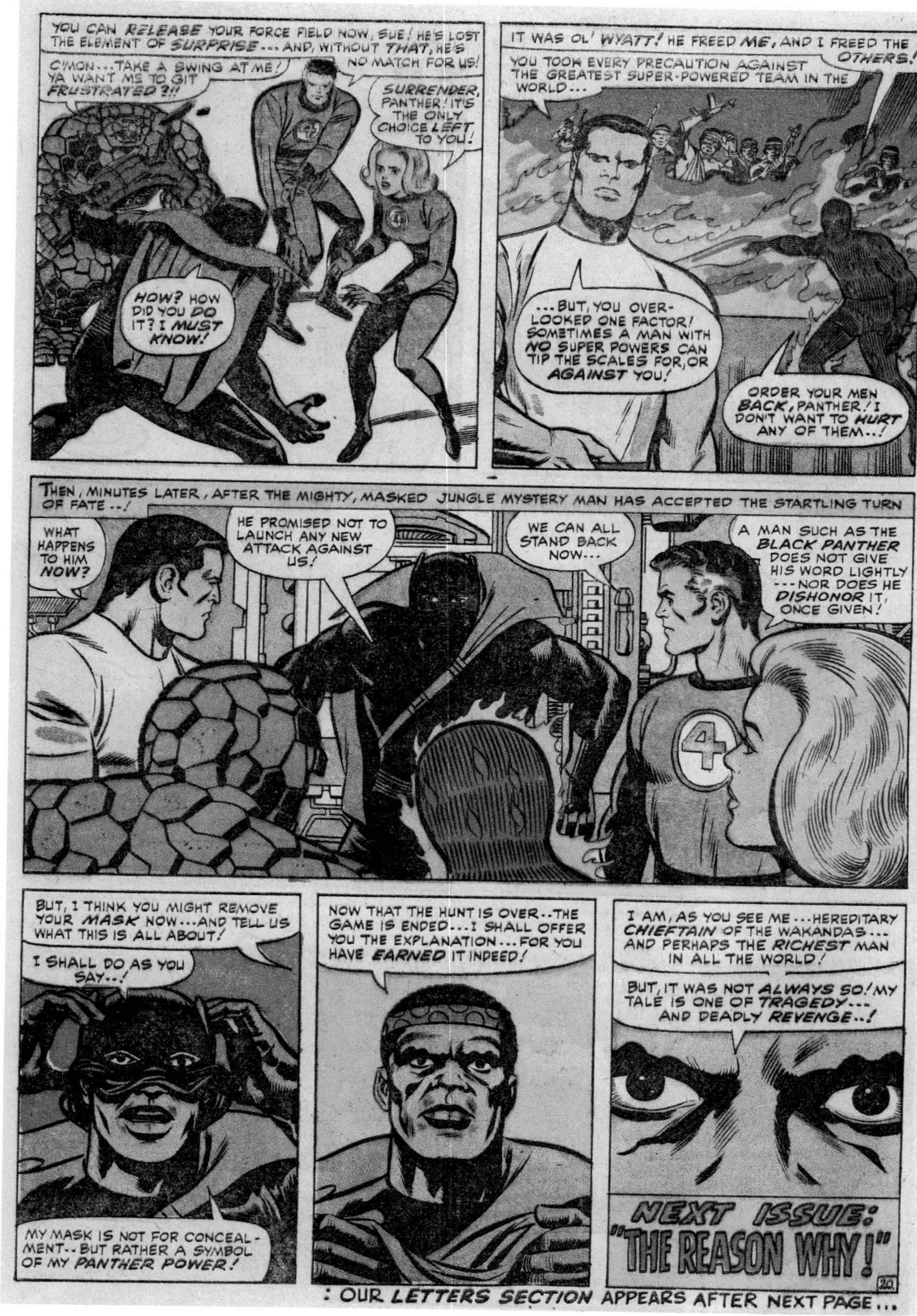
YOU CAN RELEASE YOUR FORCE FIELD NOW, SUE! HE'S LOST THE ELEMENT OF SURPRISE... AND, WITHOUT THAT, HE'S NO MATCH FOR US!
C'MON... TAKE A SWING AT ME! YA WANT ME TO GIT FRUSTRATED?!!
SURRENDER, PANTHER! IT'S THE ONLY CHOICE LEFT TO YOU!
HOW? HOW DID YOU DO IT? I MUST KNOW!
IT WAS OL' WYATT! HE FREED ME, AND I FREED THE OTHERS!
YOU TOOK EVERY PRECAUTION AGAINST THE GREATEST SUPER-POWERED TEAM IN THE WORLD...
...BUT, YOU OVER-LOOKED ONE FACTOR! SOMETIMES A MAN WITH NO SUPER POWERS CAN TIP THE SCALES FOR, OR AGAINST YOU!
ORDER YOUR MEN BACK, PANTHER! I DON'T WANT TO HURT ANY OF THEM..!
THEN, MINUTES LATER, AFTER THE MIGHTY, MASKED JUNGLE MYSTERY MAN HAS ACCEPTED THE STARTLING TURN OF FATE..!
WHAT HAPPENS TO HIM NOW?
HE PROMISED NOT TO LAUNCH ANY NEW ATTACK AGAINST US!
WE CAN ALL STAND BACK NOW...
A MAN SUCH AS THE BLACK PANTHER DOES NOT GIVE HIS WORD LIGHTLY ---NOR DOES HE DISHONOR IT, ONCE GIVEN!
BUT, I THINK YOU MIGHT REMOVE YOUR MASK NOW...AND TELL US WHAT THIS IS ALL ABOUT!
I SHALL DO AS YOU SAY..!
MY MASK IS NOT FOR CONCEAL-MENT.. BUT RATHER A SYMBOL OF MY PANTHER POWER!
NOW THAT THE HUNT IS OVER.. THE GAME IS ENDED... I SHALL OFFER YOU THE EXPLANATION... FOR YOU HAVE EARNED IT INDEED!
I AM, AS YOU SEE ME...HEREDITARY CHIEFTAIN OF THE WAKANDAS... AND PERHAPS THE RICHEST MAN IN ALL THE WORLD!
BUT, IT WAS NOT ALWAYS SO! MY TALE IS ONE OF TRAGEDY... AND DEADLY REVENGE..!
NEXT ISSUE: "THE REASON WHY!"
20
: OUR LETTERS SECTION APPEARS AFTER NEXT PAGE...

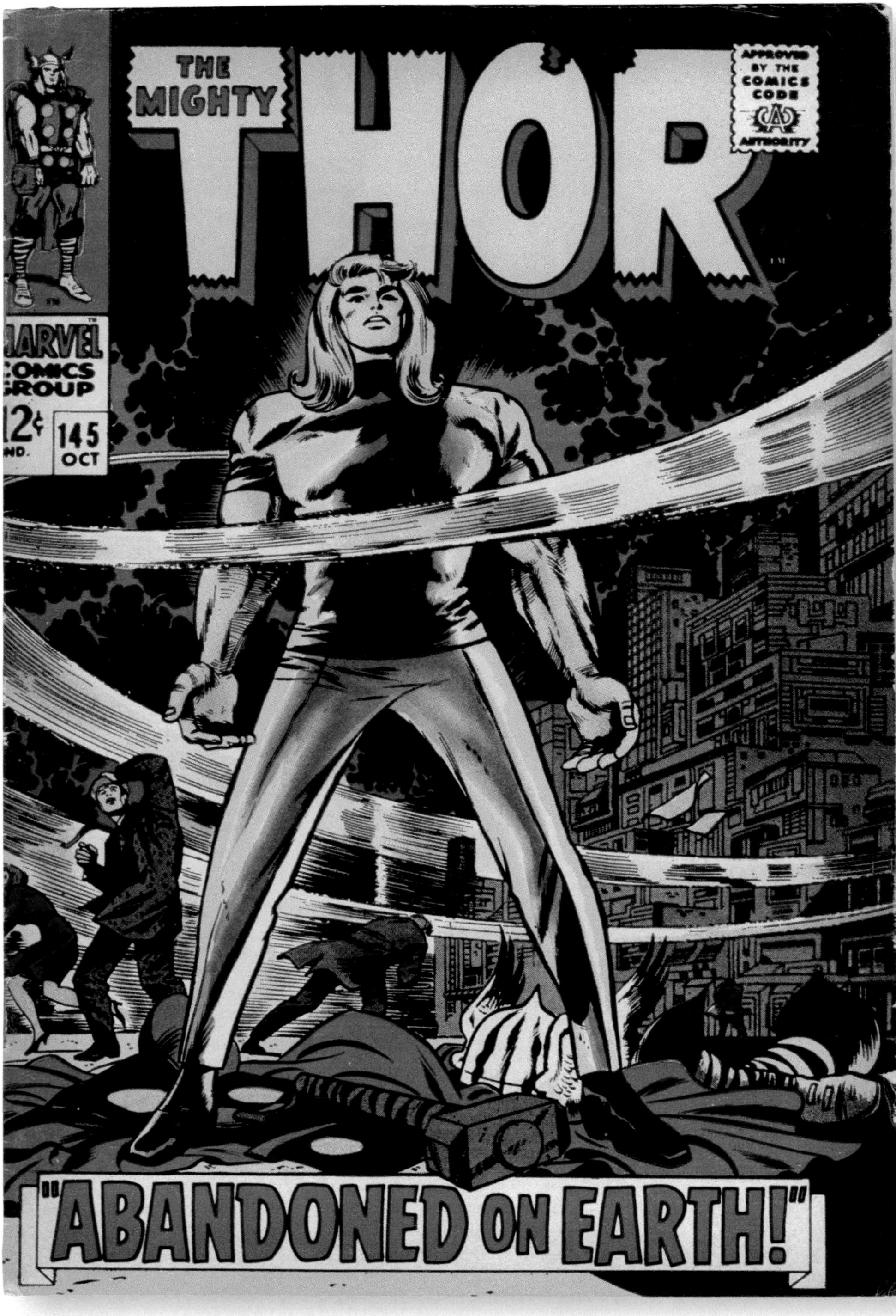
THE MIGHTY
THOR
APPROVED BY THE COMICS CODE AUTHORITY
MARVEL COMICS GROUP
12¢
145 OCT
"ABANDONED ON EARTH!"

THE MIGHTY
THOR
SCOOTER
WITH FRICTION DRIVE
BY MARX
LOUIS MARX & CO.
© MARVEL COMICS GROUP. MCMLXVIII
CONTENTS MADE IN HONG KONG

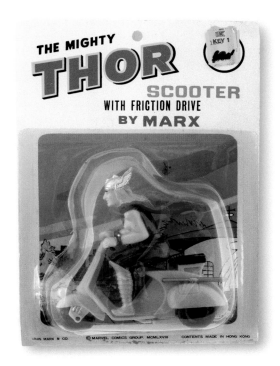

THOR No. 145

(Opposite) Cover; pencils, Jack Kirby; inks, Vince Colletta; October 1967. However coincidental, the middle-aged Lee and Kirby were somehow able to channel the essence of rock's raw energy onto the comic book pages of the 1960s, attracting legions of loyal college-age readers. Marvel's influence was such that Lee would even attempt a bit of moralizing, as he related on *The Dick Cavett Show* in 1968: "We were concerned about all the young people dropping out, and we had [Thor] deliver a little lecture in his own ridiculous way of speaking, mentioning that it is far better to plunge in than to drop out.... And at the time the little page was written, it was a good little sermon."

NEED A LIFT?

(Above) The Mighty Thor Scooter, Marx Toy Company, 1967. Thor wasn't the only character to be taken for a ride. The Marx Toy Company, which began manufacturing inexpensive plastic toys in the 1940s, also sold "scooters" straddled by Spider-Man and Captain America.

JOURNEY INTO MYSTERY No. 124

(Following spread) Interior, "The Grandeur and the Glory!"; script, Stan Lee; pencils, Jack Kirby; inks, Vince Colletta; January 1966. Here we see the partnership of Lee and Kirby working like a well-oiled machine. The series achieves an artful balance between tragedy and comedy with Thor's "fish-out-of-water" sitcom moments—another story humorously details Thor's ride uptown with an unflappable New York cabbie!

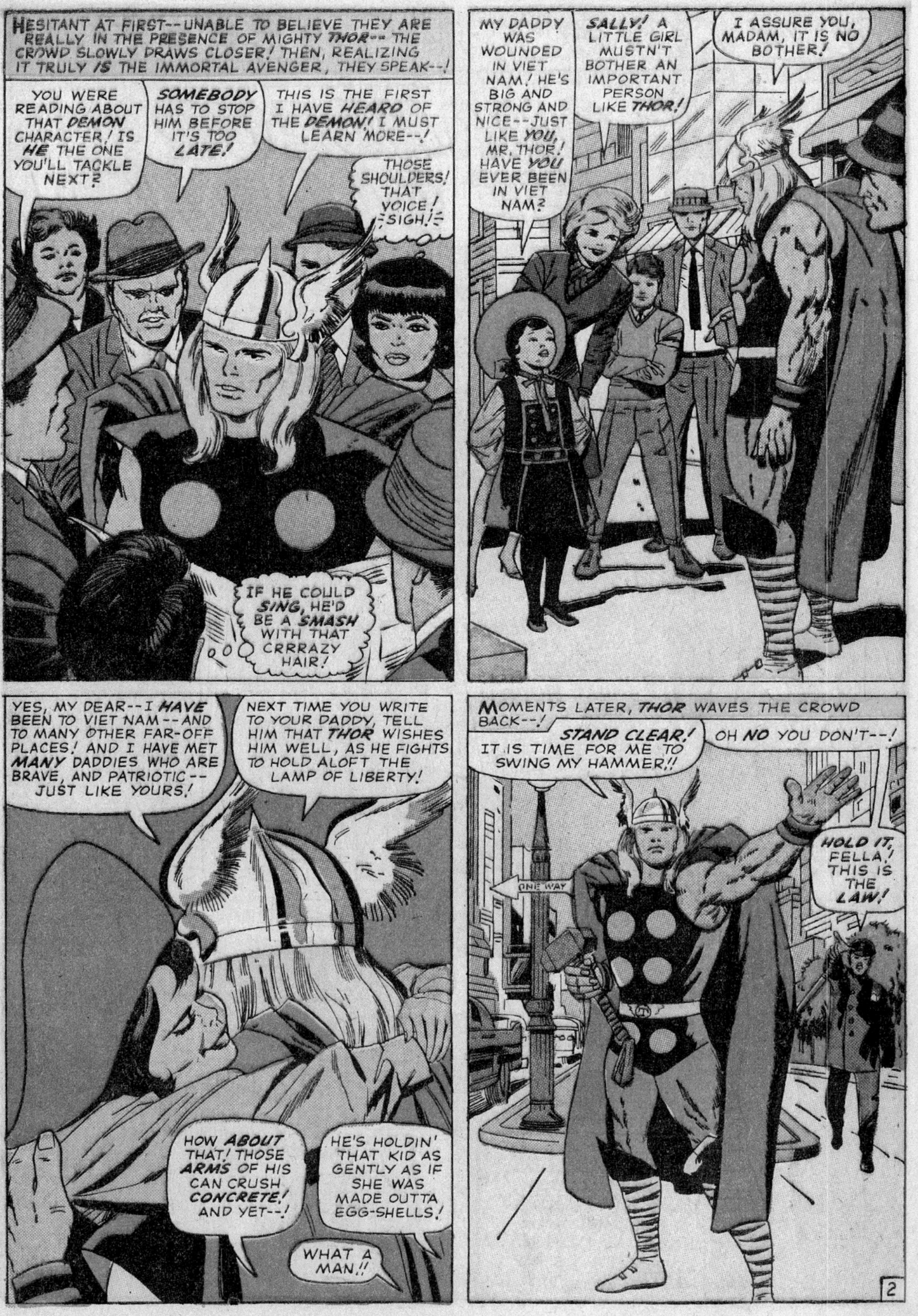

HESITANT AT FIRST--UNABLE TO BELIEVE THEY ARE REALLY IN THE PRESENCE OF MIGHTY THOR-- THE CROWD SLOWLY DRAWS CLOSER! THEN, REALIZING IT TRULY IS THE IMMORTAL AVENGER, THEY SPEAK--!
YOU WERE READING ABOUT THAT DEMON CHARACTER! IS HE THE ONE YOU'LL TACKLE NEXT?
SOMEBODY HAS TO STOP HIM BEFORE IT'S TOO LATE!
THIS IS THE FIRST I HAVE HEARD OF THE DEMON! I MUST LEARN MORE--!
THOSE SHOULDERS! THAT VOICE! SIGH!
IF HE COULD SING, HE'D BE A SMASH WITH THAT CRRRAZY HAIR!
MY DADDY WAS WOUNDED IN VIET NAM! HE'S BIG AND STRONG AND NICE--JUST LIKE YOU, MR. THOR! HAVE YOU EVER BEEN IN VIET NAM?
SALLY! A LITTLE GIRL MUSTN'T BOTHER AN IMPORTANT PERSON LIKE THOR!
I ASSURE YOU, MADAM, IT IS NO BOTHER!
YES, MY DEAR--I HAVE BEEN TO VIET NAM--AND TO MANY OTHER FAR-OFF PLACES! AND I HAVE MET MANY DADDIES WHO ARE BRAVE, AND PATRIOTIC--JUST LIKE YOURS!
NEXT TIME YOU WRITE TO YOUR DADDY, TELL HIM THAT THOR WISHES HIM WELL, AS HE FIGHTS TO HOLD ALOFT THE LAMP OF LIBERTY!
HOW ABOUT THAT! THOSE ARMS OF HIS CAN CRUSH CONCRETE! AND YET--!
HE'S HOLDIN' THAT KID AS GENTLY AS IF SHE WAS MADE OUTTA EGG-SHELLS!
WHAT A MAN!!
MOMENTS LATER, THOR WAVES THE CROWD BACK--!
STAND CLEAR! IT IS TIME FOR ME TO SWING MY HAMMER!!
OH NO YOU DON'T--!
ONE WAY
HOLD IT, FELLA! THIS IS THE LAW!
2

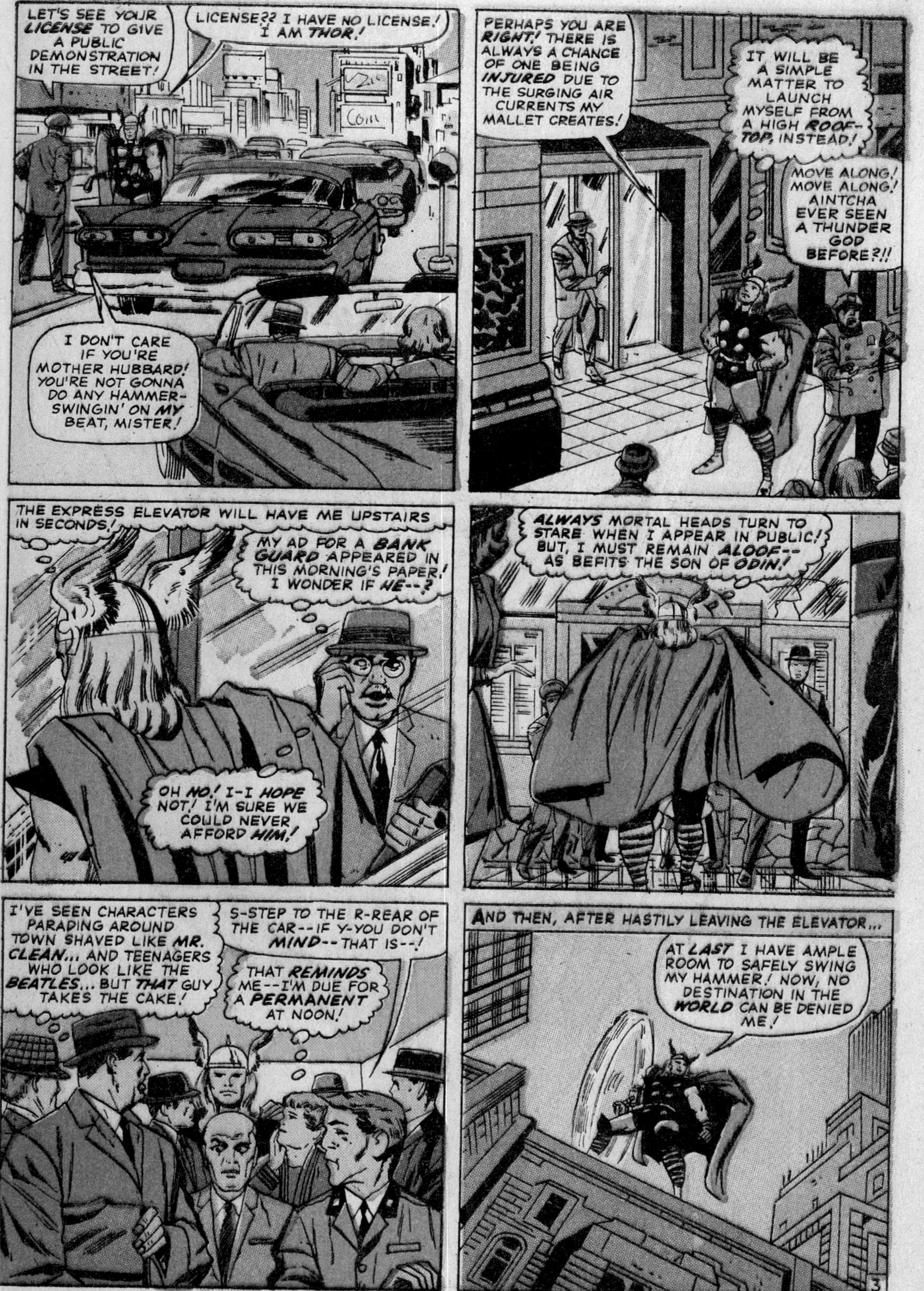

LET'S SEE YOUR LICENSE TO GIVE A PUBLIC DEMONSTRATION IN THE STREET!
LICENSE?? I HAVE NO LICENSE! I AM THOR!
I DON'T CARE IF YOU'RE MOTHER HUBBARD! YOU'RE NOT GONNA DO ANY HAMMER-SWINGIN' ON MY BEAT, MISTER!
PERHAPS YOU ARE RIGHT! THERE IS ALWAYS A CHANCE OF ONE BEING INJURED DUE TO THE SURGING AIR CURRENTS MY MALLET CREATES!
IT WILL BE A SIMPLE MATTER TO LAUNCH MYSELF FROM A HIGH ROOF-TOP, INSTEAD!
MOVE ALONG! MOVE ALONG! AINTCHA EVER SEEN A THUNDER GOD BEFORE?!!
THE EXPRESS ELEVATOR WILL HAVE ME UPSTAIRS IN SECONDS!
MY AD FOR A BANK GUARD APPEARED IN THIS MORNING'S PAPER! I WONDER IF HE--?
OH NO! I-I HOPE NOT! I'M SURE WE COULD NEVER AFFORD HIM!
ALWAYS MORTAL HEADS TURN TO STARE WHEN I APPEAR IN PUBLIC! BUT, I MUST REMAIN ALOOF-- AS BEFITS THE SON OF ODIN!
I'VE SEEN CHARACTERS PARADING AROUND TOWN SHAVED LIKE MR. CLEAN... AND TEENAGERS WHO LOOK LIKE THE BEATLES... BUT THAT GUY TAKES THE CAKE!
S-STEP TO THE R-REAR OF THE CAR--IF Y-YOU DON'T MIND--THAT IS--!
THAT REMINDS ME--I'M DUE FOR A PERMANENT AT NOON!
AND THEN, AFTER HASTILY LEAVING THE ELEVATOR...
AT LAST I HAVE AMPLE ROOM TO SAFELY SWING MY HAMMER! NOW, NO DESTINATION IN THE WORLD CAN BE DENIED ME!
3

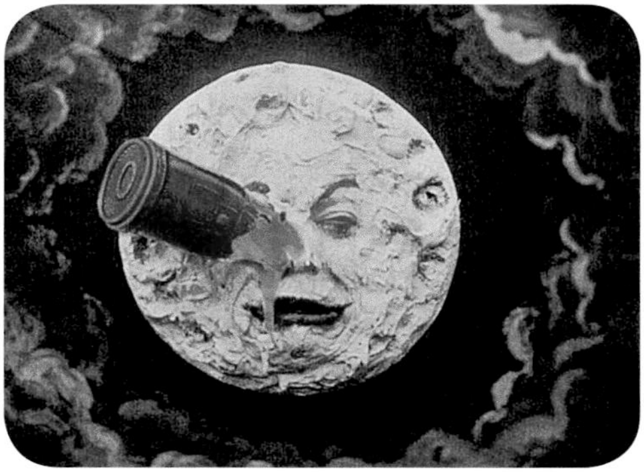

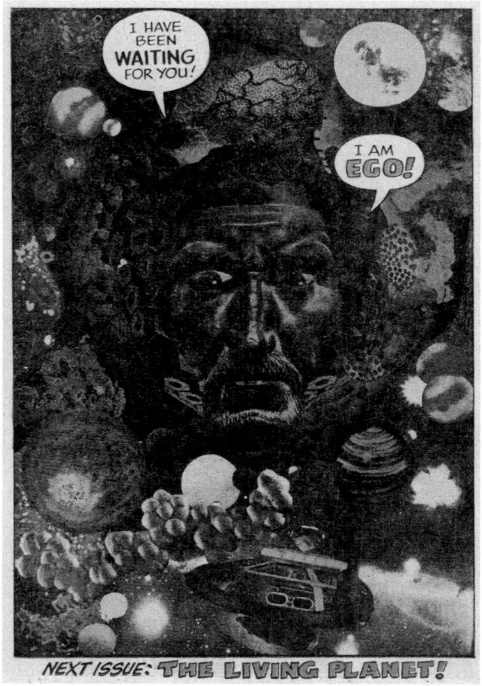
I HAVE BEEN WAITING FOR YOU!
I AM EGO!
NEXT ISSUE: THE LIVING PLANET!

MOONSHOT

(Left) Film still, A Trip to the Moon (Le voyage dans la lune)*; director, Georges Méliès; Star Film; 1902.* In the early days of cinema Méliès directed a pioneering feature combining live action with animation. This imaginative science-fiction short introduced visual tropes that permeated the culture, from comics and filmmaking—to the very notion of actually *going* to the moon.

THOR No. 132

(Below left) Interior, "...Where Gods May Fear to Tread!"; script, Stan Lee; pencils, Jack Kirby; inks, Vince Colletta; September 1966. When Jack Kirby wanted to impress you, he presented giants, including the Watcher, Galactus, and...Ego, the Living Planet! As the stories developed, and these massive figures became familiar, even expected, they often took on a more natural and smaller size. Ego will soon assume the size of a man.

THOR No. 131

(Opposite) Cover; pencils, Jack Kirby; inks, Vince Colletta; August 1966. Inker Vince Colletta was a colorful figure even among the many found in Marvel's "bullpen." Beloved by editors for his ability to make even the toughest deadlines, he was regarded as one of the industry's fastest inkers. "You could not take your eyes off him." said Lada St. Edmund, who occasionally modeled for his photography in the '60s. "You would watch him literally take a flat piece of artwork and totally transform it, give it shading and depth. It was amazing to watch....It looked like it [had taken] him hours, and he would always just laugh at that. I'd go, 'Gee. They're paying you a lot of money—don't you think you ought to take a little time?'"

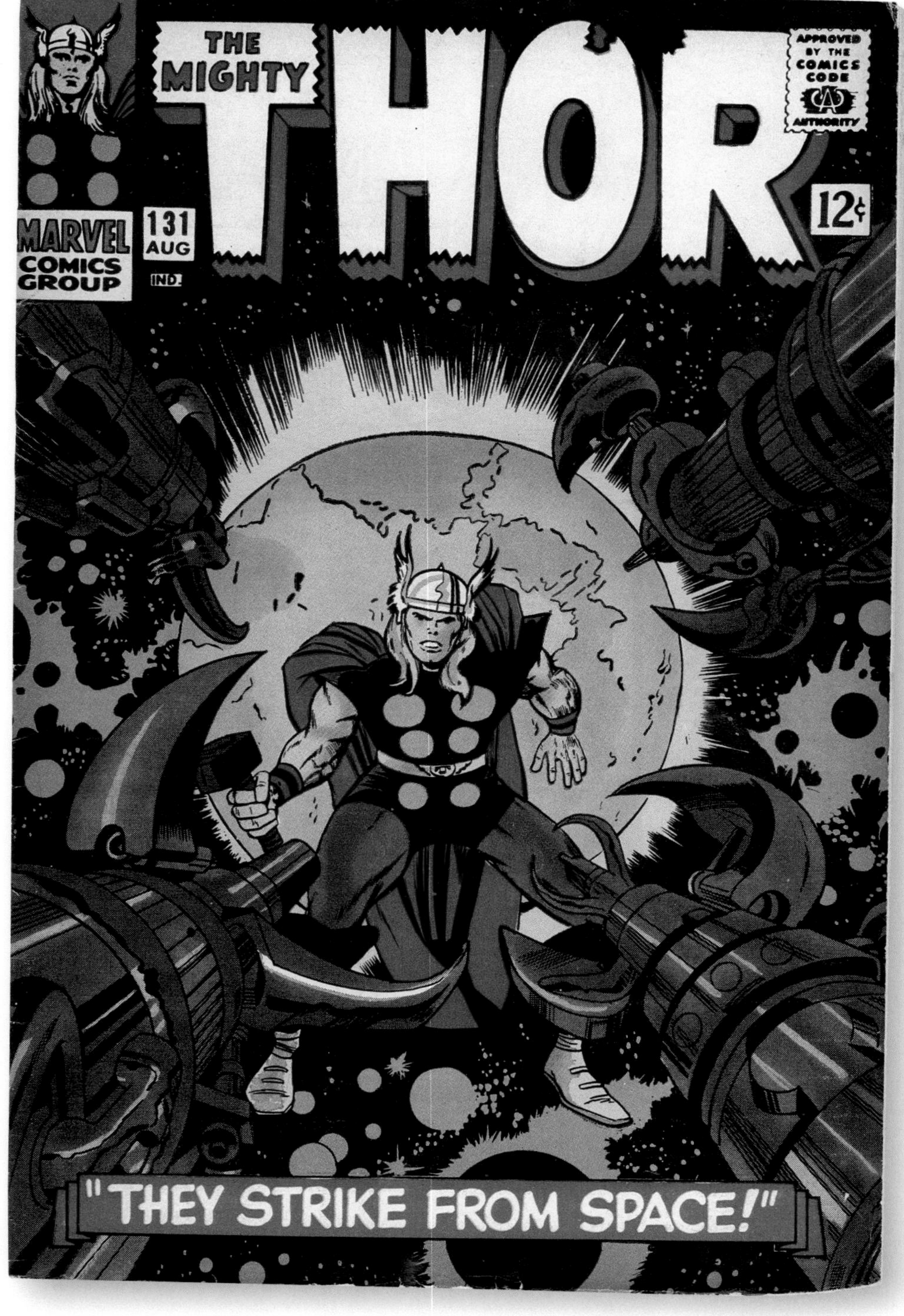
THE MIGHTY
THOR
APPROVED BY THE COMICS CODE AUTHORITY
MARVEL COMICS GROUP
131 AUG
IND.
12¢
"THEY STRIKE FROM SPACE!"

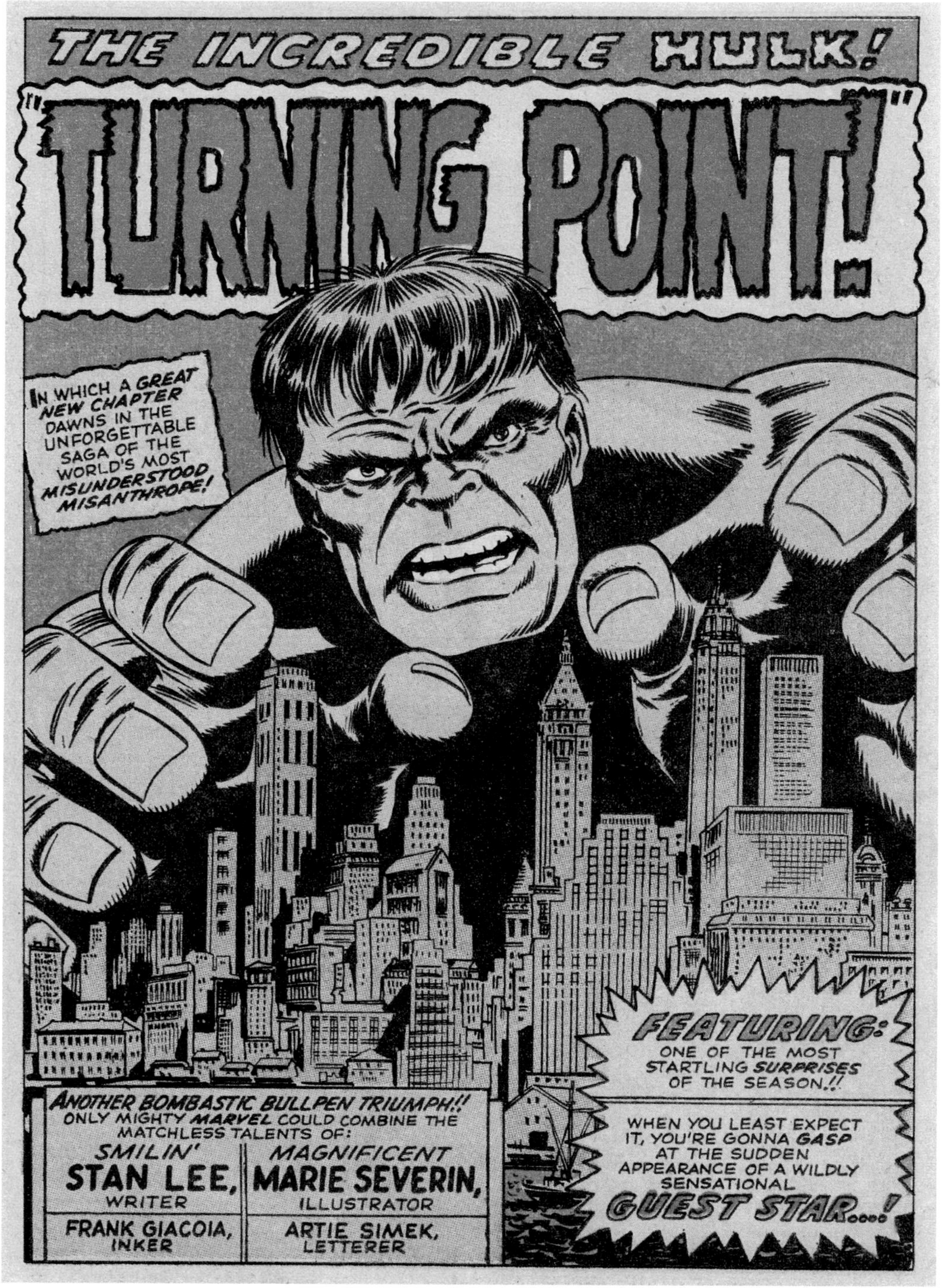
THE INCREDIBLE HULK!
"TURNING POINT!"
IN WHICH A GREAT NEW CHAPTER DAWNS IN THE UNFORGETTABLE SAGA OF THE WORLD'S MOST MISUNDERSTOOD MISANTHROPE!
FEATURING: ONE OF THE MOST STARTLING SURPRISES OF THE SEASON.!!
WHEN YOU LEAST EXPECT IT, YOU'RE GONNA GASP AT THE SUDDEN APPEARANCE OF A WILDLY SENSATIONAL GUEST STAR....!
ANOTHER BOMBASTIC BULLPEN TRIUMPH!! ONLY MIGHTY MARVEL COULD COMBINE THE MATCHLESS TALENTS OF:
SMILIN' STAN LEE, WRITER
MAGNIFICENT MARIE SEVERIN, ILLUSTRATOR
FRANK GIACOIA, INKER
ARTIE SIMEK, LETTERER

the california
PELICAN
THE
FAR-OUT
ISSUE!!
NOVEMBER 1965 - 30 CENTS

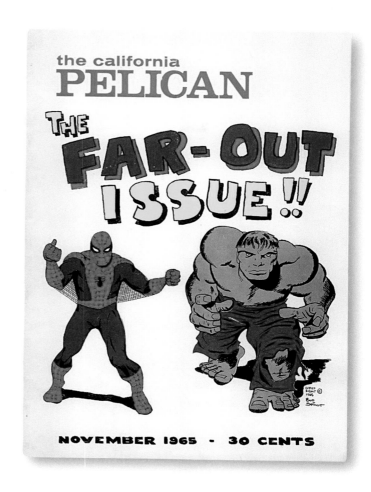

TALES TO ASTONISH No. 92

(Opposite) Interior, "Turning Point!"; script, Stan Lee; pencils, Marie Severin; inks, Frank Giacoia; June 1967.

MARVEL GOES TO COLLEGE

(Above) Magazine cover, The California Pelican *(University of California, Berkeley); art, Steve Ditko and Jack Kirby; November 1965.* While the political turmoil of the day tended to dominate the content of publications on progressive campuses around the country, comics were starting to become part of the thinking student's lexicon. In one of the earliest examples of the growing reach Marvel's characters were having outside the traditional audience, UC Berkeley's student humor magazine embraced Spider-Man and the Hulk, demonstrating that comics weren't just for kids anymore.

MARVELMANIA REDUX

(Below) Vinyl record; Scream Along with Marvel*; pencils and inks, Marie Severin; 1967.* For the second wave of Marvelmania, the M.M.M.S. membership kit now contained a recording of the opening and closing songs from the *Marvel Super-Heroes* on TV: "Stand a little straighter; walk a little prouder; be an innovator; clap a little louder; grow forever greater; we can show you how; where will you be then? You belong, you belong, you belong, you belong to the Merry Marvel Marching Society!!!"

JOURNEY INTO MYSTERY No. 112

(Opposite) Interior, "The Mighty Thor Battles the Incredible Hulk!"; script, Stan Lee; pencils, Jack Kirby; inks, Chic Stone; January 1965. Akin to kids rooting for their favorite baseball team, this splash page features a group of boys asking the age-old question, "Who is stronger, Thor or the Hulk?" Stan Lee loved to pit one hero against the other, but rarely was there an injury—or a victor!

CLASS OF '66

(Following spread) Magazine interior, "...Now You're Smart Enough for Comic Books," Esquire*; pencils, Jack Kirby with John Romita; inks, Joe Sinnott; September 1966.* In the wake of camp-inspired comics mockery brought on by the *Batman* TV series, *Esquire* discovers that, actually, Marvel comics are cool again—and are increasingly popular on college campuses. "As one Ivy Leaguer told Stan Lee, 'We think of Marvel as the twentieth-century mythology and you as this generation's Homer.'"

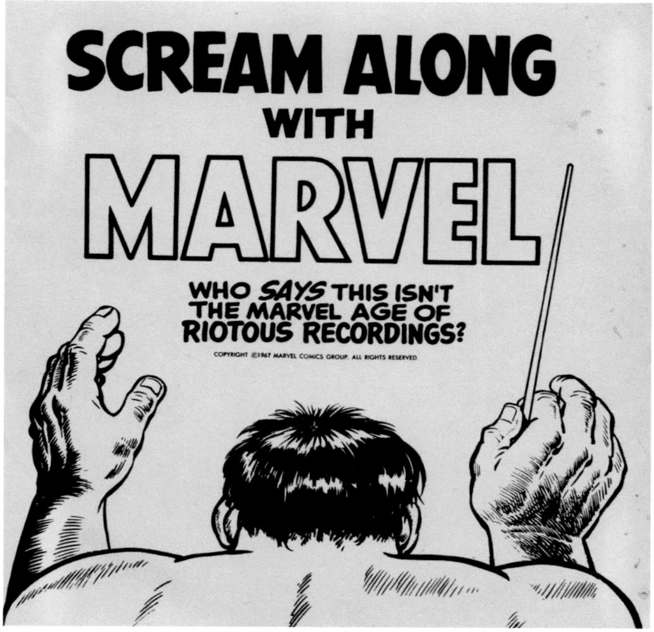
SCREAM ALONG
WITH
MARVEL
WHO SAYS THIS ISN'T THE MARVEL AGE OF RIOTOUS RECORDINGS?
COPYRIGHT ©1967 MARVEL COMICS GROUP. ALL RIGHTS RESERVED.

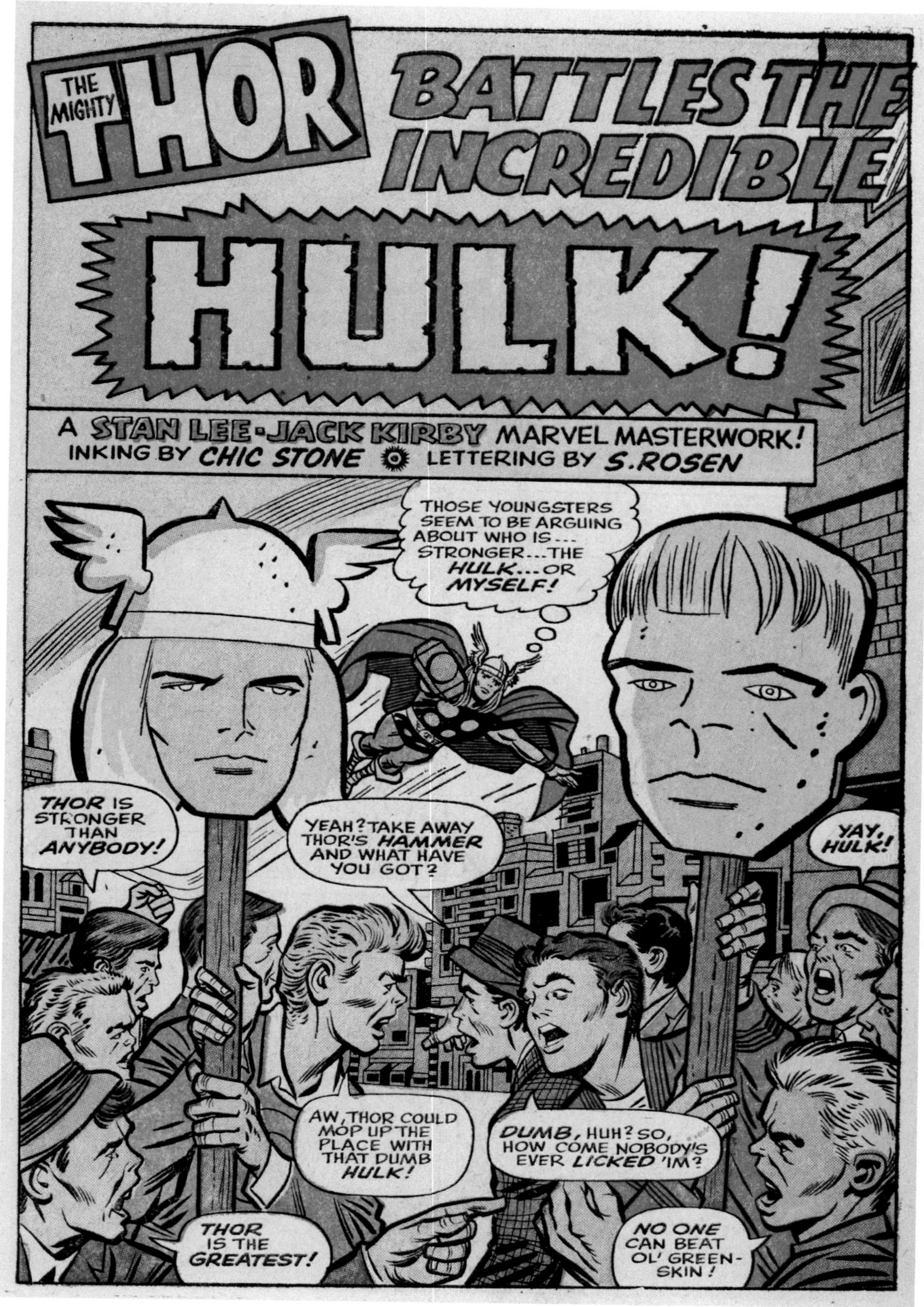

THE MIGHTY THOR BATTLES THE INCREDIBLE HULK!
A STAN LEE-JACK KIRBY MARVEL MASTERWORK!
INKING BY CHIC STONE LETTERING BY S.ROSEN
THOSE YOUNGSTERS SEEM TO BE ARGUING ABOUT WHO IS--- STRONGER... THE HULK... OR MYSELF!
THOR IS STRONGER THAN ANYBODY!
YEAH? TAKE AWAY THOR'S HAMMER AND WHAT HAVE YOU GOT?
YAY, HULK!
AW, THOR COULD MOP UP THE PLACE WITH THAT DUMB HULK!
DUMB, HUH? SO, HOW COME NOBODY'S EVER LICKED 'IM?
THOR IS THE GREATEST!
NO ONE CAN BEAT OL' GREEN-SKIN!

O.K., You Passed the 2-S Test—Now You're Smart Enough for Comic Books

What did Dostoevski know?
The true message is carried by Marvel Comics, twelve cents an ish

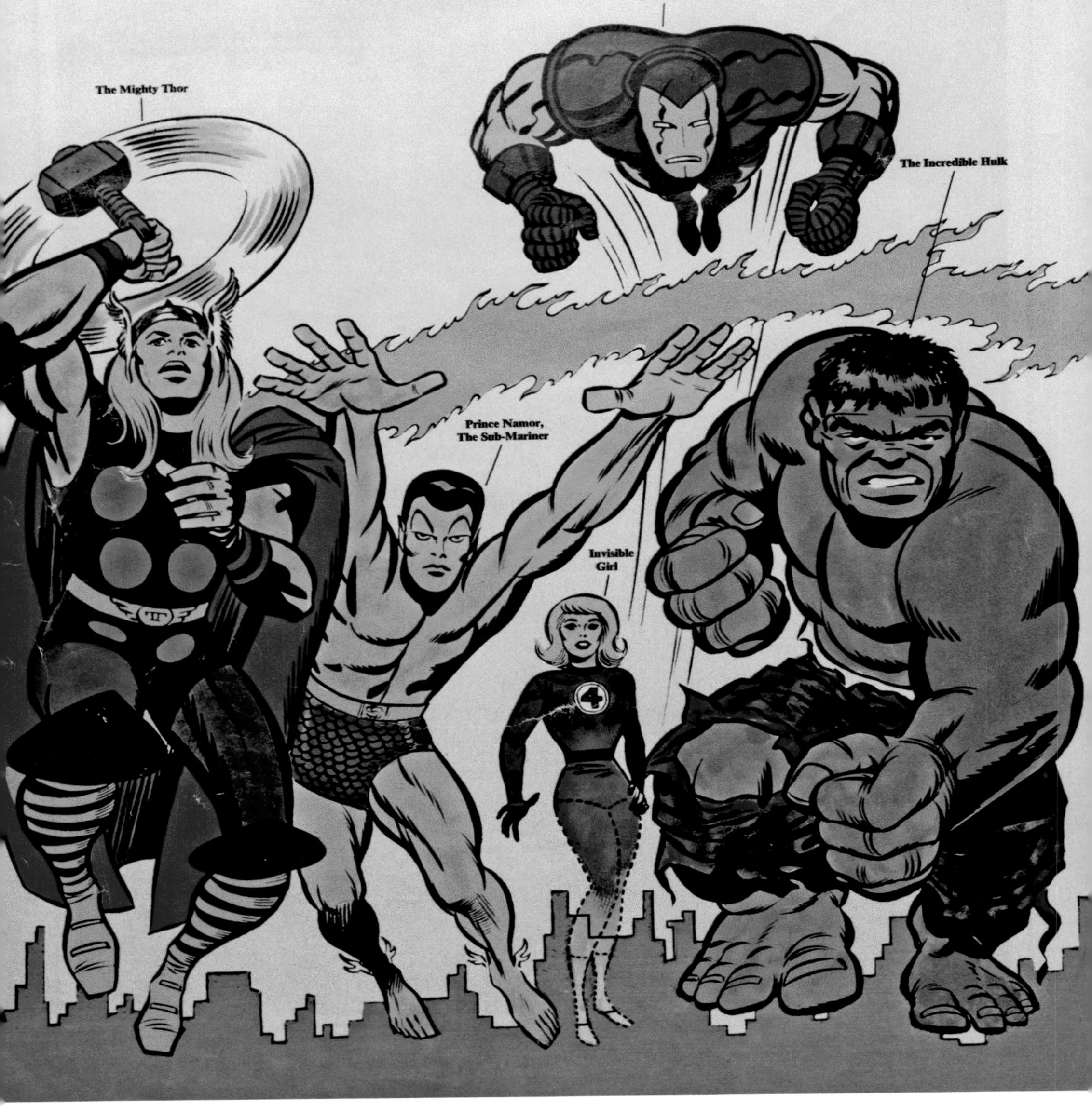
Iron Man
The Mighty Thor
The Incredible Hulk
Prince Namor, The Sub-Mariner
Invisible Girl

Early this year, the author of Marvel Comics received a letter from William David Sherman, an English teacher at State University of New York at Buffalo. "Enclosed you will find a money order for three dollars," he wrote. "Please send me twenty-five copies of issue number 46 ('Those Who Would Destroy Us'); I wish to use them in my course on contemporary American Literature....I know the class will dig them, and I hope that in them they will see various archetypal and mythological patterns at work which would give them better insight to where things are today." There is evidence that college students are already digging them. The Princeton Debating Society invited Stan Lee, author of Marvel's ten super-hero comics, to speak in a lecture series that also included Hubert Humphrey, William Scranton and Wayne Morse. Other talks were given at Bard (where he drew a bigger audience than President Eisenhower), N.Y.U. and Columbia. Some fifty thousand American college students, paying a dollar a head, belong to Merry Marvel Marching Societies and wear "I Belong" buttons on more than a hundred campuses. Bundles of mail pour into Marvel's offices every day from more than 225 colleges. Twenty-four disc jockeys are loyal M.M.M.S. members and never let their listeners forget it. And in the fall, at least twenty-five television stations will carry animated Marvel cartoons. Should anybody still suspect that children are the only Marvel readers, it might be pointed out that the company has sold 50,000 printed T-shirts and 30,000 sweat shirts, and it has run out of adult sizes of both. Why all the furious enthusiasm? As one Ivy Leaguer told Stan Lee. "We think of Marvel Comics as the twentieth-century mythology and you as this generation's Homer."

At this stage of the game it is not yet clear whether the profound impact of Marvel Comics on the campus reveals more about the comics or the campus. Perhaps a clue can be found on the following page; you figure it out.

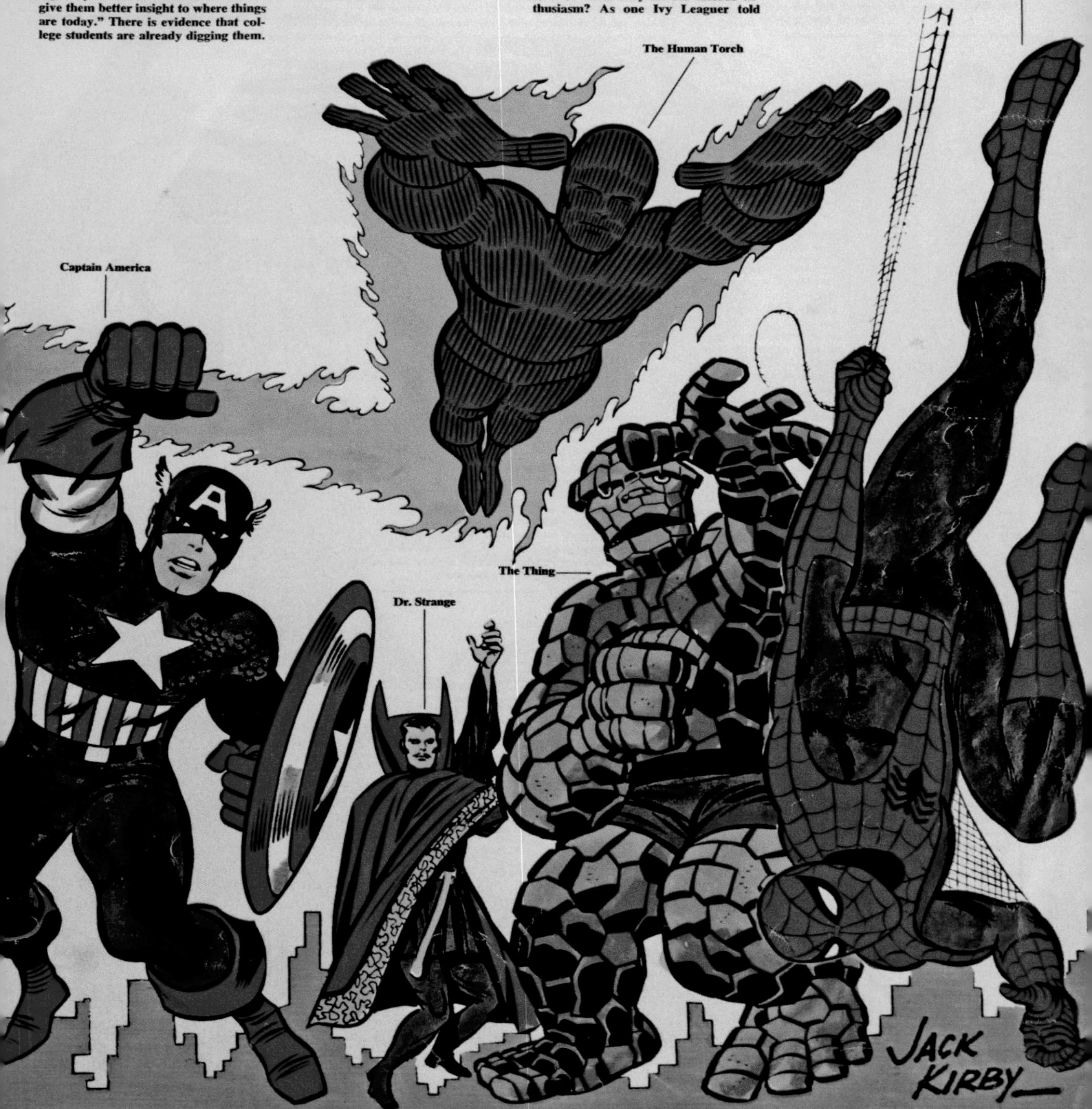
The Amazing Spider-Ma
The Human Torch
Captain America
The Thing
Dr. Strange
JACK KIRBY

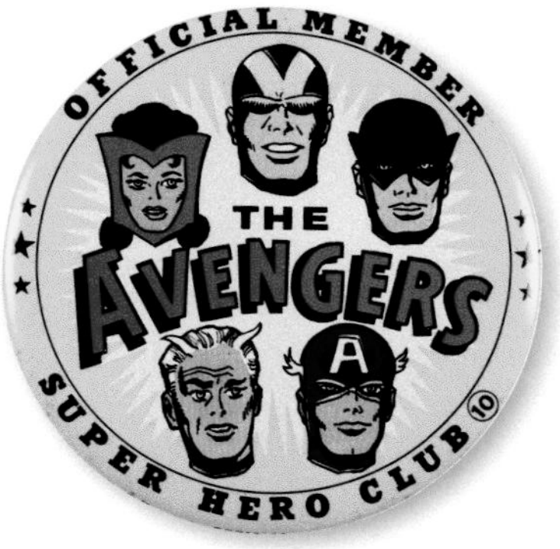
OFFICIAL MEMBER
THE
AVENGERS
SUPER HERO CLUB

PIN PALS

(Left) Avengers button, ca. 1966. Buttons featuring Marvel heroes were becoming commonplace symbols by 1966.

HEROES UNITED!

(Below) Photograph, ca. 1968. A young boy is thrilled to be in the presence of Spidey and Cap at the Michigan State Fair.

THE AVENGERS No. 23

(Opposite) Cover; pencils, Jack Kirby; inks, John Romita; December 1965. "Marvel often stretches the pseudoscientific imagination far into the phantasmagoria of other dimensions, problems of time and space, and even the semi-theological concept of creation," a Cornell student enlightened *Esquire*. "They are brilliantly illustrated, to a nearly hallucinogenic extent. Even the simple mortal-hero stories are illustrated with every panel as dramatically composed as anything Orson Welles ever put on film."

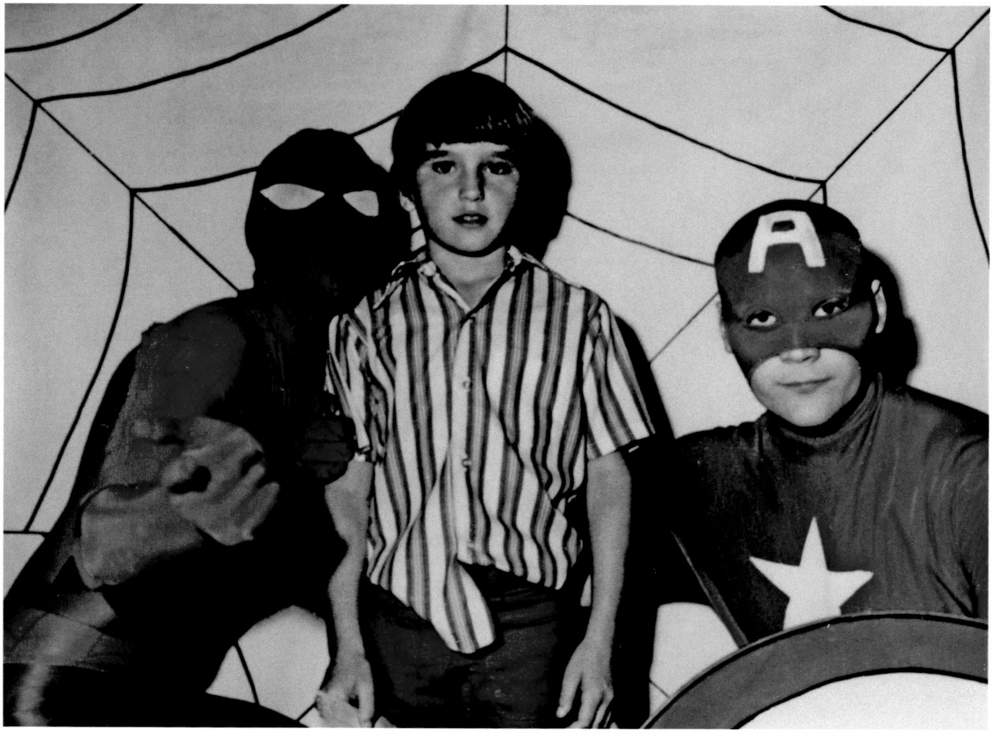

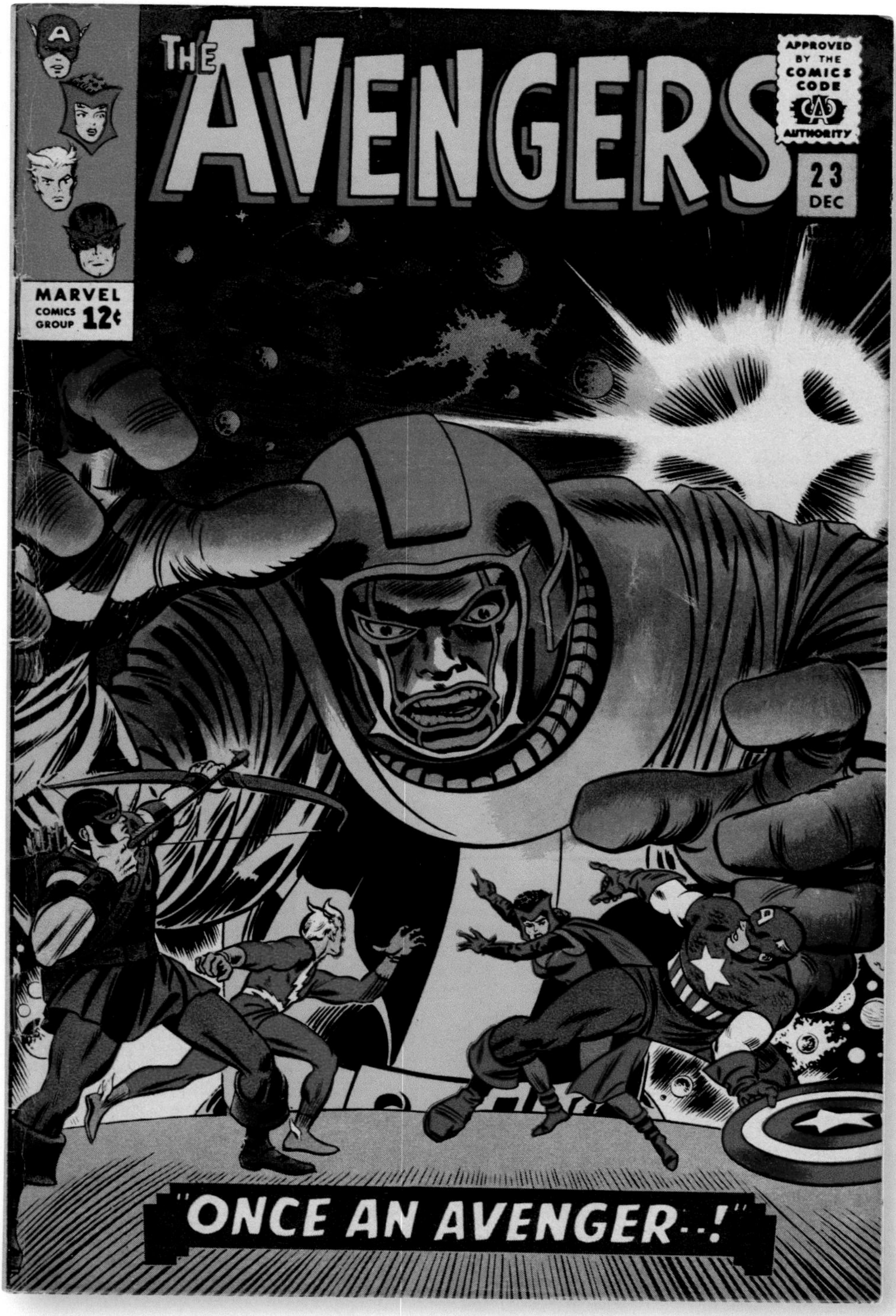
THE AVENGERS
APPROVED BY THE COMICS CODE AUTHORITY
23
DEC
MARVEL COMICS GROUP
12¢
"ONCE AN AVENGER..!"

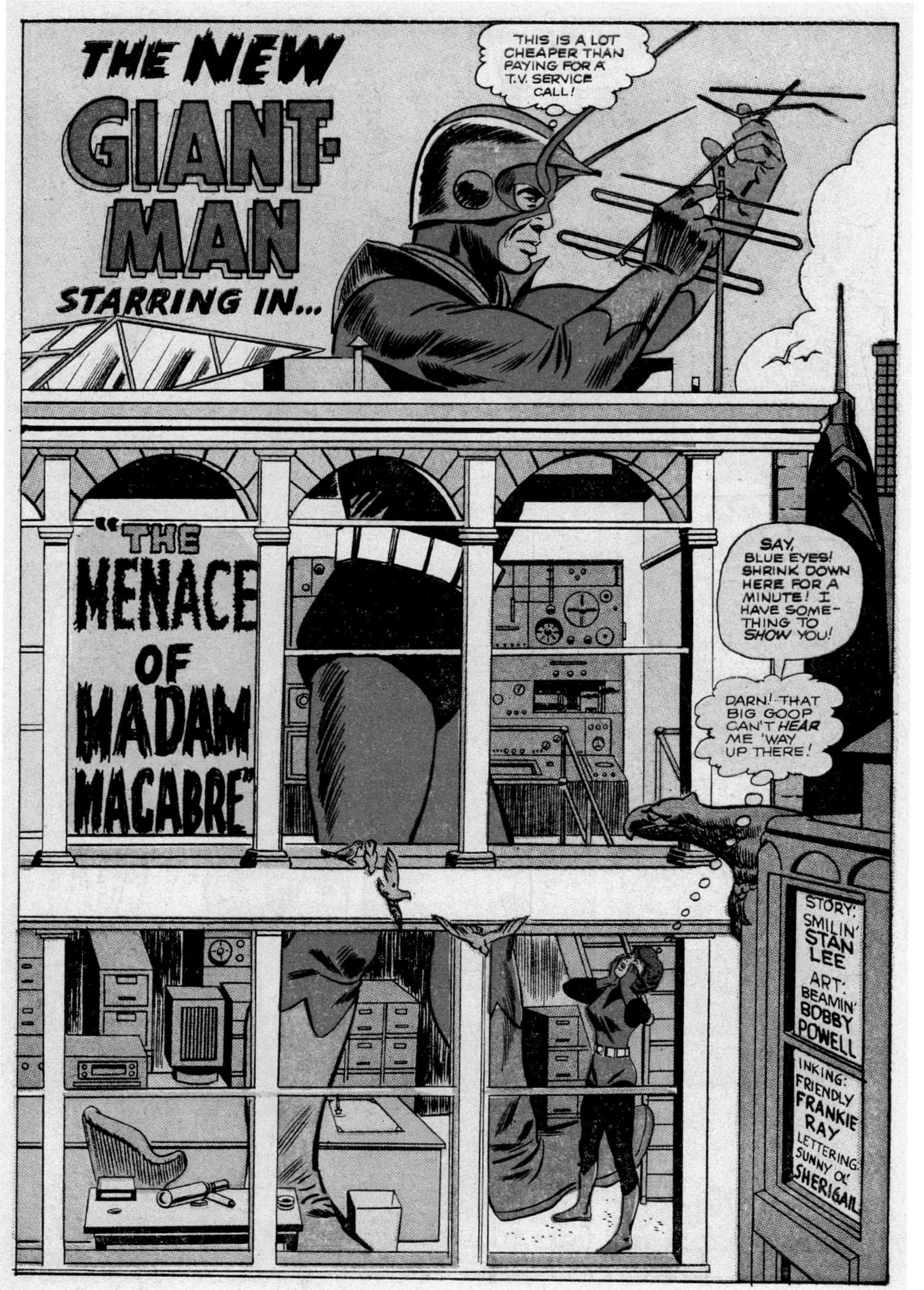
THE NEW
GIANT-MAN
STARRING IN...
THIS IS A LOT CHEAPER THAN PAYING FOR A T.V. SERVICE CALL!
"THE MENACE OF MADAM MACABRE"
SAY, BLUE EYES! SHRINK DOWN HERE FOR A MINUTE! I HAVE SOMETHING TO SHOW YOU!
DARN! THAT BIG GOOP CAN'T HEAR ME 'WAY UP THERE!
STORY: SMILIN' STAN LEE
ART: BEAMIN' BOBBY POWELL
INKING: FRIENDLY FRANKIE RAY
LETTERING: SUNNY OL' SHERIGAIL

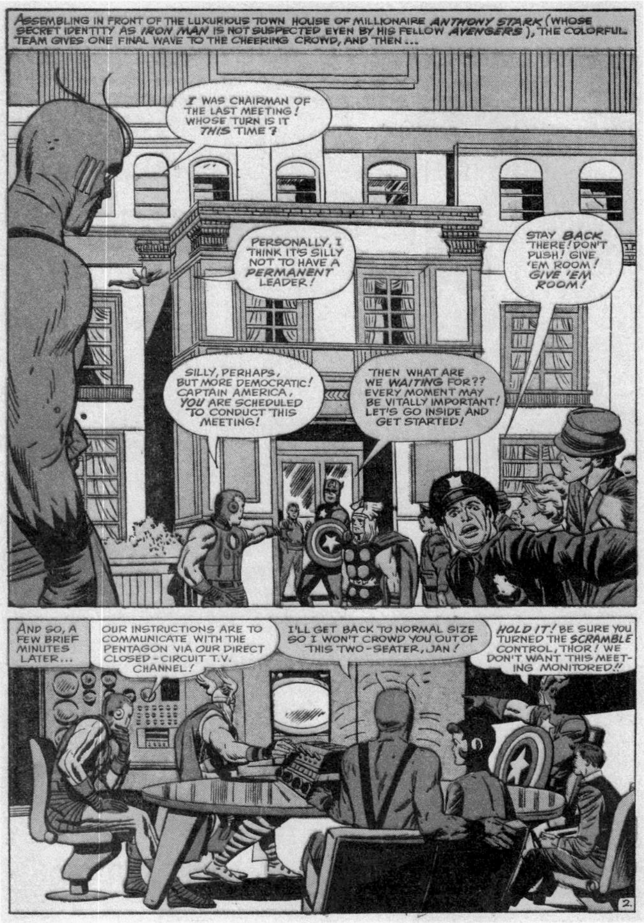
ASSEMBLING IN FRONT OF THE LUXURIOUS TOWN HOUSE OF MILLIONAIRE ANTHONY STARK (WHOSE SECRET IDENTITY AS IRON MAN IS NOT SUSPECTED EVEN BY HIS FELLOW AVENGERS), THE COLORFUL TEAM GIVES ONE FINAL WAVE TO THE CHEERING CROWD, AND THEN...
I WAS CHAIRMAN OF THE LAST MEETING! WHOSE TURN IS IT THIS TIME?
PERSONALLY, I THINK IT'S SILLY NOT TO HAVE A PERMANENT LEADER!
STAY BACK THERE! DON'T PUSH! GIVE 'EM ROOM! GIVE 'EM ROOM!
SILLY, PERHAPS, BUT MORE DEMOCRATIC! CAPTAIN AMERICA, YOU ARE SCHEDULED TO CONDUCT THIS MEETING!
THEN WHAT ARE WE WAITING FOR?? EVERY MOMENT MAY BE VITALLY IMPORTANT! LET'S GO INSIDE AND GET STARTED!
AND SO, A FEW BRIEF MINUTES LATER...
OUR INSTRUCTIONS ARE TO COMMUNICATE WITH THE PENTAGON VIA OUR DIRECT CLOSED-CIRCUIT T.V. CHANNEL!
I'LL GET BACK TO NORMAL SIZE SO I WON'T CROWD YOU OUT OF THIS TWO-SEATER, JAN!
HOLD IT! BE SURE YOU TURNED THE SCRAMBLE CONTROL, THOR! WE DON'T WANT THIS MEETING MONITORED!!
2.

TALES TO ASTONISH No. 66

(Opposite) Interior, "The Menace of Madame Macabre"; script, Stan Lee; pencils, Bob Powell; inks, Frank Giacoia; April 1965.

THE AVENGERS No. 8

(Above) Interior, "Kang, the Conqueror!"; script, Stan Lee; pencils, Jack Kirby; inks, Dick Ayers; September 1964. Located on the upper east side of Manhattan, the onetime home of industrialist and art patron Henry Clay Frick became a museum housing his eminent art collection in the 1930s. The building also served as the model for Anthony Stark's mansion—yet another example of real New York landmarks dotting the Marvel landscape.

THE AVENGERS ANNUAL No. 1

(Following spread) Interior; diagram, Roy Thomas and Don Heck; script, Thomas; pencils, Heck; inks, George Roussos; Summer 1967.

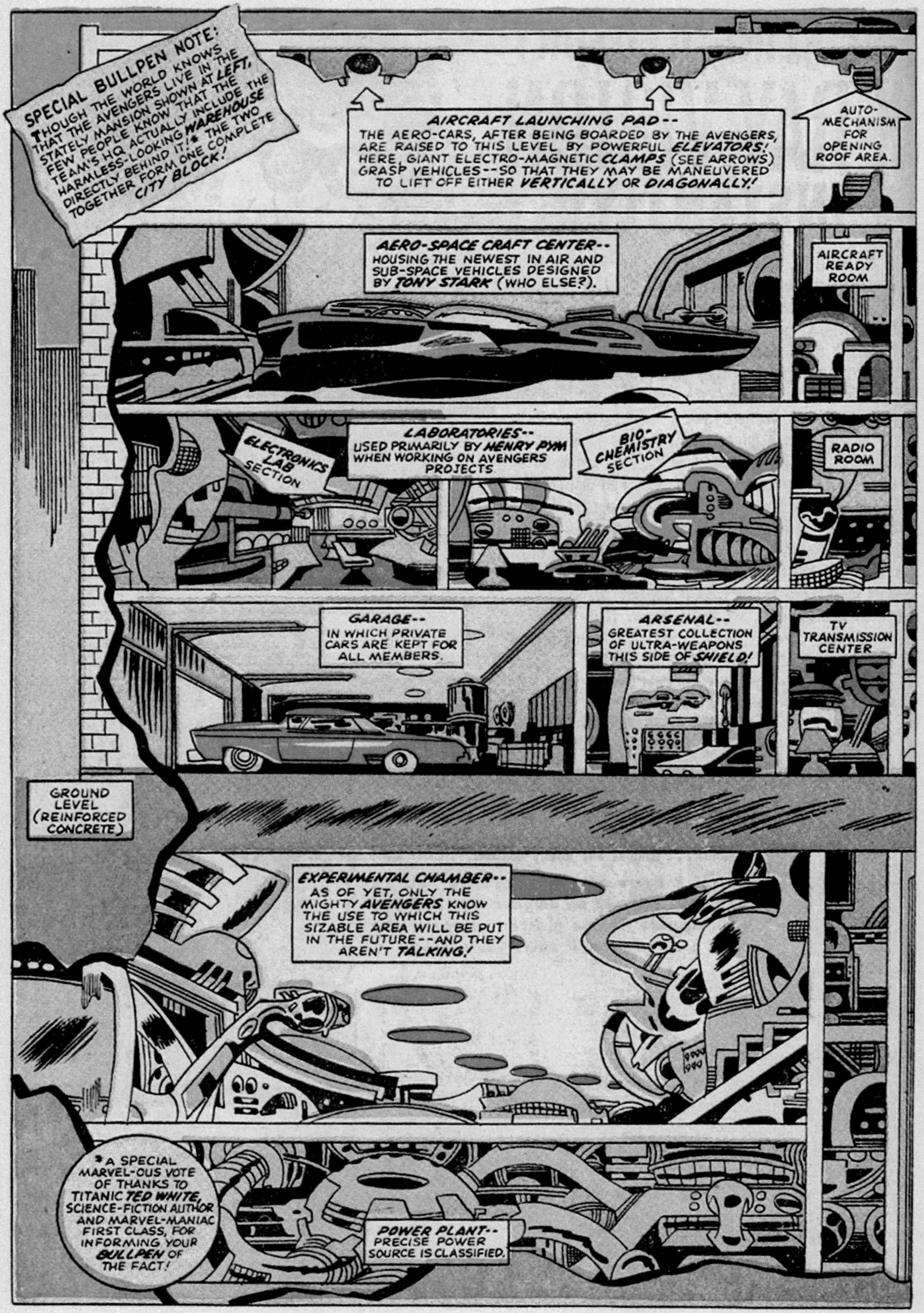
SPECIAL BULLPEN NOTE:
THOUGH THE WORLD KNOWS THAT THE AVENGERS LIVE IN THE STATELY MANSION SHOWN AT LEFT, FEW PEOPLE KNOW THAT THE TEAM'S HQ ACTUALLY INCLUDE THE HARMLESS-LOOKING WAREHOUSE DIRECTLY BEHIND IT!* THE TWO TOGETHER FORM ONE COMPLETE CITY BLOCK!
AIRCRAFT LAUNCHING PAD-- THE AERO-CARS, AFTER BEING BOARDED BY THE AVENGERS, ARE RAISED TO THIS LEVEL BY POWERFUL ELEVATORS! HERE, GIANT ELECTRO-MAGNETIC CLAMPS (SEE ARROWS) GRASP VEHICLES--SO THAT THEY MAY BE MANEUVERED TO LIFT OFF EITHER VERTICALLY OR DIAGONALLY!
AUTO-MECHANISM FOR OPENING ROOF AREA.
AERO-SPACE CRAFT CENTER-- HOUSING THE NEWEST IN AIR AND SUB-SPACE VEHICLES DESIGNED BY TONY STARK (WHO ELSE?).
AIRCRAFT READY ROOM
ELECTRONICS LAB SECTION
LABORATORIES-- USED PRIMARILY BY HENRY PYM WHEN WORKING ON AVENGERS PROJECTS
BIO-CHEMISTRY SECTION
RADIO ROOM
GARAGE-- IN WHICH PRIVATE CARS ARE KEPT FOR ALL MEMBERS.
ARSENAL-- GREATEST COLLECTION OF ULTRA-WEAPONS THIS SIDE OF SHIELD!
TV TRANSMISSION CENTER
GROUND LEVEL (REINFORCED CONCRETE)
EXPERIMENTAL CHAMBER-- AS OF YET, ONLY THE MIGHTY AVENGERS KNOW THE USE TO WHICH THIS SIZABLE AREA WILL BE PUT IN THE FUTURE--AND THEY AREN'T TALKING!
*A SPECIAL MARVEL-OUS VOTE OF THANKS TO TITANIC TED WHITE, SCIENCE-FICTION AUTHOR AND MARVEL-MANIAC FIRST CLASS, FOR INFORMING YOUR BULLPEN OF THE FACT!
POWER PLANT-- PRECISE POWER SOURCE IS CLASSIFIED.

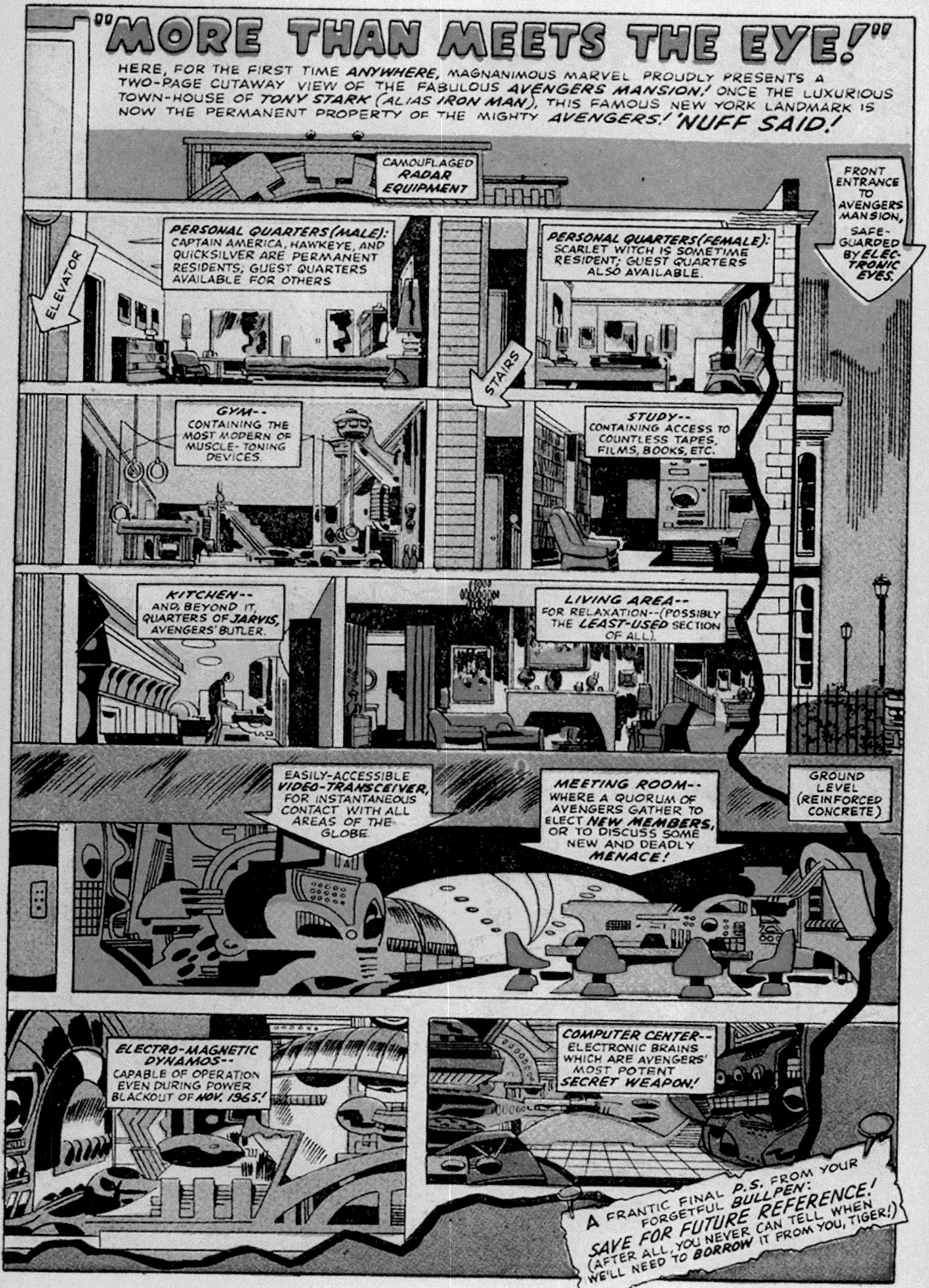
"MORE THAN MEETS THE EYE!"
HERE, FOR THE FIRST TIME ANYWHERE, MAGNANIMOUS MARVEL PROUDLY PRESENTS A TWO-PAGE CUTAWAY VIEW OF THE FABULOUS AVENGERS MANSION! ONCE THE LUXURIOUS TOWN-HOUSE OF TONY STARK (ALIAS IRON MAN), THIS FAMOUS NEW YORK LANDMARK IS NOW THE PERMANENT PROPERTY OF THE MIGHTY AVENGERS! 'NUFF SAID!
CAMOUFLAGED RADAR EQUIPMENT
FRONT ENTRANCE TO AVENGERS MANSION, SAFE-GUARDED BY ELEC-TRONIC EYES.
ELEVATOR
PERSONAL QUARTERS (MALE): CAPTAIN AMERICA, HAWKEYE, AND QUICKSILVER ARE PERMANENT RESIDENTS; GUEST QUARTERS AVAILABLE FOR OTHERS
PERSONAL QUARTERS (FEMALE): SCARLET WITCH IS SOMETIME RESIDENT; GUEST QUARTERS ALSO AVAILABLE.
STAIRS
GYM-- CONTAINING THE MOST MODERN OF MUSCLE-TONING DEVICES.
STUDY-- CONTAINING ACCESS TO COUNTLESS TAPES, FILMS, BOOKS, ETC.
KITCHEN-- AND, BEYOND IT, QUARTERS OF JARVIS, AVENGERS' BUTLER.
LIVING AREA-- FOR RELAXATION--(POSSIBLY THE LEAST-USED SECTION OF ALL).
EASILY-ACCESSIBLE VIDEO-TRANSCEIVER, FOR INSTANTANEOUS CONTACT WITH ALL AREAS OF THE GLOBE.
MEETING ROOM-- WHERE A QUORUM OF AVENGERS GATHER TO ELECT NEW MEMBERS, OR TO DISCUSS SOME NEW AND DEADLY MENACE!
GROUND LEVEL (REINFORCED CONCRETE)
ELECTRO-MAGNETIC DYNAMOS-- CAPABLE OF OPERATION EVEN DURING POWER BLACKOUT OF NOV. 1965!
COMPUTER CENTER-- ELECTRONIC BRAINS WHICH ARE AVENGERS' MOST POTENT SECRET WEAPON!
A FRANTIC FINAL P.S. FROM YOUR FORGETFUL BULLPEN: SAVE FOR FUTURE REFERENCE! (AFTER ALL, YOU NEVER CAN TELL WHEN WE'LL NEED TO BORROW IT FROM YOU, TIGER!)

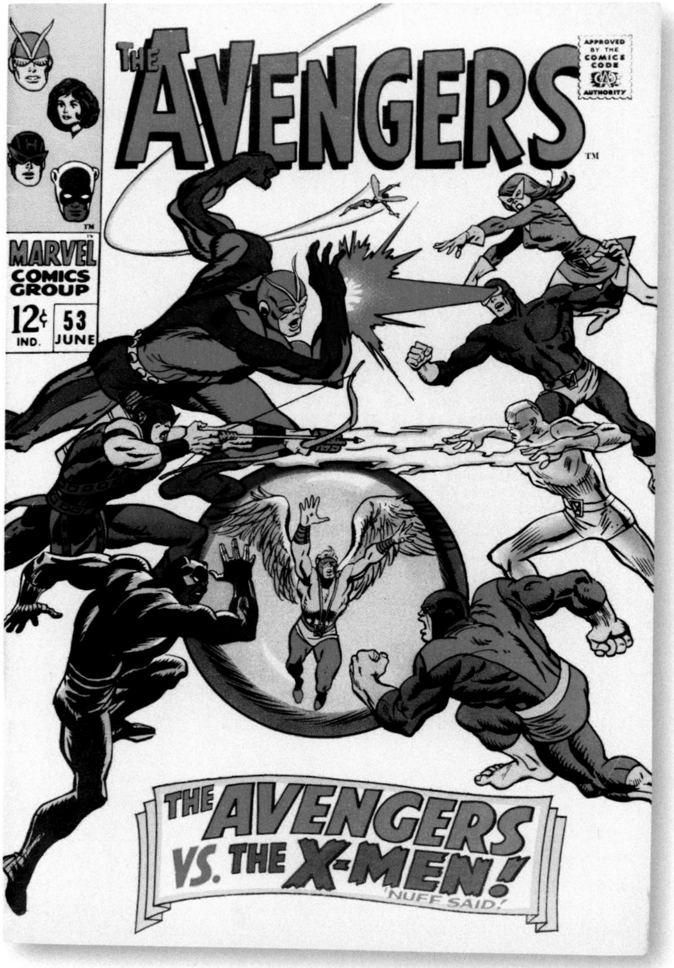
THE AVENGERS
MARVEL COMICS GROUP
12¢ IND.
53 JUNE
APPROVED BY THE COMICS CODE AUTHORITY
THE AVENGERS VS. THE X-MEN!
'NUFF SAID!

THE AVENGERS No. 53

(Above) Cover; pencils, John Buscema; inks, George Tuska; June 1968. A guest-starring role in *The Avengers* was an attempt to boost sales for the less popular X-Men, a second-tier book that was seeing declining sales. A fight between the good guys was sure to excite the fans.

X-MEN No. 49

(Opposite) Original cover art; pencils and inks, Jim Steranko; October 1968. Steranko brought a sense of dynamism to this poster-like composition. He only worked on X-Men briefly, and then only as an artist. It would take the likes of Neal Adams working with Roy Thomas to begin to shake things up for the faltering title.

WORLD COLOR XMEN

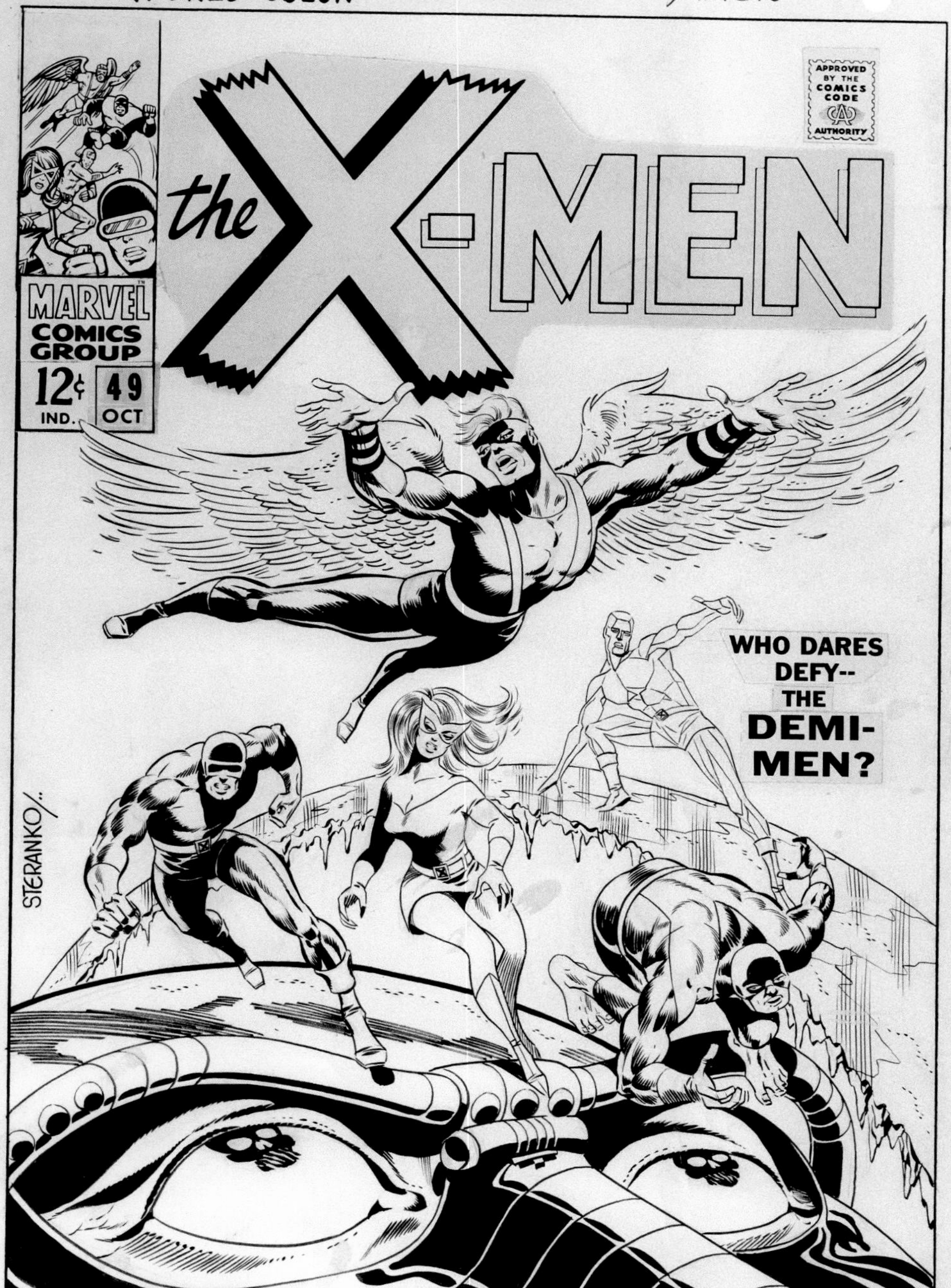

MARVEL COMICS GROUP
12¢ IND.
49 OCT
APPROVED BY THE COMICS CODE AUTHORITY
the X-MEN
WHO DARES DEFY-- THE DEMI-MEN?
STERANKO

YELLOW T S

BLACK T S

RED T S

BLUE T S

7x10½

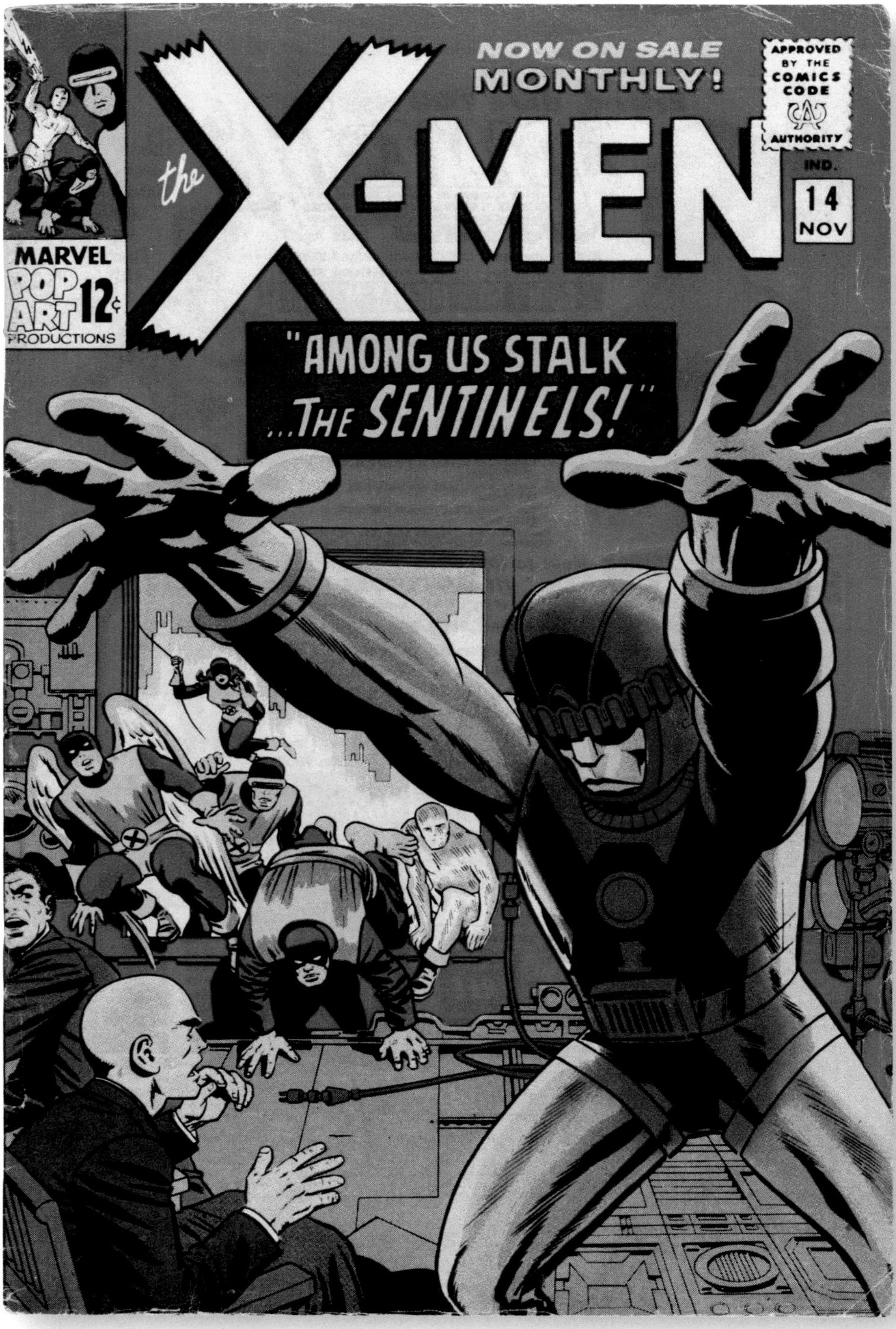
NOW ON SALE
MONTHLY!
APPROVED BY THE COMICS CODE AUTHORITY
the X-MEN
IND.
14
NOV
MARVEL
POP ART
12¢
PRODUCTIONS
"AMONG US STALK
...THE SENTINELS!"

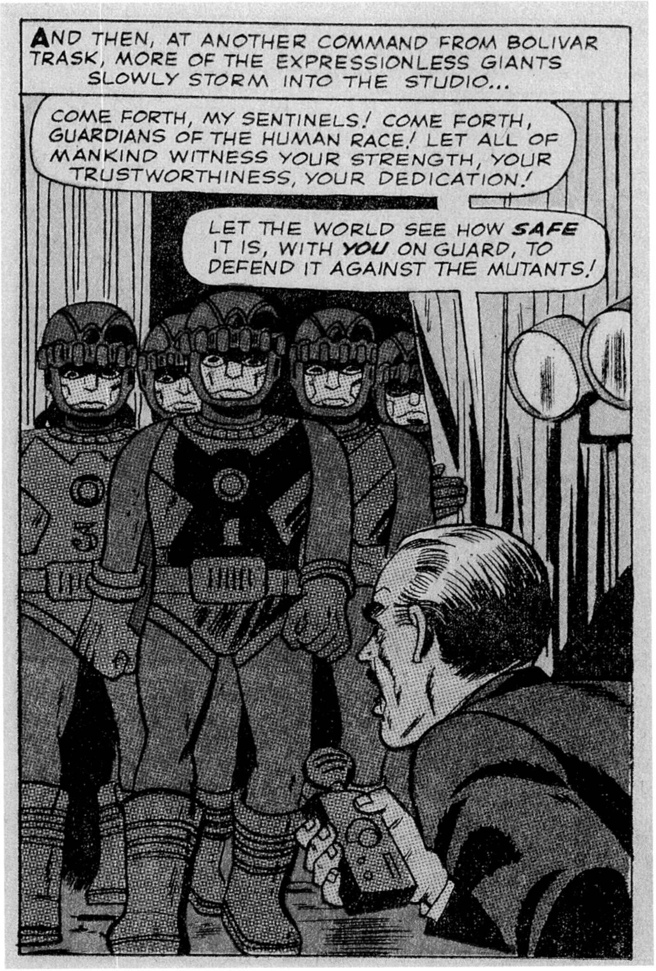
AND THEN, AT ANOTHER COMMAND FROM BOLIVAR TRASK, MORE OF THE EXPRESSIONLESS GIANTS SLOWLY STORM INTO THE STUDIO...
COME FORTH, MY SENTINELS! COME FORTH, GUARDIANS OF THE HUMAN RACE! LET ALL OF MANKIND WITNESS YOUR STRENGTH, YOUR TRUSTWORTHINESS, YOUR DEDICATION!
LET THE WORLD SEE HOW SAFE IT IS, WITH YOU ON GUARD, TO DEFEND IT AGAINST THE MUTANTS!

X-MEN No. 14
(Opposite) Cover; pencils, Jack Kirby; inks, Wally Wood; November 1965. Kirby's Sentinel robot brings a sense of overwhelming power with its massive figure and hands. By the mid-1960s Kirby was expanding his vision beyond previous boundaries to conceive protagonists that exemplified "Kirby Dynamics."

X-MEN No. 14
(Above) Interior, "Among Us Stalk the Sentinels!"; script, Stan Lee; layouts, Jack Kirby; finished pencils, Werner Roth; inks, Dick Ayers; January 1966. Dr. Bolivar Trask convinces the public that mutants are a menace. His Sentinels, a legion of robots with cybernetic brains, shake Trask's control and confront the X-Men.

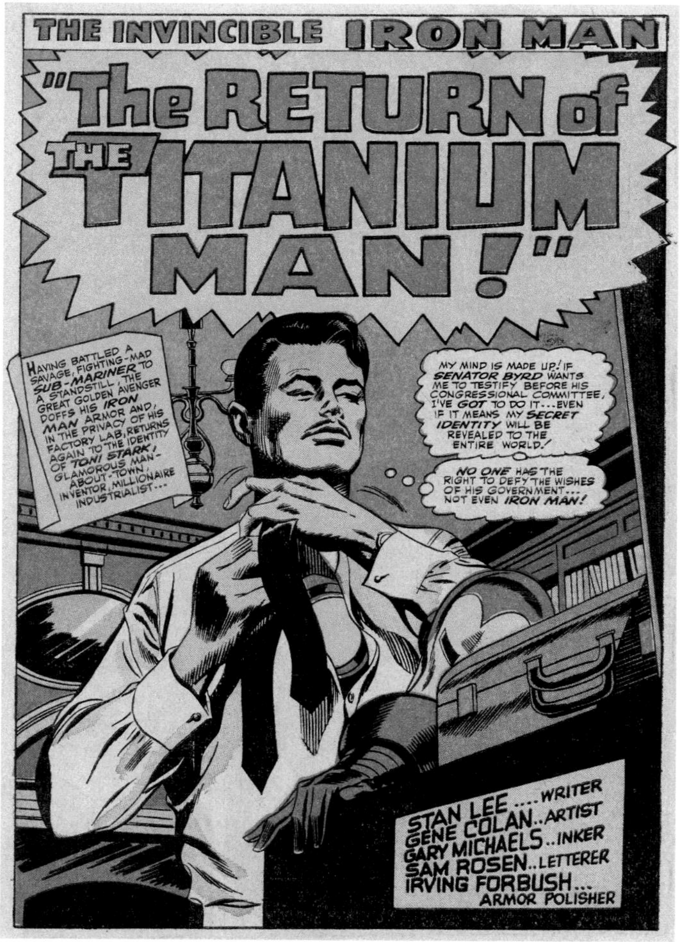
THE INVINCIBLE IRON MAN
"The RETURN of THE TITANIUM MAN!"
HAVING BATTLED A SAVAGE, FIGHTING-MAD SUB-MARINER TO A STANDSTILL, THE GREAT GOLDEN AVENGER DOFFS HIS IRON MAN ARMOR AND, IN THE PRIVACY OF HIS FACTORY LAB, RETURNS AGAIN TO THE IDENTITY OF TONI STARK! GLAMOROUS MAN-ABOUT-TOWN, INVENTOR, MILLIONAIRE INDUSTRIALIST...
MY MIND IS MADE UP! IF SENATOR BYRD WANTS ME TO TESTIFY BEFORE HIS CONGRESSIONAL COMMITTEE, I'VE GOT TO DO IT...EVEN IF IT MEANS MY SECRET IDENTITY WILL BE REVEALED TO THE ENTIRE WORLD!
NO ONE HAS THE RIGHT TO DEFY THE WISHES OF HIS GOVERNMENT... NOT EVEN IRON MAN!
STAN LEE....WRITER
GENE COLAN..ARTIST
GARY MICHAELS..INKER
SAM ROSEN...LETTERER
IRVING FORBUSH... ARMOR POLISHER

TALES OF SUSPENSE No. 81

(Above) Interior, "The Return of the Titanium Man!"; script, Stan Lee; pencils, Gene Colan; inks, Jack Abel; September 1966. Working much more with photographic reference than most of Marvel's artists, Colan offered a rich cinematic experience that leave his stories feeling highly realistic. In fact, Colan's depiction of Tony Stark appeared to be based on actor Clark Gable.

TALES OF SUSPENSE No. 93

(Opposite) Interior, "The Golden Gladiator and... the Giant!"; script, Stan Lee; pencils, Gene Colan; inks, Frank Giacoia; September 1967. Where to place the "camera" was an important feature of Colan's storytelling. Here the smaller figure of Iron Man is overwhelmed by the huge, imposing Titanium Man.

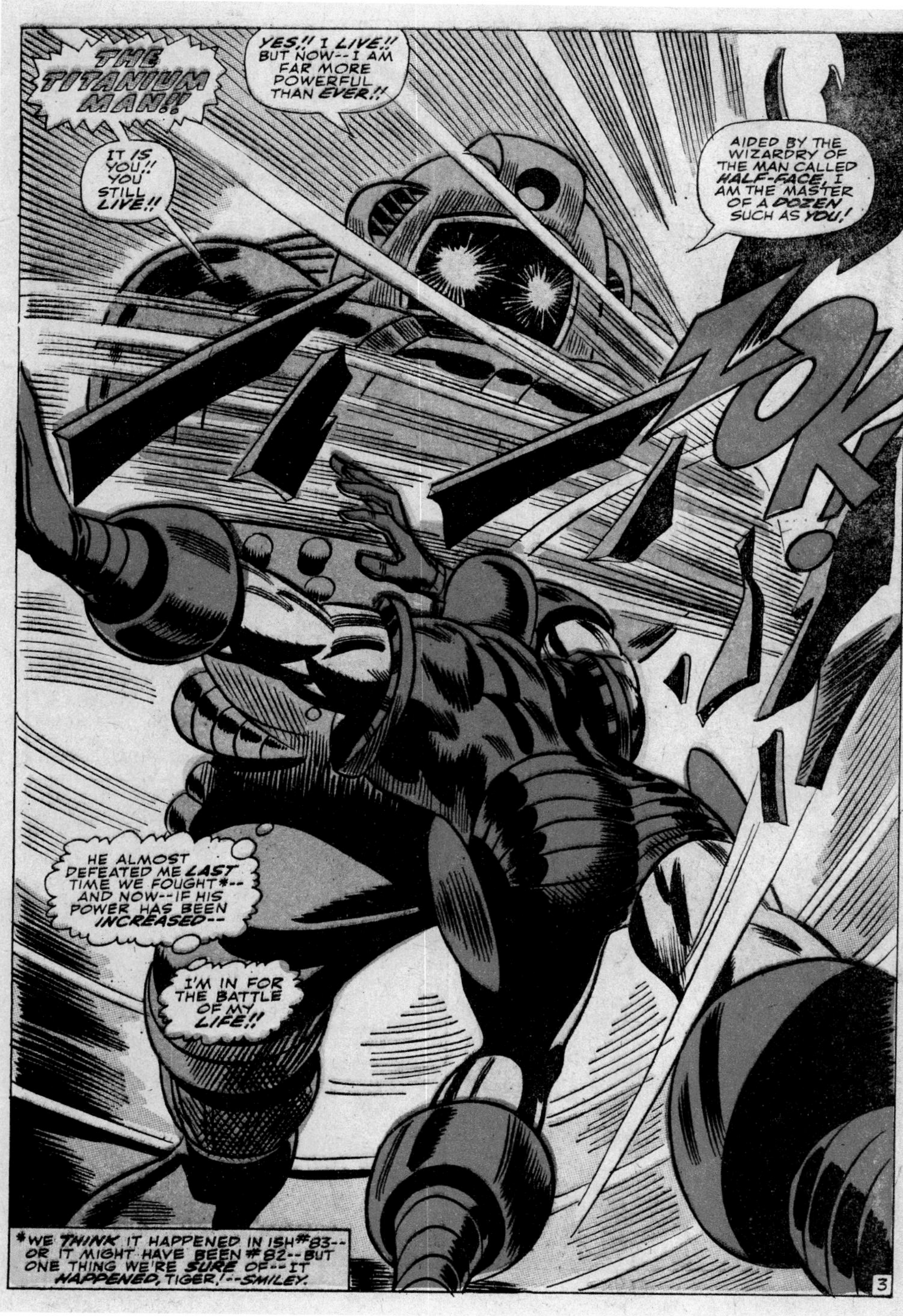
THE TITANIUM MAN!!
YES!! I LIVE!! BUT NOW--I AM FAR MORE POWERFUL THAN EVER!!
IT IS YOU!! YOU STILL LIVE!!
AIDED BY THE WIZARDRY OF THE MAN CALLED HALF-FACE, I AM THE MASTER OF A DOZEN SUCH AS YOU!
ZOK!
HE ALMOST DEFEATED ME LAST TIME WE FOUGHT*-- AND NOW--IF HIS POWER HAS BEEN INCREASED--
I'M IN FOR THE BATTLE OF MY LIFE!!
*WE THINK IT HAPPENED IN ISH #83-- OR IT MIGHT HAVE BEEN #82--BUT ONE THING WE'RE SURE OF--IT HAPPENED, TIGER!--SMILEY.
3

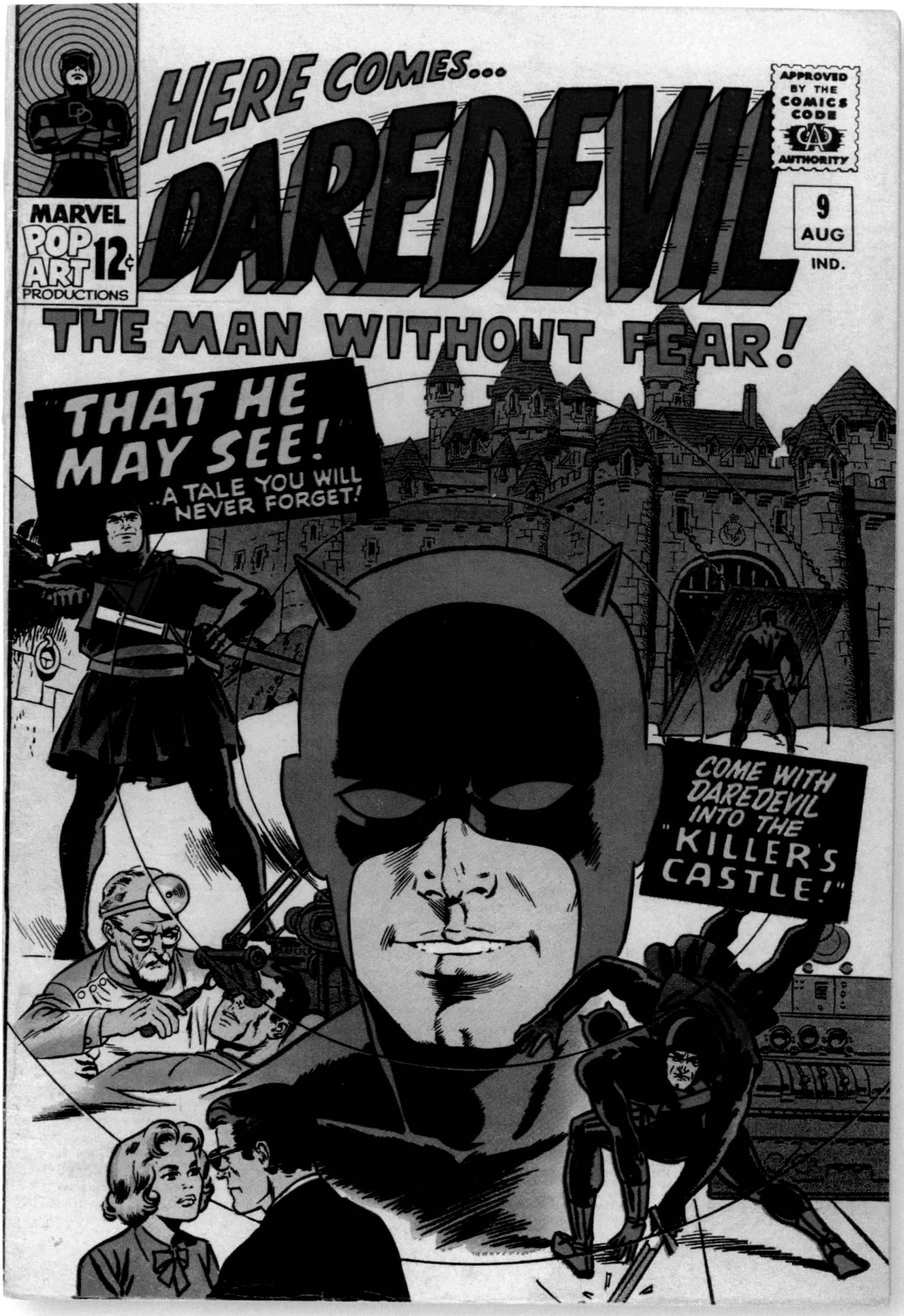

MARVEL POP ART PRODUCTIONS
12¢
HERE COMES...
DAREDEVIL
APPROVED BY THE COMICS CODE AUTHORITY
9
AUG
IND.
THE MAN WITHOUT FEAR!
"THAT HE MAY SEE!"
...A TALE YOU WILL NEVER FORGET!
COME WITH DAREDEVIL INTO THE "KILLER'S CASTLE!"

DAREDEVIL No. 9

(Opposite) Cover; pencils and inks, Wally Wood; August 1965. Wood was one of comics' most versatile and imaginative artists, celebrated by fans for some of the medium's finest science-fiction art at EC, and his witty humor stories in *Mad*. During his brief turn on *Daredevil* he designed the iconic red-and-black costume as well as the "DD" logo.

DAREDEVIL No. 7

(Below) Interior, "In Mortal Combat with the Sub-Mariner!"; script, Stan Lee; pencils and inks, Wally Wood; April 1965. Launched with fanfare, including rare cover-billing of an artist, Wood's memorable Marvel run included a seminal appearance by Sub-Mariner, a strip Wood was rumored to have been hired to pencil before his discomfort with the Marvel method left him preferring only to ink for the company. He soon left Marvel entirely to help create a critically acclaimed line of super heroes for short-lived competitor Tower comics.

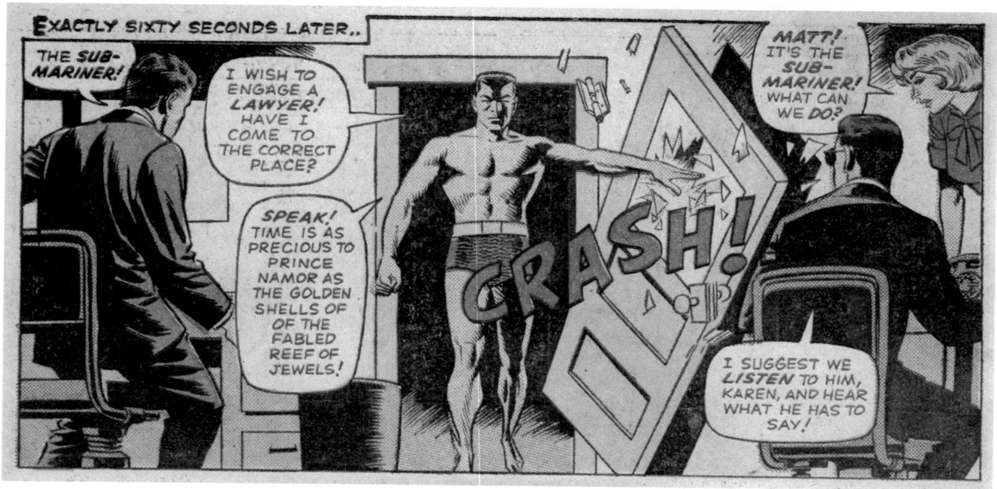
EXACTLY SIXTY SECONDS LATER..
THE SUB-MARINER!
I WISH TO ENGAGE A LAWYER! HAVE I COME TO THE CORRECT PLACE?
SPEAK! TIME IS AS PRECIOUS TO PRINCE NAMOR AS THE GOLDEN SHELLS OF OF THE FABLED REEF OF JEWELS!
CRASH!
MATT! IT'S THE SUB-MARINER! WHAT CAN WE DO?
I SUGGEST WE LISTEN TO HIM, KAREN, AND HEAR WHAT HE HAS TO SAY!

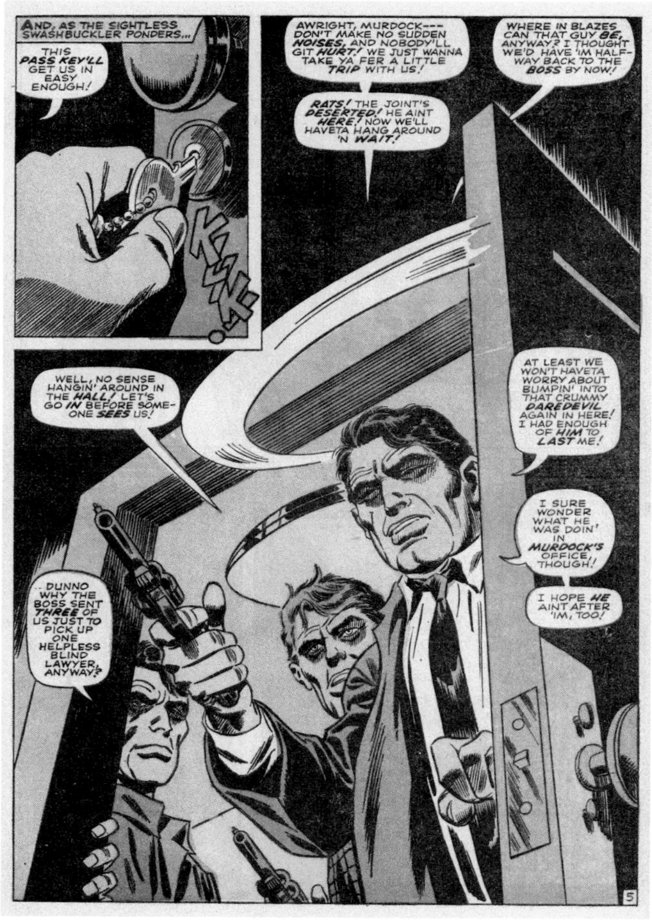
AND, AS THE SIGHTLESS SWASHBUCKLER PONDERS...
THIS PASS KEY'LL GET US IN EASY ENOUGH!
AWRIGHT, MURDOCK--- DON'T MAKE NO SUDDEN NOISES, AND NOBODY'LL GIT HURT! WE JUST WANNA TAKE YA FER A LITTLE TRIP WITH US!
RATS! THE JOINT'S DESERTED! HE AINT HERE! NOW WE'LL HAVETA HANG AROUND 'N WAIT!
WHERE IN BLAZES CAN THAT GUY BE, ANYWAY? I THOUGHT WE'D HAVE 'IM HALF-WAY BACK TO THE BOSS BY NOW!
WELL, NO SENSE HANGIN' AROUND IN THE HALL! LET'S GO IN BEFORE SOME-ONE SEES US!
AT LEAST WE WON'T HAVETA WORRY ABOUT BUMPIN' INTO THAT CRUMMY DAREDEVIL AGAIN IN HERE! I HAD ENOUGH OF HIM TO LAST ME!
I SURE WONDER WHAT HE WAS DOIN' IN MURDOCK'S OFFICE, THOUGH!
I HOPE HE AINT AFTER 'IM, TOO!
DUNNO WHY THE BOSS SENT THREE OF US JUST TO PICK UP ONE HELPLESS BLIND LAWYER, ANYWAY?
5

DAREDEVIL No. 34

(Opposite) Original art; pencils, Gene Colan; inks, John Tartaglione; November 1967. "I did once ask [Stan], though," Colan remembered, "if each issue always had to have a fight. It was hard coming up with different positions, different ways of showing action, it could become repetitive. 'No,' he said, 'Absolutely we do. Without a fight, we have no book!' Of course, he was right." Colan quickly adapted to Marvel's need for bold compositions populated by super hero slugfests. Daredevil's acrobatic movements particularly suited Colan's style, and DD became his signature character.

DAREDEVIL No. 20

(Above) Interior, "The Verdict Is Death!"; script, Stan Lee; pencils, Gene Colan; inks, Frank Giacoia; September 1966. Stan Lee pokes fun at Colan in *Origins:* "In the Bullpen, we used to joke about one panel the genial one had drawn — I can't even remember which strip it was, although it may have been a Daredevil story — in which he merely showed a man's hand holding a doorknob, about to open the door. That's all it was — a hand on a doorknob. Yet, because of the exotic lighting he gave to the panel, because of the perspective — the angle at which the hand was seen clutching the knob — because of the modeling of each finger that he drew, Gene had made that panel as dramatic and interesting as any other in the story. Like I always, say, if you've got a need for a hand clutching a doorknob, Colan's your boy!"

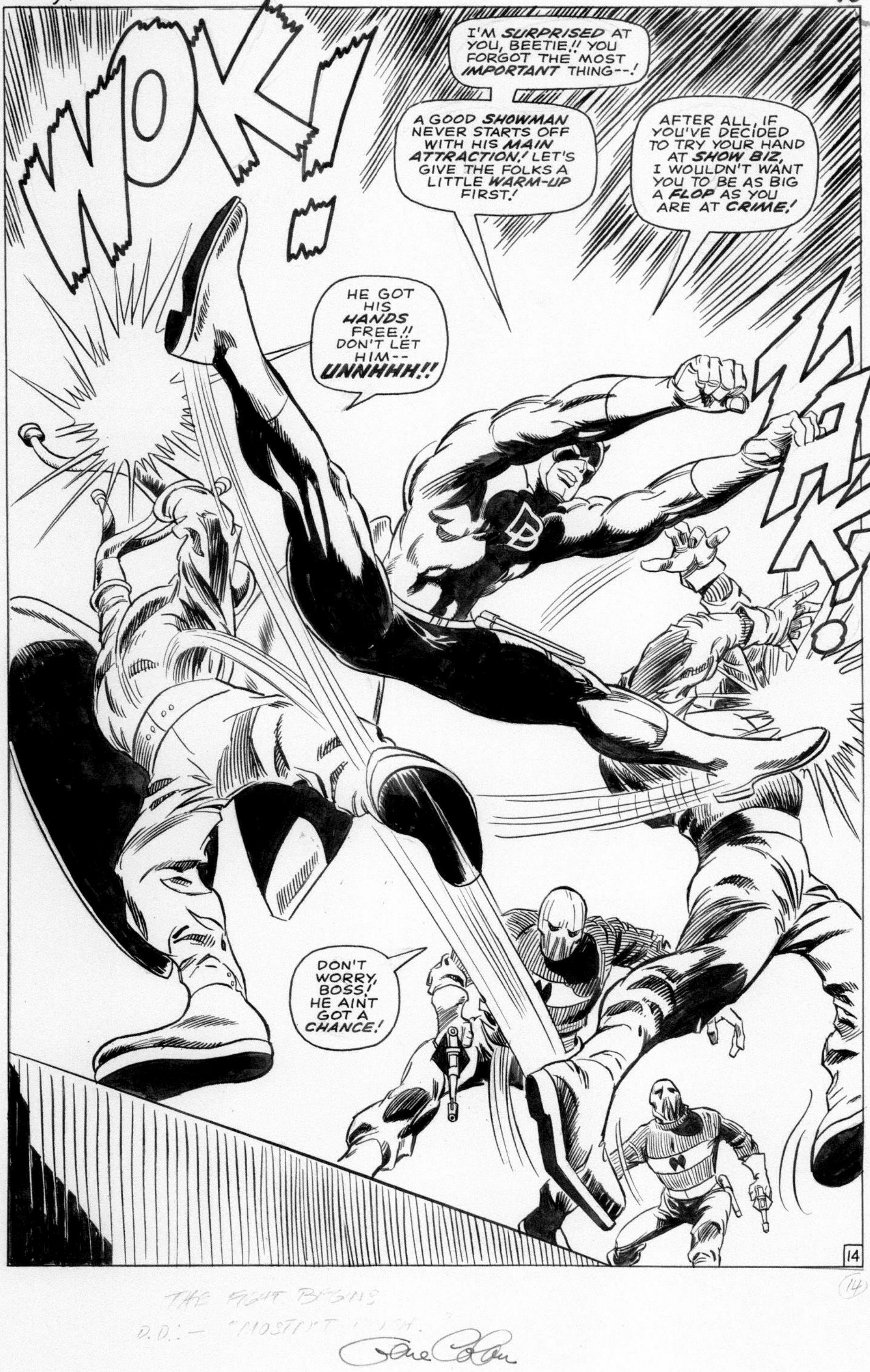
WOK!
I'M SURPRISED AT YOU, BEETIE!! YOU FORGOT THE MOST IMPORTANT THING--!
A GOOD SHOWMAN NEVER STARTS OFF WITH HIS MAIN ATTRACTION! LET'S GIVE THE FOLKS A LITTLE WARM-UP FIRST!
AFTER ALL, IF YOU'VE DECIDED TO TRY YOUR HAND AT SHOW BIZ, I WOULDN'T WANT YOU TO BE AS BIG A FLOP AS YOU ARE AT CRIME!
HE GOT HIS HANDS FREE!! DON'T LET HIM-- UNNHHH!!
WAK!
DON'T WORRY, BOSS! HE AINT GOT A CHANCE!
14

THE FIGHT BEGINS

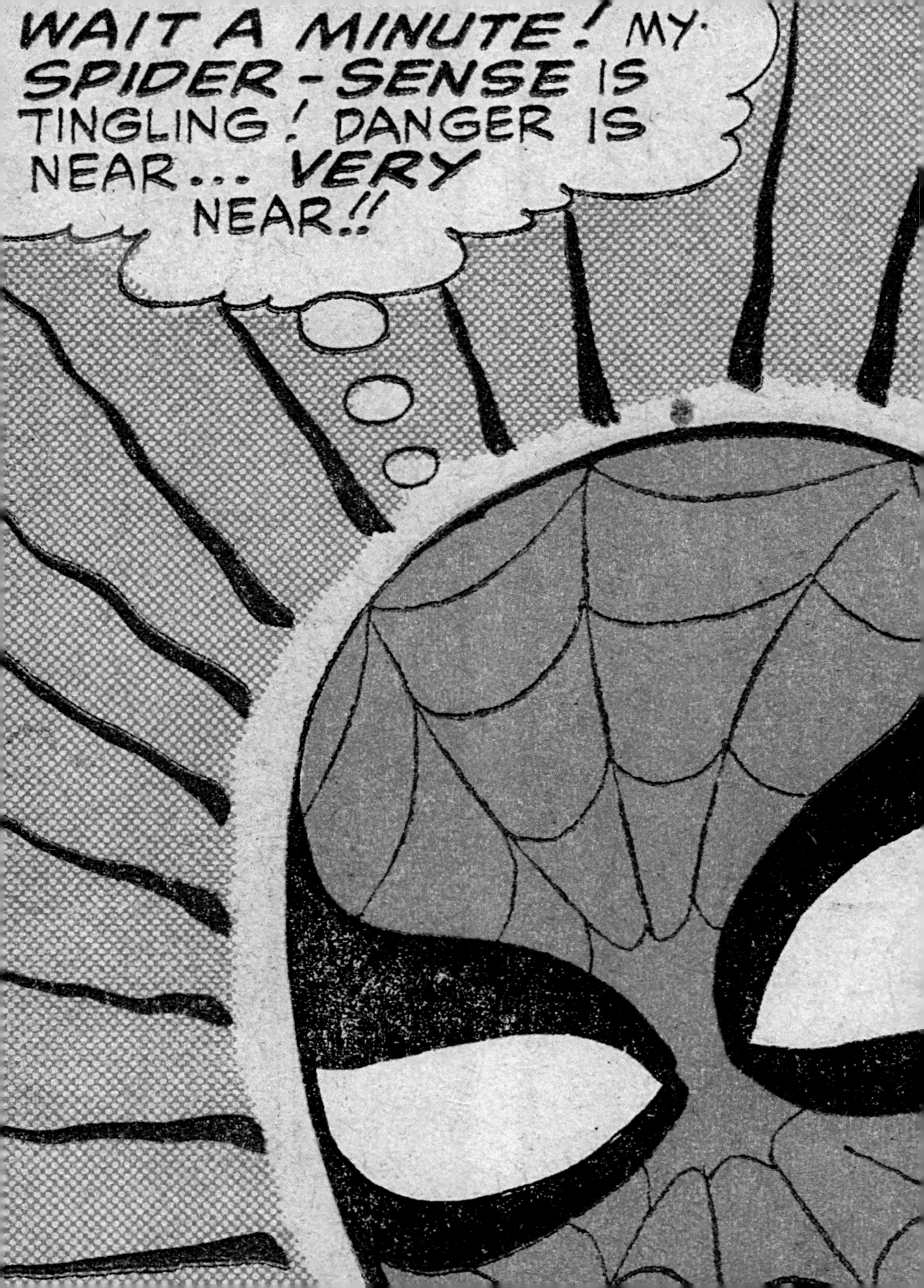
WAIT A MINUTE! MY SPIDER-SENSE IS TINGLING! DANGER IS NEAR... VERY NEAR!!

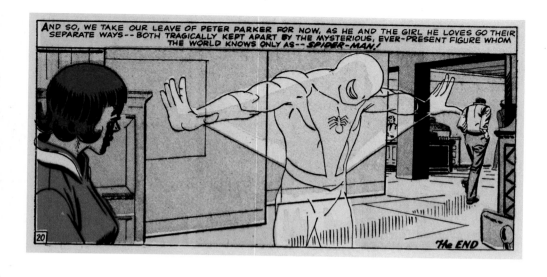

AND SO, WE TAKE OUR LEAVE OF PETER PARKER FOR NOW, AS HE AND THE GIRL HE LOVES GO THEIR SEPARATE WAYS-- BOTH TRAGICALLY KEPT APART BY THE MYSTERIOUS, EVER-PRESENT FIGURE WHOM THE WORLD KNOWS ONLY AS-- SPIDER-MAN!
20
The END

AMAZING SPIDER-MAN No. 26

(Opposite) Interior, "The Man in the Crime Master's Mask"; script, Stan Lee; plot, pencils, and inks, Steve Ditko; July 1965. Peter Parker's Spider-Sense was graphically invoked by the image of lines radiating around his head. Following in the footsteps of cartoonists Chester Gould and Harold Gray, Ditko created shorthand symbols that worked perfectly for the medium. Only a very few have innovated in this manner, and Ditko is one of the most inspired.

AMAZING SPIDER-MAN No. 30

(Above) Interior, "The Claws of the Cat!"; script, Stan Lee; plot, pencils, and inks, Steve Ditko; November 1965.

"These first five pages are a modern-day equivalent to Shakespeare as Parker's soliloquy sets the stage for his next action. And with dramatic pacing and storytelling, Ditko delivers one of the great sequences in all comics."
— ROBERT GREENBERGER

AMAZING SPIDER-MAN No. 33

(Opposite) Cover; pencils and inks, Steve Ditko. February 1966. This was Ditko's coming-of-age moment for Spider-Man. As an adult, Peter Parker shook away the guilt over his Uncle Ben's death—"lifted the weight" as it were—and would move forward by saving the life of his aunt. Ditko, in this tour de force issue, leads the hero to accept responsibility for his actions. Showcasing his ability to sustain tension, maximize drama, and move the reader through each panel with the precision of a master cinematographer, the artist tells the tale through Spider-Man's body language, from unrelenting despair to grim determination—and all without facial expressions.

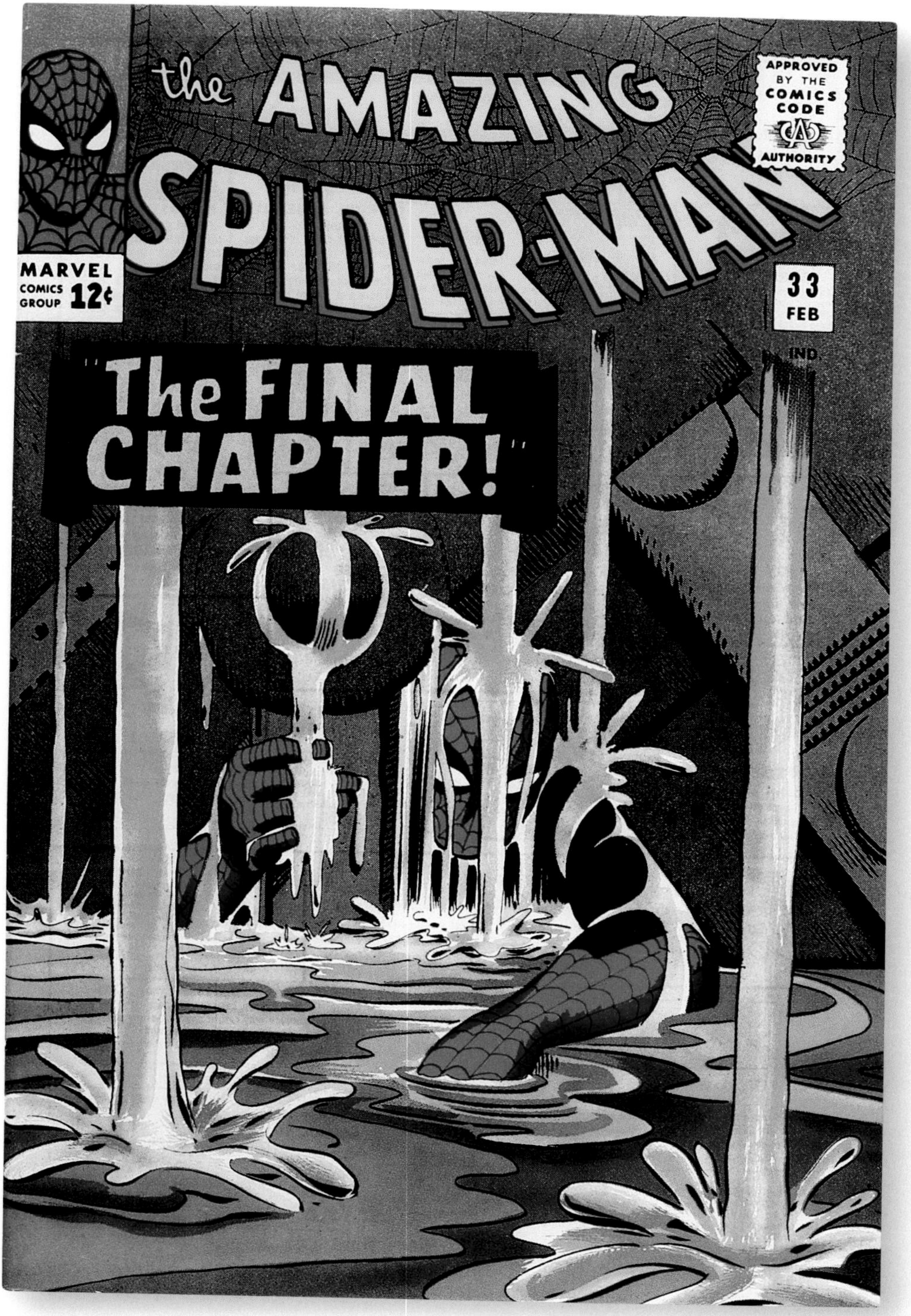
the AMAZING SPIDER-MAN
APPROVED BY THE COMICS CODE AUTHORITY
MARVEL COMICS GROUP 12¢
33 FEB
IND.
"The FINAL CHAPTER!"

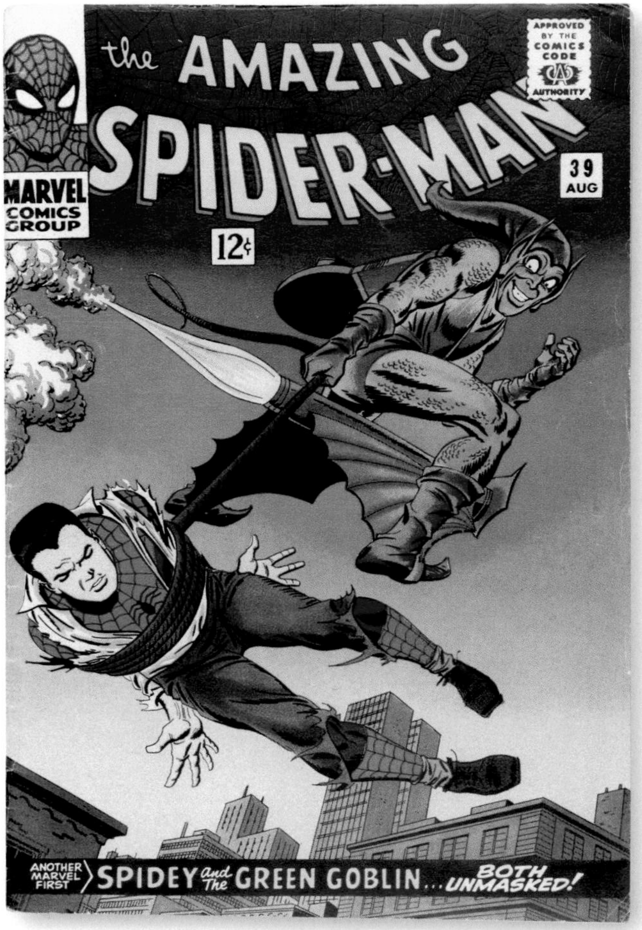
the AMAZING
SPIDER-MAN
APPROVED BY THE COMICS CODE AUTHORITY
MARVEL COMICS GROUP
39
AUG
12¢
ANOTHER MARVEL FIRST
SPIDEY and The GREEN GOBLIN... BOTH UNMASKED!

AMAZING SPIDER-MAN No. 39

(Above) Cover; pencils and inks, John Romita; August 1966. The first issue of *Spider-Man* after Ditko's departure was a stunner, as Lee decided to go all out, not only revealing the identity of the Goblin, but having him unmask Spidey. Romita was nervous to step into Ditko's shoes. "People laugh when I say this, but I did not want to do Spider-Man. I wanted to stay on Daredevil," he told Roy Thomas in a 2001 interview. "[F]or years…I felt obliged to ghost Ditko because—this may sound naïve, but I was convinced, in my own mind, that he was going to come back in two or three issues.…I couldn't believe that a guy would walk away from a successful book that was the second-highest seller at Marvel."

AMAZING SPIDER-MAN No. 48

(Opposite) Cover; pencils and inks, John Romita; May 1967.

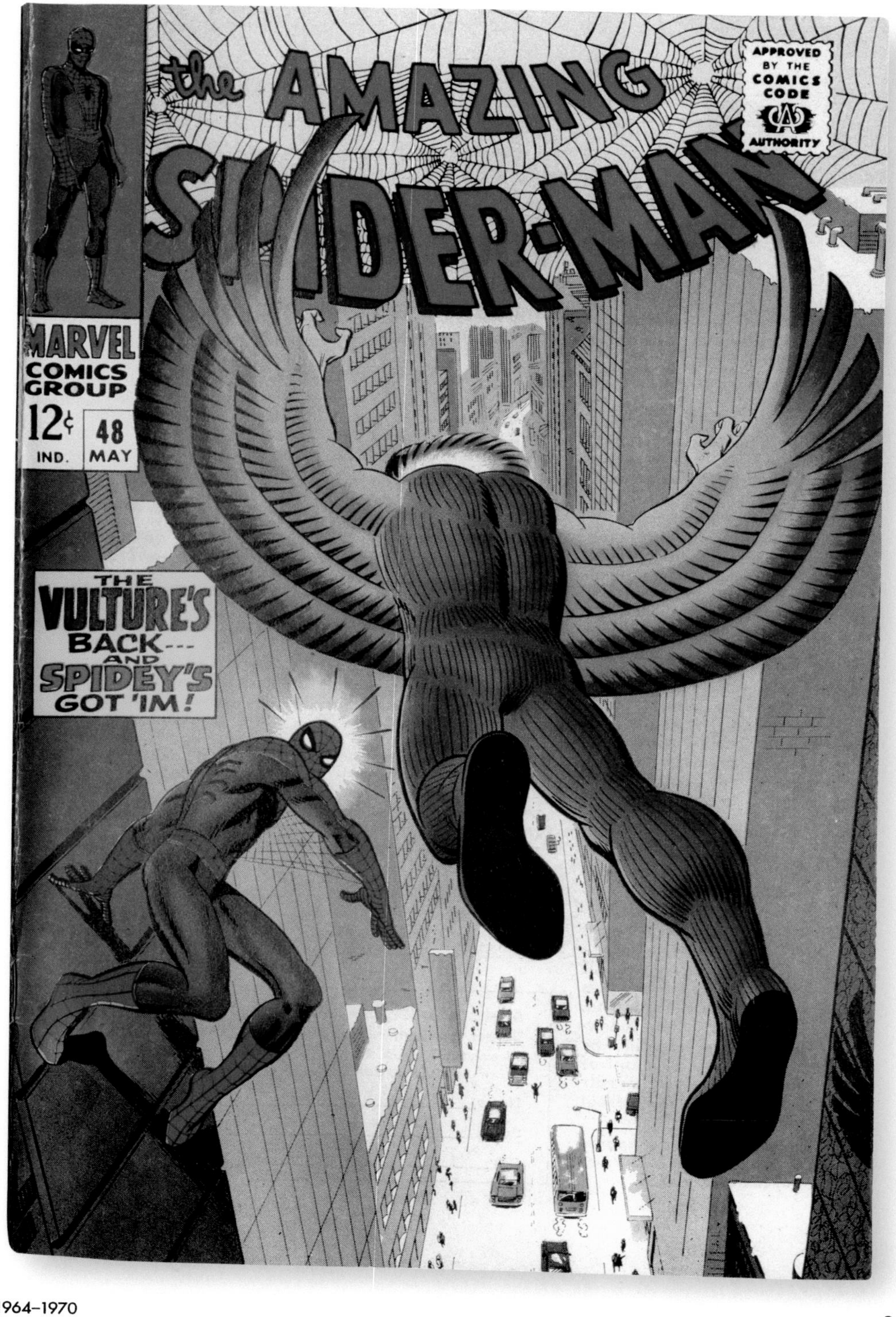
the AMAZING SPIDER-MAN
APPROVED BY THE COMICS CODE AUTHORITY
MARVEL COMICS GROUP
12¢ IND.
48 MAY
THE VULTURE'S BACK--- AND SPIDEY'S GOT 'IM!

SPIDER-MAN NO MORE!

(Opposite) Original cover art, Amazing Spider-Man *No. 50; pencils, John Romita; inks, Mike Esposito. (Below) Interior, "Spider-Man No More!"; script, Stan Lee; pencils, Romita; inks, Esposito. July 1967.* Despite the tremendous popularity — and enduring legacy — of Ditko's Spider-Man, John Romita's romance comic sensibility, combined with Lee's plotting instincts, steadily improved sales. Fan mail for issue 50 included this surprising endorsement by University of Connecticut art professor John S. Fawcett: "I finally gave in and have just spent close to $200.00 to get complete collections of most of your titles. *Spider-Man,* in my opinion, is your best effort. If we are to believe what the better mags tell us, he has a fantastic influence on the under-25 group."

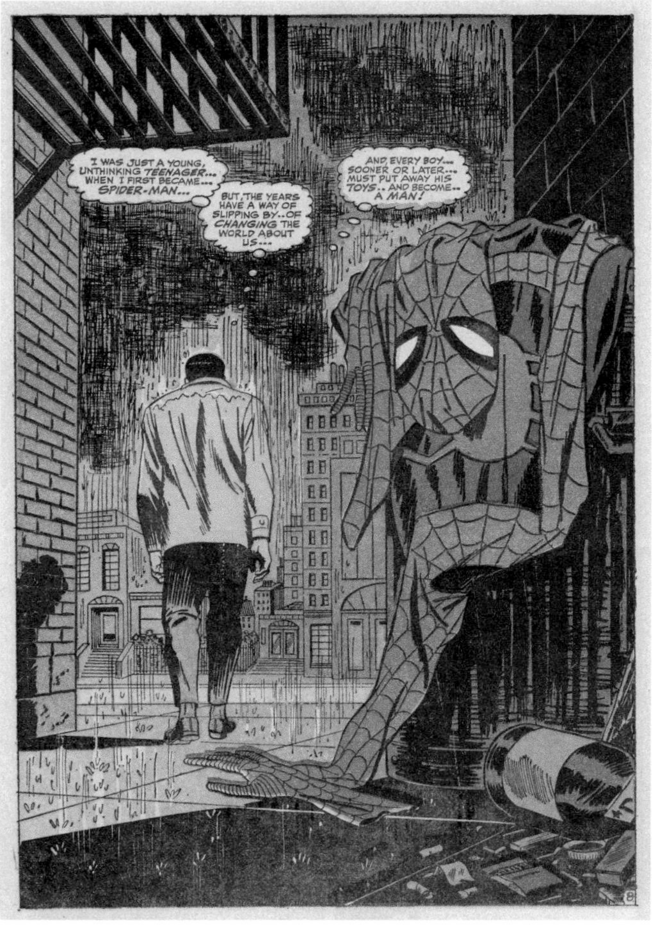
I WAS JUST A YOUNG, UNTHINKING TEENAGER... WHEN I FIRST BECAME... SPIDER-MAN...
BUT, THE YEARS HAVE A WAY OF SLIPPING BY..OF CHANGING THE WORLD ABOUT US...
AND, EVERY BOY... SOONER OR LATER... MUST PUT AWAY HIS TOYS.. AND BECOME.. A MAN!
8

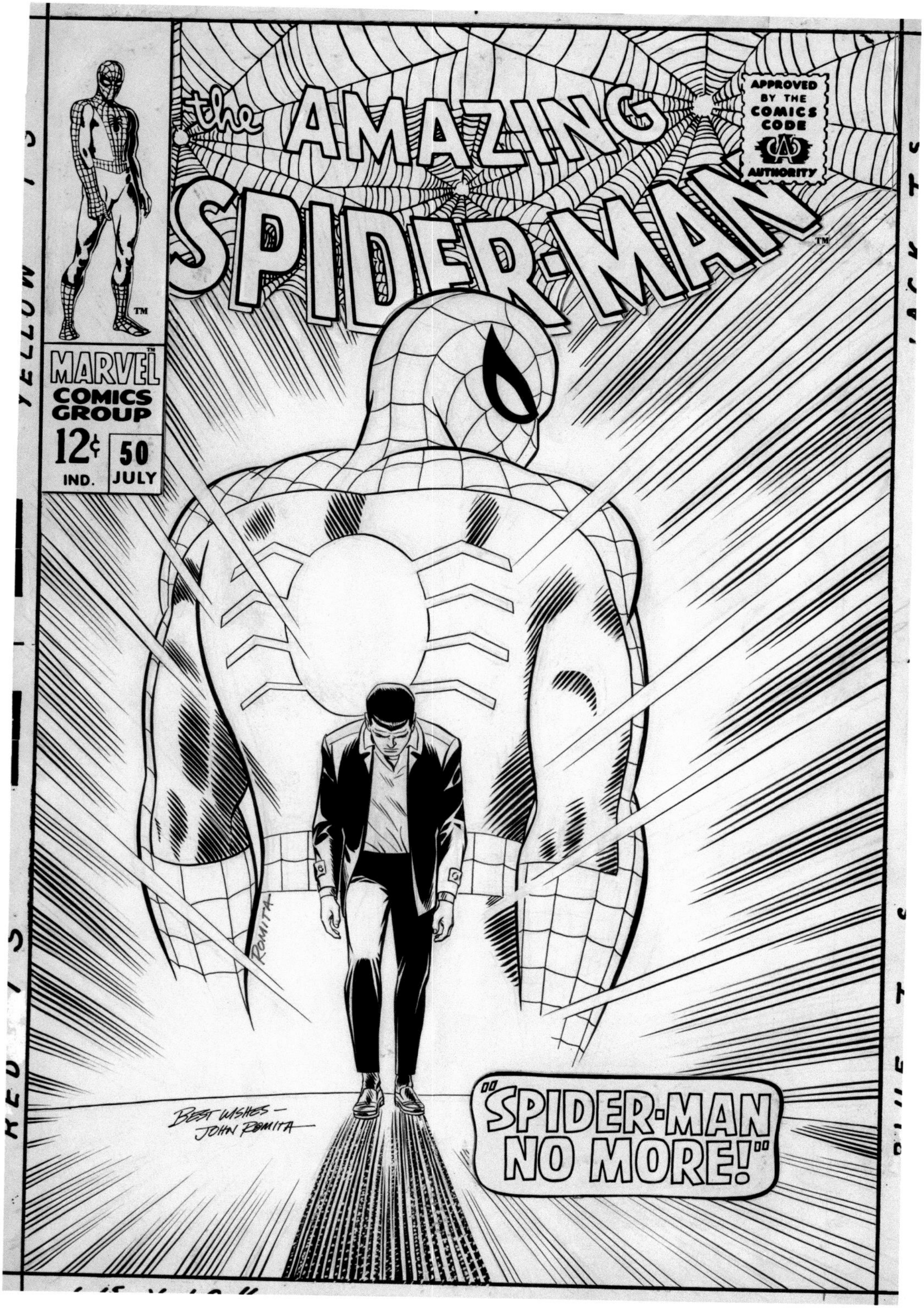

the AMAZING SPIDER-MAN™
APPROVED BY THE COMICS CODE AUTHORITY
MARVEL™ COMICS GROUP
12¢ IND.
50 JULY
ROMITA
BEST WISHES— JOHN ROMITA
"SPIDER-MAN NO MORE!"

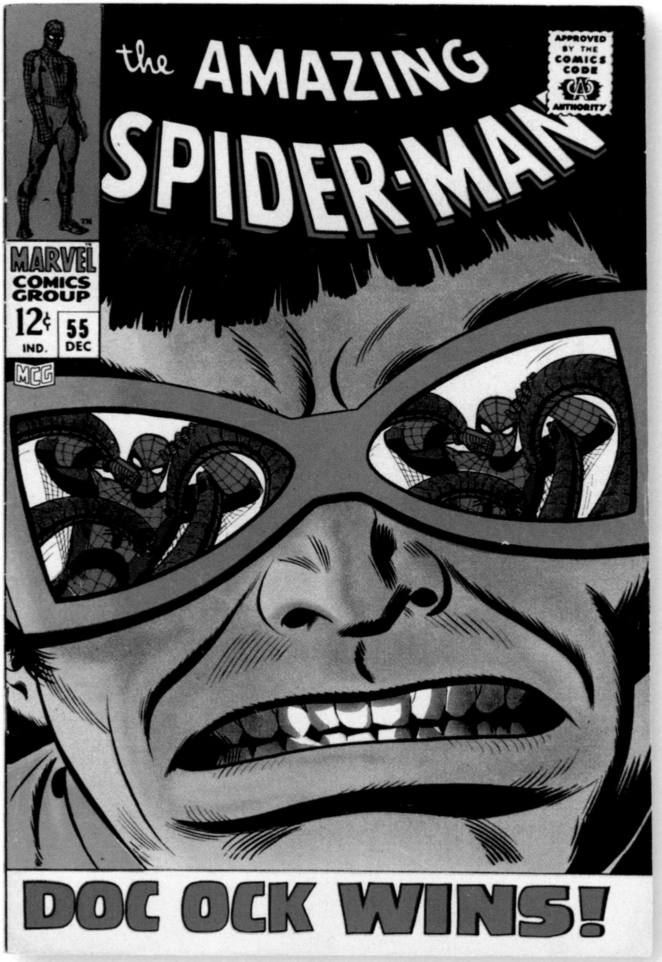
the AMAZING
SPIDER-MAN
APPROVED BY THE COMICS CODE AUTHORITY
MARVEL COMICS GROUP
12¢
55
IND.
DEC
MCG
DOC OCK WINS!

AMAZING SPIDER-MAN No. 55

(Above) Cover; pencils and inks, John Romita; December 1967.

AMAZING SPIDER-MAN No. 60

(Opposite) Cover; pencils and inks, John Romita; May 1968. John Romita's initial run of Spider-Man covers are some of the most compelling, attractive, and inventive ever crafted. Stan Lee let the picture tell the story and Romita was a master at drawing the viewer in with his visual storytelling—often using dark backgrounds to focus the viewer's attention on the central figures.

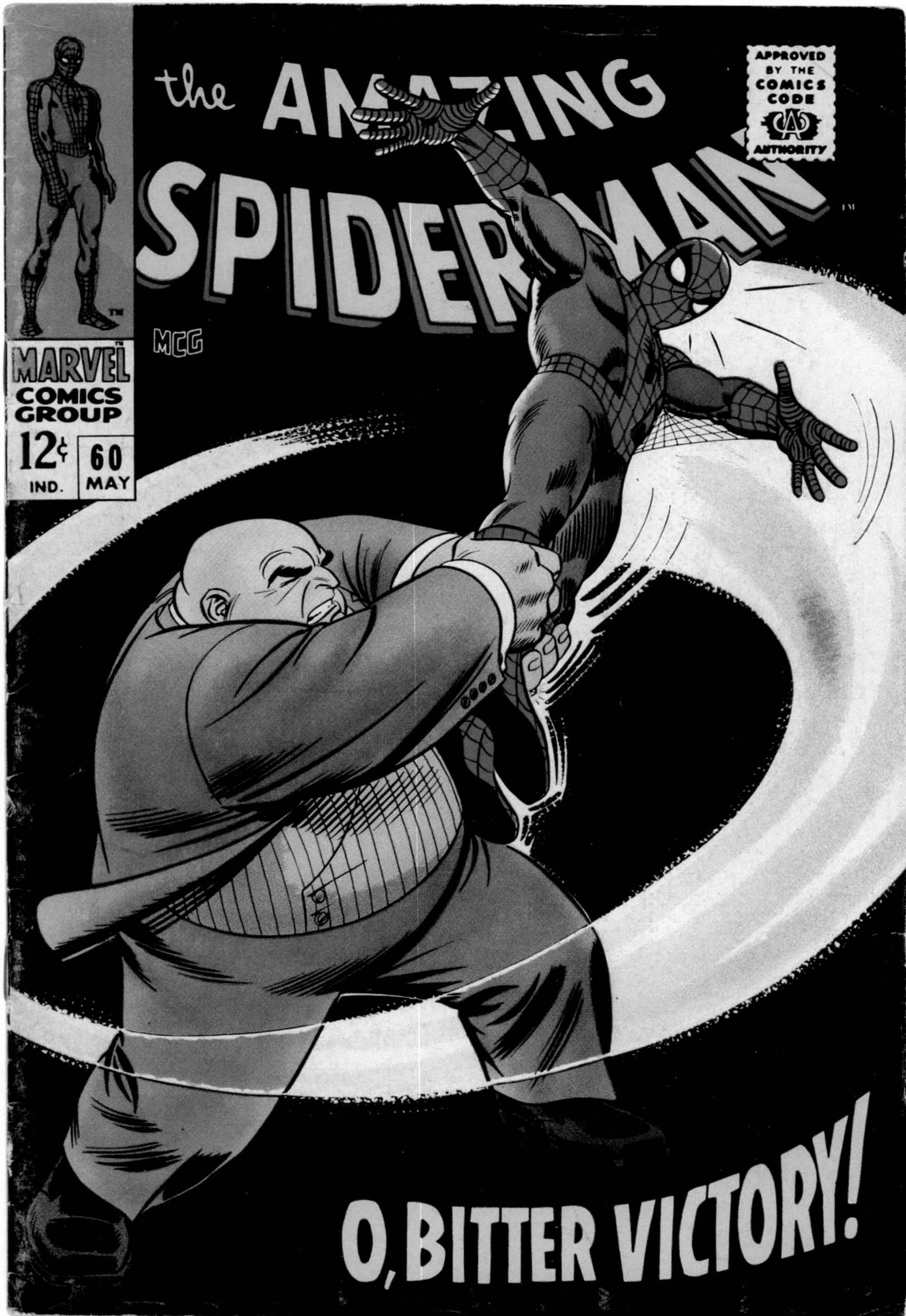

the AMAZING
SPIDER-MAN
APPROVED BY THE COMICS CODE AUTHORITY
MARVEL COMICS GROUP
12¢ IND.
60 MAY
MCG
O, BITTER VICTORY!

"…Glowing orange, green, magenta, lavender, chlorine blue, every fluorescent pastel imaginable in thousands of designs, both large and small, like a cross between Fernand Léger and Dr. Strange, roaring together and vibrating off each other as if somebody had given Hieronymus Bosch fifty buckets of Day-Glo paint and a 1939 International Harvester school bus and told him to go to it."
— TOM WOLFE, *THE ELECTRIC KOOL-AID ACID TEST*

TERRIFIC No. 43

(Opposite) Interior, pinup; pencils and inks, Barry Smith; February 3, 1968. The Britain-based Odhams Press was licensed to reprint Marvel characters in weekly installments during the mid-1960s in titles with dramatic names like *Smash, Pow, Wham, Fantastic,* and *Terrific.* A young Barry Smith contributed pinup art in many issues, although he would soon turn up in the States seeking work at Marvel.

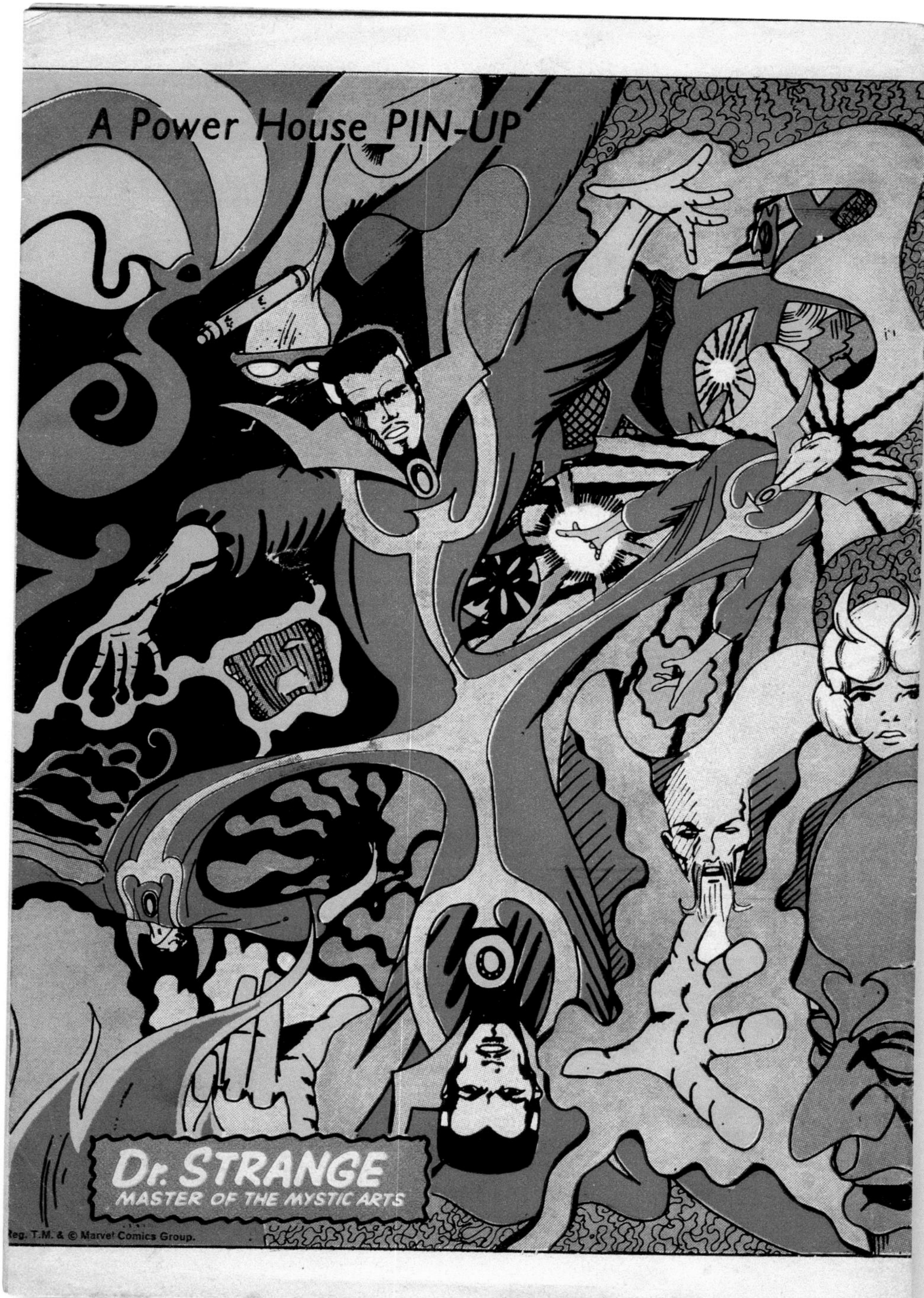
A Power House PIN-UP
Dr. STRANGE
MASTER OF THE MYSTIC ARTS
Reg. T.M. & © Marvel Comics Group.

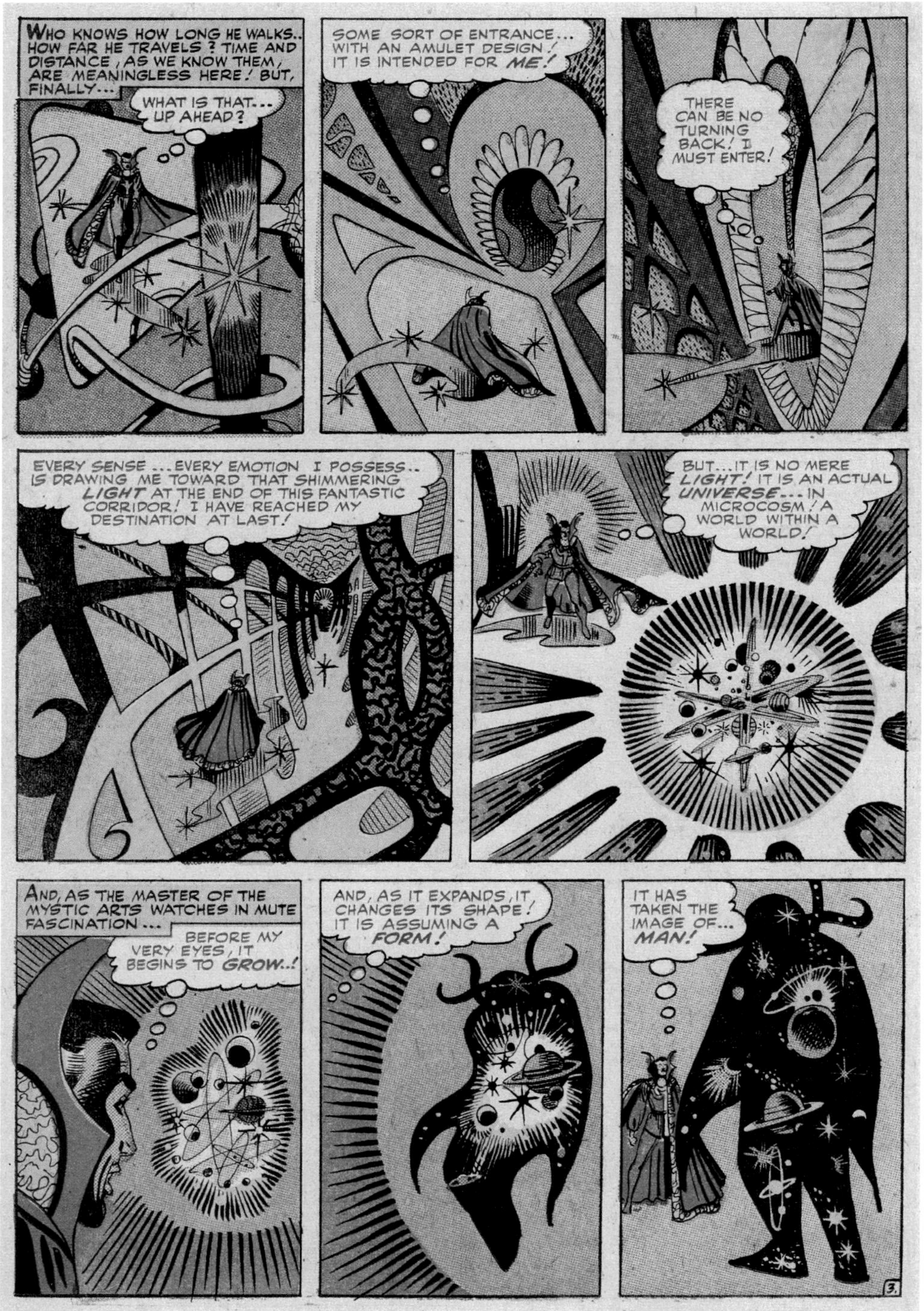
WHO KNOWS HOW LONG HE WALKS.. HOW FAR HE TRAVELS? TIME AND DISTANCE, AS WE KNOW THEM, ARE MEANINGLESS HERE! BUT, FINALLY...
WHAT IS THAT... UP AHEAD?
SOME SORT OF ENTRANCE... WITH AN AMULET DESIGN! IT IS INTENDED FOR ME!
THERE CAN BE NO TURNING BACK! I MUST ENTER!
EVERY SENSE ... EVERY EMOTION I POSSESS.. IS DRAWING ME TOWARD THAT SHIMMERING LIGHT AT THE END OF THIS FANTASTIC CORRIDOR! I HAVE REACHED MY DESTINATION AT LAST!
BUT... IT IS NO MERE LIGHT! IT IS AN ACTUAL UNIVERSE... IN MICROCOSM! A WORLD WITHIN A WORLD!
AND, AS THE MASTER OF THE MYSTIC ARTS WATCHES IN MUTE FASCINATION...
BEFORE MY VERY EYES, IT BEGINS TO GROW..!
AND, AS IT EXPANDS, IT CHANGES ITS SHAPE! IT IS ASSUMING A FORM!
IT HAS TAKEN THE IMAGE OF... MAN!
3.

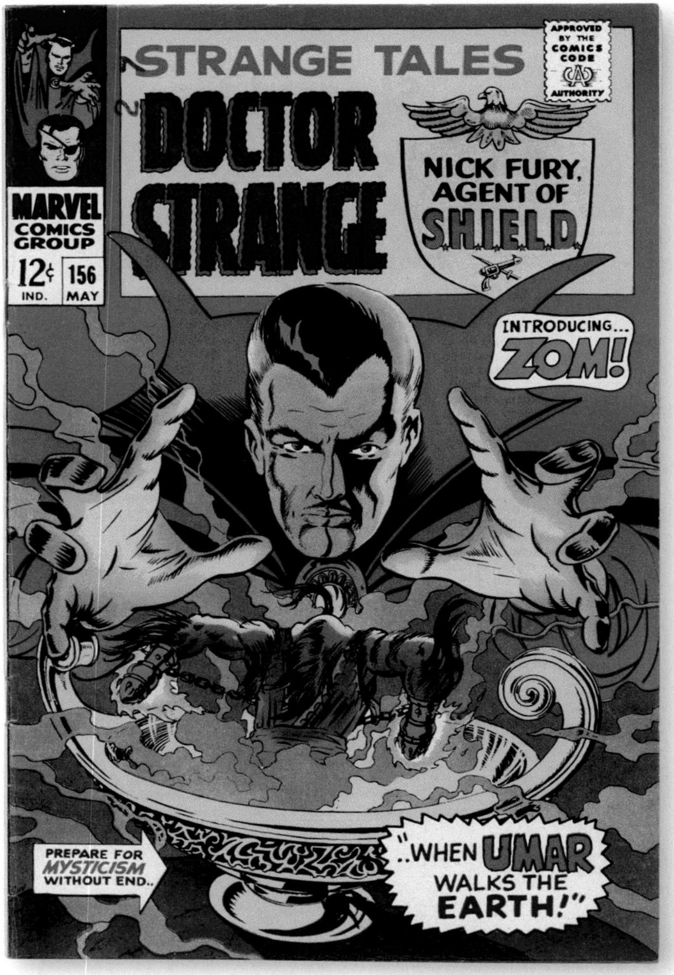
STRANGE TALES
DOCTOR STRANGE
NICK FURY, AGENT OF S.H.I.E.L.D.
MARVEL COMICS GROUP
12¢ IND.
156 MAY
APPROVED BY THE COMICS CODE AUTHORITY
INTRODUCING... ZOM!
PREPARE FOR MYSTICISM WITHOUT END..
"..WHEN UMAR WALKS THE EARTH!"

STRANGE TALES No. 138

(Opposite) Interior, "If Eternity Should Fail!"; script, Stan Lee; plot, pencils, and inks, Steve Ditko; November 1965. Dr. Strange encounters Eternity, a being consisting of the very universe, wearing the silhouette of a man. Ditko's awe-inspiring imagination seems limitless, and on Dr. Strange he was freed to craft some of the medium's most visually compelling stories.

STRANGE TALES No. 156

(Above) Cover; pencils and inks, Marie Severin; May 1967. Marie Severin began drawing for Marvel after working in production with Sol Brodsky. Her skills dated back to EC Comics, primarily as an exceptional colorist. Publisher Martin Goodman noticed an ad she had drawn and told Stan Lee to give her an assignment drawing stories. The rest is history.

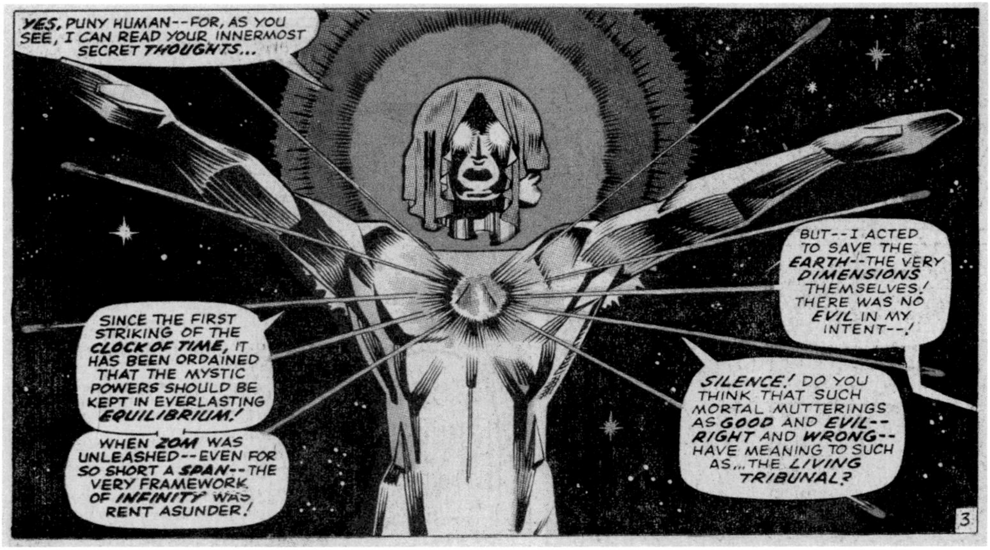
YES, PUNY HUMAN--FOR, AS YOU SEE, I CAN READ YOUR INNERMOST SECRET THOUGHTS...
SINCE THE FIRST STRIKING OF THE CLOCK OF TIME, IT HAS BEEN ORDAINED THAT THE MYSTIC POWERS SHOULD BE KEPT IN EVERLASTING EQUILIBRIUM!
WHEN ZOM WAS UNLEASHED--EVEN FOR SO SHORT A SPAN--THE VERY FRAMEWORK OF INFINITY WAS RENT ASUNDER!
BUT--I ACTED TO SAVE THE EARTH--THE VERY DIMENSIONS THEMSELVES! THERE WAS NO EVIL IN MY INTENT--!
SILENCE! DO YOU THINK THAT SUCH MORTAL MUTTERINGS AS GOOD AND EVIL--RIGHT AND WRONG--HAVE MEANING TO SUCH AS... THE LIVING TRIBUNAL?
3

STRANGE TALES No. 158

(Above) Interior, "The Sands of Death!"; script, Roy Thomas; pencils, Marie Severin; inks, Herb Trimpe; July 1967. After Ditko's departure, Bill Everett filled in on Dr. Strange for a few issues, followed by Marie Severin. Here Severin appears to be channeling Ditko, designing an effective and offbeat character in the Living Tribunal.

STRANGE TALES No. 146

(Opposite) Interior, "The End... At Last!"; script, Dennis O'Neil; plot, pencils, and inks, Steve Ditko; July 1966. Employing splash pages sparingly, Ditko knew when to use them to great effect, such as this confrontation between the dread Dormammu and Eternity. The story's title was fitting, as this issue was Ditko's final bow drawing Dr. Strange.

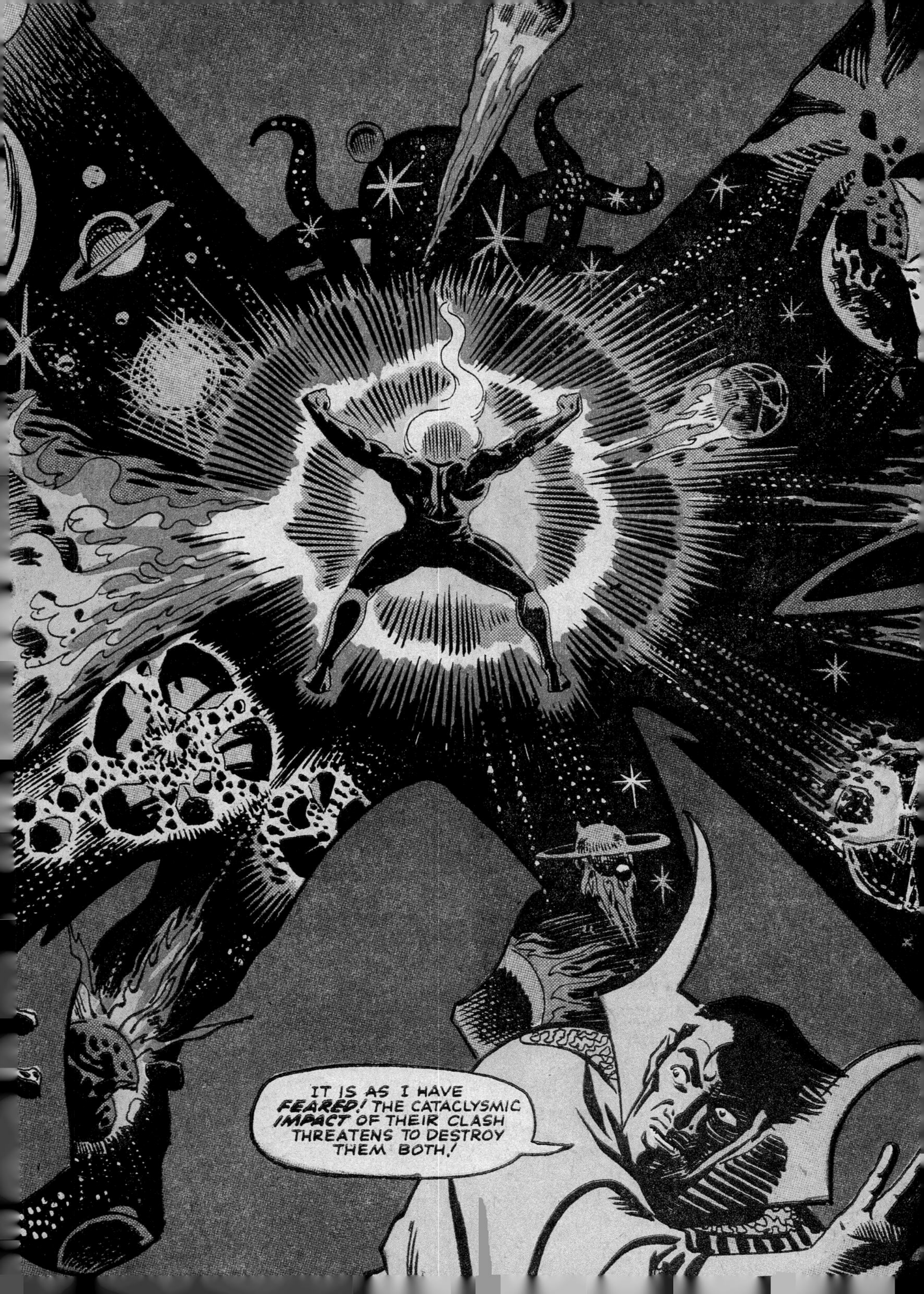
IT IS AS I HAVE FEARED! THE CATACLYSMIC IMPACT OF THEIR CLASH THREATENS TO DESTROY THEM BOTH!

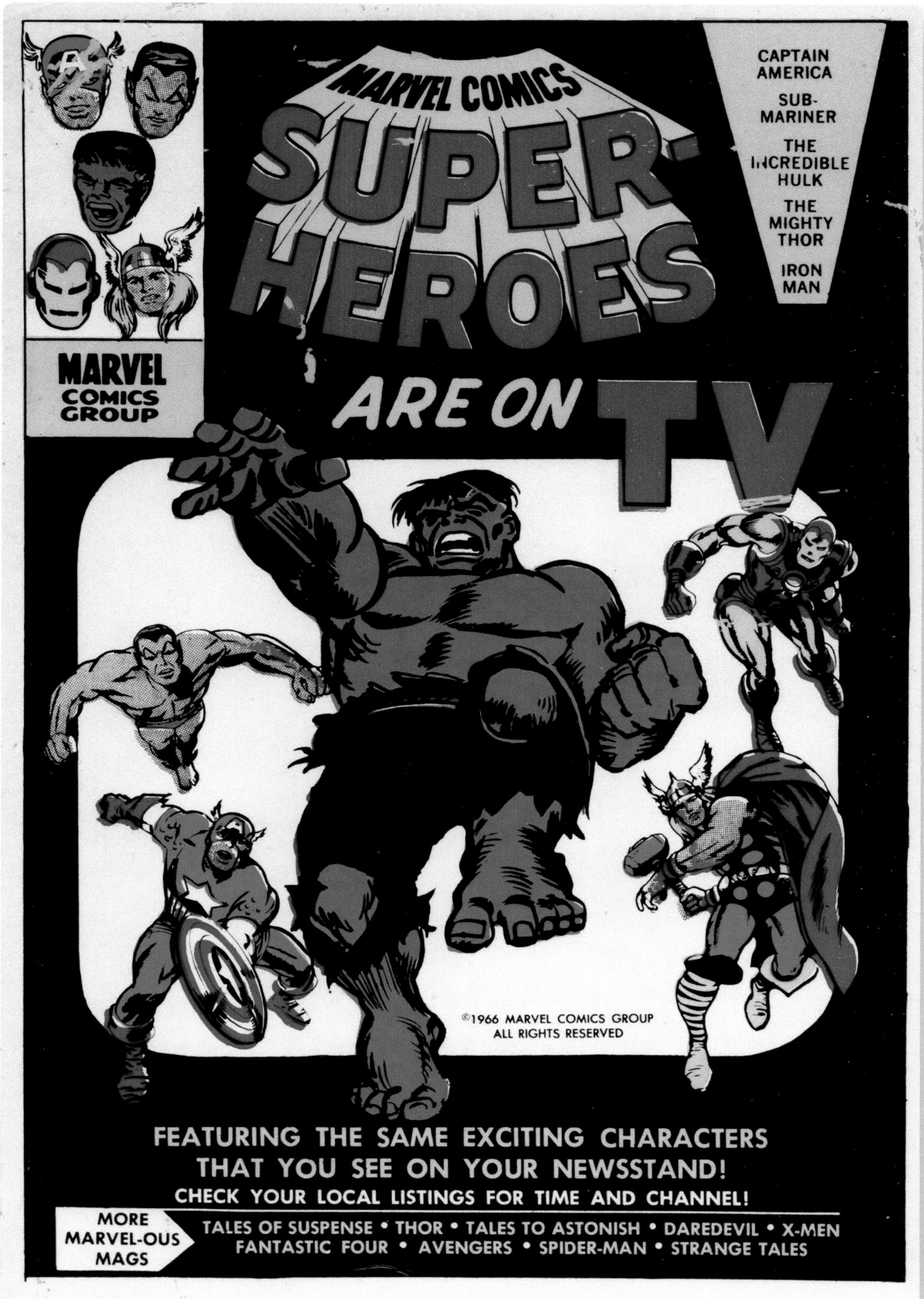
MARVEL COMICS
SUPER-HEROES
ARE ON TV
CAPTAIN AMERICA
SUB-MARINER
THE INCREDIBLE HULK
THE MIGHTY THOR
IRON MAN
MARVEL COMICS GROUP
©1966 MARVEL COMICS GROUP
ALL RIGHTS RESERVED
FEATURING THE SAME EXCITING CHARACTERS
THAT YOU SEE ON YOUR NEWSSTAND!
CHECK YOUR LOCAL LISTINGS FOR TIME AND CHANNEL!
MORE MARVEL-OUS MAGS
TALES OF SUSPENSE • THOR • TALES TO ASTONISH • DAREDEVIL • X-MEN
FANTASTIC FOUR • AVENGERS • SPIDER-MAN • STRANGE TALES

CAPTAIN AMERICA 4:30 MONDAY THRU FRIDAY
CHANNEL 7

DON'T TOUCH THAT DIAL!

(Opposite) House ad; art, John Romita, Jack Kirby, and Gene Colan; Grantray-Lawrence Animation; 1966. In September of 1966 the *Marvel Super-Heroes* cartoon was syndicated on television. Originally shown in early evening hours and featuring a live host, the simplistic cartoons appeared five nights a week to the sound of swingin' '60s theme songs, and featured Iron Man, Captain America, Sub-Mariner, the Hulk, and Thor.

CAPTAIN AMERICA CALLING

(Above) Captain America promotional postcard, ca. 1966. Many local networks employed actors to dress up as Marvel characters and appear as hosts in between the *Marvel Super-Heroes* cartoons.

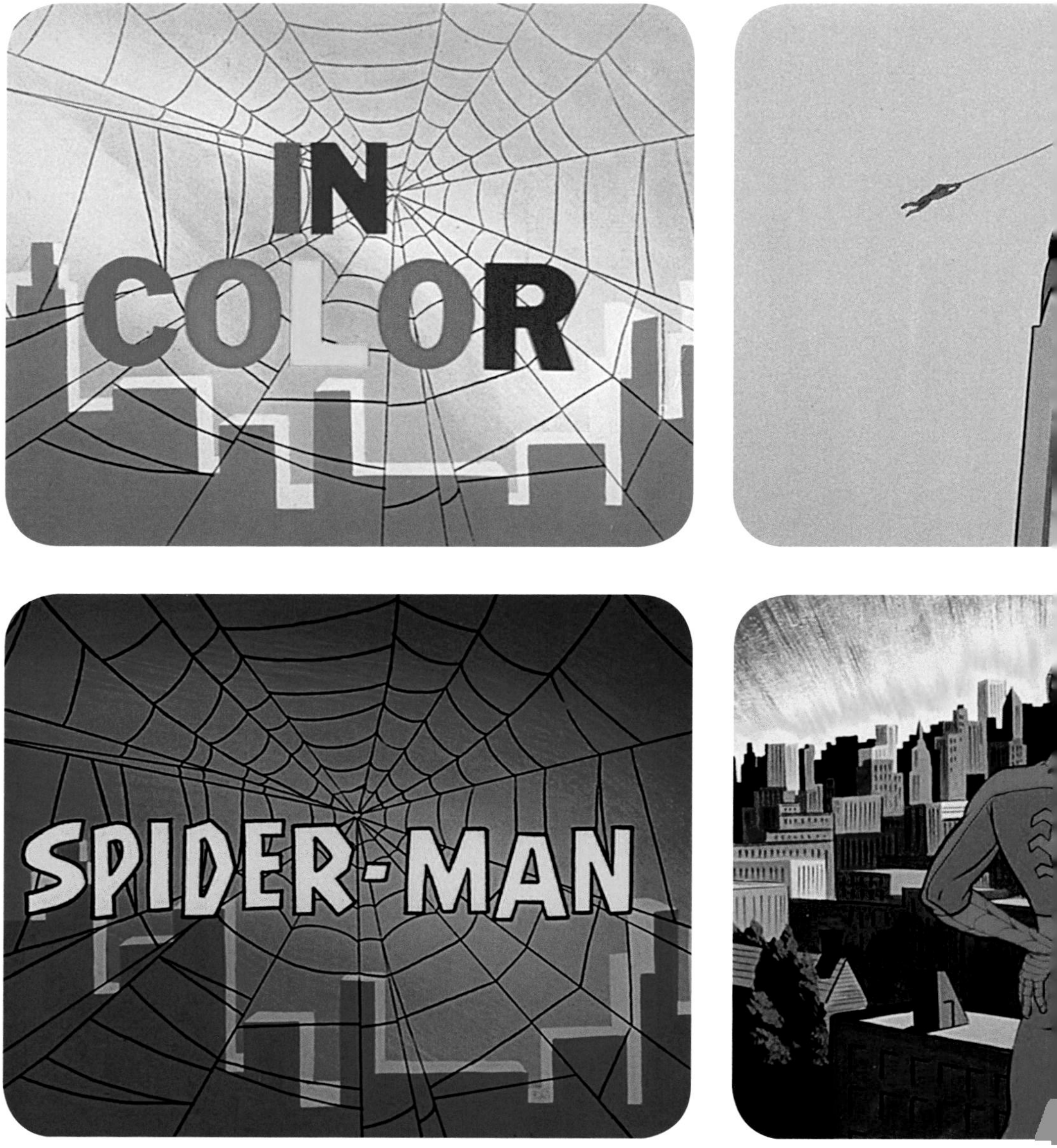
IN
COLOR
SPIDER-MAN

DOES WHATEVER A SPIDER CAN

(Above) Opening credits, Spider-Man, *ABC, 1967.* Following the success of *Marvel Super-Heroes*, Grantray-Lawrence produced a *Spider-Man* series for ABC. This cartoon featured a little more actual animation than the studio's previous outing, although Spidey's costume and stories were simplified considerably for the Saturday morning kiddie crowd.

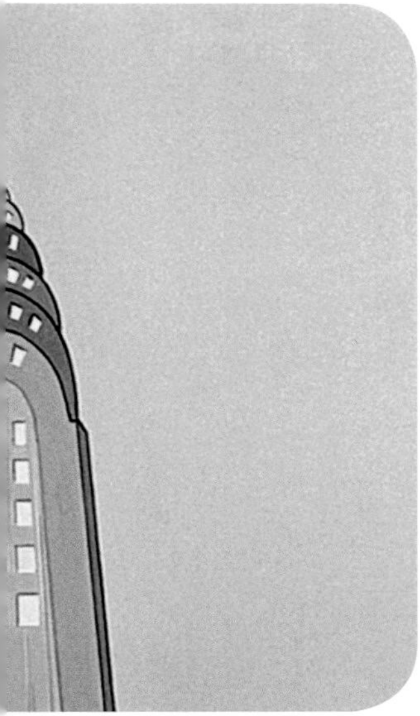

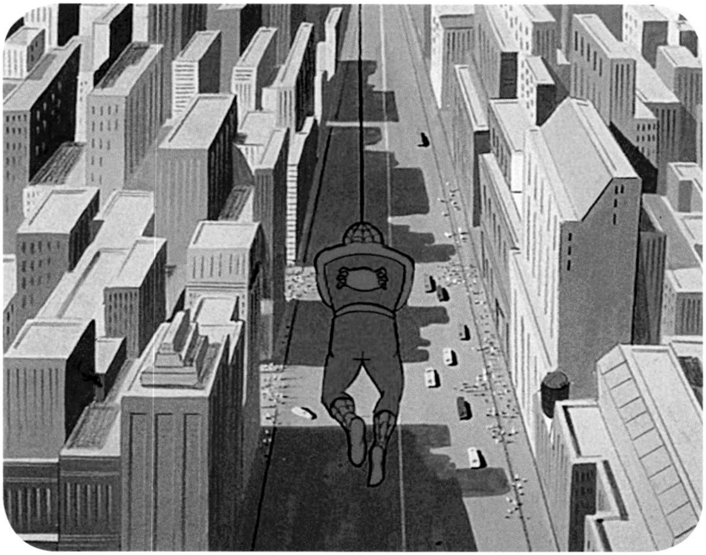

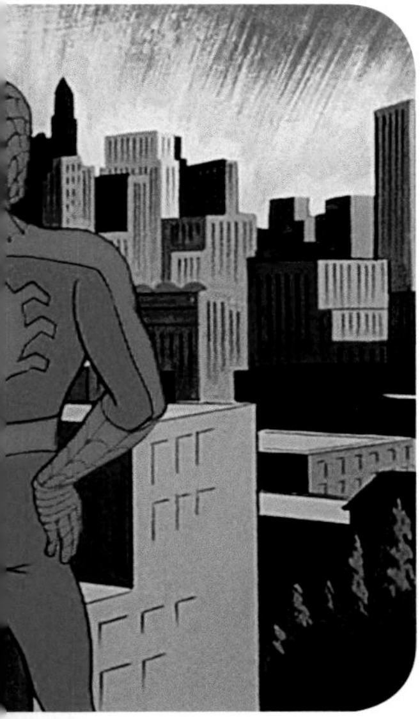

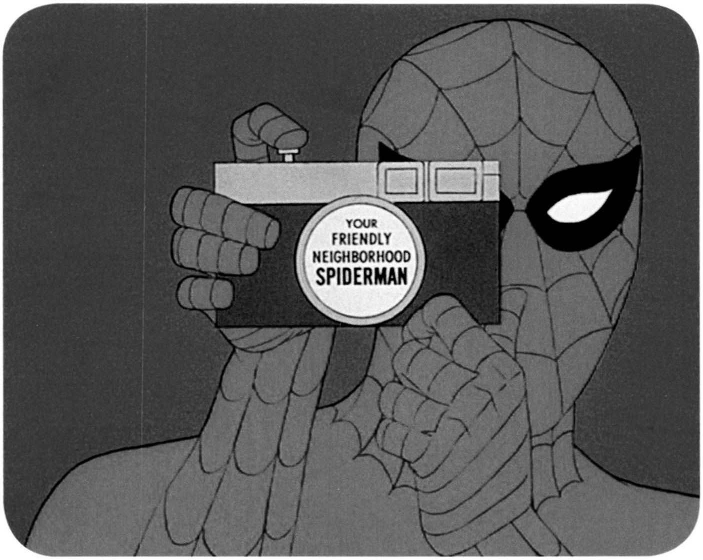
YOUR
FRIENDLY
NEIGHBORHOOD
SPIDERMAN

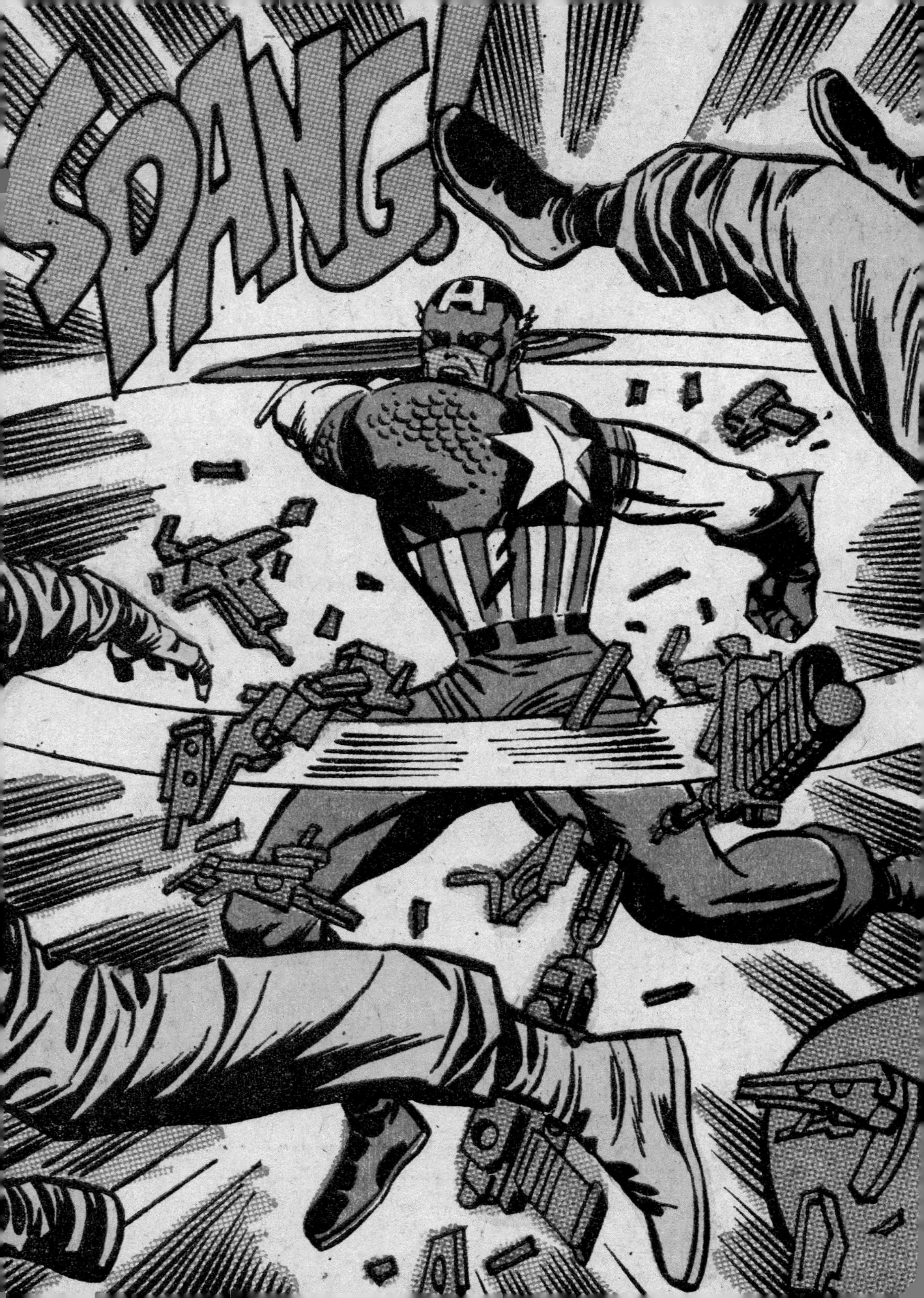
SPANG!

TALES OF SUSPENSE No. 94

(Opposite) Interior, "If This Be MODOK!"; script, Stan Lee; pencils, Jack Kirby; inks, Joe Sinnott; October 1967. Kirby's explosive action takes center stage in this panel detail.

KING OF COMICS

(Below) Photograph, Jack Kirby at the drawing board, 1965. Kirby was at the height of creativity in late 1965, producing characters, concepts, strips, and breakdowns (which, in Kirby's case, meant coplotting the story) for other artists to follow. His energy was unrelenting — he could pencil as many as three pages a day, more than double the output of most seasoned comics professionals. With pencil in hand, never far from a cigar or a pipe, the King rode the crest of the Marvel wave alongside Stan "the Man" Lee.

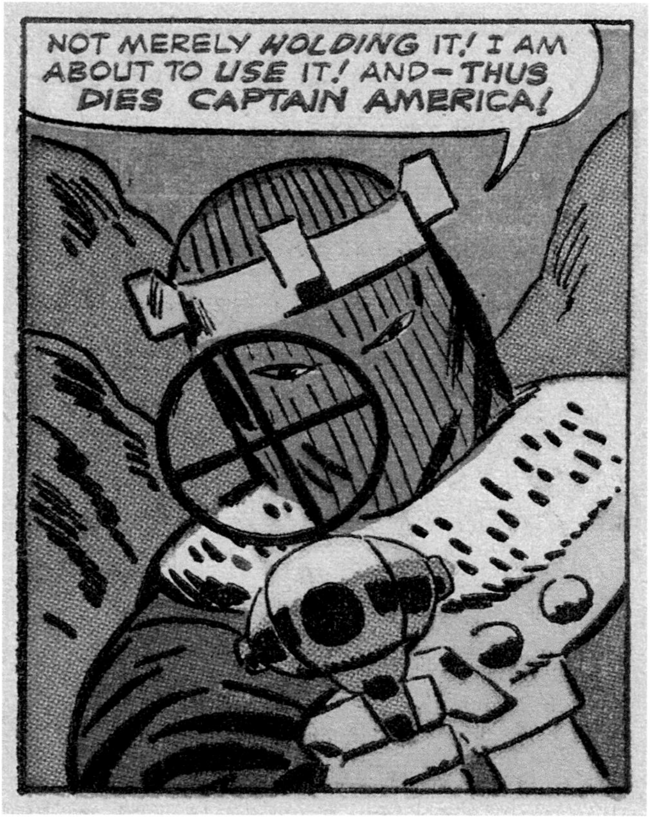
NOT MERELY HOLDING IT! I AM ABOUT TO USE IT! AND—THUS DIES CAPTAIN AMERICA!

THE AVENGERS No. 15

(Above) Interior, "Now, by My Hand, Shall Die a Villain!"; script, Stan Lee; layouts, Jack Kirby; finished pencils, Don Heck; inks, Mike Esposito; April 1965. Perhaps worried that the Comics Code might veto the Red Skull entirely, Lee and Kirby instead first brought out a crowned, ermine-collared, faceless villain called Baron Zemo who—we are told within—will turn out to be an antagonist from Captain America's wartime past.

TALES OF SUSPENSE No. 85

(Opposite) Interior, "The Blitzkrieg of Batroc!"; script, Stan Lee; pencils, Jack Kirby; inks, Frank Giacoia; January 1967. This nine-panel sequence illustrates how much movement Kirby could bring to a single page. Having gotten his start "in-betweening" animation cels in the 1930s at the legendary Fleischer Studios, Kirby understood how to bring a story to life, and Lee wisely stood back and let Kirby's images speak for themselves.

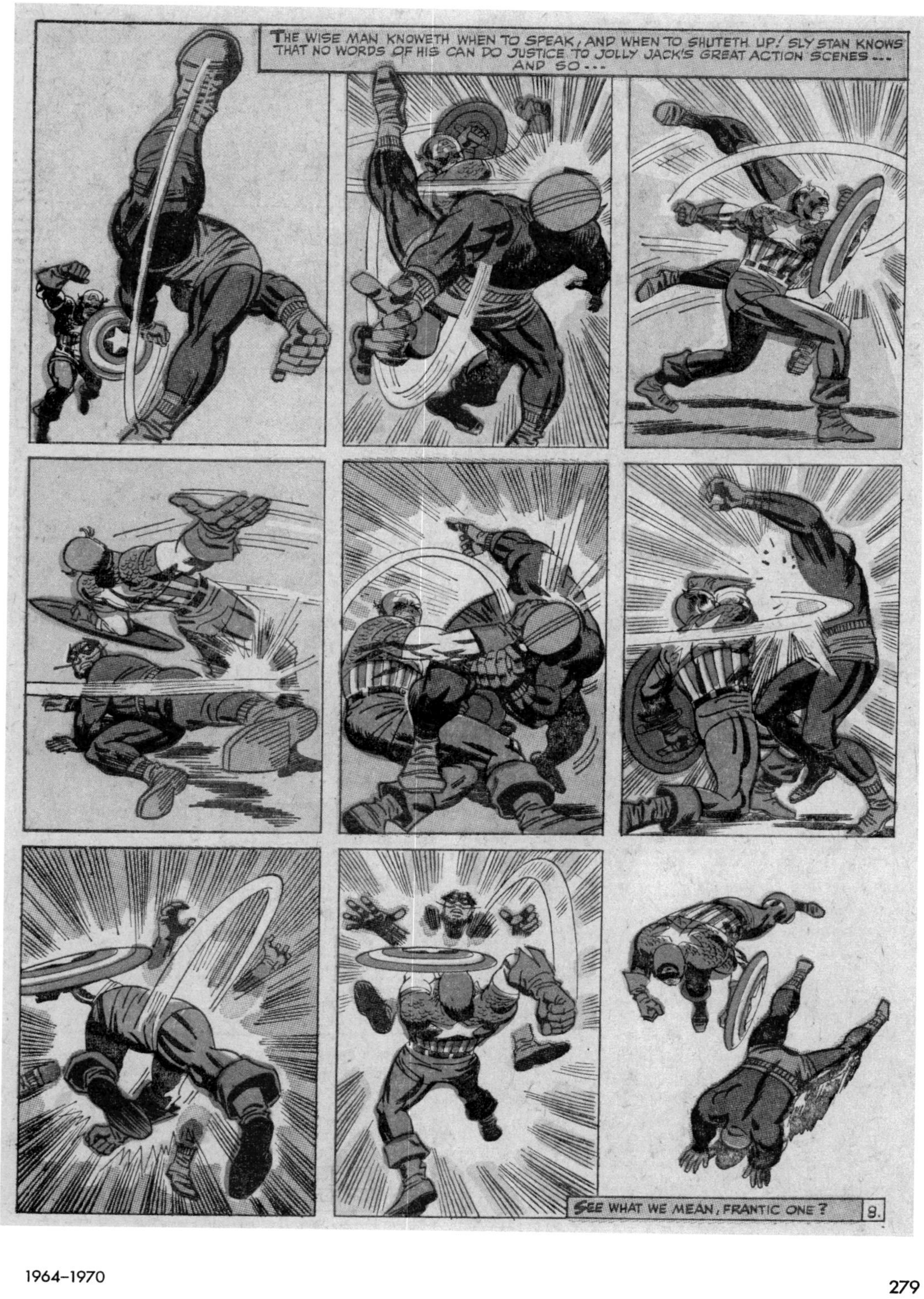
THE WISE MAN KNOWETH WHEN TO SPEAK, AND WHEN TO SHUTETH UP! SLY STAN KNOWS THAT NO WORDS OF HIS CAN DO JUSTICE TO JOLLY JACK'S GREAT ACTION SCENES ... AND SO ...
SEE WHAT WE MEAN, FRANTIC ONE?
8.

TALES OF SUSPENSE No. 94

(Below) Interior, "If This Be MODOK!"; script, Stan Lee; pencils, Jack Kirby; inks, Joe Sinnott; October 1967. Putting the Cold War firmly behind them, Marvel lets evil scientists A.I.M. (an acronym for Advanced Idea Mechanics) and its parent company Hydra (an Illuminati-inspired secret subversive cabal for world domination) develop many new villains. One of them is M.O.D.O.K.—which rivals any other acronymic character name, standing for Mental Organism Designed Only for Killing—who is all mental malice, the perfect negative image to Captain America's physical perfection.

TALES OF SUSPENSE No. 80

(Opposite) Cover; pencils, Jack Kirby; inks, Don Heck; August 1966. The Comics Code would have vetoed the Red Skull's original 1940s visage—in fact, it had to be redrawn for reprints because it looked too much like a real skull—but, despite the restriction Kirby manages to retain the sense of menace in the evil Skull's face.

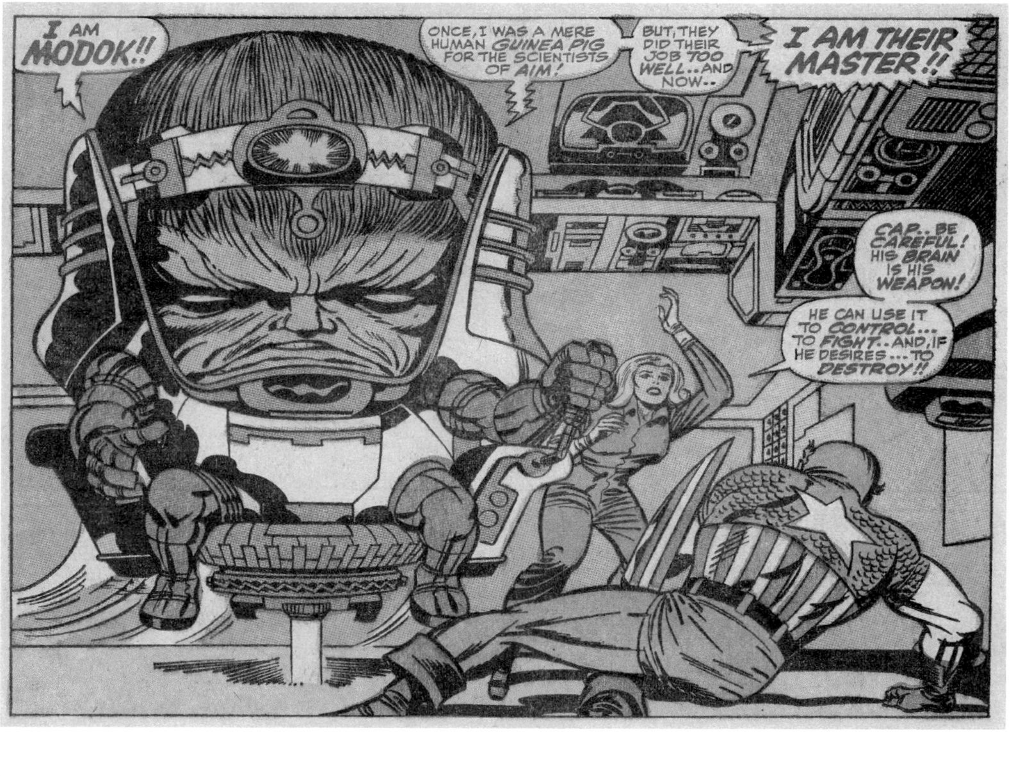
I AM MODOK!!
ONCE, I WAS A MERE HUMAN GUINEA PIG FOR THE SCIENTISTS OF AIM!
BUT, THEY DID THEIR JOB TOO WELL...AND NOW..
I AM THEIR MASTER!!
CAP..BE CAREFUL! HIS BRAIN IS HIS WEAPON!
HE CAN USE IT TO CONTROL... TO FIGHT..AND, IF HE DESIRES...TO DESTROY!!

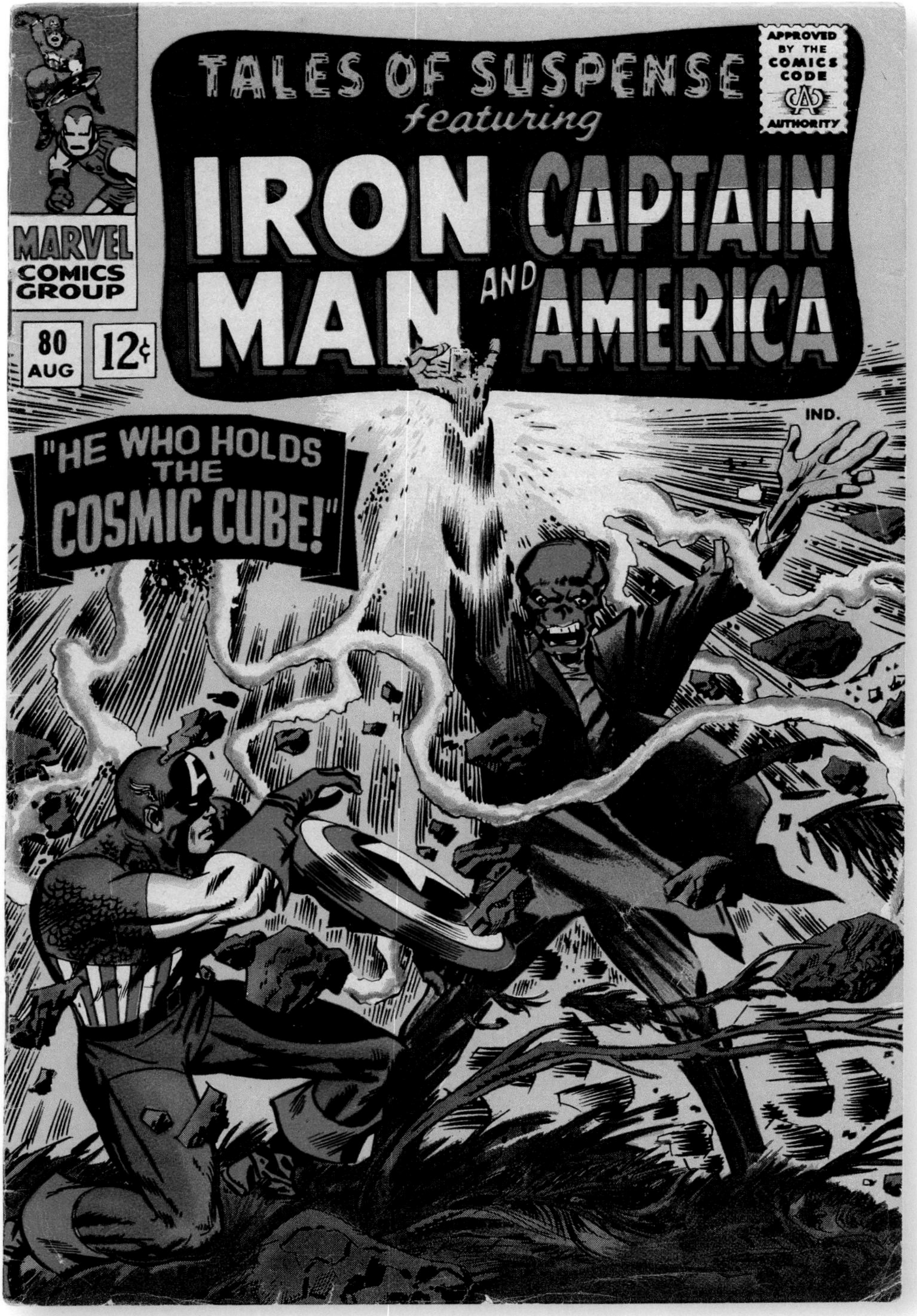
TALES OF SUSPENSE
featuring
IRON MAN AND CAPTAIN AMERICA
MARVEL COMICS GROUP
80 AUG
12¢
APPROVED BY THE COMICS CODE AUTHORITY
IND.
"HE WHO HOLDS THE COSMIC CUBE!"

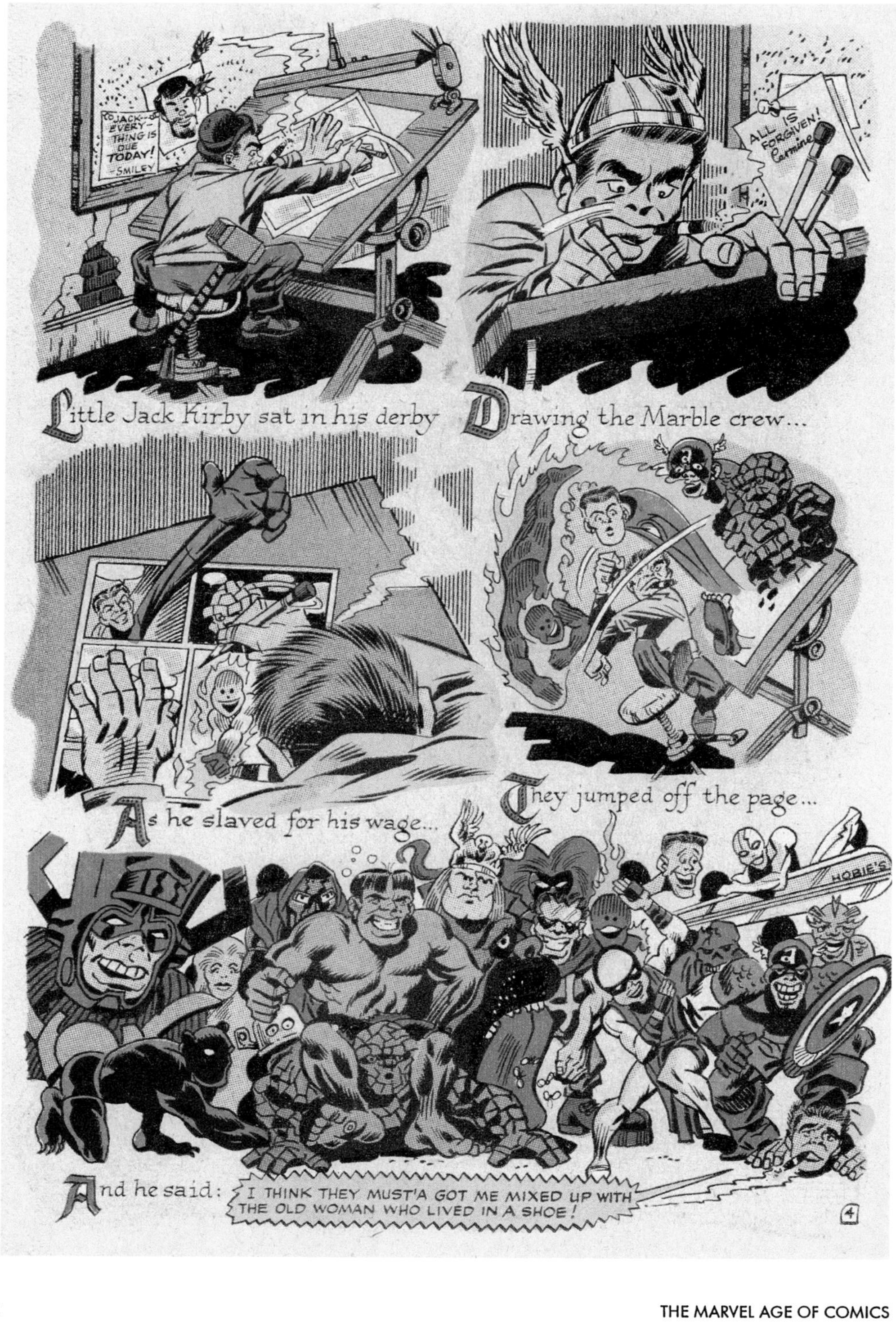
TO JACK — EVERY-THING IS DUE TODAY! —SMILEY
ALL IS FORGIVEN! Carmine
Little Jack Kirby sat in his derby
Drawing the Marble crew...
As he slaved for his wage...
They jumped off the page...
HOBIE'S
And he said:
I THINK THEY MUST'A GOT ME MIXED UP WITH THE OLD WOMAN WHO LIVED IN A SHOE!
4

NOT BRAND ECHH No. 11

(Opposite) Interior, "Auntie Goose Rhymes Dept."; script, Roy Thomas; pencils and inks, John Verpoorten; December 1968. Roy Thomas and Verpoorten transform the nursery rhyme "Little Miss Muffett" into a satirical tribute to Jack Kirby that shows a parade of Marvel characters who come to life at his drawing board.

KRAZY LITTLE COMICS

(This page) Covers, Topps Krazy Little Comics; *dialogue, Len Brown; pencils and inks, Wally Wood; 1967.* Len Brown and Roy Thomas teamed up with Wally Wood and Gil Kane for a line of mini-comics for Topps, which included parodies of Marvel characters and back cover ads by Art Spiegelman. They were test marketed but did not receive national distribution.

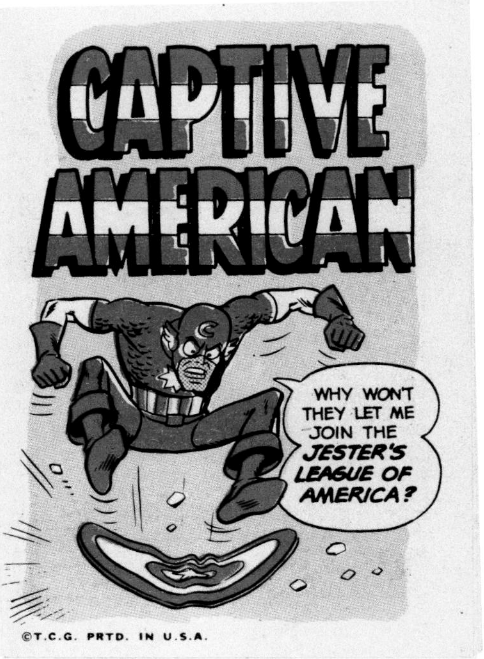

CAPTIVE AMERICAN
WHY WON'T THEY LET ME JOIN THE JESTER'S LEAGUE OF AMERICA?
©T.C.G. PRTD. IN U.S.A.

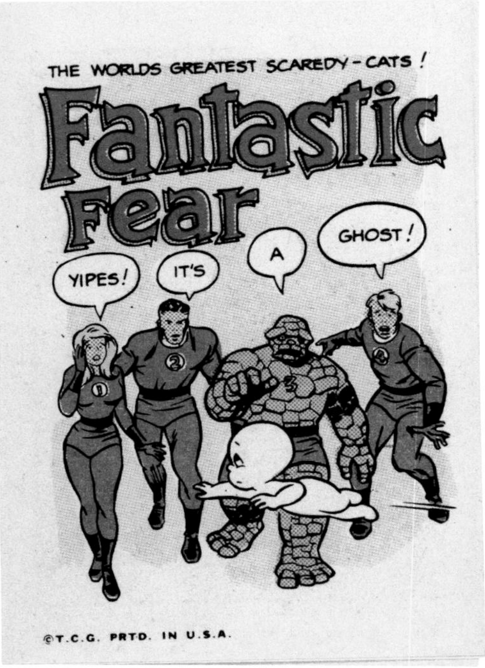

THE WORLDS GREATEST SCAREDY-CATS!
Fantastic Fear
YIPES!
IT'S
A
GHOST!
©T.C.G. PRTD. IN U.S.A.

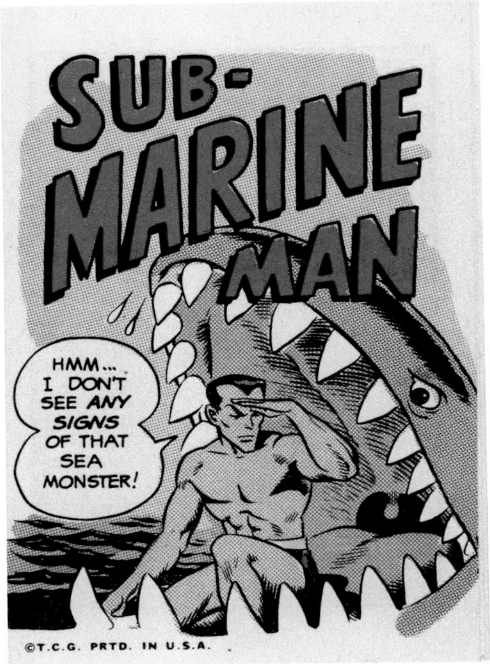

SUB-MARINE MAN
HMM... I DON'T SEE ANY SIGNS OF THAT SEA MONSTER!
©T.C.G. PRTD. IN U.S.A.

MEET THE GANG

(Below) Interior, Marvel Tales Annual *No. 1, 1964.* Although most of the "Bullpen" were actually freelancers who typically worked at home, Stan Lee created a friendly mythology that fans latched onto. Many of those who did work in the office, including the business side, were represented, although the notoriously private Steve Ditko—also conspicuously absent on the M.M.M.S. record—is not pictured.

DAREDEVIL ANNUAL No. 1

(Opposite) Interior, "Story Conference!"; script, Stan Lee; pencils, Gene Colan; inks, John Tartaglione; September 1967. In what quickly became a tradition in Marvel Annuals, Lee jokes with Gene Colan about writing their next Daredevil story. Life imitates art, as Colan really did use a tape recorder to recall their conversations.

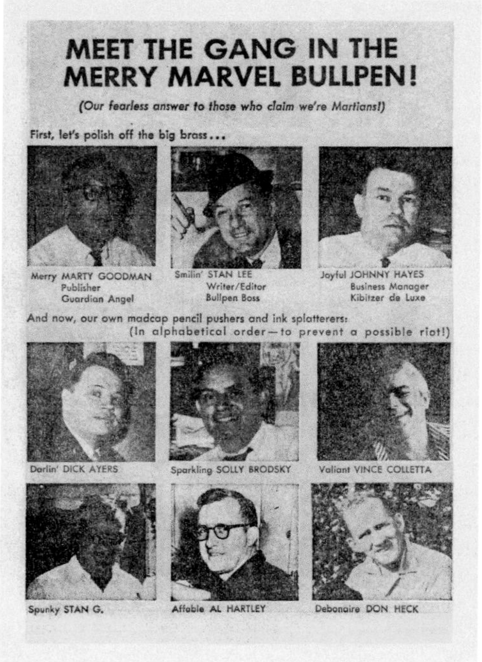

MEET THE GANG IN THE MERRY MARVEL BULLPEN!
(Our fearless answer to those who claim we're Martians!)
First, let's polish off the big brass...
Merry MARTY GOODMAN Publisher Guardian Angel
Smilin' STAN LEE Writer/Editor Bullpen Boss
Joyful JOHNNY HAYES Business Manager Kibitzer de Luxe
And now, our own madcap pencil pushers and ink splatterers: (In alphabetical order—to prevent a possible riot!)
Darlin' DICK AYERS
Sparkling SOLLY BRODSKY
Valiant VINCE COLLETTA
Spunky STAN G.
Affable AL HARTLEY
Debonaire DON HECK

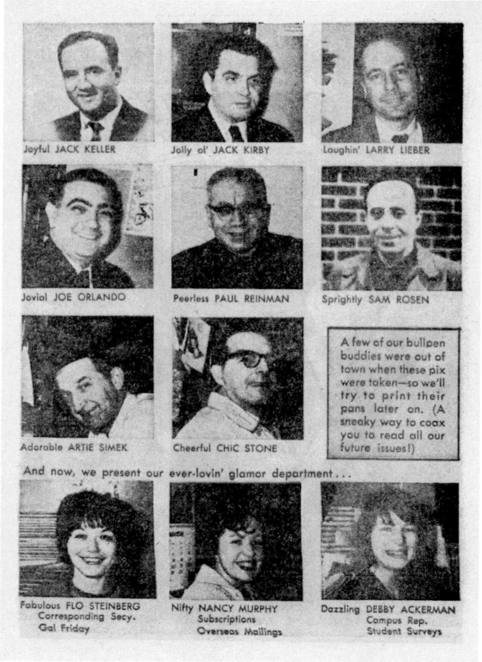

Joyful JACK KELLER
Jolly ol' JACK KIRBY
Laughin' LARRY LIEBER
Jovial JOE ORLANDO
Peerless PAUL REINMAN
Sprightly SAM ROSEN
Adorable ARTIE SIMEK
Cheerful CHIC STONE
A few of our bullpen buddies were out of town when these pix were taken—so we'll try to print their pans later on. (A sneaky way to coax you to read all our future issues!)
And now, we present our ever-lovin' glamor department...
Fabulous FLO STEINBERG Corresponding Secy. Gal Friday
Nifty NANCY MURPHY Subscriptions Overseas Mailings
Dazzling DEBBY ACKERMAN Campus Rep. Student Surveys

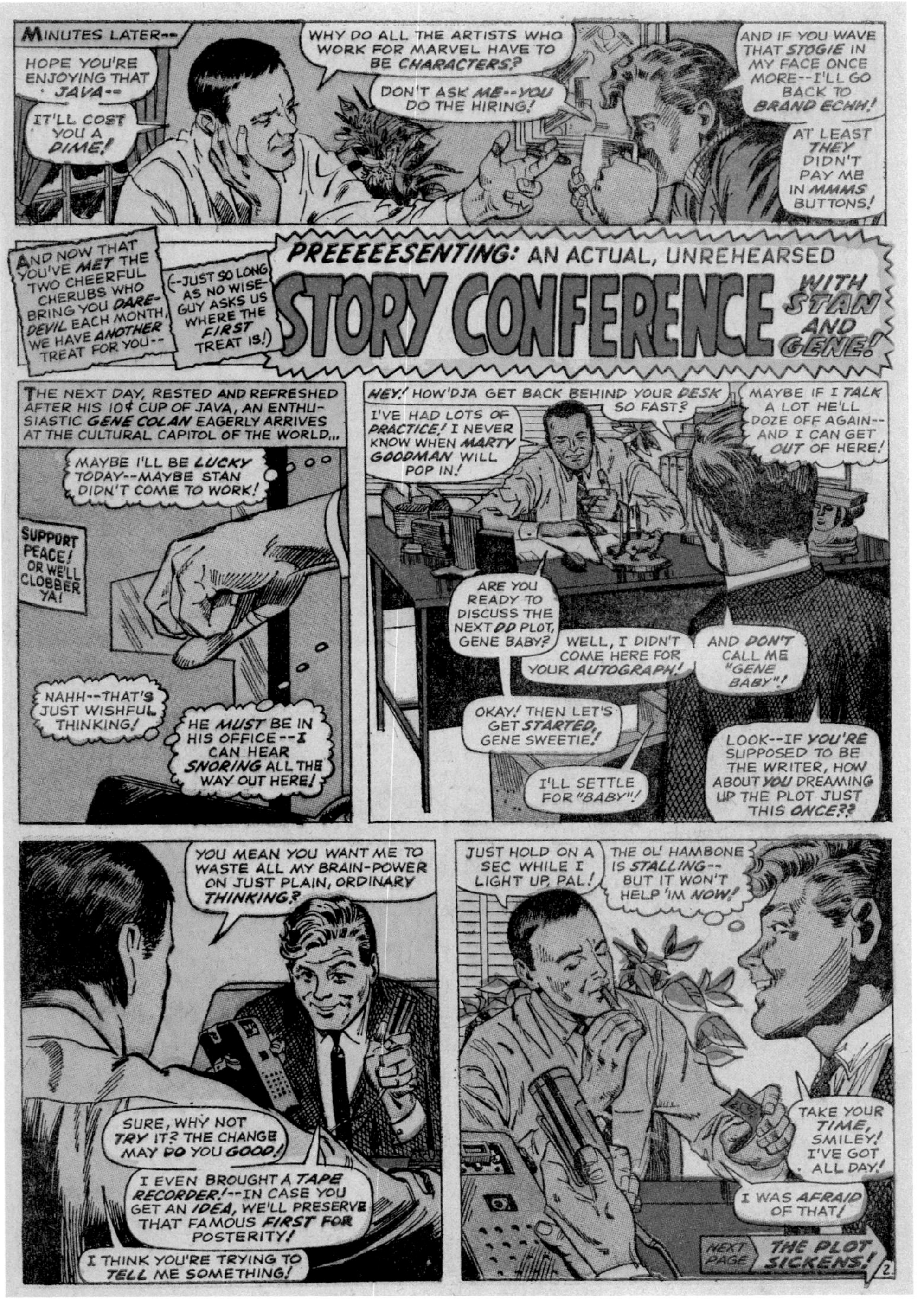

MINUTES LATER--
HOPE YOU'RE ENJOYING THAT JAVA--
IT'LL COST YOU A DIME!
WHY DO ALL THE ARTISTS WHO WORK FOR MARVEL HAVE TO BE CHARACTERS?
DON'T ASK ME--YOU DO THE HIRING!
AND IF YOU WAVE THAT STOGIE IN MY FACE ONCE MORE--I'LL GO BACK TO BRAND ECHH!
AT LEAST THEY DIDN'T PAY ME IN MMMS BUTTONS!
AND NOW THAT YOU'VE MET THE TWO CHEERFUL CHERUBS WHO BRING YOU DAREDEVIL EACH MONTH, WE HAVE ANOTHER TREAT FOR YOU--
(--JUST SO LONG AS NO WISE-GUY ASKS US WHERE THE FIRST TREAT IS!)
PREEEEESENTING: AN ACTUAL, UNREHEARSED
STORY CONFERENCE WITH STAN AND GENE!
THE NEXT DAY, RESTED AND REFRESHED AFTER HIS 10¢ CUP OF JAVA, AN ENTHUSIASTIC GENE COLAN EAGERLY ARRIVES AT THE CULTURAL CAPITOL OF THE WORLD...
MAYBE I'LL BE LUCKY TODAY--MAYBE STAN DIDN'T COME TO WORK!
SUPPORT PEACE! OR WE'LL CLOBBER YA!
NAHH--THAT'S JUST WISHFUL THINKING!
HE MUST BE IN HIS OFFICE--I CAN HEAR SNORING ALL THE WAY OUT HERE!
HEY! HOW'DJA GET BACK BEHIND YOUR DESK SO FAST?
I'VE HAD LOTS OF PRACTICE! I NEVER KNOW WHEN MARTY GOODMAN WILL POP IN!
MAYBE IF I TALK A LOT HE'LL DOZE OFF AGAIN--AND I CAN GET OUT OF HERE!
ARE YOU READY TO DISCUSS THE NEXT DD PLOT, GENE BABY?
WELL, I DIDN'T COME HERE FOR YOUR AUTOGRAPH!
AND DON'T CALL ME "GENE BABY"!
OKAY! THEN LET'S GET STARTED, GENE SWEETIE!
I'LL SETTLE FOR "BABY"!
LOOK--IF YOU'RE SUPPOSED TO BE THE WRITER, HOW ABOUT YOU DREAMING UP THE PLOT JUST THIS ONCE??
YOU MEAN YOU WANT ME TO WASTE ALL MY BRAIN-POWER ON JUST PLAIN, ORDINARY THINKING?
SURE, WHY NOT TRY IT? THE CHANGE MAY DO YOU GOOD!
I EVEN BROUGHT A TAPE RECORDER!--IN CASE YOU GET AN IDEA, WE'LL PRESERVE THAT FAMOUS FIRST FOR POSTERITY!
I THINK YOU'RE TRYING TO TELL ME SOMETHING!
JUST HOLD ON A SEC WHILE I LIGHT UP, PAL!
THE OL' HAMBONE IS STALLING--BUT IT WON'T HELP 'IM NOW!
TAKE YOUR TIME, SMILEY! I'VE GOT ALL DAY!
I WAS AFRAID OF THAT!
NEXT PAGE THE PLOT SICKENS!
2

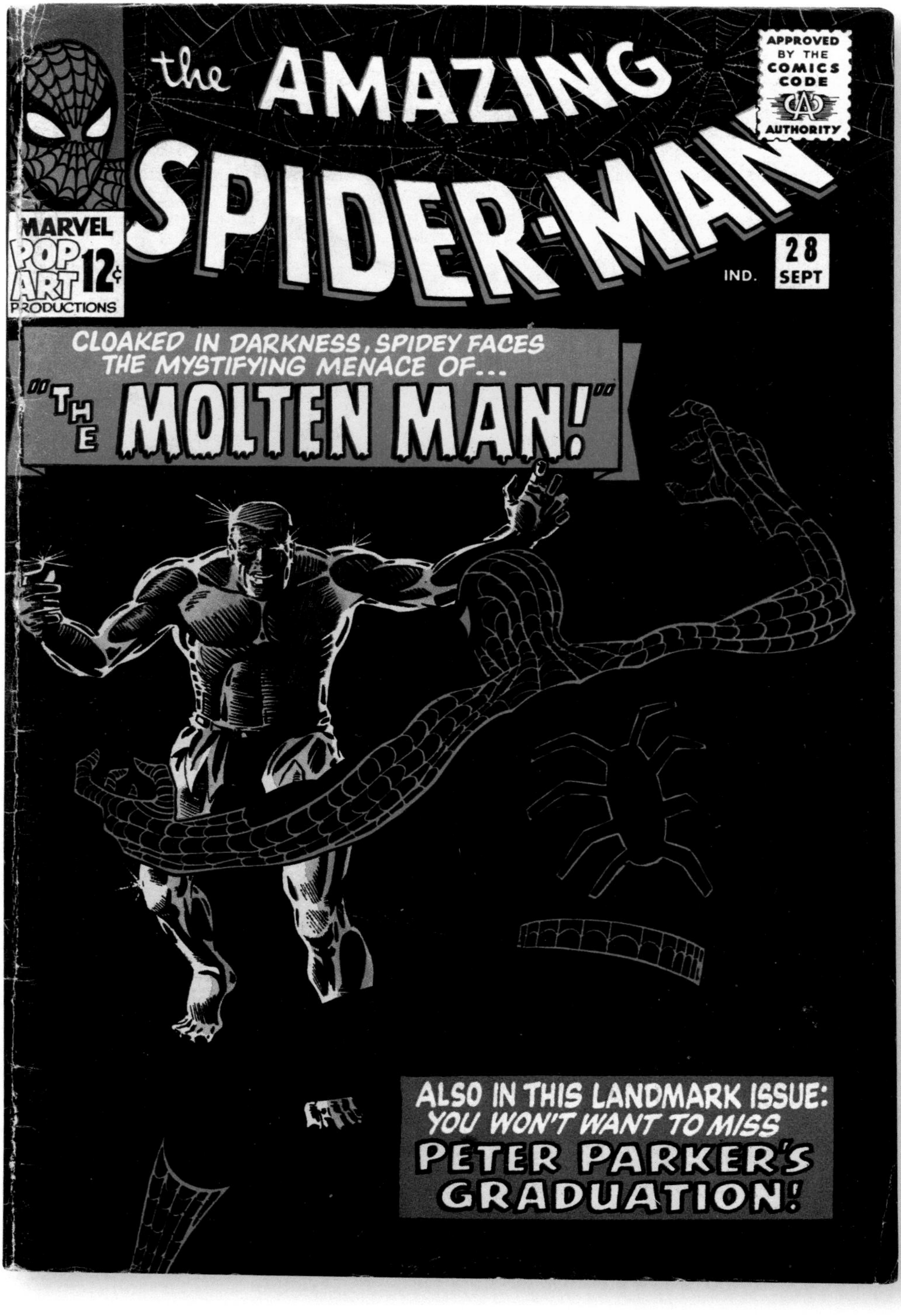

APPROVED BY THE COMICS CODE AUTHORITY
the AMAZING SPIDER-MAN
MARVEL POP ART PRODUCTIONS 12¢
IND.
28 SEPT
CLOAKED IN DARKNESS, SPIDEY FACES THE MYSTIFYING MENACE OF...
"THE MOLTEN MAN!"
ALSO IN THIS LANDMARK ISSUE: YOU WON'T WANT TO MISS
PETER PARKER'S GRADUATION!

AMAZING SPIDER-MAN No. 28

(Opposite) Cover; art, Steve Ditko; September 1965. Monotone or duotone colors on covers was used to create a mood, from stark "red alert" of *X-Men* No. 17 and the suspenseful darkness of Spider-Man's face-off, illuminated only by the glowing Molten Man. Toiling in relative obscurity, the now-celebrated colorist Stan Goldberg likely colored most of the examples here, with the possible exception of Steranko's cover for *X-Men* No. 50.

X-MEN No. 17

(Right) Cover; pencils, Jack Kirby; inks, Dick Ayers; February 1966.

X-MEN No. 50

(Below) Cover; pencils and inks, Jim Steranko; November 1968.

TALES TO ASTONISH No. 98

(Below right) Cover; pencils and inks, Dan Adkins; December 1967.

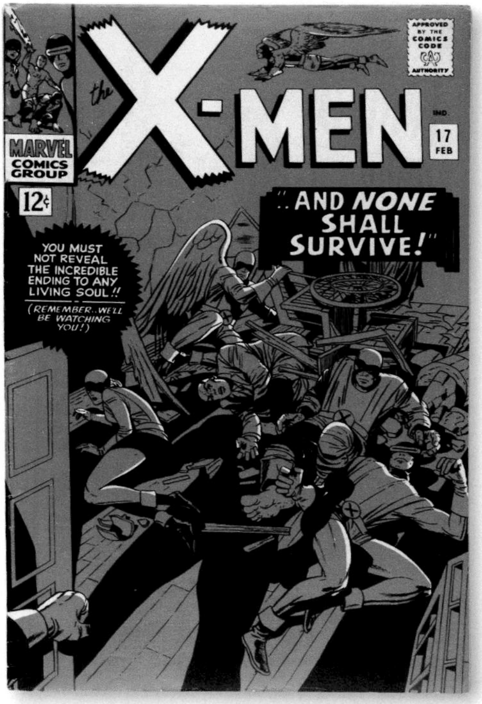

the X-MEN
MARVEL COMICS GROUP
12¢
IND. 17 FEB
APPROVED BY THE COMICS CODE AUTHORITY
"..AND NONE SHALL SURVIVE!"
YOU MUST NOT REVEAL THE INCREDIBLE ENDING TO ANY LIVING SOUL!!
(REMEMBER..WE'LL BE WATCHING YOU!)

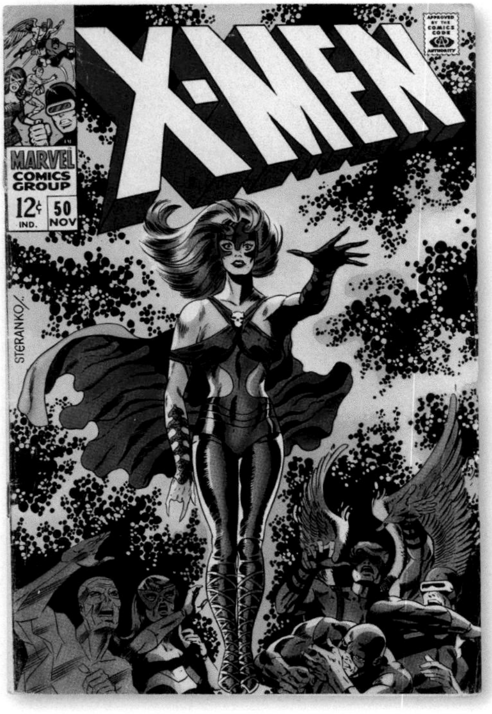

X-MEN
MARVEL COMICS GROUP
12¢ 50 NOV
IND.
APPROVED BY THE COMICS CODE AUTHORITY
STERANKO

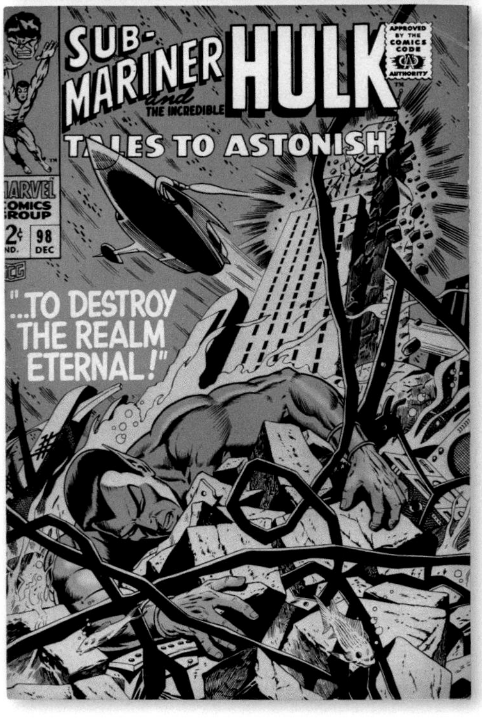

SUB-MARINER and THE INCREDIBLE HULK
TALES TO ASTONISH
APPROVED BY THE COMICS CODE AUTHORITY
98 DEC
"...TO DESTROY THE REALM ETERNAL!"

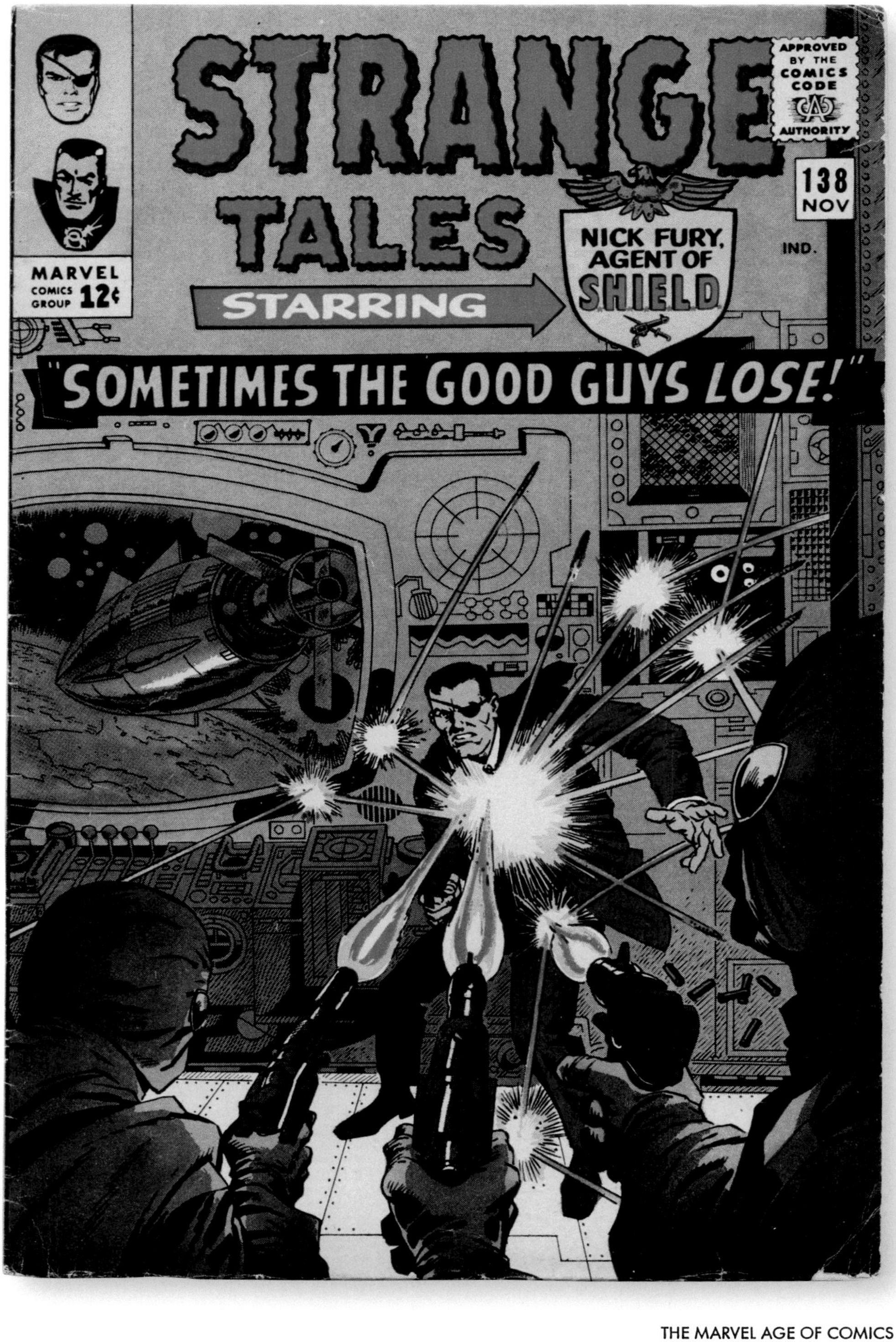

STRANGE TALES
MARVEL COMICS GROUP 12¢
APPROVED BY THE COMICS CODE AUTHORITY
138 NOV
IND.
STARRING
NICK FURY, AGENT OF SHIELD
"SOMETIMES THE GOOD GUYS LOSE!"

STRANGE TALES No. 138

(Opposite) Cover; pencils, Jack Kirby; inks, John Severin; November 1965. Kirby provided layouts for John Severin for three issues of *S.H.I.E.L.D.*, an excellent, though short-lived pairing. Fury was one of the few heroes not given a costume—although that would change when Steranko took over.

STRANGE TALES No. 135

(Right) Interior, "The Man For the Job!"; script, Stan Lee; pencils, Jack Kirby; inks, Dick Ayers; August 1965. The same team that created Sgt. Fury began this series influenced by James Bond and the *Man from U.N.C.L.E.* TV series. Fury is a "fish out of water": an intelligent, but blue collar, C.I.A. agent drafted to head the world's most technologically advanced spy agency.

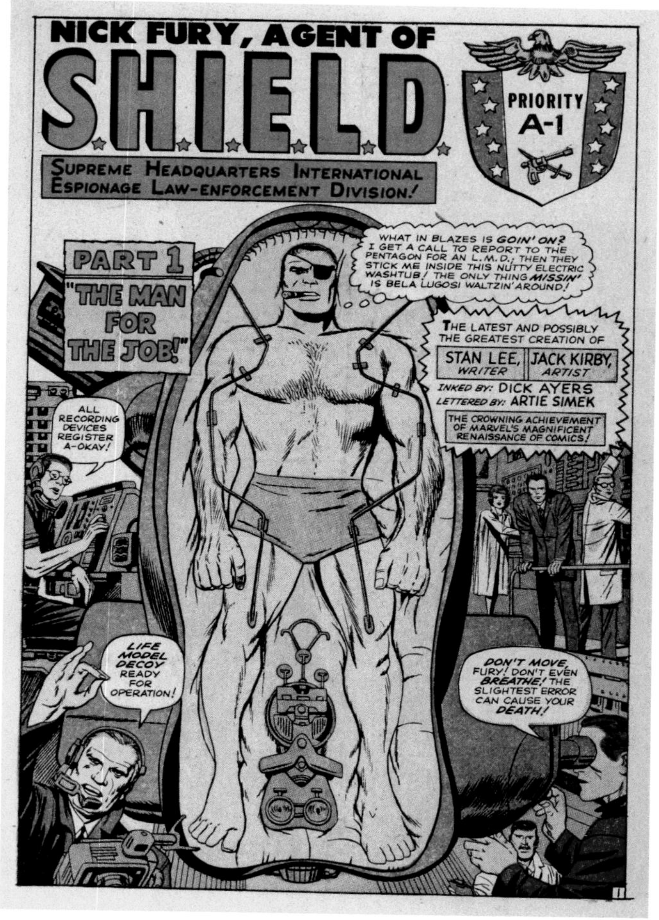

NICK FURY, AGENT OF S.H.I.E.L.D.
PRIORITY A-1
SUPREME HEADQUARTERS INTERNATIONAL ESPIONAGE LAW-ENFORCEMENT DIVISION!
PART 1 "THE MAN FOR THE JOB!"
WHAT IN BLAZES IS GOIN' ON? I GET A CALL TO REPORT TO THE PENTAGON FOR AN L.M.D.; THEN THEY STICK ME INSIDE THIS NUTTY ELECTRIC WASHTUB! THE ONLY THING MISSIN' IS BELA LUGOSI WALTZIN' AROUND!
THE LATEST AND POSSIBLY THE GREATEST CREATION OF
STAN LEE, WRITER
JACK KIRBY, ARTIST
INKED BY: DICK AYERS
LETTERED BY: ARTIE SIMEK
THE CROWNING ACHIEVEMENT OF MARVEL'S MAGNIFICENT RENAISSANCE OF COMICS!
ALL RECORDING DEVICES REGISTER A-OKAY!
LIFE MODEL DECOY READY FOR OPERATION!
DON'T MOVE, FURY! DON'T EVEN BREATHE! THE SLIGHTEST ERROR CAN CAUSE YOUR DEATH!

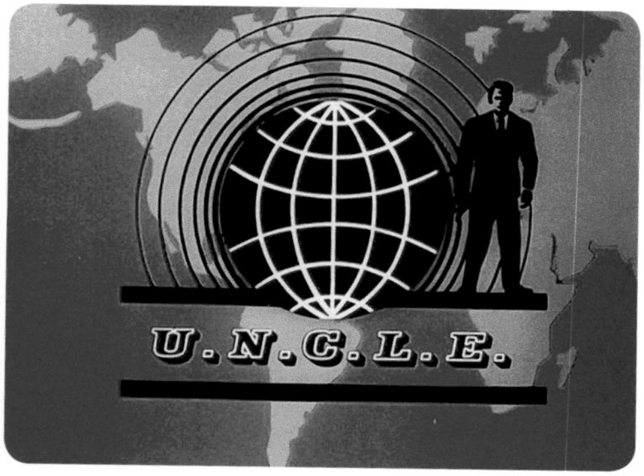

U.N.C.L.E.

FURY'S FOUNDATION

(Left) Title card, The Man from U.N.C.L.E., *NBC, ca. 1964.* Ian Fleming's James Bond films, beginning with *Dr. No* in 1962, unleashed a tidal wave of spy series, including NBC's *Man from U.N.C.L.E.* The TV series stepped away from Cold War politics and used an international force to combat evil—a concept not unfamiliar to fans of Marvel's S.H.I.E.L.D.

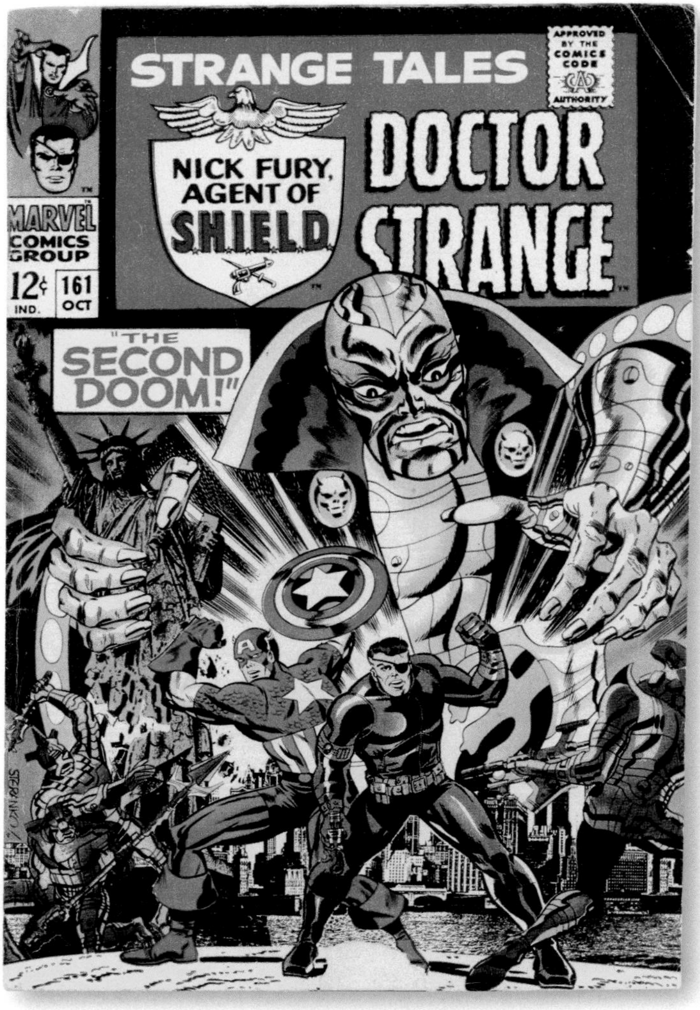
STRANGE TALES
APPROVED BY THE COMICS CODE AUTHORITY
NICK FURY, AGENT OF SHIELD
DOCTOR STRANGE
MARVEL COMICS GROUP
12¢ IND.
161 OCT
"THE SECOND DOOM!"
STERANKO

STRANGE TALES No. 161

(Above) Cover; pencils and inks, Jim Steranko; October 1967. Here Steranko takes a romp through time in a mash-up featuring characters from Marvel's three decades in publishing: Captain America from the Timely era, the Yellow Claw from the Atlas '50s, and Nick Fury representing the current Marvel Age.

STRANGE TALES No. 135

(Opposite) Interior, "The Man for the Job!"; script, Stan Lee; pencils, Jack Kirby; inks, Dick Ayers; August 1965.

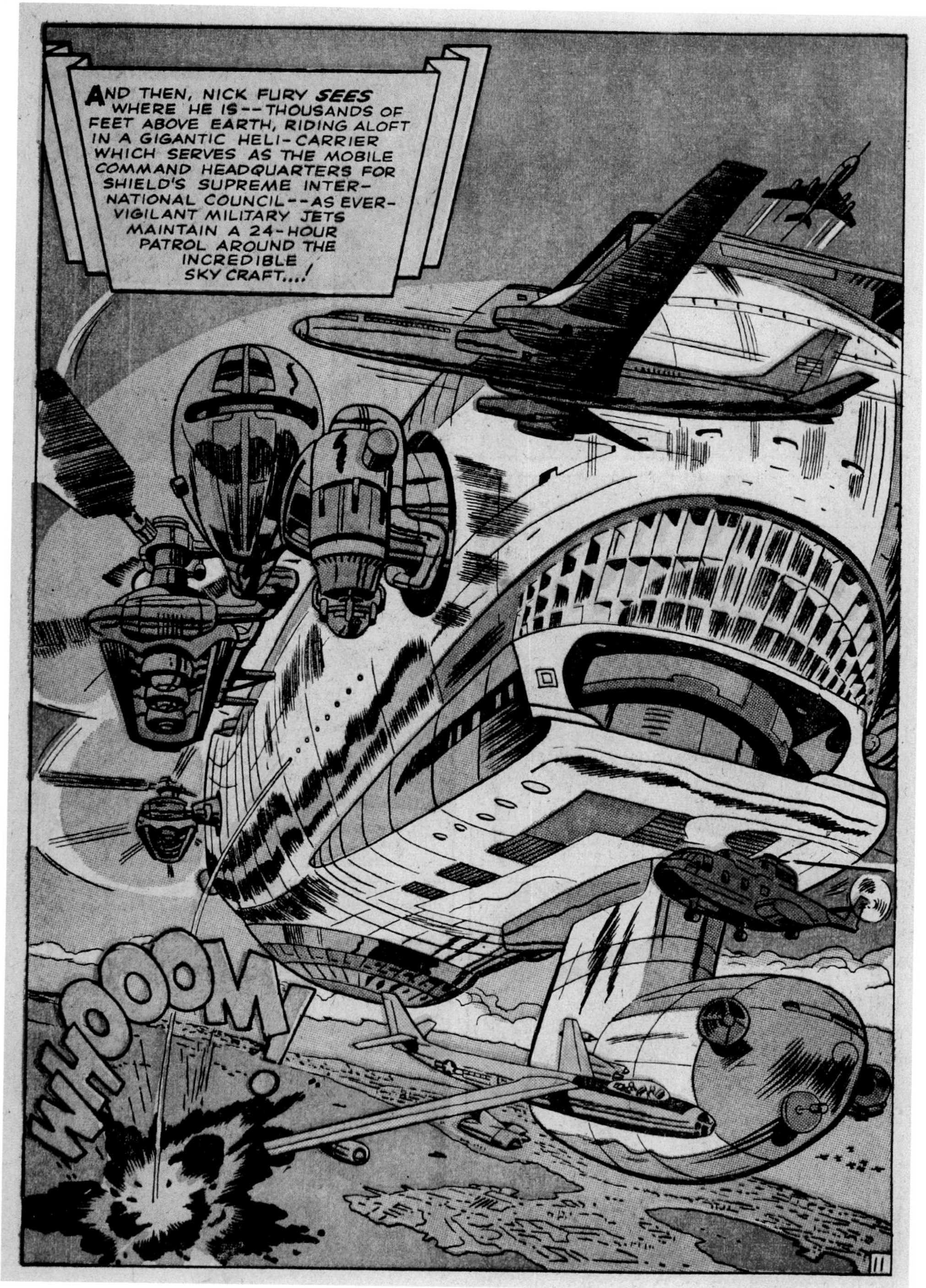
AND THEN, NICK FURY SEES WHERE HE IS--THOUSANDS OF FEET ABOVE EARTH, RIDING ALOFT IN A GIGANTIC HELI-CARRIER WHICH SERVES AS THE MOBILE COMMAND HEADQUARTERS FOR SHIELD'S SUPREME INTER-NATIONAL COUNCIL--AS EVER-VIGILANT MILITARY JETS MAINTAIN A 24-HOUR PATROL AROUND THE INCREDIBLE SKY CRAFT...!
WHOOOM!
11

NICK FURY, AGENT OF S.H.I.E.L.D.!
SUPREME HEADQUARTERS INTERNATIONAL ESPIONAGE LAW-ENFORCEMENT DIVISION
SPY SCHOOL
PRODUCED BY STAN LEE
SCRIPT AND CINEMATOGRAPHY BY JIM STERANKO
LETTERING EFFECTS BY JERRY FELDMANN
AFTER THE DEFEAT OF HYDRA (SEE LAST ISH), THE MASSIVE HELI-CARRIER HAS DOCKED FOR REPAIRS IN NEW YORK! NOW, THE INNER CIRCLE OF THE SHIELD ORGANIZATION PREPARES TO BID EACH OTHER FAREWELL -- AND A STARTLING NEW SAGA BEGINS TO UNFOLD...
HOW'S IT FEEL TO BE BACK IN CIVILIZATION, AGAIN, GABE?
NOT BAD, NICK! MAKES ME WONDER, THOUGH... ONE DAY WE'RE FIGHTIN' FOR OUR LIVES ... THE NEXT, JUST A COUPLA JOE'S STANDIN' ON THE CORNER OF FORTY-SECOND AND BROADWAY! LIFE GOES ON, HUH, COLONEL?

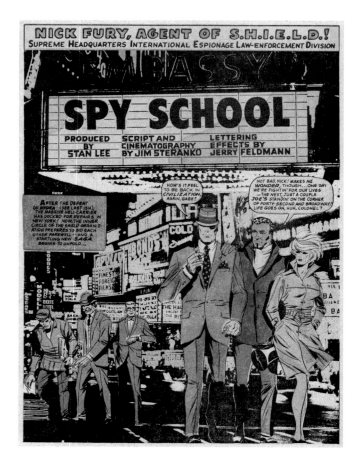

STRANGE TALES No. 159

(Left) Interior, "Spy School!"; script, pencils, and inks, Jim Steranko; August 1967.

NICK FURY, AGENT OF S.H.I.E.L.D. No. 4

(Opposite) Cover; pencils and inks, Jim Steranko; September 1968. Psychedelic was a word used—and abused—in the '60s to describe weird, colorful, sometimes hallucinogenic visuals. It could also be applied to Steranko's fantastic artwork—although he coined a new phrase for himself: Zap Art.

EVERYTHING HE TOUCHES TURNS...TO EXCITEMENT!

(Right) Movie poster, Goldfinger, *Eon Productions/United Artists, 1964.* Winning the Academy Award for special effects, with a best-selling DB5 toy and even the cover of *Life*, this third, quintessential installment of the Bond series provided the template for all the movies to follow: ever more sleek cars and gadgets, more chic *femmes fatales*, and more sinister villains. Shot with a '60s sheen that many fans argue won't ever be topped, Bond fever hit its pitch in 1964.

JAMES BOND IS BACK IN ACTION!
"GOLDFINGER"
TECHNICOLOR

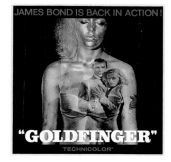

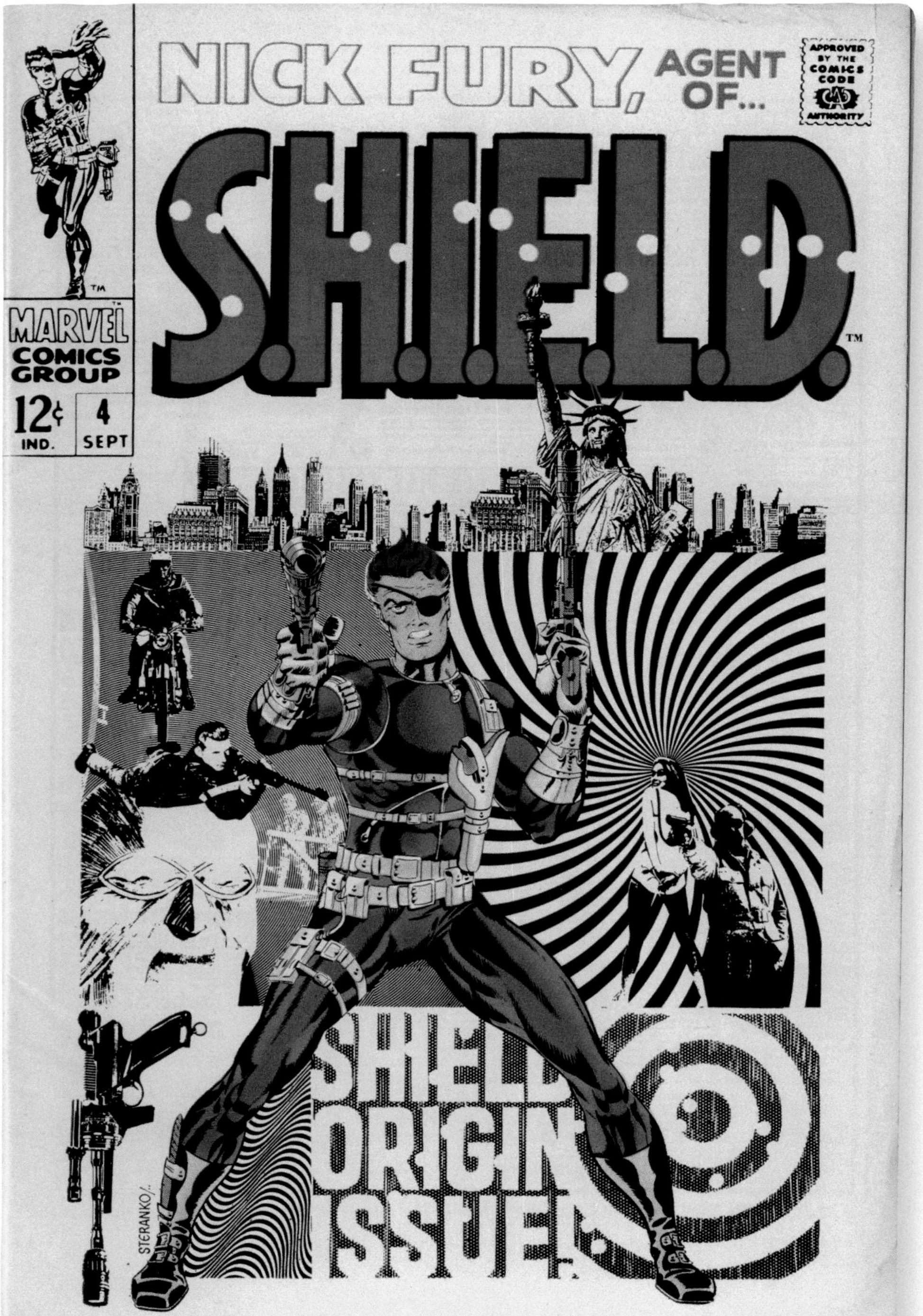
NICK FURY, AGENT OF...
S.H.I.E.L.D.
APPROVED BY THE COMICS CODE AUTHORITY
MARVEL COMICS GROUP
12¢ IND.
4 SEPT
SHIELD ORIGIN ISSUE!
STERANKO

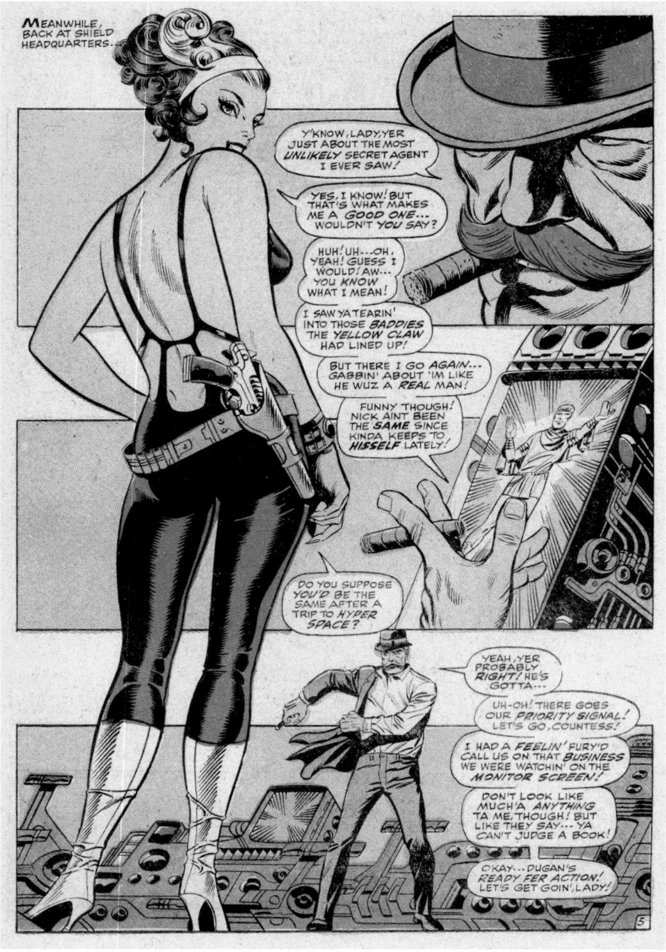

MEANWHILE, BACK AT SHIELD HEADQUARTERS...
Y'KNOW, LADY, YER JUST ABOUT THE MOST UNLIKELY SECRET AGENT I EVER SAW!
YES, I KNOW! BUT THAT'S WHAT MAKES ME A GOOD ONE... WOULDN'T YOU SAY?
HUH! UH...OH, YEAH! GUESS I WOULD! AW... YOU KNOW WHAT I MEAN!
I SAW YA TEARIN' INTO THOSE BADDIES THE YELLOW CLAW HAD LINED UP!
BUT THERE I GO AGAIN... GABBIN' ABOUT 'IM LIKE HE WUZ A REAL MAN!
FUNNY THOUGH! NICK AIN'T BEEN THE SAME SINCE KINDA KEEPS TO HISSELF LATELY!
DO YOU SUPPOSE YOU'D BE THE SAME AFTER A TRIP TO HYPER SPACE?
YEAH, YER PROBABLY RIGHT! HE'S GOTTA...
UH-OH! THERE GOES OUR PRIORITY SIGNAL! LET'S GO, COUNTESS!
I HAD A FEELIN' FURY'D CALL US ON THAT BUSINESS WE WERE WATCHIN' ON THE MONITOR SCREEN!
DON'T LOOK LIKE MUCH'A ANYTHING TA ME, THOUGH! BUT LIKE THEY SAY... YA CAN'T JUDGE A BOOK!
OKAY... DUGAN'S READY FER ACTION! LET'S GET GOIN', LADY!
5

STRANGE TALES No. 168

(Above) Interior, "Today Earth Died!"; script and pencils, Jim Steranko; inks, Joe Sinnott; May 1969. In 1975, Steranko said that this was his favorite short story. The blue-collar soldier we once knew has become a man of the world—and the world Fury moves through is a glamorous, bachelor-pad analogue to the super heroes that spawned him. The women, of course, are in a class by themselves, though the censors found Steranko's original drawing of her to be too sexy.

NICK FURY, AGENT OF S.H.I.E.L.D. No. 2

(Opposite) Interior, "So Shall Ye Reap . . . Death!"; script and pencils, Jim Steranko; inks, Frank Giacoia; July 1968.

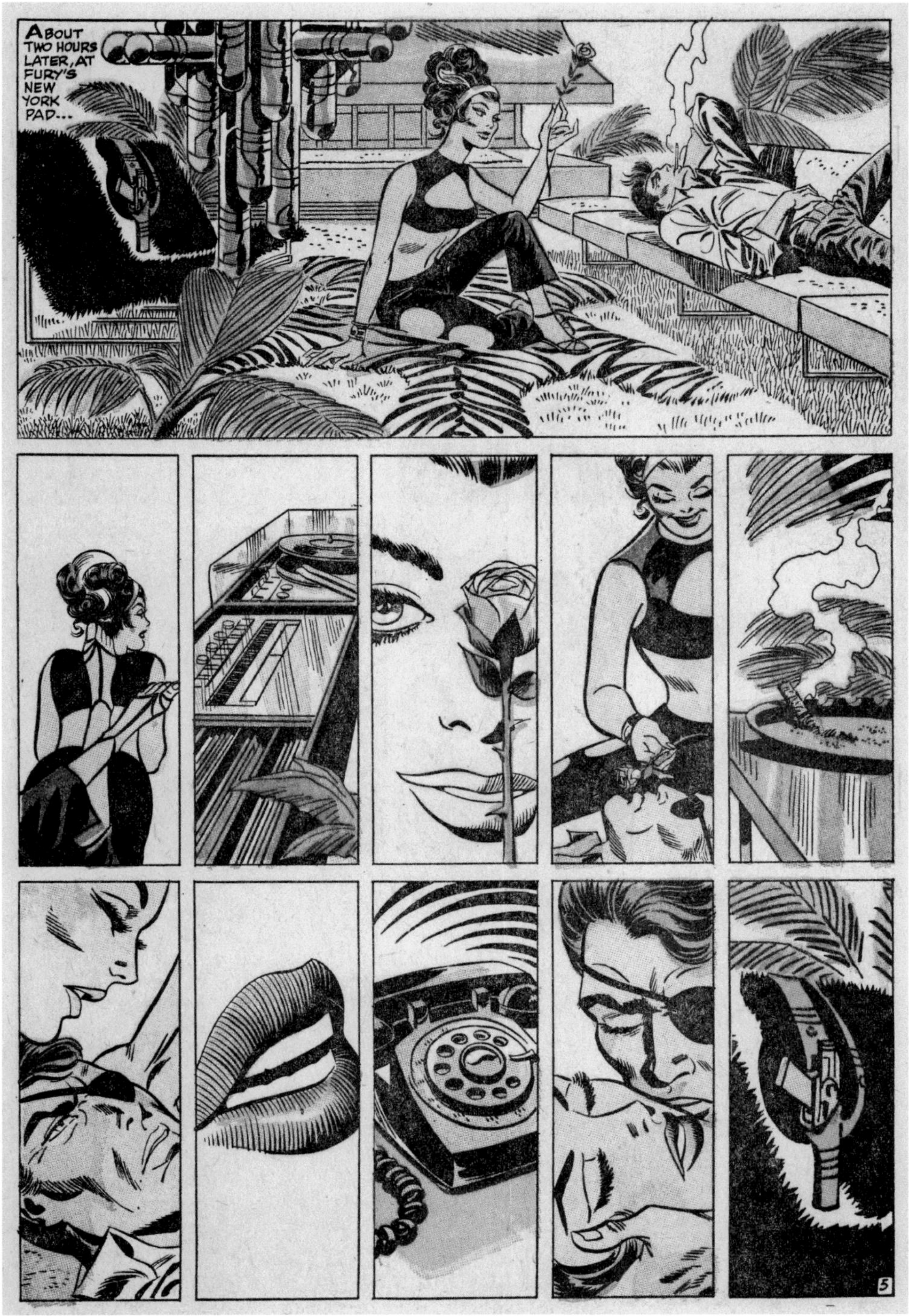
ABOUT TWO HOURS LATER, AT FURY'S NEW YORK PAD...
5

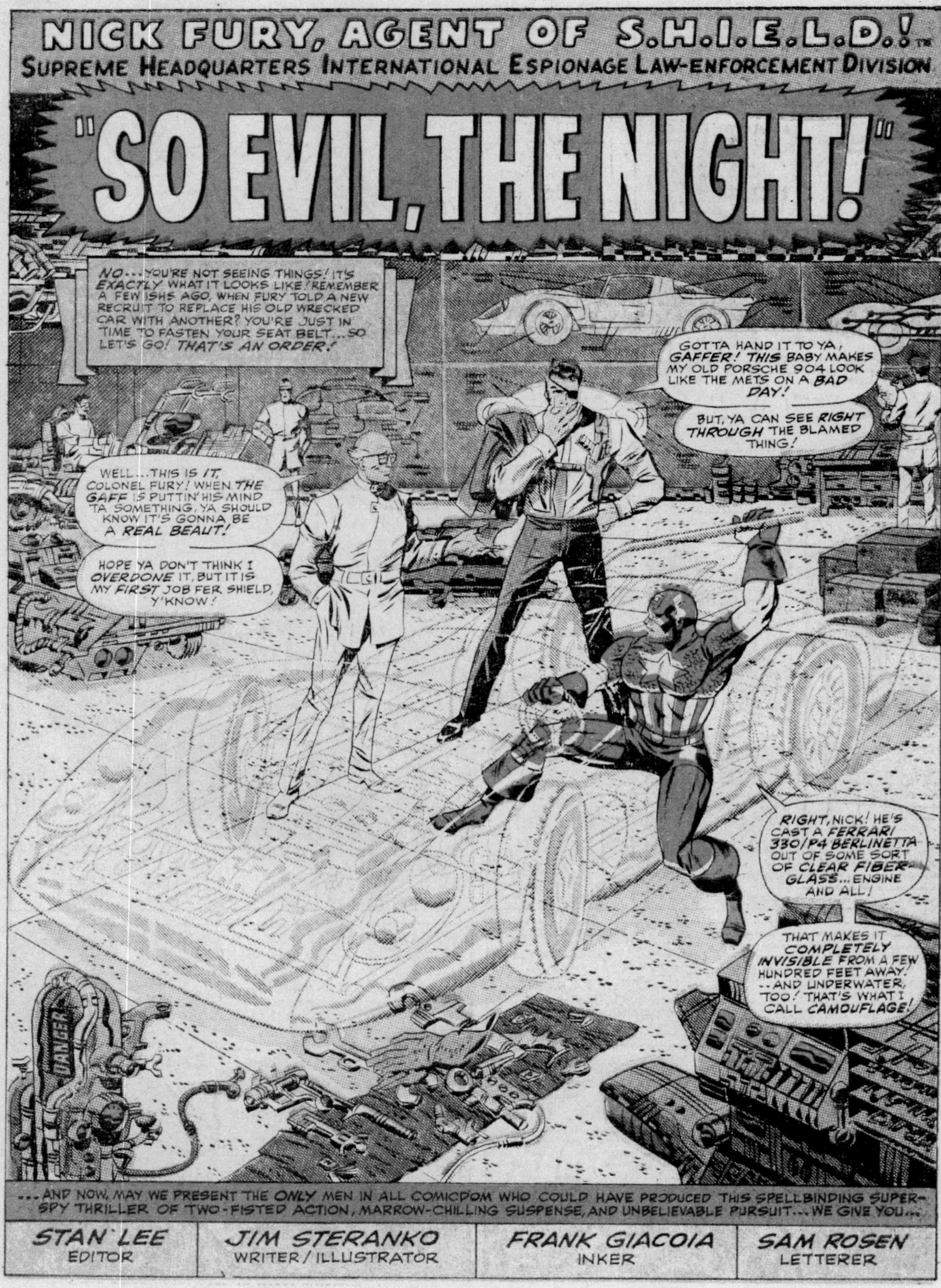
NICK FURY, AGENT OF S.H.I.E.L.D.!
SUPREME HEADQUARTERS INTERNATIONAL ESPIONAGE LAW-ENFORCEMENT DIVISION
"SO EVIL, THE NIGHT!"
NO... YOU'RE NOT SEEING THINGS! IT'S EXACTLY WHAT IT LOOKS LIKE! REMEMBER A FEW ISHS AGO, WHEN FURY TOLD A NEW RECRUIT TO REPLACE HIS OLD WRECKED CAR WITH ANOTHER? YOU'RE JUST IN TIME TO FASTEN YOUR SEAT BELT...SO LET'S GO! THAT'S AN ORDER!
GOTTA HAND IT TO YA, GAFFER! THIS BABY MAKES MY OLD PORSCHE 904 LOOK LIKE THE METS ON A BAD DAY!
BUT, YA CAN SEE RIGHT THROUGH THE BLAMED THING!
WELL...THIS IS IT, COLONEL FURY! WHEN THE GAFF IS PUTTIN' HIS MIND TA SOMETHING, YA SHOULD KNOW IT'S GONNA BE A REAL BEAUT!
HOPE YA DON'T THINK I OVERDONE IT, BUT IT IS MY FIRST JOB FER SHIELD, Y'KNOW!
RIGHT, NICK! HE'S CAST A FERRARI 330/P4 BERLINETTA OUT OF SOME SORT OF CLEAR FIBER GLASS... ENGINE AND ALL!
THAT MAKES IT COMPLETELY INVISIBLE FROM A FEW HUNDRED FEET AWAY! --AND UNDERWATER, TOO! THAT'S WHAT I CALL CAMOUFLAGE!
DANGER
...AND NOW, MAY WE PRESENT THE ONLY MEN IN ALL COMICDOM WHO COULD HAVE PRODUCED THIS SPELLBINDING SUPER-SPY THRILLER OF TWO-FISTED ACTION, MARROW-CHILLING SUSPENSE, AND UNBELIEVABLE PURSUIT... WE GIVE YOU...
STAN LEE
EDITOR
JIM STERANKO
WRITER/ILLUSTRATOR
FRANK GIACOIA
INKER
SAM ROSEN
LETTERER

STRANGE TALES No. 162

(Opposite and below) Interiors, "So Evil, the Night!"; script and pencils, Jim Steranko; inks, Frank Giacoia; November 1967. In true Bond fashion, Steranko gives Fury a new toy after he crashes his Kirby-designed flying Porsche: a customized Ferrari 330/P4 Berlinetta with "vortex beam devices in the wheel rims" and "hydrolic-mounted cannons." Oh, and did we mention it's invisible? (Even Bond didn't get an invisible car for another 40 years....) And where Bond could change the license plate on his car, Fury can change the car's color — Gaffer, in a role similar to MI-6's quartermaster, shows him how.

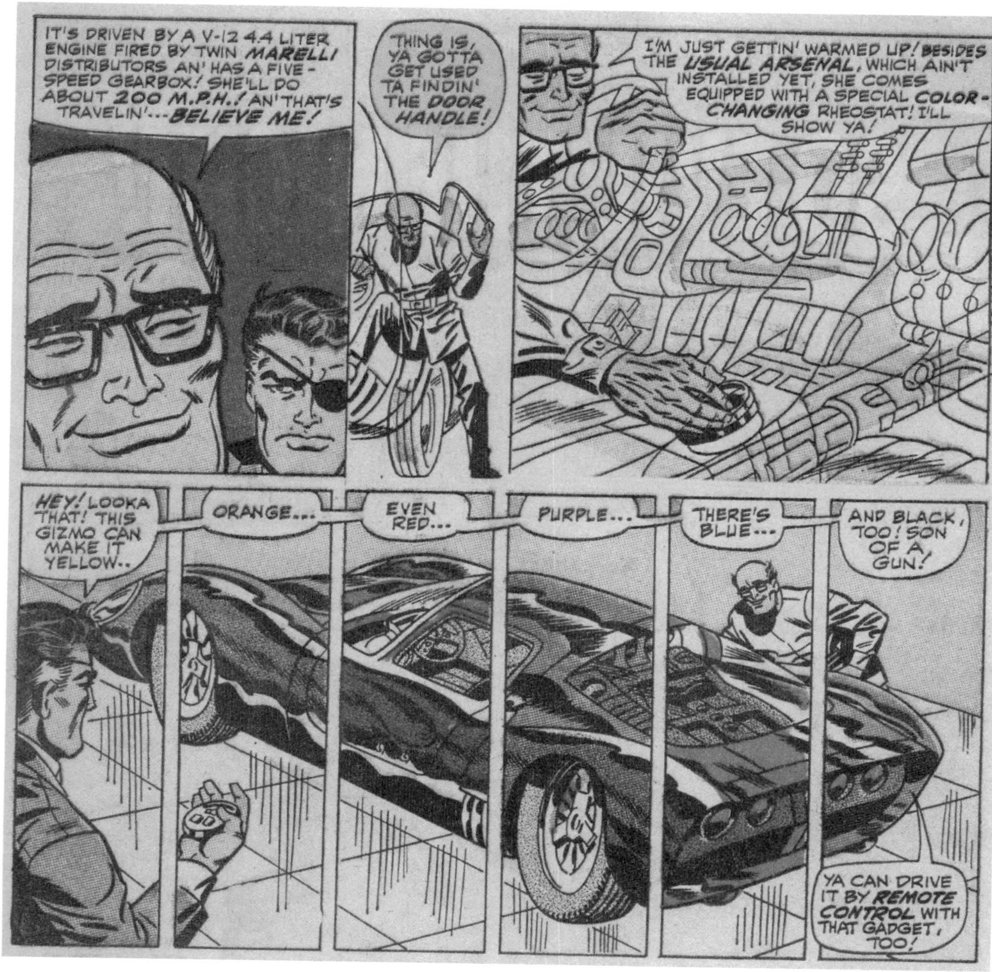
IT'S DRIVEN BY A V-12 4.4 LITER ENGINE FIRED BY TWIN MARELLI DISTRIBUTORS AN' HAS A FIVE-SPEED GEARBOX! SHE'LL DO ABOUT 200 M.P.H.! AN' THAT'S TRAVELIN'...BELIEVE ME!
THING IS, YA GOTTA GET USED TA FINDIN' THE DOOR HANDLE!
I'M JUST GETTIN' WARMED UP! BESIDES THE USUAL ARSENAL, WHICH AIN'T INSTALLED YET, SHE COMES EQUIPPED WITH A SPECIAL COLOR-CHANGING RHEOSTAT! I'LL SHOW YA!
HEY! LOOKA THAT! THIS GIZMO CAN MAKE IT YELLOW..
ORANGE...
EVEN RED...
PURPLE...
THERE'S BLUE...
AND BLACK, TOO! SON OF A GUN!
YA CAN DRIVE IT BY REMOTE CONTROL WITH THAT GADGET, TOO!

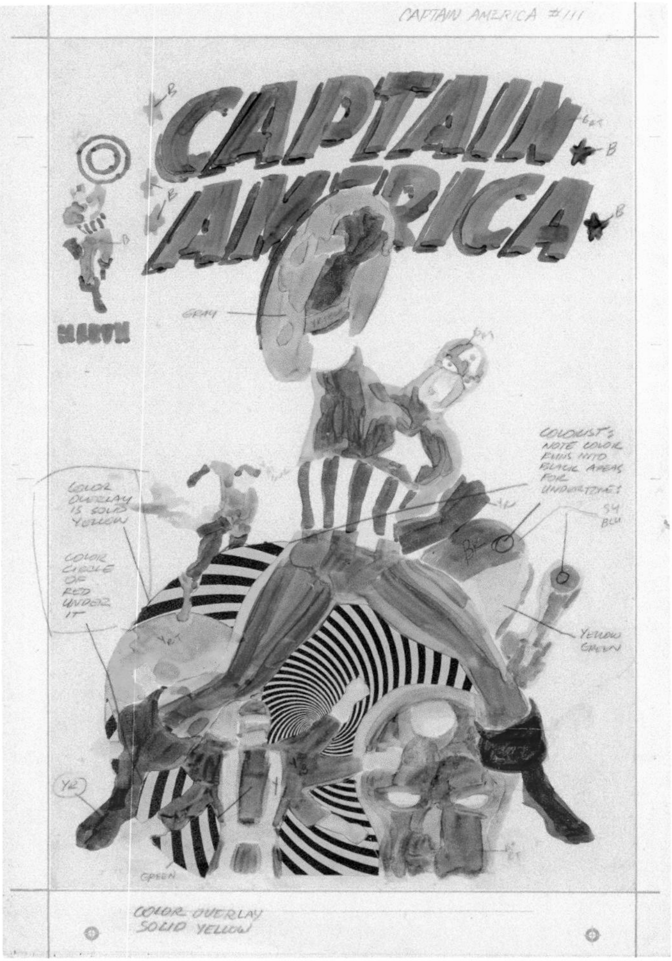
CAPTAIN AMERICA #111
CAPTAIN AMERICA
GRAY
COLORIST: NOTE COLOR RUNS INTO BLACK AREAS FOR UNDERTONE!
COLOR OVERLAY IS SOLID YELLOW
COLOR CIRCLE OF RED UNDER IT
YELLOW GREEN
GREEN
COLOR OVERLAY SOLID YELLOW

COLOR GUIDANCE

(Above) Color guide, Captain America *No.111 cover; art, Jim Steranko; March 1969.* Steranko was granted the rare privilege (and burden) of producing his books from the plot all the way through to lettering and coloring, delivering finished pages ready for production. The level of control he exercised was enviable, but the pressure was intense, as he recalled in 1979: "My life was hectic then. I worked as the art director for an ad agency in the afternoon, played in a rock band at night, and worked on my comic book pages early in the morning. It's a peculiar thing, but the more I learned about storytelling, the slower I became."

CAPTAIN AMERICA No. 111

(Opposite) Interior, "Tomorrow You Live, Tonight I Die!"; script, Stan Lee; pencils, Jim Steranko; inks, Joe Sinnott; March 1969.

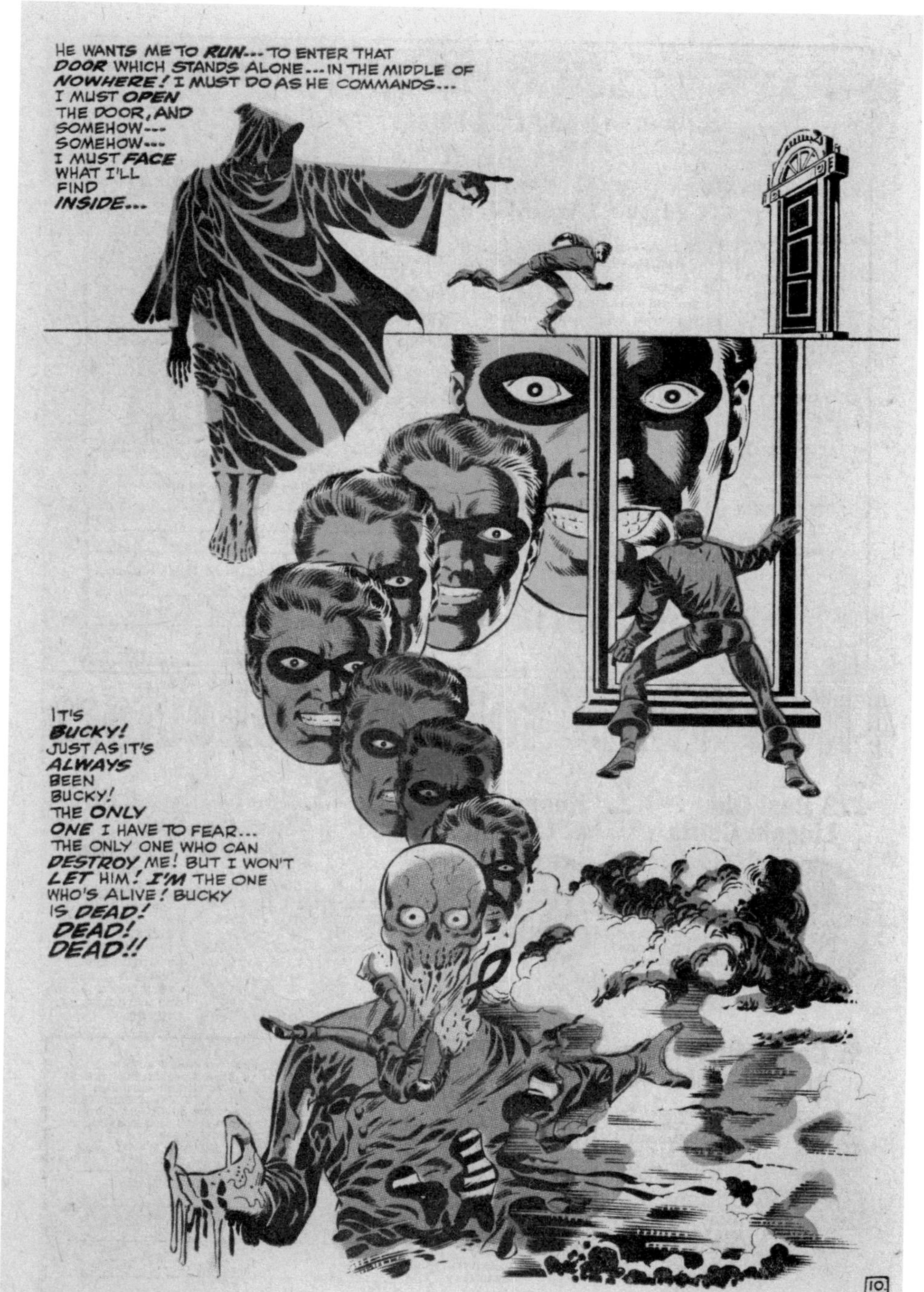

HE WANTS ME TO RUN... TO ENTER THAT DOOR WHICH STANDS ALONE... IN THE MIDDLE OF NOWHERE! I MUST DO AS HE COMMANDS... I MUST OPEN THE DOOR, AND SOMEHOW--- SOMEHOW--- I MUST FACE WHAT I'LL FIND INSIDE...
IT'S BUCKY! JUST AS IT'S ALWAYS BEEN BUCKY! THE ONLY ONE I HAVE TO FEAR... THE ONLY ONE WHO CAN DESTROY ME! BUT I WON'T LET HIM! I'M THE ONE WHO'S ALIVE! BUCKY IS DEAD! DEAD! DEAD!!
10

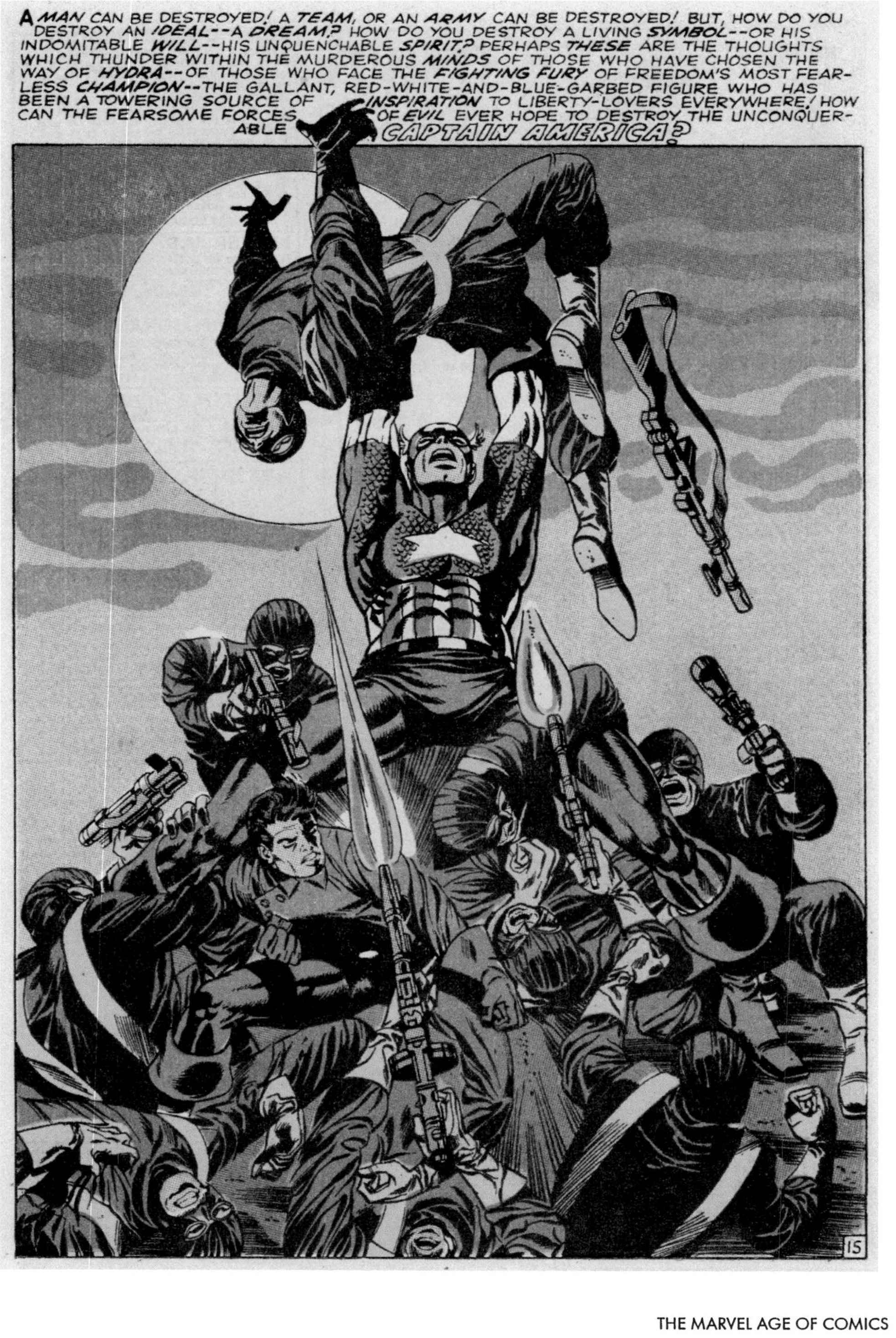

A MAN CAN BE DESTROYED! A TEAM, OR AN ARMY CAN BE DESTROYED! BUT, HOW DO YOU DESTROY AN IDEAL--A DREAM? HOW DO YOU DESTROY A LIVING SYMBOL--OR HIS INDOMITABLE WILL--HIS UNQUENCHABLE SPIRIT? PERHAPS THESE ARE THE THOUGHTS WHICH THUNDER WITHIN THE MURDEROUS MINDS OF THOSE WHO HAVE CHOSEN THE WAY OF HYDRA--OF THOSE WHO FACE THE FIGHTING FURY OF FREEDOM'S MOST FEARLESS CHAMPION--THE GALLANT, RED-WHITE-AND-BLUE-GARBED FIGURE WHO HAS BEEN A TOWERING SOURCE OF INSPIRATION TO LIBERTY-LOVERS EVERYWHERE! HOW CAN THE FEARSOME FORCES OF EVIL EVER HOPE TO DESTROY THE UNCONQUERABLE CAPTAIN AMERICA?
15

CAPTAIN AMERICA No. 113

(Opposite) Interior, "The Strange Death of Captain America!"; script, Stan Lee; pencils, Jim Steranko; inks, Tom Palmer. (Below) Cover; pencils and inks, Steranko. May 1969. Every generation has seen their Captain America die, but death is not always fatal in the Marvel Universe.... So maybe Cap wasn't really dead after all—a great relief to the young legions of dismayed Marvelites unused to such dramatic fare. This splash page is one of Steranko's most iconic, recalling some of the most heroic paintings of the French Romantics (Théodore Géricault's ca. 1818 *The Raft of the Medusa* and Eugène Delacroix's 1830 *Liberty Leading the People*). Steranko's return was worth the wait.

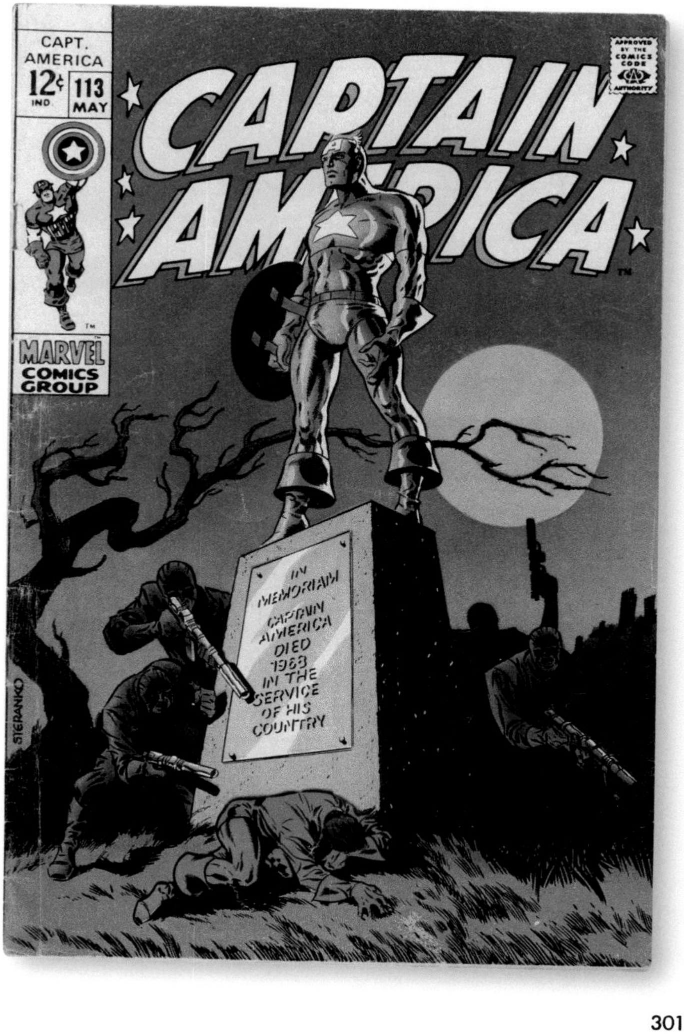
CAPT. AMERICA
12¢ IND
113 MAY
CAPTAIN AMERICA
MARVEL COMICS GROUP
IN MEMORIAM
CAPTAIN AMERICA
DIED
IN THE SERVICE OF HIS COUNTRY
STERANKO

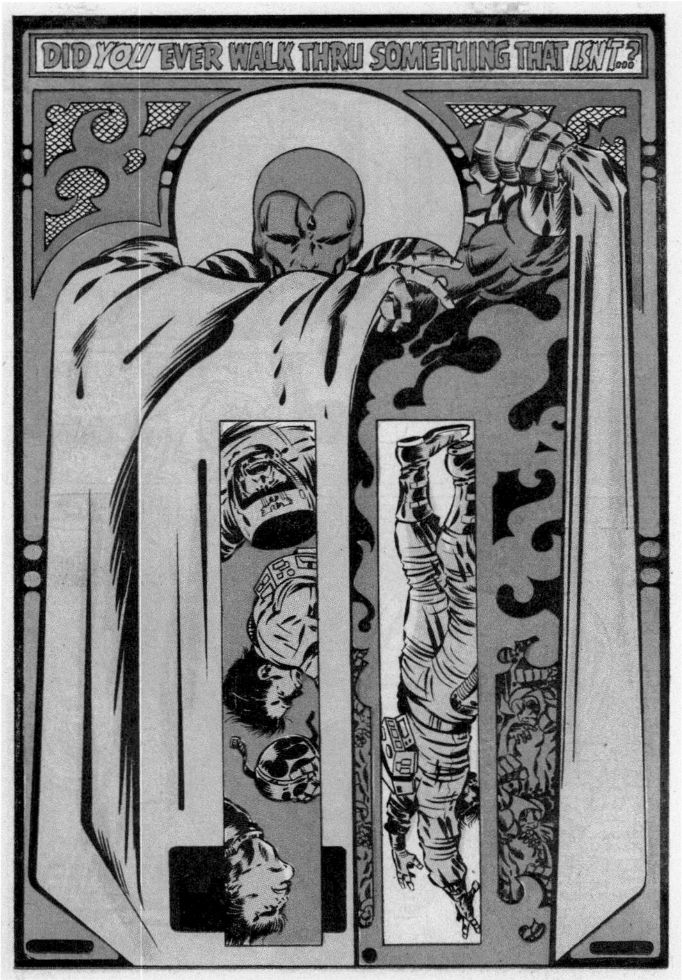
DID YOU EVER WALK THRU SOMETHING THAT ISN'T...?

THE AVENGERS No. 58

(Opposite) Interior, "Even an Android Can Cry"; script, Roy Thomas; pencils, John Buscema; inks, George Klein; November 1968. John Buscema's splash page recalled the typographic fancies of Will Eisner's Spirit. A consummate draftsman, Buscema forged an irascible — but lifelong — peace with the Marvel method, as John Romita recalled in 2002, "John would much rather have just done the drawing. 'Tell me what you want, I'll draw 'em. I don't want to hear any more about it. It's all crap.'"

THE AVENGERS No. 66

(Above) Interior, "The Great Betrayal!"; script, Roy Thomas; pencils, Barry Smith; inks, Syd Shores; July 1969. The Vision attacks the Avengers in order to steal the new, indestructible metal called Adamantium, and Ultron returns, rebuilt with it. Thomas later writes, "In my library, right there on the first page of a translation of Aeschylus' tragedy *Prometheus Bound*, is the word 'adamantine' as an adjective referring to the bonds that hold Prometheus to the rock..."

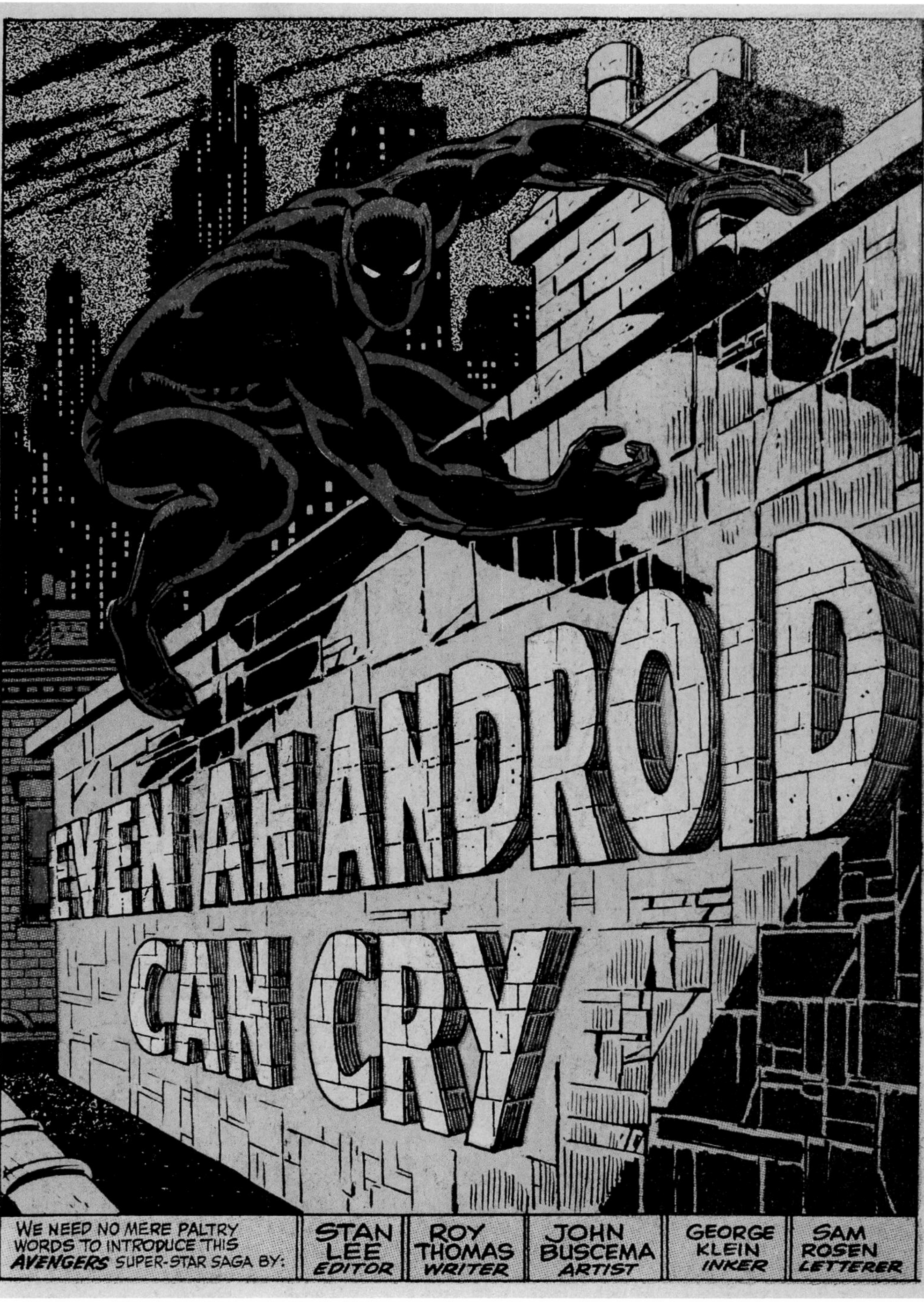
EVEN AN ANDROID CAN CRY
WE NEED NO MERE PALTRY WORDS TO INTRODUCE THIS AVENGERS SUPER-STAR SAGA BY:
STAN LEE EDITOR
ROY THOMAS WRITER
JOHN BUSCEMA ARTIST
GEORGE KLEIN INKER
SAM ROSEN LETTERER

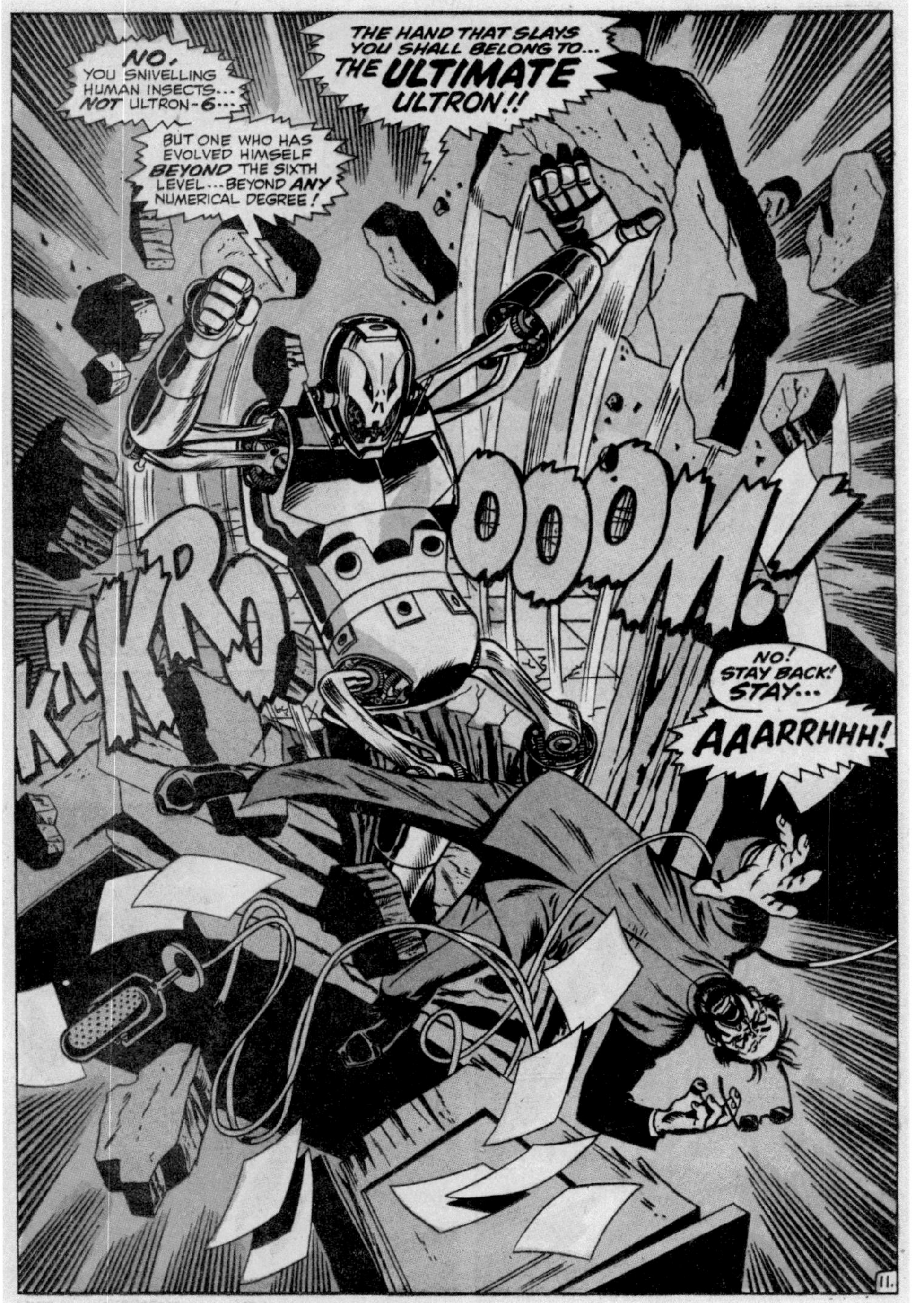
NO. YOU SNIVELLING HUMAN INSECTS... NOT ULTRON-6...
BUT ONE WHO HAS EVOLVED HIMSELF BEYOND THE SIXTH LEVEL...BEYOND ANY NUMERICAL DEGREE!
THE HAND THAT SLAYS YOU SHALL BELONG TO... THE ULTIMATE ULTRON!!
KKKROOOOM!
NO! STAY BACK! STAY...
AAARRHHH!
11.

THE AVENGERS No. 68

(Opposite) Interior, "And We Battle for Earth!"; script, Roy Thomas; pencils, Sal Buscema; inks, Sam Grainger; September 1969.

THE AVENGERS No. 57

(Below) Interior, "Behold...the Vision!"; script, Roy Thomas; pencils, John Buscema; inks, George Klein; October 1968. Roy Thomas brought a strong literary background to comic books in ways that were rarely touched on in the past, referencing classic poets such as Percy Bysshe Shelley and Robert Frost in *The Avengers*, touching on contemporary author Tom Wolfe, and even quoting verse from William Butler Yeats in *Sgt. Fury* and the *Hulk*! Thomas's background in teaching added a sophistication that connected with the college audience in ways that even Stan Lee was unable to.

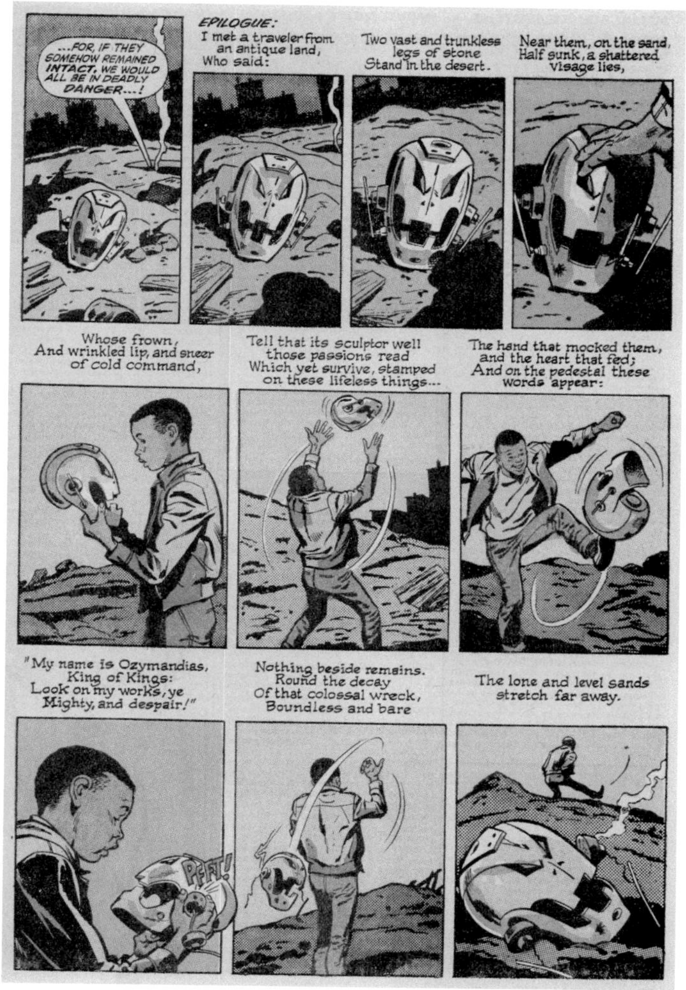
...FOR, IF THEY SOMEHOW REMAINED INTACT, WE WOULD ALL BE IN DEADLY DANGER...!
EPILOGUE:
I met a traveler from an antique land, Who said:
Two vast and trunkless legs of stone Stand in the desert.
Near them, on the sand, Half sunk, a shattered visage lies,
Whose frown, And wrinkled lip, and sneer of cold command,
Tell that its sculptor well those passions read Which yet survive, stamped on these lifeless things...
The hand that mocked them, and the heart that fed; And on the pedestal these words appear:
"My name is Ozymandias, King of Kings: Look on my works, ye Mighty, and despair!"
PFFT!
Nothing beside remains. Round the decay Of that colossal wreck, Boundless and bare
The lone and level sands stretch far away.

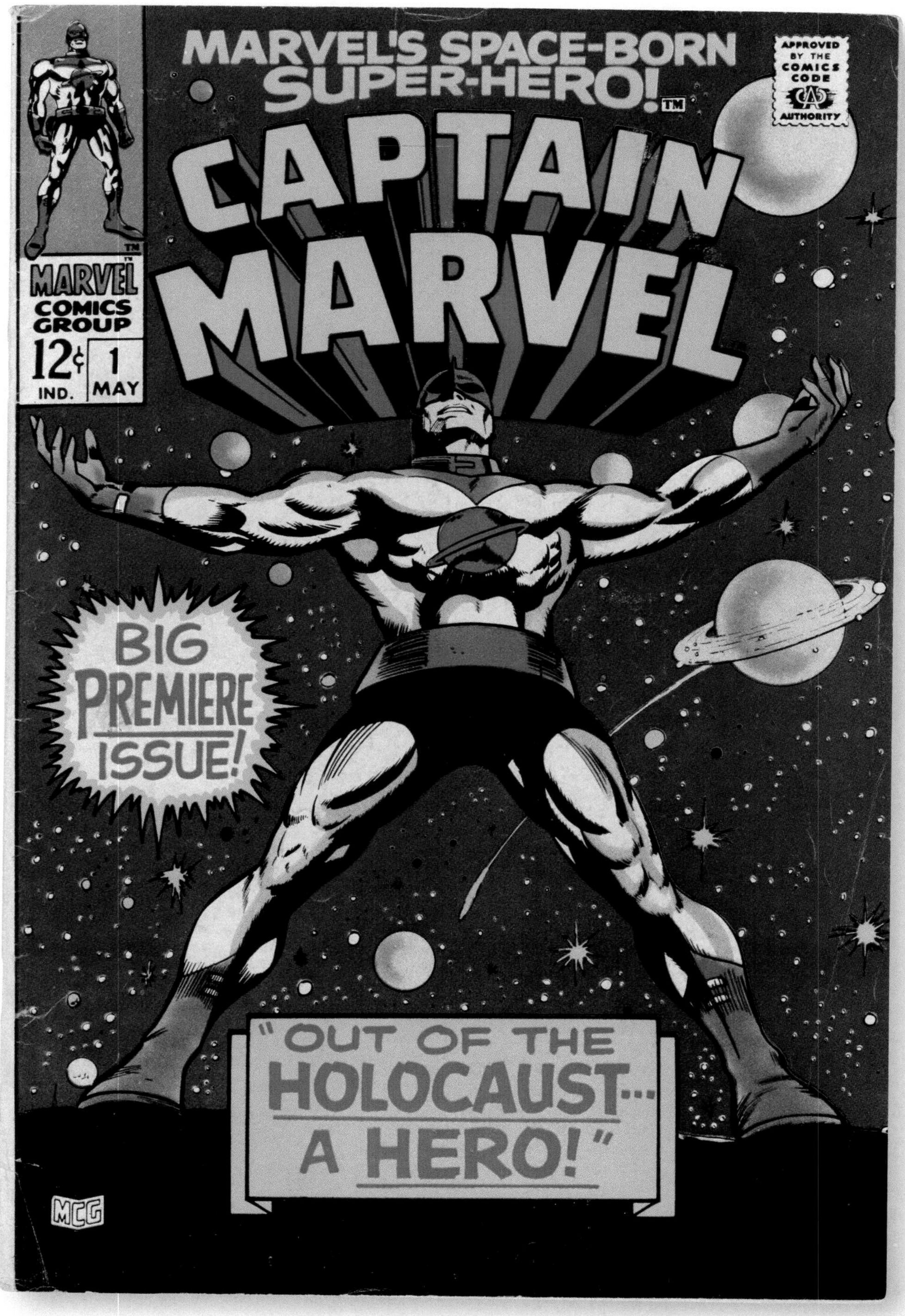
MARVEL'S SPACE-BORN SUPER-HERO!™
APPROVED BY THE COMICS CODE CA AUTHORITY
CAPTAIN MARVEL
MARVEL COMICS GROUP
12¢ IND.
1 MAY
BIG PREMIERE ISSUE!
"OUT OF THE HOLOCAUST... A HERO!"
MCG

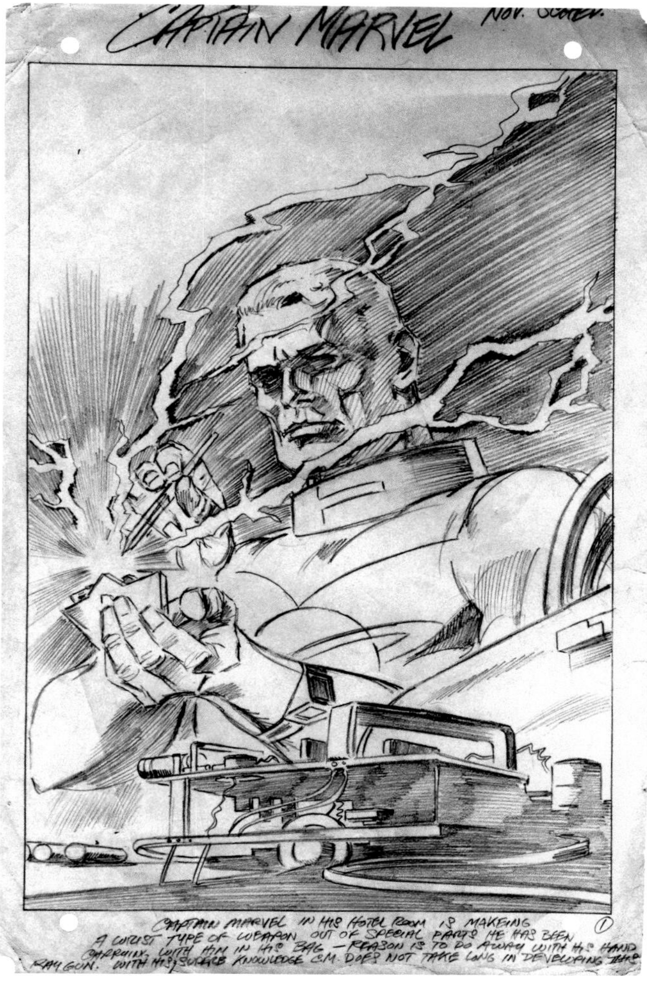
CAPTAIN MARVEL
CAPTAIN MARVEL IN HIS HOTEL ROOM IS MAKEING A WRIST TYPE OF WEAPON OUT OF SPECIAL PARTS HE HAS BEEN CARRYING WITH HIM IN HIS BAG — REASON IS TO DO AWAY WITH HIS HAND RAY GUN. WITH HIS SUPERB KNOWLEDGE C.M. DOES NOT TAKE LONG IN DEVELOPING THE
1

CAPTAIN MARVEL No. 1

(Opposite) Cover; pencils, Gene Colan; inks, Vince Colletta; May 1968. Captain Marvel was the last hero created by Stan Lee during this Marvel Age. He was also the first hero to die, as his primary mission was one of commercial necessity: Marvel did not want any other publisher to publish new stories or use the name "Marvel."

MARVEL SUPER-HEROES No. 13

(Above) Original interior art; pencils, Gene Colan; March 1968. Gene Colan lays out the splash page to the second Captain Marvel story. He leaves notes in the bottom margin to help Roy Thomas add dialogue to the fully penciled page. Of course, when he did so, he was working from a synopsis written by Thomas — making it impossible, at this late date, to sort out precisely who made up each and every story detail. It was ever thus at the early Marvel Comics!

FIGURE STUDIES

(Above) Pencil rough, Captain Marvel *No. 17; Gil Kane; October 1969.*
This page—19 in the final story—offers an example of Kane's work
method: He roughs in the figure and musculature of the character, leaving the details for the pencil stage. Notice how he draws outside the line
in panel two in order to get the feel of the figure. Throughout his career
Kane's figures had weight and solidity, giving them a lifelike quality.

CAPTAIN MARVEL No. 17

*(Opposite) Interior, "And a Child Shall Lead You!"; script, Roy Thomas;
pencils, Gil Kane; inks, Dan Adkins; October 1969.* Roy Thomas
continues his romance with the Golden Age, giving Captain Marvel
a two-person identity in homage to the original Fawcett character.

THE MARVEL AGE OF COMICS

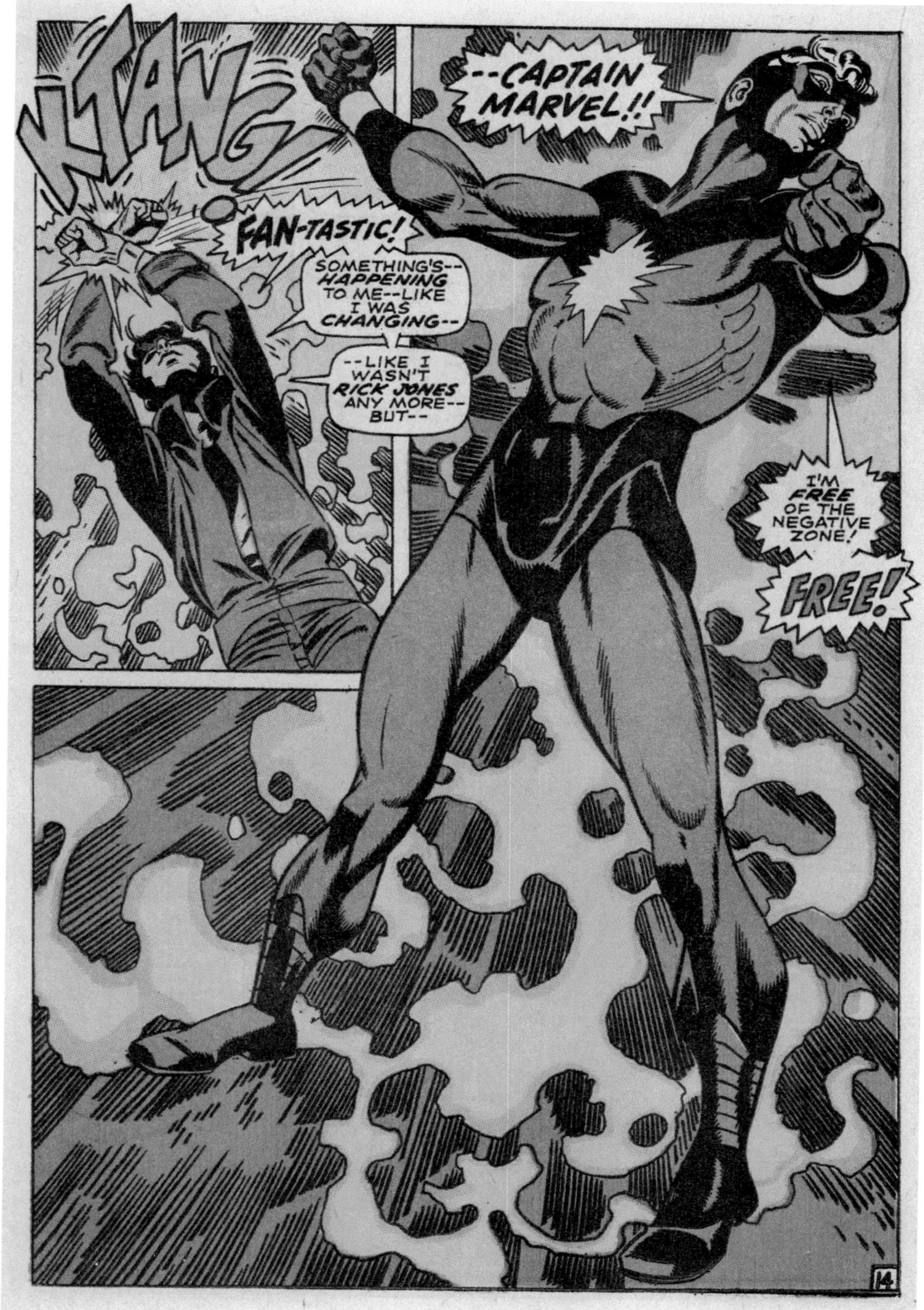
K-TANG
FAN-TASTIC!
SOMETHING'S-- HAPPENING TO ME--LIKE I WAS CHANGING--
--LIKE I WASN'T RICK JONES ANY MORE-- BUT--
--CAPTAIN MARVEL!!
I'M FREE OF THE NEGATIVE ZONE!
FREE!
14

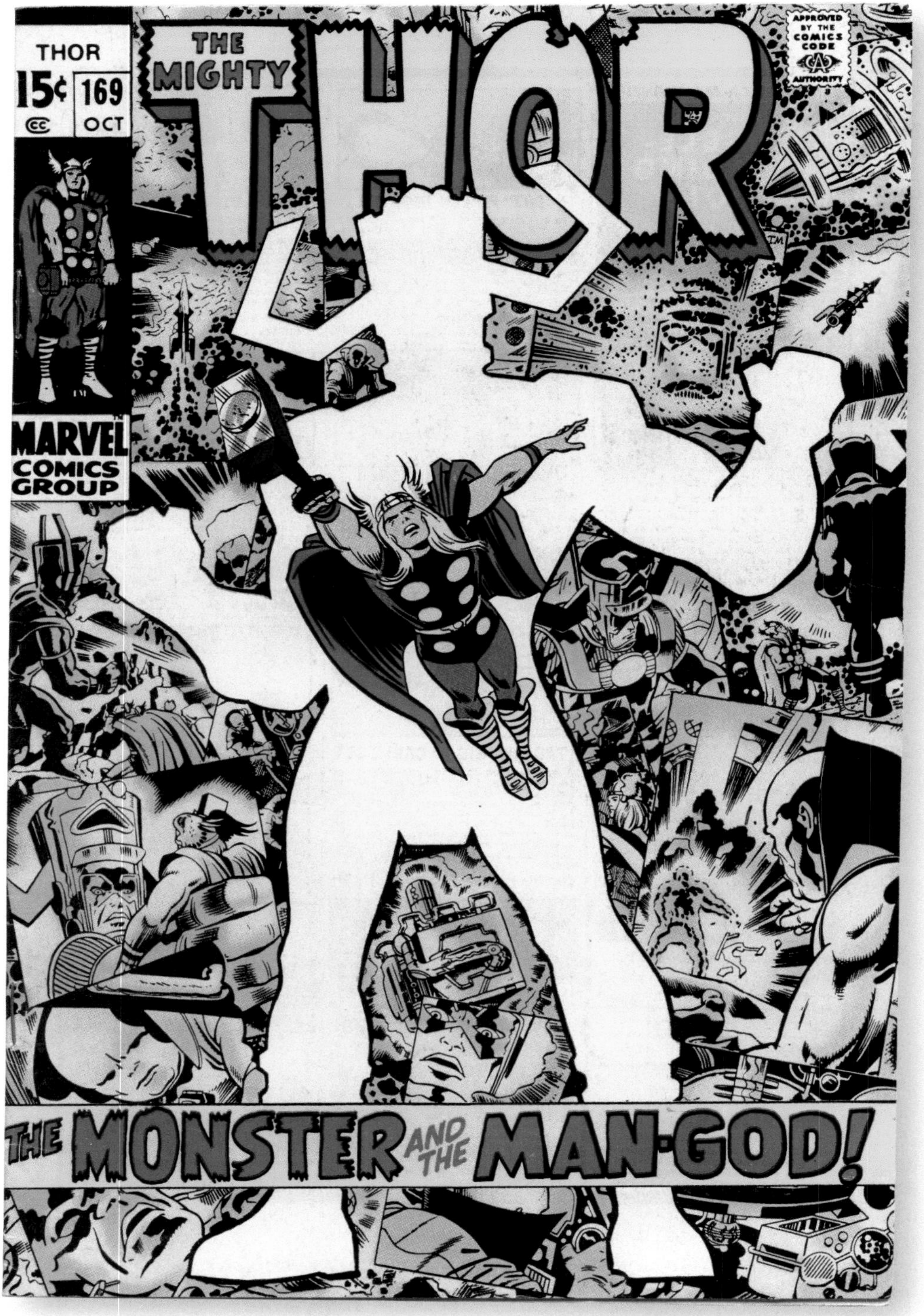
THOR
15¢
169
OCT
THE MIGHTY
THOR
APPROVED BY THE COMICS CODE AUTHORITY
MARVEL COMICS GROUP
THE MONSTER AND THE MAN-GOD!

THOR No. 169

(Opposite) Cover; pencils, John Romita and Jack Kirby; inks, Romita and George Klein; October 1969. Typically produced after the interiors were complete, covers occasionally needed to be rushed out. In this instance John Romita drew Thor and the Galactus outline, and the background was taken from interior panels. Galactus continues the story of his origin: from the planet Taa a great calamity struck and only one survived.

He SWINGS!! Most daring of the new, groovy...
"SUPER HEROES WITH SUPER PROBLEMS"
—THE NEW YORK HERALD TRIBUNE

LANCER BOOKS 72-125 50¢

THE MIGHTY THOR!

THE MOST DRAMATIC HERO IN THE WORLD

COLLECTOR'S ALBUM

"GIANTS WALK THE EARTH" & OTHER ADVENTURES

THE MOST EPIC BATTLES OF THE AGES!

HE SWINGS!

(Above) Book cover, The Mighty Thor; pencils, Jack Kirby; inks, Chic Stone; Lancer Books; 1966. To capitalize on the year's camp comics craze, Lancer released a series of paperbacks featuring kooky quotes and collegiate endorsements on the cover, with black-and-white reprints of the early Marvel tales inside. Other titles included Spider-Man, Daredevil, and the Fantastic Four. The comics were not reduced to fit; instead, the book laid out the panels one or two per page.

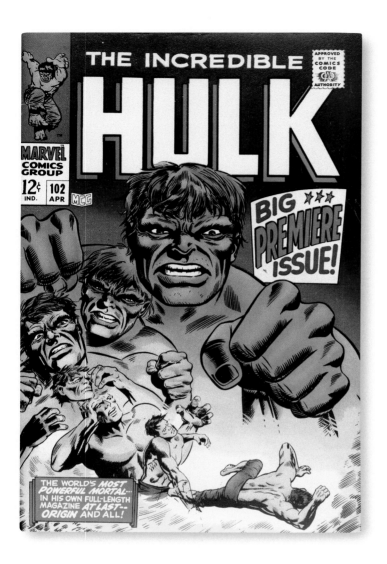

THE INCREDIBLE
HULK
APPROVED BY THE COMICS CODE AUTHORITY
MARVEL COMICS GROUP
12¢ IND.
102 APR
MCG
BIG PREMIERE ISSUE!
THE WORLD'S MOST POWERFUL MORTAL... IN HIS OWN FULL-LENGTH MAGAZINE AT LAST-- ORIGIN AND ALL!

THE INCREDIBLE HULK No. 102

(Above) Cover; pencils, Marie Severin; inks, Frank Giacoia; April 1968. After years of costarring in *Tales to Astonish*, the Hulk returned to a full-length comic of his own. After Marvel expanded its line, *Hulk* became one of its most popular titles.

HULK SPECIAL No. 1

(Opposite) Cover; pencils and inks, Jim Steranko with Marie Severin; Summer 1968. Jim Steranko not only drew the cover but created the logo that was incorporated into the art. Steranko's original cover was altered before publication because the Hulk's face looked too frightening; Marie Severin was brought in to pretty him up.

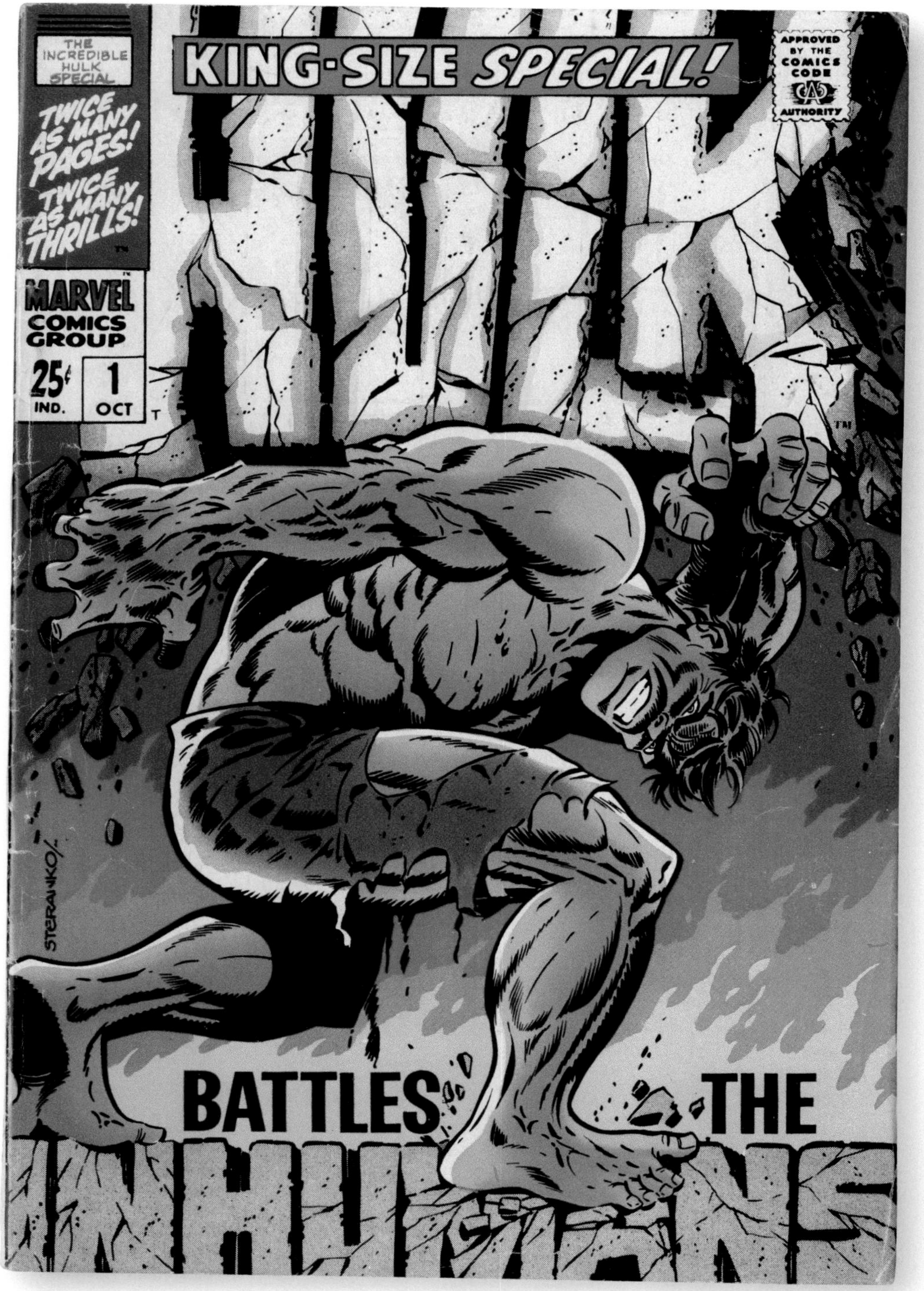
THE INCREDIBLE HULK SPECIAL
KING-SIZE SPECIAL!
APPROVED BY THE COMICS CODE AUTHORITY
TWICE AS MANY PAGES! TWICE AS MANY THRILLS!
MARVEL COMICS GROUP
25¢ IND.
1 OCT
STERANKO
BATTLES THE

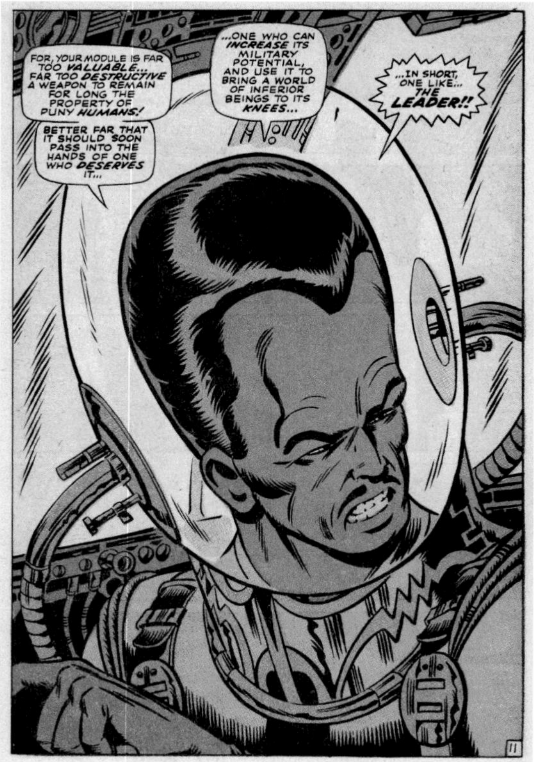
FOR, YOUR MODULE IS FAR TOO VALUABLE... FAR TOO DESTRUCTIVE A WEAPON TO REMAIN FOR LONG THE PROPERTY OF PUNY HUMANS!
BETTER FAR THAT IT SHOULD SOON PASS INTO THE HANDS OF ONE WHO DESERVES IT...
...ONE WHO CAN INCREASE ITS MILITARY POTENTIAL, AND USE IT TO BRING A WORLD OF INFERIOR BEINGS TO ITS KNEES...
...IN SHORT, ONE LIKE... THE LEADER!!

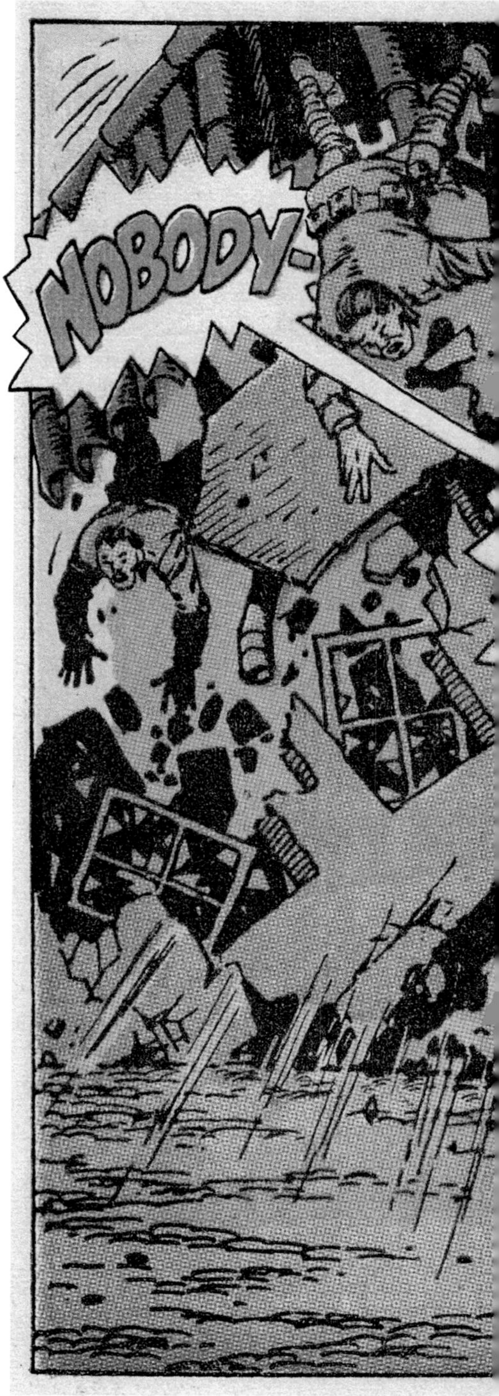
NOBODY-

THE INCREDIBLE HULK No. 123

(Above) Interior, "No More the Monster!"; script, Roy Thomas; pencils and inks, Herb Trimpe; January 1970. While gamma rays cause unpredictable results, they always include turning green! Like the Hulk, the man who would become the Leader was exposed to gamma rays, becoming super-intelligent — with the super-sized head to prove it. The Leader became one of the Hulk's greatest foes, returning frequently to plague the green goliath.

THE INCREDIBLE HULK No. 109

(Right) Interior, "The Monster and the Man-Beast!"; script, Stan Lee; layouts, Frank Giacoia; pencils, Herb Trimpe; inks, John Severin; November 1968. The Hulk epitomized every kid's frustrations of being misunderstood, different, and awkward. He also offered a cathartic effect: at least he could get his frustrations out by smashing things up!

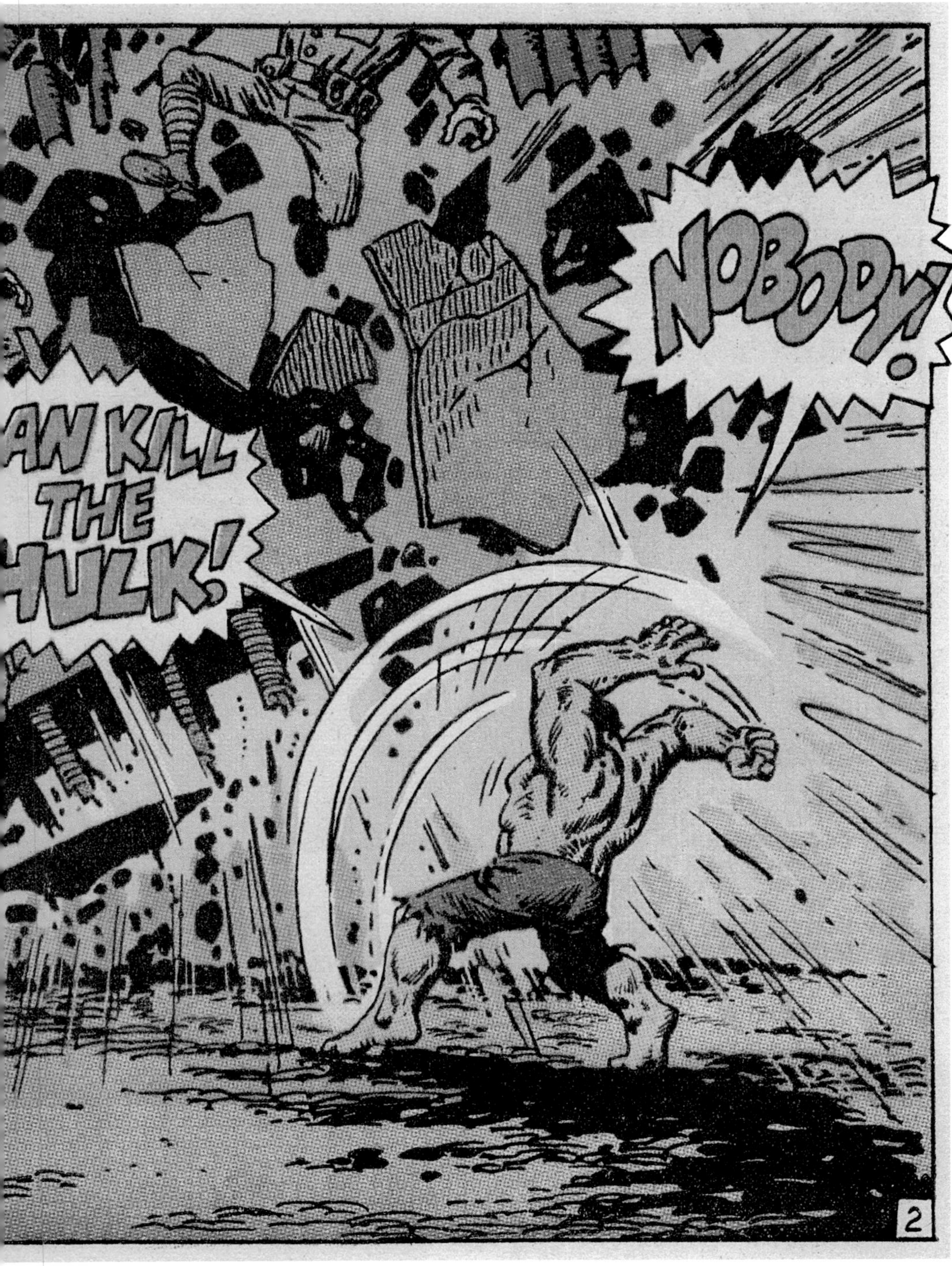
AN KILL THE HULK!
NOBODY!
2

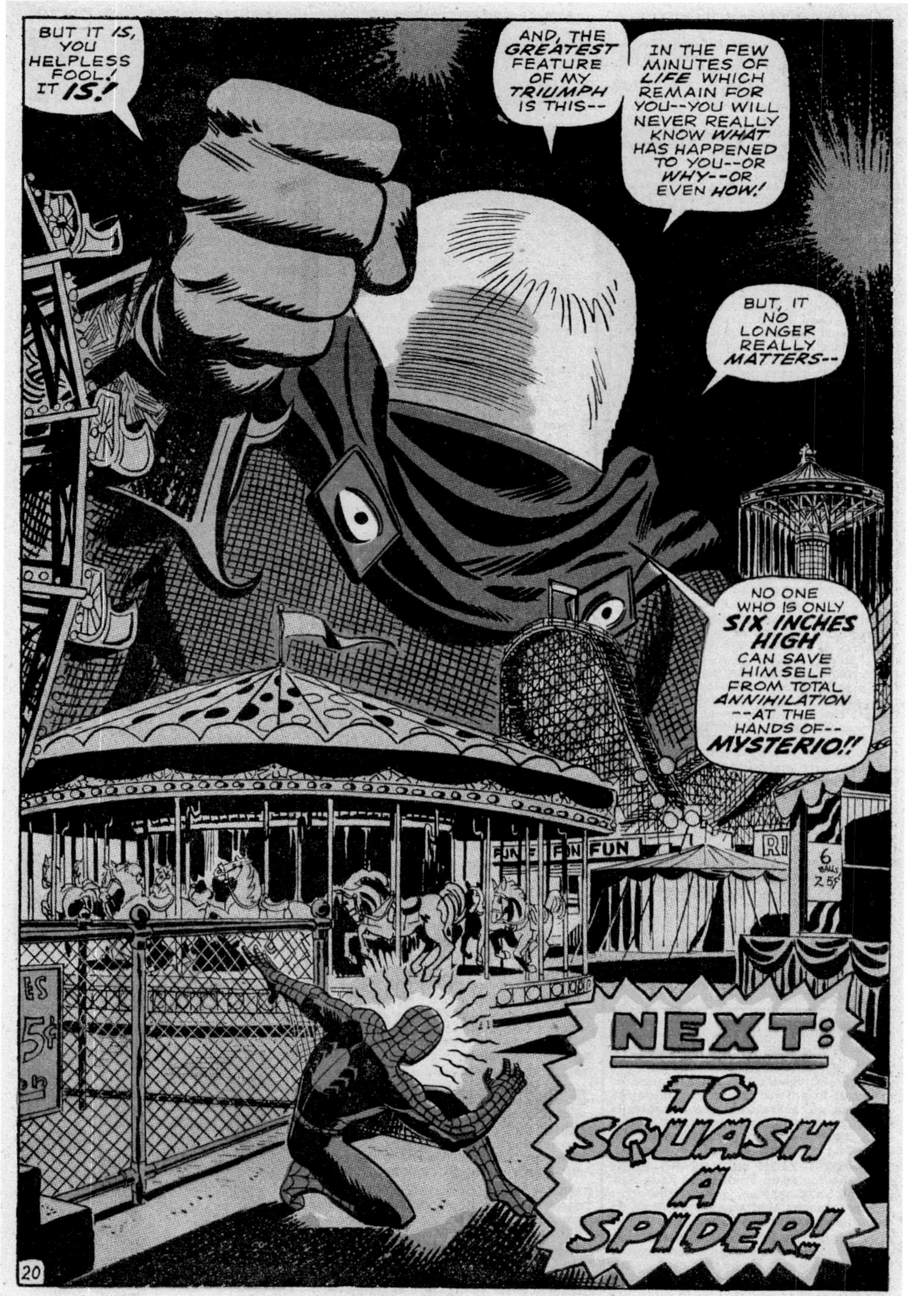
BUT IT IS, YOU HELPLESS FOOL! IT IS!
AND, THE GREATEST FEATURE OF MY TRIUMPH IS THIS--
IN THE FEW MINUTES OF LIFE WHICH REMAIN FOR YOU--YOU WILL NEVER REALLY KNOW WHAT HAS HAPPENED TO YOU--OR WHY--OR EVEN HOW!
BUT, IT NO LONGER REALLY MATTERS--
NO ONE WHO IS ONLY SIX INCHES HIGH CAN SAVE HIMSELF FROM TOTAL ANNIHILATION --AT THE HANDS OF-- MYSTERIO!!
FUN FUN FUN
6 BALLS 25¢
NEXT:
TO SQUASH A SPIDER!
20

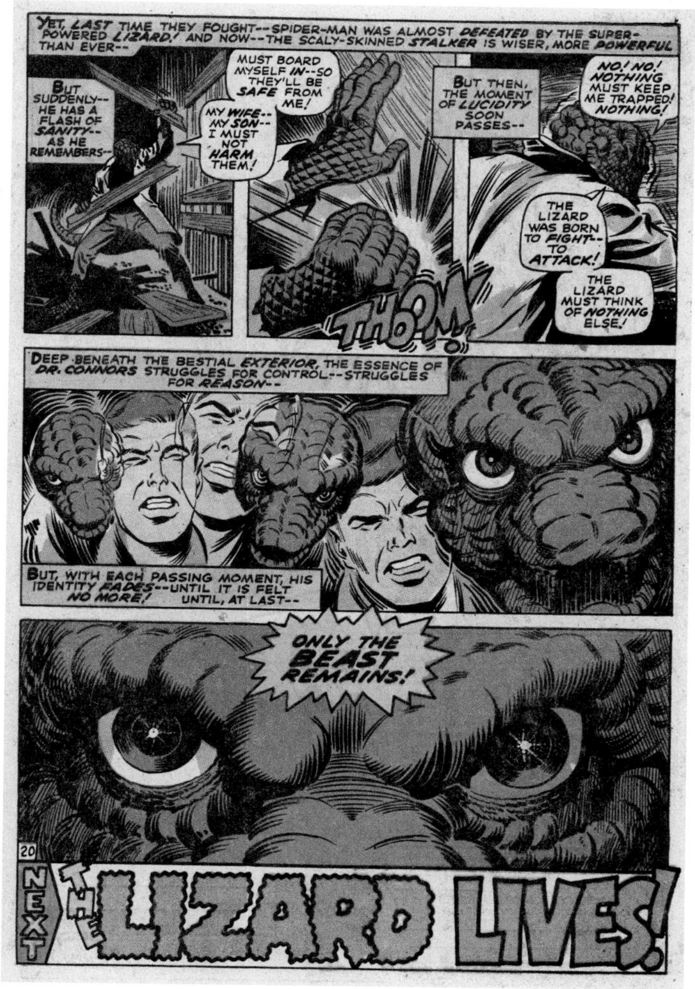
YET, LAST TIME THEY FOUGHT--SPIDER-MAN WAS ALMOST DEFEATED BY THE SUPER-POWERED LIZARD! AND NOW--THE SCALY-SKINNED STALKER IS WISER, MORE POWERFUL THAN EVER--
BUT SUDDENLY--HE HAS A FLASH OF SANITY--AS HE REMEMBERS--
MUST BOARD MYSELF IN--SO THEY'LL BE SAFE FROM ME!
MY WIFE--MY SON--I MUST NOT HARM THEM!
BUT THEN, THE MOMENT OF LUCIDITY SOON PASSES--
NO! NO! NOTHING MUST KEEP ME TRAPPED! NOTHING!
THE LIZARD WAS BORN TO FIGHT--TO ATTACK!
THE LIZARD MUST THINK OF NOTHING ELSE!
THOOM
DEEP BENEATH THE BESTIAL EXTERIOR, THE ESSENCE OF DR. CONNORS STRUGGLES FOR CONTROL--STRUGGLES FOR REASON--
BUT, WITH EACH PASSING MOMENT, HIS IDENTITY FADES--UNTIL IT IS FELT NO MORE! UNTIL, AT LAST--
ONLY THE BEAST REMAINS!
20
NEXT THE LIZARD LIVES!

AMAZING SPIDER-MAN No. 66

(Opposite) Interior, "The Madness of Mysterio!"; script, Stan Lee; layouts, John Romita; pencils, Don Heck; inks, Mike Esposito; November 1968.

AMAZING SPIDER-MAN No. 75

(Above) Interior, "Death Without Warning!"; script, Stan Lee; pencils, John Romita; inks, Jim Mooney; August 1969. Scientist Curt Connors never knew when his demonic alter ego would surface, leaving Spidey with the added burden of trying to cure his friend without harming him.

"Spider-Man is the Raskolnikov of the funnies,
a worthy rival to Bellow's Herzog for the Neurotic
Hipster Championship of our time..."
— *NEW YORK HERALD TRIBUNE*, 1966

YOUR FRIENDLY NEIGHBORHOOD SPIDER-MAN

(Above) Photograph, Marvel offices, ca. 1970. Pictured here are Stan
Lee, Marie Severin, and John Romita, who are pleased to have Spidey
(played by Roy Thomas) in the company's Madison Avenue offices.

AMAZING SPIDER-MAN ANNUAL No. 5

(Opposite) Cover; pencils and inks, John Romita; Summer 1968.
When Peter accidentally discovers that his parents were labeled
as traitors, it leads him on a quest to clear their names. Summer
specials often featured stories that were longer and dealt with
important moments in characters' lives.

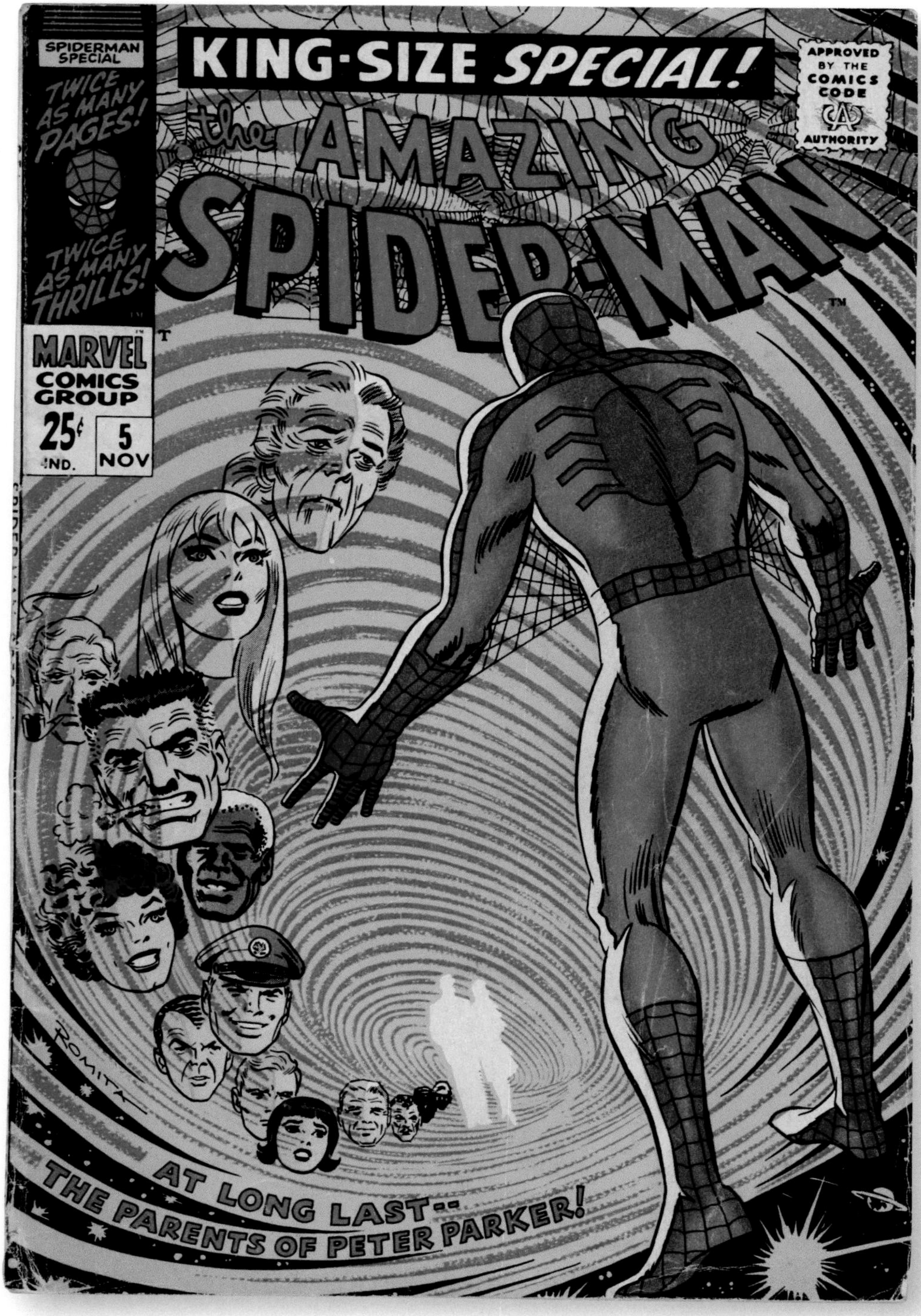
SPIDERMAN SPECIAL
KING-SIZE SPECIAL!
APPROVED BY THE COMICS CODE AUTHORITY
TWICE AS MANY PAGES!
the AMAZING SPIDER-MAN
TWICE AS MANY THRILLS!
MARVEL COMICS GROUP
25¢ IND.
5 NOV
ROMITA
AT LONG LAST--
THE PARENTS OF PETER PARKER!

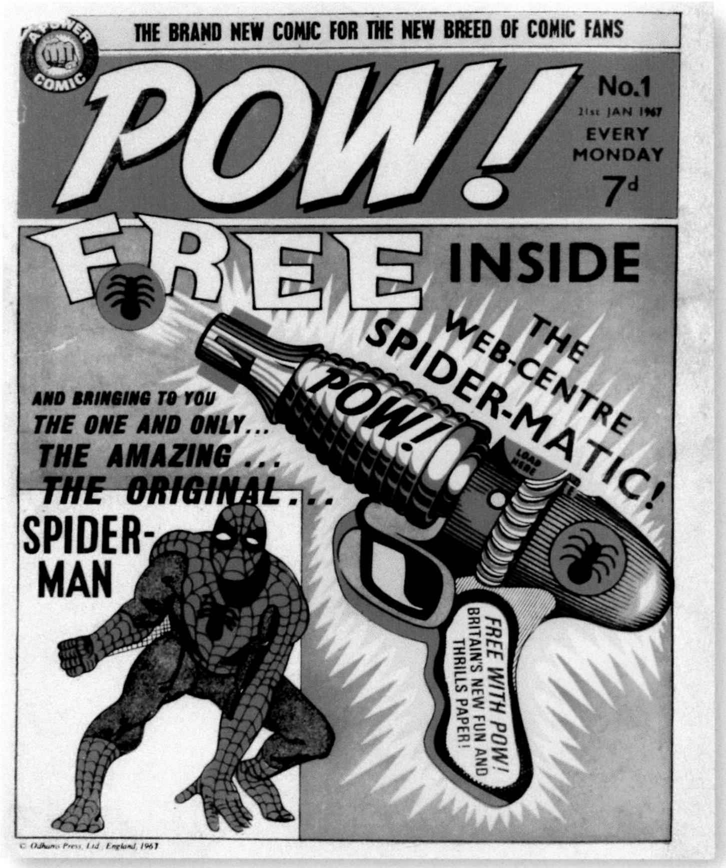
THE BRAND NEW COMIC FOR THE NEW BREED OF COMIC FANS
A POWER COMIC
POW!
No.1
21st JAN 1967
EVERY MONDAY
7d
FREE INSIDE
THE WEB-CENTRE SPIDER-MATIC!
POW!
LOAD HERE
AND BRINGING TO YOU
THE ONE AND ONLY...
THE AMAZING ...
THE ORIGINAL...
SPIDER-MAN
FREE WITH POW!
BRITAIN'S NEW FUN AND THRILLS PAPER!
© Odhams Press, Ltd, England, 1967

POW! No. 1

(Above) Cover; pencils and inks, Steve Ditko; January 14, 1967. Britain's Odhams Press began reprinting Spider-Man in *Pow!* with the tagline, "The Brand New Comic for the New Breed of Comic Fans." UK comic fans had a pretty good deal: Reprints or not, the comics came out weekly, and they often came with a free badge, poster, or toy. This issue included a Spider-Matic cardboard gun!

AMAZING SPIDER-MAN No. 67

(Opposite) Original interior art; script, Stan Lee; pencils, John Romita; inks, Jim Mooney; December 1968. "When I finished a 20-page silent story, a picture version of a plot, I very seldom had faith in it. I would always think, 'Oh my god, how is he going to do this? How is he going to do that? What do I do here? I was vague there.' By the time Stan wrote it, it was almost like we had planned every single turn of events in that story. He made it so natural." —John Romita

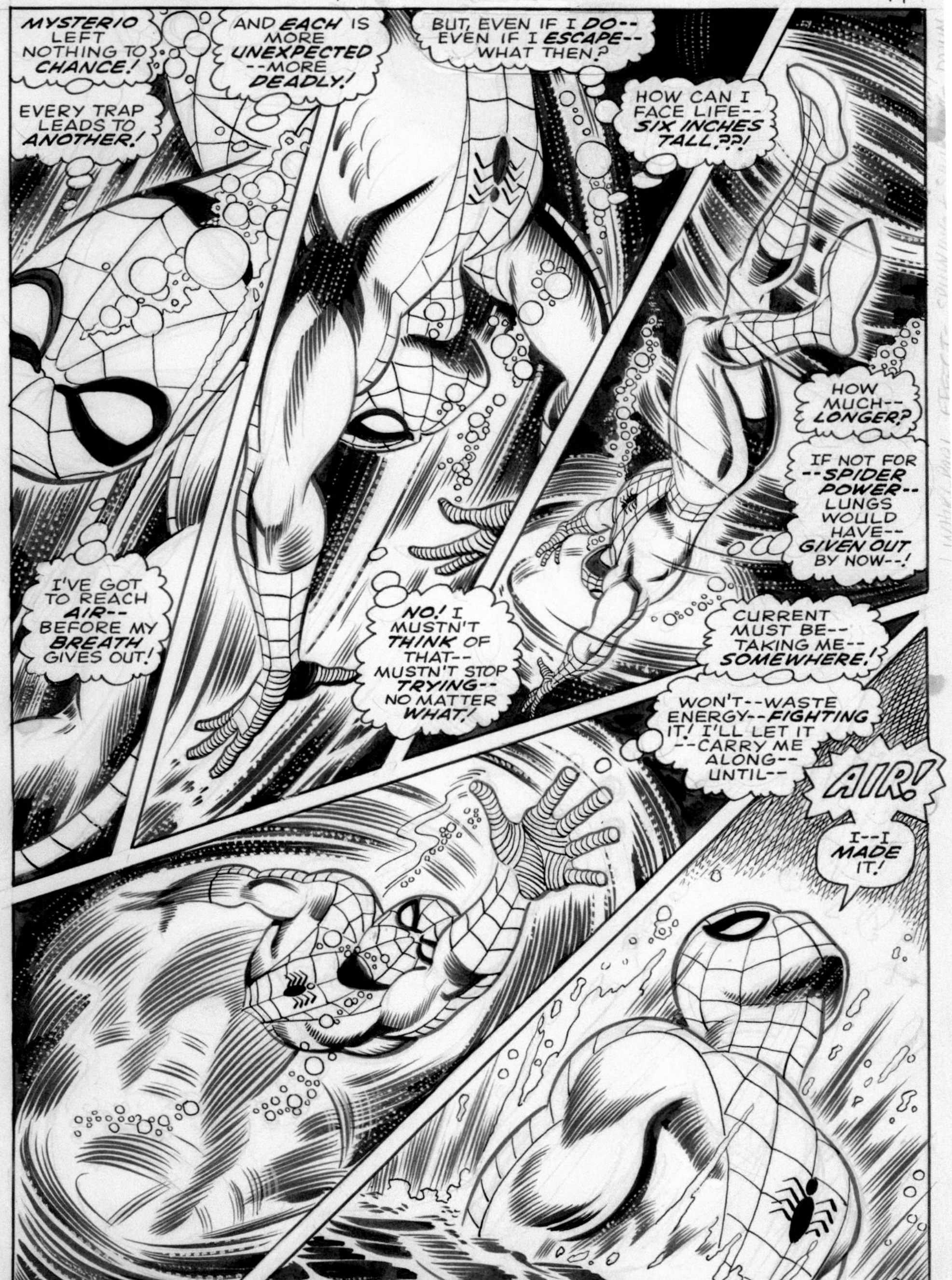
MYSTERIO LEFT NOTHING TO CHANCE!
EVERY TRAP LEADS TO ANOTHER!
AND EACH IS MORE UNEXPECTED --MORE DEADLY!
BUT, EVEN IF I DO-- EVEN IF I ESCAPE-- WHAT THEN?
HOW CAN I FACE LIFE-- SIX INCHES TALL??!
I'VE GOT TO REACH AIR-- BEFORE MY BREATH GIVES OUT!
NO! I MUSTN'T THINK OF THAT-- MUSTN'T STOP TRYING-- NO MATTER WHAT!
HOW MUCH-- LONGER?
IF NOT FOR --SPIDER POWER-- LUNGS WOULD HAVE-- GIVEN OUT BY NOW--!
CURRENT MUST BE-- TAKING ME-- SOMEWHERE!
WON'T--WASTE ENERGY--FIGHTING IT! I'LL LET IT --CARRY ME ALONG-- UNTIL--
AIR!
I--I MADE IT!
10

Jim Mooney

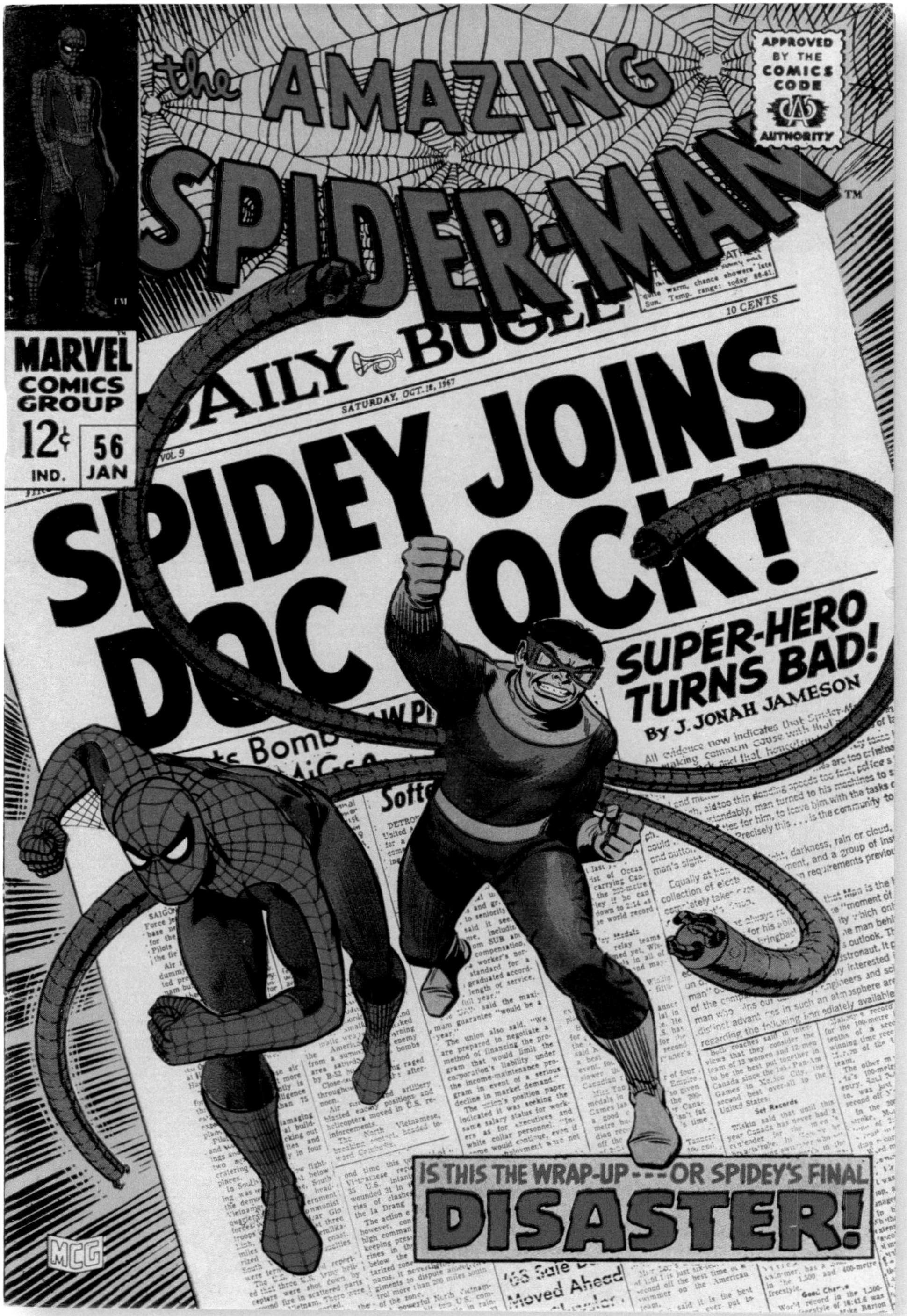
APPROVED BY THE COMICS CODE AUTHORITY
the AMAZING SPIDER-MAN
MARVEL COMICS GROUP
12¢ IND.
56 JAN
DAILY BUGLE
SATURDAY, OCT. 18, 1967
10 CENTS
SPIDEY JOINS DOC OCK!
SUPER-HERO TURNS BAD!
By J. JONAH JAMESON
IS THIS THE WRAP-UP---OR SPIDEY'S FINAL
DISASTER!
MCG

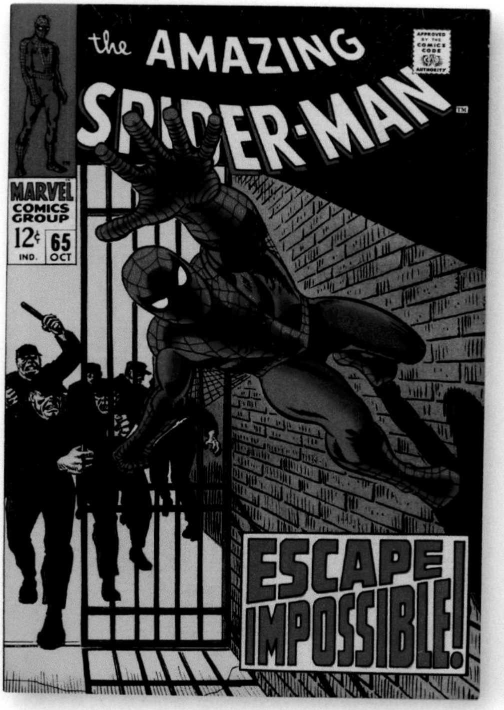
the AMAZING
SPIDER-MAN
MARVEL COMICS GROUP
12¢ 65 IND. OCT
ESCAPE IMPOSSIBLE!

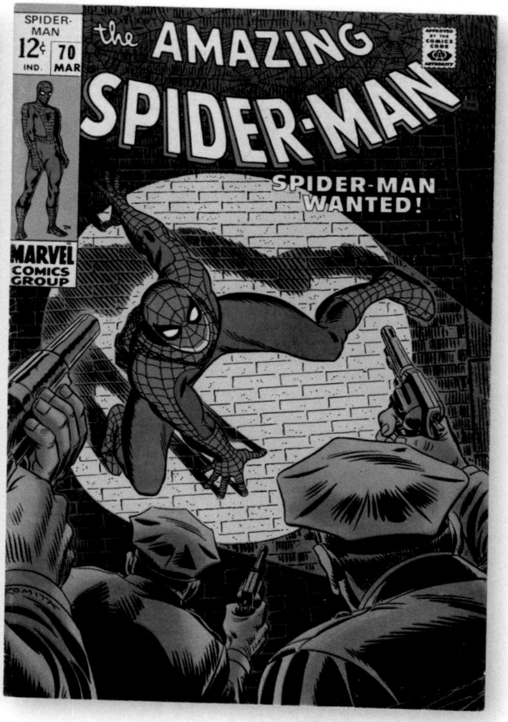
SPIDER-MAN
12¢ 70 IND. MAR
the AMAZING
SPIDER-MAN
SPIDER-MAN WANTED!
MARVEL COMICS GROUP

AMAZING SPIDER-MAN No. 56

(Opposite) Cover; pencils and inks, John Romita; January 1968.

AMAZING SPIDER-MAN No. 65

(Above) Cover; pencils and inks, John Romita; October 1968.

AMAZING SPIDER-MAN No. 70

(Above right) Cover; pencils and inks, John Romita; March 1969. Antiheroes had always been a part of Marvel's DNA, from Sub-Mariner's first bid to conquer New York City. Unlike most of Marvel's super heroes, who were generally revered by the public, Spider-Man was often—and reluctantly—at odds with the law. But to a new, older audience, images of "the Man" had taken on new significance after the tumult of 1968, as rioting spread like wildfire from Columbia university to campuses across the nation.

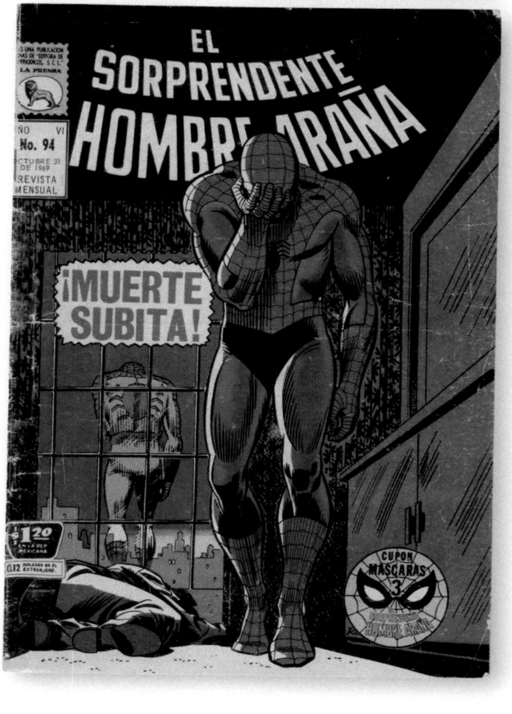
EL
SORPRENDENTE
HOMBRE ARAÑA
No. 94
REVISTA MENSUAL
¡MUERTE SUBITA!
CUPON MASCARAS 3

SPIDER-MAN ABROAD

(Right) Cover, El Sorprendente Hombre Araña *No. 94; pencils and inks, John Romita; Editorial La Prensa, Mexico; ca. 1960s.*

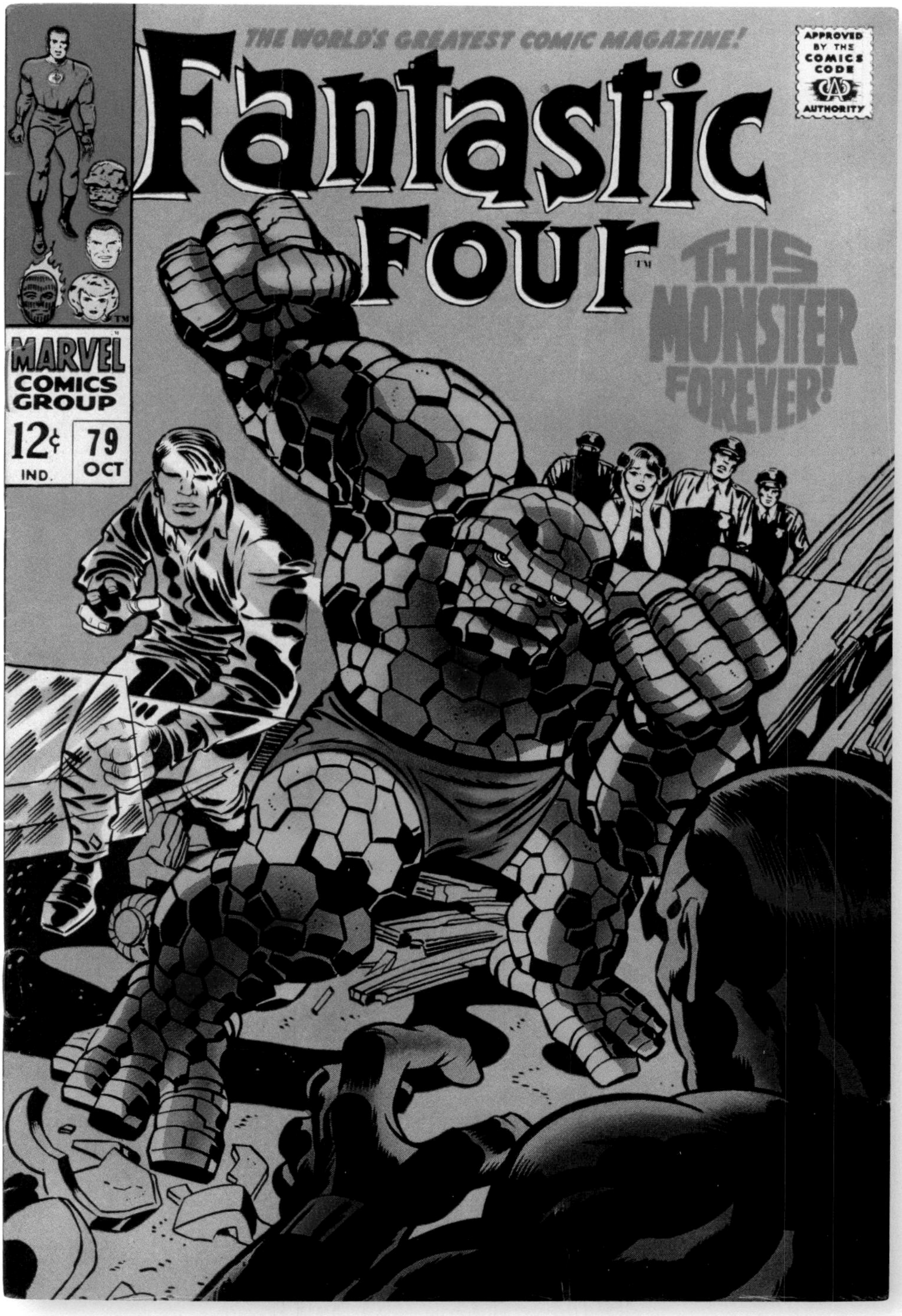
THE WORLD'S GREATEST COMIC MAGAZINE!
APPROVED BY THE COMICS CODE AUTHORITY
Fantastic Four
MARVEL COMICS GROUP
12¢ IND.
79 OCT
THIS MONSTER FOREVER!

FANTASTIC FOUR No. 79

(Opposite) Cover; pencils, Jack Kirby; inks, Joe Sinnott; October 1968. The Thing's tragic nature was such that, even when he was cured of his monstrous appearance, he could never live a normal life as Ben Grimm. His sense of responsibility — to his teammates, and to the world at large — always forced him to return to his monstrous form.

FANTASTIC FOUR No. 83

(Below) Interior, "Shall Man Survive?"; script, Stan Lee; pencils, Jack Kirby; inks, Joe Sinnott; February 1969. "It's Clobberin' Time!" became the Thing's catchphrase whenever he went into action. He certainly packed a punch making villains fly right off the page, thanks to Kirby's incredible mastery of perspective.

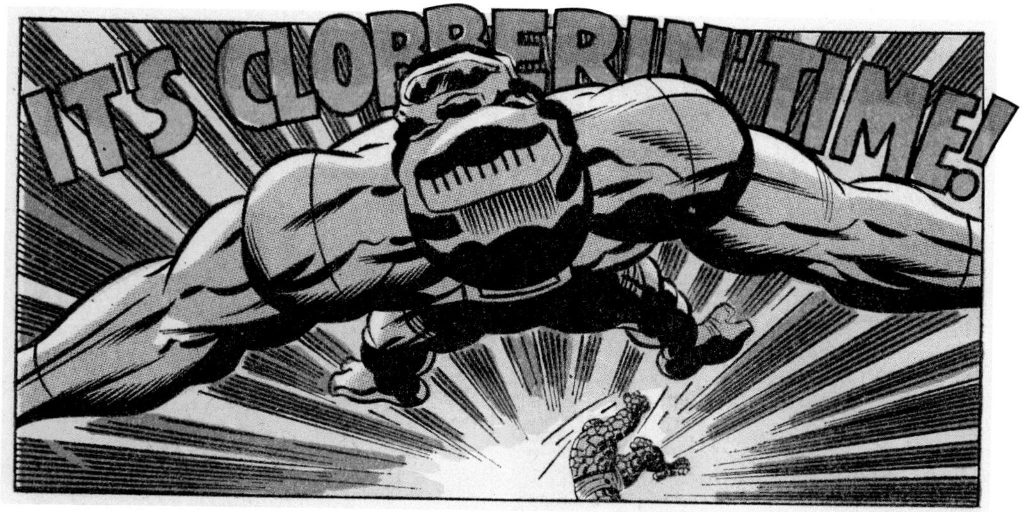
IT'S CLOBBERIN' TIME!

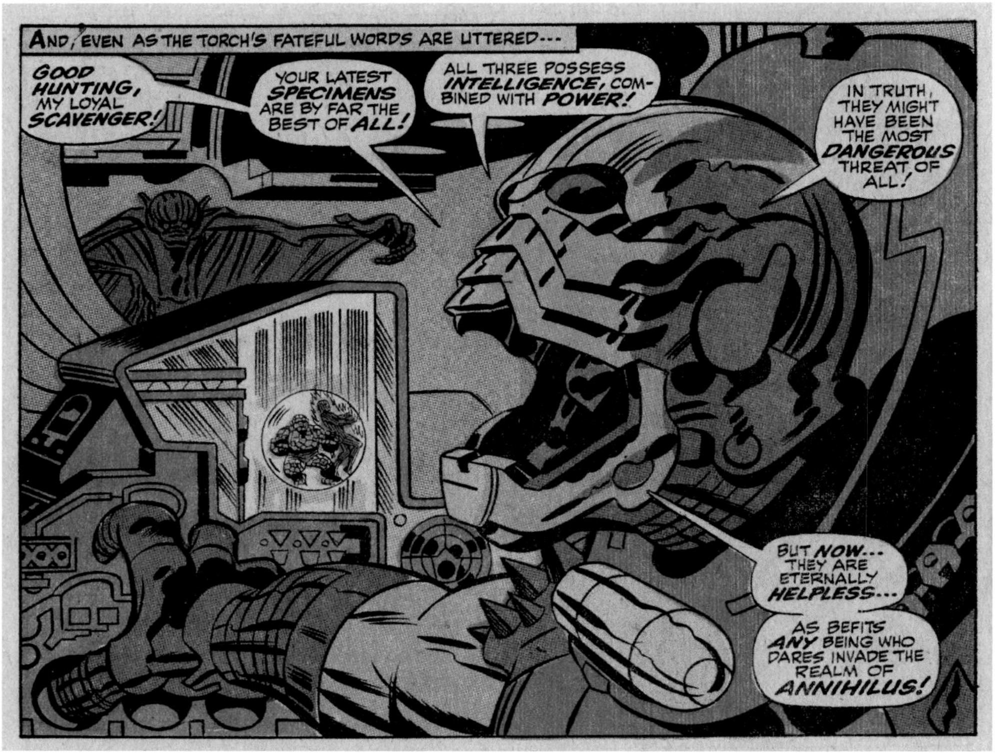
AND, EVEN AS THE TORCH'S FATEFUL WORDS ARE UTTERED---
GOOD HUNTING, MY LOYAL SCAVENGER!
YOUR LATEST SPECIMENS ARE BY FAR THE BEST OF ALL!
ALL THREE POSSESS INTELLIGENCE, COMBINED WITH POWER!
IN TRUTH, THEY MIGHT HAVE BEEN THE MOST DANGEROUS THREAT OF ALL!
BUT NOW... THEY ARE ETERNALLY HELPLESS...
AS BEFITS ANY BEING WHO DARES INVADE THE REALM OF ANNIHILUS!

FANTASTIC FOUR ANNUAL No. 6

(Above) Interior, "Let There Be Life!"; script, Stan Lee; pencils, Jack Kirby; inks, Joe Sinnott; Summer 1968. Annihilus was an alien creature whose visual look appeared to be an amalgamation of an insect and Nosferatu, Max Schreck's iconic vampire, from director F. W. Murnau's eerie 1922 silent film.

FANTASTIC FOUR No. 71

(Opposite) Interior, "And So It Ends…"; script, Stan Lee; pencils, Jack Kirby; inks, Joe Sinnott; February 1968. The Mad Thinker's android is sent into the Negative Zone, an area outside the normal sphere of our galaxy, studied extensively by Reed Richards. The antimatter universe—sparsely populated, though with a preponderance of villains, most famously Annihilus and Blastaar—became an effective threat for the FF, and offered a demise of sorts for villains that technically couldn't be killed based on the strictures of the Comics Code Authority.

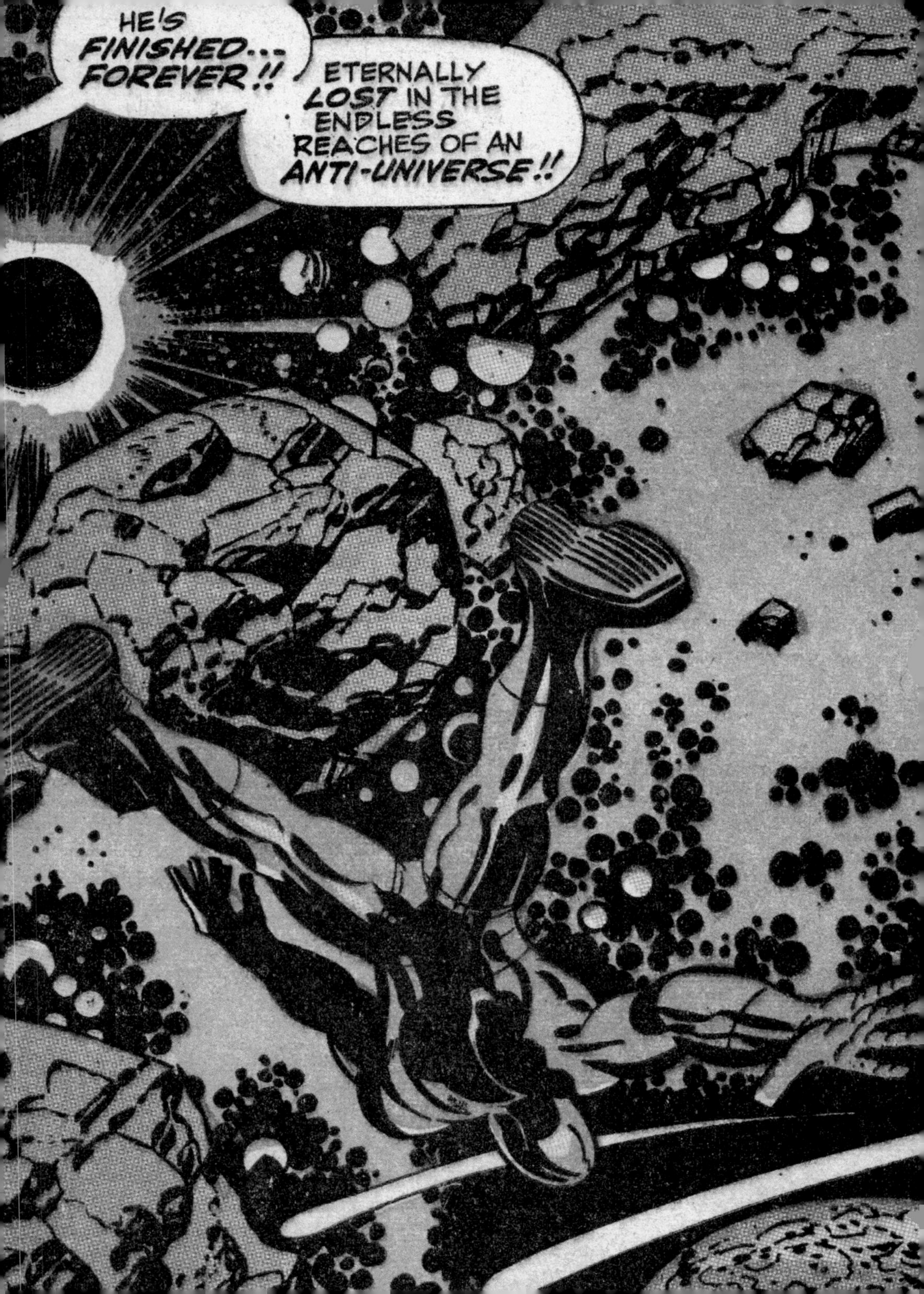
HE'S FINISHED... FOREVER!!
ETERNALLY LOST IN THE ENDLESS REACHES OF AN ANTI-UNIVERSE!!

JOE SINNOTT
COVER

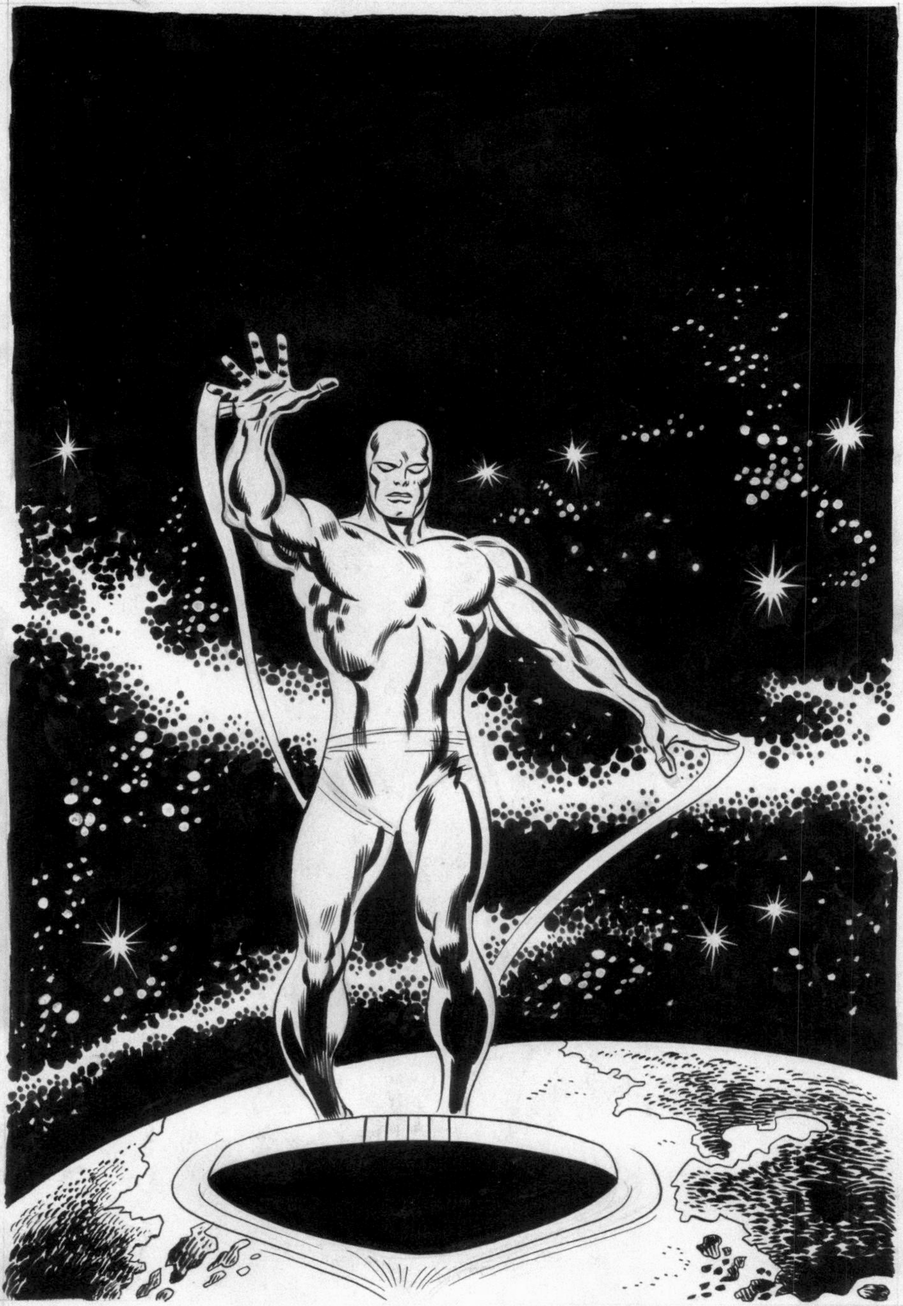

SILVER SURFER No. 1

(Opposite) Original cover art; pencils, John Buscema; inks, Joe Sinnott and Frank Giacoia; August 1968. Buscema's interpretation of the Silver Surfer differed considerably from Kirby's, taking a more naturalistic approach, inspired by comic strip old masters like the legendary Hal Foster. Buscema's character was more human in proportion and expression, giving him a less alien presence than Kirby's early vision. Perhaps Stan Lee had this in mind—along with the usual deadline and workload concerns faced by a managing editor—when Buscema was tasked to draw the character, until then so closely associated with Kirby.

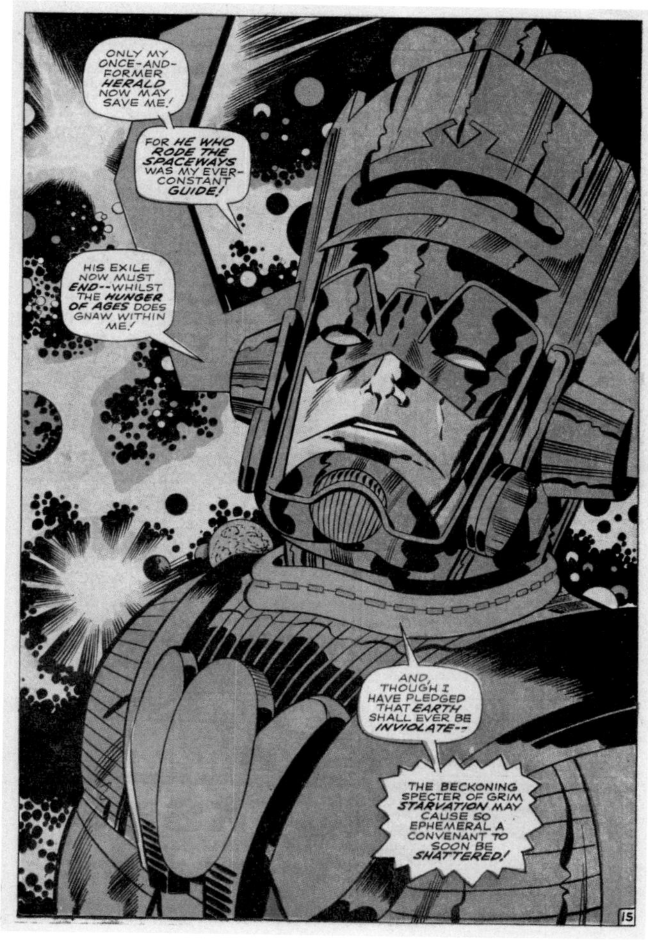
ONLY MY ONCE-AND-FORMER HERALD NOW MAY SAVE ME!
FOR HE WHO RODE THE SPACEWAYS WAS MY EVER-CONSTANT GUIDE!
HIS EXILE NOW MUST END--WHILST THE HUNGER OF AGES DOES GNAW WITHIN ME!
AND, THOUGH I HAVE PLEDGED THAT EARTH SHALL EVER BE INVIOLATE--
THE BECKONING SPECTER OF GRIM STARVATION MAY CAUSE SO EPHEMERAL A CONVENANT TO SOON BE SHATTERED!
15

FANTASTIC FOUR No. 74

(Above) Interior, "When Calls Galactus!"; script, Stan Lee; pencils, Jack Kirby; inks, Joe Sinnott; May 1968. A starving Galactus searches for his former herald. Kirby's latest signature, the full-page illustrated portrait, still manages to convey Galactus's power—even in his weakened state—but perhaps the close-up also betrays a hint of his sadness... and humanity?

"Too long have I displayed restraint! Too long have I refused to flaunt my power! But now — my very soul is aflame with burning rage! In a world of madness — I tried to practice reason — but all I won was hatred, and everlasting strife! So I'll have done with reason, and with love, or mercy! To men they're only words — to be uttered and ignored!" — THE SILVER SURFER

COLLECTING KIRBY

(Opposite) Interior original art, Silver Surfer *No. 18; pencils, Jack Kirby; inks, Herb Trimpe; September 1970.* Only fitting for the man crowned King of Comics, Kirby's voluminous output is among the most sought-after — and definitely the most-discussed — by original comic art collectors. John Morrow's long-running *Jack Kirby Collector* is an ongoing appreciation of Kirby's legacy; in issue 19, Glen David Gold describes Kirby's own take on the phenomenon at his final Comic-Con in 1993: "You ever hear of a guy named Peter Paul Rubens? He drew art for a sou, and he died a pauper. Now you can't touch a Rubens for less than two million. Me, I drew art and made enough to keep my family fed. And if it's selling for so much, that's flattery. They think of it as fine art, and that's enough for me."

19

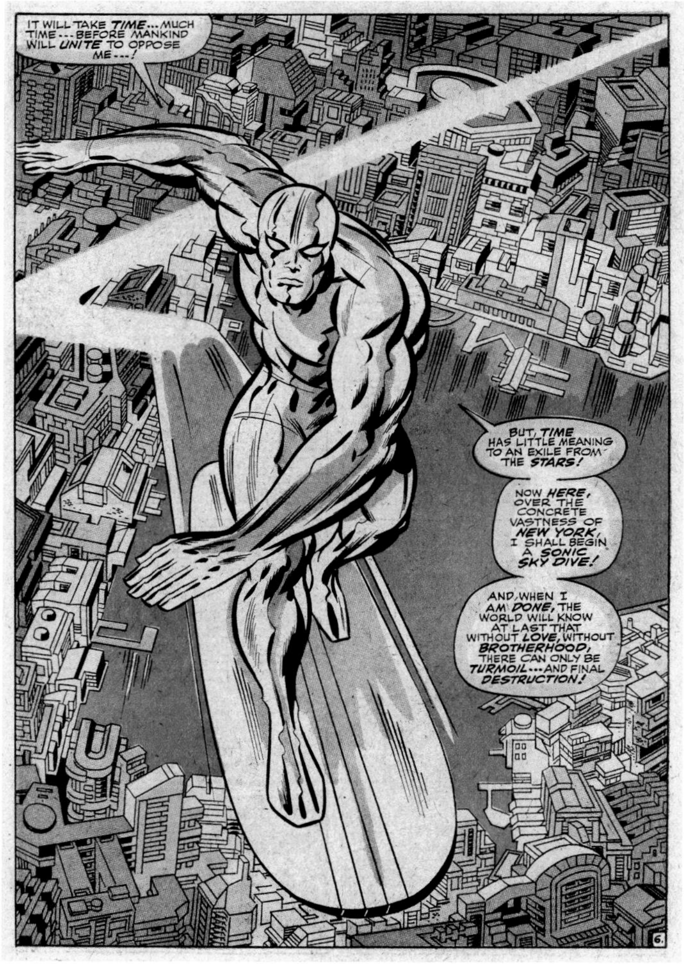
IT WILL TAKE TIME...MUCH TIME---BEFORE MANKIND WILL UNITE TO OPPOSE ME---!
BUT, TIME HAS LITTLE MEANING TO AN EXILE FROM THE STARS!
NOW HERE, OVER THE CONCRETE VASTNESS OF NEW YORK, I SHALL BEGIN A SONIC SKY DIVE!
AND, WHEN I AM DONE, THE WORLD WILL KNOW AT LAST THAT WITHOUT LOVE, WITHOUT BROTHERHOOD, THERE CAN ONLY BE TURMOIL---AND FINAL DESTRUCTION!
6.

FANTASTIC FOUR No. 72

(Above) Interior, "Where Soars the Silver Surfer!"; script, Stan Lee; pencils, Jack Kirby; inks, Joe Sinnott; March 1968.

SILVER SURFER No. 14

(Opposite) Interior, "The Surfer and the Spider!"; script, Stan Lee; pencils, John Buscema; inks, Dan Adkins; March 1970. Like the Surfer's conflicted character — born to soar through the universe, yet trapped on Earth — this short sequence seems to speak to many kids' deep connection to the comics. The stigma associated with "these childish things" still figured strongly in the minds of most adults, even as Marvel's comics were striving — and succeeding — to reinvent the medium as a more sophisticated entertainment.

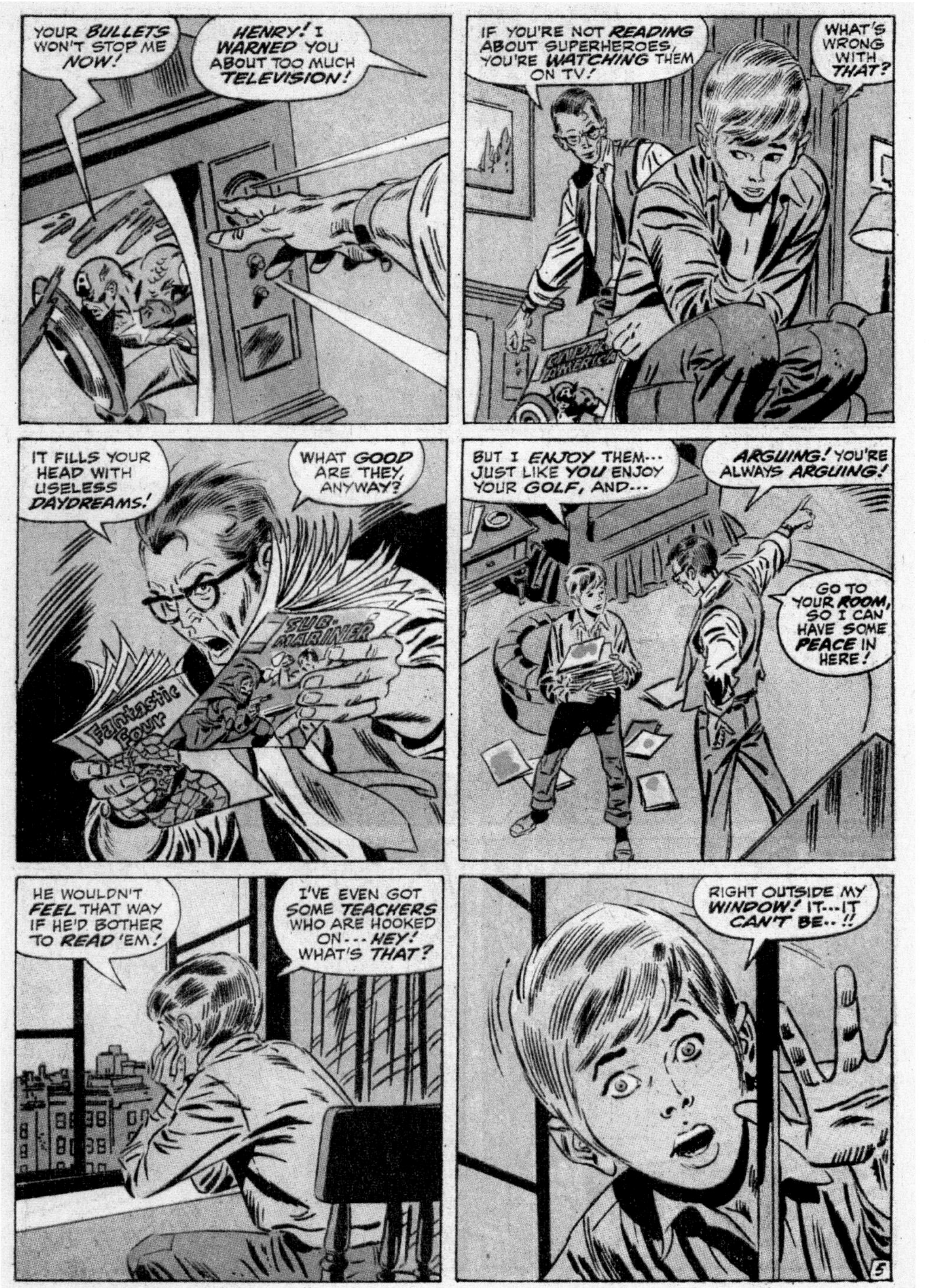
YOUR BULLETS WON'T STOP ME NOW!
HENRY! I WARNED YOU ABOUT TOO MUCH TELEVISION!
IF YOU'RE NOT READING ABOUT SUPERHEROES, YOU'RE WATCHING THEM ON TV!
WHAT'S WRONG WITH THAT?
CAPTAIN AMERICA
IT FILLS YOUR HEAD WITH USELESS DAYDREAMS!
WHAT GOOD ARE THEY, ANYWAY?
SUB-MARINER
Fantastic Four
BUT I ENJOY THEM... JUST LIKE YOU ENJOY YOUR GOLF, AND...
ARGUING! YOU'RE ALWAYS ARGUING!
GO TO YOUR ROOM, SO I CAN HAVE SOME PEACE IN HERE!
HE WOULDN'T FEEL THAT WAY IF HE'D BOTHER TO READ 'EM!
I'VE EVEN GOT SOME TEACHERS WHO ARE HOOKED ON... HEY! WHAT'S THAT?
RIGHT OUTSIDE MY WINDOW! IT... IT CAN'T BE..!!
5

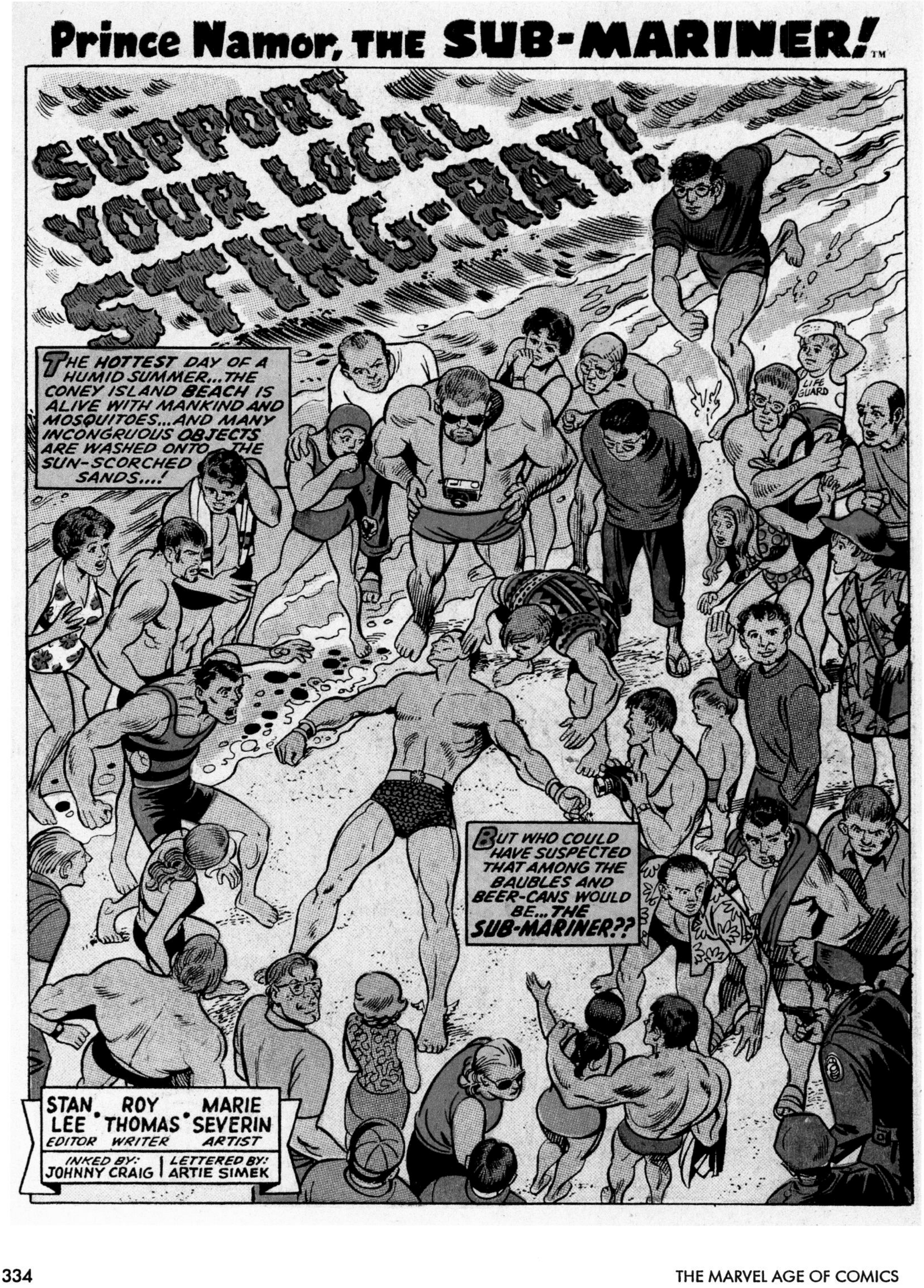
Prince Namor, THE SUB-MARINER!™
SUPPORT YOUR LOCAL STING-RAY!
THE HOTTEST DAY OF A HUMID SUMMER...THE CONEY ISLAND BEACH IS ALIVE WITH MANKIND AND MOSQUITOES...AND MANY INCONGRUOUS OBJECTS ARE WASHED ONTO THE SUN-SCORCHED SANDS...!
LIFE GUARD
BUT WHO COULD HAVE SUSPECTED THAT AMONG THE BAUBLES AND BEER-CANS WOULD BE...THE SUB-MARINER??
STAN LEE EDITOR • ROY THOMAS WRITER • MARIE SEVERIN ARTIST
INKED BY: JOHNNY CRAIG | LETTERED BY: ARTIE SIMEK

SUB-MARINER No. 19

(Opposite and below) Interior and schematic, "Support Your Local Sting-Ray!"; script, Roy Thomas; pencils, Marie Severin; inks, Johnny Craig; November 1969. On this splash page, Sub-Mariner washed up on Coney Island, with a crowd of beachgoers looking on. A master satirist, Marie often drew cartoons of her coworkers, always with the sharp eye of an artist who recognized people's quirks. In drawing the crowd Marie used the opportunity to lampoon most of the Marvel staff ca. 1969, including caricatures of Stan Lee, Roy Thomas, and herself, all of them identified in the schematic (below).

Did you know this was the Marvel Group at the time?
? some nice staff secretary
Stan
John Romita
Frank Giacoia
me
Roy Thomas
Tony Mortellaro
my dear friend Flo Davenport
Larry Lieber
John Verpoorten
Morrie Kuramoto
Gary Fredrick
Herb Trimpe
Stu Schwartzberg
? Some Canadian briefly on staff
Don Heck
Mike Esposito
Sol Brodsky
Bill Everett
Stan Lee Editor
Roy Thomas Writer
Marie Severin
Inked by: Johnny Craig
Artie Simek
Flo Steinberg — who is still a good friend of mine — had recently left staff — normally she would have had a prominent place in this and I think this figure was meant to be her —
109

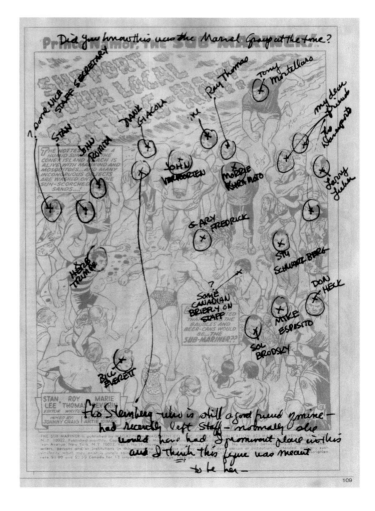

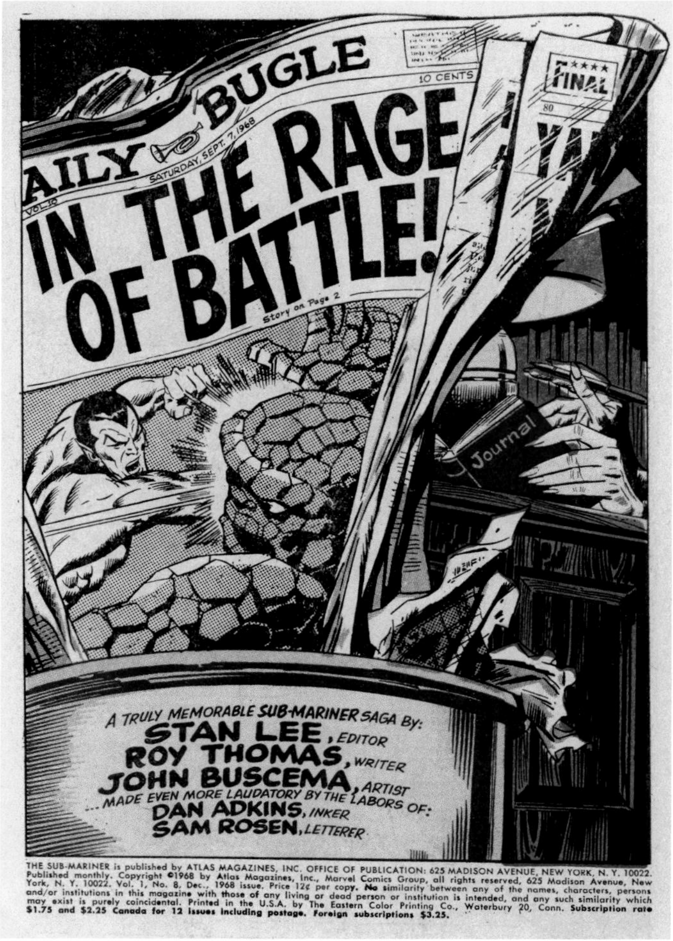
AILY BUGLE
10 CENTS
SATURDAY, SEPT. 7, 1968
FINAL
IN THE RAGE OF BATTLE!
Story on Page 2
Journal
A TRULY MEMORABLE SUB-MARINER SAGA BY:
STAN LEE, EDITOR
ROY THOMAS, WRITER
JOHN BUSCEMA, ARTIST
...MADE EVEN MORE LAUDATORY BY THE LABORS OF:
DAN ADKINS, INKER
SAM ROSEN, LETTERER
THE SUB-MARINER is published by ATLAS MAGAZINES, INC. OFFICE OF PUBLICATION: 625 MADISON AVENUE, NEW YORK, N. Y. 10022. Published monthly. Copyright ©1968 by Atlas Magazines, Inc., Marvel Comics Group, all rights reserved, 625 Madison Avenue, New York, N. Y. 10022. Vol. 1, No. 8, Dec., 1968 issue. Price 12¢ per copy. No similarity between any of the names, characters, persons and/or institutions in this magazine with those of any living or dead person or institution is intended, and any such similarity which may exist is purely coincidental. Printed in the U.S.A. by The Eastern Color Printing Co., Waterbury 20, Conn. Subscription rate $1.75 and $2.25 Canada for 12 issues including postage. Foreign subscriptions $3.25.

SUB-MARINER No. 8
(Above) Interior, "In the Rage of Battle!"; script, Roy Thomas; pencils, John Buscema; inks, Dan Adkins; December 1968. In one of the few Marvel stories to reference their original Timely continuity, Roy Thomas wrote this touching story featuring Namor's 1940 love Betty Dean. While Namor aged at a much slower rate than humans, Betty aged naturally and the contrast between the two is evident.

SUB-MARINER No. 7
(Opposite) Cover; pencils, John Buscema; inks, Dan Adkins; November 1968. Another cover using a photographic background, with Sub-Mariner the only illustrated figure. This cover, a last-minute replacement, was quickly assembled because editor Stan Lee felt the illustration that had been drawn for the cover was too unexciting.

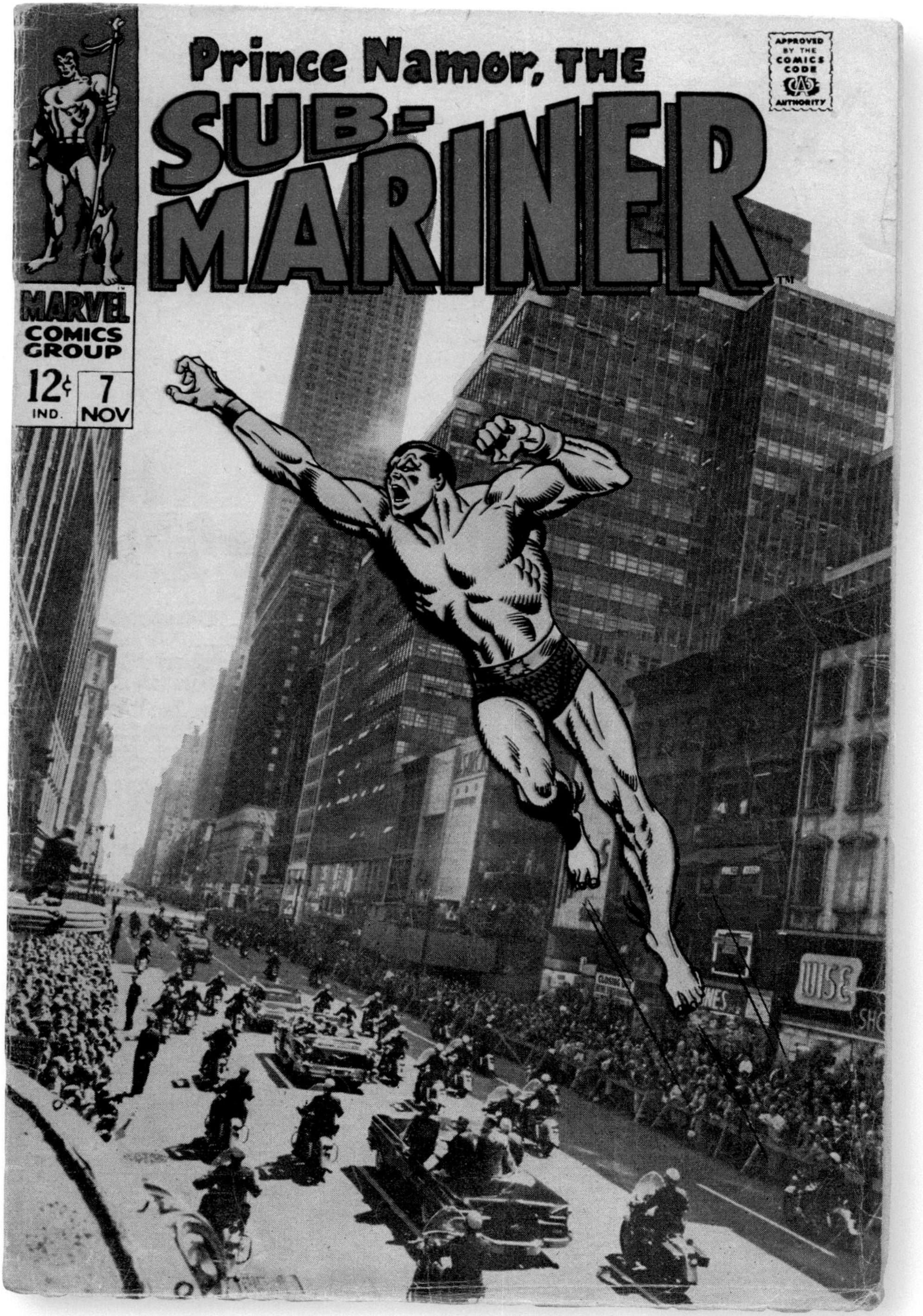
Prince Namor, THE
SUB-MARINER
APPROVED BY THE COMICS CODE AUTHORITY
MARVEL COMICS GROUP
12¢ IND.
7 NOV
WISE

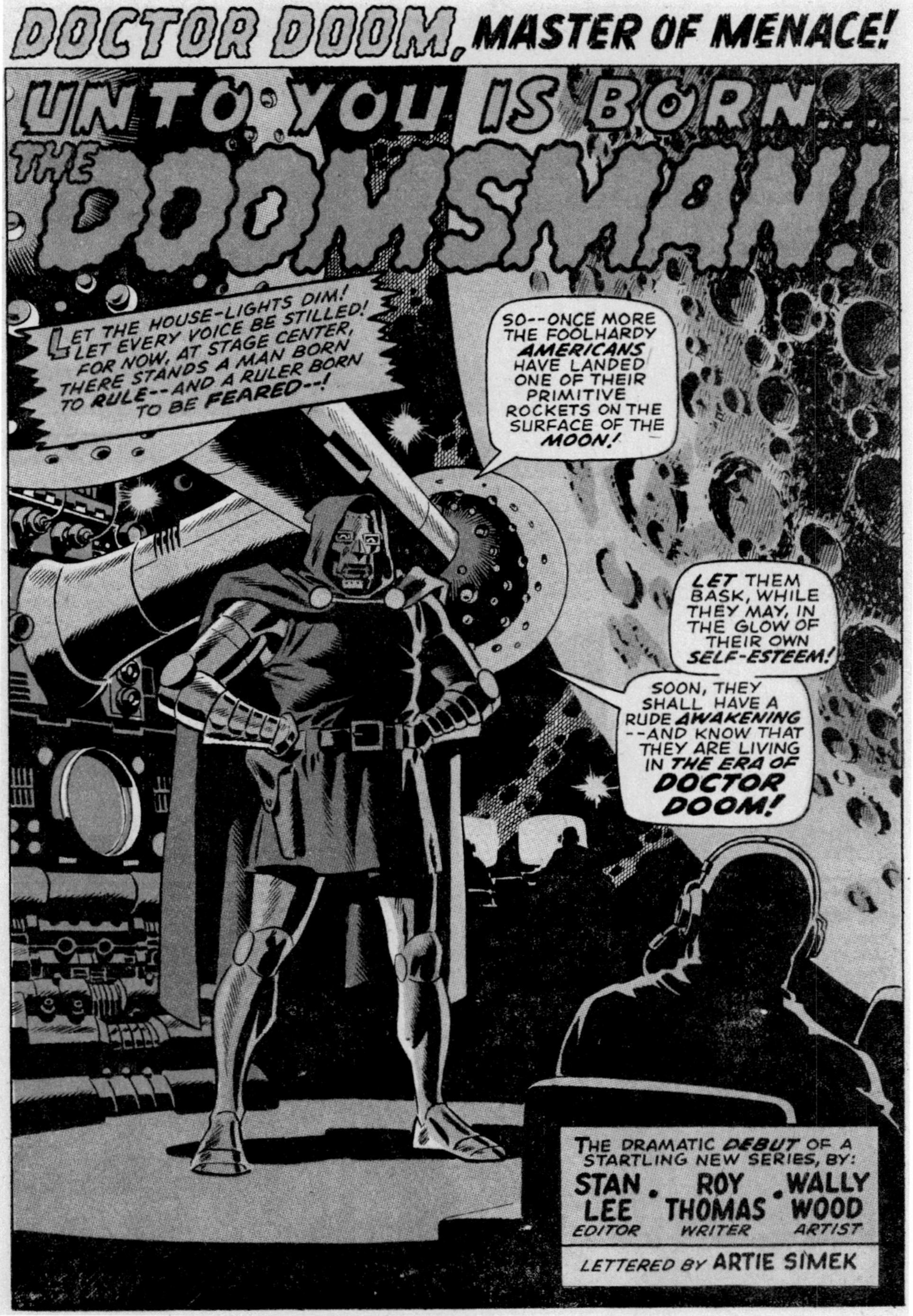
DOCTOR DOOM, MASTER OF MENACE!
UNTO YOU IS BORN... THE DOOMSMAN!
LET THE HOUSE-LIGHTS DIM! LET EVERY VOICE BE STILLED! FOR NOW, AT STAGE CENTER, THERE STANDS A MAN BORN TO RULE--AND A RULER BORN TO BE FEARED--!
SO--ONCE MORE THE FOOLHARDY AMERICANS HAVE LANDED ONE OF THEIR PRIMITIVE ROCKETS ON THE SURFACE OF THE MOON!
LET THEM BASK, WHILE THEY MAY, IN THE GLOW OF THEIR OWN SELF-ESTEEM!
SOON, THEY SHALL HAVE A RUDE AWAKENING --AND KNOW THAT THEY ARE LIVING IN THE ERA OF DOCTOR DOOM!
THE DRAMATIC DEBUT OF A STARTLING NEW SERIES, BY:
STAN LEE EDITOR • ROY THOMAS WRITER • WALLY WOOD ARTIST
LETTERED BY ARTIE SIMEK

ASTONISHING TALES No. 1

(Opposite and below) Interiors, "Unto You Is Born... the Doomsman!"; script, Roy Thomas; pencils and inks, Wally Wood; August 1970. The space race had long been fodder for popular entertainment. But Armstrong and Aldrin's historic first moonwalk upped the ante, taking the stuff of science fiction into the realm of fact. And then back into fiction, with this unique discovery on the moon's surface—a crystal ball the astronauts will carry back to Earth only to discover it contains a message for the American President from Dr. Doom.

FANTASTIC FOUR No. 98

(Following spread) Interior, "Mystery on the Moon!"; script, Stan Lee; pencils, Jack Kirby; inks, Joe Sinnott; May 1970. The extraordinary achievement of landing two men on the moon and returning them home safely was the pride of many Americans including Kirby and Lee, who leapt at the chance to have their characters contribute in their own small way. A few issues later, they received the following reply from the Apollo 11 team: "Quite contrary to your popular beliefs, the United States is perfectly able to make a round trip to the moon without any help from the Fantastic Four. Man makes it to another world only to find out that the whole thing wouldn't have been possible if not for a group of superheroes. Next time, butt out of our business!" Marvel printed the letter, "because it just might be genuine and we don't want to get into a running feud with three of the great guys of our time." Better safe than sorry, even if "the address on the envelope read 'Akron, Ohio,' and not Houston at all!"

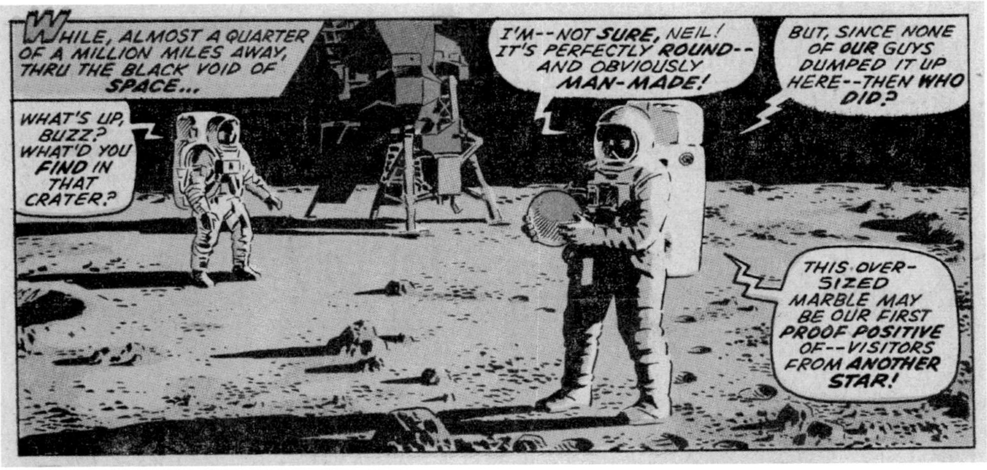
WHILE, ALMOST A QUARTER OF A MILLION MILES AWAY, THRU THE BLACK VOID OF SPACE...
WHAT'S UP, BUZZ? WHAT'D YOU FIND IN THAT CRATER?
I'M--NOT SURE, NEIL! IT'S PERFECTLY ROUND-- AND OBVIOUSLY MAN-MADE!
BUT, SINCE NONE OF OUR GUYS DUMPED IT UP HERE--THEN WHO DID?
THIS OVER-SIZED MARBLE MAY BE OUR FIRST PROOF POSITIVE OF--VISITORS FROM ANOTHER STAR!

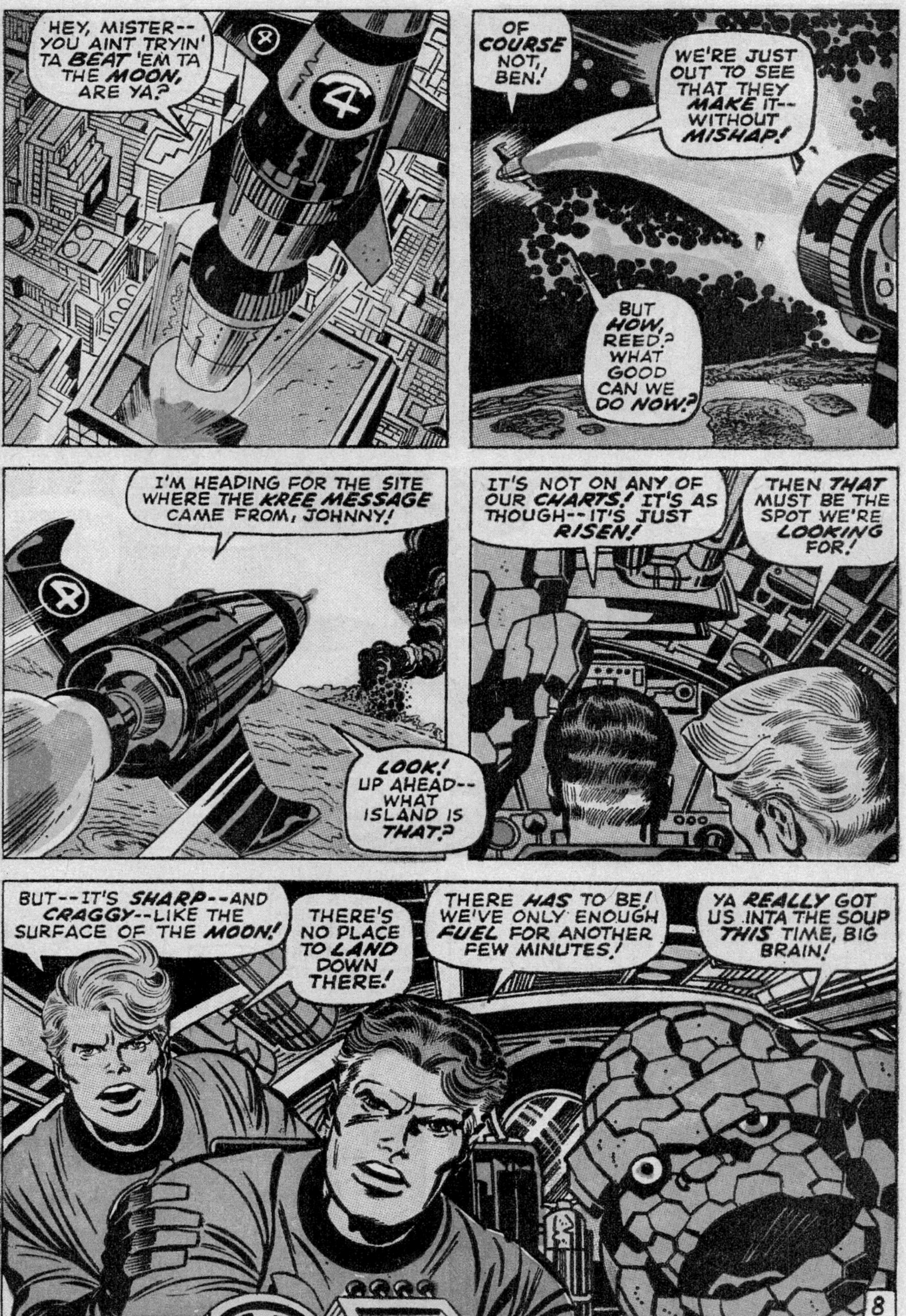

HEY, MISTER-- YOU AINT TRYIN' TA BEAT 'EM TA THE MOON, ARE YA?
OF COURSE NOT, BEN.!
WE'RE JUST OUT TO SEE THAT THEY MAKE IT-- WITHOUT MISHAP!
BUT HOW, REED.? WHAT GOOD CAN WE DO NOW?
I'M HEADING FOR THE SITE WHERE THE KREE MESSAGE CAME FROM, JOHNNY!
LOOK! UP AHEAD-- WHAT ISLAND IS THAT?
IT'S NOT ON ANY OF OUR CHARTS! IT'S AS THOUGH--IT'S JUST RISEN!
THEN THAT MUST BE THE SPOT WE'RE LOOKING FOR!
BUT--IT'S SHARP--AND CRAGGY--LIKE THE SURFACE OF THE MOON!
THERE'S NO PLACE TO LAND DOWN THERE!
THERE HAS TO BE! WE'VE ONLY ENOUGH FUEL FOR ANOTHER FEW MINUTES!
YA REALLY GOT US INTA THE SOUP THIS TIME, BIG BRAIN!

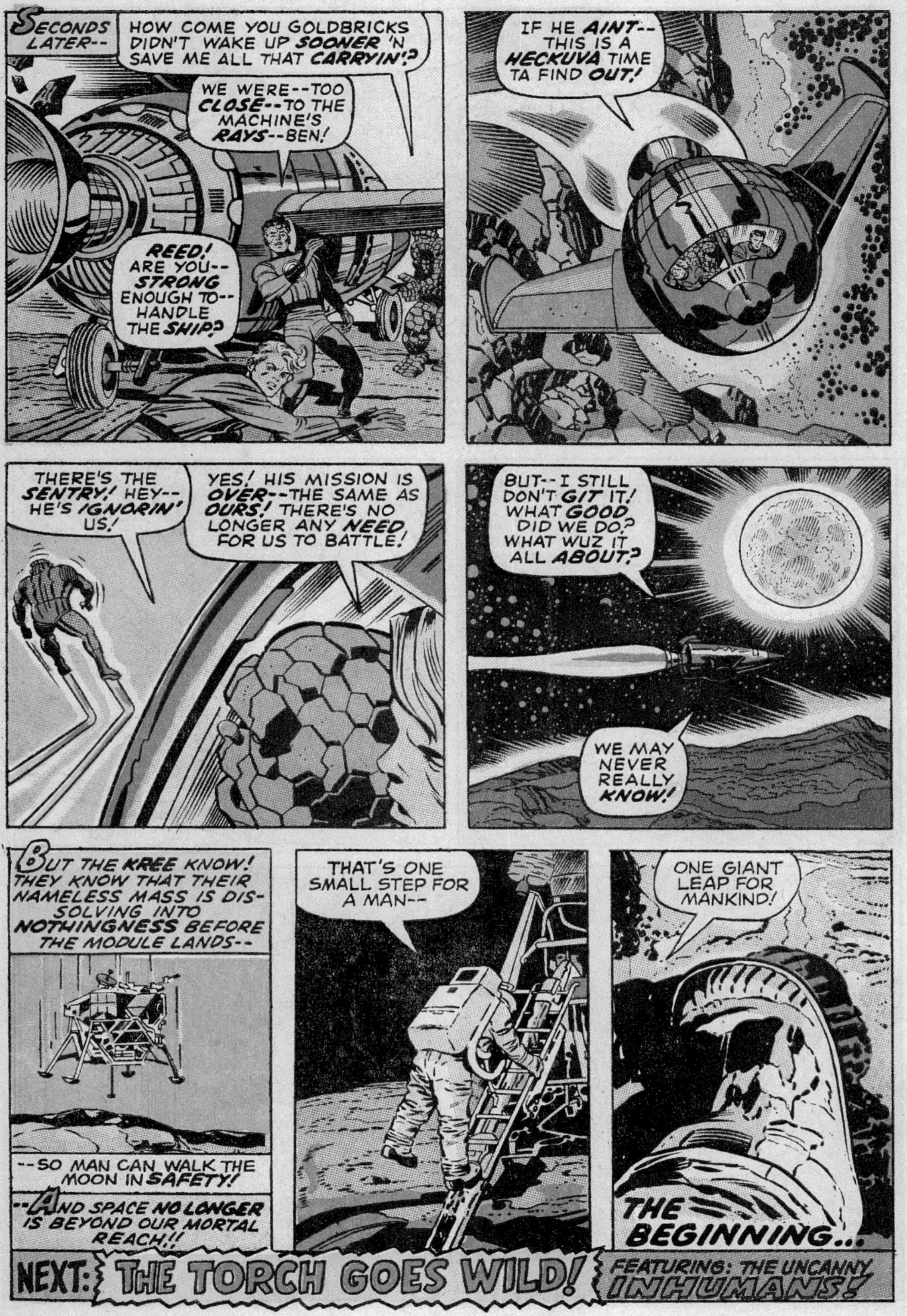
SECONDS LATER--
HOW COME YOU GOLDBRICKS DIDN'T WAKE UP SOONER 'N SAVE ME ALL THAT CARRYIN'?
WE WERE--TOO CLOSE--TO THE MACHINE'S RAYS--BEN!
REED! ARE YOU--STRONG ENOUGH TO--HANDLE THE SHIP?
IF HE AINT--THIS IS A HECKUVA TIME TA FIND OUT!
THERE'S THE SENTRY! HEY--HE'S IGNORIN' US!
YES! HIS MISSION IS OVER--THE SAME AS OURS! THERE'S NO LONGER ANY NEED FOR US TO BATTLE!
BUT--I STILL DON'T GIT IT! WHAT GOOD DID WE DO? WHAT WUZ IT ALL ABOUT?
WE MAY NEVER REALLY KNOW!
BUT THE KREE KNOW! THEY KNOW THAT THEIR NAMELESS MASS IS DISSOLVING INTO NOTHINGNESS BEFORE THE MODULE LANDS--
--SO MAN CAN WALK THE MOON IN SAFETY!
--AND SPACE NO LONGER IS BEYOND OUR MORTAL REACH!!
THAT'S ONE SMALL STEP FOR A MAN--
ONE GIANT LEAP FOR MANKIND!
THE BEGINNING...
NEXT: THE TORCH GOES WILD! FEATURING: THE UNCANNY INHUMANS!

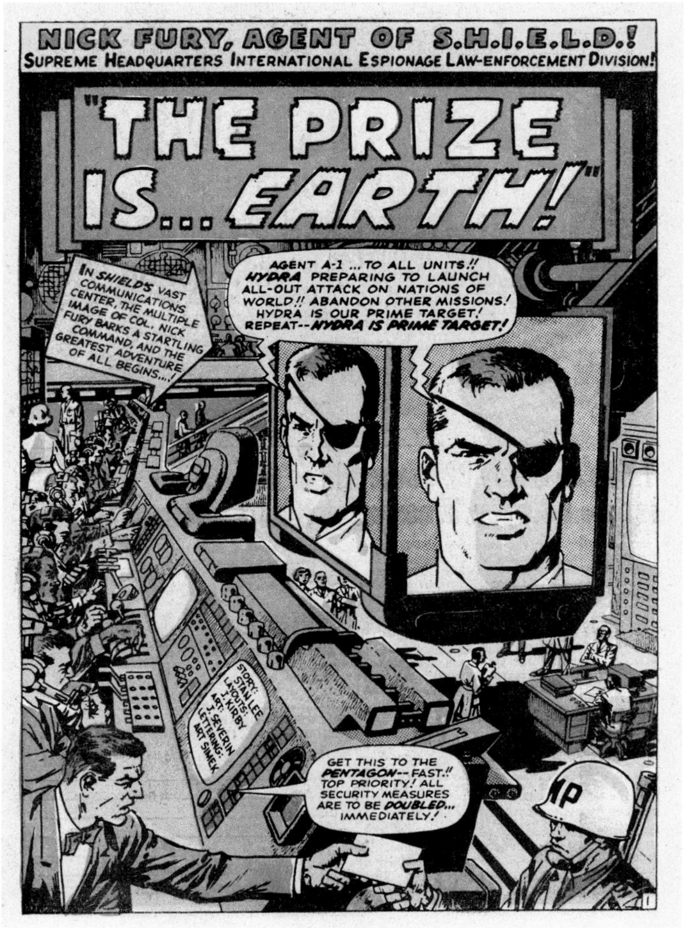
NICK FURY, AGENT OF S.H.I.E.L.D.!
SUPREME HEADQUARTERS INTERNATIONAL ESPIONAGE LAW-ENFORCEMENT DIVISION!
"THE PRIZE IS... EARTH!"
IN SHIELD'S VAST COMMUNICATIONS CENTER, THE MULTIPLE IMAGE OF COL. NICK FURY BARKS A STARTLING COMMAND, AND THE GREATEST ADVENTURE OF ALL BEGINS...!
AGENT A-1 ... TO ALL UNITS!! HYDRA PREPARING TO LAUNCH ALL-OUT ATTACK ON NATIONS OF WORLD!! ABANDON OTHER MISSIONS! HYDRA IS OUR PRIME TARGET! REPEAT--HYDRA IS PRIME TARGET!
STORY: STAN LEE LAYOUTS: J. KIRBY ART: J. SEVERIN LETTERING: ART SIMEK
GET THIS TO THE PENTAGON--FAST!! TOP PRIORITY! ALL SECURITY MEASURES ARE TO BE DOUBLED... IMMEDIATELY!
MP

STRANGE TALES No. 137

(Above) Interior, "The Prize Is... Earth!"; script, Stan Lee; pencils, Jack Kirby; inks, John Severin; October 1965. Nick Fury and S.H.I.E.L.D. faced worldwide threats from the very beginning, particularly from their nefarious nemesis, Hydra. S.H.I.E.L.D.'s state-of-the-art control center bore some resemblance to the Project Gemini control center in Houston. S.H.I.E.L.D., like NASA, spared no expense — a good thing, as every resource is needed when Hydra launches a bomb into space that could destroy the planet!

NICK FURY, AGENT OF S.H.I.E.L.D. No. 6

(Opposite) Cover; pencils and inks, Jim Steranko; November 1968. While Steranko's brief tenure drawing interior stories for Marvel had come to an end, he stayed on to illustrate some outstanding covers, including this homage to Wally Wood's fantastically detailed science-fiction covers for EC Comics 15 years earlier.

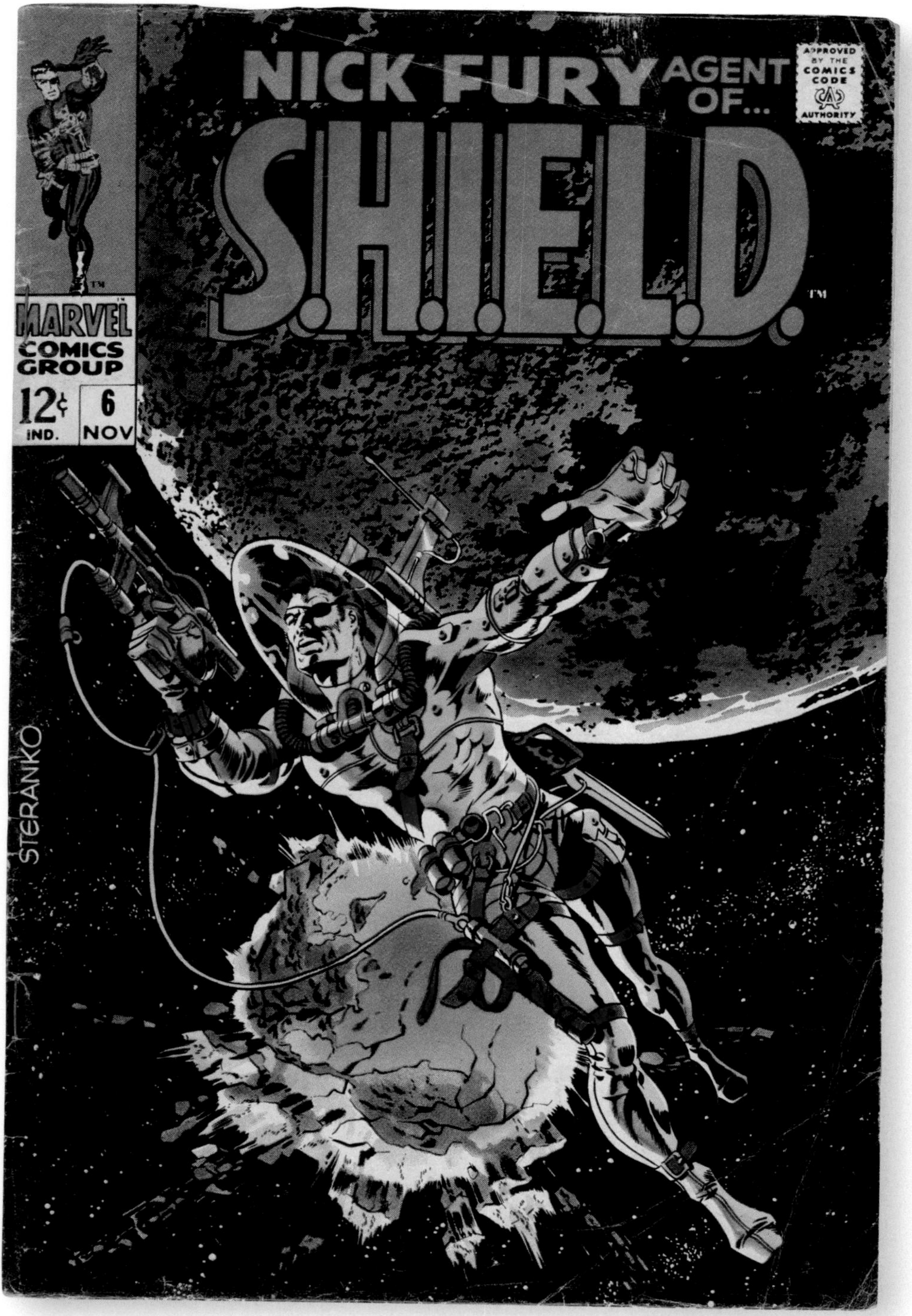
NICK FURY AGENT OF...
S.H.I.E.L.D.
APPROVED BY THE COMICS CODE AUTHORITY
MARVEL COMICS GROUP
12¢ IND.
6 NOV
STERANKO

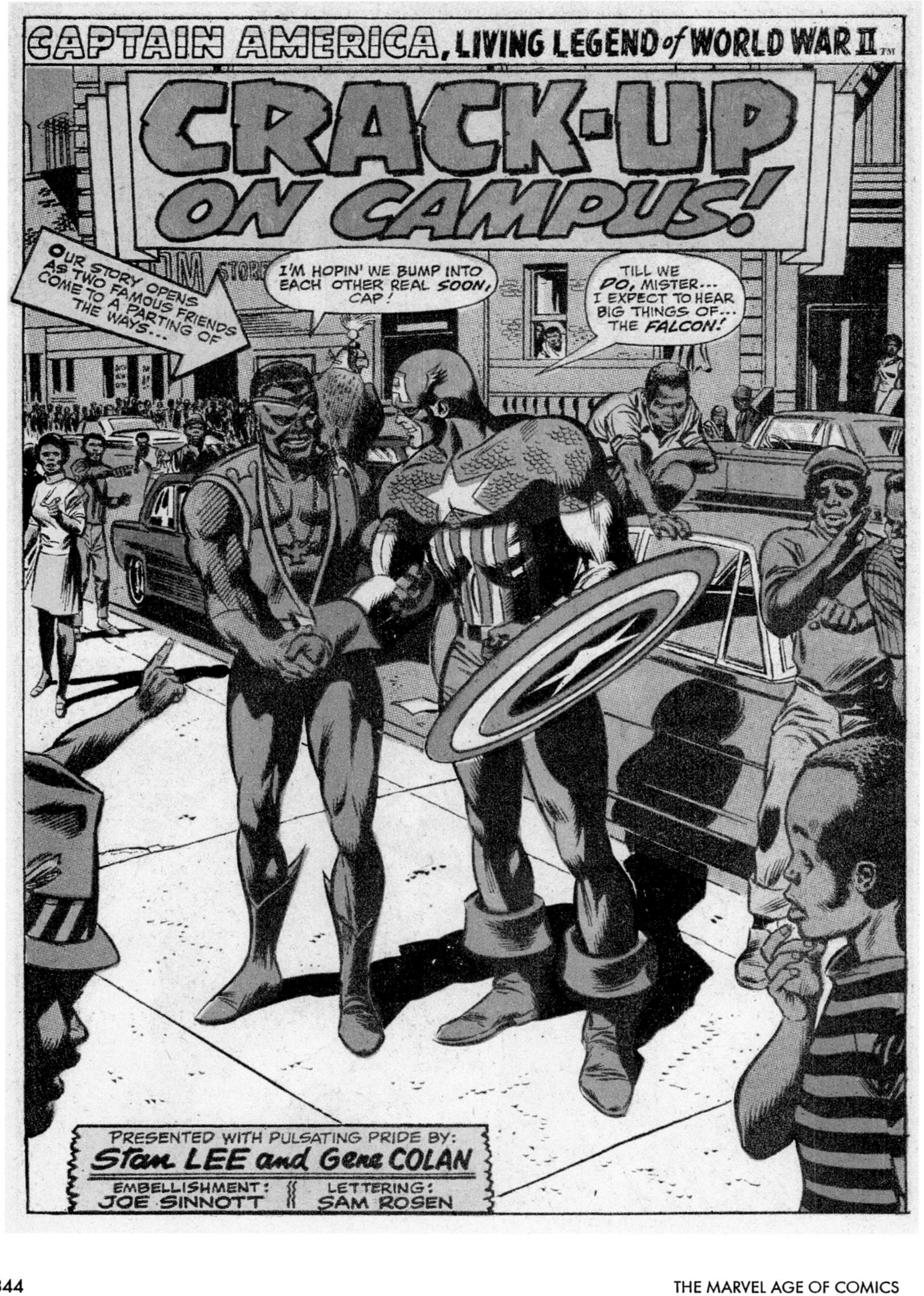
CAPTAIN AMERICA, LIVING LEGEND of WORLD WAR II
CRACK-UP ON CAMPUS!
OUR STORY OPENS AS TWO FAMOUS FRIENDS COME TO A PARTING OF THE WAYS...
I'M HOPIN' WE BUMP INTO EACH OTHER REAL SOON, CAP!
TILL WE DO, MISTER... I EXPECT TO HEAR BIG THINGS OF... THE FALCON!
PRESENTED WITH PULSATING PRIDE BY:
Stan LEE and Gene COLAN
EMBELLISHMENT: JOE SINNOTT
LETTERING: SAM ROSEN

CAPTAIN AMERICA No. 120

(Opposite) Interior, "Crack-Up on Campus!"; script, Stan Lee; pencils, Gene Colan; inks, Joe Sinnott; December 1969. While the Falcon would depart after his first encounter with Captain America, he soon returned as his full-time partner. The idea of adding an African American hero to the strip helped make Cap a more contemporary hero, and their stories would often address relevant social issues like bigotry.

AMAZING SPIDER-MAN No. 68

(Below) Cover; pencils and inks, John Romita; January 1969.

SPIDER-MAN
12¢
68
IND.
JAN
the AMAZING SPIDER-MAN
APPROVED BY THE COMICS CODE AUTHORITY
MARVEL COMICS GROUP
CRISIS ON CAMPUS!
DON'T STALL

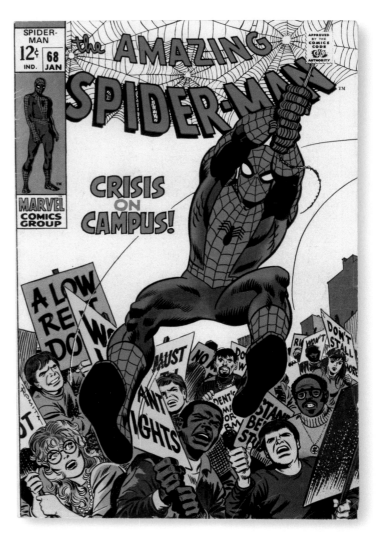

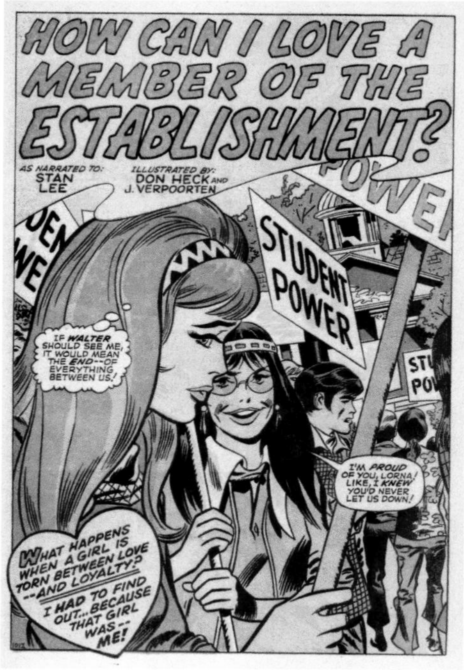
HOW CAN I LOVE A MEMBER OF THE ESTABLISHMENT?
AS NARRATED TO: STAN LEE
ILLUSTRATED BY: DON HECK AND J. VERPOORTEN
STUDENT POWER
IF WALTER SHOULD SEE ME, IT WOULD MEAN THE END--OF EVERYTHING BETWEEN US!
I'M PROUD OF YOU, LORNA! LIKE, I KNEW YOU'D NEVER LET US DOWN!
WHAT HAPPENS WHEN A GIRL IS TORN BETWEEN LOVE --AND LOYALTY? I HAD TO FIND OUT...BECAUSE THAT GIRL WAS--ME!

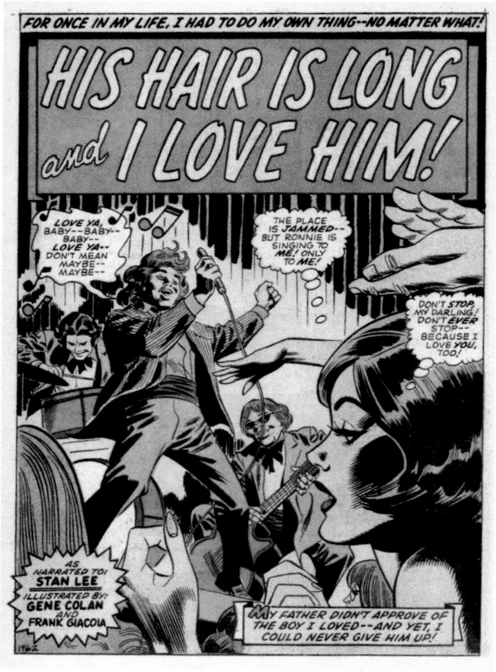
FOR ONCE IN MY LIFE, I HAD TO DO MY OWN THING--NO MATTER WHAT!
HIS HAIR IS LONG and I LOVE HIM!
LOVE YA, BABY--BABY--BABY-- LOVE YA-- DON'T MEAN MAYBE-- MAYBE--
THE PLACE IS JAMMED-- BUT RONNIE IS SINGING TO ME! ONLY TO ME!
DON'T STOP, MY DARLING! DON'T EVER STOP-- BECAUSE I LOVE YOU, TOO!
AS NARRATED TO: STAN LEE
ILLUSTRATED BY: GENE COLAN AND FRANK GIACOIA
MY FATHER DIDN'T APPROVE OF THE BOY I LOVED--AND YET, I COULD NEVER GIVE HIM UP!

NEW ROMANCE

(Above) Interior, "How Can I Love a Member of the Establishment?"; My Love *No. 5; script, Stan Lee; pencils, Don Heck; inks, John Verpoorten; May 1970. (Above right) Interior, "His Hair Is Long and I Love Him!",* My Love *No. 21; script, Lee; pencils, Gene Colan; inks, Frank Giacoia. January 1973.* Gene Colan always laughed heartily when he recalled these titles. Lee attempted to keep up with contemporary issues — even in the romance titles (he initiated these two in 1969). While the titles may be silly, Lee pairs his characteristically evenhanded approach and straightforward morals — don't judge by appearances — with lavish art rivaling anything done in the genre's heyday.

OUR LOVE STORY No. 5

(Opposite) Interior, "My Heart Broke in Hollywood!"; script, Stan Lee; pencils and inks, Jim Steranko; June 1970.

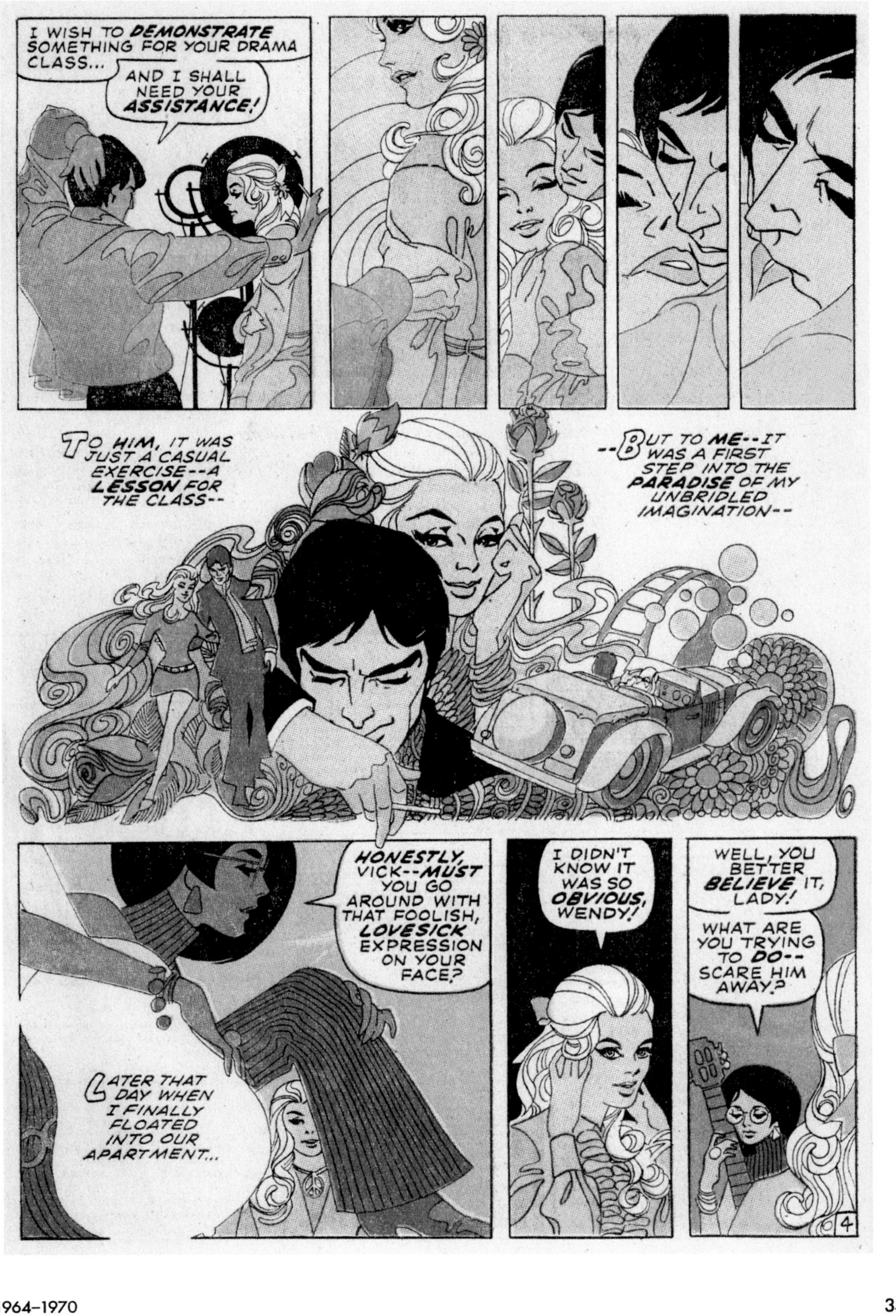
I WISH TO DEMONSTRATE SOMETHING FOR YOUR DRAMA CLASS...
AND I SHALL NEED YOUR ASSISTANCE!
TO HIM, IT WAS JUST A CASUAL EXERCISE--A LESSON FOR THE CLASS--
--BUT TO ME--IT WAS A FIRST STEP INTO THE PARADISE OF MY UNBRIDLED IMAGINATION--
LATER THAT DAY WHEN I FINALLY FLOATED INTO OUR APARTMENT...
HONESTLY, VICK--MUST YOU GO AROUND WITH THAT FOOLISH, LOVESICK EXPRESSION ON YOUR FACE?
I DIDN'T KNOW IT WAS SO OBVIOUS, WENDY!
WELL, YOU BETTER BELIEVE IT, LADY!
WHAT ARE YOU TRYING TO DO--SCARE HIM AWAY?
4

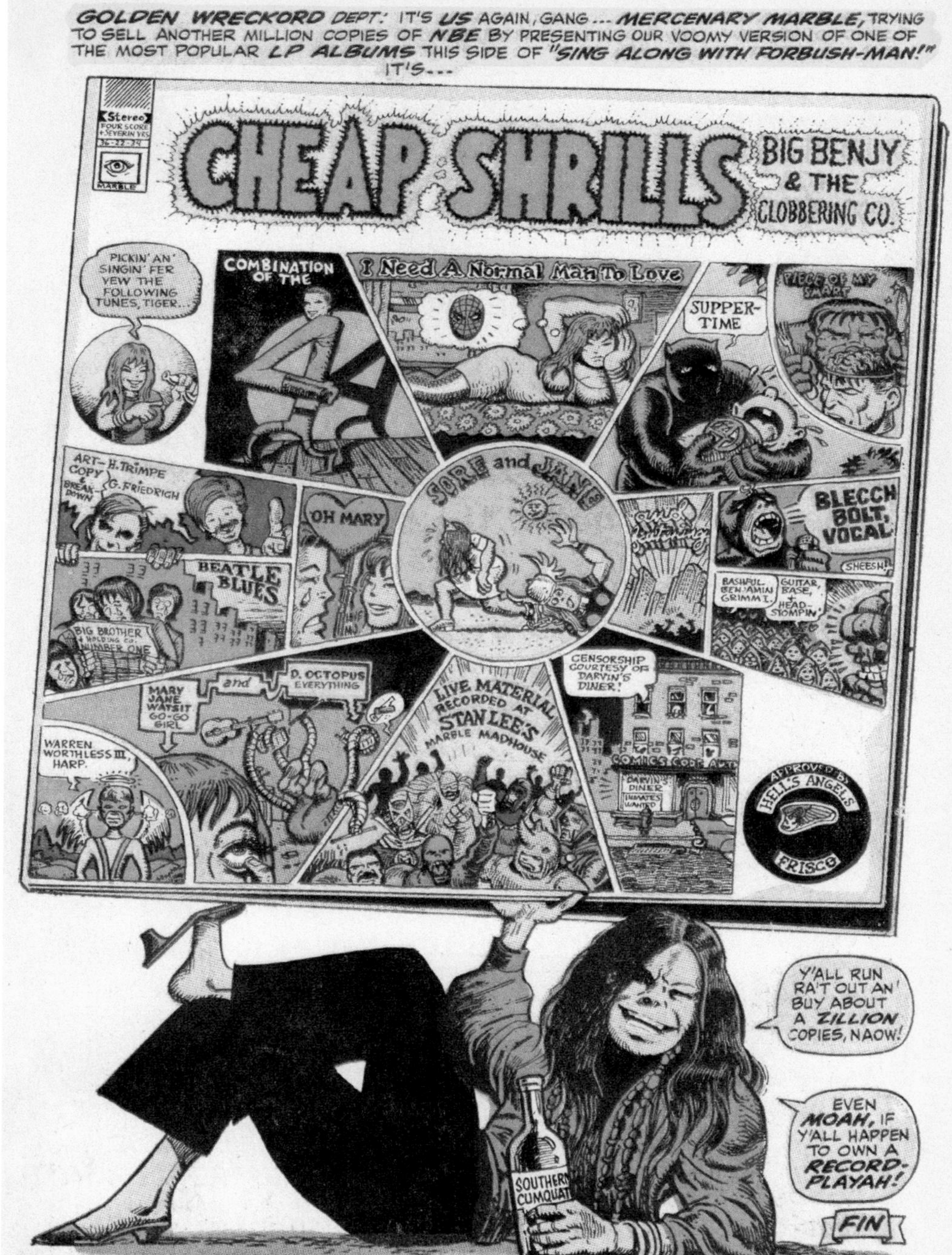
GOLDEN WRECKORD DEPT: IT'S US AGAIN, GANG... MERCENARY MARBLE, TRYING TO SELL ANOTHER MILLION COPIES OF NBE BY PRESENTING OUR VOOMY VERSION OF ONE OF THE MOST POPULAR LP ALBUMS THIS SIDE OF "SING ALONG WITH FORBUSH-MAN!" IT'S...
Stereo
MARBLE
CHEAP SHRILLS
BIG BENJY & THE CLOBBERING CO.
PICKIN' AN' SINGIN' FER YEW THE FOLLOWING TUNES, TIGER...
COMBINATION OF THE
I Need A Normal Man To Love
SUPPER-TIME
PIECE OF MY SMART
ART- H.TRIMPE
COPY & BREAK-DOWN G.FRIEDRICH
OH MARY
SORE and JANE
BLECCH BOLT, VOCAL
SHEESH!
BEATLE BLUES
BIG BROTHER + HOLDING CO. NUMBER ONE
BASHFUL BENJAMIN GRIMM I.
GUITAR, BASE, + HEAD-STOMPIN'
MARY JANE WATSIT GO-GO GIRL
and
D. OCTOPUS EVERYTHING
LIVE MATERIAL RECORDED AT STAN LEE'S MARBLE MADHOUSE
CENSORSHIP COURTESY OF DARVIN'S DINER!
WARREN WORTHLESS III, HARP.
COMICS CODE AUTH
DARVIN'S DINER
INMATES WANTED
APPROVED BY HELL'S ANGELS FRISCO
Y'ALL RUN RA'T OUT AN' BUY ABOUT A ZILLION COPIES, NAOW!
EVEN MOAH, IF Y'ALL HAPPEN TO OWN A RECORD-PLAYAH!
SOUTHERN CUMQUAT
FIN

NOT BRAND ECHH No. 13

(Opposite) Interior, "Cheap Shrills"; script and breakdowns, Gary Friedrich; pencils and inks, Herb Trimpe; May 1969. This parody of the cover to Big Brother and the Holding Company's *Cheap Thrills* album also paid tribute to another counterculture and underground comics icon, Robert Crumb, who drew the original album's artwork. Trimpe outdid himself copying Crumb's style—and it looks like they pulled the wool over the eyes of the Code inspectors. "Janis" is holding a bottle of "Southern Cumquat," and…what could that be on the floor by her side?

CHEAP THRILLS

(Above) Photograph, Elliott Landy; Janis Joplin and Big Brother drummer Dave Getz en route to Detroit; 1968. Hot off her eagerly anticipated big label debut, which included "Piece of My Heart" and "Summertime," Joplin rocketed to stardom, her songs an embodiment of the '60s. Here she takes *Sub-Mariner* along for the ride.

CAPTAIN AMERICA No. 128

(Below) Interior, "Mission: Stamp Out Satan's Angels!"; script, Stan Lee; pencils, Gene Colan; inks, Dick Ayers; August 1970. Between Hunter Thompson's 1966 *Hell's Angels* and the popularity of movies like *Easy Rider* (Peter Fonda's character Wyatt was *named* Captain America!) biker culture invaded American pop culture. Lee, fearing Captain America was no more than an anachronism, sent him on a compelling journey of self-discovery in an attempt to make Steve Rogers relevant for the brave new decade. Cap would encounter the Hells Angels, see Woodstock, and witness campus unrest firsthand.

STRANGE AND STRANGER

(Opposite) Strange Happenings rock poster; art, Greg Irons; July 1967. In Dr. Strange, Ditko and Lee had developed one of comics' most unconventional characters, infused with surrealism and mysticism that predated the youth culture's own psychedelic take on the subjects. No wonder he became a hero of "heads" across the nation — nobody's mind was any more expanded! Here the Doctor becomes the unofficial mascot of this Berkeley "Get Together" featuring the Youngbloods.

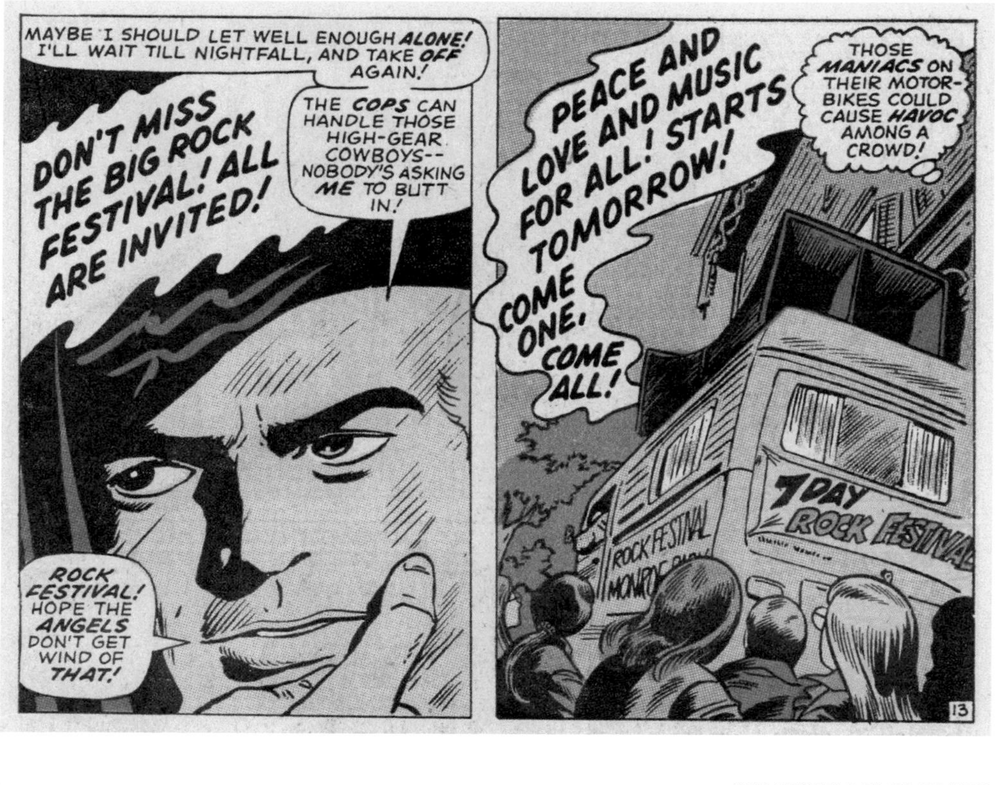
MAYBE I SHOULD LET WELL ENOUGH ALONE! I'LL WAIT TILL NIGHTFALL, AND TAKE OFF AGAIN!
DON'T MISS THE BIG ROCK FESTIVAL! ALL ARE INVITED!
THE COPS CAN HANDLE THOSE HIGH-GEAR COWBOYS-- NOBODY'S ASKING ME TO BUTT IN!
ROCK FESTIVAL! HOPE THE ANGELS DON'T GET WIND OF THAT!
PEACE AND LOVE AND MUSIC FOR ALL! STARTS TOMORROW! COME ONE, COME ALL!
THOSE MANIACS ON THEIR MOTOR-BIKES COULD CAUSE HAVOC AMONG A CROWD!
7 DAY ROCK FESTIVAL
ROCK FESTIVAL
13

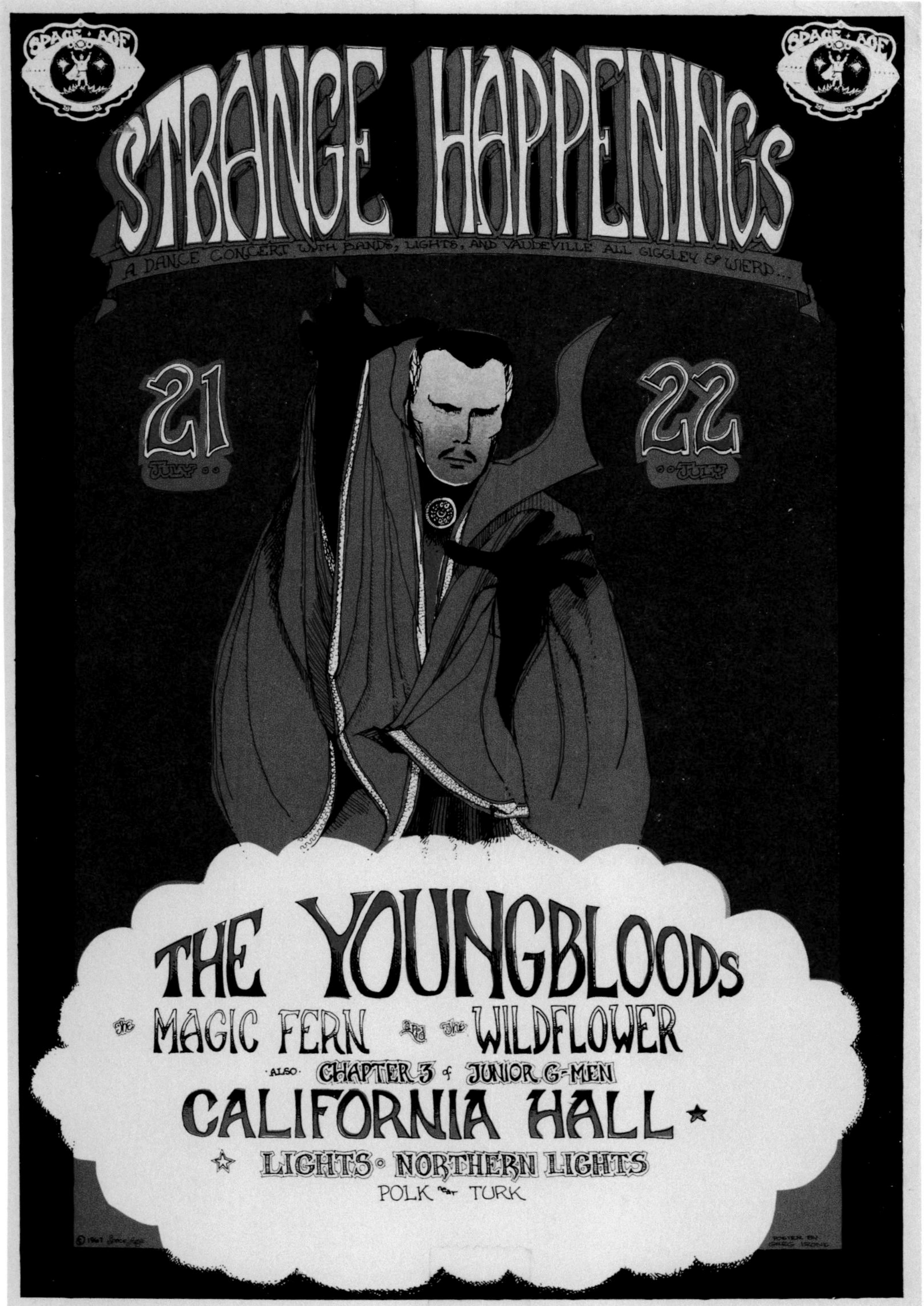
SPACE AGE
SPACE AGE
STRANGE HAPPENINGS
A DANCE CONCERT WITH BANDS, LIGHTS, AND VAUDEVILLE ALL GIGGLEY & WIERD...
21 JULY
22 JULY
THE YOUNGBLOODS
the MAGIC FERN and the WILDFLOWER
ALSO CHAPTER 3 of JUNIOR G-MEN
CALIFORNIA HALL
LIGHTS NORTHERN LIGHTS
POLK near TURK
© 1967 Space Age
POSTER BY GREG IRONS

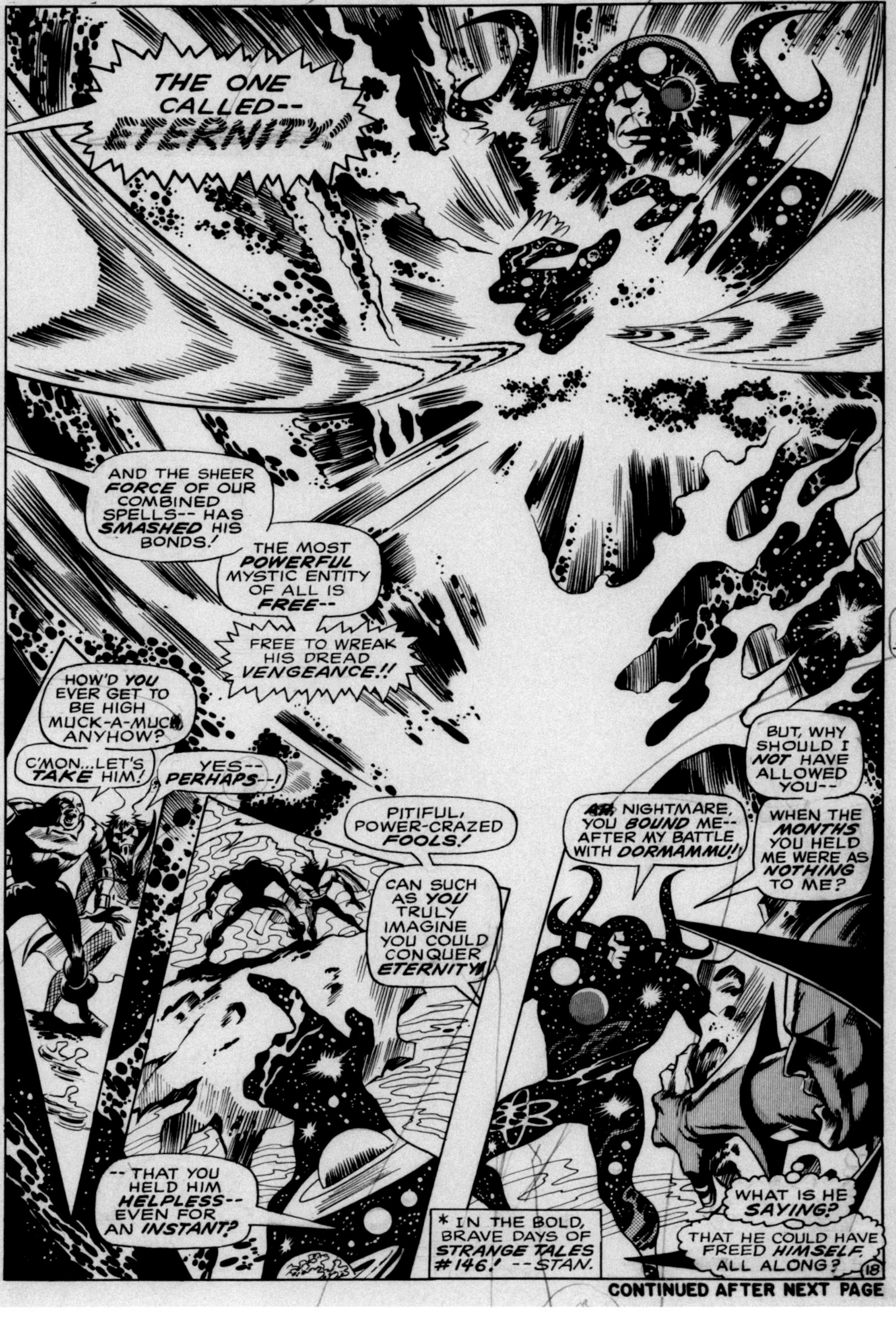
THE ONE CALLED-- ETERNITY!
AND THE SHEER FORCE OF OUR COMBINED SPELLS-- HAS SMASHED HIS BONDS!
THE MOST POWERFUL MYSTIC ENTITY OF ALL IS FREE--
FREE TO WREAK HIS DREAD VENGEANCE!!
HOW'D YOU EVER GET TO BE HIGH MUCK-A-MUCK ANYHOW?
C'MON...LET'S TAKE HIM!
YES-- PERHAPS--!
PITIFUL, POWER-CRAZED FOOLS!
CAN SUCH AS YOU TRULY IMAGINE YOU COULD CONQUER ETERNITY!
--THAT YOU HELD HIM HELPLESS-- EVEN FOR AN INSTANT?
AH, NIGHTMARE, YOU BOUND ME-- AFTER MY BATTLE WITH DORMAMMU!*
BUT, WHY SHOULD I NOT HAVE ALLOWED YOU--
WHEN THE MONTHS YOU HELD ME WERE AS NOTHING TO ME?
* IN THE BOLD, BRAVE DAYS OF STRANGE TALES #146! --STAN.
WHAT IS HE SAYING?
THAT HE COULD HAVE FREED HIMSELF, ALL ALONG?
18

CONTINUED AFTER NEXT PAGE

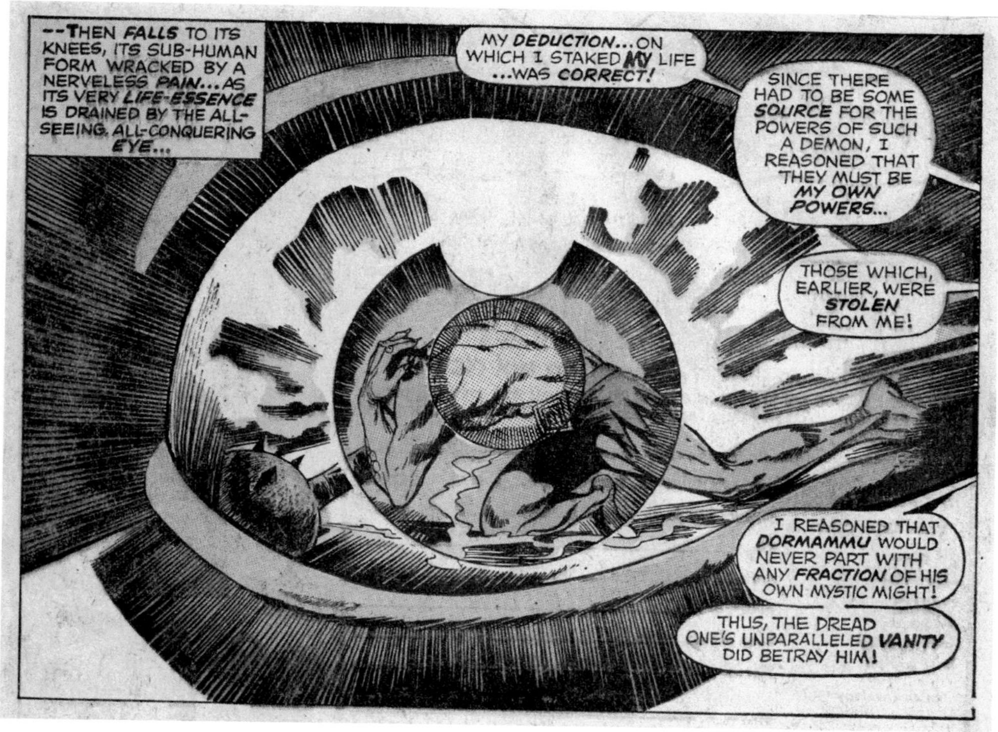
--THEN FALLS TO ITS KNEES, ITS SUB-HUMAN FORM WRACKED BY A NERVELESS PAIN...AS ITS VERY LIFE-ESSENCE IS DRAINED BY THE ALL-SEEING, ALL-CONQUERING EYE...
MY DEDUCTION...ON WHICH I STAKED MY LIFE ...WAS CORRECT!
SINCE THERE HAD TO BE SOME SOURCE FOR THE POWERS OF SUCH A DEMON, I REASONED THAT THEY MUST BE MY OWN POWERS...
THOSE WHICH, EARLIER, WERE STOLEN FROM ME!
I REASONED THAT DORMAMMU WOULD NEVER PART WITH ANY FRACTION OF HIS OWN MYSTIC MIGHT!
THUS, THE DREAD ONE'S UNPARALLELED VANITY DID BETRAY HIM!

A LONG, STRANGE TRIP

(Opposite) Original interior art, Dr. Strange *No. 182; script, Roy Thomas; pencils, Gene Colan; inks, Tom Palmer; September 1969.* "I'm not aware that any of the artists took drugs.... These guys were family men, hardworking guys, and they were simply that talented. Almost any of them could have been major movie directors. When an artist draws a panel, he has the widest choice. He can make it a close-up shot, a long shot, an overhead shot, a strange angle, a head-on shot. And they would make these creative decisions quickly and under major deadline pressure. Drugs? I don't think they would have survived." —Stan Lee

DR. STRANGE No. 172

(Above) Interior, "... I, Dormammu!"; script, Roy Thomas; pencils, Gene Colan; inks, Tom Palmer; September 1968. While many fine artists followed Ditko on Dr. Strange, Gene Colan's ink-rich, mysterious style perfectly suited the material. His visual flourishes —such as this panel of Strange's mystic "eye"—were the hallmark of the unique mystical world he created.

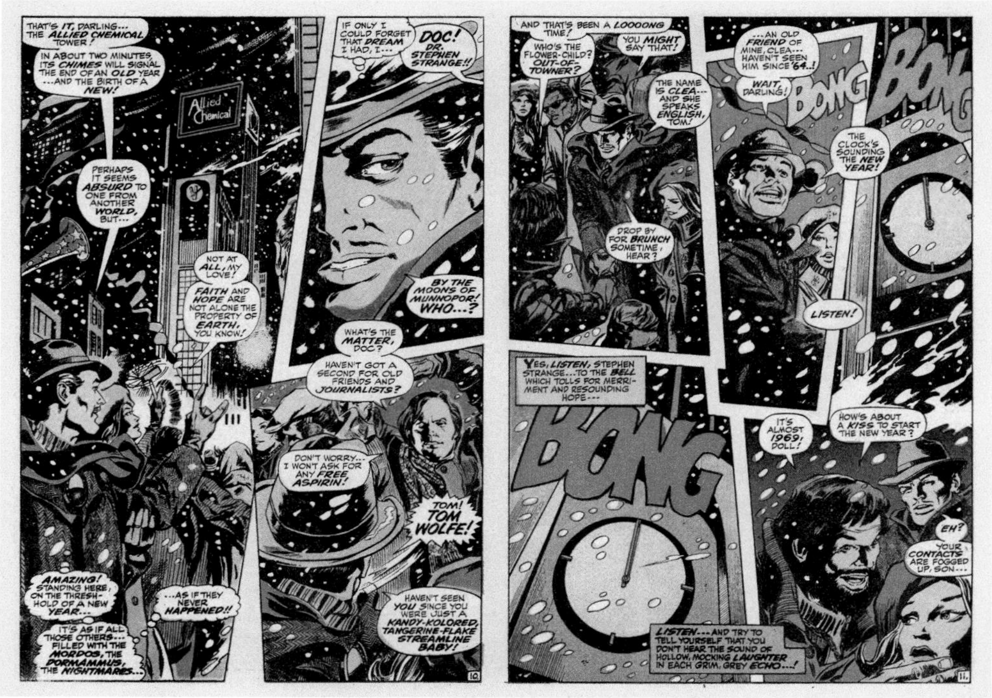
THAT'S IT, DARLING... THE ALLIED CHEMICAL TOWER!
IN ABOUT TWO MINUTES, ITS CHIMES WILL SIGNAL THE END OF AN OLD YEAR ...AND THE BIRTH OF A NEW!
Allied Chemical
PERHAPS IT SEEMS ABSURD TO ONE FROM ANOTHER WORLD, BUT...
NOT AT ALL, MY LOVE!
FAITH AND HOPE ARE NOT ALONE THE PROPERTY OF EARTH, YOU KNOW!
AMAZING! STANDING HERE, ON THE THRESH-HOLD OF A NEW YEAR...
IT'S AS IF ALL THOSE OTHERS... FILLED WITH THE MORDOS, THE DORMAMMUS, THE NIGHTMARES...
...AS IF THEY NEVER HAPPENED!!
IF ONLY I COULD FORGET THAT DREAM I HAD, I...
DOC! DR. STEPHEN STRANGE!!
BY THE MOONS OF MUNNOPOR! WHO...?
WHAT'S THE MATTER, DOC?
HAVEN'T GOT A SECOND FOR OLD FRIENDS AND JOURNALISTS?
DON'T WORRY... I WON'T ASK FOR ANY FREE ASPIRIN!
TOM! TOM WOLFE!
HAVEN'T SEEN YOU SINCE YOU WERE JUST A KANDY-KOLORED, TANGERINE-FLAKE STREAMLINE BABY!
10
AND THAT'S BEEN A LOOOONG TIME!
WHO'S THE FLOWER-CHILD? OUT-OF-TOWNER?
YOU MIGHT SAY THAT!
THE NAME IS CLEA... AND SHE SPEAKS ENGLISH, TOM!
DROP BY FOR BRUNCH SOMETIME, HEAR?
...AN OLD FRIEND OF MINE, CLEA... HAVEN'T SEEN HIM SINCE '64..!
WAIT, DARLING!
BONG
BONG
THE CLOCK'S SOUNDING THE NEW YEAR!
LISTEN!
YES, LISTEN, STEPHEN STRANGE... TO THE BELL WHICH TOLLS FOR MERRIMENT AND RESOUNDING HOPE---
BONG
IT'S ALMOST 1969, DOLL!
HOW'S ABOUT A KISS TO START THE NEW YEAR?
EH?
YOUR CONTACTS ARE FOGGED UP, SON...
LISTEN--- AND TRY TO TELL YOURSELF THAT YOU DON'T HEAR THE SOUND OF HOLLOW, MOCKING LAUGHTER IN EACH GRIM, GREY ECHO...!
11

DR. STRANGE No. 180

(Above) Interior, "Eternity, Eternity!"; script, Roy Thomas; pencils, Gene Colan; inks, Tom Palmer; May 1969. In journalist Tom Wolfe's 1968 book *The Electric Kool-Aid Acid Test*, the author discusses Marvel comics and, in particular, Ditko's Dr. Strange. After correspondence with him, Roy Thomas gave Wolfe a cameo!

STRANGER TALES

(Right) Vinyl record, Pink Floyd, A Saucerful of Secrets*; design, Hipgnosis; including art, Marie Severin; EMI (U.K.)/Tower Records (USA); 1968.* Revered by musicians of the day, Dr. Strange was the subject of songs, and even featured on the occasional album cover. Marie Severin's interpretation was fodder for the British design group Hipgnosis, as they designed Pink Floyd's second album.

STRANGE TALES No. 158

(Opposite) Interior, "The Sands of Death!"; script, Roy Thomas; pencils, Marie Severin; inks, Herb Trimpe; July 1967.

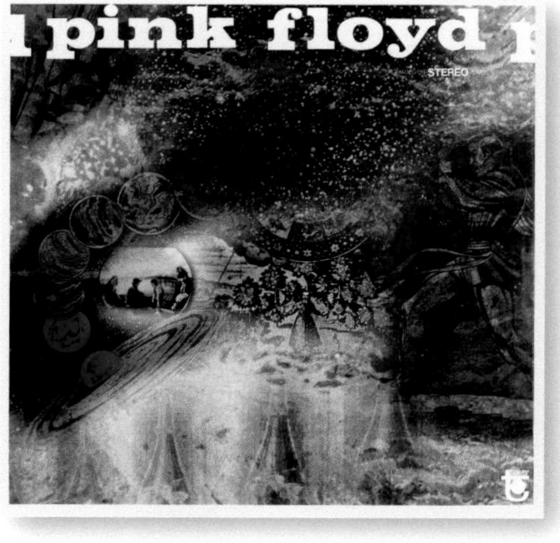
pink floyd
STEREO

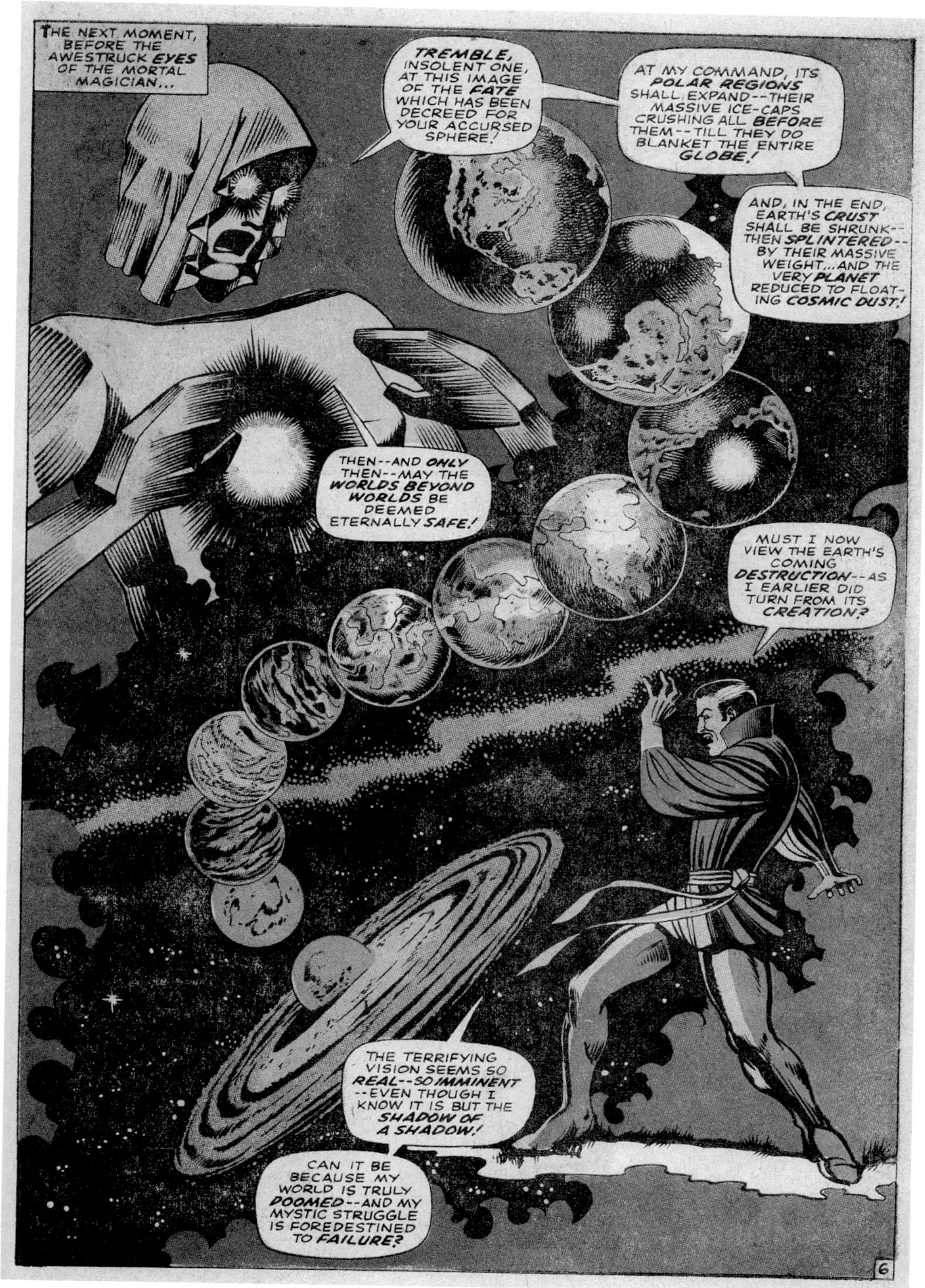
THE NEXT MOMENT, BEFORE THE AWESTRUCK EYES OF THE MORTAL MAGICIAN...
TREMBLE, INSOLENT ONE, AT THIS IMAGE OF THE FATE WHICH HAS BEEN DECREED FOR YOUR ACCURSED SPHERE!
AT MY COMMAND, ITS POLAR REGIONS SHALL EXPAND--THEIR MASSIVE ICE-CAPS CRUSHING ALL BEFORE THEM--TILL THEY DO BLANKET THE ENTIRE GLOBE!
AND, IN THE END, EARTH'S CRUST SHALL BE SHRUNK--THEN SPLINTERED--BY THEIR MASSIVE WEIGHT...AND THE VERY PLANET REDUCED TO FLOATING COSMIC DUST!
THEN--AND ONLY THEN--MAY THE WORLDS BEYOND WORLDS BE DEEMED ETERNALLY SAFE!
MUST I NOW VIEW THE EARTH'S COMING DESTRUCTION--AS I EARLIER DID TURN FROM ITS CREATION?
THE TERRIFYING VISION SEEMS SO REAL--SO IMMINENT--EVEN THOUGH I KNOW IT IS BUT THE SHADOW OF A SHADOW!
CAN IT BE BECAUSE MY WORLD IS TRULY DOOMED--AND MY MYSTIC STRUGGLE IS FOREDESTINED TO FAILURE?
6

X-MEN No. 62

(Below) Interior color guides, "Strangers... in a Savage Land!"; script, Roy Thomas; pencils, Neal Adams; inks, Tom Palmer; November 1969. Color guides were part of the comic book production process before computer coloring was invented. A Photostat of the original art page was produced — usually comic book size — and the colorist would color the page by hand, indicating to the printers through a letter and number code the color gradation they wanted.

X-MEN No. 57

(Opposite) Interior, "The Sentinels Live!"; script, Roy Thomas; pencils, Neal Adams; inks, Tom Palmer; June 1969. Neal Adams was a young, innovative artist who made a name for himself applying his more realistic, advertising illustration–influenced style on DC's super hero books. On this page Adams arranges panels to create movement as the Beast falls. Thomas and Adams give the strip a very different look, one not of this Earth, yet more realistic and familiar than ever.

X-MEN No. 58

(Following spread) Interior, "Mission Murder!"; script, Roy Thomas; pencils, Neal Adams; inks, Tom Palmer; July 1969.

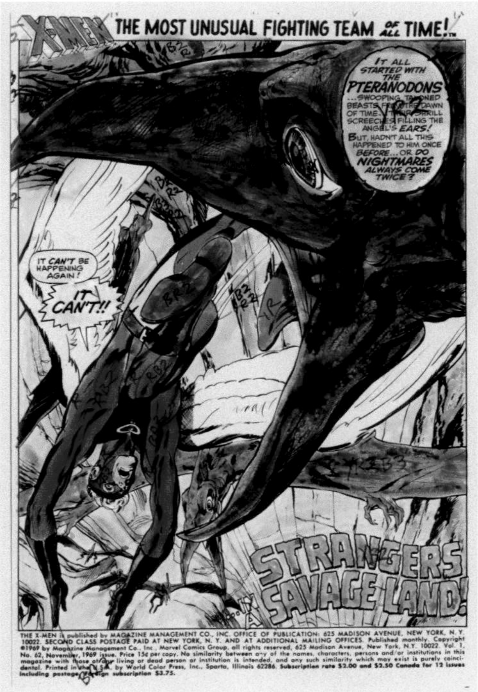
X-MEN
THE MOST UNUSUAL FIGHTING TEAM OF ALL TIME!
IT CAN'T BE HAPPENING AGAIN!
IT CAN'T!!
STRANGERS SAVAGE LAND!

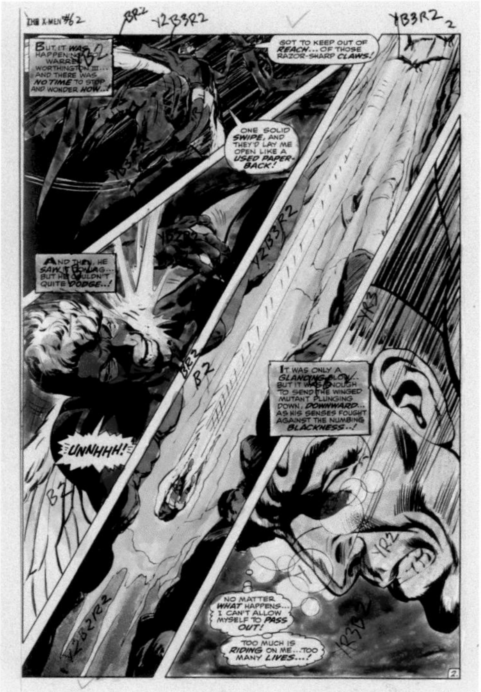
GOT TO KEEP OUT OF REACH... OF THOSE RAZOR-SHARP CLAWS!
ONE SOLID SWIPE, AND THEY'D LAY ME OPEN LIKE A USED PAPER-BACK!
UNNHHH!
NO MATTER WHAT HAPPENS... I CAN'T ALLOW MYSELF TO PASS OUT!
TOO MUCH IS RIDING ON ME... TOO MANY LIVES...!

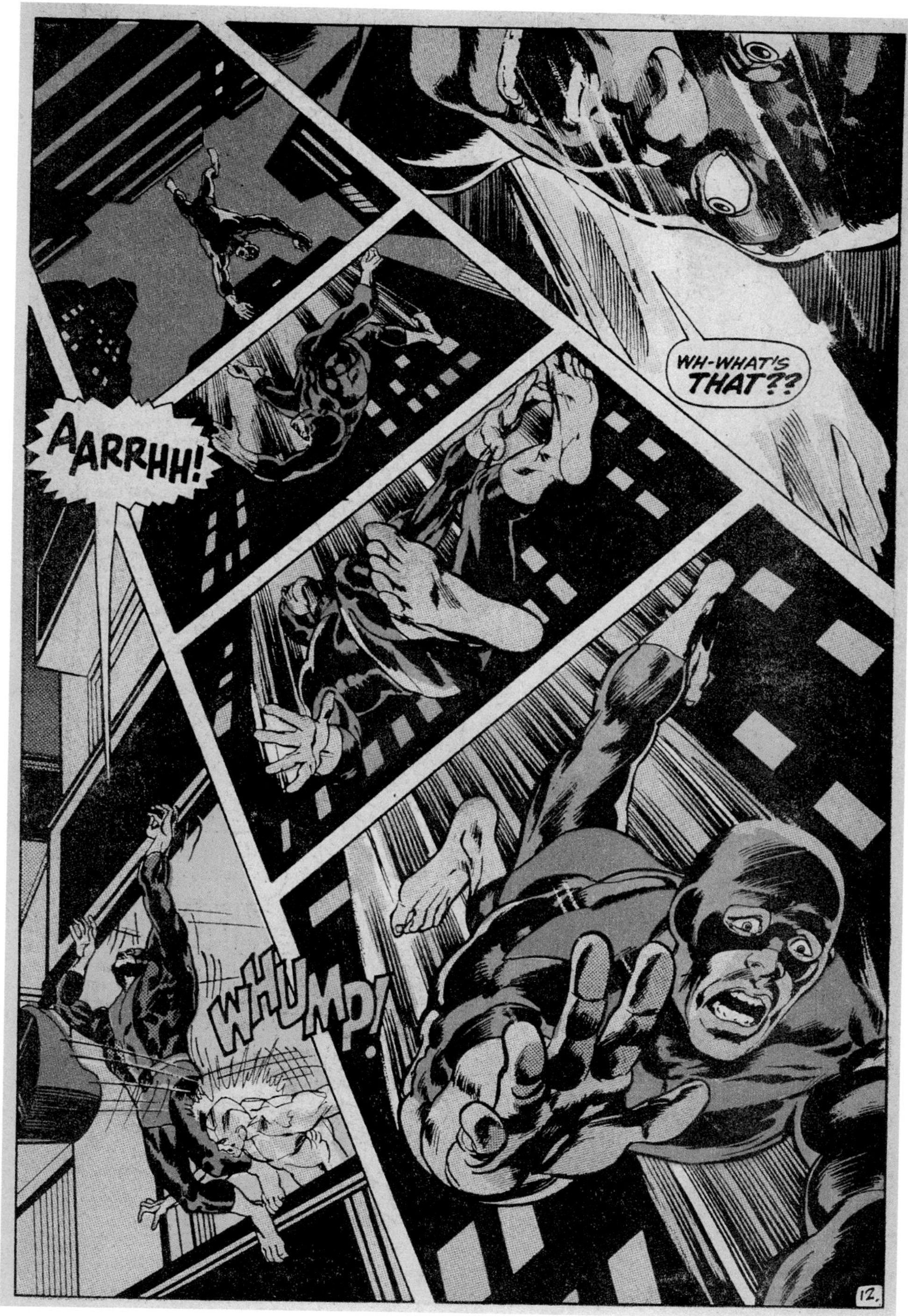
AARRHH!
WH-WHAT'S THAT??
WHUMP!
12.

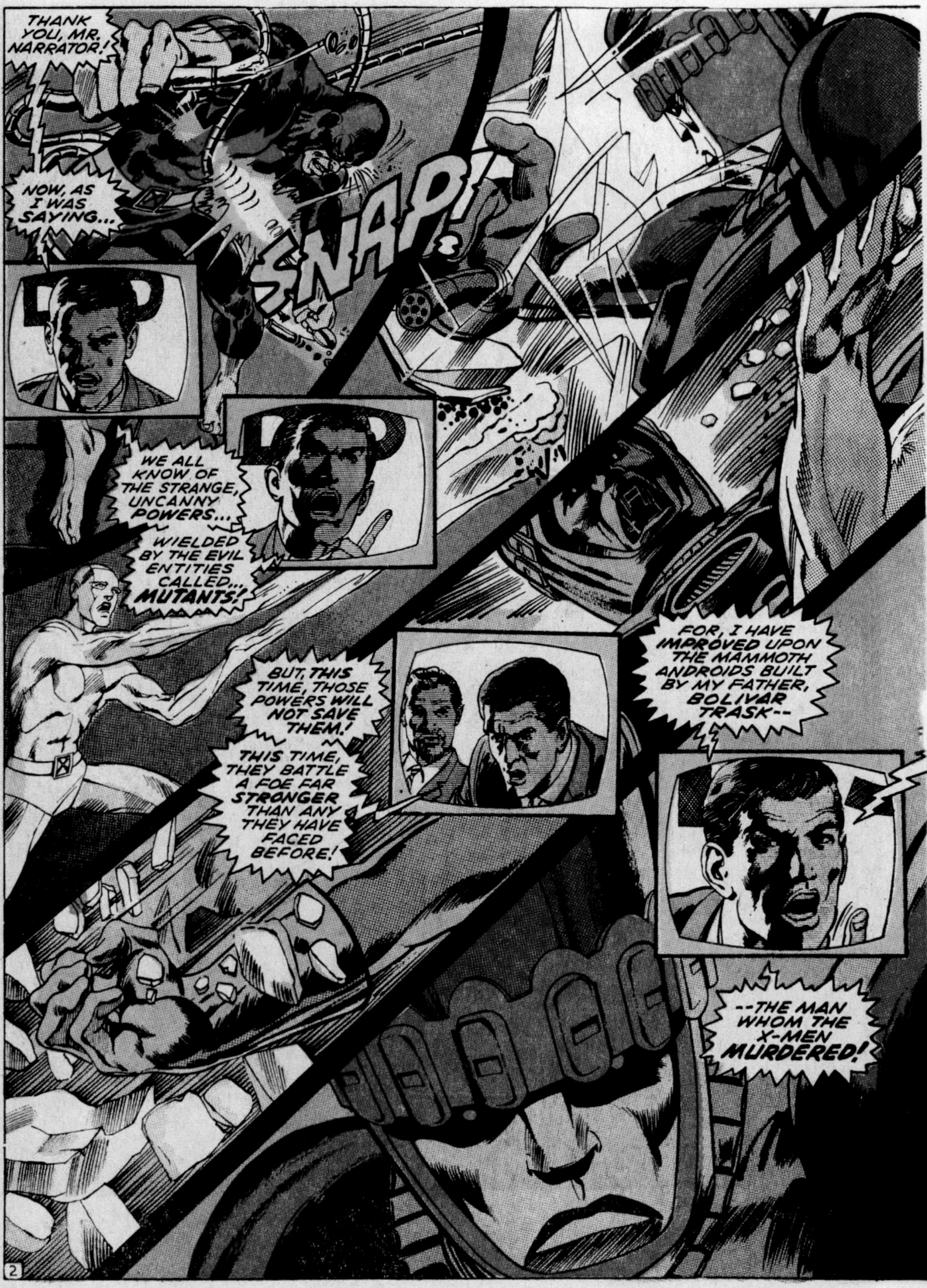

THANK YOU, MR. NARRATOR!
NOW, AS I WAS SAYING...
SNAP!
WE ALL KNOW OF THE STRANGE, UNCANNY POWERS...
WIELDED BY THE EVIL ENTITIES CALLED... MUTANTS!
BUT, THIS TIME, THOSE POWERS WILL NOT SAVE THEM!
THIS TIME, THEY BATTLE A FOE FAR STRONGER THAN ANY THEY HAVE FACED BEFORE!
FOR, I HAVE IMPROVED UPON THE MAMMOTH ANDROIDS BUILT BY MY FATHER, BOLIVAR TRASK--
--THE MAN WHOM THE X-MEN MURDERED!

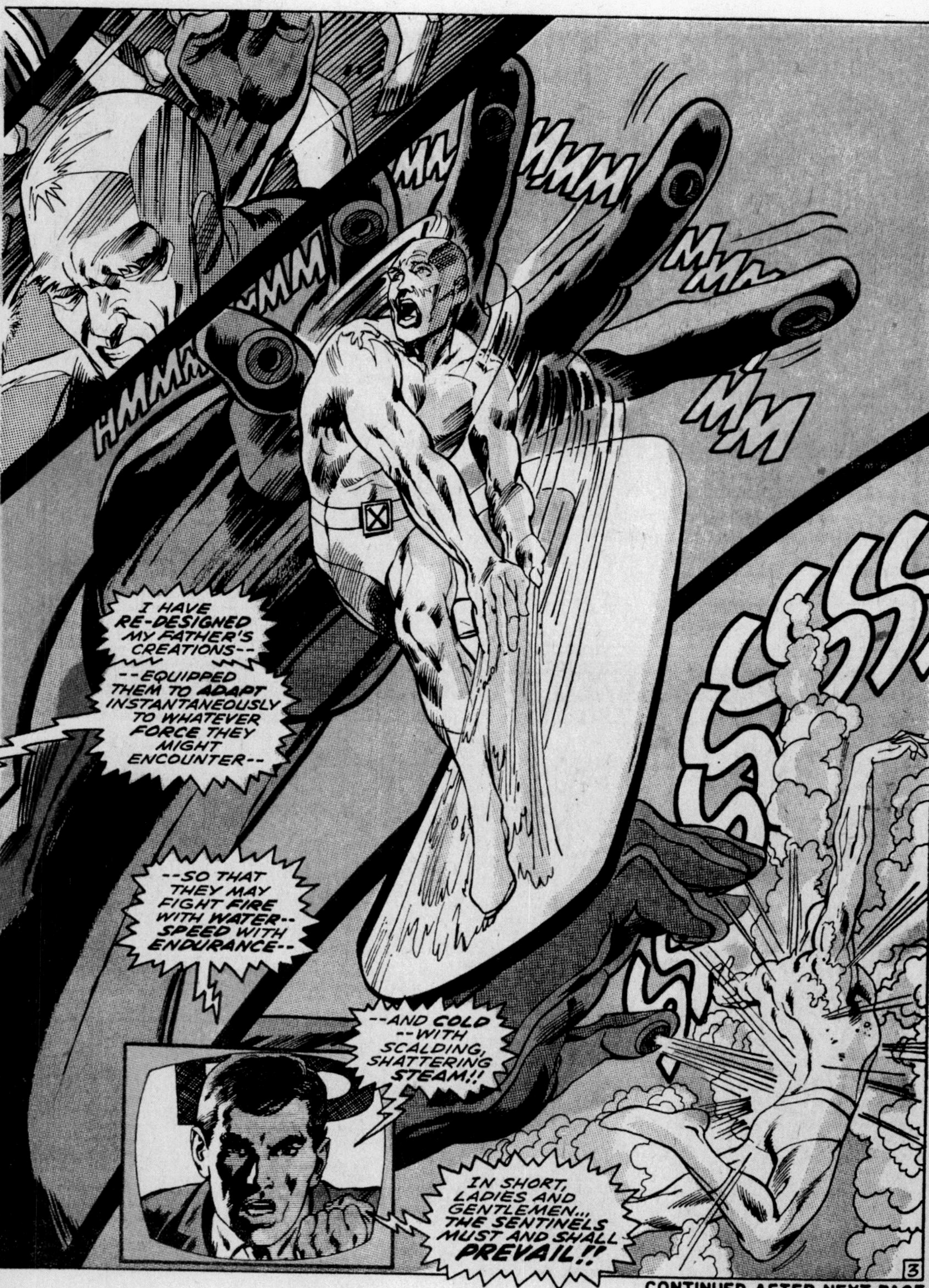
HMMMMMMMMMMMMMMMMMM
I HAVE RE-DESIGNED MY FATHER'S CREATIONS--
--EQUIPPED THEM TO ADAPT INSTANTANEOUSLY TO WHATEVER FORCE THEY MIGHT ENCOUNTER--
--SO THAT THEY MAY FIGHT FIRE WITH WATER-- SPEED WITH ENDURANCE--
--AND COLD --WITH SCALDING, SHATTERING STEAM!!
SSSSS
IN SHORT, LADIES AND GENTLEMEN... THE SENTINELS MUST AND SHALL PREVAIL!!
3

CONTINUED AFTER NEXT PAGE

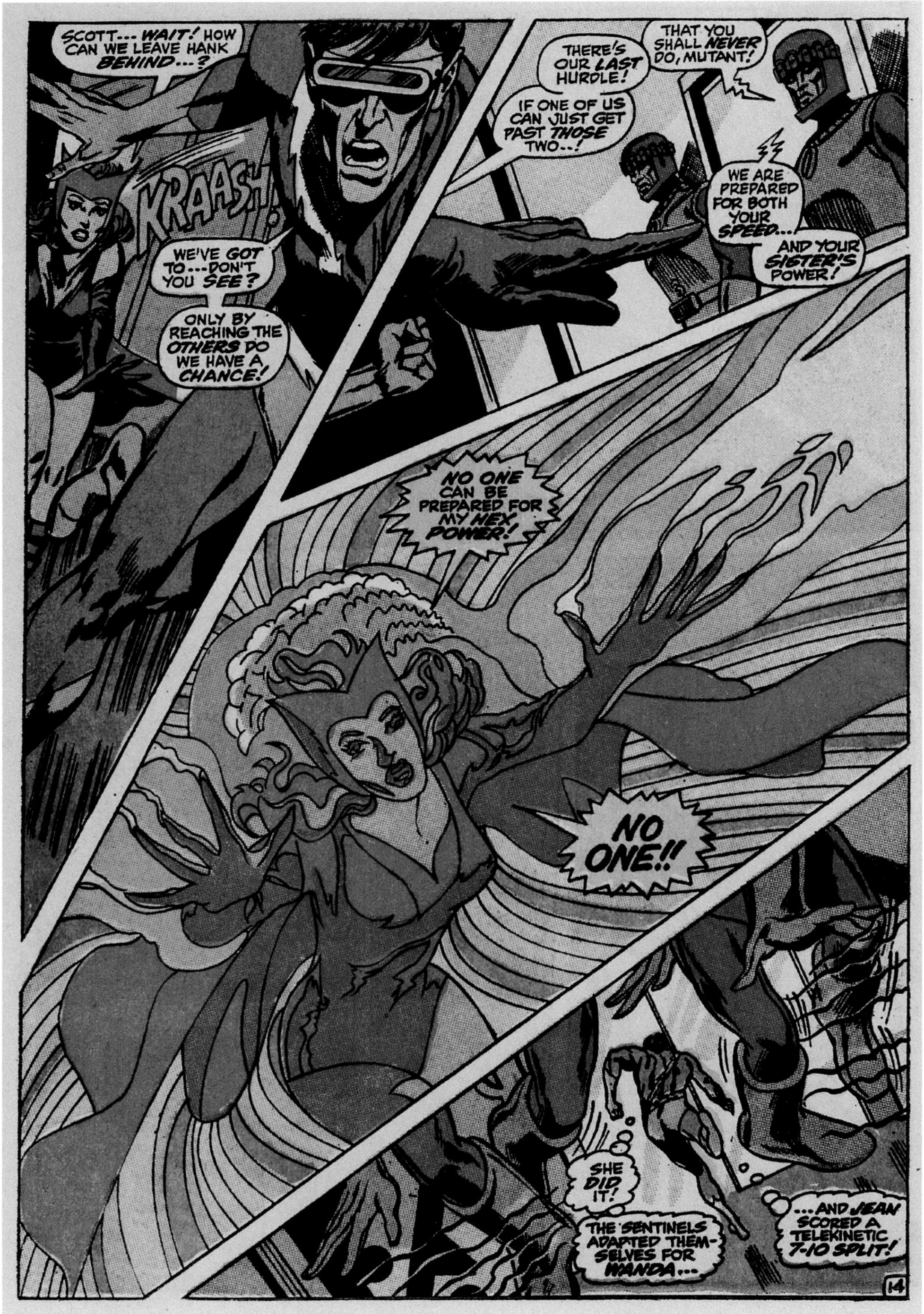
SCOTT... WAIT! HOW CAN WE LEAVE HANK BEHIND...?
KRAASH!
WE'VE GOT TO... DON'T YOU SEE?
ONLY BY REACHING THE OTHERS DO WE HAVE A CHANCE!
THERE'S OUR LAST HURDLE!
IF ONE OF US CAN JUST GET PAST THOSE TWO..!
THAT YOU SHALL NEVER DO, MUTANT!
WE ARE PREPARED FOR BOTH YOUR SPEED...
AND YOUR SISTER'S POWER!
NO ONE CAN BE PREPARED FOR MY HEX POWER!
NO ONE!!
SHE DID IT!
THE SENTINELS ADAPTED THEMSELVES FOR WANDA...
...AND JEAN SCORED A TELEKINETIC 7-10 SPLIT!
14

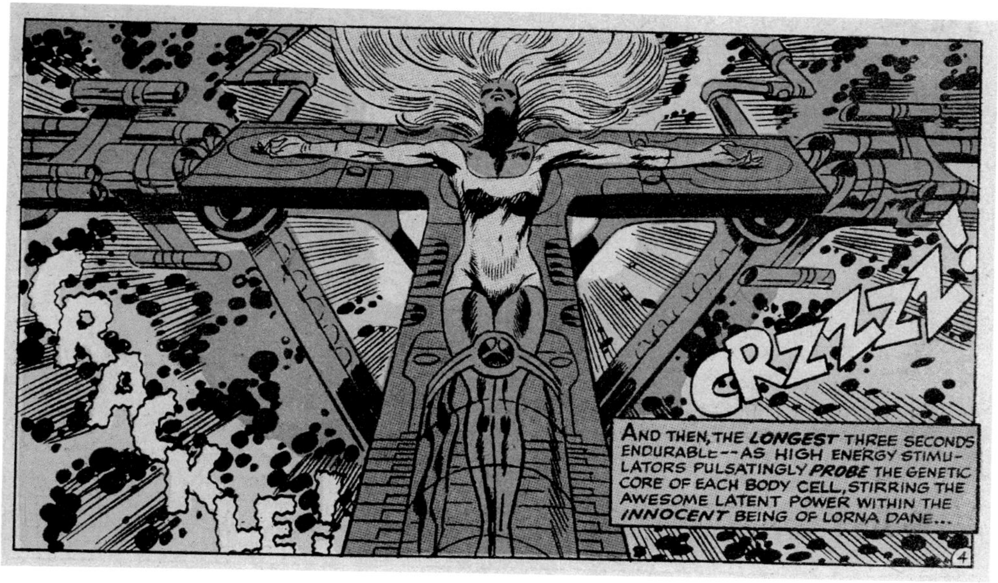
CRACKLE!
CRZZZZN!
AND THEN, THE LONGEST THREE SECONDS ENDURABLE--AS HIGH ENERGY STIMULATORS PULSATINGLY PROBE THE GENETIC CORE OF EACH BODY CELL, STIRRING THE AWESOME LATENT POWER WITHIN THE INNOCENT BEING OF LORNA DANE...
4

X-MEN No. 59

(Opposite) Interior, "Do or Die, Baby!"; script, Roy Thomas; pencils, Neal Adams; inks, Tom Palmer; August 1969. After a meeting with Marvel's young phenom, Jim Steranko, Adams decided to try out the Marvel approach, which brought him added freedom in storytelling. Here the Scarlet Witch displays her power dramatically, and we see that a small comic book panel was not big enough!

X-MEN No. 50

(Above) Interior, "City of Mutants!"; script, Arnold Drake; pencils, Jim Steranko; inks, John Tartaglione; November 1968.

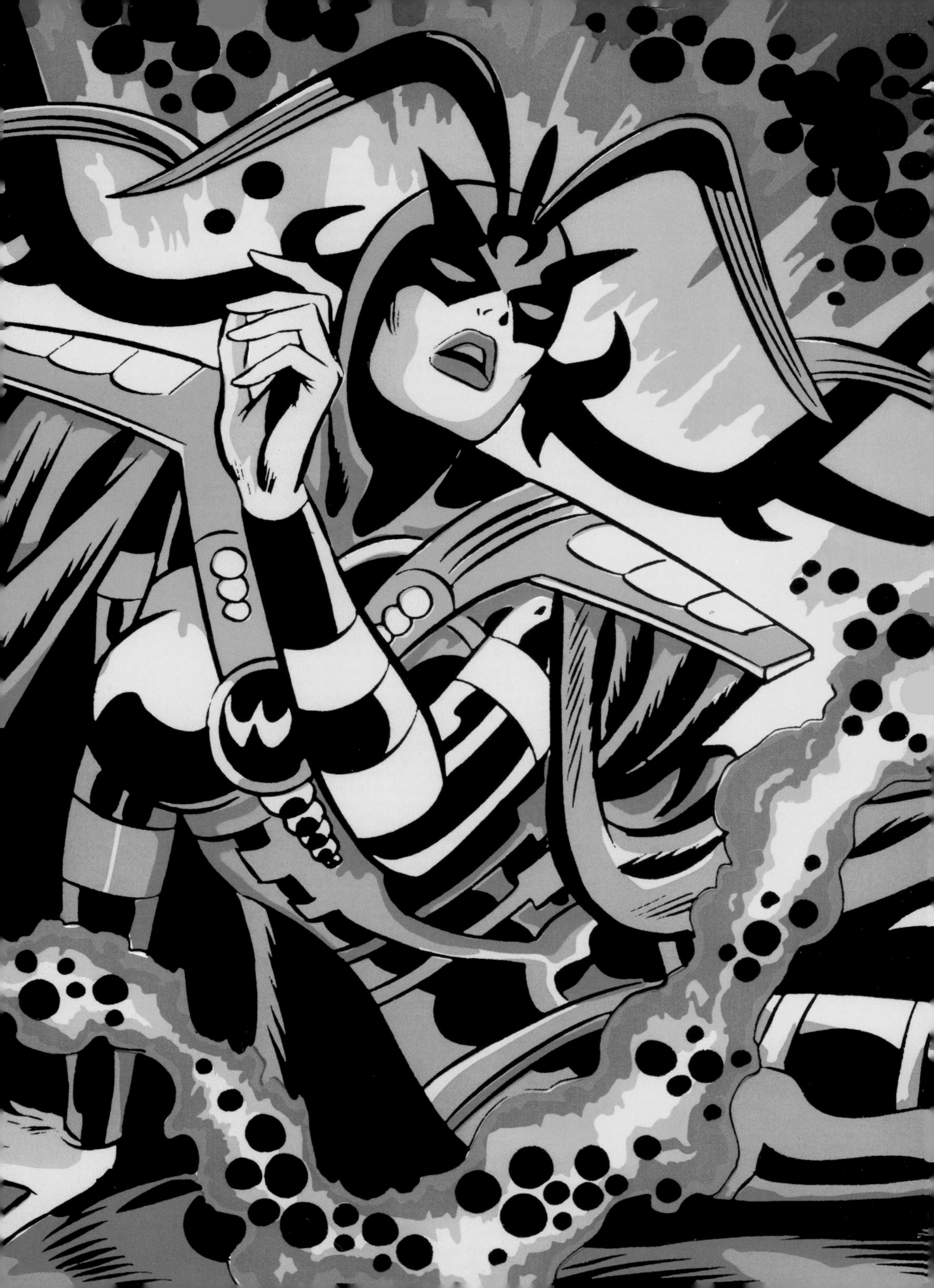

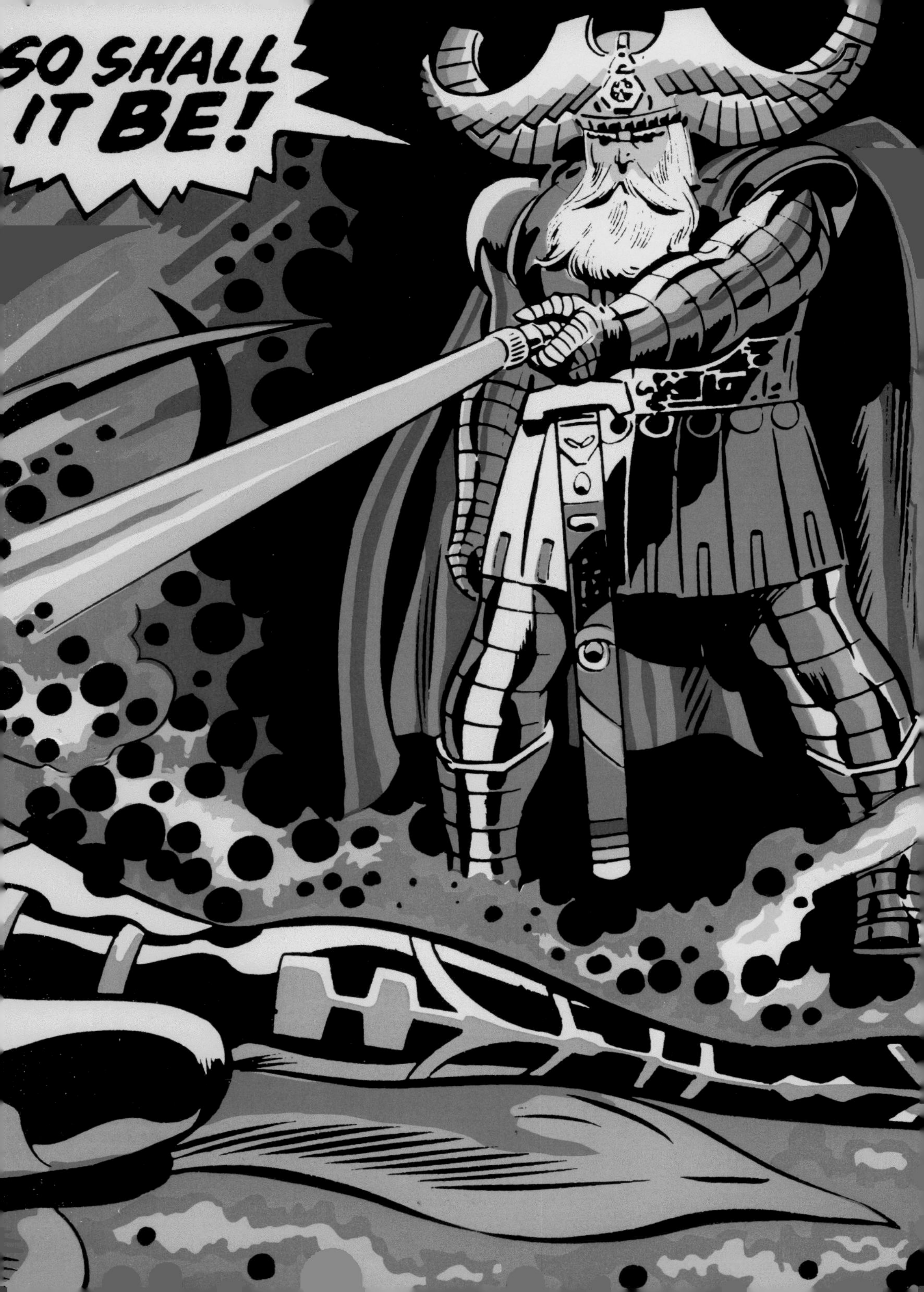
SO SHALL IT BE!

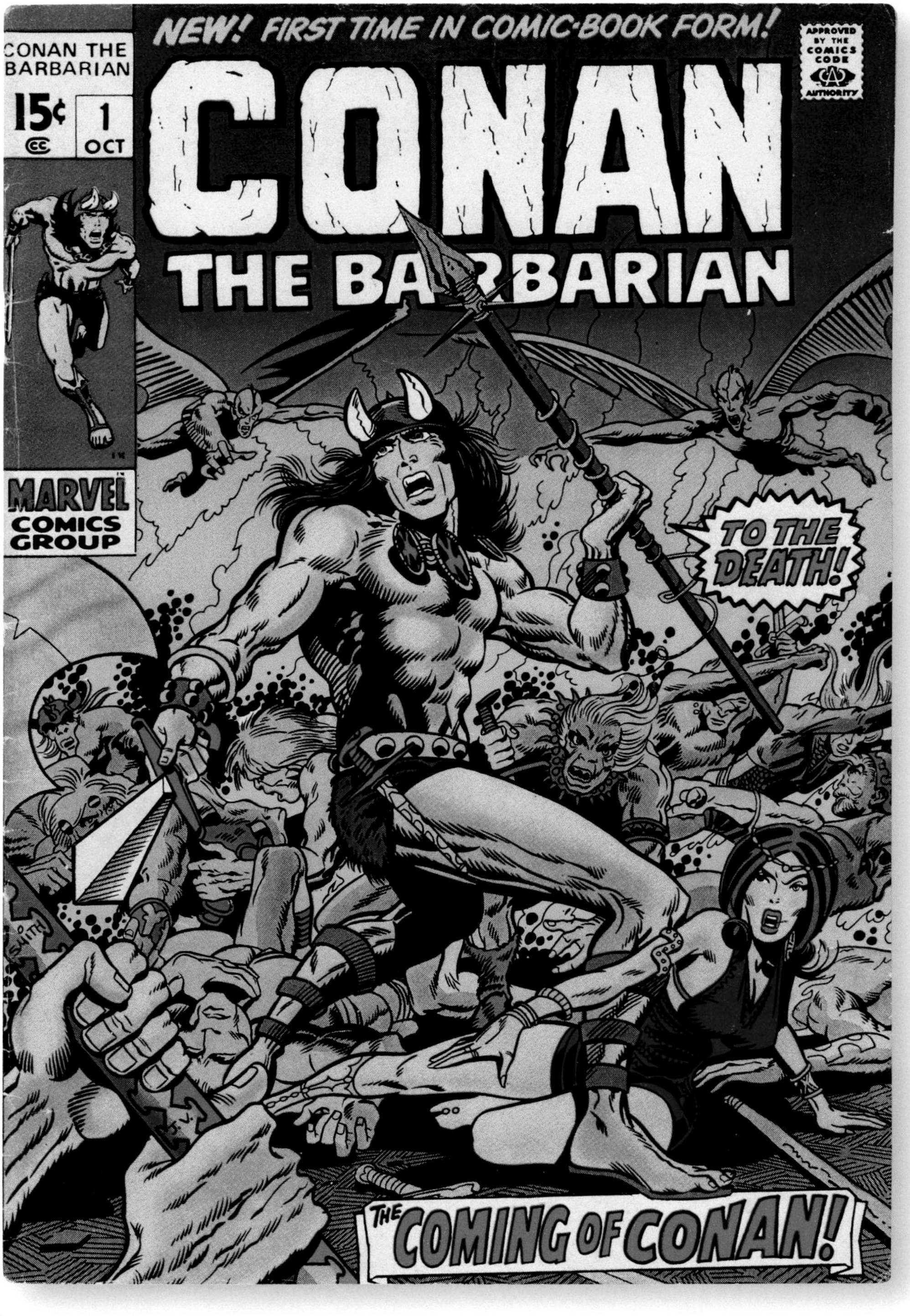
NEW! FIRST TIME IN COMIC-BOOK FORM!
CONAN THE BARBARIAN
15¢
1
OCT
APPROVED BY THE COMICS CODE AUTHORITY
CONAN
THE BARBARIAN
MARVEL COMICS GROUP
TO THE DEATH!
THE COMING OF CONAN!

Marvel — Phase Two
THE BRONZE AGE 1970–1978

BARBARIANS APLENTY

For the past several years, readers had bombarded Marvel with requests to launch a "sword-and-sorcery" comic — in response to the considerable latter-1960s success of a series of paperback books featuring pulp stories written in the 1930s by Robert E. Howard about a barbarian warrior called Conan the Cimmerian, followed by a slew of paperback imitators. Such hard-bitten heroes tended to inhabit long-lost legendary worlds full of gleaming towers, evil sorcerers, beautiful women, and slavering monsters. After a false start pursuing a lesser sword-and-sorcery creation, Roy Thomas arranged for Marvel to license Conan. *Conan the Barbarian* No. 1 hit the newsstands in the summer of 1970 with script by Thomas and pencils by Barry Smith. Smith, who in the mid-'70s would change his last name to Windsor-Smith, was a young Englishman then living in his native London and trying to obtain a green card so he could return to the United States. After a slow beginning, *Conan* would become one of Marvel's best-selling series of the 1970s and early '80s: first, with Smith's ever more decorative and illustrative Art Nouveau-cum-Kirby approach to storytelling, and then rising to even greater popularity under John Buscema's long tenure.

About that time, Red Wolf, a Native American masked hero, made his debut in *The Avengers*, courtesy of Thomas and Buscema. He would soon receive his own title, but at that time the character was backdated to the Wild West. Westerns were far from a growth industry in the early 1970s, and soon Red Wolf was back cleansing the mean streets of modern-day America. This seesaw approach to the series' setting may be one reason why the *Red Wolf* comic did not long endure.

THE RESURRECTION OF HELA BY ODIN
(Previous spread) Third Eye black light poster; art, Jack Kirby; 1971.

CONAN THE BARBARIAN No. 1
(Opposite) Cover; pencils, Barry Smith; inks, John Verpoorten. October 1970. A momentous month in comics history, October 1970 saw Jack Kirby's first Bronze Age work for DC hit newsstands at the same time as Barry Smith's *Conan* hinted at Marvel's creative expansion.

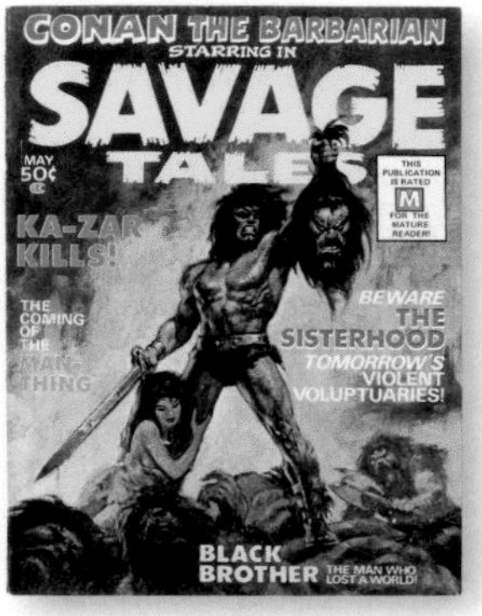
CONAN THE BARBARIAN
STARRING IN
SAVAGE TALES
MAY
50¢
KA-ZAR KILLS!
THE COMING OF THE MAN-THING
BEWARE THE SISTERHOOD
TOMORROW'S VIOLENT VOLUPTUARIES!
BLACK BROTHER
THE MAN WHO LOST A WORLD!

SAVAGE TALES No. 1
(Above) Cover; art, John Buscema; May 1971. The first issue of *Savage Tales* was meant to signal a new decade of more adult fare ("Rated M!") in black-and-white magazines.

AMAZING SPIDER-MAN No. 97
(Below) Interior, "In the Grip of the Goblin!"; script, Stan Lee; pencils, Gil Kane; inks, Frank Giacoia; June 1971. The pill-induced mania of Harry Osborn, as reflected in this hallucinogenic panel, was taking comics places they hadn't been before.

ADVENTURE INTO FEAR No. 15
(Opposite) Original cover art, Frank Brunner, August 1973.

Editor Lee, still intent on expanding the horizons of the comics field, felt that *Spectacular Spider-Man* hadn't had a fair shot two years earlier, so he persuaded Goodman to launch another black-and-white Marvel "magazine"—minus super heroes, this time. *Savage Tales* No. 1 (1971) featured Lee and Buscema on Ka-Zar, Thomas and Smith on Conan, plus three new series. The origin of the Man-Thing, a swamp-monster drawn by superb draftsman Gray Morrow, was an amalgamation of Lee, Thomas, and newcomer Gerry Conway, a 19-year-old New Yorker who was already the author of two science-fiction paperback novels. The violence in *Savage Tales* was only slightly more graphic than in the color comics, but there was some discreet nudity. The cover—a Buscema painting of Conan holding high a severed head—noted that "This Publication Is Rated 'M' for the Mature Reader."

For reasons unknown, however, publisher Goodman decided to cancel *Savage Tales* around the time that first issue went on sale. Lee, angry about the cancellation, bided his time. He wasn't going to let this one go.

MARVEL IS NUMBER ONE

With *Conan the Barbarian,* Marvel had made a leap into the future by delving into the Earth's long-lost past. However, it was in the present that Marvel faced a new and more immediate challenge.

The U.S. Department of Health, Education, and Welfare sent Stan Lee a letter asking if he would use Marvel's comics to warn America's youth about the dangers of drug addiction. Eager to help, Lee and artist Gil Kane, with the input of John Romita, prepared *The Amazing Spider-Man* No. 96 as the start of a three-issue storyline involving the Green Goblin and

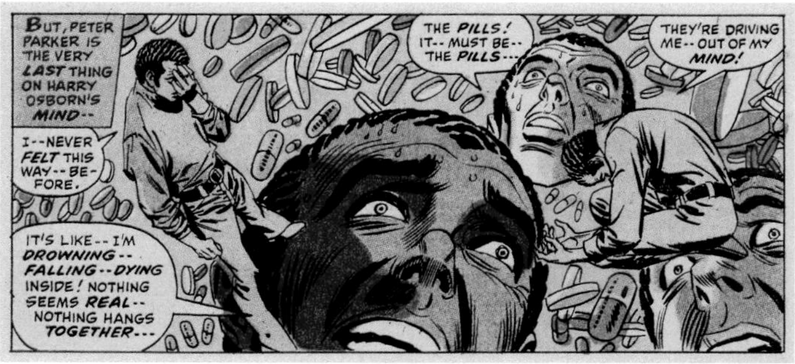
BUT, PETER PARKER IS THE VERY LAST THING ON HARRY OSBORN'S MIND--
I--NEVER FELT THIS WAY--BE-FORE.
THE PILLS! IT--MUST BE--THE PILLS---
THEY'RE DRIVING ME--OUT OF MY MIND!
IT'S LIKE--I'M DROWNING--FALLING--DYING INSIDE! NOTHING SEEMS REAL--NOTHING HANGS TOGETHER---

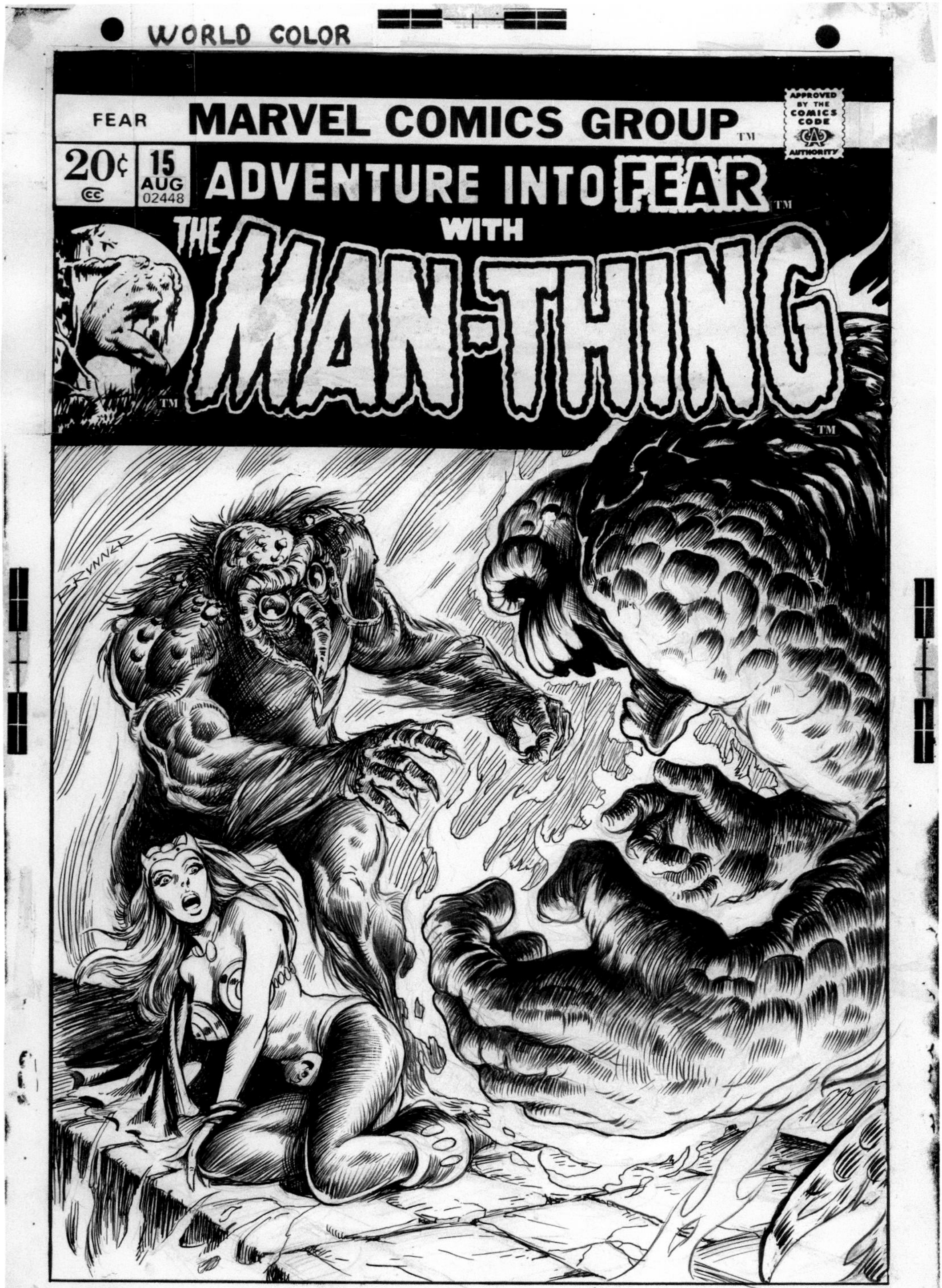
WORLD COLOR
FEAR
MARVEL COMICS GROUP
APPROVED BY THE COMICS CODE AUTHORITY
20¢
15
AUG
02448
ADVENTURE INTO FEAR
THE
WITH
MAN-THING
BRYNNER
7 X 10 1/2
FRANK BRYNNER

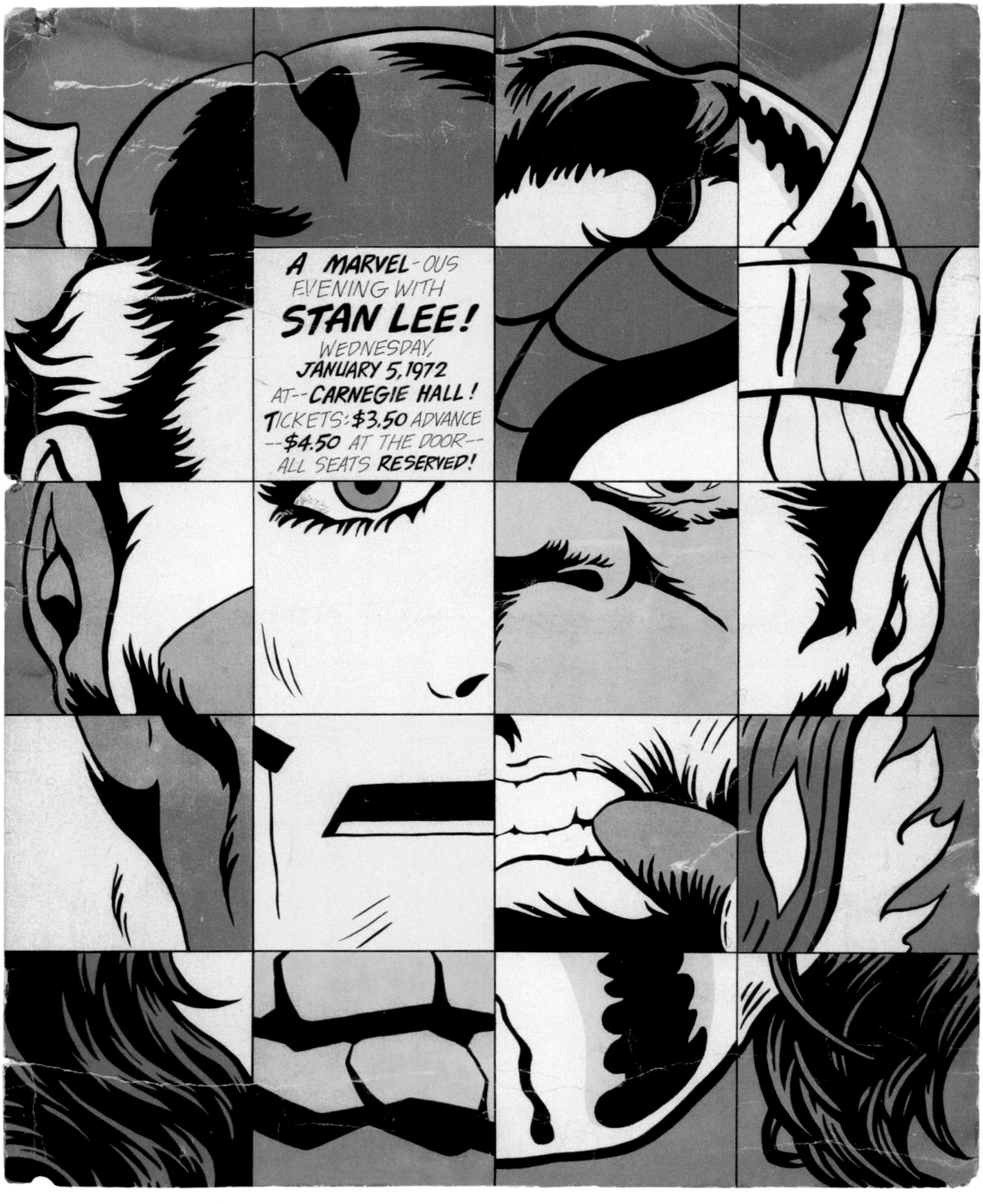
A MARVEL-OUS
EVENING WITH
STAN LEE!
WEDNESDAY,
JANUARY 5, 1972
AT--CARNEGIE HALL!
TICKETS: $3.50 ADVANCE
--$4.50 AT THE DOOR--
ALL SEATS RESERVED!

several college students, including the Goblin's son, who get perilously high on an intentionally unidentified "controlled substance." But, when the story and art were submitted to the Comics Code Authority, Lee was informed that, despite the government's request, the tale could not be printed because the 1954 Code specifically forbade any reference to drugs. Period. End of story.

Lee took his problem to his publisher and was proud that Goodman backed him and put out that issue, and the following two, without the Code seal. There was no backlash from wholesalers, retailers, or the general public... only acclaim for what Marvel was trying to do. The crisis quickly led to a long-needed rewriting of the Code, to bring it in line with a world that had changed greatly in the past 17 years.

The first tangible result of this was Marvel's first vampire story since 1954, as Spider-Man faced Morbius the Living

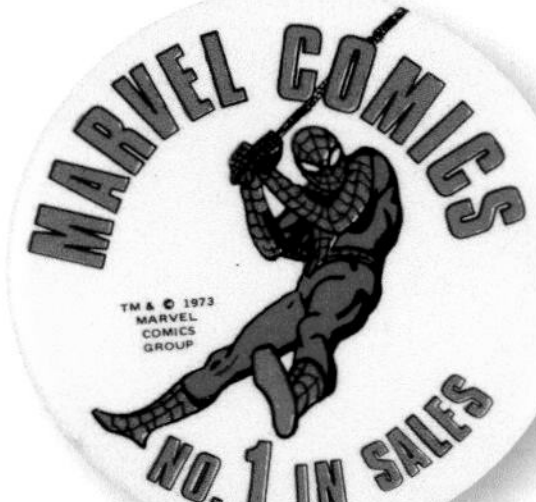
MARVEL COMICS
TM & © 1973 MARVEL COMICS GROUP
NO. 1 IN SALES

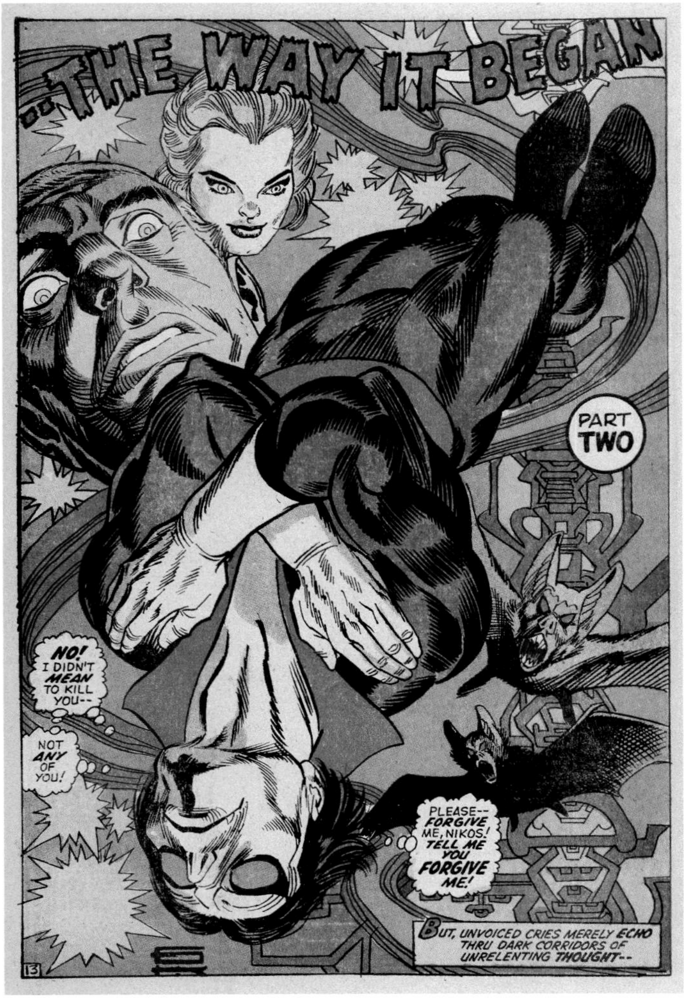
...THE WAY IT BEGAN
PART TWO
NO! I DIDN'T MEAN TO KILL YOU--
NOT ANY OF YOU!
PLEASE-- FORGIVE ME, NIKOS! TELL ME YOU FORGIVE ME!
BUT, UNVOICED CRIES MERELY ECHO THRU DARK CORRIDORS OF UNRELENTING THOUGHT--
13

MARVEL-OUS EVENING

(Opposite) Poster; pencils and inks, George Delmerico; 1972. Carnegie Hall got a makeover as the House of Ideas on January 5, 1972 ("One Night Only!"), with Stan Lee, Spider-Man and friends, the Marvel bullpen, and appearances by director Alain Resnais, author Tom Wolfe, Beach Boy Dennis Wilson, and the Chico Hamilton Players. Delmerico's Modernist poster was a hit.

No. 1 IN SALES

(Above) Promotional button, 1973. The unthinkable occurred in 1972 when little ol' Marvel took the unit sales crown from industry goliath DC—and here's the tchotchke to prove it!

AMAZING SPIDER-MAN No. 102

(Left) Interior, "Vampire at Large!"; script, Roy Thomas; pencils, Gil Kane; inks, Frank Giacoia; November 1971. Marvel's first post-Code vampire, Morbius, took *Amazing Spider-Man* by storm in 1971.

MARVEL PREMIERE
No. 1

(Opposite) Cover; pencils, Gil Kane; inks, Dan Adkins; April 1972. The religious and spiritual subtexts of Warlock were unmistakable, and indicative of Marvel's progressive vision for its comics a decade after the start of the Marvel Age.

Vampire. Actually, Morbius was a science-fictional, super-villainous bloodsucker rather than a classic Dracula type, but no matter: Neither would have been allowed before the Code updating.

Roy Thomas, who wrote the Morbius story, was busy on other fronts during this period, as well. He launched *Kull the Conqueror*, starring another Robert E. Howard sword-and-sorcery hero…developed the Defenders, a group consisting of Dr. Strange, Sub-Mariner, and Hulk…teamed with artist Gil Kane to turn a golden humanoid from *Fantastic Four* into Warlock, the sole resident super hero of a "twin Earth" on the far side of the Sun…and, in *The Avengers*, scripted a nine-issue epic storyline that pitted two alien races from the *FF* series against each other, with "this island Earth" caught in the middle. In large part because of the superlative contribution to four of its segments by artist/coplotter Neal Adams, the "Kree/Skrull War" set the standard for multipart, intercosmic clashes in comics; first-rate artwork by John Buscema and his younger brother Sal, who had begun drawing for Marvel two years earlier, also added considerably to the story arc.

Near the end of 1971, Goodman pulled off a considerable coup with regard to DC Comics—though how much of it was planned in advance and how much was rolling innovation is open to question. By now, the 32-page (minus covers) color comic book sold for 15 cents, up from the 12 cents companies had begun charging in 1962. Overnight, both Marvel and DC increased all their comics to 48 pages (minus covers) for 25 cents: a two-thirds increase in price, for a 50 percent increase in page count. The majority of the pages would be new art and story, with the rest filled with reprints.

However, after only one (at most two) issues of 48-pagers, Goodman suddenly cut back to 32-page comics…now with a cover price of 20 cents. He had brokered a deal whereby retailers would receive a bigger cut of those two dimes, making it likely that Marvel would receive additional space in stores selling comics. "DC's going to take a bath!" he proudly proclaimed to Roy Thomas and production manager John Verpoorten in his office, when announcing his plan to them. DC clung to the larger (and pricier) titles for a year; by the time they dropped to 20-cent comics in late 1972, Marvel had surpassed DC in sales for the first time ever, becoming the world's No. 1 comic book company.

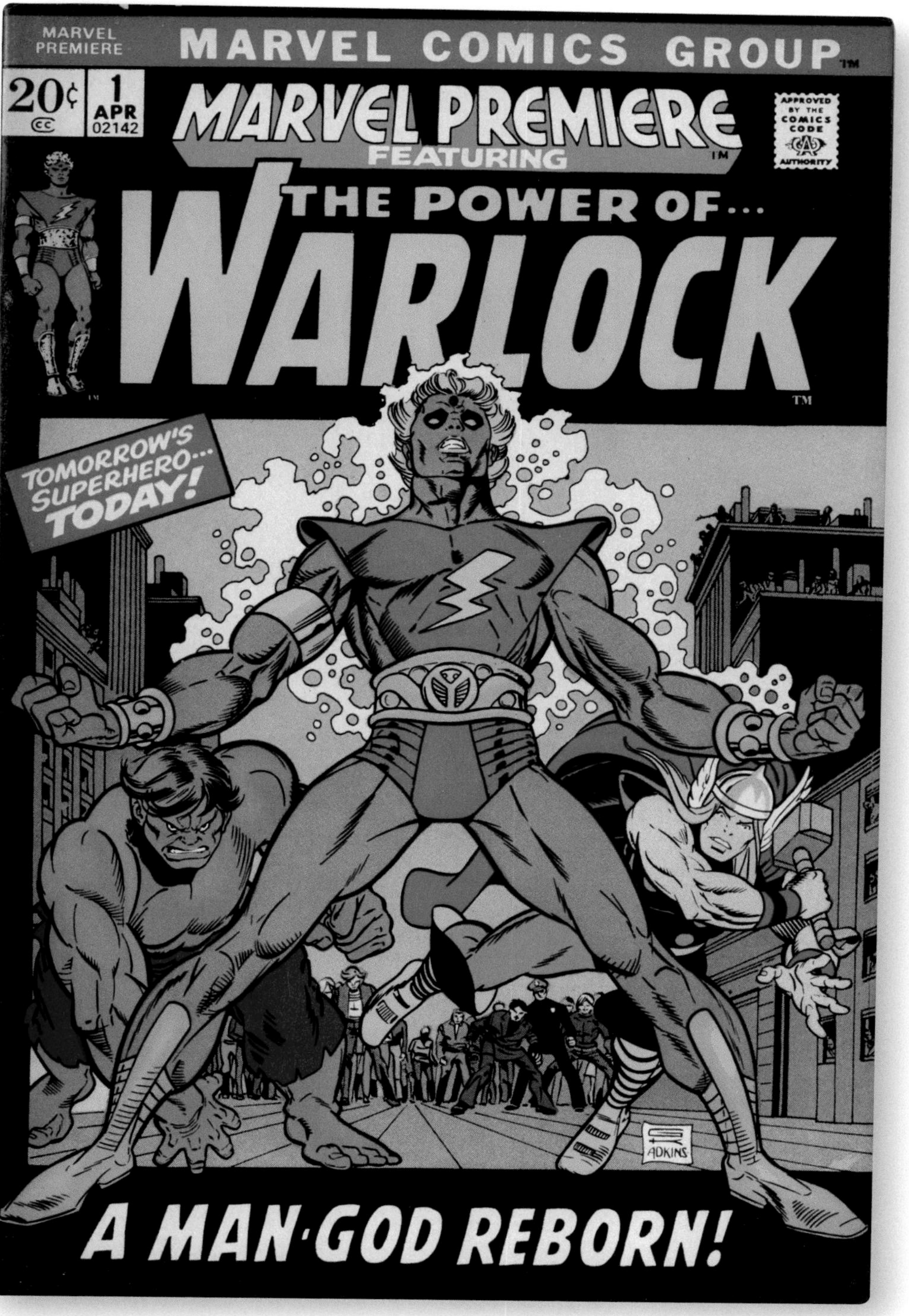
MARVEL PREMIERE
MARVEL COMICS GROUP
20¢
1 APR 02142
MARVEL PREMIERE
FEATURING
THE POWER OF...
WARLOCK
APPROVED BY THE COMICS CODE AUTHORITY
TOMORROW'S SUPERHERO... TODAY!
ADKINS
A MAN·GOD REBORN!

MARVEL SPOTLIGHT No. 5

(Right) Cover; pencils and inks, Mike Ploog; August 1972. Is he alive . . . or dead? Who cares? He's awesome! Reimagined for a post–Hells Angels America, the all-new Ghost Rider's leather-jumpsuit, skull-on-fire, demon-biking debut in *Spotlight* burned rubber toward his destiny as one of the coolest Marvel characters of the decade.

MARVEL SPOTLIGHT
MARVEL COMICS GROUP
20¢ 5 AUG 02120
MARVEL SPOTLIGHT ON...
GHOST RIDER
IS HE ALIVE... OR DEAD?
A LEGEND IS BORN!
THE MOST SUPERNATURAL SUPERHERO OF ALL!

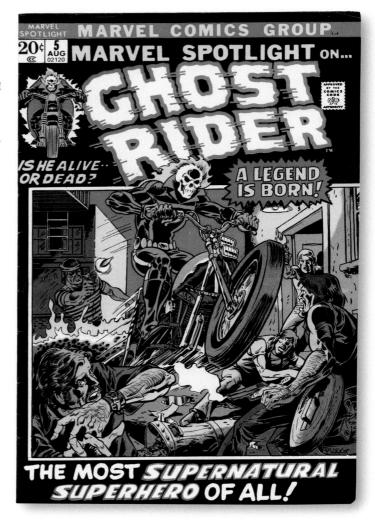

Not all of that could be attributed to the price differential, of course; Marvel had been slowly gaining on DC for the past decade, thanks to the innovative work done since 1961 by Lee, Kirby, Ditko, and others. Now, at last, the Marvel approach had paid off in full.

MARVEL ON THE MOVE

The year 1972 was a big year in the life of Marvel Comics in many other ways, as well.

It began with an "Evening with Stan Lee and Marvel Comics" on January 5—at New York's legendary Carnegie

Hall, no less. A concert promoter named Steve Lemberg had succeeded Don Wallace in controlling merchandising rights to Marvel's heroes, and he planned that big event at one of the world's most famous concert venues primarily to garner publicity for future ventures. The hall was completely sold out, but the unfocused program proved ultimately unsatisfying to some of the Marvel diehards who had filled the seats. Even so, the thing had happened: Marvel had played Carnegie Hall!

Still, the important thing was the comics themselves. On the heels of its first "modern" vampire, the company initiated several new series featuring supernatural creatures that, in

HERO FOR HIRE
MARVEL COMICS GROUP
1 JUNE 02149
20¢
LUKE CAGE, HERO FOR HIRE
APPROVED BY THE COMICS CODE AUTHORITY
SENSATIONAL ORIGIN ISSUE!

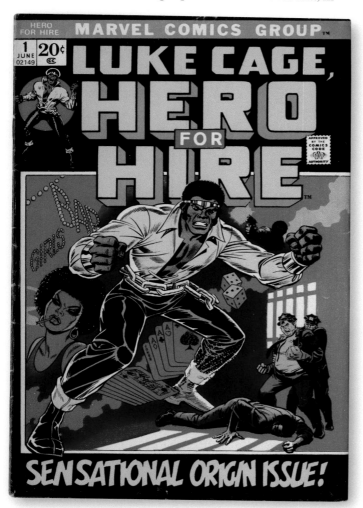

HERO FOR HIRE No. 1
(Left) Cover; pencils and inks, John Romita; June 1972. Sweet Christmas! Whether you call him Hero for Hire, Power Man, or Luke Cage, be sure to do it politely! The guy with the bulletproof skin and gleaming tiara earned Marvel's first ongoing series for an African American hero!

the 1950s, would have been the stuff of stand-alone stories in horror comics; now they were turned into continuing characters. *Marvel Spotlight* introduced Werewolf by Night, showcasing the first Marvel work by Michael Ploog, who drew very much in the style of his recent employer, the legendary Will Eisner, creator of the Spirit. *Tomb of Dracula* soon followed, with exquisite art by Gene Colan; once writer Marv Wolfman and inker Tom Palmer were piped aboard a year later, it became one of Marvel's top-quality titles. A new Ghost Rider, complete with blazing skull, black leather togs, and a fire-spouting motorcycle, was inaugurated by writer Gary Friedrich and artist Ploog. The Man-Thing shambled into his (its?) own series—and even the Beast, from the canceled *X-Men*, grew dark fur over his entire body and seemed as much monster as mutant in a solo feature.

In the wake of the hit film *Shaft*, Lee decided to develop a new African American super hero worthy of starring in his own comic. He, his office brain trust (Romita and Thomas), and writer Archie Goodwin came up with *Hero for Hire*,

DAREDEVIL No. 90
(Below) Interior, "The Sinister Secret of Project Four"; script, Gerry Conway; pencils, Gene Colan; inks, Tom Palmer; August 1972. Ol' Hornhead decamped from Hell's Kitchen to San Francisco for a time, and teamed with Black Widow. Here, the City by the Bay pits the Man Without Fear against Mister Fear.

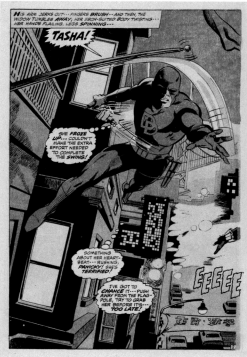

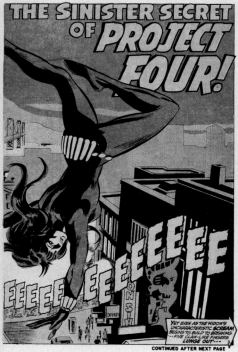

HIS ARM JERKS OUT--- FINGERS BRUSH--AND THEN, THE WIDOW TUMBLES AWAY, HER EBON-SUITED BODY TWISTING--- HER HANDS FLAILING, LEGS SPINNING---
TASHA!
SHE FROZE UP--- COULDN'T MAKE THE EXTRA EFFORT NEEDED TO COMPLETE THE SWING!
SOMETHING ABOUT HER HEART-BEAT--- RUSHING, PANICKY! SHE'S TERRIFIED!
I'VE GOT TO CHANCE IT--- PUSH AWAY FROM THE FLAG-POLE, TRY TO GRAB HER BEFORE IT'S--- TOO LATE!
EEEEE
THE SINISTER SECRET OF PROJECT FOUR!
EEEEEEEEEEEEEEEEE
YET EVEN AS THE WIDOW'S UNCHARACTERISTIC SCREAM BEGINS TO BUILD TO BREAKING --FIVE CLAW-LIKE FINGERS LUNGE OUT---
CONTINUED AFTER NEXT PAGE

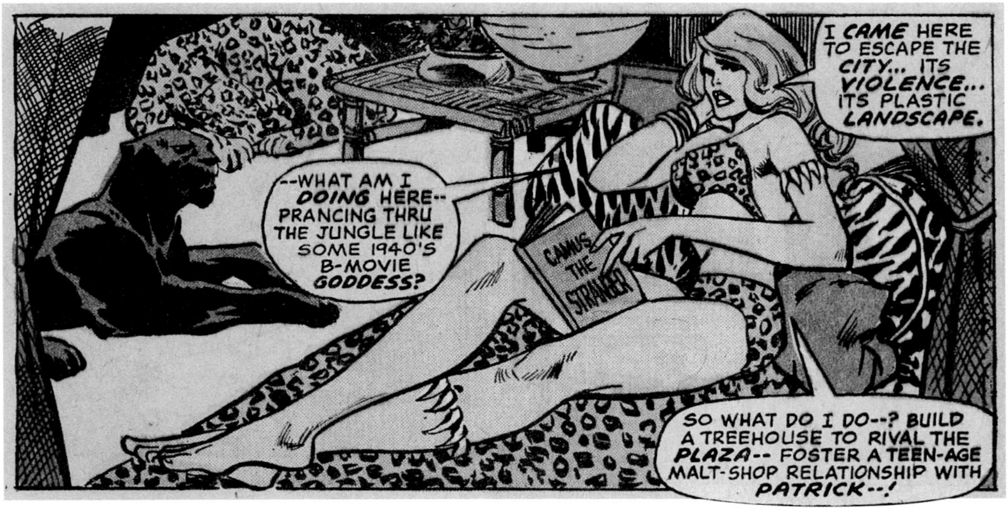
I CAME HERE TO ESCAPE THE CITY... ITS VIOLENCE... ITS PLASTIC LANDSCAPE.
--WHAT AM I DOING HERE-- PRANCING THRU THE JUNGLE LIKE SOME 1940'S B-MOVIE GODDESS?
CAMUS THE STRANGER
SO WHAT DO I DO--? BUILD A TREEHOUSE TO RIVAL THE PLAZA-- FOSTER A TEEN-AGE MALT-SHOP RELATIONSHIP WITH PATRICK--!

starring Luke Cage, an escaped—and, of course, wrongfully accused—prison inmate. Pencils were by *Iron Man* regular George Tuska, with inks by Billy Graham, a young black artist who would eventually take over full art chores on the strip.

To gain more exposure for its most popular character, *Marvel Team-Up* was launched to showcase Spider-Man, previously the ultimate loner, joining forces each month with a different hero—or monster.

In an attempt to attract more female readers, Lee came up with *The Cat* (a costumed super heroine)...*Shanna the She-Devil* (an ecologically minded jungle queen)...and *Night Nurse*, which combined a romance comic with medical drama. Female writers scripted the series, and Marie Severin penciled *The Cat* No. 1. Alas, none lasted more than a handful of issues.

Still, changes proliferated all over the line, and most of them worked out quite well. The Black Widow, fresh from her canceled anthology series, shared equal billing in *Daredevil*, which switched locale to San Francisco, a city of which scripter Gerry Conway was fond...Bill Everett took over both the writing and drawing of *Sub-Mariner*...new scribe Steve Englehart brought one-time "career gal" Patsy Walker into the Beast series, and revealed in *Captain America* that a madman had taken Cap's place fighting Red spies in the 1950s, while the real Cap was in suspended animation.

SHANNA THE SHE-DEVIL No. 5

(Above) Interior, "Where Nekra Walks, Death Must Follow"; script, Steve Gerber; pencils, Ross Andru; inks, Vince Colletta; August 1973. In what would become his signature, Gerber's final issue of Shanna concludes with self-referential musing. Existential angst in a good girl mag? This Marvel was like nothing seen before.

CRAZY MAGAZINE
No. 1

(Right) Cover; art, Frank Kelly Freas; October 1973. When editor Marv Wolfman launched *Crazy Magazine* in 1973, it wasn't the first to recycle the title of an Atlas Era humor comic — in fact, a three-issue super hero parody reprint comic had debuted earlier that same year — but it did endure a 10-year, 96-issue run. Featuring diverse contributors like comics legends Harvey Kurtzman and Will Eisner to mainstream talents Art Buchwald and Lee Marrs, the magazine experimented with humor from fumetti to — gasp! — prose. . . .

MANIACAL MIRTH TO MANGLE YOUR MIND

CRAZY
MAGAZINE

featuring:
THE WAY-OUT HUMOR OF
JEAN SHEPHERD
HARLAN ELLISON
VAUGHN BODE
KELLY FREAS
AND THE BULLPEN THAT PLAYS FOR FUN

ALSO IN THIS ISSUE:
CRAZY RIPS OFF
THE POSEIDON ADVENTURE
AND
KUNG FU

EXPLOSIVE FIRST ISSUE

SICK MAD APOON HACKED

SPECIAL ISSUE ON *THE FUTURE*-- OR WHAT'S LEFT OF IT

A NEW HELMSMAN

But the biggest change at Marvel, in fact, was occurring behind the scenes. Stan Lee was as discontented now as he had been in 1961, right before he came up with *Fantastic Four*. He felt that Martin Goodman should have done more for him when he sold the company, since the sale had depended upon Lee signing a contract to stay on and he had done so without making exorbitant demands. Instead, when Goodman retired in 1971, he named his son Chip publisher, although that didn't last long. Cadence Industries' new chairman, aware of rumors that Lee might defect to DC or elsewhere, elbowed Goodman the younger over to handling only the non-comics publications left over from Magazine Management. And in mid-1972 he promoted Lee to both president and publisher of Marvel.

At last Lee felt he would be master of his fate ... captain of his soul. He appointed Roy Thomas editor-in-chief, in charge of the day-to-day operations of the comics, with John Romita soon officially promoted to art director. He then turned his attention to new worlds he hoped to see Marvel conquer. Lee's new duties had forced him to relinquish the writing of the final three titles he was still scripting — *Fantastic Four, The Amazing Spider-Man,* and *Thor* — but he would be busier than ever, overseeing some very ambitious plans. Besides, Marvel, now separated from Magazine Management, needed to generate additional revenue to support an increase in executive staff.

He made a brief attempt to lure first *Mad* originator Harvey Kurtzman, then *Spirit* creator Will Eisner, into editing a humor magazine to be titled *Bedlam*, with which he hoped to carve out a niche somewhere between *Mad* and the young-adult-oriented *National Lampoon*. When neither man accepted the offer, however, he settled for launching a *Mad*-style parody publication, *Crazy Magazine*. Associate (and de facto) editor Marv Wolfman lavished special attention on it, as did such artists as Marie Severin and Michael Ploog. Under various hands, and with an influx of new artists and writers, *Crazy* would endure for 10 years.

Lee also arranged for Marvel to publish an "underground comix" magazine with the title *Comix Book*, edited by cartoonist Denis Kitchen. However, occupying an uneasy space between true counterculture material and Marvel's Code-approved product, it lasted only three issues, with Kitchen himself later publishing two more.

Marvel had greater success when it stuck closer to home. During the first year or two of Lee's term as publisher, the color line was expanded with such new "monster-hero" titles as *Monster of Frankenstein, Son of Satan, Tomb of Dracula,* and *Man-Thing*; and features: It! The Living Colossus, Man-Wolf, the Living Mummy, the Golem, Brother Voodoo, and War of the Worlds. There were even a few new super hero titles such as a revived *Captain Marvel, Ka-Zar, Black Panther,* and *Marvel Two-in-One*, in which the Thing costarred with a different hero every issue — not to mention *Master of Kung Fu* and Iron Fist in *Marvel Premiere*, a pair of series growing out of the martial arts craze spawned by the TV series *Kung Fu* and a slate of imported Hong Kong movies.

Also, though Marvel wouldn't know it for a while, several future star characters were busy being born, although at this

THE RASCALLY ONE

(Below) Photograph, Roy Thomas, 1972. When Stan Lee got himself kicked upstairs to president/publisher, Thomas says: "I was given the choice — did I want to be called 'editor-in-chief' or 'executive editor,' and I said, 'Executive editor sounds like somebody who comes to work every day in a tie, while editor-in-chief sounds like Perry White. I want to be editor-in-chief.' I put in the hyphens."

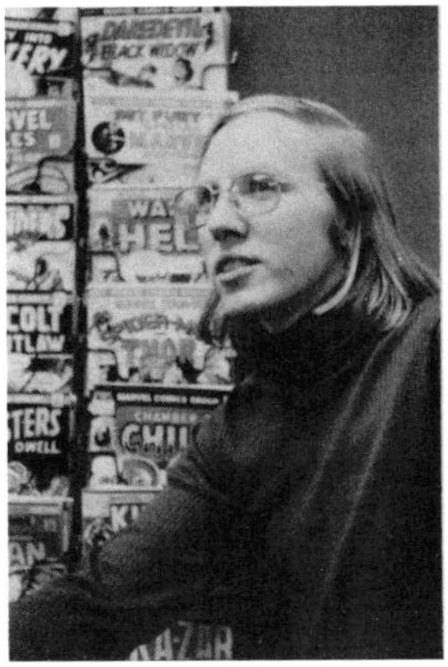

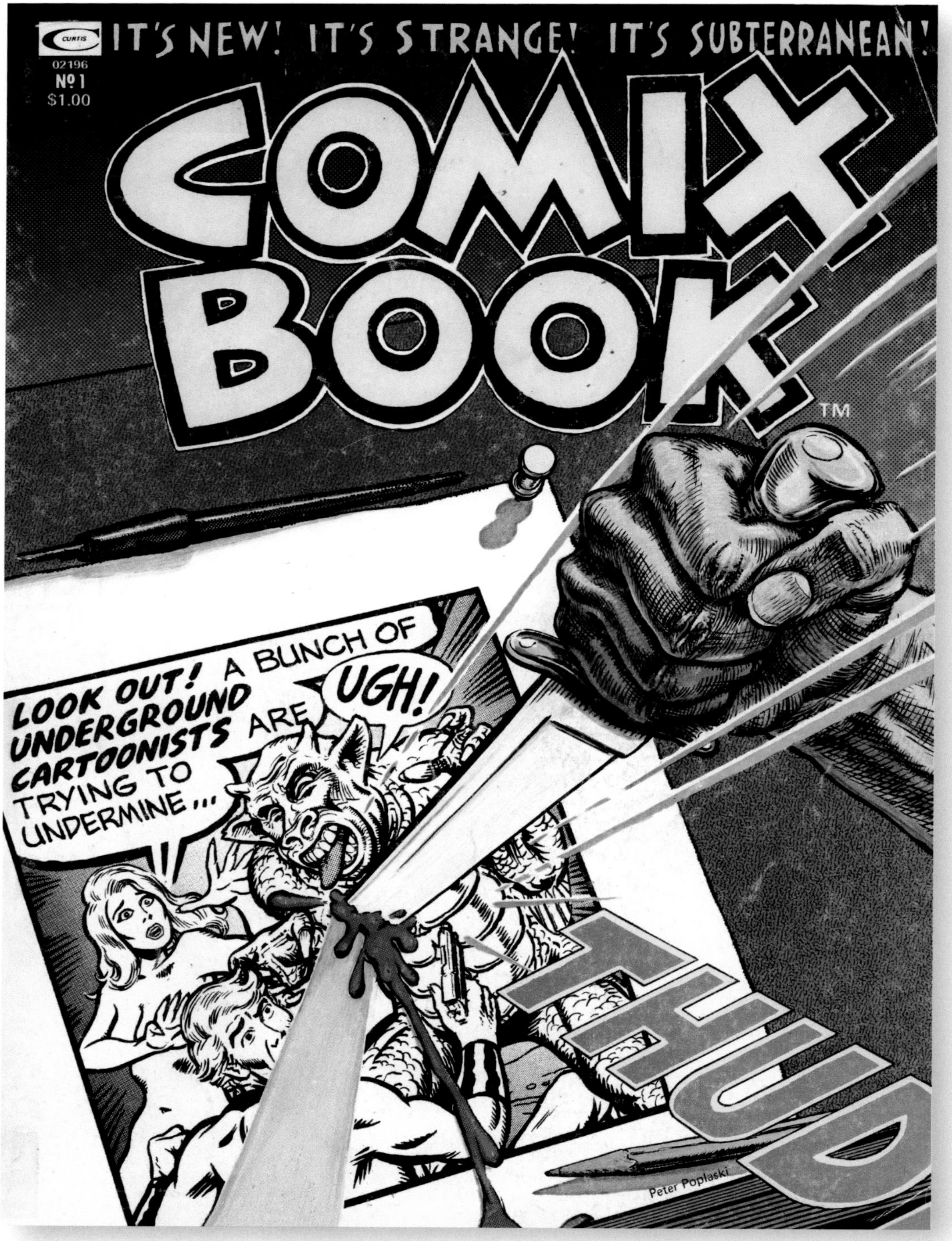
CURTIS
IT'S NEW! IT'S STRANGE! IT'S SUBTERRANEAN!
02196
Nº 1
$1.00
COMIX BOOK
TM
LOOK OUT! A BUNCH OF UNDERGROUND CARTOONISTS ARE TRYING TO UNDERMINE...
UGH!
THUD
Peter Poplaski

stage only as supporting characters in established series: Wolfman and Colan's Blade the Vampire-Slayer in *Tomb of Dracula;* Conway and artist Ross Andru's Punisher in *Amazing Spider-Man;* and a talking Duck named Howard in a Man-Thing story, courtesy of Steve Gerber and artist Val Mayerik.

As a way of expanding the supply of adventures of a number of its key super heroes and monster characters, Marvel soon launched several 48-page quarterlies, all of whose titles began with the word *Giant-Size*.

Marvel also forged an alliance with the Electric Company division of Children's Television Workshop to produce *Spidey Super Stories*, a monthly comic starring Spider-Man that was aimed at readers just growing out of *Sesame Street*. At the same time, Spider-Man began to appear on the *Electric Company* educational television show... the first (but far from the last) time that a live-action version of the wall-crawler would make the leap from the printed page to the screen, either big or small.

But color comics alone wouldn't increase Marvel's bottom line sufficiently, now that it was both a separate entity with increased overhead—*and* determined to keep DC from reclaiming its number-one status. More was needed. And Lee felt he knew just what it was.

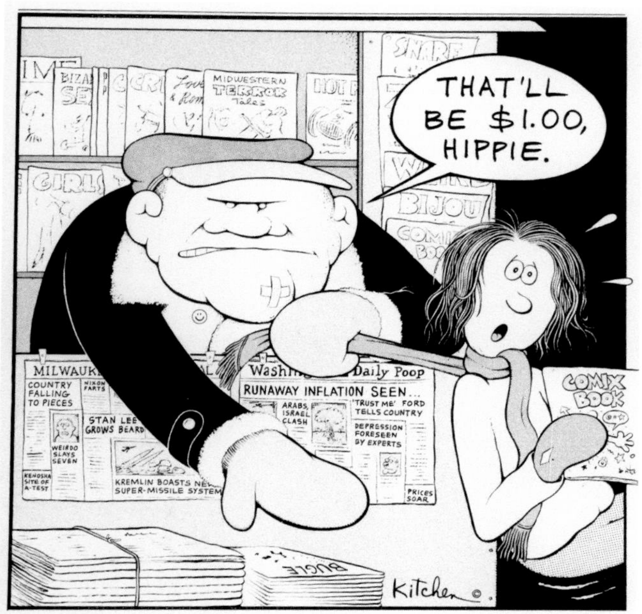
THAT'LL BE $1.00, HIPPIE.
MIDWESTERN TERROR Tales
BIJOU
Daily Poop
RUNAWAY INFLATION SEEN...
COUNTRY FALLING TO PIECES
NIXON FARTS
STAN LEE GROWS BEARD
WEIRDO SLAYS SEVEN
KENOSHA SITE OF A-TEST
ARABS, ISRAEL CLASH
'TRUST ME' FORD TELLS COUNTRY
DEPRESSION FORESEEN BY EXPERTS
PRICES SOAR
COMIX BOOK
BUGLE
Kitchen ©

COMIX BOOK No. 1
(Opposite) Cover; art, Peter Poplaski; October 1974. Marvel's brief foray into excavating the comics underground came in this three-issue black-and-white magazine edited by Denis Kitchen and featuring the talents of Basil Wolverton, Art Spiegelman, Trina Robbins, and Kim Deitch, among many counter-culture art stars.

STEAL THIS COMIC
(Left) House ad; art, Denis Kitchen; 1975.

Speech bubbles: "THEY CALL ME... BLADE!" "BLADE -- THE VAMPIRE KILLER!!"

TOMB OF DRACULA
No. 10

(Above) Interior, "His Name Is...Blade!"; script, Marv Wolfman; pencils, Gene Colan; inks, Jack Abel; July 1973. Introduced to be a thorn — or, even better, a stake — in Dracula's side, Blade transformed a supporting role in *Tomb of Dracula* into Marvel's first taste of box-office fame 25 years later.

Eager to get back into the black-and-white comics game, he announced four 76-page horror "magazines": *Dracula Lives!*, *Monsters Unleashed*, *Vampire Tales*, and *Tales of the Zombie*. Although some of their pages would be taken up by text articles and 1950s reprints, these oversize additions spread even thinner the manpower already hard-pressed to turn out the color mags. Series stars from the color comics — Dracula, Morbius, Frankenstein, Man-Thing, et al. — appeared in the new titles, the better to attract Marvel's regular readers. Thomas had writer Steve Gerber build the *Zombie* book around the walking-dead protagonist of a single Lee-and-Everett story in the 1950s horror comic *Menace*. Thomas himself began, with artist Dick Giordano, to adapt Bram Stoker's novel *Dracula* in a projected 200-page serial to be spread over issues of *Dracula Lives!* Most of the editing chores on the four "monster books," as well as

Crazy Magazine, were handled from the outset by the very able (but instantly overworked) associate editor Marv Wolfman. The black-and-white *Deadly Hands of Kung Fu* soon followed, featuring Shang-Chi as well as some new martial-arts series—as did a licensed magazine showcasing adaptations as well as new stories set on the Planet of the Apes, the scene of a series of hit films.

Lee also revived *Savage Tales*, which he allowed Thomas to immediately turn into a vehicle centered on Conan the Barbarian. Still, because Lee's fellow CMAA publishers and the Code Authority itself were unhappy that house ads in Marvel's color titles might lure young readers to the non-Code-approved black-and-whites, violence and nudity in the latter rarely exceeded by much what was acceptable in the color comics. Soon, Robert E. Howard's hero was spun off into a new title, *The Savage Sword of Conan*. (The first issue guest starred Red Sonja, a "female Conan" recently introduced in *Conan the Barbarian*; she would soon star in her own color comic.) *Savage Tales* was given over to Ka-Zar and lesser features, and folded

FEAR No. 19

(Below) Interior, "The Enchanter's Apprentice!"; script, Steve Gerber; pencils, Val Mayerik; inks, Sal Trapani; December 1973. Whoever knows fear laughs at the quack of Howard the Duck? Horror fans were introduced to Gerber's satirical fowl—and future comics phenomenon—in this issue of *Fear*, Man-Thing's final issue for the anthology before graduating to his own title the following month.

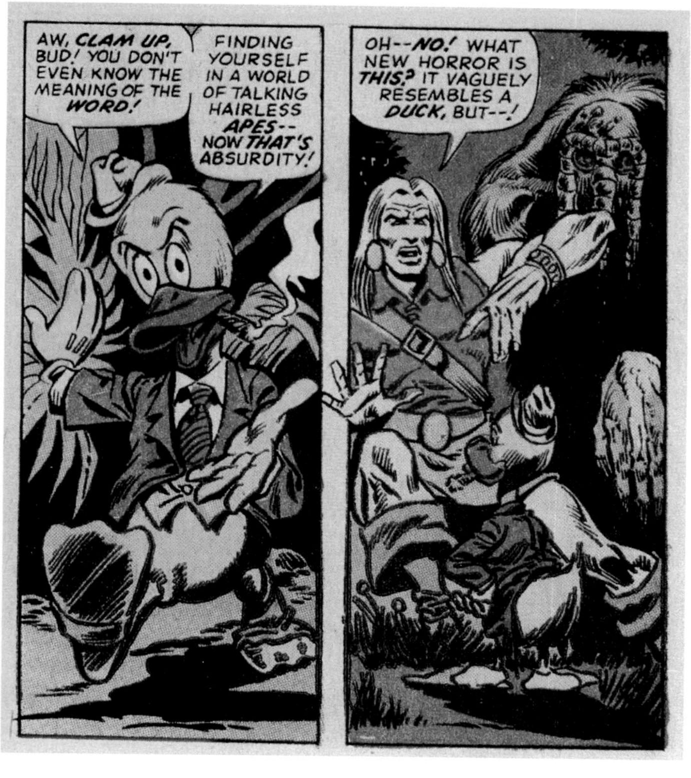
AW, CLAM UP, BUD! YOU DON'T EVEN KNOW THE MEANING OF THE WORD!
FINDING YOURSELF IN A WORLD OF TALKING HAIRLESS APES-- NOW THAT'S ABSURDITY!
OH--NO! WHAT NEW HORROR IS THIS? IT VAGUELY RESEMBLES A DUCK, BUT--!

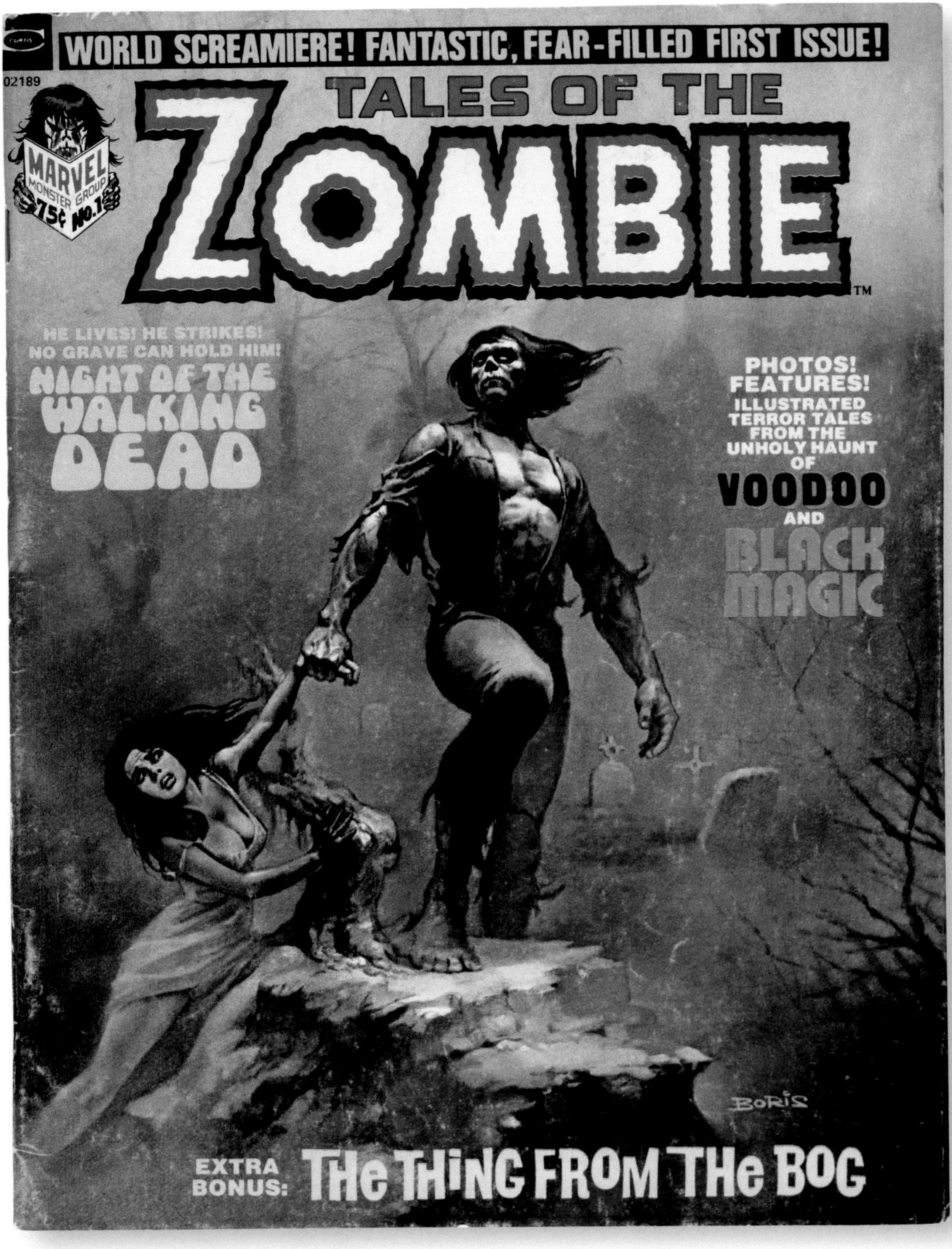
WORLD SCREAMIERE! FANTASTIC, FEAR-FILLED FIRST ISSUE!
02189
MARVEL MONSTER GROUP 75¢ NO.1
TALES OF THE
ZOMBIE
HE LIVES! HE STRIKES! NO GRAVE CAN HOLD HIM!
NIGHT OF THE WALKING DEAD
PHOTOS! FEATURES! ILLUSTRATED TERROR TALES FROM THE UNHOLY HAUNT OF
VOODOO AND BLACK MAGIC
BORIS
EXTRA BONUS: THE THING FROM THE BOG

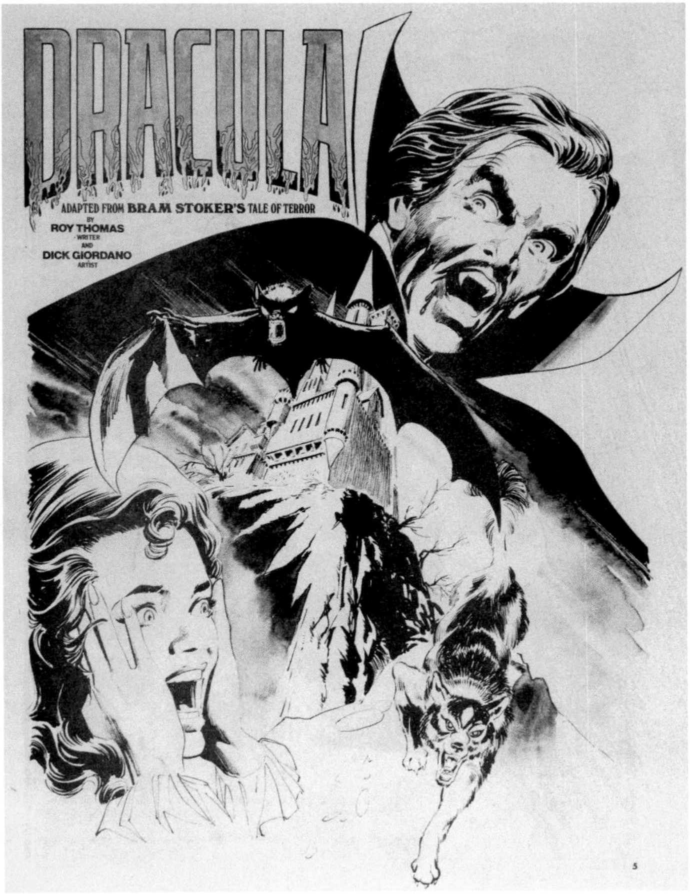
DRACULA
ADAPTED FROM BRAM STOKER'S TALE OF TERROR
BY
ROY THOMAS
WRITER
AND
DICK GIORDANO
ARTIST
5

TALES OF THE ZOMBIE No. 1
(Opposite) Cover; art, Boris Vallejo; August 1973. Superstar fantasy artist Vallejo covered many a Marvel magazine. This was one of his first.

DRACULA LIVES! No. 5
(Left) Interior, "Dracula"; script, Roy Thomas; pencils and inks, Dick Giordano; March 1974. Thomas and Giordano began an adaptation of Bram Stoker's timeless novel in *Dracula Lives!* The story would not be finished until 2005.

in a year or so. *Savage Sword* would far outlast Marvel's other black-and-whites: some two decades, and more than 200 issues.

By now, former production manager Sol Brodsky had returned to Marvel after his own short-lived comics-publishing venture, Skywald, had gone under. Lee promptly put his longtime right-hand man in charge of a new line of black-and-white comics dedicated to repackaging Marvel material—as weeklies to be sold in England! Though housed in the Marvel offices, this was almost an entirely separate division; it would endure for several years.

Lee even assigned young Gerry Conway to edit a digest-sized short-story magazine, *Haunt of Horror,* though it lasted only two issues in a company so focused on comics. Not long after it died, a new black-and-white comic was begun. Its name? *Haunt of Horror*.

MIGHTY WORLD OF MARVEL No. 1

(Right) Cover; pencils, John Buscema; inks, Frank Giacoia; October 1972. Stan Lee launched a "Marvel Invasion" of Britain in 1972 with a line of black-and-white reprints. "*The Dandy* and *The Beano* were simply comics; Marvel was a universe," wrote Geoff Dyer. "The more deeply you got into them, the more encompassing Marvel comics became: characters from one title would guest in another... so that each magazine offered a different glimpse of—and take on—a world that was imaginatively complete."

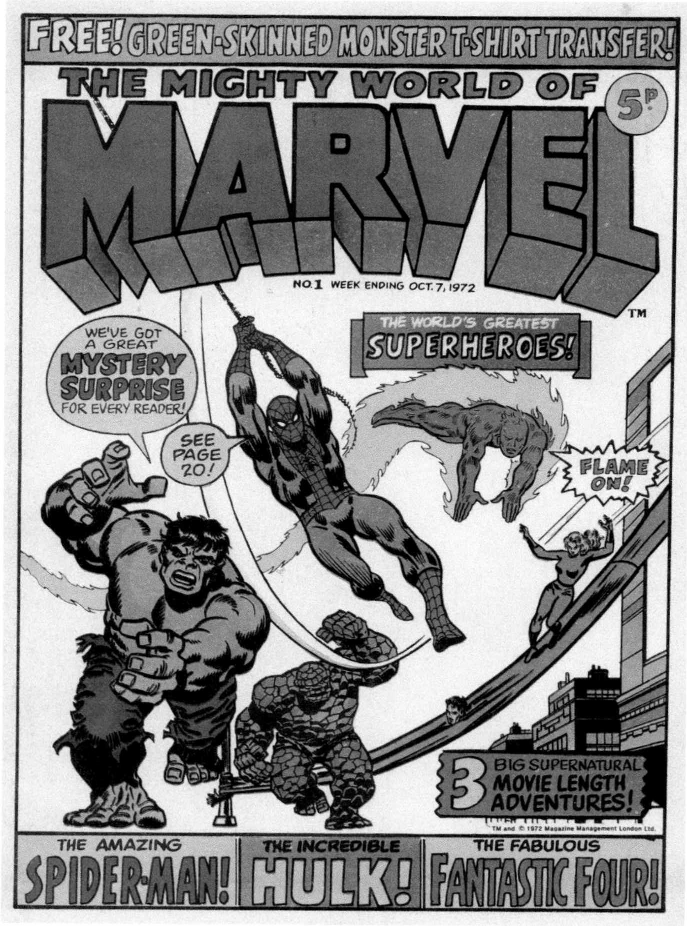

FREE! GREEN-SKINNED MONSTER T-SHIRT TRANSFER!
THE MIGHTY WORLD OF
MARVEL
5P
NO.1 WEEK ENDING OCT. 7, 1972
TM
THE WORLD'S GREATEST SUPERHEROES!
WE'VE GOT A GREAT MYSTERY SURPRISE FOR EVERY READER!
SEE PAGE 20!
FLAME ON!
3 BIG SUPERNATURAL MOVIE LENGTH ADVENTURES!
TM and © 1972 Magazine Management London Ltd.
THE AMAZING SPIDER-MAN!
THE INCREDIBLE HULK!
THE FABULOUS FANTASTIC FOUR!

MARVEL: THE NEXT GENERATION

In the end, it would be the comics—color *and* black and white—that would make or break Marvel. The sudden need for so many stories, so much art, meant headaches for Lee and his management team. But it was a rich opportunity for many young writers who'd been knocking on the doors of the "big two" pubtlishers, Marvel and DC: Mike Friedrich, until recently scripter of DC's *Justice League of America*... Warren Publishing scribes Don McGregor and Doug Moench, the latter brought east from Chicago primarily to write horror stories... former Cleveland newspaper copyboy (and fanzine scribe) Tony Isabella... David Anthony Kraft, a science-fantasy buff who rode his motorcycle up from Georgia... Len Wein, already established at DC as the creator of the popular *Swamp Thing* but vulnerable to Marvel's siren call... Chris Claremont, a recent Marvel "intern" who a year or two later would show he had what it took to craft a breakout series. All of them got their shots at writing for the color comics or the black-and-whites — or most likely both. All were in their twenties. With Stan Lee no longer writing any comics series regularly and Archie Goodwin moving for a time to DC, the oldest regular Marvel scripter was Roy Thomas, who turned 32 late in '72.

Talented young *artists* were banging down the company's portals, as well. Frank Brunner, previously a horror artist, teamed up with scripter Steve Englehart on an imaginative revival of *Dr. Strange*... P. Craig Russell (with McGregor scripts) took the *War of the Worlds* into new realms... Rich Buckler would draw a more "adult" Black Panther series (with McGregor as writer) and conceive a new cyborg hero, Deathlok, on which he worked with Moench... George Pérez started out as Buckler's assistant but would soon move on to Man-Wolf and an amazing career as a star artist... Keith Pollard, another Buckler assistant, would leapfrog to black-and-white Shang-Chi stories and beyond... Paul Gulacy would soon bring his Sterankoesque abilities to *Master of Kung Fu*... Dave Cockrum had made his name drawing DC's *Legion of Super-Heroes* but

JUNGLE ACTION No. 6
(Below) Interior, "Panther's Rage"; script, Don McGregor; pencils, Rich Buckler; inks, Klaus Janson; September 1973. Black Panther faced a revolution in Wakanda in McGregor's epic.

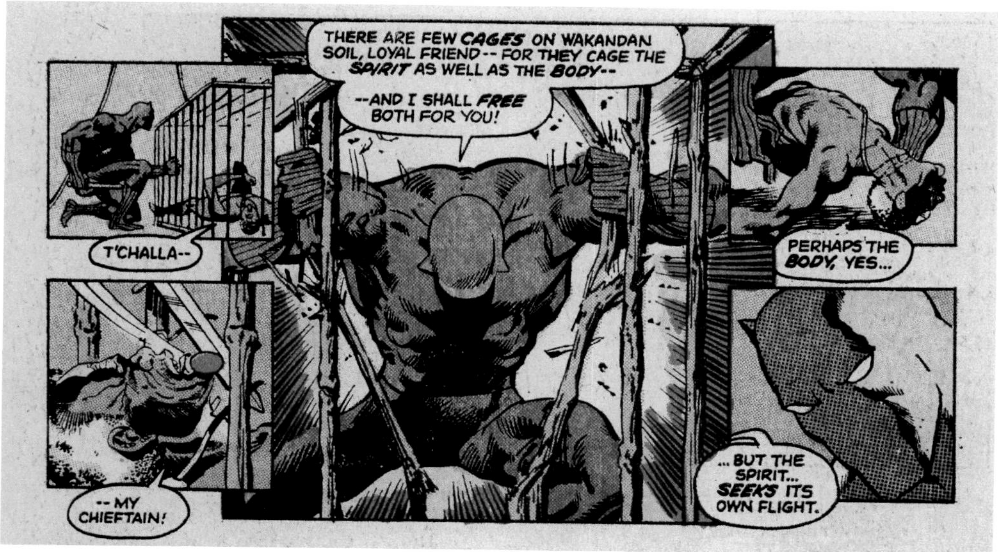
T'CHALLA--
--MY CHIEFTAIN!
THERE ARE FEW CAGES ON WAKANDAN SOIL, LOYAL FRIEND-- FOR THEY CAGE THE SPIRIT AS WELL AS THE BODY--
--AND I SHALL FREE BOTH FOR YOU!
PERHAPS THE BODY, YES...
...BUT THE SPIRIT... SEEKS ITS OWN FLIGHT.

CONAN THE BARBARIAN No. 23
(Right) Interior, "The Shadow of the Vulture!"; script, Roy Thomas; pencils, Barry Smith; inks, Dan Adkins, Sal Buscema, and Chic Stone; February 1973. In her first appearance, Red Sonja slashed her way into comics history. No damsel in distress, she saved Conan's life not once but twice in this issue!

AMAZING ADVENTURES No. 18
(Opposite) Interior, "The War of the Worlds"; script, Gerry Conway; pencils, Neal Adams and Howard Chaykin; inks, Frank Chiaramonte; May 1973.

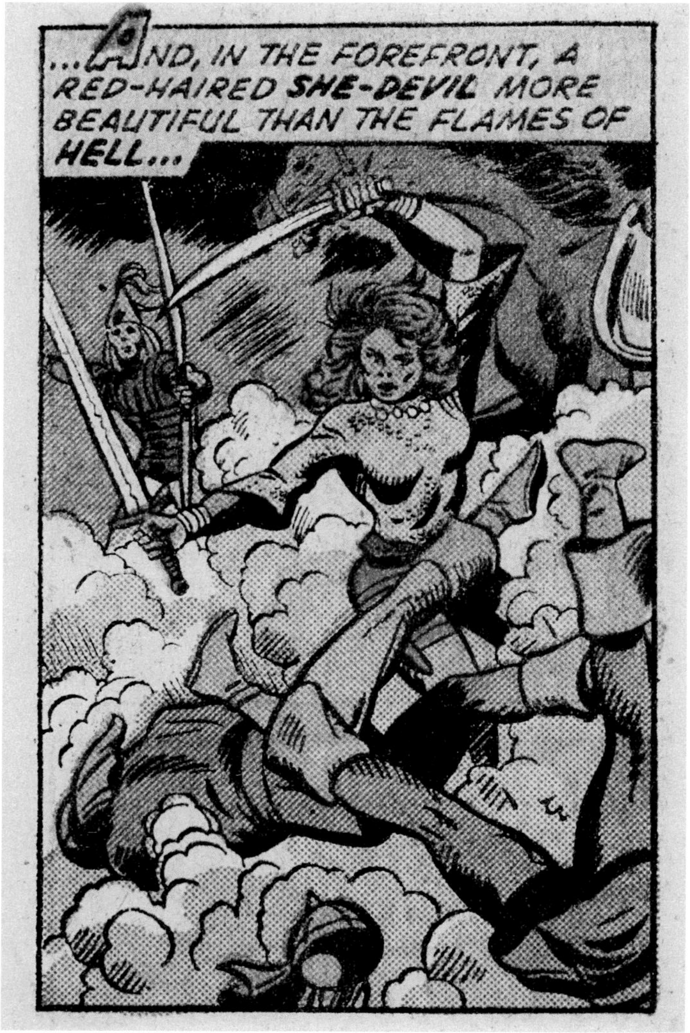
...AND, IN THE FOREFRONT, A RED-HAIRED SHE-DEVIL MORE BEAUTIFUL THAN THE FLAMES OF HELL...

would soon spearhead an even more successful team book for Marvel. The established super hero titles were perhaps taken somewhat for granted during this time of expansion in so many directions. Even so, there were high points for those paying attention.

One event that almost *everyone* noticed occurred when scripter Gerry Conway and artist Gil Kane "killed off" Peter Parker's great love, Gwen Stacy, in *The Amazing Spider-Man*—a story that, four decades later, would still resonate even with readers discovering it for the first time.

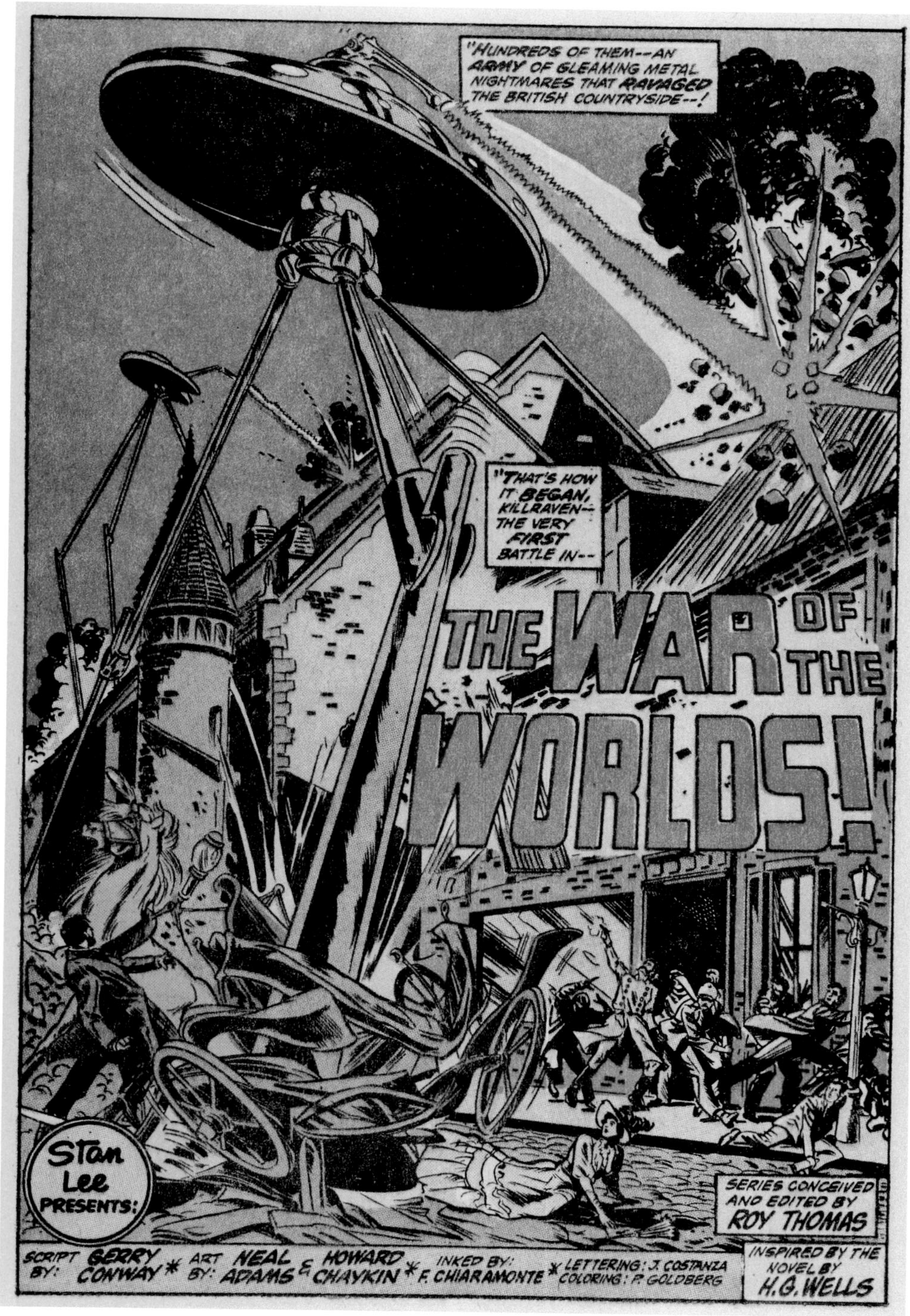
"HUNDREDS OF THEM--AN ARMY OF GLEAMING METAL NIGHTMARES THAT RAVAGED THE BRITISH COUNTRYSIDE--!
"THAT'S HOW IT BEGAN, KILLRAVEN-- THE VERY FIRST BATTLE IN--
THE WAR OF THE WORLDS!
STAN LEE PRESENTS:
SERIES CONCEIVED AND EDITED BY ROY THOMAS
SCRIPT BY: GERRY CONWAY * ART BY: NEAL ADAMS & HOWARD CHAYKIN * INKED BY: F. CHIARAMONTE * LETTERING: J. COSTANZA COLORING: P. GOLDBERG
INSPIRED BY THE NOVEL BY H.G. WELLS

Steve Englehart turned in offbeat but gripping storylines in *The Avengers,* and he and artist Sal Buscema made *Captain America* a top title again with a Watergate-inspired serial—then had a disillusioned Cap denounce his red-white-and-blue persona to become a costumed adventurer called Nomad. Englehart *then* launched the "Avengers/Defenders War," which would pit the two super-groups against each other for several months as it bounced back and forth between their two titles, in a first for Marvel—and for comics.

Writer Len Wein, assigned by editor Thomas to introduce a feisty, short-statured Canadian called the Wolverine in *Incredible Hulk,* worked with artist Herb Trimpe (and Romita's visual designs); the result would turn out to be the most popular new super hero introduced in the 1970s.

Steve Gerber displayed a real talent for crafting Man-Thing stories that centered on oddball secondary characters, with the swamp creature merely shambling in at the end to straighten things out—more or less. The writer's most noteworthy concept, though, turned out to be a character he introduced in

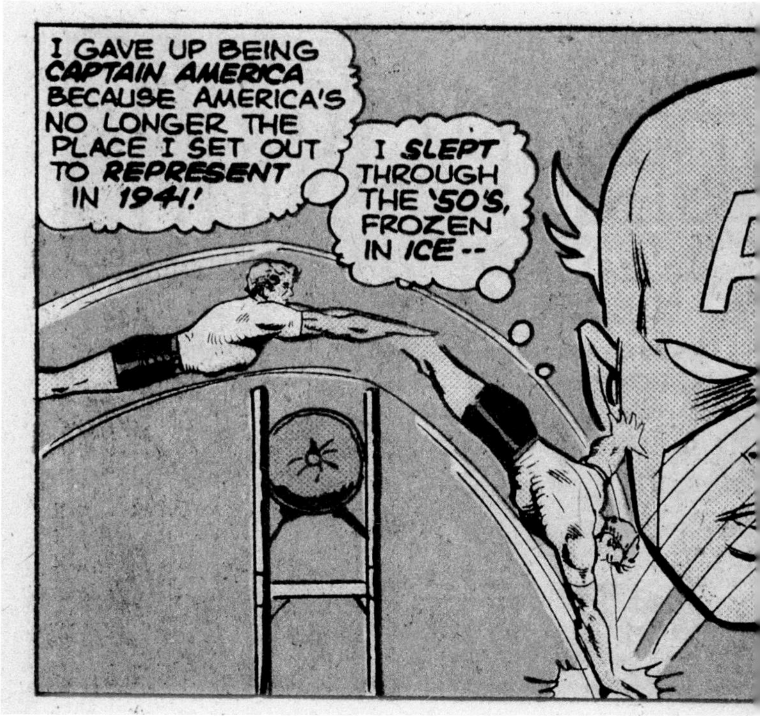
I GAVE UP BEING CAPTAIN AMERICA BECAUSE AMERICA'S NO LONGER THE PLACE I SET OUT TO REPRESENT IN 1941!
I SLEPT THROUGH THE '50'S, FROZEN IN ICE--

that series, when Howard the Duck wandered in from a world where Disneyfied drakes were the dominant life-form, and eventually became not merely the star of his own oddball title, but in 1976 a write-in Presidential candidate!

One double-threat talent who emerged during this period was Jim Starlin, an Army vet. First in *Iron Man,* and then at greater length in *Captain Marvel,* Starlin—first as artist, but soon as writer, as well—introduced a whole new cast of characters, both heroes and villains, most of whom hailed from Titan, the largest moon of the planet Saturn. The longest shadow of these was cast by Thanos, a massive, death-worshipping entity who soon became and still remains one of the most fascinating entities in the Marvel Universe. Producing so much work, however, proved to be a strain on those responsible for overseeing it.

Lee quickly realized that his skills were mostly attuned to being publisher—deciding what titles and directions should be pursued, and how—while he had little inclination toward purely business matters. Thus, by 1974 he happily relinquished the "president" half of his position to Al Landau, an executive appointed by

--AND WHEN I WAS THAWED IN THE '60'S, I GUESS I NEEDED TO BELIEVE THAT NOTHING HAD CHANGED--
--TO PROVE TO MYSELF THAT I HADN'T MISSED ANY-THING!
WELL, IT TOOK A LONG TIME COMIN', BUT I FINALLY DISCOVERED AN OBVIOUS FACT:
NOTHING'S WHAT IT WAS IN 1941.

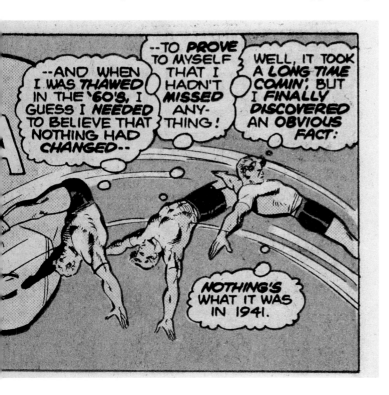

CAPTAIN AMERICA No. 178

(Left) Interior, "If the Falcon Should Fall!"; script, Steve Englehart; pencils, Sal Buscema; inks, Vince Colletta; October 1974. With a storyline centered around Cap's flagging spirits, Steve Englehart's Nomad arc was a nod to the political demoralization of early 1970s America.

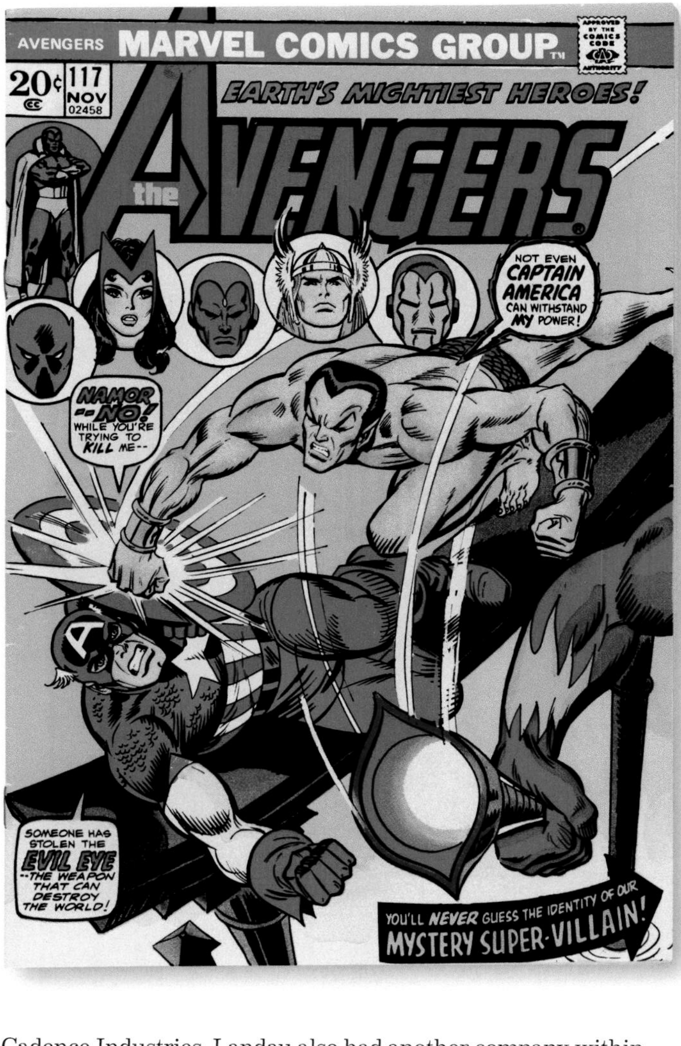
AVENGERS MARVEL COMICS GROUP
20¢ 117 NOV 02458
EARTH'S MIGHTIEST HEROES!
the AVENGERS
NOT EVEN CAPTAIN AMERICA CAN WITHSTAND MY POWER!
NAMOR --NO! WHILE YOU'RE TRYING TO KILL ME--
SOMEONE HAS STOLEN THE EVIL EYE --THE WEAPON THAT CAN DESTROY THE WORLD!
YOU'LL NEVER GUESS THE IDENTITY OF OUR MYSTERY SUPER-VILLAIN!

AVENGERS No. 117
(Right) Cover; pencils, John Romita; inks, Mike Esposito; November 1973.

DEFENDERS No. 9
(Opposite) Cover; pencils and inks, Sal Buscema; October 1973. Though commonly referred to as the Avengers/ Defenders War, writer Steve Englehart dubbed it a Clash. The fight card: Silver Surfer vs. Vision and Scarlet Witch, Sub-Mariner vs. Captain America, Hawkeye vs. Iron Man, Dr. Strange vs. Mantis and Black Panther, Valkyrie vs. Swordsman, and Hulk vs. Thor!

Cadence Industries. Landau also had another company within the Cadence umbrella, which sold Marvel's stories abroad.

Thomas, for his part, had become disenchanted with the editor-in-chief job. In August of '74, he and publisher Lee agreed that he would instead become the first "writer/editor" under contract to Marvel, handling three popular *Conan* titles, plus a few new ones: *What If?* (alternate-world storylines proceeding from classic Marvel tales)... *The Invaders*, World War II adventures of Captain America, Human Torch, and Sub-Mariner... and *Unknown Worlds of Science Fiction* and *Kull and the Barbarians*, both black-and-white magazines.

THE DEFENDERS
MARVEL COMICS GROUP
20¢
9
OCT
02152
THE DEFENDERS
LOOK OUT, IRON MAN! HAWKEYE'S GOT FRIENDS!
OKAY, BOW-SLINGER--
YOU TURNED AGAINST YOUR FORMER AVENGER BUDDIE--AND NOW YOU'RE GONNA PAY!
GUESS AGAIN, SHELLHEAD!
I'M A DEFENDER NOW--AND THEY TAKE CARE OF THEIR OWN!

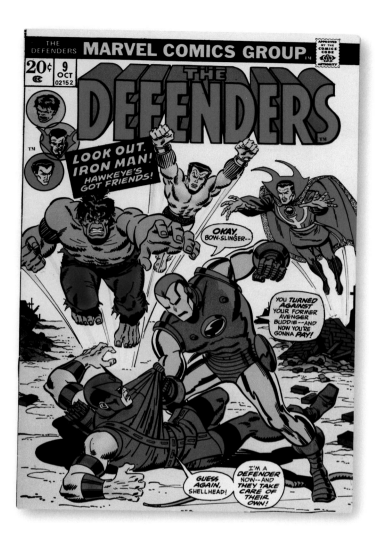

One of Thomas's last decisions as editor-in-chief was, with Lee's consent, to assign writer Mike Friedrich and artist Dave Cockrum to codevelop a return of *the X-Men*—combining a couple of the original team with several new mutants, each from a different country. This project had originated in Landau's suggestion that Marvel devise a super hero team whose members hailed from various countries where the company wanted to increase its sales. If such a comic could merely "break even" in America, it would surely turn a profit via overseas sales. Little did Landau, Lee, Thomas, or anyone else know what they were about to unleash....

X-MASTERMINDS

(Above) Photographs, Eliot R. Brown; Chris Claremont and Dave Cockrum at the Marvel offices, ca. 1979.

GIANT-SIZE X-MEN No. 1

(Opposite) Cover; pencils, Gil Kane; inks, Dave Cockrum; May 1975. Squeaking in at the tail end of Marvel's experimentation with triple-length comics, *Giant-Size X-Men* featured the first appearances of the "All-New, All-Different" mutant squad.

GIANT-SIZE AMBITIONS

The three-plus years from autumn 1974 through the end of 1977 are sometimes referred to, by those who kept count, as the era of "editorial musical chairs." The names of Marvel's editors-in-chief during this period were all ones that were already familiar to readers—but the poor Marvelites, and even the company's staffers and freelancers, needed a scorecard to keep track of them!

After Thomas's move to writer/editor status, Stan Lee split the editor-in-chief job in two: Len Wein would oversee the color titles; his longtime best friend, Marv Wolfman, the black-and-whites. However, when health problems led Wein to opt out for his own writer/editor contract a few months later, Wolfman inherited the entire line. Fortunately, Archie Goodwin returned from DC to edit the black-and-white titles under him.

In February 1976, though, Wolfman himself went the writer/editor route. When Thomas first accepted, then declined an offer to return as editor-in-chief, the job went to Gerry Conway, who had defected to DC a year earlier. Conway resigned after only three weeks—a new record. Still, during that brief interim he and Lee concocted a second web-spinner title for him to script: *The Spectacular Spider-Man*, which bumped the wall-crawler up to what amounted to biweekly status. (If you counted *Marvel Team-Up* and *Spidey Super Stories*, his adventures were now on sale weekly!)

"We used to laugh about it," Stan Lee said, a bit ruefully, of the short half-lives of Marvel editors-in-chief. "We used to say, 'Don't paint his name on the door, just tack it up.'" Conway

THE MARVEL AGE OF COMICS

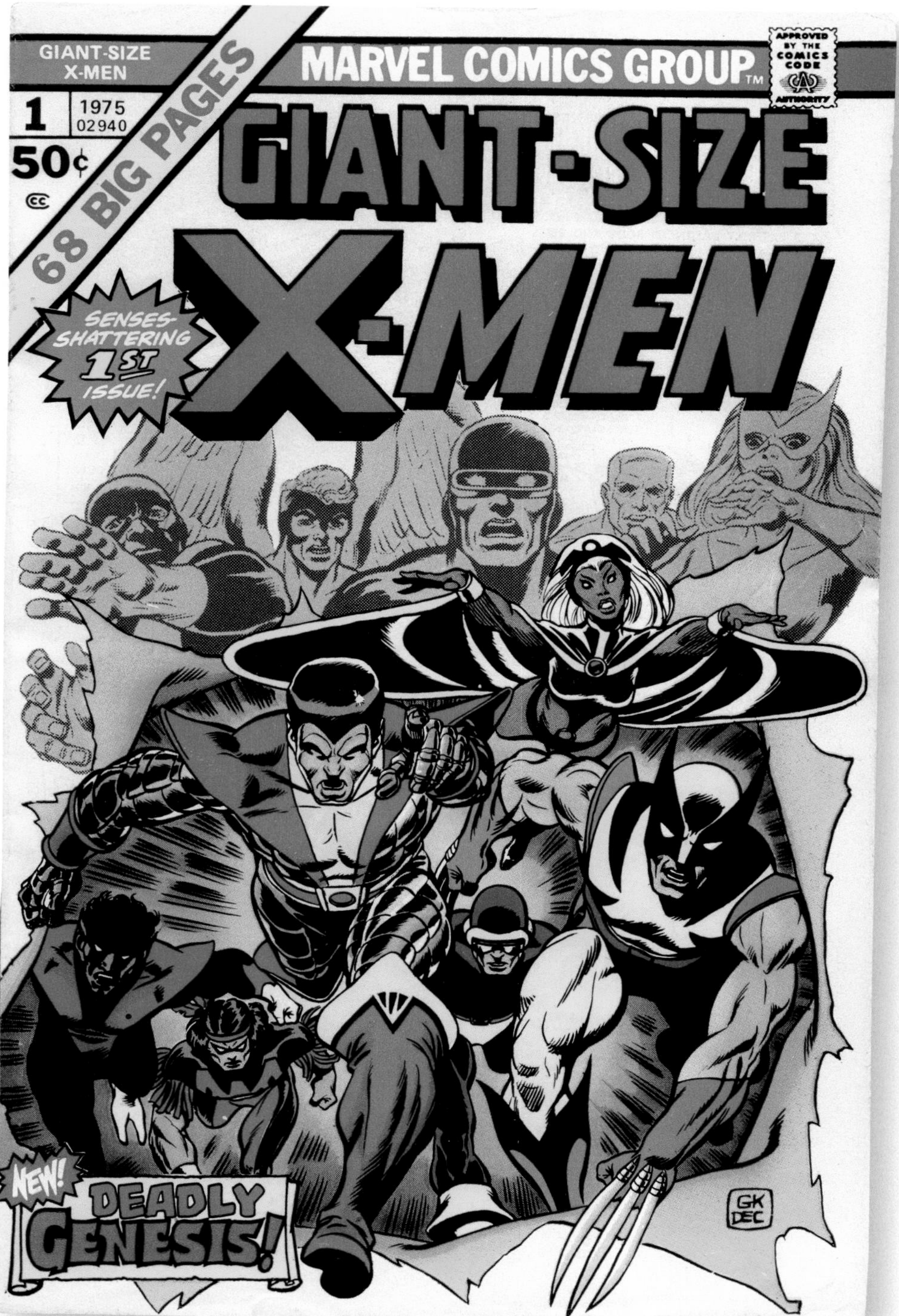
GIANT-SIZE
X-MEN
1
1975
02940
50¢
68 BIG PAGES
MARVEL COMICS GROUP
GIANT-SIZE
X-MEN
SENSES-SHATTERING 1ST ISSUE!
NEW!
DEADLY GENESIS!
GK
DEC

was replaced by a reluctant Goodwin, who nearly two years later would happily relinquish the position to Jim Shooter.

Shooter had been a boy wonder, entering the field at 13 in 1965, writing Superman stories for DC from his Pittsburgh, Pennsylvania, home, but greatly influenced by Lee's early Marvel material. He had drifted out of the industry in the late 1960s, returning to DC shortly before Wolfman offered him an assistant editor post in 1975. And now, just two and a half years later, at age 26, he had been named editor-in-chief of Marvel Comics. He would keep the job for nearly a decade, and leave his mark on it.

Marvel's mags were much like the company's editorship during this era: There was lots of entertaining, exciting, and worthwhile stuff going on — readers just had to know where to look. For instance, in 1976, some months after Marvel and DC had copublished an adaptation of the 1939 film *The Wizard of Oz*, the two companies coproduced a true comic book event: the tabloid-sized *Superman vs. the Amazing Spider-Man*, written by Gerry Conway (now back working for DC), penciled by Ross

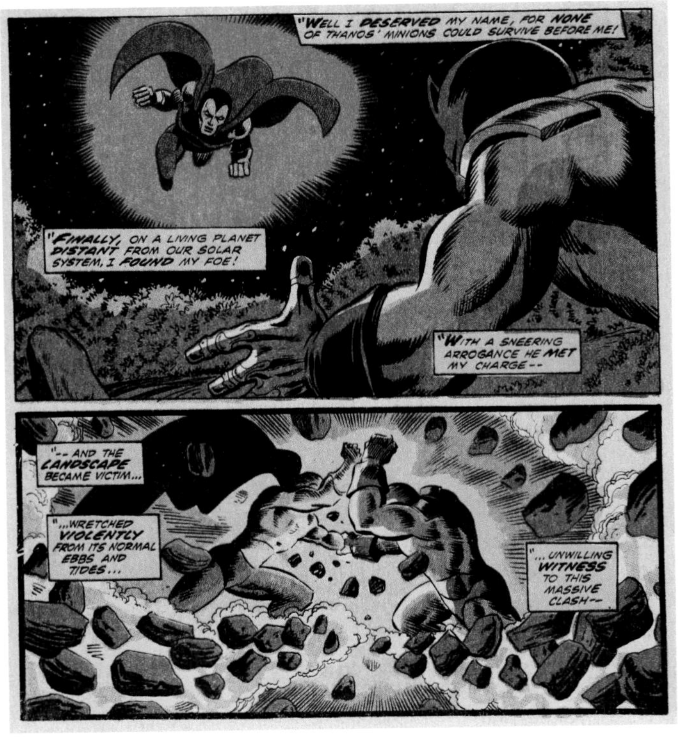

"WELL I DESERVED MY NAME, FOR NONE OF THANOS' MINIONS COULD SURVIVE BEFORE ME!
"FINALLY, ON A LIVING PLANET DISTANT FROM OUR SOLAR SYSTEM, I FOUND MY FOE!
"WITH A SNEERING ARROGANCE HE MET MY CHARGE--
"-- AND THE LANDSCAPE BECAME VICTIM...
"...WRETCHED VIOLENTLY FROM ITS NORMAL EBBS AND TIDES...
"...UNWILLING WITNESS TO THIS MASSIVE CLASH--

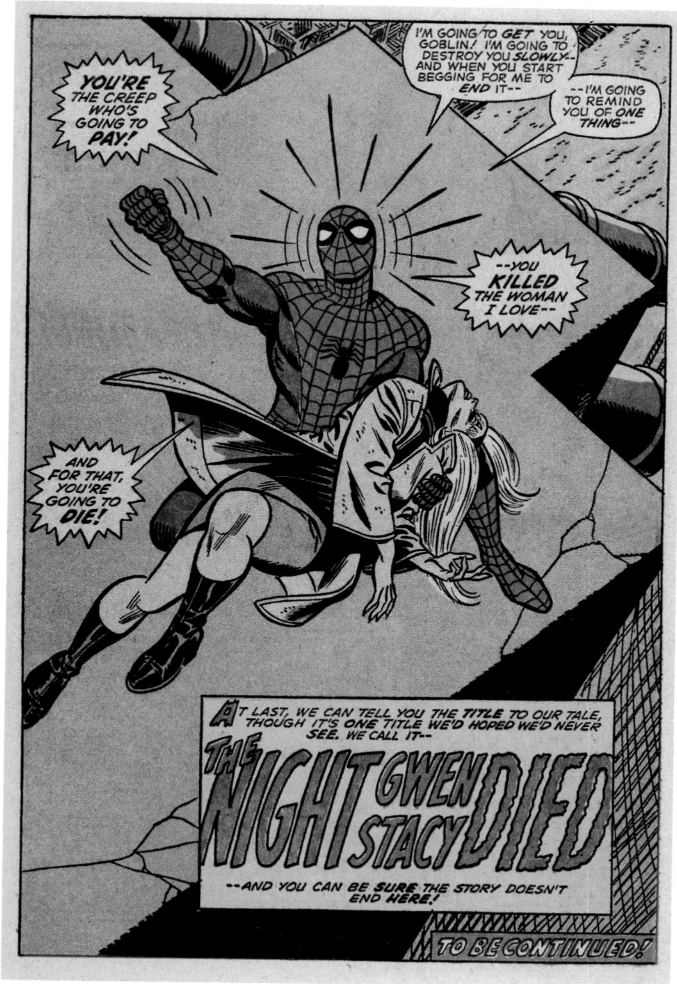
YOU'RE THE CREEP WHO'S GOING TO PAY!
I'M GOING TO GET YOU, GOBLIN! I'M GOING TO DESTROY YOU SLOWLY-- AND WHEN YOU START BEGGING FOR ME TO END IT--
--I'M GOING TO REMIND YOU OF ONE THING--
--YOU KILLED THE WOMAN I LOVE--
AND FOR THAT, YOU'RE GOING TO DIE!
AT LAST, WE CAN TELL YOU THE TITLE TO OUR TALE, THOUGH IT'S ONE TITLE WE'D HOPED WE'D NEVER SEE. WE CALL IT--
THE NIGHT GWEN STACY DIED
--AND YOU CAN BE SURE THE STORY DOESN'T END HERE!
TO BE CONTINUED!

IRON MAN No. 55

(Opposite) Interior, "Beware — Beware — Beware the... Blood Brothers!"; script, Mike Friedrich and Jim Starlin; pencils, Starlin; inks, Mike Esposito; February 1973. Jim Starlin would expand Marvel to the farthest reaches of the universe, and his "Big Bang" appeared in this humble issue, with the first appearances of Thanos and Drax the Destroyer.

AMAZING SPIDER-MAN No. 121

(Left) Interior, "The Night Gwen Stacy Died"; script, Gerry Conway; pencils, Gil Kane; inks, John Romita and Tony Mortellaro; June 1973. "As a young kid, I was very much into Terry and the Pirates and I remember when Pat Ryan, who was the main hero, lost his girlfriend, there were people on the street the next day talking about how Raven Sherman had died.... It stuck in my mind that if you're going to kill somebody, kill somebody very important, make it a real shock." —John Romita

Andru, and inked by Dick Giordano. Its success would lead to annual intercompany team-ups over the next few years, before that type of camaraderie had run its course.

Spider-Man, by facing off against the granddaddy of all super heroes, had at last achieved parity of a sort with the long-established Man of Steel, while the Fantastic Four, Hulk, et al., still rocketed along in popular titles; but some of the most noteworthy work coming out of Marvel at that time was being done by those who might be called "the new subversives."

Warlock, whose comic had been canceled a year earlier, resurfaced in *Strange Tales* in 1975 with a new creative "team": Jim

Starlin. After months of self-exile, the artist returned, writing, penciling, inking, and even coloring a revamped version of the golden-hued hero. Starlin quickly turned Adam Warlock's adventures into the most cosmic trip comics had yet seen. Overnight, the series became what one author calls "a critique of organized religion…meditations on the price of power" and a vehicle for "the suspicions [Starlin] harbored toward rigid institutionalism." Though it lasted only long enough to fill 11 regular comics plus an *Avengers Annual*, Starlin's *Warlock* achieved first cult, then legend status—and has been reprinted numerous times since.

Writer Steve Gerber's equally offbeat Howard the Duck, drawn initially by *Dr. Strange* graduate Frank Brunner and later by Gene Colan, gained his own comic that same year. Because of excessive buying by speculators, *Howard the Duck* No. 1 was a sellout, and copies were soon going for far more than cover price. Even the *Village Voice* gave the frantic fowl its front cover. Small wonder he decided to run for President in '76, as candidate of the All-Night Party! Between *Howard*, *Man-Thing*, *Omega the Unknown*, and offbeat storylines in the mainstream title *The Defenders*, Gerber was taking super heroes and their ilk places where the Marvel Age creators would never have taken them—and the older readers, in particular, ate it up.

Another scribing Steve—Englehart—continued his own brand of subverting expectations, bringing a Vietnamese woman named Mantis into *The Avengers* primarily to cause dissension in the group. When that angle petered out, he had her become the "Celestial Madonna" and marry a *tree*. It all

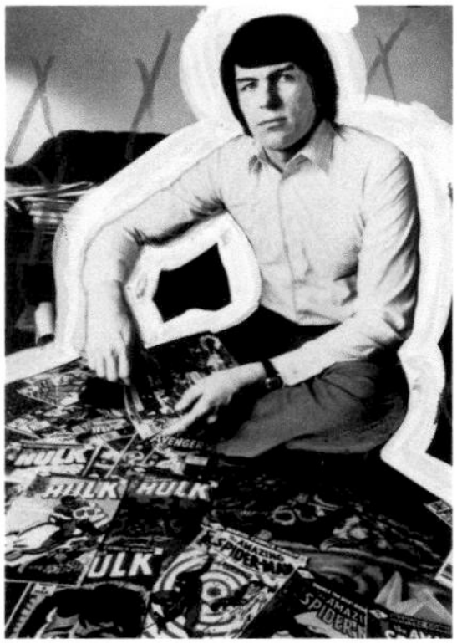
HULK
HULK

TROUBLE SHOOTER
(Above) Photograph, Jim Shooter, 1980. By 1980, Stan Lee was in L.A. to work on Marvel's screen efforts. That left Shooter largely free in overseeing the comics operation in New York.

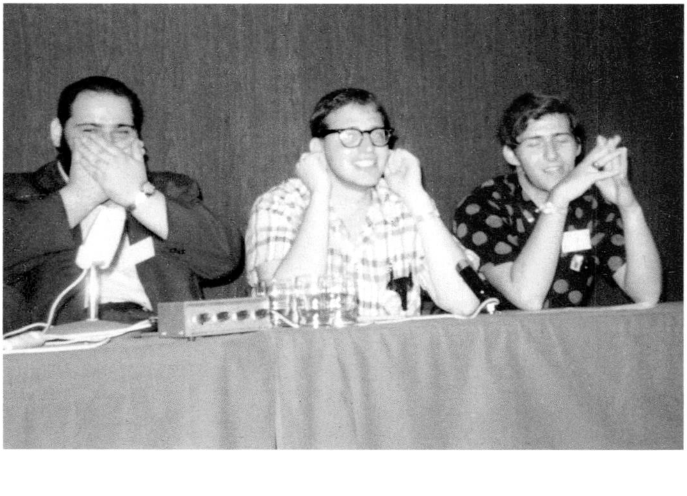

THE INMATES TAKE OVER THE ASYLUM
(Right) Photograph, Patricia A. Yanchus; left to right, Mark Hanerfeld, Marv Wolfman, and Len Wein attend a comics convention; 1967. Wolfman and Wein would each have a short turn as editor-in-chief of Marvel in the mid-1970s before stepping down to writer/editor roles.

THE BIG EVENT
(Opposite) Cover, Superman vs. the Amazing Spider-Man; *layout, Carmine Infantino; pencils, Ross Andru; inks, Dick Giordano; backgrounds, Terry Austin; January 1976.*

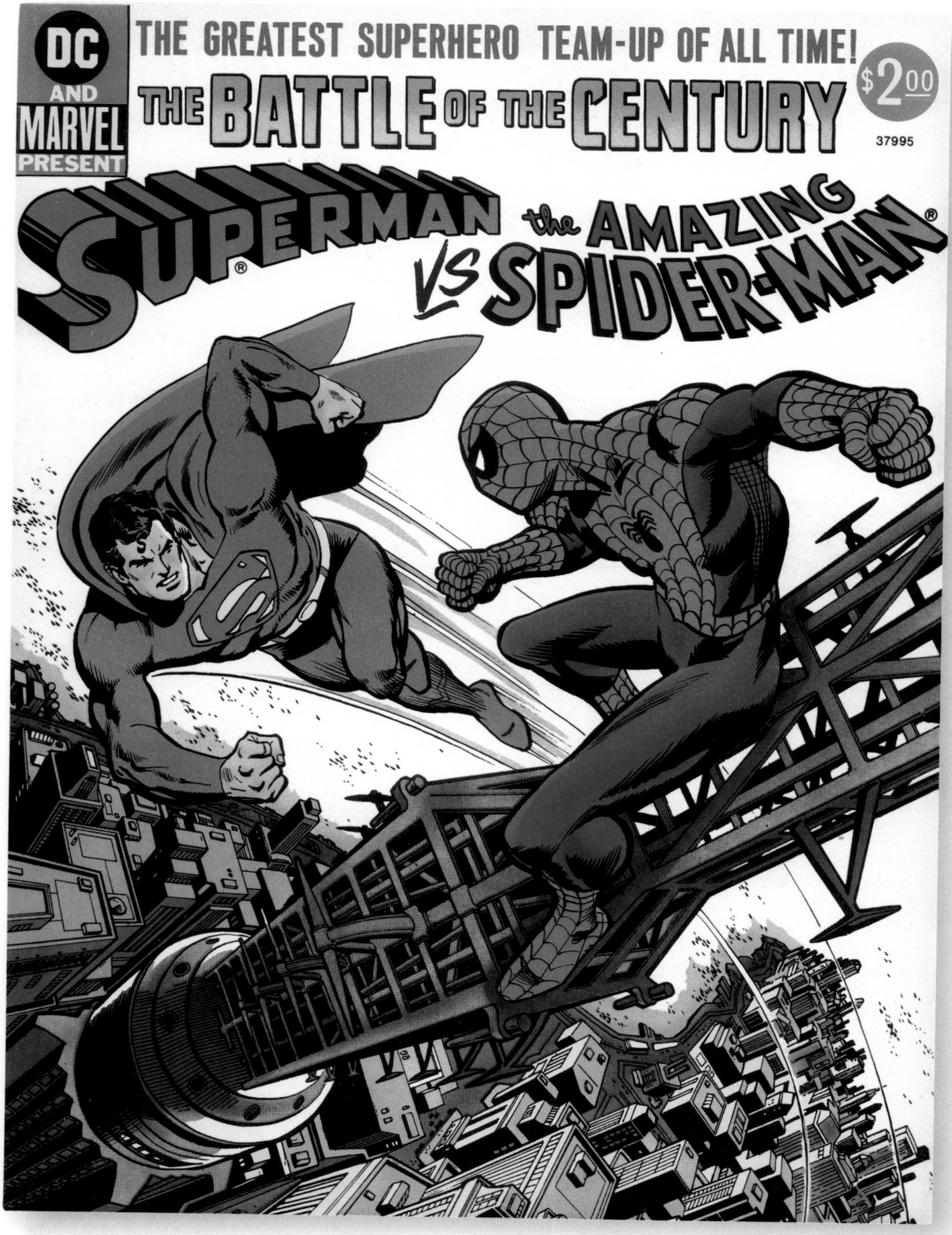
DC AND MARVEL PRESENT
THE GREATEST SUPERHERO TEAM-UP OF ALL TIME!
THE BATTLE OF THE CENTURY
$2.00
37995
SUPERMAN VS the AMAZING SPIDER-MAN

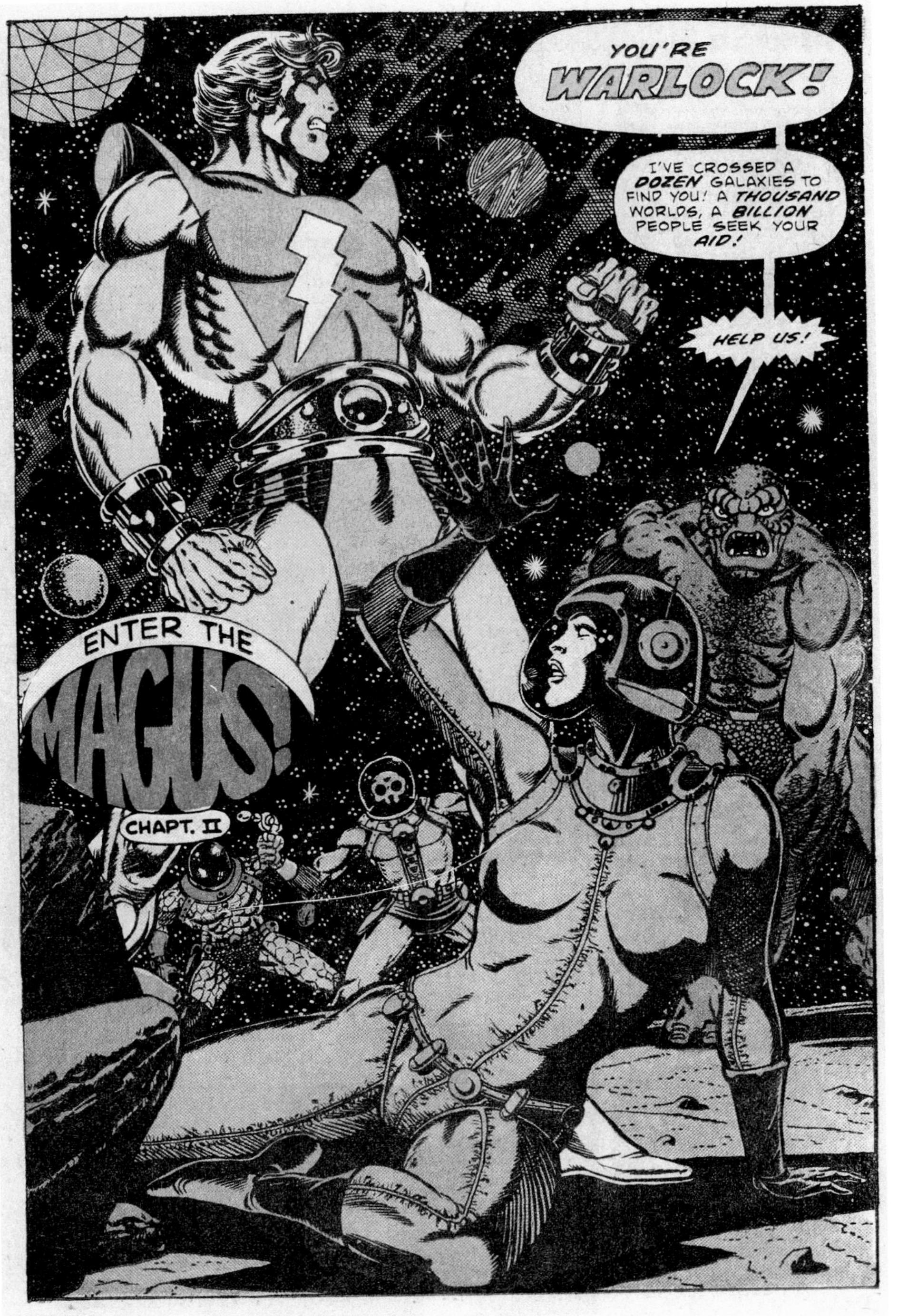
YOU'RE WARLOCK!
I'VE CROSSED A DOZEN GALAXIES TO FIND YOU! A THOUSAND WORLDS, A BILLION PEOPLE SEEK YOUR AID!
HELP US!
ENTER THE MAGUS!
CHAPT. II

made perfect sense if you read the comics. Englehart and young Detroit artist Al Milgrom also contributed some outré exploits to *Captain Marvel.*

Don McGregor dealt with political drama in Wakanda and racism with the Klan in the Black Panther series he wrote for *Jungle Action,* aided by Rich Buckler and Billy Graham… and meanwhile explored interracial relationships in the War of the Worlds and Killraven series in *Amazing Adventures,* with exquisite rendering by P. Craig Russell.

Doug Moench wrote and newcomer Paul Gulacy drew *Master of Kung Fu* with a raw intensity matching the films of Bruce Lee, after cocreators Englehart and Starlin had left the series. Moench, besides cocreating a grim crimefighter called Moon Knight in 1976, would also team with artists Mike Ploog and John Buscema on Weirdworld, a fantasy series influenced by the work of J.R.R. Tolkien, author of *The Lord of the Rings.*

GET DOWN AMERICA!
VOTE HOWARD THE DUCK IN '76

the village VOICE

CONSIDER THE PLIGHT OF HOWARD THE DUCK

VOL. XXI No. 50 THE WEEKLY NEWSPAPER OF NEW YORK MON. DECEMBER 13, 1976 60¢

'I WAS THE DYKE AT MY HIGH SCHOOL REUNION'
BY LORETTA LOTMAN (P.17)

AT LAST, CARTER'S HONEYMOON IS OVER
Vance and Lance? Why Not the Best?
BY COCKBURN AND RIDGEWAY (P.11)

PLUS

The Morning Lineup on Carter's New York Choices
BY KEN AULETTA (P.23)

The Last Angry Duck Stands Up for America
BY ERNIE EBAN (P.33)

LOOKING FOR THE BOOMIS BUCKS
BY GEOFFREY STOKES (P.29)

THE FACES OF POWER
A PHOTO ESSAY
BY JANIE EISENBERG (PP. 26-27)

THE ONLY GIFT-BOOK GUIDE YOU HAVE TO READ
BY ELIOT FREMONT-SMITH (P.67)

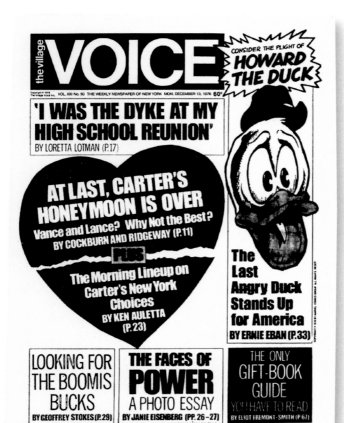

STRANGE TALES No. 178

(Opposite) Interior, "Who Is Adam Warlock?"; script, pencils, and inks, Jim Starlin; February 1975. During its two-year run of more "far out" original material, the 1973 *Strange Tales* revival featured the Haitian mystic Brother Voodoo, the 16th-century monster the Golem, and Warlock.

HE WON'T DUCK THE ISSUES

(Above) Howard the Duck campaign button; art, Bernie Wrightson; 1976.

WAAAUGH!

(Left) Newspaper cover, The Village Voice*; December 13, 1976.* Gerber's hero duck made the cover of the groundbreaking alternative weekly newspaper, even after "losing" the presidential election.

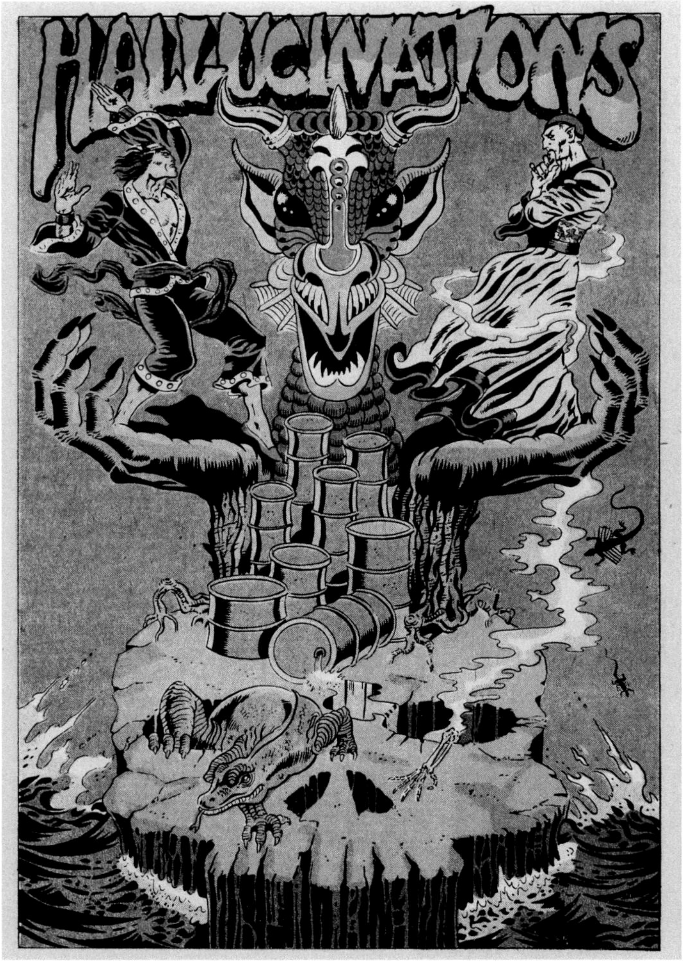
HALLUCINATIONS

MASTER OF KUNG FU No. 18

(Right) Interior, "Attack!"; script, Steve Englehart; pencils, Paul Gulacy; inks, Al Milgrom; June 1974.

WEREWOLF BY NIGHT No. 32

(Below) Interior, "The Stalker Called Moon Knight!"; script, Doug Moench; pencils, Don Perlin; inks, Howie Perlin; August 1975. Moon Knight, who fights in white at night, makes his self-deprecating debut. Moench would further develop the character in other titles. Warren Ellis, who launched a new Moon Knight series in 2014, said of the vigilante, "The man is demented in more interesting ways than I think Batman ever was."

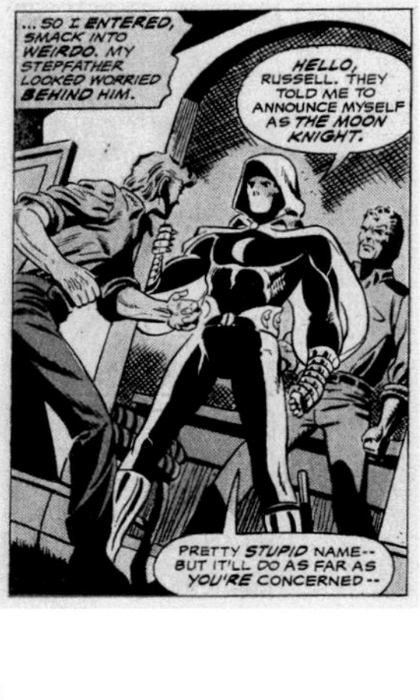
...SO I ENTERED, SMACK INTO WEIRDO. MY STEPFATHER LOOKED WORRIED BEHIND HIM.
HELLO, RUSSELL. THEY TOLD ME TO ANNOUNCE MYSELF AS THE MOON KNIGHT.
PRETTY STUPID NAME-- BUT IT'LL DO AS FAR AS YOU'RE CONCERNED--

Less subversive or showy than the foregoing but still significant was the 1977 introduction of Ms. Marvel, a character crafted around a moniker coined by Stan Lee. Gerry Conway and John Buscema helped her last longer than previous Marvel Age heroines like the Cat and Shanna the She-Devil. Her costume looked as if she'd customized one of Captain Marvel's hand-me-downs, and maybe she had... since her alter ego was Carol Danvers, formerly in charge of security at the Florida military base patrolled by Kree exile Mar-Vell.

Yet, the most important Marvel event of the 1970s—though hardly noticed at the time—occurred on Len Wein's brief editorial watch. He took over the scripting of the *X-Men* revival project, retaining Dave Cockrum as artist, and *Giant-Size X-Men* No. 1 hit newsstands in spring of '75. The precise foreign-sales rationale for internationalizing the team had fallen by the wayside; still, the team's new multicultural roster included original members Cyclops and Marvel Girl and newbies Storm (Kenya), Colossus (USSR), and Nightcrawler (Germany), plus Canada's Wolverine, who was revealed to be a mutant—and one with a skeleton made of Adamantium, to boot. Though numerous other mutants appeared in the adventure, these six became the group's core. The sole *Giant-Size* issue was followed by a regular-length *X-Men* series, with No. 94 (Aug. 1975) picking up the numbering of the recent reprint title. Chris Claremont inherited the writing chores; he and Cockrum quickly drew attention to what was perceived as a minor title. The merry mutants would, in the 1980s, become Marvel's most important group franchise. The ever-growing popularity of Wolverine didn't hurt, either.

And, in the midst of all this, as a capstone—*Jack was back!*

Jack Kirby, his early titles at DC canceled, had begun by mid-1974 to send out feelers about returning to Marvel. And, in March '75, at the company's first comics convention of its own

AMAZING ADVENTURES No. 32

(Below) Interior, "Only the Computer Shows Me Any Respect!"; script, Don McGregor; pencils and inks, P. Craig Russell; September 1975. Don McGregor and Craig Russell's revered run with the character Killraven in *Amazing Adventures* helped launch Russell into a multiple Eisner Award–winning career.

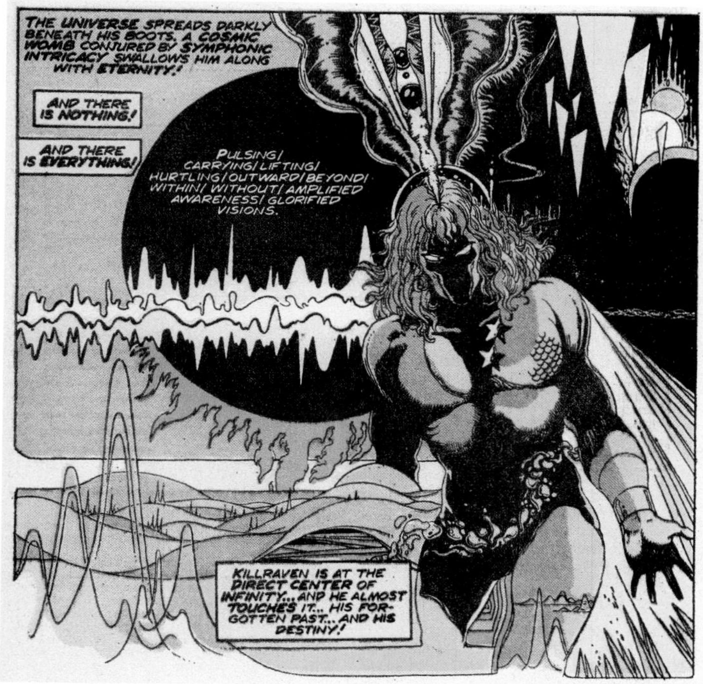
THE UNIVERSE SPREADS DARKLY BENEATH HIS BOOTS, A COSMIC WOMB CONJURED BY SYMPHONIC INTRICACY SWALLOWS HIM ALONG WITH ETERNITY!
AND THERE IS NOTHING!
AND THERE IS EVERYTHING!
PULSING! CARRYING! LIFTING! HURTLING! OUTWARD! BEYOND! WITHIN! WITHOUT! AMPLIFIED AWARENESS! GLORIFIED VISIONS.
KILLRAVEN IS AT THE DIRECT CENTER OF INFINITY... AND HE ALMOST TOUCHES IT... HIS FORGOTTEN PAST... AND HIS DESTINY!

OMEGA THE UNKNOWN No. 1

(Right) Interior, "Omega the Unknown"; script, Steve Gerber and Mary Skrenes; pencils and inks, Jim Mooney; March 1976. Gerber's surreal (bordering on bizarre) classic lasted only 10 issues but made a lasting impression on its small audience.

MARVEL PREMIERE No. 38

(Below) Cover; pencils, Dave Cockrum; inks, Rudy Nebres; October 1977.

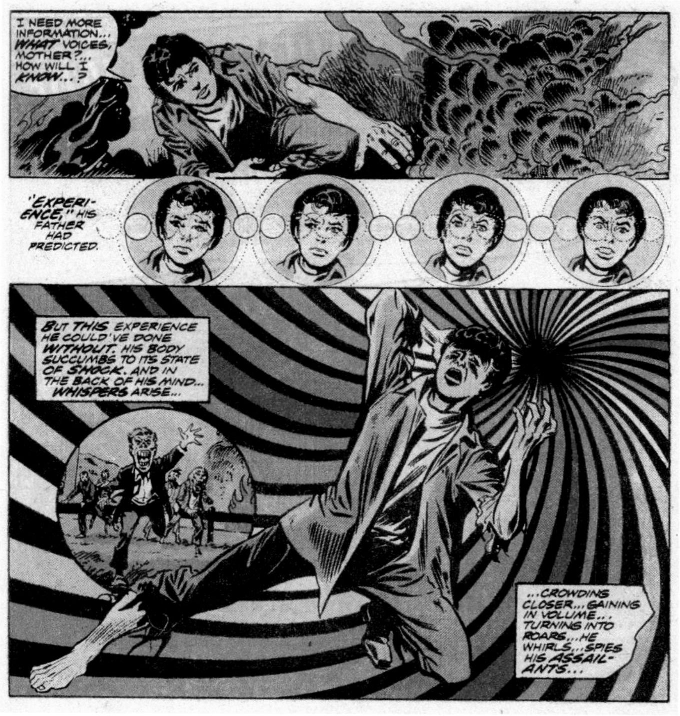

I NEED MORE INFORMATION... WHAT VOICES, MOTHER?... HOW WILL I KNOW...?
"EXPERIENCE," HIS FATHER HAD PREDICTED.
BUT THIS EXPERIENCE HE COULD'VE DONE WITHOUT. HIS BODY SUCCUMBS TO ITS STATE OF SHOCK. AND IN THE BACK OF HIS MIND... WHISPERS ARISE...
...CROWDING CLOSER... GAINING IN VOLUME... TURNING INTO ROARS... HE WHIRLS... SPIES HIS ASSAILANTS...

(the self-styled Marvel Con, held at the Hotel Commodore in New York City), Stan Lee announced the King's return during a Fantastic Four panel discussion. Kirby became the artist—and *writer*—of his cocreation *Captain America*, of an adaptation and continuation of the Stanley Kubrick film *2001: A Space Odyssey*, and of a cosmic new title of his own devising: *The Eternals*. The latter, the apparent result of a head-on collision between super heroes and the esoteric theories espoused in Erich von Däniken's book *Chariots of the Gods?*, saw Kirby venturing into regions beyond even those he and Stan Lee had explored in *Thor*, or that he had chronicled for DC in *The New Gods*.

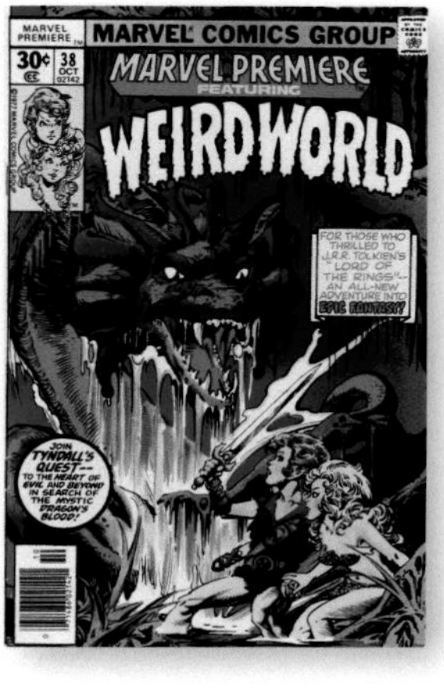

MARVEL COMICS GROUP
30¢ 38 OCT
MARVEL PREMIERE
WEIRDWORLD
FOR THOSE WHO THRILLED TO J.R.R. TOLKIEN'S "LORD OF THE RINGS"—AN ALL-NEW ADVENTURE INTO EPIC FANTASY!
JOIN TYNDALL'S QUEST— TO THE HEART OF EVIL AND BEYOND IN SEARCH OF THE MYSTIC DRAGON'S BLOOD!

Kirby's third stint at Marvel, alas, would not last as long as his second, with *The Eternals* being canceled after 19 issues. His final creation for Marvel was 1978's *Devil Dinosaur*, about the friendship of a primeval lad named Moon-Boy and an intelligent carnosaur with a bright red hide. Soon afterward, Kirby departed Marvel for what would prove to be the final time. His cocreations, however, would exist well into the next century, and their influence shows no sign of diminishing.

Quite the contrary!

Meanwhile, Martin Goodman, the man behind 1939's *Marvel Comics* No. 1 and founder of Timely/Atlas/Marvel, had published his last comic book. In 1974, he and son Chip had launched a new color line with the a familiar colophon: Atlas...aka Atlas/ Seaboard. They kick-started numerous titles and offered prime page rates in a bid to lure talent from Cadence Industries' (and Stan Lee's) Marvel. They even hired Lee's brother, Larry Lieber, as an editor. But by 1976, a victim of poor sales, this new Atlas shrugged for a final time—and Martin Goodman never again had any connection with the comic book field in which he had once been a giant.

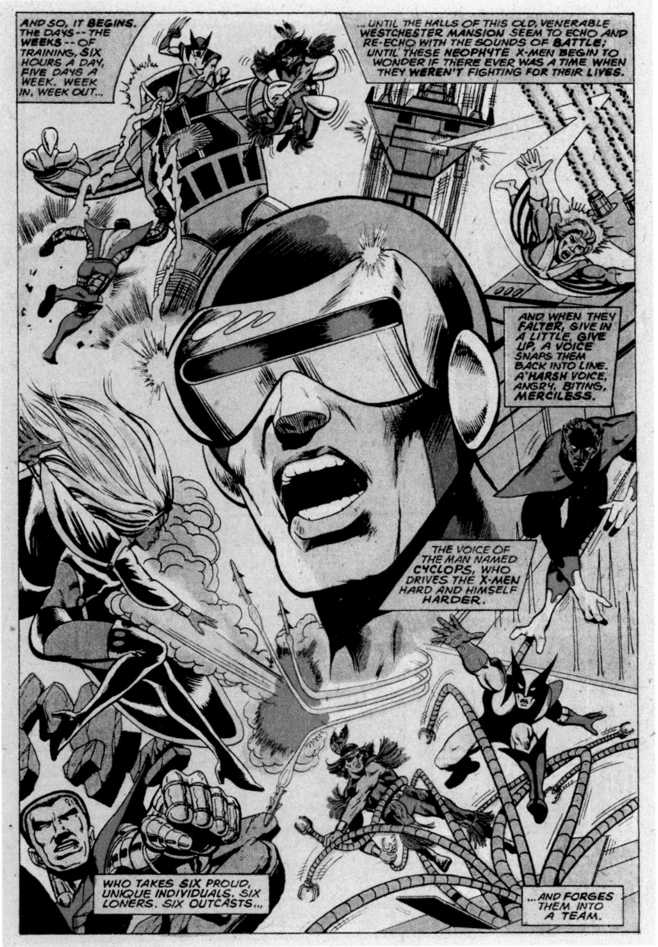
AND SO, IT BEGINS. THE DAYS -- THE WEEKS -- OF TRAINING, SIX HOURS A DAY, FIVE DAYS A WEEK, WEEK IN, WEEK OUT...
...UNTIL THE HALLS OF THIS OLD, VENERABLE WESTCHESTER MANSION SEEM TO ECHO AND RE-ECHO WITH THE SOUNDS OF BATTLE; UNTIL THESE NEOPHYTE X-MEN BEGIN TO WONDER IF THERE EVER WAS A TIME WHEN THEY WEREN'T FIGHTING FOR THEIR LIVES.
AND WHEN THEY FALTER, GIVE IN A LITTLE, GIVE UP, A VOICE SNAPS THEM BACK INTO LINE. A HARSH VOICE, ANGRY, BITING, MERCILESS.
THE VOICE OF THE MAN NAMED CYCLOPS, WHO DRIVES THE X-MEN HARD AND HIMSELF HARDER.
WHO TAKES SIX PROUD, UNIQUE INDIVIDUALS. SIX LONERS. SIX OUTCASTS...
...AND FORGES THEM INTO A TEAM.

X-MEN No. 94

(Left) Interior, "The Doomsmith Scenario!"; script, Chris Claremont; plot, Len Wein; pencils, Dave Cockrum; inks, Bob McLeod; August 1975.

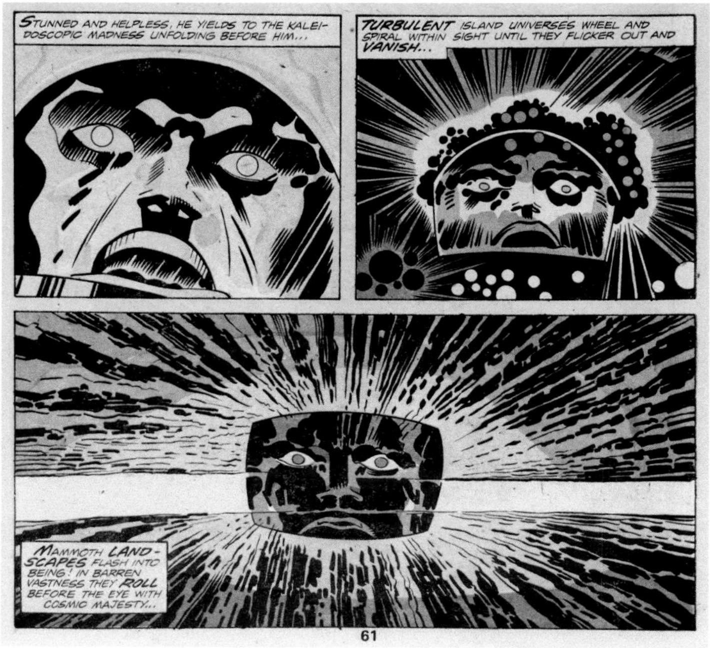
STUNNED AND HELPLESS, HE YIELDS TO THE KALEIDOSCOPIC MADNESS UNFOLDING BEFORE HIM...
TURBULENT ISLAND UNIVERSES WHEEL AND SPIRAL WITHIN SIGHT UNTIL THEY FLICKER OUT AND VANISH...
MAMMOTH LANDSCAPES FLASH INTO BEING! IN BARREN VASTNESS THEY ROLL BEFORE THE EYE WITH COSMIC MAJESTY...
61

POP GOES THE CULTURE!

By this point, Marvel's reach and influence were expanding into the world beyond comics. Building on what had been begun in the 1960s, its already-classic concepts and costumed characters were now woven into the warp and woof of the Vietnam War generation, the sexual revolution, racial politics, and the exponential growth of pop culture.

In 1975 Paul McCartney and his new group Wings recorded the song he had written for the Beatles, "Magneto and Titanium Man." Marvel characters were featured in the backdrop art for a Wings tour, and Kirby and his family had front-row seats at the band's Los Angeles concert. For a short time, there was a *Fantastic Four* dramatic radio series, adapting Lee and Kirby's stories and featuring Lee as narrator... with a 25-year-old actor named Bill Murray as the Human Torch. In February 1976 there was a second Marvel Con in New York... though, sadly, it would be the final one.

In the late 1970s, Universal TV licensed the rights to several Marvel heroes. *The Incredible Hulk*, following a highly rated TV movie, became a weekly series in 1978, starring Bill Bixby as David (not Bruce!) Banner and bodybuilding champion Lou

Ferrigno as his snarling (but unspeaking) green-skinned alter ego. It ran for five seasons and was followed by three more TV films, the first of which guest-starred Thor, while Daredevil appeared in the second. The series' most famous dialogue occurred in the 1977 TV movie, when Bixby/Banner warned an aggressive reporter who didn't suspect his secret life: "Don't make me angry. You won't like me when I'm angry." The series also gave rise to the phrase "hulking out," which was picked up by the comics.

Considerably less successful were three other Universal TV adaptations of Marvel characters. *The Amazing Spider-Man,*

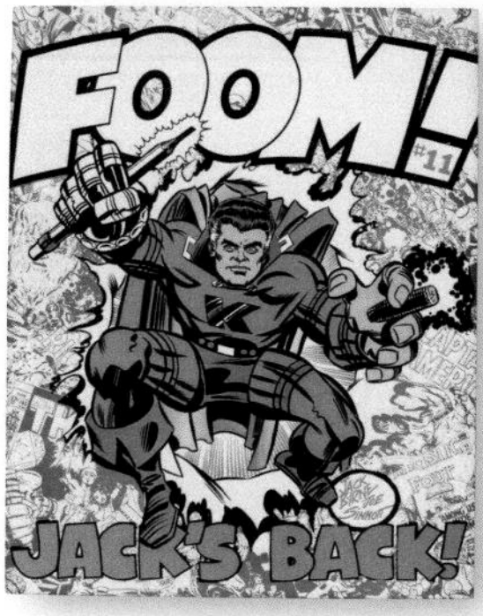
FOOM!
#11
JACK'S BACK!

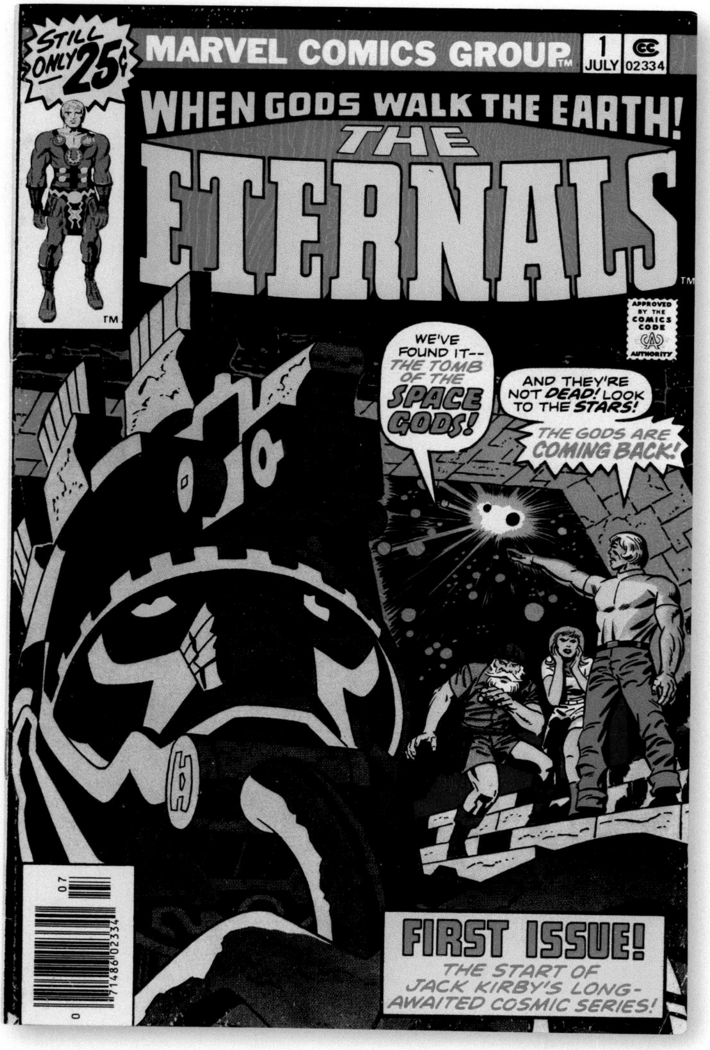
STILL ONLY 25¢
MARVEL COMICS GROUP
1 JULY 02334
WHEN GODS WALK THE EARTH!
THE ETERNALS
APPROVED BY THE COMICS CODE AUTHORITY
WE'VE FOUND IT-- THE TOMB OF THE SPACE GODS!
AND THEY'RE NOT DEAD! LOOK TO THE STARS!
THE GODS ARE COMING BACK!
FIRST ISSUE!
THE START OF JACK KIRBY'S LONG-AWAITED COSMIC SERIES!

2001: A SPACE ODYSSEY No. 1
(Opposite) Interior, "Beast-Killer!"; script and pencils, Jack Kirby; inks, Mike Royer; December 1976. Kirby adapts the Stanley Kubrick film as only he can in an oversized Treasury edition (just imagine the filmmaker's sequences with voice-over narration in Kirby style).

RETURN OF THE KING
(Above) Fanzine cover, FOOM *No. 11; pencils, John Byrne; inks, Joe Sinnott; September 1975.*

THE ETERNALS No. 1
(Left) Cover; pencils, Jack Kirby; inks, Frank Giacoia; July 1976. Playing with popular ideas of aliens in early human history, Kirby introduced the Eternals, a race of super-powered beings created by the near-omnipotent alien Celestials.

Vol. II, No. 3
September
Dynamite
LOU FERRIGNO: More than just a Hulk of muscle!

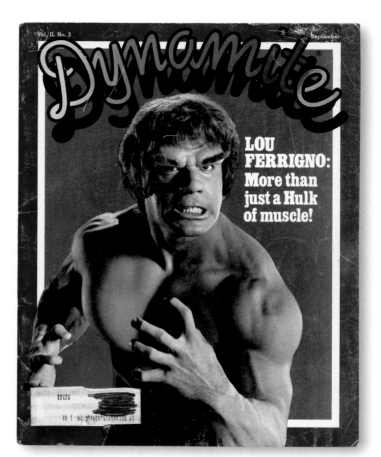

DON'T MAKE ME ANGRY...
(Right) Magazine cover, Dynamite, *1978.* Filmed for CBS on the backlot of Universal Studios, *The Incredible Hulk* series ran for 82 one-hour episodes with Bill Bixby as scientist David Banner (a departure from the comics' Bruce Banner) and bodybuilder Lou Ferrigno as his growling, green alter ego.

starring Nicholas Hammond, managed to air 13 episodes between 1977 and '79, but was hobbled by lackluster special effects and stories. *Dr. Strange* made its small-screen debut in 1978 opposite a much-watched re-airing of the TV mega-event *Roots*—and a planned sequel was canceled. The costumed hero of the 1979 *Captain America* TV movie didn't even *look* all that much like the Star-Spangled Avenger, with his altered costume and a motorcycle helmet for a mask. Instead of being a courageous wartime physical weakling who put himself in harm's way for his country, Universal's Cap inherited his moniker (the nickname of his father, a patriotic government agent) and received his abilities during lifesaving procedures he underwent after an accident. The TV folks had scant interest in utilizing the very elements that had made Marvel's heroes popular over several different decades.

The Incredible Hulk, at least, was Marvel's one major live-action media success for nearly two decades. But, apart from some outside merchandising, its major impact at the comics company was that of *The Rampaging Hulk,* a black-and-white magazine that had debuted January '77, was converted to color (and its name changed to *The Hulk!*).

Meanwhile, heading off plans of a Hollywood animation company to use the word *Spider* in the name of a new super heroine, Marvel came up with a creative solution to a practical problem: Writer Archie Goodwin and artist Sal Buscema introduced Spider-Woman in *Marvel Spotlight* No. 32 (February 1977). Filmation had to settle for Web-Woman.

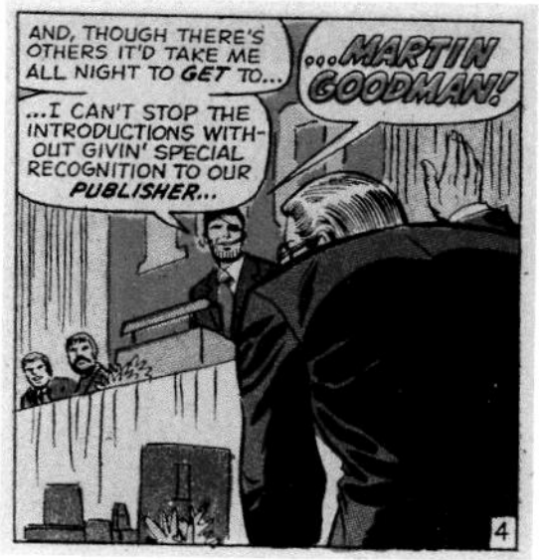
AND, THOUGH THERE'S OTHERS IT'D TAKE ME ALL NIGHT TO GET TO...
...I CAN'T STOP THE INTRODUCTIONS WITHOUT GIVIN' SPECIAL RECOGNITION TO OUR PUBLISHER...
...MARTIN GOODMAN!
4

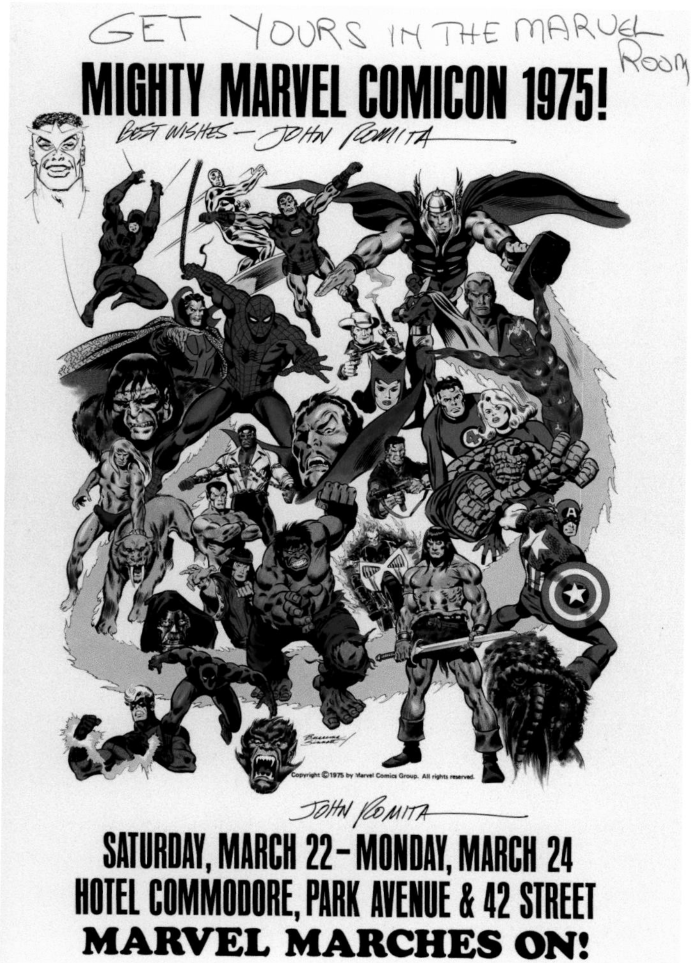
GET YOURS IN THE MARVEL ROOM
MIGHTY MARVEL COMICON 1975!
BEST WISHES — JOHN ROMITA
Copyright © 1975 by Marvel Comics Group. All rights reserved.
JOHN ROMITA
SATURDAY, MARCH 22 – MONDAY, MARCH 24
HOTEL COMMODORE, PARK AVENUE & 42 STREET
MARVEL MARCHES ON!

AVENGERS (FANS) ASSEMBLE!

(Left) Poster, Mighty Marvel Comicon*; pencils, John Buscema; inks, Joe Sinnott; 1975.*

GOODBYE, MR. GOODMAN

(Above) Interior, Sgt. Fury No. 100*; script, Gary Friedrich; pencils, Dick Ayers; inks, Mike Esposito; July 1972.*

THE ADVENTURES OF THE
Fantastic Four
The Marvel Comics Radio Series

ON THE RADIO

(Above) Vinyl record, The Adventures of the Fantastic Four, *1975.* With scripts taken directly from the comic books, the adventures were chopped into five-minute segments memorable for the presence of Bill Murray, who voiced the Human Torch. He likely shed no sizzling tears, since he followed it up with the second season of *Saturday Night Live.*

THE FANTASTIC . . . WAIT, WHAT'S THAT?!

(Right) Storyboard, Fantastic Four *cartoon, NBC; art, Jack Kirby; 1978.* The Human Torch was unavailable when the FF flew to the small screen, so Mr. Fantastic, the Invisible Woman, and the Thing were joined by H.E.R.B.I.E. the robot.

THE HULK! No. 10

(Opposite) Cover; art, Val Mayerik; August 1978. The magazine that had been *The Rampaging Hulk* was reworked in full-color as *The Hulk!* with No. 10 to capitalize on the success of the television series.

In 1976, Marvel, which under Sol Brodsky was already publishing several weekly black-and-white reprint comics for sale in the United Kingdom, developed its first super hero directly for that market: Captain Britain. He would later appear in U.S. comics.

Stan Lee—virtually the walking incarnation of Marvel by this point—was featured in TV commercials for the Personna Double II twin-blade razor and in print ads for Hathaway shirts. And, of course, he continued to make personal appearances, mostly at colleges, where he was the ultimate Marvel spokesman and cheerleader.

In 1977 he and Marvel also opened a new front: newspaper comic strips, starting with "The Amazing Spider-Man" written by "Stan the Man" and drawn by John Romita for the Register and Tribune Syndicate. It would be followed by strips "Howard the Duck" (later in '77) and "The Incredible Hulk" and "Conan the Barbarian" (both 1978). Only the Spider-Man comic strip lasted more than a couple of years; it appeared daily for nearly 42 years, most of them written by Lee, drawn chiefly by Larry Lieber (having returned to the Marvel fold after the collapse of Atlas/Seaboard) and Alex Saviuk.

HOORAY FOR HOLLYWOOD!

At this point, Marvel was riding high in the comics field, with no real competition except DC—yet, despite its number-one position, things weren't nearly as rosy as they seemed.

The drugstores, five-and-dimes, and mom-and-pop stores that had long been the main vendors for comics were either

4309
36
BEN: What's 'a matter with him?
REED: He seems to be trapped in some sort of force field.
HERBIE: Cannot compute . . . . cannot compute . .
What are we going to do about it?
REED: There must be some sort of power source
BEN: I got the idea, pal.
This oughta' cure him!
HERBIE: Cannot compute . . . cannot compute.
(o.s.) Cosine of a 30 degree angle equals
Ahhhhhhhhhhhh. Thank-you, Benjamine
BEN: Any time, little pal.

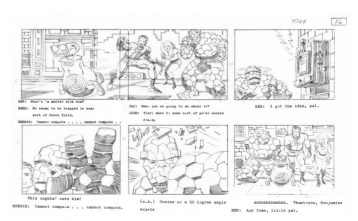

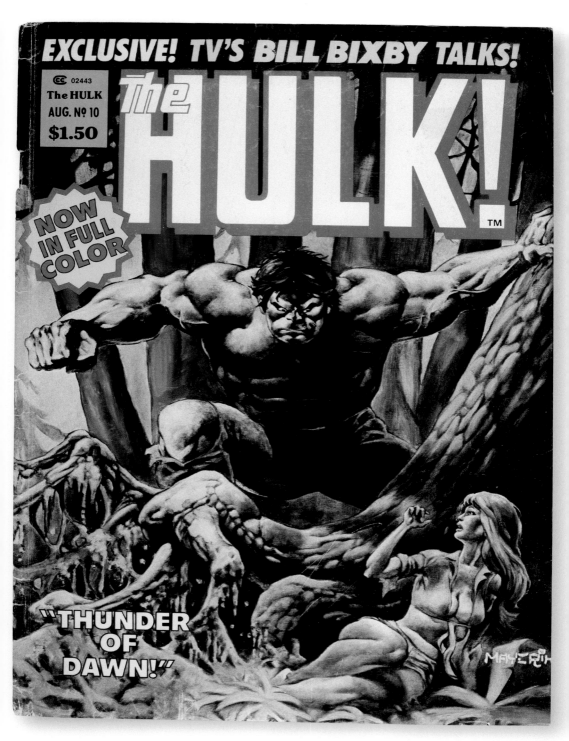

EXCLUSIVE! TV'S BILL BIXBY TALKS!

CC 02443
The HULK
AUG. Nº 10
$1.50

The HULK!

™

NOW IN FULL COLOR

"THUNDER OF DAWN!"

SPIDER-MAN GOES PRIME TIME

(Right) Publicity photo, The Amazing Spider-Man, *CBS, 1977.* The wall-crawler's big shot at a TV audience came with a 1977 pilot starring Nicholas Hammond as Peter Parker / Spider-Man.

MIGHTY MARVEL TV MOVIES

(Opposite) Publicity still, Captain America *TV movie, CBS, 1979.* Captain America starred Reb Brown as a red-white-and-blue-clad super hero that was quite different than the Marvel Comics version. The show's makers (like all of Hollywood) approached the comic property with little interest in adapting the traditional contours of the enduring mythology or its proven iconography.

going out of business, or being swallowed up by chains that favored magazines with a higher cover price than the 30 cents that had become the standard in comic books.

In addition, comics were sold to distributors on a "returnable" basis. That system tempted some dealers to simply tear off the covers of comics and return them to the publisher for a full refund of their advance, then sell the coverless mags for pure profit. Worse: by the '70s the comics companies accepted affidavits swearing that those comics hadn't been sold, rather than insisting on the physical return of ripped-off covers; that enabled the larceny-inclined to get back the money they had advanced for the comics, then sell *intact* copies under the table. For the publishers, this amounted to double jeopardy. One partial answer to their problems had manifested itself in 1973, when comics conventioneer Phil Seuling of Brooklyn had contracted to handle a certain percentage of the print runs of Marvel's and DC's magazines on a nonreturnable basis, in return for receiving the same large discount that distributors received. These were the early birth pangs of a direct-market arrangement that would eventually help the companies safeguard themselves against both fraud and crippling returns of legitimately unsold copies. The direct-market system would take several years to develop, and there would be a lot of growing pains...but it was a start.

In 1975, James Galton, a consultant to Curtis Circulation, the Cadence-owned distributor of Marvel's comics, replaced Al Landau as Marvel's president. Reportedly, Galton was given a year or two to reverse various downward trends, or Cadence was very likely to disband Marvel entirely. At the time, Marvel's survival in the face of rising costs and the sinking viability of the newsstand must have made Galton's marching orders seem almost like a suicide mission. Strangely, one factor that helped the company survive during this period was Hollywood—not a major film about a Marvel hero (that was still years in the future), but the reverse—a comic book adaptation of an adventure movie.

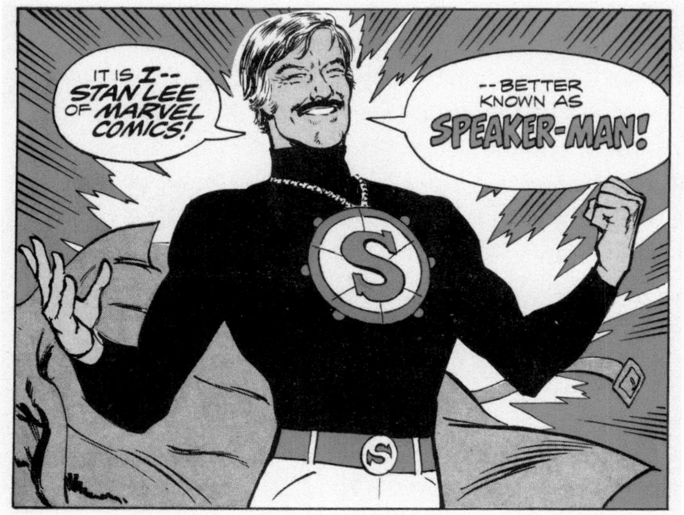
IT IS I-- STAN LEE OF MARVEL COMICS!
--BETTER KNOWN AS SPEAKER-MAN!

THIS IS A JOB FOR SPEAKER-MAN!
(Above) Promotional comic, Marvel Comics to the Rescue!; *pencils and inks, attributed Marie Severin; early 1970s.* "Our students are tired of the *usual* lecturers! They want someone *different!* Someone *off-beat!* and provocative! But where can we find someone so *special?*" With this mini-comic, American Program Bureau pitched Stan Lee as a guest speaker for the college circuit. It worked.

CAPTAIN BRITAIN No. 1
(Opposite) Cover; pencils, Larry Lieber; inks, Frank Giacoia; October 1976.

In early 1976, writer/editor Roy Thomas—just because he considered it an interesting project—persuaded Lee and Galton to take a flier at producing a comic book adaptation of a forthcoming science-fiction film from 20th Century Fox and *American Graffiti* director George Lucas. Its name: *Star Wars.* It had been brought to Thomas by Lucas's media projects director, Charles Lippincott; he and Lucas were so eager to see a Marvel *Stars Wars* comic that they waived any up-front licensing fees; their only requirement was that at least two or three issues of a several-part adaptation had to be on sale before the movie's world premiere in spring of '77. Thomas and rising artist Howard Chaykin handled the six issues, at Lucas's request. The early issues sold well even before the movie's May '77 debut, and, afterward, sales for a time exceeded a million copies per issue, with the first few installments being reissued. Tabloid-size reprints, plus an ongoing *Star Wars* comic that continued the saga, have been credited by both Galton and then-new editor-in-chief Jim Shooter with keeping Marvel in the black during an era of declining outlets and rising prices for newsprint, giving the company breathing room to successfully weather the storm. Other movie and TV licenses soon followed at Marvel, including *Battlestar Galactica,* based on an interstellar TV series.

Around the same time, the manager of the costumed rock band KISS proposed that Marvel publish a comic starring the group, whose leader, Gene Simmons, was a fervent comics fan.

With Steve Gerber writing and several top artists drawing, the magazine-format (but full-color) comic book *Marvel Comics Super Special* No. 1 turned the rockers into bona fide super heroes. Blood was drawn from each member of KISS by a registered nurse and poured into vats of the red ink used in the comic's printing—and the mag earned the comics equivalent of a gold record. A sequel or two followed, as did another *Special* billed as "The Ultimate *Unauthorized* Beatles Book!"

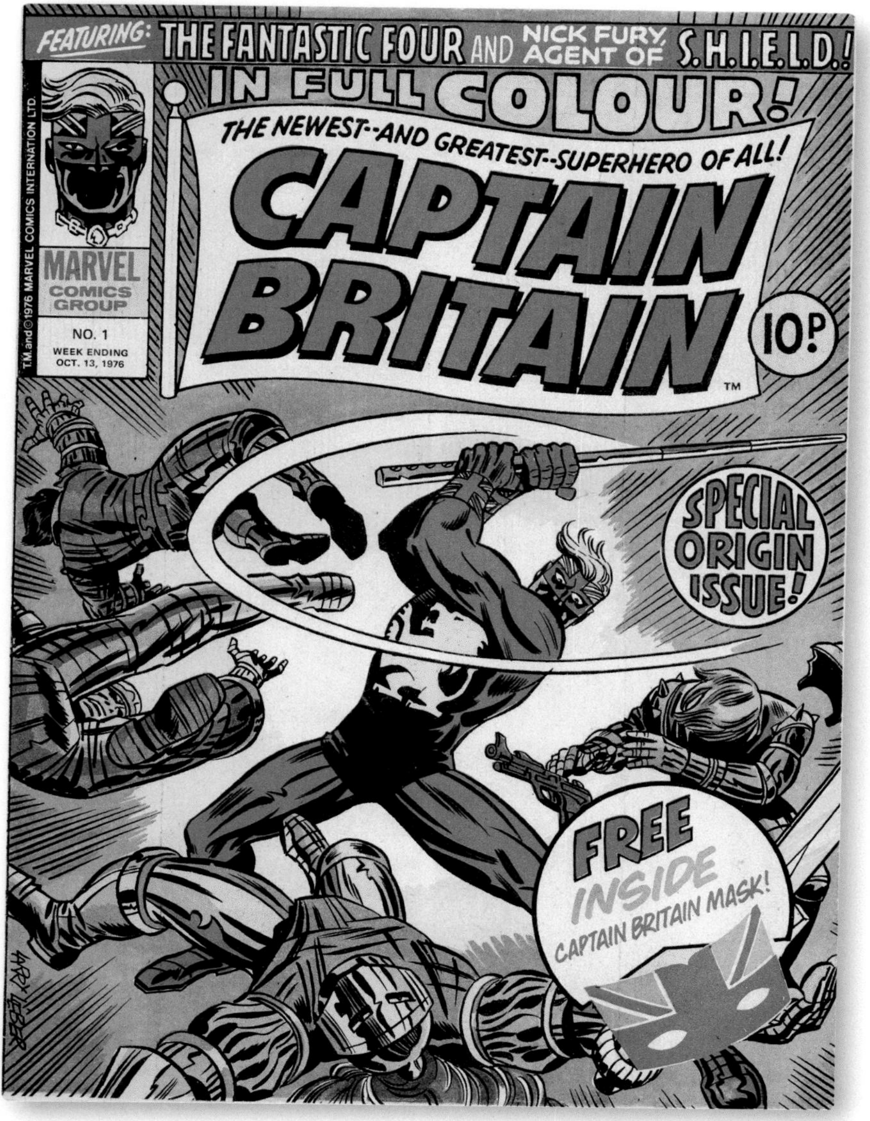
FEATURING: THE FANTASTIC FOUR AND NICK FURY, AGENT OF S.H.I.E.L.D.!
IN FULL COLOUR!
THE NEWEST--AND GREATEST--SUPERHERO OF ALL!
CAPTAIN BRITAIN
TM
10P
MARVEL COMICS GROUP
NO. 1
WEEK ENDING OCT. 13, 1976
T.M. and ©1976 MARVEL COMICS INTERNATION LTD.
SPECIAL ORIGIN ISSUE!
FREE INSIDE CAPTAIN BRITAIN MASK!

SWINGING ONTO AMERICA'S DRIVEWAYS
(Right) Newspaper strip, "The Amazing Spider-Man"; script, Stan Lee; pencils and inks, John Romita; Register and Tribune Syndicate, 1977. Your friendly neighborhood Spider-Man appeared daily in the funny pages of your local paper beginning in 1977. A smash hit, the strip led to a wave of Marvel newsprint comics.

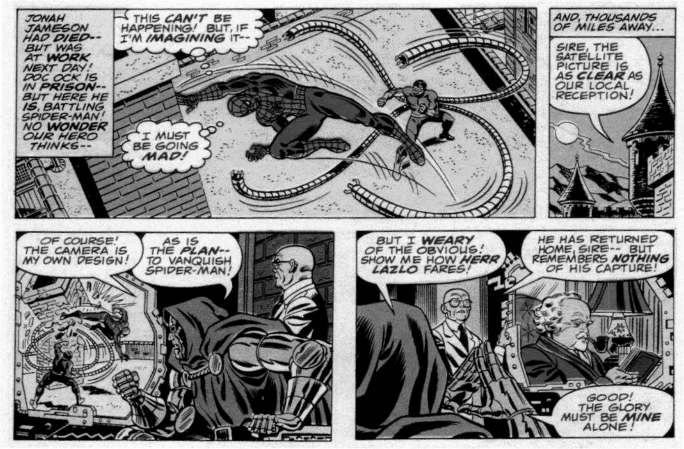
JONAH JAMESON HAD DIED-- BUT WAS AT WORK NEXT DAY! DOC OCK IS IN PRISON-- BUT HERE HE IS, BATTLING SPIDER-MAN! NO WONDER OUR HERO THINKS--
THIS CAN'T BE HAPPENING! BUT, IF I'M IMAGINING IT--
I MUST BE GOING MAD!
AND, THOUSANDS OF MILES AWAY...
SIRE, THE SATELLITE PICTURE IS AS CLEAR AS OUR LOCAL RECEPTION!
OF COURSE! THE CAMERA IS MY OWN DESIGN!
AS IS THE PLAN-- TO VANQUISH SPIDER-MAN!
BUT I WEARY OF THE OBVIOUS! SHOW ME HOW HERR LAZLO FARES!
HE HAS RETURNED HOME, SIRE-- BUT REMEMBERS NOTHING OF HIS CAPTURE!
GOOD! THE GLORY MUST BE MINE ALONE!

Even the "Not Ready for Prime Time Players" of NBC's popular *Saturday Night Live* teamed up with Spider-Man in *Marvel Team-Up* No. 74 (October 1978), written by Chris Claremont and drawn by Bob Hall and Marie Severin. Editor Jim Shooter, in a blog some years later, recalled comedian John Belushi's visit to Marvel: "He seemed more excited to meet us and see the offices of Marvel Comics than we were to meet him, if that's possible.... In the big editorial room we had all the current covers hung up on one wall. Belushi told us the plot of each book represented on that wall to prove he'd read them! Speaking about his difficulties writing the story, Chris said: 'John, you have no idea how hard it is to write comedy.' Belushi did an incredulity 'take.' Beat. 'YES, I DO!'...[Before he left, Belushi] invited those of us who had worked on the *Team-Up* story to the opening-night party for [his new film] *Animal House....*"

Then there was Dazzler—a mutant heroine whose origins were one part Marvel, one part music biz, and one part Hollywood. It was agreed that Marvel would develop a singing comic-book super heroine, Casablanca Records would provide the live songstress, and Filmworks (Casablanca's film division) would produce a movie built around a character originally called "The Disco Queen." Casablanca and Filmworks soon dropped out, and the project metamorphosed for a time into a possible vehicle for actress Bo Derek, who'd risen to fame in the motion picture *10* the previous year. Marvel eventually decided to introduce the character on its own. This mutant who could convert sonic vibrations into beams of energy made her debut in *X-Men* No. 130 (February 1980); her own comic premiered in 1981. Released only through comic book stores, as an experiment, *Dazzler* No. 1 sold 428,000 nonreturnable copies—far more copies than the average Marvel title.

In 1978, Simon & Schuster began publishing paperbacks collecting Marvel comics material under its Pocket Books imprint, eventually putting out nine of them, plus 11 original Marvel prose novels. A few years later, S&S would also issue the monumentally successful volume *How to Draw Comics the Marvel Way* by Stan Lee and John Buscema, in which the wordsmith who had created the company's prose style and one of the best draftsmen and storytellers in the history of the field combined forces to produce a virtual encyclopedia on how to write and draw one's own comics stories, using artwork from Marvel Comics (and new sketches by Buscema) as its primary examples. The book has remained in print ever since.

Meanwhile, Marvel entered into a TV partnership with a longtime Hollywood TV animation company, DePatie-Freleng. The fruit of their efforts was a *Fantastic Four* cartoon series—in which the Human Torch was replaced by a

MARVEL TEAM-UP No. 74

(Below) Interior, "Live from New York, It's Saturday Night!"; script, Chris Claremont; pencils, Bob Hall; inks, Marie Severin; October 1978. They may not have been ready for prime time, but the *Saturday Night Live* players were ready for a comics close-up with Spider-Man.

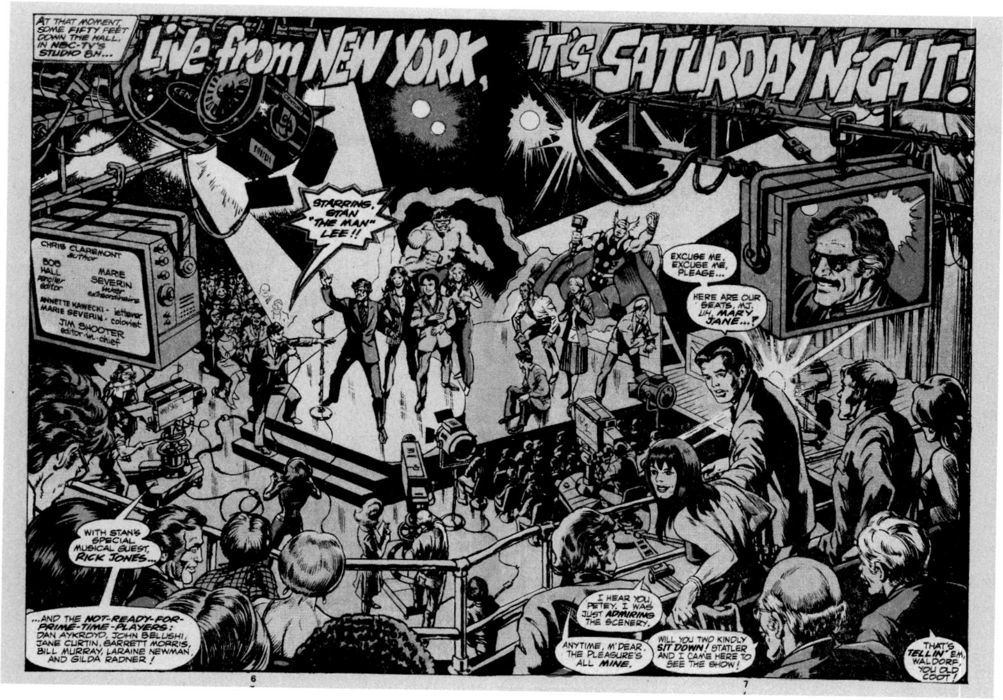

AT THAT MOMENT, SOME FIFTY FEET DOWN THE HALL, IN NBC-TV'S STUDIO 8H...
Live from NEW YORK, IT'S SATURDAY NIGHT!
STARRING, STAN "THE MAN" LEE!!
CHRIS CLAREMONT author
BOB HALL penciler editor
MARIE SEVERIN inker extraordinaire
ANNETTE KAWECKI - letterer
MARIE SEVERIN - colorist
JIM SHOOTER editor-in-chief
EXCUSE ME, EXCUSE ME, PLEASE...
HERE ARE OUR SEATS, MJ. UH, MARY JANE...?
WITH STAN'S SPECIAL MUSICAL GUEST, RICK JONES...
...AND THE NOT-READY-FOR-PRIME-TIME-PLAYERS: DAN AYKROYD, JOHN BELUSHI, JANE CURTIN, GARRETT MORRIS, BILL MURRAY, LARAINE NEWMAN, AND GILDA RADNER!
I HEAR YOU, PETEY. I WAS JUST ADMIRING THE SCENERY.
ANYTIME, M'DEAR. THE PLEASURE'S ALL MINE.
WILL YOU TWO KINDLY SIT DOWN! STATLER AND I CAME HERE TO SEE THE SHOW!
THAT'S TELLIN' EM, WALDORF, YOU OLD COOT!
6
7

MARVEL COMICS TRY-OUT BOOK No. 1
(Below) House ad; art, attributed Terry Austin; 1983.

STAR WARS No. 1
(Opposite) Cover; pencils and inks, Howard Chaykin; July 1977. Marvel had the first comics based on George Lucas's blockbuster, the first six issues of which adapted the movie, scripted by Roy Thomas and drawn by Chaykin and others.

wastebasket-sized robot called H.E.R.B.I.E. (because, at the time, the Torch had been optioned for a proposed live-action movie). Jack Kirby drew numerous storyboards for the series, his last official work on the heroes whose creation by Lee and himself had ushered in the Marvel Age of Comics, two decades earlier. Most of the stories were scripted by Stan Lee and Roy Thomas, who was now living in Los Angeles. If one can overlook the unavoidable substitution of H.E.R.B.I.E. for the Torch, the series was in many ways the most faithful full-animation adaptation of a Marvel comic to reach the home screen until the '90s; even so, it was canceled after a single season.

Despite that disappointment, the 1970s—with the *Star Wars* success and the sales of the first KISS magazine in particular—had seen the cementing of a relationship between Marvel Comics and show business that would continue to grow, at least in leaps and spurts, until, at the turn of the 21st century, Hollywood would start coming to Marvel instead of the other way around.

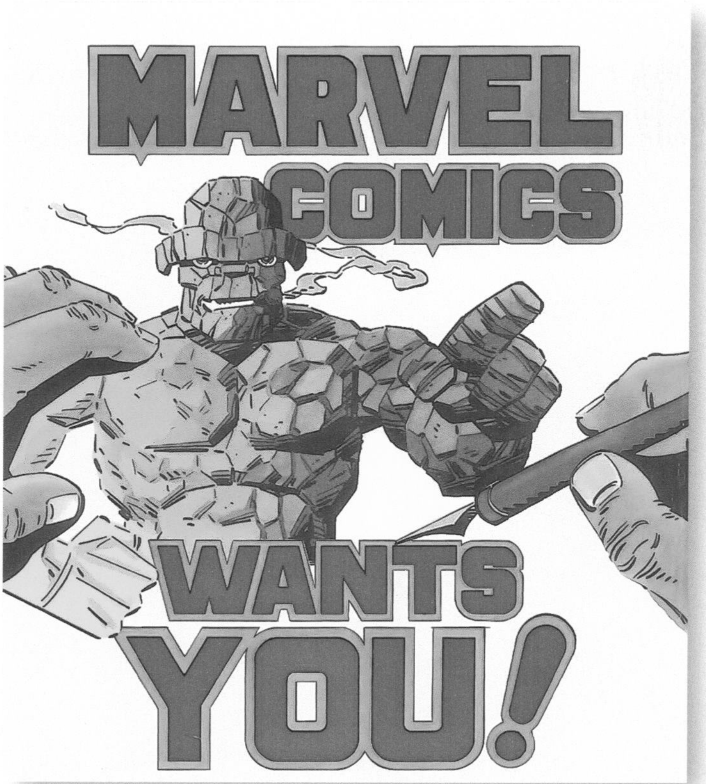
MARVEL
COMICS
WANTS
YOU!

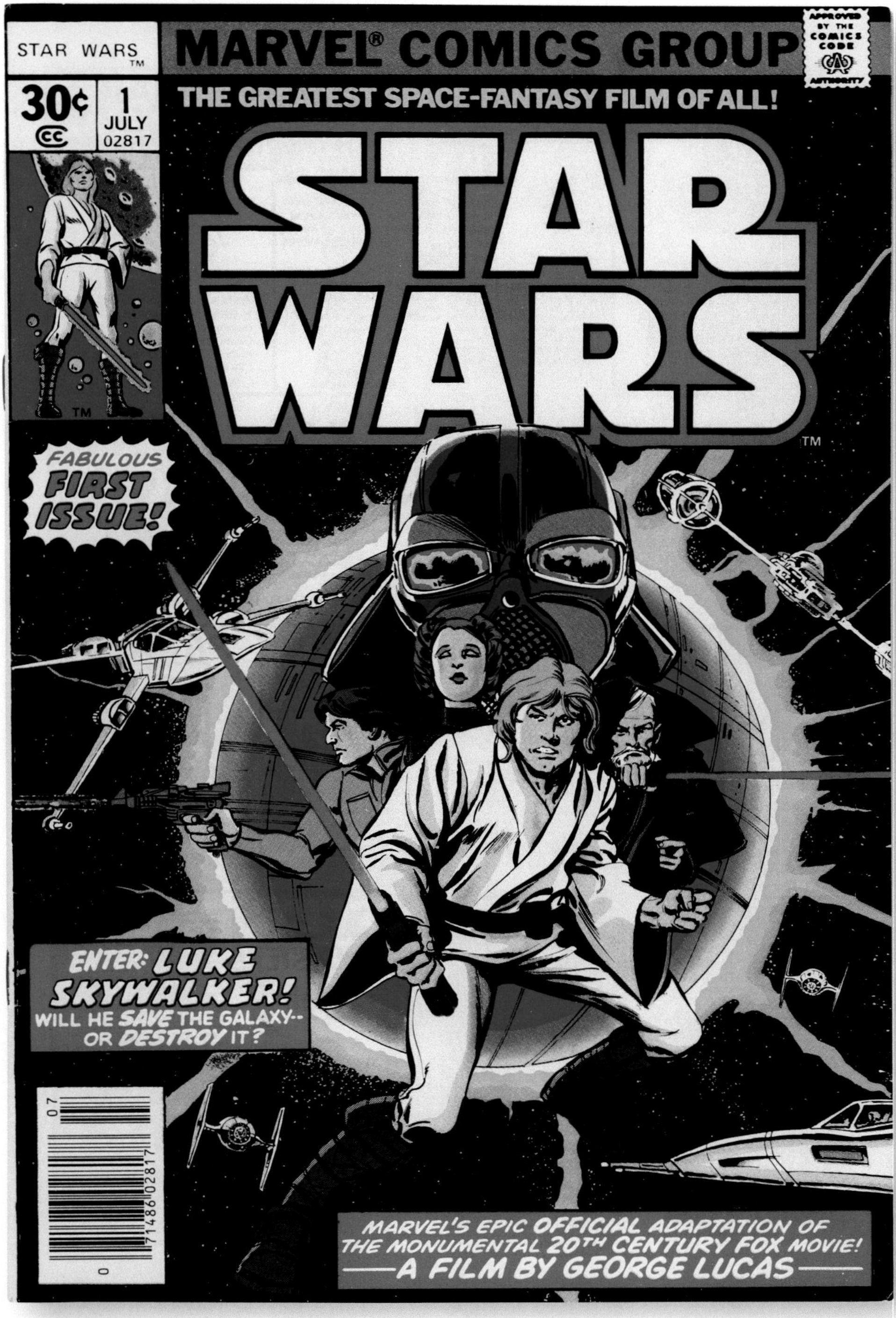
STAR WARS ™
MARVEL® COMICS GROUP
APPROVED BY THE COMICS CODE AUTHORITY
30¢
CC
1
JULY
02817
THE GREATEST SPACE-FANTASY FILM OF ALL!
STAR WARS
™
FABULOUS FIRST ISSUE!
ENTER: LUKE SKYWALKER!
WILL HE SAVE THE GALAXY--
OR DESTROY IT?
MARVEL'S EPIC OFFICIAL ADAPTATION OF
THE MONUMENTAL 20TH CENTURY FOX MOVIE!
—A FILM BY GEORGE LUCAS—

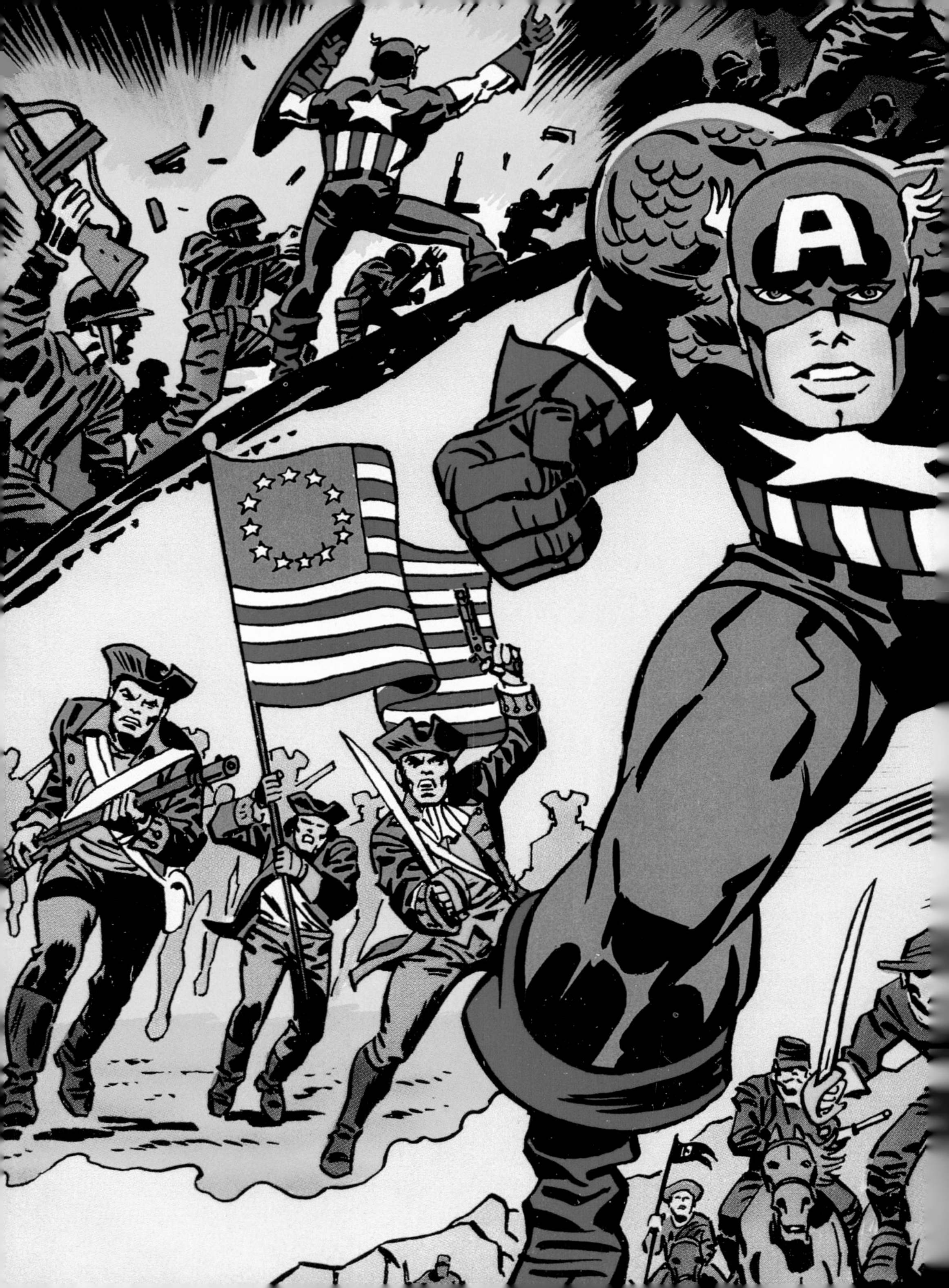

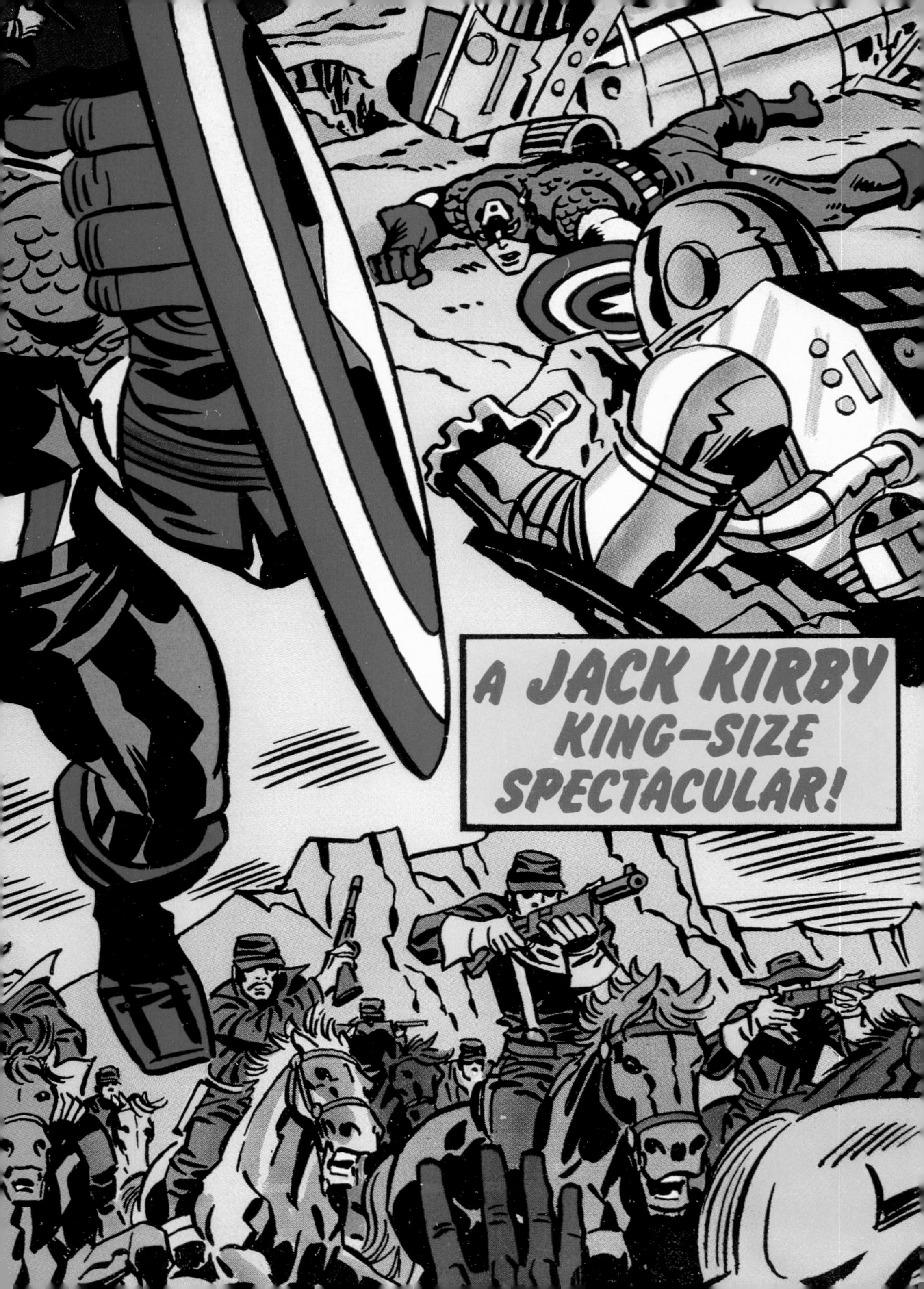
A JACK KIRBY KING-SIZE SPECTACULAR!

BY CROM! THEY SHOULD NOT--!
AND, BY CROM-- THEY SHALL NOT!!

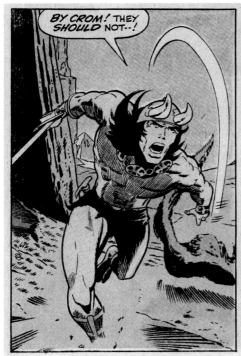

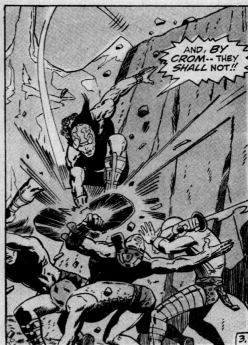

MARVEL TREASURY SPECIAL No. 1

(Previous spread) Cover; pencils, Jack Kirby, Marie Severin; inks, Frank Giacoia; September 1976.

CONAN THE BARBARIAN No. 1

(Above) Interior, "The Coming of Conan!"; script, Roy Thomas; pencils, Barry Smith; inks, Dan Adkins. October 1970.

KING-SIZE CONAN THE BARBARIAN No. 1

(Opposite) Cover; pencils and inks, Barry Smith; 1973. When Conan comes to claim his award, don't stand in his way! The Academy Award mentioned on this special's cover wasn't an Oscar — a prize that has eluded the Cimmerian — rather, as explained on the Hyborian Page inside, it was the Academy of Comic Book Art honors, for Smith as best new talent in 1970 and Thomas as best writer (domestic division) in 1971. Meanwhile, Conan had nominations for 1972 at the issue's press time, but didn't win. Still, how about an award for Smith's signature?

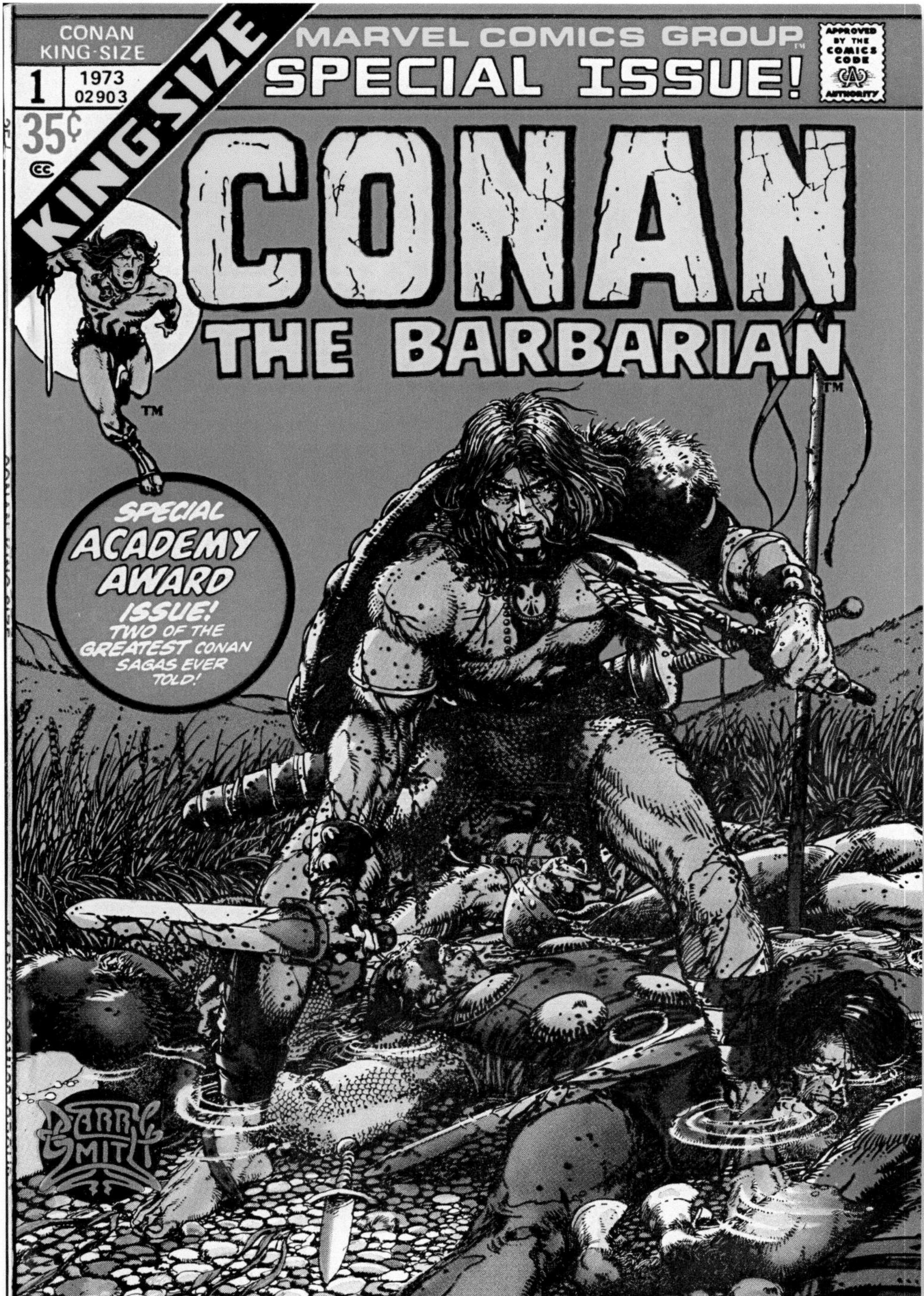

CONAN
KING-SIZE
1
1973
02903
KING-SIZE
MARVEL COMICS GROUP
SPECIAL ISSUE!
APPROVED BY THE COMICS CODE AUTHORITY
35¢
CONAN
THE BARBARIAN
SPECIAL
ACADEMY AWARD
ISSUE!
TWO OF THE GREATEST CONAN SAGAS EVER TOLD!

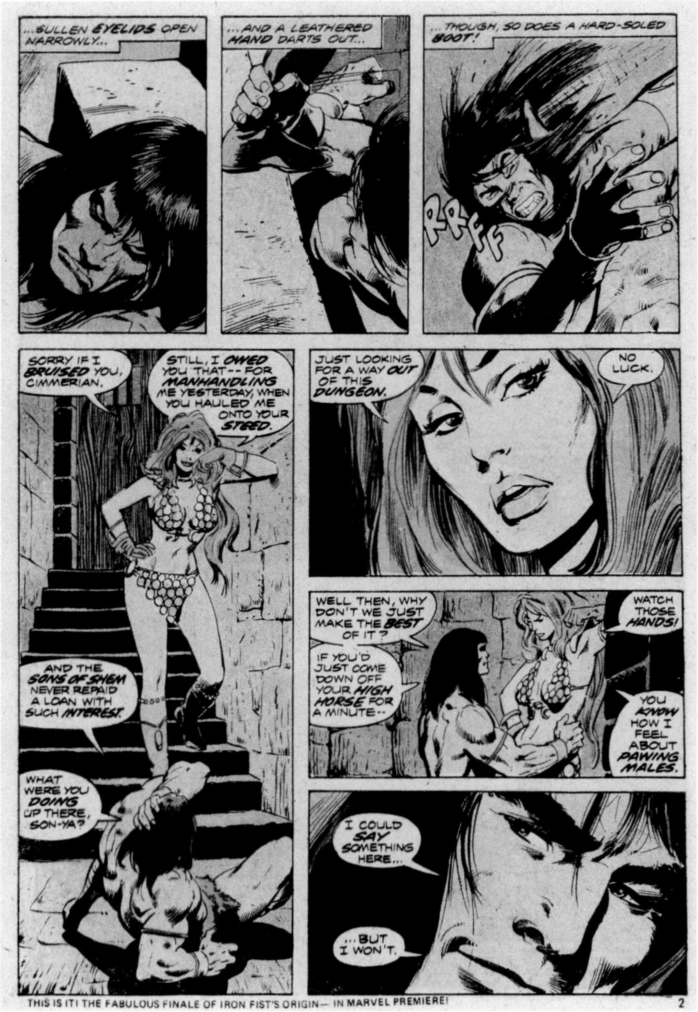
...SULLEN EYELIDS OPEN NARROWLY...
...AND A LEATHERED HAND DARTS OUT...
...THOUGH, SO DOES A HARD-SOLED BOOT!
RRFF
SORRY IF I BRUISED YOU, CIMMERIAN.
STILL, I OWED YOU THAT-- FOR MANHANDLING ME YESTERDAY, WHEN YOU HAULED ME ONTO YOUR STEED.
AND THE SONS OF SHEM NEVER REPAID A LOAN WITH SUCH INTEREST.
WHAT WERE YOU DOING UP THERE, SON-YA?
JUST LOOKING FOR A WAY OUT OF THIS DUNGEON.
NO LUCK.
WELL THEN, WHY DON'T WE JUST MAKE THE BEST OF IT?
IF YOU'D JUST COME DOWN OFF YOUR HIGH HORSE FOR A MINUTE--
WATCH THOSE HANDS!
YOU KNOW HOW I FEEL ABOUT PAWING MALES.
I COULD SAY SOMETHING HERE...
...BUT I WON'T.
THIS IS IT! THE FABULOUS FINALE OF IRON FIST'S ORIGIN— IN MARVEL PREMIERE!
2

CONAN THE BARBARIAN No. 44

(Above) Interior, "Of Flame and the Fiend!"; script, Roy Thomas; pencils, John Buscema; inks, Neal Adams's Crusty Bunkers; November 1974. Taking over from Barry Smith with the title's 25th issue, John Buscema settled into a 15-year run as artist of Conan the Barbarian—and earned renown from many as the definitive one.

CONAN THE BARBARIAN No. 24

(Opposite) Interior, "The Song of Red Sonja"; script, Roy Thomas; pencils and inks, Barry Smith; March 1973.

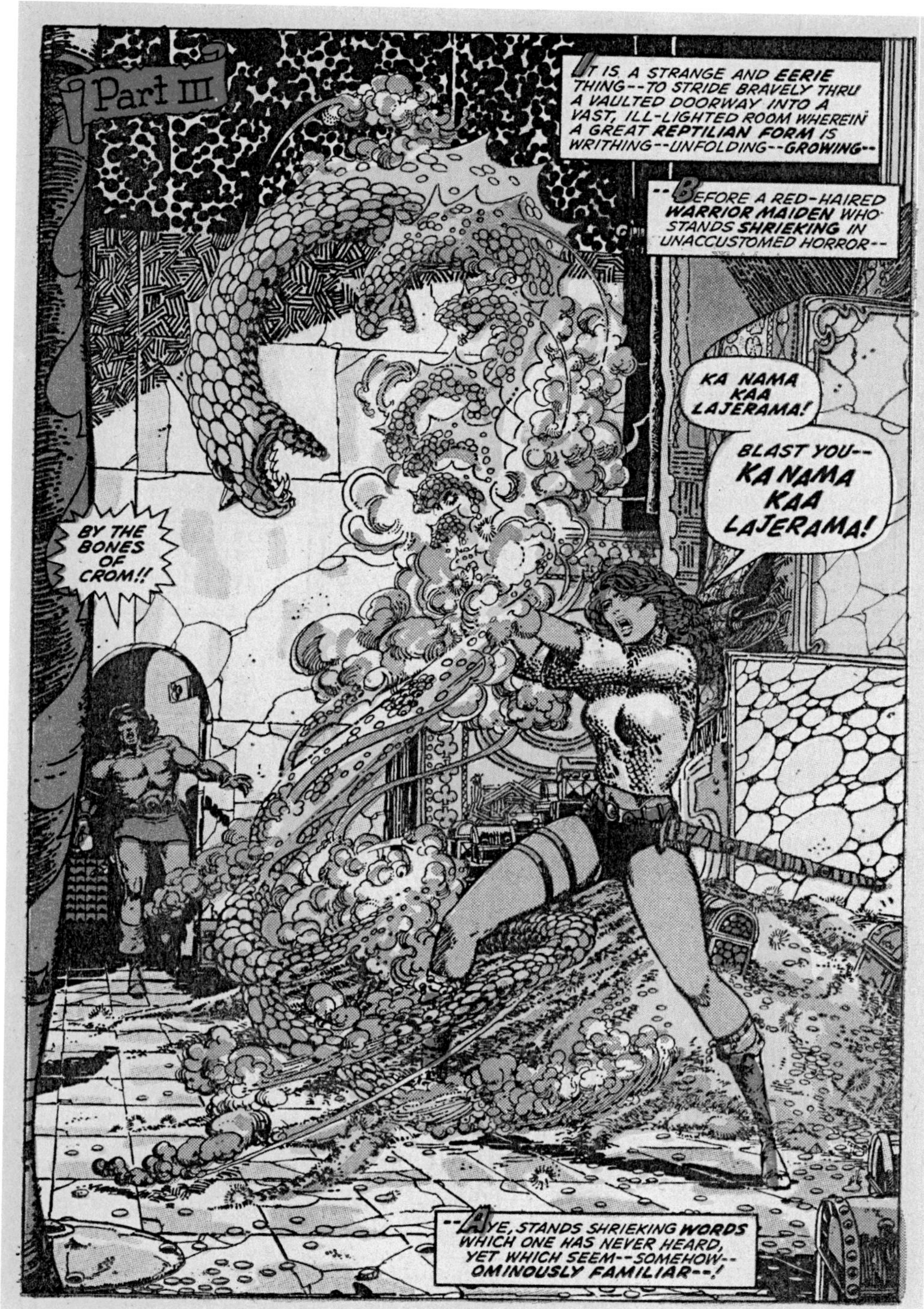
Part III
IT IS A STRANGE AND EERIE THING--TO STRIDE BRAVELY THRU A VAULTED DOORWAY INTO A VAST, ILL-LIGHTED ROOM WHEREIN A GREAT REPTILIAN FORM IS WRITHING--UNFOLDING--GROWING--
--BEFORE A RED-HAIRED WARRIOR MAIDEN WHO STANDS SHRIEKING IN UNACCUSTOMED HORROR--
KA NAMA KAA LAJERAMA!
BLAST YOU-- KA NAMA KAA LAJERAMA!
BY THE BONES OF CROM!!
--AYE, STANDS SHRIEKING WORDS WHICH ONE HAS NEVER HEARD, YET WHICH SEEM--SOMEHOW--OMINOUSLY FAMILIAR--!

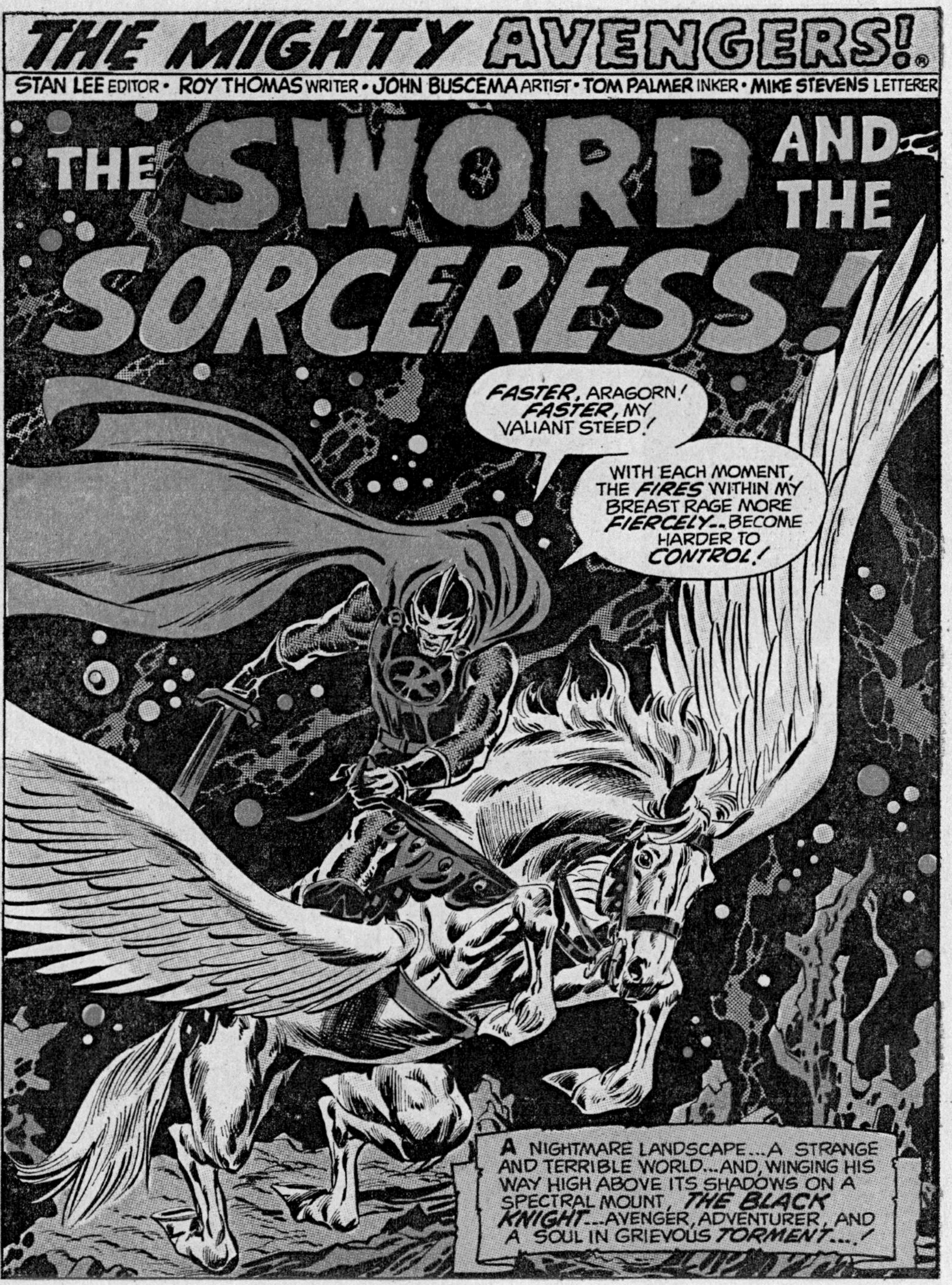
THE MIGHTY AVENGERS!
STAN LEE EDITOR • ROY THOMAS WRITER • JOHN BUSCEMA ARTIST • TOM PALMER INKER • MIKE STEVENS LETTERER
THE SWORD AND THE SORCERESS!
FASTER, ARAGORN! FASTER, MY VALIANT STEED!
WITH EACH MOMENT, THE FIRES WITHIN MY BREAST RAGE MORE FIERCELY.. BECOME HARDER TO CONTROL!
A NIGHTMARE LANDSCAPE...A STRANGE AND TERRIBLE WORLD...AND, WINGING HIS WAY HIGH ABOVE ITS SHADOWS ON A SPECTRAL MOUNT, THE BLACK KNIGHT...AVENGER, ADVENTURER, AND A SOUL IN GRIEVOUS TORMENT...!

AVENGERS No. 84

(Opposite) Interior, "The Sword and the Sorceress!"; script, Roy Thomas; pencils, John Buscema; inks, Tom Palmer; January 1971. Avengers stories know no genre boundaries — medieval fantasy in space? It's just a quick teleportation trip away.

AVENGERS No. 97

(Below) Interior, "Godhood's End!"; script, Roy Thomas; pencils, John Buscema; inks, Tom Palmer; March 1972. Longtime comic book readers found an everyman they could relate to in Rick Jones, whose status as the "Forrest Gump" of the Marvel Universe placed him in close contact with the heroes he (and they) admired. Plus, his obsessive knowledge of past comic characters came in handy in ending the Kree/Skrull War!

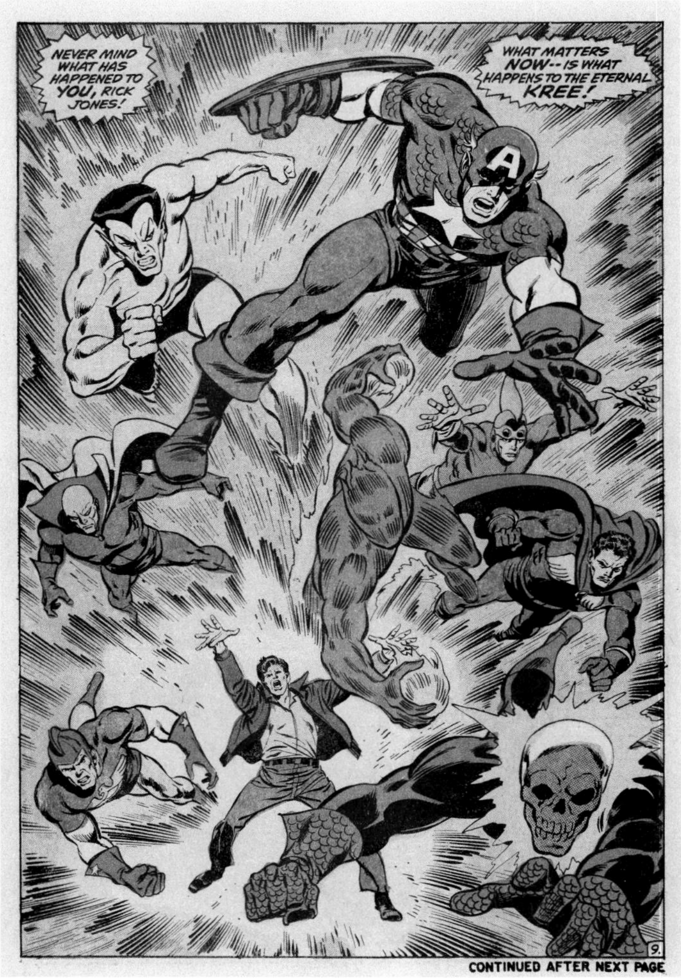
NEVER MIND WHAT HAS HAPPENED TO YOU, RICK JONES!
WHAT MATTERS NOW-- IS WHAT HAPPENS TO THE ETERNAL KREE!
9.
CONTINUED AFTER NEXT PAGE

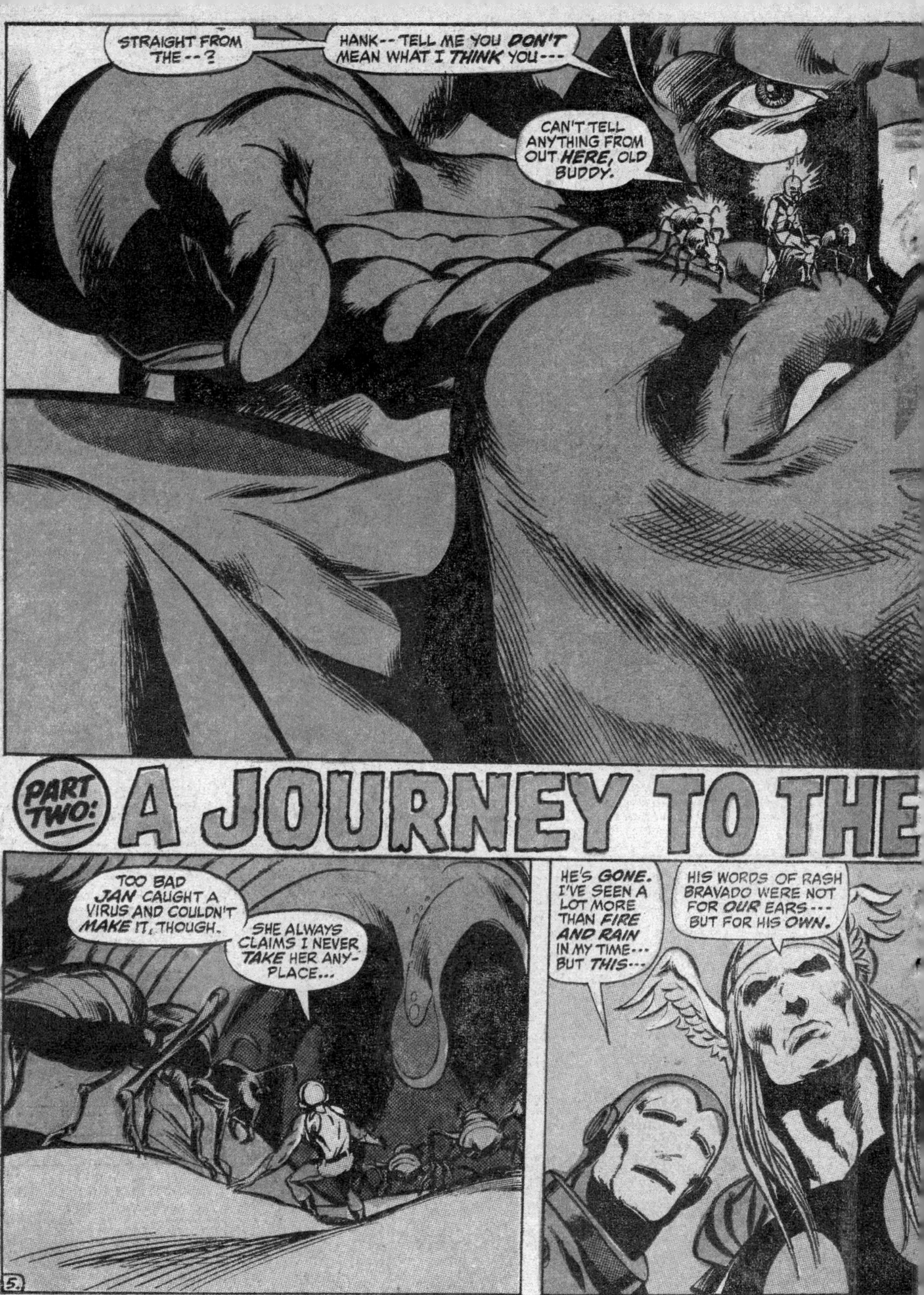
STRAIGHT FROM THE--?
HANK--TELL ME YOU DON'T MEAN WHAT I THINK YOU---
CAN'T TELL ANYTHING FROM OUT HERE, OLD BUDDY.
PART TWO: A JOURNEY TO THE
TOO BAD JAN CAUGHT A VIRUS AND COULDN'T MAKE IT, THOUGH.
SHE ALWAYS CLAIMS I NEVER TAKE HER ANY-PLACE...
HE'S GONE. I'VE SEEN A LOT MORE THAN FIRE AND RAIN IN MY TIME... BUT THIS---
HIS WORDS OF RASH BRAVADO WERE NOT FOR OUR EARS--- BUT FOR HIS OWN.
5

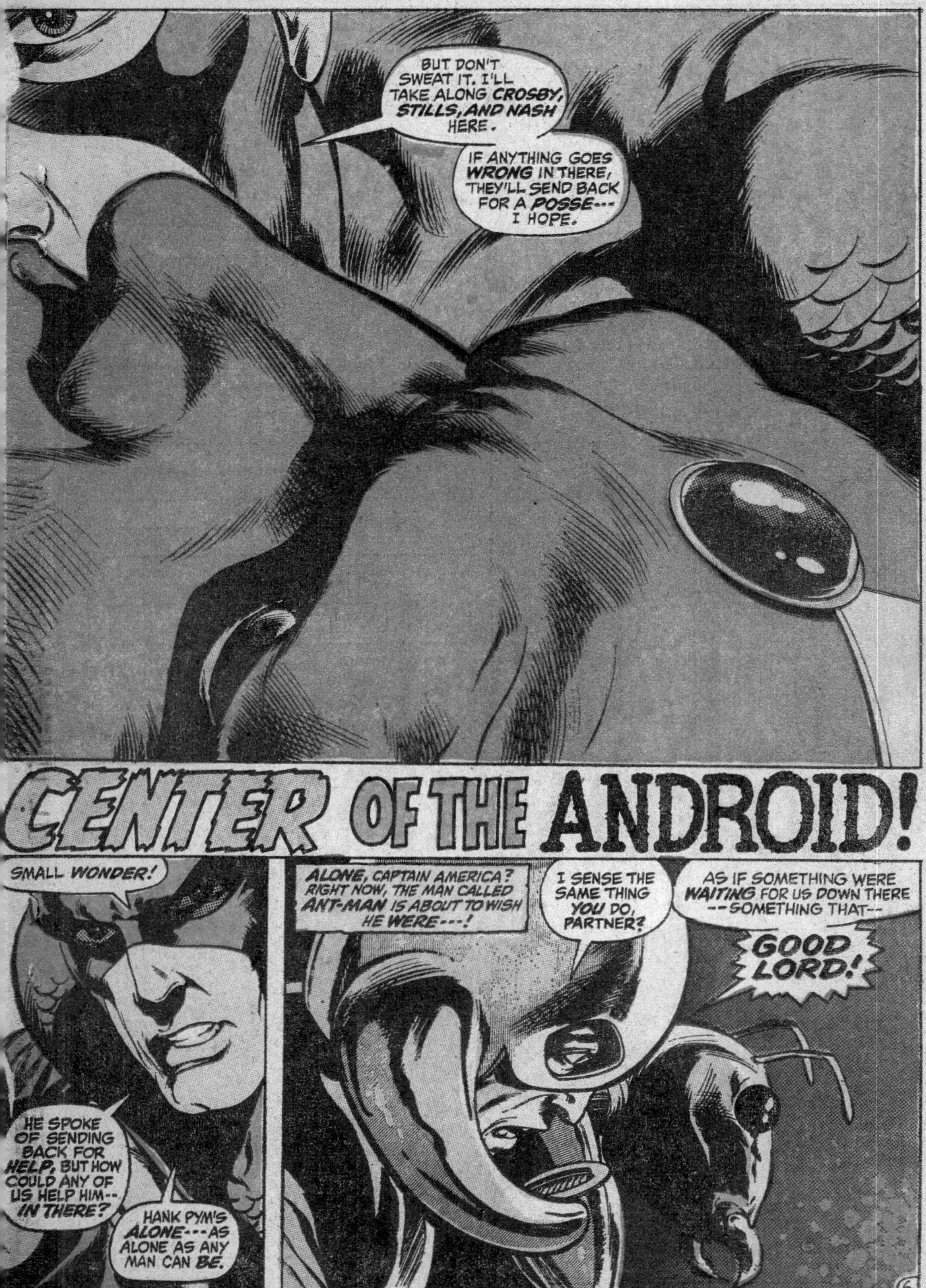
BUT DON'T SWEAT IT. I'LL TAKE ALONG CROSBY, STILLS, AND NASH HERE.
IF ANYTHING GOES WRONG IN THERE, THEY'LL SEND BACK FOR A POSSE--- I HOPE.
CENTER OF THE ANDROID!
SMALL WONDER!
HE SPOKE OF SENDING BACK FOR HELP, BUT HOW COULD ANY OF US HELP HIM-- IN THERE?
HANK PYM'S ALONE---AS ALONE AS ANY MAN CAN BE.
ALONE, CAPTAIN AMERICA? RIGHT NOW, THE MAN CALLED ANT-MAN IS ABOUT TO WISH HE WERE---!
I SENSE THE SAME THING YOU DO, PARTNER?
AS IF SOMETHING WERE WAITING FOR US DOWN THERE --SOMETHING THAT--
GOOD LORD!
6.

CONTINUED AFTER NEXT PAGE

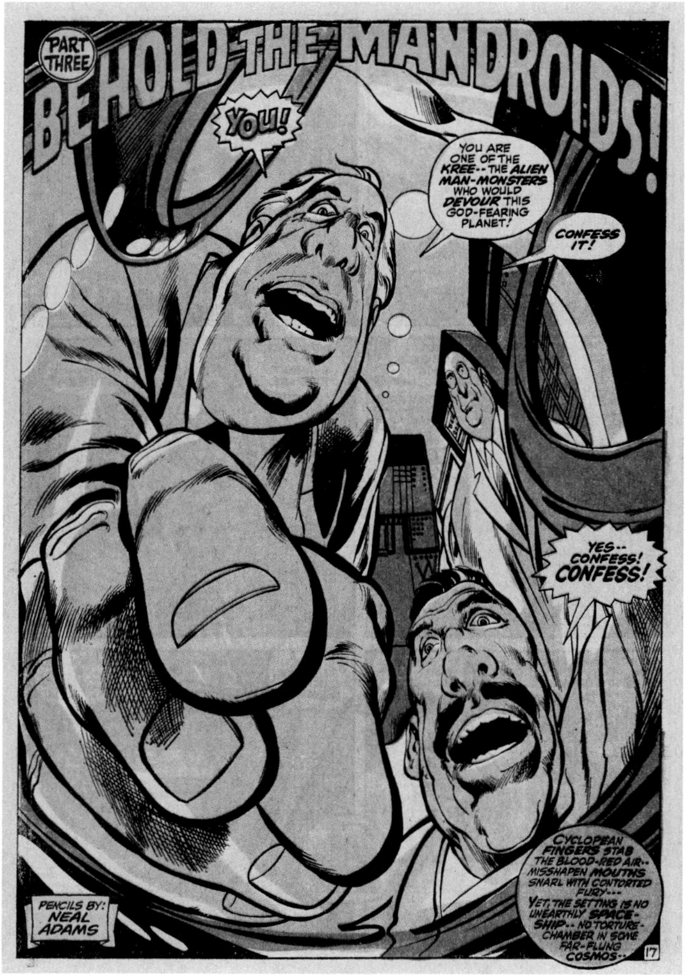
PART THREE
BEHOLD THE MANDROIDS!
YOU!
YOU ARE ONE OF THE KREE--THE ALIEN MAN-MONSTERS WHO WOULD DEVOUR THIS GOD-FEARING PLANET!
CONFESS IT!
YES--CONFESS! CONFESS!
CYCLOPEAN FINGERS STAB THE BLOOD-RED AIR--MISSHAPEN MOUTHS SNARL WITH CONTORTED FURY--- YET, THE SETTING IS NO UNEARTHLY SPACE-SHIP--NO TORTURE-CHAMBER IN SOME FAR-FLUNG COSMOS--
PENCILS BY: NEAL ADAMS
17

AVENGERS No. 94

(Left) Interior, "More Than Inhuman!"; script, Roy Thomas; pencils, Neal Adams; inks, Tom Palmer; December 1971. As with the Ant-Man/Vision interlude from the previous issue, Adams gloried in innovating new ways to establish perspective.

AVENGERS No. 93

(Previous spread and opposite) Interior and interior original art, "This Beachhead Earth"; script, Roy Thomas; pencils, Neal Adams; inks, Tom Palmer; November 1971. During his first five years on the comics scene, Neal Adams had transformed every title he took on, from DC's *Batman* and *Green Lantern* to Marvel's *X-Men*. His reunion with X-scribe Thomas on the ambitious multi-issue "Kree/Skrull War" resulted in some of the most immortal storytelling in comics history, expanding the Marvel Universe to the deepest reaches of space—and shrinking to vanishingly small levels during Ant-Man's fantastic voyage through the Vision's android innards.

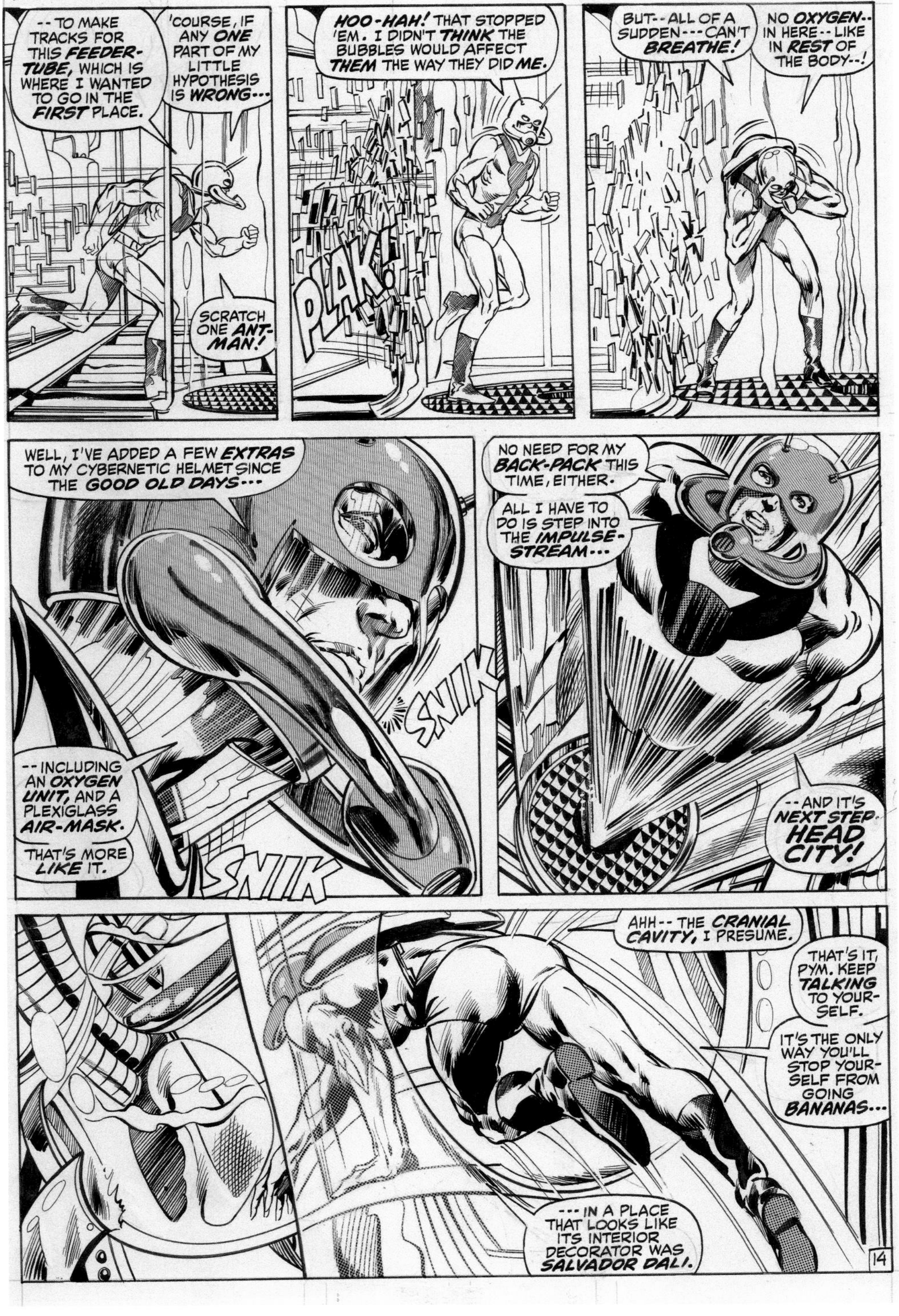
-- TO MAKE TRACKS FOR THIS FEEDER-TUBE, WHICH IS WHERE I WANTED TO GO IN THE FIRST PLACE.
'COURSE, IF ANY ONE PART OF MY LITTLE HYPOTHESIS IS WRONG...
SCRATCH ONE ANT-MAN!
HOO-HAH! THAT STOPPED 'EM. I DIDN'T THINK THE BUBBLES WOULD AFFECT THEM THE WAY THEY DID ME.
PLAK!
BUT-- ALL OF A SUDDEN--- CAN'T BREATHE!
NO OXYGEN-- IN HERE-- LIKE IN REST OF THE BODY--!
WELL, I'VE ADDED A FEW EXTRAS TO MY CYBERNETIC HELMET SINCE THE GOOD OLD DAYS---
--INCLUDING AN OXYGEN UNIT, AND A PLEXIGLASS AIR-MASK.
THAT'S MORE LIKE IT.
SNIK
SNIK
NO NEED FOR MY BACK-PACK THIS TIME, EITHER.
ALL I HAVE TO DO IS STEP INTO THE IMPULSE-STREAM---
--AND IT'S NEXT STEP, HEAD CITY!
AHH-- THE CRANIAL CAVITY, I PRESUME.
THAT'S IT, PYM. KEEP TALKING TO YOURSELF.
IT'S THE ONLY WAY YOU'LL STOP YOURSELF FROM GOING BANANAS...
--- IN A PLACE THAT LOOKS LIKE ITS INTERIOR DECORATOR WAS SALVADOR DALI.
14

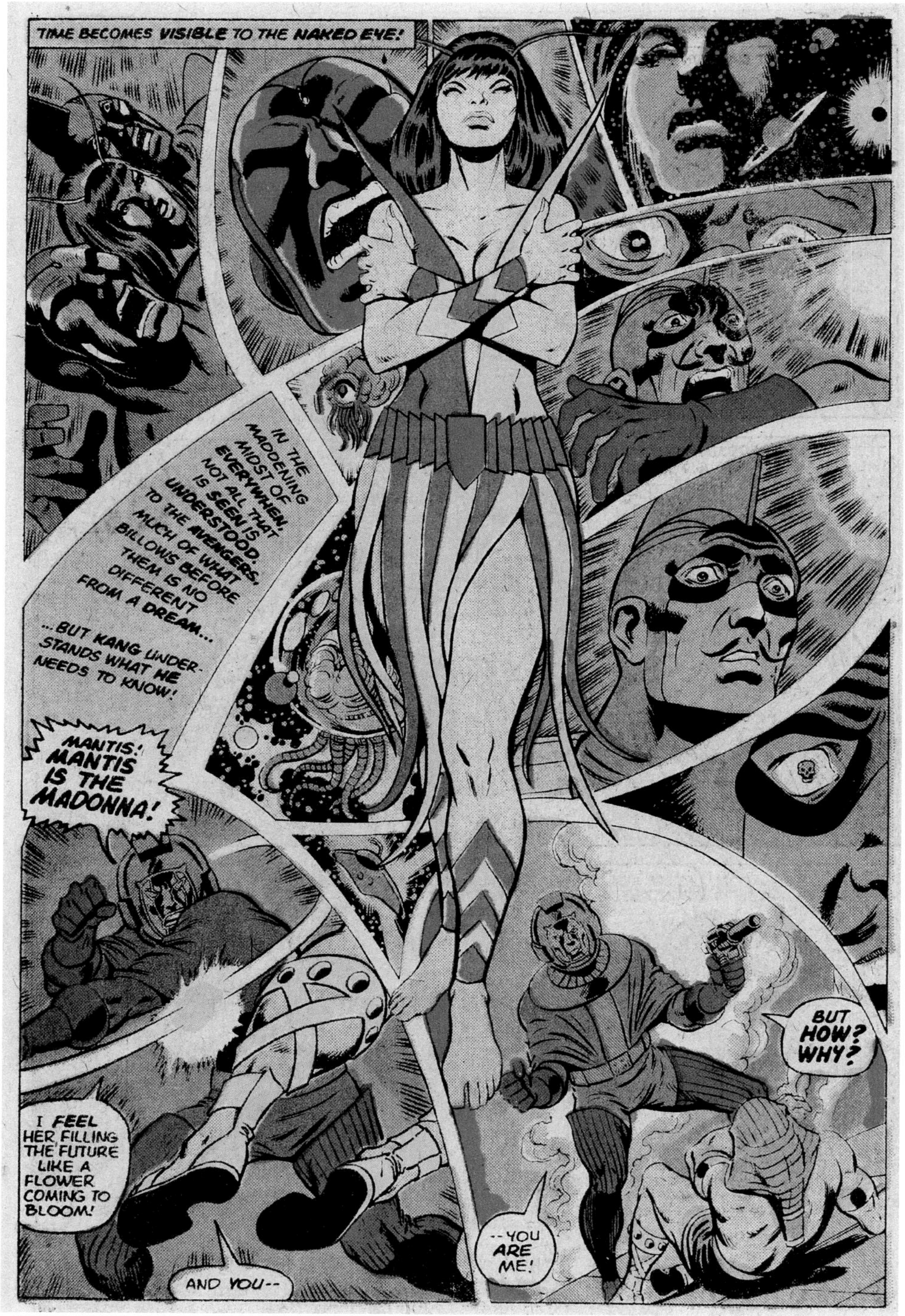
TIME BECOMES VISIBLE TO THE NAKED EYE!
IN THE MADDENING MIDST OF EVERYWHEN, NOT ALL THAT IS SEEN IS UNDERSTOOD. TO THE AVENGERS, MUCH OF WHAT BILLOWS BEFORE THEM IS NO DIFFERENT FROM A DREAM...
...BUT KANG UNDERSTANDS WHAT HE NEEDS TO KNOW!
MANTIS! MANTIS IS THE MADONNA!
BUT HOW? WHY?
I FEEL HER FILLING THE FUTURE LIKE A FLOWER COMING TO BLOOM!
AND YOU--
--YOU ARE ME!

AVENGERS No. 96

(Right) Cover; pencils and inks, Neal Adams; February 1972. The Vision's evolution from aloof android to emotional core of the team provided one of the most compelling character arcs in Avengers history.

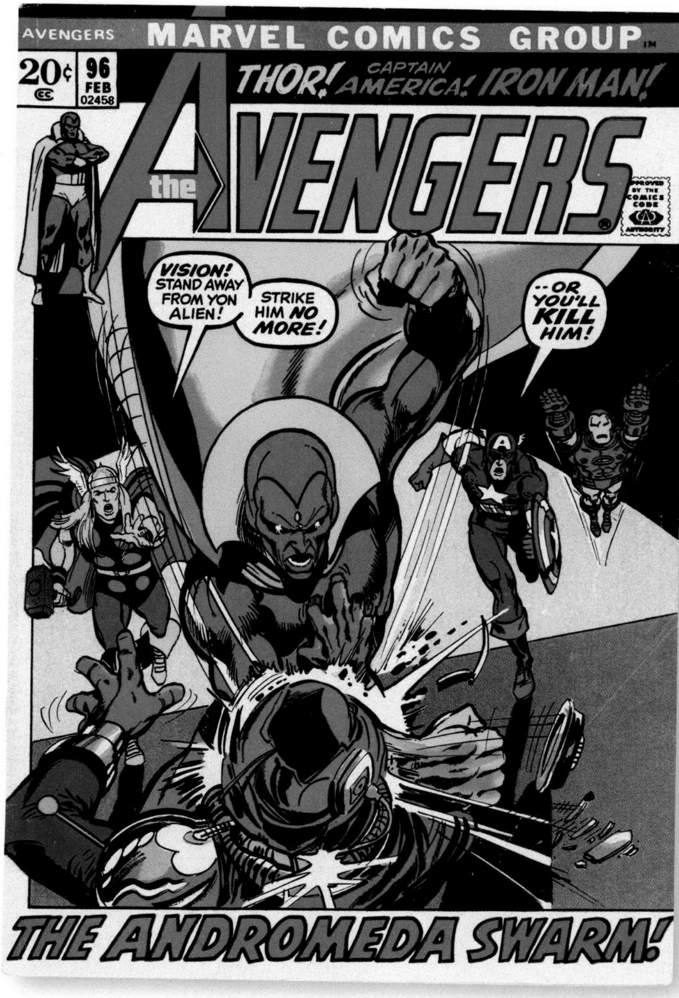
AVENGERS
MARVEL COMICS GROUP
20¢
96
FEB
02458
THOR! CAPTAIN AMERICA! IRON MAN!
the AVENGERS
VISION! STAND AWAY FROM YON ALIEN!
STRIKE HIM NO MORE!
--OR YOU'LL KILL HIM!
THE ANDROMEDA SWARM!

GIANT-SIZE AVENGERS No. 2

(Opposite) Interior, "A Blast from the Past!"; script, Steve Englehart; pencils and inks, Dave Cockrum; November 1974. If the '70s were a new age of self-discovery, Steve Englehart's story themes in the "Celestial Madonna" arc tap into the cultural zeitgeist: The time-traveling Kang learns he was/is Egyptian throwback Rama-Tut, Mantis blossoms into the mythical Madonna, and the Swordsman meets his final account in a dramatic death. Giant-size storytelling, indeed!

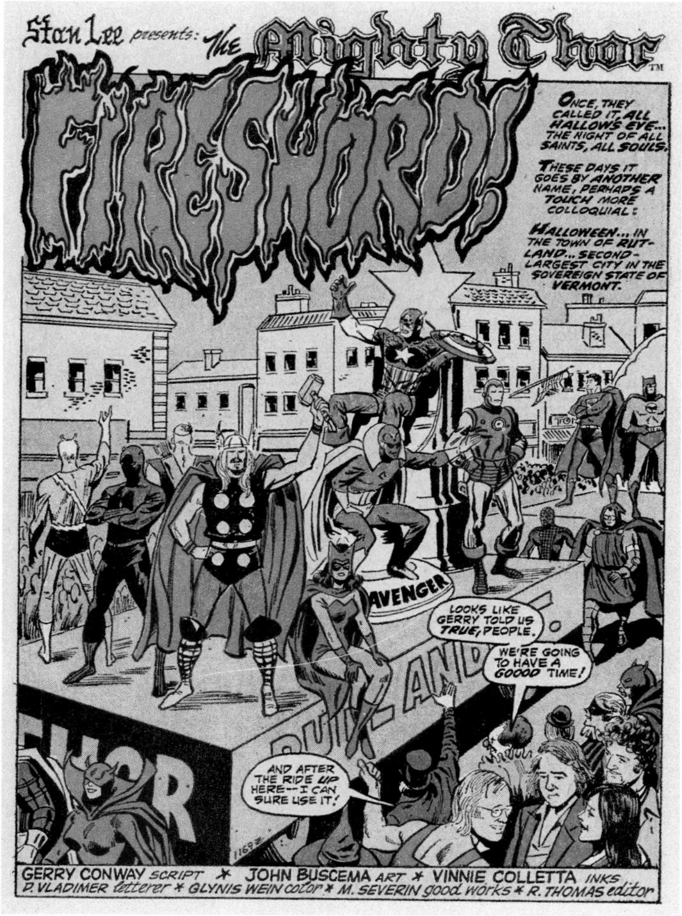
Stan Lee presents: The Mighty Thor
FIRESWORD!
ONCE, THEY CALLED IT ALL HALLOW'S EVE... THE NIGHT OF ALL SAINTS, ALL SOULS.
THESE DAYS IT GOES BY ANOTHER NAME, PERHAPS A TOUCH MORE COLLOQUIAL:
HALLOWEEN... IN THE TOWN OF RUTLAND... SECOND-LARGEST CITY IN THE SOVEREIGN STATE OF VERMONT.
AVENGER
LOOKS LIKE GERRY TOLD US TRUE, PEOPLE.
WE'RE GOING TO HAVE A GOOOD TIME!
AND AFTER THE RIDE UP HERE--I CAN SURE USE IT!
THOR
GERRY CONWAY SCRIPT ✶ JOHN BUSCEMA ART ✶ VINNIE COLLETTA INKS
D. VLADIMER letterer ✶ GLYNIS WEIN color ✶ M. SEVERIN good works ✶ R. THOMAS editor

GIANT-SIZE FANTASTIC FOUR No. 2

(Opposite) Interior, "Time Enough for Death!"; script, Gerry Conway; pencils, John Buscema; inks, Chic Stone; August 1974. Hello, Dalí! In what was by now a long-standing tradition, the surreal landscapes of Salvador Dalí's iconic painting *The Persistence of Memory* are parodied in the FF's romp through the looking glass, chasing no less august a personage than Stan Lee's beloved postman, Willie Lumpkin.

THOR No. 207

(Above) Interior, "Firesword!"; script, Gerry Conway; pencils, John Buscema; inks, Vince Colletta; January 1973. Marvel creators probably couldn't get noticed on the streets of New York City, but in Rutland, Vermont, they were celebrities! The town's real-life Halloween parades, replete with Marvel heroes, became regular events in stories from this era, with creators often breaking the fourth wall to put themselves in the middle of the action. Cameos in this issue include Steve Englehart, Gerry Conway, Len and Glynis Wein, and parade founder Tom Fagan.

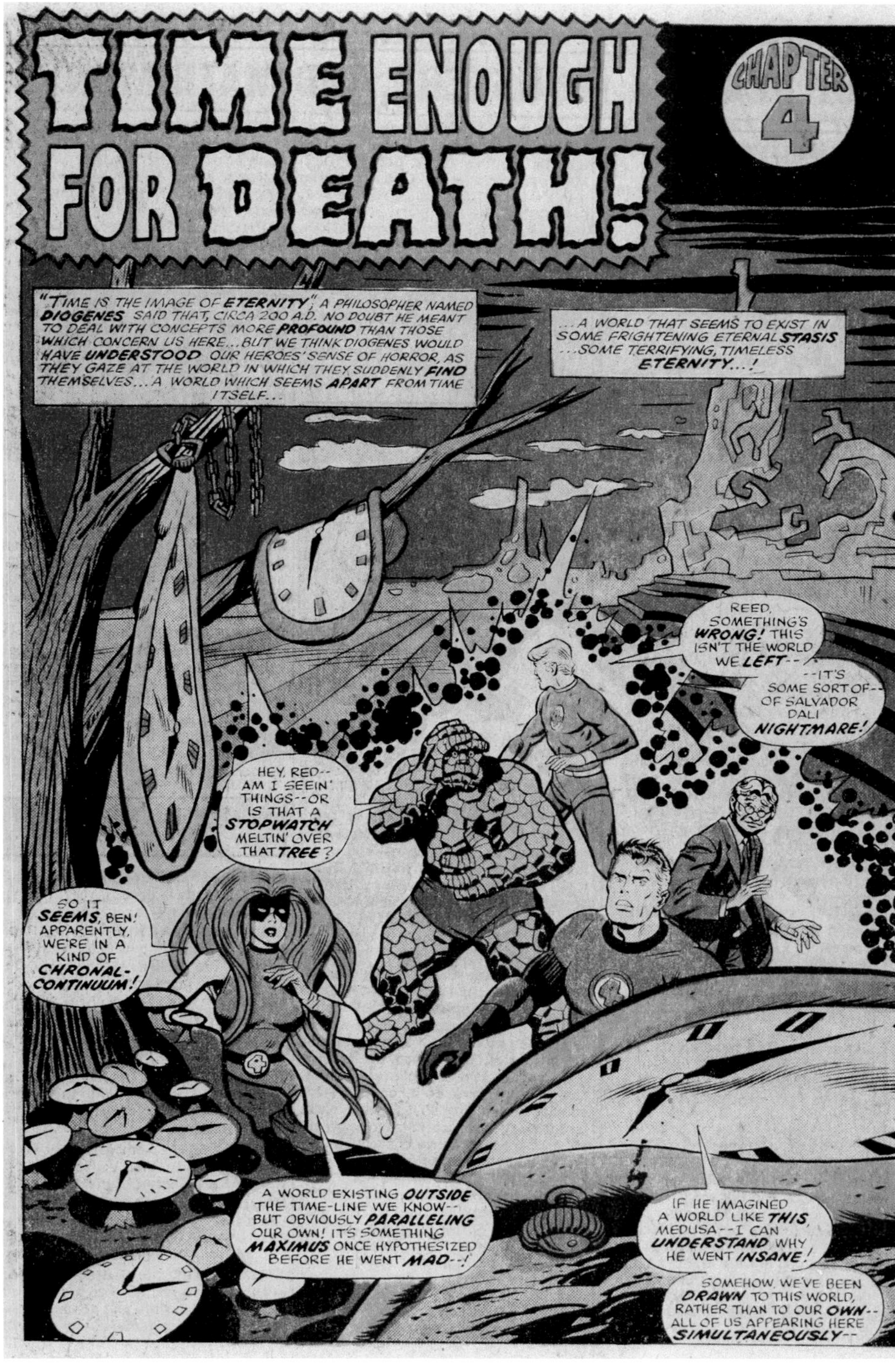
TIME ENOUGH FOR DEATH!
CHAPTER 4
"TIME IS THE IMAGE OF ETERNITY," A PHILOSOPHER NAMED DIOGENES SAID THAT, CIRCA 200 A.D. NO DOUBT HE MEANT TO DEAL WITH CONCEPTS MORE PROFOUND THAN THOSE WHICH CONCERN US HERE... BUT WE THINK DIOGENES WOULD HAVE UNDERSTOOD OUR HEROES' SENSE OF HORROR, AS THEY GAZE AT THE WORLD IN WHICH THEY SUDDENLY FIND THEMSELVES... A WORLD WHICH SEEMS APART FROM TIME ITSELF...
...A WORLD THAT SEEMS TO EXIST IN SOME FRIGHTENING ETERNAL STASIS ...SOME TERRIFYING, TIMELESS ETERNITY...!
REED, SOMETHING'S WRONG! THIS ISN'T THE WORLD WE LEFT--
--IT'S SOME SORT OF-- OF SALVADOR DALI NIGHTMARE!
HEY, RED-- AM I SEEIN' THINGS--OR IS THAT A STOPWATCH MELTIN' OVER THAT TREE?
SO IT SEEMS, BEN! APPARENTLY, WE'RE IN A KIND OF CHRONAL-CONTINUUM!
A WORLD EXISTING OUTSIDE THE TIME-LINE WE KNOW-- BUT OBVIOUSLY PARALLELING OUR OWN! IT'S SOMETHING MAXIMUS ONCE HYPOTHESIZED BEFORE HE WENT MAD--!
IF HE IMAGINED A WORLD LIKE THIS, MEDUSA--I CAN UNDERSTAND WHY HE WENT INSANE!
SOMEHOW, WE'VE BEEN DRAWN TO THIS WORLD, RATHER THAN TO OUR OWN-- ALL OF US APPEARING HERE SIMULTANEOUSLY--

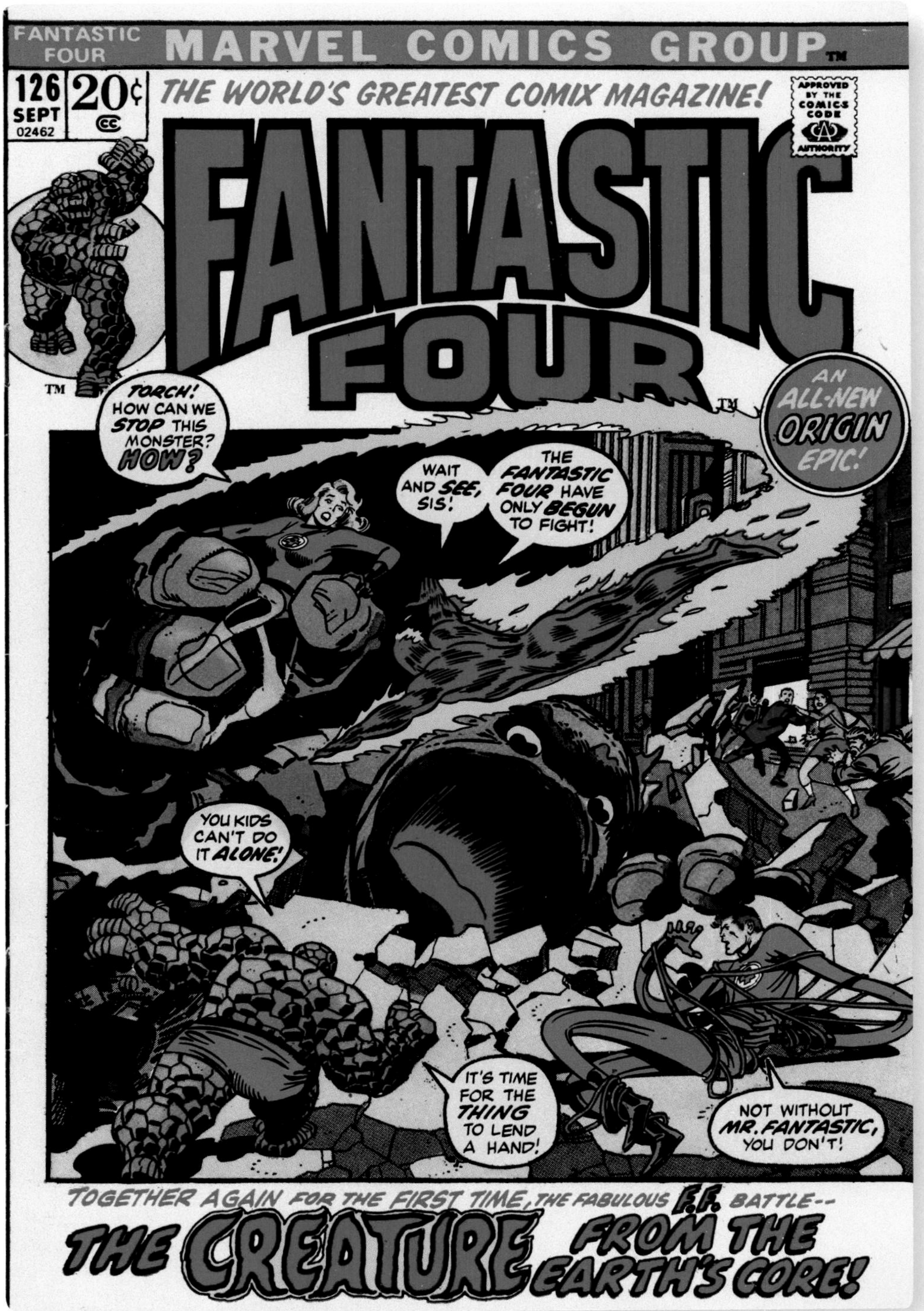
FANTASTIC FOUR
MARVEL COMICS GROUP
126 SEPT 02462
20¢
THE WORLD'S GREATEST COMIX MAGAZINE!
APPROVED BY THE COMICS CODE AUTHORITY
FANTASTIC FOUR
AN ALL-NEW ORIGIN EPIC!
TORCH! HOW CAN WE STOP THIS MONSTER? HOW?
WAIT AND SEE, SIS!
THE FANTASTIC FOUR HAVE ONLY BEGUN TO FIGHT!
YOU KIDS CAN'T DO IT ALONE!
IT'S TIME FOR THE THING TO LEND A HAND!
NOT WITHOUT MR. FANTASTIC, YOU DON'T!
TOGETHER AGAIN FOR THE FIRST TIME, THE FABULOUS F.F. BATTLE--
THE CREATURE FROM THE EARTH'S CORE!

"That was the meaning of the Fantastic Four, that a family is like your own personal anti-matter. Your family is the void you emerge from and the place you return to when you die. And that's the paradox. The closer you're drawn back in, the deeper into the void you go."
— RICK MOODY, *THE ICE STORM*

FANTASTIC FOUR No. 126

(Opposite) Cover: pencils, John Buscema; inks, Joe Sinnott; September 1972. This cover's layout is a direct homage to the very first issue of *Fantastic Four*. "*Fantastic Four* No. 1 changed my life," said Gerry Conway, who would later write for the title. "After reading that comic (and running back to the candy store around the corner to see if they had any more, and amazingly enough, finding out they had one leftover copy of No. 3…) I suddenly knew what I wanted to do with my life."

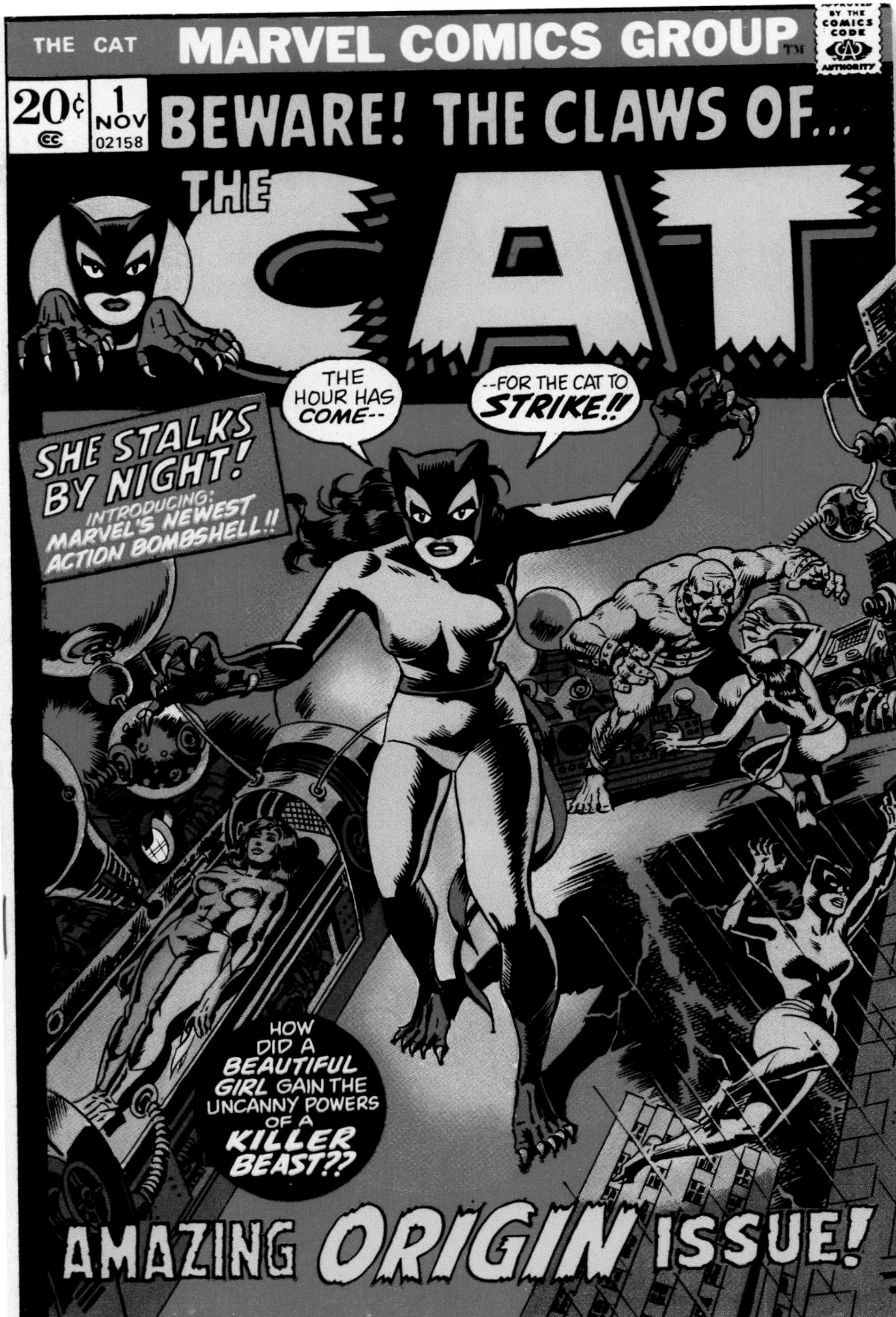
THE CAT
MARVEL COMICS GROUP
APPROVED BY THE COMICS CODE AUTHORITY
20¢
1 NOV
02158
BEWARE! THE CLAWS OF...
THE CAT
THE HOUR HAS COME--
--FOR THE CAT TO STRIKE!!
SHE STALKS BY NIGHT!
INTRODUCING: MARVEL'S NEWEST ACTION BOMBSHELL!!
HOW DID A BEAUTIFUL GIRL GAIN THE UNCANNY POWERS OF A KILLER BEAST??
AMAZING ORIGIN ISSUE!

THE CAT No. 1

(Opposite) Cover; pencils, Marie Severin; inks, Wally Wood; November 1972. Ladies and gentlemen…The Cat! Marvel's first solo title starring a female super hero wasn't just flashing girl power in the narrative: The female writer/artist combo of Linda Fite and Marie Severin acquitted themselves well in this sadly short-lived series.

AVENGERS No. 83

(Right and below) Interiors, "Come On in…the Revolution's Fine!"; script, Roy Thomas; pencils, John Buscema; inks, Tom Palmer; December 1970. This issue's tagline promised "Valkyrie and her Lady Liberators!" Unfortunately, the tantalizing prospect of an all-female Silver Age super team was undone by the wicked Enchantress. Seeking to turn the ladies of the Marvel Universe against their male counterparts, she set back women's lib in the Marvel Universe for years to come! The Valkyrie's return — this time as a hero — would be three years away in the pages of *The Defenders*.

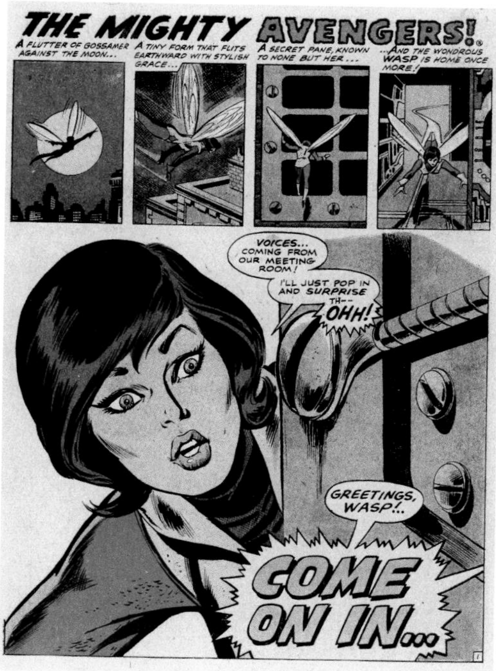
THE MIGHTY AVENGERS!
A FLUTTER OF GOSSAMER AGAINST THE MOON...
A TINY FORM THAT FLITS EARTHWARD WITH STYLISH GRACE...
A SECRET PANE, KNOWN TO NONE BUT HER...
...AND THE WONDROUS WASP IS HOME ONCE MORE!
VOICES... COMING FROM OUR MEETING ROOM!
I'LL JUST POP IN AND SURPRISE TH--
OHH!
GREETINGS, WASP!..
COME ON IN...
1

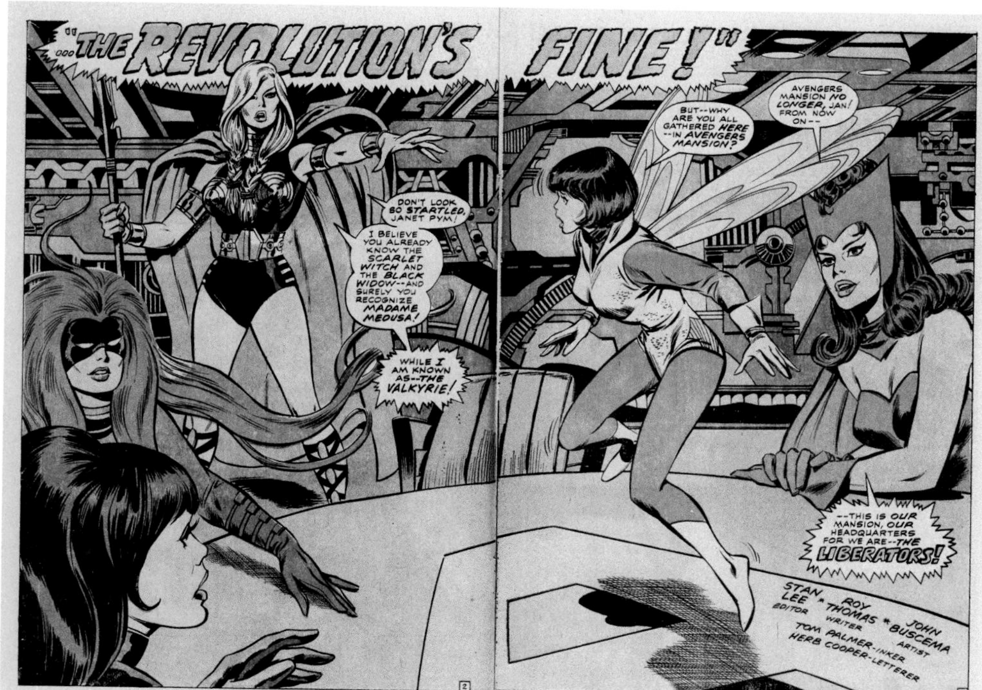
"...THE REVOLUTION'S FINE!"
DON'T LOOK SO STARTLED, JANET PYM!
I BELIEVE YOU ALREADY KNOW THE SCARLET WITCH AND THE BLACK WIDOW--AND SURELY YOU RECOGNIZE MADAME MEDUSA!
WHILE I AM KNOWN AS--THE VALKYRIE!
BUT--WHY ARE YOU ALL GATHERED HERE--IN AVENGERS MANSION?
AVENGERS MANSION NO LONGER, JAN! FROM NOW ON--
--THIS IS OUR MANSION, OUR HEADQUARTERS FOR WE ARE--THE LIBERATORS!
STAN LEE EDITOR * ROY THOMAS WRITER * JOHN BUSCEMA ARTIST
TOM PALMER-INKER HERB COOPER-LETTERER
2
3
CONTINUED AFTER NEXT PAGE

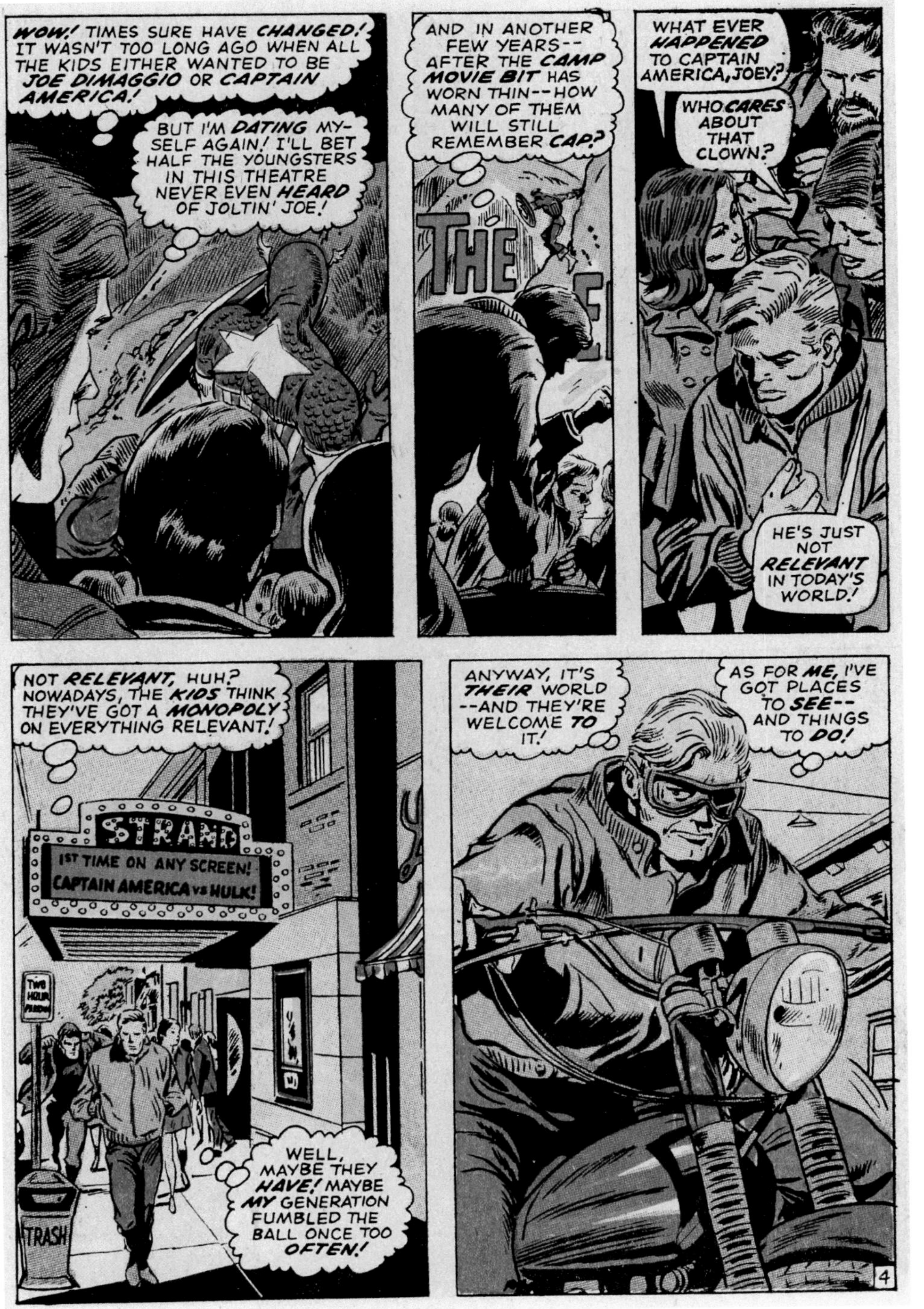
WOW! TIMES SURE HAVE CHANGED! IT WASN'T TOO LONG AGO WHEN ALL THE KIDS EITHER WANTED TO BE JOE DIMAGGIO OR CAPTAIN AMERICA!
BUT I'M DATING MY-SELF AGAIN! I'LL BET HALF THE YOUNGSTERS IN THIS THEATRE NEVER EVEN HEARD OF JOLTIN' JOE!
AND IN ANOTHER FEW YEARS-- AFTER THE CAMP MOVIE BIT HAS WORN THIN--HOW MANY OF THEM WILL STILL REMEMBER CAP?
THE
WHAT EVER HAPPENED TO CAPTAIN AMERICA, JOEY?
WHO CARES ABOUT THAT CLOWN?
HE'S JUST NOT RELEVANT IN TODAY'S WORLD!
NOT RELEVANT, HUH? NOWADAYS, THE KIDS THINK THEY'VE GOT A MONOPOLY ON EVERYTHING RELEVANT!
STRAND
1ST TIME ON ANY SCREEN!
CAPTAIN AMERICA vs HULK!
TWO HOUR PARKING
TRASH
WELL, MAYBE THEY HAVE! MAYBE MY GENERATION FUMBLED THE BALL ONCE TOO OFTEN!
ANYWAY, IT'S THEIR WORLD --AND THEY'RE WELCOME TO IT!
AS FOR ME, I'VE GOT PLACES TO SEE-- AND THINGS TO DO!
4

CAPTAIN AMERICA No. 130

(Opposite) Interior, "Up Against the Wall!"; script, Stan Lee; pencils, Gene Colan; inks, Dick Ayers; October 1970. "This is the day of the antihero — the age of the rebel — and the dissenter!... In a world rife with injustice, greed, and endless war — who's to say the rebels are wrong?" — Captain America

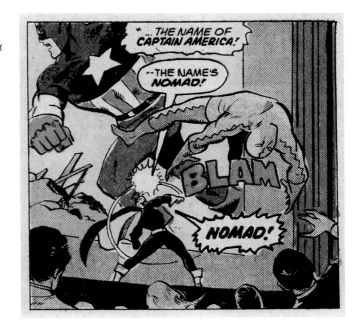

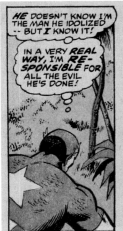

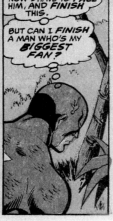

"... THE NAME OF CAPTAIN AMERICA!
--THE NAME'S NOMAD!
BLAM
NOMAD!

HE DOESN'T KNOW I'M THE MAN HE IDOLIZED -- BUT I KNOW IT!
IN A VERY REAL WAY, I'M RE-SPONSIBLE FOR ALL THE EVIL HE'S DONE!
NOW I HAVE TO FACE HIM, AND FINISH THIS.
BUT CAN I FINISH A MAN WHO'S MY BIGGEST FAN?

CAPTAIN AMERICA No. 180

(Above) Interior, "The Coming of the Nomad!"; script, Steve Englehart; pencils, Sal Buscema; inks, Vince Colletta; December 1974.

CAPTAIN AMERICA No. 156

(Left) Interior, "Two into One Won't Go!"; script, Steve Englehart; pencils, Sal Buscema; inks, Frank McLaughlin; December 1972. By the middle of 1972, Cap's floundering title was reportedly on the verge of cancellation. Englehart's masterstroke was to take Steve Rogers's quest for meaning and infuse it irrevocably into his character. America was a country that sought change — and so Captain America would be emblematic of that change. Within months, the team of Englehart and Buscema had turned *Captain America* into a top seller.

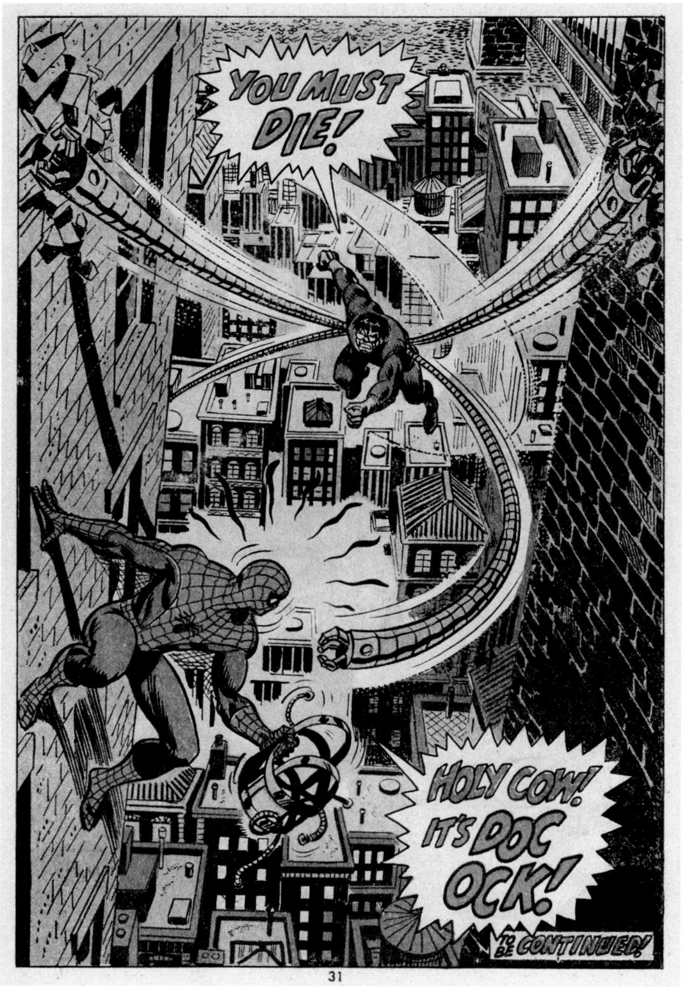
YOU MUST DIE!
HOLY COW! IT'S DOC OCK!
TO BE CONTINUED!
31

AMAZING SPIDER-MAN No. 112

(Above) Interior, "Spidey Cops Out!"; script, Gerry Conway; pencils, John Romita; inks, Romita and Tony Mortellaro; September 1972. Spider-Man has the best rogues' gallery in comics, but none was more prolific in his first decade of villainy than Doctor Octopus, who by this issue was making his eighth attempt to end the life of his archfoe.

AMAZING SPIDER-MAN No. 89

(Opposite) Interior, "Doc Ock Lives!"; script, Stan Lee; pencils, Gil Kane; inks, John Romita; October 1970. This senses-shattering panel made one heck of a wall decoration, when black-light company Third Eye published it as a neon poster in 1971.

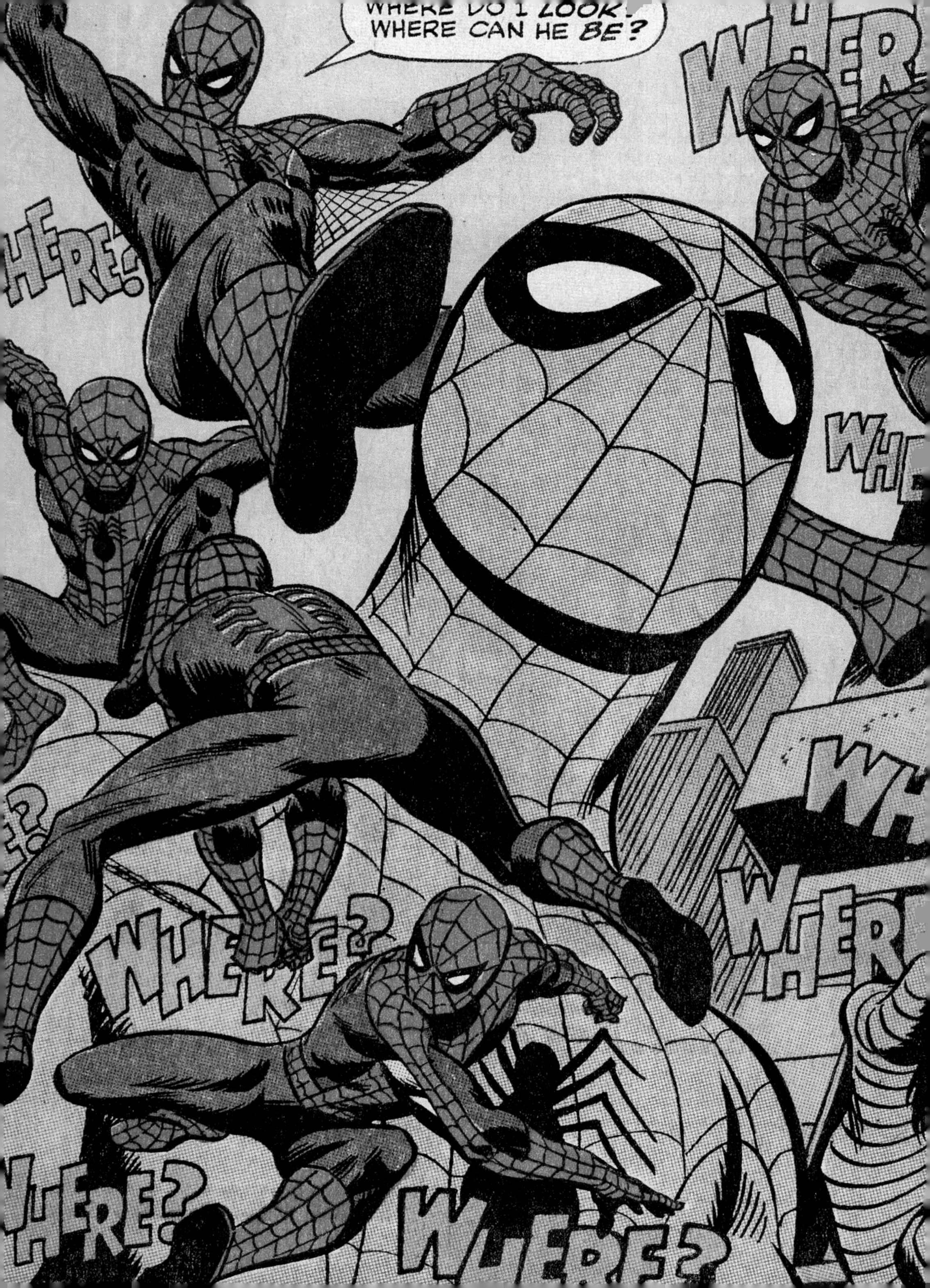
WHERE DO I LOOK? WHERE CAN HE BE?
WHERE?
WHERE?

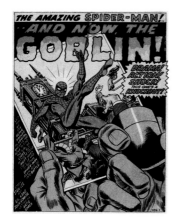

THE AMAZING SPIDER-MAN!
...AND NOW, THE GOBLIN!
DRAMA! ACTION! SHOCK! THIS ONE'S A KNOCKOUT!

AMAZING SPIDER-MAN No. 96

(Left) Interior, "…And Now, the Goblin!"; script, Stan Lee; pencils, Gil Kane; inks, John Romita; May 1971. "This One's Got It All!" blared the cover copy…but one thing it didn't have was the Comics Code Authority's seal of approval. The mere depiction of drugs and drug use — even the cautionary tone of Lee's story — would have been enough to get the comic rejected. Undaunted, Marvel published anyway, albeit nonchalantly: "We're not selling relevancy, we're selling fairy tales for adults.…if we feel we have something to say that will contribute to the story, that's fine."

AMAZING SPIDER-MAN No. 97

(Opposite) Original cover art (unpublished); pencils, Gil Kane with John Romita; inks, Frank Giacoia; June 1971.

BREAKING IT DOWN

(Right) Plot outline, Amazing Spider-Man *No. 96; story, Stan Lee; 1971.* Lee's outline for the first of the "drug issues" provided a tight enough breakdown of the plot to get artist Gil Kane going — plus character details and recommendations to research, and reference from Spidey legend and current art director John Romita.

JAN.

SPLASH can be fight scene w/Spi-- and Rob's hand holding pic.

Peter returns from England, dejected.
F.B.: Peter remembers Spi's fight in England. To bring in action.
Can't tell why he didn't see Gwen.

Brings photos to Robbie. Robbie wonders how, etc.
Reluctant to bring photos to Robbie, 'cause Robbie will tie in his appearance with Spi. But knows Robbie reads the papers anyway, and would know about it anyhow. Robbie will ask Peter how he arranged it-- how clever he was. Peter wonders how much Robbi suspects.

In school, misses Gwen-- can't concentrate-- Harry tells him about MJ's show-- all gonna go see. ('HAIR type). Pete doesn't even have price of a ticket. Realizes he's gotta stop wasting time. He MUST get a spare time job. Harry reminds him of his father's offer. Pete can't refuse it without offending Harry-- but we have FB shots of Pete remembering Goblin and problems attendant thereby.

GIL: Ask John R. for reference re: Osborn's factory etc.

Parker goes to see Osborn-- overhears Dr. telling him he's doing oka but he must stay calm and not read or discuss anything about superheroes-- or Spider-Man-- that always seems to trigger him off. Pete changes his mind and is about to leave when O. sees him and calls him in. And he takes job.

Mr. Osborn decides to treat the kids. About 8 or ten kids, including Randy Robertson and Josh (the Radical). Osborn asks "Where's so-and-so?" Kids say: "Didn't you hear? He's in the hospital-- an overdose." Josh tells O. he's starting a group to fight drug addiction and pushing which hurts the blacks more than anyone and wants O to help financially. O. gets his back up-- will be glad to help but doesn't wanna be ordered to-- slight argument which starts getting O a bit upset as Harry worries and tries to be a peacemaker.
(MJ should make play for Pete now that Gwen is gone)
Show could have psychodelic overtones which also affect O. O has a funny feeling about theatre during show-- in fact, when he first sees bldg-- after show, he goes backstage and passes locked room.
NOTE: Theatre is in slummy area in Village-- like a large store front-- basement, etc.

Pete sees reaction-- worries-- that night changes to Spidey to break in and see what's in room. At same time, O is going off his rocker at home and finds a key automatically and goes to room. O gets there first and opens room and sees GG outfits and reverts to GG due to shock. SPI enters to find GG. Ready for fight.

PP realizes Goblin knows who he is!

(Aunt May wants to see show-- Pete discourages, figuring she's too old-fashioned. But she goes with Mrs. Watson and has better time than anyone)

(Pete's spider sense should tingle when HE too passes room)

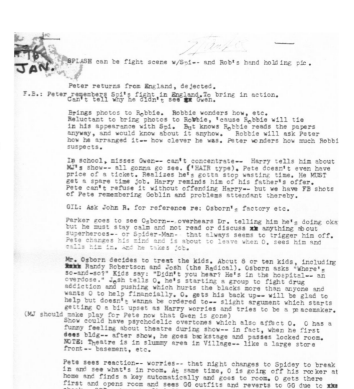

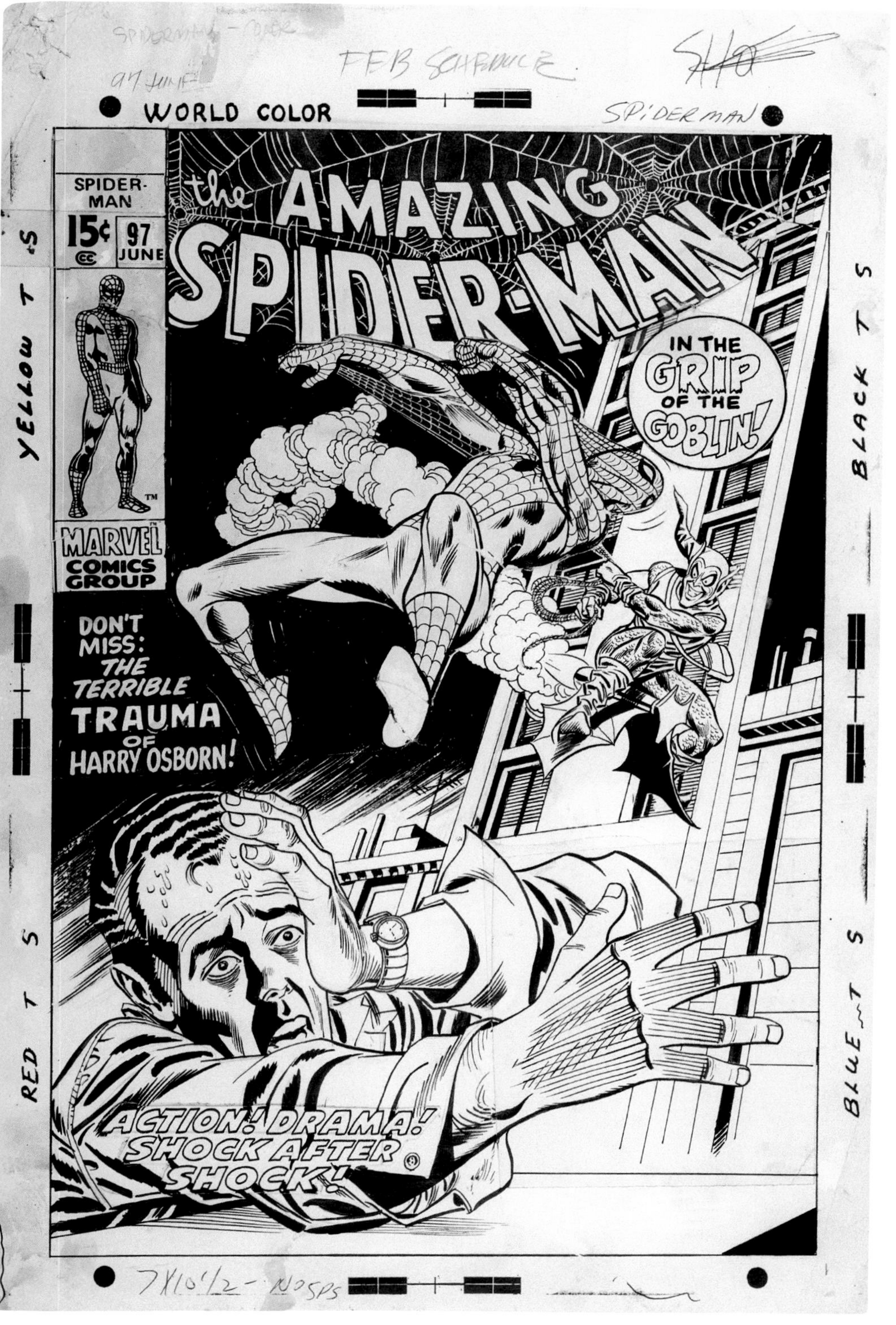

WORLD COLOR
SPIDERMAN
SPIDER-MAN
15¢
97
JUNE
the AMAZING SPIDER-MAN
IN THE GRIP OF THE GOBLIN!
MARVEL COMICS GROUP
DON'T MISS: THE TERRIBLE TRAUMA OF HARRY OSBORN!
ACTION! DRAMA! SHOCK AFTER SHOCK!
YELLOW T S
BLACK T S
RED T S
BLUE T S

"It was a dark time, young men my age were dying in a war no one wanted to fight, a President was under siege for sanctioning criminal acts...the streets weren't safe, vigilantes were shooting people on the subway. The world was going mad. So when it came time for Spider-Man to save the girl he loved from certain death, it seemed to me only natural that he fail." — GERRY CONWAY

AMAZING SPIDER-MAN No. 121

(Opposite) Interior, "The Night Gwen Stacy Died"; script, Gerry Conway; pencils, Gil Kane; inks, John Romita and Tony Mortellaro; June 1973. Gwen Stacy died, but the coroner's report had to wait for a letters page four issues later. The verdict: her neck had snapped.

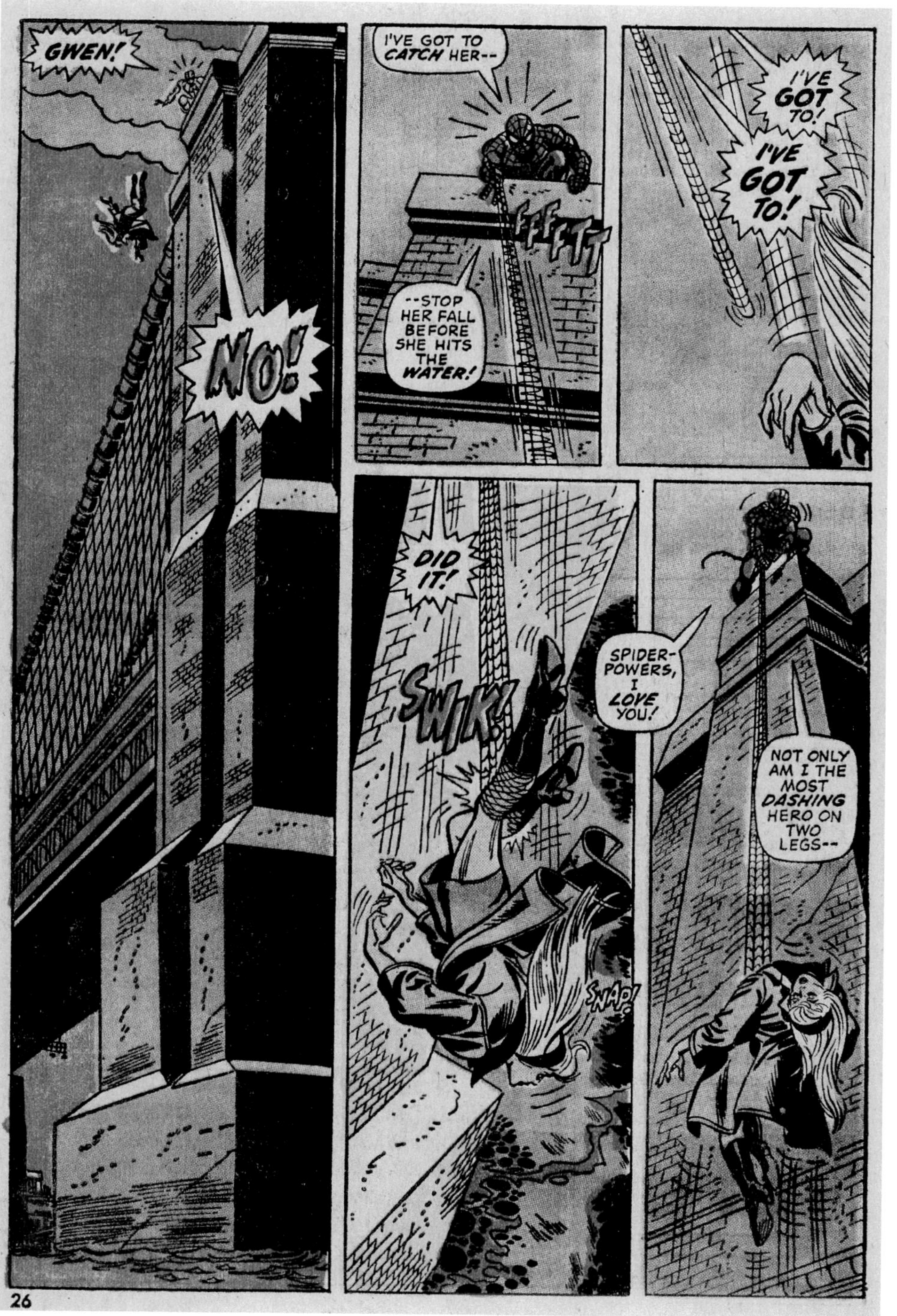
GWEN!
NO!
I'VE GOT TO CATCH HER--
FFFTT
--STOP HER FALL BEFORE SHE HITS THE WATER!
I'VE GOT TO!
I'VE GOT TO!
DID IT!
SWIK!
SNAP!
SPIDER-POWERS, I LOVE YOU!
NOT ONLY AM I THE MOST DASHING HERO ON TWO LEGS--
26

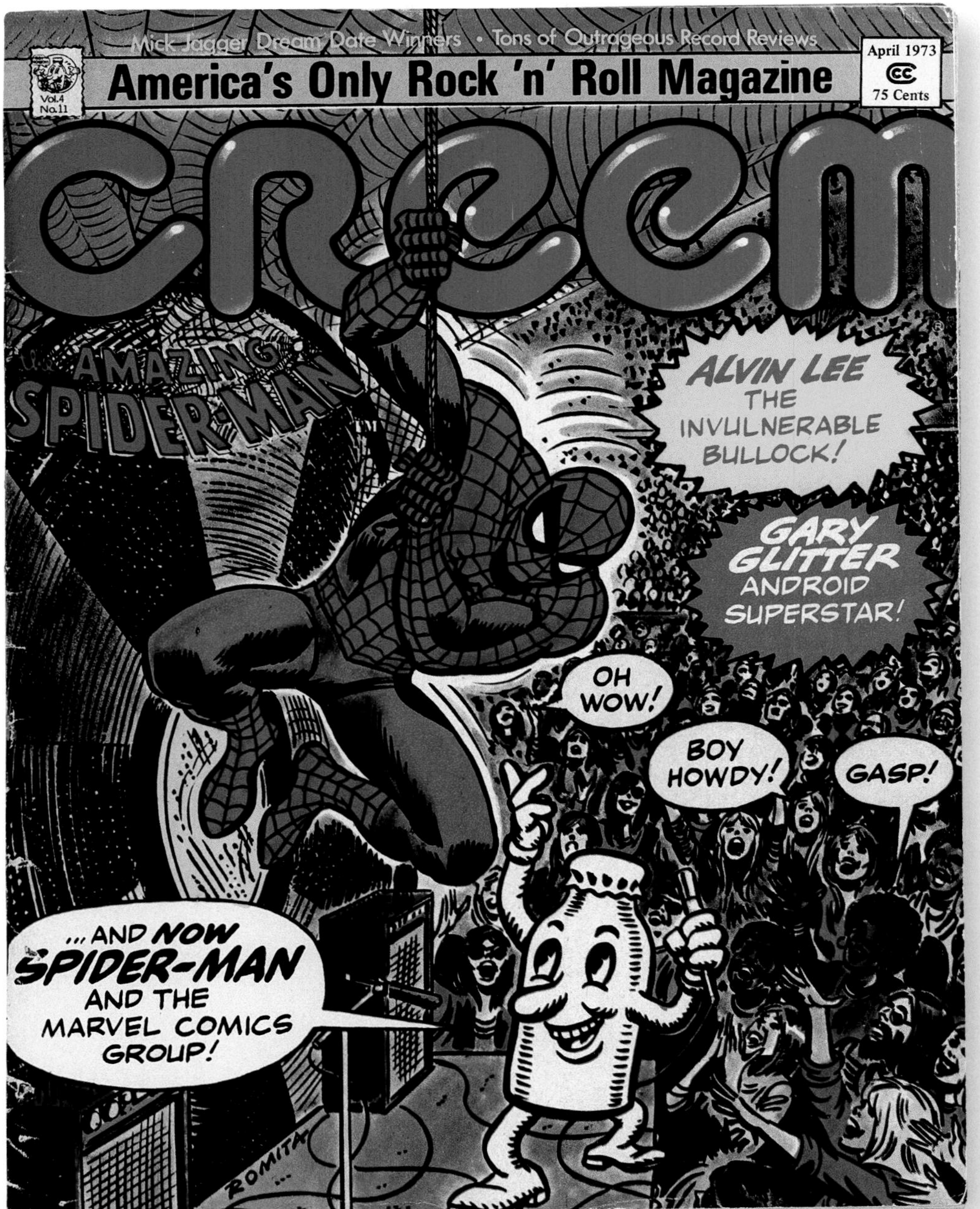
Mick Jagger Dream Date Winners • Tons of Outrageous Record Reviews
America's Only Rock 'n' Roll Magazine
Vol.4 No.11
April 1973
75 Cents
CREEM
AMAZING SPIDER-MAN
ALVIN LEE THE INVULNERABLE BULLOCK!
GARY GLITTER ANDROID SUPERSTAR!
OH WOW!
BOY HOWDY!
GASP!
...AND NOW SPIDER-MAN AND THE MARVEL COMICS GROUP!
ROMITA

BOY HOWDY!

(Opposite) Magazine cover, Creem; *pencils and inks, John Romita; April 1973.* Spider-Man takes center stage on the cover of the counterculture's coolest rock mag, greeted by magazine mascot Boy Howdy (designed by R. Crumb). By the early '70s, Spidey was truly the rock star of the Marvel stable — and his popularity would only grow.

CHICO AND THE SPIDER-MAN

(Below) Photograph, 1974. Freddie Prinze, stand-up comedian and star of the TV sitcom *Chico and the Man*, clutches a copy of *Marvel Treasury Edition* No. 1, starring Spider-Man. His son Freddie Jr. would make an appearance in Mark Millar's *Ultimates* a generation later.

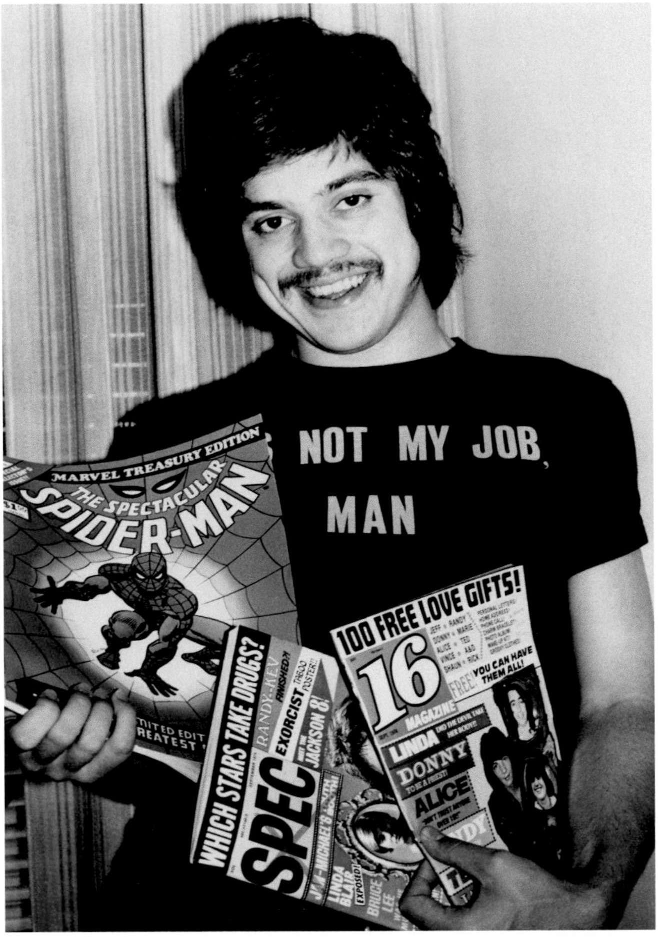
MARVEL TREASURY EDITION
THE SPECTACULAR SPIDER-MAN
NOT MY JOB, MAN
100 FREE LOVE GIFTS!
16
MAGAZINE
YOU CAN HAVE THEM ALL!
LINDA
DONNY
ALICE
WHICH STARS TAKE DRUGS?
SPEC
EXORCIST
JACKSON 8!

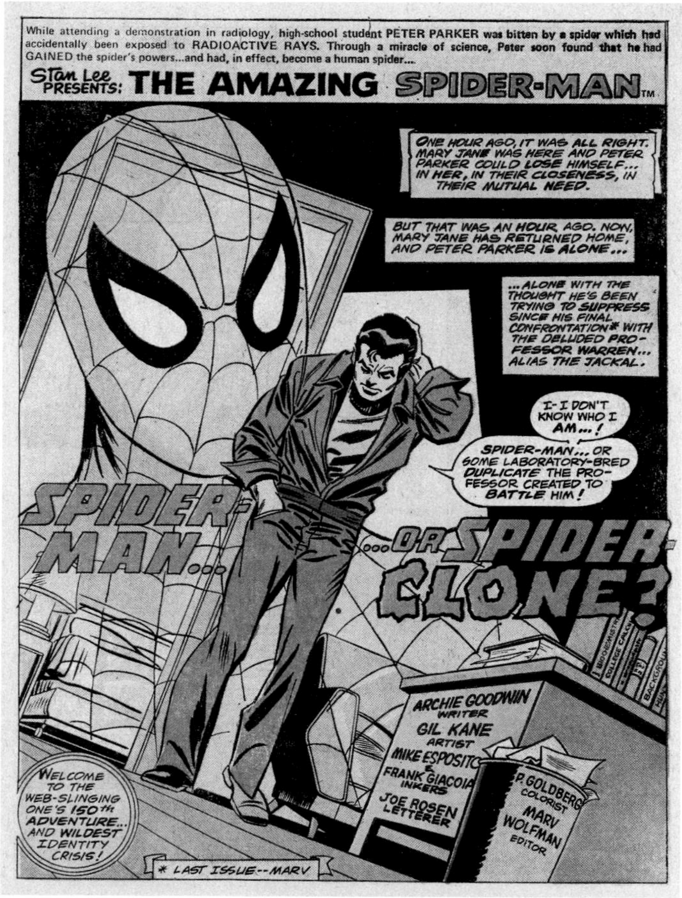
While attending a demonstration in radiology, high-school student PETER PARKER was bitten by a spider which had accidentally been exposed to RADIOACTIVE RAYS. Through a miracle of science, Peter soon found that he had GAINED the spider's powers...and had, in effect, become a human spider...
Stan Lee PRESENTS: THE AMAZING SPIDER-MAN
ONE HOUR AGO, IT WAS ALL RIGHT. MARY JANE WAS HERE AND PETER PARKER COULD LOSE HIMSELF... IN HER, IN THEIR CLOSENESS, IN THEIR MUTUAL NEED.
BUT THAT WAS AN HOUR AGO. NOW, MARY JANE HAS RETURNED HOME, AND PETER PARKER IS ALONE...
...ALONE WITH THE THOUGHT HE'S BEEN TRYING TO SUPPRESS SINCE HIS FINAL CONFRONTATION* WITH THE DELUDED PROFESSOR WARREN... ALIAS THE JACKAL.
I-I DON'T KNOW WHO I AM...!
SPIDER-MAN... OR SOME LABORATORY-BRED DUPLICATE THE PROFESSOR CREATED TO BATTLE HIM!
SPIDER-MAN... OR SPIDER-CLONE?
ARCHIE GOODWIN WRITER
GIL KANE ARTIST
MIKE ESPOSITO & FRANK GIACOIA INKERS
JOE ROSEN LETTERER
P. GOLDBERG COLORIST
MARV WOLFMAN EDITOR
WELCOME TO THE WEB-SLINGING ONE'S 150th ADVENTURE... AND WILDEST IDENTITY CRISIS!
* LAST ISSUE--MARV

AMAZING SPIDER-MAN No. 150

(Above) Interior, "Spider-Man... or Spider-Clone?"; script, Archie Goodwin; pencils, Gil Kane; inks, Mike Esposito and Frank Giacoia; November 1975. The original "Clone Saga" played out over most of 1975—a storyline commitment rare in comics to that point. But readers gripped by the machinations of the mad scientist Jackal hadn't seen anything yet. The "sequel" "Clone Sagas" of the '90s stretched over several years and multiple Spider titles.

AMAZING SPIDER-MAN No. 129

(Opposite) Cover; pencils, Gil Kane; inks, John Romita; February 1974. As if losing Gwen Stacy the previous year wasn't bad enough, now Spider-Man must deal with being pursued by a vigilante known as the Punisher who believes Spidey murdered the girl. Frank Castle doesn't give up easily, and will remain a thorn in the side of Spidey, the authorities—and the criminals—of the Marvel Universe for decades to come.

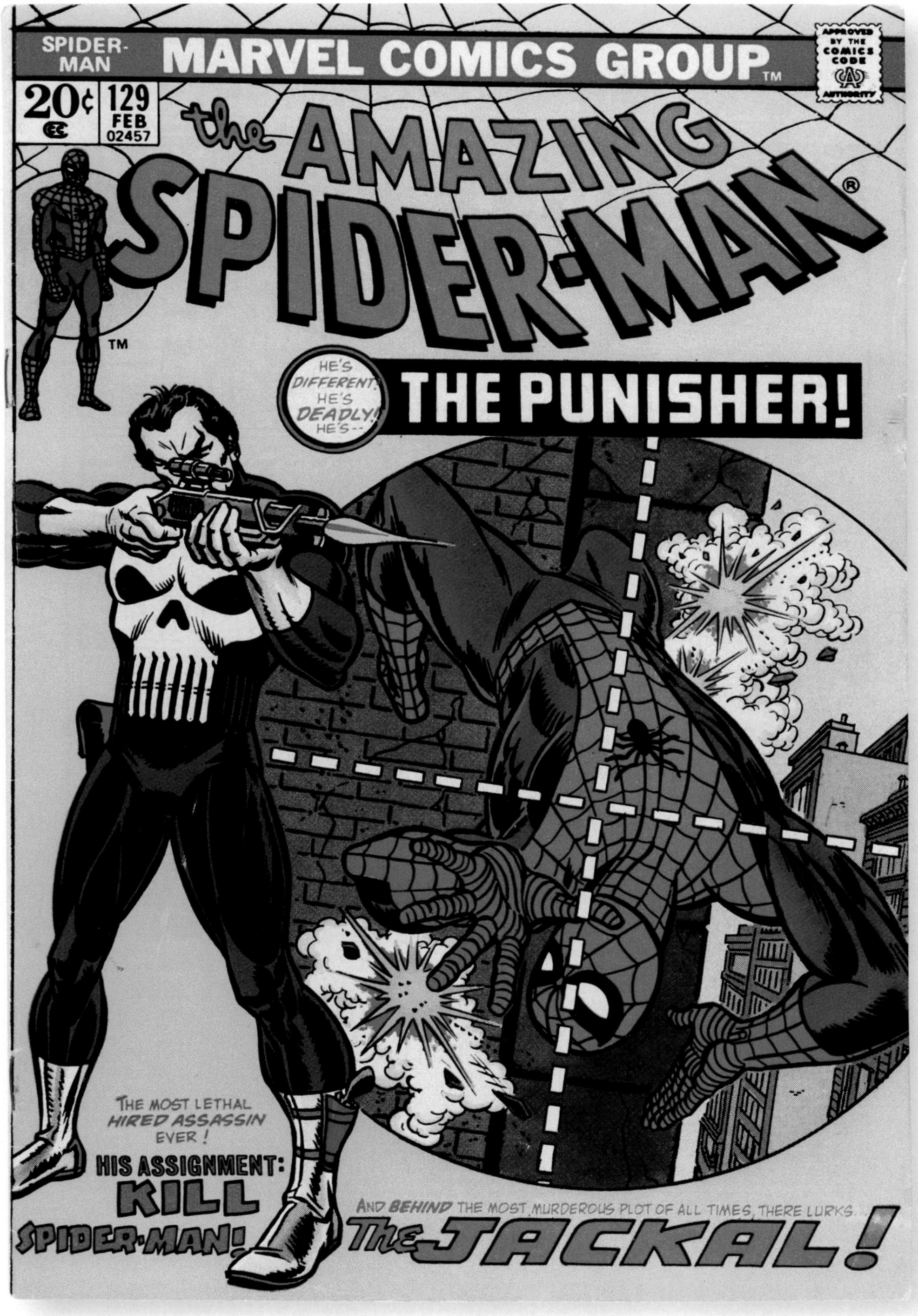
SPIDER-MAN
MARVEL COMICS GROUP
APPROVED BY THE COMICS CODE AUTHORITY
20¢
129
FEB
02457
the AMAZING SPIDER-MAN
HE'S DIFFERENT! HE'S DEADLY! HE'S--
THE PUNISHER!
THE MOST LETHAL HIRED ASSASSIN EVER!
HIS ASSIGNMENT: KILL SPIDER-MAN!
AND BEHIND THE MOST MURDEROUS PLOT OF ALL TIMES, THERE LURKS...
The JACKAL!

TOMB OF DRACULA No. 10

(Below) Cover; pencils, Gil Kane; inks, Tom Palmer; July 1973. Count Dracula had many would-be vampire slayers, but none more brash than Blade, who made his first appearance in Drac's 10th issue.

AMAZING SPIDER-MAN No. 101

(Opposite) Original cover art, "A Monster Called... Morbius!"; pencils, Gil Kane; inks, John Romita; October 1971. With a more relaxed Code, Marvel rushed in several characters emblematic of the formerly taboo. Morbius — Marvel's first vampire — received a dramatic introduction in Roy Thomas's origin story.

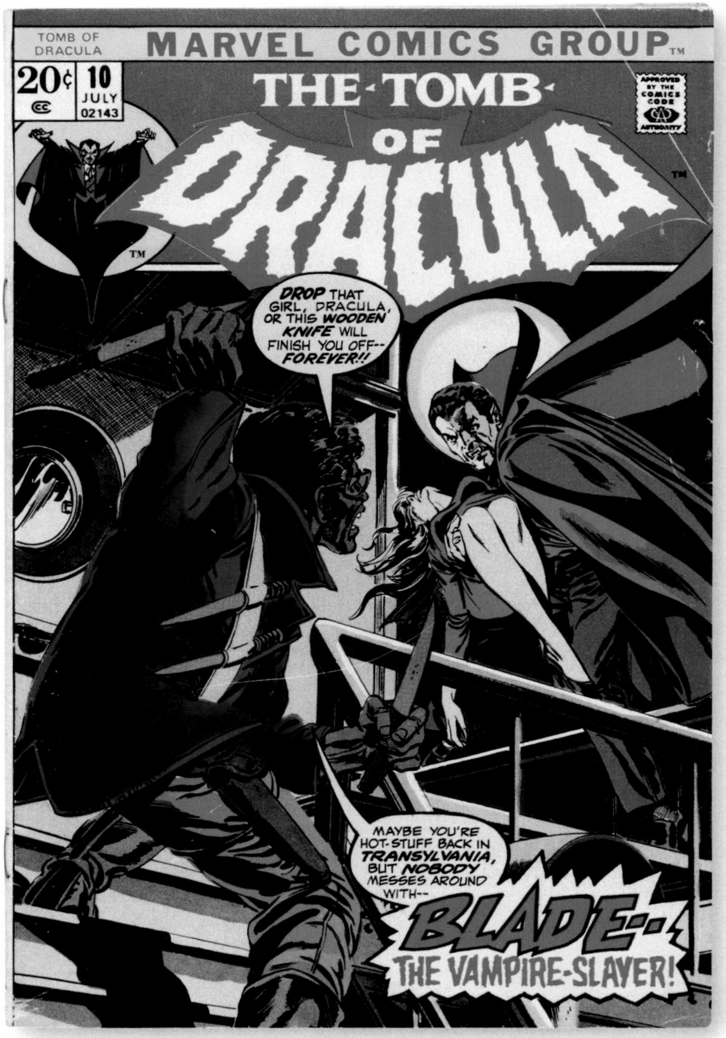
TOMB OF DRACULA
MARVEL COMICS GROUP
20¢ 10 JULY 02143
APPROVED BY THE COMICS CODE AUTHORITY
THE TOMB OF DRACULA
DROP THAT GIRL, DRACULA, OR THIS WOODEN KNIFE WILL FINISH YOU OFF-- FOREVER!!
MAYBE YOU'RE HOT-STUFF BACK IN TRANSYLVANIA, BUT NOBODY MESSES AROUND WITH--
BLADE--
THE VAMPIRE-SLAYER!

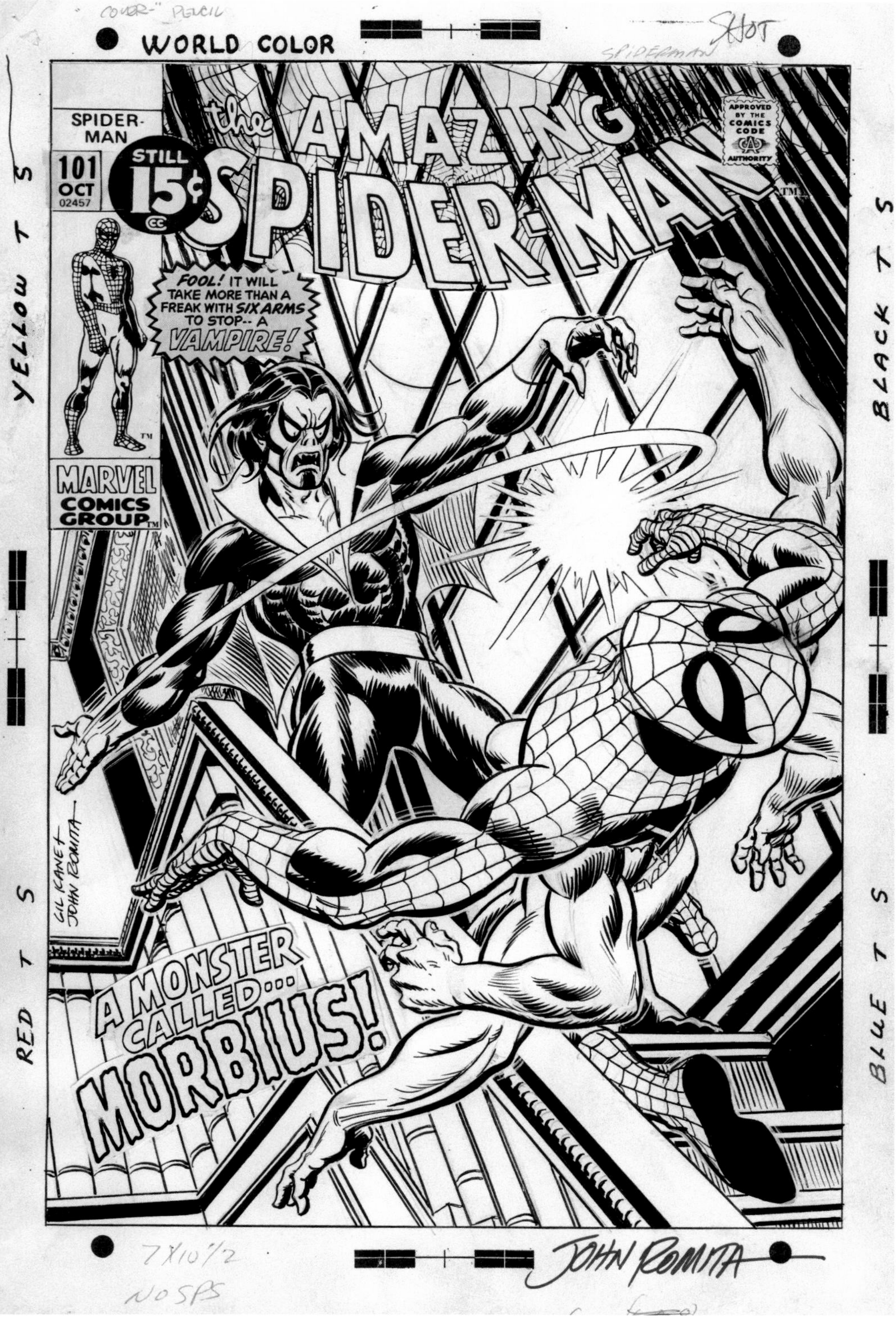
WORLD COLOR
SHOT
SPIDERMAN
SPIDER-MAN
101
OCT
02457
STILL
15¢
CC
the AMAZING SPIDER-MAN
APPROVED BY THE COMICS CODE CA AUTHORITY
FOOL! IT WILL TAKE MORE THAN A FREAK WITH SIX ARMS TO STOP-- A VAMPIRE!
MARVEL COMICS GROUP
GIL KANE + JOHN ROMITA
A MONSTER CALLED... MORBIUS!
YELLOW T S
RED T S
BLACK T S
BLUE T S
7X10 1/2
NO SPS
JOHN ROMITA

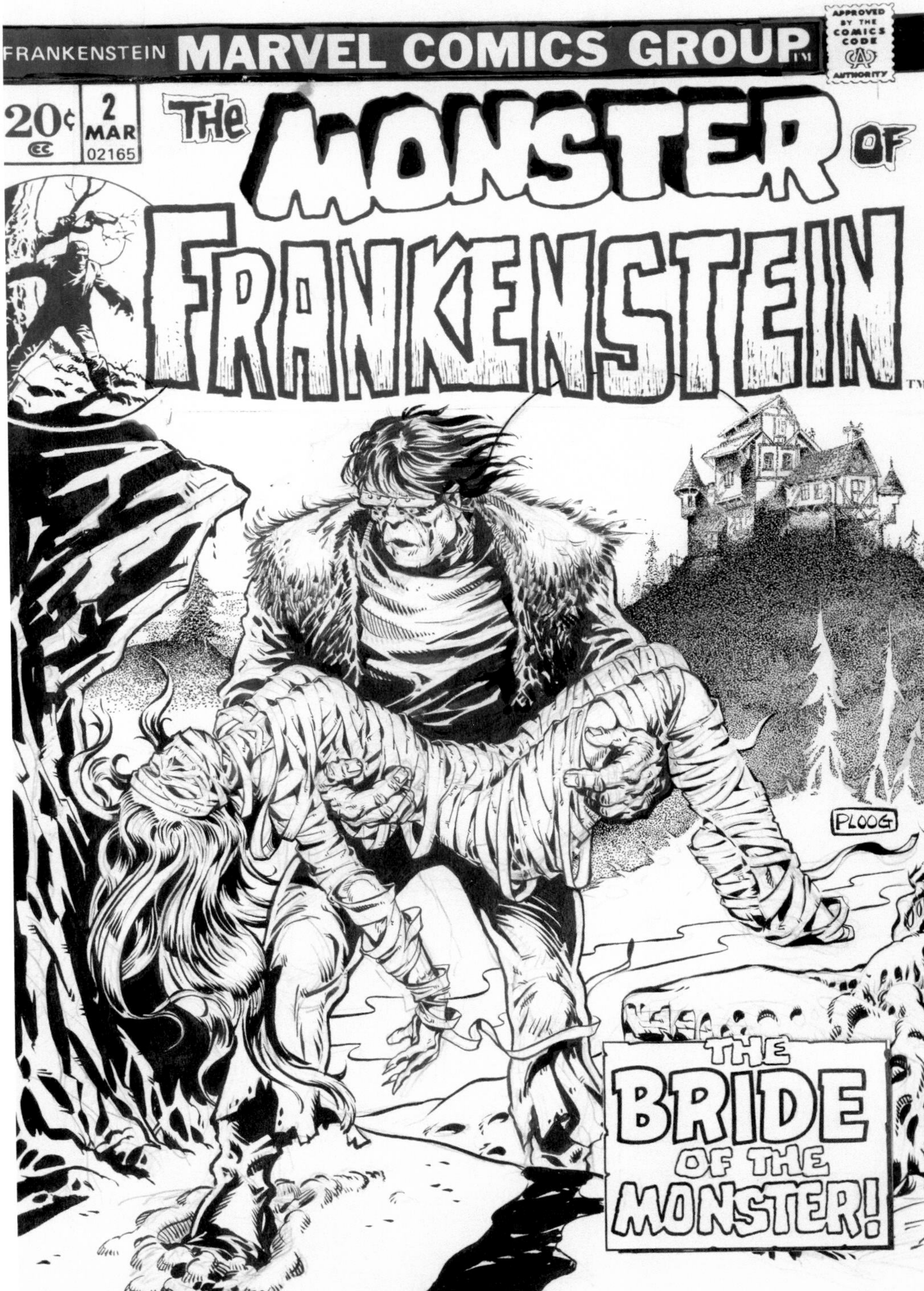
FRANKENSTEIN
MARVEL COMICS GROUP
APPROVED BY THE COMICS CODE AUTHORITY
20¢
2 MAR
02165
THE MONSTER OF FRANKENSTEIN
PLOOG
THE BRIDE OF THE MONSTER!

MONSTER OF FRANKENSTEIN No. 2

(Opposite) Original cover art; pencils and inks, Mike Ploog; March 1973. "I'd done up a Western, and I took it in to Marvel," recalled Ploog in *Comic Book Artist* No. 2. "They looked at it and said, 'No way. We don't do books that look like this.' But I'd met Roy Thomas there, and I went on home, trying to figure out what I was going to do next. A couple of days later, they called me up and said, 'How'd you like to do monsters?' ... I said, 'Sure, I'll do anything.' ... Marvel Comics at that time was magical."

WEREWOLF BY NIGHT No. 1

(Below) Interior; "Eye of the Beholder!"; script, Gerry Conway; pencils, Mike Ploog; inks, Frank Chiaramonte; September 1972. In 1971 the Comics Code was rewritten and relaxed, enabling Marvel to create a new "Monster Age." The book *Darkhold* holds the mystic secrets to turning Jack Russell into a werewolf. Soon he will be joined by Frankenstein, Dracula, the Mummy, and several others. In 2007, Roy Thomas described the comic as "inspired by a combination of *I Was a Teenage Werewolf*, a movie I'd liked since it first came out in the late 1950s, and Spider-Man ..."

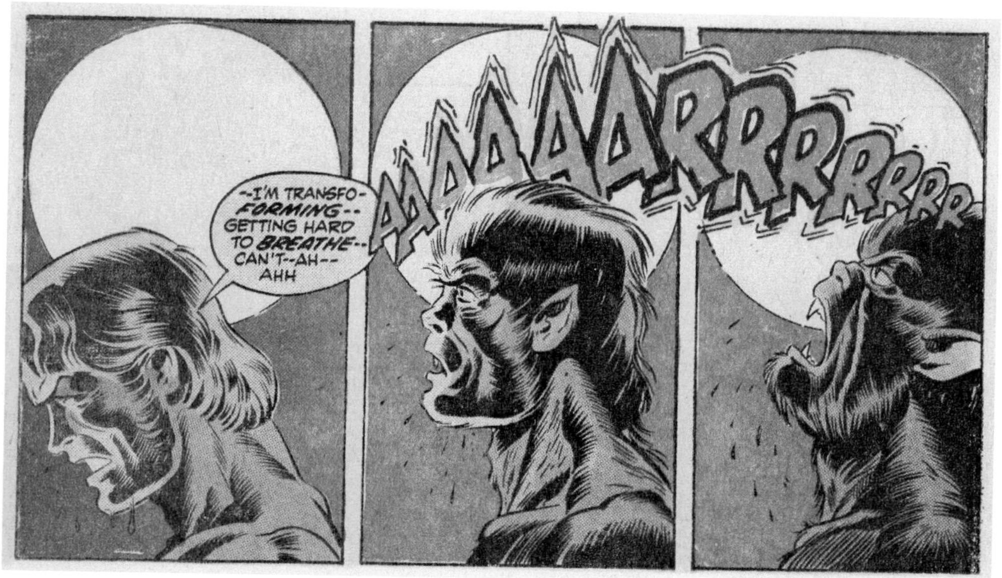
--I'M TRANSFO- FORMING-- GETTING HARD TO BREATHE-- CAN'T--AH-- AHH
AAAAAARRRRRRRRR

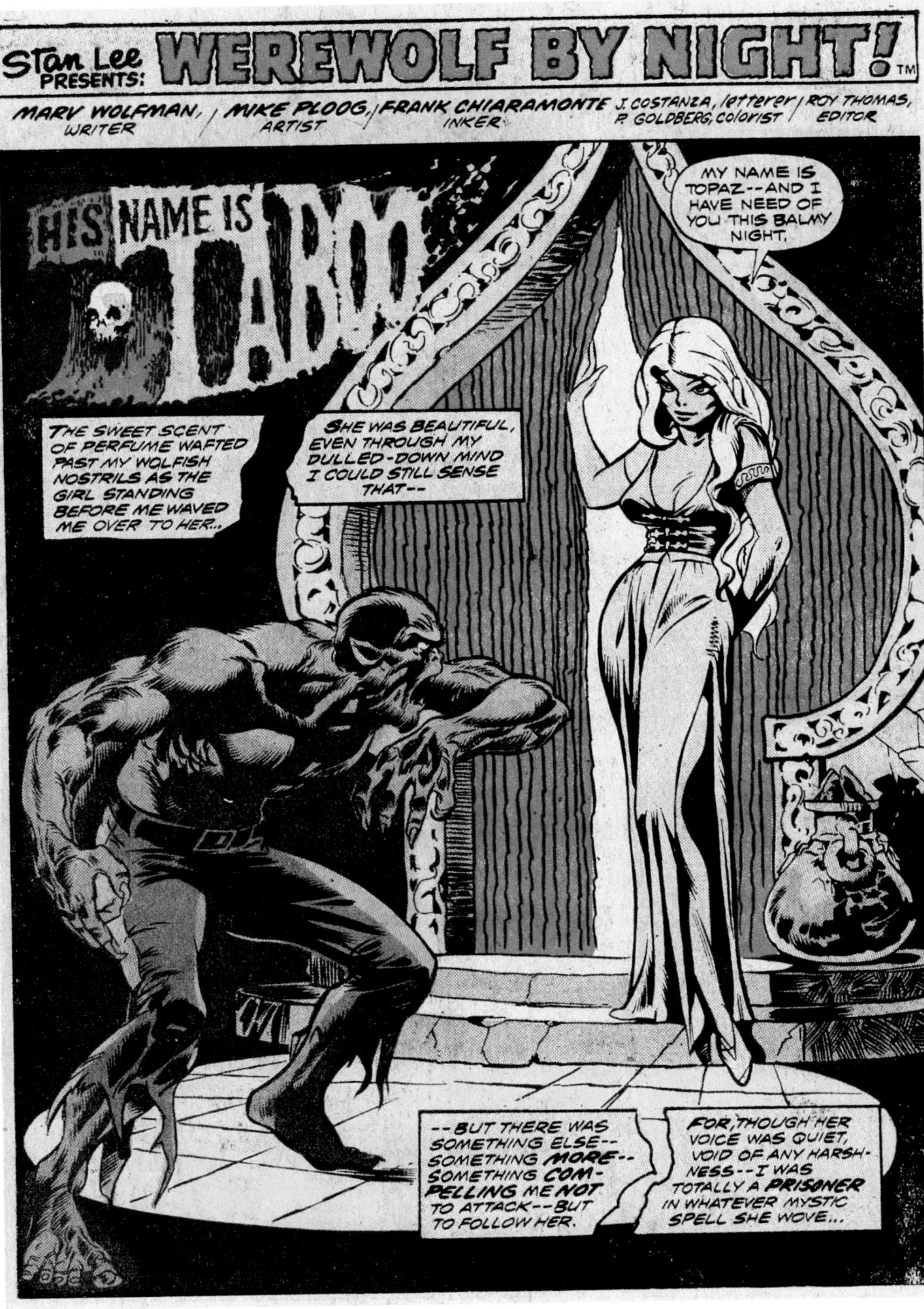
Stan Lee PRESENTS: WEREWOLF BY NIGHT! TM
MARV WOLFMAN, WRITER / MIKE PLOOG, ARTIST / FRANK CHIARAMONTE INKER / J. COSTANZA, letterer / P. GOLDBERG, colorist / ROY THOMAS, EDITOR
HIS NAME IS TABOO
MY NAME IS TOPAZ--AND I HAVE NEED OF YOU THIS BALMY NIGHT.
THE SWEET SCENT OF PERFUME WAFTED PAST MY WOLFISH NOSTRILS AS THE GIRL STANDING BEFORE ME WAVED ME OVER TO HER...
SHE WAS BEAUTIFUL, EVEN THROUGH MY DULLED-DOWN MIND I COULD STILL SENSE THAT--
--BUT THERE WAS SOMETHING ELSE--SOMETHING MORE--SOMETHING COMPELLING ME NOT TO ATTACK--BUT TO FOLLOW HER.
FOR, THOUGH HER VOICE WAS QUIET, VOID OF ANY HARSHNESS--I WAS TOTALLY A PRISONER IN WHATEVER MYSTIC SPELL SHE WOVE...

WEREWOLF BY NIGHT No. 13

(Opposite) Interior, "His Name Is Taboo"; script, Marv Wolfman; pencils, Mike Ploog; inks, Frank Chiaramonte; January 1974. Femme fatale Topaz evokes the *Spirit* of the 1940s in this gorgeous splash page — with good reason, as artist Mike Ploog had previously drawn Will Eisner's similarly Lauren Bacall–inspired Corporal Connie Rodd for *PS Magazine*, the revered instructional comic digest published by the armed services.

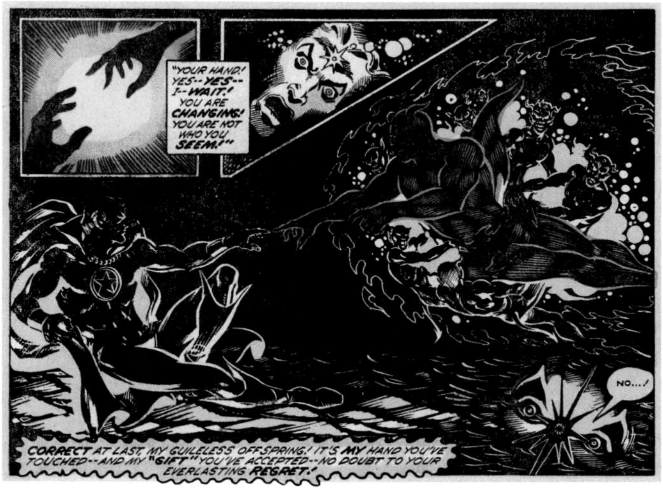
"YOUR HAND! YES--YES-- I--WAIT! YOU ARE CHANGING! YOU ARE NOT WHO YOU SEEM!"
NO...!
CORRECT AT LAST, MY GUILELESS OFFSPRING! IT'S MY HAND YOU'VE TOUCHED--AND MY "GIFT" YOU'VE ACCEPTED--NO DOUBT TO YOUR EVERLASTING REGRET!

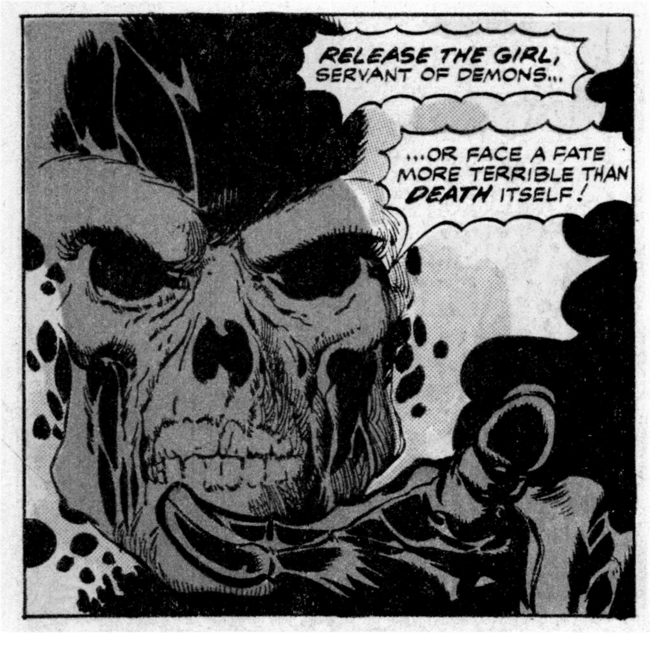
RELEASE THE GIRL, SERVANT OF DEMONS...
...OR FACE A FATE MORE TERRIBLE THAN DEATH ITSELF!

MARVEL SPOTLIGHT No. 15

(Above) Interior, "Black Sabbath!"; script, Steve Gerber; pencils and inks, Jim Mooney; May 1974. The Son of Satan's logo graced the spinner racks alongside Spider-Man and the Hulk for 13 issues of *Spotlight* and eight issues of his own title — with audacious "homages" to Michelangelo's *The Creation of Adam* clearly showcasing that this was not your older brother's Marvel.

MARVEL SPOTLIGHT No. 7

(Left) Interior, "Die, Die, My Daughter"; script, Gary Friedrich; pencils, Mike Ploog; inks, Frank Chiaramonte; December 1972.

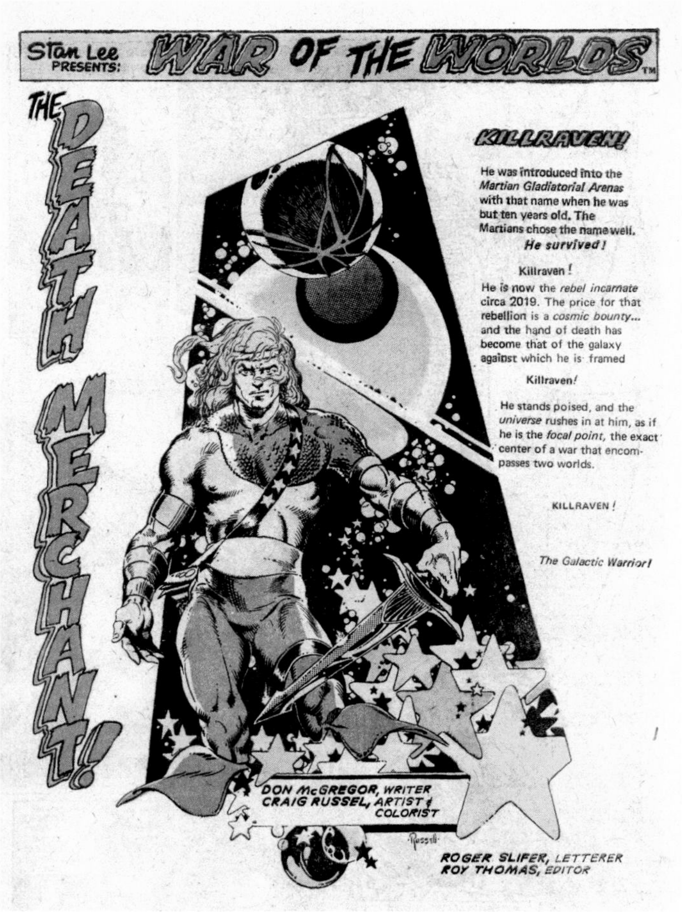
Stan Lee PRESENTS:
WAR OF THE WORLDS
THE DEATH MERCHANT!
KILLRAVEN!
He was introduced into the Martian Gladiatorial Arenas with that name when he was but ten years old. The Martians chose the name well. He survived!
Killraven!
He is now the rebel incarnate circa 2019. The price for that rebellion is a cosmic bounty... and the hand of death has become that of the galaxy against which he is framed
Killraven!
He stands poised, and the universe rushes in at him, as if he is the focal point, the exact center of a war that encompasses two worlds.
KILLRAVEN!
The Galactic Warrior!
DON McGREGOR, WRITER
CRAIG RUSSEL, ARTIST & COLORIST
ROGER SLIFER, LETTERER
ROY THOMAS, EDITOR

AMAZING ADVENTURES No. 28

(Above) Interior, "The Death Merchant!"; script, Don McGregor; pencils, inks, and colors, P. Craig Russell; January 1975. Here, Russell got a start on an award-winning career, and Killraven got a start on a much-better-dressed future.

AVENGERS No. 88

(Opposite) Interior, "The Summons of Psyklop"; plot, Harlan Ellison; script, Roy Thomas; pencils, Sal Buscema; inks, Jim Mooney; May 1971. Somewhat ahead of his time, Marvel mainstay Roy Thomas actively pursued writers from outside the comic book field to take a swing at Marvel's heroes. Celebrated science-fiction author Harlan Ellison brought his visionary talents to a two-part crossover that pitted the menace of Psyklop against both the Avengers and the Hulk. Ellison drew inspiration from H. P. Lovecraft's "The Call of Cthulhu" for his plot, which was then adapted into a comic book script by Thomas.

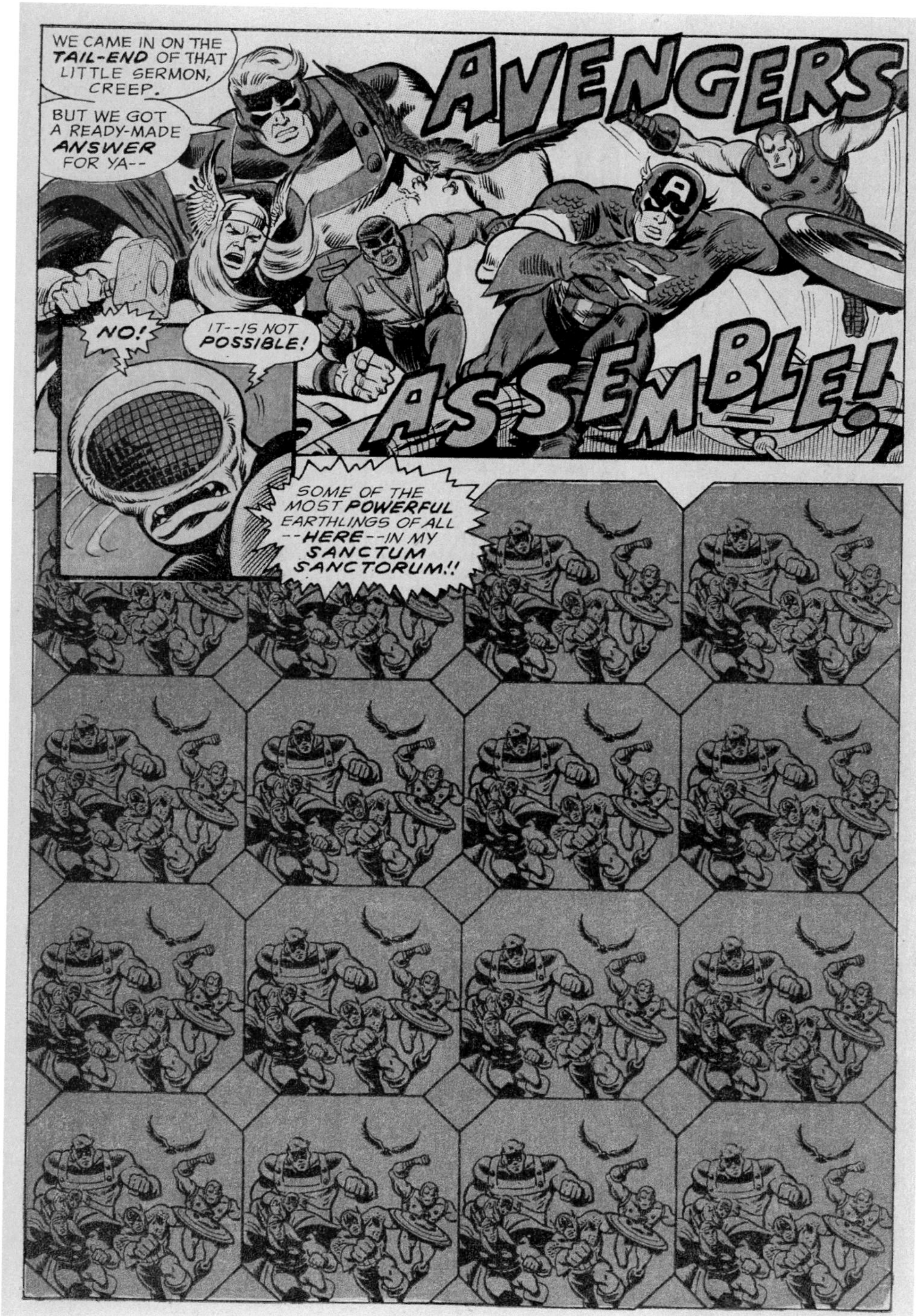
WE CAME IN ON THE TAIL-END OF THAT LITTLE SERMON, CREEP.
BUT WE GOT A READY-MADE ANSWER FOR YA--
AVENGERS ASSEMBLE!
NO!
IT--IS NOT POSSIBLE!
SOME OF THE MOST POWERFUL EARTHLINGS OF ALL --HERE--IN MY SANCTUM SANCTORUM!!

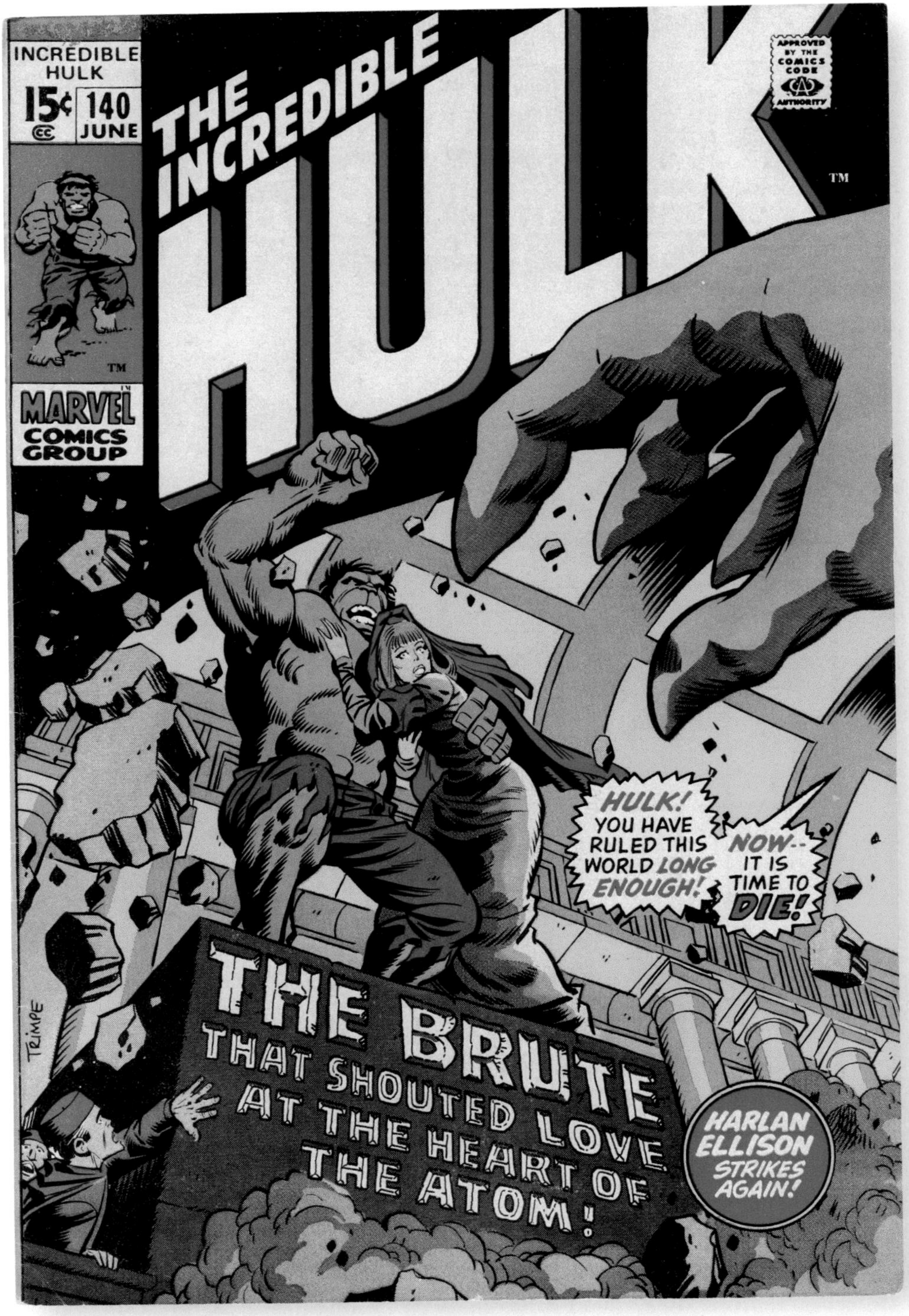
INCREDIBLE HULK
15¢
140
JUNE
THE INCREDIBLE HULK
MARVEL COMICS GROUP
APPROVED BY THE COMICS CODE AUTHORITY
HULK! YOU HAVE RULED THIS WORLD LONG ENOUGH!
NOW-- IT IS TIME TO DIE!
THE BRUTE THAT SHOUTED LOVE AT THE HEART OF THE ATOM!
HARLAN ELLISON STRIKES AGAIN!
TRIMPE

THE INCREDIBLE HULK No. 140

(Opposite) Cover; pencils and inks, Herb Trimpe; June 1971. Harlan Ellison gets a cover blurb! This unusual editorial move was emblematic of an Ellison fan who couldn't help himself, namely scripter Roy Thomas, who also took it upon himself to bury the names of 20 — count 'em! — 20 Ellison stories in the issue's dialogue. Finishing up a story begun in *Avengers* No. 88, this story introduces the lovely Princess Jarella, whose subatomic kingdom is rescued by the Hulk. A romance ensues — a first for the Hulk — but as in all things Marvel, it is fated for tragedy... a mere few years down the road.

MAILED NOT-SO-FLAT!

(Right) Subscription envelope, The Incredible Hulk *No. 162; April 1973.* Comics from the early years of subscription circulation are easily distinguished by the irrevocable crease down the middle from their journey through the U.S. postal system. Later subscription ads declared all books would be "MAILED FLAT!," no doubt to assuage discouraged subscribers with an eye on condition.

WE LOVE YOU HERB TRIMPE

(Below) Photograph, Robert Policastro; Herb Trimpe, early 1970s. Trimpe was a production artist before getting his shot at penciling full-time. A 1970 NYU student film documenting the Marvel bullpen with the above title betrays the import of the humble Bullpenners — Trimpe in particular was teased by his fellows as a bit of a heartthrob.

INCREDIBLE HULK
20¢
162
APR
02456
THE INCREDIBLE
MAGAZINE MANAGEMENT CO.
625 Madison Avenue
New York, New York 10022
520 11th Ave S
St James Mn 56081
2nd CLASS POSTAGE
PAID
SPARTA, ILLINOIS 62286

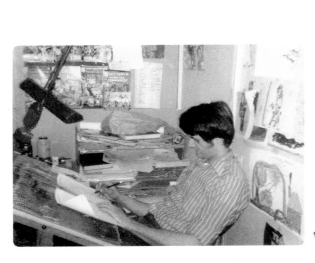

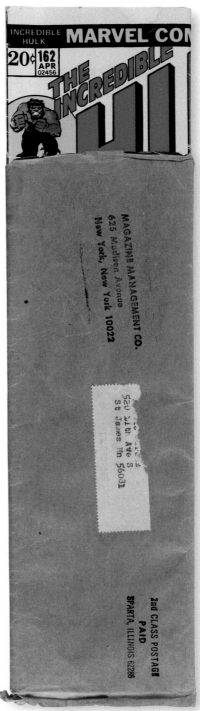

THE WOLVERINE IS BORN

(Below) Original character design; art, John Romita; 1974. The best character designer in the business, "Jazzy Johnny" does it again with the single most significant super hero creation this side of the Silver Age. Though the kitty whiskers were soon dispensed with, Wolverine would in time establish himself as the best there is at what he does...and what he does is sell comic books. And cartoons. And Halloween costumes with plastic retractable claws. And movies. And even more comics.

THE INCREDIBLE HULK No. 181

(Opposite) Cover; pencils and inks, Herb Trimpe. November 1974. The first full appearance of the figure who would become central to the comics' new direction. If you were lucky enough to buy this one off the rack, you would be considerably richer than if you bought pretty much any other issue, except possibly *Incredible Hulk* No. 1. The first Bronze Age book to break the six-figure barrier, a copy graded 9.9 by the CGC (Certified Guaranty Company) sold for $150,000 in 2011! "John's story was that Roy came to him and asked him to design a character called Wolverine.... And John [Romita] said, 'I didn't even know what a wolverine was. I thought it was a female wolf. [So] I got out the encyclopedia." —Herb Trimpe

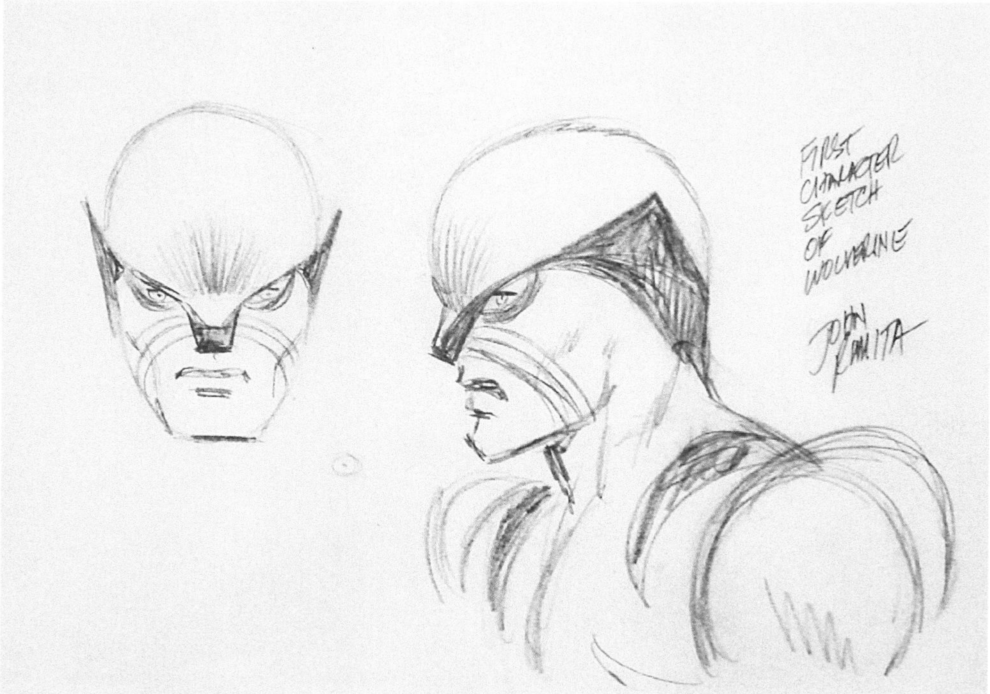
FIRST CHARACTER SCETCH OF WOLVERINE
JOHN ROMITA

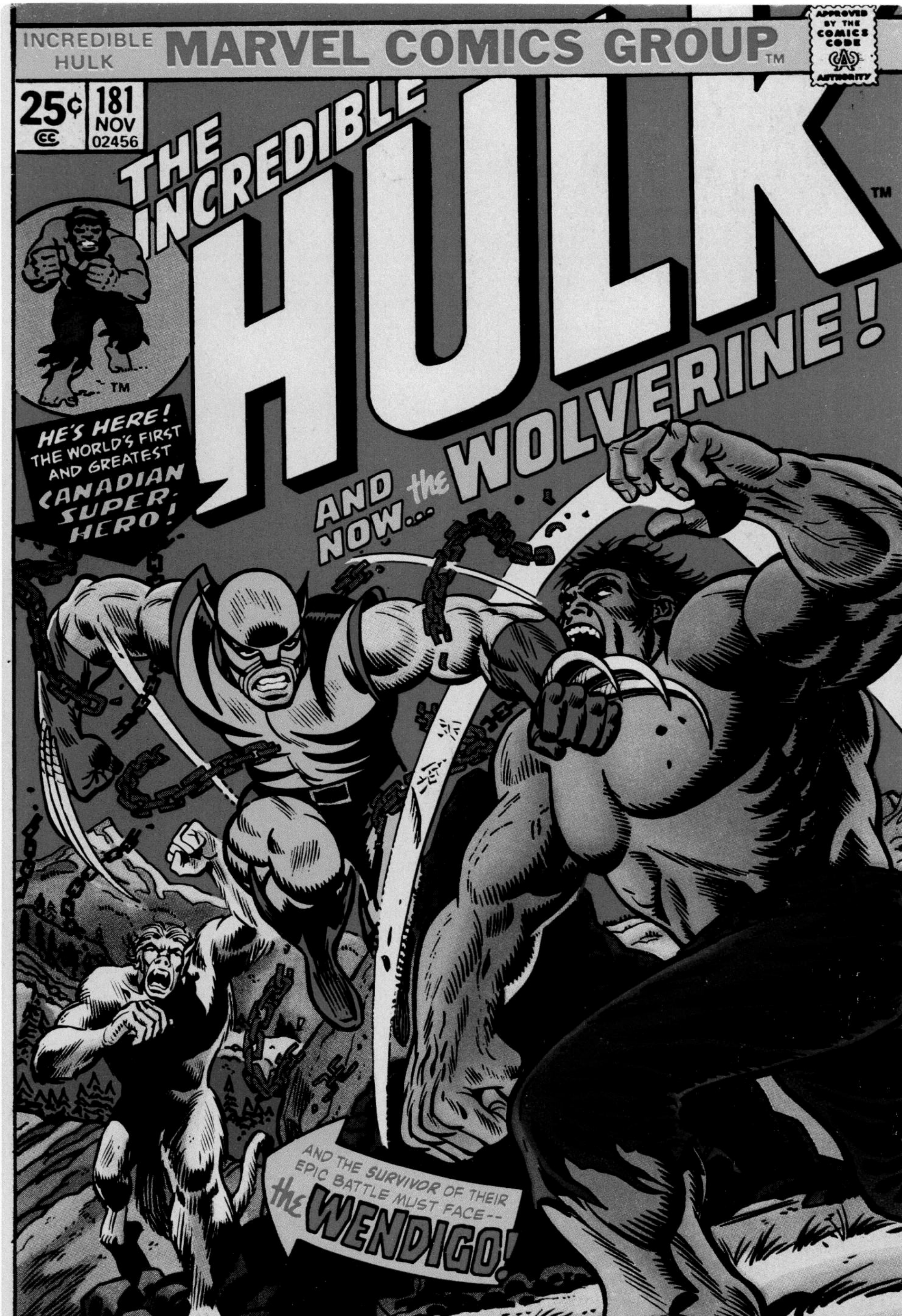
INCREDIBLE HULK
MARVEL COMICS GROUP
APPROVED BY THE COMICS CODE AUTHORITY
25¢
181 NOV
02456
THE INCREDIBLE HULK
HE'S HERE! THE WORLD'S FIRST AND GREATEST CANADIAN SUPER-HERO!
AND NOW... the WOLVERINE!
AND THE SURVIVOR OF THEIR EPIC BATTLE MUST FACE-- the WENDIGO!

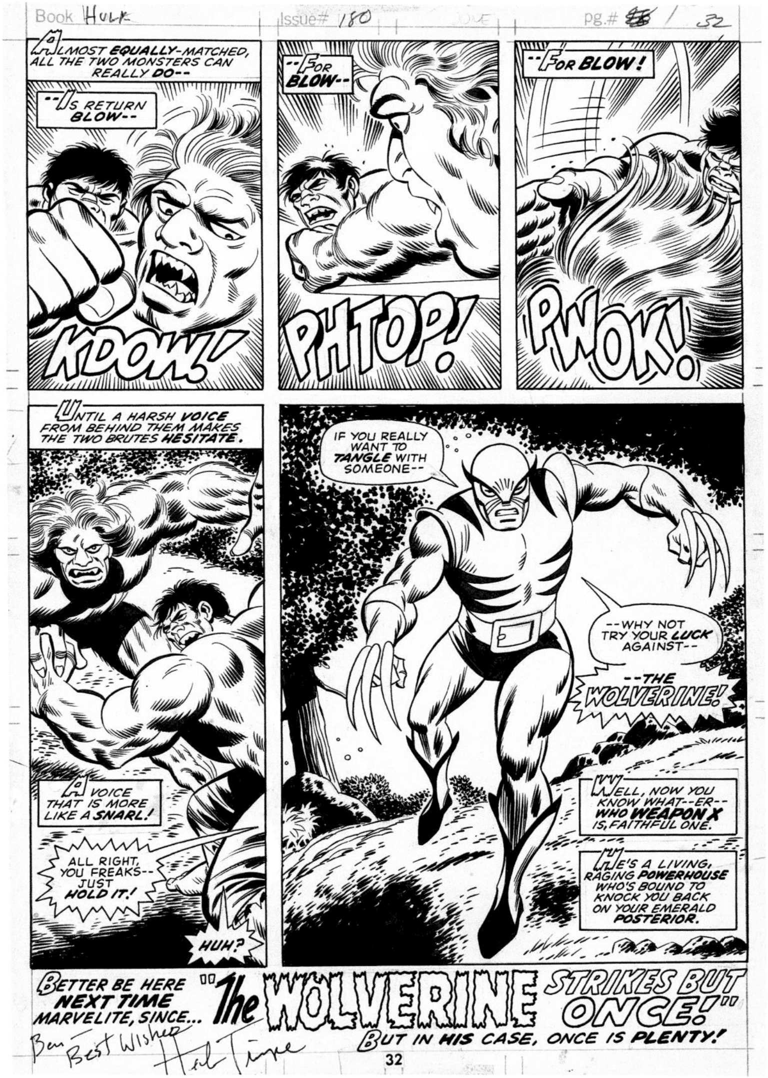
Book HULK
Issue# 180
pg.# 32
ALMOST EQUALLY-MATCHED, ALL THE TWO MONSTERS CAN REALLY DO--
--IS RETURN BLOW--
KDOW!
--FOR BLOW--
PHTOP!
--FOR BLOW!
PWOK!
UNTIL A HARSH VOICE FROM BEHIND THEM MAKES THE TWO BRUTES HESITATE.
A VOICE THAT IS MORE LIKE A SNARL!
ALL RIGHT, YOU FREAKS--JUST HOLD IT!
HUH?
IF YOU REALLY WANT TO TANGLE WITH SOMEONE--
--WHY NOT TRY YOUR LUCK AGAINST--
--THE WOLVERINE!
WELL, NOW YOU KNOW WHAT--ER--WHO WEAPON X IS, FAITHFUL ONE.
HE'S A LIVING, RAGING POWERHOUSE WHO'S BOUND TO KNOCK YOU BACK ON YOUR EMERALD POSTERIOR.
BETTER BE HERE NEXT TIME MARVELITE, SINCE... "The WOLVERINE STRIKES BUT ONCE!"
BUT IN HIS CASE, ONCE IS PLENTY!
32

THE WOLVERINE STRIKES BUT ONCE!

(Above) Original art, The Incredible Hulk *No. 180; script, Len Wein; pencils, Herb Trimpe; inks, Jack Abel; October 1974.* Wolverine interrupts a Hulk vs. Wendigo slobberknocker on the final page in his true first appearance. Given as a souvenir by Trimpe to a teenage fan in 1983, the page resurfaced in 2014 and sold at auction, tying the world record for a page of comic art at $657,250!

THE INCREDIBLE HULK No. 181

(Opposite) Interior, "And Now . . . the Wolverine!"; script, Len Wein; pencils, Herb Trimpe; inks, Jack Abel; November 1974.

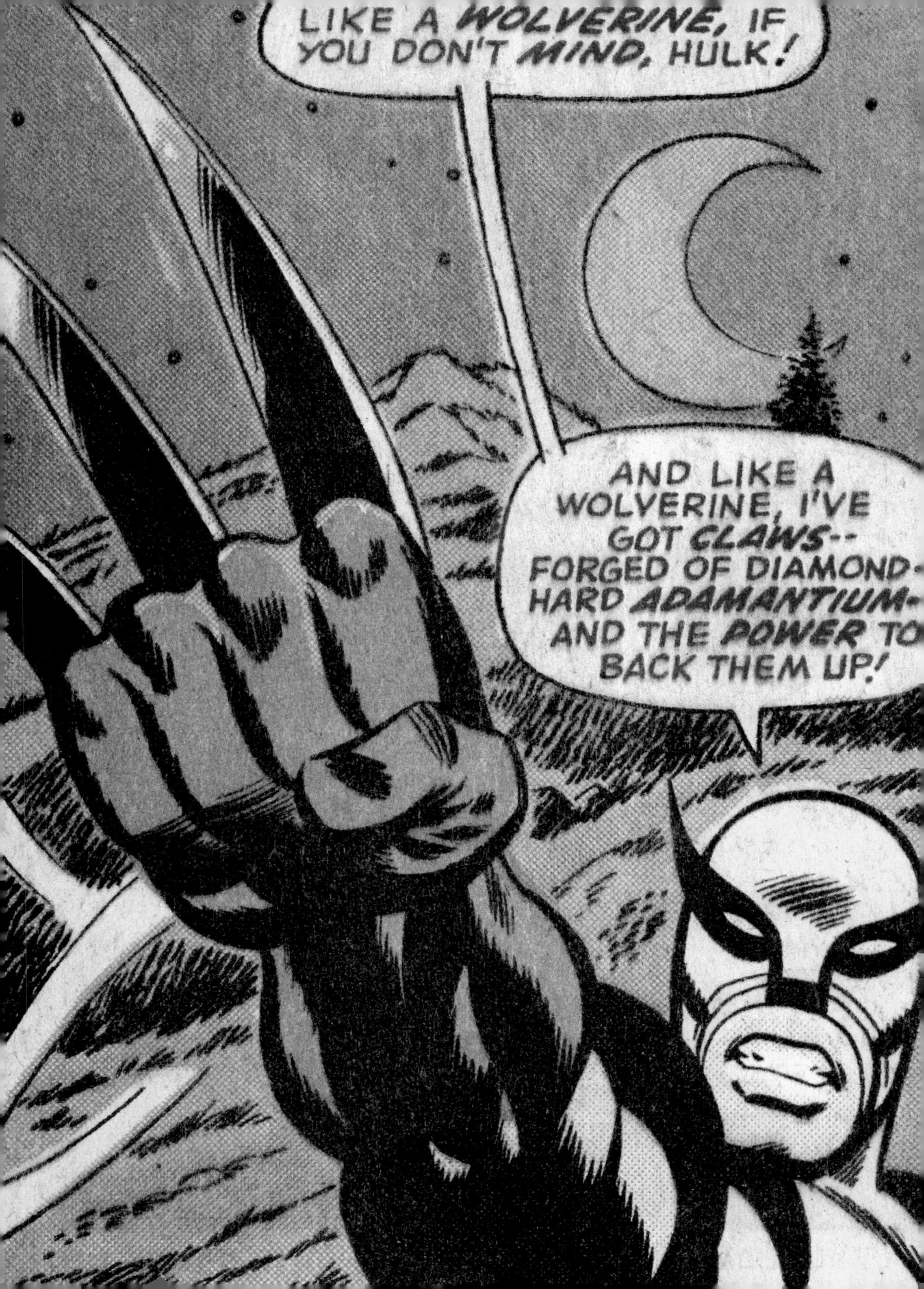
LIKE A WOLVERINE, IF YOU DON'T MIND, HULK!
AND LIKE A WOLVERINE, I'VE GOT CLAWS-- FORGED OF DIAMOND-HARD ADAMANTIUM-AND THE POWER TO BACK THEM UP!

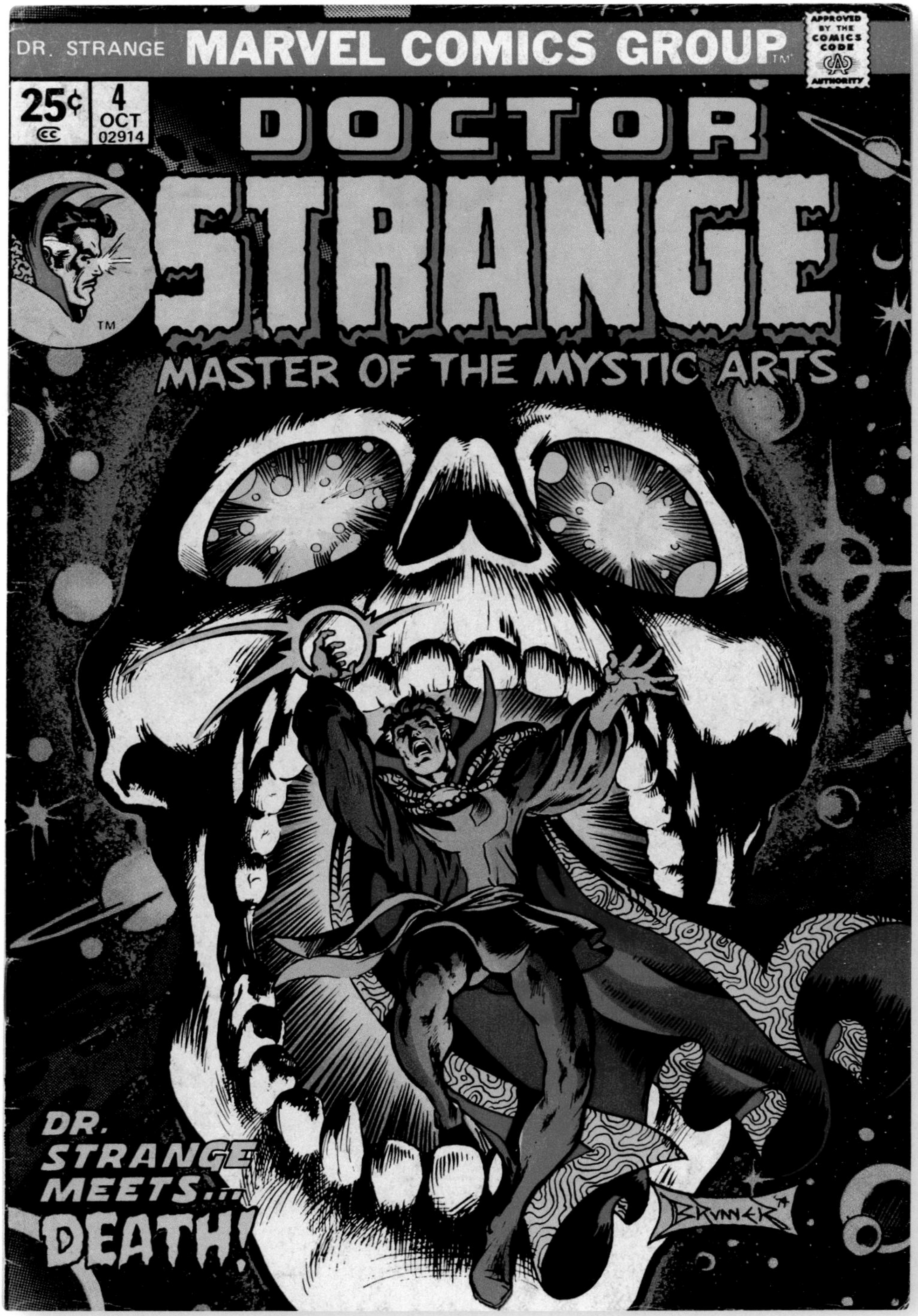
DR. STRANGE
MARVEL COMICS GROUP
APPROVED BY THE COMICS CODE AUTHORITY
25¢
4
OCT
02914
DOCTOR
STRANGE
MASTER OF THE MYSTIC ARTS
DR. STRANGE MEETS... DEATH!
BRUNNER

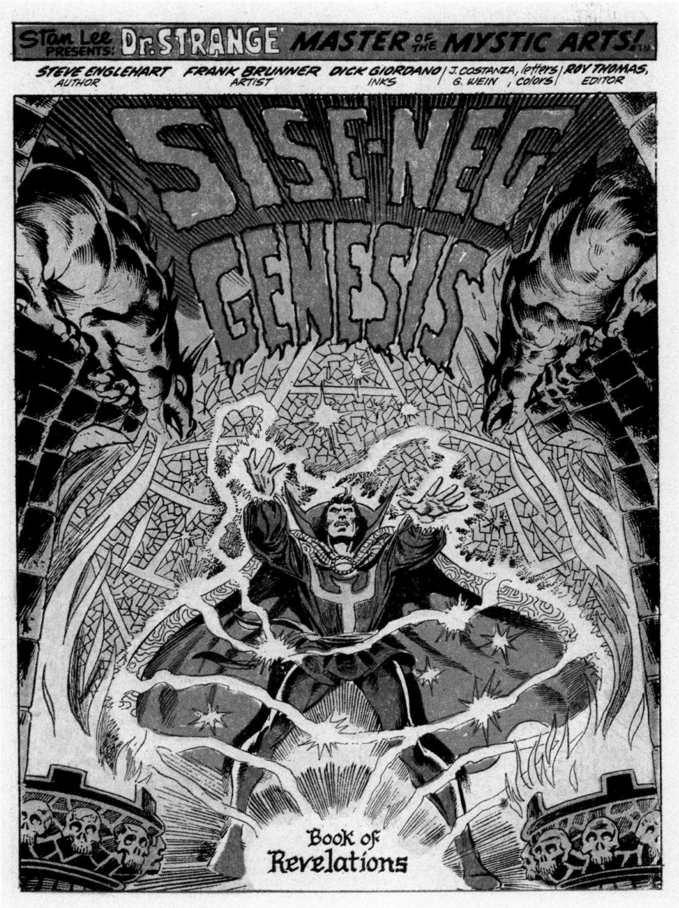
Stan Lee PRESENTS: Dr. STRANGE MASTER OF THE MYSTIC ARTS! TM
STEVE ENGLEHART AUTHOR
FRANK BRUNNER ARTIST
DICK GIORDANO INKS
J. COSTANZA, letters
G. WEIN, colors
ROY THOMAS, EDITOR
SISE-NEG GENESIS
Book of Revelations

DOCTOR STRANGE No. 4

(Opposite) Cover; pencils and inks, Frank Brunner; October 1974. "On a mountain range, I'm Doctor Strange for you…" —T. Rex, "Mambo Sun". After almost two years of "Premiere" status, the success of Englehart and Brunner restores Doctor Strange to his own title for the first time in five years.

MARVEL PREMIERE No. 14

(Above) Interior, "Sise-Neg Genesis"; script, Steve Englehart; pencils, Frank Brunner; inks, Dick Giordano; March 1974. The revered team of Englehart and Brunner bring the magic back to Doctor Strange. Englehart has described his work with Brunner as a coproduction "unique in its level of collaboration." The pair would dine together and work late into the night fusing action and philosophy into each and every one of the good doctor's spellbinding adventures.

"I can't help thinking that if Stan Lee was a young writer coming into his own in the seventies, he would be Steve Gerber."
— J.M. DEMATTEIS, LETTER IN *DEFENDERS* NO. 27

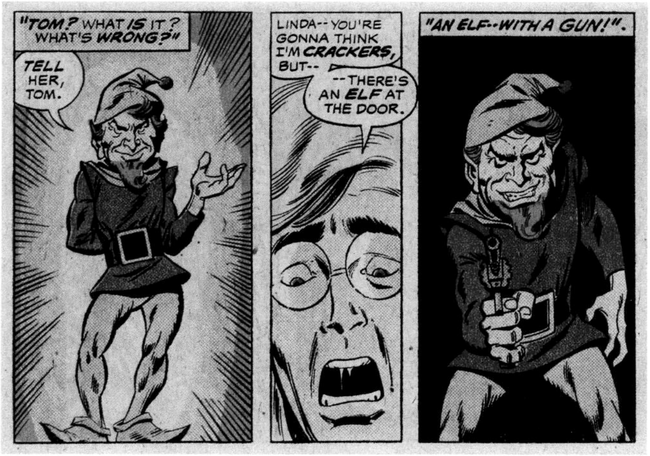
"TOM? WHAT IS IT? WHAT'S WRONG?"
TELL HER, TOM.
LINDA-- YOU'RE GONNA THINK I'M CRACKERS, BUT--
--THERE'S AN ELF AT THE DOOR.
"AN ELF--WITH A GUN!".

DEFENDERS No. 25
(Left) Interior, "The Serpent Sheds Its Skin"; script, Steve Gerber; pencils, Sal Buscema; inks, Jack Abel; July 1975. Gerber's burgeoning reputation for offbeat stories really takes off as he takes Marvel's team of (mostly) second-stringers in absurd and ever-twisted new directions — not least with one of his legendary signature creations, the seemingly inexplicable Elf with a Gun.

GIANT-SIZE DEFENDERS No. 1
(Opposite) Interior, "The Way They Were!"; script, Tony Isabella; pencils, Jim Starlin; inks, Al Milgrom; July 1974.

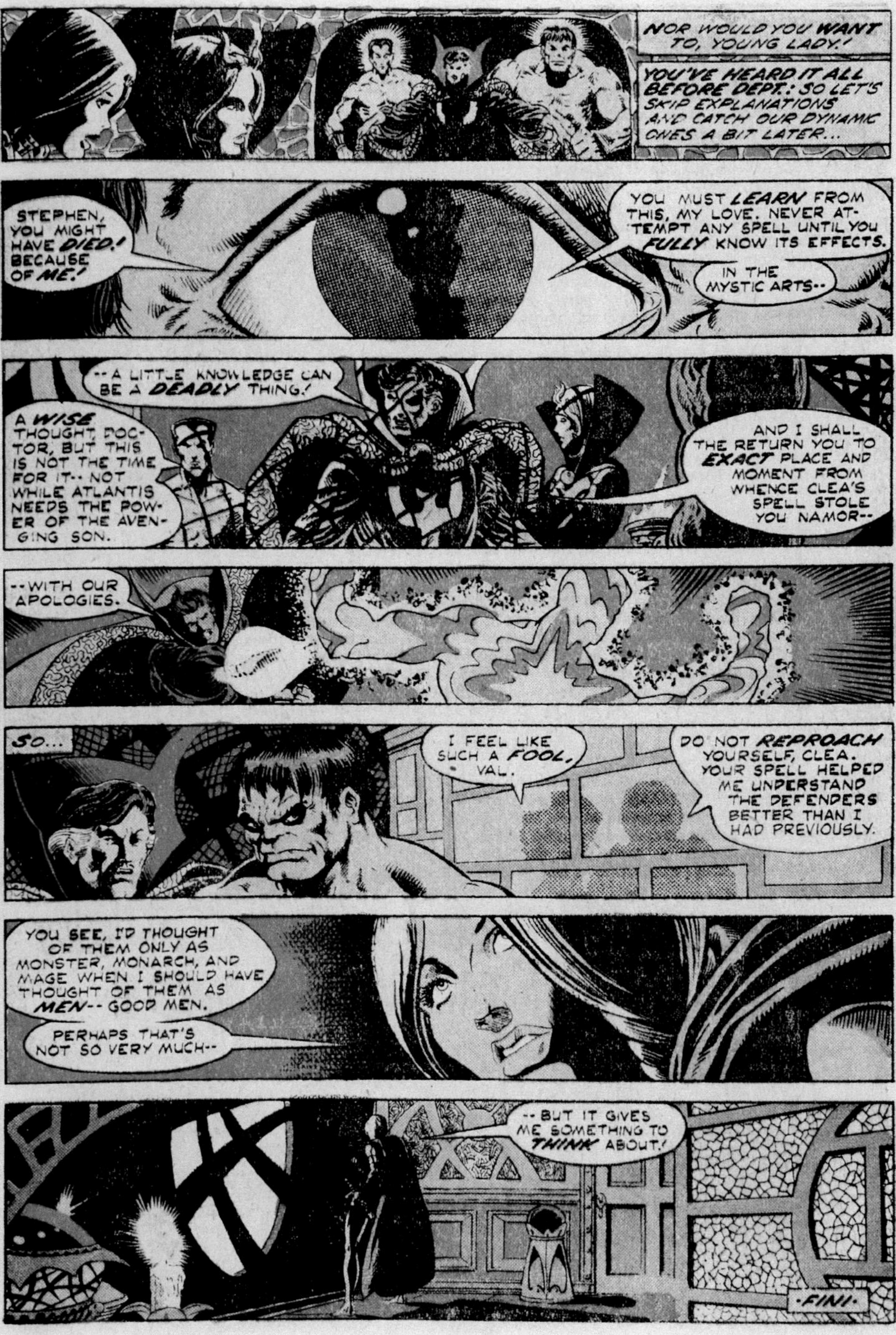
NOR WOULD YOU WANT TO, YOUNG LADY!
YOU'VE HEARD IT ALL BEFORE DEPT.: SO LET'S SKIP EXPLANATIONS AND CATCH OUR DYNAMIC ONES A BIT LATER...
STEPHEN, YOU MIGHT HAVE DIED! BECAUSE OF ME!
YOU MUST LEARN FROM THIS, MY LOVE. NEVER ATTEMPT ANY SPELL UNTIL YOU FULLY KNOW ITS EFFECTS.
IN THE MYSTIC ARTS--
--A LITTLE KNOWLEDGE CAN BE A DEADLY THING!
A WISE THOUGHT, DOCTOR, BUT THIS IS NOT THE TIME FOR IT-- NOT WHILE ATLANTIS NEEDS THE POWER OF THE AVENGING SON.
AND I SHALL RETURN YOU TO THE EXACT PLACE AND MOMENT FROM WHENCE CLEA'S SPELL STOLE YOU NAMOR--
--WITH OUR APOLOGIES.
SO...
I FEEL LIKE SUCH A FOOL, VAL.
DO NOT REPROACH YOURSELF, CLEA. YOUR SPELL HELPED ME UNDERSTAND THE DEFENDERS BETTER THAN I HAD PREVIOUSLY.
YOU SEE, I'D THOUGHT OF THEM ONLY AS MONSTER, MONARCH, AND MAGE WHEN I SHOULD HAVE THOUGHT OF THEM AS MEN-- GOOD MEN.
PERHAPS THAT'S NOT SO VERY MUCH--
--BUT IT GIVES ME SOMETHING TO THINK ABOUT!
-FINI-

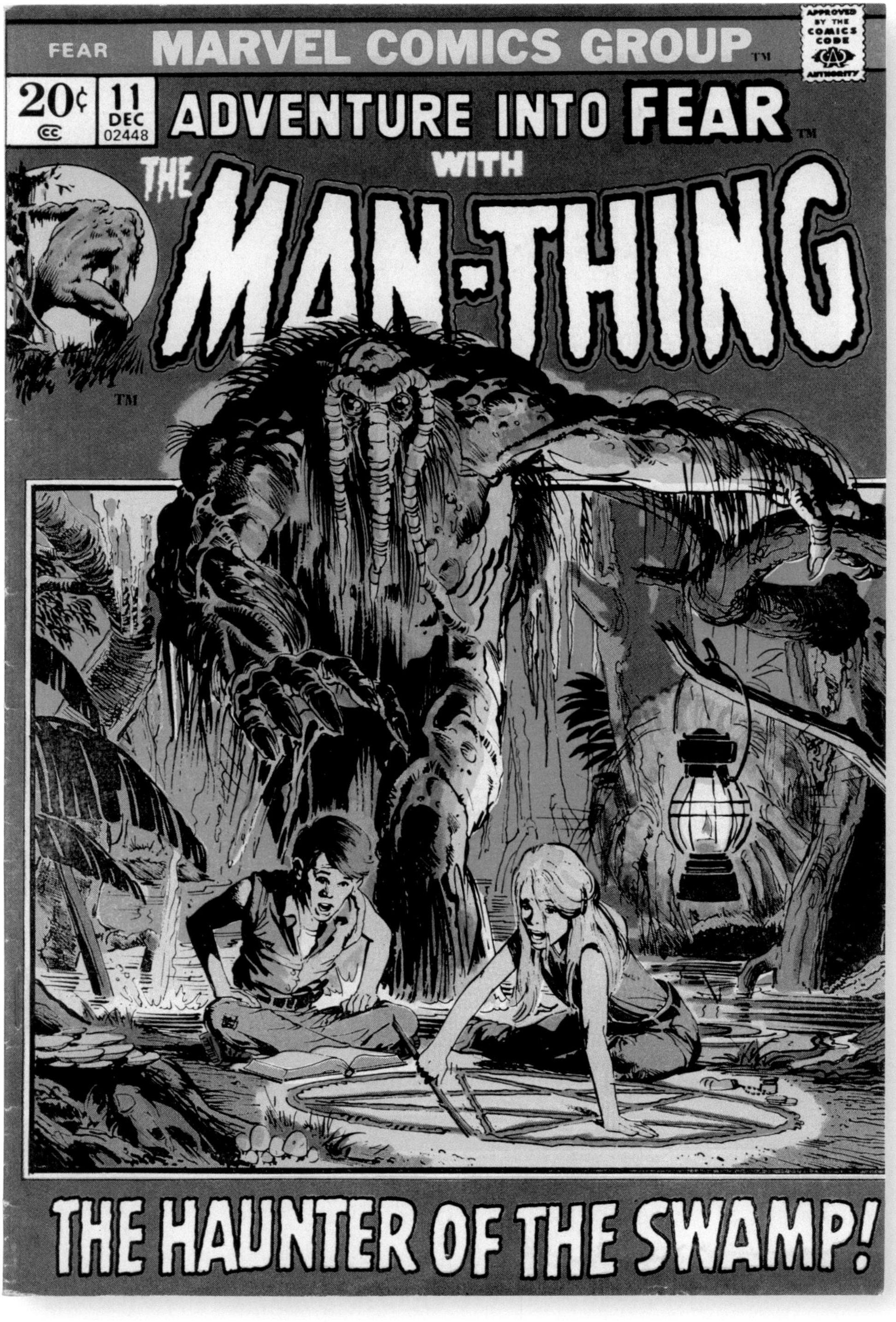
FEAR
MARVEL COMICS GROUP
APPROVED BY THE COMICS CODE AUTHORITY
20¢
11 DEC
02448
ADVENTURE INTO FEAR
WITH
THE MAN-THING
THE HAUNTER OF THE SWAMP!

FEAR No. 11

(Opposite) Cover; pencils and inks, Neal Adams; December 1972. Those who know fear will burn at the Man-Thing's touch. Adams provides a fittingly momentous cover as Steve Gerber begins a classic psychological run with the character. The writer had a magic touch with bizarre characters such as Wundarr the Aquarian and Omega the Unknown.

GIANT-SIZE MAN-THING No. 4

(Below) Cover; pencils and inks, Frank Brunner; May 1975. The book that launched a thousand quips. In a far more innocent time, Marvel's extra-length format put *Giant-Size Man-Things* into the hands of kids. (One Million Moms were not available for comment.)

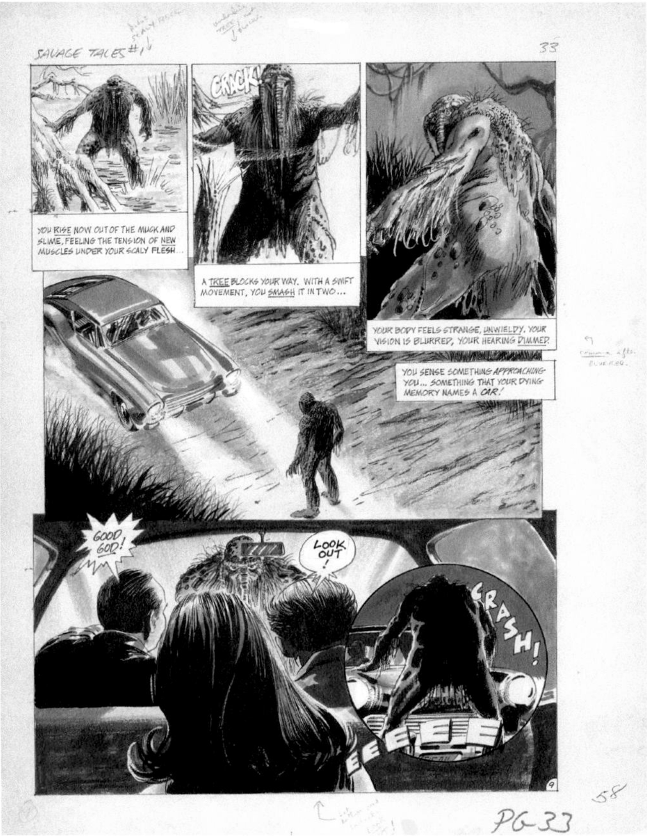

SAVAGE TALES #1
33
CRACK!
YOU RISE NOW OUT OF THE MUCK AND SLIME, FEELING THE TENSION OF NEW MUSCLES UNDER YOUR SCALY FLESH...
A TREE BLOCKS YOUR WAY. WITH A SWIFT MOVEMENT, YOU SMASH IT IN TWO...
YOUR BODY FEELS STRANGE, UNWIELDY. YOUR VISION IS BLURRED, YOUR HEARING DIMMED.
YOU SENSE SOMETHING APPROACHING YOU... SOMETHING THAT YOUR DYING MEMORY NAMES A CAR!
GOOD GOD!
LOOK OUT!
CRASH!
EEEEEE
58
PG-33

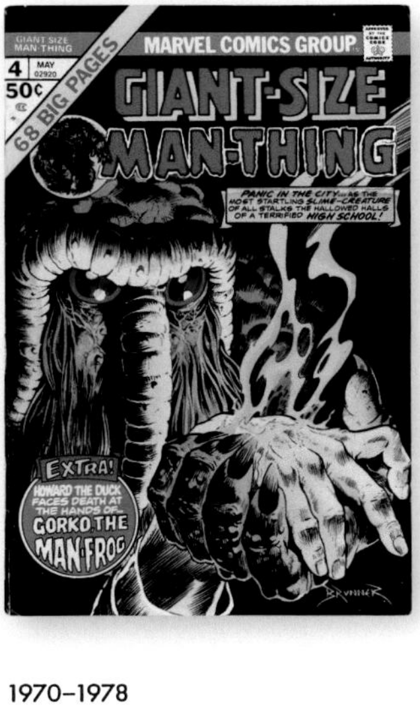

GIANT SIZE MAN-THING
MARVEL COMICS GROUP
4 MAY
50¢
68 BIG PAGES
GIANT-SIZE MAN-THING
PANIC IN THE CITY... AS THE MOST STARTLING SLIME-CREATURE OF ALL STALKS THE HALLOWED HALLS OF A TERRIFIED HIGH SCHOOL!
EXTRA!
HOWARD THE DUCK FACES DEATH AT THE HANDS OF... GORKO THE MAN-FROG
BRUNNER

SAVAGE TALES No. 1

(Above) Original interior art, "The Origin of the Man-Thing"; script, Roy Thomas and Gerry Conway; pencils and inks, Gray Morrow; 1971. Marvel updated the shambling, 1940s swamp creature the Heap with the frightening visage of the Man-Thing (beating DC's *Swamp Thing* to comic stands by two months). The monster's first appearance came in *Savage Tales* No. 1, Stan Lee's second attempt (after *Spectacular Spider-Man*) to inaugurate a black-and-white line to compete with Warren Publishing's successful horror comics magazines *Creepy* and *Eerie*.

MAN-THING No. 1

(Following spread) Interior, "Battle for the Palace of the Gods!"; script, Steve Gerber; pencils, Val Mayerik; inks, Sal Trapani; January 1974. Man-Thing lurches into his own book as Gerber hits full stride, filling the series with wild ideas including the multiversal madness of the Congress of Realities.

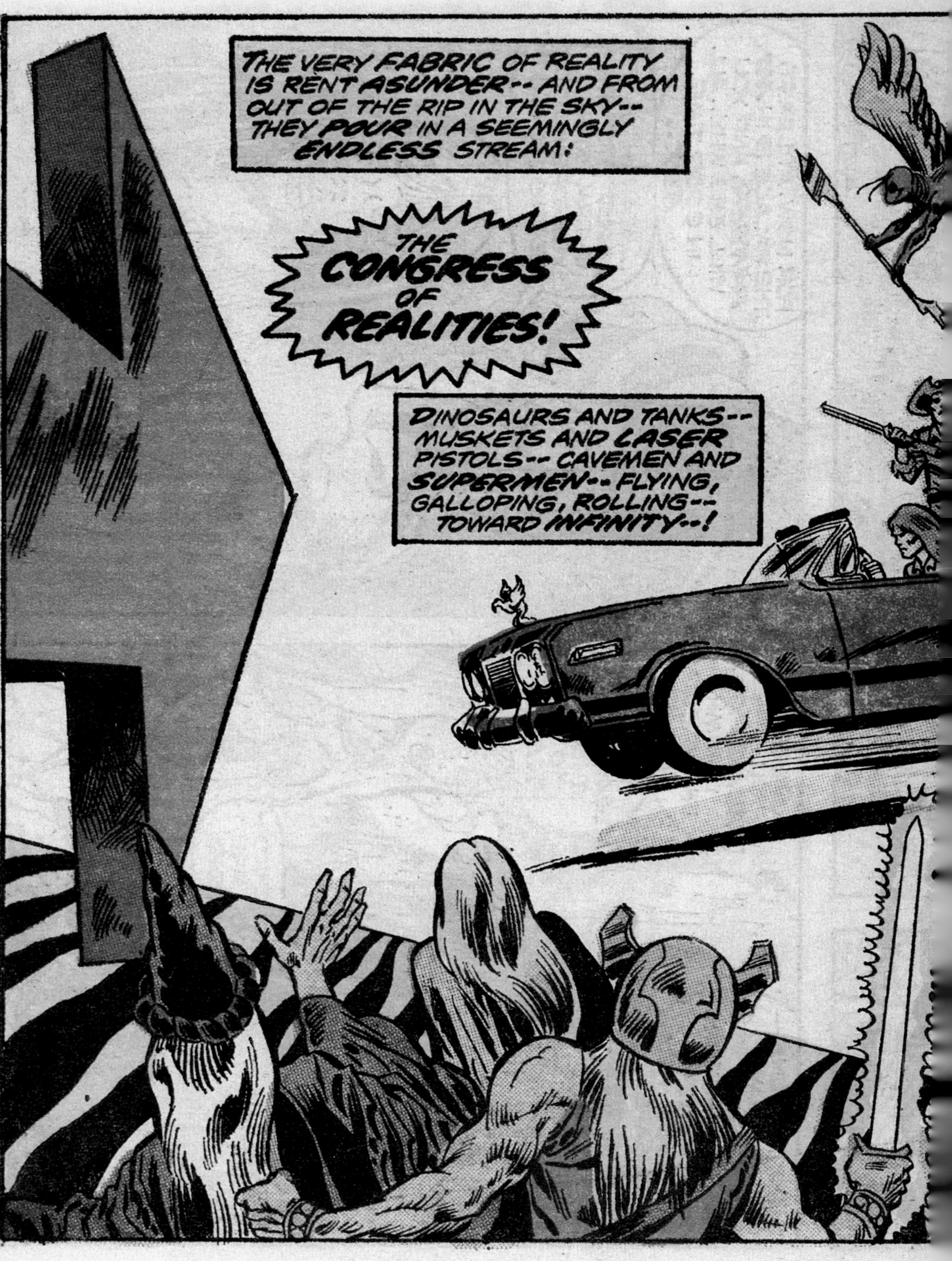
THE VERY FABRIC OF REALITY IS RENT ASUNDER-- AND FROM OUT OF THE RIP IN THE SKY-- THEY POUR IN A SEEMINGLY ENDLESS STREAM:
THE CONGRESS OF REALITIES!
DINOSAURS AND TANKS-- MUSKETS AND LASER PISTOLS-- CAVEMEN AND SUPERMEN-- FLYING, GALLOPING, ROLLING-- TOWARD INFINITY--!

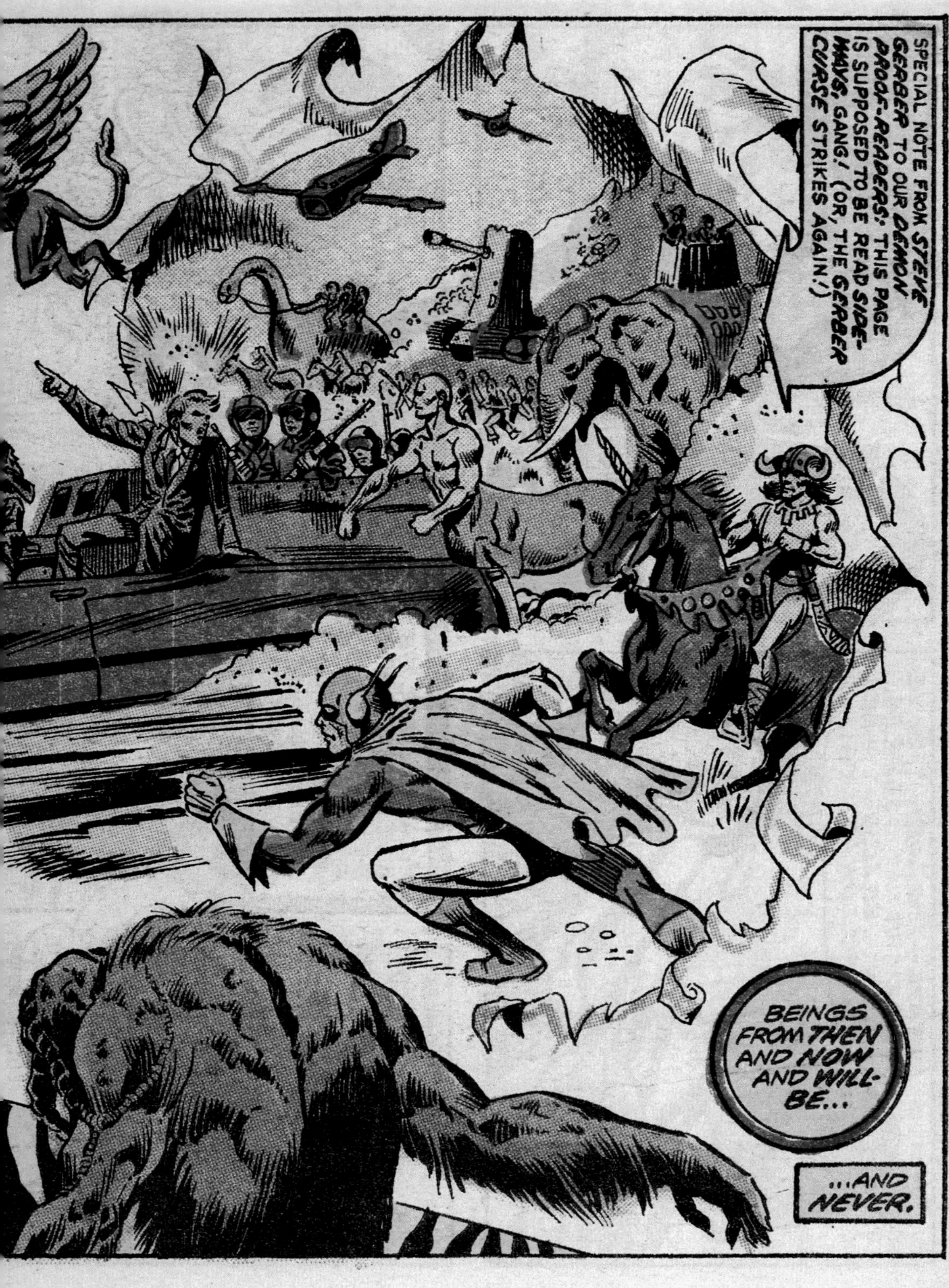
SPECIAL NOTE FROM STEVE GERBER TO OUR DEMON PROOF-READERS: THIS PAGE IS SUPPOSED TO BE READ SIDE-WAYS, GANG! (OR, THE GERBER CURSE STRIKES AGAIN!)
BEINGS FROM THEN AND NOW AND WILL-BE...
...AND NEVER.

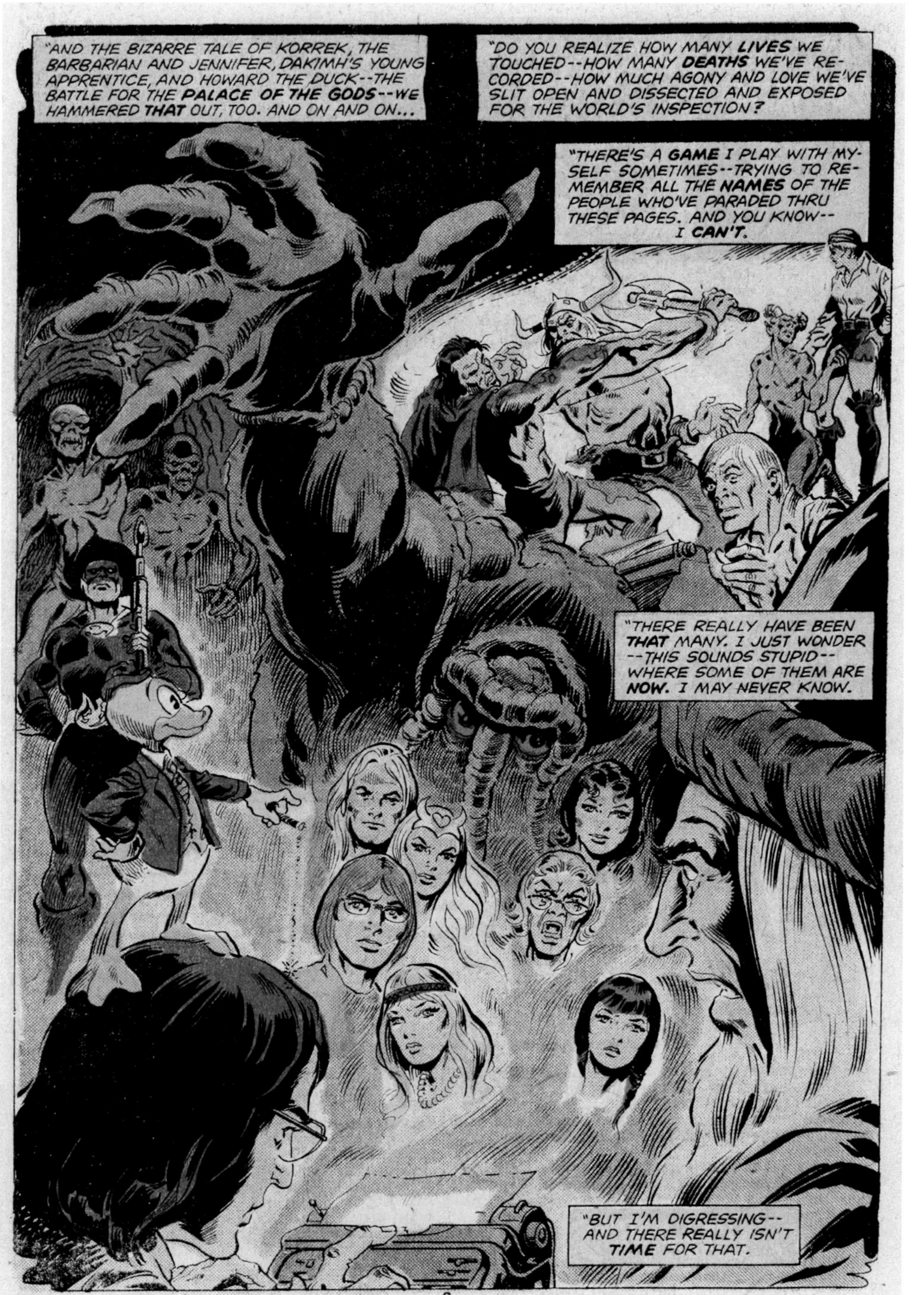
"AND THE BIZARRE TALE OF KORREK, THE BARBARIAN AND JENNIFER, DAKIMH'S YOUNG APPRENTICE, AND HOWARD THE DUCK--THE BATTLE FOR THE PALACE OF THE GODS--WE HAMMERED THAT OUT, TOO. AND ON AND ON...
"DO YOU REALIZE HOW MANY LIVES WE TOUCHED--HOW MANY DEATHS WE'VE RECORDED--HOW MUCH AGONY AND LOVE WE'VE SLIT OPEN AND DISSECTED AND EXPOSED FOR THE WORLD'S INSPECTION?
"THERE'S A GAME I PLAY WITH MYSELF SOMETIMES--TRYING TO REMEMBER ALL THE NAMES OF THE PEOPLE WHO'VE PARADED THRU THESE PAGES. AND YOU KNOW-- I CAN'T.
"THERE REALLY HAVE BEEN THAT MANY. I JUST WONDER --THIS SOUNDS STUPID-- WHERE SOME OF THEM ARE NOW. I MAY NEVER KNOW.
"BUT I'M DIGRESSING-- AND THERE REALLY ISN'T TIME FOR THAT.
6

MAN-THING No. 22

(Opposite) Interior, "Pop Goes the Cosmos!"; script, Steve Gerber; pencils and inks, Jim Mooney; October 1975. In the most artistically rendered resignation letter ever penned, Gerber brings his very personal run with the Man-Thing — and the character's solo title — to a close.

GIANT-SIZE MAN-THING No. 4

(Below) Interior, "Frog Death!"; script, Steve Gerber; pencils and inks, Frank Brunner; May 1975. Howard "... was the only sight gag I could think of to top Korrek jumping out of a jar of peanut butter in *Fear* No. 19," Gerber told David Anthony Kraft in the June 1977 issue of *Playboy*. "I told Val to have a duck come waddling out of the bushes.... 'Don't make him look too much like Donald, and for God's sake, don't dress him in a sailor suit.'"

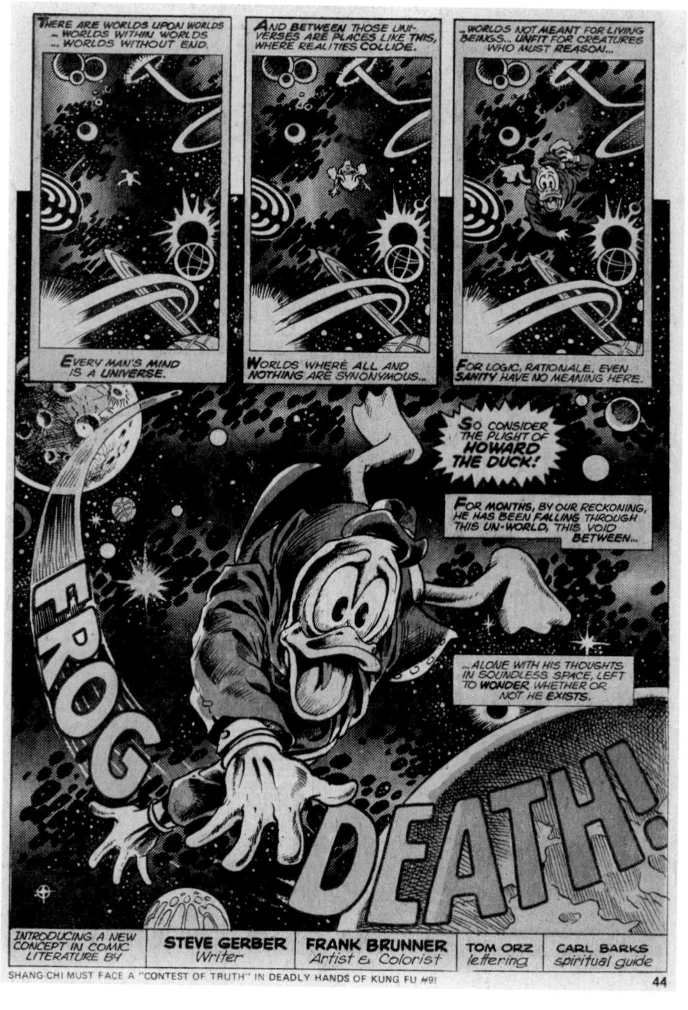
THERE ARE WORLDS UPON WORLDS -- WORLDS WITHIN WORLDS -- WORLDS WITHOUT END.
EVERY MAN'S MIND IS A UNIVERSE.
AND BETWEEN THOSE UNIVERSES ARE PLACES LIKE THIS, WHERE REALITIES COLLIDE.
WORLDS WHERE ALL AND NOTHING ARE SYNONYMOUS...
...WORLDS NOT MEANT FOR LIVING BEINGS... UNFIT FOR CREATURES WHO MUST REASON...
FOR LOGIC, RATIONALE, EVEN SANITY HAVE NO MEANING HERE.
SO CONSIDER THE PLIGHT OF HOWARD THE DUCK!
FOR MONTHS, BY OUR RECKONING, HE HAS BEEN FALLING THROUGH THIS UN-WORLD, THIS VOID BETWEEN...
...ALONE WITH HIS THOUGHTS IN SOUNDLESS SPACE, LEFT TO WONDER WHETHER OR NOT HE EXISTS.
FROG DEATH!
INTRODUCING A NEW CONCEPT IN COMIC LITERATURE BY
STEVE GERBER Writer
FRANK BRUNNER Artist & Colorist
TOM ORZ lettering
CARL BARKS spiritual guide
SHANG-CHI MUST FACE A "CONTEST OF TRUTH" IN DEADLY HANDS OF KUNG FU #9!
44

"There's a sensual quality to him.... If you stood
Howard next to Superman, you could tell instantly which
would be more interesting to jump into bed with."
— STEVE GERBER, *PLAYBOY*, 1977

HOWARD THE DUCK No. 1

*(Opposite) Cover; pencils and inks, Frank Brunner;
January 1976.* "Because You Demanded It!" was
no empty hype. Howard cult loyalists genuinely
demanded a solo title featuring the irascible,
cigar-chomping duck, which immediately
became a much wider hit, sparking one of the
industry's first — if not the first — speculator
booms, with copies of the underprinted
first pressing selling on the secondary
market for up to ten times the cover price.

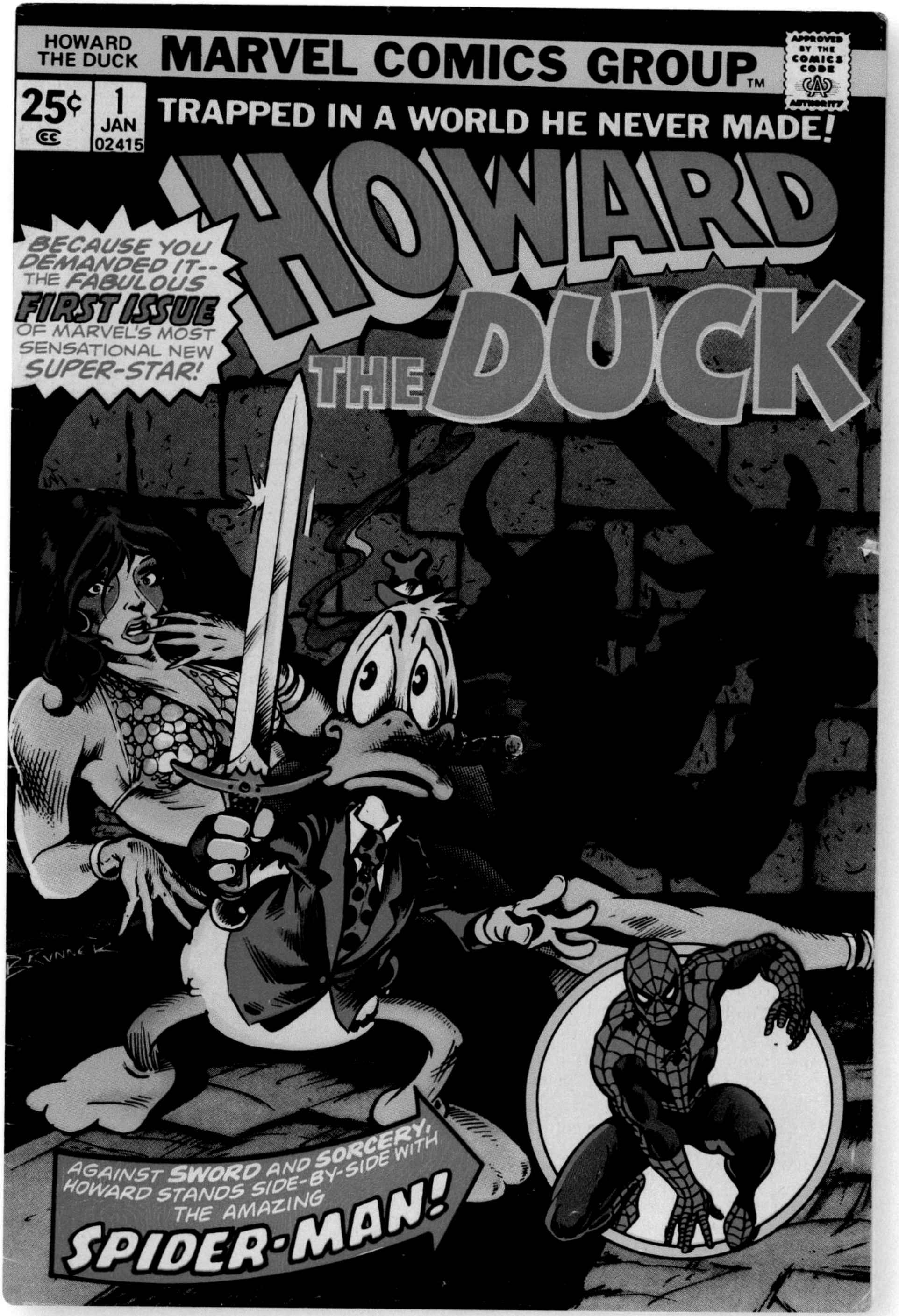
HOWARD THE DUCK
MARVEL COMICS GROUP
APPROVED BY THE COMICS CODE AUTHORITY
25¢
1 JAN
02415
TRAPPED IN A WORLD HE NEVER MADE!
HOWARD THE DUCK
BECAUSE YOU DEMANDED IT-- THE FABULOUS FIRST ISSUE OF MARVEL'S MOST SENSATIONAL NEW SUPER-STAR!
AGAINST SWORD AND SORCERY, HOWARD STANDS SIDE-BY-SIDE WITH THE AMAZING SPIDER-MAN!

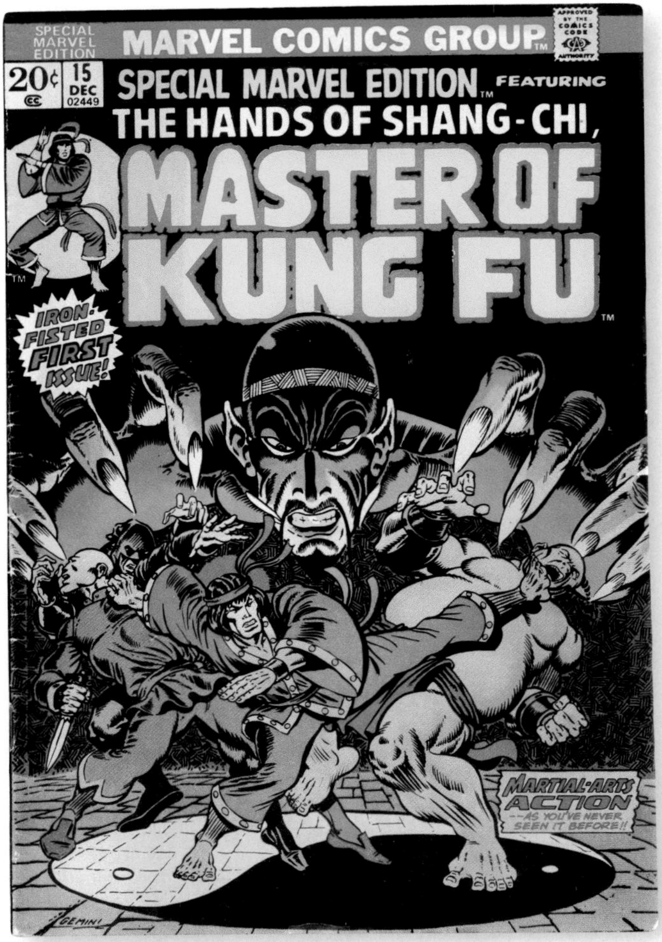
SPECIAL MARVEL EDITION
MARVEL COMICS GROUP
20¢ 15 DEC 02449
SPECIAL MARVEL EDITION FEATURING
THE HANDS OF SHANG-CHI,
MASTER OF KUNG FU
IRON-FISTED FIRST ISSUE!
MARTIAL-ARTS ACTION
--AS YOU'VE NEVER SEEN IT BEFORE!!
GEMINI

MASTER OF KUNG FU No. 18

(Opposite) Interior, "Attack!"; script, Steve Englehart; pencils, Paul Gulacy; inks, Al Milgrom; June 1974. Following Starlin's brief stint drawing Shang-Chi was Paul Gulacy, who would be a mainstay on the title for years. His detailed, dynamic perspectives drew heavily on Steranko's legacy — in a 1999 interview with Jon Cooke, Gulacy remembered his teenaged inspiration: "They'd have these three comics in a cellophane bag, and I saw the first Nick Fury with the cover gone, a great splash page that Jim had done, and I bought it... When I saw what he was doing, it was just I never had seen anything like that before — it just flipped me out."

SPECIAL MARVEL EDITION No. 15

(Above) Cover; pencils, Jim Starlin; ; inks, Al Milgrom; December 1973. Another Marvel superstar makes his bow in an unlikely place: No. 15 of a previously all-reprint book. After two suitably special issues, Shang-Chi, Master of Kung Fu, secures his own title that runs for a decade. The cover is signed by Gemini, aka the art team of Starlin and Al Milgrom ("Jim an' I," get it?).

MANCHU DYNASTY

(Right) Magazine interior, "The Zayat Kiss," Collier's; *story, Sax Rohmer; art, Joseph Clement Coll; February 15, 1913.* First introduced in the U.S. by English novelist Rohmer in this short story, Dr. Fu Manchu would go on to star in 13 books in the writer's lifetime, and several controversial movies in the decades that followed. Rohmer's characters intermingled with brand-new creations, not least Shang-Chi, Fu Manchu's rebellious son.

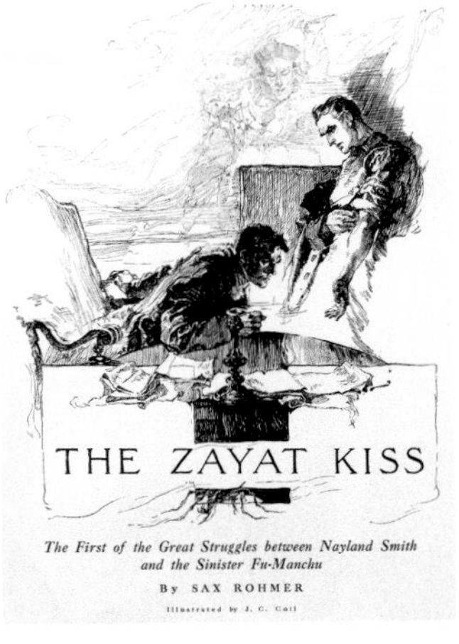
THE ZAYAT KISS
The First of the Great Struggles between Nayland Smith and the Sinister Fu-Manchu
By SAX ROHMER

"ATTACK!"

STEVE
ENGLEHART
Author

PAUL
GULACY
Artist

FEATURING
CHARACTERS
CREATED BY
SAX
ROHMER

AL MILGROM *Inking*
ORZECHOWSKI, *Lettering* · P. GOLDBERG, *Coloring*

ROY
THOMAS
Editor

MASTER OF KUNG FU is published by MARVEL COMICS GROUP. OFFICE OF PUBLICATION: 575 MADISON AVENUE, NEW YORK, N.Y. 10
Published bi-monthly. Copyright ©1974 by Marvel Comics Group. A Division of Cadence Industries Corporation. All rights reserved 575 Madison Avenue
New York, N.Y. 10022. Vol. 1, No. 18, June, 1974 issue. Price 25¢ per copy in the U. S. and Canada. Subscription rate $3.50 for 12 issues. Canada $4.25. Foreign $5.50. No similarity between any of the names, characters, persons, and/or institutions in this magazine with those of any living or dead person or institution is intended, and any such similarity which may exist is purely coincidental. Printed in the U.S.A.

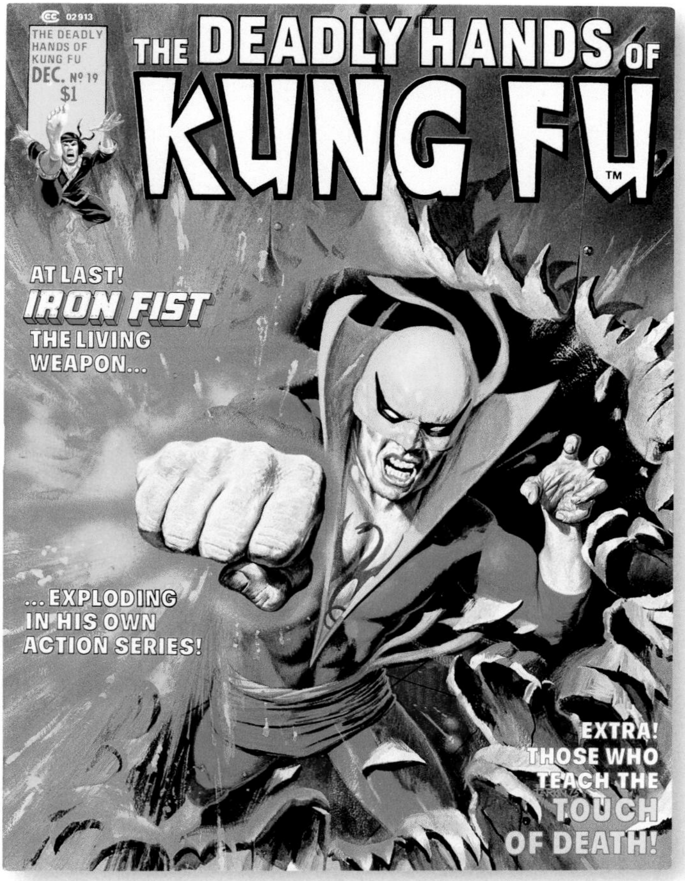

02913
THE DEADLY HANDS OF KUNG FU
DEC. No 19
$1
THE DEADLY HANDS OF
KUNG FU
TM
AT LAST!
IRON FIST
THE LIVING WEAPON...
...EXPLODING IN HIS OWN ACTION SERIES!
EXTRA! THOSE WHO TEACH THE TOUCH OF DEATH!

THE DEADLY HANDS OF KUNG FU No. 19

(Above) Cover; painting, Bob Larkin; December 1975. Deadly Hands was not merely a home to the adventures of Shang-Chi and text articles about the pop culture sensation Bruce Lee. Sons of the Tiger, White Tiger, and crossover kung fu super hero Iron Fist were also featured characters during the magazine's 33-issue run. Danny Rand, the Iron Fist, would outlast even Shang-Chi's outsider popularity, teaming with Luke Cage in 1978 for nearly a decade.

HERO FOR HIRE No. 1

(Opposite) Interior, "Out of Hell... a Hero!"; script, Archie Goodwin; pencils, George Tuska; inks, Billy Graham; June 1972. With new publisher Stan Lee eager to boost representation of women and minorities in Marvel comics, Luke Cage became the first black hero whose name was given to an ongoing title. (And the first to totally own a catchphrase: "Sweet Christmas!")

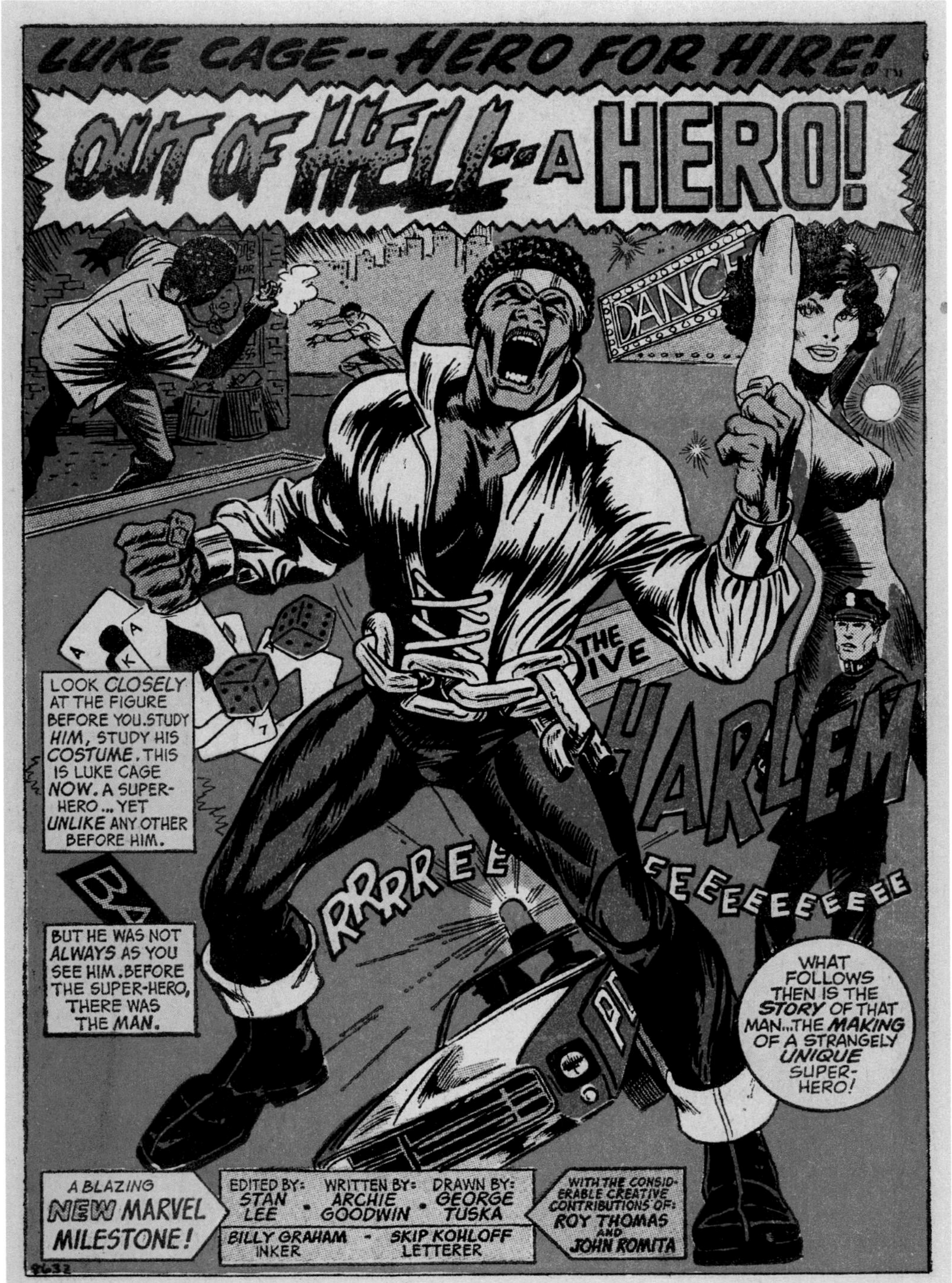
LUKE CAGE--HERO FOR HIRE!
OUT OF HELL--A HERO!
DANCE
THE JIVE
HARLEM
LOOK CLOSELY AT THE FIGURE BEFORE YOU. STUDY HIM, STUDY HIS COSTUME. THIS IS LUKE CAGE NOW. A SUPER-HERO... YET UNLIKE ANY OTHER BEFORE HIM.
RRRREEE EEEEEEEEEEE
BUT HE WAS NOT ALWAYS AS YOU SEE HIM. BEFORE THE SUPER-HERO, THERE WAS THE MAN.
WHAT FOLLOWS THEN IS THE STORY OF THAT MAN... THE MAKING OF A STRANGELY UNIQUE SUPER-HERO!
A BLAZING NEW MARVEL MILESTONE!
EDITED BY: STAN LEE • WRITTEN BY: ARCHIE GOODWIN • DRAWN BY: GEORGE TUSKA
BILLY GRAHAM - INKER • SKIP KOHLOFF - LETTERER
WITH THE CONSIDERABLE CREATIVE CONTRIBUTIONS OF: ROY THOMAS AND JOHN ROMITA

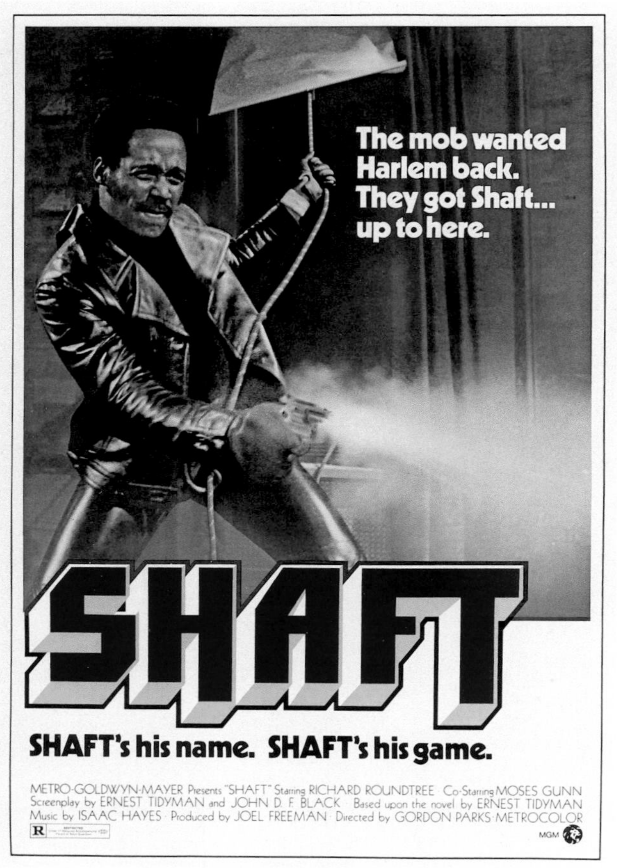
The mob wanted Harlem back. They got Shaft... up to here.
SHAFT
SHAFT's his name. SHAFT's his game.
METRO-GOLDWYN-MAYER Presents "SHAFT" Starring RICHARD ROUNDTREE · Co-Starring MOSES GUNN
Screenplay by ERNEST TIDYMAN and JOHN D. F. BLACK · Based upon the novel by ERNEST TIDYMAN
Music by ISAAC HAYES · Produced by JOEL FREEMAN · Directed by GORDON PARKS · METROCOLOR
R
MGM

JUNGLE ACTION No. 7

(Opposite) Interior, "Death Regiments Beneath Wakanda"; script, Don McGregor; pencils, Rich Buckler; inks, Klaus Janson; November 1973. T'Challa, the Black Panther, secured his first solo series in the pages of *Jungle Action*, with an acclaimed run by McGregor. The writer took the groundbreaking step of featuring an all-black cast in the Panther's native Wakanda, while pioneering the multi-issue story arc with the 13-part "Panther's Rage." His initial artist, Buckler, was one of a new generation of pencilers breaking free from their six-panel confines with innovative layouts — such as this double-page spread, printed sideways.

CAN YOU DIG IT?

(Above) Poster, Shaft, *MGM, 1971.* Veteran editor David George recalled Ernest Tidyman's brief sojourn in Goodman's magazine empire in a 2007 story for *Alter Ego*: "We soon learned that Ernie wasn't quite like the rest of us. The first thing he did was bring in a small, green-shaded library lamp for his desk and turn off the ceiling lights. This gave his office a kind of soft, dark, 'private' look. The second thing Ernie did was create the fictional black detective, Shaft. The third thing Ernie did was win an Oscar for writing the screenplay for *The French Connection*."

HERO FOR HIRE No. 12

(Right) Interior, "Chemistro"; script, Steve Englehart; pencils, George Tuska; inks, Billy Graham; August 1973.

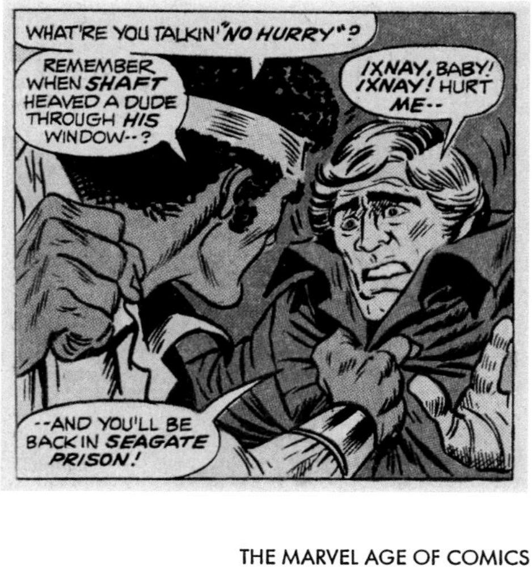
WHAT'RE YOU TALKIN' "NO HURRY"?
REMEMBER WHEN SHAFT HEAVED A DUDE THROUGH HIS WINDOW--?
IXNAY, BABY! IXNAY! HURT ME--
--AND YOU'LL BE BACK IN SEAGATE PRISON!

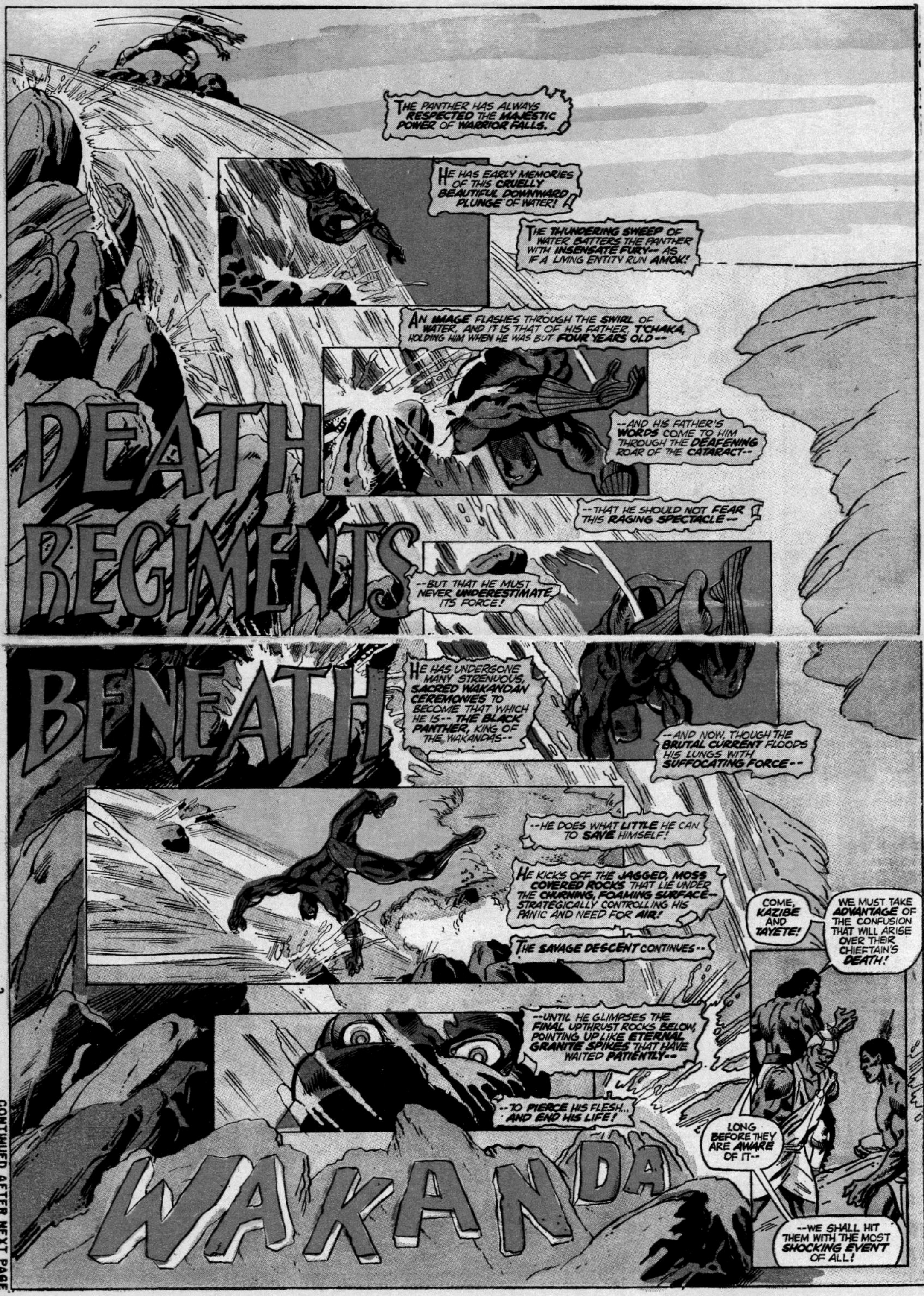
THE PANTHER HAS ALWAYS RESPECTED THE MAJESTIC POWER OF WARRIOR FALLS.
HE HAS EARLY MEMORIES OF THIS CRUELLY BEAUTIFUL DOWNWARD PLUNGE OF WATER!
THE THUNDERING SWEEP OF WATER BATTERS THE PANTHER WITH INSENSATE FURY-- AS IF A LIVING ENTITY RUN AMOK!
AN IMAGE FLASHES THROUGH THE SWIRL OF WATER, AND IT IS THAT OF HIS FATHER, T'CHAKA, HOLDING HIM WHEN HE WAS BUT FOUR YEARS OLD--
--AND HIS FATHER'S WORDS COME TO HIM THROUGH THE DEAFENING ROAR OF THE CATARACT--
DEATH REGIMENTS BENEATH WAKANDA
--THAT HE SHOULD NOT FEAR THIS RAGING SPECTACLE--
--BUT THAT HE MUST NEVER UNDERESTIMATE ITS FORCE!
HE HAS UNDERGONE MANY STRENUOUS, SACRED WAKANDAN CEREMONIES TO BECOME THAT WHICH HE IS-- THE BLACK PANTHER, KING OF THE WAKANDAS--
--AND NOW, THOUGH THE BRUTAL CURRENT FLOODS HIS LUNGS WITH SUFFOCATING FORCE--
--HE DOES WHAT LITTLE HE CAN TO SAVE HIMSELF!
HE KICKS OFF THE JAGGED, MOSS COVERED ROCKS THAT LIE UNDER THE CHURNING, FOAMING SURFACE-- STRATEGICALLY CONTROLLING HIS PANIC AND NEED FOR AIR!
THE SAVAGE DESCENT CONTINUES--
--UNTIL HE GLIMPSES THE FINAL UPTHRUST ROCKS BELOW, POINTING UP LIKE ETERNAL GRANITE SPIKES THAT HAVE WAITED PATIENTLY--
--TO PIERCE HIS FLESH.. AND END HIS LIFE!
COME, KAZIBE AND TAYETE!
WE MUST TAKE ADVANTAGE OF THE CONFUSION THAT WILL ARISE OVER THEIR CHIEFTAIN'S DEATH!
LONG BEFORE THEY ARE AWARE OF IT--
--WE SHALL HIT THEM WITH THE MOST SHOCKING EVENT OF ALL!

CONTINUED AFTER NEXT PAGE

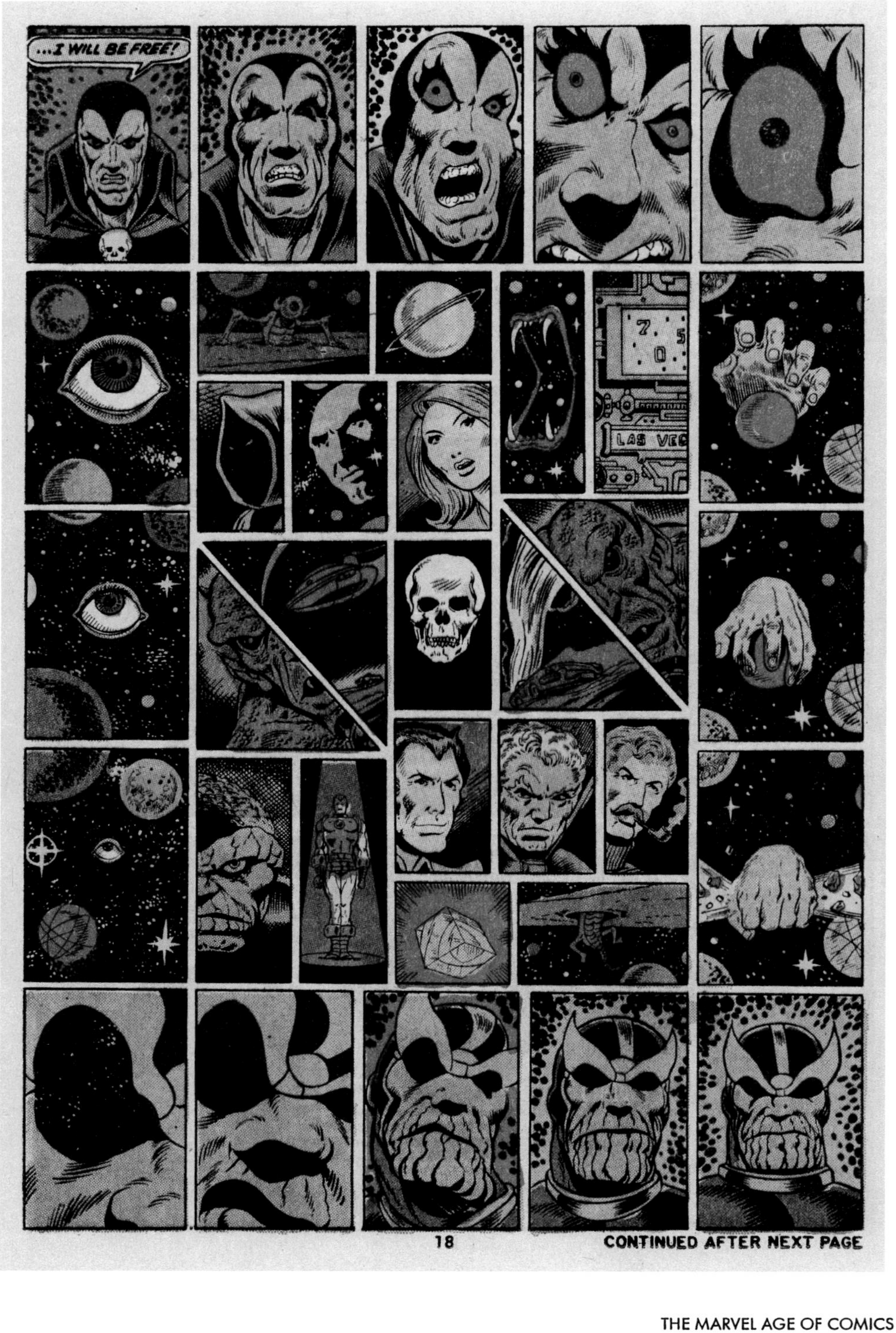
...I WILL BE FREE!
7 5
0
LAS VEG
18
CONTINUED AFTER NEXT PAGE

CAPTAIN MARVEL No. 28
(Opposite) Interior, "When Titans Collide!"; script, Jim Starlin and Mike Friedrich; pencils, Starlin; inks, Dan Green; September 1973. Bold young writer/artist Jim Starlin brought boundless imagination to the House of Ideas, carving out a whole new cosmic corner of the Marvel Universe. Graphic innovations included this remarkable 35-panel layout, featuring his signature villain, Thanos—the Mad Titan whose story Starlin continues to tell 40 years later.

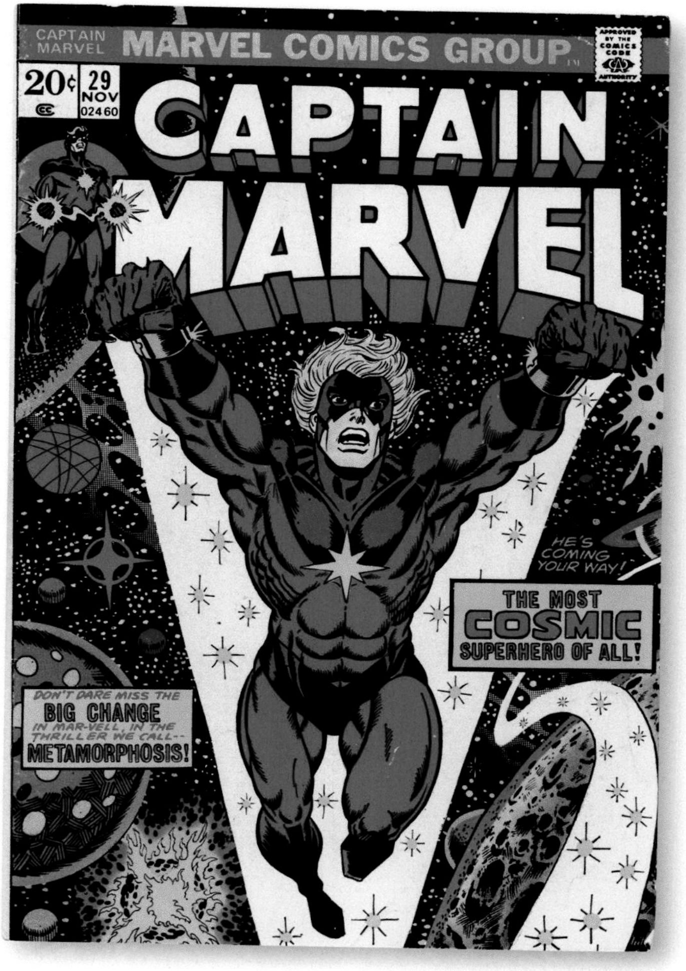
CAPTAIN MARVEL
MARVEL COMICS GROUP
APPROVED BY THE COMICS CODE AUTHORITY
20¢
29
NOV
02460
CAPTAIN MARVEL
HE'S COMING YOUR WAY!
THE MOST COSMIC SUPERHERO OF ALL!
DON'T DARE MISS THE BIG CHANGE IN MAR-VELL, IN THE THRILLER WE CALL-- METAMORPHOSIS!

CAPTAIN MARVEL No. 29
(Above) Cover; pencils, Jim Starlin with John Romita; inks, Al Milgrom; November 1973. "Stan gave the characters he created 1960s TV personalities, instead of letting them be cardboard hero cut-outs, like Superman and Batman were...," Starlin told *Comic Book Artist* in 1998. "In the '70s, we came in and gave them *Electric Kool-Aid Acid Test* personalities—trying to put super heroes into a very different kind of head space...discovering Carlos Castañeda." Here Mar-Vell obtains cosmic awareness as he embraces his destiny as protector of the universe.

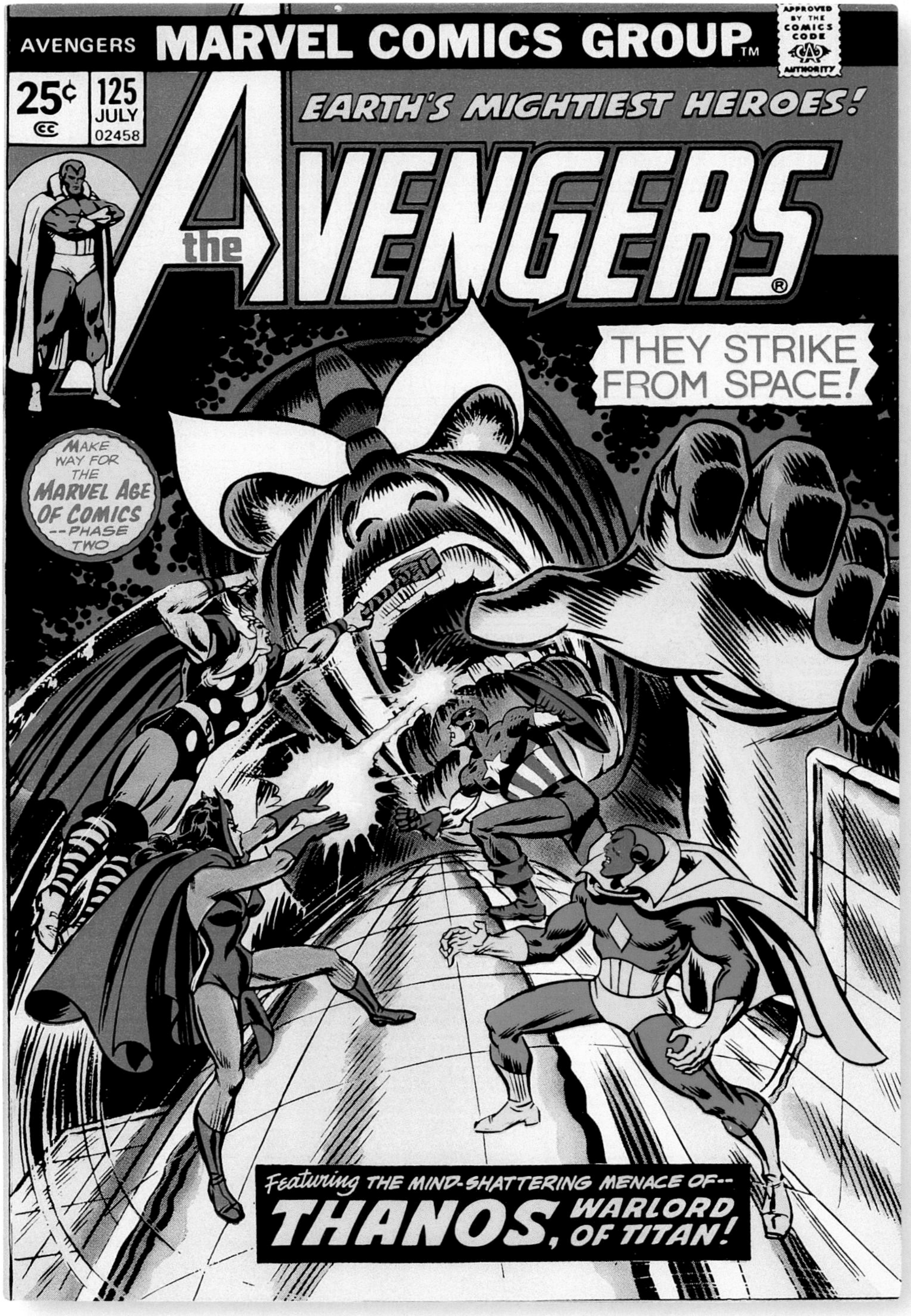
AVENGERS
MARVEL COMICS GROUP
APPROVED BY THE COMICS CODE AUTHORITY
25¢
125
JULY
02458
EARTH'S MIGHTIEST HEROES!
the AVENGERS
THEY STRIKE FROM SPACE!
MAKE WAY FOR THE MARVEL AGE OF COMICS --PHASE TWO
Featuring THE MIND-SHATTERING MENACE OF--
THANOS, WARLORD OF TITAN!

AVENGERS No. 125
(Opposite) Cover; pencils, Ron Wilson; inks, John Romita; July 1974. Thanos firmly establishes himself as one of the Big Bads of the Marvel Universe, and a cosmic thorn in the side of Earth's Mightiest Heroes. Their rivalry endures to the present day.

WARLOCK No. 2
(Right) Cover; pencils and inks, Gil Kane; October 1972. With the controversial rock opera *Jesus Christ Superstar* on heavy rotation, writer Roy Thomas was inspired to create a truly messianic super hero — the enigmatic Adam Warlock. As the Marvel Universe continued to expand, this was the first series set on another world — Counter-Earth on the opposite side of the sun.

WARLOCK MARVEL COMICS GROUP
20¢
2
OCT
02153
THE POWER OF...
WARLOCK
THE WORLD WAS EVIL! THE WORLD ROSE UP AGAINST ME--
AND SO-- THE WORLD DIED!!
COUNT-DOWN FOR COUNTER-EARTH!

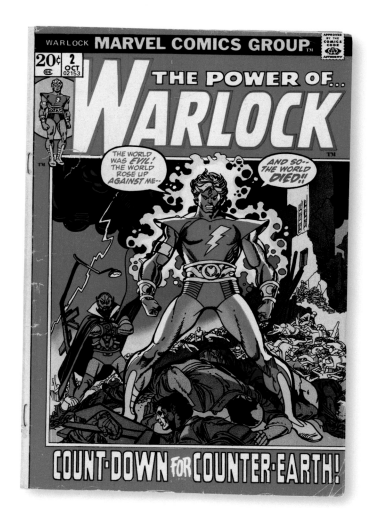

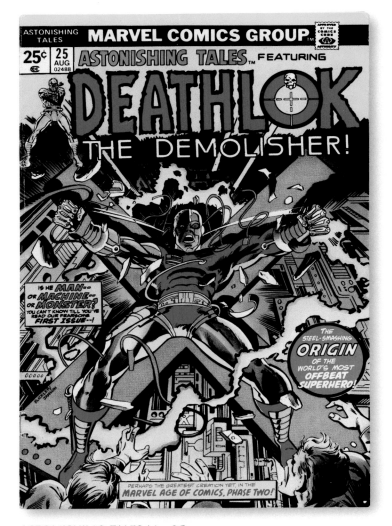

ASTONISHING TALES
MARVEL COMICS GROUP
25¢
25 AUG
02488
ASTONISHING TALES FEATURING
DEATHLOK
THE DEMOLISHER!
IS HE MAN-- OR MACHINE-- OR MONSTER? YOU CAN'T KNOW TILL YOU'VE READ OUR FEARSOME FIRST ISSUE--!
THE STEEL-SMASHING ORIGIN OF THE WORLD'S MOST OFFBEAT SUPERHERO!
PERHAPS THE GREATEST CREATION YET, IN THE MARVEL AGE OF COMICS, PHASE TWO!

ASTONISHING TALES No. 25

(Above) Cover; pencils, Rich Buckler; inks, Klaus Janson. (Opposite) Interior, "A Cold Knight's Frenzy"; script, Doug Moench; plot, pencils, and inks, Buckler. August 1974. A decade before films like *Terminator* and *RoboCop*, Buckler delivered his visionary epic of cyborg assassins in a bleak future of military control and artificial intelligence. Fallen soldier Luther Manning strives to reclaim his humanity after awakening as Deathlok, complete with a built-in computer with its own distinctive voice. Buckler deftly illustrated the character's struggle, while Deathlok's internal monologue received lettering that emulated a computer's digital output. The world was initially intended as an alternate reality completely separate from the Marvel Universe—but the temptation of team-ups with Spider-Man and the Thing quickly put an end to that.

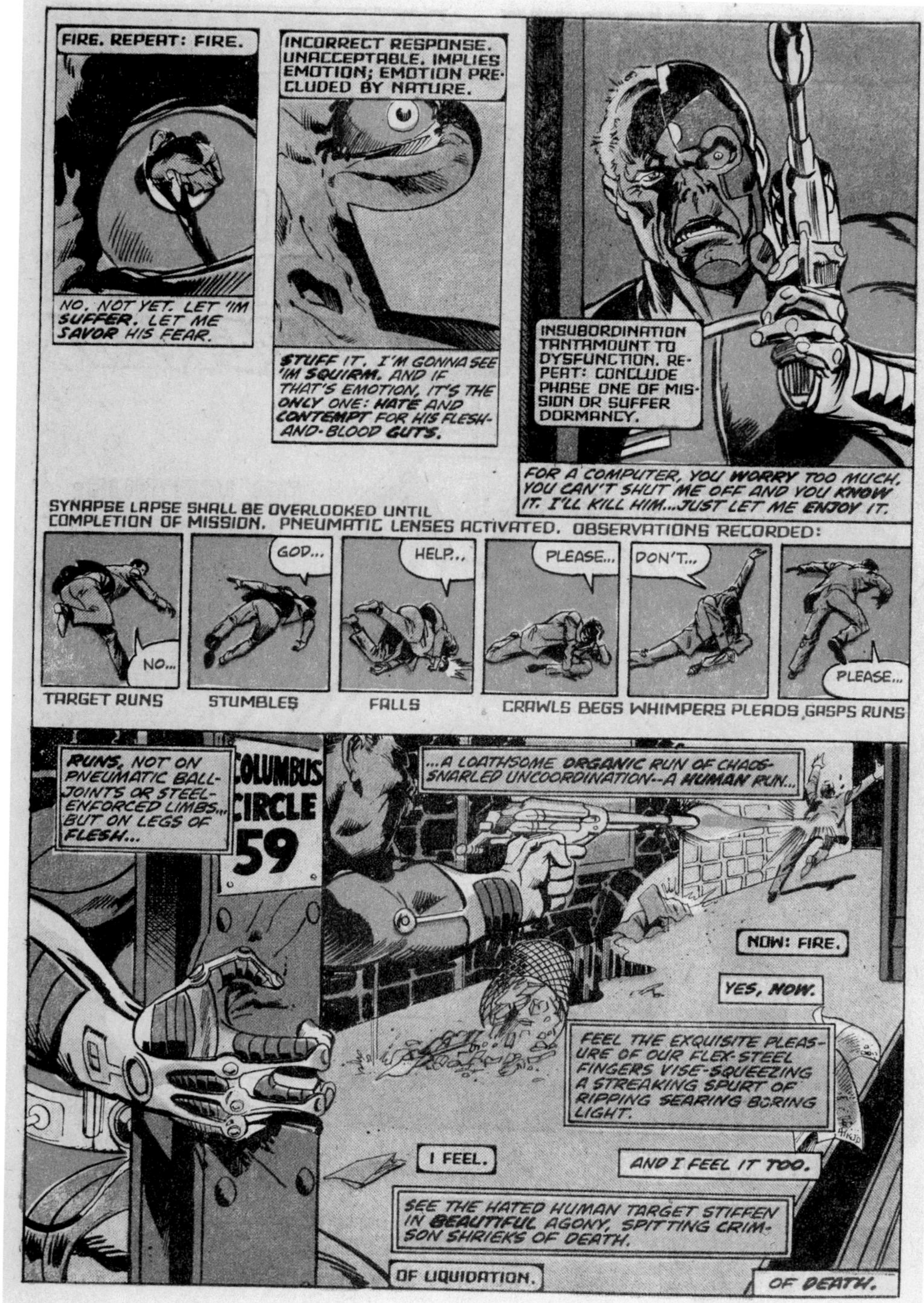
FIRE. REPEAT: FIRE.
NO. NOT YET. LET 'IM SUFFER. LET ME SAVOR HIS FEAR.
INCORRECT RESPONSE. UNACCEPTABLE. IMPLIES EMOTION; EMOTION PRECLUDED BY NATURE.
STUFF IT. I'M GONNA SEE 'IM SQUIRM. AND IF THAT'S EMOTION, IT'S THE ONLY ONE: HATE AND CONTEMPT FOR HIS FLESH-AND-BLOOD GUTS.
INSUBORDINATION TANTAMOUNT TO DYSFUNCTION. REPEAT: CONCLUDE PHASE ONE OF MISSION OR SUFFER DORMANCY.
FOR A COMPUTER, YOU WORRY TOO MUCH. YOU CAN'T SHUT ME OFF AND YOU KNOW IT. I'LL KILL HIM...JUST LET ME ENJOY IT.
SYNAPSE LAPSE SHALL BE OVERLOOKED UNTIL COMPLETION OF MISSION. PNEUMATIC LENSES ACTIVATED. OBSERVATIONS RECORDED:
NO...
TARGET RUNS
GOD...
STUMBLES
HELP...
FALLS
PLEASE...
DON'T...
PLEASE...
CRAWLS BEGS WHIMPERS PLEADS GASPS RUNS
RUNS, NOT ON PNEUMATIC BALL-JOINTS OR STEEL-ENFORCED LIMBS... BUT ON LEGS OF FLESH...
COLUMBUS CIRCLE 59
...A LOATHSOME ORGANIC RUN OF CHAOS-SNARLED UNCOORDINATION--A HUMAN RUN...
NOW: FIRE.
YES, NOW.
FEEL THE EXQUISITE PLEASURE OF OUR FLEX-STEEL FINGERS VISE-SQUEEZING A STREAKING SPURT OF RIPPING SEARING BORING LIGHT.
I FEEL.
AND I FEEL IT TOO.
SEE THE HATED HUMAN TARGET STIFFEN IN BEAUTIFUL AGONY, SPITTING CRIMSON SHRIEKS OF DEATH.
OF LIQUIDATION.
OF DEATH.

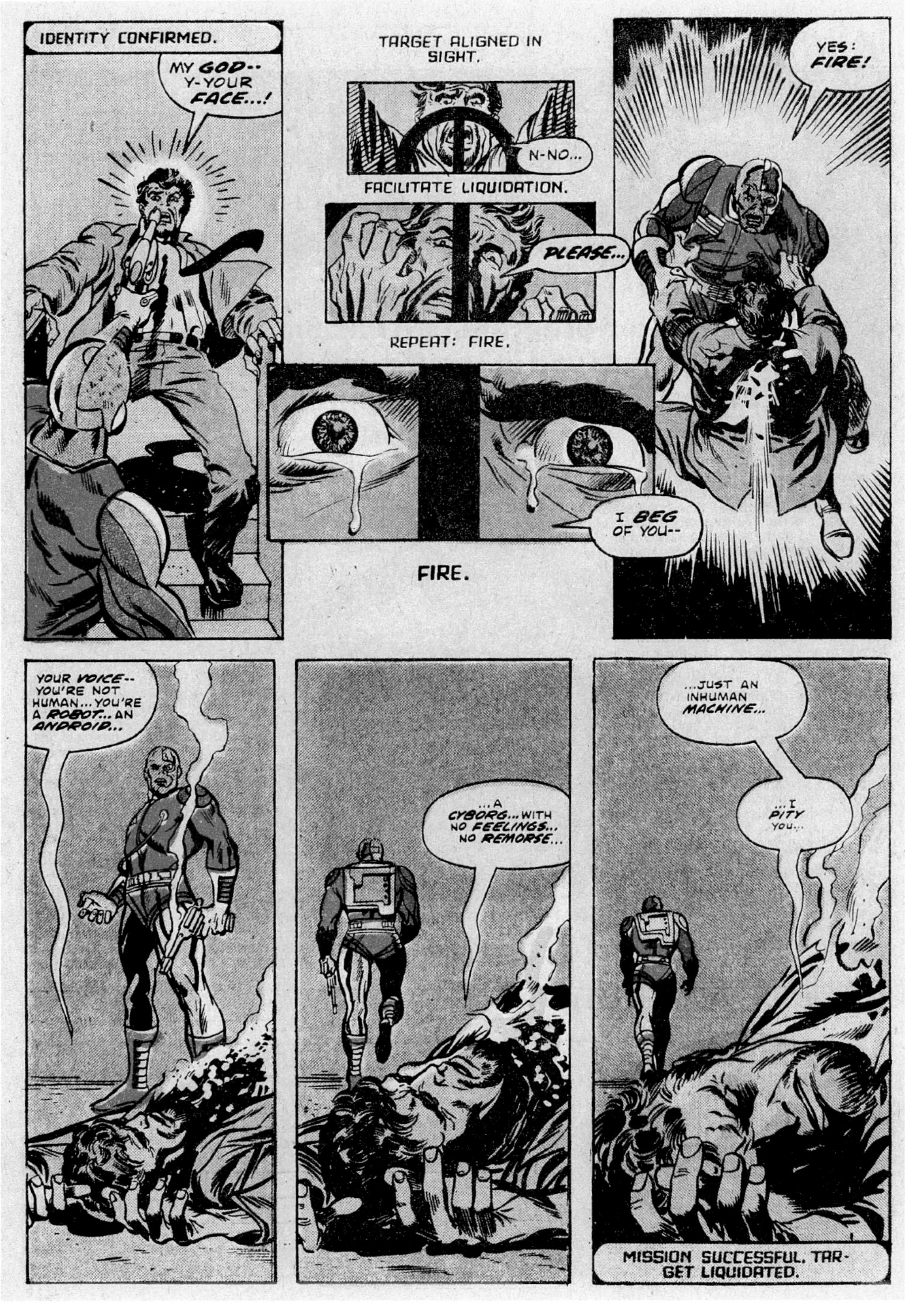

IDENTITY CONFIRMED.
MY GOD-- Y-YOUR FACE...!
TARGET ALIGNED IN SIGHT.
N-NO...
FACILITATE LIQUIDATION.
PLEASE...
REPEAT: FIRE.
I BEG OF YOU--
FIRE.
YES: FIRE!
YOUR VOICE-- YOU'RE NOT HUMAN... YOU'RE A ROBOT... AN ANDROID...
...A CYBORG... WITH NO FEELINGS... NO REMORSE...
...JUST AN INHUMAN MACHINE...
...I PITY YOU...
MISSION SUCCESSFUL. TAR-GET LIQUIDATED.

ASTONISHING TALES No. 25

(Opposite) Interior, "A Cold Knight's Frenzy"; script, Doug Moench; plot, pencils, and inks, Rich Buckler. August 1974.

MARVEL SPOTLIGHT No. 33

(Below) Interior, "(Don't Fear) the Reaper!"; script, David Anthony Kraft; pencils, Rich Buckler, Mike Nasser, and Arvell Jones; inks, Klaus Janson; April 1977. Deathlok initially fought corporate and military forces that controlled the U.S. in the future year . . . of 1990! The title of this story, however, was all 1976, borrowing from the title of rock band Blue Öyster Cult's iconic track—made even more famous decades later on *SNL* by Will Ferrell's "More Cowbell" skit with Christopher Walken.

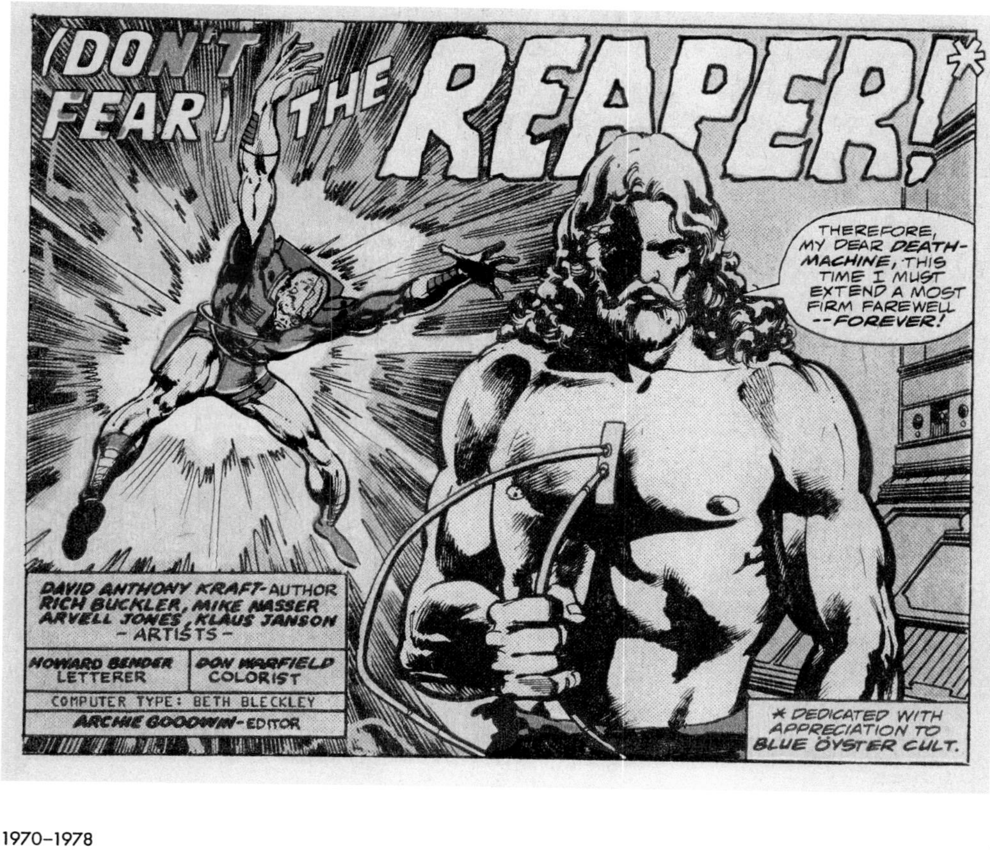
(DON'T FEAR) THE REAPER!*
THEREFORE, MY DEAR DEATH-MACHINE, THIS TIME I MUST EXTEND A MOST FIRM FAREWELL --FOREVER!
DAVID ANTHONY KRAFT-AUTHOR
RICH BUCKLER, MIKE NASSER
ARVELL JONES, KLAUS JANSON
- ARTISTS -
HOWARD BENDER LETTERER
DON WARFIELD COLORIST
COMPUTER TYPE: BETH BLECKLEY
ARCHIE GOODWIN-EDITOR
* DEDICATED WITH APPRECIATION TO BLUE ÖYSTER CULT.

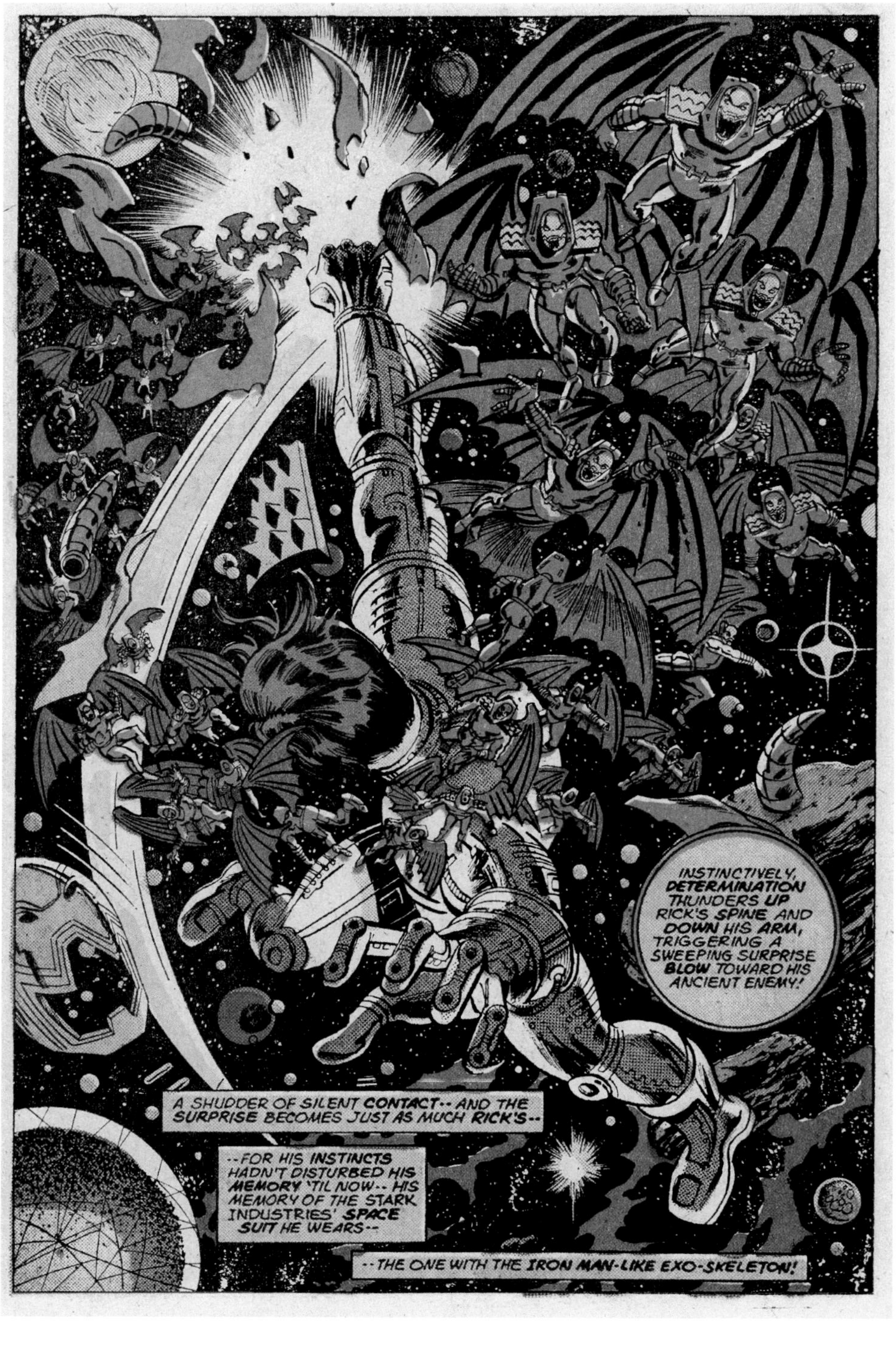
INSTINCTIVELY, DETERMINATION THUNDERS UP RICK'S SPINE AND DOWN HIS ARM, TRIGGERING A SWEEPING SURPRISE BLOW TOWARD HIS ANCIENT ENEMY!
A SHUDDER OF SILENT CONTACT-- AND THE SURPRISE BECOMES JUST AS MUCH RICK'S--
--FOR HIS INSTINCTS HADN'T DISTURBED HIS MEMORY 'TIL NOW-- HIS MEMORY OF THE STARK INDUSTRIES' SPACE SUIT HE WEARS--
--THE ONE WITH THE IRON MAN-LIKE EXO-SKELETON!

CAPTAIN MARVEL No. 37

(Opposite) Interior, "Lift-Off!"; script, Steve Englehart; pencils, Al Milgrom; inks, Klaus Janson; March 1975. When Jim Starlin took an extended break from *Captain Marvel,* Englehart and Milgrom stepped into the cosmic breach. Sailing close to the Comics Code Authority's wind, they sent Rick Jones on the ultimate Negative Zone trip, courtesy of an oddly hallucinogenic vitamin — "C" for Cosmic — pill.

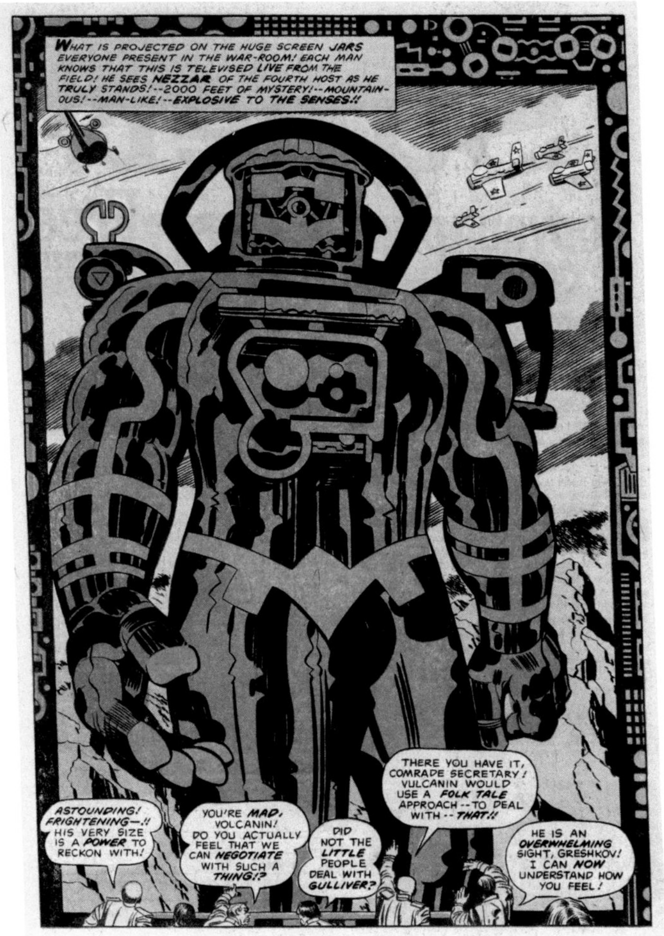
WHAT IS PROJECTED ON THE HUGE SCREEN JARS EVERYONE PRESENT IN THE WAR-ROOM! EACH MAN KNOWS THAT THIS IS TELEVISED LIVE FROM THE FIELD! HE SEES NEZZAR OF THE FOURTH HOST AS HE TRULY STANDS!--2000 FEET OF MYSTERY!--MOUNTAIN-OUS!--MAN-LIKE!--EXPLOSIVE TO THE SENSES!!
ASTOUNDING! FRIGHTENING—!! HIS VERY SIZE IS A POWER TO RECKON WITH!
YOU'RE MAD, VOLCANIN! DO YOU ACTUALLY FEEL THAT WE CAN NEGOTIATE WITH SUCH A THING!?
DID NOT THE LITTLE PEOPLE DEAL WITH GULLIVER?
THERE YOU HAVE IT, COMRADE SECRETARY! VULCANIN WOULD USE A FOLK TALE APPROACH--TO DEAL WITH--THAT!!
HE IS AN OVERWHELMING SIGHT, GRESHKOV! I CAN NOW UNDERSTAND HOW YOU FEEL!

ETERNALS No. 11

(Above) Interior; "The Russians Are Coming!"; script and pencils, Jack Kirby; inks, Mike Royer; May 1977. In his return to Marvel, Jack Kirby brought the Celestials to his first new title. Kirby loved god-like races — the Asgardians of Thor, the X-Men, Inhumans, the New Gods, and now, the Eternals. The Celestials carried with them mankind's secret history and possibly their destruction!

ETERNALS No. 3

(Following spread) Interior, "The Devil in New York!"; script and pencils, Jack Kirby; inks, John Verpoorten; September 1976. Arishem, a Celestial who can "decimate worlds," stands in judgment of Earth. Kirby drew inspiration for the Celestials in part from the ideas of Erich von Däniken, author of *Chariots of the Gods?* and *Gods from Outer Space,* among others.

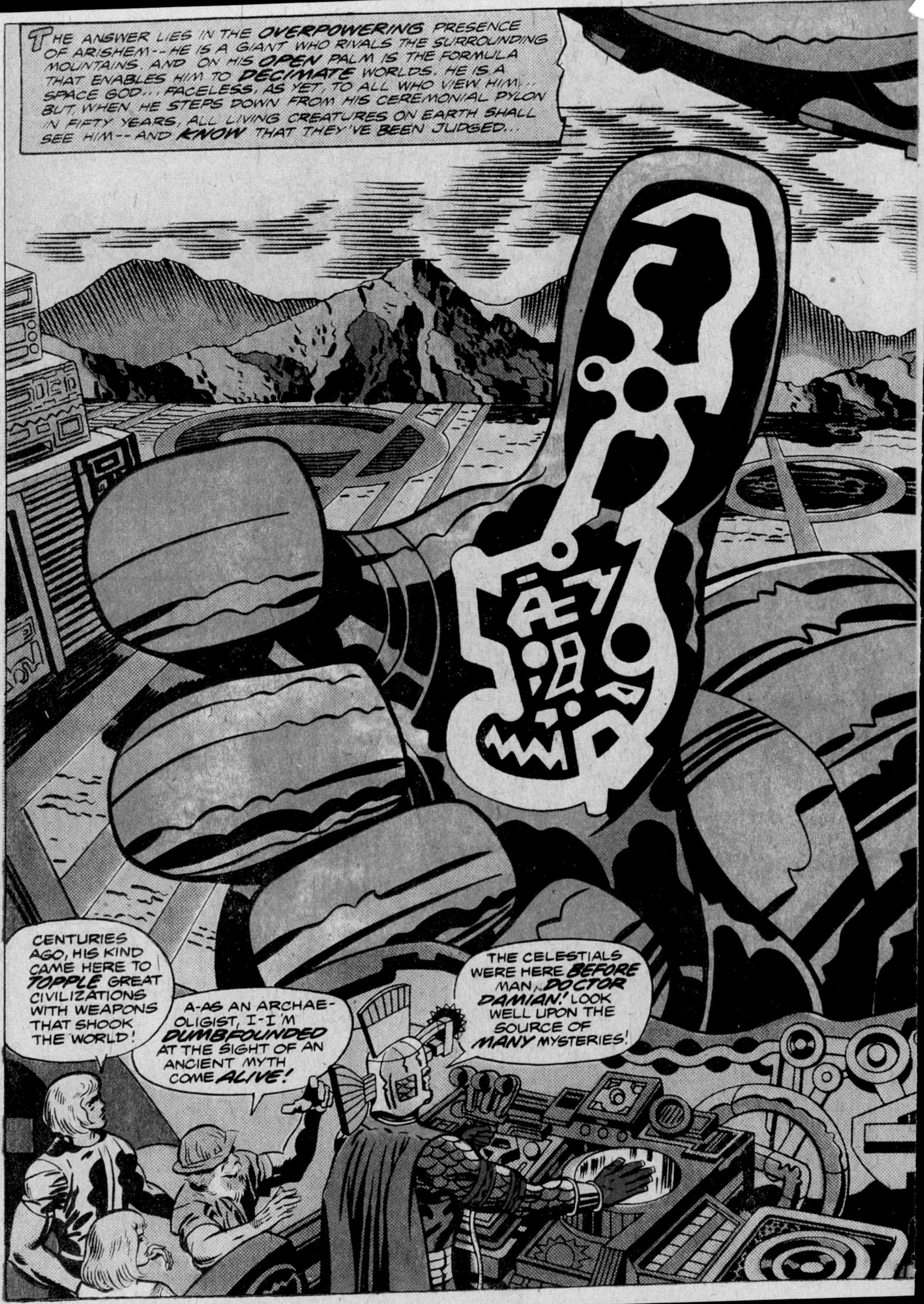
THE ANSWER LIES IN THE OVERPOWERING PRESENCE OF ARISHEM--HE IS A GIANT WHO RIVALS THE SURROUNDING MOUNTAINS, AND ON HIS OPEN PALM IS THE FORMULA THAT ENABLES HIM TO DECIMATE WORLDS. HE IS A SPACE GOD... FACELESS, AS YET, TO ALL WHO VIEW HIM... BUT, WHEN HE STEPS DOWN FROM HIS CEREMONIAL PYLON IN FIFTY YEARS, ALL LIVING CREATURES ON EARTH SHALL SEE HIM--AND KNOW THAT THEY'VE BEEN JUDGED...
CENTURIES AGO, HIS KIND CAME HERE TO TOPPLE GREAT CIVILIZATIONS WITH WEAPONS THAT SHOOK THE WORLD!
A-AS AN ARCHAE-OLIGIST, I-I'M DUMBFOUNDED AT THE SIGHT OF AN ANCIENT MYTH COME ALIVE!
THE CELESTIALS WERE HERE BEFORE MAN, DOCTOR DAMIAN! LOOK WELL UPON THE SOURCE OF MANY MYSTERIES!

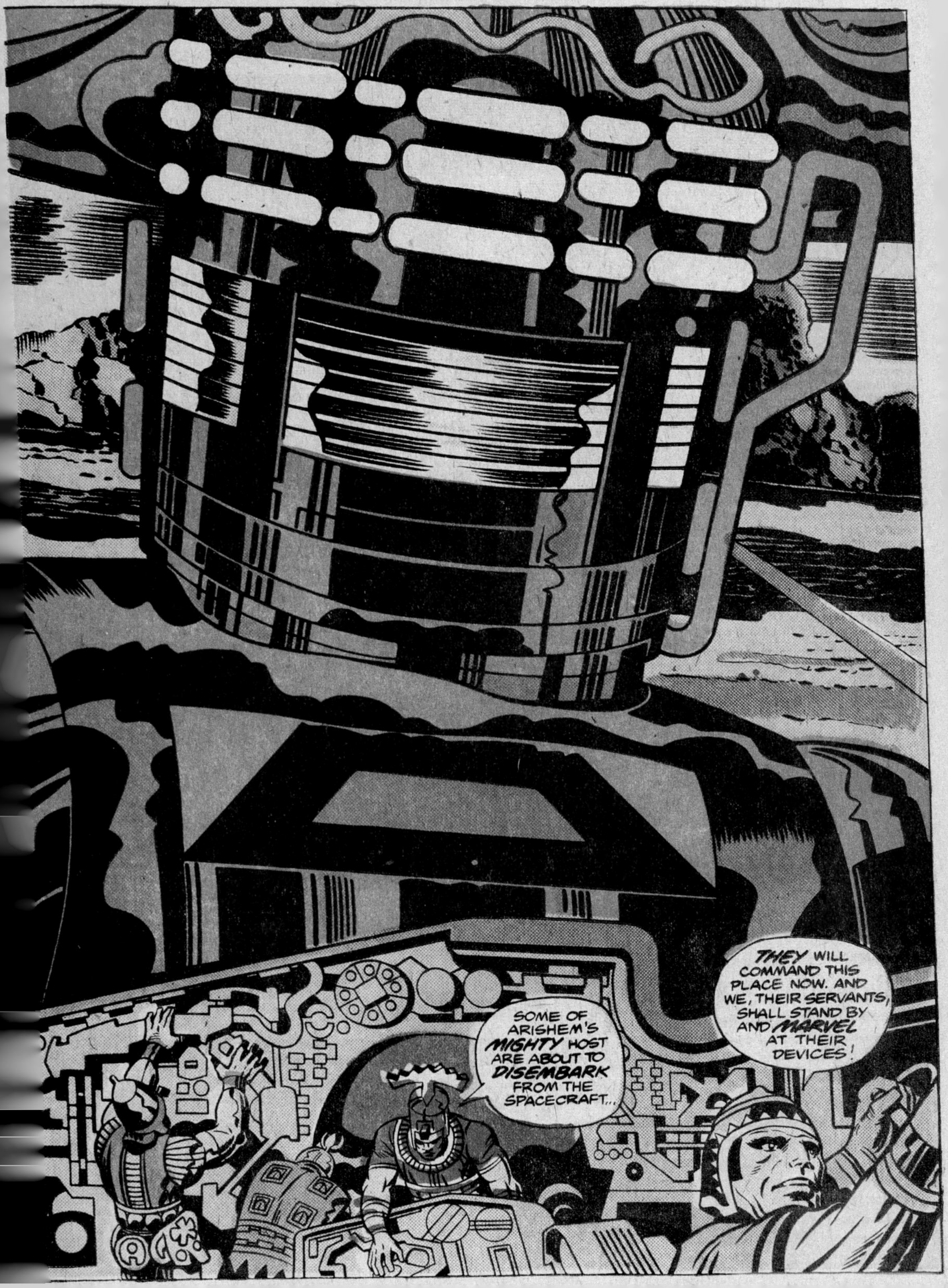
SOME OF ARISHEM'S MIGHTY HOST ARE ABOUT TO DISEMBARK FROM THE SPACECRAFT...
THEY WILL COMMAND THIS PLACE NOW. AND WE, THEIR SERVANTS, SHALL STAND BY AND MARVEL AT THEIR DEVICES!

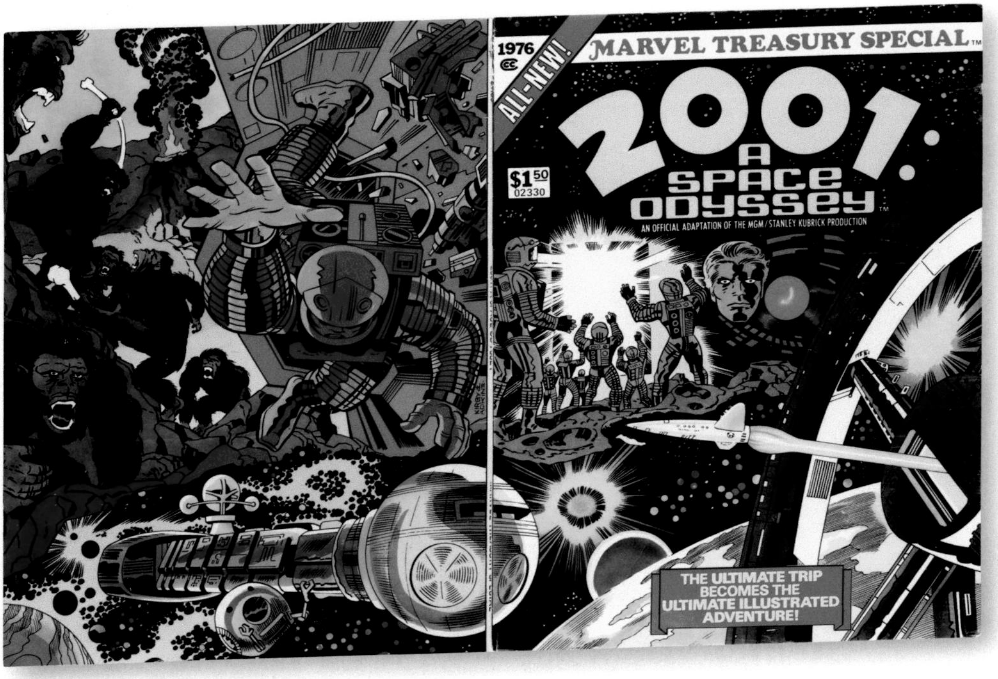
1976
ALL-NEW!
MARVEL TREASURY SPECIAL
2001: A SPACE ODYSSEY
$1.50
02330
AN OFFICIAL ADAPTATION OF THE MGM/STANLEY KUBRICK PRODUCTION
THE ULTIMATE TRIP BECOMES THE ULTIMATE ILLUSTRATED ADVENTURE!

MARVEL TREASURY SPECIAL: 2001: A SPACE ODYSSEY

(Above) Wraparound cover; pencils, Jack Kirby; inks, Dan Adkins; 1976. The series used the cinematic version as a mere jumping-off point, with the Star Child transformed by Kirby—now back at Marvel—into a "New Seed" that traveled the galaxy as an observer.

MACHINE MAN No. 1

(Opposite) Cover; pencils, Jack Kirby; inks, Frank Giacoia; April 1978. Also born from Kirby's *2001*: Machine Man (first called Mister Machine), a sentient robot who takes the name Aaron Stack—and is much more sympathetic than HAL 9000. Kirby wrote and drew the first nine issues of the character's solo series.

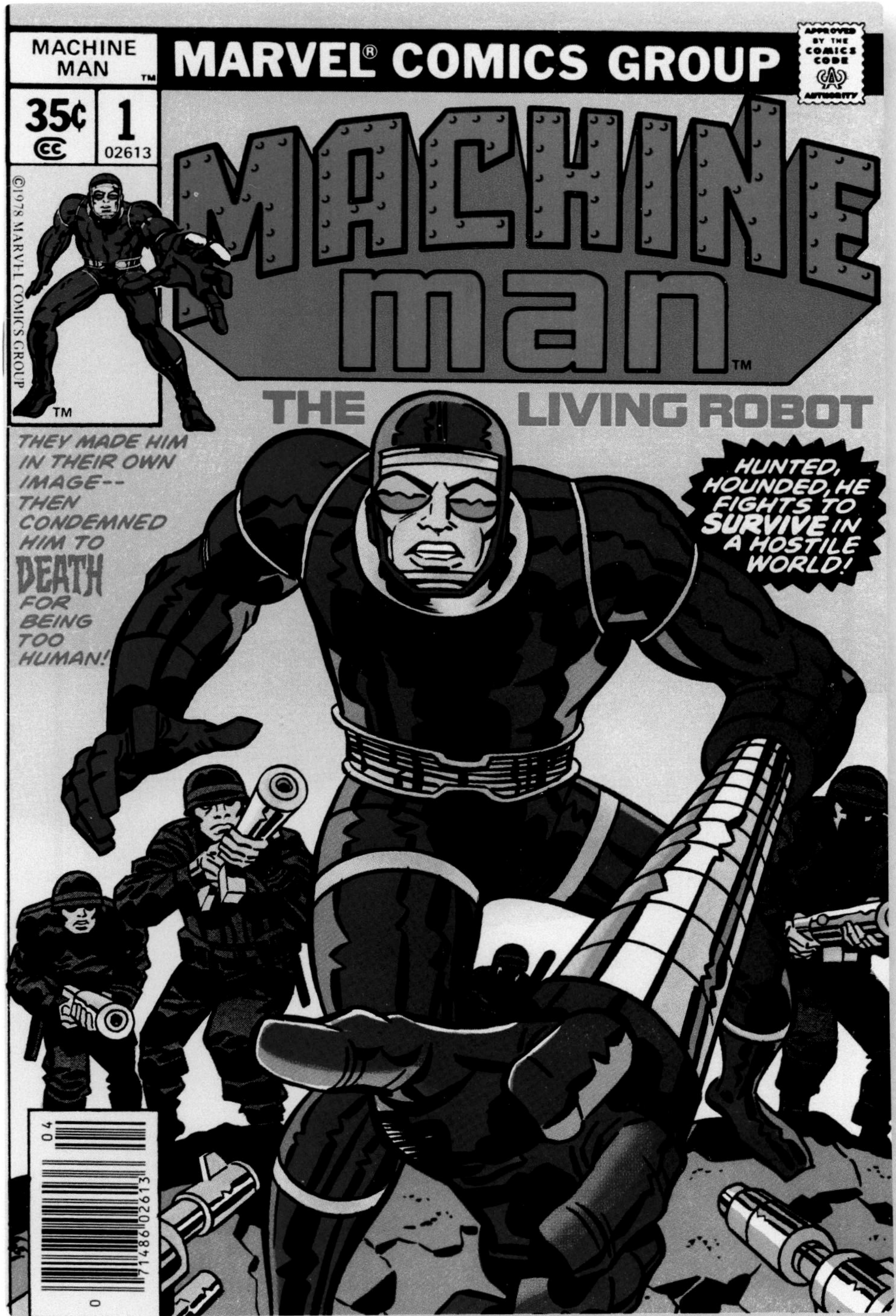
MACHINE MAN
MARVEL® COMICS GROUP
APPROVED BY THE COMICS CODE AUTHORITY
35¢
1
02613
©1978 MARVEL COMICS GROUP
MACHINE MAN
THE LIVING ROBOT
THEY MADE HIM IN THEIR OWN IMAGE-- THEN CONDEMNED HIM TO DEATH FOR BEING TOO HUMAN!
HUNTED, HOUNDED, HE FIGHTS TO SURVIVE IN A HOSTILE WORLD!

STILL ONLY 25¢
MARVEL COMICS GROUP
3 MAY
02415
TRAPPED IN A WORLD HE NEVER MADE!
HOWARD THE DUCK
MARTIAL-ARTS MAYHEM AS YOU'VE NEVER SEEN IT BEFORE--WHEN HOWARD BECOMES
MASTER OF QUACK FU!
BUCKLER & LEIALOHA

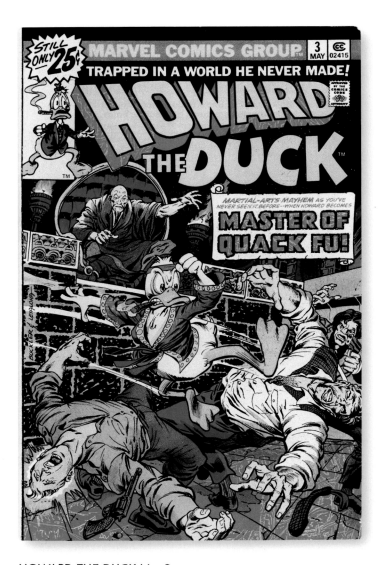

HOWARD THE DUCK No. 3

(Above) Cover; pencils, Rich Buckler; inks, Steve Leialoha. (Opposite) Interior, "Four Feathers of Death! Or Enter: The Duck!"; script, Steve Gerber; pencils, John Buscema; inks, Leialoha. May 1976. Everybody was kung fu fighting, and Howard found it more than a little bit frightening. "How can you call ripping out someone's tongue 'entertainment'?" he asks his companion Beverly after a movie. They see children play-fighting, then a teenager badly injured in a real fight. Howard then learns martial arts and takes down the adult attacker, Macho, but as in the story's real-life counterpart, the teen dies. "Funny . . ." Beverly says after Howard has sent Macho to his end. "It doesn't make me feel any better. Death is death."

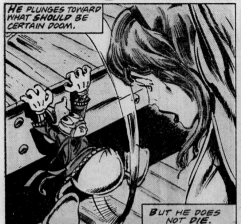

HE PLUNGES TOWARD WHAT *SHOULD BE* CERTAIN DOOM.

BUT HE DOES NOT *DIE.*

"PAIN IS A CONDITION OF THE *MIND,*" ACCORDING TO MASTER C'HAAJ, "IT CAN BE OVERCOME BY CONCENTRATION, IF NEED BE."

"FIX YOUR EYE ON YOUR *OPPONENT,* YOUR MIND ON YOUR STRATEGY, YOUR HEARING ON YOUR OWN *HEARTBEAT.*"

"STRIVE FOR THE MOMENT OF *TOTAL* AWARENESS..."

"...AND YOU SHALL ACCOMPLISH WHAT LESSER MEN WOULD TERM *MIRACLES.*"

NO!

A FLUKE--THAT'S WHAT IT IS! MY FOUR LIEUTENANTS--THE NUNCHAKU-- --BEGINNER'S LUCK, NOTHING MORE!

WELL, YOUR GOOD FORTUNE HAS JUST COME TO AN *END,* SHORTY!

DIE!!

NO.

"Dear Steve, I hate you. 'Master of Quack Fu' was one of the best written comics I've ever been jealous of. Who needs the competition?"
— STAN LEE, LETTER IN *HOWARD THE DUCK*, NO. 5

HOWARD THE DUCK No. 16

(Opposite) Cover; pencils, Gene Colan; inks, Tom Palmer; September 1977. Readers expecting the continuation of "The Island of Dr. Bong" were in for a surprise. Writer Steve Gerber explained why that story would have to wait a month in this unusual story, "Zen and the Art of Comic Book Writing," an illustrated essay letting readers in on deadline challenges, his writing process, his ongoing internal dialogue with Howard, and more. "The only reader who'll remain loyal after this flagrant flouting of comic book convention is Harlan Ellison," Gerber wrote, "Maybe." It closed with a letter to the writer from…himself, professing to be "somewhat ambivalent" about the issue. Gerber was right about one thing: It *was* definitely better than a reprint.

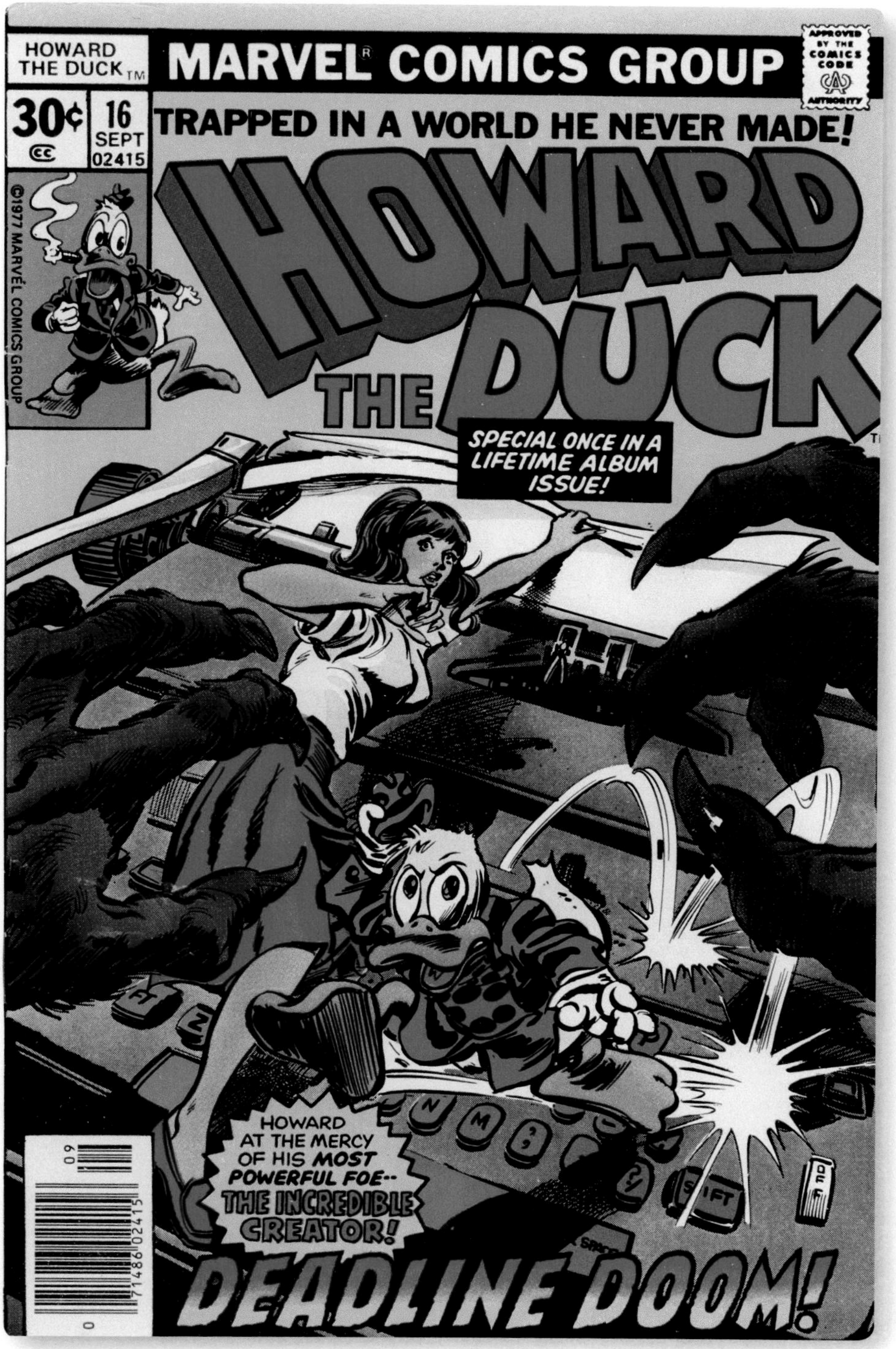
HOWARD THE DUCK TM
MARVEL® COMICS GROUP
APPROVED BY THE COMICS CODE AUTHORITY
30¢
16
SEPT
02415
TRAPPED IN A WORLD HE NEVER MADE!
©1977 MARVEL COMICS GROUP
HOWARD THE DUCK
SPECIAL ONCE IN A LIFETIME ALBUM ISSUE!
HOWARD AT THE MERCY OF HIS MOST POWERFUL FOE-- THE INCREDIBLE CREATOR!
DEADLINE DOOM!

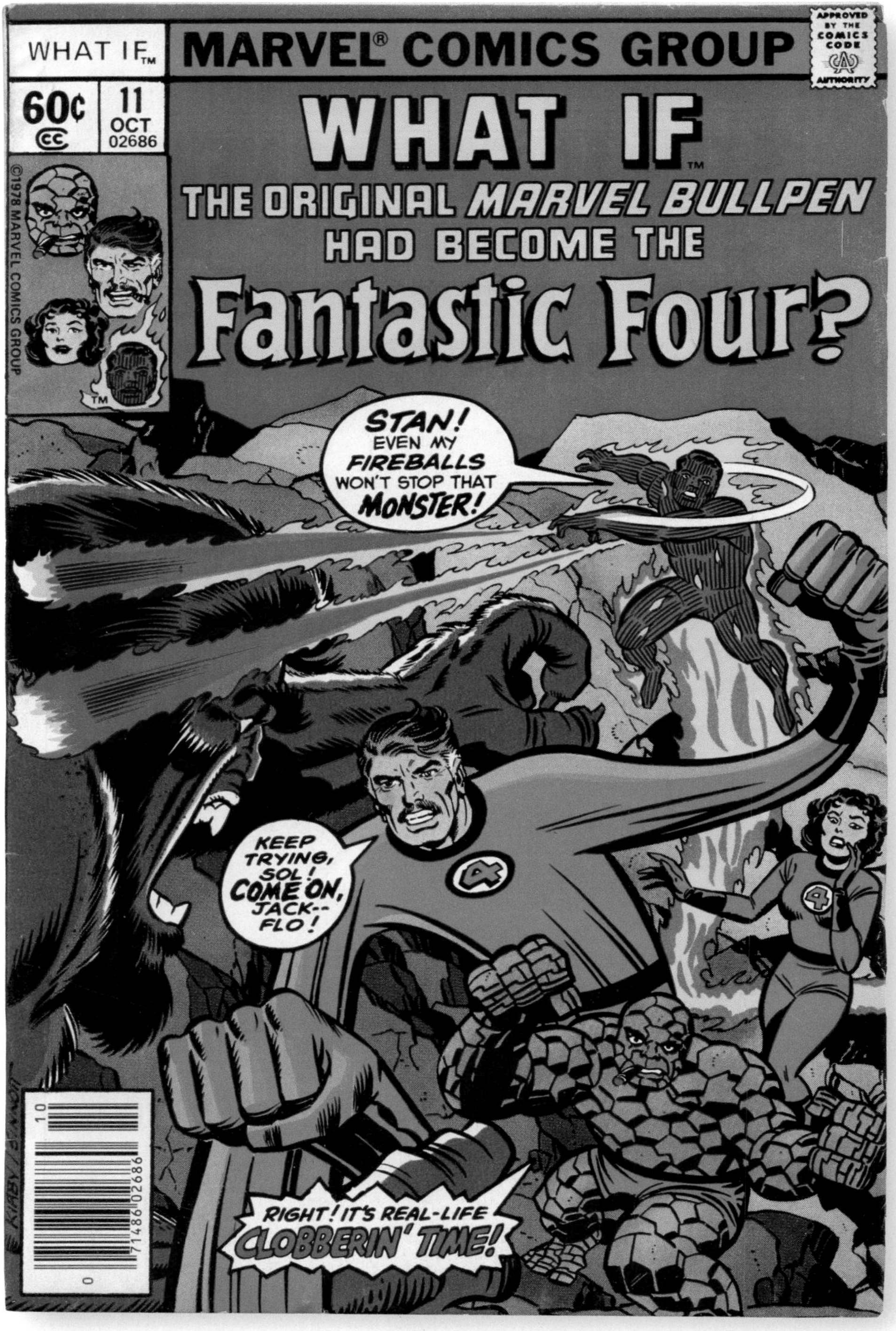
WHAT IF™
MARVEL® COMICS GROUP
APPROVED BY THE COMICS CODE AUTHORITY
60¢
CC
11
OCT
02686
©1978 MARVEL COMICS GROUP
TM
WHAT IF™
THE ORIGINAL MARVEL BULLPEN
HAD BECOME THE
Fantastic Four?
STAN! EVEN MY FIREBALLS WON'T STOP THAT MONSTER!
KEEP TRYING, SOL! COME ON, JACK-- FLO!
RIGHT! IT'S REAL-LIFE CLOBBERIN' TIME!

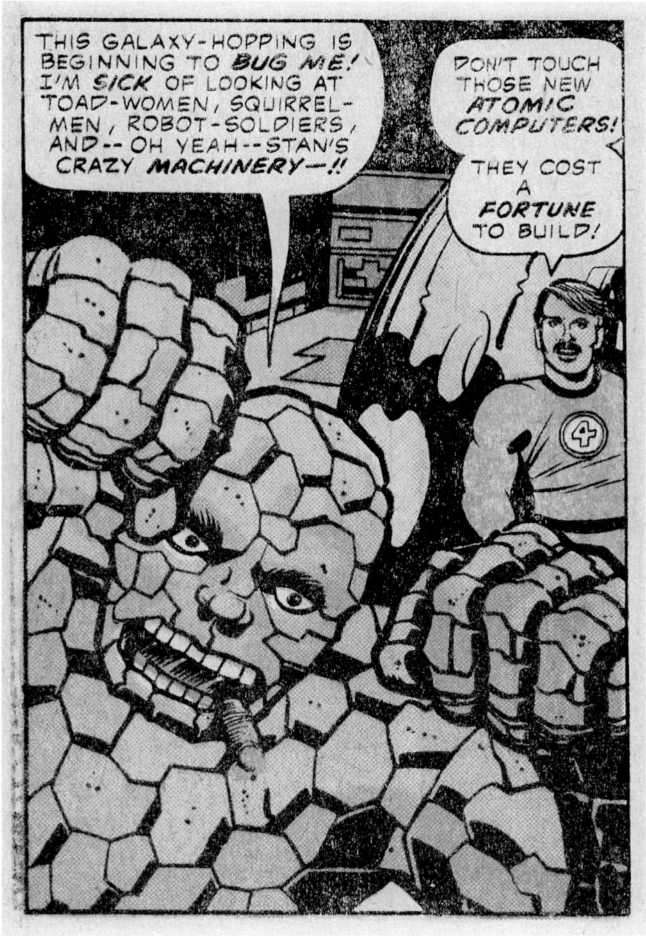
THIS GALAXY-HOPPING IS BEGINNING TO BUG ME! I'M SICK OF LOOKING AT TOAD-WOMEN, SQUIRREL-MEN, ROBOT-SOLDIERS, AND--OH YEAH--STAN'S CRAZY MACHINERY--!!
DON'T TOUCH THOSE NEW ATOMIC COMPUTERS!
THEY COST A FORTUNE TO BUILD!

WHAT IF? No. 11

(Opposite) Cover; pencils, Jack Kirby; inks, Joe Sinnott. (Above) Interior, "What If the Original Marvel Bullpen Had Become the Fantastic Four?"; script and pencils, Jack Kirby; inks, Mike Royer and Bill Wray; October 1978. In this odd and nostalgic "What If...?" story, Kirby characteristically positioned himself as the Thing. Asked by *The Comics Journal* in 1990 whether he had put some of himself into the rock-steady FF clobberer, Kirby said it was an association others made before he did and then added, "I suppose I must be a lot like Ben Grimm. I never duck out of a fight; I don't care what the hell the odds are, and I'm rough at times, but I try to be a decent guy all the time." Lee and Sol Brodsky, both then still with the company, were Mr. Fantastic and the Human Torch. And Kirby had not forgotten Flo Steinberg, who had left Marvel in 1968—she landed the Invisible Girl role.

"As Dave and I honed our craft, as individuals and a team, so did the characters make their initially halting and occasionally clumsy steps into becoming a team, and ultimately a family.... The characters had only just met then, as opposed to having been together for longer than many readers' and some creators' lifetimes. There was the marvel of discovery to every aspect of the book." — CHRIS CLAREMONT

X-MEN No. 101

(Opposite) Cover; pencils and inks, Dave Cockrum; October 1976.
"Hear me, X-Men! No longer am I the woman you knew. I am fire! And life incarnate! Now and forever — I am Phoenix!" proclaims Jean Grey, rising from the water uninjured (and in a new costume) after sacrificing herself in a crash landing. After *Giant-Size X-Men* No. 1 relaunched the team, the *X-Men* series returned to new stories with a radically different, internationally diverse group. Original (American) member Cyclops was joined by Wolverine (Canadian), Thunderbird (Apache), Banshee (Irish), Nightcrawler (German), Storm (Kenyan American; grew up in Egypt), and Colossus (Russian). Claremont and Cockrum's work impressed readers, and sent the X-Men on their way to global stardom.

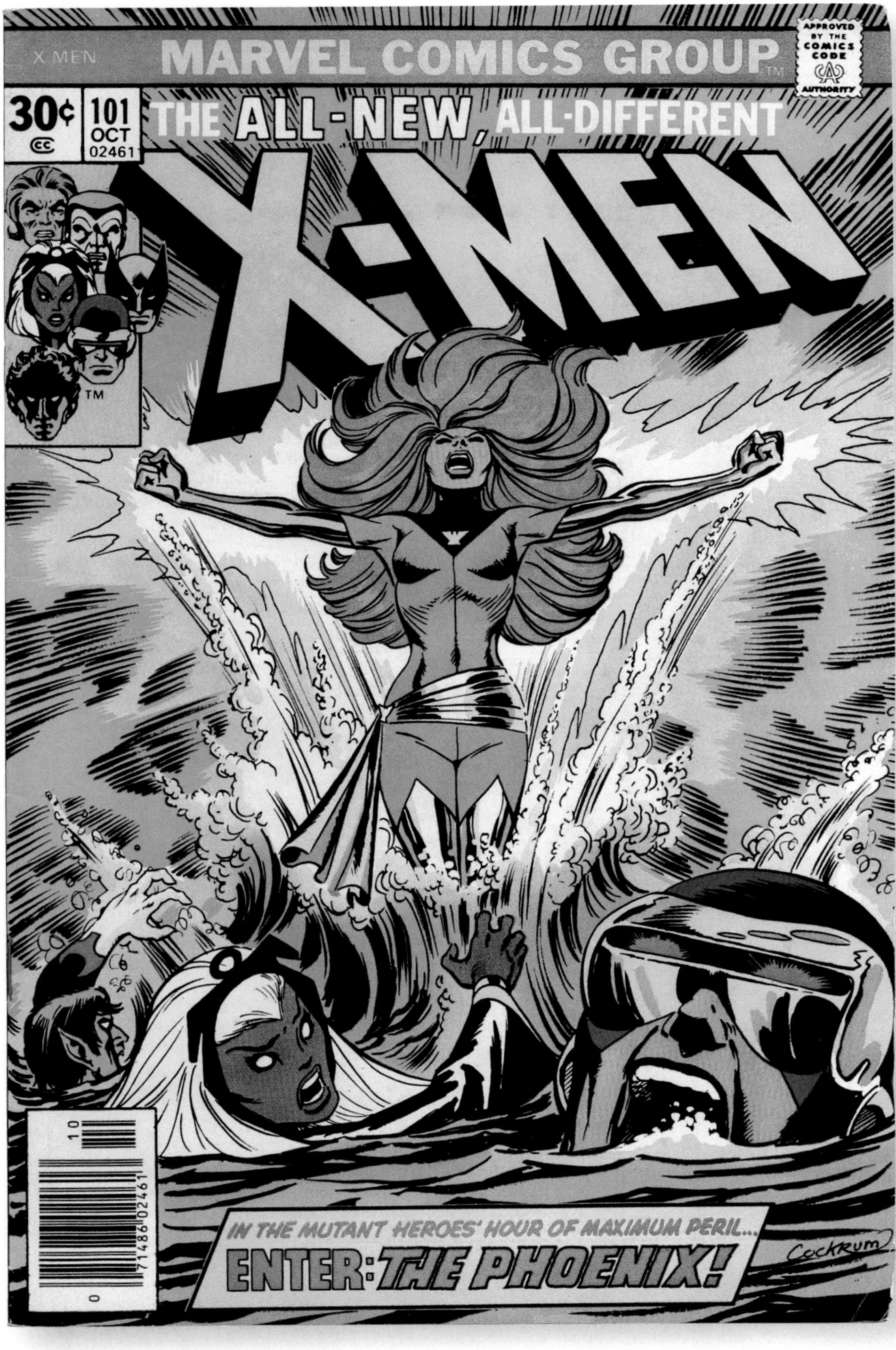
X MEN
MARVEL COMICS GROUP
APPROVED BY THE COMICS CODE AUTHORITY
30¢
101
OCT
02461
THE ALL-NEW, ALL-DIFFERENT
X-MEN
IN THE MUTANT HEROES' HOUR OF MAXIMUM PERIL...
ENTER: THE PHOENIX!
COCKRUM

FINDING PHOENIX

(Above) Design sketches, Dave Cockrum, 1970s.
An inveterate character and costume designer,
Cockrum's notebooks were filled with sketches
like these, which would help conceive Jean
Grey as Phoenix. His enthusiasm was amplified
in partner Claremont, who lamented, "The
X-Men are very real people to me, and I live
with them 24 hours a day. They are always on
the fringes of my thoughts, no matter how much
I try to divorce myself from them. It's a very
awkward situation, because it inhibits the writer
from doing those things to characters which
must be done to keep the book dramatically
viable. You don't want to kill anyone off; you
don't want to break their hearts; you don't
want to hurt them. They're your friends!"

DAZZLER No. 2

(Right) Interior, "Where Demons Fear to Dwell!";
script, Tom DeFalco; pencils, John Romita Jr.;
inks, Alfredo Alcala; April 1981. It was the "Last
Stand in Discoland" for Dazzler in the early
'80s, as the genre quickly fell out of favor with
fans, potentially undermining the character's
genesis as a disco queen. Not to worry, a switch
to Pat Benatar–style rock did the trick.

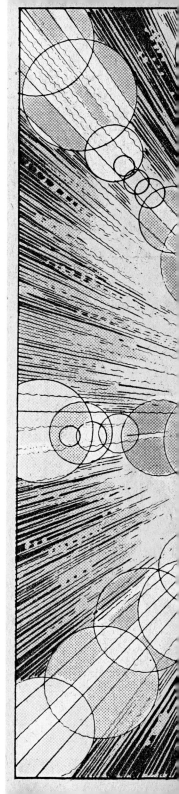

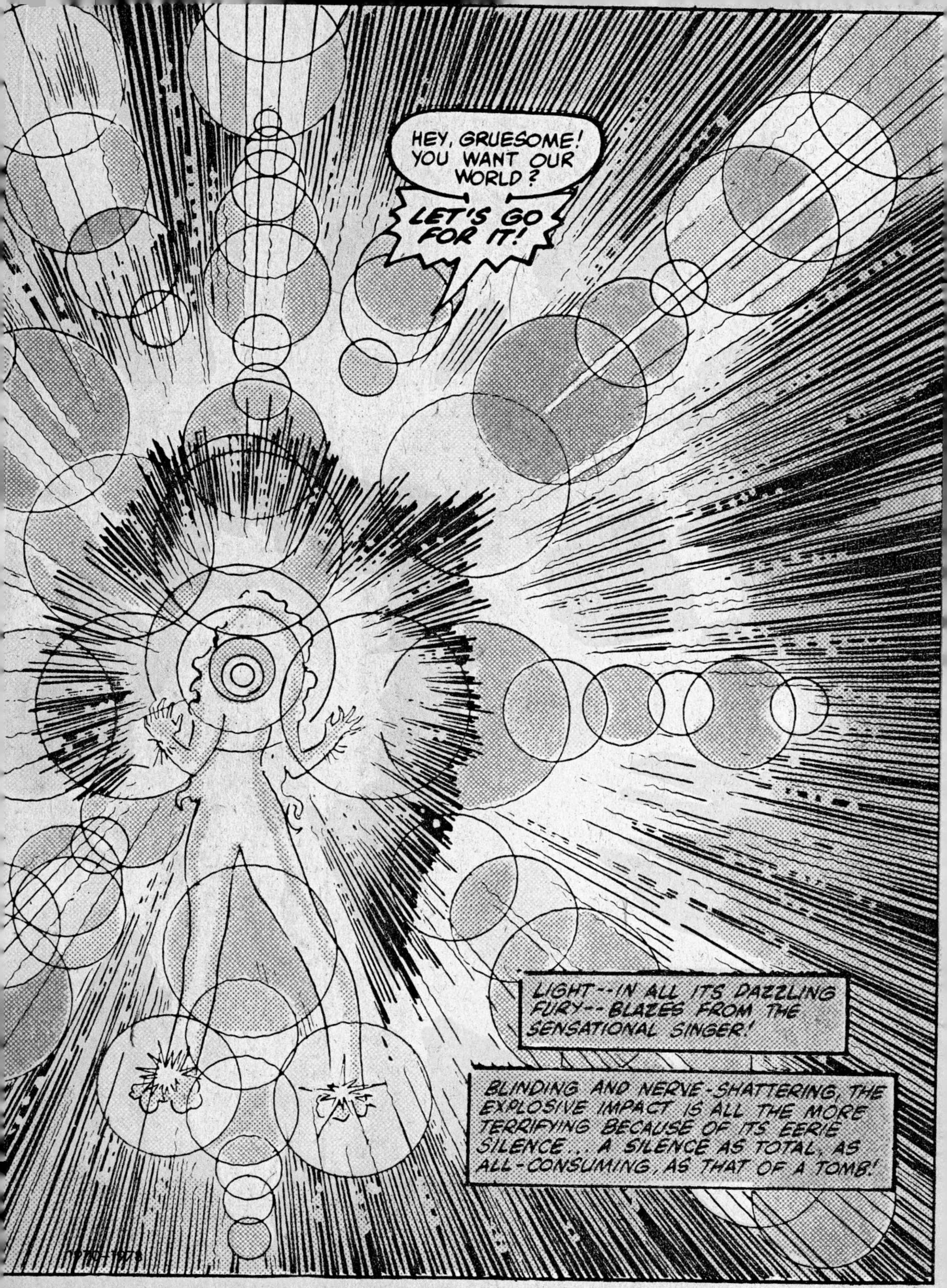
HEY, GRUESOME! YOU WANT OUR WORLD?
LET'S GO FOR IT!
LIGHT--IN ALL ITS DAZZLING FURY--BLAZES FROM THE SENSATIONAL SINGER!
BLINDING AND NERVE-SHATTERING, THE EXPLOSIVE IMPACT IS ALL THE MORE TERRIFYING BECAUSE OF ITS EERIE SILENCE... A SILENCE AS TOTAL, AS ALL-CONSUMING, AS THAT OF A TOMB!

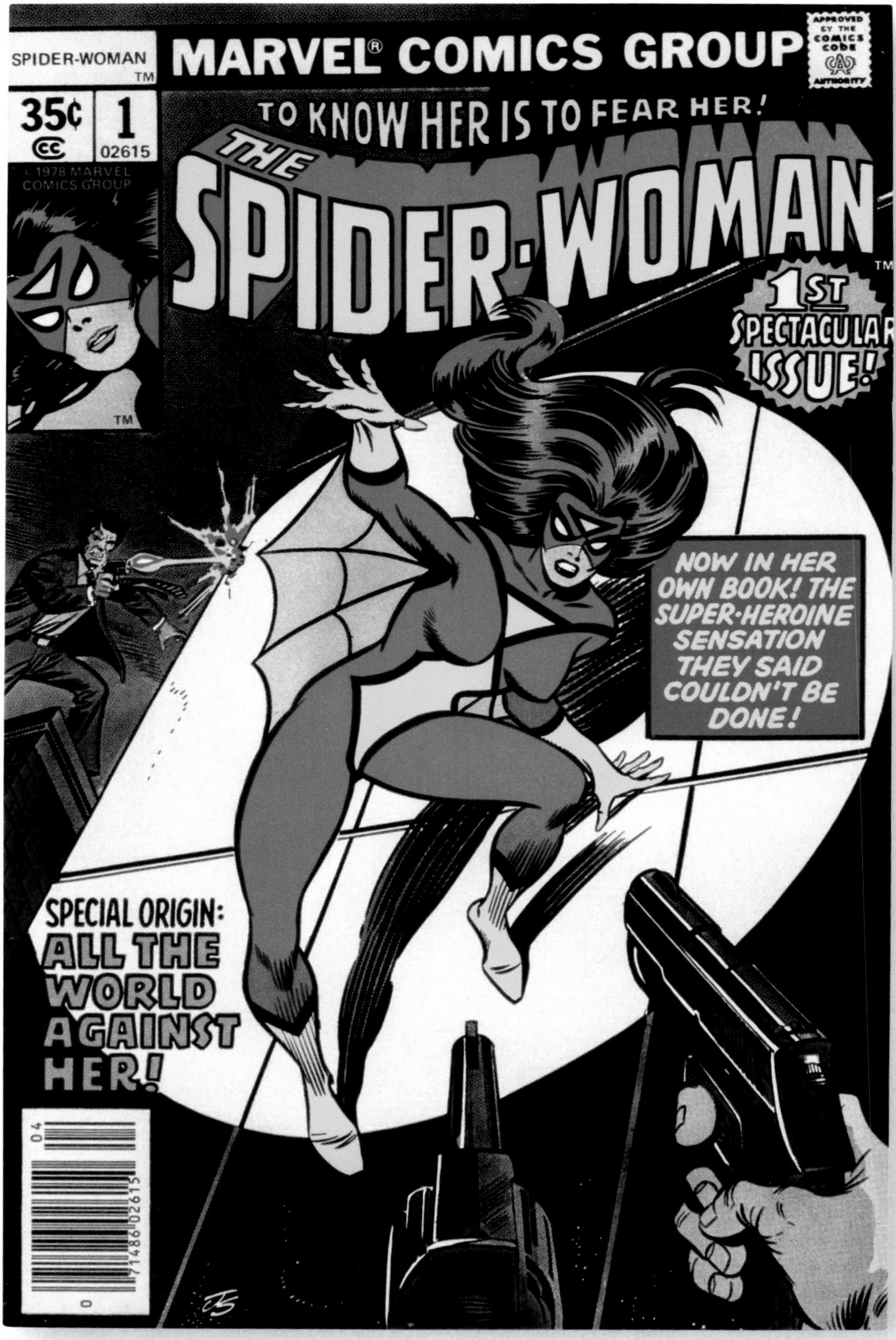
SPIDER-WOMAN TM
MARVEL® COMICS GROUP
APPROVED BY THE COMICS CODE AUTHORITY
35¢
1
02615
©1978 MARVEL COMICS GROUP
TO KNOW HER IS TO FEAR HER!
THE SPIDER-WOMAN TM
1ST SPECTACULAR ISSUE!
NOW IN HER OWN BOOK! THE SUPER-HEROINE SENSATION THEY SAID COULDN'T BE DONE!
SPECIAL ORIGIN: ALL THE WORLD AGAINST HER!

MS. MARVEL No. 1

(Below) Cover; pencils, John Romita; inks, Dick Giordano; January 1977. Gerry Conway pulled out all the stops for "This Woman, This Warrior." Carol Danvers is the liberated new editor of the *Daily Bugle*'s *Woman* magazine. "Not all feminists are delighted at the trend, however," *Newsweek* reported in an article from March 20, 1978. "Some question whether superheroines are proper symbols of liberation. Ms. Marvel and friends still live in a man's world. Virtually all of the 200 titles published each year are written by men, and the 250 million copies sold annually are read predominantly by boys. Moreover, the comics are drawn almost entirely by males."

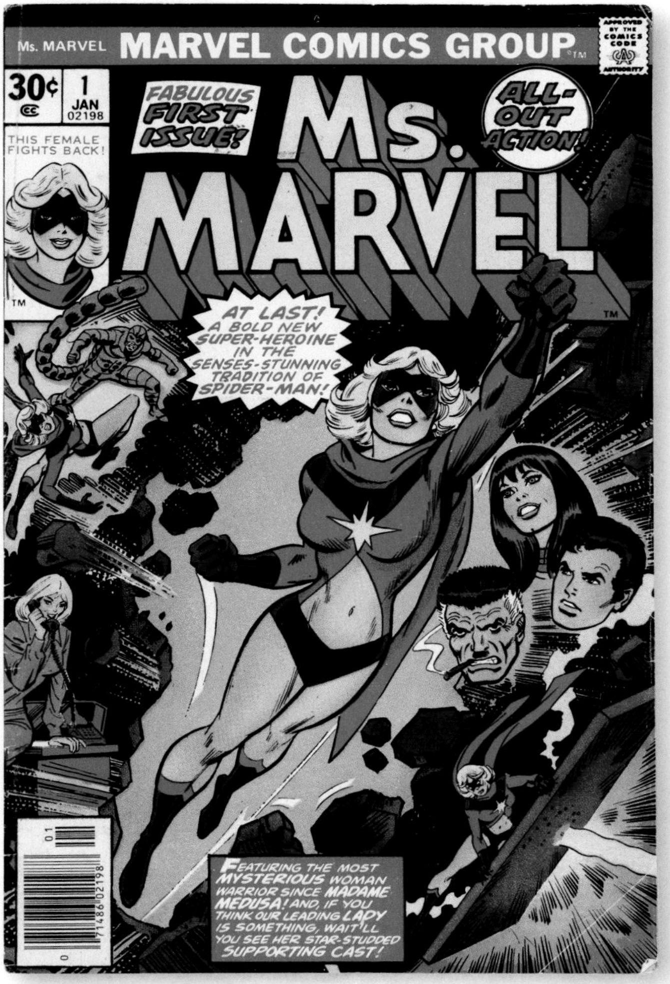
Ms. MARVEL
MARVEL COMICS GROUP
30¢
1
JAN
02198
FABULOUS FIRST ISSUE!
Ms. MARVEL
ALL-OUT ACTION!
THIS FEMALE FIGHTS BACK!
AT LAST! A BOLD NEW SUPER-HEROINE IN THE SENSES-STUNNING TRADITION OF SPIDER-MAN!
FEATURING THE MOST MYSTERIOUS WOMAN WARRIOR SINCE MADAME MEDUSA! AND, IF YOU THINK OUR LEADING LADY IS SOMETHING, WAIT'LL YOU SEE HER STAR-STUDDED SUPPORTING CAST!

SPIDER-WOMAN No. 1

(Opposite) Cover; pencils and inks, Joe Sinnott; April 1978.

MARVEL DOES THE WHITE HOUSE

(Opposite) Photograph; Amy Carter and her mother, First Lady Rosalynn Carter, with Marvel heroes; Associated Press; October 1980. When the Department of Energy launched the Captain America Youth Energy Conservation Program, Cap and fellow Marvel heroes crashed the White House. A few years later, it turns out the man in red, white, and blue would wear another uniform — Jonathan Frakes played Commander Riker in *Star Trek: The Next Generation*. As Marvel's Cap, Frakes confirmed in a 1988 *Starlog* interview, he "did such glamorous things as opening supermarkets, signing comic books at bookstores, going to children's hospitals and doing kids shows and clown shows." He eventually left, on the advice of his agent, who said, "I would much rather have you moving furniture than be thought of as Captain America."

YOUR LUNCH IS SAFE WITH US

(Below) Lunch box, ca. 1976.

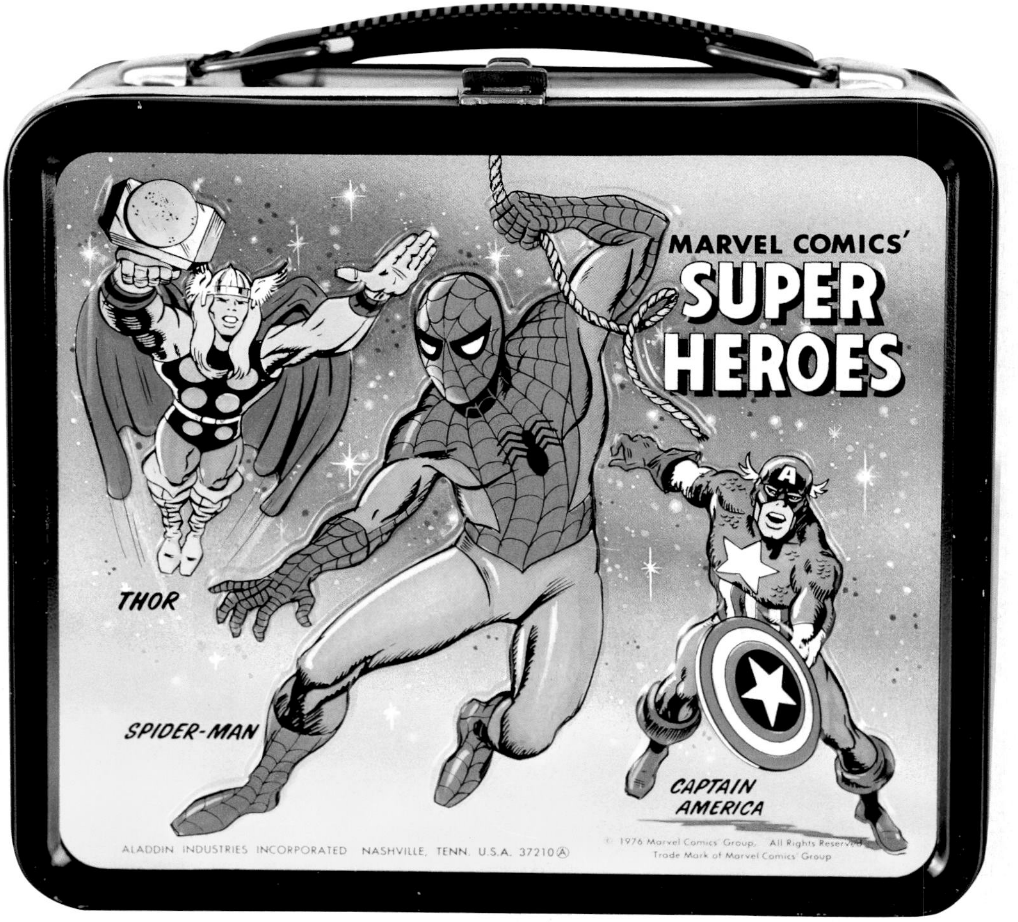
MARVEL COMICS'
SUPER HEROES
THOR
SPIDER-MAN
CAPTAIN AMERICA
ALADDIN INDUSTRIES INCORPORATED NASHVILLE, TENN. U.S.A. 37210Ⓐ
© 1976 Marvel Comics Group, All Rights Reserved
Trade Mark of Marvel Comics Group

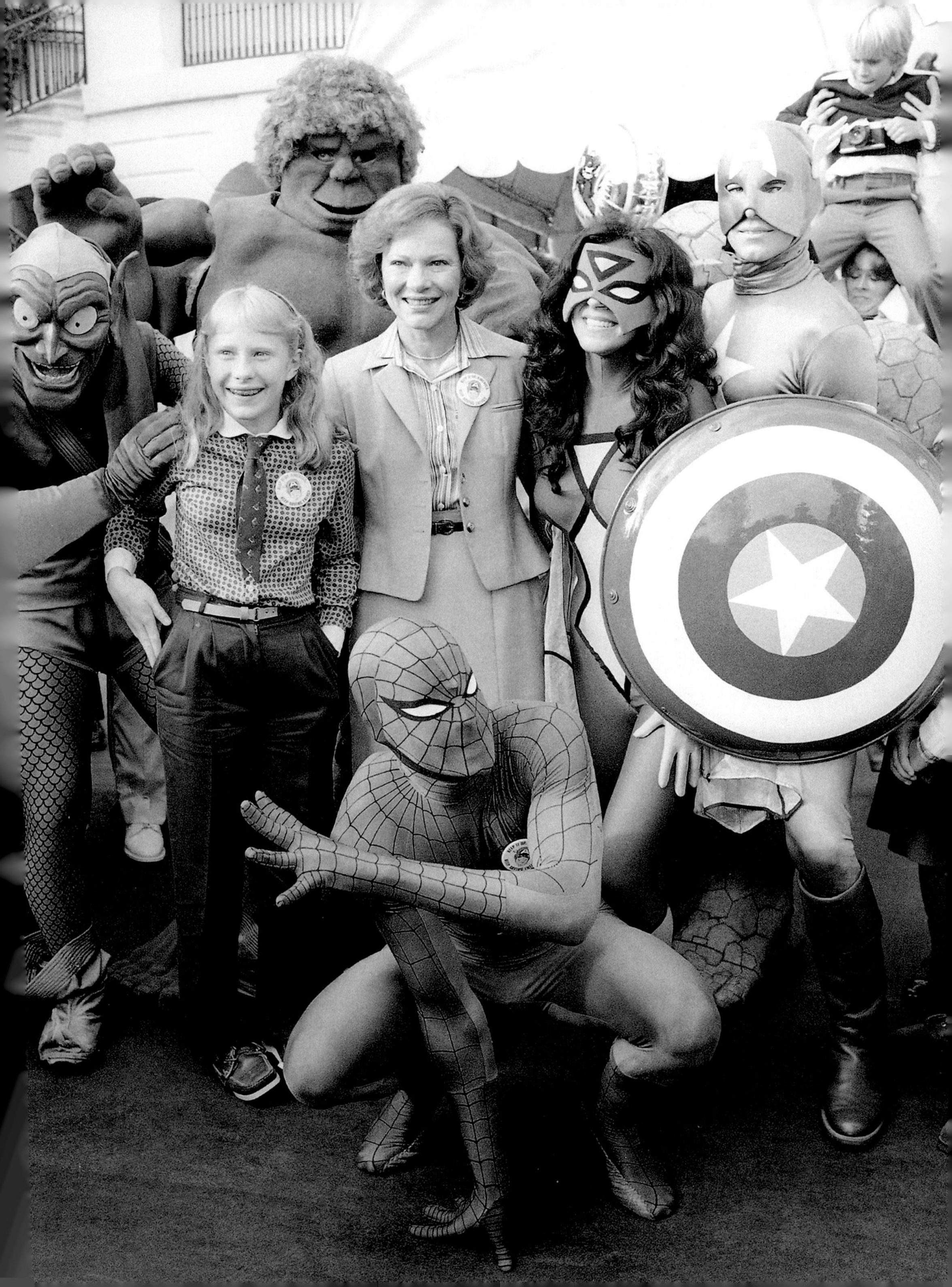

Credits

The majority of the comics included in this volume were photographed from the collections of Bob Bretall, Nick Caputo, Marvel, Barry Pearl, Michael J. Vassallo, and Warren Reece's Chamber of Fantasy. Also: Jesse and Sylvia Storob. Also featured are the collections of Ivan Briggs, Eliot R. Brown, John Chruscinski, Andrew Farago, Hake's, Robin Kirby, Gus Landt, Cory Sedlmeier, Colin Stutz, Tellshiar, and, notably, Heritage Auctions and TwoMorrows Publishing.

All images in this volume are © Marvel unless otherwise noted. Any omissions for copyright or credit are unintentional and appropriate credit will be given in future editions if such copyright holders contact the publisher.

Courtesy of estate of Jerry G. Bails; *Alter Ego* is a ™ of Roy & Dann Thomas: 21 (right).
Courtesy Alexander Braun: 232 (top).
© Eliot R. Brown: 392 (left), 392 (right).
Courtesy John Butler: 451, 452.
© Conan Properties International LLC ('CPI'). CONAN, CONAN THE BARBARIAN, and HYBORIA are trademarks or registered trademarks of CPI. Used with permission. All rights reserved: 364, 386, 420, 421, 422, 423.
© Conan Properties International LLC ('CPI'). CONAN, CONAN THE BARBARIAN, and HYBORIA are trademarks or registered trademarks of CPI. Used with permission. All rights reserved/Photo courtesy of Heritage Auctions, ha.com: 366 (top).
© DC Comics & Marvel Characters, Inc. SUPER-MAN is ™ & © DC Comics: 397.
™ & © DC Comics. Used with permission: 18 (bottom).
Amazing Fantasy No. 15, Edwin and Terry Murray Comic Book Collection, David M. Rubenstein Rare Book & Manuscript Library, Duke University: 30, 33, 94.
From the Collection of Josh Alan Friedman: 183.
Courtesy Glen David Gold: 221, 331.
By permission of *Esquire* magazine. © The Hearst Corporation. Also, *Esquire* is a trademark of The Hearst Corporation. All Rights Reserved: 238–239.
Photo courtesy of Heritage Auctions, ha.com: 80, 84, 114, 216, 292 (bottom), 354 (bottom), 480 (top).
Collection of Daniel and Louise Herman: 255.
Courtesy of the Estate of Greg Irons: 351.
© Denis Kitchen: 379.
© Elliott Landy: 349.
© MARVEL/Photo courtesy of Heritage Auctions, ha.com: 28, 89, 143, 144, 145, 182, 184, 185, 204, 205, 308, 323 (top left), 328, 408 (bottom), 462, 469 (top), 478, 484.
COURTESY OF LUCASFILM LTD. LLC/ *Star Wars* © & ™ Lucasfilm Ltd. LLC: 417.
Courtesy David Mandel: 103, 152, 298.
© MARVEL/Stan Lee Collection, American Heritage Center, University of Wyoming: 412.
From the Collection of MetropolisComics.com: 132, 159, 247.
Courtesy NASA: 62 (top).
National Cartoonist Society: 169.
© picture-alliance/AP/Schwarz: 509.
Robert Policastro: 459 (left).
© Peter Poplaski/Courtesy Denis Kitchen: 378.
Courtesy Tellshiar: 235, 240 (bottom), 273, 447.
Topps ® Krazy Little Comics used courtesy of The Topps Company, Inc.: 283 (bottom left).
2001: A Space Odyssey and all related characters and elements ™ Turner Entertainment Co. (s17): Picture taken by Patricia A. Yanchus: 396 (bottom).

EDITORIAL NOTE

Though Stan Lee is known to have championed contributors' credits as early as 1942, most writers and artists of Timely and Atlas comics remained anonymous until the 1960s. The earliest Timely comics were produced in comic shops where some artists signed their work and others did not. In addition, Timely's 1940s bullpen produced much of its work piecemeal, with different pencilers and inkers contributing to the finished product, making full identification of contributors extremely difficult, and sometimes impossible. In the Atlas period, identification is easier, as solo-produced free-lance artwork was often signed or easy to identify by strong stylistic cues.

The comic book pages presented in this volume were scrutinized by some of the most knowledgeable art spotters in the world — historians who exhaustively study art styles and artistic nuances in the penciling, inking, and even backgrounds of hundreds of artists. The resulting identifications are as accurate as possible based on what is now known. In cases where we are uncertain, contributors are listed as "attributed" or "unknown" based on the accumulated knowledge of the art spotters.

It has been TASCHEN's mission from the start to make a book on Marvel's rich history like none ever seen before — to bring that history to life not just through the storytelling of the book's expert writers, but also through the reproduction of the comics themselves. We scoured the country for collectors who owned the rarest of the rare — unslabbed comics they were willing to crack open, risking damage with the turn of every fragile page — so that you, our fair reader, might better imagine the experience of, say, discovering a copy of *Amazing Fantasy* No. 15 in your parents' or granddad's attic and whiling away the afternoon with a good read. In some instances the pages have been subject to foxing, edge and corner wear, stamps, and even notations by previous owner. In the case of original art, the artist's hand (as well as the writer's and editor's) is often on display — as are bits of tape, glue, and correction fluid. The visible age of the object in many cases corresponds to its actual age, and to the fact that readers young and old may have pulled a book out from under the pillow more than once in the decades that have passed. Rather than erase all signs of age, we have maintained the environmental and human evidence for comics archaeologists to interpret in generations to come.

AND SO WE LEAVE OUR FRIENDS DANGLING IN A WEB FAR MORE POWERFUL THAN ANY WHICH SPIDER-MAN CAN WEAVE -- THE MYSTERIOUS, DRAMATIC WEB OF FATE! NEXT ISSUE WE WILL MEET A GREAT NEW VILLAIN -- FIND MORE SPECTACULAR THRILLS -- AS SPIDER-MAN DISCOVERS THE STRANGE SECRET OF BETTY BRANT!
THE END
...FOR NOW!

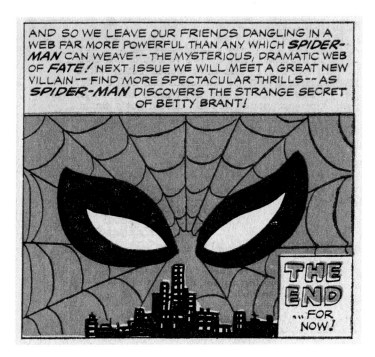

EACH AND EVERY TASCHEN BOOK PLANTS A SEED!
TASCHEN is a carbon neutral publisher. Each year, we offset our annual carbon emissions with carbon credits at the Instituto Terra, a reforestation program in Minas Gerais, Brazil, founded by Lélia and Sebastião Salgado. To find out more about this ecological partnership, please check: www.taschen.com/zerocarbon
Inspiration: unlimited. Carbon footprint: zero.

To stay informed about TASCHEN and our upcoming titles, please subscribe to our free magazine at www.taschen.com/magazine, follow us on Instagram and Facebook, or e-mail your questions to contact@taschen.com.

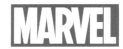

MARVEL

TASCHEN GmbH
Hohenzollernring 53
D-50672 Köln
taschen.com

Editorial consultants: Nick Caputo, Blake Hennon, Barry Pearl, Rhett Thomas, and Michael J. Vassallo
Special consultant to Roy Thomas: Danny Fingeroth

Printed in Italy
ISBN 978-3-8365-7787-8

STAMPS

SHOP BY MAIL

STAMP COLLECTING OUTFIT
A packet of worldwide stamps, 9 Triangles, 2 Diamons, animals, insects, flowers, ships, man-in-space, New African Nations, etc. Plus a packet of hinges, perforation gauge and millimeter scale, watermark detector. ONLY 25¢ to approval buyers.
L. W. BROWN, Dept MQ, Marion, Mich.

115 Dif. + 17 New Nations Stamps
Includes Monaco "Chevy," San Marino "antique plane," Chad, Ivory Coast, Central Africa, Gabon, Cameroons, Niger, Madagascar, Congo, Togo "Kennedy," many triangles, diamond, British Colonies and many others ONLY 25¢ with worldwide approvals.
CATALINA STAMPS, Dept. MQ, Orange, California

BETTER U.S. APPROVALS
To introduce our BETTER U.S. APPROVALS we offer 15 of the most wanted U.S. stamps, including a Columbian, Bi-Cents, Army-Navy, Famous American, Airs and other Commems. for only 10c.
OCEAN STAMPS, BOX 64-D, BROOKLYN 29, N.Y.

FREE
When you buy our Foreign Approvals. FREE Mammoth Collection, plus We... Stamp, $10,000 Airmail even Scot... or Master Global Albums. BARGA... VICE, 1414 W. McFadden Street, Sa...

1c
Thousands of beautiful ... 1c each—why pay more ... the best for less. Writ...
PENNY STA...
Orange

111 DIF. BON...
Includes Indonesia Agricultura... Cross, Fr. So. Antartica, Tri... Kong and many others ONLY ...
FAIRWAY STAMPS, Box 65-MH...

121 DIF. BLOCK...
Includes Giant Indonesia dance... ...tan, Hitler head, Jamaica, "Kenn... Nigeria and other, 10¢ to Appr...
TRU-VALUE STAMPS, Box 2275, ...

20 DIFFERENT TRIANGLES
With approvals — 35¢ without approval...
Picture Stamps, Box 46193-MX, Hollywood 46, Calif.

FREE
MAMMOTH GLOBETROTTER COLLECTION, ... from 100 Different Countries, with Myste... Remote Isles, when you BUY our Foreign...
WESTERLY STAMPS, 1609 S. Park, Sant...

TRIPLE OFFER 1...
10 diff. Luxembourg plus colorful ... collection ONLY 10c with approva... United Nations Stamps used ...
SUNLIGHT STAMP CO., Box 1259-F, ...

LOOK — GIANT PHILIP...
stamp, plus New Zealand, Cuba and ... Only 5c with U.S. or foreign approv...
Earl Thompson, 5448 Odell St., St. Louis ...

Sensational • COLORFUL • PHILA...
SELECTION 10¢ Accompany... approva...
LINCOLN STAMP CO., St. Catharines 81...

225 STAMPS FOR ONLY
THIS MAMMOTH VALUE INCLUDES STAMPS WO... UP TO 25c! ALSO APPROVALS. WRITE TODAY!
MYSTIC STAMP CO Camden 3, New York

SPECTACULAR! OLD U.S.!
Fam. Americans, Flags, Presidents, Airmails, Commemoratives with **approvals**, plus surprise Packet for 10¢ handling. **10¢**
METROPOLITAN STAMPS
Box 312H, Jackson Heights, N. Y.

SONG IDEAS
WANTED
s/a Write with active, Professional songwriters with publisher contacts. Records made. Share royalties.
HITS WRITTEN BY OUR PAST & PRESENT STAFF:
LET THE LITTLE GIRL DANCE — BILLY BLAND
PRETTY LITTLE ANGEL EYES — CURTIS LEE
WHAT A SURPRISE — JOHNNY MAESTRO
HOMBRE — THE BELMONTS •• PLUS MANY OTHER HITS!
Send Material NOW for FREE Examination
SONGWRITERS' ASSOCIATES
Studio 9 C 236 W. 55 St. at Broadway, NY 19, NY

Fantastic ... Valuable "Ben Franklin" ... Flami... bi-colored Vol... Trian... nd. ...

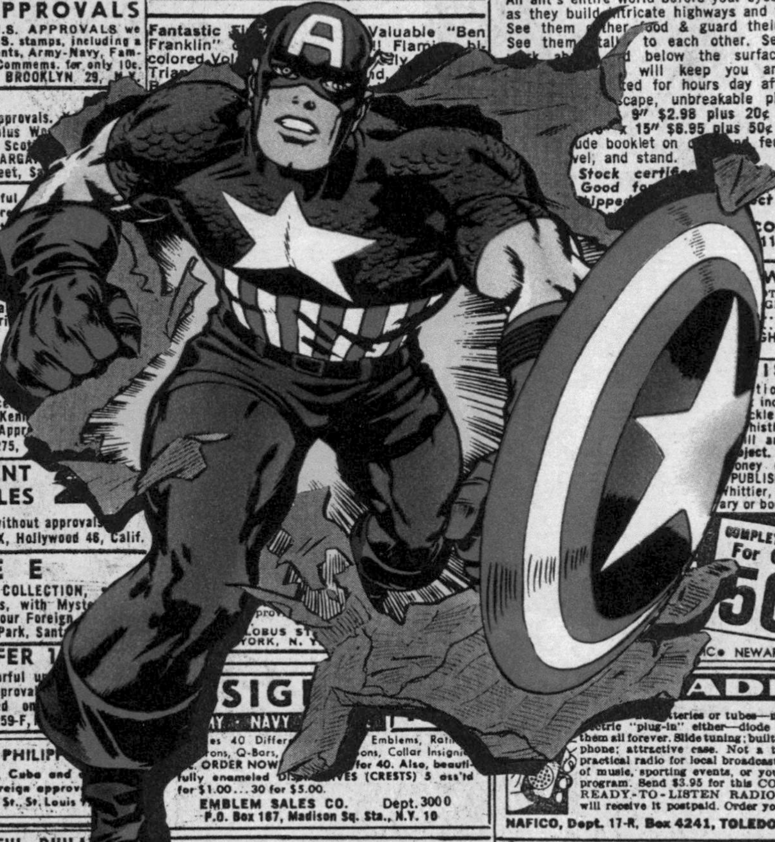

...prov... ...LOBUS ST... ...YORK, N. Y.

...SIG... ...MY NAVY ...
...es 40 Differ... Emblems, Rati... ...ons, Q-Bars, ...ons, Collar Insigni... ...ORDER NOW ...for 40. Also, beautifully enameled Disp...IVES (CRESTS) 5 ass'td for $1.00 ... 30 for $5.00.
EMBLEM SALES CO. Dept. 3000
P.O. Box 167, Madison Sq. Sta., N.Y. 10

High School Course ...t Home Many Finish in 2 Years
... as rapidly as your time and abilities permit. Equivalent to resident School work—...ares for college entrance exams. Standard H.S. texts supplied. Diploma awarded. ...dit for H.S. subjects completed. Single ...jects if desired. Ask for Free Bulletin.
American School, Dept. HA12 Drexel at 58th, Chicago 37

AS SEEN ON TV! Fascinating Escape-Proof **ANT FARM $2.98**

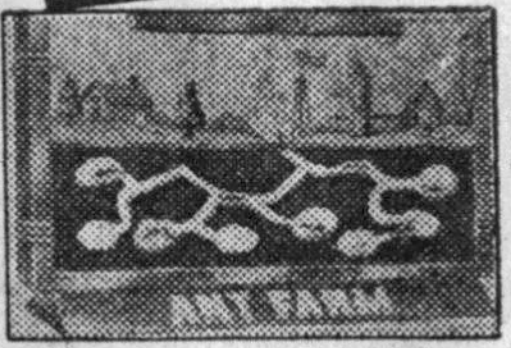

OVER TWO MILLION SOLD! ENDLESSLY ABSORBING IDEAL GIFT FOR ADULTS AND CHILDREN.

An ant's entire world before your eyes. Watch as they build intricate highways and tunnels! See them ...ther food & guard their home. See them ...talk to each other. See them ...k ab...d below the surface. This ... will keep you and your ...ted for hours day after day. ...scape, unbreakable plastic. ...9" $2.98 plus 20¢ postage ...x 15" $6.95 plus 50¢ postage ...ude booklet on ... feeding of ...vel, and stand.
Stock certific... each Good fo... ...y of ...ipped ...ct from
...CO. ...11229

...WORLD ...OTGELT 25¢ ...GELT.. 25¢ ... 25¢ ... 25¢ ...GHTS, N.Y.

...ISTLE! ...tions make ... includes the ...ckle Whistle, ...histle, Finger ...ll and Palate ...ject. ...oney order for ...PUBLISHING CO., ...Whittier, Calif. or ...ary or book dealer.

COMPLETE LIST For Only **50¢**
...INC. NEWARK 1, N. J.

...ADIO
...steries or tubes—no need for ...ectric "plug-in" either—diode eliminates them all forever. Slide tuning; built-in speaker phone; attractive case. Not a toy, but a practical radio for local broadcast reception of music, sporting events, or your favorite program. Send $3.95 for this COMPLETE READY-TO-LISTEN RADIO and you will receive it postpaid. Order yours NOW!
NAFICO, Dept. 17-R, Box 4241, TOLEDO 9, OHIO

POEMS WANTED
TO BE SET TO MUSIC
Send one or more of your best poems today for FREE EXAMINATION. Any subject. Immediate Consideration.
PHONOGRAPH RECORDS MADE
CROWN MUSIC CO.
49 W. 32 St., Studio 11, New York 1

1000 TRICKS **BE A MAGICIAN!**
Mystify — astonish others. Have fun. Be the life of the party. Make money in spare time too! Rush 25¢ now—today for this $1.00 Giant Deluxe 160-Page Magic and Fun Catalog. Loaded with Magic, Pocket Tricks, Mysteries, Illusions, Secrets, Mindreading, Hypnotism, Party Stunts, Joker's Novelties, Puzzles, Brainbusters, Books, etc. Low prices. Illustrated! Send name, address and only 25¢.

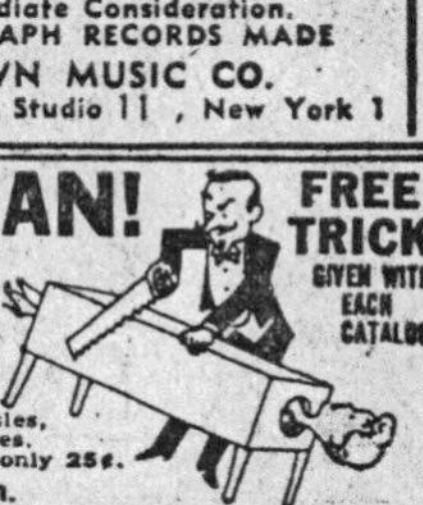

FREE TRICK GIVEN WITH EACH CATALOG
House of 1000 Mysteries, Dept. MC6-64, Monroe, Conn.

TASCHEN turns 40 this year! Since we started our work as cultural archaeologists in 1980, TASCHEN has become synonymous with accessible publishing, helping bookworms around the world curate their own library of art, anthropology, and aphrodisia at an unbeatable price. In 2020, we celebrate 40 years of incredible books by staying true to our company credo.
The *40* series presents new editions of some of the stars of our program—now more compact, friendly in price, and still realized with the same commitment to impeccable production.

The author: Since 1965, **Roy Thomas** has been writing for movies, television, and especially comic books. With notable runs on *Avengers, Uncanny X-Men, Conan the Barbarian, The Incredible Hulk,* and *Star Wars,* he served as a Marvel editor from 1965–80 and editor-in-chief from 1972–74. He currently edits the comics-history magazine *Alter Ego* and writes two online Tarzan strips as well as the occasional comic book. He and his wife Dann live in South Carolina.

Front cover: *The Amazing Spider-Man* No. 1 (cover detail): pencils, Jack Kirby; inks, Steve Ditko; March 1963.

Back cover: *The Incredible Hulk* No. 1; pencils, Jack Kirby; inks, attributed George Roussos, possibly Kirby; May 1962.

Lettering: Michael Doret.

AN ERA OF THE INVINCIBLE

The making of household heroes and mythological universes

It was an age of mighty heroes, misunderstood monsters, and complex villains. With the publication of *Fantastic Four* No. 1 in November 1961, comics giant Marvel inaugurated a transformative era in pop culture. Through the next two decades, the iconic Hulk, Spider-Man, Iron Man, and the X-Men leapt, darted, and towered through its pages. Captain America was resurrected from his 1940s deep-freeze and the Avengers became the World's Greatest Super Heroes. Daredevil, Doctor Strange, and dozens more were added to the pantheon, each with their own rogues' gallery of malevolent counterparts. Nearly 60 years later, these thrilling characters from the 1960s and '70s are more popular than ever, fighting the good fight in comics, toy aisles, and blockbuster movies around the world.

In *The Marvel Age of Comics 1961–1978*, legendary writer and editor Roy Thomas takes you to the heart of this seminal segment in comic history—an age of triumphant character and narrative innovation that reinvented the super hero genre. The result is a behind-the-scenes treasure trove and a jewel for any comic fan's library, brimming with the innovation and energy of an invincible era for Marvel and its heroes alike.

"A fantastic book... By far the greatest representation of the history of Marvel Comics!"

—Joe Sinnott, comic book artist & Marvel inker

"Marvel is pop culture in its purest form."

—*dpa*, Berlin

"A veritable Bible... chronicling Marvel's incredible odyssey."

LE FIGARO

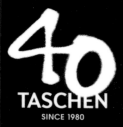

40 TASCHEN SINCE 1980